STRAVINSKY AND
THE RUSSIAN TRADITIONS
VOLUME II

Nikolai Roerich, *Shchegolikha* (painted maiden), costume sketch for *The Rite of Spring*. (Bakhrushin State Central Theatrical Museum, Moscow)

RICHARD TARUSKIN

STRAVINSKY
AND THE RUSSIAN
TRADITIONS

A Biography of the Works Through Mavra

VOLUME II

UNIVERSITY OF CALIFORNIA PRESS

Berkeley   *Los Angeles*

The publisher gratefully acknowledges the contribution provided
by the General Endowment Fund of the Associates of the
University of California Press. The publisher also acknowledges
generous subsidies from the National Endowment for the
Humanities and the American Musicological Society.

University of California Press
Berkeley and Los Angeles, California

Library of Congress Cataloging-in-Publication Data
Taruskin, Richard.
  Stravinsky and the Russian traditions : a biography of the works
through Mavra / Richard Taruskin.
    p.   cm.
  "A Centennial book"—P.
  Includes bibliographical references and index.
  ISBN 0-520-07099-2 (alk. paper)
  1. Stravinsky, Igor, 1882–1971—Criticism and interpretation.
  2. Stravinsky, Igor, 1882–1971—Sources. 3. Music—Russia—History
and criticism. I. Title.
ML410.S932T38 1996
780'.92—dc20   93-28500
                                                         CIP
                                                         MN

Printed in the United States of America
9 8 7 6 5 4 3 2 1

CONTENTS TO VOLUME II

PART III

PROGRESSIVE
ABSTRACTION

13 · RÉCLAME
(THE LOSS OF RUSSIA, I)

THE BACK IS TURNED

In naming Fokine as choreographer of "The Great Sacrifice" in 1910, Roerich made it a point that "we three"—Fokine, Stravinsky, and himself—"are all equally ablaze with this scene and have decided to work together."[1] So much a part of the game plan was Fokine that when he and Diaghilev quarreled over money at the end of the 1910 Paris season, Stravinsky became alarmed at the fate of his project. He wrote Roerich from La Baule on 12 July 1910:

> Now matters have so conjoined that Diaghilev and Fokine seem to have broken formally. I want to keep out of it altogether. Diaghilev was tactless enough to say that the question of Fokine's [contracted] participation in "The Great Sacrifice" can be resolved very simply—just pay him off and that's that. But meanwhile Diaghilev hasn't even had the notion to inquire whether you and I will want to work with anyone else. He thinks that if he cannot work it out with Fokine then he (Diaghilev) will work with [Alexander Alexeyevich] Gorsky [1871–1924, long-time ballet master of the Bolshoy Theater, Moscow], of whom I had never even heard before. For all I know Gorsky's a genius, but I don't think Diaghilev could be that indifferent to the prospect of losing Fokine.[2]

When the dispute failed to get settled, Stravinsky decided, astonishingly enough, that he would remain loyal to Fokine rather than Diaghilev. He wrote to Benois in November: "Has Diaghilev made up yet with Fokine?—That is, have they come to terms? This is a very important question, for if yes, then 'The Great

---

1. "Balet khudozhnika N. K. Rerikha," *Peterburgskaya gazeta*, no. 235 (28 August 1910); quoted in Krasovskaya, *Russkiy baletniy teatr* 1:429.
2. Vershinina (ed.), "Pis'ma Stravinskogo Rerikhu," 58–59.

Sacrifice' will be Diaghilev's, but if no, then it will go to Telyakovsky [the intendant of the Imperial Theaters in St. Petersburg], which is altogether not so good!"[3]

That is indeed something to imagine—*The Rite* at the Mariyinsky Theater, stronghold of *The Sleeping Beauty* and *The Nutcracker*! That Stravinsky could have contemplated the idea, even as a reluctant second choice, shows to what extent he still thought of himself as a Russian composer writing for a Russian audience. Even after *The Firebird* he was still very much "within the walls" of his musical upbringing.

Petrushka changed all that. The incredible lionizing Stravinsky experienced in Paris changed his attitude toward Russia, toward Fokine, and most of all, toward his own place in the scheme of things. By the middle of 1911 he was fed up with his hitherto hero-worshipped collaborator. "If you only knew what incredible efforts and unpleasantness the production of *Petrushka* cost Benois and me because of that bull-headed, despotic, and obtuse Fokine!" he wrote to Vladimir Rimsky-Korsakov shortly after the première.[4] By the next March he was writing his mother, of all people, a veritable dissertation contra Fokine. The way he peppered his prose even here with pompous Gallicisms, by no means all of them contributing any special nuance of meaning, shows more vividly than the content itself the way his environment had begun to influence him. When it came to matters esthetic, Stravinsky had begun thinking in French. "I consider Fokine *finished* as an artist," he railed. "It's all just *habileté* [skill], from which there's no salvation!" Fokine could only "arrange," not "create," whereas

> arranging things that were not meant for the stage was never our *but* [aim]—it was just something forced on us by necessity. The choreographic literature was too poor—so we[!], who had dreams of a renaissance of "movement" as a plastic art, had to content ourselves at first with remakes—*Sylphides* (Chopin), *Carnaval* (Schumann), *Cléopâtre* (everyone), *Shéhérazade* (N. Rimsky-Korsakov), etc., etc. I look upon this era of remakes as a necessary evil, a stage at which it would be unthinkable to remain. One must (or rather, one wishes to) create new forms, something that evil, grasping, if gifted Fokine has never dreamed of.[5]

Stravinsky's "we" is priceless. Who was he parroting—Diaghilev (already promoting Nijinsky as choreographic "creator") or (more likely) Benois? Still, in March 1912 he was still calling Fokine his collaborator, however reluctantly: "The only unpleasant thing" about the upcoming production of *The Rite,* he wrote to his mother, "is that it will have to be done by Fokine."[6] A letter to Benois, written

3. Letter of 3 November 1910; in IStrSM:449.
4. Letter of July 1911; in IStrSM:462.
5. Letter of 17 March 1912; in IStrSM:467–68.
6. Ibid., 467.

nine days later, reveals that the chief reason *The Rite* had to be postponed until the 1913 season was that Fokine was too busy with *Daphnis and Chloë*.[7]

In the end, what Stravinsky had dreaded came as a stroke of good fortune. *Daphnis,* which opened on 8 June 1912, was Fokine's last ballet for Diaghilev. The choreographer did go back to Telyakovsky for a while, but without *The Rite*. Paris was now irrevocably Stravinsky's base; neither the Russian stage nor the prospect of writing for Russian audiences attracted him. When Chaliapin tried to interest Stravinsky in a collaboration with Gorky on an opera about Vasiliy Buslayev, a Novgorod epic hero like Sadko, he got nowhere.[8]

But then, the Gorky project had involved an opera. The first sign of Stravinsky's overt estrangement from the milieu in which he had been reared involved the charged issue of opera versus ballet, on which Rimsky-Korsakov, as we have seen, entertained somewhat dogmatic and intransigent views. Unsurprisingly, the Rimsky-Korsakov clan viewed Stravinsky's new peer group with suspicion. Things came to something of a head—the first of many—when Stravinsky returned to Russia after the triumph of *Petrushka* and received a stern letter from Vladimir Rimsky-Korsakov, acting as a sort of family spokesman. The letter itself has not survived, but its contents may be easily deduced from Stravinsky's response, a massive rebuttal amounting to a veritable essay. In the most explicit terms, Stravinsky cast his lot with the Diaghilev venture and with its esthetic outlook—and, by implication, against that of the Rimsky-Korsakov heirs, to say nothing of his own father's legacy. Having named Benois as his mentor, he proceeded to give what amounted to a pithy précis of the latter's 1908 "Colloquy on Ballet." More ominously, he dared take a critical view of his former teacher's attitudes.

This letter was Igor Stravinsky's declaration of independence. Although couched in terms of endearment (its very length and vehemence testifying to Stravinsky's wish to persuade rather than alienate his antagonists), it was a gauntlet. The inevitable breach was under way.

Lengthy though it is, the letter demands citation practically in full, not only for the reason just given but also because it was Stravinsky's only extended *profession de foi* from the period of his early maturity. Indeed, it is the only major esthetic pronouncement Stravinsky ever made that was written neither through an intermediary nor as part of a public relations effort. The early part of the letter makes ref-

---

7. Letter of 26 March 1912; in Vershinina (ed.), "Pis'ma Stravinskogo Rerikhu," 63.

8. See Chaliapin's letter to Gorky from Milan, 25 March 1912: "I've been racking my brains about a composer for you! Glazunov will hardly bestir himself to write. Rachmaninoff, it seems to me, hasn't the temperament for it—he wouldn't take to Buslayev. There is a certain young composer—the son of the former artist Stravinsky. This young man has already written a thing or two, including, among other things, a ballet entitled *Petrushka*. This ballet was given with enormous success in Paris last year. I'm thinking of putting him in touch with you—first, of course, I'll put out a feeler and try to find out how well equipped this young man might be to take on something like Buslayev. The young fellow is now in Monte Carlo. I'll drop him a line and ask him, if he can, to come see me in Milan" (Grosheva [ed.], *Shalyapin* 1:393).

erence to two specific Diaghilev "crimes" that had aroused the Rimsky-Korsakovs' indignation: the 1909 *Cléopâtre*—in which Arensky's score had been replaced by a "salade russe" (as Nouvel sneeringly put it)[9] that included some music from Rimsky-Korsakov's *Mlada*—and the Bakst-Fokine *Shéhérazade* of 1910, which, by adapting Rimsky-Korsakov's score (minus the third movement) to a new and unforeseen scenario, had raised fundamental questions of artistic, and even legal, propriety.[10] Stravinsky answered these charges very much as a spokesman for the offending party.

Ustilug, 8/21 July 1911

Dear Volodya,

Forgive me in advance for the incoherence of this letter. I am very agitated by yours, which I was very happy to receive, but whose contents saddened me as much or more. It's not a matter of your attacks on Diaghilev—to that we're all accustomed, and it's no longer as sensitive a matter as it used to be. It's a much more serious matter that you raise—the thing we all serve together with Diaghilev, namely, the Ballet. But before I get to this, I cannot let the matter of Diaghilev go by altogether. I have said already more than once that there are deeds of Diaghilev's of which I cannot approve, like, for instance, the musical mishmash that goes by the name of *Cléopâtre*. I say this to everyone and I've said it to him more than once. But I should make it clear that it is the mixture of various authors' styles that I don't like. It's a failure from the musical standpoint. I would even rather have Arensky's worthless and stupid music all by itself. I have no objection in principle, as long as the music is good (and has integrity) and the choreographic realization shows talent. It does not offend my artistic sensibilities, which (I would like to suppose) are not in a state of decay. As regards an individual instance (like *Sheherazade*), where the subject of the choreographic composition does not correspond to the subject (if I may put it so) with which Nikolai Andreyevich prefaced the symphony, the situation is not really any different. The main thing here is not the subject, but the divine spectacle, which transports you utterly into the atmosphere of *Sheherazade*'s stupendous music. The only thing I regret is that not all four movements have been staged. This I told Diaghilev at the time, and it still disturbs me. Nor am I at all in agreement with Diaghilev in his overly blithe attitude toward cuts, just as I am not in agreement with [Eduard]

9. See Grigoriev, *Diaghilev Ballet*, 8.

10. A typescript draft for *Memories and Commentaries,* reproduced in P&D (pl. 1 facing p. 144), included the following sentence: ". . . but while [Mme Rimsky-Korsakov] attacked [Diaghilev's] production of *Sheherazade* she was delighted at the same time to receive very handsome royalties from it." The sentence was deleted in all editions of the published book. Rimsky-Korsakov's widow was only being loyal to her husband's views. A letter from the composer to his friend the Moscow hôtelier S. P. Belanovsky (8 January 1908) records his indignant reasons for avoiding the performances of Isadora Duncan: "Presumably she is very graceful, a splendid mime, Botticelli neck, etc.; but what repels me in her is that she foists her art upon . . . musical compositions which are dear to my heart and do not at all need her company, and whose authors had not counted upon it. How chagrined I should be if I learned that Miss Duncan dances and mimically explains, for instance, my *Sheherazade, Antar,* or Easter Overture! . . . When [miming] foists itself unbidden upon music, it only harms the latter by diverting attention from it" (Appendix to *My Musical Life,* 446). All in all, not so far from what a later Stravinsky might have said!

Nápravník and [Albert] Coates [the Mariyinsky conductors], who this year made a stupendous cut in the scene of the Tatar invasion in *Kitezh,* and had another cut in mind, which you all, it seems, stood firm against. However, these worthies have never been subjected to such insulting epithets as Diaghilev, who when all is said and done is doing something incomparably higher than they in artistic value—to this I can attest with complete impartiality[!]. Don't think I am just an infatuated yes-man—on the contrary, not a day goes by that I do not say something, argue, disagree, criticize. But that's one thing, and recognition of the significance of what is being created is another.

And now we come in earnest to the thing you are casting doubt upon. I mean the Ballet. Although you say that you are no enemy of ballet, later you claim that it is a "low form" of scenic art. At this everything became clear to me: from this phrase it is clear to me that you simply *do not like* ballet, and have no interest in it, that you do not attach any great significance to it. I will only say to you that it is just the opposite with me. I love ballet and am more interested in it than in anything else. And this is not just an idle enthusiasm, but a serious and profound enjoyment of scenic spectacle—of the art of animated form [*zhivaya plastika*]. And I am simply bewildered that you, who so loved the plastic arts, who took such an interest in painting and sculpture (that is, if you have not yet cooled toward them, too), pay so little attention to choreography—the third plastic art—and consider ballet to be a lower form than opera. If a Michelangelo were alive today, I thought, looking at his frescoes in the Sistine Chapel, the only thing his genius would recognize and accept would be the choreography that is being reborn today. Everything else that takes place on the stage he would doubtless call a miserable farce. For the only form of scenic art that sets itself, as its cornerstone, the *tasks of beauty,* and *nothing else,* is ballet. And the only goal Michelangelo pursued was visible beauty.

I admit I did not expect to hear such a thing from you. It saddens me terribly. It saddens me when people with whom I have been such close friends, as with you, feel completely the opposite from me. It is true that I, who am working in the choreographic sphere, have sensed the significance and the necessity of what I am doing (I am not talking only about music but about the entire work as a whole, since I am also the author of *Petrushka*'s libretto and did this work with the same love as your father, working on his operas), while you, on the one hand, see nothing but banal and even simply awful operatic productions and ugly ballets (though this year the divine *Carnaval* was presented [at the Mariyinsky]) and, on the other, out of your prejudice against Diaghilev, have not budged from your position, and, not recognizing any significance in choreography (for you have said that ballet is lower than opera, while for me all art is equal—there are not higher and lower arts, there are different forms of art—if you place one below another, it only proves that the plastic arts are less dear to you than another form of art—or else simply a thing you can do without), you dream only of artistic productions of existing operas, not giving any thought to the fact that opera is a spectacle, and a spectacle, at that, with an obligation to be artistic, and, consequently, as such, ought to have its own self-sufficient value—just as captivating gestures and movements in dance—which for some reason you place lower than recitative—are valuable, when they are created by the fantasy of a ballet master's talent, just as music, divorced from spectacle [is valuable]. These are not mere applied arts—it is a union of arts, the one strengthening and supplementing the other.

I would understand someone who opposed all unions as such: drama and music—opera, choreography and music—ballet. What can you do, it seems the fellow likes his art pure: music as music, plastic art as plastic art. But you I cannot understand, my dear, for you love the plastic arts, or always have up to now. I can understand Nikolai Andreyevich, who admitted himself that he was not "sensitive" (so what can you do—if he doesn't feel it, he doesn't feel it) to the plastic arts; but I don't understand in that case why his work took the form of opera, and sometimes even ballet, where music is deliberately united with other arts. I think that this came about not out of a lack of understanding or love for other arts, as much as it did from an insufficient immersion in or acquaintance with them. Probably it's the same with you, who have voiced this terrible heresy about "lower forms" (don't be angry at me for my brusque tone—it's not as brusque as it seems). I think that if you would attend the ballet regularly (artistic ballet, of course), you would see that this "lower form" brings you incomparably more artistic joy than any operatic performance (even the operas with your favorite music), a joy I have been experiencing now for over a year and which I would so like to infect you all with and share with you. It is the joy of discovering a whole new continent. Its development will take lots of work—there's much in store!

Well, there you have what I think about ballet, being completely in agreement with Benois and finding nothing wrong with his enthusiasm for ballet. And you are wrong to try to tear me away from Benois's sphere of influence. He is a man of rare refinement, keen to the point of clairvoyance not only with respect to the plastic arts, but also to music. Of all the artists whom by now I have had occasion to see and to meet, he is the most sensitive to music, not to mention the fact that he knows and understands it no less well than an educated professional musician. If his opinions about music are not to your taste, that does not necessarily mean that he is not competent in that area. His assertion that Diaghilev is a singer and composer should be understood simply in terms of his involvement with singing and composition; for he has studied both seriously, though in neither did he show any great abilities.[11]

Stravinsky went on to dismiss the critics (excepting Alfred Bruneau) out of hand, to assure Vladimir of Diaghilev's respect for Nikolai Rimsky-Korsakov (citing the production in 1911 of the underwater scene from *Sadko*), and to make the complaints about Fokine we have already sampled. The letter ends affectionately, as Russian letters do, with a "kiss," and with the exhortation that Vladimir "believe in my sincere friendship." But the letter contains the seeds of the dissolution of that friendship. All at once the astonishing hostility toward *Petrushka* that came pouring out of Andrey Rimsky-Korsakov's review becomes comprehensible.

Stravinsky's letters to the Rimsky-Korsakov brothers and to Steinberg maintained a fraternal and confiding tone through the period of *The Rite* and even (in the case of Steinberg) a little beyond. Increasingly present between the lines, however, is an avuncular tone that must have rankled, and comments on the Russian

11. IStrSM:459–62. Addenda made by Stravinsky in the form of footnotes have been incorporated into the text.

scene that could only have inspired feelings of inferiority and betrayal. Here, for example, is how Stravinsky informed Andrey of his plan to spend the winter of 1911–12 (when he would compose *The Rite*) in Switzerland: "You know, my dear, it's better there not just for my family but for me as well. I have to build up my strength of spirit. At home I'd become a regular neurasthenic."[12] To a September letter from Andrey that was evidently similar to the one from Vladimir which he had answered at such length in July, Stravinsky would spare only a few blithe and patronizing lines in reply: "What could be better and more wonderful than the development of established artistic forms? Only one thing—the creation of new forms. Insofar as I can see, you are sticking to the former; but since I cannot see you now, I cannot swear that you are not coming round, or perhaps have even come round, to the latter, not in words or thought (of which nobody has enough) but in feeling (of which everyone possesses all he needs). Right or wrong? Surely right! Don't keep yourself from feeling!"[13]

By the time Stravinsky wrote to Steinberg with news of the *Rite* première, wishing his old walled-in rival "the same creative ebullience," the irony can hardly be mistaken, especially since more than a year earlier Stravinsky had written Calvocoressi that Steinberg was "plunged totally into academicism," that in his last few letters he "declares that he understands nothing in my most recent compositions," ending with the query, "Is there still a chance of saving him?"[14]

The earliest letters from Steinberg in the Stravinsky Archive date from October 1912, so Stravinsky's report to Calvocoressi cannot be directly verified. But the surviving letters amply confirm the esthetic rift that had opened up between them. Early in 1913, for example, Stravinsky wrote to his teacher's son-in-law:

> Have you been to *Elektra*? [Strauss's opera had premièred at the Mariyinsky in February 1913 (o.s.) under Coates, in a translation by Kuzmin.] I've gone twice [in London] and am completely enraptured. This is his best composition. Let them speak of Strauss's perpetual vulgarities—to this I will say only that, in the

12. Letter of 8 August 1911; in IStrSM:463.

13. Letter of 24 September 1911; in IStrSM:464. In this letter Stravinsky even "assigns" Andrey some reading in the form of several articles by the German dramaturg Georg Fuchs (1868–1949), a strong proponent of choreographic adaptations à la Duncan.

14. Letter of 11 April 1912; in SelCorrII:98. The earliest surviving attestation to incipient esthetic contention between Stravinsky and Steinberg is a page bearing an eleven-bar fragment from an early, harmonically somewhat more recondite version of the "Ronde des Princesses" from *Firebird* (now at the State Institute of Theater, Music, and Cinematography in St. Petersburg), copied out in Stravinsky's hand and originally presented to Steinberg with the following friendly yet ironic inscription: "Max! Take this as a souvenir of the ballet which you still look upon (or so it seems to me) as a series of curiosities and 'Kunststück's.' Yours, Igor Stravinsky, 5 XII 1909." The leaf is printed in facsimile and thoroughly described in Abram Klimovitsky, "Ob odnom neizvestnom avtografe I. Stravinskogo (k probleme tvorcheskogo formirovaniya kompozitora)," in the yearbook of the Soviet Academy of Sciences, *Pamyatniki kul'turï: Novïye otkrïtiya* for 1986 (Leningrad: Nauka, 1987), 227–36. The contention that his musical explorations and innovations were just a bag of "clever tricks" (*Kunststücke*) was the standard anti-Stravinskian line in Russia in the period of the composer's first fame, and what had evidently started out as affectionate joshing among friends eventually reached a very public and wounding pitch with the publication of Andrey Rimsky-Korsakov's all-out attacks.

first place, if you penetrate more deeply into German art you'll see that they all suffer from this, and in the second place, time will succeed in smoothing over the lapses of taste that shock contemporaries and will reveal the work in its true light. Strauss's *Elektra* is a stupendous piece!!![15]

To which Steinberg replied (as Stravinsky must surely have expected) in terms dutifully paraphrased from what he remembered of Rimsky-Korsakov's kneejerk Straussophobia, adding for good measure his impressions of Schoenberg (whom he had met at the time of the *Pelléas* performance in December 1912):

> I heard *Elektra* at the dress rehearsal. I completely disagree with your opinion of it. I hate Strauss with all my heart. Your words, that banality is a general trait of German music, I regard as profoundly unjustified and insulting to German music, which for all its present insignificance (please don't curse me—Schoenberg is a very nice and talented man) has a transcendently brilliant past. I am completely at a loss to understand how *you* can be so enthusiastic—it must be hypnosis![16]

As for *The Rite* itself, of which Steinberg had heard the first tableau during Stravinsky's visit to St. Petersburg in September 1912, he admitted (in a postscript to his letter of 2 October):

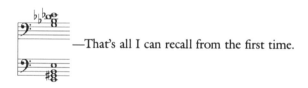

—That's all I can recall from the first time.

Stravinsky's letter to Steinberg of 16/29 July 1913 contains another *Rite*-related postscript: "Just go on playing [it]—I'm sure you'll come to feel this piece with time. Creating it gave me many of my happiest hours. And you I consider to be a man of sensitivity. Just approach this piece with an open heart. I swear to God, it's not that hard."[17] This letter has been taken as evidence of Stravinsky's candor and continued open-hearted good will toward the companions of his youth.[18] On the contrary, taken in context it can only be regarded as a taunt. In any case, it was a fruitless plea. Steinberg's response did not come until February 1914, after the Russian première, in yet another postscript: "About *The Rite of Spring* I won't write, for about this we have to talk, and talk at length."[19]

15. Letter of 17 February/2 March 1913; in IStrSM:471.
16. Letter of 4 April 1913, in the Stravinsky Archive, paraphrased in part in SelCorrI:44n.
17. IStrSM:474.
18. See Simon Karlinsky, "A Pocket Full of Buttered Figs," *Times Literary Supplement,* 5 July 1985.
19. Postcard of 18 February 1914, in the Stravinsky Archive.

They never had the talk, for with this postcard the Stravinsky-Steinberg correspondence came to an end. The only remaining item from Steinberg in the archive is poignant, a note dashed off in Paris on 16 June 1925: "Igor Fyodorovich! It is extremely deplorable that you have not found time to see me. I want very much to hear and see the ballets 'Pulcinella' and 'Chant du Rossignol.' If you can be of assistance in this I would be very glad. I am not in a position to pay the present ticket prices. My address: 7, rue Leclerc, Paris XIV chez Mme St. Choupak (métro St. Jacques). Best wishes, M. Steinberg."[20]

With Andrey Rimsky-Korsakov correspondence had broken off earlier; their friendship did not survive Andrey's attack on *Petrushka*.[21] As in the case of Steinberg, there was a poignant echo. The Stravinsky Archive preserves a letter from Andrey dated 14 January 1914, in which he apologizes to his old friend for not having sent news earlier about his marriage, and adds the following: "Permit me to make a confession to you: for me, neither our artistic differences nor the distance that separates us have extinguished my feelings of friendship toward you. Perhaps this feeling is by now an illusion, but be assured that I would give much even now for a chance to talk quietly and amicably with you." Stravinsky's "Dear John" reply is a tour de force of diplomatic yet decisive rejection:

Dear Andrey,
    We sincerely congratulate you and your wife and wish you great and long-lasting happiness in your life together. I write you this with all my heart, for I believe in the sincerity of your confession and would also not like to see our friendship become, as you say, an illusion. I am only afraid that this might happen in spite of us by virtue of the difference in our outlooks in the realm of art or by virtue of the ever more infrequent and remote contact between us. In any case, neither your venomous and thunderous writings about my works, nor your protests against my "anti-artistic" acts, ought, after your letter (whose sincerity I have no right to doubt) ever alter our good and amicable relations.
    I cannot write much, for right now I have something else on my mind—our daughter Milena was born not long ago. The delivery went satisfactorily, but afterwards, for the last twenty days and more, my wife's temperature has been slowly

20. Stravinsky's heartless reference to this episode (M&C:54/56) erroneously places it in the year 1924. His niece Tatyana Yuryevna Stravinskaya, who stayed with the composer's family in Nice from March 1925 to February 1926, corroborates the correct date in a letter she wrote home to her parents in Leningrad on 25 July 1925: "Uncle has asked me to write you the following. While he was in Paris, he was much annoyed by a relative of the Korsakovs'—Steinberg. Uncle does not like him. At first Uncle delicately avoided him, then had to resort to hints, but the latter, intentionally or not, failed to understand. Finally Uncle left Paris, but Steinberg would not leave him alone and kept writing letters. In the last of them he informed Uncle that he was going back to Piter [the old Russian nickname for St. Petersburg] and asked if he had anything to send his brother. Uncle doesn't want to have anything to do with him and asked me to warn you in case he comes to you and gives you his side of the story" (Stravinskaya, *O Stravinskom i yego blizkikh,* 63).

21. The last letter from Stravinsky to his old friend is dated 23 October/5 November 1912; see IStrSM:469.

but steadily rising. The doctors have diagnosed tuberculosis, aggravated by pleurisy. I am going through a hard time.

I embrace you. Be well, and do let us hear from you if only once in a while.

Yours, Igor Stravinsky[22]

THE METEOR TAKES OFF

The context into which all these letters have to be placed for proper evaluation includes—besides our privileged knowledge, going back to Chapter 6, of Stravinsky's long-breeding envy and *Schadenfreude*—a number of public and self-aggrandizing attacks on musical Russia and its eminent representatives that appeared in interviews Stravinsky gave both at home and abroad. These could not have failed to color the way in which the pro forma cordiality of his letters impressed their recipients.

An article on Stravinsky by Émile Vuillermoz, published in Paris early in 1912, was obviously an interview in disguise: it contained a number of inflammatory remarks that could only have originated with the composer. His resentment of the Belyayevets/Conservatory milieu boils over in Vuillermoz's account of the reception accorded the *"Funerary Chant* performed at the Belyayev Concerts, much to the despair of Rimsky's official pupils, jealous to see prolonged, as it were from beyond the grave, an artistic intimacy at which they had long taken umbrage." What did Andrey Rimsky-Korsakov or Maximilian Steinberg make of that? Or of this: "Already covertly opposed by certain of his compatriots, the young composer is overjoyed to have found in Paris the active support and enlightened dedication that alone are capable of encouraging him effectively on his audacious way."[23] Stravinsky took pains to present himself to all his French friends as one who suffered persecution at home. To Calvocoressi he sent a clipping (Fig. 13.1) from the *Peterburgskaya gazeta* (3 December 1911) in which Nikolai Bernstein tore mercilessly into a Siloti program that included the Russian première of a suite from *Daphnis et Chloë,* and added in the margin: "And after all this Mr. Bernstein still

22. Stravinsky Archive, "Copie de lettres," 25. The "anti-artistic acts" by now included Diaghilev's production of *Khovanshchina,* about which see the next chapter. The one remaining item from Andrey Rimsky-Korsakov in the archive is an invitation, sent from Leningrad on 15 June 1932, to contribute to a memorial volume for the twenty-fifth anniversary of Nikolai Rimsky-Korsakov's death (contributions were also solicited from such other émigrés and foreigners as Glazunov, Albert Coates, Osip Gabrilowitsch, Respighi, Chaliapin, and Monteux). The letter is written in French and opens with the salutation "Cher Maître," though it rather incongruously maintains the familiar second person singular. It ends, "Reçois, cher Maître, les cordiales et respectueuses salutations de ton fidèle ami et sincère admirateur."

23. "... *Chant funèbre* exécuté aux Concerts Bélaieff, au grand désespoir des élèves officiels de Rimsky, jaloux de voir se prolonger avec leur maître, au delà du tombeau, une intimité artistique dont ils prenaient depuis longtemps ombrage. . . . Déjà sournoisement combattu par certains de ses compatriotes, le jeune compositeur se félicite d'avoir trouvé à Paris les seules sympathies actives et les seuls enthousiasmes éclairés susceptibles de l'encourager efficacement dans son audacieuse carrière" (Vuillermoz, "Strawinsky," 18, 20).

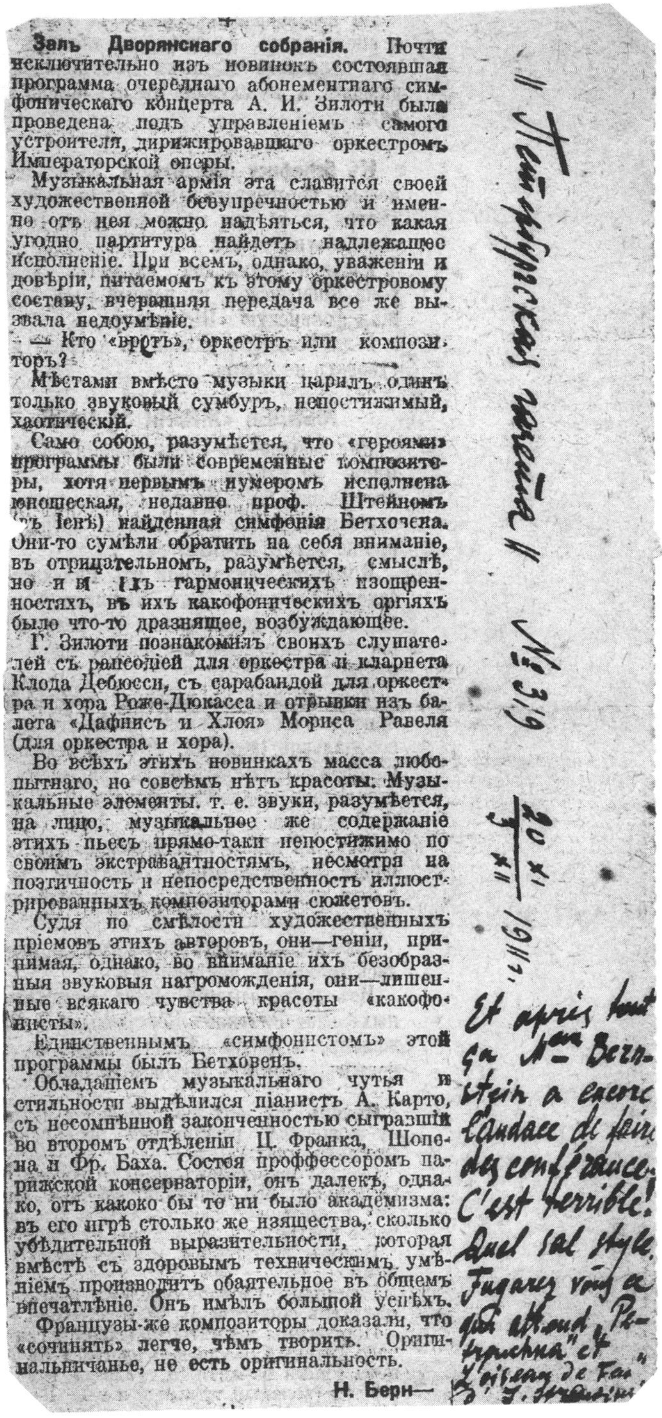

Залъ Дворянскаго собранія. Почти исключительно изъ новинокъ состоявшая программа очереднаго абонементнаго симфоническаго концерта А. И. Зилоти была проведена подъ управленіемъ самого устроителя, дирижировавшаго оркестромъ Императорской оперы.

Музыкальная армія эта славится своей художественной безупречностью и именно отъ нея можно надѣяться, что какая угодно партитура найдетъ надлежащее исполненіе. При всемъ, однако, уваженіи и довѣріи, питаемомъ къ этому оркестровому составу, вчерашняя передача все же вызвала недоумѣніе.

— Кто «вретъ», оркестръ или композиторъ?

Мѣстами вмѣсто музыки царилъ одинъ только звуковый сумбуръ, непостижимый, хаотическій.

Само собою, разумѣется, что «героями» программы были современные композиторы, хотя первымъ нумеромъ исполнена юношеская, недавно проф. Штейномъ (въ Іенѣ) найденная симфонія Бетховена. Они-то сумѣли обратить на себя вниманіе, въ отрицательномъ, разумѣется, смыслѣ, но и в[ъ] [и]хъ гармоническихъ изощренностяхъ, въ ихъ какофоническихъ оргіяхъ было что-то дразнящее, возбуждающее.

Г. Зилоти познакомилъ своихъ слушателей съ рапсодіей для оркестра и кларнета Клода Дебюсси, съ сарабандой для оркестра и хора Роже-Дюкасса и отрывки изъ балета «Дафнисъ и Хлоя» Мориса Равеля (для оркестра и хора).

Во всѣхъ этихъ новинкахъ масса любопытнаго, но совсѣмъ нѣтъ красоты. Музыкальные элементы. т. е. звуки, разумѣется, на лицо, музыкальное же содержаніе этихъ пьесъ прямо-таки непостижимо по своимъ экстравагантностямъ, несмотря на поэтичность и непосредственность иллюстрированныхъ композиторами сюжетовъ.

Судя по смѣлости художественныхъ пріемовъ этихъ авторовъ, они—геніи, принимая, однако, во вниманіе ихъ безобразныя звуковыя нагроможденія, они—лишенные всякаго чувства красоты «какофонисты».

Единственнымъ «симфонистомъ» этой программы былъ Бетховенъ.

Обладаніемъ музыкальнаго чутья и стильности выдѣлился піанистъ А. Карто, съ несомнѣнной законченностью сыгравшій во второмъ отдѣленіи Ц. Франка, Шопена и Фр. Баха. Состоя проффессоромъ парижской консерваторіи, онъ далекъ, однако, отъ какоко бы то ни было академизма: въ его игрѣ столько же изящества, сколько убѣдительной выразительности, которая вмѣстѣ съ здоровымъ техническимъ умѣніемъ производитъ обаятельное въ общемъ впечатлѣніе. Онъ имѣлъ большой успѣхъ.

Французы-же композиторы доказали, что «сочинять» легче, чѣмъ творить. Оригинальничанье, не есть оригинальность.

Н. Берн—

FIG. 13.1. Igor Stravinsky, note to Michel Calvocoressi on a review of a Siloti concert by Nikolai Bernshteyn, clipped from the *Peterburgskaya gazeta*. The program, mainly Russian premières, consisted of the "Jena" Symphony, then attributed to Beethoven; Debussy's Rhapsody for Clarinet and Orchestra; a sarabande by Roger-Ducasse; and excerpts from Ravel's *Daphnis et Chloë*. (The second half featured Alfred Cortot in works by Franck, Chopin, and Friedemann Bach.) The verdict on the modern works: "To judge by the audacity of their artistic methods these authors are geniuses; if, however, their monstrous sonic overloading is taken into account, they are 'cacophonists' devoid of all sense of beauty."

has the nerve to give lectures! It's appalling! What foul style! Just imagine what awaits *Petrushka* and *The Firebird* by I. Stravinsky."[24]

Many of the remarks in Vuillermoz's article were mirrored practically word for word in an interview Stravinsky gave the London *Daily Mail* on 13 February 1913: "Russian musical life is at present stagnant. They cannot stand me there. 'Petrushka' was performed at St. Petersburg the same day as here, and I see the newspapers are now all comparing my work with the smashing of crockery. . . . I find my only kindred spirits in France. France possesses in Debussy, Ravel, and Florent Schmitt the foremost creative musicians of the day." It might be thought that this sally was inspired by Andrey Rimsky-Korsakov's attack on *Petrushka,* but practically the same sentiments can be found in a letter from Stravinsky to Schmitt, written at Ustilug the previous September. Its tone is a heady mixture of justifiable resentment and swaggering self-advertisement:

> You realize of course that I am worth *nothing at all* in my admirable country. Even M. Siloti, who began by promoting me, has ended up declaring that my music has not produced the wished-for success, and so he has recommended that I compose something more digestible.
>
> . . . Otherwise the critics annoyed by my success abroad have declared that I have no originality, that I am not at the head of the movement (that's a low blow) but just one of those lined up behind the snob theorizers, and all this after hearing the works before *Petrushka* (which hasn't even been played at a concert in Russia).[25]

Just over a week later, Stravinsky was in St. Petersburg en route to Clarens (it would be his last visit to his native city until 1962). During this brief stopover he gave what might well be regarded as the first "typical" Stravinsky interview: arch, startling, slippery as to facts but unerring as to effect. The anonymous reviewer, who signed himself "Teatral" ("Old Theater Hand"), had come to visit Stravinsky at his family apartment, 66 Kryukov Canal. The interview is notable for the frankness with which "Teatral" seized the bull by the horns on a number of sensitive points relating to Stravinsky's position in Russian musical life, and for the disingenuousness with which Stravinsky described *The Rite,* launching, as it were, the

24. "Et après tout ça M. Bernstein a encore l'audace de faire des conférence[s]. C'est terrible! Quel sal style. Figurez vous ce qui attend 'Pétrouchka' et 'L'oiseau de Feu' d'I. Strawinski" (Collection of the author). Stravinsky's French at this point was quite insecure, as was even his command of the Roman alphabet. In the hastily scribbled note Russian letters are inadvertently substituted for Roman.

25. "Vous savez bien que je n'ai *aucune valeur* dans mon admirable pays. Monsieur Ziloti même qui commençait par me protéger a fini par déclarer que ma musique n'avait pas le succès voulu, c'est pourquoi il m'a proposé de composer une musique plus digestible. . . . D'autre part, des critiques ennuyés par mon succès en étranger me déclarent sans originalité, que je ne suis pas dans la tête du mouvement (c'est malin) mais au contraire que je me promène dans la queue des théories snobistes, et tout cela après avoir entendu les oeuvres qui précèdent *Pétrouchka* (qui n'a pas été joué encore en Russie même au concert)." The letter is given both in facsimile (first page) and in printed form in Lesure (ed.), *Stravinsky: la carrière européenne,* 19.

FIG. 13.2. "'Harum-Scarum,' A New Opera-Ballet-Cacophony by Mr Stravinsky": caricature in the *Peterburgskaya gazeta*, no. 276 (10 October 1912), evidently in response to Stravinsky's interview in the same paper two weeks earlier.

durable myth of its "abstract" conception. Most pertinent of all is the haughtiness toward his provincial homeland that suffuses Stravinsky's every word:

A famous Russian composer has come to St. Petersburg. Strange as it seems, he is far more famous abroad than he is at home, in his own country.

I am speaking of I. F. Stravinsky, son of the late singer, who has attracted the attention of all Europe with his music to the ballets *The Firebird* and *Petrushka*, which have been put on by S. P. Diaghilev.

Mr. Stravinsky looks to be a complete youth, modest, even bashful. . . .

Q: How do you explain the fact that your ballets are not given on the Imperial stage, but only on Diaghilev's?

A: By the fact that the directorate of the Imperial Theaters has never so much as approached me.

As far as *The Firebird* and *Petrushka* are concerned, they are Diaghilev's property for five years from the date of the first performance. Right now I am composing, together with the painter N. K. Rezin [*sic*], a third piece, entitled *The Rite of Spring*. Like everything I write, this is not a ballet, but simply a fantasia in two parts, like two movements of a symphony. The subject is taken from an indefinite ancient period. The first part is called "The Kiss of the Earth," the second, "The Great Sacrifice."[26]

This piece will be staged in Paris, in Gabriel Astruc's new theater on the Champs Élysées. In the construction of this theater, by the way, such outstanding artists as Maurice Denis and [Henri] Bourdelle have taken part. The former painted the ceilings, the latter did all the sculptural adornments. Right now I'm on my way to Switzerland to finish the work. I have come to St. Petersburg for only a few days, in order to see a few necessary people. At present, I, along with Diaghilev himself and the rest of the staff of the Diaghilev enterprise, am on vacation. But in November we will begin touring again, this time including Germany.[27]

Q: They say that your *Firebird* had its greatest success in London.

A: It is indelicate to speak of one's own successes, but the English press was very well disposed to me indeed. It's not the kind of "press success" you get in Paris. French critics are more frivolous.

Q: Why don't you write operas?

A: I don't know whether you recall, but I did write music to Andersen's famous tale "The Nightingale." I finished only one part and then got involved with other things. The first scene depicted a forest by the seashore, there was a little landscape music, solos, choruses. I published[!] this piece as a separate number for concert performance. But opera does not attract me at all. What interests me is choreographic drama, the only form in which I see any movement forward, without trying to foretell its future direction. Opera is falsehood pretending to be truth, while I need falsehood that pretends to falsehood. Opera is a competition with nature.[28]

Q: What is your opinion of the artists who have taken part in your ballets?

A: Both Karsavina [who, incidentally, was living at the time in the apartment immediately above the one in which this interview was being conducted] and Nijinsky were at the very pinnacle of their calling. But besides Karsavina I must mention Nijinskaya, the sister of the famous *danseur*, who has had colossal successes since she left the Imperial stage. Hers is a very great talent; she is an en-

---

26. Cf. the description given in another St. Petersburg interview, published two days earlier: "I have completed a mysterium entitled 'Le Sacre du Printemps'... There is practically no plot to it, there is only a series of dances or action in dance. How do I conceive of classical ballet at present? In general, I am an adherent of so-called choreodrama, which is bound to replace the contemporary type of ballet" (Dvinsky, "U Igorya Stravinskogo," 5; quoted in Krasovskaya, *Russkiy baletnïy teatr* 1:432).

27. Stravinsky gave another interviewer a more complete itinerary for a story published on the same day as the one being quoted in full: "No later than this coming winter, his aforementioned ballets [*Firebird* and *Petrushka*] will be mounted (in December) in the Kroll Theater in Berlin, following which they will make the rounds of such major German cities as Munich, Dresden, Leipzig, and others, and will then be given in Vienna, Budapest, and, in January, on the stage of the Covent Garden Theater in London" (*Peterburgskiy listok*, 27 September 1912; the scrapbook page that contains this clipping is photographed and inset as an illustration in *Expositions and Developments*, following p. 72/32). The interviewer goes on to make a reasonable, but in retrospect ironic, surmise about *The Rite of Spring*: "It will be put on first in Paris, and then, surely, will go from there to other big European stages as well."

28. Cf. the February 1913 *Daily Mail* interview: "I dislike opera. Music can be married to gesture or to words—not to both without bigamy. That is why the artistic basis of opera is wrong and why Wagner sounds at his best in the concert-room. In any case, opera is a backwater. What operas have been written since 'Parsifal'? Only two that count—'Elektra' and Debussy's 'Pelleas.'" These pronouncements have a particularly ironic ring in view of the opinion Derzhanovsky had expressed in print only a month before Stravinsky's last St. Petersburg visit, on the occasion of the Moscow première of the *Firebird* suite: "Russian opera, so pitifully muted since the death of Rimsky-Korsakov, must now pin its hopes on Stravinsky" ("Florestan," "Igor' Stravinskiy [k segodnyashnemu konzertu]," *Utro Rossii*, 24 August 1912).

chanting ballerina, full worthy of her brother. When she and her brother dance together, everyone else fades.... [N.B.: At the time of the interview, Nijinska was slated to dance the Chosen One in *The Rite,* but she had to surrender the role to Maria Piltz when she became pregnant.]

Q: But in St. Petersburg, on the Imperial stage, wasn't she just "one of the crowd"?

A: Yes, they didn't know how to appreciate her in St. Petersburg. That, by the way, is an old story....[29]

"Modest and bashful," indeed. Stravinsky was playing the role of a Diaghilev press agent on his own behalf, meanwhile throwing down gauntlet after gauntlet, recklessly telling a representative of the Russian musical establishment that Russia was now too small and provincial a pond for a big fish like himself.

An astonishing illustration of Stravinsky's precocious mastery of the art of *faire réclame*—no doubt picked up from Diaghilev's consummate example—is the way he managed to turn into one of the most durable legends of his early career what was in actuality a near fiasco he experienced with *Petrushka* in Vienna during the first week of 1913. The incident has been immortalized in *Chroniques de ma vie,* where we may still read of the Imperial Opera House Orchestra's "open sabotage at rehearsals and the audible utterance of such coarse remarks as '*schmutzige Musik.*'"[30] Serge Grigoriev's memoirs confirm and amplify the account: in his version, the musicians "declared they would not play it; it should receive no hearing, they said, within the sacred walls of the Vienna Opera! . . . We managed indeed to perform *Petrushka,* but only twice; and on each occasion the players duly tried their hand at sabotage."[31] It so happened that the incident was reported in the St. Petersburg press on the very day of the Russian (concert) première of *Petrushka* (11/24 January 1913)—evidently a publicity "plant" engineered by or on behalf of Koussevitzky. This version of the story, printed immediately after the fact, puts rather a different light on the circumstances that have been related and recycled in the Stravinsky literature now for over half a century:

29. "Teatral," "U kompozitora I. F. Stravinskogo," *Peterburgskaya gazeta,* 27 September 1912. In his last remark Stravinsky alludes to a controversy of long standing, between adherents of the Ballets Russes and those of the Imperial Theaters, as to which organization could truly claim to represent Russian art. Cf. these remarks by Jacques-Émile Blanche: "Those who have lived in St. Petersburg, travellers and diplomats, scorn our admiration for this phalanx of creators and interpreters [i.e., the Ballets Russes]. They stop our talk with this sentence: 'If you only knew what went on there, if you went to the opera, if you knew the Imperial Theaters and their companies, you would understand how you are being fooled; you are being given in Paris what Russia would not take.' I know a number of Russians, well respected in their colony and in the diplomatic world, who pale with rage whenever an avalanche of flowers falls at the feet of Karsavina, Nijinsky or Bakst. It would be analogous to the situation if you maintained in St. Petersburg aristocratic circles that our French expositions organized by true connoisseurs and full of Degas, Manet, Renoir and Cézanne were, far more than the Official Salons, representative of the creative force in France" ("Un bilan artistique de 1913," *Revue de Paris,* 1 December 1913; quoted in Bullard, "First Performance," 2:320). The idea of this sarcastic passage is that the Ballets Russes were not "representative" of Russian art, but far better than that.

30. *An Autobiography,* 44.

31. Grigoriev, *Diaghilev Ballet,* 78.

INCIDENT BETWEEN RUSSIAN COMPOSER
AND ROYAL VIENNA ORCHESTRA

Letters have been received from the artists of Diaghilev's troupe with information about a major incident that took place in Vienna between the orchestra of the Royal Opera there and the composer Stravinsky. When rehearsals of Stravinsky's ballet *Petrushka* began, the composer was dissatisfied with the sonority of the Vienna orchestra, and demanded that its complement be augmented. This demand of Mr. Stravinsky somehow offended the orchestra, who let it be known that they played even Wagner with their usual complement, and that no one had ever said that the Vienna Orchestra sounded bad, and that therefore under no circumstances would they agree to augment it. When Stravinsky continued to insist on his demand, all the players got up and left the rehearsal and refused to play *Petrushka*. S. P. Diaghilev managed with difficulty to smooth over the incident, but the augmentation of the orchestra even so was not achieved.[32]

Stravinsky seems to have realized the publicity value of this "incident." He wrote a letter to Florent Schmitt immediately upon his return to Switzerland: "I've just come from Vienna where the 'wonderful' orchestra of the Opernhaus sabotaged my *Petrushka*. They said such ugly, dirty music could not be played any better. You cannot imagine the insults and injuries the orchestra inflicted on me." Schmitt promptly had the letter printed.[33] The next month, Stravinsky embroidered shamelessly to his *Daily Mail* interviewer: "And what of Austria? The Viennese are barbarians. Their orchestral musicians could not play my 'Petrushka.' They hardly know Debussy there, and they chased Schönberg away to Berlin. Now Schönberg is one of the greatest creative spirits of our era. . . ."

Schoenberg, Debussy, and me. That Stravinsky could parlay the Vienna story into such a linkage of names is a testimonial to his burgeoning genius for self-promotion, even as the facts of the incident testify to the progress of the "swelled head" first noted by Mme Siloti back in 1910. Another linkage of names must have struck the Rimsky-Korsakov epigones as a particular affront, when the *RMG* came out with a special issue on 20 January 1913 devoted to "Contemporary Composers," with feature articles on Nikolai Medtner, Igor Stravinsky, and . . . Richard Strauss.

Indeed, to scan the *RMG* in the period 1910 to 1914 is to watch Stravinsky take off as if catapulted from his earlier "walled-in" milieu, which continued as before to maintain its plodding round, but only half-heartedly in the absence of its old *spiritus rector*. Reports of the Belyayev Concerts continue as before—the same poor attendance, the same listless performances, the same dull "novelties." Eventually

---

32. *Peterburgskaya gazeta*, 11/24 January 1913.
33. "J'arrive de Vienne où le 'fameux' orchestre de l'Opernhaus a saboté mon *Pétrouchka*. On a déclaré qu'une aussi laide et sale musique ne pouvait se jouer mieux. Vous ne vous figurez pas les ennuis et les injures que l'orchestre m'a fait subir" ("Les concerts," *France*, 21 January 1913; clipping in the Stravinsky Archive, Scrapbook 1912–14).

Противники героя (Heldnleben)
карр. Дж. Фрисландера.

Цѣна 20 коп.

F I G . 13.3a.   A special issue of *Russkaya muzikal'naya gazeta* (20 January 1913):
"Contemporary Composers N. Medtner, Igor Stravinsky, Rich. Strauss."

Игорь Стравинскій.

Игорь Стравинскій—блестящій талантъ, который заставилъ о себѣ говорить Западную Европу (преимущественно Францію) посѣщеніе въ 3—4 года. Тотъ фактъ, что Стравинскаго сначала удивила и озинала вся Франція, а потомъ уже собирается узнавать и Россія—нѣсупливитель, такъ какъ и въ наши дни не бываетъ пророка въ отечествѣ своемъ.

Игорь Стравинскій—сынъ знаменитаго, въ свое время, артиста Маріинской сцены, (Эстора Игнатьевича Стравинскаго (1843—1902)— родилса 5 іюня 1882 года въ Оранибаумѣ. Наслѣдственность, вѣроятно, сыграла не малую роль во взнощеніи молодого музыканта къ музыкѣ, и уже 9 лѣтъ онъ усердно занимается игрой на роялѣ. Въ 1902 году—встрѣча за границей съ Н. А. Римскимъ-Корсаковымъ—и перестройка жизни по новому плану: Стравинскій становится

Игорь Стравинскій

ученикомъ геніальнаго мастера, оказавшаго большое вліяніе на жизнь. Неустанный трудъ (между прочимъ, за это время Стравинскій сдѣлалъ ф-пі. переложеніе «Панъ-Воевода» Р-Корсакова) природное чутье и талантъ вырабатываютъ изъ ученика мастера, и уже въ 1907 г. онъ пишетъ свои первые Симфонію (не изданную) и предстоитъ свиту для голоса и фп. на текстъ Пушкина «Фавнъ и Пастушка».

Въ 1908 г. появляются: «Фантастическое скерцо», «Фейерверкъ» (фантазія для оркестра), «Погребальная пѣснь» (посвященная памяти Р-Корсакова) и также издаются четыре ф-пі. этюда, два романса («Весна—монастырская» и «Росянка—хлыстовская») и

«Pastorale для голоса и ф-пі. Въ слѣдующемъ 1909—«Сцена изъ сказки Андерсена «Соловей (для соло, хора и оркестра), и въ 1910-мъ 1911 выходятъ въ свѣтъ его балеты: «Жаръ-Птица» (сказка-балетъ) и «Петрушка» (почти въ тѣ же самые въ 4-хъ картинахъ).Послѣдніе произведенія Стравинскаго за 1911—12 г.: два пѣсни «Незабудочка» и «Голубь», кантата для хора и оркестра «Звѣздоликій» и хоородрама «Весна Священная» въ 2-хъ частяхъ.

«Жаръ-Птица»—балетъ впервые поставленъ въ парижской Большой оперѣ 25 іюня 1910 г.—декораціи Головина, костюмы по рисункамъ Бакста и Головина. Балетъ «Петрушка» поставленъ, впервые въ парижскомъ театрѣ Chatelet 13 іюня 1911 г.; декораціи и костюмы Алекс. Бенуа.

Каждое значительное явленіе искусства нельзя разсматривать, какъ нѣчто самостоятельное, явившееся само по себѣ,—напротивъ, такое явленіе имѣетъ всегда корни въ прошломъ, пуская новые молодые побѣги въ грядущее.

И талантъ Игоря Стравинскаго преврано подтверждаетъ эту мысль. Мусоргскій и Р.-Корсаковъ—духовное воспріемники его.

У перваго онъ научился правдивому, искреннему, живому языку; у второго—первоклассному мастерству, стройности, четкости и выразительности рисунка. Художественный тактъ, чувство жѣра, во-время «останавливать» поетъ разгорячённой фантазіи,—создавая изящными границы прекраснаго и прекрасному изящными беспрепятственно въ сказочный міръ, («Жаръ-Птица), а нужная для этого сосредоточенная углубенность и объективность взаимовозможность отразить въ музыкальныхъ образахъ всю плѣнительную роскошь, нежскорную фантастику и трепетную мистику сказочнаго эпоса. Вѣрнымъ, рѣзкимъ подчасъ, взмахомъ своего рѣзца высѣкаетъ Стравинскій свои дидактиче-

---

скіе контуры, они, быть можетъ, и угловаты, и недостаточно гладко этипоированы, но суть въ этомъ, да вѣдь и скалы, вымысать народный,—такова же—причудливая, неровная.

Другая сторона дарованія Стравинскаго— жуткій, подчасъ странный реализмъ, страшный по своей безпощадности, какъ бы отпарзающій завѣсу съ лица и души человѣческой («Петрушка). Какъ настоящій художникъ могъ создать Михаиломъ фонтанамъ, то известной русской душой сказать о «Жаръ-Птиц, Иван-Царевнчѣ и Царевнчѣ и Ненаглядной Красѣ, Яъ которой Жаръ-Птица особождаетотъ-чаразаго Кашеево Безсмертнаго, Царевичъ, Царевну и все спогавое Кашеево мрачное царство: Встрѣденѣ къ балету рисуетъ въ заинственныхъ трепетныхъ гармоніяхъ этосказочное царство; Но вотъ, сверкая и искрясь

Факсимиле автографа И. Стравинскаго изъ балета „Петрушка".

even Steinberg had to complain.[34] To Stravinsky's wish that he enjoy the same "creative ebullience" as the author of *The Rite of Spring,* poor Steinberg replied (from the Rimsky-Korsakov dacha at Lyubensk, which he had inherited), "Our life here is extremely monotonous: there remains only to get on with one's work. In spite of your wish, though, I can't say I'm feeling particularly ebullient."[35] Steinberg's letters show to what an extent he had assumed the mantle—indeed, the very daily existence—of his late father-in-law: onerous teaching duties, oppressive family obligations, not to mention his time-consuming labor as Rimsky-Korsakov's literary and musical executor. Having edited the *Coq d'or* Suite and the *Chronicle of My Musical Life,* he was now hard at work on Rimsky's orchestration treatise. His own creative work was at a near standstill.[36]

Meanwhile, practically every issue of the *RMG* brought news of Stravinskian triumphs and scandals in all the capitals of Europe. Grumblers like Sabaneyev could be depended upon to dismiss them as the antics of a gaudy careerist, a "composer for the modish marketplace."[37] But neither friend nor foe could gainsay the well-turned observation with which Boris Tyuneyev brought the 1913 feature article on modern composers to a close: "Mr. Stravinsky," he wrote, "has begun his career the way most composers would be happy to end theirs." The *Petrushka* première (excerpts under Koussevitzky) was greeted by the *RMG* with an unabashed puff: "This was undoubtedly an *event,* for we Russians can now boldly congratulate ourselves on the appearance of a new, outstanding talent" on the world scene.[38] Stravinsky had assumed the role of leadership that had been predicted for Steinberg, and in so doing, he had scaled the Belyayevets walls for good and all.

The inevitable backlash may be conveniently traced in the writings of Joseph Wihtol (Jazeps Vitols), Rimsky-Korsakov's distinguished Latvian protégé and a Belyayevets's Belyayevets, who has already made an occasional appearance in these pages, and who from 1898 to 1914 was the music reviewer of the *St. Petersburger Zeitung,* the Russian capital's German-language daily. He covered every local

34. "The Belyayevtsï make me just as indignant as they make you," he wrote (4 April 1913) in response to a letter in which Stravinsky had jeered at their failure to observe the centenary of Dargomïzhsky's birth, meanwhile "even as if on purpose programming 'Little-Russian Sketches' by Zolotaryov instead of Dargomïzhsky's 'Little-Russian Kazachok,' and 'Variations on a Finnish Theme' by Winkler instead of Dargomïzhsky's 'Finnish Fantasy.'" He concluded, "Shame on Glazunov, shame in all likelihood even on Lyadov" (Letter of 17 February/2 March 1913; in IStrSM:471). "But I don't know what I can do," protested Steinberg. "I have to spare Lyadov's and Glazunov's feelings, after all. Oh, if only they'd see for themselves! This second concert was simply a disgrace—I can't recall anything like it." Once again Stravinsky was baiting his old rival, rubbing his nose in the contrast between their environments. While he couldn't have cared much by this time about Dargomïzhsky's centennial, his letter is an impressive and valuable testimonial to his knowledge of the Russian repertoire he had left behind, even down to such bottom-of-the-barrel fare as Dargomïzhsky's inept and justly neglected orchestral pieces.

35. Letter of 26 June 1913; in the Stravinsky Archive.

36. See letters of 4 April and 18 May 1913 (Stravinsky Archive) in which Steinberg complains, among other things, of having piles of examinations to grade.

37. Sabaneyev, "Kontsert iz proizvedeniy Stravinskogo."

38. *RMG* 20, no. 5 (2 February 1913), col. 136.

Stravinsky première from the Symphony in E-flat to *The Rite of Spring,* and the temperature, from write-up to write-up, descended steadily from fervid to arctic. "The Petersburg school, one must hope, will with time be able to point with rightful pride to this its youngest representative," was how Wihtol greeted the symphony in 1908. The Beethoven and Musorgsky orchestrations the next year were "excellently" done. When it came to *The Firebird,* though, the critic already had his doubts: "So young and already such a know-it-all!" he exclaimed. "Where can Mr. Stravinsky go after this?" When he had his answer he reacted with unmitigated sarcasm: "I do not feel the urge to dilate particularly on *The Rite of Spring;* my sphere of operations is the art of music, and in the present instance the most competent critic would be a zookeeper."[39]

Myaskovsky captured to ironic perfection the spirit in which the denizens of his old milieu were receiving Stravinsky as early as 1911:

> One has only to strike up with anyone, but especially with a professional musician, a conversation about I. Stravinsky, and without fail you'll hear: "An uncommon talent for orchestration, astonishing technique, the richest invention, but . . . where's the music?" What kind of nonsense is this! Talent, talent, uncommon, astounding talent, and yet the very thing that provides that talent with its medium is lacking. What is this—incomprehension or disingenuousness? We can discount the latter, of course, since one encounters this opinion not only among people who are impartial and disinterested, but even among those who are close to Stravinsky. It's simply a matter of—we cannot say.[40]

As we shall see, Stravinsky managed eventually to antagonize even Myaskovsky.

THE METEOR CORRALLED

The situation was just the opposite in France, where Stravinsky was welcomed enthusiastically by the organized avant-garde—a faction that, at least in music, hardly existed at all in Russia. For them, Stravinsky was from the moment of his appearance the uncrowned tsar of Russian music, "worthy continuer of the Rimskys and the Balakirevs, who from now on makes the expression 'The Mighty Five' seem insufficient."[41] Moreover, the social prominence of the backers of the Ballets Russes gave the company's staff genius a social prestige that flattered his innate snobbery, again to a point no musician could hope to achieve in Russia. In previous chapters we have explored Stravinsky's artistic contacts and friendships among Parisian musicians. In this one we shall have a look at his involvement in

39. Vitol, *Vospominaniya, stat'i, pis'ma,* 118, 220, 228, 254.
40. Shlifshteyn (ed.), *Myaskovskiy: sobraniye materialov* 2:24.
41. ". . . Digne continuateur des Rimsky et des Balakirev, et qui, desormais, nous fait apparaître injustement insuffisante cette dénomination des 'Cinq'" ("Les concerts," *France,* 19 November 1912; clipping in the Stravinsky Archive).

the somewhat less rarefied sphere of French cultural politics, where Stravinsky found himself not only lionized, but, as we now say, "co-opted."

From the very beginning, French critics tended to see in the Ballets Russes—or, perhaps, to project onto them—the fulfillment of their own national creative aspirations. Nowhere was this viewpoint rifer than in the pages of the *Nouvelle revue française* (*NRF*), the aggressively nationalistic literary forum founded in the year of the Russian ballet's debut by a group of seven writers that included André Gide. The *NRF* went back for its motto to a program of action promulgated centuries before by Joachim du Bellay, in the title of a tract he issued in 1549 on behalf of the "Pléiade" poets, when the foundations of French literature were being laid: *Défense et illustration de la langue française*. Nothing less than a national cultural renewal was called for. It was toward that end that Jean Schlumberger parsed and updated du Bellay's slogan in his lead article for the inaugural issue of the new journal:

> *La langue* is not just language, it is culture. And if one appends *française* to it, it is not in any restrictive or exclusionary sense, but simply because our responsibility is limited to what happens among us.
>
> *Défense* no longer has the negative sense of a retrogressive reaction.—If one gives in to an ever-increasing enthusiasm for the seventeenth and eighteenth centuries, it is not without reservation.
>
> . . . Everyone is afraid of feeling lost, separated by a yawning gulf from the sure glories of French culture. But for anyone who feels himself advancing on the firm terrain of a continually developing literature, "defense" can mean no more than a psychological reaction, the response or rejoinder of a living organism to all influences, good or bad. . . . The strongest periods are those that react the most vigorously, just as they are the most avid to assimilate. . . .
>
> Finally, *illustrer* aspires less here to the sense of rendering illustrious than to that of rendering plain. Genius alone can create glory, and he appears only when he appears. But it is for each of us to define him, support him, surround him with an environment of admiration and understanding.[42]

That genius would be Stravinsky, and the explication, bolstering support, and intelligent admiration he would receive from the *NRF* as by-product of its literary politicking would ultimately seduce and profoundly influence him in turn.

---

42. "*La langue,* ce n'est pas seulement le langage, c'est la culture. Et si l'on y ajoute *française,* ce n'est point en un sens restrictif ni exclusiviste, mais simplement parce que notre responsabilité se borne à ce qui se passe chez nous.

"*Défense* n'a pas davantage le sens négatif de réaction rétrograde.—S'il faut se réjouir d'un élan toujours plus marqué vers nos dix-septième et dix-huitième siècles, ce n'est qu'après réserves faites. . . . Chez tous c'est l'anxiété de se sentir perdus, séparés par un gouffre vide, des sûres gloires de la culture française. Mais pour quiconque a le sentiment d'avancer sur le ferme terrain d'une littérature continûment développée, défense ne peut signifier que réaction physiologique, réponse, riposte d'un organisme vivant à toutes les influences bonnes ou mauvaises. . . . Les plus fortes époques sont celles qui réagissent le plus vigoureusement, tout en étant les plus avides d'assimilation. . . .

"Enfin, *illustrer* prétend moins ici au sens de rendre illustre qu'à celui de rendre évident. Le génie seul fait la gloire et il n'apparaît qu'à son heure. Mais il appartient à chacun de l'expliquer, de l'étayer, de l'entourer d'une atmosphère d'admiration et d'intelligence" (Jean Schlumberger, "Considérations," *Nouvelle revue française* [Paris, 1909; rpt. Kraus, 1968] 1:9–11).

FIG. 13.4. Jacques Rivière
(1886–1925), by Deanna Stefanek.

As enunciated in Schlumberger's editorial, the *NRF* program was above all a classicizing one, a *reprise de contact* with the firm, "sure glories" of French literature after the murky subjective vagaries of Romanticism. A year later, at the beginning of an article called "Propos divers sur le Ballet Russe," Henri Ghéon, one of the founding editors, would announce: "Our dream has been realized—and not by us."[43] The Russians' great gift to the French had been an object lesson in "two principles common to all the arts, unity of conception and respect for materials [*respect de la matière*]."[44] The exemplar of exemplars had been *The Firebird,* which "confronts us with the most exquisite miracle of equilibrium—of sound, movement, form—that we have ever dreamed of seeing. . . . Stravinsky, Fokine, Golovin are for me but one creator. . . . What imagination in the proportions, what simple gravity, what taste!" In sum: "How Russian it all is, what these Russians have made, but also how French!"[45]

Respect de la matière: if the difference between Romantic and modern art had to be boiled down to a single phrase, this one would surely be a contender. What was

43. *Nouvelle revue française* 4 (1910): 199.
44. Ibid., 200.
45. "*L'Oiseau de Feu* . . . nous propose le prodige d'équilibre le plus exquis que nous ayons jamais rêvé, entre les sons, les mouvements, les formes. . . . Stravinsky, Fokine, Golovine, je ne vois plus qu'un seul auteur. . . . Quelle fantaisie dans la mésure, quelle simple gravité, quel goût! . . . Que cela est donc russe, ce que ces Russes créèrent, mais que cela est donc aussi français!" (ibid., 210–11).

perhaps only a passing formulation by Ghéon, if a prophetic one, would be elevated to the status of a platform by Jacques Rivière (1886–1925), the literary prodigy so admired by modernists like T. S. Eliot and T. E. Hulme, who did more than anyone else to lay the groundwork for the intransigent anti-Romanticism (Cocteau's "Rappel à l'ordre"!) that would become dominant in France between the wars. By the time of *Petrushka,* Rivière's was the chief critical voice speaking from the pages of the *NRF.* The importance of his writings to Stravinsky may be gauged by the fact that close to five decades later, Rivière was the single critic to figure—as a friend, at any rate—in the "conversations" books.[46]

Rivière had an urgent program for French literature: to rescue it from subjectivity, from passivity, "to have done with the art of tired people and to produce something more vigorous and vital." That something was to be "classical" in its careful "application," its "absolutely intrinsic" beauty, and its freedom from "any sort of utilitarian, moral, or theoretical preoccupations." Rivière maintained that "all the classics were implicitly positivist." He sought an art of hard esthetic "objects" that would dispense with factitious "continuity," conventional "fluidity," and, above all, "atmosphere."[47]

He found all this and more in *Petrushka* ("a masterpiece; one of the most unforeseen, spontaneous, buoyant, and bounding [works] that I know"), and particularly in the unprecedented music of Igor Stravinsky, "this name we first learned from *The Firebird,* and that now we will never forget."[48] Rivière's description of *Petrushka* resonates clairvoyantly with the Russian cultural tendencies we examined apropos *The Rite of Spring.* Stravinsky was certainly correct when, looking back from a vantage point of nearly half a century's experience, he affirmed that Jacques Rivière "was the first critic to have had an intuition" about his music.[49] No Russian had the acuity to make comparable connections or draw comparable conclusions about Stravinsky's cultural message at that time:

This young musician knows and manages with ease our modern orchestra, so intractable and overloaded. But unlike others, he does not seek further complications; he does not wish to be original by dint of petty adjustments, tiny effronteries, fragile or unstable harmonic balances. *His audacity by contrast consists in simplifications* (there is an interlude in *Petrushka* that is nothing but enormous beatings on the big drum). He unerringly dares a thousand delectable scurrilities; he suppresses, he illuminates, *he puts down nothing but forthright, summary strokes.* He takes a trumpet

46. See Conv:60–65/56–61 (including five rather inconsequential letters, which, according to Robert Craft [P&D:661n.8], were included at Eliot's suggestion).
47. Martin Turnell, *Jacques Rivière* (Cambridge: Bowes & Bowes, 1953), 45, 46, 49.
48. ". . . Un chef-d'oeuvre; un des plus imprévus, des plus primesautiers, des plus légers et bondissants que je connaisse . . . Igor Strawinski; ce nom que nous apprit *l'Oiseau de Feu,* nous n'oublierons plus" (Jacques Rivière, *Nouvelles études* [Paris: Gallimard, 1947], 9, 10).
49. Conv:60/56.

in hand, and his great catch is in taking nothing else. He knows how to hint power-fully, *and his vigor is the result of all that he has learned to do without.*[50]

Rivière passed completely over the Russianness of *Petrushka*—the aspect that had won over the musicians—and went to the heart of its texture and design. As David Bancroft notes, "What had been conceived originally in the NRF as a lit-erary attitude became, through Rivière's integration of Stravinsky's musical atti-tude, a much broader aesthetic attitude."[51] By thus promoting Stravinsky beyond the status of First Musician to that of exemplary artist for France—indeed, for the world—Rivière was doing more than paying tribute to his genius. He was at-tempting to create a standard by means of which he could influence French artists in all media, but particularly those in his own, literary, domain.

Whatever his effect on his fellow littérateurs, it is incontestable that Rivière's overwhelming flattery heavily influenced its subject. The doctrinaire manifestos that ushered in the "neoclassical" phase of Stravinsky's career owed their greatest debt to Rivière's example, particularly his celebrated pair of essays on *The Rite,* which he made bold to characterize—at a time when everyone looked upon Stravinsky as *the* Russian Impressionist—as "the first masterpiece we may stack up against those of Impressionism," and for these magnificently expressed reasons:

> The great novelty of *Le sacre du printemps* is its renunciation of "sauce." *Here is a work that is absolutely pure.* Bitter and harsh, if you will; but a work in which no gravy deadens the taste, no art of cooking smooths or smears the edges. It is not a "work of art," with all the usual attendant fuss. Nothing is blurred, nothing is mit-igated by shadows; no veils and no poetic sweeteners; *not a trace of atmosphere.* The work is whole and tough, *its parts remain quite raw;* they are served up without digestive aids; *everything is crisp, intact, clear, and crude.*[52]

50. "Ce jeune musicien connaît et manie avec facilité notre orchestre moderne si laborieux et sur-chargé. Mais il ne cherche pas comme d'autres à se compliquer davantage; il ne veut pas être original à force de petits rapprochements, de hardiesses minuscules, de fragiles et instables équilibres harmo-niques. Son audace au contraire se marque par des simplifications (il y a dans *Pétrouchka* un interlude qui n'est fait que d'énormes coups de grosse caisse). Il ose sans broncher mille grossièretés délectables; il supprime, il éclaircit, il ne pose que des touches franches et sommaires. Il prend une trompette et sa trouvaille est de ne prendre qu'elle. Il sait sous-entendre avec puissance et sa vigueur est faite de tout ce dont il apprend à se passer" (Rivière, *Nouvelles études,* 10; here and elsewhere italics have been added to the translation in the text to underscore resonances with Stravinsky's later pronouncements).

51. David Bancroft, "Stravinsky and the NRF (1910–20)," *Music and Letters* 53 (1972): 277.

52. "La grande nouveauté du *Sacre du Printemps,* c'est le renoncement à la 'sauce.' Voici une oeuvre absolument pure. Aigre et dure, si vous voulez; mais dont aucun jus ne ternit l'éclat, dont aucune cui-sine n'arrange ni ne salit les contours. Ce n'est pas un 'oeuvre d'art,' avec tous les petits tripotages ha-bituels. Rien d'estampé, rien de diminué par les ombres; point de voiles ni d'adoucissements poétiques; aucune trace d'atmosphère. L'oeuvre est entière et brute, les morceaux en restent tout crus; ils nous sont livrés sans rien qui en prépare la digestion; tout ici est franc, intact, limpide et grossier" (Rivière, *Nouvelles études,* 73; italics added to translation; here and elsewhere translations from Rivière's *Rite* reviews are adapted from Bullard, "First Performance," vol. 2). When Rivière took over the editorship of the NRF in 1919, he wrote to Stravinsky announcing his intention "to direct the at-

If this already begins to sound like the hard-nosed "neoclassical" Stravinsky, consider the following passage, in which Rivière really warms to his subject:

> Never have we heard *a music so magnificently limited*.
>
> This is not just a negative novelty. Stravinsky has not simply amused himself by taking the opposite path from Debussy. If he has chosen those instruments that do not sigh, *that say no more than they say*, whose timbres are without expression and *are like isolated words*, it is because he wants to enunciate everything directly, explicitly, and concretely. That is his chief obsession. That is his personal innovation in contemporary music. . . . He does not wish to count on what the stream of sounds may pick up along the way by momentary fortuitous association. Rather, he turns to each thing and calls it by name; he goes everywhere; he speaks wherever he needs to, in the most exact, narrow, and literal terms. *His voice becomes the object's proxy*, consuming it, replacing it; *instead of evoking it, he utters it*. He leaves nothing out; on the contrary, he goes after things; he finds them, seizes them, brings them back. *He gestures not to call out, nor to point to externals, but to take hold and fix*. Thus Stravinsky, with unmatched flair and accomplishment, is bringing about in music the same revolution that is taking place more humbly and tortuously in literature: *he has passed from the sung to the said, from invocation to statement, from poetry to reportage*.[53]

"The classics were implicitly positivist." Stravinsky was the great classic of the new century, and Rivière did not hesitate to dub him so—"directly, explicitly, concretely." Stravinsky's work "marks an epoch not only in the history of dance and music, but in that of all the arts," he wrote, in hopes that his literary compatriots would take heed and mold their art to conform to his description of Stravinsky's.[54]

---

tention of the magazine to the anti-impressionist, anti-symbolist, and anti-Debussy movements" and asked the composer to contribute (Conv:63/59). Looking back in 1957, Stravinsky affected wonder at "the evidence in [this] letter of how quickly fashion had turned against Debussy in the year after his death" (Conv:61/57). But of course, the "anti-Debussy" sentiment of Rivière's 1913 *Rite* reviews was their most conspicuous trait, a fact that Stravinsky must have realized at the time. The reviews must surely have contributed to the cooling of the Stravinsky-Debussy relationship.

53. "Jamais on n'entendit musique aussi magnifiquement bornée. Ce n'est pas là simplement une nouveauté négative. Strawinsky ne s'est pas simplement amusé à prendre le contre-pied de Debussy. S'il a choisi des instruments qui ne frémissent pas, qui ne disent rien de plus que ce qu'ils disent, dont le timbre est une expansion et qui sont comme des mots abstraits, c'est parce qu'il veut tout énoncer directement, expressément, nommément. Là est sa préoccupation principale. Là est son innovation personnelle dans la musique contemporaine. . . . Il ne veut pas compter sur ce que la symphonie entraîne en passant, par une adhérence fortuite et momentanée. Mais il se roule vers chaque chose et la dit; il va partout; il parle partout où il faut, et de la façon la plus exacte, la plus étroite, la plus textuelle. Sa voix se fait pareille à l'objet, elle le consomme, elle le remplace; au lieu de l'évoquer, elle le prononce. Il ne laisse rien en dehors; au contraire, il revient sur les choses; il les trouve, il les saisit, il les ramène. Son mouvement n'est point d'appeler, ni de faire un signe vers les régions extérieures, mais de prendre, et de tenir, et de fixer. Par là Strawinsky opère en musique, avec un éclat et une perfection inégalables, la même révolution qui est en train de s'accomplir, plus humblement et plus péniblement, en littérature; il passe du chanté au parlé, de l'invocation au discours, de la poésie au récit" (Rivière, *Nouvelles études*, 75–76; italics added to translation as before).

54. ". . . Marque une date, non pas seulement dans l'histoire de la danse et de la musique, mais dans celle de tous les arts" (ibid., 72).

The very sounds of Stravinsky's music were models for anti-Romantic literary emulation: "They remain at all times detached, largely disengaged."[55] To Stravinsky the critic attributed his own greatest wish: "the desire to express everything to the letter."[56] His description of Stravinsky's achievement was in effect a prescription for the French literature he wished to see: "Its greatest beauty is that it is always direct. It speaks; one can only listen; it comes, it wells up, it spouts forth and leaves us nothing to do except be there."[57] Rivière was at his most clairvoyant when, dealing with the ballet's anti-individualism and its antipsychological dramaturgy, he connected with uncanny intuition *The Rite*'s ethnological sources (his sole mention of them) and its then-remote esthetic implications:

> We are witness to the movements of man at a time when he did not yet exist as an individual. These beings still mass together; they move in groups, in colonies, in layers; they are held [as individuals] in a frightening indifference by society; they are devoted to a god whom they have made together and from whom they have not yet learned to distinguish themselves. Nothing of the individual is painted on their faces. Not for an instant during her dance does the Chosen One betray the personal terror that must fill her soul. She is accomplishing a rite, she is absorbed by a social function, and *without giving the slightest sign of comprehension or of interpretation,* she acts according to the will and the convulsions of a being more vast than she. . . .[58]

This is indeed an accurate description of the esthetic stance of folk musicians, as the work of ethnographers has demonstrated many times over.[59] At the same time, it is ineluctably suggestive of the "neoclassical" Stravinsky, with his horror of "interpretation" and his veneration of tradition—something more vast than we. Between the one and the other Rivière stands as a necessary link.

Rivière's writings decisively transformed his subject's view of himself and hence

55. ". . . Elles demeurent toujours bien détachées, bien largement dégagées" (ibid., 76).
56. ". . . Le désir d'exprimer toute chose à la lettre" (ibid.).
57. "Sa plus grande beauté, c'est qu'elle est toujours directe. Elle parle; on n'a qu'à l'écouter; elle vient, elle sourd, elle jaillit et elle ne nous laisse rien à faire que d'être là" (ibid., 80).
58. "Nous assistons aux mouvements de l'homme au temps où il n'existait pas encore comme individu. Les êtres se tiennent encore; ils sont pris dans l'affreuse indifférence de la société; ils sont dévoués au dieu qu'ils forment ensemble et dont ils n'ont pas su encore se démêler. Rien d'individuel ne se peint sur leur visage. A aucun instant de sa danse, la jeune fille élue ne trahit la terreur personnelle dont son âme devrait être pleine. Elle accomplit un rite, elle est absorbée par une fonction sociale et, sans donner aucun signe de compréhension ni d'interprétation, elle s'agite suivant les volontés et les secousses d'un être plus vaste qu'elle" (ibid., 95; italics added to translation).
59. Cf. Jeffrey Mark: "The performer, whether as singer, dancer or player, does his part without giving any or much impression that he is participating in the act. And his native wood notes wild, far from giving the popularly conceived effect of a free and careless improvisation, show him definitely to be in the grip of a remorseless and comparatively inelastic tradition which gives him little or no scope for personal expression (again as popularly conceived). Through him the culture speaks, and he has neither the desire nor the specific comprehension to mutilate what he has received. His whole attitude [is] one of profound gravity and cool, inevitable intention. There [is] not the faintest suggestion of the flushed cheek and the sparkling eye. And [his performance] is ten times the more impressive because of it" ("Fundamental Qualities of Folk Music," 287–90, condensed).

contributed actively toward shaping Stravinsky's later work and thought. The composer did indeed mold his art so as to conform to Rivière's description of *The Rite of Spring,* and did indeed view his masterpiece in retrospect through a lens his French critic had provided. All the notorious writings of the Parisian neoclassical period, from the earliest ("Some Ideas About My *Octuor*" [1924], for example) to the latest and greatest (*La poétique musicale*) are obsessed with issues first broached by Rivière: limitation, purity, objectivity, intrinsicality, abstraction. "To enunciate everything directly, explicitly, concretely" became the postwar Stravinsky's motto in both word and musical deed. For attaching the phrase to a prewar composition, Rivière has been called a prophet.[60] But his was a self-fulfilling prophecy that precipitated its own realization by virtue of its impact, and that of its author personally, on Stravinsky.

One is tempted at this point to say that by hailing Stravinsky as an "anti-Debussyste" and a classicist in *The Rite,* Rivière in effect turned him into one; for we are always most profoundly influenced by those who praise us, the more so when the praise is at once so intelligent and so hyperbolic. It is not so hard to understand why, coming from a milieu in which he was ranked second to Steinberg, Stravinsky should have been susceptible to the blandishments of those who placed him higher than Debussy. He did what was necessary to keep that praise coming.

L'AFFAIRE *MONTJOIE!*

The special combination of attitudes exemplified by Rivière and the *NRF*—esthetic avant-gardism in conjunction with political, social, and religious conservatism—was deeply congenial to the Russian *dvoryanin* Stravinsky, as it was to so many other early modernists. Again the contrast with the situation back home must have been striking. These considerations may help explain Stravinsky's highly visible and personal involvement with another Parisian arts journal of the period, a clamorous, ephemeral review that reflected the policies of the *NRF* as if in a funhouse mirror.

This was *Montjoie!,* whose masthead proclaimed it the "Organe de l'Impérialisme artistique française," and whose editorial "Déclaration," reprinted wholly or in part in every issue, read as follows:

> *Montjoie!*
>
> has for its aim and for its motto THE GIVING OF DIRECTION TO THE ÉLITE, the élite whom Merchants and Barbarians of every sort have completely stymied.

---

60. Cf. Bancroft: "One is tempted to say that just as 'Le Sacre' was affirmed by many critics to be fifteen years ahead of its time, so Rivière might have been one of the few contemporary critics who could quickly assimilate the obvious novelties it had to offer" ("Stravinsky and the NRF," 278).

is the only Art Gazette of the avant-garde, which, through its literary, art, and music contributors and *by its intransigent defense of the true interests of Art*, by its great "affirmations" as by its just "demolitions," gives a precise idea of the biases and the energy of a whole generation of artists in full and vigorous bloom.[61]

The opening manifesto ("Salut") in the first issue (10 February 1913) makes repellently clear the operative definition the "organ" espoused of the "true interests of Art": "To all who are inspired by a high ideal, in art as in life, an ideal defined by the ambition of the race that would impose upon the world a basic model of culture, *Montjoie!* offers, in its pure eclecticism [*sic!*], a forum for affirmation and discussion."[62] Racism, anti-Semitism, and antidemocratic vituperation ran rampant in its pages, along with the crude nationalism proclaimed by its very name, the war cry of the ancient kings of France.[63] *Montjoie!*, in short, was a fascist rag *avant le mot*. Its combination of right-wing politics and left-wing art, plus its undeniable typographical elegance, must have made it seem to Stravinsky a revival, however tawdry, of *Mir iskusstva*.

It was Florent Schmitt, a regular contributor (later an ardent fascist) with whom Stravinsky had formed an especially close attachment, who brought him into the fold. Schmitt introduced the future composer of *The Rite of Spring* to Ricciotto Canudo, the future editor of *Montjoie!*, during the Ballets Russes season of 1912. Canudo (1879–1923) was a fantastically prolific scribbler who had even dabbled in musicology of sorts. He came by his fascination with *The Rite* and its author quite naturally, having made a reputation as a "specialist" in the musical activities of primeval man with an extended speculation on the origins of music, entitled *Le livre d'évolution de l'homme: Psychologie musicale des civilisations* (Paris: Sansot, 1907), in which he traced the evolution of music from *mouvement extatique* (learned by primitive man and woman by bodily contact in "nights illuminated by the amorous eyes of the stars"), through *mouvement orgiastique* (learned from the tumultuous rhythms of stones, "repeating, with their furious bodies, the move-

---

61. "*Montjoie!* a pour but et pour devise DONNER UNE DIRECTION A L'ÉLITE, l'élite que des Marchands et les Barbares de toute sorte ont complètement désemparée.
"*Montjoie!* est la seule Gazette d'Art d'avant-garde, qui, par sa collaboration littéraire, artistique et musicale et par sa défense intransigeante des vrais intérêts de l'Art, par ses larges 'affirmations' comme par ses justes 'demolitions,' donne l'idée précise de tendances de l'énergie de toute un génération d'artistes en pleine et vigoureuse éclosion" (*Montjoie!*, back page of no. 7 [16 May 1913]).
62. "À tous ceux qui s'inspirent d'un haut idéal, dans l'art et dans la vie, idéal défini par l'ambition de la race qui veut imposer au monde un type essentiel de culture, 'Montjoie!' offre, en pur éclectisme, une tribune d'affirmation et de discussion." For a sampling of relevant articles and extracts, see Noëmi Blumenkranz-Onimus, " 'Montjoie! ou l'héroïque croisade pour une nouvelle culture," in *L'Année 1913*, ed. L. Brion Guerry, vol. 2 (Paris, 1971), 1105n.2.
63. It was borrowed from the *Chanson de Roland* (as printed on the cover of every issue): "Ce n'est pas un bâton qu'il faut pour telle bataille / Mais le fer et l'acier doivent y être bons. / . . . / De toutes parts on entend crier: Montjoie!"

FIG. 13.5. Ricciotto Canudo (1877–1923), by Picasso (1917). The uniform is that of the Italian "Zuave" regiment in which Canudo served as a captain during the Great War. (© 1995 Artists Rights Society [ARS], New York / SPADEM, Paris)

ment of the trees, in order not to be vanquished and annihilated"), to primeval song (born of man's desire "to surpass with his own cries the cries of Nature").[64]

Canudo inevitably saw in Stravinsky's ballet the vindication of his theories. He not only commissioned "Ce que j'ai voulu exprimer dans *Le Sacre du Printemps,*" the publicity article Stravinsky later tried so hard to disavow; he actively collaborated with Stravinsky on it. This much we can tell from an urgent note (now in the Stravinsky Archive) Canudo sent the composer on 21 May 1913: "I'll telephone you to find out when and where we can meet to finish the important account of *Le Sacre. By now it's very urgent.*" Canudo's contributions to the piece seem easy enough to detect: the "grandiloquent and naïve" pronunciamentos near the beginning concerning the mounting universal sap, and so forth, obviously speak the fevered language of the *Livre d'évolution.* At the same time, as Craft has pointed out, Stravinsky's comment on his preference for the wind instruments over the strings (strings being "too evocative and representative of the human voice, . . . rich in cheap expressivity")—a passage that was picked up by Rivière and many other critics at the time—rings true and is echoed in many other of his writings, not to mention the many later works that banished or severely curtailed the presence of the string family.[65] Canudo, to the extent that he had a hand in the composition of the article, thus became only the first in a long line of Stravinskian ghostwriters.

Correspondence—with Canudo himself, with Derzhanovsky, and even with Maximilian Steinberg—removes any doubt that Stravinsky not only participated in the writing of "Ce que j'ai voulu . . . ," but stood firmly by it at the time. He did not attempt to disavow the piece until the period of the *Chroniques.*[66] Two days before the *Rite* première, Canudo wrote to Stravinsky about "your [not 'our'] article" and asked him to stop by and read proof. Later, Stravinsky sent Derzhanovsky a copy of the article for publication (over his name) in *Muzika.* On its appearance there, Stravinsky was appalled at the translation and expressed himself forcefully on the matter both to Derzhanovsky and to Steinberg.[67] In both cases he refers to the piece as "my letter." Stravinsky's own copy of the offending translation survives to this day in the Stravinsky Archive (Fig. 13.6b). Directly on it the composer began a correction that he tried to get Derzhanovsky to promise to print. Meeting with refusal, Stravinsky gave up his corrective. His emendations, in any case, were niggling: they in no way affected the sense of the article, only the ac-

---

64. See Warren Dwight Allen, *Philosophies of Music History* (New York: Dover, 1962), 130–31.

65. P&D:524.

66. Indeed, Rivière may even have had something to do with Stravinsky's embarrassment over the piece, since in his *Rite* review he referred to its "plusieurs naïvetés" (*Nouvelles études,* 74), which might just as well have been a sally at Canudo and *Montjoie!* This evaluation, however, did not prevent Rivière from quoting from the piece at his convenience (particularly the part about the winds and strings) and confidently basing conclusions as to Stravinsky's intentions on its authority.

67. Letters to Derzhanovsky, 12 August 1913 (original in IStrSM:476; translation in SelCorrI:55) and to Steinberg, 29 September/12 October 1913 (IStrSM:478).

curacy of certain lexical equivalents.[68] Unquestionably, then, "Ce que j'ai voulu exprimer dans *Le Sacre du Printemps*" is an authentic document—as authentic, at any rate, as the *Chroniques,* the *Poétique,* or the "conversations" books.[69]

But the article (or letter) was only one of several contributions by Stravinsky to *Montjoie!* To no other publication was he ever so faithful. The same issue (29 May 1913) that carried the letter also contained an autograph page from the score of the ballet (the beginning of the Spring Khorovods—and why, one wonders, did Stravinsky choose one of the tamest pages from *The Rite* for such a purpose?) signed to Canudo "avec toute sympathie artistique" (Fig. 13.6c). The very last issue of *Montjoie!*[70] carried an autograph page from *The Nightingale,* also dedicated to Canudo, along with a wild-eyed futuristic appreciation of that opera by Canudo himself, and a cubist portrait of Stravinsky by Albert Gleizes (Fig. 13.7a–b). Stravinsky was thus closely identified with *Montjoie!* throughout the brief and tumultuous period of its existence.

And he read it, too. A favorite *Montjoie!* theme was raillery against "cabotins" and "cabotinage." These terms of opprobrium, derived from the name of a seventeenth-century comedian, were the French equivalent of "ham" and "ham-acting."[71] Within *Montjoie!*'s "nouvelle dogmatique," their meaning was expanded to take in all that related to bourgeois philistinism and the kind of gaudy art that pleased such taste—perhaps "chintz" or "tinsel" come closest. Canudo's editorials crusaded indefatigably against "les nouveaux Barbares que sont les cabotins,"[72] and the issue preceding the one that carried "Ce que j'ai voulu" contained a vitriolic article by Georges Batault entitled "Le règne du 'cabotin'" (it faced another, equally bilious, called "Le juif au théâtre").[73] Almost immediately, the word began

---

68. They are reproduced in SelCorrI:54.

69. Craft has written (P&D:523) that on 5 June 1913 "Stravinsky disavowed the interview in a letter to *Montjoie!* (hand-delivered there by Maurice Delage, since by this time Stravinsky was ill with typhus), published there without Canudo's knowledge." This never happened, nor was there such a letter. Craft's account is based on a misconstruction of several documents in the Stravinsky Archive, including a pained letter (dated 5 July—not June—1913) in which Canudo complained of Stravinsky's "denial . . . of an announcement that appeared the other day." This referred not to "Ce que j'ai voulu exprimer dans *Le Sacre du Printemps*," but to a notice Canudo had leaked to the newspaper *Excelsior,* announcing that he and Stravinsky were collaborating on a theatrical work to be called "Block of Ice." *Excelsior* (no. 962 [4 July 1913]) carried the following on its "Theater and Music" page, under the heading "A Handful of News" ("Poignée de nouvelles"): "M. Igor Stravinsky has asked us to say that he is not collaborating with M. Canudo on the 'Block of Ice'" ("M. Igor Stravinsky nous prie de dire qu'il ne collabore avec M. Canudo, à propos du 'Bloc de Glace'"). Canudo wrote Stravinsky, "I did not deserve that, and I certainly did not expect it from you. Adieu, my dear Stravinsky" ("Je ne méritais pas cela, certes je ne m'attendais pas à cela de vous. Adieu mon cher Strawinsky"). But it was by no means the end of their relationship. (On the very same day Canudo sent a postcard to Stravinsky apologizing for his letter in view of the composer's illness, of which he, Canudo, had just learned.)

70. *Montjoie!* 2, nos. 4–6 (April–June 1914).

71. The translators of *La poétique musicale*—in the sixth lesson of which ("De l'exécution") the terms are very prominent—render them as "exhibitionist" and "exhibitionism"; see *Poetics of Music,* 162 (*cabotinage*), 170 (*les cabotins*).

72. Blumenkranz Onimus, "'Montjoie!'" 1110.

73. *Montjoie!* no. 7 (16 May 1913).

PREMIÈRE ANNÉE. — N° 8.   29 MAI 1913

ʒMONTJOIE!ʒ

ORGANE DE L'IMPÉRIALISME ARTISTIQUE FRANÇAIS.

Gazette bimensuelle illustrée
sous la direction de Canudo.

Ce n'est pas un bâton qu'il faut pour telle bataille
Mais le fer et l'acier doivent y être bons.
De toutes parts on entend crier : Montjoie !
Chanson de Roland.

DIRECTION ET ADMINISTRATION :
38, Chaussée d'Antin, 38 - PARIS (IX°)
Les Manuscrits ne sont pas retournés.
Tous droits de reproduction et de traduction, même partielles, sans citation et de la source, sont rigoureusement réservés pour tous pays.

ABONNEMENTS :

	UN AN	SIX MOIS	TROIS MOIS
Paris	8	4 50	2 50
Départements	10	5 50	3 50
Étranger	13	7 »	5 »

Il est fait de *MONTJOIE* un tirage de luxe
au prix de 25 francs pour toute la France et 30 francs
pour l'Étranger, envoyé sous enveloppe fermée.
MONTJOIE ne publie que des œuvres littéraires, artistiques
et musicales inédites.
La Direction reçoit le lundi de 5 heures à 7 heures

Gloires et Misères du Théâtre Actuel

Les périodiques commémorent cette année le centenaire de Richard Wagner. Nous haïssons comme il convient ces manifestations réglées par le calendrier artistique à l'usage des faiseurs de toute série.

Nous rendons hommage au génie de Richard Wagner en honorant, dès sa naissance, le chef-d'œuvre d'un jeune musicien dont l'influence est déjà très grande sur l'élite : Igor STRAWINSKY.

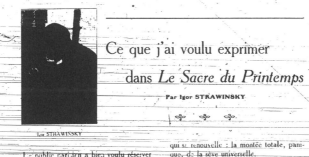

Ce que j'ai voulu exprimer

dans *Le Sacre du Printemps*

Par Igor STRAWINSKY

Igor STRAWINSKY

Le public parisien a bien voulu réserver un bon accueil, depuis quelques années déjà, à mon *Oiseau-de-Feu* et à *Pétrouchka*. Mes amis ont remarqué l'évolution de l'idée animatrice, qui de la fable fantastique de l'une de ces deux œuvres va à la généralisation toute humaine de l'autre. Je crains que le *Sacre du Printemps*, où je ne fais plus appel à l'esprit des contes de fée ni à la douleur et à la joie toute humaines, mais où je m'efforce vers une abstraction un peu plus vaste, ne déroute ceux qui m'ont témoigné, jusqu'ici, une sympathie chère.

Avec le *Sacre du Printemps*, j'ai voulu exprimer la sublime montée de la nature qui se renouvelle : la montée totale, panique, de la sève universelle.

Dans le Prélude, avant le lever du rideau, j'ai confié à mon orchestre cette grande crainte qui pèse sur tout esprit sensible devant les choses en puissance, la « chose en soi », qui *peut* grandir, se développer indéfiniment. Un frêle son de flûte peut contenir cette valeur en puissance, s'élargissant dans tout l'orchestre. C'est la sensation obscure et immense que toutes les choses ont à l'heure où la nature renouvelle ses formes ; et c'est le trouble vague et profond de la puberté universelle. A mon orchestration même, et aux jeux mélodiques, j'ai demandé de l'évoquer.

Tout le Prélude est basé sur un « mezzo-forte » toujours égal. La mélodie s'y développe selon une ligne horizontale, que seules les masses des instruments — le dynamisme intense de l'orchestre et non la ligne mélodique elle-même — accroissent ou diminuent.

Par conséquent, j'ai exclu de cette mélodie les cordes trop évocatrices et représentatives de la voix humaine, avec leurs crescendo et leurs diminuendo — et j'ai mis au premier plan les bois, plus secs, plus nets, moins riches d'expressions faciles, et par cela même plus émouvants à mon gré.

En somme, j'ai voulu exprimer dans le Prélude la crainte panique de la nature pour la beauté qui s'élève, une terreur sacrée devant le soleil de midi, une sorte de cri de Pan. La matière musicale elle-même se gonfle, grandit, se répand. Chaque instrument est comme un bourgeon qui pousse sur l'écorce d'un arbre séculaire ; il fait partie d'un formidable ensemble.

Et tout l'orchestre, tout cet ensemble, doit avoir la signification du Printemps qui naît.

Dans le premier Tableau, des Adolescents se montrent avec une vieille, très vieille femme, dont on ne connaît ni l'âge, ni le siècle, qui connaît les secrets de la nature et apprend à ses fils la Prédiction. Elle court, courbée sur la terre, mi-femme mi-bête. Les Adolescents à côté d'elles sont les Augures printaniers, qui marquent de leurs pas, sur place, le rythme du Printemps, le battement du pouls du Printemps.

FIG. 13.6a.   Front page of *Montjoie!*, 29 May 1913, showing the controversial article "Ce que j'ai voulu exprimer dans *Le Sacre du Printemps*."

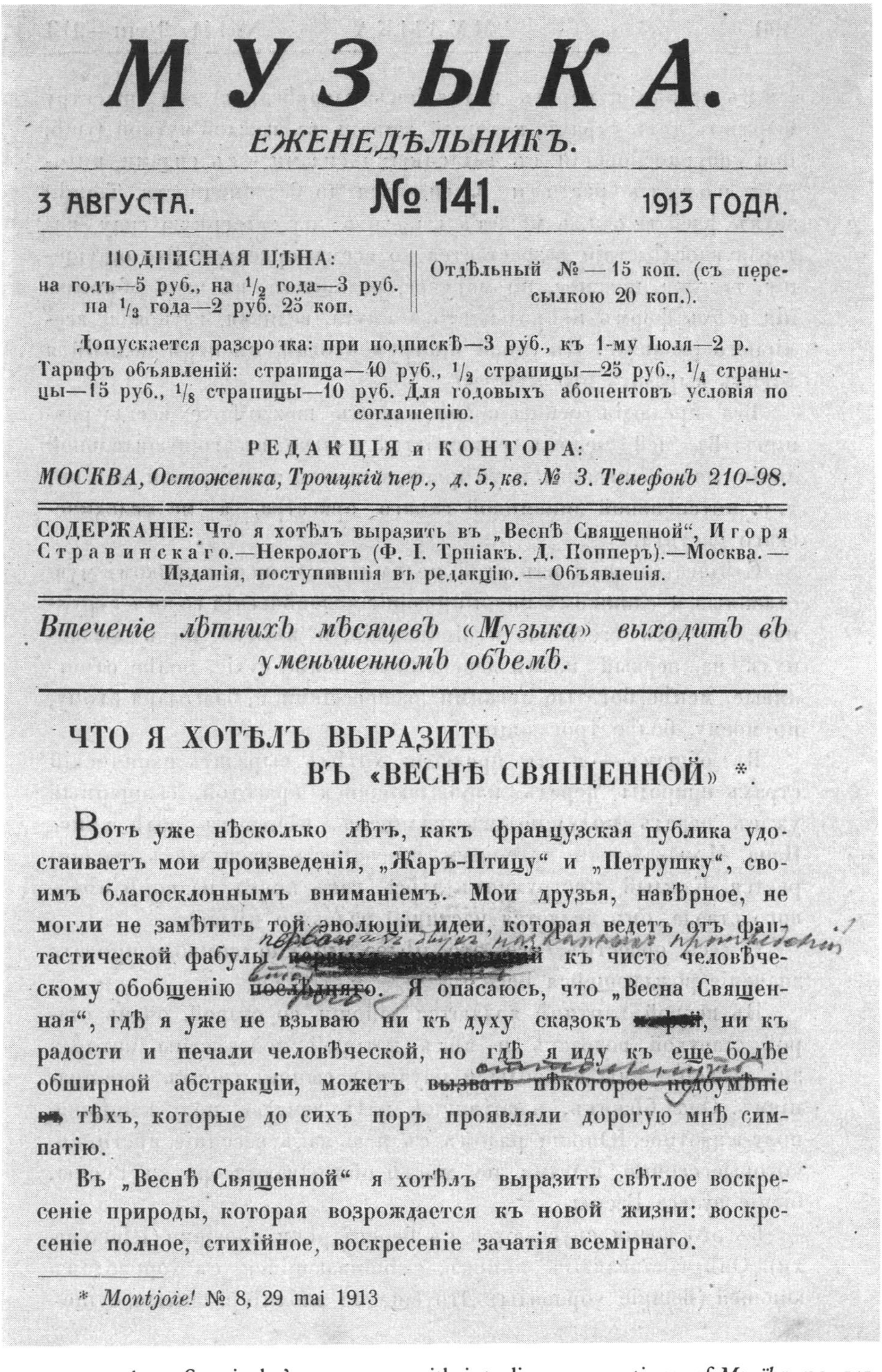

МУЗЫКА.

ЕЖЕНЕДѢЛЬНИКЪ.

3 АВГУСТА. № 141. **1913 ГОДА.**

ПОДПИСНАЯ ЦѢНА:
на годъ—5 руб., на ½ года—3 руб.
на ⅓ года—2 руб. 25 коп.

Отдѣльный №—15 коп. (съ пересылкою 20 коп.).

Допускается разсрочка: при подпискѣ—3 руб., къ 1-му Іюля—2 р.
Тарифъ объявленій: страница—40 руб., ½ страницы—25 руб., ¼ страницы—15 руб., ⅛ страницы—10 руб. Для годовыхъ абонентовъ условія по соглашенію.

РЕДАКЦІЯ и КОНТОРА:

МОСКВА, Остоженка, Троицкій пер., д. 5, кв. № 3. *Телефонъ* 210-98.

СОДЕРЖАНІЕ: Что я хотѣлъ выразить въ „Веснѣ Священной“, Игоря Стравинскаго.—Некрологъ (Ф. I. Трпіакъ. Д. Попперъ).—Москва.— Изданія, поступившія въ редакцію. — Объявленія.

Втеченіе лѣтнихъ мѣсяцевъ «Музыка» выходитъ въ уменьшенномъ объемѣ.

ЧТО Я ХОТѢЛЪ ВЫРАЗИТЬ ВЪ «ВЕСНѢ СВЯЩЕННОЙ» *

Вотъ уже нѣсколько лѣтъ, какъ французская публика удостаиваетъ мои произведенія, „Жаръ-Птицу“ и „Петрушку“, своимъ благосклоннымъ вниманіемъ. Мои друзья, навѣрное, не могли не замѣтить той эволюціи идеи, которая ведетъ отъ фантастической фабулы ~~первыхъ произведеній~~ къ чисто человѣческому обобщенію ~~послѣдняго~~. Я опасаюсь, что „Весна Священная“, гдѣ я уже не взываю ни къ духу сказокъ ~~и фей~~, ни къ радости и печали человѣческой, но гдѣ я иду къ еще болѣе обширной абстракціи, можетъ ~~вызвать~~ нѣкоторое ~~недоумѣніе~~ въ тѣхъ, которые до сихъ поръ проявляли дорогую мнѣ симпатію.

Въ „Веснѣ Священной“ я хотѣлъ выразить свѣтлое воскресеніе природы, которая возрождается къ новой жизни: воскресеніе полное, стихійное, воскресеніе зачатія всемірнаго.

* *Montjoie!* № 8, 29 mai 1913

FIG. 13.6b. Stravinsky's own copy, with interlinear corrections, of *Muzïka*, no. 141 (August 1913), featuring a Russian translation of the *Montjoie!* article: "Chto ya khotel vïrazit' v 'Vesne svyashchennoy.'" (Paul Sacher Stiftung, Basel)

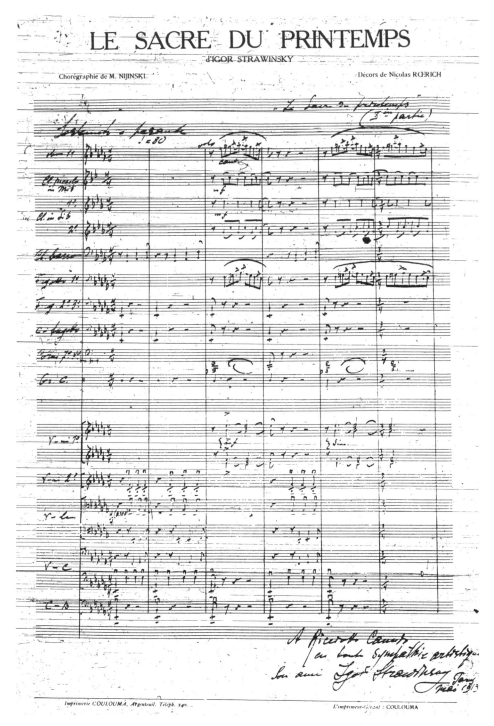

FIG. 13.6c. *Montjoie!*, 29 May 1913, back page.

cropping up in Stravinsky's correspondence, particularly with Benois (whom he could trust to understand it). In August 1913 he wrote to Benois that his *Nightingale,* on which he had just resumed work, was contrived so as to "evade all that might fuel the 'dramatic *cabotinage*' of the actors and singers."[74] And as late as April 1915 he would vent his spleen at Scriabin's *Mysterium* by calling it (also in a letter to Benois) "the 'mystic' revelations of provincial cabotinage."[75]

Like the *NRF, Montjoie!* promoted Stravinsky as the premier artist of the day. Both journals opposed Stravinsky to Debussy. *Montjoie!* did so in very pointed terms through its coverage of *The Rite* and *Jeux.* The same reviewer covered both premières—the twenty-two-year-old Alexis Roland-Manuel, the very one who, a quarter century later, would ghostwrite the *Poétique musicale.* The review of *Jeux* was buried in the back pages of the same issue in which the big puff-piece on *The Rite*—introduced with a leader by Canudo identifying the work as "le chef-d'oeuvre d'un jeune musicien dont l'influence est déjà très grande sur l'élite"—occupied the whole front page. Debussy's ballet was dismissed with praise that could scarcely have been fainter: "M. Claude Debussy's music is charming. . . . Some, naturally, declare themselves dissatisfied, wanting a second *Pelléas;* they could not await with enjoyment the first fruits of a harvest perhaps nearer than they realize."[76] Most of the space went to analyzing what went wrong with M. "Wijinsky's" choreography, blatantly at odds with the score. Not much of an event, this.

Roland-Manuel's review of *The Rite* in the next issue was delirious. Like Rivière (whose review had not yet appeared), Roland-Manuel acutely located Stravinsky's great innovation in "the robust simplicity of a work that is unspoiled by rhetoric." It was a simplicity that transformed:

> To impart to his score its rather harsh *éclat,* the enormous power of these primitive rites, much older than the Dionysiac revels, the musician—like the choreographer—had to break with hallowed canons, he had deliberately to change the color not only of his music but of all music. Igor Stravinsky, with a simplicity that one can call without exaggeration the product of genius, has accomplished this marvel: the musical material is superbly new, as new as that burst of sap it glorifies.[77]

74. IStrSM:476.

75. IStrSM:510. Stravinsky spelled the word *cabotinage* in Russian letters, which is why it has not been italicized in translation.

76. "La musique de M. Claude Debussy [!] est charmante. . . . D'aucuns, toutefois, se déclarent mal satisfaits, désireux du second *Pelléas;* ne peuvent-ils attendre en se délectant aux prémices d'une moisson peut-être plus proche qu'ils l'imaginent" (*Montjoie!* no. 8 [29 May 1913]: 6).

77. ". . . La robuste simplicité d'une oeuvre que ne dépare aucune rhétorique. . . . Pour communiquer à son oeuvre l'éclat un peu dur, l'énorme puissance de ces rites primitifs, très antérieurs aux élans dionysiaques, le musicien—comme le chorégraphe—devait briser les canons consacrés, il devait délibérément changer la couleur de *sa* musique et de *la* musique. Igor Strawinsky avec un simplicité dont il ne semble pas exagéré de dire qu'elle est géniale, a fait ce prodige: la matière musicale est superbement neuve, neuve comme cette poussée de sève qu'il a glorifiée" (*Montjoie!* nos. 9–10 [14–29 June 1913]: 13).

NOTRE ESTHÉTIQUE

A propos du "ROSSIGNOL" de Igor STRAWINSKY

Je supplie immédiatement le lecteur de ne pas s'attendre ici à un morceau de « critique ». La vague littéraire journalistique, que l'on appelle du titre déprécié de « critique », s'est répandue comme elle l'a pu sur l'œuvre dernière du jeune compositeur slave. Tous les critiques « ont donné ». Ils ont cuisiné rapidement leur bouillon sacré, en l'honneur ou non du musicien, ne s'oubliant pas jusqu'à faire de la vraie critique musicale. Ils ont fait de la littérature, *leur* littérature.

M. Émile Vuillermoz et M. Reynaldo Hahn ont parlé de temps et d'espace, afin peut-être que les charmantes fidèles de M. Bergson les comprissent, et, soucieux de couleur locale, ils ont évoqué le bambou opiagène. M. Louis Laloy, l'impayable chinoiserisant Lâ-Louâ-Chà, a parlé naturellement des Chinois, tout en se pâmant d'extase, devant la « musique céleste » (sic) du *Rossignol*, comme une religieuse devant le torse nu du Christ. M. Alfred Bruneau lui-même, véritable musicien, le seul qui ait le droit absolu de « critiquer » ses confrères, c'est-à-dire de « juger » une œuvre musicale, s'est laissé choir dans la littérature. Les autres, aussi. Pauvre Rossignol !

Assez, donc, de « critique ». Assez de mal-morts. Ouvrons les fenêtres.

Ouvrons les fenêtres sur ces domaines âpres et lumineux, où Igor Strawinsky s'avance, point seul, mais avec toute sa génération, avec les peintres, les sculpteurs, les poètes de notre génération. Regardons la petite phalange des créateurs nouveaux. Dédaignons le but de chacun, et leur but collectif, s'il en est un. Oublions leur point de départ, les mille points de départ de tout l'art contemporain, que l'on peut fixer avec certitude dans n'importe quelle époque de notre histoire de l'Art. Seule leur geste présente une importance véritable et sûre ; elle est esthétique comme celle de Roland fut épique, héroïque comme elle. Et l'affirmation de chacun nous éclairera sur le fatum esthétique incomparable de notre temps, nous montrera combien naturelle et noble est notre marche dans la montée sans sommet que l'art impose aux hommes toujours nouveaux.

Le *Rossignol* de Igor Strawinski nous aidera à comprendre nombre de formes artistiques contemporaines. Il participe de notre esthétique : du Cubisme, du Synchromisme, du Simultanisme des uns, et de la toute nerveuse Arythmie prosodique des autres.

On connaît le double scandale suscité par le *Sacre du Printemps*. Le premier scandale, logique autant que féroce, en rapport avec l'incompréhension générale et le misonéisme instinctif des foules, fut celui du ricanement des riches gens du monde, appelés au théâtre des Champs-Elysées pour les premières auditions de l'œuvre, et des journalistes qui les flattent. Le second scandale, plus indéfinissable, plus dédaignable, a été celui des ovations fanatiques faites à l'œuvre et au musicien, lors des Concerts Monteux, par des tourbes orientées vers l'enthousiasme, enthousiastes sans préparation, sans connaissance, sans droit. Les uns et les autres : des snobs. Les uns et les autres : le troupeau humain, synthèse du vulgaire, que le parti-pris ou la suggestion ambiants mènent au gré de l'heure.

ALBERT GLEIZES
Dessin pour le Portrait d'Igor Strawinsky

Toutefois, le rôle joué par le *Sacre du Printemps* sur les esprits les plus anxieux, ou les plus inquiets, ou les plus créateurs, a été très beau. Un rôle de libération, une affirmation de santé sans bornes, de courage que la force précède. Hardiesses harmoniques ; liberté intransigeante dans le choix, les superpositions et la simultanéité des sonorités et des rythmes ; mouvante et émouvante décomposition des contours mélodiques, sous l'impulsion des consonances frénétiques, des dissonances extatiques ; extrême subtilité de l'idée *sonore*, de l'expression *sonnante* ; tout un ensemble, enfin, *fortissimo*, toute une éclosion instrumentale implacable jusqu'à la fin, tel fut le *Sacre*. Tel fut le *Sacre* pour ceux qui, dans tous les

arts, recherchent justement : les harmonies hardies ; les agglomérations rythmiques tendres ou cruelles, inattendues ; la décomposition ultime du vers ou de la ligne ; la frénésie et l'extase des accords nouveaux des mots ou des couleurs, enfin la suprême abstraction de la pensée qui se concrète en elle-même, hors de toute sentimentalité.

Le *Rossignol* a bouleversé à son tour, de fond en comble, en deux soirées, le château du Prince Igor que les artistes les plus dignes avaient élevé en leur âme et conscience. Ils s'attendaient à quelque chose d'aussi formidable, d'aussi puissamment *en dehors* que le *Sacre*. Et voilà que le compositeur leur donne une œuvre tout *en dedans*, un *dolcissimo* tout en nuances et en finesses intérieures. Que penser ? Les préoccupations des meneurs de danses ne leur ont pas donné la possibilité de ce savoir, en leur octroyant, pour leur joie ou pour leur étude, deux représentations seulement de l'œuvre.

Mais la leçon du *Rossignol* a été pourtant entendue. L'apparition fort opportune de la partition a aidé les plus curieux. Et l'on a compris.

On a compris surtout la perfection de la volonté de ce musicien qui, en renouvelant sans cesse son esthétique, trouve immédiatement ses moyens nouveaux d'expression. On a compris que sa pensée métaphysique, déjà dans le *Sacre* plus mystique que métaphysique, devient plus profondément mystique, plus voluptueuse et moins sensuelle, plus cérébrale et moins intellectuelle : plus cérébriste.

Que l'on ne nous parle pas de magie des sons, de fumeries d'opium, de vertus de l'esprit et du cœur. Balivernes indignes de Strawinsky ! Que l'on nous dise l'admirable composition du « petit orchestre », où guitares, mandolines, celesta, harpes, instruments à vent, concourent à arracher pendant une heure à l'ambiance sa plus profonde vertu sonore, ainsi qu'un formidable appareil électrique saurait lui arracher ses plus intenses puissances de lumière et de chaleur.

ALEXANDRE BENOIS
Croquis inédit pour les décors du « Rossignol »

FIG. 13.7a. Canudo's paean to *The Nightingale* in the last issue of *Montjoie!*

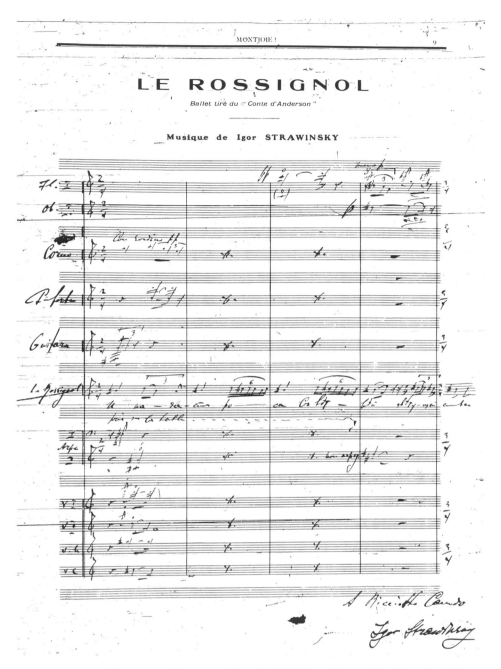

FIG. 13.7b. An autograph excerpt from the *Nightingale*'s Act III aria, printed in the final issue of *Montjoie!* with a dedicatory inscription from the composer to the editor.

What could be more seductive than praise like this? The composer of *The Rite of Spring* must have sensed what a colossal exception was being made for him: he, a foreign artist, was being hailed as a savior by what was in most other respects a chauvinistic, even xenophobic avant-garde (Schmitt: "Igor Stravinsky, I firmly believe, is the Messiah we have awaited since Wagner, for whom Musorgsky and Claude Debussy, as well as Richard Strauss and Arnold Schoenberg, now seem to have prepared the way");[78] and his work, an evocation of primitivism like no other, was being forcefully promoted by esthetes who otherwise considered that "all those primitivists of painting and literature are as odious as those bourgeois drunks who play the big baby."[79] Only too happily did he allow himself, in return for such prestige, to become the plaything of the "organe de l'Imperialisme artistique française." By imperceptible degrees, Stravinsky came to resemble his hosts and exploiters.

THE RITE RECEIVED

It was the *Rite* première, of course, that lifted controversy about Stravinsky to a new plateau and finally made the distance between him and Russia impassable. Or rather, the *Rite* premières: for there were distinct phases to the ballet's reception, starting with the noisy evening of 29 May 1913 and ending the next spring with the no less noisy triumph of the score as a concert piece. In between came the Moscow and St. Petersburg performances under Koussevitzky. With each successive event the lines were drawn more firmly and intransigence was exacerbated. The avant-garde critiques we have been sampling tell only one side of the story.

The first showing of *The Rite of Spring* is one of the most appallingly, nay absurdly, overdocumented events in the history of music. Each of the myriad published eyewitness accounts of that legendary evening conflicts with every other one; the result is sheer murk and confusion. One single confrontation of witnesses ought to suffice to indicate how futile would be the task of reconstructing the sequence of events. According to Bronislava Nijinska, "the noise and tumult continued, and it was not until near the end of the ballet, when Maria Piltz began to dance her solo, that the public quieted down";[80] while, according to Marie Rambert, "after the interlude things became even worse, and during the sacrificial dance real pandemonium broke out."[81] The weight of contradictory testimony is

78. "Igor Strawinsky est, je crois bien, le Messie que nous attendions depuis Wagner et dont Moussorgsky et Claude Debussy, comme aussi Richard Strauss et Arnold Schoenberg, semblent avoir préparé les voies" (*La France,* 4 June 1913; in Bullard, "First Performance," 3:82).

79. ". . . Tous les primitivistes de la peinture et de la littérature sont odieux comme des bourgeois saouls qui jouent aux gros bébés" (Canudo in *Montjoie!* no. 6 [1913]; quoted by Blumenkranz-Onimus, "'Montjoie!'" IIII).

80. Nijinska, *Early Memoirs,* 470.

81. Rambert, *Quicksilver,* 64.

hopeless, and we shall pass the famous story over *sans regret,* except for Stravinsky's own laconic report to Steinberg: "The performance went off in very stormy fashion: things got as far as fighting."[82] More colorful and detailed accounts of the antic proceedings may be read in Richard Buckle's biographies of Nijinsky and Diaghilev.[83] A meticulous, exhaustive, and unremittingly sober attempt to chronicle, moment by moment, what happened on the night of 29 May at the Théâtre des Champs Élysées in Paris may be found in Truman C. Bullard's dissertation on the *Rite* première.[84]

Two points do emerge clearly from this documentary miasma. First, the role of Stravinsky's music in bringing about the scandal has been systematically exaggerated. As one Paris critic wrote the next day, "at the end of the Prelude the crowd simply stopped listening to the music so that they might better amuse themselves with the choreography."[85] Indeed, many of the reviews fail even to mention Stravinsky's contribution beyond naming him as composer. Second, the stormy response had been manipulated and to a large extent provoked by Diaghilev; Cocteau was quite right to observe that "the audience played the role that had been written for it."[86] A huge press coverage was assured,[87] a durable legend created, but it is nonetheless very much of an exaggeration to regard the event as a "decisive moment in the history of music, of the dance, and of the cultural life of Europe and the world."[88] Far from exerting a decisive influence, *The Rite,* for all the shouting, seemed at first a quite ephemeral phenomenon. After a mere half-dozen performances in May and June of 1913, Nijinsky's choreography disappeared into Lethe, but for a handful of photographs and Valentine Gross's immortal pastels and (especially) action drawings, reproduced in a myriad of secondary sources.[89] Although valiant attempts have been made at reconstructing it, culminating in the

82. Letter of 20 June/3 July 1913; in IStrSM:474. He went on: "Nijinsky's choreography is incomparable. But for a very few spots everything was just the way I wanted it." Stravinsky's inconsistent testimony on Nijinsky as a collaborator vividly reflects the vacillating politics of the Ballets Russes, and later, the vicissitudes of international modernism. He was very hard indeed on Nijinsky in the *Chroniques* (see *An Autobiography,* 40–43), but reconsidered at the very end of his life. According to Vera Krasovskaya (*Nijinsky,* trans. John E. Bowlt [New York: Schirmer Books, 1979], 243), Stravinsky told the Soviet choreographer Yuriy Grigorovich that Nijinsky's, after all, had been "the finest embodiment of *Le Sacre.*"

83. Buckle, *Nijinsky,* 292–304, including a detailed resumé of what could be reconstructed as of 1971 from the choreography, a summary of Jacques Rivière's review, an account of the opening-night scandal, and a sampling of reviews; and idem, *Diaghilev,* 252–55, a little masterpiece of pithy reportage, drawing telegraphically on a wide variety of sources.

84. Bullard, "First Performance," 1:142–55.

85. Louis Vuillemin, "Le Sacre du Printemps," *Comoedia* 7, no. 2068 (31 May 1913); in ibid., 1:144.

86. *Cock and Harlequin,* trans. Rollo Myers (London: Egoist Press, 1921), 49.

87. Volumes 2 and 3 of Bullard's mammoth compilation provide every Paris and London review in the original and in English, together with copious annotations and supporting documents.

88. Truman C. Bullard, "The Riot at the Rite: Not So Surprising After All," in *Essays on Music for Charles Warren Fox,* ed. Jerald C. Graue (Rochester: Eastman School of Music Press, 1979), 206.

89. E.g., Siohan, *Stravinsky,* 49; Buckle, *Nijinsky,* insert before 271, also 296–97; Krasovskaya, *Nijinsky,* 271; Mina Lederman, ed., *Stravinsky in the Theater* (New York: Dance Index, 1949; rpt. Da Capo Press, 1975), 30; Alexander Schouvaloff and Victor Borovsky, *Stravinsky on Stage* (London: Stainer & Bell, 1982), 67, 74; Pasler (ed.), *Confronting Stravinsky,* 75–79 (including four-page color insert after 76).

Joffrey Ballet's production of 1987,[90] Nijinsky's contribution, for all its historic shock value, does not form any part of the enduring legacy of *The Rite*.

As for Stravinsky, though he recalled feeling exhilaration after the première,[91] he was keenly disappointed in the reception of the work, however it may have enhanced his notoriety and his standing with the avant-garde. He had looked forward to a great popular triumph with *The Rite* such as he had experienced with *The Firebird* and *Petrushka*, not a mere *succès de scandale*. Upon finishing the score he had exulted in advance to Roerich: "From all indications I can see that this piece is bound to 'emerge' in a way that rarely happens!"[92] But emerge it did not. That first night no one even heard it. The production was discontinued after the 1913 London tour, a casualty of Diaghilev's break with the newlywed Nijinsky. The ballet would not be revived until 1920 (in Massine's choreography). The full score would not be published until even later,[93] which meant that apart from Monteux (who directed the première) and Koussevitzky (the publisher himself) no conductor had access to it.

The disruption of musical organizations during the war did its considerable bit to retard *The Rite*'s progress as well. Thus, although Monteux's concert performance in Paris on 5 April 1914 was remembered by Stravinsky for the rest of his life as "a triumph such as *composers* rarely enjoy,"[94] the music would not be heard again for almost seven years, that is, for the whole duration of Stravinsky's so-called Swiss period. Throughout that time, for all that it was instantly his most notorious work, thoughts of *The Rite* were tinged for Stravinsky with thoughts of failure. Briefly despondent in the fall of 1913, he unburdened himself in a remarkably—nay, uniquely—self-revealing letter to Benois, a letter that betrays not only the extent of Stravinsky's emotional dependence on Diaghilev, but also the extent of his fear about his own creative future in the wake of the *Rite* fiasco.

> I knew nothing about Nijinsky's wedding, since I've not been reading the papers lately and learned about it only from Seryozha [Diaghilev]. Hard though it is to believe, there is nothing for it but to believe it! Needless to say, this will turn ev-

---

90. On this reconstruction and its sources, see Millicent Hodson, "The Fascination Continues: Searching for Nijinsky's *Sacre*," *Dance Magazine* 54, no. 6 (June 1980): 64–66, 71–75; idem, "Nijinsky's New Dance: Rediscovery of Ritual Design in *Le Sacre du Printemps*" (Ph.D. diss., University of California, Berkeley, 1985); idem, "Nijinsky's Choreographic Method: Visual Sources from Roerich for *Le Sacre du Printemps*," *Dance Research Journal* 18, no. 2 (Winter 1986–87): 7–15; idem, "*Sacre*: Searching for Nijinsky's Chosen One," *Ballet Review* 15, no. 3 (Fall 1987): 53–66; Arlene Croce, "Footnotes in the Sands of Time," *New Yorker*, 23 November 1987; Robert Craft, "*The Rite*: Counterpoint and Choreography," *Musical Times* 129, no. 1742 (April 1988): 171–76 (but also R. Taruskin, Letter to the editor, *Musical Times* 129, no. 1746 [August 1988]: 385).

91. "After the performance we were excited, angry, disgusted and . . . happy" (Conv:48/46).

92. Letter of 1/14 December 1912; in Vershinina (ed.), "Pis'ma Stravinskogo Rerikhu," 62.

93. And after revisions had been made, creating a nightmare for textologists. See Robert Craft, "*Le Sacre du Printemps*: The Revisions," *Tempo* 122 (1977): 2–8; Van den Toorn, *Stravinsky and "The Rite*," 39–56; and esp. Louis Cyr, "*Le sacre du printemps*: petite histoire d'une grande partition," in Lesure (ed.), *Stravinsky: études et témoignages*, 91–147.

94. E&D:164/143.

erything—literally *everything* that concerns us—upside down, and you can predict for yourself all the consequences—for him it's all over; for me the possibility has been taken away—perhaps for a long while—of seeing something worthwhile in the realm of choreography, and what is even *more important,* of seeing my baby, whose scenic realization had cost such incredible effort. Ah, my dear, this last off-spring of mine even now gives me not a moment's peace. What an incredible storm of teeth-gnashing rages about it! Scryozha gives me horrible news about how people who were full of enthusiasm or unwavering sympathy for my earlier works have turned against this one. So what, say I, or rather, think I—that's how it ought to be. But what has made Seryozha seem to waver himself toward *Le Sacre?*—a work he never listened to at rehearsals without exclaiming, "Divine!" He has even said (something that by rights ought to be taken as a compliment) that this piece ought to ripen a while after completion, since the public is not yet ready for it—but why then did he *never before* mention such a procedure, either in the *Mir iskusstva* days or since? To put it as simply as possible, I'm afraid that he has fallen under bad influences—strong not so much from the moral as from the material point of view (and *very* strong). . . . To tell the truth, reviewing my impressions of his attitude toward *Le Sacre,* I am coming to the conclusion that he will not encourage me in this direction. This means I am deprived of my single and truest support in the matter of propagandizing my artistic ideas. You will agree that this completely knocks me off my feet, for I cannot, you understand, I simply *can not* write what they want from me—that is, repeat myself—repeat anyone else you like, only not yourself!—for that is how people write themselves out. But enough about *Le Sacre.* It makes me miserable.[95]

The score finally began to make its way only in the twenties, beginning with Stokowski's American première (Philadelphia, 3 March 1922). By the end of the decade it had been played everywhere from Leipzig (under Furtwängler!) to Budapest (under Dohnányi) to Buenos Aires, and had been established as a—perhaps *the*—twentieth-century classic.[96] That future, however, hardly seemed assured in 1913.

The first word of the first-night reception to reach Russia was a telegram from Guriy Stravinsky to Steinberg. Either it carried an ambiguous message or Guriy was hiding the truth from the folks back home, for Steinberg sent Stravinsky felicitations on "*Sacre*'s enormous triumph."[97] Derzhanovsky, under a similar misapprehension, sent a similar message from Moscow.[98] The real story broke in the Russian press with a trio of ecstatic eyewitness reviews. They were the work not of musicians but of balletomanes, among whom a genuine avant-garde faction did exist. They focused on Nijinsky's work, bringing up Stravinsky's contribution

95. Letter of 20 September/3 October 1913; in IStrSM:477–78.
96. For a selective résumé of *Rite* premières through 1935, see Lesure (ed.), *Stravinsky: "Le sacre du printemps,"* 9.
97. Letter of 18 May/1 June [*sic*] 1913; in the Stravinsky Archive.
98. "I rejoice with all my heart at the brilliant success of *The Rite of Spring*" (Letter of 19 May [1 June] 1913; Stravinsky Archive).

only secondarily, even incidentally. Nevertheless, they effectively abetted the mounting anti-Stravinsky backlash.

The first of these essays to appear was an altogether remarkable account by Nikolai Kostïlyov entitled "Our Art in Paris," which appeared in the newspaper *Russkaya molva* on 24 May/6 June 1913. It began with an appreciation of Diaghilev's role as a cultural trendsetter who always managed to stay ahead of his competitors and emulators both at home and abroad. For the first time in history, the critic proclaimed, Russia was in advance of Europe: "Here is something for us Russians to ponder, something in which to take pride and something to value in contemporary art." Both *Jeux* and *The Rite,* he admitted, were "efforts distinguished more by daring than by success or perfection, but," he added, "in both of them there spouts the same spring of inspiration, which makes them infinitely to be valued: you find lots to criticize in them but all the same you are transported with delight." Summing up, the critic acknowledged the heated reception, but saw in that a sign of vitality:

> The novelties of the current season are a far cry from the success and perfection of *Sheherazade* or *Petrushka,* or even last year's *Tamara* [by Fokine to music by Balakirev]. . . . So far they have been lambasted heartily, and many are reproaching the Diaghilev troupe for their excessive audacity, even calling it their mockery of the public. I myself find that they ought to work things out to a greater degree and give us something more perfected. There can be no doubt that they are in a hurry to meet their deadlines and that this is harming their creative work. But all the same, if you compare them with what is being done all around them, their work sparkles like a pure diamond amid artificial stones. It has that elusive thing we call life in art, living inspiration. And this is something that is sensed not only by artists in all categories, who speak of the Diaghilev spectacles with boundless enthusiasm; it is sensed by the public at large, who fill the Théâtre des Champs Élysées despite the insane prices. At the first performance of *Jeux* and *The Rite of Spring,* part of the audience, it is true, was bewildered and even expressed disapproval[!], but another part applauded warmly, and in this applause one sensed gratitude for that strength and freshness of impression that only youthful creations, full of life, can give. Here we have, I repeat, something to think about! Every age has its art, and it is better to value it than to mourn lost forms of creative expression. Neither in architecture, nor in sculpture, nor in painting (at least in the classical varieties of the latter) can we compare with our predecessors. But in the area of decorative fantasy, not only in the theater but in life itself, our time has spoken a new word, and in this realm we Russians have turned out to occupy the first place. This is an undeniable strength and we can only take pride in it.[99]

The eminent dance critic "N. Minsky" (real name Nikolai Maximovich Vilenkin) published a "Letter from Paris" on what he called the "Festival of Spring" ("*Prazdnik vesnï*"—an attempt at direct translation of *Le sacre du printemps*) in the

99. N. Kostïlyov, "Nashe iskusstvo vo Parizhe," *Russkaya molva,* 24 May 1913.

newspaper *Utro Rossiyi* on 30 May/12 June. He, too, emphasized the controversial aspects of the latest Diaghilev presentations, but if anything he was even more emphatic in his positive assessment of the modernistic trend they represented, flinging the hostile reception back in the teeth of the protesters:

In the fate of the Diaghilev enterprise the biblical story of Pharaoh's dream has come true. Seven clamorous, full-blooded ballets produced by Fokine brought Diaghilev seven years [only four, really] of glory and full houses. But all at once into the repertoire of the Russian Ballet the *raffiné,* modernistic conceptions of Nijinsky have intruded—and fear has arisen lest the lean cows consume the fat. It seems as if the individual voices of recognition and wonder have been swallowed up in a growing chorus of protest.

It is curious that the European critics acclaimed Diaghilev as a bold innovator and reformer of choreography precisely when he was staging old ballets, Romantic in plot and classical in technique, adorned and quickened by Fokine's temperament, Bakst's taste, and the inspiration of Borodin and Rimsky-Korsakov. But as soon as Nijinsky, and, following him[!], Stravinsky, set themselves the task of radically reforming the technique and content of ballet, the public took flight and the critics began to speak of northern barbarians.

Nijinsky's first ballet, produced last year—*The Afternoon of a Faun*—already called forth light protests from the public, who however quickly became reconciled to it, persuaded that the eccentricities of movement and grouping in this ballet were prompted by ancient Greek bas-reliefs and vases—in a word, by something ancient, sanctified by the ages, recognized and esteemed by all. Nijinsky's second ballet, *Jeux,* produced this year, was already greeted by loud protests; and as concerns *The Rite of Spring,* produced the other day, the first performance of this ballet went off against an uninterrupted chorus of whistles, catcalls, singing, and laughter from the offended spectators—and ecstatic applause from a little band [*kuchka!*] of admirers.

There follows an unconditional and fairly fulsome paean to Nijinsky's talents and his "neorealism," meaning his break with "classical routine and romantic falsehood." The critic distinguishes his coinage from unprefixed "realism" in a perceptive passage that could, in light of our investigations of Stravinsky's ethnological sources and his treatment of them, be applied in a sophisticated and revealing way to the music as well.

If the starting point of his ballet is purely real, its goal is esthetic through and through. By means of rhythm he tears real movement from reality and makes it not only an object of art, but artificial, almost automaton-like. Here the whole matter is one of quality, in the nature of the rhythm, and if we could define the essence of this rhythm we would not only understand Nijinsky himself, we would illuminate this whole complicated artistic incident.[100]

100. N. Minsky, "Pis'mo iz Parizha: prazdnik vesnï," *Utro Rossiyi,* 30 May 1913.

But in fact no critic approached Stravinsky's music with this kind of subtlety, least of all Minsky. After devoting columns to Nijinsky, he tacked on one short and facile paragraph about the music in which he blandly assured his readers that "everything I have said about Nijinsky's dances applies fully to Stravinsky's score." He concluded by observing, in a phrase that must have been read with especial displeasure back at 28 Zagorodnïy Prospekt in St. Petersburg, where the Rimsky-Korsakovs still lived, that the "young musicians" of Paris "have unanimously greeted Stravinsky as a musical genius and the creator of a new polyphony and polyrhythm."[101]

Four days later, Russia's foremost balletomane, Andrey Levinson, writing in *Rech'*, added his voice to the gathering chorus in praise of "the latest effort, noteworthy and vivid if not triumphant, of our ballet abroad, an effort that is virtually magnificent in its willful audacity." Levinson wrote with great perception about depersonalization of action and expression, about the discomfort the ballet succeeded all too well in radiating into the audience, and—mirabile dictu!—about the music, "Igor Stravinsky's cyclopean poem."

> The source of this ancient witchcraft that has so obsessed with its power of suggestion the most accomplished theatrical artists of the present day—that is, the Russian dancers—is secreted in the music of Stravinsky, eccentric and demonic (in it are many sonorities familiar from *Petrushka*), piercing the earwith unbearable discordances, excruciating and imperious rhythms. If Stravinsky's effort has been a failure—and this seems likely—what a dazzling failure it is! So rich is the musical fabric, so intense and independent is his creative will, such is his immersion in the primeval soul, slavish and pathetic. True, the magnificent colors of *Fireworks* and *The Firebird* are replaced here by crude rags and tatters of barbaric melody. The woodwind instruments sound forth at times naïvely, like the panpipes of the earliest shepherds, and the bassoons, like perforated skulls in the nimble fingers of cannibal improvisers.
>
> I know of nothing more recondite than this Hottentot music.[102]

In Levinson's description of the "dazzling failure" he witnessed in Paris we recognize the *Rite* that was and is, rather than the wishful projections of the Paris critics who so profoundly impressed and influenced the composer. Here is Levinson's marvelous evocation of the Sacrificial Dance, one that surpasses in pithy accuracy of observation any that has been written since:

> To the sound of ferocious rhythmic pounding, deafened by the piercing tonalities of the orchestra, she crumples and writhes in an ecstatic angular dance. And once again the icy comedy of this primeval hysteria excites the spectator with its unprecedented impression of tortured grotesquery.[103]

101. Ibid.
102. A. Levinson, "Russkiy balet v Parizhe," *Rech'*, 3 June 1913.
103. Ibid.

"Icy comedy of primeval hysteria"—no one has ever captured more of *The Rite* in fewer words. Levinson is renowned today as Diaghilev's chief critical antagonist,[104] but clearly, he understood the Ballets Russes better than its friends. No artist could hope for a finer appreciation than Nijinsky ("and, following him, Stravinsky") received from Messrs. Levinson, Minsky, and Kostïlyov.

But then came the music critics, and everything Stravinsky ever told Calvocoressi, Vuillermoz, Schmitt, or his London interviewers was depressingly confirmed.

Only three music reviews, properly so called, appeared in the Russian press in the immediate aftermath of the *Rite* première. Two were by eyewitnesses. The cellist Yevsey Belousov was one. He sent this brief report back to the Moscow newspaper *Russkiye vedomosti:*

> Stravinsky's music is unique. Such music had never existed before. And that is not only because it has been written in such a way as to destroy all criteria of harmony and counterpoint, or because at times it consists of nothing but a chaos of cacophonous noises, but because he has succeeded in combining this sonic chaos and cacophony with a vivid psychic expressivity. The music tears even the deafest ear; it reminds one at times of the creaking and squeaking of a hundred unoiled cart wheels. There is not a single melody in it, but only vague and fuzzy embryos of tunes. It is wild and unexpected—but nevertheless, at times it is shattering and projects both the savage energy of a youthful humanity not yet sundered from the umbilical cord that unites them with Mother Earth, and the force of the dark, ill-defined sensations that possess them.[105]

Belousov's comments have the virtues of immediacy and disinterestedness, and for all its bafflement at the music *qua* music, his review does put a finger on the special quality of *The Rite* and its effect on its earliest audiences, who found the work at once incomprehensible and irresistibly exciting.

Not so the other two reviews. The second eyewitness was none other than Andrey Rimsky-Korsakov, who had gone to Paris for the express purpose of protesting the Diaghilev production of *Khovanshchina* (see the next chapter). He also caught some late performances of *The Rite,* and sent back an open letter about it (dated 7/20 June 1913) to the same newspaper in which Kostïlyov's rapturous report of Nijinsky's choreography had already appeared. Although he purported to write in sorrow rather than in anger, Rimsky-Korsakov's animus showed through clearly enough to be remarked back home with bewilderment.[106] He saw fit to couch his strictures against *The Rite* as a defense of the unruly audience:

104. See Susan Cook Summer, Introduction to Levinson, *Ballet Old and New,* ix–xii. The book, originally published in 1918, is a compilation of journalistic reviews; the 1913 *Rite* review is included.

105. Y. Belousov, "Muzïkal'naya khronika," *Russkiye vedomosti,* no. 115 (1913).

106. Derzhanovsky to Stravinsky, 24 July 1913: "I don't know what is happening with [Andrey Rimsky-Korsakov], but a certain personal enmity is evident in his writing" (SelCorrI:51).

The passions this work has aroused were so great that not only at the première, which turned into a salty scandal, but even at the third performance the audience did not allow the music, at times, to be heard. They whistled, they stamped, they expressed their indignation with loud laughter. Some, more cautious, or else wishing to be progressive critics at all costs, have attempted in their articles to expose the philistinism of such behavior on the part of the public and the absence in the author of the ballet of any intention to mock the public. And surely there can be no talk of mockery. But it seems to me that the *Sacre* does give one cause to speak of a great delusion, and perhaps even of the decline of the musical talent of its author, I. Stravinsky. The gulf between the preceding works of Stravinsky—*Petrushka* and *The Firebird*—and the *Sacre* is so great that one is forced to doubt the naturalness of its author's stylistic development. It occurred to me that Stravinsky's dizzying successes have created in him and around him a sort of inflated atmosphere, an atmosphere of artificially exalted artistic self-consciousness and a creative self-confidence that knows no restraint or doubt. His artistic development has gone not along a broad path of immanent growth, but along chance detours and tangled paths dictated by ephemeral enthusiasms. As a result the composer has shaken from his feet the dust of all harmonic foundation, preserving, in any strictly musical sense, only rhythm, dynamics, some pitiful hints of melodic design and a luxuriant orchestral coloration. With the abolition of harmonic foundations, polyphony and musical form are likewise brought to nought. For one cannot call polyphony an assortment of tones brought together by dint of sheer authorial fiat. *The Rite of Spring* is not music if by music is meant the art of harmonious conformities of tone. It is more some kind of barbaric art of noises, not always tolerable at that!

One might ask what the difference is between "authorial fiat" and the creative will that establishes new artistic values, and how I can be so sure of the harmonic nihilism of Stravinsky's latest undertakings. The answer is that what is wrong is not that Stravinsky writes the way he pleases without reckoning on anything but his own creative will, but rather the contrary: what is wrong is that he is excessively conscious not of what comes from within but of what comes from without. Under the influence not of real creative experience but of a simple act of will he has rejected all laws and declined all responsibility of self-limitation in the sphere of musical harmony. Without noticing, he has thrown the baby out with the bath water. In such a way no truly fruitful revolution in art has ever taken place. Neither Beethoven nor Wagner strove to abolish all prior foundations of musical art. The new they created did not abolish the old, but only widened artistic perspectives and possibilities. Therefore their work signified a genuine *growth* of art. All the expressive strength of music is founded on the principle of self-limitation and selectivity.

Only the path of self-limitation gives one the chance to become free of what is irrational in artistic thought. Therein lies the reality of the evocative and expressive means of art. The "freedom" Stravinsky has achieved is no freedom in any positive sense, but its antithesis, the tyranny of arbitrary rule. And the same thing has happened to Stravinsky as to so many other representatives of modernism. Fighting for freedom and individuality and in their false understanding of freedom rejecting all self-limitation, they deprive themselves by their own hand of the means of expression to assert their personal *I*.

Arbitrariness does not and cannot have an individual force. Is that not why all the futurists, for example, are as alike as twins?

The highest expression of creative individuality is always the "form" of the human personality in the Aristotelian meaning of the word, that is, a law of its personal existence and self-affirmation, which it makes for itself.

L'homme—c'est le style, one might rephrase the famous maxim. But Stravinsky's music in *The Rite of Spring* is devoid of the most precious—an individual style. One can hardly view as a *testimonium individualitatis* the mere fact that it is "like nothing else" or that it has the ability to provoke scandals![107]

What redeems this presumptuous salad of non sequiturs and double standards is our knowledge of the personal anguish and the feelings of betrayal that lay behind it, an anguish that actually had far more to do with *Khovanshchina* than with *The Rite,* the ostensible subject under review. There can be no redeeming the third Russian review of 1913. It came from the poison pen of Leonid Sabaneyev and it was surely the most captious notice *The Rite* ever received. It reeks of envy, bias, spite, and a wholly specious moral indignation. It levels insulting, baseless, irrelevant charges. It fails to observe even the most elementary rules of fair play. It is, in short, an unabashed hatchet job, transparently motivated by the writer's fanatical loyalty to Scriabin, from whom Stravinsky was stealing the headlines. As a paradigm of Stravinsky's sorry reception at home, it merits quotation far beyond its actual deserts as criticism. What must be borne in mind throughout is that Sabaneyev had not seen the production, only the four-hands piano score. That did not prevent him from writing the following:

> If the artistic merit of a work were measured by the amount of noise, talk, and more talk the given work aroused, then without doubt, the new creation that is the product of the joint efforts of Roerich, Stravinsky, and Nijinsky would have to be recognized as a work of genius.
>
> The new ballet had not even been born before they began to write about it; it had not even been staged, but already they were praising the production. And finally, like the closing chord, the grandiose scandal at the first performance. The real thing—a big "Paris" scandal! The kind every composer dreams about in his heart of hearts, the kind that stamps a work with the seal of glory and in the midst of which all motives of service to art are forgotten.
>
> Up to now such "big" scandals in Paris have been few. Just a few throughout the whole length of "Parisian" musical history. They have all been historic scandals through and through. The Gluckists and Piccinnists with their bloody battles, the failure of *Tannhäuser* on the stage of the Grand Opéra—and that's it. Stravinsky and Nijinsky have clearly fallen among good company. Does it follow, however, that "Holy Spring" [*Vesna svyashchennaya*] will in time become just as "holy" a work for all musicians as the operas of Gluck and Wagner?

107. Andrey Rimsky-Korsakov, "Russkiye opernïye i baletnïye spektakli v Parizhe," *Russkaya molva,* 27 June 1913.

But let us go to the heart of the matter. First of all, the subject of the ballet. It turns out there is no subject at all. I cannot count as a subject an assortment of scenes with practically nothing to unite them, the mere arbitrary product of Vaslav Nijinsky's creative fancy. They are all individually highly colored bits of ancient Slavic life, ancient rites, ancient dances—the absence of any "idea" in a work of art has never, perhaps, so boldly confronted the eye. Everything is for the sake of externals. The dances, the ethnological excursuses, the music, the art of the Russian choreographers, are all only pretexts for creating vivid "spectacles," exceptionally lavish visual displays of an obligatory "exotic" coloration—spectacles whose sole purpose is to shock the jaded sensory organs of the Parisians. How they are shocked—pleasantly or unpleasantly—makes no difference. The important thing is to display oneself as a true barbarian, since barbarians are à la mode right now—they inspire interest.

I have already indicated, in writing of *Petrushka,* that Stravinsky is obviously rolling down an inclined plane toward a calculated art of the marketplace. The culprit here, of course, is Diaghilev, who hitched the young composer to his enterprise and who has become bloated with his work—work that is not "artistic," but only what is required at the moment by Diaghilev the entrepreneur. The idea of the "Diaghilevshchina" is to demonstrate a barbaric Russian art to the *raffiné* Parisians. That Russian art might in fact not be barbaric at all, that it might be just as refined as the French—this is something Diaghilev either does not know or does not wish to know. Russian art must be barbaric—period! And now he has found himself a composer who can supply this barbaric art in any quantity, just the sort demanded by the virtually insatiable appetite of the entrepreneur. He writes a ballet every year. Why, you ask, necessarily a ballet!? Why not operas, why not symphonies? The answer is very simple. It is because Russian "barbaric" art became modish thanks to ballet, the incomparable Russian ballet, whose refinement has sent the *"raffiné"* Parisians into ecstasy. One must take advantage of this mood. The whole enterprise is founded very cannily and cloaked magnificently in a mantle of affected philosophizing, of sonorous propaganda for Russian art and all the rest. . . .

I have examined the music of this new creation of Stravinsky's. I will admit that I have never had a particularly high regard for this author's compositional (read: "musical") talent. In his music this young author is as calculating as any banker. Nothing with him is ever immediate, inspired, intuitive. It is all the fruit of cerebration, of reliable and successful calculations and construction. The early fruits of his creativity—if one may use so exalted a word to designate activity like Stravinsky's—were very similar to Rimsky-Korsakov, but without the latter's gentleness and fantasy. Then came the period of "Frenchification." Stravinsky began copying the methods of Ravel and Debussy. But once again the imitation was infinitely weaker than the original. Finally, beginning with *Petrushka,* Stravinsky has given us something seemingly "his own." But how uncongenial I find this "own" of his to be!

An ostentatious complexity, behind which lurks an inner poverty. The utter, irremediable absence of any "insides" to the music, which is to say its treasurable essence, its psychology. The music of Stravinsky amounts to no more than a game of jackstraws in sound. And it is false even at that, "made up," worn out. The harmonies seem at first blush to be unusual, but upon closer inspection it turns out that this unusualness is just a window dressing that hides the most threadbare simplicity. They live no inner life, as do the harmonic innovations of authentic talents; they are stricken with rickets, impotent. It is intolerable to spend any time in this atmosphere of deliberate falseness, calculatedly and circumspectly conglomerated. I cannot describe the hopelessness that arose in me as I read through and examined the new ballet. I will be told, "What about the colors, what about the sonorous luxuriance? Can one really judge Stravinsky's color without hearing him in the orchestra?"

I know this too. But I also know that they said the same thing to me about *Petrushka*. And I heard *Petrushka* in the orchestra in an excellent performance by an excellent orchestra under a first-class conductor, who, it seemed, sincerely liked the work. And so? The coloring was just coloring, and the poverty of the conception remained poverty. There was not more music, it turned out, just because its absence was indicated not by a single pianoforte but by many musicians. And so I remain an unbeliever.

And I am an unbeliever for the additional reason that I know the sorry fate of those composers who were touted in their day as "colorists." I know the fate of the dead-and-dried Berlioz. Stravinsky is a new Berlioz in his weird unmusicality. But Berlioz was a fantasist; he was full of ideas even if he could not realize them in his works owing to a lack of technique and a lack of authentically musical imagination. But withal, this was a person infinitely devoted to art. While Stravinsky—he's just a fabricator of newfangled ballet scores.

In *The Rite of Spring,* compared with *Petrushka,* there is very little that is new. It is even falser, even more primitive, even more obtrusive. The poetry that suffuses ancient Slavic life, the ineffably poetic Slavic pantheism—this Stravinsky has not transmitted at all. All the outward attributes of "pantheism" and ancient life are reproduced with the exactitude of a pedant or an archeologist. Little birds sing in the orchestra, and with fastidious accuracy other sounds of nature are likewise reproduced. But the "essence" is lacking. That essence, which Korsakov caught with genius in *Snegurochka;* that essence, which is in Beethoven's *Pastorale* and Wagner's "Forest Murmurs." And again one recalls the ill-fated Berlioz with his fastidious "storm" in the *Fantastic Symphony,* where four timpanists try with all their might to reproduce thunder in the concert hall. The result, far from verisimilar, is laughable.

No, this is no contribution to musical literature. More decisively than ever before one can now pronounce sentence on the fallacious, infinitely fallacious art of Stravinsky, an art of the ephemeral marketplace, brought into being by a chance correlation of circumstances. It will die a natural and ignominious death when the demand for it dries up, when Diaghilev will have disappeared, and with him the fashion for Russian ballet in Paris, when the *"raffiné"* Parisians will have grown tired of barbarity and will demand the classics (or something) in their musical restaurants. Then Stravinsky will have to close up his factory for modernized *lubki* and get to work on something else.[108]

---

108. L. Sabaneyev, " 'Vesna svyashchennaya,' " *Golos Moskvï,* 8 June 1913.

One has to admire the sheer brass of a critic who bases his review of *The Rite of Spring* on a four-hands reduction and then calls Stravinsky an opportunist. Nor was this the only moral innuendo to be directed at *The Rite* and its composer by outraged music journalists in Russia who had not yet seen or heard the work. To everything else, the *RMG*, in a gossip column called "Russian Music Abroad," added the charge of venality: "Despite the scandal that accompanied the mounting of the ballet, the people who 'create the theatrical weather' in Paris are pleased with the whole incident. In the words of Mr. Cherepnin, who has returned to St. Petersburg, the composer of the ballet has supposedly announced that 'now (i.e., post-scandal) we are assured of 38 thousand francs a night.' "[109]

Malicious talk like that stirred up anti-Stravinsky sentiment among many who might have known better. Even Myaskovsky, in a letter to Derzhanovsky, confessed himself put off by "the matter of the 38 thousand francs." In the same letter, however, he defended Stravinsky against the attacks of Andrey Rimsky-Korsakov and Sabaneyev, saying that "it seems to me that Stravinsky is a more musical phenomenon than they think, and it also seems to me that I will soon find links in a logical chain that will lead me naturally to *The Rite*, though I lack them now. I feel that I am gradually beginning to comprehend Stravinsky in his latest phase."[110] Derzhanovsky immediately began to scheme. He wrote directly to Stravinsky, quoting the foregoing passage from Myaskovsky's letter and also a passage in an earlier letter to the effect that "all the music in *The Rite* is stylistically characteristic and consistent, which to me is the chief objection to the accusation that Stravinsky is inorganic, contrived, put-on."[111] He offered Myaskovsky ("I have a critic who understands your work probably better than anyone else") as an antidote to Andrey Rimsky-Korsakov and Sabaneyev. The only hitch: "No score is available here; without the score, of course, one cannot write about the work."[112] Stravinsky rose to the bait and offered to send a score of the first part of the ballet for Myaskovsky's perusal.[113] This score, a copy in the hand of Catherine Stravinsky, ended up in the collection of André Meyer. Stravinsky's penciled inscription may still be clearly read at the top left: "To Nikolai Yakovlevich Myaskovsky. I urgently request that you return this score to me no later than 14 August (Old Style) and that you show it to no one except Vl. Derzhanovsky."[114]

109. "Russkaya muzïka za granitsey," *RMG* 22, nos. 24–25 (16–23 June 1913), col. 573 (unsigned).
110. Letter of 2 July 1913; in Shlifshteyn (ed.), *Myaskovskiy: stat'i, pis'ma, vospominaniya* 2:328.
111. Letter of 20 June 1913; in ibid., 326. Derzhanovsky left out another passage in which Myaskovsky had written that "*The Rite* seems in places to be exceedingly weak in invention: he'll think up some harmony and then he'll mark time with it for whole numbers at a stretch."
112. Letter of 24 July 1913; in SelCorrI:52.
113. Derzhanovsky's postcard thanking Stravinsky for the proposal (28 July) and Myaskovsky's letter acknowledging receipt of the score (7 August) are given in translation in SelCorrI:53.
114. The page on which the inscription is entered has been reproduced in Siohan, *Stravinsky*, 48. At the bottom Stravinsky wrote, "This score is a copy made from my mansucript before performance." Boris Yarustovsky, judging hastily from the listing of the manuscript in Mme Fromrich-Bonéfant, ed., *Collection musicale André Meyer* (Abbéville: Imp. Paillart, 1961), which did not contain illustrations,

Derzhanovsky further proposed that Stravinsky send proof sheets of his music in advance of publication so that Myaskovsky might review the whole work in *Muzïka*.[115] This gave Stravinsky an idea of his own. He sent Myaskovsky a telegram proposing that the latter come to Ustilug and actually correct the proofs of the Symphony in E-flat, *The Rite of Spring,* and *The Nightingale* (vocal score). Myaskovsky understandably took umbrage at being thus turned into a factotum and protested to Derzhanovsky. Stravinsky apologized to the latter in a letter from Ustilug (12/25 August 1913):

> Well it seems I've caused you trouble with my telegram to Myaskovsky. Forgive me, for God's sake. It's just that I have such an endless amount of work that I alone simply cannot cope with the proofreading side of things. So that's why I decided to turn to Myaskovsky, knowing his ability to orient himself swiftly in other people's scores. I would very much like to meet him personally and speak with him about this, since I would like to entrust to him not only the task I have in mind at present, but several others as well. . . . Perhaps he might yet decide to come, for there is much to talk over—one can't say everything in a letter.[116]

Derzhanovsky tried to smooth things over with Stravinsky and also tried to bring Myaskovsky around.[117] He only made matters worse between the two composers. "Why should I think myself less busy than Stravinsky?" Myaskovsky wrote back to Derzhanovsky in a rage. "The whole business with Stravinsky makes me sick. . . . Apparently he doesn't even know how to read proofs; before, Steinberg used to do it for him, and now he wants to saddle me with it so that he can go gallivanting abroad—well, let him sit at home for a change."[118] He agreed to read the *Nightingale* proofs only as a way of becoming familiar with a hitherto unknown piece. But when he heard from Derzhanovsky (10 September 1913) who explained that Stravinsky had been ill with typhus, was behind schedule, and needed

concluded that Stravinsky had actually dedicated *The Rite* to Myaskovsky (see IStrSM:164, 206). It became a persistent legend of Soviet Stravinskiana, embroidered quite fancifully at times, as when Igor Blazhkov, annotating Stravinsky's Russian letters, relates the ostensive dedication to Myaskovsky's enthusiastic review of *Petrushka* in *Muzïka* (no. 59 [14 January 1912]; quoted in Chapter 10): "One may suppose that Stravinsky, anything but spoiled by the Russian music critics, was so touched upon reading the above-mentioned publication that he placed a dedication to Myaskovsky on the score of the first part of *The Rite of Spring*, 'The Kiss of the Earth,' which he had just completed in February 1912" (IStrSM:511). *The Rite* is actually dedicated to Roerich.

    115. SelCorrI:52.

    116. IStrSM:476.

    117. See his letter of 16/29 August, in SelCorrI:56.

    118. Letter of 8/21 September 1913; in Shlifshteyn (ed.), *Myaskovskiy: stat'i, pis'ma, vospominaniya* 2:521. The reference to Steinberg gives a hint why Stravinsky maintained outwardly cordial relations with his old rival even after breaking with the Rimsky-Korsakov sons: Steinberg, in material need and eager for a Diaghilev commission of his own (see the next chapter), had become a willing aide. Besides proofreading, Stravinsky sent him on such errands as procuring a trumpet in D and a piccolo kettledrum for the *Rite* première (see his letters to Steinberg of 17 February/2 March and 3 May 1913 in IStrSM:471, 473; also Steinberg to Stravinsky, 11 January and 31 May 1913, excerpted in SelCorrI:44n).

to be spared the task of correcting proofs, Myaskovsky exploded again and refused even to do *The Nightingale*. And that was not all:

> My dear Derzhanushechka, I am very sorry that you have understood my long letter in a fashion so advantageous to Milord Stravinsky; still, I do not give up hope that your conscience will speak and that you will give a thought not only to the convenience of the aforementioned businessman, but also to that of this ordinary mortal, your Petersburg servant, who, you can be sure, has no great love for correcting his own proofs, let alone someone else's.... In a word, I just plain do not give a damn about Stravinsky and his commercial operations, his need to "create further" and so on (excuse me); let him read his own proofs (look at history—Bach, for all his productivity, still did his own engraving) or look at Glazunov, Lyadov, Steinberg, or any of your other pals. As for health, the only ones hurting now are the ones with no money, and besides, I don't think he's any worse off in Clarens than in his own dukedom [Ustilug]. And anyhow, I think that if he has to miss some deadline and is forced to quit his hurrying, it would only do him good—he'll do some real creative work. I don't mean by this that he is writing badly (he's too talented for that), but his work is definitely getting poorer and thinner, despite all its awesome exterior. So, no more about Stravinsky. As for you, you may in all innocence advise him to turn to Steinberg—they're friends, as you know from his dedications, and so on.... As long as you mentioned the *Rite of Spring* piece, I must remind you of one of our Moscow conversations, where I hinted that I have grown so cool to this *Spring* that I not only don't want to but actually can't write about it. I am completely indifferent to it. How long this feeling toward it will last I cannot say. I took a look at it here a while ago, approved of it all right, but my insides were not aquiver from it, and despite all wishes to the contrary (more yours than mine by now) I am in no mood to write about it at present—after all, it's no great bibliographical affair. For the wish to write even two words about it to reappear in me, someone would have to attack it with a special cruelty. Only then, perhaps, would I respond out of indignation. But in the meantime I'm deaf and dumb.[119]

Derzhanovsky now had to break the news to Stravinsky that Myaskovsky would not work for him. He did so, with consummate tact, in a letter of 3 November 1913.[120] And then he had to plead with Myaskovsky to honor his promise to write about *The Rite* for *Muzïka*. He managed to prevail upon his friend, but the article was not what it might have been had "Milord Stravinsky" been less lordly. Myaskovsky sent it in to Derzhanovsky on 9 January 1914 with a covering letter: "I am sending you a placid but unquestionably benevolent (if nothing more) notice on *The Rite*. From it you may conclude that I have personally departed rather far from Stravinsky, and that it would be in your best interests if he and I collided no

---

119. Letter of 12 September 1913; in Shlifshteyn (ed.), *Myaskovskiy: stat'i, pis'ma, vospominaniia* 2:329–30. The joshing salutation "Derzhanushechka" is derived from *dushechka*, Russian for "darling."
120. SelCorrI:60.

more—at the very least I would have to say that when I look through his music, no particular personal feeling stirs within me."[121]

The article appeared in *Muzïka* on 1 February 1914, as part of the advance publicity for the Russian première under Koussevitzky. Compared with Myaskovsky's articles on *The Firebird*, on *Petrushka*, or even on the Symphony in E-flat, its tone was "placid" indeed. It was the last extended Stravinsky review Myaskovsky would write. Its aim, clearly, was no more than "audience-softening," but Myaskovsky was incapable of writing unperceptively:

> As far as we have heard thus far, in the majority this work evokes great irritation, mockery, and only in the best instance bewilderment, chiefly because of its enigmatic harmonies, and partly because of its extremely motionless formal structure, which itself arises out of the monotony of harmonic content in many parts of *The Rite*. It is true that the harmony in this work is such that you won't make it out at one fell swoop. Much here is so unusual that one cannot grasp it immediately either with the ear or with the mind. But like all Stravinsky's previous work, *The Rite* contains so much vital fluid, so much immediacy, creative pressure, its thematic elements are so salient and characteristic, that one has only to surmount the fierce torture of first acquaintance so as later not only to return to *The Rite* with ever-increasing frequency, but to feel toward it the sincerest—well, maybe not love, but at any rate, good will.

There follows a conventional and rather tame *razbor* (descriptive commentary) of the score, number by number, and at the end Myaskovsky says a few words on "the place of *The Rite of Spring* among Stravinsky's other works." Here he attempts to redeem the pledge he had made to Derzhanovsky the year before on "finding," with the help of the score, "the links on a creative chain" that would render sensible Stravinsky's creative path. The compressed account he finally gives is somewhat cursory, but its conclusion—by which Myaskovsky seeks to justify the work and its composer—is surprising:

> Its lack of harmonic precedent is such that for a long time we not only could not comprehend *The Rite*, but, mainly, could in no wise connect it with the works that preceded it: *Petrushka*, *The Firebird*. Only by going to the trouble of attentively pursuing all of Stravinsky's works, not excluding the minor ones—the songs, *Zvezdolikiy*—did we succeed at last in catching the missing links in the line of development of the composer's harmonic thought. . . .
> Having no wish to enter into a technical description of the harmonic and other devices of Stravinsky's style, we will say only this: the foundations of his harmony apparently have much in common with the harmonic thinking of Arnold Schoenberg. The latter, of course, as a German, is far more intricate, the texture of his

---

121. Shlifshteyn (ed.), *Myaskovskiy: stat'i, pis'ma, vospominaniya* 2:499.

works is considerably more complex and refined, but on the other hand Stravinsky has the edge in his powerful blaze of temperament.

One circumstance deriving from this parallel is absorbing: traveling different paths—Schoenberg from Wagner, touching Mahler in passing; Stravinsky from Korsakov and Scriabin by way of the French—the two have come nonetheless to almost identical results.

Does this not speak better than any defensive shouting in favor of the organicism of their development and in support of their music's right to recognition (especially Stravinsky's, since he works in the slippery realm of the stage) as having an absolute, autonomous significance?[122]

All in all, a dignified assessment, but far from what Stravinsky surely hoped to get from Myaskovsky. It was a game defense, but Myaskovsky was clearly no longer about to go on the offensive for Stravinsky's sake. The whole Stravinsky/Myaskovsky affair can be taken as a paradigm of the growing estrangement between the Russian musical establishment, even its most progressive wing, and this arrogant cosmopolite who had emerged from their midst. In this charged atmosphere, anything Stravinsky said and did could be held against him. His recklessness with the press and his offhand, even high-handed relations with his Russian counterparts (he hardly treated them as colleagues) seemed to justify suspicion, as did his unswerving loyalty to Diaghilev. He was now one of those "who create the theatrical weather in Paris." What did he care about the atmospheric conditions back home?

THE RITE REJECTED

Russian musicians finally had their chance to judge the music of *The Rite* at first hand in February 1914, when Koussevitzky performed it as part of his regular subscription series in both capitals (Moscow on the fifth, St. Petersburg on the twelfth). The program consisted otherwise of French music: Franck's *Chasseur maudit,* Dukas's *Apprenti sorcier,* and Chausson's *Poème* played by Lucien Capet, who also performed a "Poème symphonique" of his own for violin and orchestra.

What kind of performance did *The Rite* receive on this occasion? For the first time we may fairly ask the question, because for the first time there was a qualified witness in the house. Myaskovsky, the only man in Russia who had seen the full score (of the first part, at least), was present (there had been no such qualified critic in Paris!), and he filed a report for *Muzïka* that began with a veiled warning to his fellow reviewers:

---

122. N. Y. Myaskovsky, "O 'Vesne Svyashchennoy' Ig. Stravinskogo," *Muzïka,* no. 167 (1 February 1914): 106–7, 111–12. Justification (or condemnation) of Stravinsky's music by superficial comparison with Schoenberg's has been a persistent strand in twentieth-century critical and analytical thinking. As recently as 1978, Allen Forte embarked on his survey of the harmonic organization of *The Rite* by observing that "in *The Rite of Spring* Stravinsky employed extensively for the first time the new harmonies that first emerged in the works of Schoenberg and Webern around 1907–08" (*Harmonic Organization,* 19).

To judge the work from this performance would be a bit rash. One can say only that *The Rite* is a vivid, original work that carries one away with its lively rhythm; it is strong practically throughout, and at times captivating. But actually all this one felt more than one really heard it, for the impression was full of distortions.

The Introduction did not come through at all. In the "Augures printaniers" and the "Rondes printanières," all the themes practically disappeared. The same fate was met by the Introduction to Part 2 and in part by the concluding dance. The "Danse de la terre," the "Jeu du rapt," and "Glorification de l'élue," and the "Cortège du sage" frequently turned into sonic porridge. The end was beyond Mr. Koussevitzky's powers. In general the music went at exaggerated tempi, with the brasses bellowing and the percussion crackling the way Mr. Koussevitzky loves it. But all the same, despite the mess called forth by Mr. Koussevitzky's magic wand, one could catch a whiff of the true beauty of *The Rite:* the peculiar charm of its harmonies (how sweetly the harmonies sounded in the "Cercles mystérieux des Adolescentes," these at first sight strange simultaneous combinations of major and minor triads, or the melody that goes in sevenths against a background of trills, and much else besides; one must not omit, on the other hand, that some things in *The Rite* are inadmissible, like the layers of parallel major seventh chords in the "Rondes printanières," which one can boldly consign to that class of phenomena that arise not out of the ear's demand, but directly under the fingers at the piano), its heroic rhythm, the nervous impetuosity of the music, and the themes which at first glance seem not to belong to it, but to have been transformed and personally colored for the occasion—short, simple, and at the same time expressive.

Serge Koussevitzky could not cope with *The Rite,* but we won't hold that too much against him, for he did perform *The Rite* after all.[123]

And what of the reception? "Don't be alarmed," Stravinsky had warned his mother, "if they hiss the *Sacre*—that's in the nature of things."[124] For the actual, somewhat surprising, reception in the hall, we may rely on Nikolai Bernshteyn's report in the *Peterburgskaya gazeta* (14/27 February): "After the first part, the conductor, had he acknowledged the applause, would have bowed, it is true, to the backs of fleeing spectators; but at the end there could be no doubt that the applause was strong . . . and friendly!" A catty letter from Benois, who heard both performances, corroborates Bernshteyn's report and adds an ironic nuance: "The success, alas, was rather big, in spite of the hundred people who walked out after the first part. I say 'alas' because the audience applauded in advance, in defiance of Paris, and also because *that* audience applauds Bach, Beethoven, Wagner, Rachmaninoff, and Stravinsky in equal measure. . . . A success with such an audience is nauseating. I am very glad that Nurok liked it, however; and that the Rimsky-Korsakov clan hissed it violently is also a consolation."[125] César Cui, sole anachronistic survivor of the original mighty kuchka, was in the audience, too, and re-

123. "Peterburgskiye pis'ma," *Muzïka,* no. 171 (1 March 1914); in Shlifshteyn (ed.), *Myaskovskiy: stat'i, pis'ma, vospominaniya* 2:155.

124. Letter of 20 December 1913; in IStrSM:480.

125. Letter of 14–17 February 1914; in M&C:131–32/140.

corded his reaction in one of his letters to Maria Kerzina: "Recently Sergey Koussevitzky has performed Stravinsky's *Rite of Spring,* which has broken all records for cacophony and hideousness. It is a treasure chest in which Stravinsky has lovingly collected all sorts of musical filth and refuse. In French I would put it that 'M-r Stravinsky est un vendangeur musical [a musical vintage-gatherer].' This 'Rite' has been booed everywhere abroad, but among us it has found some applauders—proof that we are ahead of Europe on the path of musical progress."[126]

Despite Cui's disgusted dismissal, and despite their own revulsion, the professional critics of St. Petersburg were quick to notice—indeed, to overdraw—*The Rite*'s obvious connection with the nineteenth-century Russian music that was by now their "classical" tradition. Thus Koptyayev, who had made similar observations about *Petrushka:* "When it comes to cacophony, the young author has run rings around all the modernists and futurists. There is, however, an essential difference between him and them: they are 'without a past'; he, on the contrary, esteems the tradition of nationalism and wishes to be the expresser of a national style. I have already spoken once about his commonfolk [*prostonarodnïye*] tendencies: it's a modernized Serov."[127] And the anonymous reviewer of the *Peterburgskiy listok,* who severely chastised the composer for his overweening "aspiration to hyperoriginality," nonetheless allowed that "it is highly remarkable that, despite all its excesses, *The Rite of Spring* is all the same a purely Russian work. About it one can say, forsooth, 'Here dwelleth Russia; it smells of Russia' [*Zdes' Rus' zhivyot; zdes' Rus'yu pakhnet*]."[128]

By and large, the journalistic reception of Stravinsky's "ballet-mysterium" was predictable enough. The lack of an organized musical avant-garde in Russia was only too obvious. Almost comically, the Russian reviewers found themselves saying many of the same things the French littérateurs had been saying the previous year, but from the opposite perspective and with the opposite intention. It was a case once more of *oproshcheniye* versus *uproshcheniye, kul'tura* versus *stikhiya.* An anonymous review in the newspaper *Den'*—very likely the work of Victor Kolomiytsev (1868–1936), the paper's then music editor (who had collaborated indirectly with Stravinsky on the orchestral setting of Beethoven's "Flea" for Siloti)—was typical: "One cannot deny that the music of the 'Spring' is imbued with 'primeval savagery,' but this savagery is altogether inartistic. From the standpoint of *cultured* art, it represents a counterpull toward the *savagery of chaos,* toward elemental *noises.* And if the art of music in our day is really destined to achieve utter chaos, then it will only remain for it to be born again out of the same original kernels [as before]."[129] One phrase in this review has a chilling resonance: "Stravin-

126. Letter of 16 February/1 March 1914; in Cui, *Izbrannïye pis'ma,* 446.
127. *Birzheviye vedomosti,* 14/27 February 1914.
128. *Peterburgskiy listok,* 14/27 February 1914.
129. Undated clipping in the Stravinsky Archive, Scrapbook 1912–14.

sky's music—or rather, that sonic muddle [*sumbur*] he has given us in his 'Spring' instead of music [*vmesto muziki*]—is a monstrosity through and through." "*Sumbur vmesto muziki*": this was the title of the infamous unsigned *Pravda* editorial of 28 January 1936, nominally directed against Shostakovich's *Lady Macbeth of the Mtsensk District,* that ushered in the period of severest repression in Soviet arts policy, when a spirit of provincial bourgeois philistinism (what in Russian is called *meshchanstvo*) was elevated to the status of official dogma in the USSR. The *Den'* review of *The Rite* and the *Pravda* excoriation of *Lady Macbeth,* though they seem artifacts of different civilizations, were actually written only twenty-two years apart. Could the two anonymous authors have been one?

The nadir was plumbed by a man who knew Stravinsky very well indeed. Victor Valter (Walter, 1865–1935) was an occasional writer on music whose main profession was violin playing. Trained by Leopold Auer, he was from 1890 to 1919 the concertmaster of the Mariyinsky Theater Orchestra. Thus his acquaintance with Stravinsky went all the way back to the latter's "mascot" days,[130] and he had also taken part in the Siloti-led premières of the *Scherzo fantastique, Fireworks,* and the *Firebird* suite. His "answer" to Tolstoy's *What Is Art?*—a brochure called "In Defense of Art" ("*V zashchitu isskustva*" [St. Petersburg, 1898])—had endeared him to Rimsky-Korsakov,[131] and he had maintained his ties with the family after the composer's death. It is possible that Valter wrote his lengthy attack on *The Rite* as a self-styled (or, conceivably, even designated) spokesman for the Rimsky-Korsakovs.

Whatever its circumstances, it was a thing of well-nigh incredible obtuseness and pretension. Valter, who had graduated from the University of Kharkov in mathematics before pursuing his musical career, fancied himself—like Andrey Rimsky-Korsakov, who taught philosophy at the Gurevich Gymnasium—an "*intelligent*" (as, with hard *g*, the Russians say). He took *The Rite* as a pretext for a sententious philosophical inquiry into revulsion and repellence in life and art. Here is a sample:

> The causes of [physical] revulsion are of three kinds. In the first place, there are phenomena and objects that are intrinsically repulsive, for instance odors, tactile sensations, certain sounds (scratching on glass); I cannot think of any intrinsically repulsive visual sensations: certain combinations of colors can be unpleasant, but not to the point of revulsion. In the second place, any sensation may become painful when experienced for too long a time. This applies particularly to tastes, visual sensations, and sounds, even ones that are pleasant in small doses. Finally, in the third place, any sensation may achieve a high degree of repellence if taken to a high level of intensity, even when experienced for a short period. This we experience in all sensory domains, but especially in the domain of hearing, since the intensity of sounds may be easily brought to intolerable levels.

130. Stravinsky actually recalled him from this period (E&D:47/43) as one with whom he had been "especially friendly" in his teen-age years.
131. Yastrebtsev, *Vospominaniia* 2:39.

> Upon encountering phenomena that evoke our revulsion, we may rid ourselves
> of them in two ways: either by removing the phenomenon itself or by avoiding it.

Et cetera. It is only too easy to see where all this is heading, but it takes Valter thousands of words to work his way around to his real subject, meanwhile belaboring truisms such as the distinction between actual objects of revulsion encountered in life (he christens them "first-order phenomena") and "artificial" ones encountered in works of art ("second-order phenomena"). Music, he claims, with the negligible exception of onomatopoeic imitations of natural sounds in programmatic works, "is a first-order phenomenon, and here, just as in the domain of smell, we categorically reject the repellent." And here, of course, is where *The Rite of Spring* comes in. It is a physically repulsive phenomenon that—it may be objectively demonstrated—cannot be tolerated by a normal human organism.

> I have nothing against any dissonance at all, so long as it is musically logical, that
> is, when it exists as the antithesis of consonance. But when my ears are racked
> with dissonances for a long time and with the strength of a steamboat whistle,
> then I do object: this is no longer an esthetic perception, but physical torture.
> There are people who like such torture, since for them music that does not burst
> a drumhead is too weak and they are unaffected by it. But such people need to be
> cured. Stravinsky's music . . . evokes in us an unpleasant pressure on the ear, which
> goes all the way to the point of revulsion. This revulsion, as explained above, is
> not an esthetic revulsion, but a painful sensation of the most actual sort, evoked by
> the use of physical force on our sense of hearing. . . . When you listen to Stravinsky's music performed on the piano (four-hands), you get the impression of an
> absurd musical nonsense, as if some sort of insignificant music were being played
> on two pianos tuned a half-step apart. In concert, this music, thanks to the force
> of the orchestra's sonority, evokes a physically painful sensation of which we can
> be rid, as stated above, in two ways: either by removing the music from ourselves
> or ourselves from the music. Both of these methods were employed by the Paris
> audience when the ballet was mounted in the spring of 1913.[132]

Q.E.D. But even the friendliest Russian critics were taken aback at the dissonance level of Stravinsky's music—something about which we nowadays may even need a reminder.[133] Vyacheslav Karatïgin, St. Petersburg's lonely "official modern-

132. V. G. Valter, "O 'Vesne svyashchennoy' Igorya Stravinskogo," *Birzheviye vedomosti*, 22 February/7 March 1914.

133. An effective one is Arnold Whittall's article "Music Analysis as Human Science?" Having surveyed various approaches to the score over the couple of decades ending in 1982, Whittall deplores the lack of cognizance taken by analysts (of all persuasions) of this most elemental feature of *The Rite* and suggests that in its insensitivity to the physical experience of sound analysis may have become dehumanized: "Dissonance may indeed be emancipated in that it is no longer subject to rules requiring and prescribing preparation and resolution. But the effect of that emancipation within a work where consonances remain to be heard from time to time is an enhancement of dissonance as a structural focus, and not an elimination, an emasculation of that focal role, with dissonances being transformed into 'polychords,' or some such neutral construct" (51).

ist," in a preliminary notice that preceded his full-length critique of the work, imparted to his readers the breathless news that "from beginning to end there is not a single pure triad."[134] The actual review, printed two days later, is an extremely interesting document: a detailed record of the impression made by Stravinsky's masterwork on perhaps the most receptive musical mind in the Russian capital.

His disclaimers notwithstanding, Karatïgin's interpretation of *The Rite* was a patently "futurist" one that set the tone for the Russian modernist reception of Stravinsky, such as it was, through Asafyev.[135] Karatïgin's opening paragraphs rival Rivière's for "intuition." The critic associates the "psychic stenography" of "impressionism" (understood in the large, transcending specific artistic schools and movements) with the Blokian *uproshcheniye* the French littérateurs had fastened upon (ironically, in opposition to what *they* called Impressionism, more narrowly construed) as Stravinsky's signal contribution. But of course, Karatïgin's stance was far more disinterested than theirs, and his perceptions, therefore, all the more accurate and valuable.

> Motors, moving pictures, telephones, aeroplanes, radium, a whole series of discoveries and improvements in all areas of art, science, culture as a whole—each more unusual than the last, all following upon one another with greater and greater rapidity. . . .
> I am far from holding with the "futurists," who have posited the latest advances in technology as the only worthy subject for the latest art. But can one doubt that motors and aeroplanes are bound to introduce—have in fact introduced—definite modifications in the whole psyche of contemporary man, that the breakneck speed of technological progress in our day is bound to find response in a certain general nervousness, a heightened pressure in the whole cultural atmosphere that surrounds us? Can one be surprised that the resources of the latter are bound in the end to resonate in some way even with that which is furthest from any technology and freest from the direct impact of motors and aeroplanes—that is, with the strings of our souls, the very things that manage the secrets of artistic creativity and perception? The influence, of course, is collateral and extremely complex, and the results might be extremely various. But, by virtue of the interconnectedness of all spheres of our psychological organism, this influence is bound to exist, and in fact it does. It is in the well-known quickening and sharpening of all our experiences, the well-known "impressionization" of the whole structure of our souls. The transformation of psychological impressionism into creative imagery assumes various guises, is manifested in various alterations and complications; sometimes it is even accompanied by tendencies that, strangely enough, directly contradict impressionism, inclining rather toward classic limpidity and elegance of structure,

---

134. V. G. Karatïgin, "Sed'moy kontsert Kussevitskogo," *Rech'*, 14 February 1914.
135. For Asafyev's extension of Karatïgin's viewpoint on Stravinsky into an all-encompassing theory of modern music that saw Stravinsky as the seminal force bringing music out of the period of Romantic "hypnosis" into an era of wide-awake alertness, of actuality, of the assertion of the "dynamics of contemporary life," see *A Book About Stravinsky*, 97–99.

aspiring toward a second simplicity. In such cases, obviously, the law of psychological contrasts is called into play. The artist, reflecting in art his fragmented soul, split up into nervous impressions, at the same time feels fatigued by nervous tensions and already seeks an antidote to them in a deliberate return to simplicity.[136]

Karatïgin amplified these remarks brilliantly in a somewhat later essay, composed with benefit of reflection, entitled "Music Old and New." The following paragraphs, in which Stravinsky's "futurism" is explicitly justified and reconciled with his "primitivism," still make suggestive reading. Karatïgin's assessment of the crucial role of displacement (*sdvig*) in Stravinsky's musical esthetic, backed up with solid technical observation, is an impressive testimonial to the depth of the critic's musical perceptions—these comments, recall, were made on the basis of a single hearing of the full orchestration—and his ability to articulate them. This was by any standard the finest bit of technical writing on Stravinsky to appear anywhere in the years of the composer's first fame:

> You have all seen futurist paintings, of course, and, even if only once, you have read futurist verses. . . . And you have of course noticed that *displacement* is the characteristic feature of futurist art. Either the two eyes in a portrait have skittered to different corners of the painting, or else the letters in a word have been rearranged, mixed up. I have no intention of defending such unnatural displacements in the realms of painting, poetry, or sculpture, arts that in all likelihood will always remain more or less tied to the world of reality through their dependence on a *subject*. But music! Its content is metaphysical, it has no real objects of "depiction." In music, the one art that does not depend on reality, all manner of *displacement* is possible—displacements free of any taint of perversion, displacements fraught with the attainment of a new beauty.
>
> You can look upon the "Spring" from any angle you like. You can delight in its fantastic harmonies or else reject them. But you can't overlook one essential fact. What Stravinsky is doing in the "Spring" is founded mainly on *displacement*. Tonalities are displaced. Instead of succeeding one another in an orderly fashion, they have all at once begun to pile up on top of one another. And intervals are displaced. Octaves have suddenly slipped down into sevenths. Or else it transpires that what is major down below has shifted to minor up above; whereupon the chord in the bass, as if envying the treble's audacity, begins to shrivel and pucker until it has been transformed into a diminished or augmented harmony.
>
> And rhythms are displaced. Here a quarter, there an eighth, have detached themselves from the regular measures and calmly roam at will, or else they scatter among the neighboring measures, thereby destroying their regularity and symmetry. Everywhere and in every way there is *displacement*. Everything has been shifted and shuffled, so that at first it is hard even to tell what has happened, what "regular" scheme a given harmony had belonged to before its elements had been rearranged and scattered, or, on the contrary, had collided with one another. . . .

136. V. G. Karatïgin, "'Vesna svyashchennaya,'" *Rech'*, 16 February 1914; reprinted in Lesure (ed.), *Stravinsky: "Le sacre du printemps,"* 81.

But consider the content of the ballet. . . . It is no accident that Stravinsky has fixed upon such an archaic subject. Stravinsky is drawn to the primitive, to old modes, to bare unisons and fifths, to those musical means that belong to a far remoter antiquity than the music of viols and harpsichords. . . . In Stravinsky, in a single score, the *plusquamperfectum* and the *futurum* are united. In a single work we get both lapidary melodies that correspond in their character to the spirit of prehistoric antiquity, and harmonies that will only be assimilated by the mass consciousness after decades have passed, if not longer.[137]

Like Myaskovsky, Karatïgin professes to see a deep kinship between Stravinsky and Schoenberg—prompted in his case, no doubt, by the enthusiastic letter he had received from the Russian composer about the German (see Chapter 11, n. 88). His technical observations, quite the most detailed anyone dared attempt at the time (and—in their perceptions re "polytonality" and the relatedness of the elements combined therein—quite the most penetrating), locate Stravinsky's innovations within a familiar field of antecedents:

The complexity of Stravinsky's harmony is to a certain extent *illusory*. Most often it is the simultaneous combination of several simple chords belonging to different keys. Such "polytonal" combinations (they are not uncommon in Strauss, too) sometimes produce an impression of extraordinary cunning, but even a not overly developed ear soon catches on to their true construction, after which the given harmony is perceived not as an organic whole so much as a mixture. So be it. Suppose such harmonies are of a somewhat deceptive character. Do they therefore inspire doubt as to their artistic integrity? Not at all. Does illusion not play an important part in all art? Does one not encounter in Rimsky-Korsakov, to say nothing of Debussy, hints of the illusionary possibilities in the bitonal harmonies of *Le coq d'or*? Do the new original esthetic values put forth by our time not consist precisely in that psychological ambiguity (about which I have spoken above in general terms) with which the musician resorts to polytonal sound combinations, feeling them at once as something complex and recherché and as the sum of simple components?

Let us be fair to Stravinsky: in the realm of polytonal sound combinations he manifests astonishing resourcefulness and logic. He mixes not just any old tonalities, but always those that for one reason or another have been strongly interconnected in the mind of the listener. Such, for example, is the background pedal in the "Spring Divinations," which consists of the uniting of two triads, one a semitone beneath the other. The result is something strange, but closely related to the ordinary suspension of the diminished octave, an old device that everyone knows. In the "Games of the Two Cities" [the title under which the "Game of 'Cities'" was published], Stravinsky realizes the following plan: he takes a beautiful Russian theme and accompanies it with *diatonic* thirds (with the customary succession of major and minor thirds) in a definite key; whereupon the upper voice of the thirds is systematically doubled at the *major* sixth above, while the lower voice is doubled

137. V. G. Karatïgin, "Muzïka staraya i novaya," *Teatr i iskusstvo*, no. 9 (1914); in Kuznetsov, "V zerkale russkoy kritiki," 74. Large paragraphs have been broken down into smaller ones.

at the *minor* sixth below (the further permutation of the voices has no essential significance). The result is a most curious succession of clashes. The first and third voices glide along in sevenths where the even-numbered voices give pure octaves, which falsifies the latter, and the odd-numbered sound at the octave. In essence we have three keys here, connected, however, by the abundance of pure octaves. Or else Stravinsky unites different keys in this way: he gives—to express it in "pianistic" terms—two figurational patterns, one on the white keys, the other on the black, in the same register and as far as possible in a meter that does not correspond to that of the first pattern. It is clear that what presents itself to the ear, in the given instance, when both patterns are moving quickly, is a multiplicity of little chromatic appoggiaturas, and the sum of two diatonic figurations thus takes on as it were a chromatic aspect. One is simultaneously aware of the contrast between the two patterns, and of the "pseudochromatic" whole.

I would like to say a bit more on the development of contemporary secundal chord structures out of appoggiaturas, just as the appoggiaturas themselves had proceeded from suspensions, and about the historical evolution of the unresolved suspensions Stravinsky uses from their older, simpler forms—but I am afraid that too many technical details might try the reader's attention. I will limit myself to adducing two principles that lie at the heart of contemporary impressionism, if one looks at it from the point of view of the purely musical evolution of sound structuring. The first principle is the recognition of the consonant character that underlies chords that are defined by ever more complicated acoustical relations. This principle of harmony of the "upper overtones" has been realized in part by the French, in part by Scriabin. The other principle is the granting of an increasing independence to passing harmonies. The French impressionists are not strangers to this principle either. Stravinsky bases himself chiefly on it. *Polytonal and pseudochromatic combinations can be construed without any especial strain as individual instances of the second principle.*[138]

Given such a high level of artistic sympathy and such a stunning acuity of perception, it is all the more exasperating to see Karatïgin unexpectedly, at the very end of his lengthy review, give *The Rite* the back of his hand after all:

What are the general conclusions from all that has been said? What shall be our general artistic evaluation of *The Rite of Spring*? It seems to me that, when all is said and done, its historical, symptomatic significance outweighs its artistic significance. The best episodes, the ones that act irresistibly on the listener's imagination, I have already noted. But even in these best episodes certain unpleasant features leap to the eye: the monotony with which devices are employed, the absence of any overall development of ideas, the excessive tendentiousness in contriving harmonies, each more terrifying and venomous than the last.

The main thing is the monotony. A pedal is a good thing, but how exhausted we become when pedals stretch one after the other in an endless chain! And how many monotonously gouging rhythms there are in *The Rite of Spring!* What metric

138. Karatïgin, "'Vesna svyashchennaya,'" in Lesure, *Stravinsky: "Le sacre du printemps,"* 83–85. Large paragraphs have been broken into smaller ones.

tricks does Stravinsky not throw up—and yet, it would seem, real variety is not achieved. The final dance of the doomed victim is an out-and-out rhythmic paradox, and yet there is no rhythmic life in it; it seems that it might be successfully laid out in a duple or triple meter—with plenty of syncopations, naturally.

Worst of all, despite all of Stravinsky's harmonic and coloristic invention, despite all his really significant accomplishments in the areas of polytonality and pseudochromaticism, despite all the freewheeling temperament in this music, it remains . . . superficial. Depth, breadth, inner might, epic pathos, mystical color, all that one would so like to see in *The Rite* over and above what is given there —all this is *not* given.

How did this happen? How did it turn out that the most important and necessary creative elements are lacking in *The Rite*? Is the well-known externality and superficiality of Stravinsky's talent an organic trait? One would like to think that in future opuses Stravinsky will refute such thoughts, which incidentally are inspired not only by *The Rite,* but in part by *Petrushka* and *The Firebird* too. But even if Stravinsky never presents any refutation in this sense, his *Rite of Spring* will remain in the history of our art as an exceptionally vivid, if in many ways a flawed monument to the impressionist phase of Russian music.[139]

How did *this* happen? How did the best critical mind in Russia close to Stravinsky's masterpiece? The composer, not without reason, took extreme offense at Karatïgin's conclusion, and that was the end of their good relations. He wrote to Benois: "This omnivorous critic couldn't tell the difference between impressionism and optimism. . . . He actually lumps me, Scriabin, Debussy, Ravel all together under the same heading, impressionism! You think I'm joking? With complete assurance I tell you that it's so; I have many proofs of it in his articles. . . ."[140] The composer was now at loggerheads with every Russian critic. He and Russia adamantly turned their backs on each other, putting the seal of irony on Karatïgin's earlier declaration that "*The Rite of Spring,* whatever one may make or think of it, is an event, an event of extraordinary historical importance in the life of our Russian art." The pathetic fact remains that *The Rite* ultimately had this significance everywhere *but* Russia—a fact far more pathetic for Russia than for *The Rite*.

THE UNCROWNED KING

The last chapter in the prewar reception of *The Rite* was written in Paris two months later, when, on Sunday, 5 April 1914, Pierre Monteux led the first concert performance of the work in the French capital. Here is Vuillermoz's eyewitness account of this turning point in Stravinsky's career:

The next day Monteux gave us *Le sacre du printemps*. I will not even try to describe the throng that overran the Casino de Paris, halting traffic on the Rue

139. Ibid., 85.
140. Letter of 10 April 1915; in IStrSM:518.

de Clichy and disturbing strollers on the Place de la Trinité. It was a convulsion. The great nave was assaulted by a human cataract, and the promenades lost all rights to that title.

The performance was dazzling. Monteux and his admirable orchestra achieved miracles. Before leaving Paris, Stravinsky, in a state of rapture, immediately dashed off a letter to the doughty conductor, which he has authorized me to make public.... [141]

The performance took place in unhoped-for silence. A few interjections, quickly stifled, burst forth from the crowd in their exuberance, but the public has been tamed. At the last chord all were seized with delirium; a fever of adoration swept up the whole mass of spectators. Everyone began yelling for the composer and darting about in search of him. An unheard-of elation reigned in the hall. Applause went on to the point of giddiness. Reparations are complete and Paris is rehabilitated. *Le Sacre* being promised again on 26 April, I will put off until then a full account of this prodigious masterpiece. All I can do today, for lack of space, is salute a blessed date and offer Igor Stravinsky the homage of a boundless admiration. [142]

The no less delirious account by Jean Chantavoine adds a noteworthy detail: "*Le sacre du printemps* received the most rapturous welcome: a few scattered protests had the effect of salt upon the fire, and M. Stravinsky, recognized by a group of listeners in the street, was the object of a tumultuous demonstration."[143]

141. The letter is given, in a good English translation, in SelCorrII:59–60. Stravinsky expressed his thanks to Monteux and his musicians for "the most beautiful performance that I have heard of the *Sacre du Printemps*" and for "spontaneously placing your mastery in the service of works that, though obscure, seem to you to represent an artistic effort; and you do this voluntarily, without fear of the reactionary critics, who will attack you, perhaps openly." This last was an exaggeration, to say the least: the performance had been an ambitious and spectacularly successful gamble on Monteux's part. As he later put it to Stravinsky, "I do not forget what you did for my career in having me conduct your *Petrushka* and your *Sacre*. It was with these that I rose from the ranks, and I owe this to you" (SelCorrII:76; letter of 23 May 1957).

142. "Le lendemain Monteux nous donnait *Le Sacre du Printemps*. Je renonce à entreprendre la description de la foule envahissant le Casino de Paris, arrêtant toute circulation à la rue de Clichy et inquiétant les promeneurs de la Place de la Trinité. Ce fut une ruée. L'immense nef était battue par une marée humaine et les promenoirs avaient perdu tout droit à ce titre prometteur. L'exécution fut splendide. Monteux et son admirable orchestre ont fait des miracles. Avant de quitter Paris, Strawinsky, enthousiasmé, tint à écrire séance tenante, au courageux chef d'orchestre, la lettre suivante qu'il m'a autorisé à rendre publique.... Toute l'exécution se déroula dans un silence inespéré. Quelques interjections vite étouffées jaillissent de la foule en ébullition, mais le public est dompté. Au dernier accord le délire s'empare de l'assistance; une fièvre d'adoration soulève la masse des spectateurs. On hurle le nom de l'auteur et on se lance à sa recherche. Une exaltation inouïe règne dans la salle. Les applaudissements se prolongent jusqu'au vertige. La réparation est complète et Paris vient de se rehabiliter. *Le Sacre* nous étant promis de nouveau pour le 26 avril, je remets à cette date le compte rendu de ce prodigieux chef-d'oeuvre. Je ne puis aujourd'hui, faute de place, que saluer une date heureuse et offrir à Igor Strawinsky l'hommage d'une admiration sans limites" (*Comoedia*, 6 April 1914).

143. "*Le Sacre du Printemps* a reçu l'accueil le plus enthousiaste: quelques protestations en fait l'effet de sel sur le feu, et M. Strawinsky, reconnu par un groupe d'auditeurs, a été, jusque dans la rue, l'objet d'une tumultueuse manifestation" (*Excelsior*, 6 April 1914). This detail was embellished in Stravinsky's retelling into a story that has joined the original scandal in the folklore of modern music: "A crowd swept backstage. I was hoisted to anonymous shoulders and carried into the street and up to the Place de la Trinité. A policeman pushed his way to my side in an effort to protect me, and it was this guardian of the law Diaghilev fixed upon in his accounts of the story: 'Our little Igor now requires police escorts out of his concerts, like a prizefighter'" (E&D:165/144).

Musicians in Russia looked on in amazement. Karatïgin reported as follows:

> The *clou* of the previous Russian ballet season, Stravinsky's *Rite of Spring* . . . was just given two concert performances in Paris. After the first concert Stravinsky sent the conductor Monteux a letter with a warm expression of gratitude for his impeccable, uncommonly successful, and affecting performance of *The Rite*. Many Paris papers lost no time in reproducing the Russian composer's letter in full in their own columns. It is curious to note how sharply the attitude of the French toward *The Rite* has changed.
>
> It is possible that last year the hissing and whistling at the performances of *The Rite* were directed more at Nijinsky's staging than at Stravinsky's music. Be that as it may, now, in concert performance, *The Rite* has met with an altogether different reception from last season's. Signs of disapproval were almost entirely absent. The composer was greeted both times with noisy ovations. In the *Nouvelle revue française* a very ample article by Rivière has been devoted to *The Rite*. The author of the article calls Stravinsky's mimodrama a masterpiece worthy of being ranked alongside the best achievements of the French "impressionists."[144]

"Our little Igor," rejected at home, was now the uncrowned king of French music, who would be for two generations of French composers what Debussy had been for him. He planned a conquest of his native land the next year with *The Nightingale,* but, as we shall see in the next chapter, it was not to be. Although he did not know it yet, and even though his "Russian" style had yet to reach its peak, as a "Russian composer" Igor Stravinsky was finished.

144. V. G. Karatïgin, "Teatr i muzïka," *Rech'*, 7 May 1914.

14 · SETTLING SCORES
(THE LOSS OF RUSSIA, II)

Among the "anti-artistic acts" with which the Rimsky-Korsakov clan could charge the renegade, reprobate Stravinsky, two stood out as direct and seemingly willful transgressions against the name and memory of Nikolai Andreyevich himself. The first was the Diaghilev production of Musorgsky's *Khovanshchina* in June 1913, following immediately on the heels of the *Rite* scandal, a venture in which Stravinsky played a leading role. The other—Diaghilev's production of *Le coq d'or* a year later—was one in which Stravinsky had no hand, but of which he loudly approved both in word and in later compositional deed. Although in neither case was it Stravinsky's primary intention, it would be hard to imagine more painful slaps in the face of all that was holy in the Russia Stravinsky had left behind, or more flagrant advertisements of his perfidy.

KHOVANSHCHINA REDUX

Unlike *Boris Godunov,* which he finished twice, Musorgsky did not live to finish *Khovanshchina* even once. Again unlike *Boris,* moreover, the later opera had no literary antecedent; its action had been pieced together by Musorgsky and Vladimir Stasov directly from historical sources in a virtually unprecedented, heroic attempt at implementing realist ideals in the purest and most literal terms.[1]

---

1. The remarkable Stasov/Musorgsky correspondence on *Khovanshchina* may be found in Jay Leyda and Sergei Bertensson, eds., *The Musorgsky Reader* (New York: W. W. Norton, 1947), passim beginning on p. 185. The letters in this publication were translated from Andrey Rimsky-Korsakov's edition (*Musorgskiy: pis'ma i dokumentï* [Moscow: Muzgiz, 1932]) with the original editor's valuable annotations intact. Musorgsky gave a list of his sources in his letter of 15 July 1872 (Leyda and Bertensson [ed.], *Musorgsky Reader,* 195). A good précis of the historical events that formed the basis for the plot of the opera

With the best will in the world, one has to call the attempt a flop. The torso Musorgsky left behind at his death is a chaotic assemblage of scenes—unorchestrated but for two little excerpts (Marfa's song and the Musketeers' chorus, both in Act III), full of lacunae and inconsistencies of all sorts. The second act lacked a conclusion; the fifth act was little more than a sheaf of sketches. Characters act and express themselves either without clear motivation (Marfa) or with contradictory motives (the all-important yet unfathomable Shaklovitïy); the characters who are not inconsistently drawn are stick figures (Khovansky, Dosifey); the multiple plots are held together chiefly by means of a blatantly anachronistic glue compounded of romantic love (and what a company of strange bedfellows these lovers are!); the authors' point of view is missing, or else inscrutable.

Of course, it has proved only too easy to turn all of these defects (the love intrigues possibly excepted) into virtues by critical fiat in an age that has come to regard Musorgsky's originals as protomodernist icons. *Khovanshchina,* in which, seemingly, "impersonal forces are the chief agents,"[2] has become the icon of icons, worshipped in our day for reasons its committed, politically engaged creators would have found incomprehensible. Their views, in any case, are ultimately unavailable and irrelevant, for the raft of manuscripts on which all redactions of the opera have depended cannot be assumed to possess the authority of final intention.[3] Perhaps more than any other opera, *Khovanshchina* can be all things to all men; an "authentic" performance score, in this case, is utterly chimerical.

Rimsky-Korsakov's redaction, begun late in 1881, the year of Musorgsky's death, and finished early in 1883 (the bulk of work having been done in the summer of 1882), was the first of many labors of love carried out to insure the survival of his deceased friend's work. It set the tone for all the rest. Besides the kind of pervasive retouching that has become so notorious in the case of *Boris,* Rimsky had to do a great deal of patching as well. For the end of the second act, he decided not to supply the quintet he knew Musorgsky had planned to write,[4] but instead wrote an orchestral postlude that embodied a symbolic reprise of the "Dawn over the River

---

may be found in Isaiah Berlin, "A Note on 'Khovanshchina,'" originally written for the Covent Garden program book in 1963 and reprinted in the *New York Review of Books,* 19 December 1985, 40–42. Berlin is a less reliable guide to the opera itself and its stage history.

2. Berlin, "Note on 'Khovanshchina,'" 40.

3. On the editorial problems surrounding *Khovanshchina,* see Pavel Lamm's preface to his piano-vocal score, "Ot redaktora/Einleitung des Herausgebers," in M. P. Musorgsky, *Polnoye sobraniye sochineniy,* vol. 2 (Moscow/Vienna: Muzgiz/Universal-Edition, 1931), ix–xiv (Russian), xv–xx (German). (N.B.: In the Kalmus reprint of this work, the *Khovanshchina* score is vol. 4 of the Complete Works, not Vol. 2.) A good basic discussion of the various published redactions (Rimsky-Korsakov, Lamm/Asafyev, Shostakovich) may be found in Edward R. Reilly, *The Music of Musorgsky: A Guide to the Editions* (New York: Musical Newsletter, 1980), 19–21.

4. See Musorgsky's letter to Stasov of 16 August 1876: "and I will write the quintet ... under R. Korsakov's supervision, for its technical requirements are mischievous: alto, tenor and 3 basses" (Leyda and Bertensson [eds.], *Musorgsky Reader,* 343).

Moskva" theme from the prelude to Act I.[5] This editorial interpolation was in fact an editorial interpretation that sought to provide a unifying, melioristic point of view on the action by linking the assertion of imperial power against the claims of the militia and the Old Believers (i.e., the substance of the concluding action in Act II) with the idea of a new dawn over Russia.

That this was Musorgsky's attitude is doubtful. The change was, however, entirely consistent with the progressive, "statist" historiography associated with the name of Sergey Solovyov, the influential liberal historian whose point of view Rimsky himself had previously embodied in his only historical opera, *Pskovityanka*.[6] As to the missing end of the opera, Rimsky described the situation, and his resolution of it, in his autobiography: "For the closing chorus [i.e., the immolation of the Old Believers] there existed only the melody (recorded from the lips of some schismatics by Musorgsky's confidante [the singer Lyubov Ivanovna] Karmalina and communicated by her to Musorgsky). Availing myself of the given melody, I composed the entire chorus from beginning to end, but the orchestral figure (of the pyre blazing up) was entirely my own."[7]

Rimsky actually did a bit more than that: he crowned the chorus with some final love outbursts from Marfa and Andrey Khovansky (she for him; he for Emma, the Lutheran girl), and followed it with a dramatic reprise of the march of Peter the Great's Preobrazhensky Guards regiment, with which Musorgsky, a former Preobrazhensky officer himself, had brought the fourth act to a rousing close. Thus Rimsky epitomized (celebrated?) Peter's final triumph and so passed a judgment of sorts on the opera's historical content.[8]

Of course there were heavy cuts. Rimsky recalled that "in Acts I and II there turned up much that was superfluous, musically ugly, and a drag to the scene."[9] Accordingly, he removed from Act I a lengthy scene for the scribe and the crowd that was, of all the music in *Khovanshchina*, the closest to the realistic crowd music in recitative style found in such abundance in the original version of *Boris Godunov*. No wonder Rimsky disliked it.[10] From Act II he pruned away the brief appearance of the Lutheran pastor. For some reason, though, Rimsky failed to recall his re-

5. When the noncomposer Lamm came to edit the act, he evaded the issue of a concluding ensemble by reverting to an earlier, superseded intention of Musorgsky's: "Tableau on a single menacing chord *pp* as the curtain falls" (Musorgsky to Stasov, 6 August 1873; in ibid., 241).

6. See R. Taruskin, "The Present in the Past: Russian Opera and Russian Historiography, ca. 1870," in *Russian and Soviet Music: Essays for Boris Schwarz,* ed. Malcolm H. Brown (Ann Arbor: UMI Research Press, 1984), 90–124.

7. *My Musical Life,* 259.

8. To justify the music, Rimsky added a concluding stage direction: "Trumpeteers come out on stage, followed by the Tsar's boy regiment; they recoil in horror at the sight of the bonfire."

9. *My Musical Life,* 259.

10. Rimsky occasionally expressed his disapproval of Musorgsky's recitative style in the form of parody. See R. Taruskin, "Musorgsky vs. Musorgsky: The Versions of *Boris Godunov,*" *19th-Century Music* 8, no. 3 (Spring 1985): 250.

moving from Act III its very centerpiece, the musketeer Kuzka's strophic song to the balalaika, with chorus.[11]

This was the version of *Khovanshchina* Rimsky offered to the Imperial Theaters in 1883. It was frankly an arrangement, and Rimsky made no bones about it. "What will the rabid Musorgists do when they find out I've not only changed but added to the music of this opera?" he confided to Yastrebtsev; "Beat me, probably!"[12] Despite its very favorable portrayal of the Romanovs' role in Russian history, however, Rimsky's *Khovanshchina* was rejected by the Imperial Theaters and clung to a marginal existence in provincial and amateur performance[13] until 20 November 1911, three years after the arranger's death, when the opera was at last produced at the Mariyinsky under the baton of Albert Coates (Nápravník having refused to go near it), and with Chaliapin not only starring as Dosifey, but co-directing as well.

Chaliapin made some additional changes in the opera. Motivated perhaps by a sense of fidelity to Stasov's original conception of the drama as revolving around Dosifey rather than Peter,[14] perhaps by self-aggrandizement (or, most likely, by some complex amalgam of the two), Chaliapin sought to cast the Old Believers, with Dosifey at their head, as far as possible into the foreground.[15] He did this in the first instance by dropping the whole second scene of Act IV, which depicted the exile of Prince Golitsïn and Peter's forgiveness of the mutinous musketeers (*streltsï*). Not only were the Old Believers' rivals for sympathy thus removed from contention, but the musical antecedent that gave meaning to Rimsky's ending of the opera was eliminated. A few crucial plot developments, evidently, seemed a small price to pay for the interpretation Chaliapin wished to impose on the action, the singer no doubt holding the widely shared opinion that *Khovanshchina*'s action was incomprehensible on its face in no matter what version. The special *coup de thé-âtre* that distinguished Chaliapin's Mariyinsky production was a luridly spectacu-

11. He did note its deletion in his preface to the published vocal score (St. Petersburg: Bessel, 1883), where he remarked that the song, "added on by Musorgsky later, had the appearance of an interpolation unrelated to the rest." The scene with the pastor may have been deleted by Musorgsky himself. Although the autograph vocal score survives with its companions, the scene is omitted from the final fair copy of the libretto.

12. Yastrebtsev, *Vospominaniya* 1:131.

13. Its première, on 21 February 1886, was a private, amateur performance by the so-called Musical Dramatic Circle under E. Goldshteyn. The first public, professional performance took place in Kiev on 7 November 1892 (Loewenberg, *Annals of Opera*, col. 1121). The high point of this phase of the opera's career was the production given by Mamontov's Private Opera in the season 1897–98, with Chaliapin in the role of Dosifey.

14. "At the center of it all I thought to place the majestic figure of Dosifey, the head of the Old Believers, strong, energetic, deep-thinking and long-suffering, who masterminds all the actions of the two princes [Khovansky and Golitsïn]" (V. V. Stasov, "Modest Petrovich Musorgskiy: biograficheskiy ocherk" [1881], in *Izbrannïye sochineniy* 2:211).

15. Cf. Vyacheslav Ivanov's review of Chaliapin as Dosifey at the Bolshoy Theater in Moscow, which had hired the Mariyinsky production for a guest tour: "He puts his own part in excessive relief to the detriment of the whole, and in his own part he likewise resorts to exaggerated expressivity, thanks to which details are projected excessively into the foreground" ("O narisovannïkh glazakh: o Shalyapine i o 'Khovanshchine' v Bol'shom Teatre," *Muzika*, no. 108 [15 December 1912]: 1079).

FIG. 14.1. Fyodor Chaliapin,
self-portrait as Dosifey (1911).

lar set that apotheosized the schismatics at their culminating moment of fiery
glory. It elicited a rapturous press, even though it flatly contradicted the Petrine
apotheosis that was taking place in the pit.[16]

Diaghilev, for his part, had first voiced his wish to stage *Khovanshchina* before it
had been produced at the Mariyinsky, and even before his own controversial production of *Sheherazade*. He had presented Rimsky's version of the fifth act, the one
with the immolation chorus and its aftermath, at one of his 1907 Paris concerts. Its
reception encouraged him. (Obviously at this point he had no thought of second-
guessing the standard text.) In an interview with the ubiquitous "Teatral," published in the *Peterburgskaya gazeta* as early as February 1910, Diaghilev announced
some grandiose plans for the coming summer: a "Musorgsky season" to play at the
Paris Opera, the Théâtre de la Monnaie in Brussels, and, to finish up, Drury Lane,
for a total of some forty performances. He made a special point about *Khovanshchina,* "that wonderful Russian opera that has never played as yet on any Imperial stage." "I think," he continued:

> that the choral scenes of the *streltsï,* the singing of the Old Believers (so full of
> gripping moments), the scenes of Khovansky's murder and Dosifey's immolation,

16. For details on the Mariyinsky *Khovanshchina,* see Gozenpud, *Russkiy operniy teatr mezhdu dvukh
revolyutsiy,* 330–37.

and in general the whole characteristic national element in *Khovanshchina* will make a shattering impression in Paris. Toward that end I have permitted myself to restore to the opera certain scenes that were not included in Rimsky-Korsakov's edition but are preserved only in Musorgsky's original manuscript at the Public Library.[17]

The promise of restoration was an obvious sop in the direction of that Parisian critical faction which, to Diaghilev's consternation, had turned Musorgsky's original *Boris* into a cause célèbre in the aftermath of the 1908 Paris production, specially adapted for Diaghilev's splendiferous presentation by the venerable reviser himself. It was the protests leveled at this production, in fact, that had brought the beginnings of disrepute upon Rimsky among the Parisian avant-garde. Diaghilev now turned the tables on them,[18] and the French critics, with Calvocoressi at their head, fell right into line.[19]

At this point, it will be noted, Diaghilev's plans involved only the restoration of missing scenes. Whom he had in mind to orchestrate them is impossible to guess (though Cherepnin would have been the likeliest first choice), for the production never took place. Although Diaghilev signed an agreement with Chaliapin that specified the singer's appearance as Dosifey, both sides backed out that year (Diaghilev for lack of funds, Chaliapin so as to earn the rank of Imperial Soloist with an all-Russian tour); as we know, only ballets were given in 1910.

A few months later, Diaghilev became involved in a press skirmish with Nadezhda Rimskaya-Korsakova, who had written a letter of protest to the newspaper *Rech'* concerning the impresario's "crimes against art" in adapting her husband's *Sheherazade* to balletic purposes, and his "disrespect toward the memory of the late composer," concluding with a complaint that Russia's failure to sign the Bern copyright convention deprived her of legal recourse.[20] Diaghilev's answer, printed six weeks later in the same newspaper, was not limited to self-defense. He went on the offensive against Rimsky-Korsakov's editorial activities, with *Khovanshchina* the prime exhibit:

> All last winter I sat in the Public Library poring over the autograph manuscript of *Khovanshchina* and I saw that in the only published edition of this opera, issued under the editorship of N. A. Rimsky-Korsakov, the whole thing had been, as they say, "beaten to a pulp," that is to say, there is hardly a page of the original manuscript that did not sustain multifarious, substantive emendations and alterations by Rimsky-Korsakov.

17. Zilbershteyn and Samkov (eds.), *Dyagilev* 1:212.
18. Ironically enough, it was the posthumous publication in Russia of Rimsky-Korsakov's autobiography in 1909 that gave Diaghilev his first inkling that there were missing scenes in *Khovanshchina* to restore.
19. See Calvocoressi, *Musicians Gallery*, 227.
20. N. N. Rimskaya-Korsakova, "Otkrïtoye pis'mo S. P. Dyagilevu," *Rech'*, no. 210 (25 July 1910); in Zilbershteyn and Samkov (eds.), *Dyagilev* 2:437–38.

About *Boris* it is usually said, "Yes, but it also exists in the original version." But *Khovanshchina*? Will it thus forever remain a work of Rimsky-Korsakov? That is what the whole Paris press is saying, what they protest against "at the top of their voice," demanding now for several years that someone give them at last "the real Musorgsky, uncorrected by Professor Rimsky-Korsakov."

The French critics may be right or wrong in the present instance with respect to the author of *Sadko* "who will suffer no revisions," but a thought occurs to me: What kind of letter might Musorgsky's widow have written, if only she existed, concerning the "dispositions," the "changes," and the "revisions" that have been visited on the work of the greatest genius among Russian composers?[21]

It was probably at this point that Diaghilev began envisioning a "restored," not merely a "completed," *Khovanshchina*. Stravinsky was by the fall of 1910 his natural ally in this endeavor, for he had been catapulted to musical preeminence within the Diaghilev enterprise by *The Firebird,* he had supported Diaghilev implicitly in the matter of *Shéhérazade,*[22] and—as Diaghilev no doubt knew full well—he had his own scores to settle with the Rimsky-Korsakovs. When Chaliapin's Mariyinsky *Khovanshchina* unexpectedly fell into his lap, Diaghilev sprang into action.

The initial plan of restoration may be gauged with great accuracy, thanks to the survival of the actual copy of the Bessel vocal score (Rimsky-Korsakov version) from which Diaghilev and Stravinsky worked. From all indications, these plans were laid late in 1912, when Stravinsky had just finished composing *The Rite of Spring.*[23] The Act I and Act III cuts made by Rimsky-Korsakov and described above are designated for "insertion, orchestr. Stravinsky" (*vstavka, orkestr. Stravinskogo*). In addition, several extended passages in which Rimsky-Korsakov's editorial work had been especially heavy are marked "according to Musorgsky, orch. Stravinsky" (*po Musorgskomu, ork. Stravinskogo*). In terms of the rehearsal numbers in the Lamm vocal score, they are as follows: [98] to [111] in Act I;[24] through [14] in Act III (including Marfa's song, which had been orchestrated by Musorgsky himself; it is unclear whether his scoring was to have been reinstated); through [5] in Act IV; and [9] to [22] in Act V (including the Old Believers' "Phrygian" chorus).

In addition, Shaklovitïy's aria in Act III was rechristened "Dosifey's Aria" (so that Chaliapin would sing it) and designated for Stravinsky to orchestrate "according to Musorgsky." This reassignment from one role to another is the first of numerous indications that Diaghilev did not contemplate a straightforward restora-

21. S. P. Diaghilev, "Otvet N. N. Rimskoy-Korsakovoy," *Rech'*, no. 248 (10 September 1910); in Zilbershteyn and Samkov (eds.), *Dyagilev* 1:221–22. A production of *Sadko* at the Palais Garnier had fallen through because the Rimsky-Korsakov heirs would not consent to the cuts proposed by the management of the Paris Opera.

22. See his letter to Vladimir Rimsky-Korsakov, quoted in the last chapter.

23. The score now belongs to Mr. Oliver Neighbour, who very kindly allowed me to examine it in London on 16 May 1985. It is described in great detail by Robert Threlfall in "The Stravinsky Version of *Khovanshchina*," *Studies in Music* 15 (1981): 106–15, esp. 108–10.

24. Also, the four bars added by Rimsky-Korsakov at the end of the act were marked for deletion and the last bell chord marked for threefold repetition.

tion, but a "redaction" of his own. Nor was Stravinsky's work to be carried out with complete scrupulousness as to sources. The vocal score reveals instances where Stravinsky "corrected" Rimsky-Korsakov without consulting Musorgsky, and his version of the Act III aria, as we shall see, was not a restoration at all, but a conflation.

Paradoxically, given his stated purpose (but in fact entirely characteristically), Diaghilev made cuts that altogether dwarfed the ones perpetrated by Rimsky-Korsakov. The deletion of the second scene from Act IV was taken over from the Chaliapin production, and to match it, Act II was omitted in toto, thus eliminating the role of Golitsïn from the opera altogether. This seems at first incredible, but upon reflection it is natural, even inevitable, that Diaghilev should have so decided, given the venue of the performance and given what we know of Diaghilev's antiliterary viewpoint on opera. The second act of *Khovanshchina,* Marfa's divination alone excepted, is given over to recitative dialogue concerning subject matter that must to Diaghilev, with his terror of boring the flighty Parisians, have seemed unstageability itself. Golitsïn, moreover, represented the "European" Russia, as did the music of the scene that took place in his quarters. That Russia the French wished neither to see nor to hear—or so Diaghilev assumed.

Additional cuts in the third and fourth acts included practically the entire role of Susanna in Act III, scene iii (Lamm [14]–[29]), and most of Act III, scene viii (Lamm [111]–[118]+2). From the otherwise omitted second part of Act IV, the choral music (Lamm [33]–[37] minus the Preobrazhensky March fanfares at [34] and [35]) was transferred to Act III.[25] Thus did Diaghilev turn *Khovanshchina,* as he had turned *Boris,* from a very wordy opera of political intrigue into a choral pageant with basso obbligato. The result was a version that had even less claim than Rimsky's to the mantle of authenticity.

But of course authenticity was claimed, and loudly. The newspaper *Russkoye slovo* carried, on 12 January 1913, a press release in which it was announced that Diaghilev, "having acquainted himself with the manuscripts of Musorgsky's opera, . . . disagreed with many of Rimsky-Korsakov's views" and therefore "has decided to entrust the task of 'assembling' a new *Khovanshchina* to the well-known young composer Stravinsky."[26] As expected, this news burst like a bombshell in the Russian capital. Ten days later, the newspaper *Birzheviye vedomosti* published a poll of St. Petersburg musicians, conducted by the same M. Dvinsky (Berman) who had a few months earlier elicited a rather outspoken interview for his paper from the well-known young composer (see Chapter 12, n. 47; Chapter 13, n. 26). Now he sought to sensationalize the impending *Khovanshchina* affair:

25. For more details about these and other cuts and transfers, including a few very minor ones (e.g., during the Persian dances in Act IV), see Threlfall, "Stravinsky Version," 109–10, where all of Stravinsky's markings on the vocal score now belonging to Mr. Neighbour are translated in full.

26. "Russkaya opera dlya Yevropï," *Russkoye slovo,* no. 10 (12 January 1913); in Zilbershteyn and Samkov (eds.), *Dyagilev* 1:441.

In our musical world much talk and discussion has been inspired by the following fact.

The fashionable impresario Mr. Diaghilev, who has been popularizing Russian ballet abroad, has now turned his beneficent attention to Russian opera as well. In the Imperial Public Library he has found "manuscript material for *Khovanshchina* by Musorgsky himself" that for some reason was not used by Rimsky-Korsakov and was not included in the opera (a huge crowd scene in the second [*sic*] act and a scene with Kuzka in the second [*sic!*]).

In view of this, Mr. Diaghilev has decided to use this material and complete *Khovanshchina* with it. Besides this, he has decided to reorchestrate the whole final chorus of Old Believers, entrusting this whole job to the young composer Igor Stravinsky.

Thus, it would seem, the Rimsky-Korsakov who edited and orchestrated *Khovanshchina* is now rejected as defective. He has been judged not good enough "for the West," and must be rectified. Or so Mr. Diaghilev thinks.

We have asked several of our leading musical figures to give their opinion on this matter.

Here is what they said.

There followed eight opinions, of which the ever-unpredictable César Cui's was by far the most substantial:

I think that if new Musorgsky material has been found, why not include it? On the contrary, let the public and the musical world acquaint themselves with the newly found material and pronounce their judgment. I find Diaghilev's decision to entrust the orchestration of this material to Stravinsky to be perfectly logical. The latter is Rimsky-Korsakov's pupil and an excellent orchestrator.

But as for Diaghilev's "intention" to reorchestrate the final chorus, I must confess I am at a loss to understand it. Would Stravinsky really lift his hand to correct his own teacher? Ultimately it would be excessively brash of him to set out on such a mission. I am inclined to think that Stravinsky would never agree to redo the final chorus for Mr. Diaghilev's purposes.[27]

27. Dvinsky, "O dyagilevskoy postanovki 'Khovanshchinï,'" *Birzheviye vedomosti*, 22 January 1913. Dvinsky's roster of experts was certainly a representative sampling of old-guard opinion. Others polled included the veteran composer Nikolai Solovyov (1846–1916), whose reaction was of the "why not?" variety, though he insisted that Rimsky's version was fine as it stood; the bass singer Stanislav Gabel (1849–1924), who felt that "Rimsky-Korsakov may be reorchestrated only by one who is his equal in talent—to all others we say: Hands off!"; the theory professor Liverii (Liberio) Sacchetti (1852–1916), whose opinion was simply that "Rimsky-Korsakov is sacred"; the Belyayevets composer Nikolai Sokolov (1859–1922), who alone pointed out that the final chorus was Rimsky-Korsakov's composition, and that it was not a question of rescoring but of rewriting (but what, he worried, about the heirs to the performing rights? "I suppose that this whole episode will end in court"); and Nikolai Alexandrovich Dubasov (1869–1935), professor of piano at the Conservatory ("But why Stravinsky?"). Leonid Nikolayev (1878–1942), the pianist and eventual teacher of Shostakovich and Maria Yudina, was perhaps the most negative of all: "To say that Rimsky-Korsakov is in no need of correction or rectification would be to beat a dead horse. And if he didn't include in the opera two scenes that have now been found, it means they were not necessary. Rimsky-Korsakov had too well developed a theatrical sense and too much experience to let slip anything important or substantial in *Khovanshchina*. In any case, the whole thing is a very sorry story." Amid all these prejudiced opinions, that of Iosif Wihtol (Jazeps Vitols, 1863–1948), the Latvian Belyayevets, was a breath of fresh air: "What can I say without knowing

To Stravinsky personally, Steinberg sent an anguished request as spokesman for the Rimsky-Korsakov clan:

> You have undoubtedly heard about the newspaper reports concerning Diaghilev's production of *Khovanshchina*. Since your name figures in these reports, it would be very good if you would write an explanation, let us say for *Russkaya molva,* where Andrey [Rimsky-Korsakov] is writing. Send the letter to me and I will arrange to have it appear immediately in the paper. I personally give no credence at all to these nonsensical rumors that you have been commissioned to "correct" Nikolai Andreyevich's orchestration. The appearance of an explanation by you would be *extremely* desirable and I most urgently ask that you make one.[28]

Stravinsky's answer, three weeks later, gave scant comfort: "You know by now, or rather, you have seen S. P. Diaghilev's letter to the editor of the *Birzheviye vedomosti,* which anticipated the letter I had planned to write, after which mine seems by now superfluous."[29]

This is what Diaghilev had written:

> Esteemed Mr. Editor:
>
> Concerning the appearance in your newspaper of a questionnaire regarding the restoration of *Khovanshchina* I consider it necessary to answer the attacks that have been launched against my friend Stravinsky.
>
> Stravinsky has no intention of redoing or reorchestrating the work of Rimsky-Korsakov. But, as everyone knows, the final chorus of the unfinished opera was written by Rimsky-Korsakov on a theme by Musorgsky. At my request, Stravinsky is writing a new finale on the same theme. Which of the two is better is something the public will decide when it has had a chance to hear both works. As far as the instrumentation of the unpublished and unorchestrated pages of *Khovanshchina* is concerned, it is the first time I have ever heard that the chance to become acquainted with the hitherto unknown work of a composer of genius should be regarded as a "sorry story" from any point of view whatsoever.
>
> Sergey Diaghilev
> London, 12 February 1913 [N.S.][30]

This was worse yet. Stravinsky, it now appeared, was actually going to replace Rimsky-Korsakov's own music, not simply revise his teacher's orchestration. And yet the original plan had included wholesale reorchestration. Despite its haughty tone, then, Diaghilev's letter reveals that the original project had been considerably narrowed. Was this the result of pressure?

---

the results of Stravinsky's work? In time we'll see." Could this unexpectedly friendly disposition toward the work of his younger colleague have lain behind Stravinsky's no less unexpectedly warm reference to Wihtol in M&C:61–62/63?

28. Postcard of 28 January 1913; in the Stravinsky Archive, Scrapbook 1912–14.
29. Letter of 17 February/2 March 1913; in IStrSM:471.
30. S. P. Diaghilev, "Pis'mo v redaktsiyu," *Birzheviye vedomosti,* 4 February 1913 [O.S.].

It was, but the pressure had come neither from the press nor from the Rimsky-Korsakovs. It had come from Chaliapin. He, too, it seems, had been offended at the notion of revising Rimsky's redaction; and, as reported in the press, "since Diaghilev continues to insist on restoring *Khovanshchina*, F. I. Chaliapin has announced that he refuses to appear in the forthcoming Russian season in London and Paris. Fyodor Ivanovich finds that Rimsky-Korsakov is in no need of restoration, and protests categorically against the redoing of *Khovanshchina*."[31] The impasse was resolved by a compromise announced on 9 March 1913 after a meeting at Chaliapin's apartment: Chaliapin agreed to sing in Stravinsky's final chorus (Diaghilev having probably persuaded him that the removal of Rimsky's reprise of the Preobrazhensky March would accord better with the singer's Dosifey-centered conception of the opera), while Diaghilev agreed that the scenes in which Chaliapin would appear as Dosifey would remain as Rimsky-Korsakov had edited them.[32] It is hard not to agree with Stravinsky's indignant construal of Chaliapin's motives: the singer did not want to have to relearn his part, and the controversy engendered by Diaghilev's projected restoration had given him a pretext to back out with a great show of sanctimony.[33]

By now time was very short; at Stravinsky's request Ravel was brought into the picture. Since Stravinsky had all the Musorgsky materials, Ravel had to come to Clarens. He arrived together with his mother on the eight o'clock train on the morning of Tuesday, 18 March,[34] and took up residence in a hotel near Stravinsky's *pension*.

Just what was his role? It has been detailed as long ago as 1949, in the memoirs of Daniyil Ilyich Pokhitonov (1878–1957), choirmaster of the Mariyinsky Theater, who was invited by Diaghilev to accompany his chorus to Paris and London. Pokhitonov attended a meeting at Chaliapin's home at the beginning of April, where he received a briefing on the new music his chorus would have to learn for the production.

---

31. "Konflikt Shalyapin-Dyagilev," *Obozreniye teatrov*, 20 January 1913 (unsigned); in Zilbershteyn and Samkov (eds.), *Dyagilev* 1:442. The newspaper *Vecherneye vremya* carried the story with a curious appendage in the form of a gratuitous expression of solidarity with Chaliapin from one of his Mariyinsky colleagues, the leading contralto Yevgeniya Zbruyeva (1867–1936), who played opposite Chaliapin as Marfa in "his" *Khovanshchina*, but who had nothing whatever to do with the proposed Diaghilev version: "In any event Chaliapin is absolutely right to refuse to participate in a *Khovanshchina* whose final choruses [*sic*] will be orchestrated by the young musician Mr. Igor Stravinsky. I heard his ballet music to *Petrushka* performed by Mr. Koussevitzky's orchestra, and I must say it made little impression on me. It seems to me that this was the opinion of a whole group of musicians, headed by the violinist Prof. [Leopold] Auer, namely, that there is little music in Stravinsky, and if it is the music of the future, then it's the very distant future. And this is the composer who is entrusted with the task of redoing what has already been done once and for all by N. A. Rimsky-Korsakov! It's only natural that F. I. Chaliapin will have nothing to do with this" (Stravinsky Archive, Scrapbook 1912–14).

32. All this wrangling is what undoubtedly lay behind Stravinsky's exasperated comments about Chaliapin in Conv:66–67/60–61 ("that idiot from every nonvocal point of view, and from some of these [*sic*] . . .").

33. Conv:67/62; see also Zilbershteyn and Samkov (eds.), *Dyagilev* 1:442.

34. Ravel to Stravinsky, 15 March 1913; in SelCorrIII:15.

Felix Blumenfeld, Emil Cooper [who would conduct the première], Diaghilev, and I took part in this meeting. Diaghilev laid out his plan for performing the opera. In the first act the chorus of the people "at the billpost" [i.e., the crowd scene with the scribe] was to be inserted; in the third act it was to be the scene of the musketeer Kuzka with the chorus. These were novelties taken from the original version of the opera and orchestrated by the French composer Maurice Ravel. The finale of the opera—the immolation on the bonfire—was to be done by Igor Stravinsky without the Preobrazhensky March. Diaghilev raised the question of Shaklovitïy's aria (Act III), which he considered more appropriate on the lips of Dosifey than on those of an "archfiend," as Musorgsky himself had characterized Shaklovitïy. One could only agree. Unfortunately, Chaliapin, who had made Diaghilev a promise to sing this aria in performances abroad, failed to keep his word, and the aria was simply dropped.[35]

By this account, Ravel inherited the task of preparing the "insertions" originally assigned to Stravinsky. Very recently it has become possible to verify the accuracy of Pokhitonov's recollection: the autograph full scores of the two scenes in question, thought as recently as 1980 to be lost,[36] unexpectedly turned up in an auction sale[37] and were acquired for the Pierpont Morgan Library in New York, where they are now among the Robert Owen Lehman deposits. In these scenes Ravel did not orchestrate any music that had been previously orchestrated by Rimsky-Korsakov or by anyone else; he only filled gaps.[38] In addition, Andrey Rimsky-Korsakov reported (see below) that Ravel orchestrated Marfa's song in Act III, despite the fact—just possibly unknown to Diaghilev and his collaborators—that Musorgsky had orchestrated the song himself. Of the remaining spots where (according to the plans indicated in Diaghilev's vocal score) Stravinsky was to have replaced Rimsky-Korsakov's instrumentation with his own, two—the musketeers'

35. D. I. Pokhitonov, *Iz proshlogo russkoy operï* (Leningrad, 1949); reprinted in Kuznetsova (ed.), *Shalyapin* 2:316.

36. *New Grove Dictionary,* s.v. "Ravel" (works list, 15:620).

37. A page from Ravel's score of Kuzka's song (= Lamm ed., figs. [95]–[96]) was displayed on the cover of the Sotheby's London auction catalogue, "Music and Continental Books and Manuscripts" (11 November 1982); the score came from the ill-gotten and long-hidden collection of Serge Lifar.

38. His work involved not only orchestration but also condensation (presumably on Diaghilev's instructions). In the Act I insert, which in terms of the Lamm score extended from [56] to [82], Ravel omitted the music from [65] to [66], and from [69] to [71]. The three bars before [69], in which the scribe sings unaccompanied, were compressed into one measure:

The third through the ninth bars after [73] were omitted, as were the first five bars after [77] (the voice part having been removed from the measure before that figure). In addition, the offstage trumpet parts, chorus in Act I, and the Old Believers' "Phrygian" chorus in Act V (figs. [15]–[22])—survived Diaghilev's cuts and were also safely out of Chaliapin's way. Ravel's letter in defense of his work (see below) strongly implied that he reworked at least the second of these. Carl van Vechten, who saw the production in Paris, has reported that Ravel also replaced Rimsky's version of the first, the musketeers' chorus (he called it the "hymn to Ivan Khovansky"), as well as the ensuing duet between Emma and Andrey Khovansky (figs. [98]–[108] in the Lamm vocal score).[39]

A series of telegrams from Diaghilev to Stravinsky gives evidence that all work on *Khovanshchina* was finished by 27 April, when the impresario acknowledged receipt of Stravinsky's final chorus, the last item sent.[40] The première took place at the Théâtre des Champs Élysées on 5 June, exactly one week after the *Rite* première.

Meanwhile, controversy continued to rage. History repeated itself in another exacerbated press exchange like the one in 1910 that had brought Nadezhda Rimskaya-Korsakova into a face-off with Diaghilev himself. This time, both parties employed proxies. Andrey Rimsky-Korsakov took up the cudgels on his mother's behalf in the pages of *Russkaya molva*, the very newspaper to which Steinberg had begged Stravinsky to send his "explanation" a few weeks before. It was an all-out attack on what the writer characterized as the "shady side" of Diaghilev's activity, namely, his "unceremonious and artistically indefensible meddling with musical compositions." The tale of *Shéhérazade* was rehearsed again, along with *Cléopâtre*,

---

heralding the arrival of Khovansky and his retinue, were rewritten in more elaborate form between [81] and [82]:

At [76], Ravel's score incorporates a variant reading of the voice part listed by Lamm in a footnote (p. 56), showing that a copy of the manuscript containing it had been Ravel's exemplar. The Act III insertion corresponds to figs. [78] through [98] in the Lamm score. The music from [81] to [85] was omitted. The passage from [80] to [81] was accordingly transposed up a step so as to join in the correct key to the beginning of Kuzka's song at [85]. The joint is further covered up by superimposing Musorgsky's voice parts for the first measure after [81] over the orchestral balalaika imitation that begins at [85]. From [85] to the end of the insert, Ravel's work was a straightforward instrumentation of Musorgsky's vocal score.

39. Annotations to Rimsky-Korsakov's *My Musical Life*, 260.
40. SelCorrII:7–8.

Prince Igor, "etc., etc." "At the present time," the article continued, "according to utterly trustworthy information, S. P. Diaghilev is preparing a new musical vandalism"—*Khovanshchina.* Rimsky-Korsakov retells the story of his father's redaction, citing liberally from the account in the elder Rimsky-Korsakov's autobiography. All the places in which Nikolai Andreyevich described his extensive rewriting of Musorgsky's music are set forth in italics, so as to show, in Andrey's own italicized conclusion, that *"The 'Khovanshchina' we know must be called in all honesty the joint work of two artists"*—the point being, of course, that to touch Rimsky's work on the opera was as great a sacrilege as to touch Musorgsky's. The thundering, redundant peroration was even more paradoxical:

> I consider the pertinent question to be not whether Rimsky-Korsakov did his job well or badly, but *whether anyone has the moral or artistic right to redo that "Khovanshchina" which is,* as I have said, *the joint work of two artists.*
>
> The answer, I should think, can only be in the negative. Of course, *any* composer who thinks himself congenial to Musorgsky or, at least, who thinks his own talent equal to the other's gift, *is free to make his own redaction* of *Khovanshchina.* It would in fact be very interesting if some important artist were to do this job in his own way. But *to mutilate someone else's redaction,* as Mr. Diaghilev now wishes to do, to eliminate pieces of it, even with the intention of restoring Musorgsky's original, to recompose that which has been fully composed in the given redaction of Rimsky-Korsakov—all this strikes me as absolutely inadmissible.
>
> I consider the attempt to destroy any musical whole an act of *vandalism,* and Rimsky-Korsakov's redaction of *Khovanshchina* is just such a whole. I consider it *tasteless* to mix the original Musorgsky with a Musorgsky who has passed through Rimsky-Korsakov's hands, in the first place, and through those of Messrs. Ravel and Stravinsky—Mr. Diaghilev's minions—in the second.
>
> What kind of artistic whole could emerge from the hands of Musorgsky, Rimsky-Korsakov, Ravel, and Stravinsky?[41]

Diaghilev's stand-in was Ravel, in an article published only in Russian in the pages of *Muzïka.* His polemical approach was so similar to Diaghilev's in countering Mme Rimsky-Korsakov three years before that the conclusion is inevitable that Ravel had at the very least been coached. He began by impugning the quality of Rimsky-Korsakov's work, especially the final chorus:

> It was heard once in Paris several years ago [in Diaghilev's 1907 concert series] and left behind a generally depressing impression of something long and drawn out and at the same time half-baked. In the theater the effect of such a chorus could be fatal.... Consequently an attempt to give the opera a tolerable ending might seem reasonable.
>
> Igor Stravinsky's passionate admiration for Musorgsky—a feeling that in no wise excludes the touching reverence he feels toward his teacher—ideally equipped him for this ticklish undertaking.... This new composition seems to me to be far

41. A. N. Rimsky-Korsakov, " 'Khovanshchina' M. P. Musorgskogo i S. Dyagilev," *Russkaya molva,* no. 101 (23 March 1913); reprinted in *Muzïka,* no. 123 (30 March 1913): 230–32.

more appropriate to the character of the opera than Korsakov's. Likewise we are indebted to Mr. Igor Stravinsky for an orchestration of Shaklovitïy's aria, restored to its original form. The remaining excerpts were orchestrated by me.

Next, Ravel took up Andrey's demand that the Rimsky-Korsakov redaction of *Khovanshchina* be respected as the "joint work of two artists":

A joint work? I have never heard that Musorgsky ever entrusted anyone with the job of changing his compositions. "The two composers [wrote Andrey] remained the closest of friends for a long time." Yes, but with Musorgsky's death, as anyone might surmise, this friendship existed only as a distant memory. "Close spiritual kinship"? They were of the same nationality: that is about all they had in common. Under such a racial pretext might one propose that Glazunov finish Stravinsky's work or Saint-Saëns that of Debussy? . . . God save us from posthumous *collaborators*, especially gifted ones! . . .

Mr. Andrey Rimsky-Korsakov tells us that "it is not a question of whether my father did his job well or badly." How's that? But that is the only question! Did Rimsky-Korsakov approach Musorgsky's text with circumspection? Yes or no? The great artist himself [in his memoirs] has given us the answer.

Finally, the modernist reception of Musorgsky's style is invoked:

However inexperienced Musorgsky may have been—and his contemporaries have grossly exaggerated that inexperience—the author of *Khovanshchina* was not an ignoramus when it came to the schoolboy rules anyone can find in the first harmony textbook that comes to hand. If he did not always consider it necessary to adhere to them it was doubtless because he did not look upon them as an immutable dogma. The future has vindicated him. Many of the latest composers, whom no one would accuse of ineptness, have profited from the bold lessons they have learned from this inept composer.

These "empty" fourths, these "barbarous" fifths paint with strange and powerful effect the mystic chorus of the Old Believers. With rare strength they express the primeval soul of these fanatics. How inappropriate, alongside this defiant nakedness, do Rimsky-Korsakov's ingratiating harmonies seem! . . .

While Mr. S. Diaghilev was preparing *Khovanshchina* for production in Paris . . . he acquainted himself with the manuscript original and ascertained the fact that Rimsky-Korsakov's changes went far beyond what was admitted in his preface to *Khovanshchina*. Most of the deleted scenes seemed remarkably beautiful to Mr. Diaghilev, and those passages that underwent reworking were more interesting in the original than in the Korsakovian version. Feelings of respect and of simple justice inspired him to restore these passages in that form in which they should never have been excluded.

In restoring these passages that had been distorted or deleted by virtue of the instinct of [Rimsky-Korsakov's] genius, orchestrating them in such a way *that not a single note of the manuscript original is changed,* neither Stravinsky nor I had any thought that we were committing an act of "vandalism." We remain unconvinced of this even now.

Ravel closed his letter with a particularly stinging remark: "An accurate orchestration of [Musorgsky's] manuscript would merit preference over *any* brilliant but inaccurate arrangement." Once again the Diaghilev camp had flung the charge of vandalism back in their opponents' teeth. All at once Andrey Rimsky-Korsakov's ranting about Stravinsky's egomania in his review of *The Rite of Spring* (premièred only days after the publication of Ravel's letter) takes on new meaning.[42]

Reviewing the *Khovanshchina* performance, Andrey took up the debate exactly where Ravel had left off. After calling into question the sincerity of the tribute paid Musorgsky's memory in the guise of such heavily cut productions as Diaghilev's, the younger Rimsky-Korsakov turned to the matter of additions and revisions:

> Moreover, alongside the cuts, the opera has been augmented both by interpolations borrowed from the material that did not go into Rimsky-Korsakov's redaction . . . and by certain little bits and pieces that are played not in the standard redaction and instrumentation of Rimsky-Korsakov, but in an "accurate" instrumentation by Ravel (the expression "an 'accurate' instrumentation" is not something thought up by an illiterate dilettante, but Ravel's own; he used it in a polemic against me concerning the production of *Khovanshchina*). As a result, Marfa's wonderful song withered utterly in Musorgsky's wretched harmonization and Ravel's extremely tinny orchestration.[43]

42. All quotes from Maurice Ravel, "O parizhskoy redaktsii 'Khovanshchinï,'" *Muzïka*, no. 129 (14 May 1913 [O.S.]): 338–42. The letter is dated Paris, 4 May 1913 (N.S.). Although Ravel's letter was apparently published only in Russia and in Russian translation, Andrey Rimsky-Korsakov's rebuttal appeared in French, in the Paris arts and fashion magazine *Comoedia illustré*. He complained that Ravel had either failed or refused to comprehend his main point, which he restated in italics for the benefit of his French readers: "*I considered—and I hold to this—an act of vandalism not the endeavor to create a new version of Khovanshchina on the basis of Musorgsky's surviving sketches, but only the attempt at partial correction of the version by my father.*" ("*Je considérais, et j'y tiens, comme un acte de vandalisme, non l'essai de créer une nouvelle rédaction de Khovanchina d'après les brouillons posthumes de Moussorgsky, mais exclusivement la tentative de correction partielle de la rédaction faite par mon père.*") Following a rehash of his earlier arguments, Rimsky-Korsakov ended on a note of surpassing acidulousness, returning Ravel's closing sally with interest: "In conclusion I would draw attention to the following reflections of M. Ravel. He does not at all deny the 'striking sacrifice' my father made in the interests of a colleague who was unappreciated by the public; he even waxes eulogistic about his [i.e., Musorgsky's] 'surpassing genius,' for which only 'a respectful enthusiasm' can suffice. I can do nothing here but express my profound astonishment to find the signature of M. Ravel, such an eminent and cultivated musician, under this passage worthy of a dilettante who is not equipped to pass judgment on acts of musical creation" ("Pour finir je voudrais attirer l'attention sur les réflexions suivantes de M. Ravel. Il ne nie point 'l'abnégation frappante' qu'avait mis mon père à servir son collègue non apprécié par le public; il s'exalte même en éloge sur son 'génie excessif,' dont il suffit d'avoir 'un entousiasme respectueux.' Je ne peux pas faire autrement qu'exprimer ici mon étonnement profond de trouver la signature de M. Ravel, un musicien si éminent et raffiné, sous ce passage digne d'un dilettante, qui n'est pas en état de se rendre compte des procédés de la création musicale" ("Lettre de M. André Rimsky-Korsakow," *Comoedia illustré* 5, no. 22 [20 August 1913], 999). What is curious about this letter is that it appeared so long after the fact. In it, Rimsky-Korsakov refers to his original 23 March piece in *Russkaya molva* as having been written not five months earlier, but two. And yet it was not the editors of *Comoedia illustré* who had held the new article up: Rimsky-Korsakov's covering letter that accompanied the article's submission, which survives today in the archive of Michel Calvocoressi, is dated 17 July. (My thanks to the late Gerald Abraham for sharing this document with me.)

43. A. N. Rimsky-Korsakov, "Russkiye opernïye i baletnïye spektakli." Marfa's song is not among the Ravel-orchestrated items at the Morgan Library. Although unlikely, it is possible that Andrey Rimsky-Korsakov was mistaken and Musorgsky's own orchestration had been restored by Diaghilev.

He went on to make the standard anti-Diaghilev complaint that the latter's productions were always skewed so as to present Russia in the most barbaric, "Asiatic" light. It was not an unfounded accusation as far as it went, and certainly applied to a production of *Khovanshchina* that at once omitted the whole "European" second act and inserted Kuzka's drunken song into the third. What is at first surprising in the review is its studied avoidance of all mention either of Stravinsky or of his chorus. The explanation is simple: the critic had attended the first performance, at which—laying a diabolical trap for unwary critics—Diaghilev had tacitly substituted Rimsky-Korsakov's final chorus for the notorious Stravinsky's. This was one trap Rimsky-Korsakov's own son would not fall into. He was well aware that the performance he heard contained no music composed or even arranged by his former friend.

Almost as indignant as Andrey Rimsky-Korsakov was Calvocoressi. His complaint had less to do with the orchestrations and revisions than with Diaghilev's merciless cuts. The critic sent a report to the *RMG* to make sure that Diaghilev's countrymen knew what havoc the impresario had wrought on Musorgsky's score, notwithstanding all the posturing about authenticity. Calvocoressi stopped just short of accusing Diaghilev of fraud:

> The production was preceded by the announcement that Rimsky-Korsakov's edition had been carefully examined and checked on the basis of Musorgsky's original manuscripts, and that in all places where Rimsky-Korsakov had departed from the original the authorial text had been restored. . . . [However,] whatever benefit may have accrued from the inherently praiseworthy recourse to the original authorial text was more than outweighed, in the present instance, by the huge cuts Musorgsky's work was made to suffer. . . . Possibly the cuts were deemed necessary in view of the score's great size, either out of fear of tiring the Parisian public or with the aim of easing the difficulty of mounting the work. Be that as it may, in this aspect of the production it was evidently thought possible to dispense entirely with that very respect for the author's demands which was so loudly invoked in the matter of redaction.[44]

44. Michel-Dmitri Calvocoressi, "Novaya redaktsiya 'Khovanshchinï,'" *RMG* 20, no. 39 (29 September 1913), cols. 827–28. Another harsh critique of the production, one that Soviet writers are particularly fond of quoting, was made by Anatoliy Vasilyevich Lunacharsky (1875–1933), who later became Lenin's "Commissar of Popular Enlightenment." He wrote: "The opera is presented to the French public in a scandalously denuded form. Just imagine: the scene of Marfa's divination [in Act II], full of such a severe, pure-Russian romanticism, is cut. Shaklovitïy's wonderful song 'Sleeps Now the Nest of Musketeers' [the aria Chaliapin refused to sing as Dosifey]—cut. The execution of the *streltsï* [*sic*; in the opera they are pardoned]—cut. A multitude of details are also cut, not to mention the scene of Golitsïn's exile which is not even done at the Mariyinsky" (*Teatr i iskusstvo*, 1913, no. 23, 486; quoted in Gozenpud, *Russkiy opernïy teatr mezhdu dvukh revolyutsiy*, 338; also in Zilbershteyn and Samkov [eds.], *Dyagilev* 1:442). Lunacharsky commented on the opera's reception in a way that casts some indirect light, perhaps, on the way in which Stravinsky's chorus was received: "The first act of *Khovanshchina* was greeted noisily. The final a cappella chorus enraptured the public and was repeated. I doubt whether any other chorus has ever had such a rapturous success. But the third act [i.e., Act IV] pleased them incomparably less, and after the fourth act [= Act V], which ends, as we all know, with the scene of self-immolation, the public, after wanly clapping, made for the cloakroom" (ibid.; reprinted in *Teatr i revolyutsiya* [Moscow: Gosudarstvennoye Izdatel'stvo, 1924], 433).

Calvocoressi took pains to point out that his strictures "have nothing to do with the evaluation of the work of Stravinsky and Ravel, the authors of the new, veri-fied[!] redaction." He eagerly defended them against Andrey Rimsky-Korsakov's complaints, offering along the way what turns out to have been the only contem-porary description of Stravinsky's final chorus ever to reach print. (He even in-cluded three musical examples so that Russian musicians could weigh the charge of "vandalism" for themselves.)

That this was the only substantive review of a new work by Stravinsky seems scarcely credible, given the scandalous *Rite* première only days before, not to men-tion all the advance publicity by way of controversy that had preceded the *Khovan-shchina* production itself. Stravinsky attributed the fact to Diaghilev's opening-night ruse. He wrote to Derzhanovsky: "You asked me at some point about the final chorus for *Khovanshchina*. It turned out very well indeed and was performed three times with great success in Paris. The critics, present *in corpore* at the pre-mière, and thinking that it was my chorus that was performed (it was Rimsky-Korsakov's that was actually played!), denounced it up and down. Later they stayed away from my chorus on purpose, so as to avoid embarrassment, Diaghilev having specially announced it."[45] In fact, not even Calvocoressi reviewed the chorus as performed. He wrote:

> As for the finale written by Stravinsky, which if it was performed at all in Paris was performed only toward the end of the run [i.e., beginning on 16 June], I can judge it only on the basis of the score. That, in any case, was quite sufficient to certify that this finale is not only beautiful, but utterly agrees with the author's [i.e., Musorgsky's] conception, and makes for a fitting culmination to Musorgsky's musical creation.[46]

What the writer did not tell his readers was that he was familiar not only with the score but with the sketchbook for the chorus, which Stravinsky had presented him as a gift on 6 July 1913, the date of a visit Calvocoressi had paid the composer at the Villa Borghese, a nursing home in Neuilly where Stravinsky was convalesc-ing from his bout with typhus. It was from this sketchbook that Calvocoressi quoted the original "Raskolnik" (Old Believer) themes in the *RMG* (as we may tell from the key in which he quoted it), and it was on the basis of the contrapuntal drafts contained in the sketchbook that he was able to make the following shrewd

45. Letter written at Ustilug, 12/[25] August 1913; in IStrSM: 477.
46. Calvocoressi, "Novaya redaktsiya 'Khovanshchinï,'" col. 832. For the date of the first perfor-mance of Stravinsky's chorus, see the announcements from *Le Gaulois* and *Le Figaro*, cited in SelCorrI:56n.

observation (which, however, he was quick to contradict in his final, rather fatuous assessment of the piece):

> All this is, if you please, a bit more "constructed" than what Musorgsky was wont to do, he being inclined almost always to limit himself to the statement of his themes. But the moderation displayed here, for all the great strength of the effect it makes, is such that this stricture carries relative weight at best. Even Musorgsky's most ardent adherent would have to agree, it seems to me, that in the present instance the composer's style has been fully preserved.[47]

That, we shall presently see, was going a bit far. But before turning to the chorus itself, let us note the surprising fact that its publication in vocal score in the spring of 1914—by Bessel, who held performance rights to Rimsky's version of the opera—was greeted in Russia by a silence as total as that maintained by the French critics the year before. The edition (a particell in place of the more usual piano reduction) is now a great rarity. It may not have circulated at all in St. Petersburg, although that is where it was printed. All surviving copies seem to be located in the West.[48]

What did achieve some tiny private circulation in Russia was a manuscript full score that Stravinsky sent Derzhanovsky at the latter's request.[49] Predictably enough, Derzhanovsky sent it off to Myaskovsky, together with his equally predictable assurance that Stravinsky's version was "more interesting (more profound and severe) than Korsakov's." Myaskovsky, then at the height of his irritation with "Milord Stravinsky" (see the preceding chapter), declined to review it, returning it to Derzhanovsky with the comment, "The *Khovanshchina* chorus is a severe and beautiful piece of work, but whether it is better than Korsakov's I cannot tell, since I haven't got the latter at hand."[50]

Except among the *Muzïka* crowd, then, the *Khovanshchina* chorus seems to have been rather an unknown quantity to Russian musicians. The first and only Russian critic to write about it was Asafyev, who gave it low marks indeed in his *Book About Stravinsky*.[51] Andrey Rimsky-Korsakov could not have known it as of 1915, when he wrote his withering general account entitled "Igor Stravinsky's Ballets,"[52] a piece

---

47. Calvocoressi, "Novaya redaktsiya 'Khovanshchinï,'" col. 833.

48. Stravinsky, queried by Craft (Conv:66/61), was not even sure it had been issued by the time war and revolution put an end to Bessel's commercial activity in Russia. Only two copies of the vocal score are known to the present writer, one in the estate of Gerald Abraham (it had been Calvocoressi's), the other in the possession of Robert Craft. The plates, incidentally, bear the number 7396, not 7386 as given by Threlfall ("Stravinsky Version," 110). Upon Diaghilev's death the full score became the property of Serge Lifar, who withheld it from scholarly inspection (SelCorrII:430).

49. See SelCorrI:57 (letter of 29 August 1913).

50. Letter of 12 September 1913; for the exchange, see Shlifshteyn (ed.), *Myaskovskiy: sobraniye materialov* 2:363, 539.

51. "It is all done not so much for its own sake as for the sake of being different.... Anything but the old way (that is, Rimsky-Korsakov's way)" (Glebov, *Kniga o Stravinskom*, 89).

52. A. N. Rimsky-Korsakov, "Baletï Igorya Stravinskogo," *Apollon*, 1915, no. 1, 46–57.

entirely devoted to making Stravinsky out a renegade; for the article ranges far beyond its titular subject, and had he known the chorus, the author would surely have entered it only too happily in evidence.

It would, in fact, have been his prize exhibit, so pointed was its composer's rejection of kuchkist stylization in favor of neonationalist primitivism, going far beyond Musorgsky in directions the elder Rimsky-Korsakov had consistently characterized as "barbarous" and "musically ugly." This little-known score, then, with its prominently displayed dedication to Sergey Pavlovich Diaghilev, was nothing less than Stravinsky's official public notice that he had gone over, with enthusiasm, to the other side.

The title page of the 1914 Bessel score (Fig. 14.2) is printed in Russian, French, and English,[53] but only the Russian gives the title in its complete and telling form:

FINAL CHORUS
for "KHOVANSHCHINA"
on themes of
M. MUSORGSKY
and authentic Old Believers' [themes]
composed by
IGOR STRAVINSKY
1913

What is significant about this title is its acknowledgment that Stravinsky based his chorus not only on Musorgsky's transcription of the Old Believers' chant that was later used by Rimsky-Korsakov (Fig. 14.3a), but on two additional themes from the opera as well: the running eighth-note ostinato with which Act V begins (and which accompanies Dosifey's opening monologue), and the offstage chorus of Old Believers at the beginning of Act III (heard also behind the scenes in the second act that Diaghilev omitted).[54] In Example 14.1, all the raw material from which Stravinsky worked is laid out: first the Old Believer chants in both of the variants Musorgsky had jotted down (Stravinsky copied them out on the first page of the sketchbook; the phrases are given labels in the example for use in the discussion that will follow), then the two Musorgsky melodies, and finally a characteristic harmonic progression-cum-pedal from the "Dawn" prelude that crops up unexpectedly toward the end of Stravinsky's setting as if by way of recapitulation.

In its broad features, Stravinsky's chorus shows an effort to follow Musorgsky's original dramaturgical intentions as far as these could be ascertained. According to one of Musorgsky's last letters to Stasov, it seems that he did not think it feasible

53. The text was translated for publication into French by R. and M. d'Harcourt and into English by Rosa Newmarch.
54. This chorus was itself freely based on a khorovod from Balakirev's anthology of 1866 (no. 26, "Stoy, moy miliy khorovod"), but Stravinsky was probably not aware of its derivation; see Bachinskaya, *Narodniye pesni,* 29, 156–57.

FIG. 14.2. Title page of the *Khovanshchina* chorus, originally presented to Michel Calvocoressi. (Courtesy Gerald Abraham)

EXAMPLE 14.1

a. Stravinsky, *Khovanshchina* sketchbook, p. 1

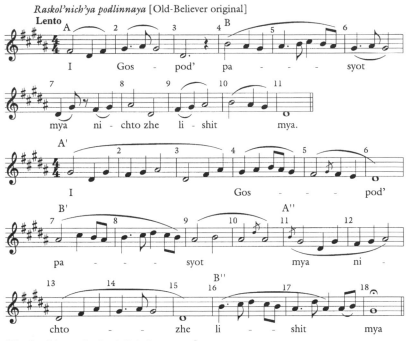

[The Lord is my shepherd; I shall not want]

b. Musorgsky, *Khovanshchina* (*Complete Works,* ed. Lamm, vol. 4), p. 314

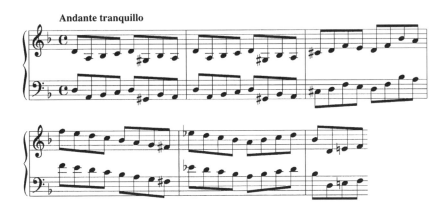

EXAMPLE 14.1 (*continued*)

c. Musorgsky, *Khovanshchina* (Lamm ed.), p. 186 (chorus)

Andantino poco sostenuto

(Ten. + Bass.) Po - sra - mi - khom, po - sra - mi-khom, pre - re - ko - khom, pre - re -

ko - khom i pre-pre-khom Ye - res' ne - che - sti - ya i

zla strem - ni - nï vra - zhi - ye!

[We will shame them, we will maul them, we will roast them, the evil, dirty heretics, devil-sent!]

d. Musorgsky, *Khovanshchina* (Lamm ed.), p. 8

F I G . 1 4 . 3 a . Musorgsky's jotting (from Lyubov Karmalina's dictation) of the Schismatics' song (two versions) on which the *Khovanshchina* finale was to be based.

to portray the Old Believers' mass suicide directly on the stage.[55] Lamm concluded from this that the composer actually "declined to show the immolation on stage, deciding rather to transfer it to the wings and have the opera end with the exit of the Old Believers as the music fades away."[56] In fact that is precisely the way Stravinsky's chorus ends: with a fade-out that must have accompanied a general exit. (The contrast to Rimsky-Korsakov's ending could not have been sharper.) Also beholden to Musorgsky's original plan was the way Stravinsky began with an unaccompanied unison melody derived not from the first but from the second variant of the source tune (phrase A' in Ex. 14.1a; a sketch for the opening is shown in Fig. 14.3b).[57]

55. 22 August 1880: "Dear généralissime, our *Khovanshchina* is finished except for a little bit in the final immolation scene: about this we'll have to put our heads together: this little rascal depends entirely on stagecraft" (Musorgsky, *Literaturnoye naslediye*, 261). In the commentary to his earlier edition of Musorgsky's letters, Andrey Rimsky-Korsakov, relying in part on his father's recollection, wrote: "One may suppose that Musorgsky found it difficult to finish the immolation scene in the last act of *Khovanshchina* without having a clear idea of how the immolation could be staged; this was long before the earliest performances in St. Petersburg . . . of Wagner's operas with their effects of fire and steam in the '*Feuerzauber*'" (A. N. Rimsky-Korsakov [ed.], *Musorgskiy: pis'ma i dokumenti*, 413).
56. Preface to the vocal score, p. xiv.
57. The sketchbook opens with a solo for Dosifey (pp. 3–4, mm. 39–45 and 53–57 in the finished chorus, an intervening choral verse splitting the two halves of what was originally conceived as a single

F I G . 1 4 . 3 b .   Page 5 of Stravinsky's *Khovanshchina* sketchbook (1913), on which he found his opening, a conflation of the melodies shown in Figure 14.3a. (Courtesy Oliver Neighbour)

Beginning with the very next phrase, however, all ostensible dependence on Musorgsky ends. The entry of the second voice joins phrase A′ of the second variant to phrase B of the first. All of Stravinsky's eventual citations of the original schismatics' tune (the so-called *raskol'nich'ya podlinnaya*) would in fact be hybrids like this one.

The outstanding feature of the second phrase is its harmonic/contrapuntal style. With its outer voices in unisons and octaves, its weird doublings and occurses, and above all the exposed fourth on the downbeat of m. 11, this harmonization (Ex. 14.2a) goes far beyond any barbarity ever committed by Musorgsky, straight into the world of the heterophonic *podgoloski* transcribed by Melgunov and Linyova. This is a chorus harmonized as if on purpose to realize Linyova's proposal (sec-

---

unbroken statement of the theme), following which there is an entrance of the whole chorus in octaves based on the first variant of the source tune. Evidently this is how Stravinsky originally meant his chorus to open. On page 5 of the sketchbook (Fig. 14.3b), however, another notation of the choral entrance is crossed out and the one finally chosen follows, headed "*Nachalo khora!*" ("*Beginning of the chorus!*"—underscoring and exclamation point original). It may have been precisely at this point that Stravinsky became acquainted with Musorgsky's original opening. As is so often the case in Stravinsky's sketches, an idea of seemingly obvious naturalness proves not to have been the initial conception but the product of a ruthless quest.

EXAMPLE 14.2

a. Stravinsky, *Khovanshchina* sketchbook, p. 5: "*Nachalo khora!*" (≈published chorus, mm. 1–15)

b. Linyova, "Opït zapisi fonografom ukraínskikh narodnïkh pesen" (*Trudï MEK*, 1), 253 (no. 5), 256 (no. 9), 260 (no. 12), 263 (no. 14), 265 (no. 16)

EXAMPLE 14.2b *(continued)*

(continued)

EXAMPLE 14.2b (*continued*)

Krï - mu   i - du - chï,   iz Krï-mui-du - chï.

onded by Stasov) that a new style of Russian art music be founded on the style of her *Peasant Songs of Great Russia as They Are in the Folk's Harmonization*. A comparison between Stravinsky's harmonization and some typical Linyova transcriptions from her first published collection (1906) will reveal the depth of his debt to her. The first song in Example 14.2b is the very "Petrivka" that was cited in Chapter 12 as a putative source melody for the Ritual Action of the Ancestors in *The Rite*.

Following this extraordinary harmonization, the *raskol'nich'ya podlinnaya* is repeated in a form that ties phrase B to phrase B″ for a "closed" ending. This time the choral harmonization (doubled in the orchestra at both the upper and the lower octave) is of the "liturgical" octave-third (⁸⁄₃) type already encountered in *Petrushka*, with antecedents both in Rimsky-Korsakov and in Musorgsky. Stravinsky employs the device in an exceedingly strict fashion amounting to a sort of parallel organum. The orchestral bass, meanwhile, is derived from Musorgsky's act-opening ostinato (Ex. 14.3; cf. Ex. 14.1b). As in numerous passages from *The Rite*, the two layers of the texture seem to take little or no contrapuntal notice of each other; the resultant harmonic clashes have an oxymoronic effect of planned fortuity, taking the "white-key dissonance" of *Petrushka* several stages further. In Example 14.3, a passage from page four of the published vocal score is laid out in the simpler fashion Stravinsky employed in a continuity draft beginning on page eleven of the sketchbook. Only the choral parts and the orchestral bass are shown.

Measures 26–30 of Stravinsky's chorus are a literal and complete citation of the theme in Example 14.1b. By dint of extensive octave doubling, Stravinsky works it into the treble register, where it then continues as an upper-voice pedal accompanying a choral phrase of Stravinsky's invention in which the trebles descend an octave through some typically Musorgskian Neapolitan-type harmonies (mm. 31–38). Next, the *raskol'nich'ya podlinnaya,* in the form given in Example 14.3, is intoned as a solo by Dosifey, each phrase answered, responsory-fashion, by the full chorus (the first response up a fifth in D-sharp minor, the second at the original pitch). It is here that the Act III chorus (Ex. 14.1c) is quoted in the form of a rough-hewn bass to each half of the Old Believer melody in turn. The latter is dou-

EXAMPLE 14.3   Stravinsky, published *Khovanshchina* chorus (St. Petersburg: Bessel, 1914), p. 4 (≈sketchbook, p. 11)

bled starkly in three octaves from bass to soprano. Example 14.4 shows the orchestra part as it is given in the Bessel vocal score.

What happens next is a stroke of neonationalist genius. The naked fourth, so conspicuous in Stravinsky's initial Linyovian harmonization of the *raskol'nich'ya podlinnaya,* is "composed out" by transposing phrase A' to C-sharp (still accompanied by the Act III choral theme, only now in the middle register instead of the bass) over a tonic pedal on G-sharp. The transposed phrase is joined directly to an untransposed concluding phrase (B'/B″). The joint is covered by an additional entrance of the Act III choral theme at the tonic pitch, overlapping with the end of the transposed statement (see Ex. 14.5 for the whole extraordinary texture).

The ending is best shown in its more compact sketch form. Evidently taking his cue from the bell-tolling progression in the Prelude (cf. Ex. 14.1d), Stravinsky works his way up to a high A-sharp tremolando, which is held thereafter as a pedal (or, as Eric Walter White aptly puts it, a "cipher")[58] to the very end, while the chorus, together with the three principals Dosifey, Marfa, and Andrey Khovansky,

58. White, *Stravinsky: The Composer and His Works,* 500.

EXAMPLE 14.4   Stravinsky, *Khovanshchina* chorus, two contrapuntal combinations

a. Measures 46–52

(Act III Chorus)

b. Measures 58–62

(Act III Chorus)

EXAMPLE 14.5   Stravinsky, *Khovanshchina* chorus, mm. 63–72

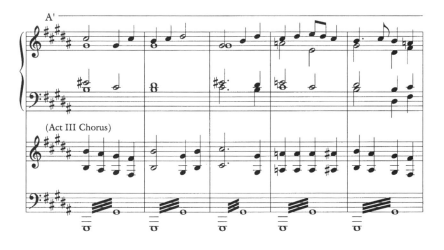

(Act III Chorus)

reach the peroration. Here, for the first and only time, Stravinsky chose the first variant of the opening phrase of the *podlinnaya* (phrase A), in majestic doubled note values. It links not with phrase B, however, but with B', returning once more to the first variant for the very characteristic falling-fourth cadence. An accordion-like harmonic oscillation (à la *Petrushka*) on a plagal cadence decorated with added sixths and sevenths (à la *Firebird*), resulting from the ubiquitous and characteristic doubling of lines at the third (à la *The Rite*), brings the chorus to an ineffably spacious, poignantly indefinite close à la *Zvezdolikiy,* the "cipher," together with the reverberating tam-tam, being the last sounds to die out (Ex. 14.6).

The opera *Khovanshchina,* in the Stravinsky/Ravel redaction of Rimsky-Korsakov's redaction, thus ends on an unresolved ninth that might have brought a blush even to the cheeky original composer. Yet the mood it strikes seems not only dramaturgically apt but also congruent with what one strongly suspects to have been Musorgsky's own pessimistic view of Russian history, so utterly traduced by Rimsky-Korsakov's banal Petrine meliorism and its gaudy orchestral apotheosis.

Its occasional circumstances, its brevity, and its obscurity notwithstanding, the *Khovanshchina* chorus marked an important stage in Stravinsky's stylistic development. As the foregoing description will have suggested, it made for a coda that rather oddly wagged the production to which it was appended, a redaction that was, for all the hoopla, preponderantly Rimsky's after all. Viewed solely in this light, Stravinsky's work, resolutely declining as it did to fit in with what preceded it, surely merited—one could even say invited—the charge of impudence.

Yet it is equally clear that on its own terms the chorus was neither parody nor travesty, but an epochal manifestation of Stravinsky's burgeoning neonationalism. No longer did it bear the slightest imprint of the walled-in "St. Petersburg school"

EXAMPLE 14.6

a. Stravinsky, *Khovanshchina* sketchbook, p. 18 (≈published chorus, mm. 74–79)

b. Stravinsky, *Khovanshchina* sketchbook, pp. 6–7 (≈published chorus, mm. 80–end)

EXAMPLE 14.6b (continued)

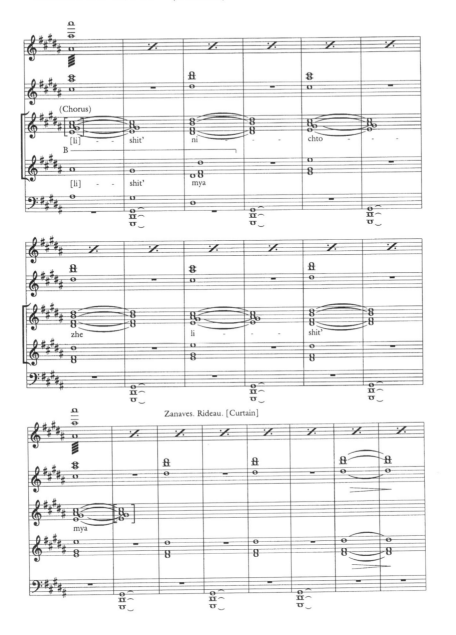

Zanaves. Rideau. [Curtain]

(continued)

EXAMPLE 14.6b *(continued)*

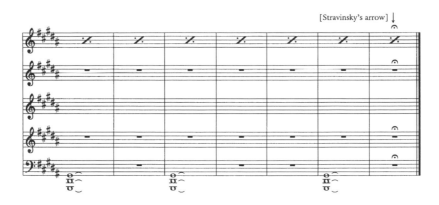

[Stravinsky's arrow]

in which its author had been educated. It was moreover implicitly anti-Western, in ways Stravinsky would develop in magnificently militant fashion over the decade that lay ahead. Following Linyova's lead, Stravinsky was effectively breathing new life into what had been, everyone agreed, of all Russian art-music traditions the most moribund. No one in Russia save Linyova herself dared dream that the Russian diatonic folkloristic idiom could be revived in any but a patently epigonal way. Having reopened this door, Stravinsky would travel a long distance down the path that now lay revealed, the path that would lead him to *Svadebka*.[59]

OPERA-BALLET

Another indispensable precedent, not only for *Svadebka* but for a host of other Stravinskian theatrical conceptions, was set a year later, on the evening of 21 May 1914, when what was surely the boldest of Diaghilev's prewar productions was unveiled. This was the notorious presentation of Rimsky-Korsakov's opera *The Golden Cockerel (Zolotoy petushok)*—or *Le coq d'or*, as it is usually called now in the West, following this very production—in the form of a ballet with voices (or, al-

59. Stravinsky's instrumentation of Shaklovitïy's aria, though a work of little consequence (nothing but an instrumentation, it was dropped from the production following Chaliapin's refusal to sing it in the character of Dosifey, and it has never been performed), nevertheless deserves a brief look. An incomplete fair copy, plus a sketch, survives in the Stravinsky Archive (the complete full score was presumably part of Serge Lifar's booty). It bears the following autograph title page:

Ariya Shaklovitogo (v redaktsii S. P. Dyagileva ariya Dosifeya) instrumentovano [*sic*] po rukopisi M. P. Musorgskogo na ½ tona vïsshe I. F. Stravinskim

Shaklovitïy's aria (in S. P. Diaghilev's version Dosifey's aria) orchestrated from M. P. Musorgsky's manuscript a half-step higher by I. F. Stravinsky

Practically everything in this *avertissement* requires qualification. For one thing, Stravinsky's score is in the same key—E-flat minor—as Musorgsky's (or Rimsky-Korsakov's). It was not transposed. (The accompanying sketch, to perhaps pointlessly complicate the matter, is written in the key of C-sharp mi-

ternatively, a cantata with mime and dance). The choreography was by Fokine, newly returned to the Diaghilev fold (for one season only) following Nijinsky's peremptory dismissal. The decors and costumes were by Natalia Goncharova, the future designer of *Svadebka,* then in her first flush of fame as fiery "*Futuristka*" of

---

nor, a whole step *lower* than Musorgsky's original.) Furthermore, and very surprisingly, at certain strategic points Stravinsky's version agrees not with Musorgsky's original (as given by Lamm in his complete vocal score, pp. 215–17), but with Rimsky-Korsakov. A symptomatic pair of such spots follows:

1. Meas. 12–13
   a. Original (Lamm, ed., p. 215)

   Akh, tï v sud'-bi - ne zlo-chast-na-ya

   b. Rimsky-Korsakov redaction (Moscow: Muzïka, 1970)
   p. 122

   Akh, tï v sud'-bi - ne zlo-chast-na-ya

   c. Stravinsky redaction (accompaniment reduced)

   Akh, tï v sud'-be [*sic*] zlo - chast-na-ya
   Fag.
   Cor.
   Cb.

2. Meas. 38
   a. Musorgsky (p. 217)

   Sto - na - la tï __ pod ya-[ryo-mom]

   b. Rimsky-Korsakov (p. 123)

   Sto - na - la tï __ pod ya-[ryo-mom]

   c. Stravinsky

   Sto - na - la tï __ pod ya-[ryo-mom]
   Cl.   Vla.
   Vc.
   Cb.

What both of these discrepancies seem to suggest is that a Musorgsky autograph of the aria may have existed in D minor, containing certain textual variants uncollated by Lamm (who in the extensive critical report to his edition cites only a single surviving manuscript source for the aria), and that both Rimsky and Stravinsky relied on it. That would be a neat explanation, but no evidence supports it. (Vyacheslav Karatïgin's survey of the sources in his article "'Khovanshchina' i yeyo avtorï [*Muzïkal'nïy sovremennik* 2, nos. 5–6 (1917): 192–218], the most extensive pre-Lamm treatment of the subject, makes no mention of any alternative ms. for Shaklovitïy's aria—which he not unjustly characterizes, by the way, as one of the opera's weakest pages [p. 211].) The only alternative explanation is that Stravinsky was tacitly eclectic in his editorial method, choosing at pleasure between Musorgsky's wares and Rimsky's. That would be entirely in character for him, even as it belies the ostensible purpose of the Diaghilev-commissioned revision.

F I G . 1 4 . 4 . Natalia Goncharova, set for Act I of *Le coq d'or* (1914).

Russian art (Fig. 14.4). All agreed, when the dust had settled, that this production had been not merely the hit of the 1914 season, but a pathbreaker and a course-charter for many seasons to come. Prince Sergey Volkonsky, Diaghilev's old boss at the Mariyinsky, thought it nothing short of epochal:

> The whimsical events of Pushkin's *skazka* went off in most whimsical fashion amid these whimsical conditions. Every role was divided in two, sung by one person and played by another. The singers sat motionless at the sides of the stage on scaffolds spreading mountainously to the right and left, dressed in crimson caftans, looking like two church choirs, head upon head in rows, like numberless saints in an ancient image. And in the middle the silent action of mimes went on. I must declare that all this was managed beautifully. Only for the first minute was one's attention divided. Thereafter the complete merger of visual and auditory impressions took over. We are living, it seems, in an interesting moment in history.[60]

Another critic who reacted with unalloyed enthusiasm was the avant-garde ballet-omane Minsky (Vilenkin), who had so rapturously welcomed Nijinsky's *Sacre du printemps*. He called his review "The Union of the Arts," and headed it with an

60. "'Zolotoy petushok' v postanovke S. P. Dyagileva," *Rech'*, no. 135 (1914); in Volkonsky, *Otkliki teatra*, 58.

epigraph attributed to Diaghilev himself: "I am now betting on ballet." Minsky's review emphasized the "theoretical," programmatic aspects of the production:

> I have no doubt that this time the inspirers of the Russian Ballet have hit upon a new form of theatrical art, one that has a huge future. It is neither ballet illustrated by music nor opera flavored with ballet, but a union of two hitherto separate art forms: a union that takes place not on the stage but in the viewer's soul. The delight of the performance consists further in that, by presenting a spectacle of singing mummies and moving dolls, *it creates an atmosphere of esthetic convention in place of the false illusionism of the old ballet and the old opera.* . . . I had a talk with Benois, who was also there, and found out that the first idea of such a musico-plastic spectacle had been his. . . . Later on, when the members of the "inner circle" decided to "balletify" Rimsky-Korsakov's opera, the thought of separating sound from movement arose in and of itself. At first they were going to put the singers in the orchestra pit, but later, on the initiative of Diaghilev, who recalled the disposition of angelic choirs in our old *lubki,* and according to Benois's designs, it was decided to seat the singers on the sides of the stage, as in an amphitheater. Benois spoke of this scenic innovation with justifiable pride and understandable excitement, and concluded his remarks with the words, "Who knows, perhaps the union of the arts Wagner dreamed about has been realized at last by us."[61]

In his memoirs, Benois did indeed take credit for the idea behind the production, though in terms more modest than those he employed in conversation with Minsky:

> I had thought long ago of splitting an operatic performance into two planes, risky though it was. But what guided me was no fatuous wish to "pull off something extraordinary" (on the contrary, throughout my long artistic career I have remained pure in this connection and have never fallen for the lure of "*épater*-ing the bourgeois"); what persuaded me to try this experiment was the fact that all too often operatic performances present an utterly unacceptable *spectacle,* and this because the criterion of vocal sonority dominates them. . . . It will suffice to recall even a wonderful singer like Felia Litvinne. Honestly, what kind of an Isolde or a Brunnhilde did she make?
>
> In the conviction that an irredeemable sin lay at the very essence of opera, I conceived the "criminal" thought of replacing the opera singers with a group of performers in whom physical deficiencies were excluded by definition. In ballet *there cannot be* outright monsters. . . . In ballet we are dealing with people who possess, if not an ideal, then at least a pleasant exterior, one that "predisposes in their favor." Another defect of opera consists in the fact that many performers appear in it who have no idea of acting, who stomp around like bears, grimacing meaninglessly. . . . Ballet dancers, on the other hand, are given instruction in "expressive deportment" as a "required subject."[62]

61. N. Minsky, "Soyedineniye iskusstv: pis'mo iz Parizha," *Utro Rossii,* 24 May 1914; italics added.
62. Benois, *Moí vospominaniya* 2:531–32.

A considerable stimulus to Benois's antioperatic theorizing must have been Mikhaíl Volkonsky's famous lampoon *Vampuka; or, The African Bride: A Model Opera in Every Way* (*Vampuka, nevesta afrikanskaya, obraztsovaya vo vsekh otnosheniyakh opera*), with music by Vladimir Georgiyevich Ehrenberg (1875–1923), a well-known musical wag who (like the fledgling Stravinsky) made a specialty of setting and "illustrating" the verses of Kozma Prutkov. A pastiche of, inter alia, *Aida* and *L'Africaine,* and with a libretto parodying all the hoariest clichés of the Italian opera, *Vampuka* opened at the Fun-House Mirror (*Krivoye zerkalo*), Nikolai Yevreynov's popular St. Petersburg cabaret theater where Ehrenberg was music director, on 17/30 January 1909, and immediately became the talk of the capital (productions—chiefly amateur—continued at least until 1927, when it reached its thousandth performance). The common noun *vampuka* became an all-purpose pejorative for everything stilted and stereotyped in theatrical productions of all kinds and even gave birth to a verb, *vampuchit'*, meaning to act with exaggerated "operatic" pathos.

The Golden Cockerel had had its first production the same year as *Vampuka,* and it was no wonder that Benois immediately fixed upon it as the perfect medium for realizing his pretty split-level scheme—"with a minimum of risk," as he put it, because it was a "showy" opera, one whose content lay on its surface without any need for "subtle psychological interpretation" or any other "literary" baggage. When in 1913 Diaghilev decided to "return to opera," Benois seized the moment and persuaded his old friend to mount Rimsky's opera in this unprecedented, guaranteed vampuka-free way.[63]

Of course, it was not really so simple.[64] Whatever Benois's original motivation might have been, the production he instigated was received as something more than a mere cosmetic improvement, as Minsky's testimony already shows. It was received not only by the critics but by the Ballets Russes insiders as an artistic breakthrough, veritably a new art form. Why?

Because it answered perfectly to their deep-seated antiliterary prejudice—this, after all, was what Diaghilev would have meant by "betting on ballet"—and at the same time it gave *plastika* an unprecedented scope. In a 1910 interview (with Minsky, as it happened), Diaghilev had stated his aims in this way: "The essence and the secret of our ballet lies in the fact that we have renounced ideas in favor of an elemental spontaneity [yes, *stikhiya*]. We wished to find an art through which all

63. Ibid., 533. On *Vampuka* see B. S. Shteynpress, *Opernïye prem'yerï XX veka* (Moscow: Sovetskiy Kompozitor, 1983), 46; also Harold B. Segel, *Turn-of-the-Century Cabaret* (New York: Columbia University Press, 1987), 283–84. Spencer Golub's *Evreinov: The Theatre of Paradox and Transformation* (Ann Arbor: UMI Research Press, 1984), a study of Nikolai Nikolayevich Yevreynov, director of the "Crooked Mirror," contains a full synopsis (152–53) and a photo of the original production (pl. 26).

64. Nor was it really unprecedented: the Benois/Diaghilev *Coq d'or* could be looked upon as a revival of the court opera-ballets of the French *grand siècle*. Given the long-standing Versailles-mania of the Miriskusniki, this is not a factor to be discounted.

the complexity of life, all feelings and passions, could be expressed apart from words and ideas—not rationally but elementally, graphically, self-evidently."[65]

Removing all bearers of words from center stage and replacing them with graphic decor and elemental gesture was the logical outgrowth of this quest for theatrical *stikhiya* (or, to put it more idiomatically in Russian, for *stikhiynïy teatr*). The imagery employed by Diaghilev and by Benois echoes the old call for *liturgichnost'*. Separating voice from movement disembodied the former and depersonalized the latter in the spirit of the new folklorism: Diaghilev's *Coq d'or* was thus a new highpoint of neonationalism, the ne plus ultra of the tendency initiated a generation earlier at Abramtsevo. As Fokine's memoirs attest, "In the dances, the poses, the groupings, the gestures, I tried to capture the style of the Russian *lubok*. . . . Besides Russian folk paintings and prints, I took inspiration from the toys of folk handicraftsmen, from the poses on old icons, the remains of frescoes, old Russian embroideries."[66] Goncharova's sets and costumes were similarly motivated and informed, and just as successful. As the young choreographer Boris Romanov (1891–1957) put it in an interview in the *Peterburgskaya gazeta,* "There was not the slightest hint of 'futurism' here, but a genuine Russian *lubok*."[67]

As by now seems almost superfluous to add, news of this production was received in Russia with a mixture of irony and indignation. In its coverage of this "latest '*boum!*' of Diaghilev's *saison russe*," the *RMG* did what it could to ridicule the whole concept:

Imagine: along the sides of the stage two raised wings with stairs have been constructed. At the raising of the curtains all the singers are in place on them. All of them, men and women alike, are dressed in identical long red caftans with big copper buttons and fur-trimmed caps. These people never make a move. It is only by their mouths, which open and close, that one can tell that they are real people, not dummies. What they sing is acted out on stage by the mimes and ballerinas. Naturally, it is very hard to achieve the full coordination of gesture with the words sung from the wings. Only Karsavina [as the Queen of Shemakha] succeeds, and then only when she is miming from a position close to the singer ([Aurelia] Dobrovolskaya) who is singing her role. This *Coq d'or* is mounted in the *lubok* style of Russian folktales. The sets and costumes justify [Goncharova's] reputation as "*Futuristka*" by the naïveté of the draughtsmanship, familiar from *lubki* and from the works of contemporary artists.[68]

Diaghilev's cousin and onetime collaborator Dmitriy Filosofov attempted a typical Miriskusnik defense of the production on the grounds that "opera has entered

65. S. P. Diaghilev, "Yeshcho o baletnïkh itogakh," *Utro Rossii,* 24 August 1910; in Zilbershteyn and Samkov (eds.), *Dyagilev* 1:214.

66. Fokine, *Protiv techeniya;* quoted in Gozenpud, *Russkiy opernïy teatr mezhdu dvukh revolyutsiy,* 270.

67. "Teatral," "Beseda s baletmeysterom B. G. Romanovïm," *Peterburgskaya gazeta,* 1 June 1914. Romanov was in Paris as choreographer for Stravinsky's *Nightingale.*

68. "Russkaya muzïka za granitsey" (unsigned).

its period of degeneracy; we are all surfeited to the point of nausea with its stylized realism. The singer has killed the composer, has killed theatrical action as well." Filosofov approved especially of the "hieratic poses" of the singers in their rows and the gravely liturgical quality of the dancers' "*plastika*."[69]

But this was decidedly a minority viewpoint. Public opinion in Russia was molded chiefly by the agonized reaction of the Rimsky-Korsakov family and by its unprecedented move legally to quash the production. After *Shéhérazade* and *Khovanshchina*, this *Coq d'or* was for them the last straw. Andrey enunciated their position in a typically humorless piece for *Apollon*. He set the family's viewpoint down in the formal guise of two main "postulates":

A. The transformation of *Le coq d'or* into a ballet-cantata can in no wise be viewed as an artistically lawful deed.

B. In particular, the staging of *Le coq d'or* presented by S. P. Diaghilev in Paris and London must be acknowledged a failure and in many respects a careless travesty.

The main point was that Diaghilev's staging "*distorted the fundamental features of the work as an operatic composition*."[70] And as usual, there had been reckless cuts.

The lawsuit, prosecuted by Mme Rimsky-Korsakov through the French courts, though successful, came too late to affect the 1914 season; all she was able to prevent were revivals. In Russia the suit was big news. A rather lengthy interview with the plaintiff appeared in the *Peterburgskaya gazeta,* of which the following is the most relevant section:

The widow of N. A. Rimsky-Korsakov, Nadezhda Nikolayevna, in answer to our question as to the reasons that have caused her to turn for protection to the French courts, says that there were two such reasons:

—"In the first place, the opera *Le Coq d'or* has been staged by Diaghilev in an utterly distorted form: some cross between a ballet and an oratorio.

"The singers are for some reason immobile and the whole opera is put through unspeakable cuts.

"For another thing, Mr. Diaghilev never even troubled to ask my permission to make these alterations, and until the last minute I did not know whether he was really putting on *Le coq d'or* or not.

"The rumors in the papers were contradictory, and only recently was I able to ascertain that *Le coq d'or* was really playing in Paris.

"This sort of treatment is what drove me to the French courts with the demand that this spectacle be halted."

—"But your ban, it seems, came too late."

69. D. V. Filosofov, "Russkaya tyazhba za granitsey," *Russkoye slovo,* 29 May 1914.
70. A. N. Rimsky-Korsakov, " 'Zolotoy petushok' na parizhskoy i londonskoy stsenakh," *Apollon,* 1914, nos. 6–7, 46, 48.

—"I don't know how many performances of *Le coq d'or* were planned, but in any case the decision of the French court will stand in the future."

—"What do you intend to do about London, where *Le coq d'or* is also scheduled to be shown?"

—"I can say nothing definite about London at this point. This is not the first time Diaghilev has allowed himself to tamper with my husband's work. A few years ago he did the same kind of thing with *Sheherazade,* but at that time we had no copyright convention with France and I had to content myself with protests in the press.

"Now, thanks to the convention, the circumstances have altered and the rights of Russian composers are protected by the French society of authors to whom I have turned for assistance. . . ."[71]

With the lone exception of Filosofov,[72] Russian journalists took great delight in taking Mme Rimskaya-Korsakova's side against the upstart Diaghilev. Anatoliy Lunacharsky, for example, wrote:

Whatever might be said in justification of this spectacle, however much it be alleged that neither Pushkin nor Rimsky-Korsakov could have objected, . . . still I deeply sympathize with the heirs of the great musician in their protest. I agree that in and of itself the show is rather interesting. How could it not be interesting to gaze upon the whole world of amusing and cunningly made toys which Mme Goncharova, like a sweet nanny, has thrown to the snobs from her apron? Isn't it piquant the way the mummified singers sing from their perches at the sides of the stage, while the ballet dancers "act out"—as often as not out of time and out of step with the music? And anyhow, Pushkin is still Pushkin and Rimsky is still Rimsky, even when they are stretched out over a Procrustean bed, "against all reason, defying the elements." Of these two giants, only torsos remain, but even their torsos are magnificent.[73]

THE NIGHTINGALE REVIVED

It was Stravinsky's opera *The Nightingale,* playing on a double bill with *Le coq d'or,* that had made all those brutal cuts necessary; and so Stravinsky was complicit with Diaghilev in the eyes of the Rimsky-Korsakovs, and whatever indignation they had formerly felt toward him now turned to hatred. Andrey Rimsky-Korsakov obviously had Stravinsky primarily in mind when he closed his protest against Diaghi-

---

71. "Teatral," "Vdova N. A. Rimskogo-Korsakova o 'Zolotom petushke'," *Peterburgskaya gazeta,* 17 May 1914.

72. He ended his review of the production by asking, "Why is it that we, the public, who have no interest in the juridical and material aspects of this lawsuit, must sacrifice the interests of art, the interests of collective creative work, to the formalized intentions of the late composer? 'Experts' (Oh God, the experts!) tell us that impermissible cuts have been made. . . . But honestly, would Wagner ever have become popular without cuts! . . . How annoying that the composer's widow, instead of turning to the court of public opinion, has summoned the court bailiff to her aid. She has risen up against youth and life, standing at death's door . . ." (Filosofov, "Russkaya tyazhba za granitsey").

73. *Sovremennik,* 1914, nos. 13–15, 261; in Zilbershteyn and Samkov (eds.), *Dyagilev* 1:466.

lev's crime with what, for all its petulance, looks now to have been a clairvoyant prediction: "In all probability, given Diaghilev's luck, plenty of composers will turn up, eager to adopt that ballet-cantata form. It might be that the example of *Le coq d'or* will inspire them to works of their own on this split-level format. Good luck to them! It is high time they got started. But why was it necessary to rape *Le coq*?"[74]

The first such new work was the very one that shared the boards with *Le coq*, the fourth Stravinsky work to be presented by Diaghilev to Paris: *The Nightingale*, newly and somewhat unexpectedly finished. The story of the opera's commissioning, which may be reconstructed from surviving documents in exceptional detail, is worth recounting for the light it throws on Stravinsky as consummate musical merchant—whose expertise in the arts of haggling and swindling was no doubt picked up directly from Diaghilev—and for the light it throws on his ambitions vis-à-vis his homeland and his place there.

The Nightingale owed its completion to the efforts of Alexander Akimovich Sanin (né Schoenberg, 1869–1956), stage director of all the Diaghilev-produced operas from *Boris Godunov* (1908) to *Khovanshchina* and *Le coq d'or*. As an actor Sanin had been trained by Stanislavsky and was the assistant stage director of the Moscow Art Theater from its founding in 1898 until 1902, when he was called to the Imperial Alexandrinsky (spoken dramatic) Theater in St. Petersburg. In 1907 Sanin joined the staff of the Antique Theater (*Starinnïy teatr*), where he became known for his adroit staging of mass scenes, including the celebrated "Street Theater" in which Benois was involved as designer and which became a powerful precedent for *Petrushka*.[75] This encounter with Benois was one of Sanin's conduits

74. A. N. Rimsky-Korsakov, " 'Zolotoy petushok,' " 54. This same prediction, expressed more in the form of a wish, was made by many of the more progressive reviewers in the Paris press. The very last issue of *Montjoie!* (vol. 2, nos. 4–6 [April–June 1914]: 22), for example, ran an interesting review by Daniel Chennevière (1895–1985), who would later make a reputation as a composer in America under the name Dane Rudhyar. Rimsky came in for considerable abuse, both for having mutilated Musorgsky and for his own failings as a composer who produced "works that are clear, neat, very orderly, very punctilious, very brilliant: a lovely surface; at bottom, nil" (". . . des oeuvres claires, nettes, très ordonnées, très rigoureuses, très brillantes: une très belle surface; au fond, rien"). The critique was frankly Futurist: "What interest can this have for modern minds, for Westerners imbued with science, mechanics, sports, who before going to see it might have been doing 100 [km] an hour in a car or an aeroplane?" ("Quel intérêt cela peut-il présenter pour les cerveaux modernes, pour des occidentaux imbus de science et d'action mécanique ou sportive, qui avant d'aller au spectacle viennent peut-être de faire du 100 à l'heure en auto ou en aéroplane?"). His conclusion called for the application of the split-action formula, not to works of the past but to those of the future: "Finally, assuming that opera is a grotesque and distorted genre, the separation of singer and mime, imagined by Fokine[!], and realized extremely well from the visual standpoint, is a fine idea. It might be whimsical to apply it to already-existing lyric dramas: as for the future, I really think that musicians will realize that drama sung on a stage is a sterile and clumsy form, and that we are soon going to turn to an abstract choreographic drama" ("Enfin, étant donné que l'opéra est un genre monstrueux et déformé, la séparation du chanteur et du mime, imaginée par Fokine, et qui fut fort bien plastiquement réalisée, est une idée heureuse. Il serait peut-être curieux de l'appliquer aux drames lyriques déjà existants: par ce qui est de l'avenir, je pense bien que les musiciens se rendront compte que la forme du drame chanté sur la scène, est une forme stérile et maladroite, et que nous en viendrons bien vite au drame chorégraphique abstrait").

75. See Benois, *Moï vospominaniya* 2:478.

to Diaghilev. Another one, perhaps the most powerful, was the director's long-standing friendship with Chaliapin, going back to the latter's Mamontov days, when many of the future artists and directors of the Moscow Art Theater were associated with the great patron's Private Opera troupe.[76]

After his success with Diaghilev had insured his European fame, Sanin was invited by his old Art Theater colleagues Konstantin Mardzhanov (Mardzhanishvili, 1872–1933) and Alexander Taírov (Kornblith, 1885–1950) to join them in founding a new house—the Moscow Free Theater—in 1913. The founders envisioned a "synthetic" theater that would become the site for all manner of adventurous spectacle both dramatic and musical. Sanin immediately thought of Stravinsky, whose major works had as yet never been performed in Russia, and saw the makings of a coup. On 17 February/2 March 1913, the régisseur wrote to the composer from St. Petersburg with the news—"*Alea jacta est:* What I was discussing with you in hypothetical terms in Paris has come to pass"—and with a plan:

> I want to approach you personally, my very dear Igor Fyodorovich, with an official request. Help us. Share your music with us. My greatest dream is to show you off to Moscow, to St. Petersburg, indeed to all of Russia. Mardzhanov agrees; he would like to commission a three-act piece from you that would make up an entire evening's program. There are no limits on character or form: employ prose, opera, dance, and mime all together as you wish in a single work. Mardzhanov is prepared to send you a certain sum immediately as an advance and to draw up an agreement with you right away concerning the purchase of the piece. We will meet all financial and artistic terms.[77]

Sanin wanted the piece for the opening of the theater, scheduled for October. At the same time he commissioned from Ravel an orchestration of the single completed act of Musorgsky's unfinished *Marriage,* after Gogol's comedy, to play on a double bill with a spectacle in which the extant music from another unfinished Gogol opera by Musorgsky, *The Fair at Sorochintsï,* would be inserted as numbers within a dramatization of the original story.[78]

Although Ravel declined the invitation, Stravinsky was eager to seize the oppor-

76. Chaliapin's *tutoyer* correspondence with Sanin goes back at least to the closing days of the nineteenth century; see Grosheva, *Shalyapin* 1:707–8; also Natalya Kinkulkina, "Pis'ma I. F. Stravinskogo i F. I. Shalyapina k A. A. Saninu," *Sovetskaya muzïka,* 1978, no. 6, 96. After the Revolution, Sanin worked at the Bolshoy Theater in Moscow until 1922, when he joined the emigration. Thereafter he enjoyed a worldwide reputation as opera director, working mainly at the Paris Opera, but with guest engagements at La Scala, the Metropolitan, the Teatro Real in Madrid, and so on.

77. SelCorrII:198.

78. See Ravel's letter to Stravinsky of 5 May 1913 in White, *Stravinsky: The Composer and His Works,* 549 (a translation appears in SelCorrIII:17–18; in both publications the annotations are inaccurate). Ravel seems to have declined the somewhat degrading commission, as the letter suggests he intended to do. A persistent rumor with respect to his phantom orchestration of *Marriage* surfaces now and then in the literature (see Lamm, preface to his edition of *Marriage* [Moscow: Muzgiz, 1931], xi; Loewenberg, *Annals of Opera,* col. 1292). In the end, *The Fair at Sorochintsï* was presented by itself on the theater's opening night, 8/21 October 1913 (see Kinkulkina, "Pis'ma Stravinskogo i Shalyapina k Saninu," 96).

tunity Sanin was offering him, and thought he had in his portfolio just the thing the new theater needed. His answer, from Clarens, was practically by return mail ([21 February]/6 March):

> Here's what's happening, my dear. I am incredibly busy and swamped with work [on *Khovanshchina*], for which reason I cannot promise to get anything together by October—but still I'll meet you halfway with the score of *The Nightingale* (Scene from the Andersen story of the same name), of which you've not yet heard. I wrote it in the *Firebird* period (what can I say? I was on some kind of ornithological streak). The story and scenario are very simple and very lyrical in an Andersenish sort of way. I worked them out together with my friend "M. S.," or rather "S. S. M." (if you must have accuracy!).

Stravinsky proceeded to give a detailed synopsis of the first act of the opera he had started five years earlier, which by then he habitually referred to as an independent scene.[79] He closed with a formal (and very canny) counterproposal: "The piece lasts about eighteen minutes. I think you will like it. Right now *The Nightingale* is in press. By the summer my publisher will be able to deliver all the material to you, even if only in the form of corrected proofs. . . . I could offer the Free Theater exclusive Moscow performance rights for a certain term in return for a certain sum. The per-performance fee you may negotiate with my publisher."[80]

Sanin, too, was a skilled negotiator. His response (from Moscow, [1]/14 March) was wily persuasion itself:

> Dear, delightful Igor Fyodorovich!
>
> Our warmest thanks for your letter. With the piece, too, we are overjoyed. Of course we will take *The Nightingale,* we will buy it. *Consider it sold.* . . . Still and all, it's just a fragment. Since you already have the foundation, you have your leitmotifs, you have the general character down, it will be *easy* for you to write one more scene so as to bring the Andersen story to its conclusion. Let it be just as short as the first, even shorter. Your librettist can knock it together for you with the greatest of ease. I mean the scene with Death and the Emperor. Death is sitting on his chest. The toy nightingale sings (imagine how utterly marvelous the comparison will be), and then the lyrical outpourings of the real nightingale! Do

79. See, e.g., the list of works appended to the *RMG* feature story that had appeared a month earlier (20 January 1913), or the interview in the *Peterburgskaya gazeta* of 27 September 1912 ("Teatral," "U kompozitora I. F. Stravinskogo,"), where he actually claimed to have published the single act as a concert number. The autograph score, now in the possession of Boosey & Hawkes, is bound within a bifolium that as it were closes it off from continuation. The title page reads "A scene from Andersen's Tale of the Nightingale / Russian text by S. S. M." With respect to the use of Mitusov's initials it is worth noting that in a letter to Benois (18/31 March 1913) in which he named his librettist, Stravinsky added: "Don't spread it around; he's keeping his name a secret" (IStrSM:472). This may be the reason why the dedication to Mitusov (see White, *Stravinsky: The Composer and His Works,* 183) has been suppressed in all published editions of the work.

80. Original in the Moscow Art Theater Museum (no. 5323/1287); published in Kinkulkina, "Pis'ma Stravinskogo i Shalyapina k Saninu," 93–94.

all this, do it however you like, do it however you feel it. But for the sake of completeness it is *essential* that you do it. . . . In my conversations with Sergey Pavlovich [Diaghilev] I feel (just between us) a certain jealousy where you are concerned. Fine. But Sergey Pavlovich is going to South America. When will Russia get to see and hear *the real Stravinsky?*[81]

Sanin followed this letter up with two prodding telegrams ([4]/17 and [14]/27 March),[82] to which Stravinsky's telegraphic reply, sent immediately on receipt of Sanin's second message, was a categorical refusal: "Absolutely impossible. Details by letter. Amicably, Stravinsky." The very next day (15/[28] March) he cabled again: "Changed my mind. Two more scenes to be written. But forced to drop all summer plans, commissions. Stravinsky."[83] Two days later (17/[30] March) Stravinsky sent the "details by letter":

> The Lord only knows, my fine fellow, what you will think of me. On receipt of your telegram I answered with a flat refusal to write one more scene and the next day I telegraph that I will be writing not one but two. But you will see the sense of it when you have been through this letter.
> The fact is, the scene from Andersen's *Nightingale* that is already in my portfolio does stand *toute seule* in a fully finished and rounded off form. By adding to it the final scene of the Chinese Emperor's illness, we would end up with something far more indistinct and monotonous, not only from the standpoint of the libretto/plot, but also from the musical point of view. The middle would be lacking, the whole kernel of the Andersen story (the contest of the artificial nightingale with the authentic one). There would be a notable lack of contrast in the music as well.
> Therefore I propose to write two more scenes for the sake of greater completeness.

There now follows a detailed synopsis of the second and third acts, pretty much as they had been planned with Vladimir Belsky's help in 1908 (see Chapter 7). Stravinsky admits as much in the conclusion of his letter to Sanin:

> I worked this scenario out in complete form while working on the "Scene from *The Nightingale.*" That is what I am now offering to compose.
> I await your answer. As you see, there will be no end of work in order to realize this plan. I will have to get right down to it as soon as the Paris season is over. We can talk over the details when we see each other in Paris. For now I just want to establish the following: I will work on these two scenes and will try to have them ready for the opening of the theater, but to be honest, I doubt I will be done before January. At one point you mention that I work slowly.[84] This is not true. I work fast. But I do not rush, for I think it better to spend one's time

81. Stravinsky Archive; the translation in SelCorrII:200 is very inaccurate.
82. SelCorrII:200.
83. Both telegrams in Kinkulkina, "Pis'ma Stravinskogo i Shalyapina k Saninu," 96.
84. This was in Sanin's first letter, in a part not quoted here; see SelCorrII:198.

working than to spend it hurrying. Thereupon I will grant the Free Theater exclusive rights for Moscow for several years—say, for three years—but I must say that in view of the exceptional pressure of this task, and in view of the fact that I shall have to turn down some very lucrative commissions, I will be forced to ask a rather hefty fee of the management of the Free Theater. That seems to be all.[85]

The next day ([18]/31 March) Stravinsky received an answer to his second telegram in the form of a telegram from Sanin: "Welcome change of mind. Hurrah. Will purchase three scenes *Nightingale*. Work on it all summer. Telegraph me immediately Free Theater terms, advance."[86] Stravinsky immediately cabled his terms, which poor Sanin must have received in advance of the warning about the "hefty fee." He was demanding 10,000 rubles in return for Moscow rights alone. (Five years earlier Diaghilev had offered Lyadov 1,000 rubles for world rights to *The Firebird*.) The money was to be paid in three installments: a 3,000 ruble advance, 3,500 upon receipt of the second scene, and the remaining 3,500 on receipt of the third. "Come to an agreement about the rest with Struve [the publisher's representative]," Stravinsky concluded breezily. "Greetings."[87]

After a few stalling telegrams,[88] Stravinsky received a counteroffer toward the end of April. "There is money, but it is not unlimited," Sanin grumbled, adding that "Konstantin Alexandrovich [Mardzhanov] agrees to everything, and can pay you the 10,000 rubles, but he does not want anyone but you to know." The conditions, however, were to be somewhat different: The three-year exclusivity would be good for St. Petersburg as well as Moscow ("since every year we will be on tour in St. Petersburg for two months"); the advance would be 2,000 rubles; another 2,000 would follow receipt of the finished score ("no later than 20 September 1913"); 3,000 would follow the day after the première or 1 February 1914, whichever came first; and the last 3,000 would be paid on 1 May 1914.[89] A short time later Mardzhanov himself cabled, imploring Stravinsky, "in light of difficult conditions," to come down to 7,500 rubles. Stravinsky replied, "Can make no concessions . . . because of option to write either opera or ballet for Diaghilev. Cable. Happy holidays."[90] Both sides now had used Diaghilev as a screw with which to apply pressure on the other. And successfully: on 21 May/4 June 1913 Stravinsky was notified by his bank that 2,000 rubles had been received from K. A. Mardzhanov, Moscow.[91] And that is how *The Nightingale* became an opera in three scenes.

Once recovered from the serious illness that had incapacitated him throughout

85. Kinkulkina, "Pis'ma Stravinskogo i Shalyapina k Saninu," 94–95. The commissions to which Stravinsky refers included that of *Svadebka* by Diaghilev (see Chapter 17).
86. SelCorrII:202.
87. Kinkulkina, "Pis'ma Stravinskogo i Shalyapina k Saninu," 96.
88. See SelCorrII:202.
89. Ibid., 202–3.
90. Ibid., 203.
91. Ibid.

the month of June and half of July, Stravinsky repaired belatedly (and for the last time) to Ustilug, where, as he promised Sanin, he "got right down to it." By the end of the month he would be writing José-Maria Sert that "I work, I eat, I sleep, and I never think of anything but *Rossignol*."[92] On the same day he informed Benois that he was "up to [his] ears" in the music of the second scene, for which he had already composed the opening as far as the "Song of the Nightingale," plus the episode with the Japanese ambassadors and the mechanical nightingale.[93] A preliminary sketch of the "Rossignol mécanique" music survives in the Stravinsky Archive, dated 19 July/1 August 1913, with the additional inscription, *"ochen' do-volen"* ("very pleased with this"). Another dated sketch, for the music of the "Night-ingale's Song to the Chinese Emperor" (scene 2) in a preliminary short score lack-ing the opening cadenza and the final slide to the high F, is signed "Ustilug 11/24 VIII 1913." Evidently, Stravinsky was not working his way through the libretto strictly in order.

Meanwhile, Sanin and Mardzhanov were planning the production, for which they engaged Roerich as designer. They were kindly indulgent when Stravinsky confessed that his health problems had made it impossible to meet the September deadline; a gentle cable from Sanin to Stravinsky's nursing home at Neuilly-sur-Seine read, "Do not worry about work. Do it when well."[94] By 18 October/1 No-vember, Stravinsky was able to send Sanin the following progress report. It con-tained, as the saying goes, good news and bad news:

> Dear Alexander Akimovich,
>
> I am finishing the second act. In a few days I'll get busy on the third. I work like a convict. I had wanted to finish it yesterday but couldn't—I had a terrible migraine. I will devote today and tomorrow to putting the final and irrevocable seal upon it—that's the hardest part—and so, there is not that much left to do. The second act was the most complicated.
>
> I still expect to come to the première of *The Nightingale* in Moscow. I look forward to this moment with the greatest impatience and joy.
>
> Diaghilev has made me very happy by changing his mind about this work. He has begun to like *The Nightingale* very much. I say he has changed his mind, since for some reason he had taken a dim view of the first act—he was indifferent to it, to say the least.
>
> Now, though, having heard the first and second acts, he has irrevocably changed his attitude toward the piece and will mount it in Paris in May and in London in June.
>
> Write me, my dear, what is doing with Roerich. Has he made anything yet for *The Nightingale*? Shall I send you something for the time being? Perhaps you'll

92. Letter of 30 July/[12 August] 1913; in Arthur Gold and Robert Fizdale, *Misia: The Life of Misia Sert* (New York: Alfred A. Knopf, 1980), 157.
93. IStrSM:475.
94. SelCorrII:203.

want to have the first act right away? It's already engraved—soon they'll begin engraving the second. I must say, the work is going very fast at the publisher's, so there will be no delays.

As ever, your
I. Stravinsky

P.S. Although I have not personally made Mardzhanov's acquaintance, I nevertheless send this outstandingly energetic figure my sincere greetings.

The greetings were in connection with the opening of the theater, which had taken place some ten days previously. On the blank outside page of the folded leaf on which the letter was written, Stravinsky scrawled, "My sincere and most hearty congratulations to all the directors and staff of the Free Theater on the occasion of its opening and its première performance."[95]

Sanin sent Stravinsky ([1]/14 November) his bemused congratulations on Diaghilev's acceptance of *The Nightingale,* but insisted that it be done first in Moscow.[96] At the same time, however, rumors began to leak that the Free Theater was not in the best of health, either artistically or financially. Stravinsky was naturally sensitive to these reports. As early as 20 September/3 October he had sought Benois's assistance in verifying them: "I ask you, friend, very confidentially, to find out what kind of shape the Free Theater is in and whether their finances threaten me. Will they still be able to stage *The Nightingale* within the current theater season? It is very important for me to find out."[97] Benois answered (28 September/[11 October]) that "I am sorry to be unable to fulfill your request completely" because the Moscow Art Theater, at which he was then employed, and the Free Theater "have become rivals, and all connections between them are broken." Still, he felt that the theater would last two years at least and that they would be able to meet their commitments to Stravinsky. "But," he hedged, "I would not promise it absolutely."[98] Derzhanovsky gave other grounds for concern: "The troupe they have assembled [at the Free Theater] is very weak. Even if *The Nightingale* is three times easier . . . than the *Japanese Lyrics,* it will still be difficult for their vocalists, [who] are yet on the level of students, and students with very dubious *musical* training at that. You would never manage Chaikovsky's harmony with such singers. . . ."[99]

A couple of weeks later (21 November/4 December), Nikolai Struve, manager of the Russische Musikverlag, joined the chorus of doubters, writing the composer that "the behavior of the Free Theater worries me." They had been stalling on

---

95. State Central Theatrical (Bakhrushin) Museum, fond. 245, no. 76213; published in Kinkulkina, "Pis'ma Stravinskogo i Shalyapina k Saninu," 96.
96. SelCorrII:205–6.
97. IStrSM:478.
98. M&C:127–28/135–36.
99. Letter of 3/[16] November 1913; in SelCorrI:60–61.

their contract, whereas Diaghilev had returned his very promptly. After another month had passed (24 December/6 January), Struve reported that Mardzhanov had twice failed to show up for business conferences at which financial matters were to be settled. By the beginning of February 1914, Struve let Stravinsky know that through Siloti he had begun negotiating behind Mardzhanov's back with the Mariyinsky Theater, since the Free Theater was in imminent danger of folding. He advised the composer to force the matter with Mardzhanov and, without necessarily waiting for a resolution from that quarter, pursue the Siloti connection on his own.[100] On [8]/21 February, Stravinsky, now living in the Swiss town of Leysin near the sanatorium in which his wife was confined with the tuberculosis that would eventually take her life, and working (now very much behind schedule) on the third scene,[101] eagerly followed Struve's advice re Siloti. He sent the following very interesting letter to his old protector:

> Dear Alexander Ilyich!
>
> Nikolai Gustavovich Struve has informed me that you have inquired about the possibility of having my *Nightingale* for the next season at the Mariyinsky. I preferred, having learned your address [Hotel Bristol, Vienna], to enter personally into correspondence with you on this matter—it will be quicker that way!
>
> First of all I will outline the state of affairs with regard to the opera. The first and second parts (scenes or acts, whatever you wish to call them) are not only engraved in piano-vocal score, but ready for the press and even translated [by Calvocoressi] into French as well. The orchestration of the first part is likewise ready. The orchestral score of the second part is now being copied, and the parts extracted, in Berlin. The third part (the shortest of the three) I am now writing and orchestrating. I hope to send it off to the publisher within a month.

This was a very optimistic forecast. On 9 March Stravinsky wrote Benois that he hoped to be done "toward the end of March."[102] Not until 28 March was he able at last to write (to Ansermet), "I have finally finished *The Nightingale*."[103] To return to the letter to Siloti:

> As to the question of obligations to which I am bound in this "Nightingale affair," they are as follows. A year ago the Free Theater commissioned me to finish the opera, the first part of which I had composed and orchestrated immediately before *The Firebird*. I confess that I agreed to this not without some hesitation, since I had not given the piece any thought (I had other things on my mind), but the financial arrangement forced me to agree, and I did agree to write the rest of it, that is, two acts more of *The Nightingale*. For exclusive rights to the opera in Moscow and St. Petersburg for a three-year period the Free Theater undertook to pay

100. Struve's letters are excerpted in SelCorrII:206–7.
101. The day before, he had written to Benois that he had got as far as the Nightingale's "*tanki*" (ritual songs), having just finished the Nightingale's first exchange with Death (IStrSM:485).
102. IStrSM:485.
103. SelCorrI:129.

me ten thousand rubles, of which two thousand were paid me last spring in the form of an advance, the rest to follow by agreement in installments within a short time. On the other side, Diaghilev has obtained from the publisher exclusive rights for one year to give the opera in Paris and London. There are the practical arrangements for your information.

Now here is how matters stand. In the Free Theater there are constant disputes, disorder, things having got to the point where, *it is rumored,* the theater will fold altogether. I personally think that this latter eventuality will not come to pass, but that various delays—it seems that they have still not signed their contract with the publisher—are inevitable. Therefore if Telyakovsky [the intendant] wishes to assume the Free Theater's responsibilities, I might immediately inquire of the theater's management why they have not signed their contract with Struve, and if I do not receive a satisfactory answer, I might inform Struve himself, who would then break off his negotiations with the Free Theater and transfer *The Nightingale* to the Imperial Theaters. I must tell you that Struve has set a minimum of five performances of *The Nightingale* in each capital (that is, 5 in St. Petersburg and 5 in Moscow).

As to the matter of sending the piano-vocal score of *The Nightingale* to Telyakovsky, I frankly think it would be worse than useless, for if this music is played in my absence—or, I should say, *by anyone but me*—no one will be able to make head or tail of it. They will say "nonsense pianissimo," as the late Nikolai Andreyevich used to say about Debussy (as opposed to "nonsense fortissimo," as he used to say of Strauss). It would be best if I played it for him myself. He does come to Paris every spring, does he not? (Though never, by the way, to a single one of my pieces.) Could I not see him there? If he is afraid to take one of my pieces without getting to know it first, then it would be best to do it there. Ah, how I'd love to play *The Nightingale* for *you!* We might perhaps do it this way. Suppose you and I got together and I played it for you, and then you could show it to Telyakovsky. What do you think of that idea? Write me, please, about all this. Besides all these matters I would like very much to see you, to chat amiably with you and firmly press your hand.

As ever, your devoted
Igor Stravinsky[104]

On 2/15 May 1914 the eventuality Stravinsky refused to foresee took place: the Free Theater, having finished its first and only season, declared bankruptcy and folded. A week earlier (24 April/7 May), Siloti had bluntly informed the composer that, sound unheard, the intendant had rejected his outlandish terms: "In light of the fact that *The Nightingale* lasts only 45–50 minutes, Telyakovsky says that 10,000 rubles is out of the question; he thinks about 4,000 would be appropriate."[105] Moreover, as Siloti informed Stravinsky, a fire at the Bolshoy Theater in Moscow, requiring the quick replacement of practically all the sets for the current repertory, precluded any new productions for the 1914–15 season.

104. Kutateladze and Raaben (eds.), *Ziloti,* 287–89.
105. SelCorrII:210.

Stravinsky was high and dry. Diaghilev alone was committed to producing *The Nightingale;* but not having commissioned the opera, he did not owe the composer any personal fee, only a per-performance royalty to be remitted to the publisher. What was to have been a killing for Stravinsky had turned instead into a financial disaster.[106] His paranoiac mercenary suspicions about Diaghilev, noted with alarm and disapproval by so many observers,[107] received a major impetus here.

OPERA WITHOUT WORDS

The canny impresario quickly snapped up the newly freed Sanin to direct *his* production of *The Nightingale*. The opera had its première in Paris after all—hurriedly, with only four stage rehearsals—on 26 May 1914, in a double bill with *Le coq d'or.* The role of the Emperor was sung by Pavel Andreyev (1874–1950) of the Mariyinsky Theater; that of the Cook by Yelena Nikoleva, also of the Mariyinsky. A star of the Moscow Bolshoy, Aurelia Dobrovolskaya, made a sensation in the virtuosic title role.

The designer was Benois—an inevitable choice, for his involvement with *The Nightingale* went back even before the Sanin commission. As soon as *Petrushka* was finished, Stravinsky began looking forward to further joint projects for himself and the artist with whom he had been working so closely and fruitfully. He had written to Benois from Ustilug as early as the summer of 1911 with the announcement that

106. Siloti and Albert Coates persisted in their efforts to place *The Nightingale* with the Imperial Theaters for the next season, Stravinsky having agreed to come down, not all the way to four thousand, but to six thousand rubles (Stravinsky to Siloti [4/17 June 1914]: "You will agree, I trust, that for me, not a rich man, it is more painful to subtract these four thousand [i.e., from ten thousand] than it is for the management to add two" [Kutateladze and Raaben (eds.), *Ziloti*, 289]). There matters rested until March 1915, when negotiations were resumed not only about *The Nightingale,* but about *Petrushka* too (see Stravinsky to Siloti, 24 March/6 April 1915; in ibid., 290; also Siloti to Stravinsky in SelCorrII:212). Telyakovsky's diary (16 March 1915) records his vacillations over Stravinsky's work: "[Nikolai] Solovyov calls Stravinsky a downright musical monstrosity, but Siloti, Cherepnin, and others were in raptures over [*The Nightingale*], and especially Coates. Besides, the opera has been successful abroad. Our musicians consider Stravinsky even more of an enfant terrible [*ozornik*] than Scriabin" (Zilbershteyn and Samkov [eds.], *Dyagilev* 2:425). On 31 March 1915 the St. Petersburg newspaper *Birzheviye vedomosti* reported that the evening before there had been an audition of *The Nightingale* (along with Coates's own *Ashurbanipal*) in Telyakovsky's apartment, at which Coates and Siloti had played the opera four-hands before the whole executive staff of the Imperial Theaters (also Meyerhold and Golovin, the prospective régisseur and designer), and that the opera was accepted (the whole news item is reproduced in IStrSM:515). On 14 May, the same newspaper ran a feature story about the opera, announcing it officially for the 1915–16 season and stating that Stravinsky would be returning to St. Petersburg that fall to supervise the production (SelCorrII:218). A contract was sent on 4 October (SelCorrII:214); Stravinsky received a three-thousand-ruble advance in February 1916 (letter to Siloti, 11 February 1916; in Kutateladze and Raaben [eds.], *Ziloti*, 293)—but the opera was not staged until 30 May 1918, after the Revolution. Needless to say, Stravinsky did not receive the stipulated remainder of his fee. Thus in the end, between 1913 and 1916 he realized a total of five thousand rubles (Mardzhanov's two thousand plus Telyakovsky's three thousand) from the "sale" of *The Nightingale*—precisely half the sum he had originally negotiated through Sanin—of which 10 percent went by subcontract to Mitusov, the librettist (see Stravinsky to Siloti, 2/15 and 6/19 July 1915; in ibid., 291–93).

107. On Stravinsky's distrust of Diaghilev, see Gold and Fizdale, *Misia,* 177–80; also Duke, *Passport to Paris,* 199–200.

plans are ripening in me for a collaboration with you, which—if all goes well—I hope to complete by the beginning of 1913. It involves Andersen's *Nightingale,* one-third of which is already written, and which I seem to recall you have heard. Write me, please, whether this prospect appeals to you or if you have any objections. Of course, it *is* an opera, toward which both of us have grown equally cool; but working with you would redeem it, and in any case I am determined to continue what I have begun. It will be great fun to create a "Chinoiserie" of this kind. Think about it, dear friend. For me it would be a great happiness.[108]

Although Stravinsky seemed to think he would finish off *The Nightingale* within two months "and then get down in earnest to 'The Great Sacrifice,' " we know that things turned out otherwise. The reason had nothing to do with Benois, of course, and the painter was glad at first to accept when Sanin, at Stravinsky's request, commissioned him to design the Free Theater production in 1913. Benois's participation, in fact—"in the role of guide, artist, designer, *costumeur, coiffeur,* etc., etc., etc.!!!"—had been one of Stravinsky's conditions.[109] It then turned out that Benois would be unavailable, being under contract at the time to the Moscow Art Theater (for a lavish production of Goldoni's *La locandiera*), from which contract Stanislavsky and Nemirovich-Danchenko would not, for the sake of their bitterly resented rivals at the Free Theater, release him. Stravinsky's response was to express his hope that he and Benois would still manage to do *The Nightingale* in Paris, "unless something new gets in the way." He went on to make some surprising comments about Roerich, who (as we know) replaced Benois as designer for the Free Theater, and with whom Stravinsky had so recently collaborated on his most important work to date:

> I have just received word from S. S. Mitusov that Roerich, who had very much wanted to do the sets and costumes for *The Nightingale,* had already come to an agreement with the management of the Free Theater about it—and all at once I am face to face with something whose meaning is about as clear to me as are the outlines of objects one looks upon with eyes asquint. I only ask, for God's sake, that this doesn't get back to Roerich, whom I like very much and consider a fine artist. But I can't see him for *The Nightingale* at all. But maybe it will turn out all right? Who knows? I had better keep an open mind!
> The whole thing is my own fault anyway. I'll tell you something about this. Feeling miserable (just before I came down with typhus) and knowing that a delay in handing in the score of *The Nightingale* was inevitable, I decided to turn to Roerich for help (keep in mind that I already knew by then that you would not be able to do the sets and so on for the Free Theater—Sanin had informed me), since he was *persona grata* there, would see them all before I would, and would put in a good word for me. That was one side of it. The other side was my strong wish not to have my piece done by some mediocre artist who would just do it as a job,

108. Letter of 30 June/13 July 1911; in IStrSM:458–59.
109. Stravinsky to Benois, 18/31 March 1913; in IStrSM:472.

not because he loved the work itself. So I told him all about *The Nightingale* and saw that he became terribly excited and that he wanted beyond doubt to do it himself. It was I who got him involved with all this. It could be that that is just fine, but after a while I began to have my doubts, and still have them. . . .[110]

Benois consoled Stravinsky in his egocentric fashion ("I believe that Roerich would achieve something miraculous with it, but some details Roerich would probably not do, and just these details would interest me enormously"),[111] as did Mitusov ("[Roerich's] Chinese materials are really very interesting—he's bought up everything Chinese—at least everything I saw").[112] The whole matter quickly became moot, but worth documenting because Stravinsky put such a false construction on it in *Memories and Commentaries,* where he cast Roerich as Diaghilev's unwelcome protégé.[113]

Benois's engagement as designer of the Paris production was announced in the *Peterburgskaya gazeta* on 28 November 1913. He and Stravinsky entered into serious correspondence on the production at the beginning of 1914—on the first of January, to be exact.[114] Like *Petrushka,* it was an exceptionally close collaboration, even by Ballets Russes standards, despite the distance that separated the two artists. Naturally enough, Benois's ideas about the separation of voice and movement told as heavily on the production of *The Nightingale* as it had on *Le coq d'or.*

According to the original conception of scene 1, the role of the Nightingale, hidden in a tree, was to have been sung by an offstage voice. It was now decided to have the Nightingale remain a disembodied coloratura soprano voice for the whole of the opera (represented on stage by a tiny, almost invisible prop bird), even when it participated in the intricate negotiations with Death in the last scene. Not only that, but Benois insisted on having the "framing role of the Fisherman split à la *Coq d'or:* sung from the pit and mimed onstage." This turned the entire first half of the first scene into a solo turn for the mime playing the Fisherman, in colloquy with the unseen Nightingale. Accompanied by two voices and orchestra, this became Stravinsky's first "ballet with singing" (*balet s peniyem,* to cite the subtitle of *Pulcinella,* its descendant). When the Fisherman reappeared to reprise his song at the end of each of the subsequent acts, what had been intended as a musical unifier now became a choreographic unifier as well.

A maximum of visual/gestic content and a minimum of words were the twin goals that ruled the construction of the new scenes. Stravinsky met with Stepan Mitusov, the librettist, early in July 1913, when he had just returned to Ustilug from his convalescent home at Neuilly.[115] Together they completely redid the libretto

---

110. Letter of 30 July/12 August 1913; in IStrSM:475.
111. M&C:126/134.
112. SelCorrI:440.
113. M&C:125/133.
114. See Benois's letter of that date in M&C:128/136.
115. Letter to Benois, 30 July/12 August 1913; in IStrSM:475.

for scenes 2 and 3, throwing out what had been written in 1909 and replacing it with a text that had been stripped to the barest verbal essentials (and perhaps even beyond).[116] To Benois, Stravinsky explained: "The role of the Chinese Emperor is almost purely choreographic; he sings very little, and when he does open his mouth to say something, what he says is accompanied at all times by primitively expressive, very slow gestures (weighty—you know what I mean, you rogue!)." He continued, in language derived knowingly from Benois's own vocabulary: "Help me, old chap, for in truth I am still afraid that some vampuka might remain despite all my incredible pains—I'm being extra frank, for I think (or rather, I continue to think) that where there is a well-learned choreographic role there will be no vampuka, and Mitusov and I have planned the whole thing (that is, *The Nightingale*) so as to hide everything that might turn, however tolerable in and of itself, into vampuka on the stage."[117]

A comparison of the 1909 scenario for scene 3 (that of scene 2 has disappeared from the Stravinsky Archive) with the final 1913 libretto will illustrate the process of devampukification. The original plan of action was as follows (strike-outs are as in the original):

—SCENE III—

The Emperor is lying down.

Whispering of evil deeds, gradually growing to a roar. The Emperor cries out: "Music, let's have music! Big Chinese drums! I do not wish to hear their words!"

"Let me hear you sing, sweet, wonderful golden bird; I have given you golden jewelry. I have hung my golden slipper around your neck. Sing, sing I say."

~~(Silence)~~

"But you are silent. There is no one to wind you up, and otherwise you cannot sing."

(Death appears)

"Oh, how hard it is for me. Who will protect me from this ~~vision? Who will help me?~~ horrible specter ~~Who will help me?~~ that gazes upon me with its ~~horrible~~ empty eye-sockets and nods its head at the words of my evil deeds?"

(The Nightingale appears)

Three songs

1) About the forest, the sunset and the Fisherman.*
2) About the Imperial gardens.**
3) About the cemetery.***

116. A letter from Mitusov in the Stravinsky Archive, datable by its contents to the period just after this meeting, attempts in touching fashion to reassure the composer of the librettist's willingness to accommodate Stravinsky's new, dogmatically antioperatic ideals: "Dear Igor, in the first place, your fear of hurting my feelings is groundless, since everything I write now I write for the greater glory of your talent. I do not enter into it, and all questions of author's pride are irrelevant. Believe me, I am happy to be able to offer even a single brick to the edifice you are erecting, and if my brick won't do, I will run off with joy redoubled in search of another."

117. Letter of 20 February 1914; in IStrSM:482. On *vampuka*, see above, n. 63.

*) After this song: "Sing, sing some more O Nightingale. I remember you, dear bird."
(The shades begin to whirl.)

**) "Thank you, thank you, dear bird! I banished you from my kingdom, but you have chased the horrible specters away from my bedside. Perhaps you will chase horrible Death away, too? Sing some more, little Nightingale! (The shades have disappeared altogether.)

***) Death flies out, leaving behind the Emperor's sword and crown.

Emperor: "You have saved my life; how shall I reward you?"

Nightingale: You have already rewarded me once and for all! I have seen the tears in your eyes. This I will never forget.

Emperor: You must remain with me always, and I will smash the artificial bird to smithereens.

Nightingale: No, I cannot live at court. But allow me only to come to you late at night to sit at your window and sing to you. My song will cheer you ~~and make you thoughtful, too~~. Farewell!!!

The Emperor watches him leave, puts on the Imperial robes, puts the crown on his head, and presses to his heart the heavy golden sword and stands in all his regal magnificence. While all this is going on the courtiers have been stealing up ~~to the doors~~ from the door and have been peering beneath the bed-canopy without finding the Emperor there. They then turn around and notice him standing at the window. They fall to the ground.

But the Emperor calls out to them: "Greetings!"

All of the above, and especially the dialogue, is lifted practically verbatim from the literary source, in time-honored Russian fashion. In the final libretto most of the speeches are gone. The first one for the Emperor is confined to the contents of his first paragraph above. He does not address the mechanical nightingale,[118] nor does he express his fear of death. The Nightingale sings only the second and third songs listed in the old scenario. Between them Andersen's little round of bargaining between Death and the Nightingale is played, the Emperor remaining silent. At the end of the second song, Death having disappeared, the Emperor sings a single *réplique*: "How beautiful, little Nightingale! My strength has returned. You're not going to fly away now, are you? I will give you the top rank at court!" All that remains for the Emperor, after the Nightingale has taken its abbreviated leave of him, is to sing his greeting ("*Zdravstvuyte!*") to the astonished courtiers. *Their* role, in contrast, is greatly expanded into a thirty-one-measure cortège (a kind of muted reprise of the Chinese March in the second scene), lasting, by Stravinsky's metronome marking, a good minute and a half, during which there is no singing at all. When it is recalled that the Nightingale's songs are sung by a disembodied voice in the pit, it is plain to what extent words have been banished from the stage, leaving little more than a "stage picture," for the success of which Stravinsky was relying very heavily on Benois: " . . . It is the riskiest of all, if you please. If in the

118. One of Mitusov's letters to Stravinsky (21 July 1913) contains a draft of the Emperor's speech that includes a six-line apostrophe to the mechanical nightingale. This Stravinsky himself crossed out in pencil, leaving the speech as we now know it from the published score.

earlier acts there had been even a minimum of movement—action, a sequence of events—here even that will be absent except for the Emperor's sun-drenched, yellow-hued '*Zdravstvuyte!*' at the end."[119]

Mitusov's frantic efforts to purge the libretto of excess verbiage are apparent in an undated letter to Stravinsky, probably written in July 1913. Thinking with his pen, Mitusov tries out three versions of the Chamberlain's speech to the palace servants to introduce the Chinese March in scene 2. What started out as a flowery quatrain ended up a single line of rhythmic prose. The three attempts, plus Mitusov's self-conscious evaluations of his handiwork, amount to a veritable treatise on opera-without-words:

Stupaite von otsyuda	Get out of here.
seychas syuda pridut	The lords and ladies are
vel'mozhi i damï ozhidat'	about to come in expectation
ego velichestva prikhoda.	of His Majesty's arrival.

That stinks. Maybe this:

Stupaite von, syuda idut Vel'mozhi	Get out; here come the lords
i damï ozhidat' ego Velichestvo.	and ladies, to await His Majesty.

Also very poor. Let me try again.

Stupaite von, syuda idut Vel'mozhi.	Get out; here come the lords.

And nothing more. The procession begins.

In keeping with the importance he now accorded the visual, Stravinsky took an exceptional interest in Benois's work, demanding full descriptions in advance of the sets and costumes[120] and reacting to them with incredibly detailed comments and suggestions, especially in the letter from which a few short excerpts have already been discussed. With no other designer did Stravinsky ever work like this. The result of all this effort was an extremely eclectic hybrid genre that may have conformed precisely to the Miriskusnik idea of operatic propriety, circa 1914, but which was in retrospect a double embarrassment to the composer. His first "critique" of it came only three years later, in 1916–18, when at Diaghilev's suggestion he completely eliminated the voices (i.e., the words) from the music of scenes 2 and 3 and turned them into a ballet pure and simple (*Chant du rossignol*).[121] For

---

119. IStrSM:482.

120. See Benois's letters of January and February 1914 in M&C:126–33/136–41; also P&D:114–18.

121. Since this piece was first performed in concert, not on stage (Geneva, 6 December 1919, under Ansermet; the Ballets Russes première took place in Paris on 2 February 1920), and remained popular with conductors, Stravinsky took to calling it a "symphonic poem" and in the *Chroniques* even stated that that was his original conception of the piece (see *An Autobiography*, 65). As so often, contemporary correspondence refutes the memoirist. A letter from Diaghilev exists (16 November 1916) virtually dictating the changes in the score (after listing twelve obligatory cuts, Diaghilev adds, "Both of the Nightingale's songs must be abbreviated and tedious places eliminated. And there is no reason for anyone to go off into a temper about this! I am a man of the theater and not, thank God, a composer"). Four days later, another letter describes plans for sets and choreography. See SelCorrII:28–30.

Stravinsky and Diaghilev as of 1916, then, *The Nightingale* was still too much an opera. The other critique, made in 1960, was at the opposite extreme. In *Memories and Commentaries* Stravinsky, having just reacquainted himself with the score by conducting (and recording) it, observed: "I now find that Act I, in spite of its very evident Debussyisms, *vocalises à la Lakmé,* and Tchaikovsky melodies too sweet and too cute even for that date, is at least operatic, whereas the later acts are a kind of opera-pageant ballet."[122] *The Nightingale,* this time around, was not opera enough. The ambivalence reflects the unresolved ambivalences in the work itself— stylistic and esthetic ambiguities that make *The Nightingale,* however delightful, one of the few Stravinsky compositions that can be heard only as a period piece.

FAUSSE-CHINOISERIE

The opera's doctrinaire antioperaticism, in other words, has dated badly. Another problem was the stylistic gap that yawned between the pre-*Firebird* act and the post-*Sacre* ones. In 1960 Stravinsky referred to "the great difficulty I experienced in returning to the opera at all after five years."[123] Benois noted at the time the "glaring incongruity of style between the first act of *The Nightingale* and the two others," claiming further that "Diaghilev tried to persuade Igor of the necessity to revise the first act as well so that the opera would take on a single general character, but the composer insisted on his way, and a certain disharmony of style remained"—mitigated, in the artist's recollection, only by his own skillfully executed designs, which made an "interesting contrast" between the lyrical nature-moods of the first act and the "courtly pomp" of the second, where Stravinsky's "fausse-chinoiserie" resonated perfectly with Benois's own.[124] Stravinsky, for his part, tried to mitigate the disparity through an emphasis (predicted by Sanin) on reprises and signature tunes such as he affected to despise in the work of other composers. Not only did the Fisherman's song return from scene 1 to bind the succeeding scenes together, but so did the little tweeting motive that continued to herald the Nightingale's every appearance (Ex. 14.7a). The Chamberlain's octatonic leitmotif (quoted in Ex. 7.8a) also returns in scene 2, and becomes the Death fanfare in scene 3 (Ex. 14.7b–c).

The term *fausse-chinoiserie* comes from Stravinsky's own letter to Benois of 30 July/12 August 1913.[125] It is just the place to begin an investigation of the music of *The Nightingale*'s new scenes. The letter actually contains an illustration in musical notation of the "black-key scale" with which the composer was experimenting; his Clarens neighbor C. Stanley Wise later recalled "the eagerness with

122. M&C:123n./131n.
123. Ibid.
124. Benois, *Moí vospominaniya* 2:534, 535.
125. IStrSM:476.

EXAMPLE 14.7

a. *The Nightingale*, [38] compared with [82]

b. *The Nightingale*, fig. [81]

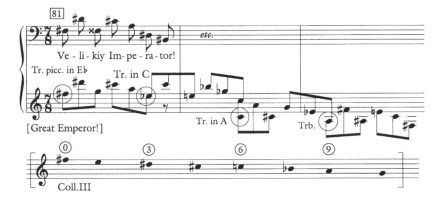

c. *The Nightingale*, 2 after [101] (also cf. 2 after [121], constructed on Collection I)

which he hurried me to the piano one day to exhibit the capabilities that he had just discovered in that Chinese pentatonic scale."[126]

The capabilities Stravinsky was investigating, if they may be judged by the results in the finished score, had not so much to do with the scale itself as with the various "polymodal" contexts in which it might be ensconced; for as Stravinsky was no doubt overjoyed to discover, the anhemitonic pentatonic pitch set is a subset both of the diatonic and (with one eminently exploitable discrepancy) the octatonic collections. One rather simple yet very crafty passage of this kind occurs at the climax of the Chinese March in scene 2 (fig. [77]), for which sketches survive

126. C. Stanley Wise, "Impressions of Igor Strawinsky," *Musical Quarterly* 2 (1916): 253.

in the Archive. The "Chinese scale" is cast as a series of four fifths that rise and fall in a *basso ostinato* pattern. Above it, a simple chromatic scale ascends and descends, as in the sketch shown in Example 14.8a. The piano part from the full score (Ex. 14.8b) shows the maximalistic, *Rite*-like harmonies with which Stravinsky contrived to flesh out this linear skeleton. The chromatic scale is doubled at the major seventh (diminished octave). The resultant frame is filled out on the downbeats with what, two chapters back, were dubbed "*Rite* chords," and on the offbeats with double-inflected (i.e., major/minor) triads. Not the least remarkable feature of this complex is the fact that it is so devised that every vertical aggregate is referable to one of the three octatonic collections, in a constant, regular circulation that reverses in the middle. Against it, one of the pentatonic march themes, hypostatized at its original pitch despite the radically altered harmonic environment, sounds forth with reckless abandon.

It was only inevitable that the composer of *Petrushka* would view the matter of chinoiserie in terms of a "white key/black key" opposition vaguely referable to the tritone polarity (C/F♯) of octatonic Collection III. The piano-vocal score of *The Nightingale*—which was no reduction of the orchestration, but preceded it— abounds in traces of Stravinsky's keyboard experiments, one hand on the "Chinese" black keys, the other on the white. The whole passage from [59] to [61] is an example of this (Ex. 14.9a), albeit concealed by the most devious orthography imaginable, with its consistent use of E-sharp and B-sharp, not to mention double sharps, that disguise the ordinary "white keys." (No wonder Stravinsky was afraid that another pianist would hash the piece in audition.) Despite the masquerade, however, it is evident that what really governs the harmony is a pair of competing scales that compose out a typical tritone axis: F♯-pentatonic in the right hand versus C-diatonic in the left (Ex. 14.9b). The black-key scale is doubled either at the second (= ninth) or third (= tenth), as the scale allows. The white-key scale is doubled at a constant perfect fourth (the tritone B/F being skipped rather than adjusted on the way up).

In the third measure of Example 14.9b, another prime Stravinskian stratagem for relating white-key and black-key collections is employed in a particularly schematic and obvious way. This is the device of acciaccatura, whereby a prominent pitch in one collection is surrounded with a pair of neighbors from the other. In the present instance, the highest note in the white-key group and its reciprocal, the lowest note in the black-key group, are both decorated in this way. These two highly schematic, "artificial" techniques—the shadowing of the "faux-chinois" pentatonic scale with concurrent diatonic white-key scales (often doubled in parallel intervals or even triads), and the use of white key/black key acciaccaturas— pervade the post-*Sacre* scenes and give them their special flavor.

The passage at [55]–[56] (repeated at [62]–[63]) is an especially telling instance of this Nightingalish "polytonality." What in the published vocal score looks like

EXAMPLE 14.8

a. *The Nightingale,* Chinese March, fig. 77 (sketch)

b. Piano part from full score, combined with pentatonic march theme

EXAMPLE 14.9

a. *The Nightingale*, figs. 59 – 61

b. *The Nightingale*, fig. 60 (without enharmonic spellings)

a virtually random assortment of ersatz triads, crazily spelled and with all kinds of multiple inflections (Ex. 14.10a), is very neatly sorted out in Stravinsky's composing draft (Ex. 14.10b). Again it is a matter of parallel fourths on the white keys, this time sandwiched inside the ninth and tenths on the black. No doubt this was one of the passages Stravinsky showed off to Wise. He must have taken a characteristic pleasure in disguising it for publication.

No connoisseur of modern Russian music could look at the upper staff of Example 14.10b and not be reminded of Scriabin's Étude op. 65/1, the famous "étude in ninths." It is therefore intriguing to discover that Stravinsky ordered Scriabin's op. 65 from Jurgenson at precisely the time he was concluding his agreement with Sanin to complete *The Nightingale*.[127] In other ways, too, Stravinsky's "chinoiserie" betrays its latent kinship with the Russian background. Pentatonic (or, more accurately, anhemitonic) melodies abound in the archaic Russian folklore Stravinsky had mined in composing *The Rite*, and some of Stravinsky's "Chinese" tunes are indistinguishable from the ostinato calendar songs in the earlier score. A good case in point is the choral dance song in the scene 2 entr'acte, harmonized there in characteristic black key/white key fashion (Ex. 14.11). In another context and with another harmonization it might just as well have served to evoke Slav antiquity. The harmonic devices applied to it here would be for Stravinsky a permanent acquisition.

At times the black-key scale is introduced into familiar Stravinskian contexts. At the beginning of the Chinese March, for example, it is inserted within a triadic *complexe sonore* referable to trusty Collection III. It occupies the F-sharp node within an (0 3 6 9) symmetrical disposition, while D-sharp is established by the churning, quasi-cadential ostinato pattern as pitch of priority. The second degree of the "Chinese scale," G-sharp, is foreign to Collection III. Far from hiding it away for this reason, Stravinsky spotlights it by the use of a typically Nightingalish double acciaccatura on the white keys (characteristically spaced as a ninth), both members of which do refer to the home collection (Ex. 14.12).

The mechanical nightingale music in scene 2 is similarly based on a Collection III complex into which a pentatonic scale has been inserted (Ex. 14.13). This time the five-tone scale is on the white keys (to distinguish "Japanese" music from Chinese?). Once again, too, the "foreign" tone (D) is given great and deliberate (in this case self-evident) prominence. The elements of the octatonic collection maintain a rigidly hypostatized (that is, "mechanical") timbral and registral distribution that harks back to some of the more "elemental" pages of *The Rite* (even as it looks as far forward as the stones-to-bread machine in *The Rake's Progress*).

Very ingenious is the octatonic/pentatonic interaction at the beginning of scene

127. Letter to Grigoriy Jurgenson, 22 March/4 April 1913; in IStrSM:473. What are apparently the very earliest surviving sketches for the later scenes of *The Nightingale* are found in the facsimile *Rite of Spring* sketchbook (London: Boosey & Hawkes, 1969), 42–45. They include the passage at [62].

EXAMPLE 14.10

a. *The Nightingale,* vocal score, fig. 62

b. *The Nightingale,* same passage as it appears in the composing draft

EXAMPLE 14.11 *The Nightingale,* fig. 56, spelling and voicing of accompaniment clarified

Og - ni, og - ni go - ryat,___ zo - lo -

tï - ye bles - - tyat____

[Fires burn, gleaming golden]

EXAMPLE 14.12

a. *The Nightingale,* opening of Chinese March

"Chinese scale"

b. Interaction of Collection III with "Chinese scale"

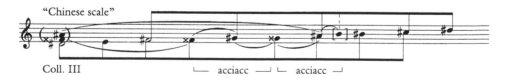

"Chinese scale"

Coll. III   └─ acciacc ─┘ └─ acciacc ─┘

EXAMPLE 14.13

a. *The Nightingale,* scene 2, mechanical nightingale music

b. "Hypostatization" of Collection III as it interacts with the "Chinese scale"

3, when the curtain goes up on the Emperor's sickroom. The chorus of specters (fig. [108]) is based on the tetrachordal partition of Collection I: the pedal D (bassoon and timpani) and the three notes of the Chorus's singsong ostinato form the lower, "structural" tetrachord of the partition; the dissonant celesta punctuations (plus two of the notes in the contrabass glissando ostinato) are drawn from the complementary, "ornamental" tetrachord. The dying Emperor's parlando counterpoint, meanwhile, is suitably based on a "Chinese scale" pitched so that it shares three pivotal pitches (the first three he sings) with the concurrent octatonic collection. The two nonreferable pitches (F-sharp and A, introduced in the measure after [109]) form a major triad with the pedal D, effecting a novel octatonic/diatonic construction (Ex. 14.14).

This analysis of the opening episode in scene 3 provides a gambit for analyzing the remarkable chord progression with which the second scene (and later, the "Chant du rossignol") begins. The famous first chord, which Stravinsky likened in retrospect to the ringing of early St. Petersburg telephones,[128] is wholly referable to octatonic Collection I, consisting of a diminished-seventh chord with two acciaccaturas (three if the E in the preliminary horn glissando is counted). Thereafter, the progression of dissonant yet stable harmonies is a rotation through the octatonic collections such as we have encountered before in *Zvezdolikiy* and *The Rite* (and in Ex. 14.8b, above). The series quickly comes to a head and then settles down into a fairly lengthy passage ([52]–[53]) that is based in characteristic fashion on a sustained if rather unusually partitioned Collection III *Petrushka* chord (its octatonic interstices having been foreshadowed in the third measure after [51]). The third chord in the series (3 after [51]) appears at first enigmatic. It contains nonreferable tones that (unlike the F-sharp in mm. 5–6 after [51][129] or the D's in the passage from [52] to [53]) cannot be explained as neighbors or as artifacts of parallel doubling. In fact, this harmony is closely related to the octatonic/pentatonic configurations in the deathbed scene: F-sharp and A are associated with D, the whole subsumed in a chord otherwise drawn from Collection I. On the analogy of the *Petrushka* chord and what we know as the *Rite* chord, this harmony could even be dubbed the "*Nightingale* chord" (see Ex. 14.15).

Octatonic/pentatonic interactions continue in scene 3 as the basis for the Nightingale's first song, addressed to the Emperor. It begins (fig. [111]) with an octatonic rotation similar to the one at the beginning of scene 2 (Ex. 14.16). Thereafter the Emperor, listening, is represented by his pentatonic scale, which skims the surface of the cascading figures that introduce each stanza of the song ([112], [113]−2, [115]). The stanzas themselves are strictly octatonic, referable respectively to Col-

128. E&D:32/30.
129. The F♯'s were an afterthought born of Stravinsky's predilection for parallel ninths on the black keys. As shown in Ex. 14.15, early sketches for this pair of measures are fully referable to Collection I.

EXAMPLE 14.14

a. *The Nightingale,* figs. 108 – 110 in vocal score

EXAMPLE 14.14a (*continued*)

Specters:

> We are all before you, we have all come here.
>
> O, think back on us! Think back! We are all your deeds.
>
> We are here to stay, we will not leave.
>
> O, think back on us! Think back!

Emperor:

> What is happening? Who are they? I don't know you!
>
> I do not wish to hear you! Ah, bring some music
>
> quickly, some music! The big Chinese drums! Ah,
>
> music, music!

b. Embedding of "Chinese scale" within tetrachordal octatonic framework

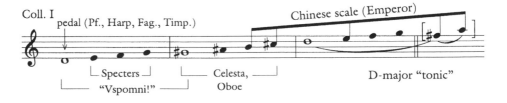

EXAMPLE 14.15 *The Nightingale*, figs. 51 – 52 , harmonic abstract
showing pedigree of "*Nightingale*-chord"

EXAMPLE 14.16 *The Nightingale*, figs. 111 – 112

(*continued*)

EXAMPLE 14.16 *(continued)*

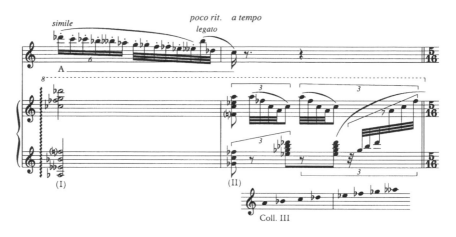

lections III ([112] + 1), I ([113] − 1), and back to III ([115] + 2), so that the whole is tied up in a neat little ABA package.

The Nightingale's remaining songs in the second and third scenes are cast in a wispy, attenuated style reminiscent of the *Japanese Lyrics*. Their stylistic evolution from sketch to score is noteworthy. The very first notation for the song with which the Nightingale wins back the Emperor's soul from Death in scene 3 was made on a loose sheet containing three rough drafts of the text in Mitusov's hand. The little phrase sketched here eventually became the main theme of the song (Ex. 14.17a). Predictably enough, it derives (but for the opening D) from Collection III. The same spot in the finished score has been deliberately teased out of its initial octatonic shape (Ex. 14.17b), Stravinsky having hit on the idea of modeling it on the slithery music to which the Kitchen Maid describes the Nightingale—and the effect of its singing—in scene 2 (Ex. 14.17c).

Taken as a whole, the role of the Nightingale itself is the one seemingly least beholden to Stravinsky's habitual harmonic symmetries and partitions. Thanks to a massive dose of ornamental passing tones and acciaccaturas, the music of the artist-bird seems to glide freely (perhaps allegorically) in the chromatic ether, in the lingering spirit of *Mir iskusstva*. The cadenza by which the Nightingale makes its spectacular unseen "entrance" in the second scene can serve as paradigm. For all its apparent freedom, the structure of the melodic line is nevertheless heavily dependent on the support of Collection II pitches, as Example 14.18 will illustrate. (Non-octatonic notes are indicated by strike-outs.)

This cadenza is also more overtly derivative of some of the best-known pages from *Le coq d'or* than anything else in *The Nightingale*. Sung by the same singer who was performing the role of the Queen of Shemakha that very season (often that very evening), the resemblance did not escape even the reviewers' notice. The

EXAMPLE 14.17

a. The Nightingale's song, scene 3 (early sketch)

[The mournful moon is shining]

b. *The Nightingale,* fig. 124 bis

c. *The Nightingale,* fig. 63

[No, little grey birdie.]

notice in one of the London papers drew up quite an elaborate bill of particulars linking Stravinsky's opera with that of his teacher:

> The story from Hans Andersen . . . is banal to the point of ineptitude—herein closely resembling that of Rimsky-Korsakov's "Le Coq d'Or," heard earlier in the week. The parallels between the two works are indeed curiously close. Each is, for instance, founded on a fairy-tale. In each there is a sort of "chorus" to comment on the action (the Astrologer in Rimsky-Korsakov's work and an old fisherman in

Stravinsky's). And in each case, too, the extravagance of the story seems, as has been hinted, more remarkable than its dramatic point and value.[130]

The impression of dramatic ineptitude may have been as much due to the manner in which *The Nightingale* was presented as to its intrinsic qualities. The great satisfaction in the production recorded both by Benois and by Stravinsky in their respective memoirs testifies forcefully to the total sacrifice of conventional dramatic values to "painterly" ones in their shared conception of opera as an art form.[131] That impression is negatively confirmed by Stravinsky's friend Wise, who attended one of the London performances and was appalled by what he saw:

Each act should last about twelve [*recte* 15] minutes; at Drury Lane the intervals between the acts extended each of them to about twenty minutes. The composer

130. *Westminster Gazette,* 19 June 1914; clipping in Stravinsky Archive, Scrapbook 1912–14. For another parallel between Stravinsky's opera and Rimsky's, compare the Japanese Nightingale's music at 3 before [93] (oboe I) and that of Tsar Dodon's parrot in the first act of *Le coq d'or* (flute at [61] + 3 et seq.).

131. Benois: "When all of this was repeated at the performance itself in all the vividness of the fanciful costumery under the enormous dark blue lantern-chandeliers, against a background of white and blue porcelain columns, when from beneath his parasol his Imperial Majesty appeared all glittering with gold and jewels and his assembled subjects all prostrated themselves before him, the effect of it all had a force that I myself did not expect; and for perhaps the first time in my whole theatrical career I had the experience of being touched to the quick by my own creation" (*Moí vospominaniya* 2:536). Stravinsky: "Scenically, thanks to Alexander Benois who designed the costumes and sets, it was the most beautiful of all my early Diaghilev works" (M&C:124/132).

has indicated in the score no such intervals whatever, and if it was found needful to drop the curtain for a few seconds the breaks should have been made as short as possible. Then a considerable portion of the second act is directed to be played behind a gauze curtain, so that the scenic impression may be to a certain extent that of moving tableaux;—at the production in London the picturesque Chinese courtiers bustled about and posed like an Italian opera chorus. The singer, too, who took the part of the Nightingale faced the audience and bowed her acknowledgments of the applause with which her fine vocalization was greeted just as appropriately as an average operatic tenor; and the final curtain—enjoined to be lowered very slowly—came down with a run, so that the fisherman sang his philosophical epilogue while the puzzled audience wondered whether the opera was finished or not![132]

What Wise describes does seem a veritable travesty, if the assumptions of the "illusionist" theater are taken, as Wise took them, for granted.[133] Yet precisely before the London performances Stravinsky came out more strongly than ever against such assumptions, in an interview with Calvocoressi that contained the promise that *The Nightingale* would be not only his first opera but his last. "I can write," yet again he said, "music to words, viz., songs; or music to action, viz., ballets. But the cooperation of music, words, and action is a thing that daily becomes more inadmissible to my mind." In a less familiar vein, responding to his interlocutor's wonder at his exceeding "policy of conciseness and speed" as a dramatic composer (as Calvocoressi put it, "the score *semper ad eventum festinat*"), Stravinsky delivered himself of a pronouncement so obviously parroted from Rivière's reviews of *The Rite* as to make any suggestion in the previous chapter concerning that critic's influence on the composer seem understated. On the evidence of this interview, that impact was not only profound but virtually immediate:

> I want neither to suggest situations or emotions but simply to manifest, to express them. I think there is in what are called "impressionist" methods a certain amount of hypocrisy, or at least a tendency towards vagueness and ambiguity. That I shun above all things. And that, perhaps, is the reason why my methods differ as much from those of the impressionists as they differ from academic conventional methods. Though I often find it extremely hard to do so, I always aim at straightforward expression in its simplest form. I have no use for working-out in dramatic nor in lyric music. The one essential thing is to feel and to convey one's feelings.[134]

132. Wise, "Impressions," 254.

133. In particular the performance he describes flouts Stravinsky's carefully calculated "segues" from scene to scene: on the one hand, the surprise explosion of post-*Sacre* harmony after the quiet close of scene 1, and, on the other, the seamless flow from the end of scene 2 into the rather traditionally leitmotivic entr'acte music preceding the scene 3 curtain (indeed, the latter spot is explicitly marked "Enchaîner" in all published scores).

134. Michel-Dmitri Calvocoressi, "M. Igor Stravinsky's Opera: 'The Nightingale,'" *Musical Times* 55 (1 June 1914): 372, 374.

Given Stravinsky's later—and oh so celebrated—squeamishness about the use of the word *express,* this statement may seem ironic or paradoxical. In fact, it is a direct adumbration of the later position. The essence of both is the idea of *actuality:* manifestation over description or suggestion. What Stravinsky here rather crudely calls expression he would later call "the realization of the present" (*Chroniques*), and later still "speculation in terms of sound and time" (*Poétique*). The evolution Rivière set in motion within Stravinsky that led from the earliest formulation of this musical actualism to the latest is precisely that "progressive abstraction" which the present group of chapters will trace.

BURNING THE LAST BRIDGE

The final performance of Diaghilev's 1914 London season took place the evening of 25 July. Three days later Austria and Serbia were at war. By the time the company got around to shipping its rented music back to the Russische Musikverlag in Berlin, France, England, and Russia had all joined with Serbia against Germany, Austria's main ally. *The Nightingale* nearly became an early casualty of the conflagration. In the theatrical gossip column of the newspaper *Golos Moskvï,* the following item appeared on 26 August/8 September:

> Before the war many newspapers carried stories about the impending production in Moscow of Igor Stravinsky's *The Nightingale,* which had gained a noisy celebrity in France and England through Diaghilev's operatic productions. Now, however, unforeseen circumstances have altered all plans. *The Nightingale* is lost. The score, the parts, and the piano arrangements of this opera, following its London performances, were sent to Berlin, where the central office is located of the company that has undertaken to publish Stravinsky's *Nightingale.* At this very time the war broke out, and our countryman's opera did not get to Berlin. The composer has kept neither rough drafts nor copies of the opera. He is beside himself with grief. To restore the whole opera from memory will not be possible.[135]

The embroideries were fanciful. Not only had Stravinsky retained copious sketches and drafts, which may be seen to this day in his archive, but the vocal score of *The Nightingale* had been printed at least two months earlier. Indeed, the *RMG* thoughtlessly picked up this sensational story from *Golos Moskvï* and ran it in their issue of 7–14 September, which on another page carried an advertisement for the opera.[136] Yet Stravinsky must have suffered a genuine fright, and it must have contributed to his decision to sit out the war in a neutral country, for the sake of his business affairs as much as for the sake of his consumptive spouse's health. And that is how Russia lost Stravinsky in fact as well as spirit.

135. "Brut" (pseud.), "Okolo teatra," *Golos Moskvï,* no. 195 (26 August/8 September 1914): 6.
136. "Raznïye izvestiya," *RMG* 21, nos. 36–37 (7–14 September 1914), col. 714.

It would not do to close the account of Stravinsky's loss of Russia, though, without telling one last tale, that of poor Maximilian Steinberg and his belated attempt to ride Stravinsky's coattails to international fame. This will be the story of Stravinsky's old Russian ties in their very severing.

We have seen that for a time Stravinsky maintained outwardly cordial relations with Steinberg even after the explosive rifts with the rest of the Rimsky-Korsakov clan. Steinberg did not contribute to any of Andrey Rimsky-Korsakov's exercises in mudslinging, nor did he ever refer to them in his correspondence with Stravinsky. He also made himself available for all kinds of tasks, from proofreading to the procurement of special instruments and mutes for the *Rite* première. The reason for all this paradoxical solicitude was simple: in 1912 Steinberg had begun composing a ballet of his own; he desperately wanted to get Diaghilev to produce it, and was counting on Stravinsky's good offices. Stravinsky, for his part, evidently relished the ironic twist events had given his relationship with the rival who had always outshone him at home, and he heartlessly let Steinberg dangle through two whole seasons. Then he cynically persuaded Diaghilev—despite the latter's not unjustified reluctance—to mount the piece, thus setting up his old confrere for a humiliating failure. Thanks to the survival of numerous letters and documents, the story can be told in interesting detail.

What Steinberg had composed was a ballet in three tableaux entitled *Metamorphoses: A Triptych in Music and Mime after Ovid,* op. 11—a sort of companion piece to Cherepnin's *Narcisse.* Its three scenes were devoted to the fables of Semele, Midas, and Adonis in turn. It was finished in piano score by the middle of September 1912.[137] On 2/15 October, Steinberg sent Stravinsky, who had just departed St. Petersburg for Switzerland, the following news:[138]

> Yesterday I played my ballet at Diaghilev's. I was told that you had written him about the ballet's existence, for which reason I hasten to thank you for your friendly cooperation. Present were Bakst, Nouvel, and Cherepnin. As far as results, as yet I have no idea. To judge by the reception I was given, I cannot think they were entirely negative, but since nobody made any definite comment about the music (Cherepnin likes it very much, though—I had played it for him earlier) I cannot be at all sure of the opposite—that is, positive results—either.

Stravinsky received this letter in Berlin, where the Ballets Russes was touring. "When I see Diaghilev I'll speak to him about *Metamorphoses* and I'll insist on his accepting the piece for production," he assured its composer. "But maybe this won't be necessary," he teased; "maybe he's already decided to take it. Write me

---

137. See Stravinsky's letter to Steinberg (Ustilug, 13 September 1912), in Galina Kopïtova, "Iz pisem k Rimskim-Korsakovïm i M. Shteynbergu," *Muzïkal'naya akademiya,* 1992, no. 4, 143.

138. In the account that follows, all letters to Stravinsky are quoted from the originals in the Archive.

everything that happens, all the rumors, everything you're doing."[139] The onus having been thrust back upon poor Steinberg, he wrote two weeks later (20 October/2 November) to complain: "From Diaghilev I've had no answer yet; this kind of uncertainty would be unpleasant for anyone, and I am in terrible spirits. Why can't you even write me a single line? Belsky [Rimsky-Korsakov's old librettist] is very pleased with the music, which cheers me a great deal. Please write and tell me what you think of all this."

Steinberg had won a friend for his project in Bakst, who—unbeknownst to the composer—wrote an enthusiastic letter about it to Stravinsky. Bakst had recently heard the "Pan" episode from the second tableau of *Metamorphoses,* which was played from manuscript at a Siloti concert on 27 October/9 November 1912.[140] On 17 November, just arrived in Paris, Bakst wrote Stravinsky about his impressions:

> At the rehearsal I was just delighted (the orchestration is marvelously fresh, no end pleasing; there is much that was unexpected, and in general it shows great gifts). The first time through, at the piano, I couldn't make out much. I liked it anyway, though, especially the finale. But then Seryozha [Diaghilev] made me back down with some imperiously sarcastic remark. The second time it was just me and Steinberg and I entered completely into the piece and loved it. I told Seryozha—he scolded me for my "musical understanding." Normally nothing is easier than to make me back down by kidding me about my musical understanding, but this time I didn't give in. At the rehearsal I was completely enchanted by the sound of the orchestra, and I can assure you that you can have no idea what this piece is like just from the piano. I am happy for him; he worked so touchingly well together with me in Paris. He is enamored of his art in a quiet yet fervent and definite way.

Bakst, whose weakness for "Greek" subjects was proverbial, made Steinberg's project his own. As he had done with *Daphnis et Chloë* and *Narcisse,* he not only undertook to design the production, but also had a hand in the scenario. Stravinsky telegraphed Steinberg about Bakst's enthusiasm, and on 20 November/5 December he cabled again: "Diaghilev has accepted *Metamorphoses*. Letter follows."[141] In the letter, dated the next day, Stravinsky claimed to have moved heaven and earth to get Diaghilev to accept yet another "Greek" ballet designed by Bakst (after *Narcisse, Daphnis, L'après-midi d'un faune,* and Roger-Ducasse's "mimodrame" *Orphée,* then under discussion). "Diaghilev will be in St. Petersburg in ten days' or a fortnight's time," Stravinsky informed his old rival, "and then you can come to him and work out the details."[142] Steinberg answered (3/16 December) that although he still had not had a word from Diaghilev, "after your second telegram I

---

139. Stravinsky to Steinberg (Clarens, 18 October [N.S.] 1912); "Iz pisem," 144.
140. Kutateladze and Raaben (eds.), *Ziloti,* 319.
141. "Iz pisem," 145n.30.
142. Stravinsky to Steinberg (Berlin, 4 December 1912); "Iz pisem," 144.

was able to get to work with a mind at peace on the final preparations for printing Nikolai Andreyevich's *Principles of Orchestration* (the book will come out, at last, in January)."

By year's end Steinberg realized that it would now be too late to mount his *Metamorphoses* during the 1913 season, "but still not a peep out of Diaghilev." He could not get back to work on the ballet until the spring, as he informed Stravinsky in a letter dated 4/17 April. He was hoping to have the music completely orchestrated and submitted to Edition Belaïeff by the middle of May, and to meet with Diaghilev in London at the beginning of June to make final arrangements for the production the following year. "I am really hoping that you will be there, too, and rejoice that at any rate I'll get to hear *Firebird* and *Petrushka* (and maybe even *Sacre?*)," he wrote Stravinsky. Then came a rather pathetic request: "Please do something for me, namely, tell me how one must present oneself in London, that is, in what attire. I am completely ignorant of the customs there, and I hear they're extremely strict. You are no doubt way past this by now." Steinberg also asked that Stravinsky make some time to consult on some unspecified professional matter before *Metamorphoses* would be handed in to the publisher. "Here there is only Cherepnin," he confided. "Glazunov, it seems, has given up on me." It seems incredible to recall that less than four years earlier Stravinsky was writing the very same kind of letter to Steinberg, his better-connected fellow Belyayevets (see Chapter 6, cited at n. 99).

In a letter of 18 May/1 June 1913, Steinberg expressed trepidation about the London meeting ("Will they really have time for me in the midst of all that will be going on?"), and in the end he did not go, partly because he heard from Catherine Stravinsky about Igor's illness, which would prevent her husband from being in London to escort his old friend. Things now returned to where they had been before, with Steinberg complaining in letter after letter about Diaghilev's silence and begging Stravinsky to intercede. After one particularly disconsolate note from Steinberg, Stravinsky wrote from Ustilug (16/29 July 1913): "Don't be sad! The fact that the Directorate doesn't answer—that's nothing. I am keeping it in mind (that is, the *Metamorphoses*), and as soon as I find out Diaghilev's address, I'll speak to him about it and write you."[143]

A postcard from Stravinsky (29 September/12 October) informed Steinberg that "Diaghilev will be coming to St. Petersburg in a few days; you will certainly be seeing him, since he will be staging *Metamorphoses* in Paris and London this season."[144] Steinberg responded to this news with gratitude (2/15 October), but in his next letter (4/17 November) complained that Diaghilev had deigned only to talk to him on the telephone; he still would not see him.

143. IStrSM:474.
144. IStrSM:478.

Steinberg did not write again until 18 February/3 March 1914. After expressing his relief that Catherine Stravinsky was better and his congratulations at the birth of the Stravinskys' daughter Milena, he added: "About my own affairs I will not write, since I think they are more or less known to you. Unfortunately everything has been arranged in a manner far from what I would have wished, and I don't even know whether to rejoice or lament. I do look forward to our meeting, though—then we will talk from the heart about everything." The arrangements to which Steinberg referred were these: After keeping the composer in suspense for a year and a half, Diaghilev had declined to produce the *Metamorphoses* in full. Only the second tableau (or "panneau"), *Midas,* was accepted. Moreover, Bakst was committed to designing the costumes for two ballets in 1914 (Strauss's *Josephslegende* and Fokine's *Papillons* to Schumann's piano piece in Cherepnin's orchestration) and would not be available, despite all previous assurances, to design Steinberg's. Mstislav Doboujinsky, in his single Ballets Russes season, was assigned to it instead. Unlike Stravinsky, Steinberg could wield no clout whatever within the councils of the Ballets Russes, and had to accept these conditions as the price of the production.

He came glumly to Paris in May. Stravinsky dutifully shepherded him around to his musical friends (on whom Steinberg made no impression at all) and even introduced him to Canudo, who rather incongruously printed a page from the gentle score of *Midas* in the riotous pages of *Montjoie!* (Fig. 14.5).[145]

The production, to use Grigoriev's blunt but accurate word, was "stillborn."[146] Treated as a stepchild from the start by one and all, *Midas* had no chance at all. It was handed to an exhausted Fokine as the very last item on his huge list of assignments, and the choreography was, accordingly, perfunctory. The comic aspects of the story were ill reflected in the music, which, though well orchestrated,[147] was pallid stuff indeed by comparison with what Diaghilev's audiences had come to expect. Pan's very characteristic flute melody, for instance, represented the kind of diluted octatonicism that even within Rimsky-Korsakov's lifetime would have been considered tame. The diminished octaves followed their textbook resolutions, and Steinberg had caught a bad case of his father-in-law's sequence disease (Ex. 14.19a). Apollo's stately lyre melody, purely diatonic in the approved Russian manner, is worth quoting for all its triteness, since its general features may have stuck in Stravinsky's memory and resurfaced when, much later, he came to write a "Greek" Apollonian ballet of his own (Ex. 14.19b).[148]

145. *Montjoie!* 2, nos. 4–6 (April–June 1914): back cover.
146. Grigoriev, *Diaghilev Ballet,* 99.
147. Even the extremely uncharitable Prokofiev had to acknowledge that Steinberg had made some "discoveries" in the instrumentation department; see Kozlova and Yatsenko (eds.), *Prokof'yev i Myaskovskiy: perepiska,* 172.
148. The most interesting music in the *Metamorphoses* was in the Semele tableau and went unheard in Paris or London.

MIDAS

Ballet de Léon BAKST et Maximilien STEINBERG

FIG. 14.5.   Autograph score page from Steinberg's *Midas*, printed in *Montjoie!* on the reverse of Stravinsky's *Nightingale* extract (see Fig. 13.7b).

EXAMPLE 14.19

a. Steinberg, *Midas*, 5 after ⬚115⬚ ("Pan plays his pipes, as the forest and mountain deities, laughing the while, take up the dance")

b. Steinberg, *Midas*, fig. ⬚125⬚ (Apollon)

Musicians and critics hardly noticed the piece—or if they did, it was only to make invidious comparisons. Prokofiev, for example, wrote to Myaskovsky that *Midas* "was created so as to make us appreciate *Firebird* and *Petrushka*."[149] And one of the London critics had this to say: "The second novelty [after *The Nightingale*] was slight almost to insignificance, being a mythological 'panel' of no great interest. M. Max Steinberg's music claims attention solely on the grounds that he is a pupil of Rimsky-Korsakov and shows him to be an ardent admirer of Stravinsky's methods, which, however, are best at first hand."[150]

Now *that* must have made up for a lot.

———————————

Steinberg went back to Russia to lick his wounds without visiting London. He and Stravinsky never met again, and, as we have seen, Stravinsky went far out of his way to snub his old friend eleven years later, on the latter's last trip west. Stravinsky's *Schadenfreude* at having bested his teacher's old pet shows through many passages in his memoirs, including his gratuitous description of the final

149. Letter of 12/25 June 1914; in Kozlova and Yatsenko (eds.), *Prokof'yev i Myaskovskiy: perepiska*, 116.
150. *Morning Post*, 19 June 1914; clipping in the Stravinsky Archive, Scrapbook 1912–14.

round in 1925.[151] It is therefore worth noting that Steinberg never published a hostile word about Stravinsky (even in memoirs that were written for publication in Stalinist Russia), and on a visit to Russia in 1934, Eric Walter White could not get Steinberg to utter a single negative comment about his former friend. The Leningrad professor expressed nothing but dignified regret over the loss of Stravinsky to the emigration.[152]

The contrast between Stravinsky's lifelong rage and Steinberg's reserve testifies better than anything else to the nature of their relationship and the respective status they had enjoyed during their formative years. It was a humiliation for Stravinsky that no amount of success could later assuage; while Steinberg, the favored son, in the course of thirty-eight years as professor of theory and composition at the Petrograd/Leningrad Conservatory, felt secure enough to use Stravinsky's music (*The Rite, Oedipus Rex, Symphony of Psalms*) as classroom material.[153] On the other hand, Steinberg's widow, the former Nadezhda Nikolayevna Rimskaya-Korsakova ("the younger," as Yastrebtsev used to call her to distinguish her from her mother), refused Stravinsky's invitation to hear him conduct *Fireworks,* the piece he had dedicated to her on her wedding, during his eightieth-birthday trip to the USSR, "because she had always known that I. S. was not fond of her husband, the composer Maximilian Steinberg, or, for that matter, herself."[154]

Though not a composer in whom one can take much intrinsic interest, Steinberg exerts an undeniable fascination in conjunction with his old rival, and by no means exclusively as the object of useless invidious comparison. One cannot help wondering what sort of career Stravinsky would have made if Diaghilev had never happened to him, or what kind of music he would have spent his life composing had he not found himself abroad at the time of the Revolution. Of course it is possible that, like so many other Russian artists and intellectuals (especially those who were members of his exalted social class), Stravinsky would have emigrated anyway, along with his wealthy Belyankin and Yelachich in-laws. Yet the surviving members of his immediate family did not emigrate. His mother came out only in 1922, and only because her son was abroad, while his architect brother Yuriy remained in Leningrad until his death in 1941, shortly before the blockade.

For an idea of Stravinsky as a Soviet composer, then, we might briefly consider the later works of Steinberg, who came out of the identical artistic milieu and who shared Stravinsky's pre-Diaghilev stylistic orientation completely, as his *Prélude symphonique* in memory of Rimsky-Korsakov made especially clear (see Chapter 6). It will not surprise us to find that his technical modus operandi continued throughout his life to be one of "octatonic-diatonic interaction" (so did Stravin-

---

151. M&C:54/56. The date there is given, incorrectly, as 1924.
152. See White, *Stravinsky: The Composer and His Works,* 14.
153. A. Guseva, "Pamyati M. O. Shteynberga," *Sovetskaya muzika,* 1984, no. 12, 133–34.
154. D&D: 259.

EXAMPLE 14.20

a. Steinberg, Symphony No. 3, I, first theme

b. Steinberg, Symphony No. 3, IV, reprise of first theme

sky's, after all), but that his esthetic outlook took on a heroic-expressionist aspect that was as in keeping with Soviet esthetics as it was at odds with Stravinskian. Nonetheless, Steinberg's Third Symphony, op. 18 (1928), dedicated to Myaskovsky, could well be compared with Stravinsky's somewhat later *Symphony in Three Movements* both as to technique and as to expression, though it is of course far more conventional in form.

The main theme of the first movement is a diatonic G-minor melody (Ex. 14.20a). Its development takes on a greater and greater octatonic coloration as the climaxes approach, culminating in a "cyclic" return in the fourth movement, accompanied by an (0 3 6 9) sequential panoply right out of *Sadko* (Ex. 14.20b). This may be "epigonism" of an academic sort—but what else was a Soviet composer to write? One can't shake the notion that it is precisely the sort of thing Stravinsky would have been turning out had he been living in his native city in 1928—and *surely* by 1938!—rather than in Paris.

Or again, like Stravinsky, Steinberg turned to folklore for inspiration in his post-Rimskian years. But in this case their two paths were altogether dissimilar. Stravinsky used folklore voluntarily as an instrument of creative self-liberation. Steinberg's folklorism was of a certain prescribed Soviet variety, in which Russian composers were forced to go out "into the field" and incorporate into European classical forms the folklore of non-Russian Soviet peoples, ostensibly as an example to native musicians of the artistic exploitation of their national heritage, but really as an instrument of Russian cultural imperialism.

The prime example of this trend in Steinberg's work was his Fourth Symphony (1933), subtitled "Turksib" after the Turkestan Siberian railway completed that year. It is based on the themes of Kazakh and Kirghiz songs. Then during the Second World War Steinberg was evacuated along with the rest of the Leningrad Conservatory staff to Tashkent, where he produced his Fifth Symphony, based on Uzbek themes, containing parts for indigenous folk instruments and describing "various periods in the history of Uzbekistan, beginning with ancient times and Tamerlane's invasion and ending in our own days, when the Uzbek people are participating in the struggle against Hitlerite Germany,"[155] in recognition of which he was made people's artist of the Uzbek SSR in 1944, two years before his death. Other large-scale works of Steinberg's Soviet period include four suites of folk songs of various Soviet peoples (including Jewish songs) for voice and orchestra (1930–31, 1936), commissioned by the well-known Byelorussian folk singer Irma Yaunzem; a capriccio for orchestra entitled *In Armenia* (*V Armenii*, 1940); and a ballet, *Till Eulenspiegel* (1936, commissioned by the Kirov—formerly Mariyinsky—ballet), which uses Spanish and Flemish folk songs for themes. He also composed a cantata for the Pushkin centenary in 1937 and a march for the Red Army's silver jubilee.[156]

Steinberg's position in the world of music, like that of all the Soviet composers of his generation, became more and more provincial as his life went on. His centennial in 1983 passed practically without notice in his homeland's musical press, save one pathetic little blurb in the more "popular" of the two major Soviet music journals, which described a purely local celebration: "The Leningrad musical community has observed the centenary of the birth of the prominent Soviet composer and pedagogue, Honored Art Worker of the Russian Soviet Federated Socialist Republic, M. O. Steinberg (1883–1946), who worked for forty years in the Lenin-

---

155. Composer's program note, quoted in Igor Boelza, "Communication from Moscow," *Musical Quarterly* 30 (1944): 357–58.

156. On Steinberg's folkloric works see I. P. Yaunzem, "Rozhdeniye pesni," *Sovetskaya muzika*, 1963, no. 8, 27–30. Another article in the same issue—L. B. Nikolskaya, "Opït khudozhnika," 30–32—contains extracts from an essay by Steinberg on the use of folklore as a resource for art music.

grad Conservatory and trained many outstanding musicians."[157] There but for the grace of God, one has to think, went I. F. Stravinsky.

But I. F. was luckier. With the severing of his connection with Steinberg he had broken his last tie with the musical environment in which he had been reared. He was free to discover Russia in his own way—and a "rejoicing discovery" it would be.

157. "Tol'ko faktï," *Muzikal'naya zhizn'*, 1984, no. 6, 3.

TURANIA

In his great oration on Pushkin, Fyodor Dostoyevsky declared that had the poet not died so young, "he might have revealed great and immortal images of the Russian soul which would be intelligible to our European brethren; he might have attracted them to us much more than they are attracted to us at present; perhaps he might have explained to them the whole truth of our aspirations, and thus they would comprehend us better than at present and might foresee our destiny; they would cease to look upon us as suspiciously and haughtily as they still do."[1] These tasks were left to Igor Stravinsky. In the years of his so-called Swiss exile, alienated from the Russia that was, he created in his art the Russia of his dreams. So persuasive and beguiling were these dreams that all Europe did seem to become Russian for a while.

Only in Russia did Stravinsky continue to meet with haughtiness and suspicion among the tastemakers. In January 1915, Andrey Rimsky-Korsakov published his most sustained attack on the composer who five years earlier had dedicated to him his first masterpiece. Especially dispiriting to Stravinsky must have been the fact that this blanket dismissal of his work appeared in *Apollon,* at the time the most prestigious of all Russian arts journals, and a conspicuous arbiter of progressive taste. The only thing that Andrey's now-famous article, "Igor Stravinsky's Ballets," succeeded in proving was that in music there simply was no Russian progressive wing. At its peroration, the composer of *The Firebird* was formally read out of the rolls of the Russian National School:

1. Fyodor Dostoyevsky, "Pushkin (A Sketch)," in *The Diary of a Writer,* trans. Boris Brasol (Santa Barbara: Peregrine Smith, 1979), 980.

FIG. 15.1a. Andrey Rimsky-Korsakov
in the 1920s.

By his musical education Stravinsky belongs to the school of Rimsky-Korsakov.
In orchestration and in compositional technique he did doubtless receive a great
deal from his teacher. Nonetheless, from the time of *Petrushka* he has broken decisively with the traditions of this school and made himself over with a whole new
set of ideals. Thus, he places a deliberate and artificial pseudonationalism (*lzhe-
natsionalizm*) above the spirit of true nationality (*narodnost'*); he is ready to sacrifice music for the benefit of spectacle and dance; he exchanges a naïve and chaste
approach to art for a sensualistic savoring of all that is narrowly specific, illus-
trative, entertaining. . . . To rest a case for the comparability of Stravinsky and
Rimsky-Korsakov on instrumentation alone as the *tertium quid* would be wrong.
For many of Rimsky-Korsakov's methods have long since become common property; on such grounds one might as easily link Rimsky-Korsakov's name with
Stravinsky as with Debussy, Ravel, or many others.[2]

Stravinsky, in fine, was henceforth to be regarded by Russians as an alien. Andrey put it quite literally: *Petrushka* was "the work of an impressionable foreigner
who happens to come to Russia and is captivated 'from afar' by the richness and
violence of 'Russian' manners." Even Stravinsky's kinship with Scriabin is denied,
on grounds that Scriabin was "neoclassic"(!).[3]

2. A. N. Rimsky-Korsakov, "Baletï Igorya Stravinskogo," 54–55.
3. Ibid., 50. Stravinsky's annoyance at this piece found expression in a letter to Benois (10 April
1915): "The fact is, my art is the polar opposite, the deadly enemy of those princples on which the quasi-
esthetic outlook of A. Rimsky-Korsakov and his clan is based. Besides, this article is written not so
much against my compositions, I think, as against all contemporary art, against all contemporary seeking and striving" (quoted in Stravinskaya, *O Stravinskom i ego blizkikh*, 63n.).

FIG. 15.1b. Stravinsky, Prokofiev, and Pyotr Suvchinsky, by then known as Pierre Souvtchinsky (Paris, 1929).

Shortly after publishing this diatribe, the younger Rimsky-Korsakov founded a journal of his own, *Muzïkal'nïy sovremennik* (the *Musical Contemporary*). The editorial board consisted of Andrey and his wife, the composer Yuliya Veysberg (Weisberg; 1879–1942), along with Vyacheslav Karatïgin, the old Rimsky-Korsakov hands Alexander Ossovsky and Ivan Lapshin, the composer and critic Yuliy (Joel) Engel (1868–1927, best remembered for his incidental music to Ansky's *Dybbuk*), and the up-and-coming "Igor Glebov" (Boris Asafyev), who joined a bit later than the rest.

The youngest member of the staff of the *Muzïkal'nïy sovremennik* was the twenty-three-year-old Pyotr Petrovich Suvchinsky (1892–1984), "a stout blond fellow, . . . a connoisseur of Kastalsky and a friend of Kashkin (Chaikovsky's old crony), passionate lover of music, a serious connoisseur of Russian poetry and literature, and also a man of well-rounded general education," as Asafyev recalled him from those early days.[4] A moneyed dilettante from the Ukraine, the heir to an immense sugar fortune, Suvchinsky had taken piano lessons from Felix Blumenfeld and aspired to a career as an operatic tenor. He was listed on the new journal's masthead as "co-publisher." In fact he was its patron.

4. Boris Asafyev, "O sebe," in A. N. Kryukov, ed., *Vospominaniya o B. V. Asaf'yeve* (Leningrad: Muzïka, 1974), 492.

The very first issue of the *Muzïkal'nïy sovremennik* (September 1915) carried an article by the editor-in-chief on Stravinsky's *Nightingale*. Its tone and substance is everything one might expect. Stravinsky is accused of caprice, of cynicism, of tawdriness, and even (in the first act) of "an immature timidity and derivativeness." His tragedy, Andrey proclaims, is that of the "flawed talent," whose audacities stem "not from self-confidence but from doubt"—doubt, that is, as to the "purely musical" worth of his inspirations. By the period of *The Rite* and *The Nightingale*, Andrey asserts, "it is clear that one can no longer even think of finding their essence in their purely musical aspect," so "debased" had that side of Stravinsky's talent become. The article ends with a caustic valedictory, an avuncular reprimand addressed as if to a misbehaving child:

> Taking a close look at Igor Stravinsky's works, one cannot avoid the conclusion that, were he to take himself sternly in hand and attend to his habitual shortcomings instead of pursuing his noisy, ephemeral, premature success, . . . his talent might yet bear fruit free of wormholes, fruit without flaw. After all, in all that is truest and best in him (all that has unfortunately been receding more and more from view), I. Stravinsky is the son—a "prodigal son," to be sure, but no less a genuine son—of the New Russian School, and it is only behind an assumed mask that he has taken furiously to trampling the green mother-earth that nurtured him.
>
> May he not complain at the severe words this article has flung his way. Behind them lurks an equal measure of love for his creative potential (albeit a love poisoned by the bitter pang of thwarted hopes)—a love not one whit weaker than the kind that zealously advertises itself by showering endless compliments. Of him to whom much is given much is demanded.[5]

Four and a half decades later, I. Stravinsky was still smarting. He went out of his way in conversation with Craft to single out Andrey's long-forgotten journal for its "very unsympathetic" editorial stance.[6] At the time, his response was private and ironic. In the fall of 1915 he was working on his *Baika* (a.k.a. *Renard*). In his article on *The Nightingale*, Andrey had referred sententiously to Stravinsky's "salto mortale," meaning his capitulation to Parisian taste. Stravinsky gleefully inscribed the phrase in the score of the *Baika* at the two points where the Cock jumps into the clutches of the Fox.

After the first issue, anti-Stravinskianism in the *Muzïkal'nïy sovremennik* shifted over from explicit hostility to a simple boycott. The journal as such was a learned monthly devoted to research and theoretical discussion—in effect, Russia's first "musicological" periodical. New music was covered in a separately published weekly (later biweekly) supplement known as the *Chronicle* (*Khronika*), and here

---

5. A. N. Rimsky-Korsakov, "O 'Solov'ye' Igorya Stravinskogo," *Muzïkal'nïy sovremennik* 1, no. 1 (1915–16): 80, 84, 88, 94–97.
6. E&D:154/135.

Stravinsky's name was very conspicuous in its absence. The only Stravinsky performance the *Khronika* covered during the two years of its existence was one of *The Faun and the Shepherdess* as sung by Nadezhda Obukhova at a posh Russian Musical Society concert under Nikolai Malko (12 December 1915). The anonymous reviewer (who else but Andrey?) did not fail to voice "regret that this period in Mr. Stravinsky's work already belongs to his distant past."[7]

Thereafter, the only references to Stravinsky in the *Muzïkal'nïy sovremennik* were those Karatïgin smuggled in as footnotes to articles on Musorgsky. One, in an article on *Khovanshchina*, was a predictable rehash of Andrey Rimsky-Korsakov's strictures on the 1913 Diaghilev production. It began with the curious announcement that "I did not get to see *Khovanshchina* in this form; but such a circumstance hardly deprives me of the right to object in principle."[8] In an essay on *Sorochintsï Fair* that touched upon Lyadov's orchestration of some instrumental excerpts, Karatïgin seized the pretext offered by the mention of his name for a digression about the recently deceased Lyadov's opinions on a wide variety of subjects, Stravinsky's music among them. This sally must have stung particularly, since Stravinsky had loved and trusted Lyadov in his prentice years: "On Stravinsky's harmony [Lyadov] expressed himself negatively. 'Stravinsky has a bad ear,' said Anatoliy Konstantinovich, 'and many of his innovations are acceptable only to those whose ears are similarly underdeveloped' (one recalls that Rimsky-Korsakov was inclined to treat Stravinsky's harmonic spiciness similarly, more as the result of a bad ear than as any new musical achievement)."[9]

The anti-Stravinsky boycott took more concrete and practical forms as well. During the season 1915–16 the *Muzïkal'nïy sovremennik* sponsored a series of six Thursday concerts of contemporary Russian music at the St. Petersburg (by then Petrograd) Conservatory, to raise money for the relief of war refugees. Evenings were devoted to the memory of the recently deceased Scriabin and Taneyev. Nikolai Medtner played a recital of his own works. Mikhail Gnesin was given a retrospective. The remaining pair of programs were omnibus gatherings in which a total of fifteen composers were represented, from Cherepnin and Myaskovsky down to such worthies as Karnovich, Aisberg, Gubenko, and Pashchenko. (Staff members Weisberg and Karatïgin were represented ex officio.) A special bordered announcement on the series prospectus explained, as if to forestall inferences, that "the new compositions of S. S. Prokofiev that were announced for performance cannot be performed, owing to circumstances over which the directors of the concerts have no control." For the far more conspicuous absence of another name, no apology was offered.

7. "Simfonicheskoye sobraniye I.R.M.O.," *Khronika zhurnala Muzïkal'nïy sovremennik*," no. 12 (1915): 15 (unsigned).

8. Karatïgin, "'Khovanshchina' i yeyo avtorï," 217.

9. Ibid., 195. The scurrilous parenthetical comment was surely spurious: Karatïgin had never been close enough to the elder Rimsky-Korsakov to have been privy to such a remark. It could only have originated with Andrey.

All this would be trivial to relate were it not for the split within the editorial ranks of the *Muzïkal'nïy sovremennik* that forced the Stravinsky matter into the open, and Andrey Rimsky-Korsakov onto the defensive. The proximate cause was a review by Asafyev of a Russian Musical Society concert (14 January 1917)—the program consisted of *Petrushka*, Myaskovsky's Second Symphony, and Prokofiev's First Piano Concerto—in which the critic made the following pointed comments on the composers represented:

> By now all three are known quantities: each travels his accustomed path, you can recognize each by his style, his character, simply on the basis of aural impressions, without any analysis of form or technique, so distinct are their individualities. One can love them or not, recognize them or not, believe in them or not, but fail to reckon with them one cannot. To do the last would be to turn away *from contemporary life, from the forms in which it manifests itself,* from attributes formed by its influence—in a word, from the whole chain of cause and effect that has produced the barbaric art of Prokofiev (barbaric, that is, from the standpoint of pure estheticism and true-blue academicism—in this instance they have merged), the tortured lyricism of Myaskovsky, with his stubborn efforts to know himself, and finally, Stravinsky's sharp inclination toward the ultra-refined materialization of sound.[10]

Andrey refused to print this in his *Khronika;* whereupon Asafyev resigned from the staff of the *Muzïkal'nïy sovremennik*—and took Suvchinsky with him, leaving the journal without its Maecenas. (The two of them immediately founded a new, frankly avant-garde journal called *Melos,* which lasted in the midst of revolution for only two issues.) Thus Boris Asafyev was the catalyst that brought "Pierre Souvtchinsky" (as he was known in the emigration and in the Stravinsky literature, and as we shall call him henceforth) into the modernist—and quite specifically Stravinskian—camp. And it was from this moment that Stravinsky would be for Asafyev the Russian critical touchstone—a view he expressed in the form of an ultimatum when he came to publish his celebrated *Book About Stravinsky* a decade or so later: "To wall ourselves off from him would mean turning musically into seventeenth-century Muscovy once more."[11] Prophetic words.

The seventeenth-century Muscovite position was enunciated by Andrey Rimsky-Korsakov, in an editorial response to the scandal the defection of Asafyev and Souvtchinsky had created for his struggling journal. This was its conclusion:

> We joyfully greet the manifestation and abet the self-determination of young talents, *however daring.* We strive to give them practical support by organizing concert-exhibitions of their work. But we are guided in our evaluations not by

10. Quoted from a proof sheet belonging to Roman Gruber in Ye. M. Orlova, *B. V. Asaf'yev* (Leningrad: Muzïka, 1964), 42; italics original.

11. Asafyev, *Kniga o Stravinskom* (Leningrad: Muzïka, 1977), 19 (cf. Asafyev, *A Book About Stravinsky,* 5).

tendentious or partisan concerns, but only by *the serious and responsible attitude on the part of creators toward their art*. We deliberately shy away from the premature canonization of young authors who are as yet only beginning their creative careers. We carefully restrain ourselves from fanning the flames of their immature egos. We parry such overrating, no matter what the reason for it—whether it be narrowly personal tastes, the blandishments of artistic politics, or the rationalistic, arbitrary application of a schema to living reality. . . .

We consider that in Russia, at the present time, *academicism*, as an actual threat to our musical life, *does not exist*. We consider the legacy of the New Russian School, far from outdated, to be as yet simply unassimilated. It has not become part of our flesh and blood. For many it is literally the art of the future. If in Western art one can discern signs of decline and fatigue, . . . such traits are absent from Russian music at the present time. We have strength and soundness to burn! . . . Not to speak of those deceased yet in the truest sense spiritually *alive*— profoundly contemporary creators like Dargomïzhsky, Musorgsky, Borodin, Rimsky-Korsakov—we have a whole slew of creators who are living or have only just departed at the height of their powers. Let us name only the biggest names: Scriabin, Taneyev, Lyadov, Glazunov, Rachmaninoff. In such circumstances, to turn the person of an artist from a self-sufficing entity into a weapon, a mere pawn in the struggle with the windmills of academicism or some such bugbear, would be a great sin. . . . We need no artificial fertilizers or, what is worse, the premature forced opening of half-formed buds, but the quiet, tender nurturing of gifts, the wish and the ability to distinguish the best and most authentic "I" in them from the dross and weeds that inevitably accumulate in the process of growth and development, that are not to be cultivated with the help of obliging well-wishers, but resolutely overcome.

"Thou shalt not make idols for thyself" [Leviticus 26:1]—this fundamental commandment of all authentic spiritual life we firmly remember and we stand ever ready to recall it to all who wish to take upon themselves the difficult task of serving the living God of art.[12]

But when all was said and done, Rimsky-Korsakov had come up with only two living names, and one of them belonged to the head of the Petrograd Conservatory. The "biggest name" in this discussion was unnamed, and did not have to be named in order to dominate it completely. Asafyev and Souvtchinsky mocked Andrey's editorial in the leader they published over the signature "Igor Glebov" in the first issue of *Melos*. Written in the spring of 1917, though not published until September, it was called "Temptations and How to Overcome Them" ("*Soblaznï i preodoleniya*") and carried Leviticus 26:1 as an epigraph—the idols in this case being academicism, estheticism, and dilettantism.[13] The influence of Souvtchinsky, the "well-rounded" intellectual, can be felt in the heavy dependence on Bergson and his doctrine of *élan vital*—the same Bergson whose philosophy would later inform

12. "Ot redaktora," *Muzikal'nïy sovremennik* 2, no. 4 (December 1916): 12–13.
13. I. Glebov, "Soblaznï i preodoleniya," *Melos*, no. 1 (1917): 4.

Souvtchinsky's own essay, "La notion du temps et la musique" (*Revue musicale*, 1939), the contents of which are now known to all musicians through Stravinsky's celebrated digest in *La poétique musicale*.

Nor was that Souvtchinsky's only major contribution to Stravinsky's mature thinking and (ghost)writing. The notorious fifth chapter of the *Poétique*, "Les avatars de la musique russe," was partly his.[14] "He has always fed books to me," wrote Stravinsky in his ninth decade of this "oldest living friend, [who] knew me more closely than anyone else in my later years in Paris."[15] Documentation of their personal relationship goes back to 1922, when Souvtchinsky, who had emigrated during the Russian civil war, was living in Berlin and saw a lot of Stravinsky during the latter's stay in the German capital awaiting his mother's arrival from Soviet Russia.[16]

What they talked about at this time is easy to guess, for it was precisely the period of Souvtchinsky's greatest involvement with the "Eurasian" movement. Two years earlier, while living in Sofia, Bulgaria, along with many others who had escaped from Russia by way of Turkey, Souvtchinsky had founded the Russo-Bulgarian Publishing House (*Rossiysko-bolgarskoye knigoizdatel'stvo*), whose first emission was Prince Nikolai Trubetskoy's violently anti-Western tract *Europe and Humanity* (recall his "pangermanoromanic chauvinism," sounded as keynote in the Introduction to this book). In 1921, Souvtchinsky issued a second volume, *Exodus to the East (Iskhod k Vostoku)*, a collection of essays in which he himself appeared as author, along with Trubetskoy and a couple of other scholars. This work marked the formal, official launching of a movement that played a considerable role in the intellectual life of the Russian émigré community between the wars. The introduction to *Exodus to the East* concluded with the proclamation that "Russians and those who belong to the peoples of 'the Russian world' are neither Europeans nor Asiatics. Merging with the native element of culture and life which surrounds us, we are unabashed to declare ourselves *Eurasians*."[17]

Some Eurasian writers (principally Trubetskoy and George Vernadsky) went

14. See SelCorrII, App. L ("Roland-Manuel and La Poétique musicale"), 505ff.

15. T&E:42, slightly paraphrased in T&C:48–49. Stravinsky was not the only eminent Russian composer of the period to value Souvtchinsky as a friend. In 1918 Souvtchinsky wrote the libretto of an unrealized opera Myaskovsky was to have composed on Dostoyevsky's *Idiot* (Myaskovsky to Derzhanovsky [3 May 1918]: "I have found a collaborator, better than whom, probably, I shall never have. In the first place, all our plans coincide *exceptionally* well; in the second place, he is a real Russian who passionately feels and understands Dostoyevsky; in the third place, he has great literary taste and gifts; in the fourth place, he has fire in his soul; in the fifth place, he is sincerely and even excessively interested in my musical activities" [in Shlifshteyn (ed.), *Myaskovskiy: sobraniye materialov* 2:408]). Souvtchinsky's relationship to Prokofiev may be gauged by the fact that the latter's Fifth Piano Sonata (1923) was dedicated to him.

16. See Souvtchinsky to Stravinsky, 21 November 1922, in P&D:658.

17. Pierre Souvtchinsky, ed., *Iskhod k Vostoku* (Sofia: Rossiysko-bolgarskoye Knigoizdatel'stvo, 1921), vii.

even further, coining the term *Turanian* for use interchangeably with *Eurasian*. The word is a derivative from Turan, the Persian name for the landmass beyond the Oxus River to the north of Iran, a huge territory extending, like the modern Russian state, from the Carpathians to the Pacific. Linguists will recognize the adjective *Turanian* as an obsolete denomination for what are now called the Ural-Altaic languages. What Eurasian writers meant by the word, however, had nothing to do with this signification. Rather, it appealed to them as a convenient way of conveying a sense of *ur*-Russianness without having to advert to the rejected existing cultures of Europe or Asia. In this limited meaning it seems worth reviving to denote the imaginary *ur*-Russia that Stravinsky conjured up in the music of his "Swiss" period—without any implication that Stravinsky's music was Turkic or Iranic in style or inspiration. Indeed, the proper noun Turania was not used by Eurasianists or linguists of any kind; coined for this book, it will refer specifically and exclusively to the land of Stravinsky's musical imagining.

Another Eurasian symposium, also edited by Souvtchinsky, followed in 1922. Entitled *On the Trails* (*Na putyakh*), it was published in Berlin by Abram Vishnyak's Helicon Press. At the time of Souvtchinsky's first meeting with Stravinsky, two more volumes were in preparation (they would be issued in 1923). One was the first of three books entitled *Eurasian Chronicle* (*Evraziyskiy vremennik*); the other was an especially vociferous collection directed against the Roman Catholic church, *Russia and Latinity* (*Rossiya i latinstvo*). It was surely to these projects and concerns that Souvtchinsky was referring when he wrote to Stravinsky, "The knowledge that you live on this earth helps me to go on."[18]

Why the phenomenon of Stravinsky should have so inspired the Eurasians will be evident from a pithy summary by Charles Halperin, a leading contemporary student of the movement, of their "Turanian" political and cultural outlook:

Russia's troubles derived from a misperception of its identity, i.e., an identity crisis. The problem dated from the wrongheaded cultural westernization of Peter the Great and found its culmination in the catastrophe of Russian involvement in the petty European squabbles which produced the First World War and the Revolution, Russia's downfall. Europe belonged to the Latino-Germanic peoples. Roman law made their whole outlook on life legalistic. The false dogma of Catholicism and the doctrinal anomaly of Protestantism induced secularism, irreligion, materialism, and decadence. Religion, meaning Russian Orthodoxy above all, constituted the essence of Eurasian/Russian being. European political forms could not be adapted to Turanian political culture. Russians/Eurasians congenitally believed in obedience to absolute authority. Democratic, parliamentary structures could not be grafted onto Eurasian political structures, as Russia's recent constitutional experiments had proven. Because of the errors of its religious, political, intellectual, cul-

18. P&D:658.

tural and moral foundation, Europe was declining; it could be saved only by Russia.[19]

As may be readily inferred from this description, Eurasianism was a peculiar amalgam of elements from nineteenth-century Slavophilism, with its concept of an "organic" society, and early-twentieth-century "*Skifstvo*," all brought to a boil by the cataclysmic events of 1914–17 and the attendant forcible uprooting and dispersal of large segments of the Russian intelligentsia. In a particularly apt phrase, Halperin characterizes the Eurasianists as unfortunate exiles who "lived in a Europe they despised and wished to return to a Russia which no longer existed."[20]

There could be no better characterization of the "Swiss" Stravinsky. Just how "Eurasian" *avant le mot* his wartime attitudes were is startlingly revealed in Romain Rolland's report of a conversation with the composer on 26 September 1914, a couple of months after the commencement of hostilities—almost precisely the point at which we left him in the last chapter. (Rolland's physical description, while not our present concern, is too vivid to be missed):

> A long visit with Igor Stravinsky. We spend three hours chatting in the garden of the Hotel Mooser. Stravinsky is about thirty; he is small, has a puny, ugly appearance, a yellow complexion, a weak, exhausted look, a narrow brow, thin, receding hair, eyes wrinkling behind his glasses, a fleshy nose, thick lips, a disproportionately long face. He is very intelligent and direct; he speaks easily, though he sometimes has to search for his words in French, and everything he says is personal and considered (whether true or false). The first part of our conversation had to do with politics. Stravinsky declares that Germany is not a barbarian state, but a decrepit and degenerate one. He claims for Russia the role of a splendid, healthy barbarism, heavy with germs that will inseminate the thinking of the world. He is counting on a revolution to follow the war, which will topple the dynasty and found a Slavic United States. Moreover, he attributes the cruelties of the tsarist system in part to German elements that have been incorporated into Russia and run the main wheels of the government or the administration. The attitude of German intellectuals inspires him with boundless contempt. Hauptmann and Strauss, he says, have the souls of lackeys. He touts the Old Russian civilization, unknown in the West, the artistic and literary monuments of northern and eastern cities. He also defends the Cossacks against their reputation for brutality....[21]

19. Charles J. Halperin, "Russia and the Steppe: George Vernadsky and Eurasianism," *Forschungen zur osteuropäischen Geschichte* 36 (1985): 93.
20. Ibid., 97.
21. "Longue visite de Igor Strawinsky. Nous passons trois heures à causer dans le jardin de l'hôtel Mooser. Strawinsky a la trentaine environ; il est petit, d'aspect chétif, laid, la figure jaune, maigre et fatiguée, le front étroit, les cheveux hauts et rares, les yeux plissés derrière un lorgnon, le nez charnu, les lèvres grosses, la longueur du visage disproportionnée au front. Il est très intelligent et simple de manières; il parle facilement, bien qu'en cherchant parfois ses mots français; et tout ce qu'il dit est personnel et réfléchi (vrai ou faux). La première partie de notre entretien a trait aux questions politiques. Strawinsky déclare que l'Allemagne n'est pas un état barbare, mais décrépit et dégénéré. Il revendique pour la Russie le rôle de belle et saine barbarie, grosse de germes nouveaux qui féconderont la pensée du monde. Il compte qu'après la guerre une révolution, qui déjà se prépare, renversera la dynastie et

But for the explicitly religious component (which would come in time), every one of the tenets in the Eurasian platform is adumbrated here, plank by plank: the decrepitude of the West, the messianic role of a newly purified Russia of which the Cossacks were the avatars, and all the rest.

Nor was Stravinsky's "Eurasianism" merely a matter of lip service paid in facile conversation with a friendly writer. It began, in profound and surprising ways, to affect his musical thought and practice, his very way of composing. By substituting *musical* for such words as *political* or *parliamentary* in a few of Halperin's sentences as quoted above, we can come close to the Stravinskian esthetic of the Swiss years: "European musical forms could not be adapted to Turanian musical culture, . . . could not be grafted onto Eurasian musical structures, as Russia's recent musical experiments [viz., kuchkist, Belyayevets, etc.] had proven."

Nineteenth-century Russian composers, however "nationalist," had always implicitly accepted European musical institutions, media, and genres. Once one is writing, let us say, for the symphony orchestra, one's basic commitment to the musical Europeanization of Russia—"Westernization," to put it in terms of the classic dualism of nineteenth-century Russian intellectual history—has been made and shown.

As for Stravinsky, known the world over as a master of that symphony orchestra, between *The Nightingale* (1914) and *Pulcinella* (1919) he would write no new orchestral music at all (excepting only his balletic arrangement of the former); nor did he compose for any standardized "Western" ensemble during this period, save only a few minor works, of which one, the Three Pieces for String Quartet of 1914, was written as thoroughly and willfully against the traditions of the medium as possible. More characteristic of the period were compositions that used "four musicians, one of whom can only be found in Honolulu, another in Budapest, and the other two God knows where!" as Diaghilev cracked to Ansermet in mock exasperation one day in 1919.[22] These weird assortments of instruments (some "live," others mechanical) were expressly chosen and deployed, as we shall see, to make quite specifically "Turanian" noises.

Then there was the matter of genre. Up to 1914 Stravinsky was a purveyor of radical "content" within established forms. During the Swiss years, his works took shapes that baffled even him. In a letter to Struve, Stravinsky tried to give his old editor an idea of *Svadebka* (*Les noces*): "a cantata or oratorio, or I do not know

fondera les États-Unis slaves. Il attribue d'ailleurs, en partie, les cruautés du tsarisme aux éléments allemands incorporés en Russie et maîtres de principaux rouages du gouvernement ou de l'administration. L'attitude des intellectuels allemands lui inspire un mépris sans bornes. Hauptmann et Strauss, dit-il, ont des âmes de laquais. Il vante la vieille civilisation russe, qu'on ne connaît pas en Occident, les monuments artistiques et littéraires des villes du nord et de l'est. Il défend aussi les Cosaques contre leur réputation de férocité" (Romain Rolland, *Journal des années de guerre, 1914–1919* [Paris: Éditions Albin Michel, 1952], 59).

22. P&D:155.

what, for four soloists and an instrumental ensemble that I am in too great a hurry to describe." Writing to Ansermet a few months later, he called it "a *divertissement* (for it is not a ballet)."[23] Far easier to say what a thing is not than to say what it is, if your vocabulary is European but the thing you are trying to describe is Turanian.

Turanian, too, were the words Stravinsky set to music during the period of his Swiss exile. Between 1913 (*Souvenirs de mon enfance*) and 1919 (*Quatre chants russes*) he wrote no fewer than eight compositions (including two large-scale concerted works) on Russian folk texts. There was a great quantity of this material in print, collected by the Slavophile philosophers and ethnographers of the mid–nineteenth century (much of it published posthumously), but very little of it had been set to original music by the Russian "nationalist" composers of the same period, for to do so would have violated their conception of what "art" was. In particular, no work in any of the "large" forms ("cantata, oratorio, or I do not know what") had ever been set to folk verse in provincial dialects (*govori*) until Stravinsky entered his Turanian phase at the outbreak of the First World War.

Even in their visual aspects, Stravinsky's manuscripts of the Swiss years were Turanian. He copied the titles and texts in an archaistic calligraphy modeled on the pre-Petrine Slavic alphabet—that is, the true old-Bulgarian *kirillitsa,* the alphabet of SS. Cyril and Methodius that had been introduced to Russia along with Christianity in the tenth century but was replaced in the eighteenth by a streamlined, deliberately romanized style of writing (the so-called *grazhdanskiy shrift,* or "civil hand") that has remained current. These manuscripts symbolize what must be deemed a deliberate effort to excrete all that was European and to cultivate that "splendid, healthy barbarism, heavy with germs that will inseminate the thinking of the world" (for a sample, see Fig. 15.2).

Stravinsky's eschewal of the standard orchestra has often been viewed as an accommodation to the realities of wartime, when the large orchestras of the European capitals had been decimated by conscription. This cannot have been the case. Stravinsky did not lack for orchestral outlets during the war. His friendship with Ernest Ansermet (1883–1969), who was exceedingly active all through this period—with the Kursaal orchestra at Montreux (1911–15), the Geneva Symphony Orchestra (1915–18), and finally with his own Orchestre de la Suisse Romande—vouchsafed Stravinsky many orchestral performances, and even opportunities to conduct (for the first time) himself.[24] Nor did the Ballets Russes cease their operations during the war. Diaghilev commissioned the *Chant du rossignol* while the war was raging, and Stravinsky did not hesitate to comply: he wrote the piece in

23. Letters of 6 April and 23 July 1919; in P&D:154.
24. He led the Kursaal orchestral through a rehearsal of his Symphony in E-flat in April 1914; his public podium debut was with the Geneva orchestra at a charity matinée for the Red Cross (20 December 1915; Stravinsky conducted the 1910 *Firebird* suite, plus Berceuse and Finale); see White, *Stravinsky: The Composer and His Works,* 31, 37.

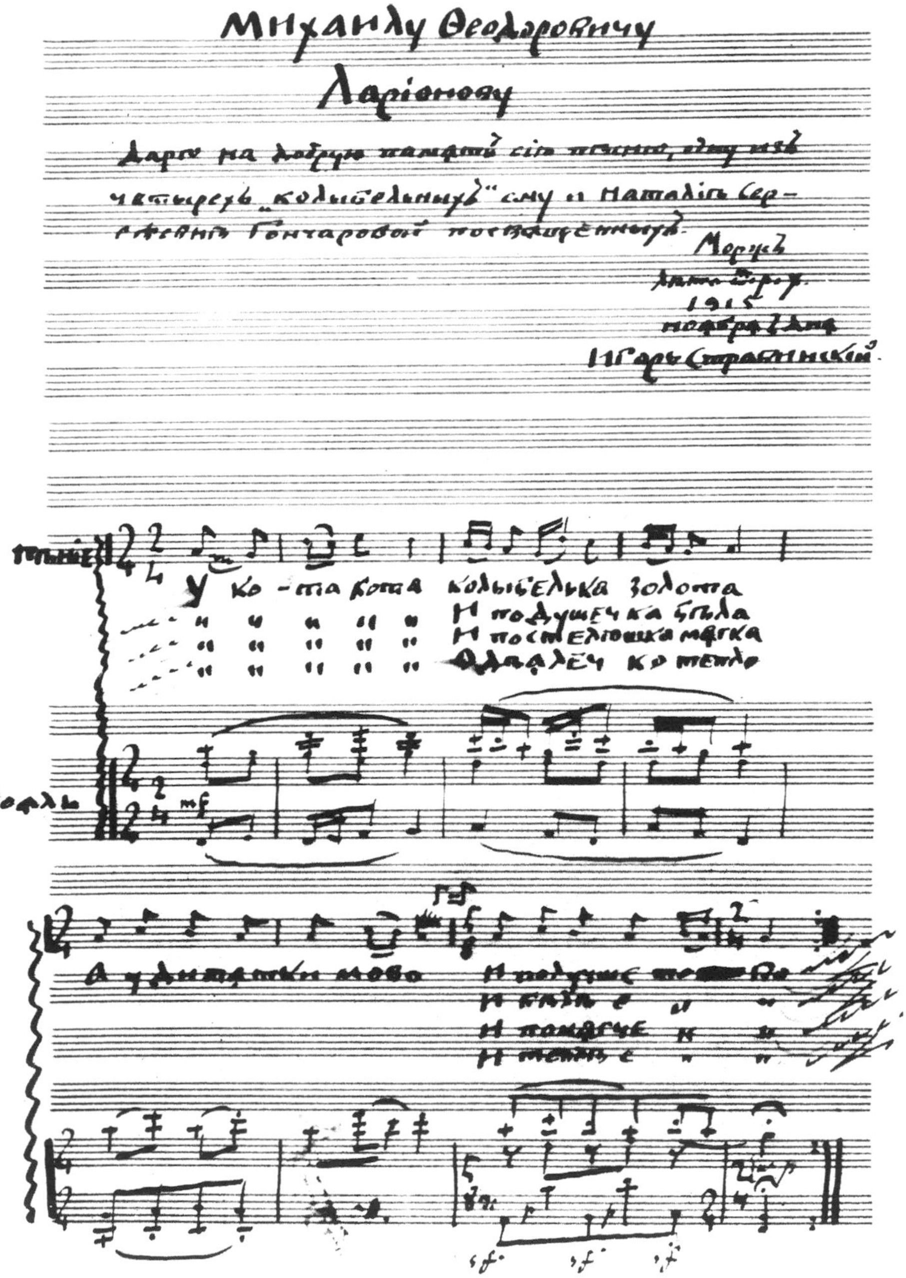

FIG. 15.2. *Berceuses*, no. 4, presentation copy to Laryonov (1915) with archaistic inscription.

the early months of 1917, fully expecting a speedy première.[25] Finally, the fact that many of the "Turanian" pieces of the Swiss period had their première performances only after the war was over—for example, *Pribaoutki* in May 1919; *Renard* in May 1922—and were published only with the help of a subsidy, shows that the impetus to write them had not been an exclusively practical one, let alone mercenary. Neither was the impulse to scale the *Svadebka* orchestra down from a *Sacre*-sized ensemble to a group of pianos and percussion entirely practical, since the final scoring was decided upon at a time when the *Sacre*-sized band would again have been available. No, the "Turanian" tendency had come about not merely through force of circumstance, but by dint of what Stravinsky, with reference to another stylistic revolution, termed "an irresistible pull within [his] art."[26]

Where had this pull come from, precisely? It was, of course, already implicit in Stravinsky's prewar "neonationalist" work, just as Eurasianism was implicit in the earlier Slavophile and Scythian trends. Stravinsky's famous book-buying expedition to Kiev in the summer of 1914, through which he fortified his library with the folklore collections that would nourish his work over the next five years, actually predated the outbreak of the war. Correspondence with Mitusov shows that he had already been looking for the 1911 publication of Kireyevsky's wedding songs, on which *Svadebka* would be based, in 1913.[27] Correspondence with Sanin suggests that the idea of *Svadebka* had come to him perhaps a year earlier still.[28]

Nevertheless, the work (and thought) of the wartime and revolutionary years showed a sudden intensification in the way these prior tendencies were actualized, amounting to a difference not merely in degree but one in kind. As Stravinsky put it in the *Chroniques,* "my profound emotion on reading the news of war, which aroused patriotic feelings and a sense of sadness at being so distant from my country, found some alleviation in the delight with which I steeped myself in Russian folk poems."[29] Along with patriotism went a dollop of crude anti-Germanism (something for which there was, after all, a considerable tradition among Russian musicians),[30] so pronounced in Stravinsky's case that Rivière called the composer a one-man "Russian front ... forcing Germany to the rear."[31] At Rolland's request, Stravinsky penned an open letter that read in part: "It is ... in the highest common interests of all nations that still feel the need to breathe the air of their healthy and age-old culture to come down on the side of Germany's enemies and

25. In the event, the ballet première was postponed until 2 February 1920; Ansermet had given the piece its première as a "symphonic poem" with the Orchestre de la Suisse Romande two months earlier (6 December 1919).
26. Conv:127/113. The topic of reference there was "atonality."
27. SelCorrII:437–38.
28. See Sanin's letter to Stravinsky of 17 February 1913; in SelCorrII:197–98.
29. *An Autobiography,* 53.
30. See, inter alia, Ridenour, *Nationalism, Modernism, and Personal Rivalry,* 176; Taruskin, "Some Thoughts on the History and Historiography of Russian Music," 336.
31. Letter of 29 June 1918; in SelCorrII:179.

to remove themselves once and for all from the intolerable spirit of that enormous, bloated Teutonic Order that is menaced by deadly symptoms of moral decay."[32] At Bakst's urging, he contributed a wicked little "Souvenir d'une marche boche" to Edith Wharton's charity gift-book, *Le livre de sans foyer* (*Book of the Homeless*).[33]

Yet as Prince Trubetskoy insisted, a Russian could not be anti-German without rejecting the West in its totality, and Stravinsky's case bears this point out in reverse. When his time came to embrace the "panromanogermanic chauvinism" of Western Europe, his embrace encompassed the *boche*, too. His Eurasianism was in the first instance born not of a rejection of anything, but of a craving that he shared with his many uprooted countrymen. It was a craving to compensate for the loss of Russia, as Nicholas Riasanovsky has poignantly observed: "In a sense, Eurasianism constituted a desperate bid to reestablish vanished Russia, to transmute fragmented and rootless existence in a foreign society into an organic and creative life at home. The scope of the dream corresponded to that of the loss."[34]

It is hard to assess the extent to which Stravinsky actively participated in the intellectual currents that coalesced around Eurasianism, though his creative evolution certainly paralleled that of the Eurasianists, perhaps even furnishing some of them with a model. In the later phases of the movement, Stravinsky was prominently enshrined in its pantheon. The last and most distinguished of the major Eurasianist journals was *Vyorstï*, published in Paris from 1926 to 1928 under the editorship of the ubiquitous Souvtchinsky, in collaboration with Prince Dmitriy Svyatopolk-Mirsky and Sergey Efron, "with the close cooperation," as the masthead proclaimed, of Alexey Remizov, Marina Tsvetayeva (then Efron's wife), and Lev Shestov. The very first issue contained a lengthy article called "The Music of Igor Stravinsky," by the newly emigrated Arthur Lourié—apparently the only major piece ever published by the Eurasianists on music or a musician.

Lourié's thrust is typical of the movement: Stravinsky had been transformed from a "Russian" composer into a "universal" one precisely because he successfully rid himself of what was covertly European in his ostensibly nationalist style. "In Russia *The Nightingale* already evoked a howl of despair," he wrote, "so completely did it withdraw from the Korsakovian pseudonational opera, which had risen from a German yeast." The kuchkists had "poured Russian wine into German bottles," and this made them mere purveyors of exotica. It had remained for Stravinsky to "break the ties that connected Russia with Western Europe," as a result of which

---

32. "Il est . . . du plus haut intérêt commun de toutes les nations qui sentent encore le besoin de respirer l'air de leur saine et ancienne culture de se mettre du côté des ennemis de l'Allemagne et de se soustraire une fois pour toujours à l'intolérable esprit de cette colossale et obèse Germania qui est menacée de funestes symptômes de décomposition morale" (Rolland, *Journal*, 61).

33. Letter of 17 August 1916; in SelCorrII:88.

34. Nicholas V. Riasanovsky, "The Emergence of Eurasianism," *California Slavic Studies* 4 (1967): 71.

"for the first time Russian music lost its 'provincial,' 'exotic' quality and . . . has become a thing of capital significance, at the very helm of world music."[35]

Stravinsky's earliest contact with proto-Eurasianist thinking would surely have come by way of Lev Platonovich Karsavin (1882–1952), brother of Diaghilev's prima ballerina and a precociously eminent professor of philosophy and religion in St. Petersburg. He lived with his sister in the same building on the Kryukov Canal as the Stravinsky family in the years of the composer's first (local) fame, and later, in the emigration, he became closely associated with the Eurasianist press in Berlin. His daughter Marianna became Pierre Souvtchinsky's wife. Karsavin was briefly very close to Stravinsky in the days preceding the première of *Petrushka* (see Chapter 10). Riasanovsky calls him the "principal religious thinker of the movement."[36]

The last book Karsavin published before leaving Russia was *The East, the West, and the Russian Idea*,[37] which presented a viewpoint entirely congruent with that of Prince Trubetskoy's classic: Russian culture was opposed to that of Europe; where European culture was a contradiction—at once legalistic and individualistic—Russian culture was organic, a whole in which the individual fulfilled himself as part of the "higher symphonic personality" of the culturally unified group, whose classless unification would eventually result in the building of a new "symphonic society."[38] While this dream does seem to conjure up visions of a Utopian Bolshevism without benefit of Marx (hence the provisional misguided acceptance by many Eurasians of the Bolshevik revolution as a first step toward the de-Europeanization of Russian society), it has been pointed out that Karsavin's views paralleled "the early idealistic conception of fascist corporation," as well as "the same philological mysticism that possessed Nazism in its early 'runic' stages."[39]

This romantic philologism rooted in Slavophilism was one of the defining traits of the movement:

> In field after field and topic after topic Russian scholars were discovering a new
> and largely "non-Western" richness in the Russian and "pre-Russian" past, and its
> connections with other civilizations. Archeology, history of art with its discovery
> of the "Scythian style," music, literature with its new links between Kievan epos

35. Arthur-Vincent Lourié, "Muzïka Stravinskogo," *Vyorsti,* no. 1 (1926): 124, 126, 134.

36. Riasanovsky, "Emergence of Eurasianism," 47. Later, Karsavin accepted an appointment to the University of Kaunas in then-independent Lithuania. He perished in a Soviet labor camp.

37. L. P. Karsavin, *Vostok, zapad i russkaya ideya* (Petrograd: Ogni, 1922).

38. See Dmitri Sviatopolk-Mirsky, "The Eurasian Movement," *Slavonic and East European Review* 6 (1927–28): 316–17. Karsavin's ideas seem to derive in part from the defense of Russian autocracy in Gogol's notorious *Selected Passages from Correspondence with Friends,* where a harmonious society is likened to an orchestra under the baton of a conductor (see N. V. Gogol, *Polnoye sobraniye sochineniy,* vol. 8 [Moscow: Izdatel'stvo Akademii Nauk SSSR, 1952], 253).

39. Billington, *Icon and Axe,* 760. This affinity, noted by today's scholars with benefit of hindsight, became much clearer between the wars. On Stravinsky's interwar flirtation with fascism and his lifelong anti-Semitism, see Taruskin, "Dark Side of Modern Music," 28–34; Craft, "Jews and Geniuses," 35–37 (and in *Small Craft Advisories,* 274–81); R. Taruskin and R. Craft, "Jews and Geniuses: An Exchange," *New York Review of Books,* 15 June 1989, 57–58; R. Taruskin, "Only Time Will Cover the Taint," *New York Times,* Arts and Leisure, 26 January 1992, 25.

and those of Persia and the Turkic peoples, investigations of folklore, history, and much else, all contributed to a fuller appreciation of Russia as a cultural and historical entity and suggested to some the need for a new scholarly synthesis.[40]

To others it suggested the need for an artistic synthesis; for among the books that laid the foundations for the new Turanian image of Russia were the very ones that formed the basis of Stravinsky's "Swiss" style.

The most fundamental distinguishing feature of the new image was its intense preoccupation with what have been termed the "lower strata of culture."[41] Beginning with the semilegendary Kirsha Danilov in the eighteenth century, the early collectors of what is known in Russian as "oral literature" (*ustnaya slovesnost'*) had emphasized the most elaborate of its forms and genres, the ones most compatible with and assimilable to eighteenth- and nineteenth-century ideas of high art: epics (*bilini*), historical songs (*istoricheskiye pesni*), "lyrical" (i.e., personally expressive) songs (*liricheskiye pesni*), spiritual verses (*dukhovnïye stikhi*), and the like.[42]

It was the Slavophile collectors who began systematically culling the poetic and prosaic manifestations of the "Daily Life of the Russian People" (*Bït russkogo naroda*), to cite the title of Tereshchenko's huge compilation, on which Stravinsky would draw. By the early twentieth century a wide assortment of this grass-roots stuff was available in print, all the way from the extremely copious liturgy of the Russian peasant wedding ritual (Sakharov, Tereshchenko, Kireyevsky) through the prose folk tales, sayings, and jingles collected by Afanasyev, down to the "lowest" stratum of all, that of children's rhymes and games (Sheyn). Much of this material, when it was sung at all, was sung to unprepossessing melodic formulas (*popevki*) or simple tunes (*napevï*), and musicians in the high-art tradition were slow to take notice of it. Only very late in the nineteenth century were the tunes even collected: first by musicians hired by the Imperial Geographical Society in St. Petersburg to accompany the philologist Fyodor Mikhailovich Istomin (1856–1920) on his collecting expeditions, and somewhat later by the members of Russia's first real ethnomusicological organization, the Musico-Ethnographic Commission (the so-called MEK), sponsored by the Imperial Society of Friends of Natural History, Anthropology, and Ethnography of Moscow University.

A composer who could call the collections of Afanasyev and Kireyevsky "great argosies of the Russian language and spirit,"[43] and who would draw upon the Istomin publications and those of the MEK for musical inspiration, was one whose fundamental outlook on Russia and its people had changed drastically under the

40. Riasanovsky, "Emergence of Eurasianism," 45.
41. See ibid., 43–45.
42. See, for example, the collection *Russian Folk Literature,* ed. D. P. Costello and I. P. Foote, in the series Oxford Russian Readers (Oxford: Clarendon Press, 1967), where these are cited as "the genres which offer most in the way of literary and historical interest" (ix).
43. E&D:130 (original ed. only).

impact of Eurasianism. For the great argosies had sailed right by the musicians of the nineteenth century, who viewed folk songs as highly finished and inviolable *objets d'art*. Afanasyev's and Kireyevsky's cargoes were unrefined ore at best—or, to use the typically Romantic "vegetative" (*rastitel'noye*) metaphor of Apollon Grigoriev, a writer whose views had influenced many nineteenth-century Russian musicians, they carried the soil (*pochva*) in which the flower of really artistic folk song thrived.[44] Stravinsky no longer wished to pluck the flower, as Rimsky-Korsakov or Chaikovsky had done. He wanted to get down into the mud itself and mold a new Russian culture from the ground up. "It is so wonderful to be of one's country, to be attached to one's land like the humblest of peasants!" Debussy had written him, exhorting him to be not just a great artist, but to "be, with all your might, a great Russian artist!"[45] It was Stravinsky's forced separation from his native soil that finally attached him to it in this way. Not even Debussy, though, could have guessed how deep Stravinsky would sink his roots.

THE ''SWISS'' SONGS:
MATTERS OF PHILOLOGY AND ETHNOGRAPHY

A good deal of confusion—some of it, regrettably, sown by the composer himself—surrounds the music Stravinsky created on the basis of Russian folk poetry. The compositions are listed, and their sources identified, in Table 2. As will be evident at a glance, the various sets of "Swiss" songs are by no means as discrete as they appear to be in their published form. Their chronology as set forth in the table, moreover, is somewhat misleading. Some of the sets (i.e., *Pribaoutki, Berceuses du chat, Podblyudnïye, Trois histoires*) were published in an order different from that of composition. It is also clear that Stravinsky did not always plan the various sets as such, but accumulated them piecemeal as "studies" during the period when his *Baika* (*Renard*) and *Svadebka* were gestating. Many of them (particularly the children's songs and the peasant choruses) were evidently composed as personal greetings or as family entertainments, perhaps with no immediate thought of publication.[46] The order of actual composition of songs during the period from late 1914 through 1917 was as follows:

A.   "*Shchuka*" (*Podblyudnïye*, no. 3)

44. See his review of Mikhaíl Stakhovich, *Sobraniye russkikh narodnïkh pesen* (Moskvityanin, no. 15 [August 1854]); quoted in Taruskin, *Opera and Drama in Russia*, 144–45.
45. "C'est si beau, d'être de son pays, d'être attaché à sa terre comme le plus humble des paysans! . . . [Soyez] de toutes vos forces, un grand artiste russe!" (Letter of 24 October 1915; in *Avec Stravinsky*, 203).
46. Some, like a lullaby for Stravinsky's daughter Lyudmila (Mikushka) or a little children's waltz for piano—both composed in 1917—were not published until years later: the waltz in *Le Figaro* (Sunday, 21 May 1922), the lullaby in the Faber edition of *Expositions and Developments* (London, 1962). A *Valse des fleurs* for piano four-hands, dated 30 October/12 November 1914, was published only in 1983 (ms. facsimile in Robert Craft, *A Stravinsky Scrapbook, 1940–1971* [London: Thames & Hudson], 146–47). For more on the two waltzes, see Chapter 18.

B. *"Puzishche"* (*Podblyudnïye,* no. 4)

C. *"Kot na pechi"* (*Kolïbel'nïye,* no. 2)

D. *"Bai-Bai"* (*Kolïbel'nïye,* no. 3)

E. *"Spi kot"* (*Kolïbel'nïye,* no. 1)

F. *"U kota kota"* (*Kolïbel'nïye,* no. 4)

G. *"Pesenka medvedya"* (*Detskiye pesenki,* no. 3)

H. *"U Spasa v Chigisakh"* (*Podblyudnïye,* no. 1)

I. *"Ovsen'"* (*Podblyudnïye,* no. 2)

J. *"Tilim-bom"* (*Detskiye pesenki,* no. 1)

K. *"Gusi-lebedi"* (*Detskiye pesenki,* no. 2)

The advantage of listing the songs in terms of the collections as published is that in this way Stravinsky's rationale for grouping is best revealed. The groupings were based largely on folkloristic source: thus the *Pribaoutki* and the *Detskiye pesenki* come (with one exception) from Afanasyev, the *Kolïbel'nïye* from Kireyevsky, the *Podblyudnïye* from Sakharov. But even here there are hidden spillovers. For example: besides the four songs in the set actually entitled *Pribaoutki,* Stravinsky set three additional items from the collection of jingles under the heading *Pribautki* in the last volume of Afanasyev's *Russian Folk Tales.* One went into the *Baika,* another into the *Detskiye pesenki,* while the third, which went into the *Kolïbel'nïye,* was actually the very next text Stravinsky set after completing the group of so-called *Pribaoutki.* This seems a significant factor in the genesis of the *Kolïbel'nïye:* it is likely that Stravinsky had the idea of composing a group of lullabies when he noticed the concordance between Afanasyev's group of *pribautki* and Kireyevsky's group of *kolïbel'nïye*—a concordance involving a text he had probably chosen in the first place for inclusion in the *Pribaoutki.*

Nomenclature for these songs (that is, simply, what to call them) presents a formidable problem. The set called *Tri pesenki (iz vospominaniy yunosheskikh godov)* was the last Stravinsky composition to be issued by Koussevitsky's Russische Musikverlag before the war interrupted Stravinsky's association with that firm (it would be resumed in 1921 with the *Chant du rossignol*). The wartime works published by Henn (Geneva) and J. & W. Chester, which include all of the other items in the table, were (except for the large-scale concerted items) published without Russian title pages. In the case of the *Berceuses du chat,* the Trois histoires pour enfants, and the *Quatre chants russes,* the French titles given by Charles Ferdinand Ramuz have become standard. The Russian titles listed by Beletsky and Blazhkov (respectively *Koshach'i kolïbel'nïye pesni, Tri istorii dlya detey,* and *Chetïre russkikh pesni*) are unauthorized back-translations from the French.

The titles given in Table 2 have been extracted in every case from autograph

TABLE 2

Stravinsky's Settings of Russian Folk Texts

Title (Russian / French or English)	Place and Date of Composition	Documentation	Folklore Sources
Tri pesenki (iz vospominaniya yunosheskikh godov) / [*Trois petites chansons (Souvenir de mon enfance)*]			
1. *"Sorochenka"* / "La petite pie" / "The Magpie"	Ustilug, July 1913 (Fair copy dated 6/19 October, according to EWW, 182)	Complete pencil draft in Archive among sketches for *Nightingale*, sc. 2 (cf. Shepard, "Checklist," 747)	Family tradition (but cf. Sheyn, no. 65)
2. *"Vorona"* / "Le corbeau" / "The Rook"	[Clarens, ca. October 1913]	Early draft in Archive, Sketchbook B (Shepard, "Checklist," 742, 747)	Family tradition
3. *"Chicher-Yacher"* / "Tchicher-Yatcher" / "The Jackdaw"	Clarens, October–November 1913	EWW, 182	Family tradition (cf. Symphony in E-flat, IV, mm. 237–40)
[*Pribautki*] / *Pribaoutki (Chansons plaisantes)*			
1. *"Kornilo"* / "L'Oncle Armand"	Salvan, [5]/18 August 1914	P&D:127 (MS. coll. Paul Sacher; cf. Shepard, "Checklist," 738)	Afanasyev, *Skazki*, III, no. 543; tune: Istomin/Lyapunov, 108
2. *"Natashka"* / "Le four"	Salvan, [31 July]/13 August 1914		Afanasyev, *Skazki*, III, no. 550
3. *"Polkovnik"* / "Le colonel"	Salvan, 16/29 August 1914		Afanasyev, *Skazki*, III, no. 544
4. *"Starets i zayats"* / "Le vieux et le lièvre" / "The Old Man and the Hare"	Salvan, 16/29 September 1914		Afanasyev, *Skazki*, III, no. 547
[*Kolïbel'nïye*] / *Berceuses du chat*			
1. *"Spi kot"* / "Sur le poêle"	Morges, 29 August/11 September 1915	Signed draft in Archive, Sketchbook D (photo in P&D:136–37; cf. Shepard, "Checklist," 738)	Kireyevsky, no. 1107

2. "Kot na pechi" / "Intérieur"	[Chateau d'Oex, ca. January–March 1915(?)]		Kireyevsky, no. 1106; Afanasyev, *Skazki*, III no. 538 (*Pribautki*)
3. "Bai-Bai" / "Dodo"	Clarens, 5/18 April 1915	Meyer catalogue, pl. 80	Kireyevsky, no. 1108
4. "U kota kota" / "Ce qu'il a le chat"	Morges, 2 November 1915	Meyer catalogue, pl. 79	Kireyevsky, no. 1104 (adapted)
Baïka pro Lisu, Petukha, Kota da Barana. Vesyoloye predstavleniye s peniyem i muzikoy / Renard. Histoire burlesque chantée et jouée / Fable of the Vixen, the Cock, the Cat, and the Ram. A merry performance with singing and music	Chateau d'Oex, January 1915–Morges, September 1916	Letter to Anna Kirillovna Stravinskaya (mother), 11 September 1916 (IstrSM: 498). For details on MSS., see Chapter 16.	Afanasyev, *Skazki*, I: nos. 14–17, 21, 23, 37–39, 52, 65, 68, 71; III: no. 542 (*Pribautki*). All freely conflated, occasionally adapted
Tri podblyudnïkh pesni i odna pesn' Ovsenyu [usual Russian title: *Podblyudnïye*] / *Four Russian Peasant Songs* [original Russian title translated: "Three Dish-Divination Songs and One Song to Ovsen"]		Cary 393	
1. "U Spasa v Chigisakh" [*sic*] / "In Our Savior's Parish at Chigasï"*	Morges, 22 December 1916	Archive, pencil draft in Sketchbook A (Shepard, "Checklist," 732, 742)	Sakharov, III, 12; Kireyevsky, no. 1063; Tereshchenko, VII, 159
2. "Ovsen"	[Morges], 1 January 1917 (N.S.)	Archive, untitled fair copy (R34)	Sakharov, III, 260

*Stravinsky consistently mistranscribed the name of the town (Chigisï for Chigasï), beginning with the earliest sketches (Sketchbook A).

Title (Russian / French or English)	Place and Date of Composition	Documentation	Folklore Sources
3. "Shchuka" / "The Pike"	Clarens, 13/26 December 1914	Archive, untitled fair copy (R34)	Sakharov, III, 13; Tereshchenko, VII, 158; Afanasyev, *Poèticheskiye vozzreniya*, II, 158
4. "Puzishche" / "Pot-Belly" (or "Mr. Portly")	Chateau d'Oex, January 1915	Archive, untitled fair copy (R34)	Sakharov, III, 11
Detskiye pesenki / Trois histoires pour enfants			
1. "Tilim-bom"	Morges, 22 May 1917	Archive, pencil draft (R28) BL Loan 75/40 (Chester deposit)	Sheyn, no. 130, adapted
2. "Gusi-Lebedi" / "Les canards, les cygnes, les oies . . ."	[Morges], 21–28 June 1917		Afanasyev, *Skazki*, III, no. 537 (*Pribautki*)
3. "Pesenka medvedya na derevyashke" / "Chanson de l'ours" / "Song of the Bear with the Wooden Paw"	Morges, 30 December 1915 (o.s.)	Archive, fair copy (in E-flat) (R26)	Afanasyev, *Skazki*, I, no. 57 (complete tale, of which song is central episode)
Svadebka/Les Noces	Clarens, 1914–Morges, 29 September/11 October 1917 (short score with complete voice parts)	For details of dated MSS., including orchestrations through 1923, see Chapter 17. The short score (particell), which represents the *terminus ante quem* of actual composition, is located in RS:64/2 (cf. Sheppard, "Checklist," 734-35)	

1. Tableau I: *U nevestï (Kosa)* / At the Bride's (The Braid)

Kireyevsky, nos. 13, 269, 421, 564, 568, 635, 646, 671, 714, 721; Sakharov, III, no. 164; Tereshchenko, II, 160, 304

2. Tableau II: *U zhenikha* / At the Groom's

Kireyevsky, nos. 125, 454, 481, 485–86, 495–97, 569, 629, 636, 678, 712, 794, and citations from spoken formulas on pp. 51, 243; Dahl, *Tolkovïy slovar'*, s.v. "*malina*"

3. Tableau III: *Provodï nevestï* / The Departure of the Bride

Kireyevsky, nos. 125, 137, 243, 749, 828, 884, 887

4. Tableau IV: *Krasnïy stol* / The Wedding Feast

Kireyevsky, nos. 142, 177, 199, 396, 407, 438, 447–48, 451, 458, 465, 491, 493, 510, 514, 571, 591, 668, 803, 823, 1009, 1021, and citations from spoken formulas on pp. 44, 200; Tereshchenko, II, 322; Istomin/Dyutsh, p. 161 (melody at fig. [110])

TABLE 2
(continued)

Title (Russian / French or English)	Place and Date of Composition	Documentation	Folklore Sources
[No Russian title] *Quatre chants russes*			
1. "*Selezeñ (Khorovodnaya)*" / "Canard (Ronde)"	Morges, 28 December 1918	Archive, Sketchbook F (Shepard, "Checklist," 728, 743)	Sakharov, III, 48 (two variants conflated)
2. "*Zapevnaya*" / "Chanson pour compter"	Morges, 3/16 January 1919	Archive, Sketchbook E (Shepard, "Checklist," 728, 743)	Kireyevsky, no. 1150 (designated *igra*, "game")
3. "*Podblyudnaya*" / "Le moineau est assis"	Morges, 10/23 January 1919	Archive, Sketchbook F (Shepard, "Checklist," 734, 743)	Kireyevsky, no. 1074 (cf. Sakharov, III, 15)
4. "*Sektantskaya*" / "Chant dissident"	[Morges], 1 March 1919	Archive, Sketchbook F (Shepard, "Checklist," 729, 743; photo in SelCorrI:425)	Rozhdestvensky/Uspensky, no. 351

LEGEND

A. Folklore sources (texts)

1. Alexander Nikolayevich Afanasyev, *Narodnïye russkiye skazki* (Russian Folk Tales), issued 1855–64 in eight installments. Citations given here are to the three-volume Soviet edition by M. K. Azadovsky, N. P. Andreyev, and Y. M. Sokolov (Moscow, 1936–40). Stravinsky (who began sketching the *Pribaoutki* before his book-buying expedition of July 1914) probably used the fourth edition, ed. A. E. Gruzinsky (Moscow, 1913), in which all the *pribaoutki* are given as alphabetized subentries under no. 251 (V, 235–41).

2. Afanasyev, *Poéticheskiye vozzreniya slavyan na prirodu* (The Slavs' Poetic Outlook on Nature), vol. 2 (Moscow, 1868). On p. 158 is found a partial citation and interpretation of "*Shchuka*" (*Podblyudnïye*, no. 3).

3. Vladimir Ivanovich Dahl (Dal'), *Tolkovïy slovar' zhivogo velikorusskogo yazïka* (Explanatory Dictionary of the Living Great-Russian Language), 4 vols. (1863–66). A saying used to illustrate the word "raspberry" is quoted in the second tableau of *Svadebka*.

4. Pyotr Vasilyevich Kireyevsky, *Pesni sobrannïye P. V. Kireyevskim. Novaya seriya. Izdanï Obshchestvom Lyubiteley Rossyiskoy Slovesnosti pri Imperatorskom Moskovskom Universitete* (Songs Collected by P. V. Kireyevsky. New Series. Published by the Society of Lovers of Russian Literature at the Imperial University of Moscow), vol. 1: *Pesni obryadovïye* (Ritual Songs), ed. V. F. Miller and M. N. Speransky (Moscow, 1911).

5. T. S. Rozhdestvensky and M. I. Uspensky, *Pesni russkikh sektantov mistikov* (Songs of the Russian Mystic Sectarians), Zapiski Imperatorskogo russkogo geograficheskogo obshchestva po otdeleniyu étnografii (Notes of the Ethnographic Division of the Imperial Russian Geographical Society, vol. 35) (St. Petersburg, 1912).

6. Ivan Petrovich Sakharov, *Skazaniya russkogo naroda* (Legends of the Russian People), 3d. ed., vol. 1 (Books 1–4) (St. Petersburg, 1841).

7. Pavel Vasilyevich Sheyn, *Velikorus v svoikh pesnyakh, obichayakh, verovaniyakh i t. p.* (The Great-Russian in His Songs, Customs, Beliefs, etc.) (St. Petersburg, 1898).

8. A. V. Tereshchenko, *Bït russkogo naroda* (Manners and Customs of the Russian People), 7 vols. (St. Petersburg, 1848).

B. Folklore sources (music)

1. Istomin/Dyutsh: *Pesni russkogo naroda, sobrani v guberniyakh Arkhangelskoy i Olonetskoy v 1886 godu. Zapisali slova F. M. Istomin, napevï G. O. Dyutsh* (Songs of the Russian People, Collected in the Archangel and Olonets Provinces in 1886. Words transcribed by F. M. Istomin, tunes by G. O. Dyutsh) (St. Petersburg: Imperial Russian Geographical Society, 1894).

2. Istomin/Lyapunov: *Pesni russkogo naroda, sobrani v guberniyakh Vologodskoy, Vyatskoy i Kostromskoy v 1893 godu. Zapisali slova F. M. Istomin, napevï S. M. Lyapunov* (Songs of the Russian People, Collected in the Vologda, Vyatka, and Kostroma Provinces in 1893. Words transcribed by F. M. Istomin, tunes by S. M. Lyapunov) (St. Petersburg: Imperial Russian Geographical Society, 1899).

C. Documentation sigla

1. Archive. The Stravinsky Archive, consisting of all MSS., letters, and memorabilia that were in the composer's possession at the time of his death, had been catalogued for sale by Sigmund Rothschild in 1970, but remained unsold until 1983, when it was acquired by the Paul Sacher Stiftung, Basel, Switzerland. The "R" numbers in the table refer to the listing in this catalogue, which is available for consultation at the Music Division of the New York Public Library at Lincoln Center (temporary

custodian of the Archive from April to August 1983). During the period of the library's custodianship, an inventory of the musical manuscripts was drawn up by John Shepard, a member of the Special Collections staff who served as curator pro tem of the Archive, and published under the title "The Stravinsky Nachlass: A Provisional Checklist of Music Manuscripts" (MLA Notes 40, no. 4 [June 1984]: 719–50). Shepard correlated the Rothschild listings, as far as possible, with the much earlier catalogue of the MSS. assembled by Robert Craft, published as Appendix C in White's Stravinsky [EWW below]. Though a convenience for those who have no access to the Rothschild catalogue, the correlation is tentative, and has not been followed here (if it had been, the first entry in the table, for "Sorochinka," would have had to read, for example, "C2b or 2c"). However, Shepard's alphabet designations for the ten omnibus sketchbooks in the Archive ("Checklist," 742–43) have been followed in preference either to the Rothschild listings, which do not distinguish sketchbooks from other types of MS., or to the Roman-numeral designations employed in the catalogue prepared by the Kunstmuseum, Basel, for its 1984 exhibit of the Paul Sacher holdings that now encompass the Archive (Stravinsky: Sein Nachlass, sein Bild [Basel, 1984]), which are vague and incomplete. Presumably, the Sacher Stiftung will eventually issue a Stravinsky catalogue of its own.

2. BL Loan. The British Library in London houses two important loan deposits of Stravinsky autographs. Under the siglum Loan 75 are MSS. belonging to J. & W. Chester, and under the siglum Loan 84 are MSS. belonging to Boosey & Hawkes, representing the holdings of the Éditions Russes de Musique at the time the latter firm was acquired by the former.

3. Cary: The Mary Flagler Cary Music Collection at the Pierpont Morgan Library, New York.

4. EWW: Eric Walter White, Stravinsky: The Composer and His Works (Berkeley and Los Angeles: University of California Press, 1966). The "Register of Works" in this volume contains many descriptions of MSS., and transcriptions of dates therefrom. Many have proved inaccurate, making White's register a somewhat risky source. The single instance in which it was found necessary to rely on it for the present table was the very first entry. Though White states explicitly (p. 182) that the MS. of the Tri pesenki is in the possession of Boosey & Hawkes, only the score of the expanded and orchestrated version of the set ("transcrite et légèrement agrandies," Nice, 1929–30) is to be found at present in the British Library (Loan 84/17). White's date is contradicted by autograph material in the Archive in the case of "Sorochinka," the first song in the set; the dates for the others are therefore to be treated with caution.

5. Meyer catalogue: Collection musicale André Meyer (Abbéville, 1973). An album of 251 plates illustrating the holdings of André-Charles Meyer (1884–1974), a French industrialist and avocational musicologist.

6. P&D: Vera Stravinsky and Robert Craft, Stravinsky in Pictures and Documents (New York, 1978). Together with the 1984 Basel exhibition catalogue, this volume is the most extensive source of Stravinsky autograph reproductions (many in color), representing all periods of the composer's career.

7. RS: Rychenberg Stiftung at the Stadtsbibliothek, Winterthur (Switzerland). This collection houses the music autograph holdings of Werner Reinhart, the patron of Histoire du soldat, to whom Stravinsky gave or sold a number of Swiss-period MSS., including that of the Svadebka particell. The Stiftung also possesses the autograph fair copies of the two works dedicated to Reinhart—the Histoire and the Three Pieces for Clarinet Solo—as well as that of the Octuor for wind instruments.

8. SelCorrI: Igor Stravinsky, Selected Correspondence, ed. Robert Craft, vol. 1 (New York, 1982). All three volumes in this series contain copious appendices by Craft, many devoted to richly illustrated chronologies of various individual works.

material. No fair copy of the full score to the *Berceuses* is at present accessible,[47] but the presentation copies in the Meyer collection of the third and fourth songs (in voice and piano arrangement) inscribed by Stravinsky to their dedicatees (Natalia Goncharova and Mikhaíl Laryonov) reveal that the Russian title was simply *Kolïbel'-niye,* "Lullabies," corresponding to that of the section in the Kireyevsky anthology—pp. 300–304, comprising songs nos. 1101–8—from which the texts were drawn.[48] The full Russian title of the *Trois histoires* is found in the manuscript fair copy deposited by J. & W. Chester at the British Library (Loan 75/40). It reads: *Detskiye pesenki dlya odnogo golosa s soprovozhdeniyem f.-p.* (Little Children's Songs for solo voice with pianoforte accompaniment). The *Quatre chants russes,* the last group to be published, seem never to have been given a collective title in Russian; the autographs on deposit at the British Library (Loan 75/48) carry individual headings only. As for the *Baika* (*Renard*), its full Russian title nowhere appears in the sketch material, where the piece is normally referred to as *Lisa i petukh* (The Vixen and the Rooster). The title given in Table 2 is derived from a letter from Stravinsky to his mother, cited there. It is, moreover, by no means clear why Ramuz, in translating the text, saw fit to change Afanasyev's ram (*baran*) into a billy goat (*bouc*), or why Stravinsky let him do so. By the time he dictated his octogenarian memoirs of *Renard,*[49] Stravinsky evidently thought the goat was original (even though the ram survived in the garbled version of the original full title he gave Craft on that occasion).

Dates on these fair copies in every case coincide with and corroborate those in the sketchbooks (given in the table),[50] establishing as a fact Stravinsky's habit of

47. One belongs to the estate of Ernest Ansermet (see SelCorrIII:521); another was sold by Stravinsky to Princess Violette Murat in 1917 (P&D:137–38).

48. The inscriptions, in a deliberately artificial, archaic style reminiscent of Musorgsky's letters and dedications, read as follows: no. 3, "*Nataliye Goncharovoy ot predannogo sochinitelya sey pesni—odnoy iz Kolïbel'nikh, ey i Mikhaílu Laryonovu posvyashchonnikh*" ("To Natalia Goncharova from the devoted creator of this song—one of the Lullabies dedicated to her and Mikhail Larionov"); no. 4, "*Mikhaílu Fyodorovichu Laryonovu daryu na dobruyu pamyat' siyu pesnyu, odnu iz 'kolïbel'nikh' emu i Nataliye Sergeyevne Goncharovoy posvyashchonnikh*" ("To Mikhail Fyodorovich Laryonov I present as a keepsake this song, one of the four 'lullabies' dedicated to him and Natalia Sergeyevna Goncharova"). The date on the latter ms. was misread by White. It maintains the stilted diction of the inscription, as follows: "*Morzh / leto ot r. Kh. / 1915 / Noyabrya 2 dnya / Igor' Stravinskiy*" ("Morges, in the year of our Lord 1915, on the second day of November, Igor Stravinsky"). In the stock phrase *leto ot r. Kh.* (literally, "year from the birth of Christ"), the old-Russian word "year" is cognate to the modern Russian word for "summer." From this, plus the date of the sketch for the first song and the date given on the Goncharova inscription—also misread (Stravinsky gives a typical Russian double date "18/5 April 1915"; White took the second number to refer to the month and ignored the actual month Stravinsky named)—White came up with four dates for the price of three: "The sketch for the first song is dated Morges 11 September 1915. . . . According to the Catalogue of the *Collection Musicale André Meyer* (Abbéville), the others are dated 18.5.1915, summer 1915 [*sic*] and 2 November" (*Stravinsky: The Composer and His Work,* 201). No ms. of the second song in the set is at present accessible, and it cannot be precisely dated. But if it is true, as White has it, that the *Berceuses* were begun at Château d'Oex, it must date from the early months of 1915. The first edition carried the date "1915–16," and this has been followed by virtually all writers. Yet it cannot be correct. The dedicatory inscription to Laryonov, penned in November 1915, already refers to the complete set of four songs.

49. E&D:119/135.

50. The only discrepancy is that the date of the "*Sektantskaya*" ("Mars 1919") is less precise.

repeating the date on which actual composition was completed on all subsequent copies.[51] Thus, with few demonstrable exceptions,[52] the dates on Stravinsky's fair copies can be relied upon for purposes of chronology. This remains the rule even when considerable revision is involved. A remarkable case in point is *"Tilim-bom,"* the first of the *Detskiye pesenki*. Its unpublished original version is only half the length of the one that has become so well known. Not only that, but the piano part is extremely simple: except for the refrains it consists of nothing but the left-hand ostinato, bringing to mind the "Song of the Bear" in the same set and suggesting the intriguing possibility that Stravinsky originally intended his "Little Children's Songs" actually to be sung and played by children—such as his seven-year-old "fils cadet," Svetik (Soulima), to whom the set is dedicated (see Ex. 15.1). Whatever the case, this primitive version of the song carries the same date as the draft in the Stravinsky Archive listed in Table 2, in which the piece is fitted out with more verses (by the composer) and an adult pianist's right hand is kept very busy throughout.[53]

A particularly rich lode of widely read and quoted misinformation surrounds the *Pribaoutki*, the first set of "Swiss" songs to have been composed. In *Expositions and Developments*, Stravinsky compared them with limericks and claimed that "according to popular tradition they derive from a type of game in which someone says a word, which someone else then adds to, and which third and fourth persons develop, and so on, with utmost speed."[54] No ethnographic or lexicographic source corroborates this statement, and given the abundance of casual ad hoc pronouncements in the Conversations books, one cannot accord it the benefit of the doubt.[55] Meanwhile, the redoubtable *Explanatory Dictionary of the Living Great-Russian Language (Tolkovy slovar' zhivogo velikorusskogo yazïka)* by Vladimir Dahl (Dal'), the richest "argosy" of all and exactly contemporary with Stravinsky's sources, indicates that the word *pribautka* is derived from *bayat'*, a rural dialect form of the verb

51. This is again a habit he had in common with Musorgsky; see Taruskin, " 'Little Star,' " 73–77.
52. One may be *"Sorochenka,"* the first entry in Table 2, if White is correct as to the date of the fair copy.
53. The extra verses consist in part of a repeat of the opening ones, with *"lyudi"* (people) standing in for the animals originally named. A letter from Stravinsky to Henry Kling of J. & W. Chester (19 January 1924; in P&D:618n.219) seems to imply that the expanded text was concocted for the just-completed orchestrated version of the song. This is not the case: the version for voice and piano published by Chester in 1920 is textually identical to the orchestrated version.
54. E&D:137/121.
55. Yet Stravinsky's authority is such that not even Soviet researchers have questioned it. Yuriy Paísov, for example, merely notes that "there is no such explanation in the major reference works and studies of folklore" and conjectures that "the composer might possibly have received this information from one or another of his friends (e.g., from S. Mitusov), who knew folk customs" ("Russkiy fol'klor v vokal'no-khorovom tvorchestve Stravinskogo," in G. S. Alfeyevskaya and I. Y. Vershinina, eds., *I. F. Stravinskiy: Stat'i, vospominaniya* [Moscow: Sovetskiy Kompozitor, 1985], 98n.1). How, one wonders, did Mitusov, a Leningrad piano teacher, get promoted to such a status of ethnographical expertise?

EXAMPLE 15.1 (*continued*)

ko - ziy dom. Be-zhit ku-ri - tsa s ve-drom za - li-vat' ko-ziy dom. A

za ne-yu pe-tu-shok, zo-lo-toy gre-be-shok, ta-shchit le -

- sen-ku, po-yot pe - sen-ku: Ti - lim bom

Ti - lim bom Mï po - tu-shim ko - ziy dom.

[Ding dong bell / Ding dong bell / The goat shed caught fire / The goat leaped out, / Its eyes were bulging, / The goat shakes its tail, / Calls people to help. / The kitty-cat rings the bell, / Summons all to come running to the fire. / "Ding dong bell / Ding dong bell / Save the goat shed!" / The hen comes running with a bucket / To douse the goat shed. / And after it the cock, / golden-comb, / hauls a stepladder, / sings (this) song: / "Ding dong bell, / Ding dong bell, / We'll put out / the goat shed!"] (Trans. RT)

"to say," which would make it a cognate to the more standard *prigovorka,* which has two pertinent meanings: a literal, etymological one, denoting speech accompanying action; and one derived by analogy from *prislov'ye,* an expression inserted into peasant speech purely for euphony, for embellishment, or for comic effect.[56]

Even in Stravinsky's outrageous explanation of the *Pribaoutki* set there is a phrase that suggests he recalled Dahl (or even consulted him): "It means 'a telling,' 'pri' being the Latin 'pre'[!] and 'baout' deriving from the Old Russian infinitive 'to say.' "[57] Dahl gives *skladnaya prigovorka* ("well-turned phrase" or "neat turn of phrase") as his primary standard-Russian cognate for *pribautka,* but then cites a wealth of secondary applications within a specifically peasant context: "A saying, a witty remark in the guise of an aphorism, a rhetorical flourish [*priskazka*]; sometimes it is a meaningless but amusing assortment of words. . . ."[58]

The little garland of thirty *pribautki* that Dahl appended to his huge collection entitled *Sayings of the Russian People* defines the genre by example much better than any dictionary could do in the abstract. Most of these depend on plays of words, on fortuitous rhymes, on onomatopoeia, on alliteration, most of all on assonance. Here is one that will appeal to musicians; it belongs to a type used by storytellers to finish up a skazka with a flourish:

> Gúsi v gúsli, útki v dúdki, voróni v koróbi, tarakáni v barabáni, kozá v sérom sarafáne, koróva v rogózhe, vsekh dorózhe.[59]

> Geese [playing] gusli, ducks [playing] bagpipes, ravens [beating] baskets, cockroaches [beating] drums, a nanny goat in a grey skirt, a cow wrapped up in burlap will cost you the most of all.

In English we might call this a jingle, which will do as well as any other word as a simple equivalent for *pribautka,* at least for the ones Stravinsky set. Many *pribautki,* including the twenty-two collected by Afanasyev, belong to a type other folklorists (e.g. Sheyn) designate *poteshki,* that is, jingles sung by or for the amusement of children. We would call them nursery rhymes (except that many of them do not rhyme), and they encompass such subcategories as tongue twisters (cf. "*Polkovnik,*" the third in Stravinsky's set),[60] riddles (cf. "*Starets i zayats,*" Stravin-

---

56. See S. G. Barkhudarov et al., *Slovar' russkogo yazïka* (Moscow: Akademiya Nauk SSSR, Institut Russkogo Yazïka, 1959), s.v. *Prislov'ye,* 3:598.

57. E&D:137/121.

58. V. I. Dahl, *Tolkovïy slovar' zhivogo velikorusskogo yazïka* (1863–66; rpt. Tokyo: Tachibana Shoten, 1934; and Tokyo: Nauka Reprint Co., 1984), s.v. "*Pribautka,*" 3:1035. A longer entry, under "*Bautka*" (1:138), gives examples of both the meaningful and the nonsense variety.

59. V. I. Dahl, *Poslovitsï russkogo naroda* (St. Petersburg, 1862), 1095.

60. Indeed, Edward J. Dent, reviewing the first British performance of the *Pribaoutki* (20 July 1920 at Wigmore Hall, with Olga Haley and an ensemble conducted by Ansermet), noticing the P-alliteration in the Russian text (though the songs were sung in French) and taking it all (not entirely without reason) as the height of dada, made merry over the spectacle of "an eminent Swiss conductor, a distinguished English singer, eight of the finest instrumental players in London, an audience representing the élite of Chelsea, of Mayfair, of Bloomsbury—and all for the sake of the Russian equivalent of 'Peter Piper picked a peck of pickled pepper'!" (*Athenaeum,* 30 July 1920, 153).

sky's no. 2), counting and choosing games (cf. the "*Zapevnaya*" in the *Quatre chants russes*).

Far from the kind of ephemeral, improvised thing Stravinsky described to Craft in *Expositions and Developments,* these are precious antiques, folkloric shards and remnants perpetuated in oral tradition over generations, even centuries. As such they especially appealed to Afanasyev, proponent of the "mythological school" of folklore, ever on the lookout for atavisms of ancient rites and customs: "*Pribautki,*" he observed, "in the form in which one hears them now on the lips of the people, apparently comprise excerpts from a variety of folk verbal prototypes: the songs, stories, and [even] the laments that accompany [popular] games and rituals."[61] While not exactly verse, *pribautki* are nonetheless distinguished, according to Afanasyev, by their strongly rhythmic character, their sporadic resort to rhyme, and the alliteration and assonance already observed and illustrated. He concludes: "Many expressions of a verselike character such as one finds especially often in animal tales [e.g., the 'Song of the Bear,' no. 3 in Stravinsky's *Detskiye pesenki*], have gone over into proverbs and jingles [*poslovitsï i pribautki*]. From certain jingles one can surmise that in addition to the animal tales that have been collected up to now, others of a similar kind exist, or at least have existed, among the people."[62]

The way Stravinsky's *Baika* (*Renard*) gradually emerged from sketches for jingles (*pribautki*) and children's songs (*detskiye pesenki*)—a process we shall trace in detail in the next chapter—shows not only that he had read these suggestive words of Afanasyev, but that they confirmed the idea of organic artistic creation on a bed-rock of folklore that ruled the creative quests of his "Turanian" period.

Bedrock of another sort is represented by the *Kolïbel'nïye,* the lullabies Stravinsky set for voice and clarinet ensemble and published under Ramuz's title as *Berceuses du chat.* The texts in this set had all appeared as illustrations to an article, "Lullabies of the Commonfolk" ("*Prostonarodnïye kolïbel'nïye*") by one V. Passek, that had appeared in the Slavophile journal *Moskvityanin* in the 1850s. The editor, Mikhaíl Pogodin, had sent the article to Pyotr Kireyevsky, who incorporated it in its entirety into the book from which Stravinsky made his selection.

In presenting his collection of lullabies to his readers, Passek had made the interesting point that such songs are the first music anyone hears. That notion must have appealed to Stravinsky, preoccupied as he was with finding a "degree zero" from which to build a style. "The lullabies of all peoples contain the kernel, the primal image [*pervoobraz*] of a people's character and life," wrote the collector. Further, he associated that kernel, in the case of the Russian people, with the ubiq-

61. A. N. Afanasyev, *Russkiye narodnïye skazki,* 4th ed., ed. A. Gruzinsky (Moscow: Tip. Tovari-shchestva I. D. Sïtina, 1913–14), 5:240.
62. Ibid.

uitous image of the petted or otherwise pampered kitty-cat (*kotin'ka*), whose purring is taken as symbolic of the mother's tenderness and the infant's security.[63] This relation must have determined the choice of a soft, susurrant trio of clarinets to accompany Stravinsky's settings.

Yet the French title is a misnomer withal, for the lullabies are sung neither to nor by a cat. Their felinity is strictly metaphorical: only in no. 4 is the cat a bit more concretely present, as an object of comparison with the baby. Here is the text as given by Kireyevsky (Stravinsky's setting omits lines 5 and 6):

U kotá, kotá	The cat has, he has
Kolïbél'ka zolotá,	A golden cradle,
A u dityátki movó	But my dear child has
I polúchshe tovó:	A still better one than that:
Lyúlya tóchenaya,	His cradle is finely-chiseled
Pozolóchenaya!	[And] gilded!
U kotá, kotá	The cat has, he has
I podúshechka belá,	Also a little white pillow,
U movó-li u dityá	But my own child has
I beléye tovó.	A whiter one than that.
U kotá, kotá	The cat has, he has
I postélyushka myagká,	Also a nice soft bed,
U movó-li u dityá	But my own child has
I pomyágche tovó.	An even softer one than that.
U kotá, kotá	The cat has, he has
Odeálechko tepló,	A nice warm blanket,
U movó-li u dityá	But my child has
I tepléye tovó.	An even warmer one than that.[64]

In no. 3 there is no cat at all. Yet as in the case of the so-called "Saucers" (about which below), the aging Stravinsky, esthetically remote from his earlier music and indifferent to it, only compounded the misnomer. Misled by the standard title, forgetting it was not his, he perpetrated (or let pass) a completely irrelevant English counterpart: "Cat's Cradle Songs," a title first used on Stravinsky's 1964 recording of the set (Columbia MS 7439) and now firmly ensconced in Eric Walter White's gazeteer and the New Grove work list, is a deplorable solecism that introduces a wholly extraneous and cheapening coyness altogether at variance with the tender originals. As we have seen, Stravinsky had at first intended simply to call the songs "Lullabies." That wish might as well be respected.

The text of "*Selezeň*," the first of the *Quatre chants russes,* is a conflation of two variants, both published by Sakharov, of a khorovod-type song (*khorovodnaya*) that

---

63. See P. V. Kireyevsky, *Pesni, sobrannïye P. V. Kireyevskim. Novaya seriya,* vol. 1: *Pesni obryadnïye,* ed. V. F. Miller and M. N. Speransky (Moscow: A. I. Snegiryova, 1911), 300–302.

64. This and—unless otherwise specified—all the other folk texts in this chapter have been kindly translated for this book by Simon Karlinsky.

accompanied a special game of tag Stravinsky might have known from childhood. It is commonly played by Russian children to this day. As Sakharov described it:

> In the evening the players gather in a meadow and make a circle, in the center of which two players assume their place: the Drake and the Duck. The circle dancers sing the song, moving around the Drake and the Duck, joining hand to hand, while the Duck begins diving out of the circle. The players turn her back; the Drake tries to catch the Duck. The diving and chasing continue until the Drake catches the Duck. It often happens that the players, wishing to continue the game, restrain the Drake. This they call "getting his dander up" [*podzadorivai zador*]. The Duck makes fun of the Drake.[65]

The text of "*Gusi-lebedi*" (*Detskiye pesenki*, no. 2) is also related to a game of tag. A bunch of children sing, "Gúsi-lébedi domóy / Sériy volk pod goróy" ("Geese and swans run home! The grey wolf is down the hill!"), after which the child playing the wolf chases the others; the one caught becomes the wolf in turn.[66]

Finally, the text of the "*Sektantskaya*," the last of the *Quatre chants russes*, returns us to the world of the mystic sects of *khlïstï* and *skoptsï*, with which Stravinsky had flirted in the past through a filter of Symbolist verse (Gorodetsky, Balmont). Now he engaged it directly. The song Stravinsky chose was, as might by now be expected, a *pesnya obryadovaya*, a ritual song. It expresses a yearning for the *radeniye*, the ecstatic whirling dance of the *khlïst* liturgy, and a sense of isolation from one's brothers and sisters in the sect, with whom one shared a love at once carnal and spiritual:[67]

Yálitsa-myatélitsa	The barren blizzard led me astray,
Zav'yála-zamyatélila	It covered with snow and swept snow
Vse putí moí dorózhen'ki;	On all my paths and roads.
Nel'zyá proytí i proyékhati	I cannot walk nor can I drive
K rodímomu bátyushke,	To my own Father,
K moyemú tsaryú nebésnomu.	To my King in Heaven.
U rodímogo u bátyushki	At my own Father's
Vse syóstrï i brát'ya lyubóvnïye,	Are all my loving brothers and sisters,
Vse lyubóvnïye i dukhóvnïye,	They are all loving and spiritual,
Svyatím Bógom ízbrannïye.	Selected by the Holy God.

The doxology formula at the end of Stravinsky's setting—

---

65. I. P. Sakharov, *Skazaniya russkogo naroda*, 3d ed. (St. Petersburg, 1914), 3:76.
66. Simon Karlinsky, personal communication, 14 December 1986.
67. See T. S. Rozhdestvensky and M. I. Uspensky, *Pesni russkikh sektantov mistikov*, Zapiski Imperatorskogo russkogo geograficheskogo obshchestva po otdeleniyu ètnografii, vol. 35 (St. Petersburg, 1912), xliii. Stravinsky distorted the text in setting it by imposing the *akaniye* pronunciation he had encountered in Kireyevsky's transcription of the "*Podblyudnaya*" (*Quatre chants russes*, no. 3; see below).

Bógu sláva, chest', derzháva　　　　Glory to God, and honor and power,
Vo vekí vekóv amín.　　　　　　　For ever and ever, amen.
Tebyá Góspodu blagodarím　　　　We give thanks to Thee O Lord

—was a standard one the composer found in the same anthology of sectarian verse as the "*Sektantskaya*" itself. He substituted "to Jesus Christ" for "honor" (thus: "Glory to God, power to Christ").

Stravinsky first intended the song for a trio consisting of voice, flute, and cimbalom.[68] He had first used the Hungarian cabaret instrument as a substitute for gusli in the *Baika*. It had the same significance in the "*Sektantskaya*," for the gusli symbolized the Psalmist's harp in *khlüst* literature.[69] References in sectarian texts (or, for that matter, in Balmont's *Zelyonïy vertograd*) to playing or hearing gusli were "a symbolic expression signifying vatic prophecy, resounding like a heavenly music over the sectarian *radeniye*."[70]

Stravinsky's "*Sektantskaya*," with its prevailing mood of nostalgia and homesickness, is often justly viewed as symbolic of the spirit that motivated what we have been calling the composer's Turanian phase, which in fact it closed. But all the music Stravinsky wrote during the half-decade that followed *The Nightingale* answered precisely to the needs articulated by Prince Trubetskoy: to forge—after having first acknowledged the inauthenticity of "European efforts to go native"[71]— an unprecedented, truly Russian high culture out of the most irreducibly Turanian elements in the "lower strata" of Russian folk art, literature, and music.[72]

''SONGS SUNG IN THE PRESENCE OF THE BOWL''

The *Four Russian Peasant Songs* for women's chorus (*Podblyudnïye*), though they were scheduled for publication by Chester along with the rest of Stravinsky's wartime output,[73] were not issued at the time. Ten years later, on 16 December 1929, Chester assigned German rights to B. Schott's Söhne in return for a small

68. For a discussion of this version, and a facsimile of Stravinsky's sketches for it, see App. I in SelCorrI:421–29.

69. Hence the aptness of Stravinsky's later transcription of the song (as "A Russian Spiritual") in his *Four Songs* of 1954, where the cimbalom part is largely taken over by the harp.

70. Rozhdestvensky and Uspensky, *Pesni russkikh sektantov*, xxiv.

71. Trubetskoy, *Yevropa i chelovechestvo*, 6.

72. See also Trubetskoy, "Verkhi i nizï russkoy kul'turï," in Souvtchinsky (ed.), *Iskhod k Vostoku*, 86–103; and idem, "O turanskom èlemente v russkoy kul'ture," in Souvtchinsky (ed.), *Yevraziyskiy vremennik*, 351–77; both are reprinted in N. S. Trubetskoy, *K probleme russkogo samopoznaniya* (Paris: Yevraziyskoye Knigoizdatel'stvo, 1927), 21–33, 34–53, respectively.

73. According to White (*Stravinsky: The Composer and His Works*, 211), Stravinsky signed a contract with the firm in December 1919; an article in the *Music Student*, no. 13 (December 1920), announced that they were "shortly to be published by J. & W. Chester."

consideration.[74] The Schott edition actually preceded Chester's. It came out in 1930, with Russian and German text and a curious German title: *Unterschale: vier russische Bauernlieder für Frauenchor und eine Solostimme a cappella.*

The neologism *Unterschale* was a misbegotten adaptation of a note Stravinsky had written on a table of queries he was sent by the publisher: "Der Generaltitel dieser 4 russischer Bauernlieder ist 'Podblyudnïye' [written in Russian letters] d.h. Unterschale-Warsagelider [*sic*]."[75] The Schott editors unfortunately disregarded the second term, which is an accurate designation of *podblyudnïye*—that is, sooth-saying songs—and chose instead Stravinsky's clumsy attempt at a cognate: "Under-the-Bowl Songs." This rendering is not merely meaningless without reference to the ritual the songs accompany (about which see below), it is incorrect. In the present context the prefix *pod-,* which usually means "under," as Stravinsky here assumed, actually means "in the presence or environs of." A properly literal (if still inscrutable) rendering would be "songs sung in the presence of the bowl."

The problem was compounded, with dire results for English speakers, when Stravinsky discussed the choruses, and the meaning of their title, in *Expositions and Developments* some three decades later. His memory—and, perhaps, his Russian—having begun to weaken, he evidently misconstrued the Russian title through the German one as referring to saucers, forgetting that *Unterschal* had been his own coinage (the German word for saucer being *Untertasse*), and manufacturing an imaginary Russian equivalent by analogy to the German: *pod* (*unter*) + *blyudo* (*Schal*) = "*podblyudo*" (forgetting that the actual Russian word for saucer was *blyudtse*). He suggested "Saucer-Readings" or "Saucer-Riddles" as a title for the set (in subsequent writings, both he and Craft continued to refer to the choruses simply as "Saucers"), and proceeded to justify his mistranslation with a bit of preposterous ad hoc ethnography.[76] For a last bit of disinformation, Stravinsky named Afanasyev as the source of the texts.

The best English rendering for the term *podblyudnïye pesni* is probably the one Nabokov came up with in the commentary to his translation of Pushkin's *Eugene Onegin:* "dish-divination songs."[77] The ceremony they accompanied was given a matchless description by Ivan Sakharov, the compiler of the book from which Stravinsky drew his texts, in the course of a description of the old-time Russian Yule (*russkiye svyatki*):

---

74. My thanks to Dr. Peter Hauser of B. Schott's Söhne for a copy of the Memorandum of Agreement. A letter from Stravinsky to Willy Strecker of Schott's (27 December 1929) gives some background: "I am glad it occurred to me, the last time I was in London, to speak to you about my a cappella choruses, which have been in the safe at the glorious J. & W. Chester Ltd. for ten solid years now. Had you not intervened, they would have spent another ten in that dirty flea bin . . ." (SelCorrIII:222).

75. Note dated Nice, 30 December 1929; in the Schott Archives. Thanks again to Peter Hauser for a copy.

76. See E&D:134–35/118–19.

77. See *Eugene Onegin: A Novel in Verse by Aleksandr Pushkin, Translated from the Russian, with a Commentary, by Vladimir Nabokov,* Bollingen Series 72 (New York: Pantheon Books, 1964), 2:496.

FIG. 15.3. *Lubok* (1856) showing maidens playing guessing games during the *svyatki*, including (at left rear) the ceremony of "dish divination" at which *podblyudnïye* are sung.

When all the festivities were done they would carry in a table and set it down in the middle of the room. The old men and women would get up and make room for the young and the betrothed of both sexes. The chief matchmaker would appear with a tablecloth and cover the table. The oldest dry-nurse would bring in a serving dish [*blyudo*] full of water and place it on the table. The young maidens, the marriageable girls, the old women, and the betrothed would take off their rings, earrings, and other trinkets and put them on the table, meanwhile "guessing their fate" silently over them. The hostess would produce another tablecloth and the matchmaker would cover the dish with it. The guests sat themselves round in a circle. In the middle of the circle the matchmaker would sit down directly opposite the dish. The dry-nurses would put little pieces of bread and salt on top of the covering cloth, and three little pieces of coal. The matchmaker would sing the first song: "Bread and Salt" ["*Khleba da soli*"]. All the seated guests would chant along in an undertone. At the end of the first song the matchmaker would raise the covering cloth and drop the bread, the salt, and the three pieces of coal into the dish, and the guests would put in their things. The dish would be covered again. After this would begin the singing of the yuletide dish-divination songs [*svyatochnïye podblyudnïye pesni*]. During the singing the matchmaker would stir the things in the dish and at the end of the song would shake it. Every song had its own meaning, although these meanings varied from place to place. Thus in various places the same meaning might be given to different songs, depending on the local custom. These meanings were: a quick marriage, a meeting, marriage to an equal, marriage to a person of high rank, a proposal of marriage, poverty, a comfortable life, a wedding, wealth, the granting of one's wish, a merry life, a husband for the girls, a wife for the youths, good fortune, a journey, a love marriage, financial gain, marriage to a courtier, misfortune, death, illness, joy. At the end of each song a special refrain was sung:

Da komu mï speli, tomu dobro. Slava!
Komu vïnetsya, tomu sbudetsya. Slava!
Skoro sbudetsya, ne minuyetsya. Slava![78]

For whom we have sung we wish the best. Glory!
Whoever draws it out, for that one will it come true. Glory!
It will soon come true, there is no escaping it. Glory!

At this point a trinket is drawn from the dish, and the owner's fate is the one vouchsafed by the preceding song—all in all an apt preface, one might say, to *Svadebka*. The description by P. V. Sheyn puts a slightly different and (with reference to *Svadebka*) an even apter slant on the proceedings: "On New Year's Eve the girls gather together and habitually foretell their future husbands in this way: they place a cup or bowl of water on the table and put their rings and earrings in it, then cover it up with a table cloth. All sit down at the table without crossing themselves, and the women who know the songs the best begin to sing, while each maiden tries to fish out her ring to the strains of that verse of the song corresponding to her heart's desire."[79]

In any case, the songs have absolutely nothing to do with saucers, and Stravinsky's howler, which has unhappily entered musicians' and even scholarly parlance as an ersatz title for the choruses, ought to be discarded. Since, as we shall see, not all of the choruses in Stravinsky's set are true *podblyudnïye,* the best solution might be to revert to the title under which Chester finally got around to publishing them in 1932. Although the choruses appeared in this edition with Russian, French, and English texts, no Russian title was given to the whole (the Chester editors no doubt finding the *Podblyudnïye/Unterschale* farrago unfixable), and Schott's subtitle was translated in its place: *Four Russian Peasant Songs/Quatre chants paysans russes.*

What was doubtless the original Russian title is found today on the title page of a fair copy Stravinsky presented in 1917 to Vasiliy Kibalchich, the conductor of the first performance. This manuscript (no. 393 in the Mary Flagler Cary Collection at the Pierpont Morgan Library, New York) presents the songs in order of composition rather than that of eventual publication. This was likely the order in which they were performed under Kibalchich by the choir of the Russian church in Geneva. The title (given in Russian in Table 2) very accurately describes the contents of the set: "Three Dish-Divination Songs and One New Year's Song," *Ovsen* being the name of one of the avatars of the Russian sun deity, to whom calendar songs were addressed at New Year's. A label (now loose, originally pasted to the flyleaf) translates *pesni podblyudnïye* as "Chants des jeux de Noël"—which, it turns out, is how Calvocoressi rendered the phrase in his translation of the texts in the nearly contemporaneous French reprint of the Rimsky-Korsakov folk song anthol-

78. Sakharov, *Skazaniya russkogo naroda* 3:8.
79. Sheyn, *Russkie narodnye pesni,* pt. 1: *Pesni plyasovïye i besednïye,* 372.

ogy, which contains several *podblyudnïye*. Stravinsky must have been Calvocoressi's source for this phrase, since he would have been far likelier than Calvocoressi to know that dish-divination songs were performed during the "twelve days of Christmas," known in Russian as the *svyatki* (so that an alternate term for *podblyud-nïye pesni* was *svyatochnïye pesni*). At any rate, the title page on the Morgan Library manuscript is the only one we have in Stravinsky's hand for the set as it stands, and should be regarded as definitive. (The manuscript fair copy in the Archive, from which the dates given in Table 2 for the second, third, and fourth choruses were derived, is untitled.)

The qualification "as it stands" is necessary because a third fair copy of the choruses is known to exist (though its whereabouts are at present unknown), and its title page gives tantalizing testimony to the existence of an unpublished fifth chorus. This manuscript was the one Stravinsky submitted to Chester as printer's exemplar in 1919. Its title page, together with the first page of "*Puzishche*" (the last in the set as published), were reproduced as illustration to an article by Edwin Evans entitled "The Stravinsky Debate," which appeared the next year in Percy Scholes's magazine the *Music Student*.[80] As in the Morgan Library score, the choruses are listed in order of composition, with the song to Ovseñ separated from the *pod-blyudnïye* (Fig. 15.4). The *podblyudnïye* as a whole are dedicated to Ruzhena Vla-stimilovna Khvoshchinskaya, the wife of one of the attachés at the Russian embassy in Rome.[81] The song to Ovseñ is dedicated to Kibalchich.

The last title listed under the heading "*Podblyudnïye*" (directly above the ornamental bird design in the middle of the page) is one that does not belong to the published set: "*Na korïte sizhu*" ("I'm Sitting on the Trough"); and sure enough, a text with that incipit is found among the *podblyudnïye* in Sakharov's *Skazaniya russkogo naroda*, immediately following "*Shchuka*" (as usual, the exclamation "*Slava!*"—"Glory!"—follows each line of the text):

Na korïte sizhú,	I'm sitting on the [overturned] trough,
Ya korísti glyazhú,	I'm looking for some advantage,
Ya yeshchó posizhú,	I'll sit some more,
Ya yeshchó poglyazhú;	I'll look some more;
Ya glyad'-poglyád'	I glance here and there,
I koríst' prishlá na dvor,	And advantage came to [our] homestead,
I koríst' na dvor,	There's advantage at our home,
Zhenikhí za stol.[82]	There are suitors at our table.

Sketchbook D in the Archive (as Shepard lists them; see the legend to Table 2)

80. Edwin Evans, "The Stravinsky Debate," *Music Student*, no. 13 (December 1920): 141, 143; see also n. 73.
81. P&D:617.
82. Sakharov, *Skazaniya russkogo naroda* 3:13.

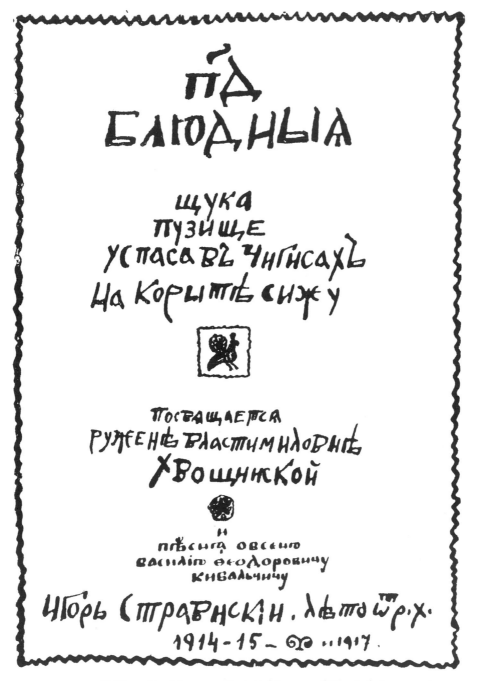

FIG. 15.4. Calligraphic title page of a lost fair copy of Stravinsky's peasant chorus, listing a fifth setting, at present unknown: "*POD* / *BLYUDNÏYE* / *Shchuka* / *Puzishche* / *U spasa v Chigisakh* / *Na korïte sizhu* // Dedicated to Ruzhena Vlastimilovna / Khvoshchinskaya // and / a song to Ovseñ / [dedicated to] Vasiliy Fyodorovich / Kibalchich // Igor Stravinsky, AD / 1914–15—... 1917."

opens with the *podblyudnïye* texts all copied out—and this one is among them.[83] Finally, in Sketchbook A, the music of the chorus is sketched out, preceded by a notation of its main tune (marked "*k podblyudnïm*," "for the *podblyudnïye*") that bears the earmarks of a copied-out source melody, the only such among the *podblyudnïye* materials in the Archive (Ex. 15.2).

The "*Na korïte*" sketch is found after the dated sketches for "*U Spasa v Chigisakh*," as listed in the table. Thus the "new" chorus would indeed have been the last of the *podblyudnïye* (properly so called, as distinct from the New Year's song) to be composed. The fact that it was listed on the calligraphic title page of the fair copy Stravinsky sent Chester for printing seems virtually unassailable prima facie evidence that he had in fact completed the song (though after he had given the Morgan Library manuscript to Kibalchich) and intended at one time to publish it.[84]

The three *podblyudnïye pesni* Stravinsky did publish have been variously interpreted in the ethnographic sources. No. 1 is unquestionably the best known of all the dish-divination songs on record—except, that is, for the famous "Glory" song in the Coronation scene from *Boris Godunov*, which, despite the use to which Musorgsky put it, is really just a lowly *podblyudnaya* that would never have been sung at a royal coronation. Stravinsky's no. 1 runs as follows:

83. In the last line Stravinsky substituted *sto rubley* (a hundred rubles) for *zhenikhi* (suitors). Another unused text in the sketchbook is a "Song to Ovseñ" that is found in Sakharov one page before the one Stravinsky did set (in the transliteration that follows, the stresses are shown as Stravinsky marked them):

Ai vo bóre, bóre,	In the forest, the pine-forest,
Stoyala tam sosná,	There stood a pine-tree,
Zelená, kudryavá.	Green and shaggy.
Oy Ovseñ! oy Ovseñ!	Oh, Ovsen! Oh, Ovsen!
Yekhali boyare,	The Boyars came,
Sosnu srubili,	Cut down the pine,
Doshchechki pilili,	Sawed it into planks,
Mostochik mostili,	Built a bridge,
Suknom ustilali,	Covered it with cloth,
Gvozd'mi obivali.	Fastened it with nails.
Oy Ovseñ! oy Ovseñ!	Oh, Ovsen! Oh, Ovsen!
Komu-zh, komu yekhat'	Who, who will go
Po tomu mostochku?	Along that bridge?
Yekhat' tam Ovsenyu	Ovsen will go there,
Da novomu godu.	And the New Year.
Oy Ovseñ! oy Ovseñ!	Oh, Ovsen! Oh, Ovsen!
[—Sakharov, *Skazaniya* 3:259]	—Ralston, *Songs of the Russian People*, 202–3

84. The manuscript depicted in Figure 15.4 is not at present in the possession of J. & W. Chester, as I was informed upon personal application on 15 May 1985. The Chester deposit at the British Library contains only a copyist's score of the four published songs (Loan 75/39). Nor has the ms. been located at the Schott Archive (communication from Eva Schneider of B. Schott's Söhne, 2 August 1985, pursuant to personal inquiry on 28 May of the same year). The "new" song may yet reside with the heirs to Mme Khvoshchinskaya's estate. Its musical material may have been reworked into the "*Podblyudnaya*" from the *Quatre chants russes*, which would account for its never having been published.

EXAMPLE 15.2

a. Source melody in sketchbook ("for the *podblyudnïye*")

K podblyudnïm

b. Sketch for "*Na korïte sizhu*"

1. Na ko - rï - te si - zhu ya ko - rïs - ti glya - zhu
2. Ta yeshch - o po - si - zhu ya yeshch - o po - glya - zhu
3. I ya glyad'_____ po - glyad' ko - rïst' pri - shla na dvor
4. I ko - rïst' na dvo - or sto - ru - bley na stol___

Soprani:

Alti: sla - va sla - va

U Spasa v Chigasakh za Yauzoyu, Slava! — At Our Savior's Church in Chigasï beyond the Yauza, Glory!

Zhivut muzhiki bogatïye, Slava! — Live wealthy peasants, Glory!

Grebut zoloto lopatami, Slava! — They rake in gold by the shovelful, Glory!

Chisto serebro lukoshkami. Slava! — Pure silver by the basketful. Glory!

According to Tereshchenko, this song foretells "marriage to a wealthy man,"[85] while Nabokov, prompted by Pushkin's own interpretation of the song in *Eugene Onegin* (V:8, note 29), read it as portending "death for elderly people."[86] Stravinsky may well have fastened on this most famous of all *podblyudnïye* for its reverberations with Pushkin's beloved novel.

"*Shchuka*" (Stravinsky's no. 3), with its gold, silver, and diamonds, has been universally interpreted as a promise of wealth and contentment (*sïtost'*):[87]

Shchuka shla iz Novagoroda, Slava! — A pike swam from Newtown, Glory!

Ona khvost volokla iz Belaózera, Slava! — It dragged its tail from Whitelake, Glory!

Kak na shchuke cheshuyka serebryanaya, Slava! — That pike had scales of silver, Glory!

Chto serebryanaya, pozolochenaya; Slava! — They were of silver [and] gilded; Glory!

Kak u shchuke spina zhemchugom spletena, Slava! — The pike's back was plaited with pearls, Glory!

Kak golovka u shchuki unizanaya, Slava! — The pike's head was embroidered with gems, Glory!

A na mesto glaz dorogoy almaz. Slava! — And in place of eyes it had precious diamonds. Glory!

85. A. V. Tereshchenko, *Bït russkogo naroda* (St. Petersburg, 1848), 7:159.
86. Commentary to Pushkin, *Eugene Onegin* 2:497.
87. Tereshchenko, *Bït russkogo naroda* 2:158; Afanasyev, *Poèticheskiye vozzreniya* 2:158.

"*Puzishche*" (no. 4), transmitted only by Sakharov, who offers no specific interpretations, might seem by virtue of its sacks of lice and fleas to bode no good,
but in fact the latter are metaphors for sowing grain, and the song foretells a
good harvest:

Uzh, kak vïshlo puzishche na repishche, Slava!	Now what a huge belly came out on the turnip field, Glory!
Vïneslo puzishche osminu vshey, Slava!	The huge belly brought enough lice to sow a third of an acre, Glory!
Osminu vshey, pol-osminï blokh. Slava!	Lice for one-third, fleas for one-sixth. Glory!

As for Stravinsky's "fifth" chorus, "*Na korïte sizhu*," Tereshchenko states that it
presages "marriage for money."[88]

Besides these, Stravinsky set yet another dish-divination to music. "*Sidit varabey
na chuzhoy garadbe*," the second of the *Quatre chants russes* of 1919 ("Le moineau est
assis"), is a particularly gnomic oracle, cast in a rather extreme form of the peasant
"*akaniye*" dialect, in which O's become A's. Its interpretation is based on its imagery of distance and alienation, spelling long sojourns in strange lands:[89]

Sidit varabey na chuzhoy garadbe, Slavna!	A sparrow is perched on someone else's fence, Glorious!
Glyadit varabey na chuzhuyu storonu, Slavna!	The sparrow looks at someone else's homestead, Glorious!
Kurïchka ryaba na zavalinki navoz gryabla, Slavna!	The speckled hen raked manure for the *zava-linka*,[90] Glorious!
Ishcho pogrebla, kalechika vïgribla. Slavna!	She raked some more [and] dug up a [precious] ring. Glorious!
Za dezhoy sizhï, pityarey vazhï. Slavna!	I sit by the vat and bring in the drinkers. Glorious!
Lezhit valchisha na pavetisha.	A whale of a wolf is stretched out over a whale of a district.
Atkinul khvost' na pyatnadtsat' vyorst. Slavna!	Its tail is flung fifteen versts away. Glorious!

One can hardly imagine anything more fitting than this text as a metaphor of
Stravinsky's own condition, cut off from his native country and flung, like the
wolf's tail, many versts away, where he peered over alien fences at alien terrains.
Taken in conjunction with the more overtly nostalgic "*Sektantskaya*," the song as
set is about the closest thing we have to an autobiographical confession from this
most tight-lipped of composers.

88. Tereshchenko, *Bït russkogo naroda* 2:158.
89. See Propp, *Russkiye agrarnïye prazdniki*, 110.
90. A *zavalinka* is a mound of earth that runs along the outside walls of a hut, with a wooden board
on top or else enclosed in wooden boards. It reaches a level convenient for sitting and is often used as
an outdoor bench (Simon Karlinsky, Personal communication, 14 December 1986).

It is precisely the aptness of his textual choices that proves—however little he may have remembered or cared about the texts he set when it came time to give his most widely noticed testimony about them—that at the time of writing Stravinsky's interest in his sources was lively and his knowledge of them detailed and accurate. The label he fastened in the flyleaf of the *podblyudnïye* score now at the Morgan Library not only connected the dish-divination songs correctly with the *svyatki,* but also quoted as an epigraph the all-important second line of the *podblyudnaya* refrain as given by Sakharov: *"Komu vinetsya, tomu sbudetsya."*[91] A dozen years later, in response to Schott's inquiry, Stravinsky was still able to recall that his "Unterschale-Warsagelider" were "Weihnachtslieder die von Weiber gesungen werden bei der Warsagung [*sic*]; dabei werden von den umgeküpten Unterschalen verschiedene Sachen herausgenomen [*sic*]."[92]

At the same time, however, he made a serious error by calling Ovseñ, the deity after whom the second song was named, the "Gottheit des Herbsten" (autumn deity). Stravinsky confused the name with *oseñ,* the Russian word for autumn, and the Schott editors compounded his error by actually changing *Ovseñ* to *oseñ* on the word's every appearance in the printed music. In folklore, Ovseñ has nothing to do with autumn. The name, which Afanasyev derives from the Sanskrit *ush,* signifies the god who lights the solar wheel and thereby makes the world a yearly gift of light. If there is a season to which *oVSeÑ* is etymologically linked, it is not *oseñ* but *VeSNa*—spring.[93] Songs to Ovseñ are New Year's songs, originally sung when the old agrarian calendar year began in March, and later transferred, along with the New Year itself, to January. They belong to the genre known as *obryadnïye* (or *obryadovïye*) *pesni,* ceremonial or calendar songs of the solar cycle, which they in fact initiate, preceding the *vesnyanki* that figure so significantly in *The Rite of Spring* (see Chapter 12). In more recent times, songs to Ovseñ became New Year's carols (also known as *kolyadki*), sung door to door in return for presents that stood in lieu of the ancient sacrifices to propitiate the gods and vouchsafe a good hunt.[94] The text Stravinsky chose to include with the *podblyudnïye* is exactly of this type:

Ovseñ, Ovseñ! ya teteryu gonyu,	New Year, New Year! I'm hunting a black grouse,
Ovseñ, Ovseñ! polevuyu gonyu;	New Year, New Year! I'm hunting the field[-bred] one;

91. Stravinsky's immediate source for the line may well have been Dahl, who quotes it all by itself in his discussion of the songs in his *Tolkovïy slovar'* (s.v., *Podblyudnïy*).

92. "Christmas songs that were sung by women at fortune telling; while singing them various objects were drawn out of a covered bowl" (notation on an editor's inquiry now in the archive of B. Schott's Söhne, Mainz; courtesy Peter Hauser). Stravinsky's notation, in a paraphrase that distorts the meaning as it improves the German, may still be read as a footnote in the Schott score: "Wahrsagelieder, Weihnachtslieder der Frauen, die gesungen werden bei der Wahrsagung, während unter dem umgestülpten Unterschalen allerhand Gegenstände hervorgeholt werden" (Fortune-telling songs, Christmas songs for women, that were sung at fortune telling, while all kinds of items were fetched out from under an inverted bowl).

93. See Afanasyev, *Poèticheskiye vozzreniya* 3:747–48.

94. See Ralston, *Songs of the Russian People,* 206.

Ona pod kust,	It [hid] under a shrub,
A ya za khvost';	But I [grabbed it] by the tail;
Mne nachla khvost',	I thought it was the tail,
An deneg gorst'.	But [lo and behold] it was a handful of money.

As set by Stravinsky, the "Song to Ovseñ" amounts to a kind of singing New Year's card, and—lo and behold!—the Archive fair copy of the song carries the date "1 January (N.S.) 1917." Indeed, all the Peasant Choruses—and the "*Podblyud-naya*" in the *Quatre chants russes* as well—carry dates in December and January (that is, around the time of the *svyatki*). It is therefore more than possible that their original impulse was personal or domestic: to serve as the musical greetings of a great Turanian composer to friends and family.

TURANIAN MUSICAL STYLE

Before Stravinsky, only two composers worth mentioning had been drawn at all to the kind of sources he now found indispensable. Musorgsky was the first—in one lone composition, the "Clapping Game," which he wrote in 1871 for insertion into the second act of his revised *Boris Godunov*. In a fashion unprecedented within his circle, he cobbled the words out of no fewer than eight nonsense songs in P. V. Sheyn's huge compendium of Russian *bït*—the first edition of which had come out under the title *Russkiye narodnïye pesni* (*Russian Folk Songs*) in 1870—and set them to his own music. Seven of the eight were from the first section of Sheyn's work, which was itself something unprecedented: an assemblage of 285 children's songs, broken down into four subcategories: Lullabies and comic songs (*Kolïbel'nïye i poteshnïye*); Sung nonsense rhymes and jingles (*Pesennïye pribautki i progovorï*); Sung choosing-up rhymes at the start of games (*Zhereb'yovïye pesennïye pribautki pred nachalom igrï*); Children's games with sung accompaniments (*Detskiye igrï s pesennïmi progovorami*). At the time all this was virgin territory for art music; indeed, for ethnography as well. Sheyn's anthology opened up the whole world of Russian children's culture to study and artistic adaptation. Its contents have endless Stravinskian resonances; in fact, the song that served Musorgsky as the basic source for the "Clapping Game" is a close cousin to the *pribautka* with which Stravinsky finished off his *Baika* (see Chapter 16).[95]

The line thus initiated by Musorgsky was taken up by Lyadov, who between 1887 and 1890 wrote three sets of *Children's Songs* (*Detskiye pesni*) on folk texts (opp. 14, 18, 22). Each set contained six songs, for a total of eighteen, of which thirteen were drawn from Sheyn. Lyadov's settings were unquestionably the model for Stravinsky's *Tri pesenki* of 1913, three songs that, according to the composer, were reworkings of pieces he had composed during his tutelary period, when Lyadov was alive

95. For details of Musorgsky's appropriations from Sheyn, see the Appendix ("Folk Texts in *Boris Godunov*") in Taruskin, "Musorgsky vs. Musorgsky," 266–70.

and in frequent contact with Stravinsky at Rimsky-Korsakov's *jours fixes*. It takes but a glance at Lyadov's op. 18/1, "*Ladushki*" (in comparison with "*Sorochenka*," the first of Stravinsky's *Tri pesenki*) to confirm the relationship (Ex. 15.3). There are also numerous thematic links between Lyadov's choice of texts and Stravinsky's (though no exact concordance): viz., "*Soroka*," op. 14/2 (cf. *Tri pesenki*, no. 1); "*Koli-bel'naya: Bayushki-bayu*," op. 14/6 (cf. *Kolibel'niye*, no. 3); and "*Kolibel'naya: U kota, kota*," op. 18/3 (cf. *Kolibel'niye*, no. 4).[96] Closest of all are Lyadov's op. 18/4 and the first of Stravinsky's *Detskiye pesenki*: both are variants of a nonsense song (*poteshka*) that is known to every Russian child:[97]

Bom, bom, bom!	Ding-dong, ding-dong!
Zagorelsya koshkin dom:	The cat's house is aflame;
Bezhit kuritsa s vedrom	The hen comes running with the bucket
Zalivat' koshkin dom. . . .	To extinguish the [fire in the] cat's house. . . .

This is Sheyn's no. 22, which the collector printed with a note: "*kogda zabavlyayut detey*" (for amusing children). From this phrase Lyadov invented an ersatz genre (*zabavnaya*, "fun song"), by which term he designated several other songs in his sets as well. Stravinsky, for his part, took off from a version he found in the later, expanded edition of Sheyn's anthology, in which the cat has become a goat:

Tilim-bom, tilim-bom	Ding-dong bell, ding-dong bell
Zagorelsya kozïy dom:	The goat shed is on fire:
Koza vïskochila,	The goat leapt out,
Glaza vïtarashchila. . . .	His eyes were bulging. . . .

Yet the surface congruence only serves to emphasize the enormous gulf that separates Lyadov and the maturing Stravinsky. The older man paints the text in typical art-song colors, depicting its semantic content with tortuously spreading, chromatic tongues of flame (Ex. 15.4). Stravinsky "says the song straight," as Linyova's peasants would have put it. His melodic line emulates the plainness of those unprepossessing, unrhetorical *napevï*—lately available for inspection in the publications of Istomin and the MEK—with an accompaniment of the strictest functionalism and diatonicism (the lone deviation—F-sharp in the refrain—being rigidly hypostatized and therefore modally "regular").[98] Impersonality of execution is

96. Despite the identical incipits, the last pair of texts are not the same. Both make use of the common formula, already illustrated in the case of Stravinsky, whereby the cat's possessions are compared with the better ones belonging to the child who is being lulled to sleep.

97. Besides Lyadov and Stravinsky, at least three other composers published settings of this song: I. S. Tezavrovsky (1903), N. S. Potolovsky (1905), and V. S. Ruzhitsky (1905). See G. Ivanov, *Russkaya poèziya v otechestvennoy muzike* 1:406.

98. For an ingenious analysis of the harmony of "*Tilim-bom*," see Van den Toorn, *Music of Igor Stravinsky*, 182, 477n.4. Van den Toorn sees the song as a paradigm of a technique of stacked Dorian hexachords, which he identifies as central to the harmonic idiom of such Swiss-period works as *Renard* and *Histoire du soldat*.

EXAMPLE 15.3   Lyadov, *"Ladushki"* (Pat-a-cake), op. 18/1

["Pat-a-cake, pat-a-cake, / Where have you been?" / "To grandma's." / "What did you eat?" / "Porridge." / "What did you drink?" / "Home-brewed beer." / The porridge is sweet, / The beer makes you tipsy. / Whoosh! Let's fly!] (Trans. RT)

EXAMPLE 15.4   Lyadov, *"Bom, bom, bom,"* op. 18/4

(*continued*)

EXAMPLE 15.4 *(continued)*

[Boom, boom, boom! The cat's house has caught fire: the hen comes running
with a bucket to douse the cat's house. Boom, boom! Boom, boom!] (Trans. RT)

assured by an ostinato of the most adamant sort (which, extending from one end
of the song to the other, already prefigures the double bass in *Histoire du soldat*).[99]
In a way that Lyadov's conventionally folkish setting never tries for, Stravinsky's is
a "created folk song" of purest Turanian pedigree (compare Ex. 15.4 with Ex. 15.1
above).

Although the folkloric verisimilitude of the narrow, short-breathed, resolutely
diatonic *napevï* and *popevki* that inform all of Stravinsky's "Swiss" songs is patent,
and although the way they are "harmonized" is heavily reliant on the example of
the peasant *podgolosochnoye mnogogolosiye* ("sing-along polyphony," as R. S. Beckwith aptly translates the untranslatable)[100] made available in the phonographic
field transcriptions of the MEK ethnographers, it would be a mistake to confuse

99. The jolting quarter rest that Stravinsky introduced before the last phrase in the 1954 version of
the song to telegraph the ending, while cute, shows how remote he had become from the esthetic that
motivated th riginal (see Igor Stravinsky, *Four Songs* for Voice, Flute, Harp, and Guitar [London: J.
& W. Chester, 1953], no. 4).

100. See Robert Sterling Beckwith, "A. D. Kastal'skii (1856–1926) and the Quest for a Native Russian Choral Style" (Ph.D. diss., Cornell University, 1969), chap. 3.

Stravinsky's "created folk songs" with imitation folk songs. The folk influence went much deeper than that, into very basic matters of style and technique, where Stravinsky's response to the stimulus of folklore often took novel turns that could not have been predicted simply from knowledge of the model.

From folk *napevï*, for example, Stravinsky cannily abstracted a principle of diatonic modality according to which tone centers are not determined a priori by the mode (as they are in the major/minor system) but are established contextually, even factitiously by virtue of a peremptory termination. In this sense, Stravinsky's diatonic *napevï* do not have functional tonal centers, only unpredictable finals. Nor do his dissonant "harmonizations" offer much help, as a rule, in determining tone centricity—or if they do, it is in ways (the use of acciaccatura, for example) that one must learn to "read" from the idiom of the songs themselves. For reasons like these, Stravinsky's "Swiss" songs, for all their apparent melodic simplicity and their obvious relationship to folklore, evince a tough, aggressive modernity that has not mellowed with age. It is not their Russian archaism but their belligerent rejection of Europe—the denial of "panromanogermanic" common practice—that has remained their most conspicuous feature.

———————

Later in life, when Stravinsky came to feel that these songs, and the intentions they embody, were vulnerable to misinterpretation—or worse, correct interpretation—he became very squeamish about them. He insistently denied any direct reliance on folklore, maintaining rather that "if any of these pieces *sounds* like aboriginal folk music, it may be because my powers of fabrication were able to tap some unconscious 'folk' memory."[101] This requires even more qualification than usual. Stravinsky's folklorism at this time was anything but unconscious, and what he tapped was not always memory.

A case in point is "*Kornilo*" (*Pribaoutki*, no. 1), of which the opening tune was borrowed from the Istomin/Lyapunov anthology, a most appropriate source for "low strata" melodies and the very one that four years earlier had furnished the *Ivanovskaya* tune that went from "The Great Sacrifice" into *Petrushka* (Ex. 15.5). With this identification firmly in hand, another, somewhat less obvious one may be confidently proposed. The melody of "*Polkovnik*" (*Pribaoutki*, no. 3) is modeled on a particular class of tunes in Istomin/Lyapunov, of which the one given in Example 15.6 is perhaps closest to Stravinsky's. In both instances the copies maintain the pitch level of the models, and in the first case Stravinsky even adopted Lyapunov's barring scheme. The evident care with which these borrowings were made suggests—just as it did in the case of *The Rite*—that other borrowed tunes lurk not only in the *Pribaoutki* but in the other sets of "Swiss" songs as well.

Yet there is a very telling difference between these appropriations and the ones

101. M&C:92/98.

EXAMPLE 15.5

a. Opening of *"Kornilo"* (*Pribaoutki,* no. 1)

f pesante Nu — tko, dya - dyush - ka Kor — ni - (i — i) - lo,

Za - (a — a) - prya - gai — ko tï ko - bï - (ï — ï) - lu

b. Devichnik song, *"Oshshe khto po sadu khodit"* (Istomin/Lyapunov, *Pesni russkogo naroda,* p. 108)

O — oosh - she khto po sa - du kho — dit,

O — oosh - she khto po sa - du kho — dit,

in Stravinsky's earlier work. Where previously the composer had sought out folk artifacts with a good kuchkist eye for ethnological suitability, here he gleefully weds his authentic texts to wildly incongruous authentic tunes. The first of the *Pribaoutki* is a carousing jingle to be recited glass in hand and followed by a down-the-hatch:

Nútko, dyádyushka Kornílo,	Well, then, Uncle [i.e., Old Man] Kornilo,
zapryagái-ko tï kobílu,	why don't you harness the mare,
u Makár'ya na peskú	so that near Macarius's Fair on the sands
prirazmích' goryó-toskú:	you might dispel your sorrow and boredom:
stoít brázhka v tuyaskú,	there stands some homemade beer in a birchwood pitcher;
brázhka p'yánaya-p'yaná,	this drunken beer makes you drunk,
veselá khmel'náya golová!	[your] inebriated head feels happy!
Brázhku pornyái vïpivái! . . .	Drink this beer in good health! . . .

The melody Stravinsky chose to carry these words was a stately *devichnik* (bridal shower) song with a text that would have been right at home in the first tableau of *Svadebka.* He underscores the incongruity by closing his song with what the delighted Prokofiev called "the gurgle of an emptying bottle" in the oboe and clarinet.[102]

102. See his letter to Stravinsky, written from New York on 10 December 1919, published in M&C:67–68/69–70; P&D:132; and, more reliably translated, in Natalia Rodriguez and Malcolm Hamrick Brown, "Prokofiev's Correspondence with Stravinsky and Shostakovich," in *Slavonic and Western Music: Essays for Gerald Abraham,* ed. M. H. Brown and R. John Wiley (Ann Arbor/Oxford: UMI Research Press/Oxford University Press, 1985), 295. Prokofiev also praised the coda (*otïgrïsh*) of the last

EXAMPLE 15.6   Rekrutskaya, *"O-oy da èdak na sinem-to morye"*
(Istomin/Lyapunov, *Pesni russkogo naroda*, p. 81), for comparison with *"Polkovnik"*
(*Pribaoutki*, no. 3; see esp. Ex. 15.33b below)

O - oy da è - dak   na   si - nem-to   mor - ye,

The third of the *Pribaoutki*, a merry tongue-twister, is set to a melodic pattern found only in, and therefore signifying, ritual laments (*prichotï*; the one shown in Example 15.6 is a *rekrutskaya*, a condolence song for an unwilling conscript and his family).

This burlesque incongruity is the esoteric side of what Stravinsky described to Romain Rolland as the root idea of these nonsense songs. As Rolland reported the description, the distinguishing feature of what he called Stravinsky's "Dicts," then still in progress, was their nonlinear, disjunctive, and alogical form: "Right now, Stravinsky is writing a suite of very short pieces for voice and orchestra, called 'Sayings' (a very ancient form of Russian folk poetry, a series of practically meaningless words that are linked only by chance couplings of imagery or sound; in Russia they are recited before or during games). The fun for him is in passing brusquely in music from one image to another that is completely different and unexpected."[103]

The discordance of imagery of which Rolland speaks can be seen most clearly in the text of the second song in *Pribaoutki*, with its two completely unrelated sentences (the second of them obviously related to the model *pribautka* jingle discussed on p. 1148). Stravinsky set the piece in two completely unrelated halves:

Natáshka, Natáshka!	Natashka, Natashka!
sladyóñka kulázhka,	[Here's some] sweet porridge,
sladká medováya,	sweetened with honey,
v pechí ne bïvála,	'twas never in the oven,
zharú ne vidála.	never saw [any] heat.
Zaigráli útki v dúdki,	Ducks began playing on bagpipes,
zhuravlí poshlí plyasát',	cranes fell to dancing,
dólgi nógi vïstavlyát',	pushing forward their long legs,
dólgi shéi protyágivat'.	stretching out their long necks.

This was Russian *drobnost'* at its Turanian fount. In text and music alike, block suc-

---

song, whose acciaccaturas (clarinet G/A, English horn A-flat) he calls "Marvelous! insolent!" He obviously remembered it twenty years later—minus the insolence, to be sure—when he composed the beginning of his *Alexander Nevsky* music.

103. "Strawinsky écrit en ce moment une suite de pièces très courtes, pour orchestre et une voix, des *Dicts* (une forme de poésie populaire russe très ancienne, une suite de mots qui n'ont presque aucun sens et ne se rattachent entre eux que par des associations d'images ou de sons; on les dit en Russie par jeu, avant les jeux). L'amusement est pour lui de passer brusquement en musique d'une image à une image tout à fait différente et qu'on n'attendait pas" (Rolland, *Journal*, 60).

ceeds block without transition or progression. A text draft for "*Natashka*" in the Archive (Sketchbook C in Shepard's listing) shows how directly the impetus toward this kind of musical shaping grew out of analysis of the words. The text is written out, as above, like a poem (Afanasyev prints it as a paragraph of prose). The first five lines are labeled "*Dactyl'i*" (the last—Cyrillic—letter of this word making it plural), and the four lines of trochees that follow are labeled "*jamb*." In Stravinsky's setting, the 3/8 dactyls (*recte* amphibrachs) in an acciaccatura-enriched E-flat give way to the 2/4 "iambs" (*recte* trochees), which descend to a final cadence on D. Precisely the same tonal relationship—an acciaccatura writ large, perhaps—governs the equally disjunct first song.

The text of the fourth song is structurally and semantically just as much of a non sequitur as the rest:

Stoit grad pust,	There stands an empty town,
a vo grade kust;	and in the town there is a shrub;
v kuste sidit starets	in the shrub there sits an old sage,
da varit izvarets;	who is cooking broth;
i pribezhal k nemu	and to him there came running
kosoy zayats	a cross-eyed hare
i prosit izvarets.	and asked for [some] broth.
I prikazal starets	And the old man commanded
besnogomu bezhat',	the legless man to run,
besrukomu khvatat'	and the armless man to grab
a golomu v pazukhu klast'.	and the naked man to hide [things] under his clothes.

Stravinsky's setting observes the same structural jolt as does the poem after the seventh line of text. But then, a little disappointingly, the composer tries to reclaim "unity" by means of an apologetic reprise of the opening instrumental music, as if a ritornello. It is as unsatisfactory a half-measure here as it would be, let us say, in a da capo aria, if for the opposite reason: it leaves the aria half full, the *pribautka* only half empty of conventional formal gestures. The reversion to formal convention bespeaks a minor lapse of faith. Stravinsky had not yet entirely shaken Europe.

In harmonic texture, though, the *Pribaoutki* are Turanian through and through, picking up exactly where the harmonic idiom of *The Nightingale* had left off. As the foregoing analysis has already perhaps suggested, the settings are, throughout, a veritable study in acciaccaturas. This can best be seen in the second and fourth songs, the first sections of which are thematically related (see Ex. 15.7). The G-sharp violin pedal in the fourth song (especially in conjunction with the nearly-as-frequent F in the bassoon) is easily related to what we know to be characteristic *Rite* harmony, in which minor-tetrachord *napevï* are accompanied by their octatonic complements.[104] Viewed as an acciaccatura (the one alternative by no means

104. For a penetrating analysis along these lines, see Van den Toorn, *Music of Igor Stravinsky*, 40–41.

EXAMPLE 15.7

a. Opening of *"Natashka"* (*Pribaoutki,* no. 2)

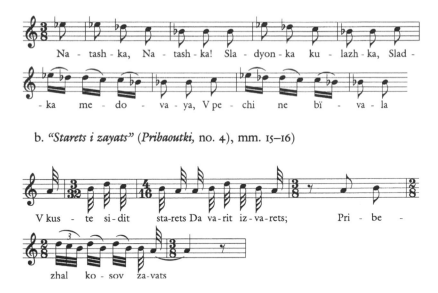

b. *"Starets i zayats"* (*Pribaoutki,* no. 4), mm. 15–16

excluding the another), the pedal is very much of a piece with the opening sonority in *"Kornilo"* (*Pribaoutki,* no. 1), an opening that bears comparison with countless other Stravinskian gambits over the next four decades and more, reaching an epitome with *Agon.*

The double acciaccatura in *"Natashka"* (*Pribaoutki,* no. 2), D-plus-E encircling the opening E-flat of the tune on its every occurrence, is the direct outgrowth of the white key/black key oppositions in *The Nightingale* (cf. the Chinese March ostinato). As for *"Kornilo,"* acciaccatura provides practically the sole source of harmony, at least in the opening (folk song–derived) section. The effect of all these acciaccaturas, so frequently encountered in all the "Swiss" music, is sooner one of heightened monophony or heterophony (cf. *podgolosochnaya mnogogolosiya*) than of harmonization. The tonally enigmatic "chug-a-lug" coda that so delighted Prokofiev in *"Kornilo"* is wholly governed by acciaccaturas. The oboe line dwells mainly on the pitches that encircle the components of the clarinet's Db/G tritone tremolo: C-plus-D encircling the D-flat, Gb-plus-Ab encircling the G. The four notes thus generated are joined in an octatonic scale: C D Eb F Gb Ab A B (Ex. 15.8).[105]

105. It is octatonic, that is, if the prevailing signature of three flats is applied to the oboe part from which it has been erroneously omitted in the published score. A sketch page (printed as an illustration in P&D:131) shows that E-flat (D-sharp) should replace E-natural.

EXAMPLE 15.8

a. *"Kornilo,"* oboe cadenza as printed

b. Sketch for same (P&D:131), showing use of E-flat, referable to Collection II

After the spiky *Pribaoutki,* the *Kolïbel'nïye* (*Berceuses*) make a very suave impression. They are all strophic as to form (the last one in the set even being written out that way). Modally, too, they are highly consistent and integrated: except for the last they are all centered on D. A typical acciaccatura idea governs the harmonic texture of the first song: the trill on the *subsemitonium* and its fifth (C♯/G♯) purrs through the song in a steady undertone, coloring what is otherwise a relatively straightforward diatonic mode.[106] The text of the song makes it clear that the foreign tones do indeed represent the purring of the metaphorical kitty-cat:

Spi, kot, na pechke	Sleep, cat, on the stove[-shelf][107]
Na voílochke,	On a nice felt [mat],
Lapki v golovkakh,	Paws at the head of the bed,
Lis'ya shubka na plechakh.	Fox-fur coat on your shoulders.

In the second song, the mode is rendered somewhat more ambiguous by oscillations of F with F-sharp and C with C-sharp—though there is nothing un-European about that. More interesting is the neighboring D-sharp that recurs independently in the little flourishes that mark the end of the first and second lines of text: the rather conventional major/minor opposition here picks up a whiff of octatonic flavoring as the roots D and B contend along the minor-thirds axis. The

106. Two tones are unstable: a Phrygian E-flat oscillates with E in the voice and the first clarinet, while there is some play between the signature B-flat and its "Dorian" counterpart B-natural in the second clarinet.

107. About the "stove-shelf" Karlinsky writes: "Behind or to the side of masonry-built, wood-burning stoves in peasant huts, there was a masonry shelf that stayed warm through the night. This was the favorite sleeping place for aged people. A cat, if there was one in the household, would quickly select that shelf as its favorite place to rest" (Personal communication, 14 December 1986).

most noteworthy aspect of the song is its texture. Only cadences are "harmonized"; elsewhere the voice and the first clarinet are paired heterophonically, exactly like *podgoloski*. The ensemble is deployed at full strength for only four measures near the end. Even there a sense of extreme leanness is maintained by an avoidance of triads and by an application of acciaccaturas so pronounced as to suggest the as yet uncoined term "clusters." The ending of the song is especially characteristic: the C-sharp (lowest note of the A clarinet) is heard retrospectively, by ears conditioned to the first song and to the *Pribaoutki*, not as a "tonal," tugging leading-tone, but as a harmonically stable acciaccatura to the final. This is in keeping with the text, which describes total contentment and family bliss:

Kot na pechi	The tomcat on the stove[-shelf]
Sukhari tolchot.	is grinding breadcrumbs.
Koshka v lukoshke	The mother cat in a bast basket
Shirinku sh'yot,	is sewing a kerchief.
Malen'ki kotyata	The tiny little kittens
V pechurkakh sidyat,	All sit in [their] little stoves,
Chto na kotika glyadyat,	while they look at the nice tomcat
I sukhariki edyat.	and eat the breadcrumb cookies [which he is making for them].

The third *Berceuse* is one of those Stravinsky pieces that lend themselves most readily to a superficial "bitonal" analysis. The vocal line is pure D-Dorian (or "Russian minor," as Balakirev had christened it half a century before), while the second and third clarinets (the first still heterophonically paired with the voice) are just as rigorously confined to a diatonic scale encompassing all the black keys, filled out with F and B to provide a couple of intersections with the voice part. Actually, the music is patterned on a pair of diatonic extensions of the familiar octatonic partition into tritone-related tetrachords (see Ex. 15.9). This technique of diatonically extending octatonic tetrachords (or, alternatively, diatonic surface projections of an octatonic background) would be the primary means by which Stravinsky organized the tonal relations in *Svadebka,* the magnum opus of his Swiss period (see Chapter 17). In the third lullaby the conceptual origins of the harmony are apparent in the consistent use of parallel fourths in the accompanying clarinets—a constant reminder that the tetrachord, not the triad, is the defining harmonic/melodic unit of "Turanian" music.

Further harmonization is governed by the acciaccatura rule. One of the notes in the clarinet fourths (usually the lower) is always in semitonal conflict with the melody note, except at cadences, where consonance is asserted by accompanying the melodic D with the fourth F♯/B, producing a fleeting specious tonic (B minor) that is never tonally confirmed (Ex. 15.10). The opening C♯/F♯ is acciaccatura-related both to the F and to the D of the vocal melody. When the melody moves up a step to E, the accompanying fourth does likewise, so as to provide that note,

EXAMPLE 15.9 *"Bai-bai"* (*Berceuses du chat*, no. 3), analytical sketch showing relationship of musical surface to octatonic background collection

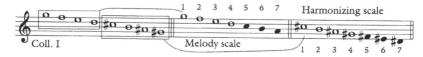

EXAMPLE 15.10 *"Bai-bai,"* mm. 1–4, without doubling line (clarinet I), showing confinement to and exhaustion of melody and harmony scales (boxed harmony is the "specious tonic")

too, with a shadow (D-sharp). The final melodic D in m. 1 anticipates the return of the acciaccatura-fourth that had originally accompanied it (the published score is confusingly misaligned here). The resulting suspension exposes the melodic D to a pair of "encircling" acciaccaturas (D♯/C♯) such as we have encountered as far back as *The Nightingale*. That this is the correct (or, at least, the intended) interpretation of the harmony is confirmed in the next bar, when the consonant "specious tonic" is quitted through the same pair of encircling acciaccaturas around D. The status of D as operative tonal center is never in the slightest doubt; which is why the harmonic language of the song cannot be meaningfully described as "bitonal." Instead we have an elaborate shadowing device, whereby one pitch collection acts as background, or setting, for another, all of its elements functioning as acciaccaturas. It is as if the "total chromatic" had been filtered through a prism, or through a polarizing lens.

Before discussing the fourth *berceuse*, an excursus is warranted to take account of *"Gusi-lebedi"* ("The Geese and the Swans"), the third of the *Detskiye pesenki*, in which the acciaccatura principle is brought to a peak. The melody is again in the "Russian minor," and it is accompanied as if on the *lira*, the Russian hurdy-gurdy, by a drone sustained in a perpetual left hand/right hand tremolo that gives the timbral effect of balalaika strumming. This D-drone is shadowed at all times by encircling acciaccaturas. In the right hand it is C-sharp from beginning to end; in the left hand the C-sharp alternates with its D-encircling counterpart, E-flat. At its first intrusion (m. 4), the E-flat resolves back to C-sharp by way of an escape tone, F, wittily inserted so as to mimic at the tritone the melodic cadence (A-B-G), thus producing a little whole-tone zephyr that relates the song to another indigenous Russian (nonfolk) tradition. Thereafter, the E-flat is associated with its fifth (B-flat), adding a characteristically Dorian sixth-degree ambiguity to the tonal mix. An extension of this idea, beginning on the second eighth note in m. 8, produces a five-eighths ostinato in which the acciaccatura E-flat resolves back to D through a series of stacked fifths. This ostinato is played out against the six eighths of the prevailing meter in a hemiola covering four measures (mm. 9–12), making up the B section of the song's modified ternary design. To speak of harmony here would be beside the point; Stravinsky's setting is pure Turanian heterophony. It is stylistically so close to the 1914 *Pribaoutki,* with which it shares its text source, that one strongly suspects that "*Gusi-lebedi*" was originally sketched for inclusion in the earlier set, though no document survives to corroborate.

In contrast to all the songs discussed so far, the fourth *berceuse* is set in an idiom that resolutely eschews all chromatic embellishment in quest of a radically severe ethnic authenticity. For unalloyed white-key purity, this song could be compared only with some of Balakirev's doctrinaire folk song harmonizations, made half a century earlier. The melody, too, is of such a pure Russian breed that if Stravinsky did actually compose it (not just copy it down), he must have had more than an "unconscious 'folk' memory" to guide him; he must have had some theoretical knowledge of the modal structure of Russian songs. The melody exhibits the so-called *peremenniy lad* (mutable mode), whereby tunes in the "Russian minor" alternate cadences on the note comparable to the Western tonic and on that tonic's lower neighbor. In most authentic tunes of this type it is the penultimate phrase that exhibits the modal mutability (*peremennost'*). A considerable number do have it at the very end, though, just like Stravinsky's.

The polyphony is the closest imitation of actual *podgoloski* Stravinsky had composed since the *Khovanshchina* chorus two years earlier. Conscious reliance on the model, once again, is most obvious in the way the first clarinet doubles (but not quite!) the voice. The freedom of "white-key dissonance" in the part-writing, while it contains no individual combination without precedent in the published "phonographic" transcriptions we know Stravinsky owned and consulted, has evolved by now beyond the limits of his models into uncharted Turanian terrain. No field-collected polyphonic folk song quite so sedulously avoids thirds in favor of Stravinsky's deliberately archaizing fourths and fifths. And while "unprepared" and even parallel sevenths can be found, as in the Don Cossack songs collected by Alexander Listopadov and published alongside Linyova's work in the papers of the

MEK,[108] no field-collected song has such a series of sevenths as we find in mm. 5–6 of Stravinsky's.

Nevertheless, a sampling of songs from Listopadov's collection can serve as exemplars of the style from which Stravinsky was obviously taking off. The end of Example 15.11a, a *vesnyanka*, is a particularly good specimen of the kind of modal occursus—the strong, independently linear approach of each voice to the final, producing a rough but well-directed unison cadence—that is a special hallmark of Russian folk polyphony, and which Stravinsky caught so well at his phrase endings (even though he approached fifths, not unisons). Example 15.11b shows the freedom with which the harmonically stable fourth is treated (compare Stravinsky's ending), while Example 15.11c exhibits parallel sevenths, and also, in its alternate cadences on G and F, the modal mutability discussed above (cf. Stravinsky's alternation of A and G).

Listopadov's songs, all for women's voices, naturally bring Stravinsky's Peasant Choruses to mind, even as they may have prompted the composer to adopt their medium. The sketches for "Shchuka" (no. 3), preserved in exceptional abundance in the Archive (Sketchbook D), give surprising and ultimately inspiring evidence of creative struggle. The starkly homorhythmic texture of the choruses, and of the fourth *berceuse*, though the lineal descendent of a folk prototype, was something attained not by facile or slavish copying of Listopadov or any other source, but by a ruthless process of elimination.

The first notations for "Shchuka" (Ex. 15.12) were made directly facing the preliminary copying-out of the text. The opening phrase, notated a fifth higher than its eventual pitch level, contains all the notes of the final version (marked with crosses), plus an infix that was pruned away along with the decorative eighth-note pairs. The setting of the word *pozolochennaya* in the fourth line of the text, meanwhile, corresponds to the final version (at the final pitch) in its middle voice, which eventually became the top. The other two voices in the sketch—a legato countermelody above and a sort of broken-chord figure below—are utterly at odds with the texture of the finished song, and startlingly conventional by comparison with it.

Following these earliest jottings are two consecutive drafts, both given in Example 15.13, that show the composer tackling the poem phrase by phrase. Both curiously stop after the fifth phrase (out of seven), and the first draft is missing the first phrase, possibly because a leaf has slipped out of the sketchbook. The fourth phrase required special attention both times.

---

108. A. M. Listopadov, "Narodnaya kazach'ya pesnya na Donu. Donskaya èkspeditsiya 1902–1903 gg.," *Trudï MEK* 1:159–218; idem, "Zapisi narodnïkh pesen v 1904 godu. Poyezdka v Donskuyu oblast' dlya sobiraniya kazach'ikh i malorusskikh pesen i zapisi velikorusskikh pesen Orlovskoy i Penzenskoy guberniy. S prilozheniyem 30 pesen v narodnoy garmonizatsii," *Trudï MEK* 2:341–63.

EXAMPLE 15.11   Songs from the Listopadov collections in *Trudï MEK*, showing voice leading and cadential characteristics of *"podgolosochnoye mnogogolosiye"*

a. *Vesnyanka (igrovaya),* *"Dremi, drema"* ("Narodnaya kazach'ya pesnya na Donu" [*Trudï MEK,* Vol. 1], no. 14)

b. *Rukobit'ye* (bridal contract) song, *"Cherez rechku ryabinka"* (ibid., no. 10)

c. *"Ne slobodushka-slavnaya Moskva"* ("Zapisi narodnïkh pesen v 1904 godu [*Trudï MEK,* Vol. 2], pt. 3: "Pesni Orlovskoy i Penzenskoy guberniy", no. 8)

EXAMPLE 15.12   *"Shchuka,"* first drafts (entered directly on text)

a.

[Shchu - ka   shla   iz   No - va - go - ro - da]

b.

po - zo - lo - chen - na - ya

EXAMPLE 15.13   *"Shchuka,"* two drafts from "Sketchbook D"

Draft I, phrase 2

O - na khvost vo - lo - kla   iz   Be - la   o - ze - ra   SLA - VA

O - na khvost vo - lo - kla iz   Be - la   o - ze - ra

Phrase 3

Kak   u   shchu - ki che - shuy - ka se - re - bryan - na - ya

- shuy - ka se - re - bryan - na - ya   Sla - va!

EXAMPLE 15.13 (*continued*)

(*continued*)

EXAMPLE 15.13 (*continued*)

EXAMPLE 15.13 (*continued*)

In the first draft, only the fifth phrase looks anything at all like its counterpart in the finished chorus, and it evidently served as model for the second draft. The rest is unrecognizable, and the setting of phrases 2 and "4a" are bizarre: syncopated, "hemiolic" cross accent and imitation are both so foreign to the nature of these choral songs as we know them that it is astonishing to encounter them at the embryonic stage. How much more "European" these relatively fancy early thoughts seem than the ascetically plain version we know, and how ruthless and deliberate, therefore, the process of de-Europeanization these sketches document for us.

The second draft, which begins just where the first leaves off, looks more familiar except for the dactyls in all the odd-numbered phrases, left over from the first draft, which mirror Sakharov's stress marks quantitatively as well as "tonically." This draft is still fancier than the final version: the even-numbered phrases are set in contrasting sharp-filled "keys" (the fourth phrase being deliberately transposed an extra sharp's distance from the original pitch field). All these fussy modulations are gone from the published version, in which the cadences of the odd and even verses oscillate between A and B in a typically Russian *peremennost'*, but with a stabilized "white-key" pitch vocabulary (except for the C-sharps through which the cadential B's are approached). Indeed, the odd phrases and the even phrases have grown so like one another as to give the impression of a lection tone, or, given the *peremennost'* factor, a sort of *tonus peregrinus*.

It is this gravely inexorable, *liturgical* quality that imparts to the finished song its aura of unassailable purity. It seems not so much an original composition as an authentic artifact of an imagined culture, of a created Turanian reality. It is only by knowing the sketches that we can see the plainness of this music for the "second simplicity" it is and appreciate the merciless repression of spontaneous "instinct" in pursuit of a higher truth. Ultimately both the received folkloric model and the unmediated personal response have been refined away, leaving behind a "small, dry thing" such as T. E. Hulme, that great prophet of modern art, foretold as the vessel of a new beauty he called Classical. What is so inspiring about the sketches is that they show how clearly Stravinsky saw through his first impressions, how firmly he possessed Hulme's artistic sine qua non: "the faculty of mind to see things . . . apart from the conventional ways in which you have been trained to see them, . . . the concentrated state of mind . . . to prevent one falling into the conventional curves of ingrained technique."[109] The creator of the Peasant Choruses was already the *musicien type* of the twentieth century.

109. Thomas Ernest Hulme, "Romanticism and Classicism," in *Criticism: The Major Texts*, enlarged ed., ed. Walter Jackson Bate (New York: Harcourt Brace Jovanovich, 1970), 570. Of course Stravinsky was as ignorant of Hulme (1883–1917; his essays were published posthumously in 1924 as *Speculations*, ed. Herbert Read) as Hulme evidently was of Stravinsky. Robert Craft, assuming Stravinsky knew Hulme, mentioned him in one of his first letters to the composer. Stravinsky replied (29 August 1947), "What is Speculations by T. E. Hulme, have no idea" (SelCorrI:330).

Stravinsky put his highly purified Turanian style to an unexpected but especially characteristic use in April 1917, when he was commissioned, in the aftermath of the February Revolution and the abdication of Nicholas II, to orchestrate the familiar "Volga Boatmen's Song" ("*Ey, ukhnem*") as a Russian hymn to replace Lvov's "*Bozhe, Tsarya khrani*" ("God Save the Tsar"). It is commonly assumed and written that this commission came from Diaghilev.[110] In fact it came directly from the Russian Provisional Government, in response to a movement that had been spearheaded by none other than Andrey Rimsky-Korsakov.

Musicians in Russia were understandably exercised over the idea of a new, post-tsarist national anthem. A young pianist and organologist named Pyotr Niko-layevich Zimin (1890–1972) wrote a letter to the *Muzïkal'nïy sovremennik* proposing a pair of contests to pick, first, the text for a new anthem, and then the best setting of it, with juries "to be selected from the ranks of Russian poets and musicians." Andrey Rimsky-Korsakov printed Zimin's letter in his *Khronika*, together with an impassioned rebuttal of its premises. A national anthem, he argued, should not be "a purely artificial entity in which the decisive role is played not by the musical content, but by a text and its formal adoption by some organ of power"; rather it should be "a melody created by the people," that is, a folk song. Moreover, it should be

a tune that reflects [the people's] heroic countenance [*ispolinskiy lik*], and it should be one that is already *recognized* by the whole Russian land. Artists might be entrusted at best with arranging such a theme. The text of the song has no right to play a determining role when the music itself is already stamped with might, sweep, freedom, and beauty. In our view, precisely these spiritual traits of our nation have poured forth with force and brilliance from the wonderful song known as "*Ey ukhnem*." . . . [It] is not a gloomy melody but a sternly majestic one. It has the beauty of boundless strength. It is not a feeling of calm joy, or one of peaceful celebration, that this song inspires in one's soul, but a feeling of terrible might, of sweeping freedom. This is truly a festive *revolutionary* song. And how close it is to the people's heart, how akin to them! With what enthusiasm will they sing it!

Do we need any other hymn? Let's leave well enough alone.[111]

Andrey had an arrangement in mind, of course: a 1905 setting for chorus and orchestra by (who else?) Glazunov. It had unassailable "revolutionary" credentials; like the elder Rimsky-Korsakov's arrangement of another barge hauler's song, "*Dubinushka*," it was written to show solidarity with participants in a general

---

110. Stravinsky implies as much himself in the *Chroniques* (see *An Autobiography*, 66).

111. A. N. Rimsky-Korsakov, "O novom narodnom gimne," *Khronika zhurnala "Muzïkal'nïy sovremennik,"* no. 18 (21 March 1917): 2–3.

strike. But its style was strictly, safely orthodox ("strangely German and academic for a revolutionary song," as Stravinsky would later put it of Rimsky's setting).[112] The younger Rimsky-Korsakov must have been gratified when within days his proposal was adopted by the Duma, the newly empowered Russian parliament, but aghast when the president of that body, Mikhaíl Vladimirovich Rodzyanko (1859–1924), who had distant family connections with Diaghilev, commissioned the new anthem from Stravinsky as part of a package that included Diaghilev's appointment to the cabinet of the Provisional Government as minister of fine arts.[113]

It is also safe to assume that the Rimsky-Korsakov clan would have recoiled in horror from the *Hymne à la nouvelle Russie,* scored for augmented orchestral winds and brass, that Stravinsky dictated to Ansermet at the Rome villa of Gerald Tyrrwhit (the future Lord Berners) through the night of 8–9 April for a performance on the morrow. It is evident that Stravinsky scored the song with Balakirev's famous harmonization of the 1860s at his elbow (Ex. 15.14a).[114] For one thing, he retained Balakirev's "Phrygian" key signature, despite the fact that he transposed the song (Balakirev had cast it in B-flat minor with six flats; Stravinsky used F-sharp minor with two sharps); within this unusual signature, both Balakirev and Stravinsky observed the strictest diatonic purity. For another thing, he adopted Balakirev's idiosyncratic chord spacings, turning the octave/third idea that, confined to the bass, had become a "sternly majestic" Russian specialty of sorts (Musorgsky's "Bydlo," Rimsky-Korsakov's *Kitezh,* Stravinsky's *Petrushka*) into a veritable *Grundgestalt,* generating the entire harmonic texture. The result was a harmonization that bore a relationship to Balakirev's comparable to that of Balakirev's to the German academic style of his day; and Balakirev's successors would have been as quick to call it "Ganz falsch" as the old Prague professor had been upon being shown Balakirev's work.

For we may imagine another book at Stravinsky's elbow, or at least very much on his mind, as he worked: the first volume of Linyova's *Great-Russian Songs in Folk Harmonization,* which contained a striking transcription of "*Dubinushka*" as sung by a group of actual barge haulers in Nizhniy-Novgorod.[115] This folk "harmonization" (Ex. 15.14b) contains not a single full triad: it is rather a matter of uni-

112. To Ansermet, 14 July 1932; in P&D:48.

113. See Paul Morand, *Journal d'un attaché d'ambassade, 1916–1917* (Paris: Gallimard, 1963), 209: "Diaghilev is related to Rodzyanko who has telegraphed him in Rome to offer him [the portfolio of] Fine Arts. The whole clan—Gorky, Argutinsky, Benois, Bakst—is coming to the fore! They have ordered from Stravinsky, who is in Rome, a national anthem on the theme of the 'Volga Boatmen's Song'" ("Diaghilew est parent de Rodzianko qui lui a télégraphié à Rome pour lui offrir les Beaux-Arts. Tout le clan Gorki, Argoutinski, Benoît [*sic*], Bakst, passe au premier plan! On commande à Strawinski, qui est à Rome, l'hymne national sur le thème des *Bateliers de la Volga*").

114. M. A. Balakirev, *Sbornik russkikh narodnikh pesen* (St. Petersburg: Johansen, 1866; rpt. Leipzig: Belaïeff, 1895), no. 40.

115. Stravinsky's ownership of this book, and his intense interest in it, are attested by his letter to his mother of 10/23 February 1916; in IStrSM:488.

EXAMPLE 15.14

a. "Volga Boatmen's Song" ("*Ey, ukhnem*"), arr. Balakirev (*Sbornik russkikh narodnïkh pesen,* no. 40)

(continued)

EXAMPLE 15.14a *(continued)*

ai - da, da, ai - da, ra - zo - v'yom mï ku - drya - vu!

b. *"Dubinushka,"* third verse (Linyova, *Velikorusskiye pesni v narodnoy garmonizatsii* [St. Petersburg, 1904], 1: no. 18)

Da vï, re - bya - ta, de - ri glot - ku. Nam kho -

zya - in dast - na vod - ku. Èkh, du - bi - nush - ka,

ukh - nem! Vot ze - lyo - na-ya sa - ma poy-dyot, I -

dyot, i - dyot, i - dyot, i-dyot, i - dyot, i-dyot!

EXAMPLE 15.14 (continued)

c. Stravinsky, *Chant des bateliers du Volga (Hymne à la nouvelle Russie)*, reduced

son singing colored by a descant in thirds, fifths, and sixths. Nor is it likely a coincidence that Linyova's transcription carries the key signature of Stravinsky's arrangement of its more famous cousin.

Whatever its sources, Stravinsky's harmonization (Ex. 15.14c) is "inartistic" in a way Balakirev could never have dreamed of allowing. It consists of a two-part counterpoint in the outer voices at the octave, sixth, and tenth à la Linyova, with both voices doubled at the octave and filled in by a third à la Balakirev, whether below the upper note ("upper-third position") or—as Balakirev had it exclusively—above the lower note ("lower-third position"). At major cadence points (but not at the end!), the thirds give way to perfect intervals. The outer-voice motion is full of "bad" part-writing (parallel octaves in mm. 6, 25–27; "hidden" octaves passim).

More important, the normative function of the triad is denied. Full triads emerge out of the part-writing at harmonically and metrically random spots (marked by asterisks in the example; an asterisk in parentheses marks full triads that are functionally even less potent because they appear off the beat in a second-species texture, or because—as in mm. 3 and 9—they appear to have the function of unstable auxiliaries). They happen most frequently when outer voices at the octave are filled in simultaneously with upper-third and lower-third doublings (mm. 3, 4, 6, 9, 10, 21, 25, 26, 27, 29, 31). Because it is the outer-voice counterpoint that is most forcefully directed, these triads (which can never occur in root position) are scarcely even heard as such.

No chord occurs that can be called a dominant. Under the specified conditions only plagal and Phrygian cadences can occur, and of these, only the one at mm. 27–28 (introduced by the first full-beat triad in root position to be heard anywhere in the piece) has anything like a conventional structure. The manner in which the cadential octaves at the peroration are filled in (mm. 30, 32) deliberately evades the expected tonic harmony, lending final confirmation to the nonessential, embellishing status of the inner voices throughout the setting.

Thus Stravinsky's *Hymne à la nouvelle Russie* was a declaration of independence from "Europe," an assertion of the rights of the peasantry, so to speak, against the bogus Enlightenment of post-Petrine Russia. It viewed the Russian Revolution from a patently post-Slavophile, Eurasianist perspective, Stravinsky seeing "la nouvelle Russie" (or "notre chère Russie liberée [*sic*]," as he called it in a telegram to his family)[116] in incongruously archaic terms that ill accorded with the liberal constitutional republic the Provisional Government was trying to establish. As a musical response to the February Revolution, Stravinsky's "Volga Boatmen's Song" was just as far off the mark as the rosy prediction he had made to Rolland about

116. Telegram of 24 May 1917; in IStrSM:489.

"les États-unis slaves," or the high hopes he expressed to C. F. Ramuz when word of the revolution first reached his ears:

> The true Russia was going to appear at last on the face of the earth, a new Russia, but at the same time the ancient one,—hatched at last, opened out, roused from her long slumber, resurrected from her own death. The Great Russia of all the great Russians, of Pushkin, of Gogol, of Musorgsky, even of Tolstoy, of the *Journal of a Writer* [i.e., Dostoyevsky's, which contained the oration on Pushkin from which our discussion took off], the Holy Russia of the Orthodox, a Russia rid of its parasitical growths: its bureaucracy imported from Germany, a certain English liberalism that had become fashionable among the nobility, its scientific spirit (alas!), its "intellectuals," their silly, bookish belief in progress;—the Russia that had been before Peter the Great and before all Europeanism, which would thus at first go backward so as better to go forward, having renewed contact with its foundations; a peasant Russia, but Christian above all, and the only truly Christian land in Europe.[117]

That was the Russia Stravinsky created, superbly and compellingly, in his music. It existed nowhere on earth, and far less did it exist after the Revolution than before.

———

The songs that made up the *Quatre chants russes*—composed after the *Baika* and the *Histoire du soldat*, after *Svadebka* was complete but for the scoring, and after Kerensky's Russia had given way to Lenin's—mark the terminal phase of Stravinsky's Swiss/Turanian period. His next work would be the *Piano-rag-music*, a close stylistic kin to these last Russian songs, and after that there would be *Pulcinella*. Of all the "Swiss" songs, the *Quatre chants russes* are the ones in which the Russian peasant idiom is most intimately wedded to the most irreducibly indigenous elements of the tradition in which Stravinsky had received his training. The synthesis was Stravinsky's final Turanian testament.

The first five measures of "*Selezeñ*" ("The Drake") set up octatonic Collection II as the referential tonality, much as "Chez Pétrouchka" had done with Collection III. The collection is partitioned this time in a way that would not have occurred

---

117. "La vraie Russie allait paraître enfin à la face du monde, une Russie nouvelle, mais qui serait en même temps l'ancienne,—éclose enfin, épanouie, tirée de son long sommeil, ressuscitée de sa propre mort. La Grande Russie de tous les grands Russes, celle de Pouchkine, celle de Gogol, celle de Moussorgsky, celle même de Tolstoï, celle du *Journal d'un Écrivain*, la Sainte Russie des Orthodoxes, une Russie débarrassée de ses végétations parasites: sa bureaucratie venue d'Allemagne, certain libéralisme anglais fait à la mode dans la noblesse, son scientisme (hélas!), ses 'intellectuels,' leur croyance assez niaise et tout livresque au progrès;—celle d'avant Pierre le Grand et d'avant l'européanisme, qui ainsi irait d'abord en arrière, mais pour mieux aller de l'avant, ayant retouché à ses bases; une Russie paysanne, mais avant tout chrétienne, et véritablement la seule terre chrétienne de l'Europe" (C. F. Ramuz, *Souvenirs sur Igor Strawinsky*, in *Oeuvres complètes*, vol. 14 [Lausanne: H. L. Mermod, 1941], 68).

to Stravinsky in 1910. The pianist's two hands and the voice each has its own assigned, hypostatized domain: the left hand is given the empty ninth C/D, the right hand an anhemitonic *napev* consisting of the pitches D♯-F♯-G♯-B (in order of appearance), and the voice mediates between the two, sharing C and D with the left hand and B with the right (see Ex. 15.15). Thereafter, either the original right-hand partition or one of the constituent tetrachords of the octatonic background set sprouts diatonic scales. It is from a series of modulations among these that the piece develops its tonal trajectory. The "voice finals" (i.e., the concluding pitches of the various sections as demarcated by the modulations) describe the same relationship—and on the very same pitches—as was observed in the first two songs of *Pribaoutki:* a composing-out of the acciaccatura relation that is of such defining importance to the Swiss/Turanian harmonic idiom.

Actual harmonic acciaccaturas also abound, of course. The little "B-flat minor" phrase in mm. 6–7 is doubly a case in point: the ending of the phrase provides an acciaccatura to accentuate the return of the right-hand *napev,* and the D-flat is an acciaccatura-in-reverse—an infix encircled by the pitches of the left-hand ostinato. (See also the relationship between voice and piano in mm. 9–13, illustrated in Example 15.15.) The end of the song is a marvelous surprise. The bass note of the concluding chord is the original voice final, while the voice in the last phrase unexpectedly takes over the original right-hand *napev.* The sudden reversal of roles gives a real sense of resolution to the concluding chord.

The "*Zapevnaya*" (no. 2) is actually a *shchitalka,* a counting-and-elimination exercise like eeny-meeny-miney-mo. Kireyevsky calls it simply a "game" (*igra*):

Na komomne, na volom[n]e,	On the hors-ity, on the ox-ity,
Na Bozhiye rose,	On God's dew,
Na popove polose	On the priest's plot [of land]
Pashot d'yakon	The deacon is ploughing
Chernïm uglyom:	With black coal:
Charka—gorelka,	The goblet is for vodka,
Medok—sostrok,	The mead is for [?],
Turban von,	Fatface, you're out—
Na Nikolin dvor,	Off to Nick's homestead;
Futka—Marfutka	Phooey on Martha,
Svyazeñ—Andryushka,	Andy's imprisoned,
Alyoshka—bog!	Alex is god!

Stravinsky's setting embodies a diabolically simple tonal progression that refines ("chooses up") the pitch material from a seven-tone diatonic collection into a five-tone anhemitonic one. The song begins "on the white keys," with D once again the pitch of priority (encircled in the voice part by a pair of the usual chromatic acciaccaturas). At the *più mosso,* which corresponds to the second little section of the text ("*Charka—gorelka...*") the voice part shifts to a four-note diatonic scale seg-

EXAMPLE 15.15   *"Selezeň"* (*Quatre chants russes,* no. 1), summary of tonal flow

ment in which the D now functions as lower neighbor to E (its importance weakened further by a contradicting D-sharp acciaccatura in the piano). The vocal line is a threefold reiteration of a pair of phrases in which the second is an anhemitonic childish singsong as familiar in the real West as in Stravinsky's imagined Russia ("It's raining, it's pouring . . ."). It is created here by exchanging D for its acciaccatura, C-sharp. After the shouted climax the piano postlude reverts to the singsong motif, the D now categorically banished. The ostinato A in the left hand completes the pentatonic pitch collection. So convincingly does Stravinsky partition this set between the hands into two independent linear planes that it would surely occur to no listener to interpret the last simultaneity even as an "F-sharp minor triad," let alone a tonic. What one hears is a functional melodic cadence to C-sharp (another composed-out acciaccatura with respect to the opening of the song) over a static, nonfunctional consonant embellishment—in other words, a heterophonic amplification (Ex. 15.16). In the jargon of the song one might say that D is off to Nick's homestead, F-sharp is imprisoned, and C-sharp is god.

The main *napev* in the third song, "*Podblyudnaya*" (Ex. 15.17b), is related to, perhaps derived from, the mysterious source tune marked "*k podblyudnïm*" (or "for the *podblyudnïye*") in Sketchbook A, the very one Stravinsky had used for "*Na korïte sizhu,*" the sketched but unpublished "fifth" chorus of that earlier set (Ex. 15.17a). Lighting upon the striking double inflection in the melody, Stravinsky composed it out in the accompaniment in a characteristic linear heterophony. A single double-inflected degree is found thereafter in all the pitch fields employed in the song, as is the use of G-sharp in acciaccatura clash with A. The latter pitch is the final of all the verses save the last, alternating with E in the "*Slavna*" interjections. The last "*Slavna,*" like the concluding line of "*Selezeñ,*" witnesses a transformation of these assigned roles. The G-sharp becomes a harmonic tone (inflected to G-natural in the voice's final outburst), and in fact forms a part of the concluding chord, which in this song does have the quality of a chord of resolution (yes, a tonic), lending the setting a sense of harmonic arrival which the previous song had notably, and just as remarkably, lacked (see Ex. 15.17c).

The "*Sektantskaya,*" on which—to judge from both the quantity and the nature of the surviving sketches—Stravinsky lavished special effort, follows a very different model from its companions in the *Quatre chants russes*. In its snaking, melismatic vocal line it is unique among the productions of the Swiss years. To do justice to the mystical religious text he had selected, Stravinsky adopted as his template the recitative-like "spiritual verse" (*dukhovnïy stikh*) as performed by the blind mendicant musicians known as *lirniki* or *kobzari* (≈*bandurïstï*) because they accompanied their songs on the hurdy-gurdy (*lira*) or on the lutelike Ukrainian instrument known as the *kobza* (in its present-day form, the *bandura*) (Fig. 15.5a). These singers, who proliferated in Little Russia until Stalin finally stamped them out in the 1930s, were well known to Stravinsky, who had had himself photographed with one in Ustilug a decade or so before he composed his stylization of their song.[118] In addition, a transcription of a *lirnik* spiritual verse was featured in Linyova's Ukrainian collection of 1903, published in the first volume of the papers of the MEK (Fig. 15.5b).

Lirniki and *kobzari* were often persecuted as beggars. This treatment, coupled with their blindness, gave them a special romantic aura for folklorists. Linyova, who evidently revered them as quasi-vatic beings, described them in a way that already evokes the mood of Stravinsky's "*Sektantskaya*" (though sectarian verse, being a Northern Russian product, had nothing to do, either thematically or stylistically, with the music of the Ukrainian mendicant singers in real life):

---

118. This picture was first published in T. Strawinsky, *Catherine and Igor Stravinsky,* n.p. (the twenty-third photograph in the album); it is reproduced in Taruskin, "Russian Folk Melodies in *The Rite,*" 507.

EXAMPLE 15.16   "*Zapevnaya*" (*Quatre chants russes,* no. 2), summary of tonal flow

EXAMPLE 15.17

a. Source melody for "*Na korïte sizhu*" (cf. Ex. 15.2), transcribed to pitch of "*Podblyudnaya*" (*Quatre chants russes,* no. 3)

b. "*Podblyudnaya,*" first line of melody

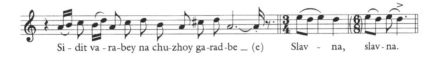

Si - dit va - ra-bey na chu-zhoy ga-rad-be _ (e)   Slav - na,   slav - na.

c. "*Podblyudnaya,*" summary of tonal flow

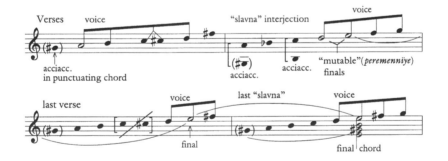

Deprived of the ability to see, to receive impressions of life from without, they go deep into their own inner world, in which they live more intensely than those who can see. A deep feeling is hidden within the outbursts of their songs, which at times resemble [spoken] declamation, while the simple, unpretentious accompaniment on the *bandura* or the *lira* further strengthens the impression. When the blind singer becomes absorbed and gives himself completely over to his song, when its groaning strains of complaint at the world's injustice pour forth from his soul, only a hard heart will remain unmoved.[119]

119. Linyova, "Opït zapisi fonografom," 231.

FIG. 15.5a. A. Podtïkanïy, *bandurist* with his guide boy, from Linyova's Ukrainian field collection (*Trudï MEK* I [1906]). Like *lirniki,* who played hurdy-gurdies, *banduristï* were blind bards who wandered western Russia and the Ukraine.

FIG. 15.5b. Melismatic spiritual verse (*dukhovnïy stikh*) accompanied by *lira* (hurdy-gurdy), transcribed by Linyova (*Trudï MEK* I). Songs of this kind were the model for Stravinsky's "*Sektantskaya*" ("Chant dissident") in *Quatre chants russes* (1919).

It was the strummed *kobza* (*bandura*) standing in for the gusli of sectarian lore, rather than the continuous sounds of the *lira,* that Stravinsky imitated in his accompaniment, at first with the cimbalom, and later, as published, with piano.[120] The song may be divided into four parts, articulated by changes in the accompanying ostinati. The first and second ostinati are related by the octatonic circle of minor thirds (referable to Collection II); the third is an acciaccatura of the usual sort that ultimately establishes B as pitch of priority. When the latter gives way to the final ostinato for the last long (unmeasured) passage in the song, we encounter that Stravinskian rarity, a perfect authentic cadence (Ex. 15.18a). The voice part is equally unusual; it unfolds over the first drone/ostinato in an unprecedented way: working from the middle outward, it gradually covers the entire chromatic spectrum within the range of the half-octave F♯–C. The method by which this singular unfolding is accomplished is nevertheless familiar. It consists of a series of "infixes" of a chromatic *tertium quid* between the notes of encircling major seconds—what in previous descriptions has been termed "acciaccatura in reverse" (Ex. 15.18b).

More conventional acciaccatura relations are many and various, and virtuosically handled. In the long stretch from m. 18 to m. 38, the minor ninth given as the third ostinato in Example 15.18a is struck a total of thirty-four times. The spelling given in the example emphasizes its function within the overall tonal plan of the song, in which B is the actual pitch of prolongation. On its first appearance, however, and several times thereafter, the ninth is spelled B♭/C♭, and the lower note is clearly the harmonic tone. Still given to orthographic self-analysis, Stravinsky fastidiously shifts his spelling of all the notes in the texture from sharps to flats and back again, to reflect the shifting harmonic emphasis of the fulcrum-ostinato (Ex. 15.18c).

Just as often, however, Stravinsky's orthography can be deceptive. When, much later, he finished *Threni* he compared it with the Renaissance music on which he had modeled it, finding one of its chief technical novelties in its ametrical tactus pulse, which is merely "counted out" rather than "beaten."[121] There are passages of this kind in the "Swiss" music too, where, possibly taking a leaf from Satie, Stravinsky suspends the barline altogether and counts the music out by means of an ostinato tactus-pulse. Both the "*Zapevnaya*" and the "*Podblyudnaya*" from the *Quatre chants russes* have passages of this kind, but the most extended one is found at the end (the Doxology) of the "*Sektantskaya,*" lasting fifty-nine eighth notes as measured by the irregularly grouped *basso ostinato.* The other parts, too, are cast in irregular, overlapping ostinati. Each part is confined to its own highly restricted diatonic pitch collection. These three apparently competing modal groups are laid

120. The rescoring of the "*Sektantskaya*" (retitled " A Russian Spiritual") as the second of the *Four Songs* of 1954, with the cimbalom part rewritten for harp and guitar in tandem, was surely the one that motivated the whole set. It restored the symbolic evocation of the *kobza/gusli,* and had perhaps less to do with the wish to emulate Webern (e.g., the songs op. 15, with harp, or op. 18, with guitar) than some writers have assumed (e.g., Heinrich Lindlar, "Die frühen Lieder von Strawinsky," *Musica* 23 [1969]: 120).
121. Conv:18/21.

EXAMPLE 15.18   *"Sektantskaya"* (*Quatre chants russes*, no. 4),
analytical sketches

a. Summary of tonal flow

b. Melodic "infixes"

c. Enharmonics

d. Composing-out of final chord in last section

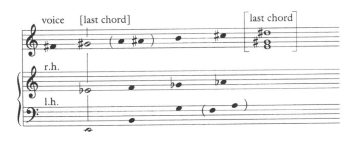

out in scalar form in Example 15.18d. The whole twittering, noodling complex re-
duces not to the wildly polytonal mélange Stravinsky's notation suggests to the
eye, but to a linear composing-out of a single, static, eminently tonal concluding
chord, the sum of the three finals. The process of this chord's unfolding brings the
whole development of Stravinsky's "Turanian" technique of linear heterophony—
and with it, a whole period in his art—to their culmination.

Although he never returned to folk texts, Stravinsky's passionate involvement
with them, however brief when viewed in terms of his exceptionally long career,
was the essential crux in his development. His artistic thinking, his style, and even
his compositional technique were all so thoroughly transformed by this Eurasian-
izing experience that except in light of it the remainder of his creative output is in
certain fundamental ways incomprehensible.

THE "SWISS" SONGS AND BEYOND:
MATTERS OF DECLAMATION

To demonstrate the truth of what may seem an overly sweeping assertion, let us
end this chapter by focusing rather narrowly on an aspect of Stravinsky's style and
technique that many have indeed found literally incomprehensible: his notorious
habits of text declamation, perhaps the one aspect of Stravinsky's work that remains today as controversial as it was when his music was new. Most often attacked
are his settings of English, a language he spoke poorly, where British and American critics have felt confident that the composer's lapses could be attributed to
ineptitude.

And not only critics. Later disclaimers notwithstanding, it is well known that
W. H. Auden and Chester Kallman were at first appalled at the way Stravinsky had
mauled their libretto for *The Rake's Progress* and proposed numerous "revisions" as
a way of salvaging a proper scansion.[122] Robert Craft, who was originally hired by
Stravinsky in 1948 expressly to read that libretto to him so he could hear it pronounced by a native speaker of English, was also nonplussed. For publication Craft
tactfully surmised that "the claims of English stress and accent did not trouble
[Stravinsky] very deeply,"[123] but letters to friends are full of despair at Stravinsky's
apparent incompetence and his unwillingness to hear about it.[124]

And not only English. "I can still see the Princess's salon," recalled Stravinsky of
the first run-through of *Perséphone* at the home of the princesse de Polignac, "myself groaning at the piano, Suvchinsky singing a loud and abrasive Eumolpus,

---

122. The chief disclaimer was Auden's obituary memoir ("Craftsman, Artist, Genius") in the *Observer,* 11 April 1971; the relevant passage is reproduced in P&D:406. For an example of revision-
as-salvage, see Auden's letter to Stravinsky of 23 November 1948, printed together with a fascinating
musical facsimile in SelCorrI:307.
123. Craft, "A Personal Preface," *The Score and I.M.A. Magazine,* no. 20 (1957): 8.
124. E.g., to Sylvia Marlowe, 4 October 1949.

Claudel glaring at me from the other side of the keyboard, Gide bridling more noticeably with each phrase."[125] What gave offense to the French littérateurs was Stravinsky's "disregard," as Craft put it, "of the *spoken* verbal requirements of accentuation or stress." He continued: "Stravinsky's argument was that to duplicate verbal rhythms in music would be dull; but the conflict that sometimes arises in his treatment of syllables as independent sounds, rather than as components of words, continues to disconcert part of his audience."[126]

This is an accurate statement of Stravinsky's mature attitude toward text setting, and a far clearer one than the composer's own notorious "explanation," a classic Stravinskian smokescreen:

> I would call the public's attention to a word that contains a whole agenda: "syllable," and hence the verb "to syllabify."
> That is what mainly preoccupies me.
> In music, which is ordered time and sound, as opposed to the chaos of sound that exists in nature, there is always the syllable. Between it and the generalized sense—the mood that bathes the work—there is the word, which channels scattered thought and shores up rational meaning. Yet words, far from helping, constitute for the musician a burdensome intermediary. All I want for *Perséphone* is syllables, fine strong syllables.[127]

Where did these strange ideas come from, which so many still find unacceptable? The answer lies in the Russian text settings of the Swiss years, for every prosodic transgression one can find in *The Rake's Progress* or *Perséphone* has its counterpart in the *Baika* or *Svadebka*, where there can be no question of ineptitude. Under the impact of Eurasianist thinking, Stravinsky made a complete about-face with respect to the prosodic traditions in which he was reared, an especially strict canon born of nineteenth-century Russian realism. It is another tale of self-liberation, and of playing a Russian tradition newly valued as authentic against one newly rejected as spurious.

––––––––––––

The older tradition was given its classic formulation by César Cui, doyen of "progressive" Russian musical criticism, in a testamentary article composed when Igor Stravinsky was nine years old:

125. D&D:20; *Dialogues*, 36.
126. App. B ("*Perséphone:* The Evolution of the Libretto") in SelCorrIII:478.
127. "Je dois . . . attirer l'attention du public sur un mot qui contient tout un programme: 'syllabe' et ensuite le verbe 'syllaber.' Là réside ma préoccupation principale. Dans la musique, qui est temps et ton réglé, par opposition au son confus qui est dans la nature, il y a toujours la syllabe. Entre elle et le sens tout à fait général—le mode qui baigne l'oeuvre—il y a le mot qui canalise la pensée éparse et fait aboutir le sens discursif. Or le mot, plutôt qu'il ne l'aide, constitue pour le musicien un intermédiaire encombrant. Je ne voulais pour Perséphone que des syllabes, de belles, fortes syllabes" ("M. Igor Strawinsky nous parle de 'Perséphone,'" *Excelsior* 29 [April 1934]; reprinted in White, *Stravinsky: The Composer and His Works*, 534).

True vocal music is written to a preexisting text, to a work of artistry, of poetry, capable of inspiring a musician. It is moreover essential that the music faithfully transmit the general mood of the poetical work and that it serve as its beautiful and well-fitting attire. It is essential that in quantity the music correspond to the dimensions of the poem, so that the music does not dangle on it like a gown on a hook, so that the text need not be artificially prolonged by repeating stanzas, verses, or individual words, and so that by such repetitions the artistic and elegant form of the poem be not distorted. It is essential that, in singing, the pronunciation of every word be suitably rendered, and that the phrasing of the text and the observance of its punctuation be correct. Besides that, the rhythm of the music and its meter must be in direct correspondence with the meter of the verse, the length of the musical phrase with the length of the text phrase, and, in fine, the music must in every way blend with the word so as to form with it one indissoluble, organic whole.[128]

Like all such dogmatic pronouncements of Cui's, these are framed as rules dictated by sheer Ciceronian common sense, yet the author attaches an explicitly programmatic significance to them when he notes that "remarkably, before the present time a majority of composers and of the public did not realize the importance of all the foregoing and willingly deprived themselves of this powerful force of expression and impression." It was a specifically Russian and a specifically realist esthetic Cui was summing up, one that had found its prime exponent in Musorgsky, and which was exemplified par excellence in a style of vocal writing Cui had long ago labeled "melodic recitative"—a kind of infinitely flexible, madrigalian arioso with which anyone who has seen *Boris Godunov* is very familiar. "The most accomplished and inspired scene" in that opera, wrote Cui, was the scene in the inn at the Lithuanian border (Act I, scene ii, in the version of 1872):

The music is so closely, so indissolubly bound with the word that it is as impossible to recall a phrase of text without the corresponding music as it is to recall a phrase of music without the accompanying text. . . . The whole scene is written in so lively, so true, and so formally free a fashion, . . . the music and text reinforce one another to such a degree, that the scene makes a far stronger impression with the music than without, despite all its lofty purely literary distinction.

Here Cui adverts to the fact that Musorgsky had set a scene from Pushkin's tragedy practically verbatim, and a prose scene at that. He is quick to caution, though, that despite Musorgsky's success, prose is far from an ideal medium for music:

In music a definite and regular rhythmic continuity is desirable. It augments the force of the impression [the music makes]. Of course, in no case should correctness of declamation be sacrificed to this rhythmic regularity. But if the one can be

128. C. A. Cui, "Neskol'ko slov o sovremennïkh opernïkh formakh" (1889), in *Izbrannïye stat'i* (Leningrad: Muzgiz, 1952), 406–8.

combined with the other, so much the better. And this is entirely possible given the tonic [accentual] quality of our [Russian] verse, with its regular and monotonous succession of stresses. A text that contained phrases now long, now short, consisting of an inconsistent, even fractionated number of verses, would evoke in the music a phrase structure correspondingly devoid of symmetry, which would reflect unfavorably on the absolute value of the music. One should not magnify this disadvantage through a constant rhythmic irregularity. Rhyme is not needed. Short verses with a rich rhyme scheme can often actually impart a rather insipid quality to the music. But regular verses in a beautiful meter are indeed highly desirable. In French verse, on the other hand, rhyme is utterly indispensable. It can, albeit to a limited extent, conceal the unsuitability for music of a syllabic [i.e., numerable] versification. Without rhyme such verses would ultimately turn into prose.[129]

For this reason among many others, Cui's paradigm of perfected operatic style was Dargomïzhsky's *The Stone Guest,* set verbatim, like the Inn scene from *Boris,* to a preexisting play by Pushkin, but one cast in elegant iambic pentameters, not prose.

All this was passed along to Stravinsky as a catechism, and he at first accepted it as uncritically as would any Rimsky-Korsakov pupil. Besides, as we know, Stravinsky had been brought up in a family that had exceptionally close ties with Cui himself and with the Russian operatic traditions he represented. Vladimir Stasov had dubbed Fyodor Stravinsky the great "realist" of the Russian operatic stage, praised him above all for his powers of truthful declamation, and saw in him the ideal portrayer of Leporello, the basso role in *The Stone Guest.*[130] Cui seconded Stasov's judgment of Stravinsky père's artistic qualities in a slew of fine notices.[131] And although—inevitably—heavily barbed, Igor Stravinsky's 1960 memoir of Cui was quite surprisingly revealing. After dismissing the old kuchkist's sterile anti-Wagnerism, his nationalism, and his orientalism with a sneer, he confided:

> Cui did help me to discover Dargomïzhsky, however, and for that I am grateful. *Rusalka* [after Pushkin's water-nymph play] was the popular Dargomïzhsky opera at the time, but Cui considered *The Stone Guest* the better work. His writings drew my attention to the remarkable quality of the recitatives in the latter, and though I do not know what I would think of this music now, it has had an influence on my subsequent operatic thinking.[132]

That is certainly putting it mildly. As long as he lived even part-time in Russia, Stravinsky's thinking on the text-music relationship was altogether dominated by

---

129. Ibid., 412. The tonic character of Russian stress is so marked that even prose displays a kind of metric evenness, with accented syllables spaced regularly, and unaccented ones arranging themselves in formations of short equal values like gruppetti between accented ones. See Taruskin, "Handel, Shakespeare and Musorgsky."

130. See V. V. Stasov, "K yubileyu Stravinskogo" (1980), in *Stat'i o muzïke* 5a:160–62.

131. For examples, see Cui, *Izbrannïye stat'i,* 309, 403, 442.

132. M&C:59/61.

the melodic-recitative ideal. He had a particularly formative experience on 4 January 1906, when, in honor of Stasov's eighty-second birthday, Rimsky-Korsakov arranged a performance at his home of the then-unpublished and all but unknown setting Musorgsky had made in 1868 of the opening scenes of Gogol's comedy *Marriage,* the most uncompromisingly realistic recitative opera ever attempted. Stravinsky's brother Guriy was among the performers, and the budding composer, accompanied by his fiancée, Catherine (they were married one week later), joined an audience of thirty-five of St. Petersburg's leading musicians (Chaliapin and Glazunov among them) to hear this legendary "experiment in dramatic music in prose."[133]

The results of this exposure may be heard in *The Nightingale,* not only in the first (pre-*Firebird*) act, but especially in the third, composed as late as 1914. The Chinese Emperor, suffering his death agony against a ritual chorus of unseen spirits (a situation reminiscent of the onstage death of Boris Godunov), sings a passage that could have come straight out of *Marriage* (Ex. 15.19). It has all the special earmarks of realistic speech-song à la Musorgsky: careful observation of the intonational contour and tempo of Russian conversational speech (in this case highly agitated) and, above all, extreme care in the handling of the tonic accent. Stressed syllables fall on the beats, while the unstressed syllables arrange themselves freely into gruppetti. Where words begin with unaccented syllables, the beginnings of beats are occupied by rests, producing an abundance of what Russian writers call "mute endings" (*glukhiye okonchaniya*), that is, the interruption of a string of short unaccented note values by a rest on the beat. At the one spot where an accented syllable does fall off the beat (the final "*muziki*"), Stravinsky fastidiously marked an accent, even though the high E-flat would hardly be sung without one. Stravinsky was well aware of the source of these prosodic practices. While at work on the first act he wrote in his diary, "Why should I be following Debussy so closely, when the real originator of this operatic style was Musorgsky?"[134] One in fact finds far less of Debussy and far more of Musorgsky in the post-*Sacre* acts of *The Nightingale* than in the pre-*Firebird* one.

As for *The Stone Guest,* it is certainly striking to discover a loose sheet among the *Nightingale* sketches in the Stravinsky Archive, on which the first six lines of Pushkin's dramatic poem (which had served unchanged as Dargomïzhsky's libretto) are noted down in Stravinsky's hand as an object lesson in prosody (Fig. 15.6). Careful scanning of the text he set would remain a prominent feature of Stravinsky's compositional process, however unconventional or seemingly inept the eventual result.

The works Stravinsky composed during his brief flirtation with Russian Sym-

133. For a full account of the occasion, see Yastrebtsev, *Vospominaniya* 2:370; an abridged version may be found in Yastrebtsev, *Reminiscences,* 379–80.
134. M&C:125/133.

EXAMPLE 15.19

a. *The Nightingale,* scene 3, Emperor's deathbed scene

[Specters: Think back! We are all your deeds. We are here to stay! O think back.
Think back on us!
Emperor: What's this? Who are they? I don't know you! I don't want to listen to you!
Quick, some music! Music, music! Bring on the big Chinese bass drums! O music,
music!]

b. Musorgsky, *Marriage,* a typical replique

Da ved', sam zhe pri-stal: zhe-ni, ba-bush-ka da i tol'-ko!

[Fyokla: You pestered me yourself: find me a wife, old woman, that's all I ask!]

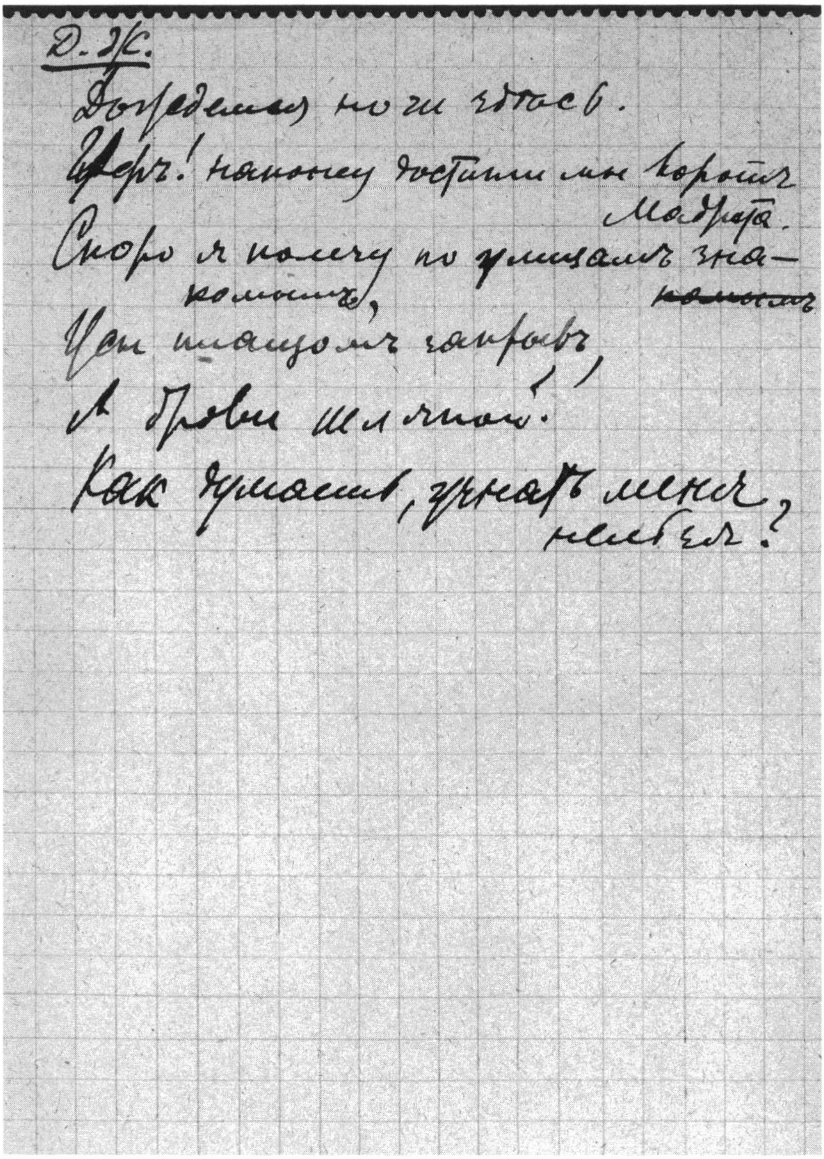

Д.-Ж.

Дождемся ночи здесь.
Уфъ! наконецъ достигли мы воротъ
Мадрита.
Скоро я полечу по улицамъ зна-
комымъ,
Усы плащомъ закрывъ,
А брови шляпой!
Какъ думаешь, узнать меня
нельзя?

FIG. 15.6. First six lines from Pushkin's "The Stone Guest," copied out for prosody study (amid *Nightingale* sketches). (Paul Sacher Stiftung, Basel)

EXAMPLE 15.20　"The Dove," first line, with hypothetical version in equal eighths

Gó - lub' k té-re-mu   pri - pál.   Gó - lub' k té - re-[mú] pri - pál.

[The dove pressed itself to the tower.]

EXAMPLE 15.21　*Zvezdolikiy*, fig. ⑪ to end, chorus parts only

Na né - be a - lé-li iz - ló-mï   i

sém' zo-lo-tïkh se-mi-zvéz - diy   ve - lí nas k pre-dé-lam pu - stín'.

[The sky was streaked with red, and seven golden constellations led us to the end of the desert.]

bolist poetry show a comparable, typically Russian fastidiousness in declamation. The setting of the opening line of "The Dove" ("*Golub*"), the second of the Balmont songs of 1911, can serve, in its fussy accuracy, as paradigm (Ex. 15.20). So as to keep the unaccented last syllable of "*k teremu*" off the third beat, the word is set as a triplet, with a typically Musorgskian "mute ending" voiding the third beat.

Even *Zvezdolikiy* was set in a thoroughly "realistic" fashion as to declamation, the composer evidently bending every effort toward realizing Cui's behest that "in singing, the pronunciation of every word be suitably rendered, and that the phrasing of the text and the observance of its punctuation be correct"—even when the text in question is one whose meaning is deliberately veiled, and whose intelligibility is beyond the power of any composer to vouchsafe. "I couldn't tell you even now [*sic!*] exactly what the poem means," wrote Stravinsky half a century after setting it, "but its words are good, and words were what I needed, not meanings."[135] But this was the composer of the *Canticum sacrum* and *Threni* speaking, not the composer of *Zvezdolikiy*. Every aspect of the Balmont setting belies such a remark, as a glance at all the mute endings and gruppetti in the musical scansion of the closing section (Ex. 15.21) will confirm.

So careful was Stravinsky's attention to Russian prosody that it was possible to state with confidence (in Chapter 9) that his first ostensible settings of a foreign language, the *Poèmes de Verlaine* of 1910, were composed not to Verlaine's text at all

135. M&C:78/83.

but to Mitusov's Russian translation. The musical scansion was in perfect accord with the Russian words, in hideous misalliance with the French. And so it is really one of the major ironies of Stravinsky's career that within a few years of the Verlaine settings he transformed himself into a vocal composer as far from the Cui ideal as it was possible to be. The texts he chose to set, beginning in 1913, were often very far from what is normally considered "artistic." His settings of them, moreover, are characteristically misaccentuated, distorted as to phrasing and punctuation, dislocated in meter vis-à-vis that of the text. In fine (to paraphrase César Cui), they are so calculated as in no way to blend with the word or to permit the formation of "an indissoluble, organic whole."

The earliest work in which we found deliberate and conspicuous departures from the norms of correct Russian declamation was the set of *Japanese Lyrics,* composed in 1912–13 (see Chapter 11). But that essay in "linear perspective" was rather a specialized experiment and a cul-de-sac. Although the *Lyrics* show Stravinsky willing to experiment in areas that were to most Russian composers strictly taboo, his prosodic innovations were contrived: literally imposed on the settings in the course of work, not the principled, "organic" procedure he claimed they were.

As in so many other ways, what finally led Stravinsky out of the blind alley and out of bondage to the constricting Russian realism in which he had been reared was his new and unprecedented approach to Russian folklore. Over and above the ideological and patriotic impulses to which he confessed at the time, what attracted Stravinsky to folk poetry was the same thing that had attracted musicians to the Symbolists and to Balmont in particular, and something, moreover, that Russian Post-Symbolists like Gorodetsky had long since recognized and appropriated from folk poems: namely, "verbal music."

Just how important this play of lingual sounds became to Stravinsky at this particular creative juncture may be gauged from the fact that his observations in *Chroniques de ma vie* on what he called the "sequences of words and syllables" in folk poetry "and the cadence they create, which produces an effect on one's sensibilities very closely akin to that of music,"[136] immediately precede, and indeed furnish the springboard for, the celebrated diatribe on music and expression—that "overpublicized bit" Stravinsky would try so hard to live down when in later life it became important to him to forge a retrospective link with the Expressionist-based music of the New Vienna School,[137] but that remains the linchpin of his postwar modernism. It was precisely the dissociation of sound from meaning

136. *An Autobiography,* 53.
137. See E&D:114–16/101–3. The retraction amounts to little more than an equivocating tautology: "Music expresses itself" (to which, in a filmed interview, Stravinsky once quaintly added, "eloquently").

EXAMPLE 15.22   *"Akh vï, seni, moí seni,"* 3d stanza (beginning)

Uzh kak   po mo-stú, po   mo-stú, po shi - ró - ko-mu mo-stú

[Along the bridge, the wide bridge]

(present to some degree in all poetry, as it were by definition) that provided Stravinsky with a reassuring validation and a powerful weapon in his avowed campaign, if one may put it so, of finally dismantling the *Gesamtkunstwerk.*

Where folk poetry went much further in this dissociation than that of the Symbolists (and in directions Stravinsky could never have taken when he was actually setting the Symbolists) was in its distentions of verbal stress patterns, something fully revealed only in singing. The best possible illustration of this phenomenon comes in a song Stravinsky obviously knew very well, having cited it in *Petrushka.* The third stanza of *"Akh vï, seni, moí seni"* (Ex. 15.22) begins with a triple shift on the phrase *"po mostú"* (along the bridge). All three syllables in turn receive the musical ictus.[138]

Stravinsky took explicit note of this phenomenon when, forty years after the fact, he recalled the pleasure he took in setting folk poems to music. "One important characteristic of Russian popular verse," he wrote, "is that the accents of the spoken verse are ignored when the verse is sung." This is not quite accurate, since the verses he set are never spoken, only sung, and hence are not subject to distortion in quite the way Stravinsky implied, but merely representative of that distortion. Nonetheless, the differences between sung and spoken accentuation were manifold in Russian folklore, and vastly suggestive to Stravinsky: "The recognition of the musical possibilities inherent in this fact was one of the most rejoicing discoveries of my life; I was like a man who suddenly finds that his finger can be bent from the second joint as well as from the first."[139] The discovery was quite remarkably specific and concrete. No less so were its effects on Stravinsky's work.

Prosodic distortions in Russian folk singing are of a very different order from those of the *Japanese Lyrics,* for the heavy tonic stress is not suppressed, merely shifted. The end product is no less authentically and endemically a Russian prosody than the fetishistic realism of Dargomïzhsky and Cui. Nor do we encounter the phenomenon of shifting stress only in Russian folk singing; it is probably a universal trait in the folk singing of tonically stressed languages. English speakers may be inclined to assume or assert, for example, that English and Anglo-American folk songs show "a close structural correspondence between words and

138. My thanks to Simon Karlinsky for this tidbit, which, as he informs me, "the late Roman Jakobson liked quoting to his students" (Personal communication, 8 June 1983).
139. E&D:138/121.

music," that "at various levels—stanza, line, verse foot, and musical measure—units of words and music correspond closely," and that "stressed syllables are set to musically stressed notes";[140] yet a glance at any field-collected anthology of such songs will turn up numerous counterexamples. Of the first ten of Cecil Sharp's famous collection *One Hundred English Folksongs,* for example, misaccentuations occur in more than half (see Ex. 15.23). The one in Sharp's no. 9 is especially telling, as it might so easily have been avoided. The others arise as a result of shoehorning refractory words into an overriding metrical pattern born of the dance. The frequency of this practice, amounting in its paradoxical way to regularity, may be the reason Sharp never called attention to it in the descriptive commentary to his collection.

Nor was Stravinsky the first Russian composer to notice the misaccentuation of Russian words in singing. It was well known to the kuchkists. Balakirev, whose position in Russian folk song collecting was quite comparable to Sharp's in England, faithfully transmitted, in his seminal anthology of 1866, a number of striking instances of stress shift within a single song, something extremely common in dance songs and ritual songs, the very types that would furnish Stravinsky with most of his Swiss-period models (see Ex. 15.24). Ten years later Rimsky-Korsakov published a version of the first of the songs cited by Balakirev, and also arranged it in simplified form as the opening chorus of his opera *May Night* after Gogol (1878). In both versions the accentual shift is maintained without adjustment (Ex. 15.25a–b). This rhythmic quirk remained a permanent feature of Rimsky's folk choruses, as in Example 15.25c, from *The Legend of the Invisible City of Kitezh,* every step of whose creation Stravinsky had witnessed at close hand. A special mark of Rimsky's sensitivity to folk accentuation can be found in a number of his operas, for example the Prologue to *Snegurochka* (1881), where folk choruses alternate with dramatic dialogue and the same characters participate in both. When singing an "impersonal" folk song, they treat the text one way; when singing "personally," they treat it very differently.

So Stravinsky's "rejoicing discovery" had ample precedent. It was something he had long known, only didn't know he knew it. For until he himself turned seriously to folk texts, these shifts of stress had little or no esthetic significance for him. They were merely among the superficial decorative trappings of *le style russe,* which advanced musical minds in Russia thought passé. We have already seen how Rimsky's youngest generation of pupils held folklore at arm's length. The closest Stravinsky came to it in his prentice days was in his songs to Gorodetsky's folkish poems from *Yar',* and that was not very close. The middle section of "*Vesna (Monastïrskaya)*" does seem to contain a characteristic Russian stress shift (see Ex.

140. Bruno Nettl, "Words and Music: English Folk Songs in the United States," in Charles Hamm, Bruno Nettl, and Ronald Byrneside, *Contemporary Music and Music Cultures* (Englewood Cliffs, N.J.: Prentice-Hall, 1975), 198.

EXAMPLE 15.23 From Cecil Sharp, *One Hundred English Folksongs* (1916)

#1: Henry Martin

There were three bro - thers in mer - ry Scot - land,

#3: The Knight and the Shepherd's Daughter

Who should ride by but Knight Wil - liam And he was drunk with wine.

#4: Robin Hood and the Tanner

Bold Ar - der went forth one sum - mer morn - ing,

#6: Lord Bateman

He sail - ed East, he sail - ed West, He sail - ed un - to proud Tur - key. There he was tak - en and put in pri - son, Un - til his life was quite wea - ry.

#8: Little Sir Hugh

It rains, it rains in mer - ry Lin-coln,

#9: Geordie

It's six pret-ty babes that I have got, The sev-enth lies in my bo-dy;

EXAMPLE 15.24 From Balakirev, *Sbornik russkikh narodnikh pesen* (1866)

a. No. 9, Khorovodnaya, *"A mï proso seyali"* ("Oh we sowed the millet")

A mï pró - so sé - ya - li, sé - ya - li. Oy, did Lá - do!

sé - ya - li, sé - ya - li!

EXAMPLE 15.24 (*continued*)

b. No. 39, Khorovodnaya, *"U vorot batyushkinïkh"* ("At Daddy's gates")

U vo-rót, vo-rót, vo-rót, da vo-rót bá - tyu-shki-nïkh,

ai Du-nái moy, Du-nái, ai, ve-syó-lïy Du-nái!

EXAMPLE 15.25

a. Rimsky-Korsakov, *100 Russian Folk Songs,* no. 42: *"A mï proso seyali"*

A mï pró-so sé - ya-li, sé-ya - li. Oy, did Lá-do! sé- ya - li, sé-ya - li!

b. Rimsky-Korsakov, *May Night* (1880), opening chorus

A mï pró-so sé - ya - li, sé-ya-li! Oy, did Lá-do! Sé - ya- li, sé-ya-li!

c. Rimsky-Korsakov, *Legend of the Invisible City of Kitezh,* Act II, chorus of drunkards

S kem ne ve-le - nó stre-vát'-sya? S brázh-ni-kom, s brázh-ni - kom.

Ko-mu vsyá-kiy po-sme-yót-sya? Brázh-ni-ku, brázh-ni-ku.

EXAMPLE 15.26 *Vesna (Monastïrskaya),* op. 6/1, middle section

Molto sostenuto

p Akh, tï pól-ye, mo-ya vó - lya, Akh, do-ró-ga do-ro - gá!

[Oh, field, my freedom, oh path thou art so dear.]

15.26). But the shift is only seeming; it is actually a sophisticated pun. *Doróga* means road, path, or journey; *dorogá* is a feminine predicative form of the Russian adjective *dorogóy,* "dear" or "precious." So what looks like a playful Russian stress shift in fact creates a meaningful utterance: "My path is precious." It is a typical Symbolist effect and far from the world of folk poetry. Rimsky-Korsakov sensed this clearly when he dismissed Gorodetsky's poem as "decadent, impressionistic lyricism [cast in] an artificially folklike Russian" and declared that he, personally, could not see "what pleasure there could be in setting [such] verses."[141]

More evidence that the freedom of accentuation in Russian folk song was not completely new to Stravinsky in 1914 can be found in the *Tri pesenki* (Three Little Songs), subtitled "Recollection of My Childhood," which he had composed during the previous summer and fall.[142] According to the *Chroniques,* they were based on tunes he used to amuse his friends with "in earlier years."[143] In a later memoir he claimed to have played them to Rimsky in 1906;[144] and indeed, the tunes could well have been among the "very sweet and witty musical jests" with which Stravinsky entertained the assembled guests at Rimsky-Korsakov's birthday party not in 1906, but in 1903, when he had just begun to frequent the Korsakovian *jours fixes.*[145] The tunes in any case were Stravinsky family trinkets: according to the composer's Clarens neighbor, C. Stanley Wise, the "Three Little Songs" consisted of "tunes by himself when a kid, p.f. written for *his* kids in the nursery."[146] The third in the set ("*Chicher-Yacher*") had been quoted as a kind of in-joke in the finale of the Symphony in E-flat, and the 1913 settings were dedicated to each of the composer's three children in turn, according to their pet names, from youngest to oldest: "*Sïnku Svetiku*" (To my dear little son Svetik [Svyatoslav, a.k.a. Soulima]), "*Dochke Mikushke*" (To my dear little daughter Mikushka [Lyudmila]), "*Sïnku Fediku*" (To my dear little son Fedik [Fyodor]). As the voice part to the first of the set shows (Ex. 15.27a), these jingles are full of accentual distortions. But as the effect is faux-naïf and parodistic, the result of imitating childish sing-song, little esthetic or technical significance need be attached to their scansion, even if in Lyadov's children's song about a magpie (op. 14/2, dedicated to "Andryusha Rimsky-Korsakov") the name of the bird (*soroka*) is carefully set with an upbeat (Ex. 15.27b).

---

141. Yastrebtsev, *Vospominaniya* 2:453; idem, *Reminiscences,* 427.

142. Most sources (e.g., White, *Stravinsky: The Composer and His Works,* 182; Beletsky and Blazhkov, "Spisok," in *Dialogi,* 379), following the dates on the autograph fair copies now on deposit at the British Library, give the date of composition as October–November 1913; however, a virtually complete draft of "The Magpie" ("*Sorochen̄ka*") is found in the midst of the sketches for *The Nightingale,* Act II (it is actually entered on the reverse of a sheet of sketches for the "Chinese March"), which suggests that it was composed in late July or August. See Table 2.

143. *An Autobiography,* 50.

144. E&D:137n./120n.

145. Yastrebtsev, *Vospominaniya* 2:279; idem, *Reminiscences,* 328.

146. Unpublished letter to Percy Scholes, January 1938, now housed in the Scholes Collection at the National Library of Canada, Ottawa.

EXAMPLE 15.27

a. *"Sorocheñ'ka"* (*Tri pesenki,* no. 1)

So - ró-cheñ' ka chi, chi, chi Na yó-loch-ku ne ska-chí.

Vsko-chí-la na yó-loch-ku, Slo-mí-la go - ló-vu-shku. Dái-te mne ve-

ryó - voch-ku Za-vya-zát' go - ló - vush-ku.

[Little magpie, don't leap up into the fir tree. She did, and broke her head.
Give me some string to tie her head.]

b. Lyadov, *"Soroka,"* op. 14/2

So - ró - ka - be - lo - bó - ka na po-róg ska -

- ká - la, go - stéy pod-zhi-dá - la, ká - shu va - rí - la, dé - tok kor - mí -

la.

[Magpie whitesides hopped on the threshold, was expecting guests, was cooking
Kasha, was feeding her young.]

So it appears we may take Stravinsky's word that his rejoicing discovery took place just when he said it: when he began thinking seriously about *Svadebka.* It was fundamentally bound up with his Turanian revolt and with his post-*Sacre* determination to depersonalize his art. And, just as in the case of Stravinsky's earlier neonationalism, our effort to take its measure will lead us back to the work of Yevgeniya Linyova.

If Balakirev was the Russian Cecil Sharp, Linyova—the first Russian musical ethnographer to use the phonograph for field research—was the Russian Bartók. She was also the first researcher to make explicit observations as to the unusual rhythmic and prosodic traits earlier students of Russian folklore had taken for granted. In the following extract she touches not only upon the mutability of accent, but also on the metrical irregularities peasant singers habitually introduced into the songs they sang, often—unlike the kinds of distension we have so far observed (such as those in Cecil Sharp)—decidedly at variance with the prevailing poetic or dance meter.

From the rhythmic standpoint folk song has a property that especially hampers its transcription into fixed notation. This property is the freedom with which accent is displaced in word and verse. The accent in folk song moves from one syllable to another within a word or from one word to another within a verse, according to the demands of sense in verse or melody, which are closely bound together and mutually influential. In this mobility of accent one feels the urge to destroy monotony, for example: *lúchina, luchína, luchiná* [normally *luchína*, torch or kindling wood], or *góri, gorí* [normally *góri*, mountains]. As a result of this mobility and mutability of [what we may call] the *logical* accent of folksong, it is often very difficult to reconcile it with the *metrical* accent of contemporary art music (as marked by bar lines), *which strives for mechanical regularity in the counting of time units.* When taking a song down by hand little rhythmic compromises are possible—one can steal an eighth note here, a quarter there, and in this way smooth over the apparent rough spots and bring the recalcitrant, capricious tune into conformity with a general mold. But . . . the phonograph insistently claims its due and will not admit such errors.[147]

Linyova goes on to pinpoint two very specific characteristics of Russian folk verse, both of which became characteristics, too, of Stravinsky's Swiss-period music:

(i) The number of syllables per hemistich in a folk verse is not constant. On the contrary, the inequality of the number of syllables in the hemistichs, each of which has one *chief* accent, is one of the characterizing traits of folk song.

(ii) The accent in the verse of a folk song is not *tonic* (that is to say mechanically regular, falling on a certain syllable of the verse), but *logical* [*logicheskoye*], mutable (changing position only occasionally for reason of sense, but nonetheless in no

147. Linyova, *Velikorusskie pesni* i:xvi. Stravinsky would have found ample confirmation of these remarks in the collection of wedding songs by Kireyevsky on which he drew for *Svadebka* (Kireyevsky, *Pesni. Nova seriya,* vol. i: *Pesni obryadnïye*). Here are a few examples of displacement as Kireyevsky noted them down as early as the 1830s:

No. 183:   Zhurila govórila,
            Govoríla, sama plakala
No. 192:   Boyarí-li vï, boyári!
No. 742:   Vesélaya sem'ya, veseláya.
No. 918:   Yasna sókola vo chistóm polye,
            Vo chístom polye vo zelyonem,
            Sazhala ego na belú rúku,
            Prinosila k rodnoy matushke:
            Matushka moya, gosudarïnya!
            Izlovila ya yasna sokolá!"
            Uzh kak tot-li sokól,
            Uzh kak tot-li yasyon,
            Tï, Seluyan gospodin,
            Seluyan, sudar' Fedotovich!

In the last example, every one of the syllables of the word *sókola* ("of the hawk") receives a stress at some point, and the metrical count is in constant flux. Melgunov, too, had noticed the mutable stress in his time, and had called attention to it in his usual belligerent fashion: "It is not surprising that to a regular musician [*zapisnomu muzïkantu*] many aspects of folk music-making will seem wild and incomprehensible. One will always find grammarians who will regard as impossible the arrangement of stress patterns in a song, e.g., on the words '*sinyó more*' [blue sea], or '*retivó serdtse*' [ardent heart] instead of *retívo*, as in fact the people arrange these accents in their songs" (Melgunov, "O ritme i garmonii russkikh pesen," 395).

Na I - vá - nu - shke cha-pán   Chort po mé-sya - tsu ta-skál.

Slï-shish' - li tï, I-vá - nu - shka, vé-rish' - li, leg-ká nó - zhen'-ka?

way arbitrary). Therefore, although *in general* any song, even the rhythmically most wayward, can be divided into measures, nonetheless, owing to the changing position of the accent and the insertion of one, two, or even three syllables into one strain or another (depending on the sense, or simply on the individual inclination of the singer toward exclamations—*èkh, ai no, pravo, da vot,* and so on), one will frequently encounter departures from the divisions (i.e., the meter) one has adopted.[148]

As she relates, Linyova briefly considered adopting the transcription method developed by the Ukrainian composer and folklorist Pyotr Sokalsky (1832–87) in his posthumously published folk song collection (1903) and his important theoretical treatise (published in 1888) on "Great Russian" and "Little Russian" folk music.[149] This method meant giving up all pretense of regular metrical barring, using bar lines only to mark the major divisions of the verses (the "hemistichs"). She decided against this, however, for the reason that in practice it obscured the rhythmic structure of the music. She preferred a system of irregular barring that placed all "chief accents," as she called them, on downbeats.[150]

Once again we should note that the early Russian nationalists, the kuchkists, armed with sharp ears and open minds, had anticipated the scientific ethnographers of the next generation. Balakirev's anthology contains notable instances of Linyova-like irregular barring, including one transcription (no. 17) that instinctively adopts Sokalsky's hemistich method (Ex. 15.28). And in Rimsky-Korsakov's anthology there is a wedding song (already cited in Ex. 12.11c) that looks for all the world as if Stravinsky had composed it.

Alongside these general remarks of Linyova's there is one other important source to be identified before we can look at the impact of Stravinsky's rejoicing discovery on his music—a source even more specifically and directly related to Stravinsky's "Swiss" compositions. This was Ivan Sakharov's *Legends of the Russian*

148. Linyova, *Velikorusskiye pesni*, xvii.
149. Sokalsky, *Russkaya narodnaya muzïka, velikorusskaya i malorusskaya.*
150. Linyova, *Velikorusskiye pesni*, xvi–xvii.

People (*Skazaniya russkogo naroda*), a huge miscellany first published in 1838 and reprinted thereafter many times. It is occasionally mentioned in connection with *Svadebka*,[151] but it was actually the source of the texts for the Peasant Choruses of 1914–17.[152]

Like most early Russian folklorists, Sakharov published only the texts of his songs, not the melodies. But in the case of the *podblyudnïye,* he felt constrained to comment obliquely on the tunes, precisely because of the way the texts were distorted in singing. His comments are quite ambiguous; it would be difficult to figure out exactly what he was driving at in the extract that follows without our knowledge of Balakirev, Rimsky-Korsakov, and especially Linyova:

> The Russian yuletide (*svyatochnïye*) songs we call *podblyudnïye* or *igral'nïye* from their adaptation to games [*igrï*] or *obryadnïye* [from *obryad,* ritual] belong without doubt to very remote times that we have no factual basis for determining exactly. As creations of folklore, these songs carry a peculiar imprint in the form of a tune that differs from all other kinds in its slow, regular, and economical [Sakharov evidently means syllabic] disposition in tones.
>
> Russian yuletide songs come in the following meters: anapestic, dactylochoric with tribrachic endings, choric, dactylic, iambic. Or else they are made up of anapestopyrrhic feet. Lines are found with two, three, or four feet. Here are examples.[153]

And what is the very first example? None other than "*Shchuka*" ("The Pike"), the third in Stravinsky's set of Peasant Choruses, but the first to have been composed. It was completed before the year 1914 was out, and the conclusion seems inescapable that Sakharov's prosodic analysis was what piqued Stravinsky's interest in setting the text. Look upon Figure 15.7b and behold Stravinsky's rejoicing discovery.

What Sakharov had sought in his pedantic way to prove was that this song was sung in "anapestic trimeters with tribrachic endings." What he actually did prove

151. See Craft, *Prejudices in Disguise,* 248; reprinted in P&D:132. Also White, *Stravinsky: The Composer and His Works,* 33. In both cases the bibliographical citations are defective.

152. Stravinsky forgetfully gave Afanasyev (the source of the *Pribaoutki, Baika,* and *Histoire du soldat*) as the source of these texts as well (E&D:135/119), and he has been followed by most subsequent writers and bibliographers, including White (*Stravinsky: The Composer and His Works,* 209) and Dominque René de Lerma (*Igor Fedorovitch Stravinsky: A Practical Guide to Publications of His Music* [Kent, Ohio: Kent State University Press, 1974], 78). Craft cited not the familiar Afanasyev *skazki* collection, but his lesser-known *Poèticheskiye vozzreniya slavyan na prirodu* (The Slavs' Poetic Attitudes Toward Nature), 2:194, as the source for these texts (P&D:604); but what one finds there is only a description of the divination ceremonies for which these texts were appropriate, together with a footnote reference to Sakharov. The most widespread of the four *podblyudnïye* texts—"*Shchuka*" ("The Pike"), the third in Stravinsky's set—can in fact be found in the Afanasyev volume cited by Craft (*Poeticheskiye vozzreniya* 2:158), as well as in Tereshchenko's *Bït russkogo naroda* 7:158, which was also in the elder Stravinsky's library. Both "*Shchuka*" and "*U Spasa v Chigasakh,*" the first in Stravinsky's set, can be found in Kireyevsky, *Pesni. Novaya seriya,* vol. 1: *Pesni obryadnïye* (nos. 1059 and 1063, respectively). But Sakharov alone contains all four texts (*Skazaniya russkogo naroda* 3:11, 12, 13, 260) and is moreover the unique source of Stravinsky's nos. 2 and 4.

153. Ivan Sakharov, *Skazaniya russkogo naroda* 3:10.

F I G . 15.7a. Ivan Petrovich Sakharov (1807–63).

was what is by now a familiar story: that the melody distorted the natural accentuation of the words. Most telling is the fact that the second syllable of the word *Novagóroda,* which is not even a normal part of the name of the ancient Russian city of Novgorod, but merely an archaic infix stemming from the old-Russian system of noun declensions, falls on an accented note in the melody. If read, rather than sung, the three lines given by Sakharov would be accented as follows:

Shchúka shlá iz Novagóroda. (Sláva!)
Oná khvost voloklá iz Bela-ózera. (Sláva!)
Kák na shchúke cheshúyka serébrannaya. (Sláva!)

A perfect example of Rimsky-Korsakov's dual manner of treating texts, alluded

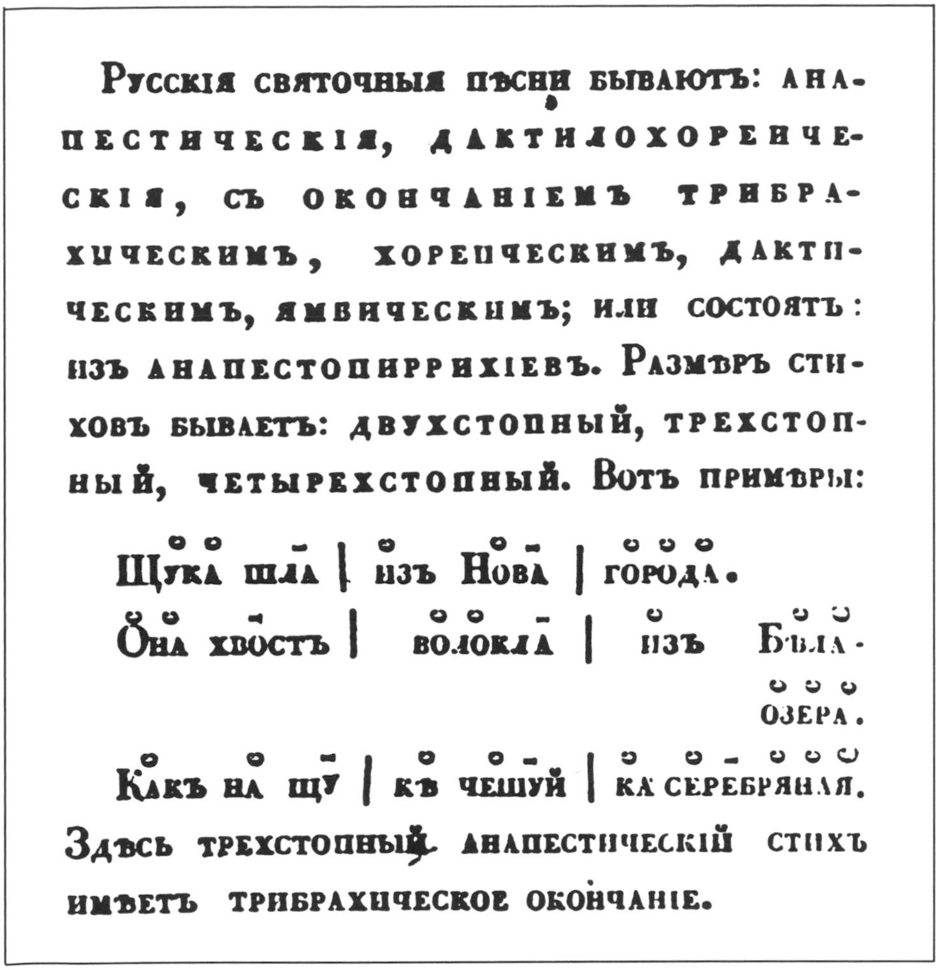

Русскія святочныя пѣсни бываютъ: АНА-
ПЕСТИЧЕСКІЯ, ДАКТИЛОХОРЕИЧЕ-
СКІЯ, СЪ ОКОНЧАНІЕМЪ ТРИБРА-
ХИЧЕСКИМЪ, ХОРЕИЧЕСКИМЪ, ДАКТИ-
ЧЕСКИМЪ, ЯМВИЧЕСКИМЪ; ИЛИ СОСТОЯТЪ:
ИЗЪ АНАПЕСТОПИРРИХІЕВЪ. РАЗМѢРЪ СТИ-
ХОВЪ БЫВАЕТЪ: ДВУХСТОПНЫЙ, ТРЕХСТОП-
НЫЙ, ЧЕТЫРЕХСТОПНЫЙ. ВОТЪ ПРИМѢРЫ:

Щука шла | изъ Нова | города.
Она хвость | волокла | изъ Бѣла-
озера.
Какъ на щу | къ чешуй | ка серебряная.
Здѣсь трехстопный анапестическій стихъ
имѣетъ трибрахическое окончаніе.

FIG. 15.7b.   Text of "*Shchuka*" ("The Pike"; Russian Peasant Choruses, no. 3) as scanned by Sakharov in *Skazaniya russkogo naroda*.

to above in connection with *Snegurochka*, can be drawn from the multifarious settings given the word *Novgorod* in its various grammatical forms in the opera *Sadko*, which takes place in that city. In the opening chorus, when the men of Novgorod sing as individuals expressing their own thoughts in colloquial language, the poeticized form of the name (in locative case) is given a conventionally "accurate" declamation (Ex. 15.29a). In the sixth scene, which portrays a betrothal ceremony, a wedding song is sung in a depersonalized, ritual context. The song is a close relative of Sakharov's "Pike," and it is given a regularized—that is, ritualized—scansion in anapests that forces the particle -*a*-, just as in Sakharov's example, onto the strong beat (Ex. 15.29b). Another relevant example may be found in the old *Gusel'ki* collection (described in Chapter 2 in connection with "How the Mushrooms Mobilized for War"). A fascinating hybrid, it consists of a setting of a variant of

EXAMPLE 15.29

a. Rimsky-Korsakov, *Sadko* (1897), opening chorus

V No-ve - gó - ro - de ve - lí - kom u nas vsyak se - bé sám,
[In great Novgorod everyone is his own boss.]

b. Rimsky-Korsakov, *Sadko,* scene vi, Wedding Song

Rïb - ka shla, plï - la iz No - va - go - ro - da, a i

Khvost vo - lo - kla iz Be - la o - ze - ra.

c. *Gusel'ki,* no. 64: *"Uzh kak shchuka-to shla iz Novagoroda"*

Uzh kak shchu-ka - to shla iz No - va - go-ro - da; Sla - va!

"*Shchuka*" to a tune familiar to everyone from its association with the most cele-brated *podblyudnaya* of them all, the "*Slava*" from the Coronation scene in *Boris Godunov.* Once again we may observe the archaic scansion of the genitive form, *Novágoroda* (Ex. 15.29c). And once again we observe that Stravinsky's "rejoicing discovery" was more a rejoicing rediscovery in the context of a new set of cultural values and desiderata.

That said, how does his setting of "*Shchuka*" relate to Sakharov's scansion? If we look only at Stravinsky's fair copy, prepared in 1917 (Fig. 15.8), we will be disap-pointed. Not only is the second syllable of *Novagoroda* apparently unaccented and thereby conventionalized, but the final syllable of the word (a mere genitive case ending) is set to a long note, vitiating Sakharov's "tribrachic ending."

But now compare the sketches of 1914. The first phrase of "Draft II" (as in Ex. 15.13 above) conforms in every way to Sakharov's classification of the meter ("anapestic with tribrachic endings"), and if one applies his scansion marks to it

FIG. 15.8. Fair copy of "*Shchuka*" (1916).

one finds that Stravinsky's barring follows Linyova's "logical accent." In a later sketch, which approaches the rhythm of the final version, dotted bar lines are used to mark off the feet, again by applying Linyova's methods to Sakharov's scansion: once again, the telltale -*a*- of *Novagoroda* occupies the position of a "logical accent" (Ex. 15.30).

Strangely enough, to find a published version of "*Shchuka*" that corresponds exactly with Sakharov's analysis of its meter, we must look to the 1954 version of the chorus, with the added horn parts (omitted in Ex. 15.31). We now have a perfect transcription of the song as scanned by Sakharov by means of a method adapted from Linyova. The bars are so arranged that *all* the anapestic "longs" (including the -*a*- in *Novagoroda*) fall on downbeats, and the "tribrachic endings" are set as

EXAMPLE 15.30 *"Shchuka,"* sketch on loose sheet with painted title, inserted in "Sketchbook D"

EXAMPLE 15.31 *"Shchuka,"* version of 1954

Once a pike swam out of Nov-go - rod.   Glo - ry!   Flick'd her
[Shchú-ka   shlá   iz Nov-[a]-go-ro - da.   Sla - va!   O - ná

tail, shot straight down from Bie - la-o-ze - ro.   Glo - ry!
khvost vo - lo - klá   iz Be-la-o-ze - ra.   Sla - va!

As she   dart-ed by, all her scales shone sil-ver bright,   Glo - ry!
Kak u   shchú-ki che-shúy-ka se - ré-bran-na - ya.   Sla - va!]

staccato eighths. The paradox is that this version, which fits the quirky Russian model better than any other, was published with English text only, and one that bears no discernible relationship to the new barring. That barring, as a matter of fact, is quite consistent with other rebarrings of the period (such as the "Evocation" and the "Danse sacrale" from *The Rite*), and reflects Stravinsky's lately-arrived-at conviction that short measures promoted accuracy in execution. In revising the chorus, Stravinsky must have gone back to his early sketches for guidance.[154]

154. He certainly did not go back to Sakharov; as n. 152 implies, he had forgotten that source entirely.

Something similar can be observed when comparing the 1954 version of "Selezeñ"—arranged for voice, flute, harp, and guitar as one of *Four Russian Songs*—and the original version for voice and piano, composed in 1918 as part of the *Quatre chants russes*.[155] The text, a conflation of two variants found in Sakharov side by side, runs as follows (Roman numerals refer to Sakharov's variants; Arabic to lines therein):

I:1		Sélezeñ, sélezeñ,	Drake, [my] drake,
	II:1	Siz golúbchik sélezeñ,	[My] dear dove-blue drake,
2	2	Khokhlátïy sélezeñ!	[My] crested drake!
3		Tï viïdi, sélezeñ,	Come out, drake,
4		Tï posmotrí, sélezeñ,	Have a look, drake,
5		Gde útushka tvoyá?	Where is [your] dear duck?
6		Gde sémero utéy?	Where are [your] seven ducklings?
7	3	Sélezeñ dogonyái útku,	Drake, chase [your] duck,
8	4	Molodóy dogonyái útku,	[My] young one, chase [your] duck,
9	5	Podí* útushka domóy,	Dear duck, go home,
10	6	Podí* séraya domóy!	[My] grey one, go home!
11	7	U te sémero utéy,**	You have seven ducklings,
12	8	Os'móy sélezeñ.	The eighth one is the drake.
	9	Búdet útushka nïryát'	The dear duck will dive
	10	Po polyám, po norám,	Through fields, through burrows,
	11	Po kustám, po izbám,	Through bushes, through [peasant] huts,
	12	Po chuzhím seleznyám	To other drakes,
	13	Po zayézzhim gostyám.[156]	To visiting merchants.

One of Stravinsky's sketches for the song (in "Sketchbook V") shows an interesting metrical palimpsest: a phrase originally notated in 2/4 time is preceded by a rest and rebarred in 3/4 (Ex. 15.32a). The three-beat barring was used in the original publication; in 1954, Stravinsky reverted to his original conception, as may be seen in Example 15.32b. As a result of the breakup of the 7/8 bars into pairs of measures in 3/8 and 2/4 (and vice versa), the declamation in the 1954 version is closer to a conventional spoken scansion of the text, in that a higher proportion of stressed syllables now fall on explicit downbeats. This must have been intentional: witness the high A-sharp on *domoy*, where in 1954 Stravinsky expressly departed from his usual method of breaking up the bars, or so it seems, in order to place the accented note on a downbeat.

155. Despite the unfortunate congruence of their titles, the two sets are not identical. The 1954 set contains two of the older *Quatre chants russes* ("Selezeñ" and "Sektantskaya," the latter rechristened "A Russian Spiritual" but best known under the title "Chant dissident") and two of the *Detskiye pesenki* of 1917 ("Gusi-lebedi," retitled "Geese and Swans," and "Tilim-bom").

156. Sakharov, *Skazaniya russkogo naroda* 3:48. Stravinsky wrote out his conflated text in "Sketchbook VI" (as numbered in *Strawinsky: sein Nachlass, sein Bild;* "R57" in the Rothschild catalogue). He introduced two variants, as indicated by asterisks in the texts: "Padi" for "Podi" (*); *detey* (children) for *utey* (ducklings) (**).

EXAMPLE 15.32

a. Metrical palimpsest for *"Selezeň"* (*Quatre chants russes,* no. 1) in "Sketchbook
F," written out as two separate entries

b. *"Selezeň,"* 1918 and 1954 voice parts aligned

EXAMPLE 15.32b (*continued*)

Despite these adjustments, the declamation remained sufficiently offbeat to merit a gentle remonstrance from Stravinsky's editor at J. & W. Chester, who wrote to the composer that "it would be a great help if some accent sign could be put in places where the word accentuation is different from the musical one," noting in particular that "there is nothing to indicate to the English singer that the word 'Selezeñ' is accentuated strongly on the first syllable since in some bars the syllable 'zeñ' appears on the strong musical beat." His prescription: "I would suggest the sign '`', which is often used in dictionaries to denote tonic accent, as if the musical sign '>' is used on the music itself, the singers might overdo the accentuation and distort the musical line." Stravinsky's reply to this, red-penciled in the margin—"no '`' or '>' needed because *my baring* [sic] *of the music* takes care of it"—shows that he had come habitually to regard the bar line, in Linyovian terms, as the marker of the "logical," as opposed to the tonic, or the metric, ictus. His editor, unacquainted with the scholarly folkloristic tradition on which Stravinsky's method rested, failed to understand the composer's purpose and continued his attempt to restore what Stravinsky had deliberately superseded, citing the authority of native Russian speakers to whom he had appealed. To this Stravinsky could only reply, "Excuse me, but I am too a Russian."[157]

An exceptionally explicit documentation of the way Stravinsky assimilated the principle of the "logical accent," and used it as a method of implementing his rejoicing discovery, can be found among the sketches for the *Pribaoutki*. A sample page of sketches for the third of the set (Fig. 15.9) will vividly illustrate how Stravinsky turned Sakharov's analytical method, via Linyova's transcription method, into a creative tool.

As we know, *pribautki*, more than any other type of folk text, represent the kind of pure "mouth music" that was Stravinsky's post-1913 ideal. And as we have seen, rhythm, alliteration, and assonance are far more important in them than sense.[158] No wonder they were the first texts Stravinsky chose to set after making his rejoicing discovery. Particularly characteristic is the third song, "The Colonel" ("*Polkovnik*"), a perfect Russian analogue (as Edward Dent immediately noticed) to our own tongue twister "Peter Piper picked a peck of pickled peppers." It is not about a colonel, not about a quail. It is about the letter *P* and (in the second half) about subtly differing rhythmic groups that all end in the vowel *A* (or, to be more precise, a schwa):

Poshól polkóvnik pogulyát',	The colonel went for a stroll,
poymál ptíchku-perepyólochku;	he caught a little bird, a quail;
ptíchka-perepyólochka	the little bird, the quail
pít' pokhotéla,	became thirsty,
podnyalás'-poletéla,	it rose [in the air] and flew off,
pála-propála,	it fell, it vanished,
pod lyod popála,	it found itself under the ice,
popá poymála,	it caught a priest,
popá popóvicha	a priest [who was] the son of a priest
Petrá Petróvicha.	[named] Peter, son of Peter.

Here the *pribautka* is set out not in prose, the way Afanasyev printed it, but with each clause as a line in itself approximating verse, the way Stravinsky did it in his sketchbook page reproduced in Figure 15.9. Turning now to the sketch, we find Sakharov's scansion marks set next to each line, and above the "poem," three musical drafts (the two-line sketch at the top of the sheet is for the oboe-clarinet duet

---

157. This correspondence, comprising a number of undated typed letters from "P.T.O." of Chester with terse colored-pencil replies in the margins, is preserved along with the autograph (in blueprint reproduction) and corrected proof of the 1954 *Four Russian Songs* among the Chester deposits at the British Library (Loan 75/56).

158. Just how little sense mattered in Stravinsky's scheme of things is apparent from the case of the so-called "*Zapevnaya*," the second of the *Quatre chants russes*. Kireyevsky himself had no idea what it meant, or whether his transcription was correct. Various meaningless words are followed by a parenthetical question mark. This fact did not deter Stravinsky from setting the text just as it stood; on the contrary, the nonsense words were very likely what attracted him. See Kireyevsky, *Pesni. Novaya seriya*, vol. 1: *Pesni obryadnïye*, 317 (no. 1150).

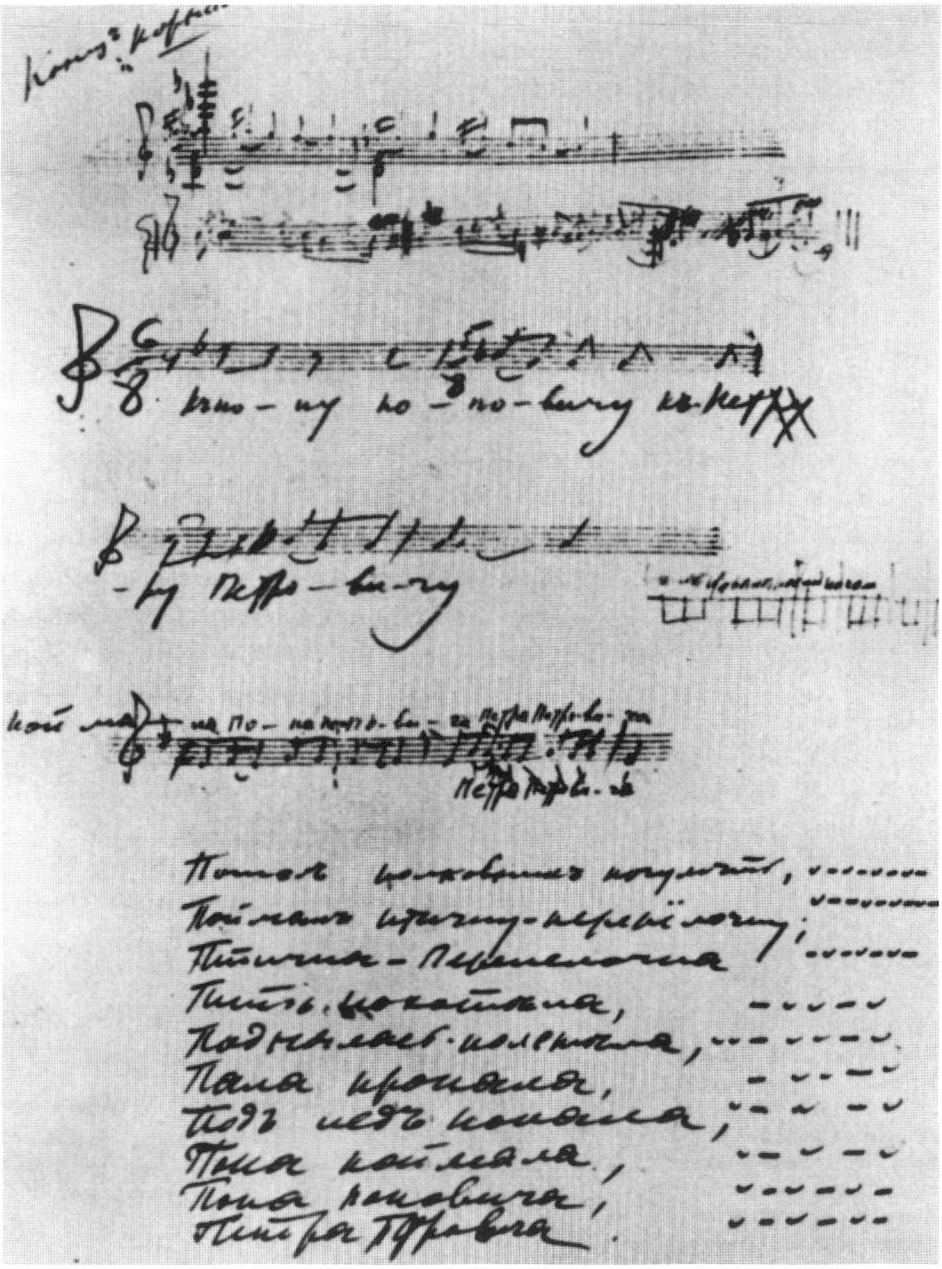

FIG. 15.9.   Sketch for "*Polkovnik*" ("The Colonel"; *Pribaoutki,* no. 3).

at the end of "*Kornilo*"). The two pitched sketches are both for the ending of the song, and both differ considerably from the final version. In the first, the grammatical case is changed for some reason from the genitive to the dative, suggesting that at first Stravinsky may have intended to paraphrase Afanasyev's text rather than set it as it stood (Ex. 15.33a). The most important way in which this sketch differs from the final version, however, is prosodic. Stravinsky at first distinguished the accented syllables from the unaccented ones by lengthening them: they are set either as quarters or as "ligatures" of two slurred eighths. In the second draft of the ending, Afanasyev's text is set without departure, and the melodic figure corresponds to one that is found in the finished song, though not at these words (Ex. 15.33b). Accented syllables are still lengthened here.

The most revealing sketch by far is the one that has obviously been added as an afterthought, most likely after the poem had been copied out and scanned at the bottom of the page. It is a purely declamational sketch, showing no pitches, just durations and barrings (Ex. 15.33c). Here Stravinsky hit upon the method he was to employ in the end for the whole song, and in many other settings as well: with only three exceptions, every syllable in the published setting carries the same duration—an eighth note (or, occasionally, a pair of slurred sixteenths)—and accentuation is achieved solely by means of what Linyova called the "logical stress," correlated with the shifting bar line. The declamational sketch (Ex. 15.33c) extends onto the facing recto in the sketchbook. In the example, it is copied out in full so that Stravinsky's first idea for the rhythm of the ending may be seen.

The section of the song corresponding to this declamation sketch seems to have given Stravinsky more trouble than the rest of the song to compose. A continuity draft that immediately follows the sketchbook page shown in Figure 15.9 corresponds more or less to the layout of the "poem" in the illustration. Through "*pala propala*" it corresponds closely with the final version (the only significant difference being an even more rigorously isochronous rhythm). At the final section, however, Stravinsky became rather fussy, marking the "logical stress" with acciaccaturas (thus bringing out the parallelism latent in *propala/popala*), and at the end he fell back on a cliché "modal" cadence he must have regretted as soon as he had penned it (Ex. 15.34a).

The next sketch shows Stravinsky characteristically confusing the upbeat/downbeat issue by sticking an accented high note on all the pickups. He must have quickly realized that this defeated the whole idea of "logical accent" (Ex. 15.34b). Before he scrapped the high-note idea, though, he sketched a version of the whole passage he liked well enough to think definitive for a while: he signed and dated it ("Salvan, 16/29 August 1914"). The *style russe* cliché at the end is gone now, but there is a conventional ritardando to a spurious long note on an unaccented final syllable (Ex. 15.34c).

The ghost of César Cui may have reared up and menaced Stravinsky at this

EXAMPLE 15.33   Transcriptions from Fig. 15.9: sketches for *"Polkovnik"*
(*Pribaoutki,* no. 3)

a.

k po - pú po - pó - vi-chu k Pet - rú   Pet-ró - vi - chu

b.

poy-má-la po-pá po-pó - vi-cha Pe - trá-Pe-tró vi - cha

c.

pá-la pro-pá-la pod lyod po-pá-la [po-pá poy-má-la po-pá po-

pó-vi-cha Pe - trá Pe-tró-vich-(a)]

EXAMPLE 15.34   More sketches for *"Polkovnik"* ("Sketchbook C")

a.

Po-shol pol-kov-nik   po-gu-lyat'

Poy - mal   ptich - ku   pe - re - pyol - och - ku

Ptich - ka   pe - re - pyol - och - ka   pit'   po-kho-te - la

pod-nya-las' po-le-te-la   pa-la pro-pa-la

pa-la pro-pa-la   pod lyod po-pa-la   po-pa poy-

po-pa po-po-vi-cha Pe-tra Pe-tro-vi-cha.

EXAMPLE 15.34 (*continued*)

b.

pa - la pro - pa - la pod lyod po - pa - la po - pa poy - ma - la

c.

pa - la pro - pa - la pod lyod po - pa - la po - pa poy - ma - la po -

rit.

pa po - po - vi - cha Pe - tra Pe - tro - vi - cha.

EXAMPLE 15.35   *"Polkovnik,"* complete voice part, incorporating scansion marks from Fig. 15.9

Po-shól pol - kóv-nik po - gu - lyát',   Poy-mál ptích-ku pe - re-pyó-loch-

- ku;   Ptích - ka   pe - re - pyó-loch-ka Pit' po-kho-té - la,

Pod - nya - lás' - po - le - té - la,   Pá - la pro - pá - la, Pod

cf. Ex. 15.33c   **Doppio movimento**

lyód po - pá - la, Po - pá poy - má - la, Po -

- pá po - pó - vi - cha, Pe - trá Pe - tró - vich - a.

point, for in the final, published version of the song (see Ex. 15.35) he adjusted the final measure with a gruppetto and a mute ending so as to take the stress off the last note; some Old Russian prosodic habits died a hard death, after all, even in a mind as determined to kill them off as Stravinsky's. But lest we be misled into thinking that Stravinsky was still beholden to old mentors, consider the setting of the words *podnyalas'-poletela* in the third phrase, where, as Stravinsky put it, "the accents of the spoken verse are ignored when the verse is sung"—or when it is set by a Stravinsky who is happy to allow a purely musical sequence to take priority over the verbal accent. And now consider the sprung rhythm at the words *poymál ptíchku* at the beginning of the second phrase, where the unique succession of two stressed syllables is overridden by the music for the sake of a parallelism with the first phrase. Stravinsky was beginning to think like a folk singer.

Perhaps the most inspiring aspect of Stravinsky's final version is the way the setting of "*pala-propala...*" is refined and simplified to the point of virtually reproducing, with its single repeated pitch, the declamation sketch given above in Example 15.33c. One might have supposed that such a solution would have been prompted immediately by the declamation sketch; and yet we see, having traversed all the sketches for "The Colonel," that it was the same "second simplicity" we have already encountered in "The Pike," something achieved through hard work and ruthless self-criticism. Nicolas Nabokov's evocation of Stravinsky at work on the *Symphony of Psalms*—fretting, pacing, erasing, muttering "Pas de pitié" the while—comes vividly to mind, as does Balanchine's recollection of the lesson he learned from *Apollon Musagètes:* "It seemed to tell me that I could dare not to use everything, that I, too, could eliminate."[159]

The opening of the song is willful to the point of being enigmatic. What is the role of the accents, which never return? Evidently they are meant to countermand the tonic stress on the second syllable (perhaps a carryover from the "Russo-Japanese" declamation Stravinsky had toyed with a year earlier) and turn the whole measure into an upbeat. There being no readily available sign for the suppression of a stress, Stravinsky seems to have intended to surround the natural stress with ersatz stresses, thus, by equalizing the stress, in effect neutralizing the stress.

But the tonic stress remains very much in force, even when honored in the breach rather than in the observance. Stravinsky's post-1914 prosody remained profoundly authentic in its Russianness, only now it was a different Russian tradition to which he pledged his allegiance. As in so many other ways, Stravinsky was playing the Russian folk-music tradition against the art-music tradition, and using it as his passport to freedom from the academic postrealist milieu in which he had been reared.

159. Nicolas Nabokov, *Bagazh* (New York: Atheneum, 1975), 168–69; George Balanchine, "The Dance Element in Stravinsky's Music," in *Stravinsky in the Theatre*, ed. Minna Lederman (New York: Da Capo Press, 1975), 81.

He would go far in this direction. The shaping of the prosody in the third of the *Berceuses* (which we may trace in detail thanks to the fortuitous inclusion of a batch of sketches for it in the published *Rite of Spring* sketchbook) shows that by 1915 the kind of peasant-singerish prosodic effects that are just beginning to emerge in the setting of "The Colonel" have become basic to Stravinsky's compositional method. No prosody is accepted anymore as a linguistic "given"; instead, the words are subjected to a searching process of experimental mauling until a shape is found that accords with Stravinsky's musical intuitions.

Again some prescient words of T. E. Hulme come to mind. "Suppose," he wrote in an attempt to define what it is an artist does, "you have a springy piece of steel of the same types of curvature" as one finds in an architect's template. "Now the state of tension or concentration of mind, if [the artist] is doing anything really good in this struggle against the ingrained habits of technique, may be represented by a man employing all his fingers to bend the steel out of its own curve and into the exact curve which you want. Something different to what it would assume naturally."[160]

This is a perfect metaphor for the whole matter of text declamation as Stravinsky came to practice it. The "natural" declamation of the language, fetishized by the likes of Cui, was for Stravinsky merely the template; the task of the artist, as Stravinsky envisioned him(self), was to find the curve which *he* wanted.

The text of the third *Berceuse,* like "The Colonel," has a close English counterpart: "Hush Little Baby, Don't Say a Word." The text in Kireyevsky runs as follows:

Báyushki-bayú, pribayúkivayu . . .	Lulla-lullaby, I am lulling [you] . . .
Kach', kach', privezyót otéts kalách,	Rockaby, rockaby, father will bring a [sweet] bread twist,
Máteri sáiku, s´ín[k]u balaláiku,	For mother a wheat roll, for sonny a balalaika.
A bayú, bayú, pribayúkivayu . . .	And lulla-lullaby, I am lulling [you] . . .
Stánu ya kacháti,	Then I shall rock [you]
V balaláyichku igráti,	[And] play the pretty balalaika,
A bayú, bayú, pribayúkivati . . .	And lulla-lullaby, I shall lull [you] . . .

Discussion will focus on the refrain. Apparently, Stravinsky first sketched it in a way that respected its accentuation as marked in the text (Ex. 15.36a; Fig. 15.10a–b). But he immediately began teasing it with an eye toward exploiting a musical correspondence between the accented -*bayú* and the unaccented -*vayu*. It is difficult to decide in just what order the sketches for this song were entered; but if for purposes of argument we make the big assumption that they made a progressive approach to the version that was published, then their order is as given in Example 15.36 (b, c, and d are all layers of a single sketch).

160. Hulme, "Romanticism and Classicism," 570.

EXAMPLE 15.36   Sketches for *"Bai-bai"* (*Berceuses,* no. 3), in *Rite of Spring* sketchbook (London: Boosey & Hawkes, 1969), pp. 110–13

a.

Bá - yu - shki ba - yú, pri - ba - yú - ki - va - yu... Kach' kach'

b.

Bá - yu - shki ba - yú, ____ pri - ba - yú - ki - va - yu...

c.

Bá - yu - shki ba - yú...

d.

Bá - yu - shki ba - yú...

e.

Bá - yu - shki ba - yú, pri - ba - yú - ki - va - yu...

f.

Bá - yu - shki ba - yú... pri - ba - yú - ki - va - yu...

g.

Bá - yu - shki ba - yú, pri - ba - yú - ki - va - yu...

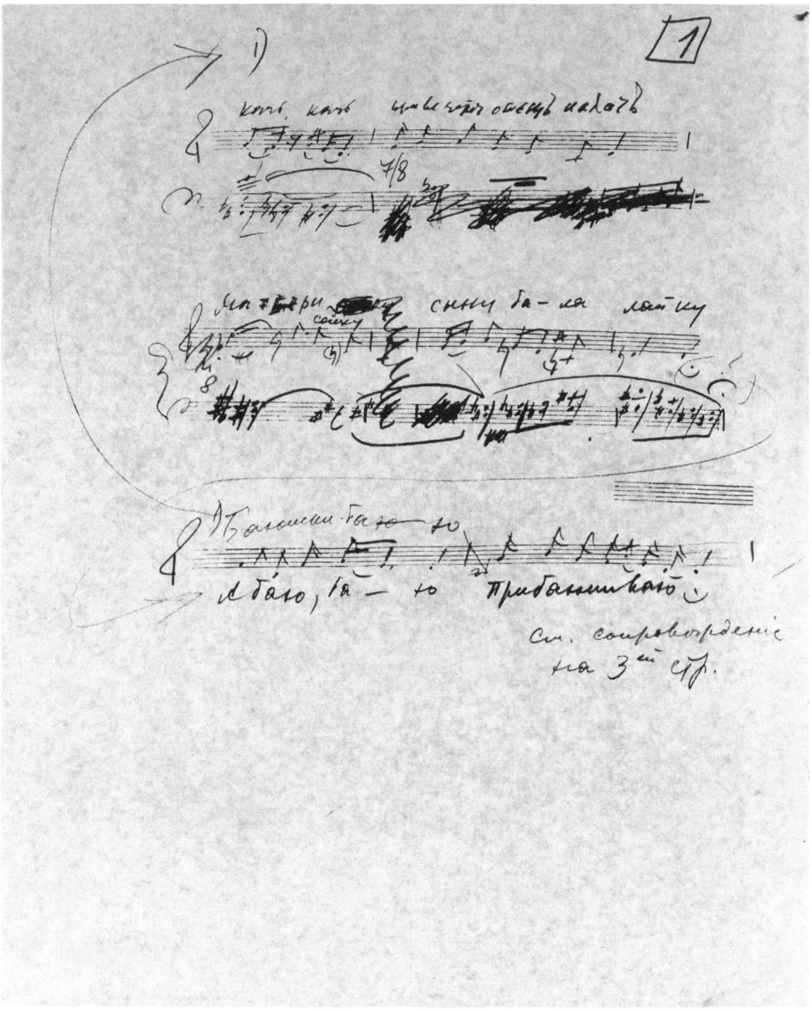

FIG. 15.10a–b.   Sketches for "*Bai-bai*" (*Berceuses,* no. 3).

The accentuation of the word *pribayúkivayu* has been utterly "bent out of its own curve" by the time the process has run its course. With respect to the final form the word assumed in the published version (Ex. 15.36g), an argument could be made that *pri-* carries an accent (since it occupies the downbeat, or "logical stress"), or that *-va-* carries an accent (since it is given an acciaccatura), or even that the final *-yu* carries an accent (since it is syncopated and lengthened, like the "sprung" *-ba-* in the first measure). But by no stretch could the third syllable be said to carry one, even though it is the normally stressed syllable in speech.

Now, to anyone who knows the later Stravinsky, this inside-out setting of *pribayúkivayu* will have a familiar ring: the famous (mis)setting of "Laudate DOMI-NUM" in the *Symphony of Psalms* leaps to mind—right down to the syncopated and lengthened, yet unaccented, final syllable (Ex. 15.37a).[161] And in turn we may be legitimately reminded of perhaps the last Stravinsky composition one would have expected to figure in the present discussion: the stress shift between the subject and the answer in the concluding fugue from the arch-neoclassical *Concerto per due pianoforti soli* of 1935. It is a purely "Turanian" invention, by way of Sakharov and Linyova (Ex. 15.37b).

Stravinsky's Turanian phase thus never really ended. A sketch page for Anne's aria, "Quietly, night," in the third scene of *The Rake's Progress* shows how English

161. The fact that the original words may have been the Slavonic Kyrie, "Góspodi pomíluy" (see P&D:295–96) does not alter the situation in the least, for Stravinsky saw fit to make no adjustments when substituting the Latin text.

EXAMPLE 15.37

a. Symphony of Psalms, III, 2 before ⟨17⟩

Lau - dá - te DÓ-MI-NUM,   lau - dá - te É - um.

b. *Concerto per due pianoforti soli,* IV, subject and answer

EXAMPLE 15.38   Anne's aria (*The Rake's Progress,* Act I, scene iii)

a. "Model stanza," transcribed from top of Fig. 15.11

Although I weep, _____ it knows of lone - li - ness

b. Published version of same line

al - though I weep, __ it __ knows, it knows of lone - li - ness.

was consciously subjected to the rule of the "logical accent." The last line of the
first stanza, "Although I weep, it knows of loneliness," was originally set in a manner that—apart from the implied accentuation of the first word, which even a native speaker might have tolerated—was impeccable as to prosody, showing that
Stravinsky was perfectly well aware of the correct scansion of the text (Ex. 15.38a).
That did not prevent him from immediately teasing it into the "inept" form in
which it was published (Ex. 15.38b), a change that can be seen explicitly entered at
the very top of the sketch page shown in Figure 15.11.

As we are well aware by now, such things were nothing new in *The Rake.*
But it was there they were noticed (as they were noticed in *Oedipus Rex* and
Perséphone), and Stravinsky was censured for them by those who tacitly, perhaps
unwittingly, approached his work with the assumptions and the prejudices of a
César Cui.

For Stravinsky, by utter contrast, once he had made his rejoicing discovery the

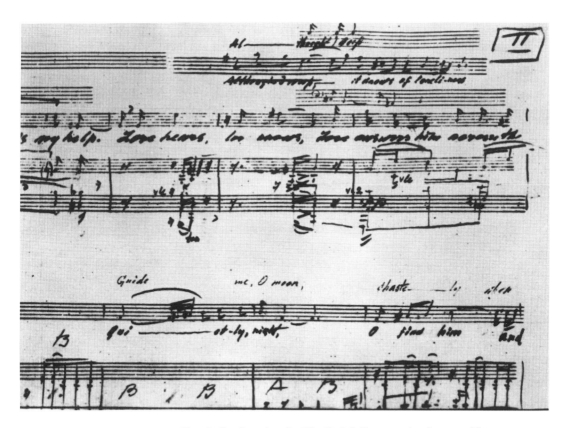

F I G . 1 5 . 1 1 .   Sketch for Anne's aria, *The Rake's Progress,* Act I, scene iii.

accents of the spoken language were there merely to be manipulated, like any other musical parameter, for the sake of musical enjoyment. "Words," we have seen him assert with reference to *Perséphone,* "far from helping, constitute for the musician a burdensome intermediary." The reason? "For music is not thought."[162] Instead, he maintained, he sought lingual sounds ("syllables, fine strong syllables") to match with musical sounds.[163] For if, as Mallarmé once put it to Degas in a phrase that so delighted Stravinsky that he quoted it twice in his published writings, "one does not create rhymes with ideas but with words,"[164] then one does not create music with words but with sounds—at least, not if one was Stravinsky. In this, as

162. "M. Igor Strawinsky nous parle de 'Perséphone,'" translated by White in *Stravinsky: The Composer and His Works,* 534.

163. One of the early musical impressions Stravinsky recorded in *Chroniques de ma vie* seems to have been "planted" in order to justify this modernist predilection. Recalling the song of an ancient, near-dumb peasant, Stravinsky describes it as having been "composed of two syllables, the only ones he could pronounce; they were devoid of meaning, but he made them alternate with incredible dexterity" (*An Autobiography,* 11).

164. The wording here follows Stravinsky, "Pushkin: Poetry and Music," in White, *Stravinsky: The Composer and His Works,* 543; also see *An Autobiography,* 117.

in so many other ways, he sought in the esthetic stance of folk artists the seeds and the validation of an authentic modernism. Although it may discountenance us that he saw fit to set the poetry of Auden or Gide as if it were a Russian limerick, that is precisely what he did, and seriously. To fail to take this aspect of his art seriously is to fail at a very basic level to understand it.

MINSTRELS RUSSIAN AND TURANIAN

The "merry performance with singing and music" originally titled *Baika pro lisu, petukha, kota da barana* (*The Fable of the Fox, the Cock, the Cat, and the Ram*), but best known by Ramuz's title, *Renard,* is one of the few Stravinsky works for which there is a distinctive critical tradition of sorts in Russia. Asafyev, writing in 1926, immediately recognized this dramatized conflation of some dozen texts from Afanasyev's tales as a *skomorosh'ye deystvo,* a minstrel show, or, as he put it, "a renaissance of the art and trade of the *skomorokh,* of the authentic 'old-time' Russian theater, a world of mockery, fun-and-games, tomfoolery, naughty satire—in sum, of a profoundly indigenous *grotesque.*"[1]

The discussion of the *Baika* is one of the really crucial arguments in Asafyev's *Book About Stravinsky.* The General Directions for Performance call for a troupe of "buffoons, ballet dancers, or acrobats" who act the story out in pantomime on a trestle-stage, which they never leave, while the singers remain seated with the instrumentalists in the rear, their voices disembodied after the fashion of Diaghilev's *Coq d'or.* Having equated Stravinsky's acrobatic mimes with the minstrels of Old Russia, Asafyev went on to substitute the former for the latter and made trenchant comparisons between the highly concentrated, exacting, and detached mental attitude demanded of acrobats and the alert, precision-tooled, objective art of Stravinsky. This further equation formed the basis of Asafyev's main, quasi-Futurist or -Constructivist thesis about Stravinsky's historical significance as the artist who brought music out of its Romantic "hypnosis" into an era of wide-

---

1. Asafyev, *Kniga o Stravinskom,* 112 (also *A Book About Stravinsky,* 105).

awake actuality and the assertion of the dynamics of contemporary social and industrial life.[2]

Asafyev's viewpoint on the *Baika,* if not his dated extrapolations from it, became well-established critical "fact" in the Soviet Union. Boris Yarustovsky asserted that Stravinsky's piece is "connected with the traditions of Russian *skomoroshestvo,* the Russian folk showmen with their allegorical depictions, often played in animal guise; no less characteristic is the grotesque wit of the skit, the abundance of songs and dances, the moralizing finale," and concluded by characterizing the *Baika* as "a revival of the forgotten practices of the folk *skomorokh* theater."[3] The viewpoint came westward in a particularly concrete and challenging form with Simon Karlinsky's pathbreaking discussion of "Stravinsky and Russian Pre-Literate Theater": "*Renard,*" Karlinsky maintained, "is a work that portrays a group of itinerant *skomorokhi* who don animal masks, perform a satirical, anti-clerical skit for a rural audience in pre-Petrine Russia and demand payment in barter at the end of the performance."[4]

This tradition of interpreting the *Baika* is at once illuminatingly correct and dead wrong. Although there is no actual mention of the *skomorokhi* either in the text of the piece or in the General Remark, Stravinsky did indeed drop unmistakable hints at their traditions, of a kind that connoisseurs of Russian art and theater like Asafyev or Karlinsky could not fail to catch: first, by subtitling the piece "A Merry Performance" (*Vesyoloye predstavleniye*), which resonates with the epithets by which the skomorokhi were known to their contemporaries—"merry folk" or "merry lads" (*vesyolïye lyudi, vesyolïye molodtsi*);[5] and second, by prominently featuring the cimbalom in the accompanying chamber orchestra, where, as the text explicitly reveals, it stood in for the gusli, the traditional skomorokh instrument.[6]

2. See the précis given on pp. 106–9 of *Kniga o Stravinskom* (or *A Book About Stravinsky,* 97–99) of a series of articles Asafyev wrote in 1924 for the Leningrad journal *Novaya muzika.*

3. Yarustovsky, *Stravinskiy,* 106, 111.

4. As read at the International Stravinsky Symposium at the University of California, San Diego, in September 1982 (quoted by Robert Craft in SelCorrI:42in.). As revised for publication in *19th-Century Music* 6, no. 3 (Spring 1983): 236, under the title "Stravinsky and Russian Pre-literate Theater," the passage is even more specific and assertive: "At its basic level, *Renard* depicts four skomorokhi in a pre-Petrine village who perform a satirical, anti-clerical skit about the victimization of a wealthy peasant (the Cock) by a con-woman disguised as an itinerant nun (in the Russian text the Fox is a Vixen). The Cock's two fellow-peasants, the Tomcat and the Ram, rescue him twice. Then the peasants kill the predator and blame the murder on the hounds of the local noblemen, whereupon the performers remove their masks and demand a payment in the form of a crock of butter." But this is not a description of the *Baika* "at its basic level"; it is a highly selective allegorical interpretation that rests on a great number of tempting but risky assumptions about Russian history, about the skomorokhi, about Stravinsky's learning, and about his intentions, to mention only four. Furthermore, by emphasizing that the libretto is "permeated with familiar Russian nonsense rhymes, proverbs and parodies of ecclesiastic diction and Orthodox prayers," Karlinsky seems to underestimate or ignore the extent to which Stravinsky depended on the preexisting tales in Afanasyev's *Narodnïye russkiye skazki* for his text.

5. See Russell Zguta, "*Skomorokhi:* The Russian Minstrel-Entertainers," *Slavic Review* 31 (1972): 297.

6. The very first historical reference to the skomorokhi, an entry for the year 1068 in the Kievan Primary Chronicle, already associates them with their instrument: "With all manner of enticements [the devil] draws us away from God, with trumpets and *skomorokhi, gusli,* and *rusalii* [pagan midsummer

Yet Stravinsky's merry lads are engaged in a kind of performance to which no documentary evidence attests. The "folk skomorokh theater" embodied in the *Baika* was something Stravinsky did not revive but invented. Its habitat was not pre-Petrine Russia, but the Turanian expanse of the composer's creative imagination. There could be no greater testimony to the power of that imagination and the compelling inner authenticity of its creations than the fact that so many sophisticated critics and scholars have accepted the historicity of this one.[7]

Unlike the skomorokhi of Turania, the skomorokhi of Russia are not known to have put on satirical plays, nor are Russian folktales such as Afanasyev collected known to have been acted out by professional entertainers of any kind. Although usually likened to the *jongleurs* or *Spielmänner* of medieval Europe, the skomorokhi are held by some modern scholars to be the descendents of the priests or shamans of the popular pagan cults of pre-Christian Russia.[8] When reduced to the function of festival and fairground entertainers, they nonetheless retained many of the appurtenances and customs of their shaman forefathers, including the donning of animal masks, as in Shrovetide mummery (depicted in the final tableau of *Petrushka;* see Chapter 10) or in seasonal "plays" containing survivals of pagan fertility rites that outlasted even the skomorokhi themselves, some continuing to be enacted by peasants in outlying districts into the early twentieth century. The "goat play" observed and described by the famous director and playwright Nikolai Yevreynov in Byelorussia in December 1915 (exactly when Stravinsky, in Morges, was hardest at work on his *Baika*) as part of the *kolyada* (the winter solstice festivities now sub-

games]" (ibid.). The story of Stravinsky's discovery of the cimbalom (in a Geneva restaurant to which Ernest Ansermet had brought him) is familiar. Aladár Rácz, the cimbalomist whose acquaintance Stravinsky made that day and who later became a sort of technical adviser to the composer, described their meeting in a radio interview of 1956 that has been issued on a disc (Bartok Records 929) that also includes the Valse and Polka from Stravinsky's *Trois pièces faciles,* arranged by the composer for cimbalom and piano. The talk, in Hungarian, is given in English translation on the record jacket. It was also published in a French translation in an article by Yvonne Racz-Barblan, "Igor Stravinsky vu par le cymbaliste Aladar Racz," in the special Stravinsky issue of *Feuilles musicales* (Lausanne, 1962). Some excerpts are given in English in White, *Stravinsky: The Composer and His Works,* 204. For more on the Racz-Stravinsky relationship, see György Kroó, *Rácz Aladár* (Budapest: Zenemükiadó, 1979).

It should be borne in mind that the gusli—which, like the cimbalom, existed by the late nineteenth century in a highly elaborated "concert" form on legs, modeled after the spinet piano—was essentially a psaltery, played directly by the fingers, while the cimbalom was essentially a dulcimer, played with sticks. Consequently the cimbalom produced a much louder, more percussive tone than the gusli, a quality that made it a suitable ensemble instrument for the *Baika* band. The only work of concert music with a part for the modernized gusli is Cherepnin's *Royaume enchanté,* discussed in Chapter 9. For full details about the gusli, see A. S. Famintsïn's monograph *"Gusli"—Russkiy narodniy muzikal'niy instrument,* Pamyatniki drevney pis'mennosti i iskusstva, no. 82 (St.Petersburg, 1890).

7. To his credit, Mikhail Druskin has remained skeptical. Despite Karlinsky's claim ("Stravinsky and Russian Pre-literate Theater," 236), nowhere in Druskin's 1974 monograph on the composer, *Igor' Stravinskiy,* did he mention *skomoroshestvo* in connection with Stravinsky's "merry performance." Rather, he goes out of his way to distance himself from the Asafyev interpretation, even though doing so deprives him of an easy way of characterizing the piece. In one place he calls it a "circus acrobatic presentation" and a "vulgar fairground spectacle" (*ploshchadnoye yarmarochnoye zrelishche*); in another, he classifies the piece as a "masque" (Russian ed., 74, 92).

8. See esp. Zguta, *Russian Minstrels,* for a sustained defense of this theory.

FIG. 16.1a. Fourteenth-century Novgorodian capitals showing *skomorokhi* play-ing *gusli*. The Cyrillic *D* on the right is the one adapted for the central figure in the frontispiece to Rimsky-Korsakov's *Sadko* as published by Edition Belaïeff (see Fig. 7.4b).

sumed within the Christian *svyatki*) will give an idea of what the actual Russian "folk skomorokh theater" may have been like:

> In the center of the procession walked an old man [*ded,* lit. "grandfather"] with a staff in his hand. He led a "goat." The latter was impersonated by a boy clad in a goat-skin. He wore a mask made of birch and pine bark, representing a goat's head. The horns were made of straw and the beard of flax. The other characters were two "gypsies" represented by girls in men's clothes. Their faces were black-ened by soot. Singers and musicians followed suit.
>
> The essence of the drama was the sudden death of the goat and its revival. When the "goat" fell "dead" on the ground, the actors feigned dismay. Then the chorus advised the "grandfather" to press the goat's "vein." By that the organ of copulation was meant. The "grandfather" did as he had been told, and the "goat" rose up and began to dance. The audience rejoiced.[9]

"An abundance of song and dance," to be sure, but no "moralizing finale" here. While an allegory, the goat play is ritual presentation, not narrative representation, clearly descended from the seasonal *khorovodi* of old, in which the skomorokhi had always assumed a leading role.

In the period of the Christian chronicles, the skomorokhi are recorded as gusli players (*guslyari*) singing wonder tales and epics to their own accompaniment, as

9. Quoted in Vernadsky, *Origins of Russia,* 153.

FIG. 16.1b. "Modern" spinet-type *gusli* Stravinsky knew and imitated with the cimbalom. (From A. S. Famintsïn, *"Gusli"—russkiy narodnïy muzïkal'nïy instrument* [St. Petersburg, 1890])

acrobats, as tightrope walkers, jugglers, conjurers, and dancers. As one modern researcher sums it up,

> The skomorokh entertained both high and low and catered for all tastes. At the royal court and the houses of princes he played the *gusli,* sang songs and told tales; in the village market places and on the streets his humour was cruder and broader, his antics unrestrained, his songs often bawdy, and his dancing obscene. He was a perennial favorite at village festivities, taking an active role in all the available types of entertainment, training and leading bears and playing the music for their clumsy dances, showing puppets and, at Christmas and Shrovetide, leading the games, dressed in the traditional animal mask.[10]

The skomorokhi also participated in domestic rituals like weddings, their role surviving in that of the *druzhko,* the wedding jester and master-of-ceremonies.[11] Historians know them in particular to have entertained Ivan the Terrible with their singing and dancing (especially "historical songs" glorifying the tsar's own exploits). Lastly, the skomorokhi seem to have played the decisive role in preserving the ancient heroic epos of Kievan Rus (the *bïlinï*), which survived into modern times only in the far north of Russia, where the skomorokhi had taken refuge when driven out of Muscovy by Tsar Alexey Mikhailovich in 1648 (they were subsequently excommunicated from the Orthodox church in 1657). By the eighteenth century they were virtually extinct.

The role of the skomorokhi in thus propagating a wide variety of Russian folklore, verbal and musical, is so well established that a link between their activity and the growth of actual theater in Russia seems implicit. Yet a gap remains that no historian has been able to close except speculatively. The prime speculator on their role was Alexander Sergeyevich Famintsïn (1841–96), a minor Russian composer and music critic (best known for his run-ins with Musorgsky, Stasov, and other representatives of the New Russian School), who wrote the earliest book on the subject of the skomorokhi and who stated flat out in his preface that they were "the earliest representatives of Russian popular epos, theater, and music."[12] Although Famintsïn's hypotheses were unquestionably the cornerstone on which Asafyev and later Karlinsky tacitly laid their confident interpretations of the *Baika,* the closest one can come to "folk skomorokh theater" on the basis of reliable evidence is festival masquerading; and whereas, according to the leading Western specialist,

10. Warner, *Russian Folk Theater,* 188.
11. See Zguta, "Skomorokhi," 299.
12. Ibid., 307. Whatever the merits of this particular claim, Famintsïn's chapter headings do give a neat summary of historically verifiable *skomoroshestvo* activities: (1) singing and playing in homes, especially at feasts; (2) participating in wedding festivities; (3) "High Performance" (*Velikaya igra,* that is, narration of epics, glorification of heroes and of the mighty); (4) "Merry Performance" (*Vesyolaya igra,* song and dance); (5) mass entertainment, often seditious or obscene (street and townsquare appearances; participation in seasonal rites, memorial rites; puppeteering [i.e., the "*petrushka*"]; bear training; etc.). See Alexander Sergeyevich Famintsïn, *Skomorokhi na Rusi* (St. Petersburg, 1889).

"the step from mask to theater is small indeed," he is forced to conclude that "the skomorokhi themselves would never take it." While he cautiously leaves open the question of "the nature and structure of skomorokh 'dramatic' performances," he warns the trigger-happy that "it may never be resolved owing to a lack of relevant information."[13] Even his Soviet counterpart, who has devoted an entire monograph to an attempt to close the gap between the skomorokhi and the beginnings of a legitimate folk theater, has stated that the only "dramatized forms" that can be associated securely with the skomorokhi are the trained-bear entertainment and the *petrushka* or *vertep*—that is, the one-man puppet show.[14]

As for skazki, they were not generally the province of the skomorokhi at all, but of specialists known as *bakhari* or *kaleki,* venerable storytellers, often blind. A twelfth-century chronicle tells of a rich insomniac who employed *bakhari* to tickle the soles of his feet, strum the gusli, and recite skazki (or *basni,* as they were called before the eighteenth century).[15] Ivan the Terrible, Mikhaíl Romanov, and Vasiliy Shuysky all used *bakhari* for the same purpose.[16] Roman Jakobson traced the lineage of these storytellers practically to modern times: "Even at the close of the [eighteenth] century we find in Russian newspapers advertisements of blind men applying for work in the homes of gentry as tellers of tales; Lev Tolstoy, as a child, fell asleep to the tales of an old man who had once been bought by the count's grandfather, because of his knowledge and masterly rendition of fairy tales."[17] These references just about exhaust the documentary evidence for a professional tradition of reciting skazki in olden times.

On the basis of internal evidence, some scholars have claimed to detect "traces of professional [i.e., public] storytellers in Russian folktales," to quote the title of the classic exposition of this line of research,[18] and have identified these professionals with the skomorokhi. Many skazka texts collected from peasants during the nineteenth century have stock opening formulas that recall the invocations (*zapevï*) in the ancient *bilinï,* or the skomorokh adaptations from *bilinï* known as "historical songs." They often contain sudden bursts of nonsense patter (cf. the *pribautki* described in Chapter 15), a standard attention-grabbing device of public entertainers, such as those descendants of skomorokhi the Shrovetide carnival barkers (see the discussion of the *balagannïy ded* and the *rayoshniki* in Chapter 10).

Many if not most skazki have stock endings, "to release the attention of the

13. Zguta, *"Skomorokhi,"* 313.

14. A. A. Belkin, *Russkiye skomorokhi* (Moscow: Nauka, 1975), 140.

15. I. I. Sreznevsky, *Svedeniya i zametki o maloizvestnïkh i neizvestnïkh pamyatnikakh,* pt. 2 (St. Petersburg, 1876), 554; paraphrased in Zguta, *Russian Minstrels,* 98; and in Roman Jakobson, "On Russian Fairy Tales," commentary to *Russian Fairy Tales* (after Afanasyev), trans. Norbert Guterman (New York: Pantheon Books, 1945), 635.

16. Zguta, *Russian Minstrels,* 98.

17. Jakobson, "On Russian Fairy Tales," 635.

18. L. M. Brodsky, "Sledï professional'nïkh skazochnikov v russkikh skazkakh," *Etnograficheskoye obozreniye* 16 (1904): 2–18.

hearer, to call forth in him a smile or even a laugh, and sometimes also to turn the attention upon the storyteller himself, with the aim of receiving thanks, a treat, or a present. The ending is usually rhythmic, is spoken with a rapid 'tongue twisting,' and sometimes a rhyme."[19] Stravinsky ended his *Baika* with a very elaborate passage of this type, concluding with the line "There's a tale for you, and I get a crock of butter" ("*Vot vam skazka, a mne krinka masla*"), copied verbatim from the ninth tale in volume one of Afanasyev's skazki (there are near variants in tales no. 2 and no. 14 as well).[20] Occasionally these envois mention *molodtsï* (young lads),[21] a term that often designated skomorokhi.[22]

Some have been skeptical of associating these *skazochnïye pribautki* too hastily with the skomorokhi. Russell Zguta, for one, prefers to regard them as "an indication of editing and no more."[23] Such traces of the skomorokhi in the diction of modern-day skazka narration, in other words, may be the result of cross-fertilization of genres: the rhetoric of the *bouffonnerie* grafted to the content of the skazka over generations of retelling. This certainly seems to be true of the "skazka" that served as the linchpin of the "public storyteller" theory,[24] a longish set of nonsense verses in comically inflated epic style, pleonastically entitled "A Fable of the Olden Days of Yore" ("*Baika pro starinu starodavnuyu*"; Afanasyev, no. 428), which the editors of the Soviet Academic Edition of Afanasyev's tales identify as a parody of the *bïlina*, a genre the skomorokhi are known to have both transmitted and spoofed.[25]

But even if we do allow the possibility that the skomorokhi had a hand in the composition and dissemination of skazki, that still does not constitute any evidence for the tradition Stravinsky's *Baika* is said to exemplify, that of enacting skazki in dramatic form. The envois demanding payment or refreshment, including the one quoted at the end of the *Baika*, use the first person singular, suggesting an individual entertainer rather than a troupe.[26] Still, internal evidence does suggest other (undocumented) possibilities. A great many skazki contain obviously interpolated songs—little "arias," so to speak—which are often actually sung to a tune, or *napev*, by reciters to this day. Afanasyev sometimes distinguished them in his collection by setting them off as verse within prose. In addition, numerous skazki—often the same ones—are cast in dialogue form almost throughout.

19. Sokolov, *Russian Folklore*, 431.
20. "*Lisa-Povitukha*" ("The Fox as Midwife"), in [Afanasyev,] *Russian Fairy Tales*, 191–92.
21. Cf. Afanasyev, *Narodnïye russkiye skazki*, nos. 3, 81.
22. See Brodsky, "Sledï," 11–12.
23. Zguta, *Russian Minstrels*, 100.
24. Brodsky, "Sledï," 12–13.
25. Commentary to Afanasyev, *Narodnïye russkiye skazki*, ed. Azadovsky, Andreyev, and Sokolov, 3:457.
26. Stravinsky got around this by having the four singers in the *Baika* shout "*Vot vam skazka*" in unison, followed by "*a mne krinka masla*" by the first tenor alone. In some of the sketches, the second phrase is recast in the plural ("*a nam krinka masla*"). Jakobson ("On Russian Fairy Tales," 645) cites another common envoi: "This is the end of my tale, and now I would not mind having a glass of vodka."

While such tales lend themselves perfectly well to straight recitation ("in voices"), they could easily suggest a dramatized rendition to an ethnographer speculating on the origin and classification of genres—or to a creative artist on the lookout for material to transform.

Such an ethnographer was A. I. Nikiforov, who in an article of 1928 isolated and described what he called the "children's folktale of the dramatic genus."[27] "There are folktales," he wrote,

> that cannot be evaluated solely on the basis of their written text. Their whole artistic life, their whole significance, their generic essence is defined not so much by the text as by their manner of performance, or rather, of course, the interaction of these two factors. . . . In the course of collecting folktales in the north of Russia, I noticed that among them a certain group of tales was rather markedly distinguished by certain specific elements of a performance character as well as a certain specificity in the structure of the text itself. Owing to the predominance in both regards of peculiarities that are analogous to the peculiarities of literary works for the theatrical stage, I will go so far as to designate this group of tales as tales of the dramatic genus.[28]

It will come as no surprise, but rather as confirmation of the unerring authenticity of Stravinsky's "folk" imagination, that one of Nikiforov's prize exhibits was the tale published by Afanasyev as "The Cat, the Cock, and the Fox" ("*Kot, petukh i lisa*")—the kernel, as we shall see, from which the *Baika* germinated—and that another was the tale Nikiforov calls "The Limewood Leg" ("*Lipovaya noga*"; Afanasyev published it under the title "The Bear" ["*Medved'*"]), from which Stravinsky appropriated the central song for the third of his *Detskiye pesenki* (a.k.a. *Trois histoires pour enfants*). In both these tales, as Nikiforov emphasizes, "the central role in their performance belongs to the singing of the verses or little songs that form the basis of the crucial repetitive element of the tale."[29]

Repetition of the central action, stereotyped by means of dialogues, verses, or songs, is in fact the sine qua non of the dramatic genre as Nikiforov defines it, as well as one of the aspects that further defines it specifically as a genre of tales told either by or to children.[30] It is of course a feature conspicuously present not only in the *Baika*, where it came readymade with the textual source (this notwithstanding Stravinsky's later claim that the repetition of the Cock's seduction was his idea),[31] but also in that other Afanasyev-based minstrel show, *Histoire du soldat*, where, as we shall see, it had to be deliberately contrived.

27. A. I. Nikiforov, "Narodnaya detskaya skazka dramaticheskogo zhanra," in *Skazochnaya komissiya v 1927 g.*, ed. S. F. Oldenburg (Leningrad: Gosudarstvennoye Russkoye Geograficheskoye Obshchestvo, 1928), 49–63.
28. Ibid., 49–50.
29. Ibid., 52.
30. Ibid., 61–62.
31. E&D:135/119.

In a perceptive memoir of Stravinsky, Elliott Carter related these plot repetitions (by means of which "the characters on stage and the audience are dealt with as if they had no memory, as if living always in the present and not learning from previous events") to such basic stylistic matters as Stravinsky's characteristic "unified fragmentation" and "cross-cutting" of static blocks of material, resulting in music that "holds together in a very new and telling way."[32] These matters are indeed profoundly related, and few Stravinsky compositions display the "very new and telling" principles of Stravinskian coherence more effectively than the *Baika*. A study of its relationship to its sources in Afanasyev will underscore more boldly than ever the extent to which Russian folklore was responsible for the shaping of Stravinsky's innovative modes of musical thought.

To return to the question of the hypothetical *skomorosh'ye deystvo* and sum up: what gives the Turanian conceit known as *Baika* its compelling aura of Russian ethnographic veracity is the way it simultaneously and persuasively closes two tantalizing historical gaps. It is plausible that troupes of skomorokhi enacted plays or skits on a stage or in a public square, even if we do not know that they did so. Conversely, it is plausible that skazki, particularly the kind Nikiforov designated "dramatic," were enacted on a stage or in a public square, even if we do not know that they were so enacted. In the *Baika*, a gusli-playing band of recognizable *vesyolïye molodtsï* enact a dramatic folktale upon a stage—"with singing and music," to quote Stravinsky's subtitle. The conception is thus doubly plausible. Add the uncanny confidence and resourcefulness with which Stravinsky deployed and adapted his folkloristic sources—a process we shall trace in the pages that follow—and the result is a putative picture of life in pre-Petrine Russia that is "realer than the real."

BAIKA: THE EVOLUTION OF THE TEXT

Stravinsky came only gradually to the idea of a continuous, acted-out skazka. The earliest sketches and text drafts for what became the *Baika* were evidently made with nothing more ambitious in mind than some more children's songs and *pribautki* to go with the sets discussed in Chapter 15. Indeed, on the cover of the main sketchbook for the *Baika*, a thirty-six-page bound copybook in the Stravinsky Archive that carries no date but must belong to the latter part of 1915,[33] there is a pasted label that reads *Igor' Stravinskiy / "Detskiye pesni"* ("Children's Songs"), the same title (except not in the diminutive form) as the one used to designate the set that concludes with the "Song of the Bear," the text of which (like the ones that

32. See Carter's untitled memorial in double special edition entitled "Stravinsky: A Composers' Memorial," *Perspectives of New Music* 9, no. 2–10, no. 1 (1971): 3–5.

33. It was not catalogued by Rothschild and bore the designation "IS4" in an appendix to the Rothschild listing at the New York Public Library during the period of the NYPL's custodianship of the Archive. The sketchbook corresponds to no. 15c in Craft's checklist of Stravinsky's manuscripts, as published by White (*Stravinsky: The Composer and His Works*, app. C, 556).

would furnish the starting point for the *Baika*) was one of the many interpolated songs found in the section of Afanasyev's anthology devoted to animal tales. The Archive also contains a more elaborate and decorative painted label (one of the so-called colored drawings grouped together as item no. 2 in the Rothschild catalogue) that reads *Detskiye Pesni Igorya Stravinskogo: "Lisa i Petukh"* (*Children's Songs by Igor Stravinsky: "The Fox and the Cock"*).

So what became the *Baika* was originally conceived as just another "histoire pour enfants" out of Afanasyev. How literally this was true is revealed by an inscription on the cover of the envelope that contained the *Baika* sketchbook at the time of Stravinsky's death. It reads: *Pribautki: 1) Svetiku "Skripi noga." 2) "Gospodi pomiluy."* This suggests a projected second set of nonsense songs that would have contained both the "Song of the Bear" ("Creak, My Paw," dedicated "To Svetik," i.e., Soulima) and what, as we shall shortly observe, unexpectedly ended up as part of the concluding pattersong in the *Baika* (a much later inscription on the envelope cover, in French, identifies the "*Gospodi pomiluy*" as "*Renard: chanson finale*").

A page-by-page examination of the sketchbook will show, more concisely and graphically than can be demonstrated for practically any other major Stravinsky composition—just how what we know as "*Renard*" took shape out of a compost of children's songs and nonsense jingles.[34] The process had an uncanny, unsuspecting authenticity, moreover, which told superbly on the quality of the finished product. "We had a *skazochnitsa* like that at home named Maria Maximovna," a leading nineteenth-century folklorist and art historian once recalled of one of his family's serfs. "She had preserved in her memory an enormous supply of individual *skazka* episodes out of which she would manufacture hundreds of tales, changing the proper names and from time to time inserting comic prefaces [*priskazki*], tales-within-tales, and nonsense patter [*pribautki*]."[35] Except that he dealt with literary

---

34. For the record, the earliest surviving notation for the *Baika* is found in Sketchbook C (according to John Shepard, "The Stravinsky *Nachlass:* A Provisional Checklist of Music Manuscripts," *MLA Notes* 40 [1983–84]: 719–50), in the midst of sketches for the *Pribaoutki* of 1914; it was therefore presumably entered in the summer of that year.

The music is that of the ostinato that accompanies the Cock's song at fig. [10] and again at [42] in the finished score. The words are adapted from the ending of one of the variants of Afanasyev's tale of "The Cat, the Cock, and the Fox," the basic source of the *Baika* plot: "*Vot mï tebya, stuk v lobok da v korobok*" ("Here's what you get from us, a knock on the head and into the box"). Though it figures in some sketches as the concluding line of the *Baika* text (that is, right before the envoi: "*Vot vam skazka,*" etc.), this line was dropped from the final libretto.

35. Rovinsky, *Russkiye narodnïye kartinki*, quoted in Brodsky, "Sledï," 9.

artifacts on the printed page rather than artifacts of oral tradition stored in memory, that was precisely how Stravinsky "manufactured" the *Baika*. He became a *skazochnik* in his own right, not a mere retailer of peasant antiquities; and his *Baika* was a genuinely new skazka created out of the common stock in true peasant fashion—with names changed, with tales-within-tales, and with *priskazki* and *pribautki* galore.

Initially work was focused on the fable of "The Cat, the Cock, and the Fox." Afanasyev gives it in three versions, followed by a little appendix of references to previously published variants.[36] In each of them the Fox seduces the Cock over and over again (from two to four times) with promises of food. This repeated action, as Nikiforov observed, is the defining characteristic of the tale. All else is secondary, even the outcome. In one version, the Fox succeeds in eating the Cock (it ends—unusually for a skazka—with a moral: "This is what comes of not heeding warnings!"). In the others, the Cat (assisted in the second version by a Ram) succeeds each time in rescuing the Cock. The last time, enticing the Fox and her four daughters out of their lair with a song to the gusli, the Cat captures and kills them all.

Stravinsky did not choose this tale merely because it was one that Russian children like his Fedik, Svetik, and Mika were sure to know and love, or because Afanasyev's fox tales, however unique and indigenous in their particulars, bore a strong generic resemblance to tales beloved in Western Europe too—where, for better or worse, Stravinsky's audience now resided. (These went back to the medieval "animal epic" Reinardus Vulpes—a.k.a. Reinart de Vos, Reynard the Fox, Reineke Fuchs—by way of Chaucer's "Nun's Priest's Tale," the *Roman de renart* from which Ramuz derived *Baika*'s French title, as well as adaptations by Goethe, Grimm, Perrault, and La Fontaine.) No, his far simpler, less calculating reason was that "The Cat, the Cock, and the Fox" contained the greatest concentration in all of Afanasyev of interpolated ditties, and it was with these that he began.

The first entry in the *Baika* sketchbook comprises the texts of two of these songs, copied not from one of the three main versions of the tale as given by Afanasyev, but from his appendix, which gives variants of the songs as previously published by a certain "Mme Avdeyeva" in a collection of 1856 called *Russian Folktales for Children* (*Russkiye skazki dlya detey*). The first of them is the one the Fox uses to entice the Cock out of the house. This was an especially popular *detskaya pesnya* in its own right: it appears in the old *Gusel'ki* collection in two versions (Ex. 16.1a) and was also set by Lyadov (Ex. 16.1b). The second text in the *Baika* sketchbook is

---

36. In the prerevolutionary editions, including the one Stravinsky used, the tale is assigned the number 17 and the three versions are listed as 17a, b, and c. In the standard modern editions (ed. Azadovsky, Andreyev, and Sokolov [Moscow, 1936–40]; ed. Propp [Moscow, 1957]), the three versions are independently numbered (37–39) and the appendix of variants is omitted. The first version (i.e., no. 37 [= 17a]) is available in English in [Afanasyev,] *Russian Fairy Tales*, 86–88. Unless otherwise specified, Afanasyev's tales will be referred to here by the numeration in the Soviet editions.

FIG. 16.2. Alexander Afanasyev (1821–76), whose collection of *skazki* furnished text material for the *Baika* and the *Histoire du soldat*.

the song with which the Old Man, with whom the Cock lives in Avdeyeva's version, frees him from the Fox's clutches by playing on his little gusli (*gusel'tsï*). The lines given below in italics are the ones that survived into the finished *Baika* (at figs. [43]–[50] and [62]–[71], respectively):

1. Lisa:
   Petushok, *petushok,*
   Zolotoy grebeshok,
   Maslyana golovushka,
   Shelkova borodushka!
   Vïglyani v okoshechko:
   Vot boyare yekhali,
   Gorokh rassïpali—
   Nekomu podobrat'.

   The Fox:
   Little Cock, little Cock,
   Golden crest,
   Butter head,
   Silken beard!
   Look out the window, dearie:
   See, the noblemen have passed by,
   And let drop a pea—
   There's no one to pick it up.

2. Starik:
   Stren'-bren', moí *gusel'tsï,*
   Zolotïye moí *strunochki!*

   Old Man:
   Strum, strum, my little gusli,
   My little golden strings!

EXAMPLE 16.1

a. *Gusel'ki,* no. 20

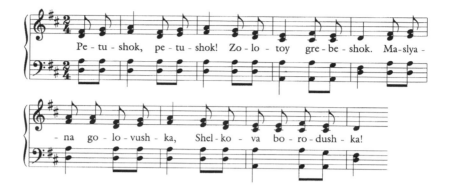

b. Lyadov, op. 14/4

Uzh kak doma li lisa,	Is Foxy not at home,
Lisa Ivanovna,	Foxy, daughter of Johnny,
So svoími malími detushkami?	With her little kiddies?
Pervaya-to doch' Chuchelka.	The first daughter is Chuchelka.
A vtoraya-to Pochuchelka.	And the second is Pochuchelka.
Tret'ya-to Podai-pirozhok,	The third is Give-us-a-pie,
A chetvyortaya Zazhmi-kulachok.	And the fourth is Shake-my-hand.

Stravinsky eventually modified the texts of both these songs by conflating the Avdeyeva variants with those found in Afanasyev's own versions of the tale (the first song mainly from no. 17a [=37], the second from 17b [=38]). This became necessary when the songs had to find a place within a continuous narrative. The important facts established thus far, then, are that Stravinsky's starting point was what is now the second encounter between the Fox and the Cock in the *Baika,* and that the imitations of gusli music, inherent in the text itself, had been part of the earliest, predramatic conception of the piece. They may indeed have provided in embryo the idea of the eventual *skomorosh'ye deystvo.*

Sure enough, the very first musical notations in the sketchbook, at the foot of the second page, include the gusli music at fig. [62].[37] A rather crude if complex concatenation of acciaccaturas (Ex. 16.2a), it was probably the product of an experimental laying-on-of-hands at the keyboard, and was considerably refined on the way to its final form (Ex. 16.2b). Over the next half-dozen pages of sketching, Stravinsky worked at the two songs concurrently. The first notation for the Fox's song (Ex. 16.3a), also at the bottom of the second page, is clearly related to the music at fig. [43], but without the characteristic triplet rhythm that (in the cimbalom) functions in the finished score as the Fox's leitmotif. That rhythm was derived from the word *kikereku* ("cock-a-doodle-do"), which occurs in the song only in Afanasyev no. 37, not the Avdeyeva version Stravinsky started out setting (Ex. 16.3b).

Signs of text conflation begin to creep in as early as the third page of the sketchbook. That page contains a draft of the music from [43]+2 to [45]−3 in pretty nearly its final form. Stravinsky substituted the epithet *chesanna golovushka* ("little combed head"), taken from Afanasyev no. 37, for Avdeyeva's *maslyana golovushka,* and so it would remain.[38] Pages 4–7 show a continuity draft of the latter part of the song to the gusli (figs. [67]–[71]). The first seven measures (the naming of the

37. This confirms Stravinsky's recollection (E&D:136/120) that "the *guzla* [*sic*] music—'plink, plink' . . . —was the first part of *Renard* to be composed." The confusion of gusli with *guzla* (a Balkan bowed-string instrument, comparable to the old-Russian *gudok*) was not, as has been often supposed, the result of the aged Stravinsky's forgetfulness. It had been Ramuz's doing, as witness the original full and vocal scores published in 1917. The mistake, therefore, was probably Craft's, in editing Stravinsky's memoirs for publication. Unable to read Russian, he must have relied on the French text in the score.

38. It is interesting to learn that when Stravinsky briefly worked at an instrumental arrangement of the *Baika* in October 1940, he again began (and, as things turned out, finished) precisely with this passage, the first to have been fully composed in 1915. See SelCorrI:415 for a description and photograph of this little-known revision.

EXAMPLE 16.2

a. *Baika* sketchbook ("IS4"), p. 2, sketch of song to the *gusli*

b. *Baika,* accompaniment at 62

p staccato sempre

EXAMPLE 16.3

a. Sketchbook, p. 2, sketch for Fox's song

Petushok, petushok

b. *Baika,* fig. 43

Tenor II

Ku - kua - re - ku pe - tu-shok, zo - lo - toy gre - be-shok!

EXAMPLE 16.4   Sketchbook, p. 5

tyuk   tyuk   gú - sel'-tsï   ba - rá - no - vï   strú - noch-ki

vixen's daughters) are notated in values twice as short as those of the final version (that is, in a sixteenth-note unit reminiscent of the "Danse sacrale"). At the spot corresponding to fig. [68], Stravinsky replaced Avdeyeva's first couplet with a text from Afanasyev no. 38 ("*Tyuk-tyuk, gusel'tsï, baranovïye strunochki*": "Plink, plink, little gusli, little sheepgut strings"). This text would remain. The shifting meters over the ostinato would later give Stravinsky some notational problems (Ex. 16.4).

The text drafts across the bottom of pages 6–7 in the sketchbook are momentous. They consist of lines of dialogue adapted from the end of Afanasyev no. 38 (plus one line from no. 39), showing that Stravinsky had by now decided to set "The Cat, the Cock, and the Fox" in its entirety, as a narrative, if not yet as a play (only one line of the following extract—the Fox's, adapted—eventually made it into the finished libretto, at fig. [71]):

[Kot i baran]: "Lisïn'ka, zhivi kharashen'ka svoím padvor'yem" [this line is
    from Af39].
Lisa: Podi, Chuchelka, posmotri—kto takuyu khoroshuyu pesnyu poyot?
Kot i baran: Vot mï tebya stuk v lobok da v korobok (èto 4 raza
    chetvïryom detyam)
    Vot mï i tebya stuka v lobok da v korobok (èto pod konets samoy lise)

[Cat and Ram]: "Foxy, live well in your homestead there."
Fox: Chuchelka, go see who is singing such a fine song.
Cat and Ram: Here's a knock on the head for you and into the box (this 4 times to
    the four children)
    Here's a knock on the head for you too and into the box (this at the end to the
    Fox herself)

If the tale was now to be set complete, rather than as two discrete set pieces, the most urgent requirement was that the Fox's seduction song to the Cock be split in two, since she now had to encounter the Cock at least twice. Accordingly, the very next opening of the sketchbook (pp. 8–9) shows two variants of the song, labeled "First time" and "Second time." They were fashioned by freely conflating elements from Afanasyev nos. 37–38. The lines crossed out in the "first time" song include one Stravinsky had apparently cobbled himself:

Pervïy raz	[Source]	First time
Kikireku Petushok	Af37	Cock-a-doodle-do, little Cock
Zolotoy grebushok [sic]		Golden crest
~~Maslyana golova~~	Af37, fn.	Butter head
~~Dai ruku ruchen'ku~~	Stravinsky?	Give me your little hand
~~Dam tebe lepyoshku~~	Af38, adapted	I'll give you a cookie
~~Chesanna golovushka~~	Af37, fn.	Little combed head
~~Maslennaya boro[. . .]~~		Little greased be[ard]
Sholkova borodushka		Little silken beard
Vïglyani v okoshku		Look out the window
Dam tebe lepyoshku	Af38, adapted	I'll give you a cookie
Na krasnoy na lozhke	Af37	On a pretty spoon[39]
Kikireku petushok		Cock-a-doodle-do, little Cock
Zolotoy grebeshok		Golden crest
(Petukh: Kto tut poyot?)		(Cock: Who's singing here?)
Vtoroy raz		Second time
Kikireku, petushok	Af37	Cock-a-doodle-do, little Cock
Zolotoy grebeshok		Little golden crest
Chesanna golovushka	Af37, fn.	Little combed head
Sholkova borodushka		Little silken beard
Krasnen'ki nosok,		Little red-nose,
Smyatennïy lobok!		Little rumpled brow!
Vïglyani v okoshko		Look out the window.
Dam tebe lepyoshku—	Af38, adapted	I'll give you a cookie—
Dam i zyornïshkov	Af37	I'll give you seeds, too.
U menya to khoromï bol'shiye		I have a big mansion.
V kazhdom uglu		In every corner
Pshenichki po merochke:		There's a measure of wheat:
Yesh', sït, ne khochu!		Eat till you're full and want no more!
Kikireku petushok		Cock-a-doodle-do, little Cock
Zolotoy grebeshok		Little golden crest!

Pursuing this new tack of filling out the plot, Stravinsky cobbled (on p. 10) a warning from the Cat and the Ram to the Cock, conflating this text, too, from Afanasyev nos. 37–38. He never set it to music, though, because a better idea occurred to him. He decided to go for the most colorful and dramatic ending possible, even if that meant incorporating lines and whole passages from other tales from Afanasyev. He began roving at will, at first through all the fox tales (later he would range further still). Page 11 of the sketchbook contains lines from three different skazki, all having to do with trapping the Fox. The first of these entries

39. "A cookie on a spoon" makes less sense than Afanasyev's original: *"Dam tebe kashki / na krasnoy na lozhke"* ("I'll feed you some groats on a pretty spoon").

is from a footnote variant in verse (what is known as a *pobasenka*) appended to Afanasyev no. 14, "The Fox, the Hare, and the Cock."[40] In this tale the tables are turned: it is the Cock who triumphs over the Fox on behalf of the Hare, whom the Fox had put out of its dwelling. The *pobasenka* Stravinsky copied out reads in its original form as follows:

Idyot petukh na pyatakh,	The Cock is at her heels,
Nesyot sablyu na plechakh	Carrying a saber on his shoulders
Khochet lisu posechi	He wants to slash the Fox
Po samï plechi.	Cleave her very shoulders.

Since the Cock was the captive in Stravinsky's version, he substituted *zveri* (the beasts—that is, the Cat and the Ram) for *petukh* (the Cock), changed the verbs first to the third person plural, then to the first person plural, and, finally, substituted a proper barnyard weapon (*kosa,* a scythe) for the saber.[41] In the end, once he had decided to disembody the singers' voices from the dancers on stage, he went back to the third person, arriving at the version that may be found in the finished score at fig. [72].

Next he turned to Afanasyev no. 21, "The Fox as Mourner" (cf. Fig. 16.3), and no. 23, "The Peasant, the Bear, and the Fox,"[42] both of which contain versions of one of the most wonderful devices to be found in the whole repertoire of Russian barnyard tales: a poetic dialogue in which the cornered Fox interrogates the various parts of her body in turn so as to discover which of them had betrayed her. Here is how Stravinsky conflated them in his sketchbook, pages 11–13:

Af23:	"Okh vï moí glazon'ki,	"Oh my little eyes,
	Chto vï smotreli?"	What did you watch?"
Af21:	"Mï smotreli, da smotreli	"We watched and watched
	Chtob sobaki lisin'ku ne s'yeli."	Lest the dogs eat up the Fox."
Af23:	"A vï ushki chto delali?"	"And you, ears, what were you doing?"
	"A mï vsyo slushali,	"We kept listening whether
	daleko li psï gonyat."	the curs were catching up."
Af21:	"Nozhki, nozhki! Chto vï delali?"	"Legs, legs! What did you do?"
	"Mï bezhali da bezhali,	"We ran and ran,
	chtob sobaki lisin'ku ne poymali."	lest the dogs catch the Fox."

40. For a translation, see [Afanasyev,] *Russian Fairy Tales*, 192–94. The translation includes only the main text, not the footnote from which Stravinsky borrowed his verses.

41. He also adopted the Cock's crow as given in Afanasyev no. 14: "*Kukureku*" (modified in the final score to "*kukuareku*").

42. [Afanasyev,] *Russian Fairy Tales,* 437–39 (no. 21), 288–89 (no. 23).

FIG. 16.3. *Lubok* (1852) showing a tale of a cock and fox. In this version, a satire on religious hypocrisy known as "The Fox as Mourner" (cf. Afanasyev no. 21), the cock, grief-stricken by the death of one of his harem of hens, flies up into a tree to devote himself to repentance and prepare for death. A passing fox lures the cock down, eats him, and then sits on a tree stump to mourn pharisaically.

"A tï, khvostishche,
   chto delal?"
"Ya po pnyam, po kustam,
   po kolodam zatseplyal,
   chtob sobaki lisin'ku
   poymali da razorvali."
[Stravinsky: ili, "Chtob
   lisu zveri khvatili da
   zakamshili."]

Af23:   "A-a kanal'ya! Tak pust'
   zhe tebya sobaki yedyat."
   (Vïsovïvayet khvost')

"And you, little tail, what were
   you doing?"
"I with stumps, bushes,
   and logs got entangled,
so that the dogs might catch the Fox
   and tear her to bits."
[Or, "So that the beasts might
   seize the Fox and finish
   her off."]

"Aha, you rascal!
   So let the dogs eat you!"
   (She sticks out her tail)

This whole dialogue, minus the exchange with the ears, and with "beasts" (*zveri*) substituted for "dogs" and "curs" throughout, can now be found at figs. [73]–[79] in the published score.[43] At this point Stravinsky reverted to the end of Afanasyev no. 38 (Beasts: "*Vot mï i tebya tyuk v lobok da v korobok!*"), added on the tag (All [to the audience]: "*Vot vam skazka, a nam krinka masla*"), and that was to have been that.

All that was needed now was to go back and fill in the actual abductions of the Cock after each of the Fox's songs. The Cock's cries for help were quickly found in Afanasyev no. 37 and jotted down on page 15 of the sketchbook. This extract is unexpectedly surrounded by two excerpts from Afanasyev no. 17, a skazka in verse that must have particularly attracted the composer's eye and inner ear by virtue of its linguistic features. A peculiar amalgam of several different tales, it begins with that of a Sow who strays from the barnyard and is devoured by a Wolf.[44] In this version the Fox then comes running up and asks the Wolf to share his meal with her. Rebuffed, the Fox scampers off to a distant town, where by good fortune she espies the Cock sitting on an oak branch. She calls out to him in ersatz "Church Slavonic":

Okh tï, petukh-petushok!	Hey there, little Cock!
Spushchaisya ty na nizyashcheye,	Come down to a lower branch,
S nisyashchego, na zemlyashche;	And from there to the ground.
Ya tvoyu dushu	I will raise your soul
Na nebesa vznesu.	Up to the heavens.

This was a perfect way to cap the Fox's blandishments to the Cock, and it found its way into the final version at fig. [50] (where the raising of the Cock's soul to heaven is risibly contradicted by the bass singer's descent from g′ in falsetto to low E). The last fifteen lines of Afanasyev no. 17 consist of the Cock's pleas to the Fox, beginning with an attempt to divert her attention and culminating in a litany to the saints that quickly degenerates into typical tale-ending patter. Stravinsky, ever on the lookout for Turanian mouth-music, found it irresistible. He turned it into the longest solo set piece in the *Baika*, the Cock's "whine," sung by the first tenor from [57] to [62], twenty-eight bars in all.[45]

---

43. Omitted from the transcription is the version of the dialogue with the tail from Afanasyev no. 23, which Stravinsky also copied out in his sketchbook but never set.

44. Cf. Afanasyev nos. 51–52, "*Svin'ya i volk*" ("The Sow and the Wolf").

45. Here Stravinsky substituted a flattering epithet of his own devising, *Lisïn'ka-lisitsa, neprochnaya sestritsa* (Foxy-Woxy, spotless sister), for Afanasyev's *Lisitsa, zheltaya knyaginya* (Foxy, yellow[-haired] princess), compounding it from an adjective associated with the Fox earlier in the verse-skazka (*neprochnaya*) plus the epithet *Lisichka-Sestrichka* (Little Sister Foxy) found in several other tales (e.g., Afanasyev no. 1: *Lisichka-sestrichka i volk* [Little Sister Foxy and the Wolf]). Also noteworthy is the fact that (as he would do in the "*Zapevnaya*" from the *Quatre chants russes*) Stravinsky did not hesitate to incorporate into his libretto words the collector, finding them dubious or possibly mistranscribed, had signaled with a question mark.

Nor did he stop there. Fascinated with this skazka-in-verse, Stravinsky worked hard to adapt Afanasyev no. 17 to his purposes in toto. (More than three whole pages in the sketchbook are devoted to this task; later, Stravinsky transcribed the adapted text on a fresh sheet that is now one of the miscellaneous *Baika* sketches grouped by Rothschild as no. 29 in his inventory of the Archive [= Craft listing no. 15d].) This meant changing the first part from an encounter between a sow and a wolf into one between the Cock and the Fox. The whole episode reads as follows in Afanasyev's original text:

1	Kak volki ozarnichali,	While the wolves made mischief,
	Sebya velichali,—	[And] extolled themselves,
	Skhodila svin'ya so dvora,	The Sow went out of the barnyard,
	Svodila za soboy makhïn'kikh i belen'kikh;	And took her little white [piglets] with her;
5	Ona dumala—po lesu-lesu,	She thought [she'd go all the way] through the forest,
	An u kolos, u ovyos.	But it was through ears of oats [she went].
	U ney bïli zubki lovki,	She had nimble teeth,
	Usyo skhvatïvala golovki.	She kept grabbing the tips.
	Podkhodila k volku blizko,	She came up close to the Wolf,
10	Poklonilas' emu nizko:	[And] bowed low to him:
	"Zdrastvuy, volk-volchok!	"Greetings, Wolfie dear!
	Ne budet li s tebya	Wouldn't you like
	Makhïn'kikh i belen'kikh?"—	My little white [sucklings]?"—
	"Ekh, ty, svinushka!	"Hey there, little Sow!
15	Ya glazami okinu—	I spy you—
	I tebya ne pokinu."	And I won't let you go!"
	Vzyal za shchetinu	He seized her by the bristles,
	I povalil na spinu	And threw her on her back
	I stal kostochki ob'yedat',	And fell to picking her bones clean,
20	A myakushko v kuchku sobirat'.	And piling the carrion in a heap.

Stravinsky copied all of this out on page 16, changing all references to a wolf or wolves to *lisa* (Fox) and all references to the sow to *kïchatok* (a south-central Russian dialect form of *kochet,* peasant vernacular for Cock, which in standard Russian is always *petukh*). All references to the sucklings (*makhïn'kikh i belen'kikh*) were replaced by the phrase *kurochka-ryabushechka* ("little speckled hen"). He found these terms in various Afanasyev skazki: *kïchatok* came from no. 39, a third and otherwise unused version of the basic tale "The Cat, the Cock, and the Fox," while *kurochka-ryabushechka* came from no. 71, another skazka-in-verse entitled "The Hen" ("*Kurochka*"),[46] a cumulative house-that-Jack-built yarn about the

46. See [Afanasyev,] *Russian Fairy Tales,* 27–28.

consequences of a lost egg. At the point where the Sow (Cock) greets the Wolf (Fox), Stravinsky inserted the previously rejected epithet *Lisitsa, zholtaya knyaginya* ("Foxy, yellow princess").

All these substitutions are entered in rough, random fashion—some directly in the text as copied, others as palimpsests or marginalia. The most revealing entry on the page is found to the right of line 9, the first word of which, *podkhodila* ("she approached") is extended as follows: *podkhodila, da podkhodila, da* . . . ("she approached, yes she approached, yes . . . ").

Although written in words, not notes, this is a musical sketch. Stravinsky's mind was already at work on the trochees and dactyls of what would eventually become the "First Song of the Cat and the Ram," as he eventually called it. And even though line 9 did not make it into the final text, the same extension device can be observed, applied to the beginning of line 7, at fig. [28] in the published score (Ex. 16.5). As Stravinsky affirmed years later, "The music of *Renard* begins in the verse."[47] A sketch like this one allows us to see how literally this was true.

The text sketch on page 16 is rounded off with a line that is not part of Afanasyev no. 17 and that looks therefore like Stravinsky's own invention: *Svinïkh roditeley pominat'* ("As a memorial to the Sow's ancestors"—a jesting reference to the mound of carrion). A marginal note ("see p. 81, skazka 'b'") is actually a reference to the source of the new line: it is the last clause in Afanasyev no. 52 (= 22b in the edition Stravinsky used), a prose version of "The Sow and the Wolf," which must have caught Stravinsky's eye after all the work he'd been doing on its verse counterpart. The clause preceding the one Stravinsky appended to Afanasyev no. 17 is a variant of line 19 as set out above: *Stal svinïye kostochki glodat'* ("He began gnawing on the Sow's bones"). Stravinsky went back and modified the already-copied line to conform with the version in Afanasyev no. 52 (meanwhile perhaps absent-mindedly substituting *glotat'*—"to gulp down"—for *glodat'*). An arrow then links the text sketch on page 16 with a whole dialogue copied out of Afanasyev no. 52, intended for insertion between lines 16 and 17 of the text given above. Although it had been printed by Afanasyev as prose, Stravinsky set it out in the form of verse to match the layout of no. 17. This was very easy to do, for the text is full of rhymes and off-rhymes:

"Zdravstvuy, milaya zhena	"Greetings, good wife
suporosnaya svin'ya!	with piggy litter in tow!
Zachem shlyayesh'sya i skitayesh'sya?	Why are you gadding about so?
Zdes' volk poyedayet ovets."	Here the wolf eats the sheep."
Prikhodit svin'ye konets.	Piggy's end draws nigh.
"Ne yesh' menya, volchin'ka,	"Don't eat me, Wolfie,

47. E&D:136/120.

EXAMPLE 16.5 *Baika*, bass I at 28

U ney bï - li da, u ney bï - li da, u ney bï - li da zub - ki lov - ki da,

ne yesh' menya, seren'koy!	Don't eat me, grey one!
[Ne budet li s tebya	[Wouldn't you like
mokhan'kikh i belen'kikh?]"	(my) little white (sucklings)]?"
"Ne khochu myastsa inova,	"I want no other meat,
khochu myastsa svinova."	I want pig meat."

The line in brackets was the composer's insertion, appropriated from Afanasyev no. 17 to replace the more prosaic *ya tebe privedu stado porosyat* ("I'll give you a whole herd of piglets") in no. 52. Stravinsky was now ready to try a continuous draft of this little tale-within-a-tale. He deleted several lines from no. 17, increased his reliance on no. 52, and even dragged in a couple of lines from no. 51, the remaining version of the tale of the Sow and the Wolf. The whole eclectic composite, as copied out on a clean loose sheet, is given below as a testimonial to Stravinsky's prowess as a *skazochnik*, a skazka-raconteur, in his own right:

1	Kak lisa ozornichala	Af17	While the Fox made mischief
	Sebya velichala:		And extolled herself:
	Skhodil kïchatok so dvora		A cock went out of the barnyard,
	Svodil kïchatok za soboy		The cock took along with him
5	Kurochku-ryabushechku.		A little speckled hen.
	Chort ego ponyos	Af51	The Devil took him
	Da v chuzhuyu polesu—v ovyos		To a strange wood—to an oatfield
	Otkul' vzyalas' lisitsa	Af52	Whence appeared a Fox
	Khvost podnyala		And raised her tail,
10	Kïchetku chelom otdala		And bowed low to the Cock.
	"Zachem shlyayesh'sya i skitayesh'sia?		"Why are you gadding about so?
	Zdes' lisa		Here the Fox
	Podzhidaet myastsa."		Awaits her meat."
	"Ne yesh' menya lisïn'ka,		"Don't eat me, Foxy,
15	Ne yesh' menya krasnaya,		Don't eat me, red,
	Ne budet li s tebya		Wouldn't you rather have
	Kurochki-ryabushechki?"		Some of my little speckled hen?"
	"Ne khochu myastsa innogo,		"I want no other meat,
	Khochu petushkinogo."		I want the Cock's."

With only a few minor changes,[48] this is the text of the "First Song of the Cat and the Ram" (or, more properly, the text sung while the Cat, the Ram, and the

48. They are as follows: line 1 is repeated with *krasnaya* (red one) in place of *lisa;* after line 2, lines 7–8 from Afanasyev no. 17, quoted above, are restored; "speckled hen" (line 5) is put in the plural

Cock do their dance on the stage after the Fox has been beaten for the first time) from fig. [27] all the way to [36], where the mouth-music gives way to wordless melisma on the last vowel of *petushkinogo*. The remainder of the text, from [39] to [41], is the remainder of Afanasyev no. 52, telling how the hypothetical Sow/Cock of the tale-within-a-tale met her end. These lines, too, went through several stages, which may be traced in a bundle of loose sheets inside a bifolium labeled "*Pervaya pesnya Kota da Barana*" ("First Song of the Cat and the Ram"):

Afanasyev no. 52 (set out in verse):

Vzyal volk svinku	The wolf seized the sow
za beluyu spinku,	by her white back,
za chornuyu shchetniku;	by her black bristles;
ponyos volk svinku	The wolf carried the sow off
za pen', za kolodu,	beyond the stump, beyond the well,
za beluyu beryozu,	beyond the white birch,
stal svin'ye kostochki glodat',	he fell to gnawing the sow's bones,
svinïkh roditeley pominat'.	in memory of the sow's ancestors.

Stravinsky, "Pervaya pesnya":

Vzyala lisa kocheta	The Fox seized the Cock
za boki,	by his sides.
ponesla ~~lisa~~ ego dalyoko,	The Fox carried him far away,
za pen', za kolodu,	beyond the stump, beyond the well,
za beluyu beryozu;	beyond the white birch;
Stala kïchetovïye kostochki glodat',	She fell to gnawing the Cock's bones,
[Myakushko v kuchku sobirat']	[piling the carrion in a heap]
kïchetovïkh roditeley pominat'.	in memory of the Cock's ancestors.

The next-to-last line, it may be recalled, was a survivor from Afanasyev no. 17, the very line Stravinsky had used as a link to no. 52 in the first place. The first five lines of the "*pervaya pesnya*" survived unchanged into the final text. Stravinsky bracketed the last three lines in the text sketch, adding a note to himself: "Instead of these three lines, these two." What follows is an adaptation from the latter part of no. 17, the part that actually deals with the Fox and the Cock. The only changes Stravinsky made here were in word order, and in the substitution of his rare find, *kïchatok,* for the common *petukh:*

Stala lisa kïchatki vertet'	The Fox started to whirl the Cock around.
Ne v moch' kïchatku stalo terpet'.	The Cock couldn't stand it.

(*kurochek-ryabushechek*); lines 6–7 (from Afanasyev no. 51) are deleted; line 8 is repeated with *krasnaya* for *lisitsa*; line 9 is changed to "*khvost podzhala*" ("her tail between her legs"); some synonyms are substituted in line 10 (*chavo* for *zachem, shatayesh'sya* for *skitayesh'sya*); in line 17, "speckled hen" is again in the plural.

Then he added a note, "following that . . . ," and drew an arrow to a pair of lines he invented himself on the basis of the vocabulary he had drawn from Afanasyev no. 39, adapted to his own dramatis personae:

Kïchet kurochek stal klikat'	The Cock started calling to the hens.
Kurï kïchatka ne slïshut.	The hens do not hear the Cock.

Stravinsky dropped the first of these couplets and boiled the first line of the second down to a brilliantly assonant phrase, *Kïchet klichet* ("The Cock cries out"), which he set, no less adroitly, in the form illustrated in Example 16.6. Nothing could have capped off the exuberant "First Song" more fittingly; Stravinsky-*skazochnik* was really on his mettle.

Nor was he finished even now with Afanasyev no. 17. One episode remained: that of the Fox's request to share the Wolf's repast and the latter's rebuff. These eight lines, with their coarse language and surrealistic reference to Yermak Timofeyevich (d. 1585), the Cossack chieftain who conquered Siberia for Ivan the Terrible, were the juiciest bit of all:

1	Bezhala neprorochnaya lisitsa:	The blameless Fox came running:
	"Okh tï, kum-kumanyok!	"Say there, old pal!
	Nekuplennoye u tebya, deshevoye;	What you've got there cost you nothing;
	Ne podelish' li myastsa?"	Won't you share some meat with me?"
5	—Ekh tï, kumushka!—	"Ahoy there, my little gal!—
	Vedayesh', Yermak	Don't you know that Yermak
	Zap[erdel] natoshchak?	Began farting [after eating] on an empty stomach?
	I tebe togo ne minovat'.—	And this you won't escape, either."

This dialogue, somewhat modified,[49] is copied out on page 18 of the sketchbook and headed by a legend: *Posle pervogo pokhishcheniya Petukha pribegayut zveri* ("After the first abduction of the Cock the animals come running up"). It is thus turned into a single threatening replique for the Cat and the Ram, by means of which they scare off the Fox (see the published score at fig. [24]). Although Stravinsky wrote out the unprintable word *zaperdel* in several musical sketches on pages 17–19, it was ultimately bowdlerized into *zatreshchal* ("crackled") in the final text (m. 157 in the published score).

The remaining text jotting on page 17 shows how alertly Stravinsky was scanning Afanasyev by now, and how eclectically he was redeploying its contents. The jotting consists of the following note to himself: "N.B.: The first time the Fox

---

49. I.e., lines 2 and 5 are consolidated: *"Ekh tï kumushka, golubushka!"* ("Hey there, old girl, sweetie!").

EXAMPLE 16.6 *Baika*, voice parts at 40

Kï-chet kli-chet da kï-chet kli-chet Ku - rï kï-che-ta ne slï-shut

steals the Cock, the latter shouts, 'You'll break the Fast, Foxy' [*Oskoromish'sya, Lisitsa*]. The Fox answers [in rough translation], 'For some it's forbidden, for us it's a treat' [*Komu skoromno, a nam na zdorov'ye*]." The lines are found in no skazka, but Afanasyev quotes them in his commentary (omitted in all Soviet editions) to the tale *Lisa-ispovednitsa,* "The Fox Confessor." They came from what the collector called the "folk parable of the Cat," as transmitted by Dahl in his collection of folk sayings (and also in his "Explanatory Dictionary," which Stravinsky used constantly, to illustrate both the words *oskoromit'sya* and *skoromniy*). It is a dialogue between a cat and a mouse:

> "Tomcat Eustace! You've had yourself tonsured?"—"I have."—And you've taken the cowl?"—"And taken the cowl."—"Then it's all right to walk by you?"—"Go right ahead." The mouse ran, and the cat pounced. "You'll break the Fast, Tomcat Eustace!"—"For some it's forbidden, for us it's a treat."[50]

In the published score the exchange (somewhat garbled) turns up after the second abduction, not the first. It really belongs with the first, though, because Stravinsky decided, rather late in the game, to base the first encounter between the Fox and the Cock on Afanasyev no. 16, one of the versions of "The Fox Confessor,"[51] and fashioned its text on pages 20–21 of the sketchbook.

It is not a tale that would have immediately struck the composer of the *Baika* as suitable to his purpose, for in it the Cock, not the Fox, ends up the victor. The Fox, who in all of Afanasyev's tales is actually a vixen, appears in the guise of a nun, spies the Cock, and invites him to confess his sins. The following dialogue ensues in Afanasyev's text (in Stravinsky's, the order of the first two paragraphs is reversed):

> II —"O Chanticleer, my beloved child! You are sitting on a tall tree and thinking thoughts that are evil and accursed. You cocks keep many wives: some of you have as many as ten of them, some twenty, some thirty, with time their number reaches even forty! Whenever you chance to meet, you fight over your wives and concubines.

50. Afanasyev, *Narodnïye russkiye skazki,* ed. Gruzinsky, 1:35.
51. See [Afanasyev,] *Russian Fairy Tales,* 72–74.

"Come down to the ground, my beloved child, and do penance. I myself
have been in distant deserts, I have not eaten nor drunk and have suffered
many hardships; and all the time I longed to hear your confession, my
beloved child."

—"O holy mother Fox, I have not fasted and I have not prayed; come some
other time."

—"O my beloved child, you have not fasted and you have not prayed, but
come down to the ground none the less. Repent, else you will die
in sin."[52]

The relevance of this dialogue to the cat-and-mouse exchange quoted above, in
which the cat is likewise disguised as a monastic, is obvious. The dialogue continues awhile in Afanasyev's version until the Cock is finally persuaded. The Fox
snatches the Cock, but before she has a chance to kill him, the Cock manages a bit
of religious hypocrisy of his own. Claiming to be a church deacon, he proposes
that the Fox become his wafer-woman (*prosvirnya*), that is, the one charged with
baking the parish's communion bread (*prosvira*). "We shall profit greatly," quoth
he, "we shall be given sweet cakes, great roasts, butter, eggs and cheeses." The Fox
falls for this and loosens her grip. The Cock flies up into the tree and mocks the
Fox: "My dear Madame Wafer-Baker, greetings! Is not the profit great, are not the
wafers sweet?" The vixen goes off sulking: "I have been all over the world, and nowhere have I seen anything so disgraceful. Since when are cocks deacons, and foxes
wafer-bakers?"[53]

It must have been finding the cat-and-mouse exchange in Afanasyev's commentary that led Stravinsky to see the possibilities in this tale, plus the fact that the
long skazka-in-verse (Afanasyev no. 17), from which he had taken so much, had
been arbitrarily classified by the collector among the Fox-Confessor tales. Stravinsky reordered the dialogue as indicated in the extract above (using his own red-
penciled Roman numerals) and modified it so that it could be used as the vehicle
to bring the Cock down into the Fox's clutches the first time (see figs. [11]–[19] in
the score).[54]

It is this forty-nine-measure passage that has given the *Baika* its unjustified reputation as being somehow "anticlerical." While the placement of the Fox-
Confessor episode near the beginning may lend it a factitious prominence in the
finished product, the creative history of the piece shows the episode to have been
in fact a late and relatively insignificant afterthought. The religious theme never
returns; in sheer running time it accounts for hardly an eighth of the whole. Nor

52. Ibid., 72.
53. Ibid., 74.
54. I.e., he prefaced the whole with a salutation, *Zdrastvuy, krasnoye chado!* ("Greetings, beautiful
child!"), and inserted an interjection for the Cock (*Podi von lisa!,* "Get out of here, Fox!"), which he
found in Afanasyev no. 14 (*Lisa, zayats i petukh,* "The Fox, the Hare and the Cock"—see [Afanasyev,]
Russian Fairy Tales, 192–94).

can "The Fox Confessor" truly be counted a satire of the clergy; the target of its fun is neither the putative nun nor the putative deacon, but hypocrites in general. Soviet scholarship has dependably made the most of the fact that when Afanasyev chose "The Fox Confessor" (no. 16) for inclusion in a later selection of tales for children (*Russkiye detskiye skazki,* 1870), it was one of twenty-four potentially "harmful" skazki listed in a memorandum submitted by a low-ranking censor to his superior officer in the tsarist Ministry of Internal Affairs.[55] But no sophisticated critic of Russian letters, tsarist or Soviet, takes the reactions of the state censorship as a guide to the nature of literary works or the designs of authors. (The point is especially futile in the present case, since the skazka in question had been published already.) Stravinsky, a sincerely, at times ostentatiously professed believer, would scarcely have selected a tale that smacked to him of the anticlericalism others have discerned in Afanasyev no. 16. Here we may take the composer's word that, as he conceived it, "*Renard* does not need symbolic overtones. It is . . . not so much satire as gentle mockery and 'good fun.' "[56]

Continuing to develop the plot as it were from back to front, Stravinsky now sketched, on pages 22–23, the rooster's music at fig. [10] (later to be repeated at [42]). The text is the composer's own, compounded from attributes of the Cock as given (somewhat contradictorily) in his main sources, Afanasyev no. 17 (where the Cock is *na dubu,* "on an oak") and no. 37 (where his master leaves him to *sterech' dom,* "stand watch over the house"). Finally, on page 24 of the sketchbook, Stravinsky reached the beginning, signaled joyously with exclamation points and multiple underscoring:

Nachalo: Podaite mne syuda!!! Podaite mne syuda!!!

Beginning: Lemme at him!!! Lemme at him!!!

Stravinsky had discovered the perfect text with which to characterize the Cock— who "swaggers on his perch" (*suyetsya na svoyey vïshke*), according to the composer's direction—and get the story started. It came from a totally unrelated skazka, "The Bear and the Cock" ("*Medved' i petukh,*" Afanasyev no. 65). The plot is complicated and irrelevant to our purpose, but the climax is a little set piece in which a cock, flapping his wings and crying at the top of his lungs, literally scares a bear to death.[57] His cry, which Stravinsky took over verbatim and in its entirety (right down to the onomatopoetic cockcrows in the first line), runs as follows:

55. See the Commentary to Afanasyev, *Russkiye narodnïye skazki,* ed. Azadovsky, Andreyev, and Sokolov, 1:521. Reference is made there to a 1924 article by V. V. Danilov entitled "The Folk Tale Before the Bar of Censorship in 1870" ("Skazka pered sudom tsenzurï 1870 goda").

56. E&D:138/122.

57. For the whole tale in English, see [Afanasyev,] *Russian Fairy Tales,* 455–56.

TABLE 3

How the *Baika* Text Was Assembled

Number	Main Source in Afanasyev	Pages in Main Sketchbook
1. March	—	—
2. "The Cock swaggers on his perch" (through [9])	Af65 (*Medved' i petukh*, "The Bear and the Cock")	22–29
3. First Encounter ([9]–[20])	Af16 ("*Lisa-ispovednitsa*, "The Fox Confessor")	19–21
4. First Abduction ([20]–[24])	(see no. 8)	(see no. 8)
5. Entrance of Cat and Ram ([24]–[27])	Af17 ("*Lisa-ispovednitsa*, "The Fox Confessor")	17–19
6. "First song of the Cat and the Ram" ([27]–[41])	[27]–[31]: Af17	16–18
	[31]–[40]: Af52 ("*Svin'ya i volk*," "The Sow and the Wolf")	
	[40]–[41]: Af39 ("*Kot, petukh i lisa*," "Cat, Cock, and Fox")	
7. Second Encounter ([42]–[53])	[42]–[50]: Af37–38, plus variants in appendix ("*Kot, petukh i lisa*," "Cat, Cock, and Fox")	1–3, 8–10, 34
	[50]–[52]: Af17 Spoken lines at [52]: Commentary (1913 ed., p. 35)	
8. Second Abduction ([53]–[57])	Af37 ("*Kot, petukh i lisa*," "Cat, Cock, and Fox")	15
9. "The Cock's whine" ([57]–[62])	Af17	15
10. Song to the Gusli ([62]–[71])	Af38, plus variants in appendix ("*Kot, petukh i lisa*")	1–2, 4–7
11. Dénouement ([72]–[81])	[72]–[73]: Af14 ("*Lisa, zayats i petukh*," "Fox, Hare, and Cock"), footnote variant	11
	[73]–[79]: Af23 ("*Muzhik, medved' i lisa*," "Peasant, Bear, and Fox") and Af21 ("*Lisa-placheya*, "The Fox as Mourner")	12–13 (original ending)
12. Final *pribautka* ([81]–[90])	[81]–[87]: Af542 (*pribautka*)	—
	[87]–[90]: Af542, footnote variant no. 2	
13. Envoi ("*Vot vam skazka . . .*")	Af9 ("*Lisa-povitukha*," "The Fox Midwife")	13

Kudá-kudá-kudá!	Whither-whither-whither!
Da podaite mne ego syuda;	Just give him to me hither;
ya nogami stopchu,	I'll trample him with my feet,
toporom srublyu!	I'll cut him up with my axe!
I nozhnishko zdesya,	A knife is here,
i guzhishko zdesya,	and a noose is here,
i zarezhim zdesya,	and we'll slaughter him here,
i povesim zdesya!	and we'll string him up here!

The skazka text as such, roughed out with many ideas for the music, was now essentially complete. Its kernel was the "second" encounter of the Fox and the Cock, from which point Stravinsky had pushed first forward to the end, then backward to the beginning, drawing along the way on a wide variety of skazka material from Afanasyev, chiefly but by no means exclusively derived from other fox, cock, and cock/fox tales.

The whole process is summarized in Table 3, which also incorporates the last step toward completing the text as we now know it, one taken at a considerably later stage of composition. Having tacked on such a wealth of prefatory material at the head of the tale, Stravinsky now apparently felt the need for an extended coda, in pure skomorokh-mountebank pattersong style, to bring his musical skit to a bravura conclusion. He therefore had the inspired idea of adapting for this purpose the *Pribautka: "Gospodi pomiluy,"* which he had previously completed as a separate and unrelated piece.

A complete draft of the *pribautka,* dated 3/16 January 1916, with a single voice part notated in the treble clef, survives in the Archive.[58] The nonsense text, which corresponds exactly to that of the *Baika* (figs. [87]–[90]), is a footnote variant to one of Afanasyev's own *pribautki* texts (no. 542 in Soviet editions; no. 251k in the edition Stravinsky used). It is closely related to the nonsense song "*Turu-turu petushok*" in Sheyn's *Russkiye narodnïye pesni* of 1870 (pt. 1, no. 44) from which Musorgsky had concocted the text of the "Clapping Game" in the revised second act of *Boris Godunov:*

Gospodi pomiluy!	Lord, have mercy!
Na konike Danilo,	Danilo's on his berth,
na lavke Flor,	Flor is on the bench,
na pechi prigovor,	this jingle's on the stove,
v pechi kalachi—	in the oven there are bread twists—
kak ogon' goryachi,	hot as fire,
pro boyar pchenï.	baked for the noblemen.

58. It is no. 30 in the Rothschild catalogue, no. 15f in Craft's checklist (see White, *Stravinsky: The Composer and His Works,* 566). Shepard, "Stravinsky *Nachlass,*" 740, erroneously gives the month as December.

Nayekhali boyare	Noblemen have arrived from all around
da sobak navezli;	and brought with them a lot of dogs;
sobaki-to vzdurili	those dogs have gone wild
da popa ukusili.	and bitten the priest.

To this set piece Stravinsky prefixed a far longer extract from Afanasyev no. 542 proper (figs. [81]–[87] in the score), setting it to the same *napev* as the preexisting *pribautka,* but very ably adapting the text (as shown in brackets) so that it proceeds nimbly from the gory conclusion of the fox tale:

Kukolka, kukolka! [Lisïn'ka-lisitsa!]	Dolly, dolly! [Foxy-Woxy!]
Glyacha dolgo ne zhila?	Why didn't you live long?
Ya boyalas' tipuna.	I feared a boil on the tip of my tongue.
A tipun-to ne sud'ya,	But a boil is no judge,
a sud'ya-to lodïga.	and the judge is a knucklehead.
Lodïginï deti	Knucklehead's children
khotyat uleteti	want to fly off
za Ivanov gorod.	beyond Ivan's town.
Oni po gramotke pishut,	They write a letter each,
na devitsu [lisitsu] dïshut.	and breathe on the girl [Fox].
Devitsa, devitsa! [Lisïn'ka-lisitsa!]	Girlie, girlie! [Foxy-Woxy!]
Podi po voditsu.	Go fetch water.
Na doroge-to volki	Along the road the wolves
gorokh molotili,	were threshing peas,
popovï [Liskinï] rebyata	the priest's [Fox's] children
popu-to [Liske-to] skazali,	told the priest [Fox],
popad'ya-to [Lisïn'ka-to] s pechi	the priest's wife [vixen] (fell off) the stove
oblomala plechi.	(and) broke off her shoulders.
Syom-peresyom	What if we try-and-try-again—
Na lopatke ispechon;	it's baked on a shovel;
muzhik pesnyu spel,	the peasant finished his song,
na kapustnik sel,	sat down to a friendly feast,
s'yel tri koroba blinov,	ate three cartons of pancakes,
tri kostra pirogov,	three cartloads of pies,
zaúlok rogulyok,	an alley-full of crescent pastries,
zakhod kalachey,	a cow's pen full of bread twists,
makinnitsu s suloyu,	a hogshead of turnip *kvas,*
ovin kiselya,	a barn full of fruit preserve,
povarenku shchey!	and a vat of cabbage soup!

The final touch was to go back and substitute the word *lisku* (the Fox) for *popa* (the priest) in the last line of the "*Gospodi pomiluy*" verse, so that the very last line of the libretto now referred back to the main tale: "The dogs went wild and bit the Fox."

With the possible exception of the framing *Shestviye* (processional/recessional), for which no sketches appear to survive, and which was probably composed after

EXAMPLE 16.7 *Lisiñ'ka-lisitsa* sketch (loose leaf collected in Rothschild no. 29)

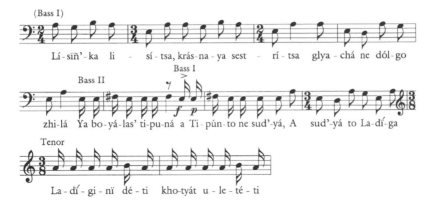

the rest of the score had already been submitted to the publisher,[59] the setting of
Afanasyev no. 542 was the last music in the *Baika* to be composed. There is no trace
of it in the sketchbook. The earliest notation for it, a loose sheet in the great bundle of miscellaneous sketches grouped by Rothschild as no. 29 (=Craft no. 15d)
suggests that the accompaniment was originally to have been far more elaborate
than the spare cimbalom-dominated background we know today. The vocal melody, too, shows some interesting differences from the final version. The beginning
pile-up of foxy epithets was to have been longer, rather obscuring the "*Gospodi pomiluy*" theme, and the 5/16 and 7/16 "subtactile" metric disruptions, such a characteristic feature of the piece as we know it, are absent (Ex. 16.7).

Less likely to be noticed is the inversion of the word order in the fourth measure: *ne dólgo* instead of *dólgo ne;* yet this is the most significant detail by far, for the
inversion shifts the accent onto a stronger musical ictus. The fact that Stravinsky
turned right around and shifted it back again in the published version raises what
is undoubtedly the most intriguing aspect of the *Baika:* the multifaceted rhythmic/
metric relationship of text and music.

BAIKA: WORDS AND MUSIC

"The music of Renard *begins in the verse."*

The sketches have already revealed the truth of this remark, but it is a complicated
truth. Stravinsky's attitude toward text setting, as we know, had become superbly

59. It is missing from the "complete" holograph vocal score, written in Stravinsky's best Turanian
hand, replete with calligraphic title page and final date (1 August 1916), now in the Paul Sacher Collection. For photographic facsimiles, see Lichtenhahn and Seebass, *Musikhandschriften* (n.p., showing
the end of the "First Song of the Cat and the Ram," figs. [38]–[41]), and *Strawinsky: sein Nachlass, sein
Bild* (p. 63, showing the end of the chase, the kill, and the beginning of the concluding *pribautka*, figs.
[78]–[82]). From the latter it appears that the seven notated screams for the singers were also an afterthought, replacing the most un-Stravinskian direction (still in the published score) that "both tenors
and both basses howl at the top of their lungs" ("*oba tenora i oba basa vopyat blagim matom*").

playful, artificial in the best sense. His prosody is full of delightful surprises, and the more familiar one is with the accentual and metrical character of his texts, the more one is able to be delighted and surprised by the setting.

It was only natural that the composer of *The Rite of Spring* should have been powerfully attracted by the specific qualities of skazka language, prose hovering on the brink of nonsense verse. Like all Russian language, it is highly accentual and therefore ineluctably rhythmic. It is full of rhymes and off-rhymes that parse it up into well-defined lines (verses) of freely varying length (cf. the *rayoshniy stikh,* discussed in Chapter 10). Already we seem to be describing the rhythmic qualities of *The Rite,* and many aspects of the following discussion may be fruitfully "read back" upon the more abstractly conceived instrumental music of the great ballet. The key to Renardian prosody, like that to the rhythm of *The Rite,* lies in the interplay of ictus and measure.

Either tonic accent or syllable count may determine the metrical structure (which is to say the implicit barring) of vocal music. In the *Baika* they function at times as alternatives, at other times in tandem, at still other times in opposition. The voices and instruments may agree or disagree. Sometimes, moreover, a pre-existent melody—either abstractly conceived or else modeled on the accent or verse structure of a specific line of text—may countermand the accentual character of a line to which it is subsequently set. These three Renardian prosodic models—accentual, syllabic, and "contrafact"—may be disengaged from one another only on the dissecting table. It is their unpredictable, fantastically inventive interaction that gives the *Baika* its special quality, the one Asafyev pinpointed so well when he spoke of a "profoundly indigenous *grotesque.*" While we may find few examples of any of these types that are completely free of interference from the others, basic distinctions can nonetheless be usefully drawn.

Conventional metrical prosody, consisting of the regular, a priori ordering of accent or quantity into isochronous measures or feet, is practically absent in the *Baika.* Ametrical prose rhythm had been accommodated by nineteenth-century musical "realists" such as Musorgsky by abandoning the a priori ordering of quantity but retaining isochrony. In a Musorgskian recitative, accented syllables mark isochronous beats, with the intervening unaccented syllables falling in between in freely variable gruppetti. We have seen how faithfully Stravinsky employed this method in his earliest music (up to *The Nightingale*). Traces of it may still be found in the *Baika,* especially in the Fox's dialogues with the Cock (Ex. 16.8).

The standard unit of isochrony in the *Baika,* however, is neither measure nor ictus, both of which are "superstructures," but the base itself—which is to say, the syllable. Accentual prosody based on isochronous syllables gives rise to a fluctuating beat pattern. The tonically accented measure is now the variable unit. The phrases given in Example 16.9 show how this works; they are short because "pure" prosodic types are so rare in this music. Even within them there are arbitrary el-

EXAMPLE 16.8 *Baika,* Fox at ⟨43⟩

Ku - kua-re - kú, pe - tu- shók,   Zo- lo- tóy gre - be- shók,

EXAMPLE 16.9

a. *Baika,* Cock at ⟨20⟩

Po - ne - slá me - nyá li - sá,   Po - ne - slá pe - tu-
- khá, Po kru-tím be- rezh - kám, Po vï - só - kim go -
rám, V chu- zhí - ye zém - li,   V da - lyó - ki - ye strá - nï,

b. Cat and Ram at ⟨27⟩

Bass I

Kak li - sá o - zór - ni - cha - la, krás - na - ya o - zór - ni - cha - la

Bass I

Bass II

I   se - byá   ve - li - chá - la.

ements: the rests separating the clauses in Example 16.9a, for example, and the placement of the fifth bar line in Example 16.9b. Extending the examples to show how they continue will reveal further refinements and extensions of the basic technique. At fig. [21], the whole verse, rather than the accentual unit, becomes the barring guide (cf. Sokalsky's hemistich method, discussed in Chapter 15); furthermore, arbitrary lengthening of accented syllables is admitted, thus bringing conventional syncopation to play in a most unconventional context (Ex. 16.10).

The music that follows the pair of measures shown in Example 16.8 abandons the Musorgskian isochronous ictus and reverts to the more endemically "Swiss-Stravinskian" isochronous syllabification. Accented syllables are placed on the downbeats (that is, following Linyova's "logical accent"), but again lengths are arbitrarily varied to enrich the rhythm and to prevent literal repetition of any accent pattern, despite the fact that each of the three phrases in the example adds up to the same eight eighth notes in length (Ex. 16.11).

EXAMPLE 16.10   *Baika*, voice parts at [21]

(go)-ram, V chu-zhí-ye zém-li,   V da-lyó-ki-ye strá-nï,   Za tri dé-vyat' ze -
- mél', V tri-dtsá - to- ye   tsár-stvo, V tri-de - syá - to - ye go-su - dár-stvo;

EXAMPLE 16.11   *Baika*, 2 after [43], voice and accompanying ostinato

ché - san-na go - ló-vush-ka,   Shél- ko-va   bo - ró - dush-ka,

Vḯ - glya-ni v o - kósh - ko.

Yet that length is by no means inviolate: the Cock immediately contravenes it in his reply. Indeed, the breaking of the pattern is obviously an element in the dramaturgy. In Example 16.12, the Cock's reply is given, together with an early version from the sketchbook (p. 34), to show how arbitrarily the length (but not the metrical position!) of the accented syllables may vary.

The reader will not have missed the five-eighths ostinato in the accompaniment (four notes plus a rest), cross-cutting the variable stresses of the vocal line it ostensibly supports. This, too, recalls *The Rite*, with its tantalizing counterpoints of fixed and mutable rhythmic elements. Stravinsky's barring generally favors the part he considered to occupy the rhythmic foreground. In the case just cited it is the variable vocal melody that governs the barring, but this is not invariably the case. The beginning of the song to the gusli (Ex. 16.13) was a troublesome spot. Stravinsky resolved the conflict here in favor of the gusli music, but provided a secondary

EXAMPLE 16.12

a. *Baika,* fig. 44 , voice and ostinato

b. *Baika* sketchbook, jotting on p. 34

EXAMPLE 16.13   *Baika,* fig. 62 (= 64 , 66)

barring to indicate for the singers their syllabic stresses. As soon as the quarter pulse in the accompaniment is abandoned, the barring is freed to follow the syllabic stress according to the Renardian norm.

The very first vocal music in the *Baika* (Ex. 16.14) is a fascinating spot where all three rhythmic/metric types—accentual stress, verse unit, ostinato—collide. The voice part, an imitation cockcrow, begins off the beat with an unaccented syllable, in preparation for the big leap to the downbeat at m. 3. (Needless to say, it is necessary to know the Russian text with its alternation of upbeats and accents—*kudá-kudá-kudá*—rather than the undifferentiated English "chuck-chuck-chuck . . ." to appreciate what Stravinsky is up to here.) The basic ostinato begins together with the voice, only it is on the beat (its beat, that is), so that its notation is one-eighth off with respect to the bar (Stravinsky fastidiously shows this by beaming the viola according to the four-note ostinato unit, contradicting the bar placement). The discrepancy is resolved by the second voice, whose part—barred to coincide with the beginning of the phrase (verse), not the accent—governs the barring of the whole for one five-eighth measure, at the end of which the ostinato is back on the beat with respect to the bar. The entrance of the clarinet and cimbalom at fig. [1], coinciding with the beginning of an ostinato unit in the strings, has the effect of a major structural downbeat, following which the ostinato is firmly in control of the rhythmic organization.

EXAMPLE 16.15   *Baika,* voice parts at 86 (note stress)

Verse-barring really comes into its own in the closing *pribautka,* the typical rapid patter (*skorogovorka*) of the skomorokhi being translated into strings of "sub-tactile" sixteenth-note bars, their lengths varying directly with the number of syllables in each successive line of text. Example 16.15 shows how Stravinsky set the last seven lines of Afanasyev no. 542. In the setting of lines 6–10 from the same text (Ex. 16.16), the correspondence between measure and verse is especially exact. Stravinsky's irrepressible playfulness is likewise especially evident: he modified the setting of the first two measures (extending the penultimate syllables) according to the syllabic texting of the last two measures, then he repeated the second measure in unmodified form. The result is a veritable tongue twister: its difficulties are contrived for the sake of the exhilaration that comes in surmounting them. That Stravinsky literally went back and contrived the difficulties in the manner suggested here will be evident if Example 16.16 is compared with the sketch for the same passage (end of Ex. 16.7).

EXAMPLE 16.16 *Baika,* voice parts at [82]

The fastidious accents marked in the last two measures of Example 16.16 would seem to imply that the bar line is meant to supersede the verbal stress. But does it? Can it? A loose sheet among the sketches in Rothschild no. 29 contains a special direction for the performance of the penultimate measure. Stravinsky did not include this direction in the final score, perhaps thinking it fussy. But it is very revealing. A bit of background may be helpful in interpreting it.

In standard Russian speech, the pronunciation of the vowel *o* depends on its placement with respect to the stress. When accented, the letter has its full value (that is, the sound represented by [ɔ] in the International Phonetic Alphabet, roughly equivalent to the *a* in *all*). When it is unaccented, *o* becomes a neutral "schwa" ([ə]). When in the so-called pretonic position, however (that is, when it occurs in the syllable directly preceding the stressed one), it is pronounced like the Russian letter *a*, comparable to the *a* in *father* or the *o* in *box*. Stravinsky's note to the second tenor and first bass reads: "*Oni* is to be enunciated like '*ani*' with a strong aspiration and an accent on '*a*' as indicated by the *fp*" (*Oni vigovarivayetsya kak "ani" s sil'nïm pridïkhaniyem i s aktsentom na "a" kak pokazano ff*). In other words, the first syllable of *oni* ("they"), while it receives a musical ictus, is nevertheless to be pronounced as though pretonic, thereby implying the normal accentuation of the word on the second syllable. The note to which it is sung is thus at once upbeat and downbeat; Stravinsky, as Pieter van den Toorn has pointed out in other contexts, is trying to "have it both ways."[60]

The final *pribautka* in the *Baika* also provides a paradigm of the "contrafact" method of setting a text, in which a thematic phrase is molded on the prosody of a model verse or stanza and then is made to carry succeeding lines strictly according to syllabification—i.e., "number"—without regard to stress. The declamation of the first two lines of the "*Gospodi pomiluy*" verse (fig. [87] in the score)—conceived, as we know from Archive material, as a separate and independent composition considerably earlier than the material immediately preceding it in the *Baika*—is prosodically impeccable. It provided the model stanza to which other lines were fitted, including the one that actually begins the song as Stravinsky finally cobbled it together (fig. [82]), the accents falling as they may (Ex. 16.17). Without detailed knowledge of the *Baika*'s creative history it would not be possible to identify the "*Gospodi pomiluy*" verse, buried as it now is, as the model stanza from which the other, prosodically distorted, verses were derived. More straightforward is the case of the "First Song of the Cat and the Ram," in which the first couplet quite obviously provides the model stanza for the rest (Ex. 16.18).

Similarly, without knowing what the sketchbook reveals—namely, that all the material up to the second encounter of the Fox and the Cock was composed roughly in reverse order—it would be difficult to guess how some of the prosodic anomalies in the first part of the *Baika* came about. To pick one example, the Cock's reply to the Fox at fig. [45] (Ex. 16.19a) is puzzling for the way the unaccented final syllables of *kúshayet* and *slúshayet* fall on downbeats. They do so because the model stanza was the Cock's replique at 2 after [49], where the accented rhyming words *glup* (stupid) and *khlup* (a bird's tail) occupy the analogous metrical positions (Ex. 16.19b).[61] The passage at [45] went through some revealing preliminary drafts in the sketchbook, Stravinsky at first unreflectingly transferring to it the scansion of the model, then having some fastidious second thoughts. The first preliminary sketch (Ex. 16.19c) seems to have been intended expressly to eliminate the end stress on *kúshayet,* while the third such sketch (Ex. 16.19e) seeks a

---

60. For a stimulating discussion of the matter, see chap. 8 of Van den Toorn, *Music of Igor Stravinsky* (bearing in mind that his ex. 51b, which treats the same passage discussed here in Ex. 16.14, perpetuates a misprint in the full score that has gone uncorrected since 1917: in the double bass part the notes and rests are reversed).

61. This replique—"The Cock is not so dumb; you won't get to gnaw my tail"—is one of the few lines of text in the *Baika* that seem definitely to have been written by the composer. He was no doubt prompted by Dahl's dictionary, which he must have had to consult for the meaning of the dialect word *khlup,* referring to that part of a fowl's anatomy sometimes called "the Pope's nose" in English. Dahl cites the proverb *Glup kak khlup* (Stupid as a bird's behind).

EXAMPLE 16.17

a. *Baika,* final *pribautka,* model stanza

fig. 87

Gó - spo - di po - mí - luy, Na kó - ni - ke Da - ní - lo

b. *Baika,* final *pribautka,* opening line

fig. 82

Lí - siñ' - ka, li - sí - tsa! Glya - chá dól - go ne zhi - lá?

c–g: Additional lines set to melody of model stanza

c.

fig. 83

Lí - siñ' - ka, li - sí - tsa, Po - dí po - vo - dí - tsu

d.

fig. 84

Lí - ski - nï re - byá - ta Lí - ske to ska - zá - li _____

e.

fig. 85 + 2

Mu-zhík pés-nyu spel... ___ Na ka-púst-nik sel. ___

f.

fig. 88

V pe - chí ka - la - chí, Kak o - gón' gor - ya - chí

g.

fig. 89

Na - ye - kha - li bo - ya - re da so - bák na - vez - lí

EXAMPLE 16.18

a. *Baika,* fig. 27 (model)

Kák li - sá   o - zór - ni - cha - la,   Krás - na - ya   o - zór - ni - cha - la

I   se - byá   ve - li - chá - la.

b. Fig. 31

Ot - kúl' vzya - la - sya   li - sí - tsa,   ot - kúl' vzya - la - sya   krás - na - ya

khvost pod - zhá - la   kï - chet - kú   che - lóm   ot - dá - la

c. Fig. 39

Vzya - lá   li - sá   kï - che - tá   za   bó - ki   Po - ne - slá   e - go   da - lyó - ko

EXAMPLE 16.19

a. *Baika,* fig. 45

Pe - túkh   kásh - ku   kú - sha - yet   li - sú   ne   slú - sha - yet.

b. *Baika,* 2 after 49

Pe - túkh   ne   ták - to   glup,   Ne   glo - dát'   te - bé   moy   khlup.

EXAMPLE 16.19 *(continued)*

c. *Baika* sketchbook, p. 34, first variant

Pe-túkh kásh - ku kú-sha-yet   I lís-ku ne   slú -   sha-yet

d. Second variant

Pe - túkh kásh- ku   kú - sha -yet   i lí -   sku ne

e. Third variant

Pe - túkh kásh - ku kú -   sha-yet   li - sú ne slú -   sha-yet.

middle ground by none-too-appropriately adopting the portamento with which Stravinsky had mocked the reference to the Cock's rear end (*khlup* in Ex. 16.19b).

These lines, in their turn, formed the model for the Cock's song that introduces each of the encounters ([42], reused at [10]). Likewise, the Cock's outburst at [13] was the model for the whole first section (through fig. [9]), and not the other way around, as the finished score would suggest. This is made clear in the sketchbook (p. 21), where the passage at [13] is sketched in a version quite like its present form, only up a minor third, while the "*Podaite mne syuda*" music is first sketched three pages later to a quite different tune (Ex. 16.20).

The sketch for [13], moreover, is a real model stanza: an archetypical example of verse-cum-accentual barring. The finished music, by contrast, has been metrically distended to fit the Procrustean bed of the eight-beat ostinato running beneath, just as in folk singing Linyova's "logical accent" might shift to accommodate an established metrical pattern (Ex. 16.21).

BAIKA:
INTERACTING PITCH STRUCTURES

The fact that the tune quoted from the sketchbook in Example 16.21 made it into the score at two pitch levels, one a minor third below the sketch, the other a minor third above, will hardly be news at this point. The trusty octatonic cycle of "nodes" remained a very efficacious governor of tonality in the *Baika,* even if the acciaccatura-enriched monody of the *Pribaoutki* and the strict white-key diatonicism of the fourth *Berceuse* or the *Hymne à la nouvelle Russie* play more con-

EXAMPLE 16.20   Sketchbook, p. 24

po - dai - te mne syu - da

EXAMPLE 16.21

a. Sketchbook, p. 21 (note relationship between bar and stress)

O má - ti mo-yá li - sí - tsa   Ya ne pó-stil-sya ne mo - líl-sya

Pri - dí v in-nó-ye vrém - ya

b. *Baika,* fig. 13, voice and cimbalom ostinato

spicuously on the music's surface. That Stravinsky was able to mingle all these
styles and techniques so successfully, meanwhile mining the old octatonic lode for
novel nontriadic partitions and linear extensions, testifies to his undiminished
resourcefulness.

There are some rather baldly displayed tone-semitone scales in the *Baika*—far
from a common occurrence in Stravinsky, for all his dependence on such scales as
a referential source. An example is the beginning of the Cock's "whine" (fig. [57]),
based on a descending Collection III succession (Ex. 16.22). The accompanying
double bass sounds an (0 11) span-defining E, which of course brings the "*Rite*
chord" to mind. The E-major arpeggio that "acoustically amplifies" the double-
bass pitch, meanwhile, turns the whole harmonic aggregate into an oblique (and,

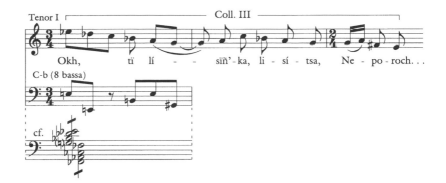

EXAMPLE 16.22 *Baika*, fig. 57, voice plus double bass in first bar to show relationship between the implied harmony and the *Gadaniya* ("Auguries") chord from *The Rite of Spring*

one is willing to wager, slyly calculated) reference to the famous "Auguries" ostinato chord in the earlier ballet.

Arpeggiated *Rite* chords permeate the twice-presented music of the Cock's abduction (figs. [20]–[24], [53]–[57]), which is based on Collection I with relatively little interference. In the passage shown in Example 16.23, the (0 11) span F–E is variously filled in with the fifth and sixth semitones, alternately or (even) simultaneously, the simultaneous fill producing a symmetrical intervallic array consisting of the *Rite* chord plus its inversion, known to Bartók scholars as the "Z-tetrachord." The concluding cimbalom/bassoon figure is also an arpeggiated *Rite* chord, referable to Collection III as a transition into the Cock's whine.

The music that follows this concluding riff on its other appearance (the entrance song of the Cat and the Ram) returns to Collection I for what is surely the most single-mindedly octatonic little number in the score, indeed in the whole Swiss decade. It is compounded of two basic elements: a theme and an accompanying ostinato. The latter, wildly arpeggiated in the cimbalom, consists of the entire collection partitioned into motivic segments deriving from the tune quoted in Example 16.20. The diatonic fifth/sixth idea is in fact a potent motivic binder that reaches a sort of apotheosis in the melismas at the climax of the "First Song of the Cat and the Ram" (Ex. 16.24).

The thematic component of the entrance song is a melodic phrase that occurred to Stravinsky in connection with the text reference to Yermak and his noisy digestive tract. Example 16.25 shows its first appearance in the sketches. Like the three-note motive from which the ostinato was constructed, this little diatonic *napev* can be transposed to the other (0 3 6 9) octatonic nodes without leaving the confines of Collection I. It makes at least one appearance at each of them: compare the bassoon and trumpet at fig. [24], the canon in the horns one bar after [25], and the first bass two bars later (Ex. 16.26).

EXAMPLE 16.23 *Baika,* fig. 21

EXAMPLE 16.24

a. *Baika,* cadential phrase at 13 (cf. Ex. 16.14)

b. Voice parts at 37

c. Cimbalom ostinato beginning at m. 157, showing derivation from phrase given in Ex. 16.24a

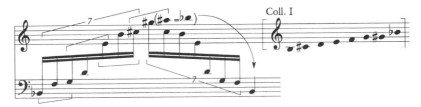

EXAMPLE 16.25   Sketchbook, p. 17

Ve – da-yesh' Yer-mak   za - per- del na - to-shchak

EXAMPLE 16.26

a. Bassoon and trumpet at 24

(Note harmonization drawn from Coll. I nodes)

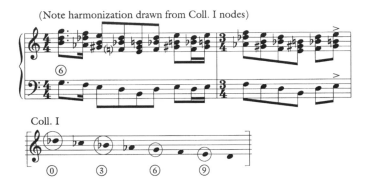

Coll. I

b. Canon in the horns at 1 after 25

c. Bass I at 3 after 25

Al'   ne ve – yesh' Yer - mak   Za - tre-shchal na - to-shchak.

Together with its transposition at the tritone, the theme exhausts the octatonic collection. As the sketches demonstrate, Stravinsky recognized this property implicitly by treating the tritone transposition as a functional equivalence. The words to which the theme is set in Example 16.25 are actually sung at the distance of a tritone in the finished score. Comparison of the voice parts in m. 157 as found in sketch and score respectively is very instructive (Ex. 16.27): the first phrase in the sketch is a tritone away in the score, while the second phrase is untransposed (or more precisely, transposed up an octave, leaving the original pitch-class content undisturbed). Transposition by an octave and by a tritone are thus shown to be functionally equivalent.

Now, the theme shown in Example 16.25 is a deliberate and obvious pun. Its constituent pitches are at once referable to Collection I and to the diatonic white-key scale. They are in fact the only pitches that can intersect in this way. *Mutatis mutandis,* the theme at its various octatonic nodal transpositions will intersect with the major scales on E-flat, F-sharp, and A. As various sketches reveal, Stravinsky at first intended to exploit the "polytonal" possibilities inherent in this situation. Example 16.28 shows an entry from page 19 of the sketchbook, in which the parallel doubling in thirds between the two bass voices introduces C as a specious tonic, while the piccolo plays a Stars-and-Stripes-Foreverish obbligato that supplies an A to complete the C-major scale. It is easy enough to see why such a cluttered texture was finally rejected. In the finished score the basses sing a version of the theme beginning on B-flat, modified (but for the neighbor-note C-flat) to conform to the major scale on E-flat. These E-flats and the solitary C are in fact the only pitches in the entire song that are foreign to Collection I.

A similar interaction between the octatonic scale (Collection III this time) and the diatonic white-key scale can be found in what is perhaps the earliest music to have been composed for the *Baika,* the "second" encounter of the Fox and the Cock (fig. [43]ff.). Van den Toorn has called attention to the way the collection is partitioned here to emphasize the apposition of the "white notes" in the voice (G-A) and the "black notes" in the instruments, particularly the "E♭-D♭ reiteration of the cello" at the antipodal tritone.[62] He stopped short of noting how, while the black notes remain hypostatized in their original position as an ostinato, the white notes spawn the full white-key scale—most conspicuously in the flute roulades, but also in the voice parts, which sound the nonoctatonic D as early as the second measure. By fig. [45] (the Cock's replique, quoted in Ex. 16.19), the D has become a veritable reciting tone, the focal pitch (though not the final, let alone the "tonic") of a typical, diatonic yet tonally nonimplicative *napev,* while the original octatonic ostinato continues to grind away below (Ex. 16.29). Also noteworthy is the play in

62. Van den Toorn, *Music of Igor Stravinsky,* 153.

EXAMPLE 16.27

a. Sketchbook, p. 17 (voice parts and cimbalom only)

b. *Baika,* bass I and tenor I (with cimbalom) at 4 after 25

EXAMPLE 16.28   Sketchbook, p. 19

EXAMPLE 16.28 (*continued*)

za - per - del na - to- shchak

EXAMPLE 16.29 *Baika,* 7 after 43 –4 after 45 (for beginning of the passage see Ex. 16.11 above)

Dam te-be go-

Vï - glya-ni v o - kosh-ko.   Ne glya - zhu   v o - kosh - ko   Ne

rosh – ku.
na – do   mne   go – – rosh - ku

Coll. III

"C - scale"

EXAMPLE 16.30

a. *Baika,* tenor I and cimbalom at 1 after 71

b. Fox's repliques at 73, 75, and 77 compared, tenor I and cimbalom

EXAMPLE 16.30 (*continued*)

c. Anacruses at 73, 75, and 77 compared

the voice parts between the exclusively octatonic B-flat and the exclusively diatonic B. The result is a harmonic/contrapuntal texture that is rooted equally in rural Russian folklore and in the no less indigenous Russian lore of symmetrical harmonic structures, St. Petersburg style. It is rooted in both but wholly beholden or referable to neither. That is what makes it so purely and authentically Turanian.

This texture may be savored at its richest in the music that immediately precedes the slaying of the Fox. The latter's interrogation of its eyes, legs, and tail (figs. [73]–[79]) takes the form of a strophic song in which the main tune, played on the cimbalom, is derived from the phrase to which the Fox, at fig. [71], had sung her response to the other animals' gusli serenade (Ex. 16.30a). At [73], the fox sings a diatonic countermelody in which the first note combines with the cimbalom's open fifth to present the important fifth/sixth motive in the form of a harmonic simultaneity. Each subsequent return of the tune, as the Fox, with increasing anxiety, addresses the parts of her anatomy in turn, is pitched a minor third higher than the last—that is, according to the familiar (0 3 6 9) octatonic rotation (Ex. 16.30b). The three motivic cells are referable to and, but for one note, exhaust the pitches of Collection II. Thus the nodal properties of that collection organize tonally the thirty-seven-bar dramatic crux of the play. The octatonic reference is strengthened by the "polytonal" anacrustic arpeggios that introduce each strophe of the song. The first violin, clarinet, and flute in each case are individually confined to triads and dominant-seventh chords with roots along the Collection II circle of nodes (Ex. 16.30c).

Besides the Fox's diatonic *napev* and the secondary, simultaneously unfolding one in the violins[63]—which taken together together constitute a six-note diatonic

63. Secondary, that is, according to a judgment Stravinsky made himself in relegating it to small type in the piano vocal score.

span that intersects with Collection II four times in each transposition, ultimately exhausting it (Ex. 16.31a)—there is an element of deliberate clash with the reigning octatonic collection in the form of a duet of double bass and viola (later cello), pizzicato. It is organized around a series of four T-S-T tetrachords (viola) descending not by minor but by major thirds, presented with their constituent dyads reversed, and accompanied by the bass's descending chromatic line (Ex. 16.31b). These instrumental parts, which exhaust the chromatic scale in strict sequence and hence are harmonically neutral, seem a purely synthetic element, a mere textural thickener or "fill." Yet they are subjected to the same strict series of octatonically motivated transpositions as the rest. (In each transposition, the middle T-S-T tetrachord is referable to the reigning octatonic collection.)

Such seemingly routine writing is not often encountered in Stravinsky, and one looks for a reason. Chromatically descending ornamental bass lines were a stock-in-trade of an earlier generation of Russian composers, especially when writing variations against a folk tune. We examined a slithery example from Borodin (Ex. 10.28b) for the light it shed on *Petrushka.* Another comes to mind in connection with the passage we are pondering from the *Baika,* for it features a progressively accumulating, hence very conspicuous, chromatic descent in the bass (Ex. 16.32). It is sung in the first act of *Prince Igor* by a character named Skula. He is a *gudochnik,* a fiddle-scraping skomorokh. That is already a connection with the *Baika,* of course; but what amplifies the resonance many times over is the fact that the role of Skula was created in 1890, with colossal success, by Fyodor Stravinsky, who remained closely identified with it throughout the remaining decade of his career. Could this strangely perfunctory bass line in the *Baika* have actually been Igor Stravinsky's final, and probably unconscious, tribute to his illustrious parent?

If so, it is not the only curious echo of "classical" Russian opera in the piece. The Fox's monklike chant in her first encounter with the Cock is not so much redolent of the Slavonic liturgy (as has often been proposed) as reminiscent of the Holy Fool's lament at the close of *Boris Godunov;* and her salutations to her prey in the second encounter call to mind various passages from the role of Varlaam (another Fyodor Stravinsky specialty) in the Inn scene from the same opera.

But of course the *Baika* is no more an opera than *Histoire du soldat,* a second *skomorosh'ye deystvo* to which the first indirectly gave birth. As Charles-Ferdinand Ramuz put it in the first draft of his libretto for the *Histoire,* "this is not a play, it is a story."[64] The *Baika* may not even be a story. It is a collage, a sublime mishmash in which the story as such (true to the old Miriskusnik ideal, only so much more so!) is intelligible only on the visual plane. The text, hovering perpetually on the

64. Robert Craft, "*Histoire du soldat* (the Musical Revisions, the Sketches, the Evolution of the Libretto)," *Musical Quarterly* 66 (1980): 333; reprinted in SelCorrIII:470.

EXAMPLE 16.31

a. Diatonic mode of Fox/violin *napevï* (white notes intersect with Collection II)

b. Tetrachordal analysis of music at ⟦73⟧, ⟦75⟧, etc.

EXAMPLE 16.32   Borodin, *Prince Igor*, Act I, "*Knyazhaya pesnya*," 8 after ⟦13⟧

Kak voz-go-vo-rit o - tets   nash ba-tyush-ka,   Vo-lo-di - mir svet

Ya - ro - sla - vich: Goy, vï p'ya - ni-tsï, slu - gi

(continued)

EXAMPLE 16.32 (*continued*)

[Thus doth speak our Little Father, Vladimir, bright son of Yaroslav:
Hey, you drunkards, faithful servants, How can I not take pity on you. . .]

brink of nonsense, dispenses with linear narrative altogether. The plot is interrupted for unannounced and unidentified digressions and flashbacks, and the characters—impersonated now by one voice, now by another, now by voices in tandem or tutti—are fragmented and absorbed into the musical texture to the point where in a concert performance (the only kind "*Renard*" gets anymore) there is no hope of following the plot in any but the most generalized terms, and then only if one has read a program note. Hence the *Baika* is as much a "cubist" rendering of a *skazka* as *Svadebka* is a "collage" of wedding scenes. Asafyev's shrewd (perhaps, as we shall see, too shrewd) comment about *Histoire* applies with greater justice to the *Baika:* "Despite the essentially syncretic plan [it] is chiefly a musical composition. Such is the fate of all attempts at artistic synthesis in the presence of music, itself the art of the movement and transformation of the energy of sound: music immediately begins to dominate."[65]

Despite the fact that it is a sung piece, whereas *Histoire* is a work of spoken theater, the music of the *Baika* is every bit as absolute. To an extent unprecedented and never again equaled by Stravinsky, he succeeded, through the methods we explored in Chapter 15, in making the words of his "merry performance" literally and indispensably *a part of the music.*

HISTOIRE DU SOLDAT: THE CONCEPT

Histoire, by contrast, is "literary" through and through. No wonder Diaghilev never showed the slightest interest in it. Stravinsky's allegations notwith-

65. Asafyev, *A Book About Stravinsky,* 162.

standing,[66] Diaghilev's indifference was no simple matter of jealousy. Diaghilev had not commissioned the *Baika* either, yet he took it over with enthusiasm from the princesse de Polignac. He rightly recognized that *Histoire* as a totality was not worthy of him—or of Stravinsky. Although it shares the superficial trappings of the *skomorosh'ye deystvo*—"to be read, played, and danced," as its subtitle proclaims, upon a trestle by a troupe of itinerants—and although its subject was mined from the same lode as that of its predecessor, this stuffy *moralité,* conventionally linear in form and complacently preachy in content, was the bastard offspring of mismatched talents in temporary opportunistic alliance. Its inauthenticity as a work of art forever condemns it to stepchild status among Stravinsky's works for the stage, even as the inspired music, unencumbered by the verbal ball-and-chain, has long since won its inevitable place among the Stravinskian evergreens.

There cannot be the slightest doubt that the concept of a narrative with musical illustrations was Ramuz's, not Stravinsky's. The work itself proclaims the fact: Stravinsky could never have had at so late a date an idea so at variance with the direction his work had taken. By the time he dictated his late memoirs to Craft, the composer, having outlived all his collaborators, was in the habit of taking credit on principle for everything and anything related to his theatrical enterprises; so he took credit for this one, too, and claimed, moreover, that he had had the general idea of a "dramatic spectacle for a *théâtre ambulant*" since the earliest days of the war. He also maintained that the specific idea of a play based on the tale from Afanasyev in which "the soldier tricks the Devil into drinking too much vodka, then gives the Devil a handful of shot to eat, assuring him it is caviar, and the Devil greedily swallows it and dies" occurred to him in the spring of 1917.[67]

This is obviously too early. It was the Bolshevik coup in Russia that created Stravinsky's material need, as he acknowledged in the *Chroniques,* and it was this need that led to the "feverish" discussions with Ramuz and Ansermet, who were in "equally straitened circumstances" and were looking, like Stravinsky, "for some means of escape" from them. In this telling, Ramuz and Stravinsky discovered the source in Afanasyev together, in "the cycle of legends dealing with the adventures of the soldier who deserted and the Devil who inexorably comes to carry off his soul."[68]

Ramuz's account, written only a decade after the fact, differs from Stravinsky's earlier version in two essential details. First, the whole project, from preliminary discussion to performance, is set in the year 1918—a fact corroborated by the fairly

66. See *An Autobiography,* 79–80.
67. E&D:101/90.
68. *An Autobiography,* 70–71. In E&D (101/90) Stravinsky claimed that he had pieced the plot together out of separate episodes in various Afanasyev soldier tales before Ramuz became involved in the project.

extensive surviving Stravinsky/Ramuz correspondence.[69] Second, Ramuz recalled that it was a single story from Afanasyev that furnished the plot, not a conflation of separate episodes: "We had only to leaf together through one of the volumes of that huge compilation by a famous Russian folklorist whose name I forget; and amid so many themes and folk maxims, in which the Devil almost always played the leading role, we immediately fastened, for all sorts of reasons (including its very incoherence), on the one about the soldier and his violin."[70]

Ramuz gracefully attributed the plan to a vague joint inspiration. The third party to the deliberations, however, did not hesitate to credit the first thought of the play to the writer: " 'What do you do,' Ramuz would say," wrote Ansermet, " 'when you can hardly count on publication, if not address the public directly in our proper role, which is, for me, telling stories, for you, Stravinsky, making music, and in such a way that our product might move any audience at all.' "[71] And it was Ramuz, according to his own account, who conceived of the ultraliterary, hence un-Stravinskian, form the work would take:

> Not being a man of the theater, I had proposed to Stravinsky that we write, not a play in the strict sense of the word, but a "story," persuading him that the theater might be conceived in much broader terms than usual and that it could adapt itself perfectly, for example (as I continue to think), to what one might call the narrative style. For Stravinsky's sake it was agreed that he would conceive his music as something that could be completely independent of the text and would constitute a "suite," which would admit of concert performance.[72]

What this arrangement really vouchsafed was the possibility for the two osten-

69. The earliest reference to *Histoire du soldat* is found in a letter of 28 February 1918, in which Ramuz implies that the real work on the project had not yet begun, though the subject had been selected (see Charles Ferdinand Ramuz, *Lettres, 1900–1918* [Lausanne: Éditions Clairefontaine, 1956], 353; also SelCorrIII:33). A letter of 10 March informs Stravinsky that Werner Reinhart's patronage had been secured, which amounted to a go-ahead to compose the score (*Lettres,* 353–54; SelCorrIII:34). While it might seem risky to rely on the dates of letters to establish chronology in a working relationship that involved frequent personal contact and telephone conversations, the fact is that ten letters from Ramuz to Stravinsky have been published dating from the period between the spring of 1917, when Stravinsky claimed to have conceived the idea, and the earlier of the letters cited above, and, while they make frequent reference to ongoing projects and, especially, to business affairs arising from those projects, they contain no hint of *Histoire.*

70. "Nous n'avons eu qu'à feuilleter ensemble un des tomes de l'énorme compilation d'un illustre folkloriste russe dont j'ai oublié le nom; et, entre tant de thèmes, dits populaires, où le Diable jouait presque toujours le rôle principal, celui du soldat et de son violon, pour toute espèce de raisons (dont son incohérence même), nous avait aussitôt retenus" (Ramuz, *Souvenirs sur Strawinsky,* 63).

71. " 'Que faire,' disait Ramuz, 'lorsqu'on ne peut plus guère compter sur l'édition, sinon s'adresser directement au public dans notre fonction propre qui est, pour moi, de raconter des histoires, pour vous Strawinsky, de faire de la musique, et de façon à ce que notre production puisse toucher n'importe quel public' " (Ernest Ansermet, "La naissance de 'Histoire du soldat,' " in Ramuz, *Lettres,* 35).

72. "N'étant pas un homme de théâtre, j'avais proposé à Strawinsky d'écrire, plutôt qu'une pièce au sens propre, une 'histoire,' lui faisant voir que le théâtre pouvait être conçu dans un sens beaucoup plus large qu'on ne le faisait d'ordinaire et qu'il se prêtait parfaitement, par exemple (je continue à le penser), à ce qu'on pourrait appeler le style narratif. Pour Strawinsky, il avait été convenu qu'il concevrait sa musique comme pouvant être complètement indépendante du texte et constitua une 'suite,' ce qui lui permettrait d'être exécutée au concert" (Ramuz, *Souvenirs sur Strawinsky,* 62).

sible collaborators to work virtually independently of each other, as is only too apparent in the lopsided shape of the product. The text is concentrated largely at the beginning, the music at the end: by the time the midpoint of the score is reached (No. 7, Petit concert), almost 90 percent of the text has been read. From a narrative with musical and scenic interludes, *Histoire* turns abruptly into a ballet pantomime with brief interludes of recitation.

The tale on which Ramuz modeled his narrative is easily identified as Afanasyev no. 154 (no. 91 in prerevolutionary editions), "The Runaway Soldier and the Devil" (*"Begloy soldat i chort"*). One of the lengthiest items in all of Afanasyev, it is obviously a pair of *skazki* combined in a chance oral redaction (hence Ramuz's comment on the story's charming incoherence). As a matter of fact, Afanasyev no. 153—"The Soldier Saves the Princess" (*"Soldat izbavlyayet tsarevnu"*), on which Ramuz and Stravinsky did not draw, Stravinsky's implication notwithstanding—is an independently transmitted variant of the second tale in the pair. So completely does no. 154 match up with the plot of the *Histoire du soldat* libretto, and even with its rhetoric (cf. the threefold repetition of "Et à present qu'est-ce que je vais faire?" as a cue for No. 3, Music to Scene II), that it is possible to interpolate the list of Stravinsky's musical numbers directly into the Afanasyev text, as follows:

THE RUNAWAY SOLDIER AND THE DEVIL

A soldier had requested leave, made ready, and set out a-marching [No. 1: *Soldier's March*]. He marched and marched, but saw no water anywhere to soak himself a breadcrust and have a bite for the road, and his belly was long since empty. There was nothing for it but to trudge further. He looked round and spied a little brook a-running. He went up to the brook, fetched three crusts from his knapsack, and set them in the water. And the soldier also had a fiddle. In his free time he would play various songs on it to stave off boredom. So the soldier sat down by the brook, took his fiddle, and started up a tune [No. 2: *Music to Scene I ("Airs by a Stream")*]. Suddenly out of nowhere the Unclean One came up to him in the guise of an old man clutching a book. "Greetings, Mr. Serviceman!" —"Hello there, kind sir!" The devil winced a bit at being called a kind sir. "Listen, old chap! Let's trade: I'll give you my book, and you give me the fiddle." —"Ha, old man! What do I want with your book? I've been in service to our sovereign for a good ten years now without being able to read. I never knew how, and now it's too late to learn!" —"Never mind, Serviceman! My book is such that whoever looks in it will know how to read it!" —"Well, let's have it. I'll give it a try!"

The soldier opened the book and started to read as if he had known how since childhood. He rejoiced and immediately exchanged his fiddle for it. The Unclean One took the fiddle, began working the bow, but it was no go. There was no sense to his playing. "Listen, pal," he said to the soldier, "come be my guest for three days or so and teach me to play the fiddle. I'll thank you for it!" —"No, old man," replied the soldier, "I am needed at home. In three days' time I'll be far from here." —"Please, Serviceman, if you come stay with me and teach me to fiddle, I'll have you home in one day. I'll drive you in a post carriage." The soldier sat and pondered: should he go or not? And as he did so he fished a crust out of the brook, for he was hungry. "Hey, Serviceman, old pal," said the Unclean One, "your food is awful. Have some of mine!" He untied his sack and brought out white bread, roast beef, vodka, and all kinds of goodies—"Eat to your heart's content!"

The soldier ate his fill, drank his fill, and agreed to stay with the old stranger and teach him to fiddle. He remained his guest three days, and then asked to go home; whereupon the devil led him out of his mansion. In front of the porch stood a team of three fine horses. "Have a seat, Serviceman, you'll be home in a flash." The soldier seated himself with the devil in the carriage. How the horses up and carried them off! The miles vanished in the twinkling of an eye! They reached their destination in a trice. "Well, do you recognize this village?" asked the Unclean One. "How could I not!" replied the soldier. "In this very village I was born and bred." —"Well, good-bye!" The soldier got down from the carriage, came to his kinfolk, started greeting them and telling them about himself, about his regiment, and about his leave. It had seemed to him that he had been visiting with the Unclean One for three days in all, but in fact he had spent three years with him. His leave had expired long ago, and in his regiment he was counted a deserter.

The soldier became frightened. He didn't know what to do! Not even the thought of carousing crossed his mind! He went out to the outskirts of the village [No. 3: *Music to Scene II ("Pastorale")*] and thought, "Where can I go? If I go back to the regiment they'll run me out of the service for sure. Hey, you devil, you've played a jolly trick on me!" He had hardly pronounced these words when the Unclean One himself appeared. "Don't carry on so, Serviceman! Stay with me. In the regiment you live pitifully, they feed you crusts and beat you with sticks, while I will make your fortune . . . Would you like me to make you a merchant?" —"Well now, that wouldn't be so bad. Merchants live well. Let me try my luck!" The Unclean One made him a merchant, gave him a big shop in the capital city with all kinds of expensive wares, and said, "Now good-bye, old pal! I'm off to the thrice-ninth realm, the thrice-tenth kingdom. The king there has a beautiful daughter, the Princess Maria. I'm off to torment her every which way!"

Our merchant lived without a care. Luck came his way of itself. He had such success in business that he could ask for nothing more! The other merchants began to envy him. "Let's ask him," they said, "what manner of man he is and where he came from. Can we strike a bargain with him? He's taken away all our trade— let him go to hell!" They came to him, began questioning him, but he replied, "Brethren! Right now I'm terribly busy and have no time to talk. Come back tomorrow—you shall learn all." The merchants went to their homes; and the soldier thought, What to do? What answer should he give? He thought and thought, and decided to give up his shop and leave town by night. So he collected all the money he had on hand and set off for the thrice-tenth kingdom [No. 4: *Music to Scene III*].

He marched and marched [No. 5: *Soldier's March (reprise)*], and came at length to the gates. "Who goes there?" asked the sentry. He replied, "I am a healer. I have come to your realm because your king has a sick daughter. I wish to cure her." The sentry told the courtiers, the courtiers told the king himself. The king sent for the soldier [No. 6: *Royal March*]. "If you can cure my daughter, I'll give you her hand in marriage." —"Your Majesty! Have them bring me three packs of cards, three bottles of sweet wine plus three bottles of fiery spirits, three pounds of nuts, three pounds of lead bullets, and three bundles of bright wax candles." —"Very well, all will be ready!" The soldier waited until nightfall, bought himself a fiddle, and went to the princess [No. 7: *Little Concerto*]. He lit the candles in her chamber, began to drink and carouse, and played his fiddle [No. 8: *Three Dances (Tango, Waltz, Ragtime)*]. At midnight the Unclean One arrived, heard the music, and fell upon the soldier. "Greetings, pal!" —"Hello!" —"What are you drinking?" —"I'm having a sip of *kvas*." —"Let's have some!" —"Certainly!" And he offered him a full glass of fiery spirits. The devil drained it, and his eyes rolled up under his forehead. "Hey, that's strong stuff! Give me something to munch!" —"Here are some nuts. Munch away!" said the soldier, but slipped him the lead bullets instead. The devil gnawed at these and broke his teeth. They fell to playing cards. What with one thing and another the time passed, the cock crew, and the devil vanished. The king asked the princess, "How did you sleep last night?" —"Peacefully, praise God!" And the next night it was the same. But toward the third night the soldier asked the king, "Your Majesty! Have them forge a ten-ton vise and make three rods of copper, three rods of iron, and three of tin." —"Very well, it shall all be done!"

At the dead of midnight the Unclean One appeared. "Greetings, Serviceman! Once again I have come to carouse with you." —"Greetings! Who is not glad to see a merry companion?" They began to drink and carouse. The Unclean One espied the vise and asked, "And what is this?" —"Oh, the king has taken me into his service and charged me with teaching his musicians to fiddle, and they all have crooked fingers—no better than yours. I've got to straighten them out in this vise." —"Say, pal," the Unclean One began to ask, "couldn't you straighten my fingers too? I still can't play that fiddle!" —"Why not? Just lay your fingers down there." The devil put both his hands in the vise. The soldier tightened it, squeezed it shut, then seized the rods and let the devil have it. As he beat him he taunted, "There's merchanthood for you!" The devil begged, the devil pleaded, "Let me go, for pity's sake! I'll never come within a hundred miles of the palace again!" But he whipped him all the more. The devil leaped and bounded, whirled and twirled [No. 9: *The Devil's Dance*], tore himself loose with all his might, and said to the soldier, "Go ahead and marry the princess, but you'll not escape my clutches. As soon as you shall travel a hundred miles from the city, then and there I'll seize you!" [No. 11: *The Devil's Song*]. He spoke and vanished [No. 10: *Little Chorale*].

So the soldier married the princess and lived with her in love and harmony. And a few years later the king died, and the soldier began to rule the entire kingdom. One time the new king and his wife went out to walk in the garden. "Ah, what a wonderful garden!" he said. "You call this a garden?" replied the queen. "Beyond the city we have another garden, about a hundred miles from here. Now, that one is something to admire!" [No. 12: *Great Chorale*]. The king got ready and set out for it with his queen. No sooner had he alighted from the carriage than the devil met them: "What are you doing here? Have you forgotten what I told you? Well, old pal, you've only yourself to blame. This time you'll never wriggle free." —"What can I do? Such, it seems, is my fate! At least let me say good-bye to my young wife." —"Say it, but make it snappy!" . . . [No. 13: *Triumphal March of the Devil*].[73]

73. Afanasyev, *Narodnïye russkiye skazki,* ed. Azadovsky, Andreyev, and Sokolov, 2:380–83.

Besides the obvious, if vague, topicality of a soldier's tale in the last horrific phases of the world war, and besides the superficial Faustian resonances that made for a pat link with a distinguished literary and theatrical heritage, what made this story the inevitable choice was the all-pervading icon of the soldier's violin. For one thing, it eased the integration of spoken words and instrumental music. It also became the means by which Ramuz sought to do something about that "incoherence" after all: its role in the libretto, much strengthened relative to the folktale, became that of formal and thematic unifier. Virtually every departure Stravinsky and Ramuz made from Afanasyev was made to enhance the violin's prominence and its status as motive force.

Where Afanasyev's soldier cured the princess by distracting the devil with a game of cards and besotting him with drink and with a meal of buckshot (the very episode Stravinsky recalled in 1962 as the tale's main attraction!), Ramuz's soldier (with the eager connivance of the Reader)[74] uses the cards and drink to win back the fiddle from the devil, and the fiddle is what cures the princess. Where Afanasyev's soldier gets rid of the devil by the use of physical torture, all Ramuz's soldier needs, once again, is his magic violin. In the end, having regained it, the devil recaptures the soldier with the same magical instrument, on which he plays a grating parody of the music by which the soldier, in the Little Concerto, had proclaimed his freedom and, in the Tango, had won the princess (Ex. 16.33).

This last stroke was Stravinsky's idea.[75] It suggests a somewhat different interpretation of the violin symbolism from what is customary—and, possibly, from what Ramuz had had in mind. The violin is usually construed in hackneyed Faustian terms as representing the soldier's soul. But it would seem—from Stravinsky's use of it in the final number and from its role in the revival of the princess—to represent, instead, a kind of liberating and health-giving *élan vital* that is in the end perverted and made the instrument of enslavement.

Stravinsky's treatment of the violin—how consciously we cannot say—harks back to a very special and distinct Russian tradition of the Silver Age in which the "agitated creativity" of a magic violin is invested with quasi-"Scythian" significance.[76] In this light, *Histoire du soldat* may be read as a parable of the Russian Revolution as viewed from afar and with dismay by a Stravinsky who had greeted the

74. Stravinsky acknowledged Pirandello's influence here (E&D:102/91), but anachronistically: the great Italian writer was only just beginning his career as a dramatist at the time of *Histoire*. The sudden direct intervention of a "Greek chorus" in a dramatic action was far from uncommon in early-twentieth-century theater, and has eighteenth-century antecedents. Meyerhold's adaptation of Carlo Gozzi's *Love for Three Oranges* contained the device, and Prokofiev incorporated it into his opera of the same name, which was written concurrently with *Histoire* (see R. Taruskin, "From Fairy Tale to Opera in Four Not-So-Simple Moves," *English National Opera Programme,* December 1989).

75. Ramuz's original plan had been to have the devil march the soldier off to the strains of the opening number (he may have been recalling the processional/recessional device in the *Baika*); see letter of 28 February 1918, *Letters,* 353; SelCorrIII:33.

76. For a discussion of this violin imagery and of instances of it in the work of the painter Casimir Malevich and the poet Nikolai Gumilyov, see Billington, *Icon and the Axe,* 477.

EXAMPLE 16.33

a. *Histoire du soldat,* Little Concerto, fig. 13

b. Tango, fig. 4

c. Triumphal March of the Devil, fig. 3

events of February 1917 as a liberation, only to see that brief interlude of freedom dashed by a coup. This would constitute a truly relevant "contemporary reference" for the action of *Histoire,* at least as interpreted through the music.[77]

Those who have inferred a connection between the play and the more general world conflagration—including, at various times, both Ramuz and Stravinsky—have never managed to specify just where that connection resides or in what it might consist. Meanwhile, Asafyev seems to have sensed the anti-Bolshevik subtext in *Histoire,* for he very sedulously avoids all discussion of source and plot in his treatment of the work in his otherwise meticulous *Book About Stravinsky*—ordinarily so vitally concerned with backgrounds—and never so much as mentions Afanasyev or Ramuz by name.

All such pointed contemporary references, along with that peculiar brand of

77. Cf. E&D:102/91.

ironizing that belongs to *Histoire* alone, can be read only in the music. Ramuz's text is a trite and schoolmasterly Everyman spiel, for the purposes of which a number of very dull contemporary allusions and genteel grotesqueries are introduced. The soldier was "dressed," in Stravinsky's recollection, "in the uniform of a Swiss Army private of 1918" and christened Joseph Dupraz, the Vaudois equivalent of John Doe. The action was reset in a vaguely Vaudois locale ("Entre Denges et Denezy . . ."). The various guises the devil assumes before finally revealing himself "en diable"—an old lepidopterist, a cattle dealer, a door-to-door pedlar woman (a procuress in early versions of the libretto), a musician *en frac*—were recognizably local and contemporary types.[78] The specifically Russian or "Oriental" content of Afanasyev's tale, such as it was, was systematically purged (though of course it seeped inexorably back into the music). Instead of a bazaar merchant, Ramuz's devil turns the soldier into a modern market-playing capitalist who wheels and deals by telephone. Instead of a troika, the devil and the soldier get around in a snazzy automobile. And on and on in this sophomoric vein.

Rarely, too, can there have been a more squirmily sententious *moralité*. The Reader steps out of his role to egg the soldier on toward his moral resurrection (the card game) not so much for the sake of *Verfremdung,* as modern commentators love to imagine,[79] as for the sake of issuing direct moral instructions to the audience. After the soldier has beaten the devil and won the princess, the Reader mounts a figurative pulpit to deliver a homily on the evils of greed—that is, of wanting (in a phrase that has become oddly timely) "to have it all" (*de tout avoir*).[80]

Ramuz contrives to endow the end of the story with moral uplift by giving it an Adam-and-Eve twist. Because Ramuz's soldier, egged on by the princess, seeks to regain his past happiness on top of his present happiness by taking his bride to visit his mother, he ignores the devil's (no, the Reader's) injunction and oversteps the boundaries of his Eden. The devil triumphs not out of devilhood, but assumes the role of some sort of avenging angel exacting (on whose behalf?) a just moral retribution upon the soldier's hubris.

What can one make of all this? What Stravinsky made of it is clear enough from the way his ludicrous "boche" chorale mocks Ramuz's solemn Reader. It is impossible to take seriously a fable that takes itself so seriously. No one who loves the

78. Writing in 1962, Stravinsky still encouraged producers to "localize the play" and update it for contemporary audiences (E&D:102/91). It has been done that way occasionally, most recently in an adaptation by Kurt Vonnegut with a Vietnam War subtext (see "Kurt Vonnegut Reinterprets 'L'Histoire du Soldat,'" *New York Times*, 8 May 1993). But the music, inextricably fixed in the "contemporary" world of 1918, invariably defeats any such attempt.

79. See, e.g., Jürgen Engelhardt, *Gestus und Verfremdung: Studien zum Musiktheater bei Strawinsky und Brecht/Weill* (Munich: Katzbichler Verlag, 1984).

80. The sermon has its admirers among the literary; see Roger Shattuck, "The Devil's Dance: Stravinsky's Corporal Imagination," in *The Innocent Eye* (New York: Washington Square Press, 1986), 330; also (much abridged) in Pasler (ed.), *Confronting Stravinsky,* 87.

Histoire pays the story much attention,[81] and neither shall we. It is the music alone that rewards close examination.

HISTOIRE DU SOLDAT: THE MUSIC

But first let us dispatch a durable set of fictions that have attached themselves like barnacles to that music. They are given a concise formulation in an oft-quoted passage from one of the conversations with Craft, though they surely did not originate there:

> My choice of instruments was influenced by a very important event in my life at that time, the discovery of American jazz. . . . My knowledge of jazz was derived exclusively from copies of sheet music, and as I never actually heard any of the music performed, I borrowed its rhythmic style not as played, but as written. . . . Jazz meant, in any case, a wholly new sound in my music, and *Histoire* marks my final break with the Russian orchestral school in which I had been fostered.[82]

The last sentence is a typically gratuitous non sequitur. What can it mean to say that a work for a chamber septet marks a break with an orchestral school? More important are the claims that *Histoire* derived its timbre and its rhythm from jazz—and falser testimony Stravinsky never gave. *Histoire* marked no break with those Russian traditions in which Stravinsky was interested at the time he composed it; moreover, it is precisely in instrumentation and in rhythmic style that the unbroken Russian connections are most manifest.

If the choice of instruments had been influenced by jazz, why, to begin with, did Stravinsky choose a bassoon? The composer tried to get around this point in *Expositions and Developments* by saying that the bassoon was his substitute for the saxophone. But the saxophone was no jazz legitimate at this time; its first jazz use

81. The proof of this is the fact that practically every commentator on *Histoire* gets it wrong. Even White, who gives a meticulous scene-by-scene synopsis (including some informative comparisons of the various versions of the libretto), incorrectly refers to the Reader's sermonizing during the Great Chorale as "narration" (*Stravinsky: The Composer and His Works*, 231). Stravinsky himself (E&D:107/95) places the first scene of Part II in a restaurant (instead of "a room in the palace") and forgets about the crucial card game. Perhaps the palm for plot-mangling ought to go to Wilfrid Mellers (*Man and His Music*, vol. 4 [New York: Schocken Books, 1969], 203), who, thinking the Chorale is the devil's hymn of triumph, goes on to observe that "of course, it is dramatically appropriate that a Devil's Chorale should invert the technique of Bach."

82. E&D:103–4/91–92. Earlier remarks ascribing a jazz style to *Histoire* can be found in Alexandre Tansman's monograph, based in part on interviews with the composer (*Igor Stravinsky: The Man and His Music*, trans. Therese Bleefield and Charles Bleefield [New York: G. P. Putnam's Sons, 1949], 196). Stravinsky's prewar writings and interviews, it should be stressed, do not make this claim (except in the case of the last of the "Three Dances," of course). The quote from the *Chroniques* adduced by Barbara B. Heyman in her article "Stravinsky and Ragtime," *Musical Quarterly* 68 (1982): 548, to the effect that "*soldat* is indicative of the passion I felt at the time for jazz" is an inadvertent portmanteau, combining the last word of a sentence about *Histoire* with the beginning of another about the *Ragtime pour onze instruments* (cf. *An Autobiography*, 77–78).

came in the Chicago bands of the 1920s.[83] Elsewhere in the same discussion of *Histoire* with Craft (in connection with the Royal March), Stravinsky recalled a *paso-doble* band he had heard in Seville during Holy Week of 1916,[84] consisting of a cornet, a trombone, and a bassoon. Right there we have three of the seven instruments in the *Histoire* ensemble, the cornet and trombone being of course "overdetermined" for a "soldier's tale" by their association with military music, where they are accompanied by drums. Ramuz was explicit on this point: "Stravinsky . . . made a large place in his little ensemble for the trombone and the cornet à pistons, dear to all our [military] fanfares; [and] an even bigger place for the big drum, the flat drum, the side drums, the cymbals, for they are no less beloved."[85] Drums and double bass in tandem have a jazz "rhythm" connotation today, but that was not the case in 1918. Indeed, the double bass was an even later addition to the standard jazz instrumentarium than the saxophone. Nor was any jazz or jazz-influenced ensemble ever complete (or even recognizably a jazz ensemble) without a piano or some reasonable facsimile thereof (let us say, a cimbalom).

As for the all-important violin, it has never been a true jazz instrument, despite the individual careers of a few conspicuous performers, beginning with Joe Venuti (1903–78). But although Venuti did have an influence on European jazz, his career had not even begun in 1918. When the "jazz violin" style took hold, moreover, it was sugar-sweet confection (think of Stephane Grappelli), at the opposite extreme from the gutsy, dirty idiom of the soldier's violin, surely one of Stravinsky's most amazing and original inspirations of the period.

It is, in fine, a vividly imagined "peasant" fiddle style, obviously conceived in the teeth of what was then (and now) known as the "Russian school" of violin playing, propagated in the teaching of the Hungarian-born Leopold Auer and the playing of his famous pupils, the Jaschas, Mischas, and Toschas. A thing of tremendous suavity and brilliance, this style had nothing to do with any truly indigenous instrumental tradition in Russia. The violin writing in *Histoire,* by contrast, has an abnormally low tessitura and is a tour de force of a different kind, full of brusque and scrappy double-stopping, *bariolage,* and zesty crisscrossing of the open strings.

This style of playing did have a model, though it was not to be found in jazz. It is an adaptation of the playing technique of the Gypsy fiddlers of Eastern Europe, and particularly of their so-called *verbunkos* style. The name is a Hungarian corruption of the German *Werbung,* "recruitment," and the *verbunkos* was originally a dance performed by soldiers who went from village to village recruiting for the army. "The musicians, mostly gypsies, tried to render the accompanying music (partly simple folk tunes) as impressively as possible, the improvised instrumental

83. See *New Grove Dictionary,* s.v. "Saxophone" (16:539).
84. For the date, see *An Autobiography,* 62.
85. "Strawinsky, de son côté, avait fait une large place dans son petit ensemble musical au trombone et au cornet à pistons, chers à toutes nos fanfares; une plus large encore à la grosse caisse, la caisse plate, aux tambours, aux cymbales, qu'elles n'affectionnent pas moins" (Ramuz, *Souvenir sur Strawinsky,* 63).

FIG. 16.4a. Early-nineteenth-century lithograph showing a *verbunkos* fiddler with accompanying cimbalom and cello.

accompaniment corresponding to the virtuosity of the recruiters' dance."[86] This obviously connects with the character who plays the fiddle in *Histoire* (primitive though his playing may have been by flashy Gypsy standards), and may even account for Stravinsky's misplaced allusion, in the *Chroniques,* to the genre of Russian folk song known as *rekrutskaya* (he spells it "*rekroutskia,*" à la française), which is not a soldier's song at all, but a formal lament sung by women—the mothers, wives, and sweethearts of those who have responded to the call to enlist (see Chapter 15).[87] Of actual *rekrutskiye* there is not a trace in *Histoire,* since there is no character in the tale who might have sung one. Most likely Stravinsky confused the Russian *rekrutskaya* with its superficial cognate *verbunkos.*

Now, the direct descendent of the *verbunkos* fiddler was the twentieth-century Gypsy cabaret musician, who by 1918 had assimilated "all genres of entertainment music: popular art songs, folk songs, . . . selections from operettas and popular operas, international dance music . . . (e.g., polka, waltz and foxtrot) and jazz" into his repertoire and adapted it to the style of playing that had been developed in the recruitment dances of a bygone time.[88] Because such performers usually worked in tandem with a cimbalom player, it is reasonable to deduce that both the idiom of

86. *New Grove Dictionary,* s.v. "Gypsy music" (7:868).
87. *An Autobiography,* 71.
88. *New Grove Dictionary* 7:868.

FIG. 16.4b. Aladár Rácz (at the cimbalom) with his wartime restaurant band (Geneva, 1916–18).

the *Soldat* violin and the idea of a contemporary dance suite (Tango-Waltz-Ragtime) had a common origin in memories of the same Geneva restaurant "with a small orchestra of string instruments including a cimbalom" where Stravinsky had made the acquaintance of the virtuoso cimbalist Aladár Rácz (1886–1958), who left such a mark on the later Swiss-period scores.[89] Whatever the source of the idea, though, the Gypsy character of the soldier's violin is certain: compare it with the arch-*gitane* violin solo in the last movement of Debussy's *Ibéria,* composed in 1910 (Ex. 16.34).

Nor is there anything inherently jazzy about Stravinsky's complex writing for the percussion. The drum part in any "jazz" score Stravinsky might have seen in 1918 would have been confined to churning out the basic pulse beat. In contrast to their function in the African music that was among the progenitors of jazz, the drums never took part in the "inner-rhythms and over-rhythms" that gave a jazz performance of that period its character.[90] Stravinsky's drums have taken back their "African" character (though not by way of Africa). For all these reasons,

89. It is perhaps telling, then, that Stravinsky used the cimbalom as piano-surrogate in the *Ragtime pour onze instruments.*
90. See Rudi Blesh, *Shining Trumpets: A History of Jazz,* 2d ed. (New York: Alfred A. Knopf, 1958), 36–37.

EXAMPLE 16.34

a. Debussy, *Ibéria,* III, fig. 61, violin solo

b. *Histoire du soldat,* Music to Scene I, 1 after 10 –2 after 11

then, it is worse than misleading to insist, as Stravinsky did in his 1962 memoir, that (except for the bassoon) "the instruments [in *Histoire*] are jazz legitimates." Only three of the seven (or, counting the percussion, perhaps three and a half) could be described that way at the time the music was written, and the focal keyboard instrument, without which no ensemble could be considered "jazz-legitimate," was lacking.

Yet even the three "legitimates" found their way into *Histoire* by a route that had nothing to do with jazz of any kind. Still excepting the bassoon, the members of the *Histoire* band were all indigenous to an altogether different kind of popular, improvising musical group, one with which Stravinsky was very familiar indeed. This was the East European village band, more particularly the Jewish variety whose members were known as klezmers (in Yiddish, *klezmorim;* Fig. 16.5). The standard klezmer band was a quartet consisting of a violin, a double bass, a clarinet, and drums, and was often expanded to include a trumpet and/or a trombone.[91] The air

91. Aron Marko Rothmüller, *The Music of the Jews,* trans. H. S. Stevens (South Brunswick, N. J.: Thomas Yoseloff, 1967), 172; Macy Nulman, *Concise Encyclopedia of Jewish Music* (New York: McGraw-Hill, 1975), 140.

F I G . 1 6 . 5 .   A troupe of Byelorussian *klezmorim* (Jewish village musicians) with a *badchan* (wedding master-of-ceremonies; cf. Russian *druzhko*), late nineteenth century. Practically the whole *Histoire du soldat* ensemble is represented: percussion, trombone, clarinet, trumpet, fiddle; most klezmer bands also had a double bass.

at Ustilug (known to its predominating Jewish population as Ustileh) must have rung frequently with klezmer music during the summers Stravinsky spent there up to 1913. What better ensemble could he have imagined to accompany his *théâtre ambulant* than one modeled on the vagabond players of the shtetl?

Thus the ensemble of *Histoire du soldat* is no jazz band, but a stylized village band compounded out of overlapping cadres of Ustilug *klezmorim,* Vaudois *fanfaristes,* and *pasodoble* players from Seville, all led by a Gypsy fiddler. The fact that they play a ragtime no more types them than the fact that they play a chorale. With the sole (partial) exception of that one little dance, their music owes nothing whatever to "jazz," whether as performed or as notated.

The very first requirement of "jazz," vintage 1918, was a steady common-time tactus pulsation against which melodic syncopations could rebound. What makes these or any syncopations intelligible and delightful (whether or not the steady pulsation is explicitly present on the musical surface at a given moment) is absolute certainty as to what is on the beat and what is off. What makes Stravinsky's rhythm fascinating and delightful, by contrast, is its metrical ambiguity—that is, the doubts the composer continually and deliberately sows ("fiendishly, sadistically," as

Van den Toorn would have it)[92] precisely about what jazz takes for granted. Further: the "jazz" or ragtime tactus is a spacious, commodious thing. It allows for, indeed depends upon, subdivision, normally notated as four sixteenths to the quarter. The characteristic Stravinskian beat, by contrast, is nervous and mutable, distinction between ground rhythm and subdivision being constantly blurred by oscillation or alternation between patterns that are coordinated, in works dating as far back as the "Abduction" and the "Rival Tribes" in *The Rite,* at the "subtactile" level.

The characteristic ragtime syncopation is not so much the stressing of a weak beat or the suppression of a strong one (as most musical dictionaries will define the term), but rather the placement of accents—or better, the attacks of the longer melody notes—on the weak subdivisions of the beat, especially the second or fourth sixteenth, and the tying of these notes over the next strong beat. These syncopations—"fooling around with the beat," in professional slang—are usually confined to patterns of no more than one or two measures' duration, and are often reiterated through melodic sequences that only enhance the absolute regularity of the underlying four-square meter. Scott Joplin's didactic études (*The School of Ragtime—Six Exercises for Piano,* 1908) ideally illustrate all these points, at the same time providing a little catalogue of ragtime clichés (Ex. 16.35).

As Joplin emphasizes over and over again, ragtime is played exactly as written, so the distinction Stravinsky draws in the extract cited above between jazz-as-played and jazz-as-written is doubtful. It cannot account for the vast difference between his rhythmic style, with its Turanian roots, and that illustrated by Joplin. Indeed, when it was truly his aim to "stylize" ragtime, Stravinsky did borrow Joplinesque clichés just like the ones in Example 16.35. The locus classicus for this sort of thing in his work comes not from *Histoire* but from the very next piece he wrote, the *Ragtime pour onze instruments,* completed on the morning of the German surrender (the composing score is dated "Jour de la délivrance. Messieurs les Allemands ont capitulé. Dimanche 10 Novembre 1918 Morges"). Relative to Joplin's notation, Stravinsky's is augmented by a factor of two. It is notated throughout in 4/4 meter without the slightest deviation, thus satisfying the conditio sine qua non for a true ragtime. (At the same time, the augmented note values, which cause each of Stravinsky's measures to equal half of one of Joplin's, facilitates a great deal of "hypermetric" irregularity that circumvents the stereotyped rigidity of ragtime phrase structure.) Allowing for the differing size of the note values, then, it will be apparent from a few citations that in this piece a Joplinesque rhythmic style is mimicked quite faithfully (Ex. 16.36).

But now compare the little Ragtime from *Histoire.* It begins faithfully enough to the model (notated at Joplin's metrical level, too) with nine measures in regular

92. Cf. Van den Toorn, *Music of Igor Stravinsky,* 225.

EXAMPLE 16.35   Scott Joplin, *The School of Ragtime,* incipits to two of six études (from Rudi Blesh, *They All Played Ragtime,* 4th ed. [New York: Oak Publications, 1971], 142–45)

EXAMPLE 16.36   *Ragtime pour onze instruments,* excerpts from pp. 6–7 of the piano reduction, marked à la Joplin

a.

EXAMPLE 16.36 *(continued)*

b.

c.

d.

duple meter and rhythms that (especially if the rests are filled in with ties) duplicate the patterns shown in Example 16.35. The dotted rhythms in the seventh and eighth bars (found in the *Ragtime pour onze instruments* as well) probably represent an adaptation by ear of the "notes inégales" style of executing the smallest subdivisions of the beat, so characteristic of jazz performance. And if this is so, even Stravinsky's claim that he had not heard jazz or ragtime by 1918, but only seen it, must be discounted.[93]

By the tenth measure of the *Histoire* Ragtime, the "jazz" idiom has been decisively challenged by a "subtactile" intruder in the form of a 3/8 bar that effectively derails the all-important downbeat pattern. From there to the end it is war between the forces of "jazz" regularity and those of Stravinskian disruption. The "jazz" pattern is recognizably reasserted twice more (figs. [31] and [36]; [33] sounds more like a sudden reprise of the Tango). In between, the meter degenerates into busy subtactile patterns, the measures often counted in odd groupings of sixteenth notes. It should be noted, though, that these odd measures are always paired (i.e., 3/16 + 7/16, 5/16 + 7/16, etc.); and since the sum of two odd numbers is an even number, the pairs are easily heard as conventionally syncopated rhythms against an implicit "jazz" pulse in eighth notes (Ex. 16.37).

Yet even this beat is subtactile vis-à-vis the 2/4 meter of the Ragtime as such, and hence Example 16.37 cannot be described as a jazz or ragtime rhythm. While Stravinsky's exposure to the irregular groupings of interstitial subdivisions in ragtime may account for the heightened incidence of subtactile metrical coordinations in *Histoire* as compared with its immediate predecessors (*Baika* and *Svadebka*), the distinction between the stimulus and the response remains essential. The foreign element of "jazz" may have irritated the Stravinskian rhythmic organism into producing a musical pearl in the *Histoire* Ragtime, yet it is precisely the interplay between jazz and nonjazz that sustains lively musical interest here—something the flabby *Ragtime pour onze* notably lacks. As wittily observed in one of the last

93. The question of just when and how Stravinsky became acquainted with "jazz" is vexed by his typically sketchy and contradictory recollections. In the *Chroniques* he wrote that his "passion for jazz . . . burst into life so suddenly when the war ended," and that "at my request, a whole pile of this music was sent to me" (*An Autobiography,* 78). He does not say by whom; but in any case, both *Histoire* and the *Ragtime pour onze instruments* were finished by war's end, so his passion must have burst a bit earlier than he reported on this occasion. In *Dialogues and Diary* (p. 87 [cf. *Dialogues,* 54]) he amplified: "In 1918 Ernest Ansermet, returning from an American tour, brought me a bundle of ragtime music in the form of piano reductions and instrumental parts, which I copied out in score. With these pieces before me, I composed the Ragtime in *Histoire du soldat,* and, after completing *Histoire,* the Ragtime for eleven instruments." It is usually assumed that the tour from which Ansermet returned was a Ballets Russes tour, but the Diaghilev company's American tours were made in the spring of 1916 and the winter of 1916–17. Ansermet participated only in the first of these, so if it was indeed he who furnished Stravinsky with his ragtime scores, it would have to have been nearly two years earlier than the composer recalled. Whatever the facts may eventually turn out to be, Heyman ("Stravinsky and Ragtime") has argued persuasively that Stravinsky must have heard "jazz" (whether or not he had seen it) considerably before the period of *Histoire.* Her best item of evidence, cited on p. 546, is an extract from an interview with C. Stanley Wise, published in the New York Tribune of 16 January 1916, in which Stravinsky is quoted as saying, "I know little about American music except that of the music halls . . . but I consider that unrivalled. It is veritable art and I can never get enough of it to satisfy me."

EXAMPLE 16.37 *Histoire du soldat*, Ragtime, bassoon at 1 after 27 , as written and in terms of syncopation

as written: as heard?

Stravinsky interviews, "whereas the 'Ragtime' in the *Histoire* is as smoothly integrated as a minuet in Mozart, the one for cleven instruments is as dated as a coonskin coat."[94]

Nowhere else in *Histoire* is the "jazz" idiom so much as broached. Much of the rhythmic writing might even be called "anti-jazz," since irregular groupings in the melody take precedence in the barring and accentuation over the regularly duplemetered bassi ostinati. In the Music to Scene I, the four-eighths double bass pattern already represents a subdivision of the notated beat, and it is further subdivided into pairs of sixteenths by the violin. The regular subdivision of the eighth note is actually the one rhythmic element that remains stable in this piece, precisely the reverse of the situation that normally obtains in "jazz." Meanwhile, the four-note ostinato is placed in the most various positions with respect to the melodic ictus.

In the Soldier's March, the basso ostinato consists of a capacious left-right-left-right oompah figure that in another context might well have governed a "jazz" or ragtime surface rhythm. It is repeatedly contradicted by a pesky subtactile figure in the melody—three eighth notes on the pitches B-C#-D—which Stravinsky consistently bars as a unit so that the arrival on the following E is always a notated downbeat, despite the misalignments that result with respect to the continuing oompah tread running beneath. Are these misalignments to be heard as syncopations? Specifically with respect to the passage given in Example 16.38, in which the 3/8 group makes two appearances, the first creating a misalignment and the second correcting it, the question arises as to whether the bar lines or the ostinato truly control the rhythm. If the latter, then the pattern could be construed in terms of "jazz." If the former, we are dealing with sheer "anti-jazz."

Pieter van den Toorn, in a trenchant discussion of this very passage,[95] concludes that owing to the conditioning the ear has received from earlier occurrences of the 3/8 figure, plus the "additional havoc" wrought by the "highly irregular stresses in the percussion," both "the steady 2/4 periodicity of the ostinato itself" and the " 'true' metric identity for the B-C#-D-(E)" fragment (i.e., as producing a synco-

94. R&C:43–44/T&C:106.
95. Van den Toorn, *Stravinsky and "The Rite,"* 80–83.

EXAMPLE 16.38 *Histoire du soldat,* Soldier's march, fig. ⑧ (tune, with double-bass vamp shown as rhythm)

pation against the ostinato) are "temporarily lost," with the result that "offbeats are for a moment no longer distinguishable from onbeats." As he further notes, however, Stravinsky's stress and slur markings on the 3/8 measure serve to preserve its character as an upbeat figure at all times. These markings are introduced only on the third occurrence of the figure (m. 49), where for the first time the figure appears displaced with respect to the tactus. The markings (and the attendant articulation in performance) serve to hypostatize the metric significance of the figure and lend it an independence from the ostinato which the ear by now has been conditioned to accept. It would therefore seem more accurate to say not that offbeats have become indistinguishable from onbeats, but (something far more teasing to the ear) that two separate layers of onbeat-ness have been contrived to coexist, a situation first encountered in *The Rite.* Such a situation could not persist over the long haul, perhaps; in any case, Stravinsky terminates it after four measures, before the ear has had a chance to decide which pattern it will choose to follow. When the second 3/8 measure cancels the effect of the first, we may note once again Stravinsky's strategy of pairing subtactile units so as to reinstate regularity where and as he chooses. The resolution (van den Toorn calls it landing "on target") is as important to the game as the disruption: it is in fact what makes it a game, and therefore delightful, not a mere indulgence in meaningless metrical "static."[96]

The essential foreignness of the whole metric-rhythmic scheme described here to the world of "jazz" or ragtime should be obvious. Nor will it occasion surprise at this point to discover its source in the mother lode of Slavic folklore. Let a single example suffice: a recently collected Ukrainian game song called "*Vorotarichku, vorotarichku*" uncannily adumbrates the whole game plan of the Soldier's March, as

96. See ibid., chap. 3 ("Stravinsky Rebarred"), for some acute generalizations about Stravinskian metrics that have greatly stimulated and clarified the foregoing discussion. The chapter has also appeared in somewhat condensed form as "Stravinsky Rebarred," *Music Analysis* 7, no. 2 (July 1988): 165–96.

EXAMPLE 16.39 *"Vorotarichku, vorotarichku,"* in *Igri ta pisni* (Kiev, 1963), p. 512 (cited by Grigory Golovinsky in Alfeyevskaya and Vershinina [eds.], *I. F. Stravinskiy: Stat'i i vospominaniya* [Moscow: Sovetskiy Kompozitor, 1985], p. 92)

may be readily observed by hypothetically accompanying the tune with Stravinsky's oompah (Ex. 16.39).

Of course, it took Stravinsky to add the ostinato; but it is clear nonetheless that the musical prosody of *Histoire*—or, to put it the way Stravinsky did in his memoir, its "rhythmic style"—has its antecedents in the same Turanian terrain as that of the Russian songs of the same period. The "American" element in *Histoire* is as much a superficial ornament or flavoring as the Spanish (Royal March), Argentine (Tango), or German (Chorale). The score's reputed cosmopolitanism, corresponding to the universalized and denatured version of the Russian folk tale on which the libretto was based, is not much more than skin deep, and its status as a watershed in the composer's development (for good or ill) has been exaggerated. The gaudy surface hues mask a musical fabric whose neutral color remains a pure, dyed-in-the-wool Turanian. Liudmila Pitoëff, who danced the princess in that one-and-only Lausanne performance of 1918, was quite right to suggest that Stravinsky's music, "with its tangle of Russian melodies, truly represents the Russian folk tale."[97] All one would like to add to that is that the Russianness of the *Soldat* music inheres not just in the melodies but in the tangle, and is expressed not just on the thematic surface, but at the most fundamental levels of rhythmic, modal, and harmonic design.

97. "Souvenirs Intimes," *Quartier latin* (1945); quoted in P&D:167.

Some of the Russian melodies may be authentic. Robert Craft, citing documents in his own possession, has identified one of the tunes the soldier plays on his fiddle in the Music to Scene I as a Russian "street song" that begins with the words "I am pretty but poorly dressed."[98] The thematic fragments in the outer sections of the same piece strongly imply derivation from an authentic prototype, since they prominently exhibit a "mutable" (*peremennïy*) cadential figure so endemic to Russian "lyrical" folk songs that Glinka himself once christened it "the soul of Russian music" (Ex. 16.40).

The "Princess" motive—which Stravinsky once claimed came to him in a dream of a Gypsy fiddler by a roadside[99]—is confined to the familiar modal tetrachord of Russian folklore (T-S-T), endemic to both diatonic and octatonic scales. Stravinsky naturally exploits both associations. On its first appearance in the Petit concert (Ex. 16.33a above), the harmony is strictly diatonic and typically ambiguous as to center. In the Tango, however (Ex. 16.33b), the ever-resourceful composer came up with a harmonization based on an unprecedented partition of the octatonic collection—and who would have thought there were any left! Instead of harmonizing the tune with its tetrachordal complement (as he might have done in *The Rite* or, more recently, in the *Baika*), Stravinsky accompanies it with a single arpeggiated triad in such a way that the whole-step/half-step ordering of the collection (the "melody scale" as defined in Chapter 4) and the half-step/whole-step ordering (the "harmony scale") are set in quasi-"bitonal" conflict (Ex. 16.41).

The C♯/D♭ ambiguity is made punningly graphic by having the passage start with these pitches at the double octave, so that they sound like a single doubled pitch. But the ear is almost immediately forced to reinterpret the interval as a dissonance (a diminished sixteenth?!) in light of the passage's two-tiered unfolding. Rarely has octave identity in music been so effectively abjured. Similarly neutralized is the tendency function of the A in the violin melody. When it comes it coincides with the stable "root" of the accompanying harmony, and the ear, prevented from interpreting it as a conventionally unstable leading tone, is deliciously confused.

The sinuous violin melody in the outer sections of the Tango is in a weird hybrid tonality compounded of an octatonic *complexe sonore* organized around A, C, and F♯, plus the key of C-minor, plus the open strings of the violin. Both the ([1, 2] "harmony") and the ([2, 1] "melody") orderings around the nodes are exploited. The first nine measures, for example, are referable to octatonic Collection II with the exception of the imported dominant, G (Ex. 16.42a). Thereafter, de-

98. In P&D:623n.280 the tune is identified with the violin music at one measure after fig. [10], but in a later account ("*Histoire du soldat*," 326; SelCorrIII:464) Craft associates it with the music at fig. [11], which later figures so prominently in the "Petit concert."
99. Conv:13/17.

EXAMPLE 16.40   *Histoire du soldat,* Music to Scene I, figs. $\boxed{1}$ and $\boxed{2}$ compared

EXAMPLE 16.41   Harmonic relationship of melody and accompaniment in Tango, fig. $\boxed{4}$

EXAMPLE 16.42

a. *Histoire du soldat,* Tango, mm. 1–9

b. Tango, measures around fig. $\boxed{3}$

c. Tango, close of first section

d. Interaction of Collection II with the scale of C ("melodic") minor

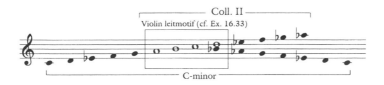

EXAMPLE 16.43

a. *Histoire du soldat,* draft of Chorale in Archive (Rothschild no. 45)
   compressed from open score to two staves

b. *Histoire du soldat,* Great Chorale, mm. 1–9

EXAMPLE 16.43 (*continued*)

c. Hexachordal analysis of harmonization

d. Opening of "*Tilim-bom*" for comparison

partures from the home collection are frequent—they consist mainly of specious dominant colorings like the first, plus some reminiscences from the Petit concert—but enough telltale passages remain to show that despite the high degree of contamination, Collection II remains the principal mode of reference (cf. Ex. 16.42b and 16.42c, noting especially the latter's "terminating convenience").

Thus, even one of the ostensibly exotic items in *Histoire* displays a basically Turanian *facture*. The same can even be said of the Chorale, for all that it is obviously modeled on Luther's "A Mighty Fortress," in all likelihood the only chorale a Russian Orthodox musician would have known.[100] Surely its most characteristic harmonic touch is the bass F-natural contradicting the F-sharp of the soprano in the second bar—an echo of the harmonization by stacked Dorian hexachords that is so common in the Russian songs of the period: compare "*Tilim-bom*," which exhibits the same double-inflected pair (see Ex. 15.1). The dichotomy persists, though not quite so conspicuously, in subsequent Chorale phrases: bass C against C-sharp in the second phrase, bass E-flat against E in the third. A comparison of the published version of the first three phrases of the Great Chorale with an early sketch in the Archive will show how deliberately the composer worked to clarify this aspect of the harmonization. In the draft, C-sharp is allowed to stand in the bass in the second phrase, and the final cadence is approached via a bass E-natural. Noteworthy, too, are the pains Stravinsky took to purge all the cadences of leading tones. Compared with the final deftly Turanianized harmonization, the original draft seems by turns academic (the second phrase) and chaotic (the third) (Ex. 16.43).

It must have been features like these that caused Gerald Abraham, in a typically shrewd evaluation, to call attention to "symptoms of *essential* Russianness" in

---

100. The only discussion of *Histoire* known to me that acknowledges Stravinsky's parody of Luther's famous hymn is the brief one in Shead, *Music in the 1920s*, 42–43.

Histoire du soldat, even where "the superficial Russianness almost or quite disappears."[101] Less discerning critics have variously damned *Histoire* as an indiscriminate "musical cocktail" that led its composer down the path of sterility toward the "form of expression which was soon to dominate all his music: the stylistic exercise";[102] or else they have praised it as the work in which Stravinsky finally "purified [his] artistic ideals" and purged his work of the "primitive popularism" of his earlier, more insularly Russian-sounding scores.[103] But if purification means Europeanization, and if stylistic exercise is code for "neoclassicism," then the seminal work was not *Histoire* but *Mavra,* an opus whose abundant "superficial Russianness" has blinded all and sundry to its essential significance.[104] Between *Histoire* and *Mavra,* meanwhile, Stravinsky would complete the two scores—one vocal and one instrumental—that brought his Turanian phase to its peak.

101. Gerald Abraham, *100 Years of Music,* 4th ed. (London: Duckworth, 1974), 254.

102. André Hodeir, *Since Debussy: A View of Contemporary Music,* trans. Noel Burch (New York: Grove Press, 1961), 30.

103. Adolfo Salazar, *Music in Our Time,* trans. Isobel Pope (New York: W. W. Norton, 1946), 291.

104. A refreshing exception is Stephen Walsh, in his monograph *The Music of Stravinsky,* 114ff.

Every form of art has its starting point in reality, and its finishing point in music.
—*Andrey Belïy*[1]

THE PROJECT

In the issue of 18 April 1915, the news-from-abroad section of *Muzïka,* Vladimir Derzhanovsky's Moscow modern music magazine, carried the following item, headed "New Works by Igor Stravinsky":

> The latest major work of Igor Stravinsky—who is now living in Clarens and who habitually entrusts the premières of his stage pieces to Diaghilev's foreign enterprises—is *Svadebka.*
>
> *Svadebka* is not an opera and not a ballet. In its conception and structure it approximates a new and specifically Russian type of spectacle that has been sketched as yet only in the imaginations of a few leading musical figures, the type Lyadov had meant to pursue in creating his "rusalia" *Leyla and Alaley* with A. M. Remizov (work was cut short by the composer's death), or Alexander Kastalsky, who is at present sketching some musical pictures to be called "Folk Festivities in Russia" [*"Narodnïye prazdnestva na Rusi"*]. *Svadebka* is more or less of the same character. It has no plot in the crudely utilitarian sense of the word. There is no "action," but nonetheless it is an *act,* the contents of which unfold before the hearer and viewer in the plain and shapely form of folk festivities. The headings of *Svadebka*'s four projected scenes will give an idea of its contents: (1) At the young man's [*U molodogo*], (2) At the young woman's [*U molodoy*], (3) The Wedding Table [*Krasnïy stol*], (4) Festivity [*Prazdnestvo*]. To this plan of action one may add that the scenes culminate in the departure of the young couple for the bedchamber, while the two matchmakers sit by the doors keeping watch.......
>
> Extraordinarily interesting is the orchestral complement in this composition, the result of the composer's new-found views on instrumentation, already discernible in embryonic form in Stravinsky's suite "From Japanese Lyrics," performed in

---

1. Andrey Belïy, "Formï iskusstva," in *Simvolizm* (Moscow, 1910; rpt. [as Slavische Propyläen, no. 62] Munich: Wilhelm Fink Verlag, 1969), 153.

Moscow last year by Mme Koposova at an "Evening of Contemporary Music." These three vocal pieces were performed by a small orchestra, the essence of which consisted in its having many voices but few performers. In other words: the orchestra had both winds and strings, but each instrument had its own independent role and none was doubled, as a consequence of which the whole body of strings was reduced to a solo quartet. The same principle forms the basis of the *Svadebka* orchestra. This orchestra will consist exclusively of *individualized* voices—the first violin part, for example, will be played by a single violinist, and so on down to the double bass. In sum: an orchestra of soloists. This, naturally, will lead to an attenuation of the scoring, its dematerialization. It goes without saying that from the purely practical point of view this amounts to a refinement in the purely artistic and material (acoustical) sense. But new colors will be introduced into this orchestra by including in its instrumental roster (which will number as many as forty) an extremely substantial part for a chorus, which will have a purely instrumental, coloristic role, and which will take part from the beginning of the score to the end (at times singing little *pribautki,* at times only separate words, and in a few instances wordlessly).

To the dispatch printed in *Muzika,* three issues back, one must make a correction: the première of *Svadebka* will take place not in Monte Carlo but in Paris, where in May of next year Diaghilev's *saisons russes* will be resumed.

Other new compositions of Stravinsky: vocal *pribautki* (born in the first instance, perhaps, as splinters off the *Svadebka* score), and a "March, Polka, and Valse" of humorous character for small orchestra.[2]

Nothing could be more fascinating or more instructive than to compare this early report—facts liberally intermixed with rumor, extrapolation, and hot air—with the "choreographic scenes" we know, premièred not in 1916, as the report so confidently predicted, but in 1923, under the title *Les noces.* The minor differences are legion, and will be mentioned as the occasion arises. The major difference is so important that it could epitomize the whole creative evolution through which Stravinsky's art passed in his "Swiss" years under the influence of Russian folklore. What was conceived in 1914 as a work for an ensemble of highly differentiated and individualized soloists was presented in 1923 in a guise that was, in the composer's devastatingly apt description, "perfectly homogeneous, perfectly impersonal, and perfectly mechanical."[3] And that is why the phrase "progressive abstraction" not only sums up the metamorphosis that this greatest of Stravinsky's wartime

2. "D. de R." (V. V. Derzhanovsky), "Za rubezhom: novïye sochineniya Igorya Stravinskogo," *Muzika,* no. 219 (18 April 1915): 262–63. In no. 216 (p. 213), Derzhanovsky had excerpted a letter from Prokofiev (over the signature "S") in which it was reported that "beginning March 1916 [Diaghilev] has a contract with Monte Carlo, where the following novelties will be presented: (1) Stravinsky's *Svadebka;* (2) his *Fireworks* [with Giacomo Balla's curtain]; (3) a staging of Neapolitan folk festivities (the last two items in collaboration with Marinetti and the Futurists); (4) a suite of pieces by Scarlatti [this would become *Les femmes de bonne humeur,* orch. Tommasini]; (5) perhaps my ballet [i.e., *Chout*]." For the full text of the letter, dated Rome, 24 February/9 March 1915, see Bïkov (ed.), *Iz arkhivov russkikh muzikantov,* 98–99.

3. E&D:134/118.

compositions underwent, but serves in this book to designate an entire phase of his career.

The source of Derzhanovsky's basic information about *Svadebka*, its subject matter, and its projected instrumentation was Prokofiev, just back from Western Europe. He had been tagging along with the Ballets Russes in hopes of wangling a second commission from Diaghilev after the rejection of his *Ala and Lolli* (to Gorodetsky's libretto; it became the *Scythian Suite*). Prokofiev heard the portions of *Svadebka* by then completed (probably the first tableau and a bit of the second) together with Diaghilev in Rome in February 1915, and some more of it (the rest of the second tableau?) in Milan on 1 April.[4] He was both astonished and amused at the intuition with which Derzhanovsky had dilated upon the information he had been given. "You've pissed up a storm about *Svadebka*," Prokofiev wrote him two days after the article appeared. "I oohed and aahed as I read it."[5] To Stravinsky himself, who had written to inquire about "a rather well informed notice about my *Svadebka*" that had appeared, he had heard, in some Russian journal ("Did it come from you?"),[6] Prokofiev wrote, "I gave some information to Derzhanovsky, on the basis of which he whipped up such an article in *Muzïka* that you'd think he had just come from the first performance."[7] This was in fact the first public notice of the existence of the work, the composition of which had only just begun.

It was still far from complete at the beginning of the next year, which did not, however, prevent Diaghilev from coolly informing a New York reporter that "Stravinsky has two new scores. One of them, which is already finished, is entitled 'Les Noces Villagoises' [*sic*]. The other, which is unfinished, is to be mystical. It is a great enterprise, on which Stravinsky and Massin [*sic*] are working together. Goncharova, a painter, granddaughter of Pushkin [!], is assisting them."[8] The "mystical" ballet—*Liturgiya*—would never get very far at all, and *Svadebka* was still eighteen months away from its completion in particell. The scoring would go through some astounding metamorphoses before the final choice was made and executed, just in time for the 1923 première. No project—not even *The Rake's Progress*—would ever occupy Stravinsky even half as long.

Its conception went back to the time of *The Rite*. The first reference to it in a surviving document is in a letter from Sanin, dated 17 February/2 March 1913 (al-

4. See Robert Craft, "Stravinsky's *Svadebka*: An Introduction," in *Prejudices in Disguise*, 251.

5. To Derzhanovsky, 30 April 1915 (in Bïkov [ed.], *Iz arkhivov russkikh muzïkantov*, 99). The vulgar expression is deleted from this edition. It is conjecturally restored: the Russian infinitive "to piss" (*pisat'*) differs only in stress from the infinitive "to write" (*pisát'*), and jocular substitutions are common.

6. Letter of 12 May 1915; in IStrSM:488.

7. Letter of 3 June 1915; in IStrSM:517.

8. "Diaghileff Talks of Soul of Ballet," *New York Post*, 24 January 1916. In a letter to Percy Scholes (19 August 1915; now in the Scholes Collection, National Library of Canada), Stravinsky's Clarens neighbor C. Stanley Wise stated that as of 16 August 1915 *Svadebka* was "about ⅓ . . . finished." This probably means Stravinsky was up to the beginning of the fourth tableau (and that he was actually, therefore, closer to half finished than two-thirds).

ready cited in Chapter 14, it was the letter in which the régisseur first proposed that Stravinsky compose something for the Free Theater in Moscow). Sanin calls the work by the name *Svad'ba,* the standard form of the Russian word for wedding, not the rustic diminutive with which it was later definitively christened.[9] Sanin recalls that Stravinsky had told him about it in person, which would seem to mean that they had discussed it during the previous *saison russe,* that is, in June 1912. In any case, he writes, "it is obvious that you have had your heart set on this piece for a long time."[10] By 6 August 1913 Mitusov was writing from St. Petersburg to Stravinsky in Ustilug to tell him that he had looked everywhere for "the book of songs" without success.[11] This must be a reference to Kireyevsky's anthology of wedding song texts. From these letters it is clear that by the summer of 1913 Stravinsky was champing at the bit to compose *Svadebka,* and that were it not for Sanin and the *Nightingale* commission he would have begun working on it then and there.[12]

The idea of the piece grew naturally out of *The Rite,* and it is strange that Derzhanovsky should not have picked up on this fact (but then, he had never seen *The Rite* on stage). *Svadebka,* too, would be, in Levinson's superb phrase, an "icy comedy"—an elegantly detached, nonnarrative presentation of a ritual action. The difference was that it would be drawn from an exceedingly well documented living tradition (or at the very least from customs that survived in living memory) rather

---

9. According to an anecdote Nicolas Nabokov claimed to have heard from Stravinsky, it was Diaghilev, the work's eventual dedicatee, who came up with the final form of the title. "In describing to Stravinsky a particularly drunken peasant marriage [i.e., wedding] Diaghilev called it a *'shal'naya svadebka'* (a crazy bout of a marriage [lit., a madcap peasant wedding]). Stravinsky beamed: 'Svadebka! Svadebka! I have it,' he exclaimed. 'This is what I need! This is the title I am looking for! It is marvelously precise!'" (Nabokov, "The Peasant Marriage," 276). The use of the diminutive here does not have to do with size but rather indicates, first, that the wedding is a rural one, much as a man (*muzh*) becomes a peasant (*muzhik*) by the use of the diminutive; a *svadebka,* then, is a *svad'ba* enacted by *muzhiki* (cf. Ramuz's French title, *Les noces villageoises,* adopted in collaboration with Stravinsky). It also indicates enjoyment, as in one of the song texts Stravinsky used in the fourth tableau (Kireyevsky no. 803; see Table 4 at fig. [117], p. 1436 below); in peasant jargon a *svadebka* is "a fine wedding." The fact that the word actually appears in the text of the piece may cast some doubt on Nabokov's account of its christening. (The word also appears in a song text that is part of Vladimir Belsky's libretto for Rimsky-Korsakov's opera *The Legend of the Invisible City of Kitezh* [Act II, fig. (104)]; as we know, this was the Rimsky-Korsakov opera with which Stravinsky was most closely acquainted.) Wherever it may have come from, the title *Svadebka* was adopted sometime between 25 June 1914 (N.S.), the date of a letter from Prokofiev to Myaskovsky in which he reported that "the novelties of the coming Diaghilev season will be two ballets: Stravinsky's *Svad'ba* and my ballet" (Kozlova and Yatsenko [eds.], *Prokof'yev i Myaskovskiy: perepiska,* 116); and 8 March 1915 (N.S.), when Diaghilev wrote to Stravinsky, "Hurry up and finish *Svadebka.* I am in love with it" (Zilbershtein and Samkov [eds.], *Dyagilev* 2:125). It was, of course, during that interim that Stravinsky procured the Kireyevsky song anthology. A sheet of text sketches probably made not too long afterward (now in the sheaf labeled R87 in the Rothschild catalogue) contains the final speech of the bridegroom, copied directly out of the book, with a note: *"samiy konets 'Svadebki'"* ("the very end of *Svadebka*").

10. Translated from the original in the Stravinsky Archive. Another translation may be found in SelCorrII:197–98. In E&D:130/114 Stravinsky states that he "became aware of an idea for a choral work on the subject of a Russian peasant wedding early in 1912."

11. SelCorrII:40.

12. This should dispose of the hardy conjecture that Stravinsky had the idea for *Les noces* while watching a Jewish wedding together with Cocteau at Leysin in 1914 (cf. P&D:150).

than from an imagined archaic lore. It would seek validation in ethnological fact, but (like *The Rite*) it would refuse to be bound by any limits such validation might imply. Its reality, like that of *The Rite,* would be one created, not received (hence—*pace* Derzhanovsky—the fatal difference between a Stravinsky and a Kastalsky). But it would be a *Rite* in black in white: the literal black and white of four keyboards. And despite its considerable clangor, not to mention the rowdy doings in its fourth tableau, it would not be a thing of primitive abandon, but more nearly the opposite.

Svadebka is the depiction of a sacrament, enacted with the "profound gravity and cool, inevitable intention" that befit any artifact of "remorseless . . . inelastic tradition," whether folkloristic or religious.[13] It is a work of dignity and reserve, and finally of exaltation: "a Christian mystery in which two persons become one in a solemn festal rite," according to a leading American Slavist, who points out that Stravinsky deliberately emphasized "the popular Christian elements in the peasant ritual . . . rather more than they would have been in a typical wedding" and adds that "those critics who . . . have emphasized the pagan and orgiastic elements in *Les Noces* are in error."[14] Above all, in keeping with his "rejoicing discovery," Stravinsky allowed himself to be guided by the words of his text so deeply into uncharted Turanian domains of style and design that even admirers of *The Rite* could feel themselves left behind.

Myaskovsky was among them. After going through *Svadebka,* he wrote disconsolately to Prokofiev: "Someday when you have the time, explain Stravinsky to me. I hardly understand a thing; although here and there some feeling comes through, it's all very dim. . . . There's something prickly and ascetic about it."[15] He understood a lot better than he knew: a better pair of adjectives for *Svadebka* was never chosen.

13. Cf. Mark, "Fundamental Qualities of Folk Music," 289.

14. William E. Harkins, "The Text of Stravinsky's *Les Noces*" (typescript originally prepared as a contribution to an unrealized facsimile edition of sketches and preliminary versions of *Svadebka* by the Harvard University Press), courtesy of the author. The critics to whom Harkins refers include, in the first instance, Asafyev. The chapter on *Svadebka,* one of the weakest in *A Book About Stravinsky,* is revealing of the limitations Soviet materialism set on even the most progressive musical outlooks of the 1920s. Asafyev calls the work an embodiment of the ancient cult of fertility and reproduction, a "feast in honor of Eros," an expression of the "epic forcefulness and Euripidian rigor of life, as expressed by the confrontation of man and his instinct for procreation," and a "Dionysian" celebration of "the invocation and excitation of the male procreative force" (chap. 6, passim). In other ways, however, Asafyev's is a reasoned and substantial discussion. For sheer vulgarity nothing can match Nicolas Nabokov's interpretation of the piece, in which Asafyev's highfalutin dichotomy of "threnodial" and "buffoon" elements is reduced to a formula: "In Russian peasant marriages and funerals, men get drunk and women weep, wail and sob." Nabokov characterizes *Svadebka* as a "primitively coarse . . . ritual of pagan origin" and a "curiously inexorable, drunken ritual" ("The Peasant Marriage," 276). The reason to dilate upon this otiose simplification is that it is by an old friend of the composer's (but would Stravinsky, who was mortally offended by Asafyev's interpretation—see Craft's foreword to the French translation, xiii–xiv—have remained Nabokov's friend after this?), one of those who, on the basis of a personal relationship to the author, have been widely accorded authority with respect to the works.

15. Letter of 7 April 1924; in Kozlova and Yatsenko [eds.], *Prokof'yev i Myaskovskiy: Perepiska,* 190.

Every Russian knows by heart the lines in which nurse Filippyevna tells Pushkin's lovesick Tatyana how she came to be wedded:

> . . . For two weeks or so
> a woman matchmaker kept visiting
> my kinsfolk, and at last
> my father blessed me. Bitterly
> I cried for fear; and, crying [*s plachem*],
> they unbraided my tress and, chanting [*s peniyem*],
> they led me to the church.
> And so I entered a strange family . . . [16]

With merciless concision, the passage succeeds in suggesting—at least from the bride's point of view—the full range of the Russian peasant wedding ritual (*svadebniy obryad*). It is a highly formalized performance (*igra*, lit., game or play); to perform a wedding in "peasant" Russian is quite literally to "play" one—*igrat' svad'bu*. The rite lasts weeks from beginning to end, has an elaborate cast of characters, and is at every turn accompanied by liturgical incantations of every sort, drawn from a vast, regionally diverse repertoire whose collected specimens, out of which Stravinsky fashioned the text for his "choreographic scenes," in his day already numbered in the thousands.

Pushkin's passage adumbrates the specific contents of Stravinsky's first and third tableaux, which suggests it may actually have helped guide the composer's imagination as he threaded his way among the songs in Kireyevsky's, Tereshchenko's, and Sakharov's immense argosies of wedding lore. A preliminary exposition of the traditional *svadebniy obryad*, drawn from these three sources plus Dahl's dictionary, will help us comprehend the *Svadebka* text and its "starting point in reality."

The most extended, systematic, and comprehensive description of the wedding ritual to be found in the literature Stravinsky is known to have consulted is the eighth chapter of the second volume of Tereshchenko's *Bït russkogo naroda:* a "Survey of Present-day Wedding Rites" ("*Obzor nïneshnikh svadebnïkh obryadov*")—present-day, that is, as of the 1840s.[17] The survey is a kind of summary abstraction of the many individual accounts of local wedding customs in a dozen Great Russian guberniyas, as well as in Byelorussia, "Little Russia" [Ukraine], and among the Don and Ural Cossacks, that are presented later in the book. Stravinsky's song selections show his method likewise to have been eclectic and schematic. In the

16. Pushkin, *Eugene Onegin,* trans. V. Nabokov, 2:162.
17. Tereshchenko, *Bït russkogo naroda* 2:116–42. All information not credited to another source in the following discussion comes from this one.

Svadebka text, songs from many different localities and in a multitude of regional dialects combine to produce a synthetic impression that may not be "authentic" with respect to any particular existing wedding rite, but that seeks to transmit, and to transform into art, something of the universal core of symbolically rendered experience in which all the various individual rites participate.

Tereshchenko begins by observing that the irreducible roster of dramatis personae in any Russian peasant wedding includes the bride (*nevesta*) and groom (*zhenikh*), their parents (or stand-ins for the latter, known as *posazhonïye*), and their friends, who form themselves into entourages and choruses for various purposes. In addition there are three essential players: two matchmakers—male (*svat*) and female (*svakha*)—and the *druzhko,* often called the best man in English, but whose multifarious functions go well beyond those of an ordinary best man. As Dahl defines him, the *druzhko* is "a young married man, the chief master-of-ceremonies, a wit, who knows the whole ritual, a glib talker, the general organizer of the entertainment, and a comedian in his own right; it is also he who leads the bridal couple off and stands watch over them during the night."[18] It is not difficult to recognize in this description a survival of the shamanistic agrarian folk religion that preceded Christianity in the Russian countryside, with the *druzhko*—sometimes called the "wedding jester"—taking the place of the skomorokh of old. As Tereshchenko notes, the two matchmakers and the *druzhko* form the essential trio that is responsible for the whole *dobroye delo,* the "good deed" of arranging and accomplishing the marriage from first to last.

The first stage in the *svadebnaya igra* is that of *svatan'ye,* the making of the match. A *svat* or *svakha* is sent by the groom's parents to those of the bride. They go through an elaborate preliminary ritual of small talk, the hosts repeatedly asking the matchmaker to sit down, the latter steadfastly declining. When the subject is at last broached and the proposal provisionally accepted, a toast is drunk. The parents must now appoint a *svat* or *svakha* of their own for further negotiations. This second matchmaker comes dressed up in conspicuous finery, but is nonetheless received by the household that initiated the proposal as a complete stranger whose purpose is unknown, the matchmaker meanwhile pretending to have gotten lost on the road and to have happened on the house of the wedding party by chance. On being asked his occupation, the matchmaker declares himself a merchant and proceeds to describe his "wares." Both sides having thus obliquely made their intentions known, the matter now proceeds to the *smotrinï* (or *glyadinï*), the ritual inspection of the bride, who is led out to be viewed by the matchmaker (or, on a special occasion, by the assembled family of the groom). She being approved, the bargain is sealed with a *rukobit'ye,* a striking of hands.

18. Dahl, *Tolkovïy slovar',* s.v. "*drug.*"

According to Tereshchenko, the *smotrinï* is the first stage of the *svadebnaya igra* at which prescribed ritual "music" is heard, in the form of a *plach,* a formal lament in which the bride pleads with her father not to send her away. The word *plach,* in common parlance, simply means crying or weeping, as in Nabokov's translation from *Eugene Onegin* quoted above. Most modern scholars (as well as Stravinsky) agree that, as it functions in the wedding ritual, the *plach* is not the spontaneous expression of feeling, but the fulfillment of a prescribed liturgical requirement, performed to a prescribed liturgical text, and sung in a prescribed liturgical manner to a prescribed liturgical formula. Pushkin, a better folklorist than his translator, used the word in this sense, and in canny apposition with *peniye,* which means something more closely resembling that which is denoted by our rougher English word *singing.* In English, both *plach* and *peniye* would be termed varieties of singing, but the Russian peasant usage distinguishes them sharply.

Stravinsky knew this well; his text notebook for *Svadebka* contains a note to himself to look up *plach* in Dahl. When he did so, this is what he found:

> a ritual of lamenting for a bride which lasts from the time of the marriage contract to that of the bridal shower, about two weeks [cf. *Eugene Onegin*]; a song of complaint, sung at bridal showers; the bride does not sing, but *wails* [*ne poyot, a pla-chot*], lamenting her maiden beauty, her raven tresses, her freedom, pleading for her mother's intercession, and so on. Afterward the bride's girlfriends lament for her, cursing the matchmaker, the wedding party, even the groom. *We wailed,* or *We wailed a wail* [means] "we sang such a song." For such laments there are countless tunes or motives, but for the *plach* that laments the deceased, which is performed particularly at dawn, practically throughout Russia there is a single monotonous motive [*napev*], the repetition of three tones, the last being stretched out.[19]

This is a completely accurate and detailed description of the opening of the first tableau of *Svadebka,* even down to the bride's melody (Stravinsky having chosen to ignore Dahl's distinction between nuptial and funerary laments).

To return to our narrative: the preliminary assent, signified by the *rukobit'ye,* leads to the *sgovor* or actual betrothal. Visits and exchanges of gifts by the bride and groom and their families are followed by a ceremony in which the *svat* and *svakha* sit both families down to a formal celebration. The bride and groom are placed side by side and gaze at each other while toasts are made and special toasting songs, known as *velichal'nïye* (lit., songs of praise), are sung to the couple, to their wedding, their dowry, their fertility, and to the bride's father. *Velichal'nïye* are often recognizable by the insertion of the names and patronymics of their addressees. The *sgovor* marks the beginning of the *svad'ba* as such.

The next stage is the appointment of *poyezzhane* (sing., *poyezzhanin*), the mem-

19. Ibid., s.v. *"plakat'."*

bers of the wedding procession or train (*poyezd*). The bride and the groom are each provided with a suite or entourage. The suites will eventually accompany the wedding couple into the church and mingle after the ceremony, but they have important individual duties to perform during the two-week period initiated by the *sgovor*. The *poyezzhane* are strictly ordered by rank. The designations of these ranks are hand-me-downs from the nomenclature of the feudal aristocracy. The wedding couple themselves are the *knyaz'* and *knyazhna* (prince and princess), the bride's title being that of an unmarried princess. As soon as the wedding ceremony is completed she assumes the title *knyaginya,* a married princess, by which she will be addressed or referred to during the wedding feast. The groom's *poyezzhane* are known as *boyare* (sing., *boyarin*), lords. Pride of place in the groom's party, after the groom himself, goes to a senior member of his family who is known as the *tisyatskiy,* the Old Russian word for a division commander (*tisyacha* being Russian for one thousand). Next, another honored male is designated the *bol'shoy barin* (great baron), followed by lesser barons, the matchmakers, the *druzhko,* and so on.[20]

In the Ukraine and neighboring territories, the first task of the *poyezzhane* is to go from door to door inviting the villagers to the wedding. It is they who will hire musicians (Tereshchenko mentions both regular violinists [*skripachi*] and *gudochniki,* players of the *gudok,* the three-stringed Russian folk fiddle, as well as bagpipers, flute-tooters, kettledrummers and tambourine men [*litavrshchiki s bubnami*]). The bride's *poyezd* helps her pack her trousseau, for which ceremony there is a special category of accompanying choral song.

We come now to the last and most elaborate of the prenuptial ceremonies within the *svadebnaya igra,* the *devichnik,* or bridal shower, which takes place shortly before the wedding itself, usually on the very eve. It is a purely female occasion: once again the bride performs her *plach,* more shrilly and tearfully than ever; her girlfriends divert her with songs of solace and affection. Candles are lit and the *korovai,* the huge and lavishly decorated wedding loaf, is displayed. The bride is seated on a high place, the maidens forming a circle around her. A chosen matron, known as the *prichital'shchitsa,* covers the bride's head with a veil and leads the singing of another form of lament, the *prichot* or *prichitaniye,* in which the maidens bewail the loss of a member of their carefree circle to marriage. Stravinsky looked up *prichot* in Dahl, too, and found it defined as being sung "in a wild monotone."[21] This definition, too, made a strong imprint on his music, and especially on that of the first tableau, which depicts the *devichnik.*

The main business of the *devichnik* is the unplaiting of the bride's braid (*kosa*), the combing out of her tress, and its redoing in two plaits (which will be wound round the head and hidden under a kerchief or headdress for the duration of her

20. Ibid., s.v. "*poyezdit'*."
21. Ibid., s.v. "*prichislyat'*."

F I G . 1 7 . 1 . *Devichnik,* plaiting ceremony, photographed in the village of Kolezhma (Karelia) in 1971. (From A. P. Razumova and T. A. Koski, *Russkaya svad'ba Karel'skogo pomor'ya* [Petrozavodsk, 1980])

married life; Fig. 17.1). A special repertoire of *plach* (for the bride) and song (for the girls) pertains to this ceremony. Her parents bless the bride, and she is led off by the matchmakers to the bath. The girls accompany each action with appropriate songs.

The next morning the girls reassemble to prepare the bride for the altar (*venets;* lit., crown or wreath). She is dressed in special finery, all the while pretending not to know why and giving vent to her biggest bout of *plach.* The *poyezzhane* gather in the courtyard. The groom's *druzhko* arrives to announce the departure of the bridal train for the church. The parents do not attend (the *posazhonïye* go in their place). The departure of the *poyezd* is the signal for the mother of the bride to perform her major set piece, a formal *plach* of leavetaking.

The wedding ceremony itself is called the *venchaniye,* because while the vows and rings are exchanged the "prince" and "princess" wear symbolic crowns. If the crowns should fall off disaster is foretold, so they are held in place by members of the bridal party. Each member of the company holds a candle, which is closely watched for omens. At the conclusion of the church ceremony the priest gives the bride and groom three sips apiece of red wine, after which the groom throws the wine cup to the ground and stamps on it. The priest bids the couple kiss in the presence of the assembled company, and they are wed.

From this point on, *plach* gives way to revelry (*vesel'ye*). The company now repairs to the groom's home, where the couple is blessed by the *posazhonïye,* their

FIG. 17.2. *Krasnïy stol* (late-eighteenth-century *lubok*): the *druzhko* toasts the bride and groom.

church godparents. The bride and groom must fall to their knees three times before the *posazhonïye,* after which they are seated at the head of the "beautiful table" (*krasnïy stol,* also known as the *knyazhenetskiy stol,* the "princely table") and the wedding feast begins. At the conclusion of the meal the *korovai* is cut. The first piece goes to the bride and groom; the second is placed under the pillow of the marriage bed and will serve the couple as their wedding breakfast on the morrow. This ceremony is accompanied by a huge commotion of beating on dishes and glasses with spoons.

Now the *druzhko* comes into his own, leading the revels with all manner of songs, toasts (*velichal'nïye*), jokes, and jingles (*pribautki*) (Fig. 17.2). The musicians hold forth to accompany strenuous, competitive male dancing (the so-called *russkaya plyaska,* familiar from *Petrushka*), which soon degenerates into girl-chasing. The merrymaking continues past midnight, often until dawn.

While the festivities are still in full swing, the newlyweds are led off by the *svat* and *svakha* to the bedchamber, which is lit by the same candles that had been held during the *venchaniye.* The couple is bedded down on a hay mattress (*sennik*). Outside, the *druzhko* circles the house on horseback for the rest of the night, saber drawn. In the morning the *svat, svakha,* and *druzhko* come to greet the couple. The bride and groom are sent to the bath, after which they consume the piece of the *korovai* that had been set aside the night before. Later in the day they visit the bride's parents, where they are received as guests, for the bride is now considered part of the groom's family, where she assumes the lowest position in the domestic pecking order, after her mother-in-law and sisters-in-law.

———————

It is because the Russian peasant wedding is so much more a rite of passage for the bride than for the groom that its ritual centers so asymmetrically around her experience and emotion. The groom's role in the *igra* is quite peripheral and nebulous compared to hers; in most areas there is no ceremony of initiation for the groom comparable to the *devichnik,* nor does he have a prescribed and formalized expressive canon to render his experience on the order of her elaborate repertory of *plach.* The *plach* and the *devichnik* are the really emblematic components of the *svadebnaya igra*—even as the *svadebnaya igra* had come to emblematize the peasant culture generally—and had echoed as such in Russian art music for more than a century before Stravinsky came to write *Svadebka.* The folksy divertissements that graced the Russian singspiels of the late eighteenth century were often representations of *devichniki,* the best known example being the one in the second act of Matinsky and Pashkevich's *St. Petersburg Bazaar* (*Sankt-peterburgskiy gostinnïy dvor,* 1782). This took the form of a little suite of seven bridal choruses on authentic folk texts, of which variants can be found in Sakharov, Tereshchenko, and Kireyevsky. The tunes are thought to be among the earliest transcriptions "from life" in the history of Russian art music.[22]

In 1809, a singspiel by Alexey Titov entitled *Devichnik; or, Filatka's Wedding* (text by Alexander Knyazhnin) played in St. Petersburg, containing similar material.[23] Fourteen years later, Alexander Varlamov published his most famous song "The Red Sarafan" ("*Krasnïy sarafan,*" words by Nikolai Tsïganov), the text of which makes explicit reference to the bridal veil and the replaiting of the tress, and which, to the consternation of ethnographers like Istomin and Melgunov, became so popular as to find a place in the actual *devichnik* ceremony, displacing the authentic songs it had originally parodied. Both of Glinka's operas contain scenes of wedding ritual. The third act of *A Life for the Tsar* portrays a *devichnik* disrupted by

22. See Bachinskaya, *Narodnïye pesni v tvorchestve russkikh kompozitorov,* 152–55 and 68, where a recent field-collected variant of the wedding song "*Letal golub, vorkoval*" (discussed in Chapter 12 in connection with the "Dance of the Earth" from *The Rite*) is set beside the tune Pashkevich set. An even earlier *devichnik* scene was incorporated into the very popular vaudeville *The Miller Who Was a Wizard, a Cheat, and a Matchmaker* (*Mel'nik—koldun, obmanshchik i svat,* 1779), by Alexander Ablesimov, modeled on Rousseau's *Le devin du village,* with a score that was a pastiche, arranged by Mikhaíl Sokolovsky, of folk and popular songs in the manner of the Gay-Pepusch *Beggar's Opera.* It lasted on the Russian operatic stage throughout the nineteenth century, and was reissued in piano-vocal score by Jurgenson as late as 1884. See Nicholas Findeisen, "The Earliest Russian Operas," trans. M. D. Calvocoressi, *Musical Quarterly* 19 (1933): 334–35; also Simon Karlinsky, *Russian Drama from Its Beginnings to the Age of Pushkin* (Berkeley and Los Angeles: University of California Press, 1985), 124–27. Both *Mel'nik* and *Sankt-peterburgskiy gostinnïy dvor* have been published in full score by Muzïka (Moscow) as nos. 10 (1984) and 8 (1980), respectively, in the series *Pamyatniki russkogo muzïkal'nogo iskusstva,* gen. ed. Yuriy Keldïsh.

23. See Ginzburg, *Istoriya russkoy muzïki* 2:31.

Ivan Susanin's abduction, and *Ruslan and Lyudmila* opens on the title characters' *krasnïy stol* (in this case, literally a *knyazhenetskiy stol*), which is disrupted by Lyudmila's abduction but resumed at the end of the opera when the nuptial pair are restored to one another. The *svadebnïy obryad* figures prominently in a number of Rimsky-Korsakov's operas, particularly *Snegurochka, Sadko,* and *The Legend of the Invisible City of Kitezh,* in the last of which the ceremony is interrupted and resumed as it is in *Ruslan.*

Staged representations of the *svadebnaya igra* pure and simple, unattached to any plot, were also common in the nineteenth century and continued into the twentieth. These form the immediate background to *Svadebka* as a theatrical spectacle. The most famous of these pageants was *A Russian Wedding at the Turn of the Sixteenth Century: A Dramatic Presentation from the Private Lives of Our Forefathers, with Choruses, Wedding Songs, and Dances (Russkaya svad'ba v iskhode XVI veka: Dramaticheskoye predstavleniye iz chastnoy zhizni nashikh predkov s khorami, svadebnïmi pesnyami i plyaskami),* put together in 1851 by Pyotr Petrovich Sukhonin (1821–84) and presented in both capitals. The music was to have been arranged by Alexander Serov,[24] but in the end the job went to Otto Ivanovich Dyutsh (1825–63), the Danish-born conductor of the Russian opera troupe in St. Petersburg, who had studied composition with Mendelssohn at the Leipzig Conservatory and whose son Georgiy would later collaborate with Fyodor Istomin on one of the Russian Geographical Society folk song anthologies Stravinsky knew so well.

Besides a virtually complete *svadebnïy obryad,* from *svatan'ye* to *krasnïy stol,* Sukhonin's *Russkaya svad'ba* contained a panoply of such other Stravinsky-related genres as *podblyudnïye* and *svyatochnïye igrï* (see Chapter 15). It ended, just as *Svadebka* would end, with the *svat* and *svakha* nonchalantly leading the nuptial pair off to the marriage bed (mid-nineteenth-century audiences found this titillating). The piece remained in the repertoire for the rest of the century, spawned countless imitations, and was even—shades of Diaghilev!—taken to Paris in 1875.[25]

One of the many latterday offshoots of its tradition was almost precisely coeval with the *Svadebka* première: *The Russian Folk Wedding Ceremony (Obryad russkoy narodnoy svad'bï),* a production of Vsevolod Vsevolodsky-Gerngross's short-lived Experimental Theater, first performed in Leningrad on 7 February 1924. The music for this spectacle was arranged by Stravinsky's quondam advocate Vyacheslav Karatïgin,[26] who relied for the most part on printed sources but who did copy down some tunes from living informants, harmonizing them with the aid of the prototypes of folk polyphony in the collections of Palchikov and Linyova.

---

24. A. Glumov, *Muzika v russkom dramaticheskom teatre* (Moscow: Muzgiz, 1955), 200.

25. For details on *Russkaya svad'ba* and its critical reception, including one hostile review that reads like Andrey Rimsky-Korsakov on the subject of *Petrushka* ("Don't disturb [Russian folklore's] waters; don't adulterate its limpid moisture with the cognac of French dramaturgy"), see Gozenpud, *Russkiy opernïy teatr XIX veka* 1:396–99.

26. See Karatïgin, *Izbrannïye stat'i,* 172.

"Vyacheslav Gavrilovich was able to approach this task with what I would call scientific scruples," wrote Andrey Rimsky-Korsakov, ever on the lookout for a stick with which to beat Stravinsky, "*consciously binding himself to the strictest criteria of folk style* as he understood them, and *rejecting flat out any free construction* of his musical data."[27]

The same could be said about Alexander Kastalsky's *Folk Festivities in Russia*, to which Derzhanovsky compared Stravinsky's as yet unwritten ballet-cantata in 1915, and the same prejudicial remarks as Andrey applied to Karatïgin's work could be justified on its behalf. After *Svadebka*'s Leningrad première, in fact, Kastalsky himself—unquestionably the greatest and most creative connoisseur of Russian folk polyphony that ever was—confided his offended reactions to his private notebook: "In *Svadebka* one occasionally comes upon interesting attempts by Stravinsky to approach the folk manner of choral singing; but he has to no good purpose laid the dissonances on excessively thick, wishing, it seems, to render the singing of a wild drunken peasant company (as if the wedding ceremony were interesting by virtue of inebriation and cacophony)."[28]

THE SOURCE

Although *Svadebka* did not lack for precedents on the Russian stage, and although these precedents surely helped prompt its conception, it did not have any musical model there. At best a collateral descendent of the Sukhonin/Dyutsh tradition of ethnographic pageantry, the work was roundly rejected by that tradition's direct heirs. For models Stravinsky had only his ethnographic sources and his own previous work: *The Rite* for the idea of a direct, nonnarrative embodiment of ritual action; the *Baika* (composed during a hiatus between the sketching of the third and fourth tableaux of *Svadebka*) for a nonlinear mode of presentation; the *Pribaoutki* and the *Podblyudnïye* for an approach to the folk texts and folkish *napevï* (as well as "the folk manner of choral singing"). *Svadebka* synthesized all these trends in Stravinsky's art, and at the same time took much further the distinctive Miriskusnik impulse toward cool creative abstraction. Thus *Svadebka* became at once the pinnacle of the Eurasian/Turanian phase of Stravinsky's career and a masterpiece of pure perceptual form that transcended its own conceptual dependence on folkloric data to an extent unprecedented in the work of any Russian musician.

27. A. N. Rimsky-Korsakov, "V. G. Karatïgin—kompozitor," in A. N. Rimsky-Korsakov et al. (eds.), *Karatïgin*, 73–74; italics original.

28. A. D. Kastalsky, "Iz zapisok," in IStrSM:208. The Russian première of *Svadebka* took place on 12 December 1926, performed by Russia's oldest chorus, the Leningrad State Academic Choir (formerly the Imperial Court Chapel Choir) under Mikhaíl Georgiyevich Klimov (1881–1937), its director since 1913. Maria Yudina and the twenty-year-old Dmitriy Shostakovich were among the pianists.

It stands as a monument to the inspired dictum of Andrey Belïy that serves as this chapter's epigraph.

For all that, Stravinsky's initial conceptual dependence on the "starting point in reality" was so great that, as he confessed more than once, he felt he could not get started on this cherished project without the proper ethnographic tools. From the way he told the story in the *Chroniques* and, even more so, in *Conversations,* one would think that he risked life and limb in the tense period between Sarajevo and the outbreak of the war just to procure a book of songs.[29] As the composer's recently published business correspondence reveals, however, the primary reason for his trip to Kiev in July 1914 was to confer with his wife's brother-in-law, Grigoriy Belyankin, who was the manager of the Russian estates Stravinsky held jointly with his wife. He also stopped, most likely, in the city of Rovno, one guberniya to the east of Ustilug on the way to Kiev, where the Azov-Don Commercial Bank, in which the composer kept his assets, was located.[30] The visit to the bookseller, where Stravinsky finally turned up a copy of Kireyevsky's wedding songs, was a secondary, serendipitous result of the trip. The fact is, the *Svadebka* text could have been fashioned quite satisfactorily without Kireyevsky—and without the lucky find in Kiev, it surely would have been: Tereshchenko, Sakharov, and Sheyn together contain upward of a thousand wedding songs from which Stravinsky could have drawn.

But the Kireyevsky anthology alone contains just as many, and for other good reasons as well it was the obvious source of choice. It was a legend. As Mikhaíl Speransky put it in his preface to the 1911 publication on which Stravinsky drew, Pyotr Vasilyevich Kireyevsky (1808–56), whose philosopher brother Ivan was the foremost theorist of Slavophilism, became the undisputed "center, around which formed a whole informal society of collectors of folk songs, monuments of folk poesy," in the 1830s and '40s, the decades that saw the heyday of Russian romantic nationalism.[31] These informal collaborators and informants included every scholarly folklorist from Dahl and Yakushkin on down, but most of all, they included the greatest living poets and writers as well.

Both Pushkin and Gogol sent song texts to Kireyevsky, and Pushkin played a famous trick on the great collector which so captured Stravinsky's imagination that the composer made a special point of recalling it in conversation with Craft forty-five years after learning of it from Speransky, who in turn had cited the memoirs of Fyodor Buslayev (1818–97), the greatest nineteenth-century historian of the Russian language. On a visit to Kireyevsky in the 1840s, Buslayev was shown the notebook that contained Pushkin's contribution to the great anthology. "Now this

---

29. See *An Autobiography,* 52–53; Conv:48–49/47.
30. See SelCorrII:203, 261–63.
31. M. N. Speransky, "P. V. Kireyevskiy i yego sobraniye pesen," in Kireyevsky, *Pesni obryadnïye,* l.

ПѢСНИ

собранныя П. В. Кирѣевскимъ.

Новая серія.

Изданы

Обществомъ Любителей Россійской Словесности при Императорскомъ Московскомъ Университетѣ

подъ редакціей дѣйствительныхъ членовъ Общества

академика В. Ѳ. Миллера и проф. М. Б. Сперанскаго.

Выпускъ I.

(Пѣсни обрядовыя).

Съ портретомъ П. В. Кирѣевскаго.

Печатня А.И.Снегирёвой Москва.
1911.

FIG. 17.3a. Title page of the main text source for *Svadebka:* Songs / Collected by P. V. Kireyevsky / New Series / Published by the Society of Lovers of Russian Philology at the Imperial / Moscow University / under the editorship of the executive officers of the Society / Academician V. F. Miller and Prof. M. B. Speransky. / Volume I. / (Ritual Songs). / With a portrait of P. V. Kireyevsky [see Fig. 17.3b]. / Moscow: A. I. Snegiryova / 1911.

F I G .   1 7 . 3 b .   Pyotr Vasilyevich Kireyevsky (1808–56).

batch," Kireyevsky told him, "Pushkin gave me himself, saying, 'Sometime when you have nothing better to do try to figure out which ones the folk sing and which ones I made up myself.' And no matter how I try to guess the answer to this riddle, I simply cannot. When this collection of mine is printed, Pushkin's songs will pass as folk songs."[32] Stravinsky, in his turn, was delighted by the thought that "perhaps a line of Pushkin's is in *Les Noces*."[33] If so, it comes at the very beginning of the fourth tableau, which contains the only text Stravinsky selected from among the thirty-four Pushkin-imparted songs Kireyevsky incorporated into his anthology under the heading "Pskov guberniya/Opochetsky District/village of Mikhailovskoye" (Pushkin's ancestral summer home).

The geographical organization was one of Kireyevsky's innovations. He took his songs just as he received them from his informants, with local dialects and regional ritual variants intact. Many of these made their way harum-scarum into Stravinsky's libretto, for the composer picked and chose eclectically from the ethnographer's carefully classified wares. Many of Kireyevsky's informants couched their songs within a narrative description of the *svadebnaya igra* as performed in this or

---

32. F. I. Buslayev, *Vospominaniya* (Moscow, 1897); quoted by Speransky in ibid., xlvi.
33. Conv:49/47.

that locality, and these descriptions, too, the collector incorporated wholesale. The result is a panorama of wedding customs throughout the length and breadth of Russia that may appear indiscriminate and redundant, but that in fact provides an unprecedentedly rich assemblage of the artifacts of Russian *bït,* life-as-lived. Stravinsky helped himself liberally to whatever slices of Russian life the legendary "argosy" had to offer, whether embodied in actual song text or not. Quite a lot of the exclamations, *druzhko* patters, and spontaneous conversation reported in Kireyevsky's descriptive narratives found their way into the *Svadebka* libretto, as often as not set to music alongside the actual songs.

As Buslayev's account of his meeting with Kireyevsky has already shown, the collector expected to publish his songs in the 1840s. The wedding songs, as a matter of fact, were to have been the first installment. According to Speransky, several of them (including the Pushkin songs) were set up in type in 1838.[34] On 5 March of that year they were passed for publication by state censor Ivan Mikhailovich Snegiryov, a leading folklorist in his own right and Kireyevsky's former professor at Moscow University.[35] But then the collector suffered an inexplicable change of heart, withdrawing, to the exasperation of his baffled colleagues and informants, into a state of *oblomovshchina,* that quintessentially Russian brand of dawdling. Although he continued to amass songs by the thousands, he never lifted a finger to bring them out. In 1848 he allowed fifty-five religious songs (*dukhovnïye stikhi;* lit., spiritual verses) to be published under the auspices of Moscow University. From then until the end of his life in 1856, Kireyevsky issued a grand total of sixteen songs, all in journals edited by his friends, and only at their importuning.[36]

After the great collector's death, and after a power struggle among his heirs in the course of which a considerable number of his papers (including, apparently, the autograph manuscripts of Pushkin and Gogol) were lost, the task of editing his vast legacy fell to his disciple Pyotr Alekseyevich Bezsonov (1828–98), who between 1860 and 1874 issued ten volumes of *Songs Collected by P. V. Kireyevsky* (*Pesni, sobrannïye P. V. Kireyevskim*), and also included Kireyevsky-collected material in his own publications, *Mendicant Pilgrims* (*Kaliki perekhozhiye,* 4 vols., 1861–64) and *White Russian Songs* (*Byelorusskiye pesni,* 1871). Bezsonov's choice of songs for publication reflected his own interests and values: historical songs, *bïlïnï,* "spiritual verses." The remainder, including the wedding songs and other songs of work and ritual that in fact made up the bulk of Kireyevsky's estate, went into a case at the Rumyantsev Museum in Moscow that remained undisturbed and forgotten for a quarter of a century.

It was the Pushkin centenary in 1899 that led to the rediscovery of this collec-

34. Speransky, "Kireyevskiy i yego sobraniye pesen," lviii.
35. G. N. Parilova and A. D. Soymonov, "P. V. Kireyevskiy i sobrannïye im pesni," in *Pesni, sobrannïye pisatelyami,* ed. D. D. Blagoy et al., Literaturnoye nasledstvo, no. 79 (Moscow: Nauka, 1968), 47.
36. Speransky, "Kireyevskiy i yego sobraniye pesen," lix.

tion. Spurred by the tantalizing reference in Buslayev's memoirs, the philologist Vsevolod Miller (1848–1913), with the assistance of S. O. Dolgov, curator of manuscripts at the Rumyantsev, ransacked the case in search of the famous "batch" in Pushkin's hand. They did not find it, but to their astonishment they uncovered over five thousand "folk lyrics, encompassing in song all aspects of popular life," the existence of which had been utterly unsuspected.[37] Publication of these, beginning of course with the wedding songs that included Pushkin's (duly labeled, but in Kireyevsky's hand), now became a cause célèbre. The much-heralded first installment of this new series of publications, including all 1,043 wedding songs Kireyevsky had accumulated, plus another 129 ritual songs of various kinds, was finally issued in 1911. This was the volume on which Stravinsky pounced at last in Kiev, and on which he would base most of the text of *Svadebka* (as well as the *Berceuses* and various other songs). Its irresistible attraction, in light of its fabulous pedigree and checkered history, will now be easy to grasp. (That history, by the way, is not over even yet: the remaining three-thousand-odd songs collected by Kireyevsky in the 1830s and '40s are still in their case in what became the old building of the Lenin Library in Moscow. Not until 1968 did any more of them see the light of day;[38] since then a tiny but steady trickle of scholarly publications has begun to tap this vast reservoir of songs, of which more than half still await release.)

PUTTING IT TOGETHER

The first stage of work on *Svadebka* was one of browsing and jotting. Stravinsky filled up a twenty-four-page notebook (no. 84/2 in the Rothschild catalogue described in Chapter 15) as well as innumerable loose sheets (grouped by Rothschild in six lots under nos. 84/1, 3–7) with text extracts, predominantly from Kireyevsky, and very occasional musical notations. As he worked in this fashion, he also essayed various outline scenarios. The earliest of these, which occupies page 2 of the notebook, consisted of three acts. The first was given over to the *smotreniye* (as Stravinsky had it, substituting a variant of the standard Russian word for "inspection" for the more specific *smotrini,* the bride show). This was a logical place to start if one was planning a really comprehensive musical depiction of the *svadebnaya igra,* since it was at the bride show, as we know, that the first ritual "singing"—that is, the first bridal *plach*—occurs.

The second act in this draft scenario was divided into three scenes. The first was entitled "*Sgovor*" ("The Betrothal") and was broken down further into two parts: "At the bride's" and "At the groom's." The latter entry bore a page reference to

37. V. F. Miller, "Pushkin kak poèt-etnograf," *Etnograficheskoye obozreniye* 11 (1899): 157.
38. The volume in which publication of Kireyevsky's legacy was resumed is the one referred to in note 35 above.

Kireyevsky, showing that Stravinsky intended to base this part of the scene on a description of the so-called *vecherina zhenikha,* a rather grave and serious sort of bachelor party, reported to Kireyevsky by an informant named Oznobishin from Toropets in the Pskov guberniya. This local rite centers on a purifying bath and an exorcism (*zaklinaniye ot porchi,* specified by Stravinsky in the scenario), in which the *druzhko,* notwithstanding the Christian trappings that clothe the ceremony, reverts distinctly to his pre-Christian role of shaman. Taking a skillet in one hand and an axe in the other, he places three stones in the skillet and, after walking twice around the perimeter of the groom's home and reciting the Creed, makes the following incantation on the third go-round:

> Be thou witch, be thou lizard, or be thou dungeon dweller, only then wilt thou take my wedding when thou hast gone to Jerusalem-town and has opened the coffin of our Lord and looked Him in the eye; and thou canst not go to Jerusalem-town and thou canst not unseal the coffin or see the Lord, and therefore thou canst not accomplish the deed. And there lies over a whirlpool, in the ocean, on the island of Buyan, a white stone; and when you find that stone, there you will find my wedding and only then will you take it.

Then the *druzhko* strikes the stones with the butt of the axe and says, "As these stones have crumbled, so shall you evil spirits scatter."[39]

This marvelous scene, with its classic manifestation of syncretic Russian folk religion (*dvoyeveriye*), was a natural for the composer of *The Firebird:* in the manner of a skazka it likens the wedding, like Kashchey's "death," to a disembodied and faraway object on the mythical island of Buyan. Although the scene never made it into the libretto, the self-contained second half of the second tableau in *Svadebka,* drawn largely from *sgovor* and *vecherina* songs, includes a lengthy litany to ward off evil spirits, clearly a vestige of "Act II, scene i, part 2" in the original draft scenario.

The second scene of Act II in the draft is also divided into two parts. The first is the *devichnik,* and the second is designated "*V banyu vedut*": "[The bride] is taken to the bath." Stravinsky's designation of the third scene—"In the bride's house before the departure for the church" ("*V dom nevestï pered ot'yezdom v cherkov'*")—retains the use of the Pskov dialect (*cherkov'* for *tserkov',* "church"), showing that this scene, too, was to have been based on the texts and descriptions imparted to Kireyevsky by his Toropets informant. Finally, the third act of the original draft scenario was to embody the *Krasnïy stol,* the wedding feast.

To summarize the scenario as first sketched in R82/2:

---

39. Kireyevsky, *Pesni obryadnïye,* 49. The inconsistent second-person number is original.

```
┌──────────────────────────────────────────────────────────────────┐
│  SVADEBKA: Fantasia in Three Acts and Five Scenes                  │
│  Act I                                                             │
│     Smotreniye                                                     │
│  Act II                                                            │
│     Scene i: Sgovor                                                │
│        a. At the Bride's                                           │
│        b. At the Groom's (Exorcism—see Kireyevsky, p. 49)          │
│     Scene ii                                                       │
│        a. Devichnik                                                │
│        b. To the Bath                                              │
│     Scene iii                                                      │
│        In the Bride's House Before the Departure for Church        │
│  Act III                                                           │
│     Krasnïy stol                                                   │
│                                                                    │
└──────────────────────────────────────────────────────────────────┘
```

It is probably no coincidence that this first-draft scenario corresponds so closely to the typological breakdown of the wedding songs in the Istomin/Lyapunov collection of 1899 on which Stravinsky had so often relied: *"Na sgovorakh"* ("At betrothals")—*"Na smotren'i"* ("At the bride show"; and note the use of Stravinsky's form of the word)—*"Na devichnike"* ("At the bridal shower")—*"Kak po nevestu priyedut"* ("When they come for the bride")—*"Posle ventsa"* ("After the church ceremony")—*"Vo vremya krasnogo stola"* ("During the wedding feast"). Stravinsky's adoption of these categories, for each of which he had a supply of appropriate and authentic songs ready and waiting, probably indicates an early intention to base the music of each section of *Svadebka* on ethnologically apposite source melodies, as he had done in certain parts of *The Rite*. The scenario in the case of *Svadebka* being far more closely based on observable and documented fact than that of the earlier ballet, it is likely that the music was at first meant to match it strictly, custom for custom and song for song.

Not only is the first-draft scenario far more inclusive and ethnographically scrupulous than the one Stravinsky finally adopted, but it is also far more conventionally representational—that is, "narrational"—in concept. This becomes especially clear when one looks further into the text notebook and discovers the extremely detailed plan for Act II, scene i, part 1: "At the Bride's." Stravinsky not only copied out song texts and incipits, but also included a number of detailed descriptions of rites, which in this context assume the function of stage directions. The first pair of descriptions were from an article, "On the Weddings and Wedding Rites and Customs of the Russian Peasants" (*"O svad'bakh i svadebnïkh obryadakh i obïchayakh russkikh krest'yan"*), by Pyotr Ilarionovich Strakhov, a professor of veterinary medicine at Moscow University, first printed in 1836. Kireyevsky had extracted the songs for his collection; the editors of the 1911 publication restored the full text of the article. What follows is the complete scenario of the scene exactly as Stravinsky jotted it down on pages 7–8 of his notebook, amplified by a few explanatory references and remarks in brackets.[40]

SECOND ACT

I

AT THE BRIDE'S

P. 241:   When they have arrived home from the bath, the father and mother meet the bride with an icon, exactly as they had seen her off to the bath. After the blessing, the bride's girlfriends seat her on a bench at the table, placing on the table before her a dish, next to which they place a comb. Each girl approaches the bride, takes the comb from the table, combs her hair, replaces the comb, and drops a few coins in the dish.

To music: "I comb, I will comb Nastasia's tress," etc. [Kireyevsky no. 635, p. 177: This is actually a *devichnik* song, and it survived into the finished score at fig. [2].]

[P. 241]: Afterward the girls take their leave of the bride, saying, "Remain behind, dear, and be happy." When the girls have gone, the bride sits down on a bench by the window under the icon stand [*krasnoye okno*] and begins howling to her mother and father:

#868, p. 238:   "My father, my own,
                 My mother, my own! etc.

[all of this is   [Where are you forcing me to go?
crossed out by   Have I not worked for you?
Stravinsky]   Have I not taken care of you?]"

        or:
#869, p. 239
        or: [similar complaints]
#880, p. 241

[Not in Strakhov's text; by Stravinsky?:]

After this the girls lead the bride to the middle of the parlor [*gornitsa*]. They themselves go up to the father and mother of the bride and bow low to them in front of the icons. Meanwhile the bride wails to her father and mother:

#876, p. 240:

Bright moon, O father mine,
Red sun, O mother mine!
I have no need for gold or silver
I ask only for your honest blessing.

Her parents bless the girl with icons. See p. 240. The bride continues to wail

---

40. In his essay on *Svadebka* (*New York Review of Books* [*NYRB*], 30; also, in somewhat abbreviated form, in *Prejudices in Disguise*, 266), Craft erroneously states that these scenario sketches were later than the three-act scenario "and intended for the four-tableaux final score," though they do not for the most part correspond to it. In fact, these transcriptions from Kireyevsky are found only a couple of pages from the three-act scenario in the notebook and obviously relate to it, as the heading "Second Act" already establishes.

#881, p. 241 (with my [i.e., Stravinsky's] changes):

> Bright moon, O father mine,
> Red sun, O mother mine!
> Teach me wisdom and reason,
> How I am to live and be in strange parts.

[Stravinsky's changes here actually involve the conflation of the formula invocation from song no. 880 with the second and third lines of no. 881. The latter is a song addressed to the mother alone, so the imperative "teach me" had to be adjusted to the second person plural.]

Her parents go up to the bride and, standing on either side of her, comfort her by pressing and embracing her by turns:

The parents [no. 882, p. 241]:

> You, my own little child,
> Go and live and grow accustomed
> To strange faraway parts,
> To a strange father and mother!

or:

Sakharov: *Songs of the Russian People*, vol. III, #229

"Answer Song to the Bride" ("*Otvetnaya neveste*")

> "Our beloved sweet
> Anna Ivanovna!" etc.
> [One must live among strangers
> with wisdom,
> with reason.
> Strangers are like the dark forest,
> Like a menacing cloud.
> The heart freezes without frost,
> The eyes produce tears without ill.
> Among strangers be:
> Both submissive
> and obedient.]

[Sakharov, *Skazaniya russkogo naroda*, vol. 1 (3d ed., St. Petersburg, 1841), p. 163. This song found its way into the finished score at fig. [9].]

With its linear sequence of events and conversation-in-song, this little scene is virtually operatic, reminiscent of Alexander Serov's folk opera after Ostrovsky known as *The Power of the Fiend* (1871), or of Sukhonin's "dramatic presentation from the private lives of our forefathers." The curious notation "to music" ("*pod muzïkoy*") before the first song text could seem to raise the question whether in this earliest conception of *Svadebka* the music was to have been continuous. More likely it was a self-conscious adaptation of peasant lingo, referring to the use of instruments, as opposed to singing (*peniye*), as in the subtitle Stravinsky eventually gave the score: *Russkiye khoreograficheskiye stsenï s peniyem i muzïkoy* (Russian choreographic scenes with singing and [instrumental] music).

While in its linear and narrative manner this scene is a virtual antithesis to the

Svadebka we know, it does establish certain creative principles that continued to operate over the whole course of composition. Extreme freedom of conflation is one: Stravinsky slapped two of Kireyevsky's songs together without a care, nor did he scruple to import a song (no. 635, the first one in the scene) from a different locality (the Oryol guberniya) and a different ceremony (the "selling of the tress" to the groom's brother, or the *svat,* after its replaiting at the conclusion of the *devichnik* ritual, equivalent to the formal "giving away of the bride") solely on the basis of its verbal resonance with the comb on the table in Strakhov's descriptive commentary.

More telling even than free conflation is free invention. Stravinsky replaced one episode copied from Strakhov via Kireyevsky with another in which the songs were authentic (though conflated) but the connecting action, while plausible enough, was imaginary. True to the old Miriskusnik ideal, Stravinsky was actively creating, not merely transcribing, his folk reality. A tension is already noticeable between the archeological accuracy of the plan and the irrepressible fantasy of the execution; and therein we have one of the secrets of *Svadebka*'s extraordinary vitality. By forcing his inventions through the hard resistance of archeological fact, Stravinsky tempered them and made them hard in turn. He managed to steer a successful course between the Scylla of dull pedantic fidelity to his sources (against which Kastalsky and the other composers associated with the Moscow Musical-Ethnographic Commission habitually foundered) and the Charybdis of purely arbitrary, hence trivial, invention (which sucked the Prokofiev of *Ala and Lolli* and *Chout* to the bottom).

At length it became clear to the composer that his initial ethnologically inclusive plan was intractable and redundant from the musical point of view. No fewer than three scenes—the *smotreniye* (Act I), the first part of the *sgovor* (Act II, scene i), and the *devichnik* (Act II, scene ii)—would have to be based on the musical style of the bridal *plach*. He toyed briefly (Notebook, p. 5) with a six-part plan adapted directly from Dahl's dictionary.[41] Dispensing with the preliminary stages (visits of matchmaker, *smotrini, rukobit'ye,* etc.), he now proposed to begin in medias res, to wit:

1. *Bol'shoy propoy* (lit., The Great Toast)—i.e., the culmination of the *sgovor* (betrothal) ritual

2. *Plach' i korovai* (lament and wedding loaf ceremonies)

3. *Devichnik* (bridal shower, plaiting of tress)

4. *Venchaniye* (the church ceremony)

5. *Otvod* (exorcism)

6. *Knyazhoy stol* (= *krasniy stol,* the wedding feast)

41. Dahl, *Tolkoviy slovar',* s.v. "*svatat',*" including entries for *svatan'ye* and *svad'ba.*

Scenes 3 and 6 correspond to the first and fourth tableaux we know. But there was still too much *plach* redundancy, and the church ceremony would have been a sticking point for musical setting. Because it stands entirely apart from the *svadebnaya igra* and has no folkloric tradition, the *venchaniye* is unrepresented in the textual and musical sources on which Stravinsky wished to draw.

Only when he abandoned altogether the idea of the wedding ritual as a fixed succession of events—a decision that rendered superfluous most of the entries in the text notebook[42]—did Stravinsky finally solve his problems with the scenario. In a momentous reversal of his initial plan, he rejected the portrayal of the surface enactment of the *svadebnaya igra* in favor of a symbolic, abstracted presentation of its essential structure and meaning. What inspired him so to reconceptualize the piece was probably a song (Kireyevsky no. 999) he never even attempted to set to music; but having encountered it on page 279 of the Kireyevsky collection, he immediately seized upon it as an epigraph to the entire composition:[43]

Dve reki sotekalisya,—	Two rivers have flowed together,—
Dve svakhi soyezzhalisya,	Two matchmakers have come together,
Dumali dumu nad rusoy kosoy:	They thought a thought about a blond tress:
"Kak nam respletat' rusu kosu?	"How shall we unbraid this tress?
Kak razlozhit' kosu na dvoye?"	How shall we divide the braid in two?"

Here at last was the *zamïsel,* the conceptual kernel he was looking for. He would strip the wedding down to its metaphorical *Grundgestalt:* he would show the "rivers," he would show their coming together, and he would do so through the abstracted sounds and poetic diction of the *svadebnaya igra* rather than through a direct representation of its action.

Out went the *smotreniye,* out went the *sgovor.* Not a single note was ever composed for the first act of the original plan, and only one song that would have been appropriate to it was ever copied into the notebook (the bride's lament to her parents—Kireyevsky no. 868, via Strakhov—already cited in the extract above; Stravinsky actually entered it into his notebook twice). He combined the first part of Act II, scene i (*sgovor*) and the next scene (*devichnik*) into a single scene where he could concentrate all the bridal *plach* together. This new scene, which retained its rather vague designation "At the Bride's," was then paired with another equally

42. These included detailed citations from passages in Kireyevsky describing the *sgovor* (for Act II, scene i), the girls' "dances in the bath" (*plyaski v bane*), possibly for use as an entr'acte between Act II, scenes ii and iii, as well as a few khorovod texts from the postwedding portion of the Kireyevsky volume, and two songs taken down from a live informant, Mikhail Nikolayevich Semyonov, an old friend of Diaghilev's who had settled in Rome, with whom Stravinsky remained on good terms through the late 1930s (see SelCorrII:263–64).

43. The sheet of paper on which Stravinsky copied out this song and enshrined it in a multicolored painted frame (with the legend "*Pered pervoy kartinoy,*" "Before the first scene") is reproduced in color in P&D: pl. 6. The epigraph is entered in situ in the earliest orchestral draft score (Stravinsky Archive, R83).

generalized scene—no longer related directly to the *vecherina zhenikha*—that retained the original designation of the second part of Act II, scene i: "At the Groom's." Thus the two rivers.

The rest of the scenario remained more or less as it was in the original draft. The third scene, like the original Act II, scene iii, took as its basis the departure for the *venchanie;* it was eventually christened "*Provodï nevestï,*" "Seeing off the Bride." It is the point in the scenario where the two rivers flow together at last—a powerful natural climax of which the composer would not fail to make the most. These three scenes would still form a single act, comparable to Act II in the original draft (it would now be called "Part I"). The *Krasnïy stol* remained in place as the concluding act (Part II), roughly equal in length to the first. The scenario had achieved something like this, its final, form by April 1915, when Derzhanovsky printed Prokofiev's description of it in *Muzïka,* the only significant difference being the order of the first two scenes.[44]

The parallelism in concept of the two opening scenes has been called into question by literalistic folklorists, for (as we have seen) there is no universally practiced symbolic ritual of preparation for the groom comparable to the *devichnik.* Yet Stravinsky's idea was not arbitrary, nor did it lack a "starting point in reality" via Kireyevsky. As the composer leafed through the massive anthology his eye was caught by two instances of just such a parallelism, both of which he copied into his text notebook at an early stage. The first of them was in fact the very first entry; its original source was Pavel Yakushkin's transcription of the *svadebnaya igra* as enacted in a small village in the Maloarkhangelsky district of the Oryol guberniya in south central Russia. When the groom's train reaches the bride's hut, the formal giving-away takes its customary form of selling the bride's replaited tress. Once the bargain has been struck, songs are sung to invoke the Virgin Mary's protection over the nuptial pair, the mother of the Savior standing in, as Simon Karlinsky has noted, for "some ancient fertility goddess."[45] The bride and groom are here represented synecdochically by their respective coiffures. The Virgin is symbolically asked to help the matchmakers replait the bride's tress and to comb the groom's curls, even though these acts had already been accomplished (in the bride's case, the previous evening) and despite the somewhat misleading headings given the songs by Yakushkin (see below). The tress (*kosa*) and the curls (*kudri*) in these texts, like the acts of plaiting and combing, are to be taken figuratively, abstractly. That Stravinsky understood this synecdoche, and that it was greatly suggestive to him, is clear from the titles the first two scenes of *Svadebka* bore on the autograph vocal score, completed in 1917: Scene 1 is entitled "*Kosa,*" and scene 2 is designated

44. We may assume that the listing of the third and fourth scenes in Derzhanovsky's account was garbled. He has the *krasnïy stol* as the third scene, followed by "*Prazdnestvo.*" But the two titles are synonymous. The "beautiful table" *is* the wedding "festivity."

45. Karlinsky, "Stravinsky and Russian Pre-Literate Theater," 236.

"*Kudri.*" These were not changed back to "At the Bride's" and "At the Groom's" until the first proofs.[46] The two songs, as Stravinsky encountered them on page 162 of the Kireyevsky collection, run as follows:

No. 568: "*Kogda neveste cheshut kosu*" "When the Bride's Braid Is Being Combed"

Prechistaya Mater',	Purest Mother,
Khodi k nam u khat'	Come to our hut
Svakhi pomogat'	To help the matchmaker
Kosu raspletat',	Unplait the braid,
Natal'inu kosu,	Natalya's braid,
Mikhailovnï rusu.	[Natalya] Mikhailovna's blond [braid].

No. 569: "*Kogda cheshut volosï u zhenikha*" "When the Groom's Hair Is Being Combed"

Prechistaya Mater',	Purest Mother,
Khodi k nam u khat'	Come to our hut
Svakhi pomogat'	To help the matchmaker
Kudri raschesat',	Comb out the curls,
Vasil'yevï kudri,	Vasili's curls,
Dimitricha rusï.	[Vasili] Dimitrich's blond [curls].

As noted, Stravinsky seized upon this striking pair of songs at the very outset of his work, showing that the bride/groom parallelism was in his mind from the beginning. It is noteworthy, moreover, that he reversed their order, copying the groom's song first into his notebook, which agrees with the order of scenes reported in *Muzïka* in 1915:

(Text notebook [R82/2], p. 1)

Cheshut volosy			Hair is combed		
Zhenikhu No. 569	⎤	str.	The groom's No. 569	⎤	p.
Neveste No. 568	⎦	162	The bride's No. 568	⎦	162

The other bride/groom pair comes from a group of songs taken down in another village in the Maloarkhangelsky district. No informant is credited, so they may have been collected by Kireyevsky himself. Although the songs in this group are not entered in their proper ritual sequence with interstitial descriptions of the ceremonies they adorn, the pair in question nonetheless shows up as a unit, leaving no doubt that in the given locality they were ritually linked. The texts, as found in Kireyevsky on page 177, are as follows:

46. See the materials on deposit from J. & W. Chester at the British Library, Loan 75/42–43.

No. 635: "*Kogda prodayut nevestinu kosu*"

Chosu, pochosu
Nastas'inu kosu,
Chosu, pochosu
Timofeyevne rusu.
A yeshcho pochosu,
A i kosu zapletu,
Alu léntu upletu,
Goluboyu perev'yu.

"When the Bride's Tress Is Being Sold"

I comb, I will comb
Anastasia's tress,
I comb, I will comb
[Anastasia] Timofeyevna's blond [tress].
And I will comb it some more,
And I will braid the tress, too,
I will weave in a red ribbon
And tie it with a blue one.

No. 636: "*Kogda stanut chesat' zhenikhovï kudrï*"

Chem chesat', chem maslit'
Da Viktorovï kudri,
Chem chesat', chem maslit'
Da Nikiticha chornï?
—Kinemsya, brosimsya,
Vo tri torga goroda,
Kupim mï, kupim mï
Porovanskogo masla,
Raschesim, razmaslim
Viktorovï kudri,
Raschesim, razmaslim
Nikiticha chornï.

"When the Groom's Curls Are Being Combed"

How shall we comb, how shall we oil
Victor's curls,
How shall we comb, how shall we oil
[Victor] Nikitich's black [curls]?
—We'll be off, we'll dash off
To three market towns,
We'll buy, we'll buy
Some oil of Paravani [a Georgian town],
We'll part, we'll anoint
Victor's curls,
We'll part, we'll anoint
[Victor] Nikitich's black [curls].

These two pairs of songs, and the rituals they describe, became the basis for the parallelism between the first and second tableaux of *Svadebka* as we know it. Their sequential nexus is broken in the process, and with it all sense of linear, narrative time. They are regrouped so that the two bride's songs are found in scene 1, while the two groom's songs form the very basis of scene 2. The songs are deployed in a multitude of interesting ways, all of which militate against a sense of linearly unfolding action. Time is frozen or telescoped. Song no. 568 (given to "the mother," according to the direction in the score, but sung by a tenor) is heard at fig. [21] in the first tableau simultaneously with a fragment of a bridal "wail" (*vopl'*) sung after a bath on the eve of the *devichnik,* as transcribed for Kireyevsky by an unidentified informant in a rural district of the Voronezh guberniya (Kireyevsky no. 721, lines 3–6, sung by a soprano). In the actual *svadebnaya igra,* the two songs would have been sung about thirty-six hours apart (and no. 568 would have been sung by a chorus). Song no. 635, meanwhile, acts as a binder: it is heard at the outset of the first scene as a refrain (figs. [2] and [7]) and returns at the end to round the scene off (fig. [24]). The opening section of the second scene, which immediately follows the reprise of no. 635, consists of an elaborate intersplicing of songs nos. 569 and 636 (figs. [27]–[35]). As in the preceding scene, one of them (no. 569) acts as a refrain, reappearing independently at fig. [44].

The effect of all these simultaneities, intercuttings, and reprises is to turn the first pair of scenes into a vertical slice through a single static instant of time. There is neither a sense of unfolding action within them individually, nor a sense of linear progression from the one to the other. Their component songs and texts have become tesserae, arranged and manipulated by the composer into patterns dictated no longer by ethnographic but by formal and symbolic concerns. The dominant impression is one of highly concentrated and contrasted essential moods—lamentation versus religious solemnity, the latter to be followed by the exuberant exaltation of the *provodï* (scene 3) as the "two rivers flow together"—abstracted from the *svadebnaya igra,* but no longer actually depicting it.

These mood essences are conveyed by the patterns themselves, by the contrasting vocal groupings and singing styles—in short, by the musical *composition,* construed in the most literal sense—rather than by the words of the text per se; for the words, as presented in the libretto that finally took shape, have become a babble. As in the *Baika*—and perhaps even more completely—the words in *Svadebka* have become part of the music. Narrative coherence is left mainly to the visual spectacle that accompanies the music. And that is how Stravinsky brought the chef d'oeuvre of his Eurasian period from its "starting point," as Belïy would have said, to its "finishing point."

THEMATIC AND TEXTUAL STRUCTURE

In keeping with the absorption of the text into the music, the matching of voice parts with characters in *Svadebka* (again as in the *Baika*) is extremely fluid. The soprano soloist is the bride at the beginning of the first tableau, the groom's mother at the end of the third (fig. [82]); meanwhile, the bride's mother (represented at [82] by the mezzo-soprano in duet with the groom's mother) had been represented in the middle of the first tableau (fig. [21], in duet with the bride) by the tenor. The groom, however, is always represented by the bass voice. On his first appearance as a "speaking" character (fig. [50]; the only other is at the very end) he is represented by a pair of bass voices in duet.

All the same, it would be forcing things considerably to insist that the text is a wholly abstract "collage." Although its narrative coherence may be minimized on the purely textual, anecdotal level, it is quite vivid on the level of musical structure. Both acts, or "parts," like those in *The Rite of Spring,* proceed inexorably to powerful climaxes that are cruxes as much of plot as of musical construction. Taken together, they epitomize the dual significance of the wedding. The first wave (initiated by the tolling ostinato that starts up halfway through the second tableau) can be said to symbolize the sacramental solemnity of the rite; the second (beginning approximately when the tuneless shouting commences in the fourth tableau) asserts its procreative, life-affirming significance.

More concretely, each of the two "rivers" in the symbolic action is personified in the text (and, lest we forget, on stage) by a hypothetical individual who is consistently identified throughout the course of the presentation. The bride and groom retain the given names and patronymics by which they are introduced on their first appearance in the text. The first personal reference to the bride occurs in song no. 635, cited above, and Nastasia Timofeyevna she remains to the end, Stravinsky diligently substituting that name for whatever others he may have found in his source texts. The groom, for his part, is arbitrarily christened Khvetis Pamfil'yevich for the duration (the given name occurs in two songs that appear in the *Svadebka* text: Kireyevsky nos. 497 and 514, both from the Tambov guberniya in south central Russia; the patronymic was apparently Stravinsky's caprice).

Chance discrepancies between texts, moreover, are generally resolved. The two texts given above relating to the combing of the groom's curls, for example, disagree as to the color of his hair. Stravinsky "corrected" this inconsistency in the *Svadebka* text so that the groom, like the bride, is always a blond.

Table 4 (appendix, pp. 1423–40) provides documentation of Stravinsky's sources for the *Svadebka,* together with a brief ethnographic characterization of the source texts, so that the relationship between the ritual actions embodied in the songs and the import of the libretto may be appreciated. Finally, the source and text information is correlated with a summary of the thematic content of the music (a theme being defined for this purpose as any tune that recurs), so as to give a preliminary indication of the patterns into which Stravinsky cast his melodic tesserae, all in preparation for the analytical discussion that follows.[47]

In Table 4, the "themes," as defined above, are given an identifying letter so that their progress can be traced. And this reveals something rather rare and wonderful about *Svadebka:* the relationship between its textual and musical units is as fluid as that between voice parts and characters. Texts and tunes do of course occasionally relate on a stable one-to-one basis; indeed, many textual reprises, especially in the first and second tableaux, are signaled by musical returns as well. No less frequently, however, and perhaps more characteristically, texts and tunes live separate lives, meeting and parting promiscuously. This becomes more and more obviously the case as the fourth tableau approaches its climax, intensifying the impression there of anarchic "lifelike" collage. But in fact nothing could be less anarchic than the way Stravinsky exploited the remarkable independence of the musical component in planning and executing the formal structure of the work.

Instances of promiscuous coupling of text and tune can be found in all the tableaux. A simple one can be found in the second, beginning at fig. [41], where two different *kudri* songs are set to the same tune (theme J) as if they were one. Some-

47. For a line-by-line translation of the text, including a more detailed ethnographic and semantic discussion of each song than is appropriate here, see "Stravinsky's *Les Noces,*" trans. and annotated by Roberta Reeder with Arthur Comegno, *Dance Research Journal* 18, no. 2 (Winter 1986–87): 31–53. For much of the information incorporated into Table 4, I am indebted to Prof. William E. Harkins, who kindly made available to me not only his study of the *Svadebka* text cited in note 14, but also his unpublished annotated translation. References to Harkins in the remarks on the table are to his annotations.

what more intricate is the interrelationship of texts and tunes in the middle section of the first tableau. Theme E, which carries most of the Tereshchenko song ("*S pod-kameskha, s podbelogo . . .*") beginning at [18] + 2, is foreshadowed in the tenor and bass at [14] + 2, while the other parts are finishing up the Sakharov text ("*Ne klich', lebedushka . . .*"), sung to theme C. The tenor and bass, though their tune is different, sing the same text as the women's voices. At fig. [18] the roles are reversed. Now the basses take up theme C to reiterate the famous opening words of the Te-reshchenko song ("*S podkameshka s podbelogo*") as a motto, while the soprano solo sings the text complete to theme E. The primary identification of the Tere-shchenko song with theme E is confirmed at fig. [70] in the third tableau, when the soprano uses a variant of the same tune (slightly altered by a chromatic inflec-tion of the fourth degree, as demanded by the local harmonic environment) to sing a variant of the same text as found in Kireyevsky. Theme C is present in the texture at this point, too, but it carries the words of a different song.

These examples illustrate the way a given tune can turn up in conjunction with a variety of texts. The converse also occurs. Two bars before fig. [97] in the fourth tableau, the bass and tenor soloists, impersonating the groom's father, strike up K458, a jocular admonition to the groom, sung to a distorted, "inebriated" tune (theme R). This song is interrupted by two others, K199 (women of the chorus) and K493 (the bride's mother), the latter being sung by the mezzo-soprano (at fig. [98]) to a tune strikingly reminiscent of the "Dance of the Earth" from *The Rite*. When the tenor chimes in two bars later, this time impersonating the *druzhko*, he resumes K458, but sings it to the melody of K493. The first song regains its orig-inal text only at [99] + 3. The most conspicuous case of this kind is the long litany (K125) that begins at fig. [46] in the second tableau and runs intermittently through the rest of the second and the whole of the third, finally providing the third tableau—and the whole "First Part" of the ballet—with its climax. On its various appearances it is sung to five different tunes, most of them reprised from other contexts where they had carried other texts.

Needless to say, only a listener as familiar with the contents of Kireyevsky's col-lection as the compiler himself—and maybe not even then—could know exactly what Stravinsky was up to here. The point is not whether the specific relationships between textual and musical units are always intelligible—though some, like the use of theme O as a fourth-tableau refrain in many different textual contexts, will strike the naïvest ear. The point, rather, is that *the music,* often acting indepen-dently of the words and at times at a fairly abstract level, *is the prime shaper of the ballet's form.* Musical articulations even contradict the ostensible divisions of the Part One into tableaux, and override them (thus anticipating an innovation widely attributed to Elliott Carter). When *Svadebka* is properly performed, observing Stravinsky's *attacca subita* directions, only the change of scene on stage marks the succession of tableaux. Meanwhile, the music tells a different story.

Of the three tableaux in Part One, only the first has a musical structure that co-incides with the actual boundaries of the scene. It falls into a fairly traditional, rounded three-part scheme, the outer sections based on themes A and B, acting at first in tandem and at last in vertical juxtaposition and conflation, with a middle section dominated by theme C. In the first section themes A and B are firmly associated with their original texts. Since A is associated with a text that unfolds, while the text of B is sung virtually complete both times, the music through fig. [9] has the character of a strophic song with refrain, rounded at the end by a reprise of the opening line.

The refrain character of B is what enables it, on its reprise at fig. [24], to effect an immediate subsumption of the whole tableau within a single rounded musical structure. What happens between figs. [9] and [24] is immediately cast in retrospect as "the middle section," however its own unfolding may have been interpreted. The recurrence of themes C and E in conjunction at fig. [18] tends to cast the nonrecurrent setting of K564 at [16] as a middle section in its own right, turning the whole scene into an arch; but that would leave the duet of the bride and her mother (fig. [21], K721 and K568 superimposed) unaccounted for.

Debate as to what predefined formal archetype best fits all the details here is as fruitless as ever; nonetheless, the basic character of the scene as a da capo design remains clear, and sets a precedent. The design is articulated musically rather than textually: the soprano (bride) does not resume her original text at fig. [25], but sings a new one to a tune that ingeniously combines recognizable elements of themes A and B (the former at its original pitch, the latter transposed up a fourth vis-à-vis its prototype, which runs concurrently beneath). Though not without ambiguities, the first tableau is thus nevertheless relatively conventional in shape.

The second is anything but conventional. Beginning with an alternation/conflation of themes G and H, similar to the treatment of themes A and B at the beginning of the first tableau, it proceeds to another such passage based on a different pair of tunes (themes K and L). Between them a number of seemingly extraneous, bewilderingly heterogeneous items intrude.

As the music thus hints, the second tableau is not really one scene, but two. Confirmation of this hunch comes from the text. Up to fig. [46] the text concerns the groom's curls, paralleling the first scene's preoccupation with the bride's tress. This much of the scene exactly mirrors the structure of the first tableau; theme G, which always returns with its text intact, performs the same rounding/refrain function as had theme B in the earlier scene, enclosing a lengthy, contrasting middle section and tying the whole into a neat da capo package.

The second part of the second tableau, from [46] to the end, is built on blessing songs and amulets drawn from the *vecherina zhenikha* and from the ceremonies attending the departure of the groom's suite on the wedding morn. This assortment of texts has direct relevance to the exorcism rite adumbrated in the first draft scenario, and probably corresponds to Act II, scene ii, part 2 of that initial plan. It has nothing to do, either textually or musically, with the first half of the second tableau, its eventual neighbor in *Svadebka*, and probably represents an earlier conception of the scene "At the Groom's."

But it has everything to do, both textually and musically, with the third tableau. The second half of the second tableau and the whole of the third are drawn from a common stock in Kireyevsky: indeed, K125, the grand climactic litany, proceeds unbroken from the one into the other. The other texts in the third tableau, like those in the latter portion of the second, are concerned with parental blessings and appeals to the saints. The musical content of the two scenes, as we shall discover, is also closely connected. What we have, then, in the second tableau of *Svadebka*, is a pair of unrelated little scenes, one of which parallels its static predecessor, while the other links up with its successor in a dynamic, overarching sweep that presses on to the end of Part One.

Characteristically, Stravinsky disguises the joint between the two independent halves of the second tableau by setting the beginning of K125 (fig. [46]) to a variant of theme G, the refrain theme of the *kudri* episode. When this is jacked up, at [48], to a higher pitch level, and when this higher pitch level is maintained at the next phrase (fig. [49]), it sounds like a climactic "development" of theme G. But what Stravinsky has really done is transform theme G into theme K, which will pursue an entirely independent course upon resumption after the mock-liturgical interruption at [50], the latter marking the apparent (though, as we have seen, not the real) break between the two halves of the scene.

Upon the resumption of theme K at fig. [55], the remainder of the second tableau is based on a single melodic/harmonic juggernaut (K′, first heard at fig. [49], where the first lines of the litany are recited for the first time). The word suggests itself because this new theme sweeps inexorably through such a rich process of growth without a single digression (though there is a seeming one at [58]) until the end is reached. This dynamic evolution quite gives the lie to those who see nothing in Stravinsky's music of the period but static "blocks."

———

Until its climax, the third tableau presents no new themes at all, but is wholly parasitic on the middle section of the first. This thematic reminiscence reflects a parallelism in setting: the first and third tableaux both take place at the bride's. The parallelism is set forth at the outset in very explicit terms, when a whole complex of thematic material from the first tableau (first heard at figs. [9]–[11]) is recapitulated by the same voice parts and at the same pitch level (figs. [65]–[68]). Only the texts are new: instead of a song of consolation, as in the first tableau, the words here embody a blessing on the bride that corresponds with the blessings on the groom in the scene just ended. A special symbolic effect is created at fig. [70], when three different tunes from the first tableau (themes C, E, and F) are sounded in counterpoint. The texts, as before, echo those of the second tableau; indeed, one of them, K125, is actually in process of continuation from the second tableau. The use of motives associated with the bride in conjunction with texts associated with the groom is an effective way of portraying the coming together of the "two rivers." The music of the third tableau is thus at once a recapitulation of the first and a dynamic continuation of the second. At fig. [75], the melodic/harmonic ideas of the second tableau are explicitly resumed. The thematic material that carries this development, however, comes from the first tableau: the ever-pliant theme C.

The climax is reached at fig. [80], the moment of the bride's departure, where the two rivers join in a magnificent musical cataract. It is a climactic textual moment as well: K125 has finally reached the end. The melodic figure that, beginning at fig. [78], carries this musical wave to its crest is the one new theme introduced in the third tableau. Only later will its full musical/symbolic import become clear: it is a much-streamlined foreshadowing of the borrowed folk melody (theme M) that will resurface in complete form around the middle of the fourth tableau (fig. [110]+2) and redirect that scene toward its own triumphant conclusion as the bride and groom are led off to the marriage bed. The theme, magnificently developed in the fourth tableau to a blazing culmination before [133], is thus associated with consummation on both its appearances.

The longest scene by far, the fourth tableau is organized at first in a manner reminiscent of the simple scheme at the beginning of Part One. The song heard at the outset—K142, set to a melody here designated theme N—acts for a while like a musical/textual refrain operating over a vast territory: it is last heard at [128]+3, some 263 measures after its first appearance. The musical structure is at first organized only very loosely by this device. For most of its progress, the fourth tableau seems a thematically casual, agglutinative affair. A considerable amount of nonrecurrent, hence nonthematic, material is heard along the way, and only occasionally do recurrences group themselves in salient patterns. The music from [93] to [104], for example, does form a sort of thematic arch (Q-R-S-R-Q, with a nonrecurrent motive inserted at fig. [97]), but the length and the musical prominence of its components are extremely variable, and the texture is full of distracting contrapuntal juxtapositions and overlaps.

This situation changes drastically as the tableau approaches its end. As the decisive moment of consummation looms, the musical texture becomes obsessed with recapitulatory gestures that provide not only a musical shape, but a symbolic commentary as well. We have seen how theme M is resumed after [110]. The introduction of this decisive musical component is strategically inconspicuous— brief, isolated from other statements of the theme, and textually parasitic on theme T, which carries the bulk of the lengthy song (K177) to which theme M is appended at the very end. Its role here is to carry the bride's direct discourse (she sings of her ties, both literal and figurative, to the groom). At [120], the theme reappears in conjunction with one of the last reprises of theme N, from which it henceforth takes over the function of chief refrain. The texture is increasingly dominated by theme M, and it forms the melodic basis for the supreme climax shortly before the end. On the way to that, it is sounded fortississimo in the one-and-only measure in all of *Svadebka* where the "music" sounds alone, without the "singing" (one bar before [125]). The theme's symbolic association with the stage action (preparing the bride and groom for the marriage bed) and with the increasingly ribald texts, is forged unmistakably.

Yet this is not the most remarkable of the recapitulations that crown the fourth tableau. As early as fig. [93], as part of the background to one of the densest motivic/contrapuntal knots in the score, the first and second pianos insinuate a modified reprise of theme A, the bridal *plach* from the very beginning of the opening tableau. Like the first statement of theme M, it is an isolated event, planted amid its more conspicuous surroundings like a sort of time bomb. It begins to detonate at fig. [114], where it is sung by the bridesmaids at its original pitch, as part of the first song that relates explicitly to the marriage bed. This could not be a more conspicuous moment, preceded as it is by an abrupt halt in the music and the *druzhko*'s shouted command, "Sing your songs!" At fig. [115], back in the piano parts, the motive accompanies theme N, still officiating as chief refrain. At [121] + 4 it resurfaces in the voices (again at its original pitch) and finally reaches the musical foreground at [122], where it is sung by the bride *sola,* in acknowledgment of her submission to her husband and his family. In this connotation, the motive links up with the meaning of the bridal *plach* whence it sprang, and the symbolic purpose of its reprise is explicitly revealed. But what is actually performed as *plach* in the first tableau (*devichnik*), replete with grace notes and glissandi, is reprised in the fourth as "singing." As Margarita Mazo has noted, the *plach,* as a manner of performance, is "not allowed to cross the wedding's main watershed into the episode of the 'krasny stol.' "[48]

Theme A′ next sounds in the pianos as accompaniment to a brief reminiscence (by the *druzhko*) of theme N, in the course of a speech on the connubial life that follows the wedding. At [131] + 4, sung by the altos, it forms one last digression

48. Margarita Mazo, "Stravinsky's *Les Noces* and Russian Folk Wedding Ritual," *Journal of the American Musicological Society* 43 (1990): 127–28.

to delay the choral climax on theme M—a last suggestion, perhaps, of the bride's hesitation.

Finally, after the choral climax has died away, theme A′ forms the melodic substance of what might be called the precoital coda, the groom's address to the bride, in which he speaks in distinctly self-centered terms of wedded bliss (adverting to his wife as "my nocturnal amusement"), while bells—also to the modified tune of the bridal *plach*—ring out eternity. *Svadebka,* no less than *The Rite of Spring,* ends on a note of pitiless virgin sacrifice, and it is Stravinsky's music, not the texts or even their juxtaposition, that drives the point home.

SETTING THE TEXTS

The freedom of interplay between text and music that made this eloquent peroration possible is all the more remarkable when one considers how narrowly circumscribed is the role of the instrumental accompaniment, the traditional playing field of leitmotif and reminiscence. Abstractly musical structuring in *Svadebka* must take place largely within the vocal—that is to say, texted—medium. The extreme flexibility with which Stravinsky was able to deploy that medium was due in part to the specific properties of the melodic material, but in larger measure to the composer's idiosyncratic habits of prosody.

Essential to an understanding of *Svadebka* prosody is the discussion in Chapter 15 of Stravinsky's "rejoicing discovery" and the methods to which it gave rise; but we must also take note of a few specific Russian art-music traditions relating to the treatment of wedding songs. The meter of these songs, as transcribed by the earliest eighteenth-century collectors, often fell into a pentasyllabic foot with the stress on the third syllable: ˘ ˘ ´ ˘ ˘. A good example is the variant preserved in the Lvov/Pratsch collection of 1790 (later taken over unchanged by Rimsky-Korsakov) of a dance song that shares its first pair of lines with a particularly famous wedding song that happens to be featured prominently in the first tableau of *Svadebka* (the interlinear refrains—"*akh lyuli lyuli*" etc.—are omitted):

Ĭz pŏd kámĕshkă, | ĭz pŏd bélŏvă,	From beneath a stone, 'neath a shining stone,
Prŏtĕkál rŭchĕy | bĕl sĕrébrănŏy . . .	Gushed a little brook bright and silvery . . .[49]

49. The skillful metrical translation is by Malcolm Hamrick Brown; see his "Native Song and National Consciousness," in *Art and Culture in Nineteenth-Century Russia,* ed. Theofanis George Stavrou (Bloomington: Indiana University Press, 1983), 76.

This meter became so widely accepted as the "authentic" meter of Russian popular verse that its employment became practically de rigueur in artistic stylizations by such early-nineteenth-century romantic poets as Aleksey Koltsov (1809–42), after whom it actually became known as the Koltsov meter (*kol'tsovskiy stikh*). One of his most famous "artificial folk songs" is the following, entitled "A Maiden's Sorrow" ("*Grust' devushki*"):

Ŏtchĕgó skăzhĭ, mŏy lyŭbímĭy sĕrp	Tell me why, my beloved sickle,
Pŏchĕrnél tĭ vĕs', chtŏ kŏsá mŏyă? . . .	Have you turned all black, my scythe? . . .

The convention remained in force long after Koltsov's time, as in these lines from the middle of a poem by Nikolai Grekov (1810–66) entitled "Where Art Thou, Little Star?" ("*Gde ti, zvyozdochka,*" best known in Musorgsky's setting):

Gdĕ tĭ, dévĭtsă, gdĕ tĭ, krásnăyă?	Where art thou, maiden, where art thou, so fair?
Ĭl' pŏkínŭlă drŭgă mílŏvă? . . .	Hast thou forsaken thy beloved?

Now, this meter presented a problem of accommodation to nineteenth-century composers and transcribers: how was it to be reconciled with the standard meters of conventional art music? Pratsch's solution (Ex. 17.1a) was to lengthen the last syllable of the foot so as to fill out the last measure of a three-bar duple pattern (Rimsky-Korsakov in his turn compressed it all into one three-quarter measure). Alexander Gurilyov (1803–58), who was to the music of "Russian songs" what Koltsov was to their verse, characteristically stretched a foot of *kol'tsovskiy stikh* over two measures of waltz time, the first beginning with a rest; thus his setting of "A Maiden's Sorrow" (Ex. 17.1b; also compare the familiar "Gypsy" tune *Ochi chornïye* ["Dark Eyes"]). Even Musorgsky, in his earliest surviving song, pulled the *kol'tsovskiy stikh* out of shape. In setting "Where Art Thou, Little Star?" he crammed the first two (unaccented) syllables into a single beat, which became the anacrusis in common time (Ex. 17.1c).

It was Glinka who broke through the barrier to an authentic rendering of this meter in art music. Each of his operas contains a wedding chorus (in Act III of *A Life for the Tsar* it is a *devichnik* song [Ex. 17.2a]; in the Prologue to *Ruslan and*

EXAMPLE 17.1

a. *Sobraniye russkikh narodnïkh pesen s ikh golosami polozhennïkh na muzïku Ivanom Prachem,* 2d ed. (St. Petersburg: Tip. Shnora, 1806), pt. 1: *Pesni plyasovïye ili skoriye,* no. 1: *"Iz pod kameshka, iz pod belova"*; compared with rhythmic notation as found in Rimsky-Korsakov, *100 Russian Folk Songs,* no. 38

b. Alexander Gurilyov, *"Grust' devushki,"* beginning

c. Musorgsky, *"Gde tï, zvyozdochka?",* middle section

EXAMPLE 17.2

a. Glinka, *A Life for the Tsar,* chorus of maidens (Act III)

EXAMPLE 17.2 *(continued)*

b. Glinka, *Ruslan and Lyudmila,* wedding chorus (Prologue)

Lel' ta - in-stven-nïy,   u - po - i - tel'-nïy!   Tï vo-stor-gi l'yosh v serd-tse nam.

Lyudmila it is a *velichal'naya* sung at the *krasnïy stol* [Ex. 17.2b]). Both are in the pentasyllabic meter of "*Iz pod kameshka*"; and in both, Glinka set the syllables isochronously, producing a quintuple meter—among the earliest such usages in Russian art music, and, of course, a powerful precedent.

It has been observed that in *Svadebka* "Stravinsky shows himself to be the direct descendent of Glinka, who has given us an amazing representation of the cult of the Russian Eros in the first act [*recte* the Prologue] of *Ruslan.*"[50] The Soviet critic who made the observation had a different agenda from ours—namely, the denial of *Svadebka*'s link with the Orthodox church—but as a statement about Stravinsky's prosody the remark holds true. Like Glinka himself Stravinsky adopted syllabic isochrony as his basic modus operandi, with the result that his prosody takes as its alpha and omega the metrical/accentual structure of the text. "In the beginning was the word," writes Robert Craft with reference to Stravinsky's process of sketching,[51] to which William Harkins adds, no less pertinently, "it is clear that the musical rhythms arise from the text far more often than they are imposed upon it."[52]

Nevertheless some important qualifications are in order; for the effect of Stravinsky's prosody, though his methods were rooted in Glinka's, is altogether distinctive and original.

In part the difference had to do with the nature of his sources. Kireyevsky, imbued with the then-novel passion to study folk songs "as a scientific object" (in the famous words of Alexander Serov),[53] admonished his informants, in an open letter published in 1837, to "take down every song word for word, no matter how nonsensical."[54] As a result it soon became clear that the metrical regularity of the pentasyllabic verse copied by Koltsov and his many imitators had been a figment of the editorial idealism of the eighteenth-century collectors, who had trimmed and pruned the songs they published the way the gardeners of their time might have

50. Belaiev, *Stravinsky's "Les Noces,"* 4.
51. Craft, "Stravinsky's *Svadebka*" (*NYRB*), 26.
52. Harkins, "Text of Stravinsky's *Les Noces*," 3.
53. Cf. A. N. Serov, "Russkaya narodnaya pesnya, kak predmet nauki" (1869), *Izbrannïye stat'i,* vol. 1 (Moscow: Muzgiz, 1950), 81–108.
54. Vulfius, *Russkaya mïsl' o muzikal'nom fol'klore,* 20.

trimmed a hedge. The songs in the Kireyevsky collection, like those presented by other nineteenth-century collectors like Sakharov and Tereshchenko, were more like the "English gardens" of a later time: a wild vegetation, luxuriant in its unruliness, and "organically grown." It was found that the meter of Russian folk poesy—and of wedding songs in particular—depended not on syllabification (number) but on stress, and equally on the dictates of melody, as we know from our investigation of Stravinsky's "rejoicing discovery" and its consequences.[55]

Modern researchers classify Russian folk lyrics not according to meter, then, but according to tonic patterns based on what the pioneering Linyova had called the "logical stress." The basic categories are single-stressed lines, double-stressed lines, and so forth.[56] To pick a familiar example, the version of "*Iz pod kameshka*" (or *kamushka*) found in Kireyevsky (K622) has an infinitely variable syllabification (shown in parentheses below at the beginning of each line). The tonic stresses, almost equally variable at the beginning, settle down to a uniformly triple-stressed pattern for the the direct discourse at the end.

It is easy enough to imagine a singer imposing a uniformly triple "logical stress" pattern on the whole song. If, having done so, we scan it musically with Glinka's *Ruslan* chorus as our model—that is, with isochronous syllables and with each measure containing one "logical accent" (on the downbeat except at the beginning of a line)—something quintessentially Stravinskian begins to emerge (Ex. 17.3). Line 5 is the only one to begin with an accented syllable. In our hypothetical musical scansion it is set as part of a single measure with the end of line 4, with a rest standing between the two accents, following the example of Stravinsky's setting of K569 at the beginning of the second tableau in *Svadebka* (see the last measure of Ex. 17.4).

(13)   *Iz pod kámushka bístraya vodá bezhála;*
        The water rushed swiftly from under the stone;
(14)   *Iz pod bérezhku bystréy ètoy yeshchó bezhála,*
        From under the bank it flowed more swiftly still,
(11)   *Vse víshen'ya, oréshen'ya podmíla.*
        Washing the cherry and nut trees.
(12)   *Pod víshen'yem, pod oréshen'yem stoít kón',*
        Under the cherry and nut trees there stands a steed,
5   (9)   *Vózle konyá stoít mólodets.* [Kireyevsky's accent]
        By the steed there stands a brave lad.
(8)   *On cheshót konyá grebeshkóm:*
        He combs the steed with a comb:
(8)   *"Uzh i kón' tï móy, voronóy,*
        "Well, black steed of mine,

55. See esp. Rudolf Westphal, "O russkoy narodnoy pesne" (1879), in ibid., 173–74.
56. Harkins, note appended to Craft, "Stravinsky's *Svadebka*" (*NYRB*), 31.

EXAMPLE 17.3 Hypothetical setting of K622 (= *Pesni, sobrannïye P. V. Kireyevskim*, n.s., no. 622)

Iz pod ká - mush - ka   bḯ - stra - ya vo - dá be - zha - la;

Iz pod bé - rezh - ku bï̈ - stréy è - toy yesh - chó be - zha - la,

Vse ví - shen' - ya, o - ré - shen' - ya pod - mḯ - la.

Pod ví - shen'-yem, pod o - ré - shen'-yem sto - it   kón',

Vóz - le ko - nyá sto - it   mó - lo - dets.

On che - shót ko - nyá gre - besh - kóm:

"Uzh i kón' tï   móy, vo - ro - nóy,

To - vá - rishch tï   móy, do - ro - góy!

Po - yé - dem - ka, kón', so   mnó - yu

V dál' - nyu - yu   ne - zna - kó - mu - yu   do - ró - gu,

Po mód - nu - yu   i spe - sí - vu - yu Po - ro - skóv' - yu!"

EXAMPLE 17.4 *Svadebka*, fig. 27 (rhythm only)

Pre - chí - sta - ya Mát'   kho - dí, [kho-di] k nam u   khát', svá-khe po - mo-

- gát',   kú - dri ras - che - sát'.

(8) *Továrishch tï móy, dorogóy!*
　　Dear comrade mine!

(8) *Poyédem-ka, kón', so mnóyu*
　　Let us go, steed, you and I,

10 (11) *V dál'nyuyu neznakómuyu dorógu,*
　　On a journey to far-off, unknown parts,

(13) *Po módnuyu i spesívuyu Poroskóv'yu!"*
　　For the well-dressed and haughty Praskovya!"

Compared with the mechanical hypothetical realization, Example 17.4 (Stravinsky's) is of course less consistent—and therefore far more imaginative and interesting. He puts two accents in the first bar, and follows the second with a rest even though the next syllable is not accented. Conversely, in the third measure he allows two accented syllables in succession without an intervening rest. Rests were evidently an area in which Stravinsky allowed himself a free hand, as we can see clearly if we compare Example 17.4 with the various recurrences of the same double-stressed quatrain later on (Ex. 17.5).

It would be well to view this sort of variation not so much as arbitrary free play, but as purposeful artistic manipulation of a convention abstracted from prior Russian prosodic practice, hypothetically reconstructed here by putting Kireyevsky and Glinka together. (There is no reason, of course, to assume that Stravinsky, heir to the practice, ever made such a studied reconstruction.) Here it is the principle of one logical stress to the bar that is manipulated for the sake of greater or lesser tension. Syllabic isochrony was also fair game. The setting of lines 18–22 of K125, which immediately follows the last appearance of K569 in the second tableau, is a case in point. The text, consisting of short-breathed double-stressed lines with variable syllable-count, is as follows:

I tï Máter' Bózh'ya,　　　　　　And you, Mother of God,
Sáma [K's accent] Bogoródicha　　The Blessed Virgin Herself,
Pód' na svád'bu . . .　　　　　　Be off to the wedding!

Example 17.6a shows a hypothetical musical scansion based on strict adherence to the "rules" developed in the foregoing discussion, while Example 17.6b shows Stravinsky's actual scansion at fig. [46]. The notation is very revealing: the *portato* marks on repeated notes, as well as the repetition of the vowels, show clearly how the syllables so notated have been arbitrarily lengthened against an implicit background of isochrony. At first the lengthening seems to be coordinated with the stress. (The treatment of the word *sama* is curious: Stravinsky's distortion of a peasant singer's distortion noted by Kireyevsky has the effect of restoring the normal stress of the word.) But by the time the word *Bogorodicha* has been reached, accent and duration are leading separate lives, subject only to Stravinsky's creative discretion. The barring is unusual for the way it gathers up whole lines into single

EXAMPLE 17.5

a. *Svadebka,* fig. 33 (rhythm)

Pre-chí-sta-ya Mát', kho-dí [kho-di] k nam u khát', svá-khe po-mo-gát'

kú - dri ras - che - sát'

b. *Svadebka,* fig. 44 (rhythm)

Pre-chí-sta-ya Mát', kho-dí [kho-di] k nam u khát' svá-khe po-mo-

-gát' kú - dri ras-che-sát'.

EXAMPLE 17.6

a. K125, lines 18–20, hypothetical scansion

I tï, Má-ter' Bó-zh'ya, sá-ma Bo-go - ró-di-cha, Pód' na svád'-bu!

b. *Svadebka,* fig. 46 (rhythm)

I tï, Má-ter' Bo - o-zh'ya, sá - ma Bo - go-ró-di-cha

Pó - od' na svád'-bu, pód' na svád'-bu!

measures (cf. Rimsky-Korsakov's barring of "*Iz pod kameshka*" in Ex. 17.1a, or Sokalsky's barring by hemistichs, first discussed in Chapter 10). But the dotted bar shows Stravinsky to have been honoring the principle of stress/bar coordination in the breach, as his markings show him to have been so honoring the rule of isochrony.

In other places Stravinsky did not bother to indicate through the notation the process of manipulation. In setting lines 11–16 of Sakharov's "Answer Song to the Bride" (figs. [12]–[16] in the first tableau), he freely introduced quarters (or "lig-

EXAMPLE 17.7

a. *Svadebka,* fig. $\boxed{12}$ (rhythm)

Khvé - tis su - dár' Pam - fíl'-ye-vich   u te - byá so-lo - véy vo sa-dú,

Va vï - só - kom té - re - mu, Va vï - só-kom Iz-u - krá-shen - nom

De - nyó-chek   on svi - stít i vsyu   nó-chen' - ku - po - yót.

b. Sketch from Rothschild no. 82 (rhythm)

Khvé - tis   su - dar' Pam - fíl' - ye - vich   u te - byá so - lo -

véy vo sa - dú,   Va vï - só - kom   té - re - mu   (etc.)

atures," slurred pairs of eighths) into a setting that is mostly articulated in the customary isochronous eighths. The barring, too, is unusual: whereas in Example 17.6b the measures contained whole lines (in their length perhaps suggesting the grandeur of the invocation to the deity), Example 17.7a allots separate bars to the anacruses, producing extra-short measures. In this case we can reconstruct the process of manipulation on the basis of a fortunately surviving sketch (Ex. 17.7b), dated November 1914, which shows that Stravinsky's original bar placement had conformed to the general prosodic guidelines we have been developing. In this early draft there is indeed one "logical stress" to the bar, and where lengthening occurs, it too is regulated by the logical stress.

Finally, *Svadebka*'s thematic structure insured that certain motives would have to carry a wide variety of texts, each with its own stress pattern. It is at these spots that one can observe most clearly how, as Westphal had put it of actual folk singing some thirty-five years before, Stravinsky's "metrics . . . are defined by the tune alone." An instance with an ironic twist in the present context is Stravinsky's setting of "*Iz pod kameshka*"—our starting point—as he found it in Tereshchenko's anthology. In this particular variant, the first word (the compound preposition *iz-pod*, "from beneath") is contracted by replacing *iz* with *s*, a less common preposition meaning "from." This results in a reduction in the numeration of the verse. What had been a pentasyllabic foot is now tetrasyllabic: *s pŏdkámĕshkă,* | *s pŏdbélŏgŏ,* as Tereshchenko spells it (the composer's spelling is more conventional).

EXAMPLE 17.8 *Svadebka,* fig. 18 (rhythm)

S pod ká-mush-ka s pod bél - o - go ru-che-yók be-zhít, ru-che-yók be-

-zhit   s pod ká-mush-ka   (s pod bél - o - go) s pod ká-mush-ka s pod bél - o - go

tsim - bá - la - mi b'yut,   I p'yut   i l'yut   v ta - rél - ki b'yut.

Stravinsky set these four-syllable phrases to the *popevka* of theme C (Ex. 17.8), never flinching when the metrics of the tune turned that of the text inside out. He even insisted on it with an accent mark!

In sum, Stravinsky arrogated to himself every prerogative of a peasant singer as regards versification, varying the stress and quantity of his texts (to quote Linyova) "according to the demands . . . of the melody, [in an] urge to destroy monotony."[57] In his basic approach and in his deviations alike, the composer followed authentic and highly specific customs, and ended up with settings closer both to the letter and to the spirit of Russian folk song than any Russian composer in the literate tradition had come before.

FINDING THE TUNES

What is true of the rhythmic structure of *Svadebka* holds equally for the melodic structure. With few exceptions, the melodies in *Svadebka* consist of what a folklorist would call *popevki*—characteristic turns and cells that are inherently static, iterative, open-ended, noncadential (hence tonally suspensive, recursive, infinitely extendable). Practically all of the themes quoted in Table 4 could serve as examples. Such themes are in essence molds into which any text may be poured, especially when textual accent, as we have observed many times over both in this chapter and in Chapter 15, is treated as independent of the musical ictus. Again with only a few exceptions, Stravinsky's themes are metrically as ambiguous—or better, as neutral—as they are tonally indeterminate. That is why they are entered in the table without bars, which vary—along with the note values and the number of repetitions of the constituent *popevki*—on practically any reprise of a given theme.

The status of Stravinsky's *popevki* as melodic molds in most cases follows obviously from their structure: what is theme B, for example, but a reciting tone? Yet what seems simple and self-evident in the finished music was, as so often the case

---

57. Linyova, *Velikorusskiye pesni v narodnoy garmonizatsii* 1:xvi, quoted at greater length in Chapter 15.

б) Лихвинскій уѣздъ с. Алфоновское.

419 (1).

Поется на дѣвичникѣ.

Растопися жарко, банюшка,
Разгорися, да и каменка,
Разсыпься, бѣлъ жемчугъ,
По столу, но скатерти,
По серебряному блюдечку!
Расплачется да и Вѣрушка
Передъ своимъ роднымъ батюшкой:
„Государь ты мой батюшка!
Ты на что вино куришь,
Ты на что пиво варишь?“
— Ты дитя мое, дитятко!
Да твоихъ гостей поить,
Да твоихъ полюбовныихъ.

420 (2).

Ты ручей, ты мой ручей,
    Ладо, ручей!
Бѣлъ, серебряный!
Какъ по томъ ли по ручью
Съѣзжалися гости
Къ Сергѣю на свадьбу.
Востужитъ, востужитъ
Сергѣева матушка:
„Чѣмъ же вѣдь намъ будетъ
Гостей потчивать?“
Возмолвитъ, возмолвитъ
Сергѣй своей матушкѣ:
„Не тужи-ка, матушка,
Не тужи, родимая!
Наварилъ я, матушка,
Девять бочекъ полпива,
Десятую вина;
Напёкъ я, родимая,
Девять печей пироговъ,
Десятую хлѣбовъ.
Упоимъ, укормимъ
Гостей полюбовныихъ!“

421 (3).

*Поется, когда женихъ пріѣдетъ за невѣстой,
чтобы ѣхать къ вѣнцу. Въ это время не-
вѣстѣ чешутъ голову.*

Не во трубушки трубятъ по зарѣ,—
Свѣтъ Марьюшка плачетъ по русой косѣ:

„Коса ль моя, косынька русая!
Вечоръ тебя косыньку матушка плела,
Серебрянымъ колечкомъ матушка вила.
Пріѣхала свашенька не милостива,
Что не милостива и не жалостива,
Начала косыньку и рвать и щипать,
И рвать и щипать, на двѣ заплетать.

422 (4).

Если женихъ или невѣста сирота.

Ужъ [1]) ты елка, ты слушка,
Зеленая сосёнушка!
Всѣ [2]) ли у тебя [3]), ёлушка,
Да и всѣ [2]) сучки, вѣточки,
Да ц·всѣ [2]) ли на макушечкѣ?
— Да и всѣ [2]) въ меня [4]) сучки, вѣточки;
Одного сучка нѣтути,
Да что самой верхушечки.—
Да и всѣ [2]) ли въ тебя [3]), Сергій сударь,
Да и всѣ ли гости съѣхались,
Да и всѣ [2]) ли полюбовные?
— Да и всѣ [2]) въ меня [4]) гости съѣхались,
Да и всѣ [2]) полюбовные;
Одного гостя нѣтути,
Что родимаго батюшки.

    [1]) южъ. [2]) юсѣ. [3]) тебе. [4]) мене. — *Поправки
П. И. К-аго.*.

423 (5).

*Поется, когда, воротясь отъ вѣнца, поѣзжане
въѣдутъ на дворъ.*

Выглянь, матка,
Во стекольчато окошко,
Какъ сынъ-соколъ ѣдетъ,
Соколушку везетъ,
Не бывалаго гостя,
Что вѣкъ не бывала,
Двора не знавала.
Посади лебедку
Подъ святые на лавку;
Начнетъ же лебедка,
Начнетъ гурковати,
Къ дому привыкати.

FIG. 17·4. The beginning of *Svadebka*.

a. Page from Kireyevsky's wedding songs containing no. 421. The text of *Svadebka*
begins with the portion at the top of the right-hand column, where the words “*Kosa l’
moya, kosin’ka rusaya!*” (“Tress, O my blond tress”) caught Stravinsky's eye.

24. Да какъ Ѳедорова матушка.

Да какъ Ѳедорова матушка,
Свѣтъ Михайловиця осударыня,
Въ воскресенье спородила,
Въ воскресенську заутреню,
На рукахъ его носила,
Ростила, ростила дитятко,
По головушкѣ гладила,
Уму-разуму уцила:
Ты рости, рости, дитятко,
Рости-ко, цядо милое,
Быдь талантливъ, быдь сцастливой,
Ко людямъ быдь оцѣсливой,
Съ господами быдь вѣжливой,
Ко невѣстамъ быдь сцастливой.
Какъ поѣдешь жанитися,
Приворацивай простатися;
Какъ приѣдешь на тёшшинъ дворъ,
Не спушшай лошадь по двору,

b. Wedding song no. 24 from F. M. Istomin and G. O. Dyutsh, *Pesni russkago naroda, sobranï v gurberniyakh Arkhangel'skoy i Olonetskoy v 1886 godu* (St. Petersburg: Imperial Geographical Society, 1894)—possibly the inspiration for Stravinsky's "grace note" style.

EXAMPLE 17.9   *Svadebka*, various early sketches for the opening
lament (1914)

a.

EXAMPLE 17.9 (*continued*)

g.

h.

with Stravinsky, the product of a ruthless process of search and refinement. We may observe this process, and gain insight into the way Stravinsky's *popevki* actually operate, by turning for a moment from the published score and comparing some of the preliminary forms the opening setting of K421 (the bridal *plach*) assumed on the way to its final shape. (For the text source, see Fig. 17.4a.)

The earliest notations (Ex. 17.9a), made in the summer of 1914, show a real cadenced phrase (*napev*), not a *popevka*. (Another surprise: the words set are not the first line of *Svadebka* as we know it, but the second.) This tune looks as if it might have been borrowed from some as yet unidentified printed source. The eventual *popevka* as we know it was obviously extracted (abstracted) from the first three notes of this tune (plus a characteristic grace note, possibly prompted by notations such as that in Figure 17.4b) at the original (crossed-out) pitch. Perhaps the earliest evidence of this abstraction is the little phrase given in Example 17.9b. Meanwhile, the setting of the first line followed its own route to the same *popevka* (Ex. 17.9c and 17.9d); line 2 was then linked up with the following lines in a way that begins to look familiar (Ex. 17.9e and 17.9f).

At this point we may shift over to the earliest "finished" form of the opening *plach* (Ex. 17.9g; see Fig. 17.5a–b), a particell of the initial projected version of the first tableau (scored as Derzhanovsky described it in *Muzïka*), made early enough

FIG. 17.5a. Early draft (1915) of the opening of what is now the first tableau of *Svadebka*. The heading reads "Act II," reflecting the original draft scenario. (Paul Sacher Stiftung, Basel)

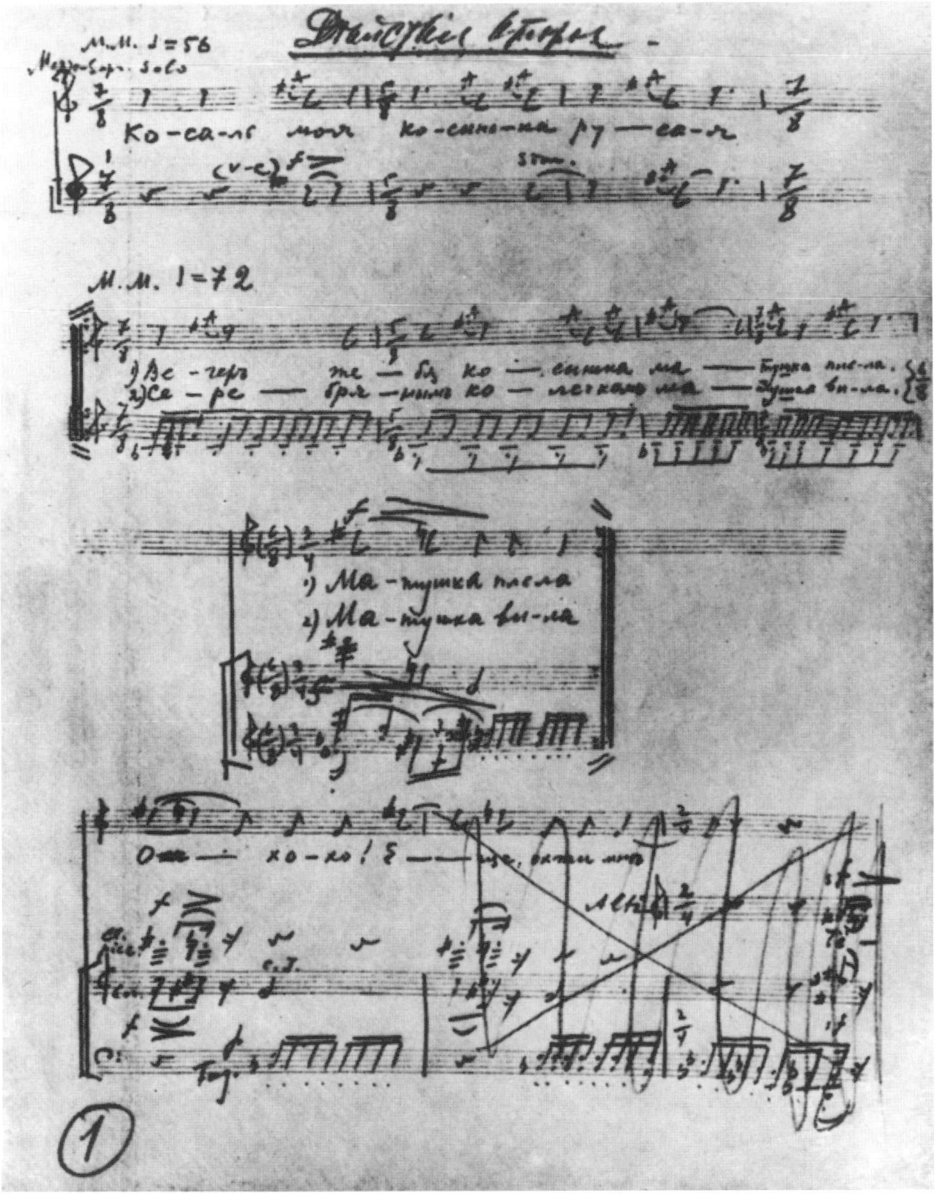

FIG. 17.5b. Same in vocal score.

that it is still designated "Act II," after the first-draft scenario.[58] Here the phrases have been considerably expanded through internal repetition. Even further expansion had taken place by the time Stravinsky arrived at the version that was eventually performed and published (Ex. 17.9h). The text has been made to accommodate this expansion by some repetition of its own, including an unusual example of *apocope,* or end-clipping, resulting from the partial repetition of *kosa* in the fourth measure. This particular form of word-mangling, described by Linyova, was widely practiced by Russian peasant singers but rarely represented in the printed collections of Stravinsky's time.

Even without tediously detailed collations, the vertical alignment will show at a glance the way Stravinsky's *popevka* technique works. Having arrived at his model trichord, the composer is free to vary the lengths of the notes practically ad libitum, to vary the order of their presentation to a considerable extent (as long as the ending is properly approached), and to insert as many internal repetitions as he likes. By using such techniques he could have set practically any text from Kireyevsky—or from the telephone book—to the chosen melodic material.

The discovery that the opening motive cell had been abstracted from a more shapely melodic context shows the radical stripping-down of *Svadebka*'s melodic idiom to have been a very deliberate decision. Hence the futility, at this stage, of attempting to trace Stravinsky's motives to specific ethnographic sources. He no longer needed them. By the time he composed *Svadebka*, the creator of *The Rite of Spring* had gone though *vesnyanki, naígrïshi,* and *khorovodï* by the cartload, and could probably think them up faster than look them up. Their authentic modal archetypes were now his stylistic second nature.

The (0 3 5) trichord on which he based theme A, for example, is represented by legions of tunes in the anthologies we know he knew and used. The pair in Example 17.10 are found on a single page of Listopadov's "Folk Songs Recorded in 1904" from the second volume of *Trudï MEK*. The first of them is actually a *devichnik* song, and it comes, like so many of Kireyevsky's tuneless texts, from the Oryol guberniya. A Kastalsky would have jumped at the chance to set Kireyevsky's text to this tune, as indeed Stravinsky himself might have done a few short years before. And in a way, of course, he did just that—only not "this tune" from "this collection," but a modal prototype that represented a whole class of tunes found in any and every collection.

Even if we did not know from his sketches precisely how Stravinsky abstracted this particular *popevka,* it would be naïve to suppose that he went looking for it in

58. Holographs of this version of the opening have been published twice in facsimile. Eric Walter White printed one, from the collection of Lord Berners, in a plate insert between pp. 64–65 of his *Stravinsky: A Critical Survey* (New York: Philosophical Library, 1948). The heading "*Deystviye vtoroye*" ("Second Act") may be plainly read. In the facsimile in P&D:144, the heading appears to read "*Deystviye pervoye*" ("First Act"), but close inspection reveals that *pervoye* has been written over *vtoroye*.

EXAMPLE 17.10

a. A. M. Listopadov, "Zapisi narodnïkh pesen v 1904 godu" (*Trudï MEK,* vol. 2), pt. 3: "Pesni Orlovskoy i Penzenskoy guberniy," no. 1 (*Sbornitsa*)

1. Sbor-ni-tsa, sbor — ni-tsa___ Dar'-yu-shka,___ so-bra-la___ svo-i-kh(ə) vsekh pod-rug. 2. So-bra-la _____ svo-i-kh(ə) vsekh pod — rug, po-sa-di-la_ i — kh(ə) vsekh za_ stol.

b. Ibid., no. 3 (*Troitskaya khodovaya*)

1. Po-duy,_ po — duy,_ ne-po-go — du-shka,_ bu-byon_ vi — tya-rok.___ 2. Bu-byon vi-tya — rok,_____ raz-duy, raz duy_
3. La — zo-ri-vai t'vet._____ Kak de — vu — shka_
tï ka-li — nu — shku,_ la-zo — ri — vai t'vet.
da na mo — lat-tsa_____ gla — za pro — da-la.___

EXAMPLE 17.11   Istomin/Lyapunov, *Pesni russkogo naroda,* wedding songs, no. 24 (p. 117, "*Posle ventsa*")

1. A Vo-stru-bi — la tru-bon'-ke Ra-no po_ za — re!_ Akh
[5.   Ve-chor mo — yu_ ko — son'-ku Ma-men'-ka ple — la,_ Akh
ra — no po za — re!
ma-men'-ka ple — la] *etc.*

a book. He was operating by now at a more essential level than his books. Thus he remained unmoved even when he encountered, in the trusty Istomin/Lyapunov anthology, a setting of a variant of his opening *plach*, K421 (Ex. 17.11);[59] for this was merely an individual Russian folk song, while Stravinsky was after more generic, elemental stuff from which to forge his own Turanian idiom.

We may gain a different perspective on this question by taking a closer look at the two known instances—one of them acknowledged—of melodic borrowing in *Svadebka*. In *Memories and Commentaries* Stravinsky admitted that "one of the themes of *Les Noces* is folk derived," but then hedged reflexively: "it is not really a folk melody but a worker's melody, a proletarian song."[60] He recalled that Stepan Mitusov had been his source, and indeed, a bifolium survives in the Stravinsky Archive with a title page in the composer's hand that testifies to the truth of this declaration: "Russian Songs imparted to me by S. S. Mitusov. I. Stravinsky, Ustilug, VII/1913" (Fig. 17.6a). Inside one finds three successive stabs, only the last one complete, at notating what is given in Table 4 as theme M, the climactic tune for both the third and fourth tableaux (Fig. 17.6b).

The surprising thing is that although Stravinsky did apparently struggle to take the tune down from Mitusov's dictation, Mitusov had not obtained it from oral tradition, but from a source Stravinsky knew all along, the Istomin/Dyutsh anthology of 1894 (Fig. 17.6c). The text, the pitch level, the note values are all just as they are in the printed book, though Mitusov evidently had a hard time recalling the middle of the song (hence the abortive efforts at transcription) and garbled the text placement, the barring, and the key signature of the original. Also at first (but only at first) surprising is the fact that it is not a "workers' melody" at all (what would

---

59. The closeness of this song's text to that of the opening *plach* in *Svadebka* is not immediately apparent in the example, since Stravinsky did not set the first pair of lines from K421. But compare the two columns below:

Istomin/Liapunov #24
Vostrubila trubon'ka rano po zare!
Rasplakálas' devushka po rusoy kose.
Da svetlaya koson'ka, rusaya kosa!
Vechor moyu koson'ku mamen'ka plela,
Zolotom, sérebrom uvivívala
Pras'kim-to zhemchugom unizívala.
Prishli-to dve svakhon'ki nemilostivï
Nachinali moyu koson'ku rvat', porïvat',
Razdelyali moyu koson'ku na shest' pryadey,
Zavivali moyu koson'ku na dva pletnya,
Nadevali na golovushku vechnoy kolpachok,
Uvivali moyu koson'ku krug golovï.

Kireyevsky #421
Ne vo trubushki trubyat po zare,—
Svet Mar'yushka plachet po rusoy kose:
Kosa l' moya, kosïn'ka rusaya!
Vechor tebya kosïn'ku matushka plela,
Serebryanïm kolechkom matushka vila,
Priyekhala svashen'ka ne milostiva,
Shto ne milostiva i ne zhalostiva,
Nachala kosïn'ku i rvat' i shchipat',
I rvat' i shchipat', na dve zapletat'.

60. M&C (UC Press ed. only): 97.

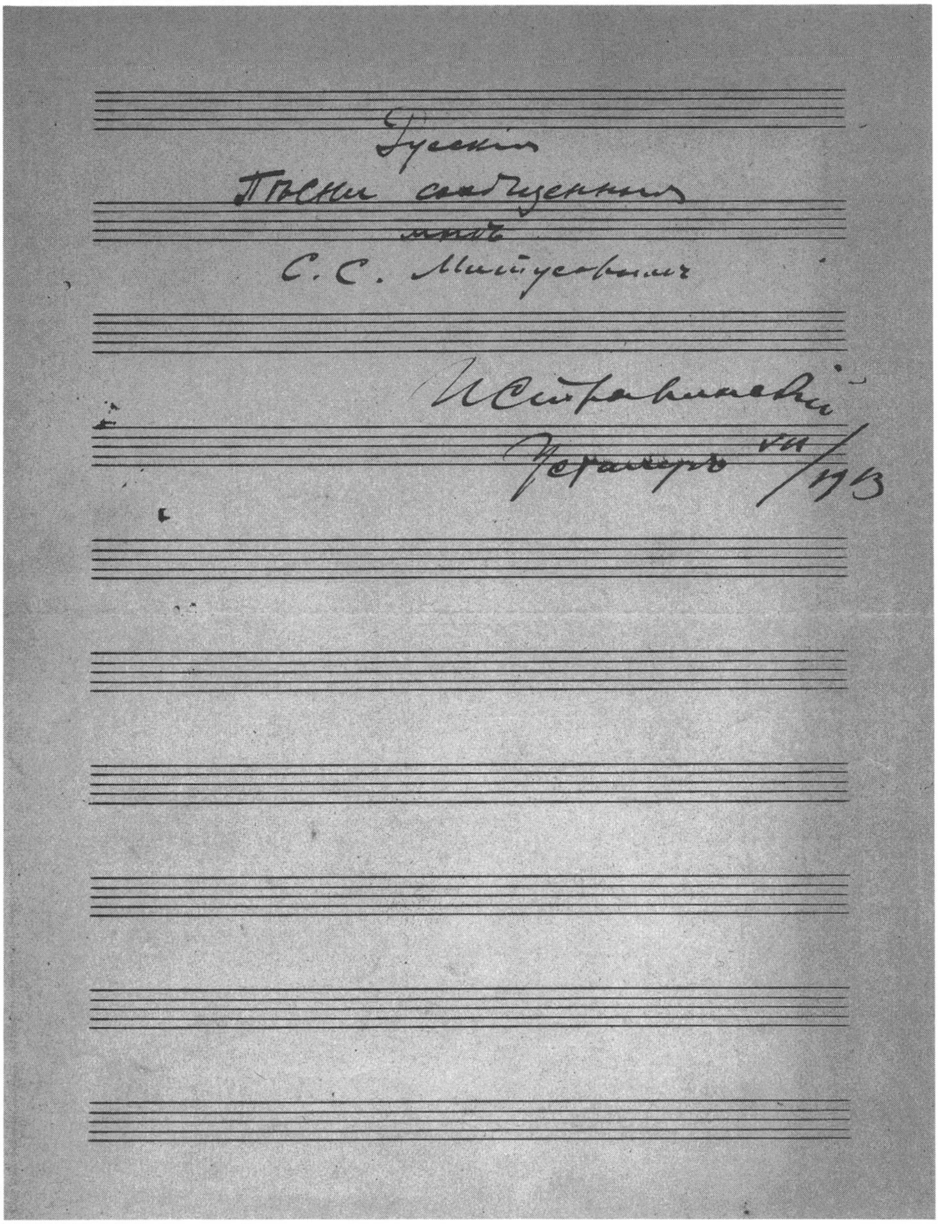

FIG. 17.6a. Cover of bifolium containing folk song taken down from Stepan Mitusov's dictation and used in *Svadebka* (fourth tableau). (Paul Sacher Stiftung, Basel)

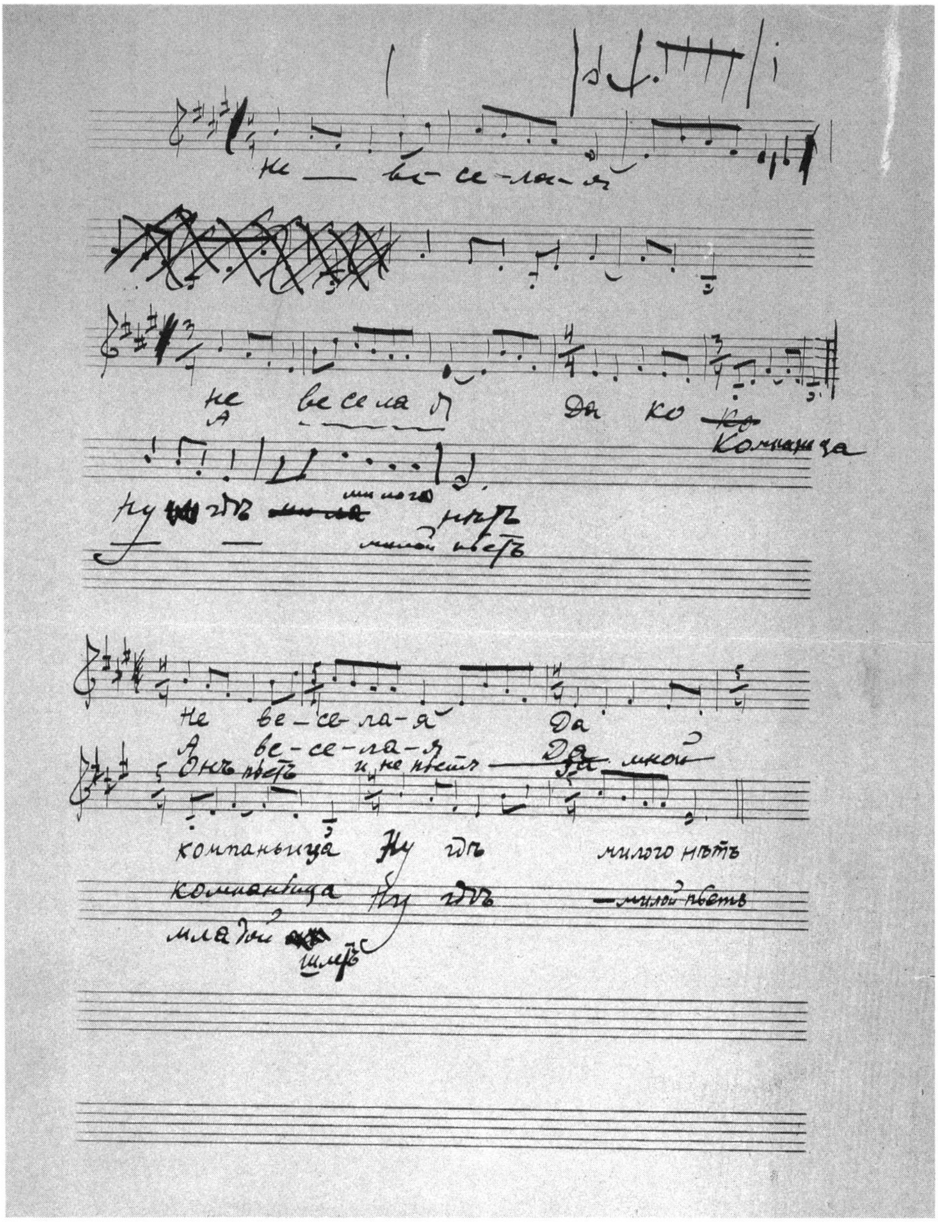

FIG. 17.6b. Inner page of same bifolium, showing three stabs at transcription.
(Paul Sacher Stiftung, Basel)

3. Не веселая да канпаньица.

FIG. 17.6C. Istomin/Dyutsh, *protyazhnaya* no. 3 ("*Ne veselaya da kanpan'itsa*").

such a thing have been doing in *Svadebka* anyway?), but a love song (*lyubovnaya*, as Istomin classified it), with a text that proclaims, "There is no joy or good company where my beloved is not."

In its elaborate three-part form, its range of a tenth, its well-defined "mutable" (*peremennïy*) cadence structure (involving what plainsong scholars would call a *commixtio*—that is, the use of a secondary final within an unchanged diatonic musical "space"), and its melismatic declamation, the song is easily identified as a *protyazhnaya*—that special genre of "drawled-out" lyrical effusion that had nothing to do with ritual or calendar, and as such is totally unlike the *popevki* that surround it in Table 4 and in the score. Its function within that score is clear: it is a linear focal point around which the *popevki* coalesce at the climax; and it is no less clear that a relatively lengthy, shapely *napev*, to be presented in toto (as it is—once only—by the bass soloist, representing the *druzhko*, at fig. [120]), is the kind of thing one is far likelier to seek in "sources," be they oral or written, than the little melodic tesserae out of which the bulk of the music is assembled.

Just as he had derived the trichordal *popevka* for the bridal *plach* from a longer tune that failed to survive the sketch process, Stravinsky abstracted a *popevka* from pitches 6–10 of the Mitusov tune (not counting a repeated note) and elaborated it into the impressive climax at the end of the third tableau. With more extensive documentation it might be possible to show that other *popevki* in *Svadebka* were similarly abstracted from specific tunes. Far from undermining the thesis propounded here, such discoveries would only confirm the basic truth: that Stravinsky was no longer interested in folk songs as such, but only in stylistic abstractions from folklore. And to say this is only to say that in *Svadebka*, the neonationalist ideal—which had conditioned Stravinsky's attitudes toward folk sources and their relationship to art from the beginning of his association with Diaghilev—had reached its pinnacle.

One little detail among Stravinsky's sketches speaks volumes about his creative methods, and about the balance, as he viewed it, between the artist's fancy and the ethnographer's conscience. One might even say it puts in a nutshell just what it was that made Stravinsky Stravinsky. On a scrap of paper (now preserved along with the Mitusov bifolium in a packet in the Archive catalogued by Rothschild as R87), Stravinsky copied the tune down at the pitch where the bass sings it straight through at fig. [120]—that is, down a step from the pitch Mitusov had given him (Ex. 17.12a). At the very end he made a typical copyist's slip: he forgot to transpose the last note (which, as is common in folk-song cadences, he had transferred to a higher octave). The tune thus ended not with a typical rising fifth, but with a rising sixth, in actual folk practice an absolutely nonoccurrent cadential interval. When he noticed this slip, Stravinsky did not routinely correct it, as a Kastalsky would have done, but seized upon it as a *trouvaille* and exploited it with gusto.

Twice he used it as a modulatory agent, linking theme M with the preparation for theme A' (at its original pitch) at fig. [121] (Ex. 17.12b) and with its own transposition at fig. [125] (Ex. 17.12c). At the very climax came the stroke of genius: four choral statements of the last phrase of theme M (with the opening "intonational thesis," as Soviet ethnomusicologists would say, expanded from a fourth to a fifth).[61] The last note (B) is held invariant, the whole rest of the tune being alternately transposed so that the cadential approach oscillates thrillingly between the original fifth and the serendipitous sixth (Ex. 17.12d).[62]

---

61. See I. I. Zemtsovsky, *Russkaya protyazhnaya pesnya: opït issledovaniya* (Leningrad: Muzïka, 1967), 7–8. It is this form of the tune, by the way, that Stravinsky quotes in M&C:91/97.

62. There is evidence that the famous "extra" bar of silence (fig. [134] + 9)—which Andrew Imbrie, in a brief but eloquent memorial essay, likened to "one measure of eternity" (in an article of the same name, *Perspectives of New Music* 9, no. 2–10, no. 1 [1971]: 51–57)—originated as a similar copying error. The measure does not appear in the 1917 particell, so that there are eight beats between the bell chords immediately before fig. [135], as everywhere else. (Mm. 3–6 after [135] are also lacking in this version.) Stravinsky revised the ending of the ballet when he prepared the piano-vocal score for publication. In the autograph fair copy of this score (now among the manuscripts deposited by J. & W. Chester at the British Library, Loan 75/42–43), the single measure of silence from the particell is the last measure of p. 184, the "extra" measure the first on p. 185. Repeated or omitted measures over a page turn being among the very commonest varieties of copying mistakes, it is altogether possible that the extra measure was introduced in this inadvertent way. But when Stravinsky prepared his final full score in 1923, he consciously chose to retain the measure, evidently regarding it as a "legitimate accident" of the kind he describes so compellingly in the *Poétique musicale*. He took it as a gift—whether to call it a gift from God or from Stravinsky's unconscious is up to us—and made us the gift of it in turn. Pierre Boulez was completely wrong to assume it was "merely" a mistake, even if it did originate as one; wrong to eliminate it from his recording of the work (Nonesuch H-71133); and wrong especially to attempt to persuade Stravinsky (as he is shown doing, with temporary success, in Rolf Liebermann's and Richard Leacock's documentary film "A Stravinsky Portrait," released in 1965) that it should be eliminated from the score for the sake of a consistency that is no less foolish for its being rational. As Imbrie makes affectingly clear, the measure, whatever its origins, is now one of *Svadebka*'s glories, and Stravinsky's insertion of it, whether a considered invention or only a decision to keep a fluky acquisition, was an utterly characteristic stroke of his artistic genius.

EXAMPLE 17.12

a. Stravinsky's notation of Theme M from Mitusov's dictation (Rothschild no. 87)

b. *Svadebka,* 4 after 120

c. *Svadebka,* 1 before 125, instruments only

EXAMPLE 17.12 (*continued*)

d. *Svadebka*, choral phrases at 3 after 130

The other source sketch for *Svadebka* consists of a long unbarred melody in the alto clef, with a text in Church Slavonic, copied out on a loose sheet (among the fragments gathered into a packet bearing Rothschild number R84). Robert Craft has identified it as a fifth-mode *dogmatik* from the *Oktoïkh*, or *Osmoglasiye*, the eight-week cycle of Russian medieval (i.e., "*znamennïy*") service chant, grouped according to the eight-mode musical system inherited in concept (if not in actual melodic content) from the Byzantine liturgy. Craft also indicated some of the ways in which Stravinsky derived the music between figs. [50] and [55] in the second tableau from this liturgical source.[63]

A *dogmatik*, or *bogorodichen* (from *Bogoroditsa*, Mother of God) is an invocation to the Virgin Mary (cf. the Greek Orthodox *Theotokion*) sung following the Doxology at the end of *Gospodi vozzvakh* (Ps. 140, "Lord, I cry unto Thee"), the opening psalm of the Slavonic Great Vespers. The particular one Stravinsky copied out comes from the Saturday evening service that inaugurates the fifth week of the *Oktoïkh* cycle, during which, as in every week of the cycle, all the proper chants share a particular fund of *popevki*. It is these, rather than a shared scale or final, that define a *glas* or mode within the musical system of the Orthodox church (cf. the Byzantine system of *echoi*). The text refers in typical fashion to Mary as a *brako-neiskusna nevesta,* a "bride undefiled," which may be what led to its selection (even

63. See Craft (with Harkins), "Stravinsky's *Svadebka*" (*NYRB*), 27–28; Craft, *Prejudices in Disguise,* 260–61; P&D:149–50.

though the bride is not mentioned in the *Svadebka* text at this point), just as the girls' invocation to the "*Bogorodicha*" (Pskov dialect) before fig. [53] was presumably responsible for the choice of a *bogorodichen* to begin with.[64]

The chant melody shown in Example 17.13a is taken not from Stravinsky's sketch directly, but from Nikolai Uspensky's transcription from the neumes of a manuscript of the late seventeenth century, now at the Leningrad Public Library.[65] The reason for the substitution is that the published transcription happens to agree with the pitch of Stravinsky's adaptations in *Svadebka*, making comparison easier. The chant is reproduced in the example up to the point where Stravinsky's copy of it (Ex. 17.13b) breaks off.

To use familiar plainsong terminology, Stravinsky has in effect "centonized" the old *znamennïy* chant, reshuffling its constituent *popevki* into a new configuration. By independent transposition of certain phrases, he has built a little responsorial *scena* from the abstracted chant motives, to which he set three different texts from Kireyevsky. This little *scena*—"which," as Craft notes, "is as close to a representation of the Orthodox service on the stage as Stravinsky ever came"[66]—was apparently intended as a whiff of the otherwise unrepresented *venchaniye*, the actual solemnizing of the marriage vows. The representation, however, is entirely in the music, not on the stage—or even in the text. Nor is the chant sung by the basses at fig. [50] any longer a recognizable Russian *dogmatik*. Rearranged and disguised, it has become part of the orthodox Turanian liturgy. Once again, to recall our epigraph, Belïy's "starting point" has been transmuted into his "finishing point" through the agency of Stravinsky's extraordinary powers of abstraction.

---

64. It is also quite possible that this sketch, and the music it spawned, were originally connected with the liturgical ballet Diaghilev commissioned from Stravinsky, Goncharova, and Leonid Massine in 1915. Despite his later vehement denials, Stravinsky did work on this piece for a time in the winter of 1915–16. The primary witness to this fact is C. Stanley Wise, both in his published "Impressions of Igor Strawinsky" (cf. p. 256: "The other important composition, to which he was giving much thought during this winter of 1915–1916, is of a religious character [*Liturgie*], but is not yet sufficiently advanced to be here described") and in an unpublished letter to Percy Scholes (cited above in note 8). The letter goes into considerable detail, the source of which could only have been the composer himself: "Miassine [*sic*] and Strawinsky . . . are collaborating in—I don't know what to call it—a sort of modern Passion Play. Strawinsky sums it up as a 'Liturgy.' It is to consist of a complete series of moving tableaux—one cannot call them ballets—giving the life of our Lord beginning with the Annunciation. The scenes will be separated from one another by vocal entr'actes (no orchestra) all of course liturgic in character which occasionally overlap the scenes. There will be something like 25 tableaux. They expect to produce this (as also 'Svadebka') in Paris next May—if war permits of performances there. I said to Strawinsky that I feared such a work might not be permitted in England (if they gave performances there too—as hoped) & he said—'I don't know about that but I am *sure* they will not allow it in Russia.' Both he and Miassine are treating it in a very reverent spirit but honestly I cannot fancy it myself—unless perhaps given all by itself with nothing even of the most serious kind either before or after it. . . . None of the music of the *Liturgie* has been written yet." This testimony from a source close to Stravinsky yet unconnected with Diaghilev gives strong credence to the latter's claim (e.g., to the *New York Post;* see note 9 above) that Stravinsky had accepted the commission. For the latter's point-blank denial, see Conv: 48/47.

65. N. D. Uspensky, *Obraztsï drevnerusskogo pevcheskogo iskusstva*, 2d ed. (Leningrad: Muzïka, 1971), 52–53.

66. Craft, "Stravinsky's *Svadebka*" (*NYRB*), 28.

EXAMPLE 17.13

a. *Dogmatik* (fifth *glas*) (trscr. N.D. Uspensky, *Obraztsï drevnerusskogo pevcheskogo iskusstva,* 2d ed. [Leningrad: Muzïka, 1971], 52–53), marked to show the use of its *popevki* in *Svadebka*

b. *Svadebka,* fig. 50, voice parts, marked to show derivation from the *dogmatik*

EXAMPLE 17.13b (*continued*)

A glance at the summary listing of themes in Table 4 will show how utterly unlike the rest of *Svadebka* this quasi-liturgical *scena* is, and again how unlikely it is that the more characteristic motifs in the work were—or needed to be—borrowed from any specific preexistent source. Except for the anomalous theme R′ (where the mode can be deduced only with considerable analytical effort), the liturgical chant as given in Example 17.13a represents the single instance in all *Svadebka* of an ungapped, fully articulated diatonic musical space.

Because of its ungapped (though incomplete) scale, and because of its seemingly closed, periodic, and cadential structure, theme F also stands out stylistically from the run of *Svadebka* tunes. The likelihood that it is a borrowed tune is very much enhanced by the notational appearance of what may be the earliest sketch for it, where it takes the form of a strophic melody set to the text of K828. The most telling aspect of the sketch is its disposition according to that peculiar lower-third doubling we have observed in the "Song of the Volochobniki" in *Petrushka,* in the "Volga Boatmen" harmonization, and in models for both of these in Rimsky-Korsakov, Musorgsky, and Balakirev. It is a specifically kuchkist device, and one Stravinsky seems to have applied mainly to borrowed material. At the pitch level shown in the sketch, and set to a truncated version of the same text, the song went into *Svadebka* at fig. [70] + 4; with the lower-third doubling (split between the choral basses divisi and the fourth piano) it turns up again at fig. [74] (Ex. 17.14).

Assuming it is a borrowed melody, what kind of melody is it? It could easily be another adapted *znamenniy* chant, which would have been appropriate to an invocation of SS. Cosmas and Damian. Although a search through the *Oktoïkh* did not turn up a melody coinciding exactly with the one Stravinsky used in *Svadebka,* a

EXAMPLE 17.14   Sketch (Rothschild no. 82) of setting of K828 (cf. *Svadebka*, fig. 21)

Ma - tush - ka, Kuz' - ma - Dem' - ya - na!   *(etc.)*

EXAMPLE 17.15   *Znamennïy* chant excerpts (from Uspensky, *Obraztsï*), transposed to pitch of Ex. 17.14

a. Preface (*Poglasitsa*) to the Invitatory Psalm (*Gospodi vozzvakh*), second *glas* (p. 25)

Le - sti-yu zmi-e - vo - yu rai - ski - ya pi - shchi li-shen.

b. *Dogmatik,* fourth *glas* (p. 45)

...na ra - mo vo-spri - i - - - - mǝ ...

c. Antiphon (*Stepenna*), fourth *glas* (p. 47)

Svya - tï - mǝ du - khom vsya - ka - ya du - sha

zhi - vi - - - tsya i chi - sto - to - yu vo-...

d. *Stikhira,* fifth *glas* (p. 52)

Che - stnï - mǝ tvo - i - - mǝ

EXAMPLE 17.16   *Bilina* melodies, transposed to pitch of Ex. 17.14

a. Rimsky-Korsakov, *100 Russian Folk Songs*, no. 1 ("*Kak vo gorode stol'no-kievskom*")

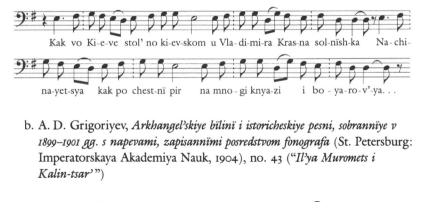

Kak vo Ki-e-ve stol' no ki-ev-skom u Vla-di-mi-ra Kras-na sol-nïsh-ka   Na-chi-

na-yet-sya   kak po chest-nï pir   na mno - gi knya-zi   i bo - ya-ro-v'-ya. . .

b. A. D. Grigoriyev, *Arkhangel'skiye bilinï i istoricheskiye pesni, sobrannïye v 1899–1901 gg. s napevami, zapisannïmi posredstvom fonografa* (St. Petersburg: Imperatorskaya Akademiya Nauk, 1904), no. 43 ("*Il'ya Muromets i Kalin-tsar'*")

Shto iz   da - le-tsya da iz tsi - sta po-lya, Iz to - go roz-dol'-ya shi-

- ro - ko-go,   Tut ne gruz-na tu-tsya pod - ni - ma - la-se, Tut. . .

wealth of *popevki* found there do conform to its modal type (i.e., [0 2 4 5] with cadence on 2). The last of the melodies given in Example 17.15 is found in the same service as the *dogmatik* on which Stravinsky drew for the second tableau.

Perhaps even closer to the *Svadebka* tune, because they are strophic, are the recitation formulas used by bards narrating the old Russian epics known as *bilinï*. Again, no exact coincidence has been uncovered, but at least two melodies Stravinsky might have known could have furnished him with a model for the tune (Ex. 17.16).

SCALE TYPES

With the exception of these liturgical and quasi-liturgical melodies, there is no tune in *Svadebka* that contains more than a single semitone. Hardly any melody in the score is ungapped, and many of the most conspicuous and characteristic ones (themes A, C, and O, for example) are anhemitonic. Even theme M, the Mitusov-imparted *protyazhnaya*, comprises a scale with only one semitone. Because its scale is gapped (at the pitch level dictated by Mitusov, the note G is missing for full diatonic representation), it is immaterial whether the key signature contains two sharps (as in Istomin/Dyutsh) or three (as Stravinsky took it down).

A whole category of tunes in *Svadebka* is of a type that might be termed "embellished anhemitonic." Their scales contain one semitone, but the pitch that creates it operates under restrictions that tend to subordinate that pitch structurally to one of its neighbors. The two widely separated melodic variants given in the table as E and E′ are both representative of an (0 3 5 8) anhemitonic scale, with an adjacency between 5 and 8 that functions either as an upper neighbor to 5 or as a descending (never ascending) passing tone. In no case is it ever approached by skip. Whether this embellishing tone is semitonally adjacent to 5 or to 8—that is, whether it should be represented as 6 (= F at the pitch level shown) or as 7 (= F♯) is immaterial to the mode's identity. That Stravinsky realized this is shown by the fact that he used these two melodies to carry two variants (one from Kireyevsky, the other from Tereshchenko) of a single song. Thus he clearly regarded the two tunes, despite the superficial difference in their scales, as variants of a single tune, representing a single anhemitonic pitch field with dissimilar embellishments.

For another example of this phenomenon, theme G belongs to the same modal type as themes E/E′. In it, the note E exists only as a descending pass between the structural, mode-defining pitches F and D. No other degree, even in this short *popevka,* is approached and quitted in only one way, which testifies to E's subordinate, embellishing status. The same can be said of the E in themes J/J′ and the B♭ in theme L. A slightly different picture is presented by themes K/K′. An initially ungapped anhemitonic trichord (0 2 4) picks up an upper semitonal adjacency as a way of marking its cadences. The basically anhemitonic character of the theme, in which the essential pitches are really only two (E and F♯, with D serving as a phrase articulator), is crucial to the way it functions in context within the second tableau.

In all cases where it is proposed that the modal type represented by a theme is "embellished anhemitonic," the theme is classified "A" (for anhemitonic) in Table 4, with the embellishing semitonal adjacency bracketed in the modal layout. It is important to note that these embellishing semitonal adjacencies are never applied to their governing pitches by direct upward step progression. That is to say, they never function as leading tones, hence never compromise the fundamentally neutral tonal status of the tunes in which they occur. As we shall see, this quality of acentric ambiguity, inherent in anhemitonic *popevki,* was especially important to Stravinsky when it came to constructing this particular score.[67] Thus there would

67. One may judge the prescience of Stravinsky's intuition in the matter of the "tonality" of Russian anhemitonic or diatonic *popevki* by comparing the remarks of the eminent Soviet ethnomusicologist Feodosiy Antonovich Rubtsov (1904–81), who in a ground-breaking essay of 1964 entitled "Principles of Modal Structure in Russian Folk Songs" promulgated as a novel theory the idea that "ordinary principles of modal structure, entailing the presence of a clear tonal center and modal tendencies that direct or restrain melodic motion, do not apply to the musical structure of ancient anhemitonic *napevi.* . . . A song melody may begin on any degree and end on any degree, depending on the meaning and purpose of the *napev*" (F. A. Rubtsov, "Osnovï ladovogo stroeniya russkikh narodnïkh pesen," in *Stat'i po muzïkal'nomu fol'kloru* [Leningrad: Sovetskiy Kompozitor, 1973], 37). Equally pertinent is Constantin Brailoiu's remarkably wide-ranging discussion of anhemitonic modes in his essay "Sur une

seem to be ample justification for the concept of "embellished anhemitony." If the category is accepted as coined for the purposes of this discussion, it transpires that most of the themes in *Svadebka* are anhemitonic. The first tableau, the modal character of which establishes the perceptual norms for the work as a whole, is in fact altogether dominated by anhemitonic themes.

Those who have noted the prevalence of anhemitony in *Svadebka* have been inclined to relate it to what they have seen as an archaizing tendency. Victor Belyayev, author of the earliest published analysis of the score, who perhaps hyperbolically asserted the (0 3 5) configuration to be "the fundamental motif from which the whole of its melos is developed," identified that melos explicitly with "the old way of Russian life."[68] Asafyev, in his turn, made much of the "union of archaic musical elements with formal principles derived . . . from the Renaissance."[69] Asafyev's reference to "Renaissance" principles has to do with his strange notion that *Svadebka* was modeled on "the old madrigal comedies of the seventeenth [*sic*] century (like the *Amfiparnasso* of Orazio Vecchi)."[70] Alfredo Casella, too, had likened *Svadebka* to *L'Amfiparnasso,* which caused Craft to wonder whether the "farfetched comparison" had not been "suggested by Stravinsky himself, who was fond of throwing out false scents of this kind."[71] The early-Soviet perspective certainly contributed to the widespread exaggeration of the archaism in *Svadebka,* which, though inherent in the subject matter, is not underscored in the music. Least of all is archaism implied by anhemitony; *The Rite of Spring,* the very locus classicus of archaistic folklore, contains far less of it than *Svadebka.*

Rather, it seems that Stravinsky's preference for anhemitony in the later score had primarily a technical stimulus. Although the anhemitonic motives in *Svadebka* may have been prompted in the first instance by Dahl's description of the three-tone *plach* (which the composer inevitably associated with the gapped minor tetrachord [0 (2) 3 5] he had already exploited so extensively in *The Rite*), what accounted for their prevalence in the end was their suitability to the all-embracing tonal system Stravinsky devised for the score, one of his greatest, if hidden, achievements. Through it, Stravinsky solved once and for all the central problem of his "Swiss" period, namely, that of forging a distinctive yet "authentic" Turanian style.

He did it by fusing all that was irreducibly non-"European" within his stylistic reach, encompassing both his newly acquired "folk" heritage and the older heri-

---

mélodie russe," in *Musique russe,* ed. Pierre Souvtchinsky (Paris: Presses Universitaires de France, 1953), 2:329–92.

68. Belaiev, *Igor Stravinsky's "Les Noces,"* table of contents and p. 2. This analysis was not published in its original language until 1972 (in V. M. Belyayev, *Musorgskiy, Skryabin, Stravinskiy: sbornik statey* [Moscow: Muzïka]). Stravinsky's predictably dismissive reactions to Belyayev's book are recorded by Craft in P&D:618n.233. What is interesting about them is that Stravinsky did not reject the terms of Belyayev's quaint harmonic analysis, but merely "corrected" its details.

69. Asafyev, *A Book About Stravinsky,* 129.

70. Ibid., 133.

71. P&D:619n.236.

tage of his Belyayevets training. The fusion took the form of an octatonic/diatonic interaction of unprecedented scope, depth, and integrity, one that governed all aspects of tonal organization within this greatest of all neonationalist scores. What made anhemitonic melodic constructs indispensable to this scheme was precisely their tonally suspensive character, the absence of semitones barring implicit cadential functions (at least in the ordinary "Western" sense), thus rendering the melodic surface of the score "non-progressive" and "non-implicative," as one perceptive writer has termed it.[72] By using melodies devoid of inherent tonal orientation at the surface of his score, Stravinsky avoided contradiction with the symmetrically conceived and apportioned ground plan it will now be our business to uncover and describe.

THE FINISHING POINT

If nothing else, the experience of composing *The Rite of Spring* taught Stravinsky to regard the (0 2 3 5) T-S-T tetrachord as the most potent agent of linearly conceived diatonic/octatonic interpenetration. Replicated disjunctly at the major second it produces what Mily Balakirev called the "Russian minor," known familiarly to the West as the Dorian mode. At the minor second the tetrachord generates the octatonic scale. The tetrachord being intervallically palindromic (that is, self-replicating or invariant when reversed or inverted), the octave species it generates are likewise self-inverting. The Dorian scale happens to be the one diatonic scale that exhibits this symmetrical structure. As in the case of the octatonic scale, all its modal properties hold true whether one "reads up" or "reads down." Here we already have the nub of the matrix that generated the melodic/harmonic texture of *Svadebka* (Ex. 17.17).

Example 17.17 is notated at the pitch of theme A, the bride's *plach*, so as to facilitate a number of preliminary observations, including the derivation of the first harmony in *Svadebka* (disregarding the percussive acciaccaturas at the very beginning). At fig. [1], the entering pianos harmonize the melody of the *plach*, whose tones are found within the upper tetrachord of the diatonic scales given in the example, with the pitches that enclose its octatonic complement, as shown in scale no. 4. The nature of the spacing here, with the fourth inverted to a fifth, suggests another sort of enclosure, or infixing—that is, the bounding of the *plach* tetrachord by the defining pitches of the complementary tetrachord, both of which are semitonally adjacent to an outer pitch of the *plach* (Ex. 17.18).

72. David Schulenberg, "Modes, Prolongations, and Analysis," *Journal of Musicology* 4 (1985–86): 324. Tonal "implication" in *Svadebka* comes about, on those rare occasions where Stravinsky resorts to it, by specific gesture. One example—possibly the only one of its kind in the score—comes after fig. [8] in the first tableau, where the bridesmaids finish K636 with an obvious cadential flourish that identifies E as the tonic of the soon-to-be-superseded first section of the piece. This gesture seems a vestige of a kind of quasi-tonal thinking Stravinsky would abandon as he worked further into the score, and as he evolved the ground plan we shall be tracing, which obviates the necessity for such explicitly cadential tonal references (see Ex. 17.34d on p. 1409).

EXAMPLE 17.17   Diatonic and octatonic scales formed from T-S-T tetrachords

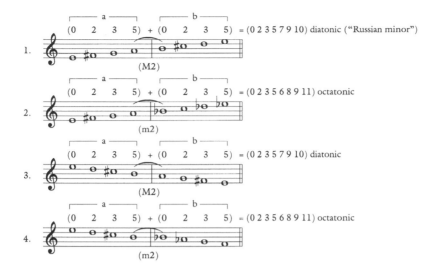

EXAMPLE 17.18   *Svadebka,* fig. 1 (tetrachordal partition of Scale 4)

EXAMPLE 17.19 An early sketch for the opening *plach* (Rothschild no. 82)

Ko - sa   mo - ya ko - sïn - ka   ru - sa - ya

EXAMPLE 17.20 An early setting of K438 (Sketchbook Rothschild no. 87)

Okh, na iz - be — zel' —— ya, Uv · ïz - be ve - sel' - ya

Thus the *plach* tetrachord is harmonically embellished by its octatonic complement even as its melodic embellishment (the grace note F♯) is drawn from its diatonic complement. In a small way this "polytonal" example illustrates the basic principle of harmonic/contrapuntal construction in this score—the superimposition of two pitch fields that intersect around the notes of the *plach*. By the time of *Svadebka* such devices were hardly finds; they were surface manifestations of an absolutely assimilated and taken-for-granted background theory of diatonic/octatonic interaction. Another such routine determined the extension of the *plach* motive, on its reappearance in the fourth tableau, through two additional pitches that just happen to complete the pentachord common to the diatonic and octatonic collections (with E as zero: 0 3 5 6 8 [see theme A′ in Table 4]; for white-key representation the zero-pitch should be B, the octatonic collection of reference then becoming Collection I). We have previously encountered this particular "pun" in the *Baika* (see Exx. 16.25 and 16.26). It is hard to say which usage came first, since the *Baika* was composed later than the first tableau of *Svadebka,* when the motive and its extensions were conceived, but earlier than the fourth tableau, when the device actually makes its appearance in the score. In any case, lest there be any lingering doubt as to whether the theme marked A′ in Table 4 is really a variant of theme A, consider Example 17.19, a very early sketch for the *plach* motive.

At the point where theme A′ is first introduced—that is, the big polythematic contrapuntal clot at fig. [93]—octatonic and diatonic melodies are indeed concatenated; moreover, diatonic and octatonic versions of a single theme (the "berry" tune, N/N′) sound simultaneously. It is surely significant that what appears to be the earliest sketch for theme N, the main unifying theme in the early stages of the fourth tableau, should have been made not at the pitch level of the finished score, but at that of our "matrix" as given in Example 17.17. The sketch (Ex. 17.20) consists of a melodic jotting entered alongside the text of K438, to which it is sung at fig. [119]. It is equally significant, of course, that the eventual pitch destination of theme N (starting on D♭/C♯) lies along the same (0 3 6 9) axis as the pitch of the sketch. The tune as given in Example 17.20 conforms to the pitch content of the diatonic collection represented by scales 1 and 3 in Example 17.17. Its octatonic variant—the unique instance of such "intercollectional" thematic transformation in the score—partakes of the pitch content of scale 4, as does theme P, the only other octatonic melody in the fourth tableau.

As for scale 2 in Example 17.17, the "ascending" octatonic extension of the focal *plach* tetrachord, it coincides with the pitch content of the most important octatonic theme in *Svadebka,* the parental lament (theme I), another *plach.* This theme (plus the piano accompaniment, which supplies in the form of an ostinato the two pitches required to exhaust the scale of reference) was incidentally the one from which Arthur Berger inferred the octatonic scale as a referential collection for Stravinsky's music in his historic article of 1963.[73] The way the collection is partitioned in this melody/accompaniment complex quite ingeniously disguises the derivation proposed in Example 17.17—that is, from the minor tetrachord on E. But the derivation is indeed demonstrable (and "functional") when the theme (in its variant form I') returns at the end of the third tableau to finish the whole "First Part" of the ballet.

It comes as a poignant coda following the magnificent choral yawp that greets the symbolic confluence of the "two rivers." That climax, we may recall, had been built on a diatonic motif abstracted from a variant of the Mitusov tune (theme M″ in Table 4), pitched so that it may be referred to the diatonic scales in Example 17.17. At the moment of the bride's departure, the chorus extends the final syllable of its song in an ecstatic melisma that consists of an oscillation between their melody's final, A, and a newly introduced B (see figs. [80]ff.). These are the boundary pitches that mark off the tetrachords of the diatonic scales in Example 17.17.

The joint between yawp and lament is signaled by an abrupt shift (at fig. [82]) to an oscillation between A and B♭—the boundary pitches between the tetrachords of scale 2 in Example 17.17. The transition between themes and between collections, coinciding with the huge emotional wrench on stage, thus takes the form of a palpable semitonal contraction, precisely as suggested by the tetrachordal schemata in Example 17.17. The tone common to both scale-defining oscillations, A, thus takes on, ineluctably, the role of a center—or at least a focal pitch—as Berger indeed noted (if for other reasons).

Having observed this much (and recalling the way the diatonic grace notes had been made to coexist peaceably with the octatonic harmony at fig. [1] on the basis of the focal status of the upper tetrachord of scale 3), we may go on to note the similar interaction that takes place between figs. [35] and [39] in the second tableau. Berger, defending his identification of the octatonic scale as the "single referential collection" accounting for the "total pitch content" of the passage domi-

73. For the relevant discussion, see Berger, "Problems of Pitch Organization," 130–31.

nated by theme I, conceded the presence of "a few exceptions so marginal as scarcely to require mention (some dozen tones, mainly ornamental)."[74] These foreign tones all occur in lines set in counterpoint against theme I, as shown in Example 17.21. It is hard to know precisely in what way these pitches are ornamental; but Example 17.17 furnishes a means of accounting for them. In Example 17.21a, the extraneous pitch (B) is part of a diatonic *popevka* referable to scale 1 and hence related to the octatonic main theme (derived from scale 2) by virtue of their common possession of the all-important T-S-T tetrachord on E. Stravinsky's contrapuntal usage here points up the kinship between the octatonic and diatonic sets as extensions of the same tonality-defining basic tetrachordal cell, precisely as illustrated in Example 17.17. In Example 17.21b, both elements, octatonic and diatonic alike, have been transposed by minor thirds (i.e., one notch along the [0 3 6 9] cycle of nodes), albeit in opposite directions. Under such a transposition, of course, the pitch content of the octatonic component is invariant. The diatonic counterpoint, while no longer referable to any single scale in Example 17.17, remains referable to scale 2 except for the newly introduced "foreign" pitch, *D* (referable to scale 1), seen now as the product of a transposition.

A similar octatonic/diatonic interaction, involving one of *Svadebka*'s most prominent anhemitonic *popevki,* may be observed at figs. [68]ff. There theme C is initiated by the bass soloist at the pitch level originally associated with theme A: that is, on an (0 3 5) configuration referable to the generating tetrachord of scale 3 in Example 17.17. The *popevka* is immediately taken through a complete (0 3 6 9) rotation that implicates and exhausts scale 4, the "descending" octatonic collection cognate to scale 3 (Ex. 17.22a). The pianos, meanwhile, are noodling an ostinato, the bass of which sums up the (0 3 6 9) nodes of scale 4 (reading up from the bottom), coinciding with the starting pitches of each transposition of the *popevka.* (The two seemingly extraneous pitches in the middle of the texture, C and F♯, are borrowed from the reciprocal "ascending" octatonic scale around the same nodes, i.e., scale 2 in Example 17.17.)

The newsworthy event here is what happens at fig. [69]: the mezzo-soprano soloist chimes in with a transposition of theme C beginning on F♯. The constituent notes of the resulting *popevka*—D♯, F♯, G♯—are not to be found in any one scale in Example 17.17. They do, however, link up with the particular transposition of the same *popevka* running concurrently above and below the "foreign" element in the soprano and tenor parts, to form an anhemitonic subset of scale 1 at an (0 3 6 9) nodal transposition precisely analogous to that of the soprano's *popevka* at [69]+2 vis-à-vis the initiating pitch level in the bass (Ex. 17.22b).

To this observation we may add the striking fact that the groom's concluding address to the bride, which is based on a cyclic reprise of the bride's opening *plach,*

74. Ibid., 132.

EXAMPLE 17.21

a. *Svadebka,* 5 after 36 (pitches foreign to scale 2 circled)

b. *Svadebka,* fig. 38 (foreign pitches circled)

EXAMPLE 17.22 Scalar derivation of music at 68 ff.

a. Scale 4

b. Scale 3, t9 (down m3)

is pitched at the level of the first transposition shown in Example 17.22a, and the tintinnabulating instrumental coda that derives from it is harmonized exclusively with pitches referable to an anhemitonic subset of the scale given in Example 17.22b. The two "ornamental" tones in the voice part—E and D, applied as an anacrusis to C♯ (cf. theme A′ in Table 4, also Ex. 17.19 above)—derive from scale 4 (see Ex. 17.23). The whole ending tonality of the score, then, is adumbrated in the mezzo's strange entrance at [69].

EXAMPLE 17.23   Ending of *Svadebka,* scalar analysis

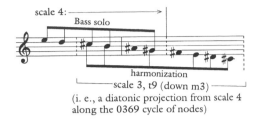

All these wide-ranging, seemingly desultory observations, drawn from all four tableaux, are actually leading in a single very interesting direction. They seem to identify the array presented in Example 17.17 as something more than just a heuristic tool. We seem, in fact, to be on the way to uncovering a master *complexe sonore,* comparable to the one discussed in connection with "Chez Pétrouchka" (Chapter 10), that governs, at both short range and long, the pitch relations of the entire work. The difference is that the octatonic/diatonic tonality-defining interactions governed by the *Petrushka* complex had mainly to do with triadic harmony, whereas those in *Svadebka* have to do with melodic configurations (i.e., "modes") based on the T-S-T tetrachord.

What we have observed so far about transpositions in *Svadebka* suggests that, unsurprisingly, Stravinsky viewed his diatonic *popevki* and their implied scales within an octatonic perspective. That is, he considered them not as discrete entities but as elements in a perpetual state of potential symmetrical rotation around the tonal matrix implied by the (0 3 6 9) octatonic nodes. Hence, in order fully to represent the *complexe sonore* governing *Svadebka,* the Dorian scales in Example 17.17 have to be conceptualized in terms of a complete fourfold (0 3 6 9) transpositional array. This complex may be looked upon as a mapping of symmetrical diatonic scales onto the octatonic background represented by the scales 2 and 4 in Example 17.17. Since the nodes of both the ascending and the descending scales are the same, either an ascending or a descending representation of the mapping process will have an identical pitch content so far as the diatonic projections are concerned (Ex. 17.24).

As newly charted in Example 17.24, the "alpha-scale" (henceforth scale α) seems to be identical to what has up to now been designated scale 1. However, scale 1 was an ascending sequence only, while scale α is more properly (and neutrally) a collection, encompassing both scale 1 and its descending counterpart, scale 3. As Example 17.24 suggests, one need only imagine an array of descending Dorian scales (replications of scale 3 at the [0 3 6 9] nodes) mapped onto scale 4 in order to have

EXAMPLE 17.24   Diatonic projections from scale 2 (identical scales descend from scale 4)

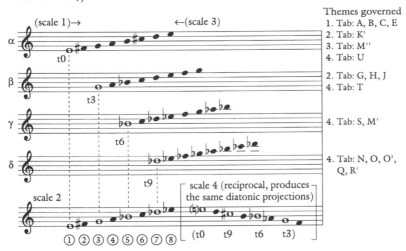

a technically complete, though in practice redundant, representation of the *complexe sonore* that governs Stravinsky's neonationalist masterpiece.

Viewed this way, the fourfold diatonic array (scales α through δ) represents not four different keys but four functionally equivalent diatonic projections of a single (0 3 6 9) matrix. Neither are the starting and finishing notes of their graphic representation (i.e., the nodal points) to be regarded as tonics a priori, since the intervallic structure of the various *popevki* derived from these scales is designed, as we have seen, to preclude such an implication. By the same token, the two octatonic scales are best regarded not as representing "Collection I" (descending) and "Collection III" (ascending), but (like the "melody" and "harmony" scales of earlier Russian practice) simply as alternative ways of filling out the same cycle of (0 3 6 9) nodes. Thus, despite the differing local pitch collections, it can be said that *Svadebka* begins and ends in the same tonality, in the sense developed for "Chez Pétrouchka" in Chapter 10, whereby an octatonic *complexe sonore* (there a complex of triads, here a complex of diatonic scales) can be viewed as a single pitch field with multiple local surface projections. By means of strategic, controlled departures and returns, such a complex can be made to comprehend a functionally unified tonal system.

A sense of tonal motion can be achieved by means of transitions ("modulations") among the diatonic nodal projections (scales α through δ). And in fact such modulation turns out to be the primary means of tonally articulating and differentiating the four tableaux, providing the "true" divisions discussed earlier, as opposed to the superficial demarcations indicated in the score. The main themes of the first (bride's) tableau—themes A, B, C, and E, plus the nonrecurrent material at fig. [12]—are all referable to scale α. Those in the first part of the second (groom's) tableau (through fig. [50])—themes G, H, and J—all refer to the "beta-scale" (scale β), representing the next "higher" notch along the (0 3 6 9) circle. The second part of the second tableau, while it contains music beholden both to scale α (theme K) and to scale β (the nonrecurrent material between [59] and [61]), also contains the most extended apparent departure from the governing *complexe sonore*—something to which we will return.

The third tableau is dominated, like the first, by scale α (we are back at the bride's), except for the octatonic/diatonic rotation between [68] and [70], already discussed, and the octatonic mothers' lament at the end. Especially noteworthy are the contrapuntal overlays of themes—all referable to scale α—between [70] and [74]. The only new theme in this tableau, Theme M″, is also composed, as we have seen, of pitches from scale α.

The fourth tableau places greatest emphasis on the "delta-scale" (scale δ), which occupies a position as far "down" the (0 3 6 9) circle from α as β is "up." It may be regarded, then, as scale β's reciprocal. Themes N and O, the ritornelli that dominate the early part of the tableau, are introduced within the tonal orbit of scale δ, though they both make appearances in other pitch fields (O′ at fig. [106] refers to scale β; N plus O at [128] + 3 refers to the elusive "gamma-scale" [scale γ]). Themes Q and R′ also being derived from scale δ, and theme A′ making both its first (fig. [93]) and its final appearances within that collection of reference (though not at the same pitch level), it is arguable that the fourth tableau is as much "in" scale δ as the first and third are "in" scale α and the second starts "in" scale β.

The harmonic rhythm of the fourth tableau is much the fastest, though, and the focal scale vies with competitors both from within the governing *complexe sonore* and from without. Scale γ makes its only appearances at the *Krasnïy stol*. The nonrecurrent melodic material following [94], although it is mainly derived from an anhemitonic (0 3 5) trichord—A♯(B♭)/C♯(D♭)/D♯(E♭)—that is held by scales γ and δ in common, must be ascribed to the latter scale because of the punctuating F♯'s, which are found only in scale δ. The material at [98] (theme S), in complement, can be referred only to scale γ. The theme is quickly involved in a regular (0 3 6 9) rotation, flanked by statements at the upper and the lower third (Ex. 17.25).

Scale γ comes briefly into its own at fig. [110], where it is entrusted with the first statement of theme M′, which will eventually support the climax of the whole ballet (see Table 4). The theme never comes back in this tonality, though, and except for the brief return of themes N and O after [128], scale γ is not heard again. The relatively short shrift given this scale in Stravinsky's deployment of his *complexe sonore* enhances the status of scale α, its tritone antipode, as first among equals, shadowed on either side by scales β ("above") and δ ("below"). By providing a point of equilibrium between its shadows, scale α comes to connote harmonic repose.

EXAMPLE 17.25   *Svadebka*, 3 after 98 (analysis of tetrachordal structure)

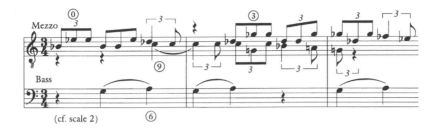

Its primacy is asserted in another way as well, one that will entail a further refinement in our representation of the *complexe sonore*. Besides the diatonic scales in their normal forms as represented in Example 17.24, which we may term "authentic," Stravinsky makes occasional telling use of modal extensions, whereby an extra T-S-T tetrachord is attached at the lower or the upper end to form a new scale (Ex. 17.26). On a loose analogy with medieval mode theory, we may designate these extensions "plagal" and "pluperfect," respectively. (On an even looser analogy with the theory of the *znamenniy* chant, they could be called "dark" and "thrice-bright.")

In principle these extensions could be applied to any of the four diatonic scales in the *complexe sonore* (or even to the octatonic ones, for all the difference it would make), and each of the four does undergo extension at some point. Theme L, for example, on its first appearance (bass solo at [53]), employs the plagal extension of scale β (see Table 4 to verify its pitch content); theme A′ appears at [131] + 4 in γ-plagal; theme D, as well as its nonrecurrent continuation beginning at fig. [16] in the first tableau, implicates δ-plagal. These are sporadic events, however, and transient, without long-range significance for the tonal structure of the ballet.

It is another matter with the basic scale, α. Its modal extensions are numerous, recurrent, and thematically significant. Moreover, they provide Stravinsky with the means to achieve a grandiose tonal climax at the conclusion of the fourth tableau.

The plagal extension is heard frequently throughout Part One of the score, encompassing the first three tableaux. Its initial appearance occurs in the tenor solo (the bride's mother) at fig. [21]. The fact that Stravinsky doubles it at the lower fourth at [23] proves its "plagal" status: the part sung by the bass is in α-authentic, and the doubling underscores the modal affinity. Not only that, but the theme is actually recapitulated within the authentic scale at fig. [74] in the third tableau. (The soprano part at [21] could be construed within α-plagal as well as α-

EXAMPLE 17.26 Upper and lower extensions of scales derived in Ex. 17.24

authentic; as long as neither member of the pair C/C♯ occurs, its status is moot.) The bride's solo at [25] is completely within α-plagal, here coexisting with the authentic scale in the choral parts. Again, the replication of melodic elements of theme B at the upper fourth demonstrates the nature of the plagal scale's affinity with its authentic prototype.

The women's responses to the bass duet at [51] and [52] can be construed as belonging to the plagal variant of the α-scale; though, being derived from a *znamenniy* chant melody, they are perhaps sooner viewed as segmenting the latter's uniquely complete white-key scale. There can be no question, though, about the modal status of the tenor solo at fig. [58], which consists of a transposition of theme L as originally stated by the bass at [53]. There the theme had invoked β-plagal; here it is α-plagal, which is resumed at fig. [62] and carries the second tableau (over a basso ostinato referable to octatonic scale 2) to its climactic conclusion.

In the third tableau α-plagal asserts itself briefly at [74]+5 in opposition to its own authentic form, and also in opposition to scale δ at [75]. This little phrase sets a powerful precedent, for it allows us to reinterpret the climax of the tableau at [78]ff. as α-plagal rather than α-authentic, despite the fact that the melody does not contain any C-naturals, by which the plagal form is most readily distinguished from the authentic. The emphasis given the pitch A, the bottom note of the downward-extending tetrachord, tends to identify the mode as plagal; besides, C-

EXAMPLE 17.27 *Svadebka*, fig. [97]

naturals are conspicuously present in the accompaniment, the harmonic structure of which strongly recalls the ostinato at the end of the second tableau. This association of endings was an important factor for interpreting the ballet's musico-dramatic meanings. Both for that reason and for reasons that will emerge from an analysis of the harmonic structure of the fourth tableau, it will be advantageous to regard the climax of the third as plagal.

The climax of the fourth tableau is very elaborately prepared. Scale δ having been established as undisputed local governor at the outset (fig. [87]), its hegemony is challenged in the remarkable passage at [92], in which choral parts based on scale α are accompanied by a bass line drawn from scale γ, its tritone antipode. (The "upper voice" of the accompaniment here consists of neutral, hence mediating, octatonic material carried over from the passage at [91], based on theme P.) By the use of α and γ in this unique conjunction, scale δ has been "encircled" (Ex. 17.27).

The choral material is obviously related to themes A/A'; indeed, once theme A' has surfaced in the choral parts at [114], it remains linked with its "home" scale (though not without admixtures—viz., the upper neighbors G–F from its octatonic parent, scale 4). Fig. [114] initiates a thirty-three-bar passage that is indubitably and exclusively referable to scale α. It includes some nonrecurrent choral material that is accompanied by theme A′ in the pianos (figs. [115]–[117]), followed by theme U at [117] (first heard at [111], also on scale α). At fig. [119] scale δ attempts a comeback via theme N, only to be rebuffed once again by theme A′ in its home scale ([121], including a nonrecurrent choral ostinato). At [122], theme A′ is unexpectedly usurped by scale γ at the antipodal tritone. It will never sound again in the home scale. Indeed, at fig. [126] (pianos), it is acquired by scale δ, with which it had formerly contended, and there it will remain (though not on the same pitches) for the groom's grand peroration at [133].[75]

Why the sudden switch? It has to do with a third element, one that since fig. [110] had been vying for thematic dominance with themes N and A′: the Mitusov tune (theme M′). At first the strategic inconspicuousness of the Mitusov tune is enhanced by its being cast in the tonally peripheral orbit of scale γ. Very quickly, though, it is brought into more central tonal ground; all future statements of the climactic theme (beginning with the bass solo at [111] + 6) will invoke scales β or α. The first statement of theme M′ on α comes at fig. [120]—right before theme A′ departs that scale. In effect, the position of theme A′ as representative of scale α has been preempted.

———————

From this point on the place of theme M′—and with it, of scale α—at center stage is vigorously upheld and reinforced. The reinforcement consists in the elaborate mirroring of scale α with its plagal and, for once, pluperfect extensions. The use of the latter, being the unique occurrence of a "thrice-bright" region in the entire score, lends the final measure of exaltation to the crowning moment, especially by comparison with the climax of Part One at the end of the third tableau, which had taken place in the plagal realm.

The mirroring process works as follows. At fig. [120], the bass soloist enters with theme M′ in the plagal extension of scale α. After two measures, half of the choral basses intrude with a continuation of the theme in the authentic scale, which runs briefly in canon with the plagal form of the tune before the two join in characteristic parallel motion at the end (Ex. 17.28a; the situation is reminiscent of the treatment of theme F at [23]). At [124] the tenor sounds the theme for the last time on scale β before it is remanded once and for all to scale α. One measure before [125], the instruments, in their one explosive solo measure, strike up the

75. It has already been observed that in between, at [131] + 5, theme A′ sounds briefly in the plagal extension of scale γ, a rare tonality chosen apparently for its local pitch variance against its immediate context; see below.

EXAMPLE 17.28   Interplay of scale forms at climax of fourth tableau

a.

b.

c.

(*continued*)

EXAMPLE 17.28C *(continued)*

tune in the plagal before shifting abruptly into the pluperfect (Ex. 17.28b; the focal note E furnishes the pivot, provided courtesy of the "erroneous" leap of a major sixth). The whole climactic passage, from [130] to [133], is devoted to multiple statements of theme M′, the latter being buffeted like a soccer ball from one modal region to another (Ex. 17.28c), sometimes with the help of pivots like the one introduced at [125]. The reiterated use of B as cadential pitch implies the culminating ascendency of the pluperfect mode.

Example 17.28c is especially revealing of the way Stravinsky exploits his modal scales as dramatic foils. Between [131] and [132] he dips unexpectedly into the plagal region, and even beyond it to scale β, meanwhile bringing in theme A′ in an extremely remote pitch area (underscoring in yet another way the dramatic situation: this is the passage construed above as the bride's precoital resistance). The harmonic region—the plagal form of scale γ—could not be more remote: the pitches to which motive A′ is sung here are not present in the authentic or pluperfect forms of scale α, to which the passage from [130] to [133] is otherwise exclusively confined (the remaining such pitch, B♭, is found in scale β, which must be why that scale is momentarily invoked right before fig. [132]). Thus the reassertion of α- pluperfect at [132] comes as a fresh jolt that enhances the sense of its brilliance beyond anything that had gone before. Scale α, the scale that had started *Svadebka* on its way, returns in glory at the end, rounding off what is tonally one of the most original and compellingly unified scores Stravinsky ever composed.

<hr/>

At the broadest level, the tonal flow of *Svadebka* may be compared with the movement of a pendulum: beginning stably within scale α (first tableau), the tonal pendulum swings out to a position of greater tension or potential energy along the (0 3 6 9) circle to scale β (first half of the second tableau); regains equilibrium by returning to scale α (end of the second tableau and into the third), its "downward" motion emphasized by the plagal region; swings out again in the opposite direction to scale δ (first part of the fourth tableau); finally regains equilibrium triumphantly at the climax of the fourth tableau, its "upward" kinetic swing dramatized by the use of the pluperfect form of the concluding tonal region.

The tones of the groom's final address to the bride, though related earlier to scale δ (then called scale 3 at t9), can also be referred to the tonally neutral descending octatonic (scale 4), out of which the opening bridal *plach* had been constructed, thus bringing things emphatically full circle. The ambiguity created by the harmonization, which refers exclusively to scale δ, can be construed as a reinforcement of cyclicity through the explicit denial of the sense of an ending, a reading amply supported by the bell sonorities, which, as so often pointed out, symbolize the everlasting cycle of church sacraments, of which marriage is but one, and thus bracket the whole foregoing action within the perpetual round of birth and death.

The tonal plan uncovered and described here must be sharply distinguished from the usual concept of a functional harmonic plan, on the one hand, and from a system of keys, on the other. It is worth reiterating that the four scales on which *Svadebka* is built have little in common with what is usually meant by a key, for there is no basis for assigning pitch priority either within the diatonic pitch collections themselves or, in most cases, within the individual *popevki* that are extracted from them. Indeed, as we know, the intervallic structure of the *popevki* is expressly designed to preclude the establishment of priority by any but factitious means; in different environments, one and the same *popevka* can admit a variety of centric assignments or scalar referents.

Individual *popevki*, moreover, can appear at various pitch levels within a given scale, sometimes with altered intervallic content, sometimes not, but such trans-

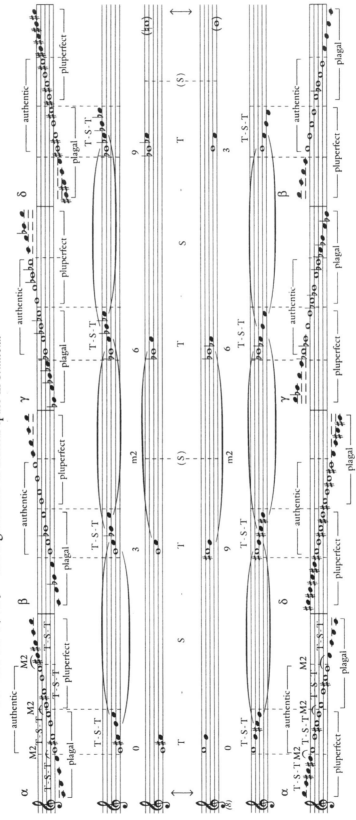

EXAMPLE 17.29   The organization of musical space in *Svadebka*

positions do not as a rule effect any change in tonal implication. Compare, for example, the various pitch levels at which "authentic" tune fragments appear before and after [131] in Ex. 17.28c, or the statements of theme C at [9] or at [11]+3 (soprano) in the first tableau.

In sum, the degrees of the four basic diatonic scales in *Svadebka*, unlike the degrees in any tonal, key-defining scale, are not functionally differentiated a priori. Rather than keys, then, the four *Svadebka* scales represent four diatonic projections from a single octatonic background matrix—four quadrants, so to speak, of a symmetrically (hence nonhierarchically) apportioned musical space, depicted at last in fully elaborated form in Example 17.29.

Thus, although *Svadebka* contains relatively little surface "octatonicism," the deeper structure that rules the variegated diatonic surface is more thoroughly and systematically derived from a single (0 3 6 9) octatonic matrix than that of any other Stravinsky composition of comparable size and scope. Background matrix and diatonic surface are linked by the ubiquitous T-S-T tetrachords. The lower tetrachord in each "authentic" diatonic scale (= the upper tetrachord in the "plagal" scales) is referable to the "ascending" octatonic background scale; the upper authentic tetrachords (= lower "pluperfect" tetrachords) refer to the "descending" background scale. One can say of the octatonics in *Svadebka* what was said in an earlier chapter about the folklorism of *The Rite:* Elements that had at first played gaudily on the surface have been submerged to work their influence at the deepest strata of structure and style; and the deeper they went—the more they thus, as it were, receded from view—the more pervasive and determinant did their influence become.

A REALIBUS AD REALIORA

Since the disposition of symmetrical musical space arises in *Svadebka* out of tetrachordal rather than triadic partitioning of the octatonic collection, it follows that the structure of the music is articulated essentially by melodic means—which is to say, by the "top line." In any analytically meaningful sense, *Svadebka* is a fundamentally monodic, or at best a heterophonic, composition. This is its most quintessentially Turanian feature and its most significant departure from the norms of traditional Western practice.

However beautifully crafted, then, however variegated, however strongly it may support or enhance the melodic parts, harmony in this score remains at all times structurally subordinate to those parts, if not altogether incidental. No aspect of *Svadebka*'s texture has less bearing on its tonal coherence than its "bass line," such as it is. With only the rarest exceptions the harmony is a surface veneer, a "color." Thus to approach the analysis of this composition with the normative assumptions one brings to the analysis of harmonically conceived music in the European tradition is virtually to guarantee bewilderment, as will any approach that insists on treating the texture of the work holistically, the way most standard analytical methodologies prescribe a priori.

But even if only an embellishment, the multifarious harmonic operations Stravinsky contrived to set off the structural surface are indeed a superb enhancement that invites and repays investigation. Five distinct harmonic idioms may be distinguished in *Svadebka*. Those most directly related to its structural principles are the ones involving the verticalization of its salient melodic formations—purely diatonic (often anhemitonic) chord configurations on the one hand, and octatonically referable "polyharmonies" on the other. A far less essential role is played by occasional, though sometimes very conspicuous, patches of triadic harmony. The familiar Stravinskian device of acciaccatura-enriched monody is also extensively used, and acciaccaturas are a ubiquitous condiment that add piquancy to the other harmonic schemes as well. Finally, there is perhaps a greater emphasis than in any other extended Stravinsky composition on parallelisms of all kinds.

Of the five idioms, the purely octatonic constructs need detain us least. By the time of *Svadebka* they were *vieux jeu*. The most salient octatonic passages have in any case already been noted: the harmonization of the bridal *plach* near the beginning of the first tableau, the passages based on theme I/I′ in the second and third, the rotation of the theme C *popevka* at figs. [68]–[72]. Also noteworthy is the harmonization of K636 near the beginning of the second tableau (figs. [29], [31], [34]), strikingly intercut with the diatonic harmonization of K569. Here, a melody referable to scale β (authentic) is accompanied by a noodling pattern mainly derived from the "ascending" octatonic collection in our matrix, with characteristic emphasis on the *Rite of Spring*–ish (0 11) span defined by the top of the T-S-T tetrachord the two scales have in common: viz., the defining C plus an auxiliary D♭, functioning in tandem as a static eighth-note pulsation (Ex. 17.30).

Two further points concerning surface octatonicism demand elaboration. First, Stravinsky was fully aware of the complementary relationship between the "ascending" and "descending" octatonic scales at the heart of his conception (scales 2 and 4 in Example 17.17), and of its potential for compositional development. Numerous passages in *Svadebka* juxtapose the two scales as a way of articulating sections. The most conspicuous such articulation comes at the very outset in the responsorial interplay between the bride's *plach* and the bridesmaids' *prichot* (Ex. 17.31). The static harmony underlying the bride's music (a "*Rite* chord," as defined in Chapter 12) is derived from the "descending" collection (scale 4), while that of the bridesmaids' response (another *Rite* chord, inverted) derives from the "ascending" (scale 2).

Complementary scales around the same (0 3 6 9) nodes were designated "melody scale" and "harmony scale" in some of our previous discussions (the earliest in Chapter 4). The terms will no longer do for *Svadebka*, and this is the second point:

EXAMPLE 17.30 *Svadebka*, fig. 31

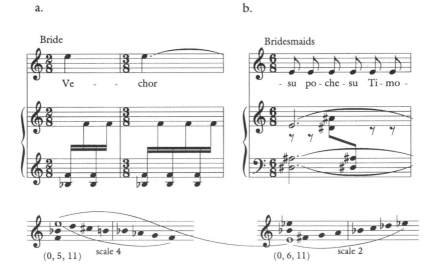

EXAMPLE 17.31 Inversion relationship between bride's and bridesmaids' repliques

EXAMPLE 17.32 *Svadebka*, fig. 76, piano IV

Stravinsky no longer shows any interest in extracting triads at the nodal points. There is only one spot in the score that even vestigially exhibits the Rimskian legacy of "triadic octatonicism" that played such a formative role in *Petrushka* and had remained such a conspicuous component of *The Rite*'s sound surface. It comes on the way to the climax of the third tableau as an accompaniment to the theme C *popevka*, and will bring the end of *Petrushka* to mind in its oscillation between triads rooted a major second apart, each admixed with octatonic confrères to produce *Petrushka* chords. These alternate at the climax of the passage with "Auguries" chords à la *Rite of Spring*, the latter making their final bow in their creator's work. The piano IV part gives an adequate précis of the total harmonic content (Ex. 17.32).

The cited passage is the zenith of a long development emanating from the first appearance of theme K, at fig. [55] in the second tableau. What had begun as a purely melodic oscillation is amplified into an oscillation of triads and thence to *Petrushka* chords in a progressive harmonic enrichment that sweeps through the two tableaux and unites them. The enrichment is only that: the basic impulse, like all basic impulses in *Svadebka*, remains melodic; triads and superimpositions thereof provide a sonorous amplification, nothing more. Thus, what had been a *Grundgestalt* in *Petrushka* has become an epiphenomenon in *Svadebka*, a fleeting surface excrescence.

More pertinent and typical is the initial harmonization given theme K at [55], as it sets out on its great march (Ex. 17.33). A glance at Table 4 will remind us that theme K begins anhemitonically, acquiring a semitone only when it reaches its ar-

EXAMPLE 17.33 *Svadebka*, fig. 55

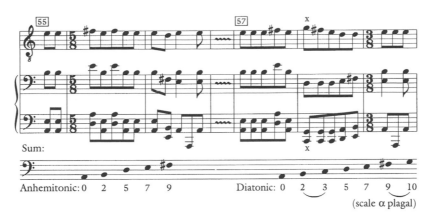

bitrarily imposed cadence. Its harmonization reflects this structure—indeed, was designed to reflect it. For most of its progress the melody is accompanied by the "open," resolutely atriadic sound of superimposed fifths, one such concatenation assigned to each note of the melody. The sum of the tones in the harmony defines one of the three possible anhemitonic selections from the pitches of scale α (the only one possible at this point, since it includes both the F♯ and the D of the melody). When the melody finally reaches the note G, thus becoming diatonic, the new pitch is harmonized with a fifth-complex that includes C and thus completes the full diatonic scale α (in its plagal extension).

The dilation of anhemitonic sets into the vertical domain is one of the most interesting aspects of *Svadebka* harmony, entailing as it does a reordering of the consonance/dissonance perspective that smacks superficially of archaism. Thirds are eschewed in favor of "Pythagorean" intervals such as fourths, fifths, and their compounds, and there are numerous instances of chords in which the major second (and/or its inversion) is treated as stable, ergo as consonant.

The static, therefore stable, vertical aggregate with which the instruments accompany one of the many statements of theme A' in the fourth tableau is a symmetricalized sum of the theme's own (0 3 5) trichord plus the inversion (Ex. 17.34a). Harmonizations of the theme as stated by the instruments themselves are uniformly constructed so as to emphasize the (0 3 5) trichord as the basis of harmony. In Example 17.34b, the resolution of the "dissonant" third to the second is especially telling. The most conspicuous instance of this kind is the plangent bell harmony at the very end of the ballet. The whole score comes to rest on a "Pythagorean" second (Ex. 17.34c). The cadence after fig. [8] in the first tableau (Ex. 17.34d), in which the second is approached by leap, demonstrates its functional consonance even more explicitly.

Yet to call this anhemitonic harmony "medieval" or "Pythagorean" is obviously

EXAMPLE 17.34 *Svadebka*, anhemitonic harmony

a.

b.

c.

EXAMPLE 17.34 (continued)

d.

fig. [8] (voices only)

Go - lu - bo - yu pe - re - v'yu!

beside the point: it is Eurasian harmony par excellence, derived from the verticalized tones of the *plach*. It is an invented Turanian style, whose authenticity has a purely internal validation. Even so, there are passages in *Svadebka* that even Kastalsky had to concede were "close to folk polyphony" in style.[76] Here we leave the realm of verticalized anhemitony; for although, as Kastalsky reminds us, harmonic fifths and fourths, "though not encountered particularly often, . . . are nonetheless characteristic" of Russian folk polyphony,[77] the really ubiquitous devices of peasant harmony consist in somewhat peculiar doublings at the third.

Let us consider a few spots Kastalsky singled out for grudging approval in the course of a generally abusive assessment of *Svadebka*. With the greatest connoisseur of "sing-along polyphony" as our divining rod, we will surely be led to those passages where Stravinsky deliberately aped that manner. One such, according to Kastalsky, comes at fig. [74], where—against a variant of theme C in the altos and tenors—the basses divisi lumber along in a reprise of theme F, which we have already had occasion to identify speculatively as a tune borrowed from the repertory of chant or epic (Ex. 17.35a; cf. Ex. 17.14). Pleased with the quasi-kuchkist doubling in thirds, Kastalsky compared this spot with Musorgsky's folkish music (although—needless to add—"Musorgsky in such cases acted more simply and nearer the truth"); but the static background harmony he condemned as "wild"—a wildness, he went on, "that is to be explained by seeking after originality at all costs."[78] The harmony is in fact one of those *plach* verticalizations that are so characteristic of this score. Combined with the anhemitonic theme C derivatives (Ex. 17.35c), the total pitch content of the passage at fig. [74] coincides precisely with "scale 1" (as defined in Example 17.17; α-authentic as defined in Example 17.24), the most essential *Svadebka* pitch collection of all.

Kastalsky also cites as faithful to the folk tradition the climactic harmonization of the Mitusov tune (figs. [130]ff.); and here, if we disregard the accompaniment

76. Kastalsky, "Iz zapisok," in IStrSM:209.
77. Ibid., 208.
78. Ibid., 209.

EXAMPLE 17.35

a. *Svadebka,* fig. 21 , basses and piano IV

b. Background harmony

c. Theme C derivatives

scale 1 (α authentic)

a, b, c   a, c   a   a, b   a, b, c   c   a, b

EXAMPLE 17.36   *Svadebka,* fig. 130

with its insistent anhemitonic sets, we do encounter something remarkably akin to the folk harmonizations recorded by Linyova et al. (Ex. 17.36). As usual in sing-along polyphony, the basic units of harmony are the third-plus-octave and fifth-plus-octave (cf. the "Volga Boatmen's Song" harmonization discussed in Chapter 15 and its models). Complete triads do not occur except as by-products of the confluence of third-doubled lines. The most powerful cadential gesture is the occursus, approached by similar motion with an octave displacement in the highest voice, on the way to which dissonances impermissible in conventional Western counterpoint regularly occur.

Example 17.36—and there are other harmonizations like it in *Svadebka* (e.g., the harmonization of K569 at the beginning of the second tableau; the beginning of K125 at fig. [46]; the vocal harmonization of A′ at fig. [114])—fits the bill, strongly confirming Stravinsky's familiarity with published *podgoloski* transcriptions. Indeed, it was while he was at work on the fourth tableau (10/23 February 1916) that Stravinsky wrote to his mother asking her to send any and all phonographically transcribed folk song collections, and specifying that he already possessed the first volume of Linyova's major work, *Great-Russian Songs in Folk Harmonization*.[79] Thus we may state with confidence that he had seen and perhaps studied the song given in Example 17.37, which illustrates all the stylistic points cited as relevant to Example 17.36.

Kastalsky actually brought himself to praise Stravinsky for his handling of certain endemically Russian traits of harmony and voice leading, like thirdless $\frac{7}{5}$ chords and (particularly) the ascending resolution of sevenths, as in the tenor and bass parts at fig. [61] in the second tableau (Ex. 17.38), a passage Kastalsky singled out for approval. He associates the resolution of the seventh in such cadences with primitively literate Eastern European musical traditions like the Polish-derived three-part sacred and secular songs (*psal'mï, kantï*) cultivated in Russia during the Petrine period (cf. Ex. 17.39a).[80] In the example from *Svadebka*, the upward-resolving seventh is incidental to the movement in parallel triads (unbroken in the women's parts). This parallelism, too, has its counterpart in *kantï* (Ex. 17.39b).

Yet one may doubt whether this homely repertoire could have been Stravinsky's model. Its rudimentary functional harmony, for one thing, is quite alien to the tonal idiom of *Svadebka*. Perhaps more to the point, *kantï* were transmitted exclusively in manuscript songbooks known as *pesenniki*. At the time Stravinsky was writing *Svadebka* there were no published anthologies of such pieces (such as the composer might have found in his father's famous library); the only existing printed transcriptions were in an article by the church musician Stepan Smolensky that sought to adapt a few selected *kantï* to the repertoire of contemporary Ortho-

79. IStrSM:488.
80. IStrSM:208.

EXAMPLE 17.37 Linyova, *Velikorusskiye pesni v narodnoy garmonizatsii,* vol. 1, no. 19 (*Soldatskaya:* "*Kak po kamne, po reke*")

EXAMPLE 17.38 *Svadebka,* fig. 61 , choral parts only

EXAMPLE 17.39 Seventeenth-century *kantï* (from Ginzburg, *Istoriya russkoy muzïki v notnïkh obraztsakh* [Moscow, 1969], vol. 1)

a. From "*Chto ponizhe bïlo goroda Saratova*" (p. 10)

EXAMPLE 17.39 *(continued)*

b. From *"Raduysya, Rossko zemle"* (p. 5)

li - kuy, ve - se - li - sya,   li - kuy, ve - se - li - sya

dox church choirs[81]—not the sort of publication Stravinsky was likely to consult.[82]

He had another model. As early as March 1914, before a note of *Svadebka* had been committed to paper, Stravinsky clipped from the pages of *Rech'* a lengthy article by the famous linguist and academician Nikolai Yakovlevich Marr (1864–1934, the very one over whose crackpot theories of Marxian linguistics Stalin would become so comically exercised near the end of his life) entitled "Thoughts on the Religious Singing of the Ancient East: On the Occasion of a Concert of Georgian Sacred Music at the Hall of Nobles on the Sixteenth of March."[83] Marr's thesis, related to his linguistic theories, which traced the origins of human speech to the languages of the Caucasus, was that "the religious singing of the Georgians and related tribes represents a vestige of the religion of the ancient Orient [i.e., the Near East], neither Semitic nor Aryan, but of the Japhetic tribes that have newly emerged as a focus of scientific research"—that is, what more recent scholars would call the hypothetical primeval "Indo-European" culture. Marr chides the scholars of the humanistic disciplines for failing to recognize this heritage the way philologists and archeologists had done, and calls upon artists to "develop these precious artifacts before they perish in obscurity."

It was a typical neonationalist plea on behalf of a cultural heritage that would hold a special appeal for an artist with Eurasianist leanings, the Caucasus being no less a part of "Turania" than Russia; in fact it was a point of special emphasis for the Trubetskoys and Karsavins to insist on the community of Eurasian cultures. Hence, it is not surprising to find that Stravinsky showed an interest in Georgian folk and religious music, or that this interest should have left its mark on *Svadebka*.

Both volumes of the *Trudï MEK* that we know Stravinsky to have used con-

81. S. V. Smolensky, "Znacheniye XVII veka i yego kantov v oblasti sovremennogo tserkovnogo peniya tak nazïvayemogo 'prostogo napeva,'" in *Muzïkal'naya starina*, vol. 5 (St. Petersburg, 1911); cited in Yu. V. Keldïsh, *Ocherki i issledovaniya po istorii russkoy muzïki* (Moscow: Sovetskiy Kompozitor, 1978), 64.

82. The first scholarly publications of *kantï* were by Nikolai Findeyzen: *Petrovskiye kantï*, in *Izvestiya Akademii Nauk SSSR* (Moscow, 1927); and *Ocherki po istorii muzïki v Rossii* (Moscow and Leningrad: Muzgiz, 1929), vol. 2.

83. N. Y. Marr, "Mïsli o religioznom penii Drevnego Vostoka: po povodu gruzinskogo dukhovnogo kontserta v zale Dvoryanskogo sobraniya 16-go marta," *Rech'*, 16/29 March 1914. The clipping is in Stravinsky's 1912–14 scrapbook, now at the Paul Sacher Stiftung, Basel.

tained studies of Georgian and other Caucasian musics, the work mainly of Dmitriy Ignatyevich Arakchiyev (Arakishvili, 1873–1953), a Georgian composer and folklorist who was in effect the Linyova of the Caucasus, being the first to investigate the local ethnic music with the aid of the phonograph. It was because he knew these publications by Arakchiyev that Stravinsky made a point, in his letter to his mother of February 1916, to request "folk songs of the Caucasian peoples that have been phonographically recorded." He placed this request first, as a matter of fact, before requesting Linyova.

His mother must have sent him the collection *Georgian Folk Songs and Verses* (*Kartuli khalkuri khimgebi* [Tiflis, 1909]) by Ia (Ilya) Kargareteli (1867–1939), because its entire musical contents, consisting of sixteen polyphonic songs calligraphically transcribed by the composer on high-quality card stock, survives today in the Stravinsky Archive, the composer having become fascinated, it seems, not just with the music but with the Georgian alphabet.[84] The contents of this beautiful document evidently came into Stravinsky's possession too late to have influenced the composition of most of *Svadebka;* but comparison with Arakchiyev's contributions to the *Trudï MEK,* particularly the group of religious songs published under the title "Georgian Canticles for the Liturgy of St. John of Damascus in Folk Harmonization," will show the source of the parallel triads that crop up now and again in Stravinsky's score, as well as the upward-resolving seventh, and will also provide an ethnographic validation for some of his characteristic anhemitonic consonances (Ex. 17.40). The passage in *Svadebka* closest to this "Japhetic" style is the one at figs. [12]–[14] in the first tableau, where the women's voices sing an extended diatonic melody in parallel major and minor triads, the pianists' left hands meanwhile thumping out acciaccaturas with a particular insistence (Ex. 17.41).

Semitonal acciaccaturas, so prevalent in the "Swiss" songs, remain a vital feature of *Svadebka*'s special idiom as well (one need only cite the very opening of the piece). Novel, however, and evidently "Japhetic," is the preoccupation with parallelism. Not that precedents are lacking in earlier Stravinsky scores: one thinks immediately of the accompaniment to the opening bassoon melody in *The Rite,* and there is an early *Svadebka* sketch that seems to take the idea over quite literally from the earlier ballet (Ex. 17.42). A catalogue of parallel doublings of this type in *Svadebka* would include the fourths and fifths in the bass accompanying theme G/ G′ intermittently throughout the first half of the second tableau; the snaking chro-

---

84. See Victor Varunts, supplementary note to Stravinsky's letters to his mother in *Muzikal'naya akademiya*, 1992, no. 4, 118. The first page of this manuscript is illustrated in P&D:44, erroneously dated "c. 1904." This date is contradicted not only by the date of Kargareteli's publication, but also by the paper Stravinsky used, which bears a Swiss watermark and which was also used for the fair copy of the Peasant Choruses of 1914–17. On the basis of these observations, this Georgian transcription would most likely date from the early months of the year 1917, when Stravinsky was hard at the fourth tableau of *Svadebka*.

EXAMPLE 17.40   Selected passages from D. I. Arakchiyev (Arakishvili),
Gruzinskiye pesnopeniya na liturgiyu sv. Ioanna Zlatoustogo v narodnoy garmonizatsii
(*Trudï MEK* 1:337–60)

a.

b.

c.

d.

EXAMPLE 17.40 (continued)

e.

(No. 18)

f.

(No. 27)

g.

(No. 30)

h.

(No. 34)

EXAMPLE 17.41 *Svadebka,* fig.  12

Khve - tis, su - dar' Pam - fil' - ye - vich u te -

- bya so - lo - vey vo sa - du, Va vï - so - kom te - re -

mu, va vï - so - kom iz - u - kra - shen - nom

EXAMPLE 17.42

a. *The Rite of Spring,* fig. 1 (composed 1911)

EXAMPLE 17.42 (*continued*)

b. Early sketch for *Svadebka*, opening lament (1914)

matic fifths accompanying theme J at fig. [41]; the triads rising by semitones in the bass at fig. [16], mixing their colors (generally into octatonically referable compounds) with the parallel triads in the voice parts that run along a diatonic track; the multiple projections of scale γ accompanying that scale's biggest moment—the introduction of the Mitusov tune at [110]+2—with a string of astringent pseudochords; the racing six-fours at [112]; the triads at [124]; the ninths at [125]. These pseudoharmonic automata flit harmlessly across the sonorous surface like so many gaudy graffiti.

— — — — — —

One such "automaton" should be singled out for cutting a bit deeper into the harmonic texture. Theme N, on its many recurrences in the fourth tableau, is usually accompanied by an octatonic hexachord, referable, like most of the notes in the theme, to "descending" scale 4, which mechanically rises and falls (just as demonstratively as the C-major scale would later do in the last movement of the 1923 *Octuor*) in counterpoint against the tune over a pedal that defines the starting note of scale δ as a specious tonic. The hexachord is doubled in parallel major triads for a new kind of octatonic/diatonic interaction—a rather pat and factitious kind, for not all the notes of the triads, obviously, can refer to the scale formed by the "roots."

One way of specifying the relationship between the scale and the chords would be to say that every second chord is referable to the governing scale, the others being "passing" harmonies; but that would not be very satisfactory, since the first chord would have to be interpreted under this construction as "passing." Another way of accounting for the complex—à la Yastrebtsev (recalling his discussions with Rimsky-Korsakov, reported in Chapter 4)—would be to say that the roots of the triads belong to one octatonic collection, the thirds and fifths to another; but this, too, is unsatisfactory, the collection invoked by the thirds and fifths being the one octatonic scale that is represented by neither the "ascending" nor the "descending" scales in our scheme, since it embodies a different (0 3 6 9) set of nodes. The complex, qua complex, therefore has no legitimate standing within *Svadebka*'s meticulously organized musical space. Better not to regard it as an octatonic/diatonic interaction at all, then, but simply as a "Japhetic" sonorous amplification of the hexachord line, the preeminence of which is well assured by its multiple doublings (see Ex. 17.43a).

The parallel construction returns with theme N on all of its recurrences (and even once without it). Each time, the texture is further augmented in some ingenious way. At fig. [89] the octatonic hexachord is shadowed by a chromatic one moving in parallel with it—a rare instance in Stravinsky of the kind of play with simultaneously unfolding "interval cycles" such as Perle and Antokoletz have identified in the work of Berg and Bartók.[85] Conceptualized in terms of beats rather than individual pulses, it can be described as a juxtaposition of the interval-3 cycle (minor thirds) and the interval-2 cycle (whole tones), the members of each linked by offbeat passing tones conforming to the structure of their respective governing scales (Ex. 17.43b). At fig. [90] the triadically sound-boosted hexachord is reinforced by a complete (0 3 6 9) triadic rotation of Collection II, shifting on and off the beat according to a 7/8 metric pattern of its own, producing a new set of "polychords"; and at [92] (this time without theme N) the whole complex (expressed in dominant sevenths) runs against its own retrograde in rigorous contrary motion, generating yet another spicy harmonic mix (Ex. 17.43c and 17.43d). These manipulations, though they invoke pitch collections of fundamental structural importance in *Svadebka,* are not for that reason any more significant than the other pseudoharmonic automata in our inventory. The most one could say for them is that, in conjunction with the melodies they accompany, they reflect on the surface, and hence dramatize, the relationship between the diatonic foreground of the piece and its octatonic background. The unshakable strength of that background is what holds together all the boisterous goings-on at the surface.

Svadebka is without a doubt the most convincing Turanian synthesis Stravinsky ever achieved. It unites all the strands that made up his multifaceted Russian heritage within a single, strictly integrated perspective. The rustic diatonic or anhemitonic *popevki* dance on the surface of a structure that is regulated in all its essential aspects by the urbane chromatic routines of the old St. Petersburg school tradition. That control lends *Svadebka* a degree of global coherence greater than that exhib-

85. See George Perle, "Berg's Master Array of the Interval Cycles," *Musical Quarterly* 62 (1977): 1–30 (including a brief discussion of *The Rite of Spring*); idem, "The Musical Language of *Wozzeck*," *Music Forum* 1 (1967): 204–59; Antokoletz, *Music of Béla Bartók*, chaps. 7–8. Antokoletz has made an attempt to apply this perspective systematically to Stravinsky in "Interval Cycles in Stravinsky's Early Ballets," *JAMS* 39 (1986): 578–614.

EXAMPLE 17.43   *Svadebka,* parallel triads over scale 4 patterns

a.

b.

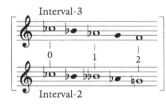

c.

EXAMPLE 17.43 (continued)

d.

Scale 4 in contrary motion

Table of Root Simultaneities ("Polyharmonies")

ited by the other masterpieces of the Russian period—where progress from point to point had been based on methods of interlocking, discretely conceived and executed "blocks"—and far beyond the reach of Stravinsky's contemporaries, as a glance at a score like Prokofiev's *Scythian Suite* will easily confirm. Where *The Rite* had been agglutinative, *Svadebka* is comprehensive. It marked the summit, not only of Stravinsky's neonationalist phase, but of neonationalism *tout court,* fulfilling to an extent undreamed of the prophecies made over the preceding dozen years, and from their vastly different standpoints, by Stasov, Bilibin, and Linyova.

Stasov, concentrating on the "starting point in reality," had called for a choral music that would have "all the truth, caprice, irregularity one finds on the lips of the people." What he would have made of the fourth tableau of *Svadebka* one cannot help but wonder, especially such passages as the one at [125], with its juxtapositions of authentic folk melody (in the instruments), actual speech (for the tenor soloist, impersonating the *druzhko*), and folklike *popevki* (for the chorus); or the passage before [127], where the traditional shout "Bitter, bitter!" ("*Gor'ko, gor'ko!*") is heard just as Stasov would have wanted to hear it, "with all the changes in the quantity of the *personnel,* some entering, others falling silent and starting up again when they're good and ready, . . . and with all kinds of shifts in *rhythm, tempo,* and even *mood,* such as characterize real people feeling and creating something 'all their own.'" Linyova, concentrating on the "finishing point in music," had called for the rebirth of folk song "in terms of *style:* free, broad, and lyric; in terms of bold and complex voice leadings, the voices interlacing and separating, at times fused with the main melody, at times departing radically from it."[86] What neither she

---

86. Stasov and Linyova citations are from Linyova, *Velikorusskiye pesni* 2:lxxiv–lxxv. They are both quoted in fuller form in Chapter 10.

nor Stasov could have dreamed was that this rebirth would be accomplished by such a complete overhaul of harmonic and tonal structure along lines associated in their day only with "fantastic" music, not folkloristic.

Nor, of course, could they have predicted that it would be accomplished only outside of Russia, by a composer whose name would be reviled within the borders of his homeland within a decade after the work's première, and whose chef d'oeuvre would be described by an official of his homeland's government as a work that "uses . . . some elements of Russian life to mock Russian customs and to please the European spectator by the express emphasis on Russian 'Asianism,' crudity, animal instincts, sexual motives."[87]

All the more queerly does this description of *Svadebka* read when we compare it with the peroration of Linyova's eulogy for Stasov, delivered at a meeting of the Musical-Ethnographic Commission in 1907 and printed in the second volume of its *Papers:* "Perhaps when *the people shall be called to life* not only in operas but in reality, then we shall hear a *song of freedom* composed by singers of the people, we shall hear 'national anthems' not written on demand but created by popular inspiration, and the idea of nationality in music for which Stasov stood will be realized more greatly than he ever dreamed."[88]

Svadebka, completed in particell between the Russian Revolution of 1917 and the Bolshevik coup—"dans ces inoubliables jours de bonheur que traverse notre chère Russie libérée"[89]—was just such a realization, the most magnificent ever accomplished. Inspired by that moment of hope, Stravinsky celebrated no Russia that is or was, and certainly no Russia that ever will be, but a Russia out of time and space, the Russia he described to Ramuz, a Russia not of the real but of the *realiora.*

The hope died quickly, and Stravinsky soon relinquished the Stasovian dream.

87. Tikhon Khrennikov, Declaration in response to the Resolution on Music of the Central Committee of the Communist Party of the Soviet Union, 10 February 1948; quoted in Slonimsky, *Music Since 1900,* 1367.
88. Ye. E. Linyova, "Mïsli V. V. Stasova o narodnosti v muzïke," *Trudï MEK* 2:384.
89. Telegram from Stravinsky to his mother, 24 May 1917; in IStrSM:489.

APPENDIX

TABLE 4

Svadebka: Summary of Ethnographic Sources, Action, and Musical Themes

Legend: K = Kireyevsky, *Pesni, sobrannïye P. V. Kireyevskim, novaya seriya, vïp. I* (Moscow, 1911).
Modal classifications: A = anhemitonic; D = diatonic; C = chromatic (chiefly octatonic)

Location	Source reference and remarks	Musical theme	Modal classification
	SCENE 1: At the Bride's (Kosa, *"Tress"*)		
[0]	**K421** (Kaluga guberniya), lines 3–5. Not actually a *devichnik* song but a lament for the maiden braid, sung the morning after the replaiting "when the groom comes for the bride to go to the altar" (remark by Kireyevsky's informant, Prince N. A. Kostrov). Stravinsky evidently chose these lines for their strong emphasis on the *kosa* itself. They probably caught his eye because the song is divided between two columns in the source book; the lines with which Stravinsky chose to begin *Svadebka* appear at the top of the page. Stravinsky's setting is a very deliberate stylization of the actual bridal *plach* as described by Dahl (a three-note formula) and as actually performed by peasant brides (viz., gliding pitch contour, glissandi, vocalized breathing—see Mazo, "Stravinsky's *Les Noces*," 126). Stravinsky evokes these performance features by the use of skipping grace notes, the performance of which requires a quick glissando like a sob. He may have drawn this from life, but there are ample clues in his sources. Dahl describes the bride's "wail" (*vopl'*) in terms not of singing but of groaning and sobbing (*stenaniye, ridaniye;* see *Tolkovïy slovar'*, s.v. *"vopiyat'"* [to wail]). Suggestive, too, is the appearance of one of the wedding songs in the Istomin/Dyutsh collection (Fig. 17.4b) in which melodic variants, entered in small print, look very much like Stravinsky's grace notes. What could seem a misreading of a source is more likely an example of this composer's happy propensity to take his inspiration where he found it. The superficial appearance of the notation may have inspired Stravinsky with a useful idea.	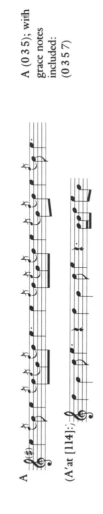 A: (A' at [114]):	A (0 3 5); with grace notes included: (0 3 5 7)

TABLE 4 (continued)

Location	Source reference and remarks	Musical theme	Modal classification
[1]+11	**K671** (Oryol guberniya), line 7. A single ejaculation of despair, lifted out of a *plach* collected by Yakushkin in 1843, sung by the bride upon being seated with the groom in the carriage that will take them to the altar. Mazo associates Stravinsky's setting of this line with the typical sound of the bridal *vopl'*.		
[2] (Brides-maids)	**K635** (Oryol guberniya), lines 1–7 (of eight). This song is translated and discussed in the main text. It is the source of the name by which the bride is known throughout. Harkins emphasizes its sibilant alliteration, "the sound perhaps suggesting the rustle of combing locks." The setting follows Dahl's description of the monotone *prichot* form of lamentation. There is also an imitation of gliding pitch, as noted by Mazo.	B	A (0 [[1] 2] 5 7 9)
[3]+5	**K13** (Archangel guberniya), line 17. Stravinsky inserts a modified version of this line to complete the preceding song, chosen for its reference to a "fine comb" (*chastiy greben*).		
[4] (Bride)	**K421**, resumed (lines 6–9), plus the ejaculation (*vopl'*) from **K671** as before.	A	
[7] (Brides-maids)	**K635**, reprised, replete with last line.	B	
[8]+2 (Bride)	**K421**, reprised, line 3.	A	
[9]	Sakharov, *Skazaniya russkogo naroda*, vol. 3 (Wedding songs), no. 164. This is the song Stravinsky cited in his draft scenario as the "*Otvetnaya neveste*" ("Answer-Song to the Bride"). A close variant is found in Kireyevsky (no. 937), but the Sakharov text corresponds to Stravinsky's almost exactly, allowing for the substitution of Stravinsky's names for the bride and groom. Sakharov	C D ([10])	A (035) D (024679)

E ([14] + 2)

(nonrecurrent)

C

E

places the text among his "Maidens' Songs at the *Devichnik*." It is an effort by the bridesmaids to console the bride.

[16] **K564** (Oryol *guberniya*), lines 10–15. Stravinsky's "*Rai rai!*" exclamation seems to be a contraction of Kireyevsky's "*Igrai, igrai skomoroshichek*" ("Play, play, dear little skomorokh"), fashioned to resonate with the common wedding-song refrain "*Rai moy rai!*," a high-spirited exclamation possibly deriving from *rai,* Russian for paradise. Dahl (*Tolkoviy slovar'*, s.v. "*rai*":2) associates the word with noisemaking. On skomorokhi, see Chapters 10 and 16. Evidently Stravinsky adopted the exclamation to intensify the mood of the preceding song of consolation.

[18] Tereshchenko, *Bit russkogo naroda* 2:160 (bottom), lines 1–3, conflated with two lines from another song in the same volume, 307, as follows:

p. 160

S podkameshka s podbelogo, rucheyek bezhit,
S podkameshka s podbelogo tsimbaliki b'yut.
Oni p'yut i l'yut
V tsimbali b'yut. } p. 307
Vot znat' moyu lyubeznuyu Yelizavetushku,
k venchaniyu vedut

From under a stone, from under a white [stone] a
  stream runs forth.
From under a stone, from under a white [stone] they
  are beating the cimbalom.
They drink and pour
And beat the cimbalom.
Thus we know my darling little Elizabeth is being led
to the altar.

Stravinsky modified these lines in various interesting ways. As usual, the name Nastasya Timofeyevna replaces "darling little Elizabeth"; Stravinsky shows his familiarity with the ways of Russian folk poetry first by forming an adroit diminutive from the bride's given name and then by separating it from her patronymic in a parallel construction: *Vot znat' nashu Nastyushku, znat' nashu Timofeyevnu. Most

TABLE 4 *(continued)*

Location	Source reference and remarks	Musical theme	Modal classification
	curious is the evidence that at the time he composed this song (late 1914 or early 1915), Stravinsky was not yet familiar with the instrument denoted by the Russian word *tsimbali* (diminutive *tsimbaliki*): none other than the cimbalom he would shortly come to know so well (as ersatz gusli) and use so often. At this point Stravinsky thought the word meant "cymbals," and actually substituted the standard Russian word for cymbals (*tarelki*) in the fourth line of the text as it appears in the score. Both of the texts Stravinsky conflated here from Tereshchenko belong to the most famous of all families of Russian wedding songs, existing in countless variants (some in Kireyevsky, but unused by Stravinsky). Tereshchenko associates "*S podkameshka s podbelogo*" with the *devichnik* as practiced in Pskov guberniya, while "*Vo gornitse vo svetlitse*," from which the third and fourth lines above were drawn—and which is found in Kireyevsky in four variants (one of them used by Stravinsky—see *K243* at [70], below)—is a *velichal'naya* to the bride, sung on the wedding morn, after she receives her father's blessing before departing for the altar.		
[21] (Bride and her mother together)	*K721* (Simbirsk guberniya), lines 3–6 (of eight) (Bride). According to the famous Moscow historian Mikhaïl Pogodin, who imparted the song to Kireyevsky in 1853, it is sung by the bride upon emerging from the pre-*devichnik* bath, while one of her bridesmaids combs and braids her hair the maiden way for the last time. The *devichnik* ceremony begins directly afterward ("often at two in the morning," writes Pogodin). *K568*, complete (Mother). Translated and discussed in the main text.	(nonrecurrent) F	D (0 2 4 5)
[24] (Brides- maids)	*K635*, final reprise, stretched out with repetitions, and ending with a line from *K13* as at [3]+5, above.	B	

A (0 3 5 7 9)

A/B

[25]
(Bride)
K714 (Simbirsk *guberniya*), lines 1–3, sung by the soprano soloist, representing the bride, while the chorus continues with *K635*. The song seems to function here as an apostrophe to the ribbon mentioned in the bridesmaids' song. Actually it is a matchmaking song sung long before the *devichnik*, not by the bride but by the chorus of maidens. It refers to a ribbon given by the bride's parents to the groom to wear "as a symbol of his rights over her and of her deflowering" (Harkins, "Text of Stravinsky's *Les Noces*"). The setting here is a superimposition of solo *plach* on choral *prichot* such as occurs regularly in the actual enactment of the *devichnik* rite (cf. Mazo, "Stravinsky's *Les Noces*," 133–34, including ex. 14).

SCENE 2: At the Groom's (Kudri, "*Curls*")

G

A (0 3 5 [7] 8)

[27]
K569 (Oryol *guberniya*), complete. Translated and discussed in main text.

H

A (0 3 5 7 [8] 10)

[29]
K636 (Oryol *guberniya*), lines 1–4. Translated and discussed in main text.

G

[30]
K569, partial reprise (lines 2–4)

H

[31]
K636, resumed and completed (lines 5–12)

G

[33]
K569, partial reprise (lines 1–4)

I

C (0 1 3 4 6 7 [9 10])

(pianos:)

[35]
K454 (Ryazan *guberniya*), lines 1–4. Kireyevsky remarks that this song is sung by the groom and his suite when they embark on the wedding morn to pick up the bride.

TABLE 4 (continued)

Location	Source reference and remarks	Musical theme	Modal classification
[36] (The groom's parents in turn)	**K712** (Simbirsk *guberniya*), lines 1–4. According to Po-godin, who collected this song, it is sung by the chorus of maidens to the groom at the culmination (*zapoy,* "toast") of the *sgovor,* or betrothal ceremony, after the formal exchange of gifts between the families of the bride and groom. It is one of a pair of toasts, the other being in honor of the bride.	I (cont'd)	
[38]	While K712 continues, the tenor soloist pronounces the actual toast: "*Kvas,* fine as raspberries, ripened ten times over!" ("*Kvas, chto malinoye, desyat'yu nalivan!*"). Its source, slightly modified, is Dahl, *Tolkovïy slovar',* s.v. "*malina*" (raspberry).	I (cont'd)	
[38]+6	**K481** (Tambov *guberniya*), lines 1–2, 4–6, 8–10. This song accompanies the kneading of the dough for the *korovai,* the wedding loaf, and implicitly compares the groom's attributes with those of the bread (e.g., twist-ing his curls = kneading the dough). In this song the groom is actually called Khvetis, and it may have been Stravinsky's source for the name.		
[41]	**K678** (Voronezh *guberniya*), lines 1–9. Although *kudri* remain its subject, this song, imparted to Kireyevsky in 1848 by one A. von Kremer, is a *velichal'naya,* sung at the wedding feast by the girls to a bachelor guest.	J	A (0 2 [4] 5 7 9)
[42]+3	**K794** (provenance not given), lines 7–12. The *kudri* phase of the second tableau reaches its climax with the groom's own apostrophe to his curls. K678, line 5, omitted at fig. [41], actually follows this song (bass and mezzo-soprano at [43]+2).	J (cont'd)	
[44]	**K569,** complete (reprise).	G	
[46]	**K125** (Pskov *guberniya*), lines 8–22, 1–2. These lines are taken from a litany sung at the *vecherina zhenikha,* the groom's bachelor party, to ward off evil spirits (cf. the	G'	A (0 2 [4] 5)

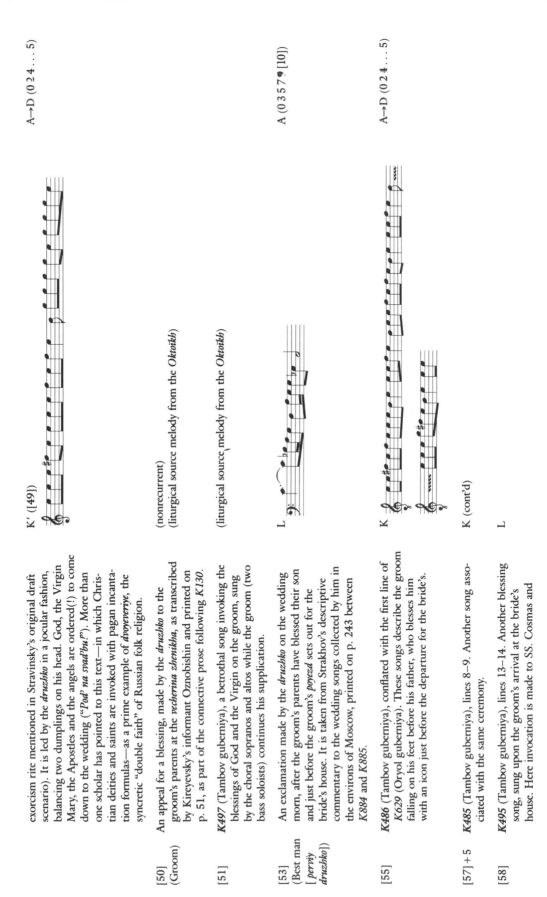

A→D (0 2 4 . . . 5)

K′ ([49])

(nonrecurrent)
(liturgical source melody from the *Oktoïkh*)

(liturgical source melody from the *Oktoïkh*)

L

A (0 3 5 7 9 [10])

K

A→D (0 2 4 . . . 5)

K (cont'd)

L

[49]

exorcism rite mentioned in Stravinsky's original draft scenario). It is led by the *druzhko* in a jocular fashion, balancing two dumplings on his head. God, the Virgin Mary, the Apostles and the angels are ordered(!) to come down to the wedding ("*Pod' na svad'bu!*"). More than one scholar has pointed to this text—in which Christian deities and saints are invoked with pagan incantation formulas—as a prime example of *dvoyeverye*, the syncretic "double faith" of Russian folk religion.

[50]
(Groom)

An appeal for a blessing, made by the *druzhko* to the groom's parents at the *vecherina zhenikha*, as transcribed by Kireyevsky's informant Oznobishin and printed on p. 51, as part of the connective prose following *K130*.

[51]

K497 (Tambov *guberniya*), a betrothal song invoking the blessings of God and the Virgin on the groom, sung by the choral sopranos and altos while the groom (two bass soloists) continues his supplication.

[53]
(Best man
[*perviy
druzhko*])

An exclamation made by the *druzhko* on the wedding morn, after the groom's parents have blessed their son and just before the groom's *poyezd* sets out for the bride's house. It is taken from Strakhov's descriptive commentary to the wedding songs collected by him in the environs of Moscow, printed on p. 243 between *K884* and *K885*.

[55]

K486 (Tambov *guberniya*), conflated with the first line of *K629* (Oryol *guberniya*). These songs describe the groom falling on his feet before his father, who blesses him with an icon just before the departure for the bride's.

[57] + 5

K485 (Tambov *guberniya*), lines 8–9. Another song associated with the same ceremony.

[58]

K495 (Tambov *guberniya*), lines 13–14. Another blessing song, sung upon the groom's arrival at the bride's house. Here invocation is made to SS. Cosmas and

TABLE 4 *(continued)*

Location	Source reference and remarks	Musical theme	Modal classification
	Damian ("Kuz'ma-Dem'yan," treated as a singular noun), physician patron saints of weddings.		
[58]+3	*K496* (Tambov guberniya). More of same. God's blessing is invoked on the godparents of the bride and groom (*posazhoniye*), who will accompany them to the altar. This and the next song are joined by Stravinsky over a conjoint octatonically derived basso ostinato suggestive of pealing church bells.	L (cont'd)	
[61]	*Kl25* (litany) resumed (lines 1–2, 5–10). Appeal is made to the physician St. Luke to unite the bride and groom and to bless their firstborn.	K	

SCENE 3: *Seeing Off the Bride* (Provodi nevesti)

Location	Source reference and remarks	Musical theme	Modal classification
[65]	*Kl37* (Pskov guberniya), lines 1–7, 10–16. Oznobishin's commentary: "When the bride enters [the *gornitsa*] in her complete wedding attire, her father and mother greet her wearing fur coats turned inside out. The former takes up an icon and a candle, the latter bread and salt. The bride and groom take their places opposite the table on a spread cloth and fall down. The [bride's] parents send them off to the altar with a blessing." This song is that blessing.	C D (tenor at [67])	
[70]	Three songs in counterpoint: a. *Kl25* (litany) resumed (lines 11–17): St. Cosmas (Stravinsky adds Damian), in his capacity as blacksmith, is ordered to "forge us a wedding" (cf. Rimsky-Korsakov, *Skazaniye o nevidimom grade Kitezhe*, Act II, fig. [104]).	C (cont'd)	
	b. *K243* (Kostroma guberniya), sung by the soprano soloist beginning at [70]+1 while the tenor continues with Kl25. Kireyevsky notes that this song is sung by the girls "after the bride has been blessed with an icon." The text is a variant of the song partially adapted from Tereshchenko (*Bit russkogo naroda* 2:307) at fig. [18] in the first tableau. Various voices will intermittently continue this song up to fig. [74]:	E'	A (0 3 5 [6] 8)

c. **K828** (provenance not given), lines 1, 6–8. Another song about SS. Cosmas and Damian collecting nails and "forging a wedding," sung by the choral basses against both of the preceding songs beginning at [70]+4.

F

[75] **K125** (litany) resumed and completed (lines 18–20, 6, 13, 21–25. Stravinsky builds the ending of this litany, which had been introduced at [46] in the middle of the second tableau, into the largest climax in the work so far—the crest, so to speak, of its first wave. The last line (Kireyevsky: "*Vilis' drug okolo druga*" ["They have become entwined the one around the other"]) is changed, ungrammatically but archaistically, to "*Vilis' drug kolo drugu*," so that the composer could have the right concluding vowel for a massive melisma (all voices from [80]). Cf. the ending of the "Dance of the Cat and the Ram" in the middle of the *Baika* (i.e., the culmination of *its* "first wave"). As the melisma dies away, the bride, groom, and all their retinue depart for the church.

C

M" ([78])

D (0 5 7 9 10 or
0 2 4 5 7)

Source melody from Istomin/Dyutsh, imparted to Stravinsky by Stepan Mitusov (for original form, see [110]+2, below)

[82] (Mothers of the Bride and Groom) **K884** (provenance not given), lines 1–5. A *plach* sung by the groom's mother just before he departs for the bride's on the wedding morn. Strakhov: "*As many of the members of the groom's suite go to harness the horses, his mother, after uttering a prayer to God, seats her son the groom on a bench, on a fur coat [that is spread there], takes a glass of beer in her hands and, with a prayer and having crossed herself, anoints the lad's head with the beer, parts his hair with a comb, and, falling on his breast, wails: 'My own child, . . . don't leave me, poor and embittered'*" (Stravinsky substitutes "wretched" [*goremichnaya*]). Stravinsky's setting is again in the recognizable style of a *plach* (see above).

I'

(pianos:)

C (0 1 3 4 6 7 [9 10])

[83] **K887** (provenance not given), lines 1–2. While the soprano (groom's mother) continues the preceding *plach*, the *mezzo*-soprano (bride's mother) enters with a lament of her own. Strakhov: "*As soon as the young couple have crossed the threshold of her hut [on their way to the church], the bride's mother seats herself in her

I' (cont'd)

TABLE 4 (*continued*)

Location	Source reference and remarks	Musical theme	Modal classification
	daughter's place, on a fur coat [that is spread there], and begins howling: 'Farewell, my own child! I have nourished you and quenched your thirst. . . .'" Stravinsky omits the first word, so that the two mothers' laments begin similarly.		
[84]	*K749* (provenance not given), lines 5–9. Both mothers now shift over to another lament collected by Kireyevsky himself. In the actual *svadebnaya igra* it is sung by the bride's mother at the *devichnik*. Both mothers end by repeating the opening line of their first song(s): "My own child" ("*Rodimoye dityatko*"). Stravinsky's superimposition of the two mothers' laments, which in the actual wedding-day ritual are sung at different times and places, is typical of his method. The atemporal telescoping is justified for the sake of abstracting an intensely concentrated mood.	I' (cont'd)	

SCENE 4: *The Wedding Feast* (Krasniy stol)

Location	Source reference and remarks	Musical theme	Modal classification
[87]	*K142* (Pskov *guberniya*), with conventional interpolations ("Ai *lyuli, lyuli*" etc.). This is the one poem Stravinsky chose from among those noted down (or composed?) by Alexander Pushkin, presumably at his father's estate at Mikhailovskoe during his exile year, 1824. It could not have been more appropriate to its specific place in the *Svadebka* proceedings: Pushkin (or Kireyevsky) tags it as a song "the girls sing when the bride returns from the church."	N O (*lyuli, lyuli* refrains)	D (0 1 3 5) A (0 2 5)
[88] (tenors)	*K447* (Ryazan *guberniya*), lines 1–2. These two lines from a *velichal'naya* sung by the maidens to the bride (noted down in 1847 by Yakushkin, who mistakenly identified it as a song sung *to* the maidens) continue the berry imagery of *K142*, which they interrupt (*K142* is resumed and completed at [89]). Harkins notes that in Russian wedding poetry berries symbolize the deflowering of the bride (cf. English/American "cherry").	(nonrecurrent)	

[89] + 4   Two lines, evidently interpolated by Stravinsky, that somewhat pedantically explain the symbolism of *K142*: "One berry is lord Khvetis, and the other berry is sweet Nastasya."

N

[89] + 2   *K451* (Ryazan *guberniya*), beginning in the bass (overlapping with the end of *K142*), taken up by the full chorus in antiphony with a comical falsetto (later hocketing) bass solo evidently representing the *druzhko* in his capacity as jester. Technically this song is a *popoynaya*, that is, a toast sung at the *gyovor* ceremony, not the wedding feast. It is sung over a drink when the fathers of the bride and groom have concluded the marriage contract. They are the two men who are named in the song. The father of the groom has "found a golden ring" (the bride) and is happy; the father of the bride has "lost the golden ring" and is sad. Stravinsky evidently did not grasp the import of this song, for, as Harkins notes, he did not adapt the names of the fathers to the patronymics of the bride and groom, as maintained throughout the *Snadebka* text. The groom's father should be Pamfili, not Fyodor; the bride's should be Timofey, not Pelagey.

P       C (0 2 3 5 6)

N' ([92] + 4)      C (0 1 3 4 6 7 9 10)

[93]   Three songs (four tunes) in counterpoint:

a. *K142* (reprise), lines 2–3 (choral sopranos).

b. Tereshchenko, *Bit russkogo naroda* 2:322 (choral tenors and basses; later the whole chorus). A *koril'naya*, or comical teasing song (sung, according to Tereshchenko's description, not at the wedding feast but at a prenuptial shower), with which the girls accompany the groom's party on its way home from the bride's. The groom and his party are compared to a pack of swift, slant-eyed borzoi hounds. The refrain "U-lyu-lyu-lyu-lyu" parodies the hunters' attack command (cf. *War and Peace*, bk. 2, pt. Four, chap. 5).

c. *K407* (Tula *guberniya*), lines 1–6. Another comic song comparing the bride to a goose in flight. This song is sung by the four soloists (*druzhki*?) through [96] + 5, while the chorus (the company), beginning at [94], interjects cries of "*Oy, lyui*," adapted from *K447* (see above). Meanwhile, the pianos adumbrate the theme that will finish the tableau: the groom's epithalamium.

N
N'

Q      A (0 2 7 10 or 0 3 5 7)

O' (choral interjections)      A (0 5 7 or 0 5 10)

A'      A→D (0 3 5 [6 8])

TABLE 4 (continued)

Location	Source reference and remarks	Musical theme	Modal classification
[96]+6	K458 (Ryazan guberniya), lines 1–4. A song sung by the bride's father as he hands her over to the groom before the church ceremony. In Stravinsky's version, spelled out in his performance directions, it is the groom's father (tenor and bass soli) who leads the assembled male guests (choral tenors and basses) in what has become a sort of koril'naya asserting the groom's rights over the bride.	R	C (0 1 2 3 5 6 7 9)
[97]+1	K199 (Tver guberniya), lines 9–10. Meanwhile, the women chime in with a mock chiding of the bride ("We told you so, Nastasya dear"), adapted from the middle of a song collected by I. M. Snegiryov in the village of Ostashkov.	(nonrecurrent)	
[98]	K493 (Tambov guberniya). Another giving-away-the-bride song, sung in folk ritual by the bride's father at the zgovor while joining the couple's hands. Stravinsky gives it to the bride's mother (mezzo-soprano soloist), who, in the stage direction, "leads her [i.e., the bride] to her son-in-law," to whom the song is addressed. It overlaps with the groom's father's song (K458), which continues until [98]+4.	S	D (0 2 3 5 7)
[99]+3	K458, resumed and completed (lines 5–8)	R'	D (0 2 3 5 7 8 10) (natural minor)
[100]+4	K407, resumed and completed (lines 7, 9–17). At [101]+4 Stravinsky inserts a line of his own ("gostey obkhodili," "went around to all the guests"), which adds to the description of filling glasses and drinking toasts. The composer may have recalled the famous wedding jester's song from Alexey Verstovsky's opera Askold's Grave (1835): "Zakhodili charochki po stoliku" ("The cups went around the table").	Q	
[104]	K1009, lines 1–9, copied by Kireyevsky out of the so-called Glazunov Songbook (Glazunovskiy pesennik), a huge (six-volume) miscellany published in St. Peters-	Q (cont'd)	

D (0 3 5 7 9 10)

T ([106])

O' (*lyuli, lyuli* refrains)

T (cont'd)

T'
O' (*lyuli, lyuli* refrains as before)
M' ("factory song" from Istomin/Dyutsh via Mitusov):

D (0 2 5 7 9 10 or 0 2 3 5 7 10)

Ne - ve - syo - la - ya Da

kom - pan' - i - tsa. Nu gde mi-lo-vo net.

A (0 3 5 7 9)

U

burg in 1819 by the house of Glazunov (founded by the famous composer's grandfather), containing folk songs of all kinds, favorite operatic airs and choruses, etc. Stravinsky changed the number of geese from plural to singular so that the song becomes a *koril'naya* addressed specifically to the groom in search of the bride (swan). This song is hooked up—without changing the tune—to:

[108] *K571* (Oryol guberniya), lines 1–4. A song sung to the bride on the way to the altar in actual folk ritual. It shares with *K1009* the bridal imagery of goose and swan. This song gives way in turn, still maintaining the same melody, to:

[109] *K177* (Tver guberniya), lines 3, 5–11, presented out of order (5–6, 3, 7–11). More swan imagery. It is in the midst of this song (line 10, fig. [110]+2) that Stravinsky introduces the "factory song" he took down from his friend Mitusov.

[111] (Match-maker) *K438* (Ryazan guberniya), lines 1–6. Another *propoy*, the text of which plays on the literal meaning of the word (from *propit'*, to "drink away," e.g., one's fortune, one's property, etc.). Although it functions here as a humorous *koril'naya* sung by the *svat* to the father of the bride, Harkins notes that "in more serious bridal laments this reproach, that he has sold her for drink, is often addressed by the bride to her father."

[111]+1 (*Druzhka*) This "typical wedding jest," as Harkins terms it, is drawn from a lengthy prose description of the "village wedding" as performed in the Olonets guberniya, on pp. 44–45 of the Kireyevsky anthology. It is shouted by the matchmakers when the groom's suite arrives to pick up the bride on the wedding morn (she being hidden

TABLE 4 (continued)

Location	Source reference and remarks	Musical theme	Modal classification
	away to be dressed): "Matchmakers, snap to it! Give the groom his bride! He's getting bored!" Transferred to the wedding feast, and shouted by the *druzhko* (tenor soloist), it obviously refers to the marriage bed. The shouting of the *druzhko* (as opposed to his singing) at the *krasniy stol* is explicitly recorded by Istomin in the preface to his second collection (with Lyapunov), p. xv. (Cf. *infra*, [114]−1, [125]−2 through [127]−3, [129]+3; it is always the *druzhko* to whom Stravinsky assigns spoken—that is, shouted—lines.)		
[112] (*Druzhko*)	*K806*, complete (including the final shouted exclamation [114]). Harkins calls this "a classic humorous apostrophe by the best man to the company" and translates it thus: "Fair maids, cooking whizzes, pot smashers, proud matrons, thin old grannies, puny brats, zany rogues and piddling scoundrels: Sing your songs!"	J'	A (0 2 [4] 5 7 9)
[114]	*K510* (Tambov guberniya), lines 1–6. A stichomythic exchange between bride and groom about the marriage bed, narrated by the girls. Stravinsky casts this in antiphonal terms, the choral sopranos and altos supplying the "he said/she said" and the soloists (minus the bass) reciting the actual repliques. The stage direction here is copied directly from the descriptive commentary preceding this song in Kireyevsky (p. 147): "The *druzhko* selects a married couple from the groom's suite, whom he sends off to warm the bed for the young couple." Harkins comments that "the original significance of this rite was a transferral of fertility to the newly wedded couple." This takes place at the conclusion of the wedding meal.	A' (soloists' repliques)	A' (0 3 5 [6 8])
[115]	*K1021*, lines 1–8. From the Glazunov Songbook. A *velichal'naya* in praise of the groom.	Instruments: A' (cont'd) Voices: N'	
[117] (Matchmaker and wedding suite)	*K803*, lines 1–6. A song of encouragement to the *druzhko* (Savel) not to relax his efforts to arrange a fine wedding (*sryazhai svadebku*) for the groom, his friend (Khvetis). This text was evidently the source for the title of Stravinsky's work. It is noteworthy that, though this	U	

song is defective in the source (Kireyevsky prints an ellipsis to show that a word—probably a name—is missing from the first line), Stravinsky unhesitatingly set it just as it stood (cf. the *zapevnaya* in the *Quatre chants russes*).

[119] (The wedding party)	*K438*, resumed (lines 7–11). The portion set here ends with the announcement that a speech is to follow; the concluding punctuation is a colon. The remainder of the song—i.e., the *druzhko's* speech—is replaced by:	N
[120]	*K803*, resumed and completed (lines 7–10). The *druzhko* responds that he has attended well to his duty and arranged a wonderful *svadebka*.	M (source melody)
[121]	*K823*, describing the bride's joining a new family, to which she will have to be submissive, but where she will be well treated.	A' N ([122] + 4
[123]	*K448* (Ryazan guberniya), lines 1–6. Sung by the male voices while the women continue with *K823*. This text describes the groom in search of his bride.	N' (octatonic variant)
[125]	*K591* (Oryol guberniya), lines 1–12. The main wedding toast. Prince Kostrov, Kireyevsky's informant, called it "The Chief Matchmaker's Sing-Song at the *Knyazhnik*," the latter (more often, according to Dahl, called the *knyazhak*) being an alternative name for the *krasniy stol*. The collector added the following note: "These jingles [*pribautki*] are uttered by the chief matchmaker when the young couple begin soliciting gifts from their relatives. Approaching the father of the groom of the bride, he says this song. Depending on whom the matchmaker, offering wine, approaches, the beginning formula will vary." Although he gives this song to the *druzhko* rather than the *svat*, Stravinsky reproduces the scene with remarkable realism. The tenor soloist, taking the part of the leader of the toast, shouts his *pribautki* in a fast, precisely notated rhythmic patter, faithful—as Stravinsky had not been in years—to the declamation of the spoken language. "The remaining best men and the women,"	M

TABLE 4 (continued)

Location	Source reference and remarks	Musical theme	Modal classification
	as Stravinsky designates the chorus at this point, respond in "sing-song," using a typical three-pitch *napev*. Beginning at [127], the best man begins shifting rapidly between speech and notated sing-song (marked "*napevaya*" by Stravinsky: "taking up the *napev*").	[127]: A' (instruments) N (voices)	
[127] + 3	Meanwhile, the bass soloist and the chorus, representing the guests, interrupt the toast with the traditional cry, "Bitter, ugh, we can't drink it," referring to the wine. The bride and groom must then kiss (they do so, according to Stravinsky's stage direction, at [127]+5), which sweetens the wine, and the toasts continue. This whole episode, including the exact form of the guests' exclamation and the exact wording of the stage direction, comes from Pogodin's description of the wedding customs of the Sirzan district (Simbirsk guberniya), given in Kireyevsky on p. 200.		
[127 (bis)]	This leering little quatrain about the bride's impending pregnancy, sung by the bass soloist (joined from time to time by his colleagues in the chorus) to the hocketing tune first heard at [91] to the words of *K451*, is the one *Svadebka* text that has so far eluded identification. Two bits of circumstantial evidence seem to point to a source within Stravinsky's own circle of family or friends, its appearance in *Svadebka* being then an in-joke on the order of the brief allusion to "*Chicher-Yacher*" in the finale of the Symphony in E-flat. One of these clues is a footnote in which Stravinsky directs that the first vowel in the indicative pronoun (the so-called è *oborotnoye*, or "backward E") be iotized, so that the word is pronounced not "èta," but "yeta." This is a common way of parodying the effects of inebriation (cf. Varlaam's song in *Boris Godunov*: "Kak yekhal yon"). In any case, Stravinsky's concern for pronunciation here suggests that he knew this song as actually sung, not just as recorded in print. The second clue is a calligraphic copy of this particular excerpt from *Svadebka* (words and rhythms only), amorously inscribed to Vera Sudeikine	P	

(the future Mme Stravinsky) in her autograph album, signed and dated Paris, 1921. It is reproduced in Craft (ed.), *Igor and Vera Stravinsky: A Photograph Album*, 53; a photograph of the album itself (open to this page), as part of a collage of Stravinsky memorabilia, can be seen in R. Craft and A. Newman, *Bravo Stravinsky*, 38–39.

[128] + 2	P	K591, resumed and completed. In the song's original context the matchmaker is soliciting gifts of money for the newlyweds. In the context created by the interpolation of the preceding song, these lines have the effect of bidding on the bride herself. The basses continue with this through [130].
[128] + 3 (*Druzhko*)	N	K491 (Tambov guberniya), lines 1–3. In the folk ritual this song is sung by the bridesmaids when the groom's party arrives at her threshold on the wedding morn. In this new context, the image of the impatient groom at the gates suggests the imminent deflowering of the bride. Where the text goes into direct discourse, it is set to the "*lyuli lyuli*" music from above (theme O).
	O ([129])	
[129] + 2 (*Druzhko*)	(spoken)	K668 (Oryol guberniya), sung, according to the compiler of the manuscript Kireyevsky copied, "when they wish to lead [the newlyweds] off to bed." It is not sung in *Svadebka*, but shouted (tenor) and answered (also in a shout) by the other soloists plus the sopranos and altos of the chorus. In Harkins's translation: "Ay, you blind best men, haven't you noticed: The girl's pushed towards her fellow and asked him to the storeroom" (that is, the unheated chamber where the marriage bed is set up).
[129] + 4	(spoken)	K438, resumed and completed (lines 12–13). Again, the lines pick up a double entendre from their context. Instead of a *propoy* (toast at the *zgovor*), it is now addressed by the *svat* (shouting) to the couple warming the bed: "We've got the girl, now give us the bed."
[130]	M	K396 (Tula guberniya), lines 1–7. Stravinsky uses this song, collected by one Afanasiy Markovich in February 1850, to accompany the following action: "The bed warmers climb out. Fetis (i.e., Khvetis) and Nastasya

TABLE 4 (continued)

Location	Source reference and remarks	Musical theme	Modal classification
	are led to the bed, tucked in, the door is closed, and they are left alone. The parents of the bride and groom seat themselves on a bench in front of the door. All face them." The composer changed the opening word of the text, *korovat'* (bed), to its synonym *pastel'ya*, to accord with the diction of the preceding (shouted) song.		
[131] + 4	*K514* (Tambov guberniya), lines 1–2. The song describes the newlyweds in bed. The descriptive commentary in Kireyevsky is evidently the source of the preceding stage direction: "An hour after the feast is ended the *druzhko* leads the newlyweds to bed and, entering the hut where the bed has been prepared, asks the married couple who have been sent to warm it, 'What sort of people are lying here?' They answer: 'We were sent by the young prince to warm the bed.' The *druzhko*: 'Having warmed it, be so kind as to climb down.' They: 'Not until we are paid for our work.' The *druzhko* hands them each a glass of beer, while the girls sing [K514]."	A'	
[132] + 2	*K465* (Kaluga guberniya), lines 4–5. The anonymous informant called this song an *obigrivil'naya*, a local variant of *velichal'naya*. The groom is praised for the way he lovingly caresses his bride. The chorus hits its climax at the point where the groom (in bed with his bride) presses her to his heart.	M	
[133]	*K514*, resumed and completed, now cast in the form of direct discourse (groom to bride). He calls her his "nightly pleasure"; whereupon, according to the descriptive commentary in Kireyevsky, "the *druzhko* urges them round one another leg to leg, with instructions not to disentangle themselves until his return; they are left alone and all go back [from the bed hut] to the house."	A'	
[133] + 9	*K465*, resumed and completed (lines 7–8). The groom caresses the bride and promises her a good life: "We will live together so well that people will envy us."	A' (cont'd)	

PART IV

ON THE CUSP OF
THE NEW CLASSICISM:
A HERITAGE REDEFINED

No other phase of Stravinsky's career was so completely given over to vocal music as were the Swiss years, when the "rejoicing discovery" of folk poetry sent its powerful Eurasian reverberations into every fiber of the composer's creative being. Nevertheless, in the period between *The Nightingale* and *Mavra* Stravinsky did manage to turn out a steady stream of minor instrumental compositions, and they are worth a look. In them we may see how features of his art that entered by way of its subject matter finally solidified into "abstract" components of its style. These compositions are listed in Table 5.

A NEW PATH?

Unlike the vocal music, so resolutely focused in the assimilation and creative transformation of the composer's native folklore, the instrumental works of the period are a motley. Many of them do exhibit national character, or at least incorporate material of determinable national origin; but in place of the ethnic purity of the vocal music we are confronted with a veritable melting pot. Alongside the expected Russian (and, possibly, Byzantine) melodies, we find Stravinsky drawing on German, Irish, French (Breton), Italian, Spanish, and even Brazilian sources, in addition to various mongrel types of North American popular music. This surface cosmopolitanism has led many commentators to locate the beginnings of Stravinsky's "neoclassicism" right here, turning these mostly unassuming little pieces into a major esthetic watershed. The fact that a few of them exhibit simple triadic harmonies, sans octatonic or "polytonal" admixtures, has led to their being looked upon as "tonal," which also seems to spell neoclassicism.

Instrumental Compositions of the Swiss Years

Title	Date	Dedicatee	First Public Performance	Publication
Trois pièces (string quartet)[a] 1. [Danse] ♩ = 126 2. [Excentrique] ♩ = 76 3. [Cantique] ♩ = 40	26 April 1914 (Leysin) 2 July 1914 (Salvan) 25–26 July [1914] (Salvan)	Ernest Ansermet	Chicago, 8 November 1915[b] (Flonzaley Quartet)	1922 (Paris, Édition Russe de Musique)
Tsvetochniy val's (*Valse des Fleurs*) (piano four-hands)	30 October/12 November 1914 (Clarens)		New York, 1949 (Chamber Art Society)	1983 (MS. facsimile in *A Stravinsky Scrapbook, 1940–1971*, 146–47)
Trois pièces faciles (piano four-hands) 3. Polka	15 November 1914 (Clarens)	Sergey Diaghilev	Lausanne, 22 April 1918 (Ernest Ansermet and Nino Rossi)	1917 (Geneva, Ad. Henn)
1. Marche 2. Valse[c]	9 December 1914 (Clarens) 6 March 1915 (Château d'Oex)	Alfredo Casella Erik Satie		
Souvenir d'une marche boche (piano solo)	1 September 1915 (Morges)			1916 (MS. facsimile in Edith Wharton, ed., *Le livre des Sans-Foyer*)
Valse pour les enfants (piano solo)	December 1916? (Morges)	"Pour les petits lecteurs du *Figaro*"		21 May 1922 (Paris, *Le Figaro*)

Work	Composition	Dedicatee	Premiere	Publication
Cinq pièces faciles (piano four-hands)[a]		Eugenia Errazuriz	Lausanne, 22 April 1918 (Ansermet and Rossi)	1917 (Henn)
1. Andante	7 January 1917 (Morges)			
3. Balalaika	6 February 1917 (Morges)			
5. Galop [orig. title "Cancan"][e]	21 February 1917 (Morges)			
4. Napolitana	28 February 1917 (Morges)			
2. Española	3 April 1917 (Morges)			
Étude (pianola)	10 September 1917 (Morges)	Eugenia Errazuriz	London, 13 October 1921 (Reginald Reynolds)	1951 (London, Boosey & Hawkes, arr. Soulima Stravinsky for two pianos)
"Lied ohne Name" (two bassoons)[f]	ca. October 1918 (Morges)		London, 30 October 1979 (John Price and Joanna Graham)	1982 (MS facsimile in SelCorrI:410)
Trois pièces (clarinet solo)		Werner Reinhart	Lausanne, 8 November 1919 (Edmund Allegra)	1920 (London, J. & W. Chester)
1. ♩ = 52	19 October 1918 (Morges)			
2. ♪ = 168	24 October 1918 (Morges)			
3. ♪ = 160	15 November 1918 (Morges)			
Ragtime pour onze instruments	10 November 1918 (Morges)	Eugenia Errazuriz	London, 27 April 1920 (Arthur Bliss, cond.)	1919 (Paris, Éditions de la Sirène)
Piano-Rag-Music (piano solo)	28 June 1919 (Morges)	Artur Rubinstein	Lausanne, 8 November 1919 (José Iturbi)	1920 (London, J. & W. Chester)

TABLE 5 (continued)

Title	Date	Dedicatee	First Public Performance	Publication
Concertino (string quartet)	24 September 1920 (Garches)	Flonzaley Quartet (MS ded. André Caplet)	New York, 23 November 1920 (Flonzaley Quartet)	1923 (Copenhagen, Wilhelm Hansen)
Symphonies d'instruments à vent	20 November 1920 (Garches)	"A la mémoire de Claude Debussy"	London, 10 June 1921 (Serge Koussevitzky, cond.)	1920 (Revue musicale, final section only, arr. piano) 1926 (Paris, Édition Russe de Musique, arr. piano by Artur Lourié) 1952 (London, Boosey & Hawkes, revised score of 1947) 1983 (Melville, N.Y., Belwin Mills, original score of 1920)

[a] The titles were added to the string quartet pieces when they were orchestrated and published as the first three of the Quatre études for Orchestra (1930).

[b] In a letter to Stravinsky (5 March 1917), Francis Poulenc noted that the string quartet pieces were "performed for the first time at the Salle des Agriculteurs by Yvonne Astruc, Darius Milhaud, et al." (SelCorrIII:198–99). This was the Paris, not the world, première.

[c] In D&D:72, Stravinsky states: "I orchestrated the Valse for seven solo instruments after composing it," and mentions an arrangement of the March for eight solo players. The latter has remained unpublished. The manuscript, dated 1915, is in the collection of the Paul Sacher Foundation, Basel. It was performed for the first (and only?) time under Robert Craft at a Stravinsky memorial concert at the Whitney Museum in New York in October 1981. The arrangement of the Valse is apparently the one found in the Suite for Small Orchestra, eventually published as "Suite No. 2" in 1925. The instrumentation is always listed as dating from 1921, yet the scoring of the Valse is for precisely seven instruments: flute, piccolo, oboe, two clarinets, bassoon, trumpet. Thus if the "Suite No. 1" is generally dated 1917–25, it appears that No. 2 should be listed as 1915–21. (For an account of the occasion that motivated the instrumentation of the second suite, see Chapter 19.)

[d] The chronology of the Cinq pièces faciles in D&D:73 is belied by the dates on the autographs. In conversation with Craft, Stravinsky let it be known that "the Española was joined to the album after a trip to Spain, the Napolitana after a trip to Naples. Two of the Russian souvenirs, the Baïalaïka . . . and the Galop, were added at a later date, and the third, the Andante, like most preludes, was tacked on last." But as the table shows, the Andante came first, not last; and the Española plus Napolitana came last, not first. The trip to Spain, incidentally, had taken place in the spring of 1916, almost a year before any of the pieces in the set were composed.

[e] See the description of Lot 118 in the catalogue "Fine Books and Manuscripts" (sale no. 5114), for items auctioned at Sotheby's on 14 December 1983.

[f] Both the title (why in German?) and the instrumental designation were added by Stravinsky to the existing MS (Sketchbook E as listed by Shepard) in July 1949.

Stravinsky was happy to abet this view, in an oft cited if apocryphal anecdote about the impression his little Polka for piano four-hands had made on Alfredo Casella, who was quick to echo that piece and the others of its ilk in his *Pupazzetti* for piano duet (as he would later echo *Pulcinella* in his *Scarlattiana* for chamber orchestra, and so on). In Stravinsky's words, "a new path had been indicated; . . . so-called neoclassicism of a sort was born in that moment."[1]

But the Polka's path had been indicated three years earlier in the third tableau of *Petrushka*—and, more than a generation before that, in the "Chopsticks" paraphrases of the Belyayevtsï (see Chapter 1). The piece that had got the paraphrases started, in fact, had been a polka (Borodin's), based, like Stravinsky's, on the humorous counterpoint of a childish ostinato with sophisticated grown-up elaborations. Closer to home—that is, to Stravinsky's home as of 1914—was Erik Satie, who had been writing pieces in a style variously known as "café-concert," "Transatlantique," or "music-hall" since the turn of the century. Stravinsky actually referred to his Polka, Valse, and Marche for piano four-hands as his "three music-hall pieces" in a letter of 1916.[2] So whatever the path Stravinsky's Polka might have indicated in 1914, it was not "neoclassicism," nor was it "born in that moment."

Nor was it "tonal." The B-flat–major vamp in the Polka could just as well have been the occasion of that famous exchange between Diaghilev and Stravinsky concerning the "Augures printaniers" from *The Rite,* as the composer recalled it for the CBS-TV camera in his eightieth year: "How long will this continue??" —"To the end, my dear!" One triad does not make a key. The *Trois pièces faciles,* along with the *Valse de fleurs* that immediately preceded them, belong, together with vast tracts of *The Rite* and many of the Swiss songs, to the special genre of "vamping pieces," as we may call them, a genre that is as inherently Eurasian in conception and facture as the most overtly folkish page in *Svadebka*.[3] Although they make conspicuous teasing reference to the phonology and morphology of tonal music, they remain altogether alien to tonal grammar and syntax.

A comparison of the waltz in the third tableau of *Petrushka,* with its genuinely functional, if primitive, harmonic accompaniment courtesy of Lanner, and the four-handed *Tsvetochniy val's* (*Valse de fleurs*) of 1914 (Fig. 18.1) will show how far

1. D&D:72/*Dialogues,* 41. There are serious discrepancies between the composer's report and other relevant documents. Stravinsky recalled that he "played the Polka to Diaghilev and Alfredo Casella in a hotel room in Milan in 1915. . . . Casella was so genuinely enthusiastic about the Polka that I promised to write a little piece for him, too. This, the March, was composed immediately on my return to Morges" (ibid.). Yet the autograph of the March is dated 9 December 1914, and the meeting in Milan could not have taken place before Casella's arrival back in Italy from France, which according to Casella's memoirs occurred "on the day of Sgambati's death," which was 14 December 1914 (Casella, *Music In My Time,* trans. Spencer Norton [Norman: University of Oklahoma Press, 1955], 123). The version of the story in the *Chroniques,* according to which the meeting with Diaghilev took place in Rome in the winter of 1915 (Stravinsky having all three pieces "in my luggage" by then) and which does not mention Casella at all, is in greater harmony with the known external facts.

2. To Ansermet; in SelCorrI:131.

3. For another suggestive Russian forerunner to Stravinsky's vamping pieces, see Vladimir Rebikov's "Strolling Musicians", op. 31/2, from the set of children's pieces for piano entitled *Silhouettes.*

FIG. 18.1. *Tsvetochnïy val's* (*Valse de fleurs;* 1914).

Stravinsky's musical imagination had retreated from Europe behind Turanian lines. For all its harping on the C-major triad, the *Tsvetochnïy val's* never once establishes its key through a cadence. Although configurations occur in the prima part that can be construed as adumbrating the dominant, the putative leading tone is, if not actually suppressed, grossly attenuated at such moments, only to return when the putative resolution is due. In m. 11, note how deliberately Stravinsky weakens the suggestion of a dominant by contradicting the implied seventh (F) with F-sharp; in mm. 22 and 24, note how the leading tone (B) is contradicted by B-flat. The harmonic rhythm never supports any tonal plan with a pattern of tension and release. Release can never be anticipated, which is why Stravinsky must create factitiously whatever impression of tonal closure he wishes to evoke, typically by means of accents. Nor does harmony serve to articulate any overall shape. The piece starts and stops, despite its apparent "tonal" orientation, without any tonally articulated beginning or ending.

It is not so much that Stravinsky denies the existence of the tonic/dominant relationship as that he is indifferent to its traditional form-generating properties. It may exist in his Swiss-period music, but only as a "clang." Even when the tonic and dominant happen to be both harmonically and rhythmically in place, as in the Valse from the *Trois pièces faciles,* they function jointly as nothing more than a drone, an inert backdrop against which the music unfolds, not the force that guides it.

Thus, for all their "tonal" and "Western" resonances, the instrumental pieces of the Swiss years are nevertheless quite of a piece with the more overtly Turanian vocal music of the period. They still exemplify—in some cases, to a surpassing degree—the characteristics of that peculiarly "Russian" modernism definitively established by *The Rite* and best described by employing a Russian vocabulary: *nepodvizhnost', drobnost', uproshcheniye.* Let us revisit these terms, one by one.

1. *Nepodvizhnost'.* The word means immobility, and it was applied by many critics to the ostinato-driven music of *The Rite.* Yet what are the "vamping pieces" of the Swiss decade if not *nepodvizhnost'* raised to an even higher power? The pieces in which "tonality" seems superficially to have made a comeback are the very ones in which "goal-oriented" form and directed voice-leading are most conspicuously in abeyance. Some of them are virtually reduced to the level of wind-up toy automata by the maintenance of a single ostinato for the duration. These most immobile pieces of all include the *Trois pièces,* the *Tsvetochniy val's,* the *Figaro* waltz, and several of the *Cinq pièces faciles* (though in the latter set, the opening Andante excepted, the ostinati are less implacable and the pieces, concomitantly, are more conventionally shaped; Robert Craft was quite right to point out that the *Trois pièces* "are landmarks in Stravinsky's art, which cannot be said of the national songs and dances" in the *Cinq*).[4]

Nor is the genre of "automata" simply coextensive with that of the "easy" or "children's" pieces. The first of the Three Pieces for String Quartet carries the device to an extreme: it presents a multiplicity of hypostatized ostinati, each having its own pitch collection and registral space, the whole making up what in the discussion below will be termed a "mobile."

That said, the *Valse pour les enfants* printed in *Le Figaro* (Fig. 18.2) can serve as a convenient paradigm to illustrate Turanian *nepodvizhnost'.* Its vamp is one of Stravinsky's characteristic "phonological" references to tonality, and an especially elusive one. Superficially it could be described as a "mixture" of tonic and domi-

---

4. SelCorrI:411.

FIG. 18.2. *Valse pour les enfants* (1916?).

nant, the bass line reaching the tonic on every second downbeat by way of the supertonic (cf. the *gapi mushka* music in *Petrushka*), the accompanying chord tones making an opposing approach to "V₇" by way of the tonic third and fifth. Yet if one takes the pattern as beginning on the second quarter in the measure (and the placement of the four preparatory notes in the melody encourages one to do so), then one has an unimpeded tonic/dominant alternation, albeit one in which the putative dominant is hobbled by the significant—and, as we have seen, characteristic—lack of a leading tone.

There is a leading tone in the piece, though: it is D-sharp, applied to E. (By contrast, the F-sharps in the melody either proceed in somewhat archaistic fashion as cadential supertonics like the A's in the bass, or are neutralized by F-naturals; they never resolve as leading tones to G, the putative tonic of the vamp.) Is the waltz, then, "bitonal"? Hardly. For one thing, the "added sixth," exemplified here by E, seems to be part and parcel of Stravinsky's idea of cadential "final" in almost all the triadic vamping pieces of the period: compare both the Polka and the Waltz Trio from the *Trois pièces faciles* (and also compare Satie's *Gymnopédies,* which loom rather large in the background). For another (more important) thing, the vamp's immobility and the circularity of the progression it unfolds preclude its participating in the articulation of the music's form. Without such shaping there is no tonality, hence no "bitonality." The harmony is denatured, "melted into air," and on this bed of air the melody floats free, unfettered by any directionality that a more dynamically articulated chordal succession might have imposed. For a true antecedent to this innocuous little waltz one must look not to Lanner or Schubert or Chopin, but to the "Augures printaniers" or the "Cercles mystérieux"—and beyond them, to the *vesnyanki* and *petrivki* of the immemorial agrarian calendar.

2. *Drobnost'.* This quality of being a sum-of-parts has been in our Stravinskian vocabulary since Chapter 2. Its witting exploitation again goes back to *The Rite* and reached its spectacular peak in the instrumental music of the Swiss years—a peak so spectacular that recent critics have felt the need anachronistically to borrow a term from Karlheinz Stockhausen's music and writings of the 1960s[5] to deal with such Stravinskian products as the second of the Three Pieces for String Quartet (1914) or the *Symphonies d'instruments à vent* (1920).[6] Here is how G. W. Hopkins summarizes Stockhausen's concept of the "moment" in *The New Grove Dictionary:* "Each individually characterized passage in a work is regarded as an experiential unit, a 'moment,' which can potentially engage the listener's full atten-

5. "Momentform" (1960), in Karlheinz Stockhausen, *Texte zur elektronischen und instrumentalen Musik,* vol. 1 (Cologne: Verlag M. Du Mont Schauberg, 1963), 189–210; also cf. *Momente* (1962) for chorus and orchestra.

6. For the concept, see Jonathan D. Kramer, "Moment Form in Twentieth-Century Music," *Musical Quarterly* 64 (1978): 177–94; on the second piece for string quartet, see Marianne Kielian-Gilbert, "Relationships of Symmetrical Pitch-Class Sets and Stravinsky's Metaphor of Polarity," *Perspectives of New Music* 21 (1982–83): 210–21. The literature relating to the *Symphonies* will be discussed below (see note 63).

tion and can do so in exactly the same measure as its neighbors. No single 'moment' claims priority, even as a beginning or ending; hence the nature of such a work is essentially 'unending' (and, indeed, 'unbeginning').”[7]

Some of Stravinsky's instrumental works of the Swiss period can indeed support this description (whether they invite it is another question). We have already associated the quality of “unending” and “unbeginning” with *nepodvizhnost'*, a quality intrinsic to unisectional, ostinato-driven pieces. When such sections are multiplied, one result is *drobnost'*.

Besides the quartet and wind pieces, we might take the Étude for Pianola as a paradigm of *drobnost'*. Inspired by a visit to Spain with the Ballets Russes in May/June 1916, the Étude, in Stravinsky's words, aimed to convey “the whimsicalities of the unexpected melodies of the mechanical pianos and rattletrap orchestrinas of the Madrid streets and the night taverns.”[8] It represents a kind of vertical slice through time, calculated to give the impression of a cacophony of simultaneous musics, the whole unfolding in a sort of instantaneous “specious present.” Thus, though inevitably sequential, the piece is not temporally “linear.” The many little sections, most of them characterized by a distinctive ostinato, conspire to produce a seemingly random pattern of intercuttings in which, just as in Hopkins's description of Stockhausen's idea, the individual sections form no perceptual hierarchy and no progression. One unlearns one's habits of drawing motivic connections from section to section when listening to music like this. When sections return, they do so without significant change. If the first of the string quartet pieces is a musical “mobile,” the Étude is a musical “collage.”

These visual-arts analogies remind us that Stravinsky's deliberately disjointed productions of the war years are often compared with analytical cubism. As cubism purports to represent multiple perspectives on a two-dimensional plane, Stravinsky's music often suggests multiple layers of a single unordered moment in time, presented in an arbitrary, nonsignificant sequence. The cubist analogy, being less anachronistic than one drawn to Stockhausen, may be a more effective way of conceptualizing a work like the Étude (though, as will be argued below, it does not fit the redoubtable *Symphonies* quite as well as is often maintained). In any event, it would be unwise to insist on a perfect fit either with respect to cubism or with respect to *Momentform*. The Étude does have a definite sense of beginning and ending (the latter is a marvelous joke, in fact). What it lacks is a sense of a middle—that is, of something purposefully connecting the beginning and the end. Yet when actually performed on a pianola, the ending takes on a quality of unsignaled interruption that human performers seem incapable of duplicating (though

---

7. *New Grove Dictionary*, s.v. “Stockhausen, Karlheinz” (18:152).
8. *An Autobiography*, 69.

in his own performances—and not only of his own music—Stravinsky certainly tried).[9] The status of an ending becomes equivocal under these circumstances.

Stravinsky's attraction to mechanical performance media went deeper than their potential for shock and amusement. He spent countless hours between 1914 and 1929 recording his works on piano rolls—everything from the Études, op. 7, to the 1924 *Sonate* for piano, encompassing the three prewar ballets as well as *Pulcinella,* the *Chant du rossignol,* and *Svadebka* (see Fig. 18.3). In addition, he at one time planned a version of the last-named piece that would have included a pianola in its actual performance roster.[10] Robert Craft has called Stravinsky's infatuation with the pianola "one of the inexplicable eccentricities of his career."[11] Yet explanation would seem to lie, at least in part, precisely in the two quintessentially Turanian qualities of Stravinsky's music that we are investigating right now: its *nepodvizhnost'* and its *drobnost'*. The impersonal and esthetically disinterested machine can—in theory, at least—perform a more neutrally regular—hence more "immobile"—ostinato than a human executant, for example; and, as the original roll of the Étude proves, it can underscore *drobnost'* with jolting disjunctures, unsignaled and unanticipated to an extent apparently unattainable by a physically involved and esthetically engaged human being.[12]

One of Stravinsky's most impressive piano rolls is that of the *Piano-Rag-Music,* rendered with a speed and "dexterity" in negotiating the nontransitions that not even Artur Rubinstein could have equaled, had he ever overcome his aversion to the piece Stravinsky had written for him and attempted to perform it. Rubinstein doubtless found it baffling, as have many since, not only because of its excessively

9. Compare the actual piano roll of the Étude, issued by the Aeolian company in 1921, with "human" performances of the piece, whether in the two-piano arrangement by Soulima Stravinsky (recorded by Paul Jacobs and Ursula Oppens on Nonesuch 71347) or as orchestrated as the concluding movement ("Madrid") in *Four Études for Orchestra* (1930). The supreme document of Stravinsky's pianolistically mechanical performance ideals remains his recording, with Soulima, of Mozart's Fugue in C minor, K426. It was made around 1938 as the filler side on French Columbia set LFX-951-3, chiefly devoted to Stravinsky's *Concerto per due pianoforti soli.* The inhumanly mechanical manner in which they execute the final cadence obviously emulates the "perfectly impersonal and perfectly mechanical" style of the player (*recte* playerless) pianos Stravinsky had experimented with in the twenties.

10. For details of Stravinsky's love affair with the player piano and a complete list of his output in the medium, see Rex Lawson, "Stravinsky and the Pianola," in Jann Pasler (ed.), *Confronting Stravinsky,* 284–301.

11. P&D:164.

12. Yet a caveat must be entered. As Rex Lawson demonstrated dramatically at the International Stravinsky Symposium at the University of California, San Diego, in September 1982 (and as Ansermet warned Stravinsky as early as June 1919; see P&D:164–65), the "mechanicalness" of the mechanical piano was not to be taken for granted, and the intervention of "interpretation" cannot be ruled out. See Lawson's remarks in "Stravinsky and the Pianola," 286, concluding with the witty observation that it was poor performances(!) that created "the mistaken impression . . . that the player piano had its own unique sound, characterized by inexorable tempi and terrace dynamics with only one terrace." Even if we assume that by Lawson's lights what Stravinsky wanted from the pianola was "bad" performances, the fact that the pianolist is able to shape the dynamics, tempo, and even the touch by means of his pedaling (plus other devices and attachments that varied from model to model) does tend rather to limit the value of Stravinsky's rolls as documentation of his performance practice (this despite what Stravinsky had to say in *An Autobiography,* 150–52).

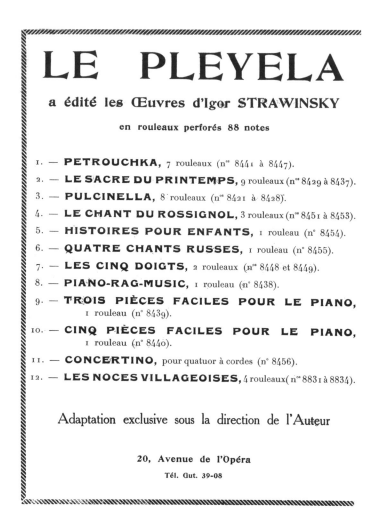

LE PLEYELA

a édité les Œuvres d'Igor STRAWINSKY

en rouleaux perforés 88 notes

1. — **PETROUCHKA,** 7 rouleaux (n⁰ˢ 8441 à 8447).

2. — **LE SACRE DU PRINTEMPS,** 9 rouleaux (n⁰ˢ 8429 à 8437).

3. — **PULCINELLA,** 8 rouleaux (n⁰ˢ 8421 à 8428).

4. — **LE CHANT DU ROSSIGNOL,** 3 rouleaux (n⁰ˢ 8451 à 8453).

5. — **HISTOIRES POUR ENFANTS,** 1 rouleau (n° 8454).

6. — **QUATRE CHANTS RUSSES,** 1 rouleau (n° 8455).

7. — **LES CINQ DOIGTS,** 2 rouleaux (n⁰ˢ 8448 et 8449).

8. — **PIANO-RAG-MUSIC,** 1 rouleau (n° 8438).

9. — **TROIS PIÈCES FACILES POUR LE PIANO,**
   1 rouleau (n° 8439).

10. — **CINQ PIÈCES FACILES POUR LE PIANO,**
   1 rouleau (n° 8440).

11. — **CONCERTINO,** pour quatuor à cordes (n° 8456).

12. — **LES NOCES VILLAGEOISES,** 4 rouleaux (n⁰ˢ 8831 à 8834).

Adaptation exclusive sous la direction de l'Auteur

20, Avenue de l'Opéra

Tél. Gut. 39-08

FIG. 18.3a. Back cover of special Stravinsky issue of the *Revue musicale* (5, no. 2 [December 1923]), advertising the composer's piano rolls.

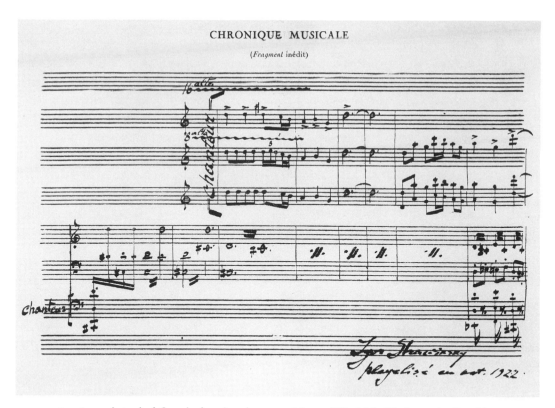

CHRONIQUE MUSICALE

(*Fragment* inédit)

FIG. 18.3b.   A typical Stravinsky pianola score: No. 2 ("*Gusi-lebedi*") from the *Detskiye pesenki* ("Histoires pour enfants" as listed in the *Revue musicale* advertisement), published in "Chronique musicale" in *Les feuilles libres,* no. 29 (October–November 1922), as a "Fragment inédit . . . pleyelisé en oct. 1922."

percussive approach to the keyboard,[13] but also because of its excessive *drobnost'*. It is even more of a collage than the *Étude,* and even as sympathetic a commentator as Eric Walter White would describe it as late as 1966 as being "rather incoherent."[14] Craft was closer to the mark when he described the *Piano-Rag-Music* as a "composed improvisation, unique in Stravinsky's work."[15] But its distinction is one of degree, not kind. Its seeming uniqueness arises from its epitomizing a quality that is in fact one of the essential and defining characteristics of Stravinsky's Turanian art, whatever the specific nature of the "objects" collaged or the harmonic vocabulary employed.

   3. *Uproshcheniye.* Both *nepodvizhnost* and *drobnost'* are part of the general strip-

13. See Arthur Rubinstein, *My Many Years* (New York: Alfred A. Knopf, 1980), 65.
14. White, *Stravinsky: The Composer and His Works,* 243. In his first book on the composer, written some three and a half decades earlier, White had expressed himself with unaccustomed heat on this entertaining little piece, calling it "a disgracefully botched piece of work which, even if perpetrated in an unfortunate moment, ought never to have been published" (*Stravinsky's Sacrifice to Apollo,* 94).
15. SelCorrII:449.

down, the radical simplification of means, known as *uproshcheniye,* which, having fomented controversy among early audiences of *The Rite,* continued apace throughout the Swiss years until it reached the point of unprecedented laconism. Those hostile to such simplification, we may recall, saw the process as one of *oproshcheniye,* going mindlessly primitive. In the vamping pieces, with harmony reduced to a single chord or oscillation, the point might seem well taken. But in the more serious works, Stravinsky's blunt straightforwardness of utterance, which had its origins and its analogues in the great Silver Age debates over *kul'tura* and *stikhiya* (see Chapter 12), made a powerful impression on many musicians. A memoir by Otto Luening, who as a teen-aged disciple of Busoni was living and working in Switzerland, is pertinent:

> I met Stravinsky in Zürich while I was a member of the Tonhalle Orchestra. We performed his *Fireworks.* . . . He conducted one rehearsal and I was not very impressed with him. He was so nervous that he was not in control of the situation.
>   I bought *Ragtime, Three Japanese Lyrics,* and *Three Pieces for Clarinet* to study and these indicated that Stravinsky was thinning out his style considerably. Rumor had it that this mysterious Russian who lived in Morges had turned his back on all previous music and had . . . reduced his musical statement to an economical, essential style just sufficient to say what he meant.[16]

The thinning out is dramatically evident in the slow progress of *Svadebka*'s instrumentation, beginning with what Stravinsky (mistakenly) recalled as a "super-*Sacre* orchestra"[17] and ending up with the black-and-white ensemble of four pianos and percussion that became such an emblem of its anti-Romantic day.

The "super-*Sacre*" scoring—for which an orchestral draft survives of the first seven pages of the first tableau, dating from late 1914 or early 1915—actually specified a far less inflated orchestra than *The Rite* (woodwinds, for example, were in pairs, not quintuplets). It was unconventional only in that there were to be two string sections (designated "Quintuor Ière" and "Quintuor II^{de}"), one bowed, the other plucked.[18]

A second preliminary version (dated Morges, 29 September/11 October 1917), with most of the first tableau written out in complete full score, and with sufficient cues thereafter in the particell to enable a conjectural reconstruction,[19] called for a highly variegated ensemble consisting of thirty-five soloists. It was this scoring that Prokofiev described to Derzhanovsky (as quoted at the beginning of Chapter

16. Otto Luening, memoir in the special issue entitled "Stravinsky: A Composers' Memorial," *Perspectives of New Music* 9, no. 2–10, no. 1 (1971): 131.

17. R&C:118/T&C:198.

18. Facsimile pages from this version are printed in P&D:144 and *Strawinsky: sein Nachlass, sein Bild,* 86.

19. This was done by Robert Craft and Ramiro Cortes and performed in 1973 by the Gregg Smith Singers and the Orpheus Chamber Ensemble under Craft. A recording was briefly available on Columbia M33201 (1974).

17), which means that Stravinsky had decided on it by the spring of 1915. A title page for this version dating from 1916 (erroneously labeled by Stravinsky years later as being "the first orchestral plan for *Svadebka*") lists the performing forces as follows:[20]

Instrumental complement

2 Flauti (Fl¹ Gr., poi Fl. pic; Fl² Gr.,; poi Fl. pic)
2 Oboi
2 Clar. (Clar. picc. mib poi Cl. gr.)
2 Fag.

3 Trombe { picc mib
          2 gr. do

2 Bugles Sib [N.B. Défense absolue de les remplacer par les cornets à pist.]
4 Corni in Fa
1 Baryton Sib
3 Tromboni
Tuba

Cimbalum hungari
Clavecino
Arpa
3 Timpani| un éxécutant
Gran Cassa et Piatti
Tambour de Basque ⌉
Tamb. milit. | un éxécutant
Triangolo   ⌋

3 Violini Soli
2 Viole Soli
2 V-celli soli
1 Contrabasso solo

N.B.
Défense absolut
de
doubler!
          —Igor Stravinsky

Vocal complement

1 soprano solo   1 Tenor solo
1 alto solo   1 Basso solo

Coro:
4 soprani
4 Alto
4 Tenori
4 Bassi

20. Title page of orchestral fair copy of the opening of the first tableau (R83 in the Stravinsky Archive). The listing is multilingual; as given in the present text, what is Russian has been translated into English, the rest left in the original French or Italian. Facsimile pages from this version of the piece may be found in P&D: pls. 6 and 7 (between pp. 144–45).

Two aspects of this scoring stand out as noteworthy. One is the expanded brass section, which includes a number of instruments normally found only in bands. The bugles called for here are of the valved type commonly known in English as flugelhorns (Stravinsky would use them again in *Threni*). The "Baryton Si♭" is the instrument developed by Adolphe Sax as part of the saxhorn family, distinguished by its narrow bore from the similarly pitched euphonium. The tiny piccolo trumpet in E-flat is a great rarity, manufactured only by the firm of Besson, and first designed around 1855 for performances of works by Bach.[21] The wide-ranged ensemble of five trumpet-type instruments was surely meant to emulate the sound of a peasant band of *rozhok* players.

Similarly motivated was the ensemble of plucked and struck strings, including the cimbalom (making its abortive debut in Stravinsky's work), along with what must be one of the earliest specified uses of the harpsichord in twentieth-century music. These two plus the harp were surely meant to constitute a conceptual gusli (cf. Glinka's harp/piano combination in *Ruslan*).[22]

It is astonishing to turn from this instrumentation to the one Stravinsky made (of the first and second tableaux only) in 1919, his last year in Switzerland. Only six musicians were now required. A pianola has taken over the lion's share of the instrumental music, the rest being given over to a pair of cimbaloms and a harmonium, with a battery of eight percussion instruments under the command of a single executant—clearly a spinoff from *Histoire du Soldat*.[23] Despite the reduction in sonority, this instrumentation suffered no loss of folk-specificity, thanks to the pair of gusli surrogates, and actually gained in rhythmic rigidity and *nepodvizhnost'* courtesy of the pianola.

The definitive instrumentation, conceived in 1921 and achieved two years later, was the ultimate *uproshcheniye*. What is particularly striking is the way the folk-specificity was now absorbed or attenuated while the *nepodvizhnost'* was further enhanced, and the way the monochromatic timbre of the ensemble accorded with the highly abstract and (classically!) simplified staging the ballet was given in its belated realization by Bronislava Nijinska. The choreographer left an unforgettable memoir of her consultations with Diaghilev before rehearsals commenced:

> "Bronia, are you ready to begin rehearsing this ballet? How do you see it? You remember the first scene. We are in the house of the bride. She sits in a big Russian armchair to one side of the stage, while her friends comb and plait her hair."
> "No, Sergei Pavlovich," I interrupted, "there must be no armchair, no comb and

21. See *New Grove Dictionary*, s.v. "Trumpet" (19:223).

22. The first *Svadebka* scoring had also included a part for the piano, as may be seen in the facsimile page in *Strawinsky: sein Nachlass, sein Bild*, 86. Whether there would also have been a harp to complete the *gusli* à la Glinka is unclear.

23. Facsimile pages from this version may be found in P&D: pl. 7; *Strawinsky: sein Nachlass, Sein Bild*, 89; and the Stravinsky memorial volume of *Perspectives of New Music* 9, no. 2–10, no. 1 (1971): 28, 57, 78, 158.

no hair!" I took a sheet of paper and sketched the bride with plaits three meters long. Her friends holding the tresses formed a group around her. Diaghilev burst out laughing—which with him was often a sign of pleasure. "What happens next? How can the girls comb such long plaits of hair?" he asked. "They won't comb them," I said. "Their dance on point and hers will express the rhythm of plaiting." I went on drawing and explaining my idea of the choreography and staging. Sergei Pavlovich got more and more amused. "A Russian ballet on point!" he exclaimed.[24]

In a similar way Stravinsky was now saying, "There must be no gusli, no *rozhki,* no solo strings; the timbres of my four grands will abstract and distill their essences." But he was after more—or rather, less—than timbres at this point. Where the previous scorings had emphasized a variegated interplay of instruments and a consequently antic, contrapuntal texture, the four pianos are hitched together in lockstep. Their deployment emphasizes doublings, and in this sense the last scoring of *Svadebka* was paradoxically the most "orchestral" of all. The doublings demand precision of execution, and precision demands rigidity—in a (Russian) word, *nepodvizhnost'.*

All the old Turanian elements were reaching their final conjoint apotheosis under the aegis of a classicizing simplicity—for which read: abstraction. Stravinsky was acutely aware of this result, and remained aware of his achievement even when he had forgotten his aim. In a very late memoir, the eighty-six-year-old composer confessed that "the final score, . . . though streamlined, stronger in volume, and instrumentally more homogeneous, is also, partly for the same reasons, something of a simplification."[25] Precisely. But what he forgot in 1969 was that in 1923 the simplification was the end, the rest the means. It was what "neoclassicism," at least at first, was all about.

For the last word in *uproshcheniye,* toward which the whole of Stravinsky's Swiss decade seems in retrospect to have been aspiring, we may pause to review the concluding "chorale" from the *Symphonies d'instruments à vent* as it appeared in advance of the rest in the pages of the *Revue musicale,* as part of a Debussy memorial supplement to the issue of December 1920 (Fig. 18.4).[26] It was just that, the *appearance* of the piece, that so distinguished it from its companions in the volume. It makes an astounding visual impression, this sparse succession of widely spaced chords in quarters and halves, absolutely devoid of expression marks, gradually shedding their sharps and flats as the final phrase, entirely on the white keys, ap-

24. Bronislava Nijinska, "Création des 'Noces,'" in *Gontcharova et Larionov,* ed. Tatiana Loguine (Paris: Klincksieck, 1971), 119; quoted in Buckle, *Diaghilev,* 410–11.

25. R&C:118/T&C:198.

26. "Dix Compositions inédites pour le piano, les instruments et la voix écrites et dédiées à la mémoire de Debussy." They were commissioned, in April 1920, by Henry Prunières (1886–1942), a remarkably versatile musicologist and critic, a disciple of Romain Rolland, who was prominently involved both in erudite research (chiefly on Lully and seventeenth-century opera) and in the propagation of new music and who was about to launch what has proved France's most durable journal of musical re-

FIG. 18.4a. Raoul Dufy's title page for the Debussy memorial supplement to the *Revue musicale* (December 1920). (© 1996 Artists Rights Society [ARS], New York / SPADEM, Paris)

FIG. 18.4b. Stravinsky's "chorale" as printed in the *Revue musicale* supplement. The first chord in the third system should have an A♯.

proaches. Full of *Luftpausen* and, toward the end, full beats and even measures of silence, it comes across as a veritable slap in the face of rhetoric.

Amid its companions, and especially for its being placed directly after Florent Schmitt's stilted, note-blackened exercise in *démodé* impressionism, Stravinsky's denuded fragment, anticipating Sartre, was "beautiful and hard as steel and [made] people ashamed of their existence." By the beginning of the third decade of the century, *uproshcheniye,* what Luening called "an essential style," had acquired a tremendous moral force. This *was* the beginning of a new classicism, of "dry hardness," to quote T. E. Hulme.[27] It proceeded, though, from the long-standing implications of Stravinsky's Turanian mode.

Whatever their ties to Stravinsky's past or their portents of his future, the instrumental pieces of the Swiss years form anything but a homogeneous corpus. They cannot be surveyed in a neat synoptic manner, only in terms of their fascinating specifics. Not every one of them needs to be individually described. Some, like the *Ragtime,* have come up already in other contexts and need no further commentary here. Others raise no fresh problems, afford no new insights. Only a few, notably the *Symphonies,* will require close scrutiny.

The omission of *Pulcinella* from this discussion, while glaring, is justified by its having been one of the rare instances (the first since the *Firebird,* in fact) in which Stravinsky accepted a commission for a project he had no hand in formulating.[28]

search and opinion. The supplement appeared in the second issue, under the title *Tombeau de Claude Debussy* (with a title page designed by Raoul Dufy). Stravinsky's "Fragment des Symphonies pour [*sic*] instruments à vent à la mémoire de C. A. Debussy" (fig. [65]–end, in terms of the score of 1947) was the seventh item in the album. The others were as follows:

1. Paul Dukas, "La plainte, au loin, du faune . . ." for piano, embodying reminiscences of the opening flute solo from the *Prélude à l'après-midi d'un faune.*
2. Albert Roussel, "L'accueil des muses" for piano.
3. Gian Francesco Malipiero, untitled piano piece, later reprinted as "A Claude Debussy."
4. Eugene Goossens, untitled piano piece, later reprinted as "Hommage à Debussy."
5. Béla Bartók, untitled piano piece, later published as the seventh of the *Improvisations on Hungarian Peasant Songs,* op. 20.
6. Florent Schmitt, "Et Pan, au fond des blés lunaires, s'accoudra" for piano.
8. Maurice Ravel, "Duo pour violon et violoncelle," later the first movement of his *Sonate* for the same combination (1922).
9. Manuel de Falla, "Homenaje pour guitare" (later orchestrated as part of a suite of *Homenajes*), incorporating quotations from "Soirée dans Granade."
10. Erik Satie, "Que me font ses vallons" (text by Lamartine), a recitative-like setting inscribed "En souvenir d'une admirative et douce amitié de trente ans" (later reprinted in *Quatre petites mélodies*).

27. Hulme, *Speculations,* 126.
28. A letter from Ansermet to Stravinsky of 10 June 1919 (quoted in Buckle, *Diaghilev,* 360) already mentions that Diaghilev and Massine were planning a "Pergolesi-Picasso" ballet. (At this time Falla was the intended composer; see Jaime Pahissa, *Manuel de Falla: His Life and Works* [London: Museum Press, 1954], 111–12.) Stravinsky was last on board the project; he received the commission for music in the fall, by which time it had become a "rush order" (R&C:118/T&C:198). The reason for the late commission completes the parallel with *The Firebird.*

Moreover, its popularity among Stravinsky's works notwithstanding (and despite much insistent propaganda to the contrary), *Pulcinella* is far less an original composition—even a "recomposition"—than a freewheeling and imaginative arrangement. At the time of its première (18 May 1920 at the Paris Opera) the ballet was listed frankly as "*Pulcinella*. Musique de Pergolési, arrangée et orchestrée par Igor Strawinsky."[29] As anyone who has actually compared Stravinsky's work with its models can attest, this is an adequate description. Over the years, the notion has spread (much abetted by the composer) that the work was a new composition, loosely based on "Pergolesi's" themes, rather than a transcription of a whole array of complete preexisting vocal and instrumental pieces (most of them, as everybody knows by now, not by Pergolesi; see Table 6).[30]

The printed piano-vocal score (J. & W. Chester, 1920) already reversed the perspective of the original programs and affiches: "*Pulcinella*. Musique d'Igor Stravinsky, d'après Giambattista Pergolesi." By then Stravinsky had already told an interviewer that the ballet had been based "on unpublished themes by Pergolesi," throwing in for good measure the outright fib that "being in Italy, I ransacked the libraries with M. Diaghilev."[31] In the *Chroniques,* Stravinsky wrote that "the material I had at my disposal [consisted of] numerous fragments and shreds of compositions either unfinished or merely outlined, which by good fortune had eluded filtering academic editors."[32] In *Expositions and Developments* he claimed even more: "I could not produce a 'forgery' of Pergolesi because my motor habits are so different"[33]—suggesting that he rebarred, desymmetricalized, or otherwise distorted the rhythm of the music, which is even less true.

This is not, however, to deny that, in Eric Walter White's words, *Pulcinella* "has a definite entity of its own produced by the careful relation of textures, dynamics, tonalities and instrumental colors."[34] But that is merely good arranging. For the rest, Stravinsky's changes may be summed up, again following White, as consisting of "elision or lengthening or repetition of phrases," and the occasional modification of the harmony "by the use of ostinati and the prolongation of certain chords." It was Ansermet, in a hagiographic *Revue musicale* article,[35] who seems to have laid the foundations for regarding *Pulcinella* as an independent work of Stravinsky, based on scattered "pages of the old Italian master, which he took as a

29. See the poster reproduced in P&D:182.

30. Attributions of the "Pergolesi" items, where they augment, refine, or correct those given by White (*Stravinsky: The Composer and His Works,* 247), follow more recent research by Ian D. Bent (as published in the liner notes to London Records OS 25978 [1966]) and Miguel Chuaqui ("Stravinsky and Distortion in *Pulcinella*" [seminar report, University of California, Berkeley, 1990]). For the Parisotti reference I am beholden to Prof. Margaret Murata, University of California, Irvine.

31. *Comoedia,* 31 January 1920; quoted in P&D:183.

32. *An Autobiography,* 82.

33. E&D:128/112.

34. White, *Stravinsky: The Composer and His Works,* 246.

35. Ernest Ansermet, "L'oeuvre d'Igor Strawinsky," *Revue musicale* 2, no. 9 (1921): 1.

TABLE 6 "Pergolesi" in *Pulcinella*

Location in Pulcinella		*Source*
Sinfonia (Overture)	(G major)	Domenico Gallo (b. ca.1730), Trio Sonata No. 1 in G, I
Scene I		
Fig. [1] Serenata (Tenor: "Mentre l'erbetta")	(C minor)	Pergolesi, *Il flaminio,* Act I: Aria (Polidoro), D minor
[9] Scherzino	(C major)	Gallo, Trio Sonata No. 2 in B-flat, I
[20] Più vivo		*Flaminio,* Act III: Canzona (Checca)
[23] Allegro	(A major)	Gallo, Trio Sonata No. 2, III
[35] Andantino	(F major)	Gallo, Trio Sonata No. 8 in E-flat, I
Scene II		
Fig. [46] Allegro	(B-flat major)	Pergolesi, *Lo frate 'nnamorato,* Act II (Overture) (B♭ major)
[61] Allegretto (Soprano: "Contento forse")	(D major)	Pergolesi, *Adriano in Siria,* Act III: Arietta (Aquilio), G major
[68] Allegro assai	(C minor)	Gallo, Trio Sonata No. 3 in C minor, III
Scene III		
Fig. [91] Allegro alla breve (Bass: "Con queste paroline")	(G major)	Pergolesi, *Flaminio,* Act I: Aria (Bastiano), G major
Scene IV		
Fig. [104] Andante (Trio: "Sento dire")	(E-flat major)	Pergolesi, *Frate 'nnamorato,* Act III (Nina, "Suo caro," E♭ major)
[108]	(E-flat major)	Ibid. (Ascanio, recit., mm. 25ff.; Nina, mm. 20ff.)
[112] (Tenor: "Chi disse")	(E-flat minor)	Ibid., Act II (Canzona di Vannella, D minor)
[114] Allegro (Soprano-tenor: "Una ti fa")	(E-flat minor)	Ibid., mm. 9–21
[117] Presto (Tenor: "Una ti fa")	(D minor)	Ibid., mm. 22ff.
[122] Larghetto	(E-flat major)	Ibid., conclusion
[123] Allegro alla breve	(G minor)	Gallo, Trio Sonata No. 7 in G minor, III
[132] Tarantella	(B-flat major)	Unico Wilhelm Graf von Wassenaer, *Concerti armonici* (The Hague, 1740), No. 6 in B♭ major, IV
Scene V		
Fig. [144] Andantino (Soprano: "Se tu m'ami")	(F minor)	Alessandro Parisotti (1835–1913), Arietta, "Se tu m'ami" (G minor), from *Arie antiche* (1885), reprinted in *Anthology of Italian Song* (New York: G. Schirmer, 1894)
[150] Toccata	(E major)	Carlo Ignazio Monza (ca.1696–1739), *Pièces modernes pour le clavecin,* Suite No. 1: Air (E major)
Scene VI		
Fig. [158] Gavotta con due variazioni	(D major)	Monza, Suite No. 3: Gavotte (D major)

TABLE 6 *(continued)*

Location *in* Pulcinella		Source
Scene VII		
Fig. [170] Vivo	(F major)	Pergolesi, Sinfonia for Cello and Basso Continuo, III (F major)
Scene VIII		
Fig. [179] Tempo di minuetto (Trio: "Pupillette, fiammette")	(F major)	*Frate 'nnamorato*, Act I (Canzona de Don Pietro, G major)
[187] Allegro assai (Finale)	(C major)	Gallo, Trio Sonata No. 12 in E major, III

point of departure." The English version quoted here comes from the New York Philharmonic program book for 8 January 1925 (the concert at which Stravinsky made his American debut as a conductor), in which Ansermet's article was reprinted "at the request of Mr. Stravinsky."[36] In any case, the proper place for a discussion of *Pulcinella* is not amid the "Swiss" pieces, but in conjunction with the style change it is so often said to have triggered. We will take a closer look in the next chapter.

THE RETURN OF THE C-SCALE

The most convenient superficial divider by which to classify the remaining instrumental output of the Swiss years is that between compositions close to the "peasant" manner cultivated in the vocal music and those alien to it.

At the one extreme we have the first of the Three Pieces for String Quartet, composed hard on the heels of *The Nightingale*. It is as straightforward a bit of imitation folklore as Stravinsky (or anyone) ever wrote, as would be perfectly evident even without the program note by Ansermet (to whom the set is dedicated, and whose somewhat simplistic words clearly carried the composer's authority), according to which it "represents a group of peasants singing and dancing against the monotonous setting of the steppes."[37] The sustained D in the viola (paired at the unaccompanied beginning and end with a characteristic acciaccatura C-sharp) is the drone of a *volïnka* (a.k.a. *duda*), the Russian bagpipe Stravinsky must have heard every day at Ustilug. The extremely recursive, "cellular" *naígrïsh* tootled up above on the chanter (first violin) might well have been a variant of the popular dance tune "Little Quail" ("*Perepyolushka*"; see Ex. 18.1), or some other of its ilk.

Beneath the folkish surface lies an interesting—and much analyzed—technical study. On the one hand, the piece develops further the rhythmic *nepodvizhnost'*, the frozen immobility, created in *The Rite* by the use of ostinati. Here there are two

36. Quoted by Howard Shanet in notes to Columbia Records MS 6329.
37. Notes accompanying performances by the London Philharmonic Quartet (February–April 1919), in SelCorrI:407.

EXAMPLE 18.1

a. Three Pieces for String Quartet, I, first violin melody, complete

b. "*Perepyolushka*" (cited from IStrSM:219); transposed, note values halved, unbarred

frozen levels: the twenty-three-beat violin tune and the seven-beat percussive pattern in the cello, which determines the barring. Since seven does not go evenly into twenty-three, the violin melody falls behind the cello pattern by the remainder, two beats, on each repetition. Since two does not divide seven evenly, the falling-behind effect crosscuts the cello pattern. Stravinsky lets the music play itself out just long enough for this phenomenon to run its course, then lets the air out of the conceptual bagpipe. The result is what we have called a mobile, consisting of (in this case) two fixed elements coursing through time (space) within independent orbits, passing in and out of phase with each other. The second violin punctuates the texture with an element all its own, just as fixed as the others, but with its recurrences unevenly distributed so as to inject a modicum of (human?) caprice in counterpoint with the impersonal automata that are in motion above and below it.[38]

While no other Stravinsky composition consists so purely and simply of a texture like this, the "musical mobile" was an important stylistic resource throughout the Swiss years and beyond. A conspicuous instance of it crops up in the "Petit concert" from *Histoire,* where (as White has described it) "a theme in an irregular

38. The second-violin pattern consists of a group of four eighth notes played once after several beats' rest and twice after resting again. The rests are the variable element. If we regard the pattern as consisting of two halves, the first ending with the single statement and the second with the double statement, the four complete patterns emerge as follows:

1. 22 ♩ (10 + 12)   2. 21 ♩ (10 + 11)   3. 21 ♩ (8 + 13)   4. 20 ♩ (8 + 12)

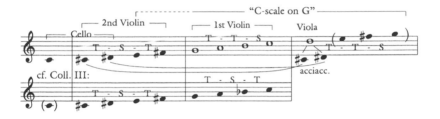

metre is accompanied by at least three different regular metres."[39] Another, as we shall see in the next chapter, is the "Russian Maiden's Song" from *Mavra*.

At the same time, the first quartet piece furthers Stravinsky's extension of St. Petersburg tonality. Its melodic material is partitioned into two tritonally related tetrachords, of which one is assigned to the first violin, the other to the second (the cello's drum pattern partaking of both and bridging them). Partitions of this kind, as we observed as early as Chapter 4, had originated in Rimskian octatonic praxis, and reached a zenith in *Svadebka*. For complete octatonic referability to obtain, of course, both tetrachords must be of the T-S-T ("minor") species. Here, the first violin music has been modified to the configuration T-T-S, coinciding with the defining tetrachord of the major scale. Substitutions of this kind were not without Korsakovian precedent (cf. Ex. 4.42); what makes Stravinsky's usage significant is the sustained D in the viola that lends harmonic support to the violin melody, completing a pentachord of the major scale which thus assumes decisive priority over the octatonic, the Eb/Db figures in the cello (spelled D#/C# in the second violin) being relegated within the total texture to the status of typically Stravinskian acciaccaturas surrounding the viola D (the more so for the way C-sharp is handled at the outset of the piece). The impression is that of a primitively expressed "C-scale on G" spiced with octatonic (Collection III) auxiliaries (Ex. 18.2).

It is a measure of the thoroughness with which Stravinsky had octatonicized his style that major-scale priority should be newsworthy. In fact, all during the Swiss years, alongside the Turanian masterpieces that brought Stravinsky's octatonic practice to a peak, the composer was turning out little pieces, chiefly of a parodistic nature, that heralded a new interest in clean diatonic—no, not just diatonic, but "C-scale"—melody.

Many of Stravinsky's C-scale melodies are well-concealed borrowings. In the second of the Three Pieces for String Quartet—which, Ansermet confided, "represents an unhappy juggler, who must hide his grief while he performs his feats before the crowd," and which Stravinsky acknowledged having intended as a portrait

---

39. See ex. 32 in White, *Stravinsky: The Composer and His Works*, 234.

F I G . 1 8 . 5 . Little Tich (Harry Relph, 1867–1928).

of Little Tich, a famous English clown[40]—the borrowed theme is a tune found to-day on a loose sheet of paper tucked into a pocket in the back cover of a sketchbook given over to the *Pribaoutki* and the *Pièces faciles* for piano duet, compositions of 1914. The tune is labeled "Breton song imparted to me by Shura [i.e., Alexander] Benois" (Ex. 18.3a) and followed by a description of the circumstances under which Benois had heard it: "And they danced, while on a rock in the rain a clarinet[tist] sat and played this song with all his might." Under this there are two more notations: the first (Ex. 18.3b) is an obvious derivation from the Breton tune,[41] while the second, labeled "Dancing Girl: Bareback Rider" ("*Tantsovshchitsa: nayezd-nitsa*"), may be a phrase taken down at the circus, possibly at the same performance at which Stravinsky saw Little Tich (Ex. 18.3c).[42]

What all three notations obviously have in common is the rising/falling-fourth motive (bracketed in Ex. 18.3), which, in the context of these tonal source melodies,

40. SelCorrI:407; M&C:89/95. Stravinsky had caught Little Tich in June 1914, when he was in London for the Ballets Russes performances of *The Nightingale*. The autograph of the second piece for string quartet is dated 2 July. On Little Tich (1867–1928, a.k.a. Little Tichborne, né Harry Relph), who was actually a dwarf, see Tristan Rémy, *Les Clowns* (Paris: Bernard Grasset, 1945), 376–80.

41. It is curious indeed that in a very late program note for *Pribaoutki* Stravinsky (or, more likely, Craft) cited this plainly labeled tune as an example of an unused Russian theme in his sketchbooks (T&E:27/T&C: 36).

42. Craft assumes (SelCorrI:408) that the Breton song had been imparted to Stravinsky by Benois when the latter visited the composer in La Baule, Brittany, in August 1910 to discuss *Petrushka*. But Stravinsky and Benois were together in London in June 1914 to view *The Nightingale*, their joint creation, and it seems more likely that Benois sang him the song then (possibly at the circus). This at least would explain why the tune is found among Stravinsky's 1914 sketches.

EXAMPLE 18.3

a. "Breton song imparted to me by Shura Benois"

b. Derivation from same in Sketchbook

c. "Dancing Girl: Bareback Rider"

←Three Pieces, II, 4–5, 9–10, 45–46

represents a progression from the fifth scale degree to the tonic and back. In the bareback-rider phrase the progression is extended to reach the tonic through a repetition of the concluding fifth degree (bracketed from beneath in Ex. 18.3c), and in this form the motive found a home in the second of the Three Pieces, as one of the motley assortment of phrases from which that notably disjointed composition is assembled. Its three appearances are at mm. 4–5, 9–10, and 45–46, the last of them especially close to Example 18.3c. (In early drafts and in the piano four-hands version Ex. 18.3c appears at this spot unaltered.) Two pitch levels are employed, as shown in Example 18.4.

There does not seem to be anything particularly noteworthy about the deployment of the little motive until one observes that the four notes thus invoked form a versatile pitch collection that may be embedded in any of three different scale formations: "white key" anhemitonic, diatonic (including the tonic scales of all the notations in Example 18.3, plus the scale with one sharp), and octatonic (Collection III). Add to this complex the ubiquitous acciaccaturas without which no Stravinsky composition of the period is complete, and one arrives at the recipe, more or less, from which this notoriously enigmatic little grotesque was concocted.

Analysis from these premises quickly reveals A to be the pitch of priority. At the outset, the A/E fifth of Example 18.4a is prepared as a stable referential sonority by virtue of its encirclement by acciaccaturas. (The part-writing, somewhat occluded

EXAMPLE 18.4   Three Pieces for String Quartet, II, tonal intersections based on transpositions of phrase bracketed in Ex. 18.3

a.

b.

c.

EXAMPLE 18.5   Harmony at beginning of Three Pieces, II, abstract showing acciaccatura relations

EXAMPLE 18.6 Three Pieces, II, mm. 13–14, 18–19, abstracted to show relationship of pitches employed to Collection III

by a voice exchange, is clarified in Example 18.5.) The next "moment" (mm. 13–14, expanded in mm. 17–19 and recapitulated in mm. 52–55) is a melody referable to Collection III, with two acciaccatura pitches, registrally disjunct from the rest, that make conventional (if delayed) appoggiatura-style resolutions to Collection III pitches within the "normal" tessitura of the tune (Ex. 18.6). This moment is intercut with another, a convulsive vamping figure (mm. 15–16, 20–21, 23), that with its bass note F might have been conceived to accompany the Benois tune in Example 18.3, but that always ends on a sustained B-flat. By analogy to the opening figure (cf. Ex. 18.5), this B-flat is heard as a tendency tone seeking resolution to A, a tendency reinforced by its reapplication as an acciaccatura to A in a new harmonic context. The new application produces yet another intercut "moment" consisting of a single chord (sounded a total of five times in mm. 22 and 24–25, and recapitulated—once only—in m. 53) with obvious (if perhaps uncalculated) affinities to the "Danse sacrale" from *The Rite*.

The long-awaited resolution (long, that is, within the time scale of this minuscule composition) comes at m. 26, which inaugurates the antic middle section of the piece. A appears in the viola, encircled as ever by its attendant acciaccaturas in the cello and second fiddle. For the next three bars the latter instrument continues to oscillate between the acciaccatura pitches, while a little "mobile" gets under way in the others: the viola noodles up and down a two-beat white-key five-finger pattern in sixteenth notes from A, while the cello takes off from its B-flat on a three-beat "interval-5 cycle" (as Perle would say; "stacked fifths" in more informal lingo) in eighth notes derived by extension from the motive in Example 18.4a. Three of the four pitches in the cello's pattern are referable to Collection III (the one remaining is the acciaccatura A-flat), so that the whole passage may be viewed as a typical diatonic/octatonic intersection around pitch-class A. The first violin figure, which punctuates the mobile running underneath with sharply articulated E's, makes pointed reference to the borrowed *ur*-motive in its original form. Each of these E's, referable to both the octatonic and the diatonic sets displayed in Example 18.4, is preceded by an acciaccatura (grace-note D-sharp) that is referable only to the octatonic. In the perspective of this passage, then, diatonic is foreground, octatonic background.

That perspective is abruptly reversed in the next passage, mm. 30–33. The E is relegated to the bottom of the texture, where it accompanies a sinuous little first-

EXAMPLE 18.7

a. Three Pieces, II, mm. 31–32

b. Harmonic abstract

violin flourish that is in fact the longest passage of unimpeded octatony in the piece. What is especially noteworthy is that the solo is confined for most of its duration to the tones that complement the two "root motives" within Collection III (as beamed in Ex. 18.4c); to put it in more familiar Stravinskian terms, it is the collection-exhausting tritonal transposition of the original anhemitonic set to the black keys. Thus, a point of maximum tonal difference is assumed so as to distinguish the middle section from the outer ones, analogous to traditional tonal modulation.

What the composer has in effect accomplished here is a new symmetrical partitioning of Collection III, so exhaustively ransacked (or so one would have thought) for such relationships in the second tableau of *Petrushka*. Partitioning of this kind being of such long-standing central concern to Stravinsky, it is hard to imagine it arising in the present context except by deliberate compositional strategy. (Even so, Stravinsky could not resist smudging the edges a bit with an acciaccatura D in the viola, infixed between the critical C♯/D♯ pair of the violin melody; see Ex. 18.7.)

Retransition is initiated by another first-violin solo that transposes the anhemitonic set along the trusty (0 3 6 9) circle of octatonic nodes to a middle ground between the white-key and black-key areas (viz., C♯-E-F♯-A). At the end of the retransition comes the phrase shown in Example 18.4b, played on the cello and viola in C-string harmonics to produce "un son étranglé." The *ur*-motive (perhaps it represents our Petrushka-like "unhappy juggler") having thus been throttled, it is the one element from the opening section of the piece that is withheld from the compressed and muted recapitulation. Stravinsky leaves the work hanging at the

EXAMPLE 18.8   *Marche* (1914), organization of pitch field

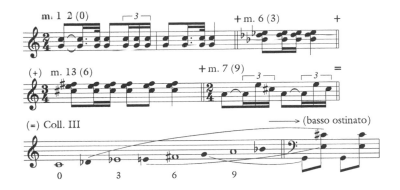

end by signing off with the least stable of its elements, the "convulsive vamp" that ends on a tendency tone.[43]

This description neither accounts referentially for every note in the piece nor explains away its disjunctures, but it does perhaps sufficiently demonstrate the role of borrowed music in the organization of its motley surface. Something similar takes place in the March from the *Trois pièces faciles,* composed later the same year (the manuscript is dated Clarens, 9 December 1914). The source tune in this case was that of "a jocular song" called "The Blacksmith and His Son," as given by P. W. Joyce in his anthology *Old Irish Folk Music and Songs* (Dublin: Hodges, Figgis, 1909), a copy of which Stravinsky purchased in London at the end of January 1913 (Fig. 18.6).[44] As in the case of the Benois tune, which it resembles, this song is never really quoted, but haunts the March in the guise of minimal motives that recur frequently, at once supplying thematic material and mapping out the composition's tonal terrain. The two-bar repercussive figure at the opening (repeated with a rhythmic variant in mm. 5–6) is the one most conspicuously employed. Its reiterations (mm. 1–2, 6, 13), plus the A-major opening of the march tune itself, neatly circumscribe the (0 3 6 9) boundaries of octatonic Collection III, from which the basso ostinato likewise derives (Ex. 18.8).

For the rest, only two other tiny motives from the source melody survive more or less recognizably in the March. One is the descending scale pattern in m. 4 of the song, quoted several times (most nearly literally at m. 30 of the March in the

43. This discussion of the second piece for string quartet owes much to some shrewd analytical remarks made by William Benjamin in the course of a review of Allen Forte's *The Structure of Atonal Music* (*Perspectives of New Music* 13, no. 1 [1974]: 179–80).

44. See Robert Craft (ed.), "Appendix: Selected Source Material from 'A Catalogue of Books and Music Inscribed to and/or Autographed and Annotated by Igor Stravinsky,'" in Pasler (ed.), *Confronting Stravinsky,* 350–51. Joyce's collection contains 842 tunes, of which the one selected by Stravinsky, on p. 269, is no. 486.

FIG. 18.6. P. W. Joyce, *Old Irish Folk Music and Songs* (Dublin: Hodges, Figgis & Co., 1909), p. 269, containing (at top) the source melody for the March from *Trois pièces faciles*.

primo's left hand); the other is the beginning of m. 7 in the song, which crops up in somewhat embellished form in Stravinsky's m. 25.

While the basso ostinato continues unperturbed, the melodic elaboration in the primo strays ever further from the (0 3 6 9) matrix staked out at the beginning. F-major arpeggios intrude as early as m. 14, and the two biggest thematic outbursts (mm. 27, 33) are also centered on F. (Could the Benois tune have reverberated here?) The jokey ending, in which the ostinato impulsively breaks off on the G, confirms the *drobnost'*-ridden "collage of keys" effect: though it is the lowest bass note, G had nowhere been heard or used as a tonic in this piece.

Collage of a more orderly kind may be seen in the Galop from the later set, *Cinq pièces faciles*. Here Stravinsky "composes out" his surface harmonic eccentricities, as if to justify them by embedding them in the music's structure. The piece begins with some trifling "wrong note" writing: the unison fanfare on G, reminiscent of the opening of the March from the earlier set of duo-piano pieces, and perceived inevitably as the dominant of C, is followed out of the blue by F-major and B-major triads before resolving.[45] The Trio, in F major, features a first strain with first and second endings precisely on these chords, each of them approached through an octatonic circle-of-thirds progression (Ex. 18.9).

Rigorous white-key diatonicism as grotesquerie, an effect pioneered in *Petrushka*, reaches its peak in the parody pieces of the Swiss decade. The epitome of unabashed *oproshcheniye* is the little *Souvenir d'une marche boche*, Stravinsky's contribution to Edith Wharton's *Livre des sans-foyer*, a gift book published in 1916 for the relief of Belgian war orphans. According to Soulima Stravinsky, the composer improvised the piece on the spot on 1 September 1915.[46] A heavy mockery of everything Teutonic, it makes a pointed jab at Beethoven's Fifth (see Ex. 18.10).

NEW AMERICAN SOURCES

Citation of a more serious and determinant kind may underlie the *Piano-Rag-Music*, by far the most successful of the ostensible "jazz" stylizations that dot the later Swiss years. The title notwithstanding, the inspiration for the piece may not have been jazz or ragtime at all. An early draft title page for the work in the Stravinsky Archive (Sketchbook F [= Rothschild 61]) reads: "Igor Strawinsky / Gran matshitch / Dedié à Arthur Rubinstein" (Fig. 18.7a). The word Stravinsky spelled "matshitch" must surely be *maxixe*, which designates a popular urban dance form from Brazil, historically derived from the polka but full of lilting syncopations. It originated in the late nineteenth century and reached its peak of pop-

45. The little stack of fourths that follows the second of these chords, banged out *sff* in the lowest register of the piano, is not heard as harmony but as percussion—and that is how it was intended, as the 1921 Suite No. 2 for Small Orchestra confirms. In the orchestrated version the chord is replaced by a thud on the bass drum, *fff*, and the stack of fourths in the piano has become a cluster at the very bottom of the keyboard.

46. Cited in Joseph, *Stravinsky and the Piano*, 60.

EXAMPLE 18.9   *Galop* (1917), composing-out of "wrong" harmonies

a.

b.

EXAMPLE 18.10

a. *Souvenir d'une marche boche* (1915), mm. 14–16

b. Beethoven, Symphony No. 5, IV, coda

FIG. 18.7a. Title page of sketch for the "Gran matshitch" (*Piano-rag-music*).

ularity around the time of the First World War, by which time it had become, like ragtime, a sublimated genre of composed piano music.

Artur Rubinstein made two Latin American tours during the war years. One of these, in September 1917, coincided with a Ballets Russes tour of Brazil and Argentina.[47] Thus Rubinstein may have been among the conduits (via the returning artists of the ballet) through which Stravinsky made contact with the various American musics that began fascinating him in the late war years. A "Gran matshitch" would have been a most appropriate gesture of appreciation toward the friend who, by commissioning it in 1918, had shown himself a benefactor in Stravinsky's hour of greatest material need.[48]

47. See Grigoriev, *Diaghilev Ballet*, 126–31; also Rubinstein, *My Many Years*, 11–16.
48. Rubinstein's account of the commission, which he recollected as having been a gift, is in *My Many Years*, 59–60. Letters relating to it may be found in SelCorrII:162, 183. The terms of the commission, arranged through Stravinsky's Chilean patron Eugenia Errazuriz, were executed between March and May 1918, although the work was not composed until over a year later.

FIG. 18.7b. "La Mattchiche" (Paris: Hachette, ca. 1903), one of many arrangements of a Latin polka that was popular in France for decades, showing up at the last in Gershwin's *American in Paris* (1928).

As the *Chroniques* attest (and as Rubinstein's horrified memoir confirms),[49] the aim of the *Piano-Rag-Music* was "to stress the percussion possibilities of the piano."[50] The writing is saturated to an unprecedented degree with familiar acciaccaturas. Some passages, indeed, consist of almost nothing else, while in others the harmony approaches tone clusters. Even the best disposed of Stravinsky's early critics were taken aback by its nonchalant but deadly mixture of *drobnost'* and *uproshcheniye*. The normally worshipful Eric Walter White found it "hard to credit any serious composer with the inanity of such passages" as the one shown in Example 18.11a.[51] Meanwhile, the sketch given in Example 18.11d indicates that the piece as published may even have been toned down a bit from the original improvisatory conception.

Piano-Rag-Music was the work that gave rise to Stravinsky's famous remark, "Fingers are not to be despised; they are great inspirers."[52] Comparison of the finished score with some of the early drafts, and of the latter with examples of actual *maxixe* rhythm, will show how Stravinsky's fingers helped him tease his work into its fascinatingly wayward shape. We shall have an unusual insight into that famously empirical process of composition at the keyboard that has in most cases left scant trace in the documents we possess.

The *maxixe* is identified with several characteristic rhythms, of which one is the typical "Latin" $3 + 3 + 2$ accompaniment ostinato (Ex. 18.12a) and another is the common syncope figure ♪♩♪ , approached, especially in pick-ups, through a tie (Ex. 18.12b).[53] Languorous rhythms like these are scarce in Stravinsky's frenetic piece, but they had been there before the composer's nervous fingers took over. Early sketches for the opening show two or three preparatory bars before the beginning of the piece as we know it, and these bars do exhibit typical *maxixe* rhythms (Ex. 18.13).

The last measure of Example 18.13c corresponds recognizably with m. 2 of the published score (though in the latter the *maxixe* rhythm has been disguised by doubled note values and the replacement of the tie by a rest). A little further along in the same sketch, we find some typical *maxixe* syncopes that are transmuted in the finished score (mm. 5–7) into an *echt*-Stravinskian sequence of irregularly grouped isochronous values (Ex. 18.14). Early sketches for one of the longish unbarred passages in the *Piano-Rag-Music* reveal a melody that must have been quoted from some piece of Latin sheet music in Stravinsky's possession. It is never allowed to appear in such complete form in the published score, however; instead it is broken into sections that often overlap at tonally contrasting pitch levels. The

49. Rubinstein, *My Many Years*, 85.
50. *An Autobiography*, 82.
51. White, *Stravinsky's Sacrifice to Apollo*, 94.
52. *An Autobiography*, 82.
53. Both examples, as well as much of the information presented here on the *maxixe*, come from David P. Appleby, *The Music of Brazil* (Austin: University of Texas Press, 1983; cf. exx. 31 and 57).

EXAMPLE 18.11   Acciaccaturas in *Piano-Rag-Music* (1919)

a. Mm. 33–36

b. Mm. 84–87

c. Beginning of m. 83 (long barless passage)

d. Sketch for same in Sketchbook G (Rothschild no. 75), p. 18

EXAMPLE 18.12   *Maxixe* rhythms

a. Accompaniment from Francisco Mignone, "Cucumbyzinho"

b. Melody from Ernesto Nazareth, "Labirinto"

EXAMPLE 18.13   Three sketches for the opening of *Piano-Rag-Music*

a. Sketchbook F, p. 3

b. Sketchbook F, p. 3

c. Sketchbook G, p. 6

EXAMPLE 18.14   Camouflage of *maxixe* rhythms in *Piano-Rag-Music*

a. Sketchbook G, p. 7

b. *Piano-Rag-Music,* mm. 5–7

EXAMPLE 18.15   Reconstruction of hypothetical *maxixe* original from *Piano-Rag-Music* sketches

a. Sketchbook G, p. 9

b. Sketchbook G, p. 15

c. Hypothetical original

telltale residual tie (despite the absence of bars!) gives a clue to the tune's original form (Ex. 18.15).

INSTRUMENTAL PROSODY

Unbarred passages are found in a number of Stravinsky works of the late Swiss period. We have already seen them, not only in the *Piano-Rag-Music,* but in the *Quatre chants russes* that date from the same year. The paradoxical thing, suggested in Example 18.15, is that in most cases the unbarred passages are just as inherently metrical as those surrounding them. There are two compositions, however, in which unbarred passages seem to contain a truly additive, nonstressed rhythm. In the *Symphonies d'instruments à vent* of 1920, the long, smooth flute/clarinet duos in the first part of the piece were sketched without bars, but published with them, since a conductor was involved.[54]

No such consideration forced Stravinsky's hand when it came to that charming appendage to *Histoire du soldat,* the Three Pieces for Solo Clarinet of 1918.[55] The second of these is Stravinsky's one and only meterless composition. Not at all coincidentally, it is also one of his most uncharacteristically legato conceptions: there are only three notes (all in the middle section) that do not fall under a slur. The reason why these two phenomena—meterlessness and legato—should be related is that in the absence of even an irregularly felt pulsation, the only unit of "grouping" available to the listener is the total phrase; it is also pertinent that the notes grouped by slurs tend to be isochronous, producing what Asafyev calls "thematic ribbons" of tone.[56] Thus, what we have in effect is typically supple Stravinskian *prosody,* the slurs taking the place of the missing verbal units such as govern grouping in *Svadebka* or the Russian songs.

It is interesting to compare the "synthetic" rhythm of the second clarinet piece with the "analytic" third, in which the note values are mixed, the articulations varied, the stresses frequent and marked—all of which tends to break the music down into terse motivic units that demand barring according to a typically subtactile ictus. The resultant scansion, with the denominator of the rhythm constantly shifting among quarters, eighths, and sixteenths, is instantly recognizable as belonging to Stravinsky's "instrumental" style (fountainhead: the "Danse sacrale"), even as

54. See Craft's description of the sketches in SelCorrII:452–58, esp. ex. 9. Just how arbitrary the published barring was may be appreciated by comparing the 1920 and 1947 versions of the spots in question. They differ radically, but the differences do not in any way affect the way the music is articulated or stressed.

55. Edwin Evans, in an article ("The Stravinsky Debate") published in the December 1920 issue of Percy Scholes's magazine the *Music Student,* asserted that these pieces had been influenced by the playing of the American jazz clarinettist Sidney Bechet (in particular, by a Bechet solo called "Blues caracteristique"). But Bechet's European tour with the Southern Syncopated Orchestra, greeted ecstatically by Ansermet in an article in the *Revue romande,* took place in 1919, and although Stravinsky's clarinet pieces were first performed in the fall of that year, they had been composed a year earlier.

56. Asafyev, *A Book About Stravinsky,* 251.

EXAMPLE 18.16   "Infixing" in Three Pieces for Solo Clarinet, III

the grouping in the second piece, based on irregularly patterned isochrony, would (if parsed with bars) remind us of the Turanian vocal idiom of the *Baika* or *Svadebka*.

Though confined to the melodic dimension, the Three Pieces for Solo Clarinet exhibit by implication many of Stravinsky's characteristic harmonic and textural devices, even acciaccaturas. The third piece unfolds largely through a process of in-fixing in which a major second is split by the insertion of the middle semitone, thus reidentifying the tones of the original major second as a pair of "encircling" acciaccaturas, now perceived as lying a diminished third apart. Or conversely, a given pitch may be surrounded by its encircling acciaccaturas as a way of expanding the tonal space by gradual semitonal increments.

The theme that opens the piece behaves in just this way (Ex. 18.16). The A-flat and B-flat of the first measure are encircled by their semitonal neighbors, so that in retrospect they sound like infixed appoggiaturas to the white-key collection. As for the device of semitonal increments, observe the way Stravinsky leads the A♭/B♭ pair by intermediate stages (A/B; A♯/B) to A♯/B♯ (B♭/C) at the climax of the first phrase group.

A much more orderly (hence perhaps less interesting) process of this kind operates over several sizable passages in the *Concertino*, composed in 1920 for the Flonzaley Quartet, who five years earlier had given the première performance of the Three Pieces. At fig. [19], for example, the cello (the leading voice by virtue of the dynamics and expression marks) plays a progression of major triad arpeggios

EXAMPLE 18.17 Infixing in *Concertino* for String Quartet (1920), fig. 19, cello

such that every third root is the semitonal infix of the preceding pair. To put it another way, the tonal space between the tonic and the dominant of C major is unfolded through major seconds ascending by minor seconds (Ex. 18.17); the device relates by analogy to the standard octatonic progression in which major thirds ascend or descend by minor thirds along the (0 3 6 9) axis.[57]

Even more strikingly than in instances previously observed (e.g., the Galop from the *Cinq pièces*), Stravinsky here plays out an essentially harmonic device in the linear dimension. No less than in tonal music viewed through the Schenkerian lens, the interpenetration of the vertical and linear gives Stravinsky's music a *background,* a sense of directed motion, of patterns completed. Or not completed: the substitution of the dominant of C major for the expected E-major chord at the end of Example 18.17 shows Stravinsky edging toward the accommodation with the trappings of functional harmony that will mark his soon-to-be-born neoclassic manner (in the present context the accommodation is perhaps a residue from *Pulcinella,* the work that immediately preceded the *Concertino*). What should be emphasized, of course, is that at this stage it is clearly the infix pattern that sets the norm, the tonal "terminating convenience" that intrudes and deviates. In no meaningful sense could the former be called a "preparation" for the latter.

57. In his review of Forte's *The Structure of Atonal Music,* William Benjamin analyzes an elusive passage in the second of the Three Pieces for String Quartet in just this way: in terms of the language of the review, the process is described as "unfolding of [pitch class set] 8–1 by means of ic [interval class] 2" (*Perspectives of New Music* 13, no. 1 [1974]: 181). In the limited context of the single piece under investigation, the remark might seem factitious; but more obvious recurrences of the device, such as we are uncovering in the pieces for clarinet and the *Concertino,* plus the analogy between it and Stravinsky's familiar octatonic rotations, all seem to confirm Benjamin's insight.

SYMPHONIES D'INSTRUMENTS À VENT: MATTERS OF GENRE AND FORM

Unquestionably, the instrumental masterpiece of the decade was the *Symphonies d'instruments à vent* in memory of Claude Debussy,[58] composed in the summer of 1920, after the Stravinskys had left Switzerland but before they had settled in Paris. The sketching took place in Carantec, a Breton fishing village where the family had rented a cottage. The orchestration was completed in the fall at Coco Chanel's estate in Garches on the outskirts of the French capital, where they would live until 1922.

As a post-Swiss, pre-Parisian composition, the *Symphonies* occupies an interesting quasi-symbolic place in Stravinsky's catalogue, poised as it is between the "Russian" and the "neoclassic" phases of his career. Indeed, Stravinsky tended to look back on the piece as the first of his "so-called classical works," as he put it as early as 1924 in a letter to Ramuz.[59] Early critics generally shared this viewpoint; in fact, the *Symphonies* was the earliest Stravinsky composition to be linked with "neoclassicism" in the press—first of all by Boris de Schloezer, in response not to any element of eighteenth-century pastiche, of which there is none in the *Symphonies,* but to the work's conspicuously "denuded, stripped-down style."[60] The *Symphonies* also became an early focal point of Stravinskian propaganda on behalf of "pure music," that shibboleth of all Parisian shibboleths. In a program note that accompanied performances in the 1920s he described the *Symphonies* as an arrangement of "tonal masses . . . sculptured in marble . . . to be regarded objectively by the ear."[61]

Its fascinating mosaic structure, in which discrete sections ("blocks") in varying but strictly coordinated tempi are juxtaposed without conventional transitions, has attracted much scholarly attention. Van den Toorn writes of how "the blocks, upon successive (near) repeats, attain a self-enclosed stability, a distinction and insulation possibly without equal in Stravinsky's universe."[62] A formidable analytical literature has grown up around the work: critics have come to see it, somewhat contradictorily, as being on the one hand a (perhaps *the*) paradigmatic Stravinsky composition offering a skeleton key to the secrets of his style and, on the other, as a harbinger of certain radical departures in the conceptualization of musical time

---

58. It is best to refer to this piece by its French name, since the English "Symphonies of Wind Instruments" is such a vague and ambiguous makeshift. The first word of the title is meant in its Greek etymological sense, for which a better English equivalent would have been the Latinate "concords" or, better yet, "concinnities."

59. SelCorrIII:83.

60. *Revue contemporaine,* 1 February 1923, 257; quoted in Scott Messing, *Neoclassicism in Music: From the Genesis of the Concept Through the Schoenberg/Stravinsky Polemic* (Ann Arbor: UMI Research Press, 1988), 129.

61. Quoted by Deems Taylor in a review of the American première under Stokowski in 1924; reprinted in *Of Men and Music* (New York: Simon & Schuster, 1937), 89–90.

62. Van den Toorn, *Music of Igor Stravinsky,* 339.

that came to fruition during the resurgence of hard-core modernism that followed the Second World War.[63]

Without wishing necessarily to challenge either the viewpoint Stravinsky himself promulgated or those later put forth by distinguished scholarly commentators, it seems nevertheless appropriate, given the terms of the present study, to propose an alternative viewpoint. It is possible to regard the *Symphonies* from a less abstract perspective, and concomitantly a less radical one. To place the emphasis on the points of contact between the *Symphonies* and Stravinsky's earlier work as well as his Russian heritage is to point up its Janus-faced aspect, poised on the cusp of what looms in retrospect—but, of course, only in retrospect—as the most marked stylistic watershed in the composer's career.

For this interpretation, too, we have the composer's authority—both implicit, as encoded in the work's original conception and purpose, and explicit, as set forth in some often overlooked pronouncements and program notes. Conceived as a *tombeau* for Debussy, the composition powerfully conveys a sense of impersonal hieratic calm. In the most literal and self-evident sense it is a chant. And that is what could only have been expected from Stravinsky, the reinventor of rites. Not from him a spontaneous lament from the ephemeral heart. He could be counted on to make his beloved friend and mentor a properly liturgical obsequy.

63. This body of work begins with Edward T. Cone's "Stravinsky: The Progress of a Method," in which the whole of the *Symphonies* is laid out in summary tabular form to show that it is made up of six separate, concurrent, and intercut musical continuities which are multiply resolved in the concluding Chorale. The "method" in question—Cone calls it "stratification, interlock, and synthesis"—is compared with Baroque ritornello technique and traced in a number of other Stravinsky compositions of the neoclassic period, notably the *Serenade en la* for piano and the *Symphony of Psalms*. László Somfai's "*Symphonies of Wind Instruments* (1920): Observations on Stravinsky's Organic Construction," *Studia musicologica* 14 (1972): 355–83, is a close analysis that aims to uncover the "organic continuity" that underlies and unites the "small elements and essentially static short episodes" which make up the composition's heterogeneous surface. Its method is akin to that of the "cellular" analysis promulgated by Messiaen in his classes at the Paris Conservatory and applied in published analyses involving Stravinsky by Boulez ("Stravinsky demeure," in *Musique russe*, ed. Pierre Souvtchinsky [Paris: Presses Universitaires de France, 1953], 1:151–224; published in English as "Stravinsky Remains," trans. Herbert Weinstock, in Boulez, *Notes of an Apprenticeship*, 72–145) and Jean Barraqué ("Rythme et développement," *Polyphonie* 3 [1954]: 47–58).

Taking a viewpoint radically opposed to Somfai's, Jonathan D. Kramer has featured the *Symphonies* prominently in two seminal articles on musical discontinuity, especially as reflected in the music and writings of Stockhausen. In "Moment Form in Twentieth-Century Music," he declares categorically that Stravinsky's *Symphonies* is "probably the first moment-form piece ever composed" (184) and a composition in which the "organic" processes sought by Somfai are renounced in favor of static blocks ("moments") that create form by virtue of sheer succession and by durational ratios. In "New Temporalities in Music," *Critical Inquiry* 7 (1981): 539–56, Kramer modifies his viewpoint to the extent that *Symphonies* is now described as an "impure moment form." He now locates its discontinuity (loosely borrowing his terminology from the vocabulary of Schenkerian analysis) in the "middleground" of the piece, while "in the foreground . . . motivic, harmonic, and voice-leading consistency produce continuity within the moments; [and] in the background, a linear, stepwise progression . . . operates over the entire piece" (553). Most recently, Kramer has devoted a lengthy chapter in his *Time and the Meanings of Music* (New York: Schirmer Books, 1988) to an exhaustive taxonomy of the *Symphonies* along lines proposed in "New Temporalities."

Finally, Christopher F. Hasty, in "On the Problem of Succession and Continuity in Twentieth-Century Music," *Music Theory Spectrum* 7 (1986): 58–74, seeks a middle way between the extremes represented by Somfai and Kramer. His detailed analysis of the opening section is based in part on methods derived from the work of Pieter van den Toorn and Allen Forte.

This much is known. In the *Chroniques,* Stravinsky speaks of the *Symphonies* as "an austere ritual which is unfolded in terms of short litanies between different groups of homogeneous instruments," mentioning specifically "the *cantilène* of clarinet and flute, frequently taking up again their liturgical dialogue and softly chanting it."[64] These remarks should be taken seriously and literally. It is when the *Symphonies d'instruments à vent* is considered as a service—and a service of a very particular kind—that its style and structure make the greatest sense.

The Russian Orthodox office of the dead, called the *panikhida,* begins with Psalm 118, intoned by the reader (priest or deacon), followed by the first of many litanies (*èkteniya*) in which the reader's prayers are answered by choral responses: *Gospodi pomiluy* (=Kyrie eleison), *Alliluiya* (in five syllables), *Podai gospodi* (=Grant it, O Lord), and so on. Readings from St. John Damascene and from the Epistle to the Thessalonians lead to the first big musico-liturgical item, the Hymn of the Departed (*Tropar' o usopshikh*), a strophic choral anthem with a refrain— "Blessed art Thou, O Lord; teach me to justify Thy ways"—that is sung after each of five three-line verses. At its conclusion votive prayers are made on behalf of the deceased to each member of the Holy Trinity in turn, and to the Virgin. The appeal to the Virgin is made at a slower tempo than the rest. The *Tropar'* culminates in a threefold *Alliluiya.*

Another small *èkteniye* separates the end of the *Tropar'* from the beginning of the second major musical item, the *Kanon,* a lengthy strophic hymn whose major sections (*heirmoi*) are marked off from one another by the interpolation of various short litanies, acclamations, and, finally, the *Kondak,* the concluding votive prayer, sung at a slower tempo than the rest. The service ends with more litanies, culminating in the threefold utterance, "Eternal remembrance" ("*Vechnaya pamyat'*"), delivered (according to an express rubric) "slowly and quietly" (*protyazhno i tikho*).[65]

In its general outlines, and in a surprising number of details, this brief description of the *panikhida* service is also a description of the *Symphonies.* The strange shape of Stravinsky's composition, which has occasioned so much analytical comment, conforms to that of the service: two major continuous musical items, tellingly referred to in the composer's sketches as *slavleniya* (doxologies),[66] are surrounded by a wealth of brief interjections and, in particular, refrains. The

---

64. *An Autobiography,* 95. In a program note for the concert (10 April 1948) at which both the revised version of the *Symphonies* and Stravinsky's long association with Robert Craft were launched, the composer put it this way: "There are various short sections, a kind of litanies in close tempo relations succeeding one another; and some rhythmical dialogues between separate woodwind instruments, such as flute and clarinet."

65. Cf. N. I. Bakhmetev, ed., *Obikhod notnogo tserkovnogo peniya,* vol. 2 (Petrograd: Pridvornaya Pevcheskaya Kapèlla, 1869), 315–30.

66. See the commentary to André Baltensperger and Felix Meyer (eds.), *Igor Stravinsky, Symphonies d'instruments à vent: Faksimileausgabe des Particells und der Partitur der Erstfassung* (Winterthur: Amadeus Verlag, 1991), 19 (German), 33 (English).

flute/clarinet "tempo secondo" music in the first half of the piece, quite explicitly strophic and punctuated by "choral" refrains (figs. [9]–[15] + 2 and [17]–[20] in the 1920 version; figs. [15]–[26] + 3 and [29]–[37] + 3 in the version of 1947), corresponds to the *Tropar'*, while the "tempo terzo" music in the second half of the piece (1920: [27]–[34], [35]–[38]; 1947: [46]–[56], [58]–[64]) represents the *Kanon*. The static, recurrent melodic and harmonic tesserae that organize the rest of the piece and provide its "tempo-primo" continuity correspond to the litanies, responses, and acclamations. The demonstratively slow-and-quiet final "chorale," the part extracted for publication in the *Revue musicale*, is the concluding *Vechnaya pamyat'*.

These general outlines are clear, and perhaps sufficient. Stravinsky's evocation of the *panikhida* in his *Symphonies* was based on impressionistic recollection, not research. It would be silly to insist that every detail of the composition should correlate with the liturgical model. Still, enough details seem to do so to warrant pursuing the matter a bit further, on the understanding that the smaller the detail, the more speculative the putative correlation.

The "tempo secondo" having been identified with the *Tropar'*, it seems reasonable to associate the music for three flutes that inaugurates that tempo (1920: fig. [4]; 1947: fig. [6]) with the introductory chanting of the *pripev* (antiphon) that precedes the actual singing of the hymn. The calm "tempo secondo" motive that concludes the first half of the composition and alternates with the rapid passages in "tempo terzo" during the second half (1920: [24], [25] + 4, [34] + 3, [38]; 1947: [41], [43], [45], [57], [64]) can be associated with the slow votive prayers in which the deceased is named, culminating in the *Kondak*, which precedes the *Vechnaya pamyat'*, already associated with fig. [65].

Finally, it seems reasonable to propose that the one musical motive that permeates the score from beginning to end is a fancied setting of a word that similarly permeates the *panikhida:* the pentasyllabic Slavonic *Alliluiya*. Here Stravinsky employs the familiar Russian octave-third spacing, an infallible symptom of his "liturgical" vein (Ex. 18.18).[67]

True, there are instances of this motive with more than five notes and with fewer. But we have seen this characteristically Stravinskian contraction/expansion device at work (in *Svadebka* and elsewhere) notwithstanding the presence, and the consequent distension, of a text. Indeed, the device has a special justification in the *Symphonies* if we regard that work as an instrumental evocation of liturgical chanting, for plainchant formulas ("tones") have acted in a typically Stravinskian fashion since time immemorial. As seen in Example 18.19a, the opening motive in the *Sym-*

67. All examples from the *Symphonies* will be cited from the 1920 score, though it is less widely circulated than the revised version of 1947, for it is the Stravinsky of 1920 who is our present subject. By the time he revised the score Stravinsky, as by now we have had ample opportunity to observe, had lost touch with the impulses and imagery of his "Russian" music. A prime symptom of this loss is the present *Alliluiya* motive; Stravinsky's 1947 articulations consistently detach the first "syllable" from the rest.

EXAMPLE 18.18   *Alliluiya* in *Symphonies d'instruments à vent* (version of 1920)

a. 2 after [1]

b. 4 after [6]

c. 2 after [25]

d. 2 after [40]

EXAMPLE 18.19

a. *Symphonies d'instruments à vent,* opening formula parsed as a chant

b. *Tropar' o usopshikh* (*Obikhod notnogo tserkovnogo peniya* [1869], p. 316)

EXAMPLE 18.20

a. *Symphonies d'instruments à vent,* concluding chorale parsed as chant

b. *Vechnaya pamyat'* (*Obikhod,* p. 330)

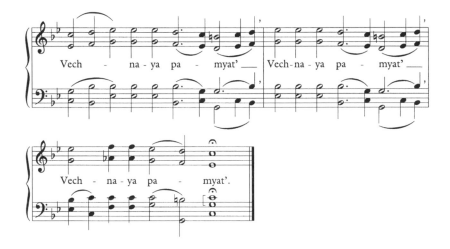

phonies, in particular, behaves precisely like a psalm or canticle tone (as well it might, since the *panikhida* opens with the reciting of a psalm): the melody can easily be parsed into a *repercussa,* a flex, and a cadential formula, of which the latter two are rhythmically fixed but the first is freely extensible to accommodate the prosody of the (imaginary) text. For comparison, a verse is given in Example 18.19b from the *falsobordone*-like harmonization of the *Tropar'* in the 1869 edition of the *Obikhod* (the Slavonic *Liber usualis*), which represents the kind of music Stravinsky, or any other Orthodox churchgoer of his generation, would have actually heard in situ. One could make a similar claim about the melodic structure in the second half of the concluding chorale (1920: [42]ff.; 1947: [69]ff.), and even relate it to the structure of the threefold *Vechnaya pamyat'* setting that was standard at the time in Orthodox practice (Ex. 18.20).

Even the halting mode of performance—made especially vivid in the second phrase of Example 18.20a by the use of rests, but present throughout the *Symphonies* in the form of *Luftpausen*—has a correlative in the Slavonic liturgy. Robert Craft has left an affecting memoir of Stravinsky's own *panikhida,* at the church of SS. Giovanni e Paolo in Venice on 15 April 1971. "The singing," he reported, "is an art of agogics, of the *kratema,* the *parakletike,* the *apoderma.*"[68] Of the three terms cited, only one actually refers to agogics: the *apoderma,* defined by Wellesz as "the sign of a short musical division [that] stands at the end of a musical phrase, [dividing] it from what follows."[69] It is this aspect of Slavonic ritual chanting that Stravinsky seems to have had in mind when he dotted his score of 1920 so liberally with *Luftpausen* and *fermate*—many of which, once again, he removed in 1947, having grown estranged from the imagic sources of his earlier music and insensitive to its expressive content.

If the *Symphonies* did represent a stylized instrumental *panikhida* service, it was not the first one Stravinsky composed. The same idea, evidently replete with citations from the liturgy, had informed the *Pogrebal'naya pesn'* for Rimsky-Korsakov, written, one recalls, and perhaps with a start, only a dozen years before. And that piece, one may further recall, had belonged to an identifiable Belyayevets genre. Clearly, the *Symphonies,* at least in the original version, belonged to it too.

SYMPHONIES D'INSTRUMENTS À VENT: MATTERS OF STYLE

Another way in which the *Symphonies* looked back had to do with the tonal plan and its harmonic elaboration. This would be the last major work of Stravinsky's to be tonally organized in ways that have become so familiar to us in the course of traversing his music since *The Rite.* For the last time Stravinsky mined the harmonic potential of the "Russian" tetrachords that had reached the peak of their governing power in *Svadebka.* As in *Svadebka,* so in the *Symphonies* they determined the octatonic/diatonic interplay that made the work cohere. Looked at from this traditional point of view, the *Symphonies* is indeed an "organically constructed" composition, as Somfai would have it, and in this very important sense the work is Stravinsky's "Russian" valedictory.

The most explicitly octatonic music in the *Symphonies* is to be found in the refrains. To take the most characteristic referential harmony first—what Allen Forte has called the "cosmic sonority,"[70] encompassing a family of chords that are bound in both halves of the work to the ubiquitous *Alliluiya* responses—we may observe

---

68. Craft, *Stravinsky: Chronicle of a Friendship,* 416.
69. Egon Wellesz, *A History of Byzantine Music and Hymnography,* 2d ed. (Oxford: Clarendon Press, 1962), 295.
70. Allen Forte, "A Hymenopteran Response," *Music Analysis* 5 (1986): 331.

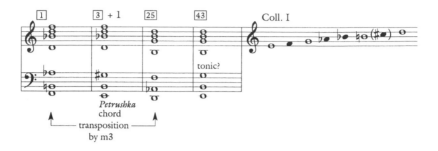

how all its varied manifestations refer to, and practically exhaust, a single octatonic collection (Ex. 18.21).

The third of these chords is the first again, transposed one notch "down" the (0 3 6 9) axis of octatonic invariance. Had this chord been altered the way the first was upon repetition (that is, had D been inflected to D-flat), Collection I would have been exhausted. Instead, the third chord is thinned out to produce the harmony at fig. [43], referable to both the octatonic and the diatonic collections, and the pivot through which modulation is effected to the rapt "white-key" sonorities of the chorale's final phrases. Without the precedents illustrated in Example 18.21, there would be scant justification for referring the harmony at [43] to the octatonic collection at all. (The chord for which it substitutes, viz., the harmony at [3]+1, is the familiar, quintessentially octatonic *Petrushka* chord, making its unobtrusive final bow in Stravinsky's work.)[71]

The "downward" transposition that governs the harmonic progression from the first half of the *Symphonies* into the second is prepared within the first half by transposing the opening refrain on its various recurrences. Its first two statements stand a minor third higher than the last three; in between comes one that conjoins them like a passing tone. Since the melodic structure involves an encircling (0 3 6) progression, and since the successive transpositions of it are by a half step and a whole step respectively, all the tones of the outer statements—and all the "structural" tones of the middle statement as well—are referable to the same octatonic collection as the form-governing chords, and ultimately exhaust it (Ex. 18.22). Thus the music of the *Symphonies* can be seen to depart from and to revert periodically to pitch configurations drawn consistently from Collection I, which thus may be said to govern the *Symphonies* the way Collection III had governed "Chez Pétrouchka,"

71. Possibly this is what prompted Serge Koussevitzky's otherwise incomprehensible remark that the *Symphonies* contain "reminiscences of *Petrushka* and *Le Sacre du printemps*, and to these pages is quite artificially attached a chorale of no artistic value" (*The Times* [London], 24 July 1921; cited in P&D:222).

EXAMPLE 18.22   Tonal progression over first section of *Symphonies d'instruments à vent*

a. Beginning

b. Fig. 6

c. 2 after 20

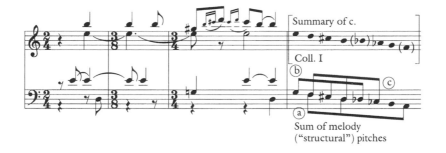

Sum of melody ("structural") pitches

the multileveled downward transpositions possibly suggesting the plagal cadences of threnodic chanting.[72]

The same collection, in its tetrachordal partition, functions referentially in the *Symphonies* very much the way it had done in *Svadebka*. It forms a background set,

72. Indeed, when one reads other passages in Craft's description of Stravinsky's *panikhida*, describing the "falling whole-tone cadences" and the "effect of trailing off to the last note, so that one is uncertain whether or not it has actually been sung" (*Stravinsky: Chronicle of a Friendship*, 416), one again thinks willy-nilly of the *Symphonies* in memory of Debussy. The first two phrases of the portion of the chorale melody set out for comparison with the *Vechnaya pamyat'* in Example 18.20a vividly illustrate both of Craft's observations: the cadences consist of falling whole tones, of which the last note is detached and clipped.

EXAMPLE 18.23 The organization of tonal space in *Symphonies d'instruments à vent* (cf. Ex. 17.29)

a. The referential set (Collection I), partitioned into T-S-T tetrachords

b. The derivative diatonic sets

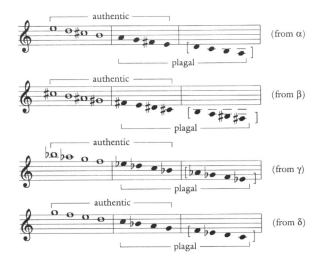

spawning symmetrical diatonic outcroppings at each of its (0 3 6 9) nodes by attaching disjunct T-S-T tetrachords at the major second to each of the T-S-T tetrachords embedded within the collection. Again as in *Svadebka,* each of these scales is given a further "plagal" extension as shown in Example 18.23.

Most of the episodic material in the *Symphonies* can be traced to these derivative scales. Thus the flute melody at fig. [4] (described above as the *pripev* or antiphon introducing the *Tropar'*) is accountable to scale β. At fig. [5], the reference shifts to scale α. When these melodies are recapitulated (in reverse order) near the end of the first half of *Symphonies,* they are both transposed "downward," in accordance with the overall plan, into the plagal region. At fig. [21] the material at [5] returns, referable to α-plagal; and at [23], the material at [4] comes back, referable to α-plagal. The music that closes off the first half of the piece (the "votive prayer" at [24]), is accountable to scale γ.

In the central episode of the first half—the strophic *Tropar',* extending from [7] to [15] and from [17] to [20]—Stravinsky conjures up a grand "pandiatonic" matrix by laying disjunct T-S-T tetrachords end to end, linking scales α and δ in what is

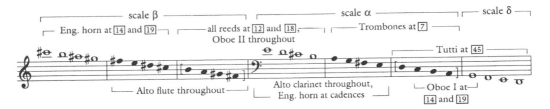

potentially a never-ending cycle. The various instruments that participate in the chanting of the *Tropar'* are each assigned to pitch classes derived from discrete diatonic segments of this matrix, so that the responses by the reeds stand out vividly against the nattering melismata of the alto flute and alto clarinet. The total texture is thus not so much a harmonic one as a traditionally Slavic multilevel monophony or heterophony. The English horn cadences at [15] and [20] leave no doubt that the focus of the matrix is scale α, establishing E as a specious tonic that conditions the pitch of the refrain transpositions at [15]+2 and [20]+2, already discussed (Ex. 18.24). At the very end of the *Symphonies,* the whole ensemble takes a final dip into the plagal region, where the white-key collection (here expressed as a symmetrical "Dorian" scale) is located. The enigmatic final chord[73] can be heard as a last descent, plunging even deeper into plagal space. Viewed from this perspective it indeed functions as a "final," if not a conventional tonic, a goal prepared by the descending whole-tone cadences shown in Example 18.20a, now transferred to the bass, which takes on its traditional (though for Stravinsky unusual) functional role as director of harmony.

The midsection of the second half—the *Kanon*—is also structured around a matrix of disjunct T-S-T tetrachords. The thematic content of the music is an elaboration of the surprising little high-speed motive that intrudes in the oboes just before fig. [3]. Not only the melody, but also the characteristic doubling at the fourth/fifth, is taken over for elaboration. The ambitus of the melody coinciding exactly with that of a T-S-T tetrachord, the doubled melody necessarily encom-

73. Van den Toorn interprets it as a C-major "terminating convenience" that gives an ersatz tonal resolution (and concomitantly, a retroactive reinterpretation) to all the preceding octatonic music, much of which (e.g., at the beginning) is organized around the G-B-D-F "dominant seventh" sonority (for which reason, among others, Van den Toorn sees the *Symphonies* as Stravinsky's first representative neoclassical composition: see *Music of Igor Stravinsky,* 337ff.); Kramer interprets the chord as nonfunctional and "open-ended," therefore "appropriate to a piece that is largely permutational rather than developmental, that is sectional more than progressive, that exists to a great extent in moment time" (*Time and the Meanings of Music,* 261); for Hasty, "the final C in the bass can be heard, without severely straining the imagination, as a Debussean added sixth" ("On the Problem of Succession and Continuity," 69). This last interpretation at least, and despite the analyst's disclaimer, does seem strained; for added sixths never occur in the bass (or rather, the sound described as an "added sixth," which is identifiable as such by virtue of the major second it forms with the fifth, cannot be constructed if the note creating it is in the bass).

EXAMPLE 18.25 Tetrachordal matrix in second part of *Symphonies d'instruments à vent*

Coll. III   α–authentic   α–plagal   δ–authentic   δ–plagal   γ–authentic

32 – 37   37   31 , 35 – 36   29 – 30   27   26 , 28

EXAMPLE 18.26 Embellishing acciaccatura harmony in *Symphonies d'instruments à vent*

a. Version of 1920 (fig. 32)

b. Version of 1947 (fig. 54)

EXAMPLE 18.27 (0 5/6 11) "*Rite* chord" constructs in *Symphonies d'instruments à vent*

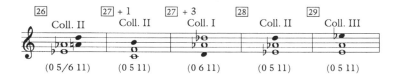

passes a complete "Dorian" or Russian-minor scale. Thus the whole passage from [26] to [38] (excepting a couple of contrasting "moments" before [27] and at [34]) amounts, melodically speaking, to a mosaic in which the pitch-class content of various scales given in Example 18.23 are abruptly juxtaposed, as schematized in Example 18.25.

That Stravinsky actually worked from a matrix like this is strongly suggested by the fact that the "highest" element in it comes at the climax ([32]–[34]), the loudest moment in the *Symphonies*. (Note, too, that the "lowest" element is darkened further by a chromatic adjustment that produces a pair of "Phrygian" tetrachords.) At the climax, in which the leading melodic role is taken by a pair of trumpets, the doubling interval is contracted to a minor third, so that the scale represented by the doubled melody becomes octatonic. In this case it is Collection III, the "ascending" tetrachordal complement of Collection I, as already observed in the discussion of *Svadebka* (see Example 17.17).

The "harmonizations" of these doubled melodies are heavily dependent on typical Swiss-period embellishing acciaccaturas. The clearest instance comes, once again, at the climax, where three of the four minor thirds in the trumpets are shadowed in the trombones and tuba by major thirds (Ex. 18.26; cf. the harmonization of the opening melody in the "Rival Tribes" from *The Rite*). Stravinsky was fully conscious of this device as a procedure for embellishing the harmony. When he revised the *Symphonies* in 1947, he made its application to the passage in question more systematic than before, and even wrote about it to Ansermet, who was about to conduct the world première of the revision in an NBC Symphony broadcast (31 January 1948): "From yesterday's telegram you know . . . that the trombones (with tuba and bassoons) now play major thirds in opposition to the minor thirds of the trumpets."[74]

Elsewhere acciaccaturas are chosen so as to combine with the doubling interval (fourth or fifth) to form octatonic-specific (0 5/6 11) *Rite* chords (see Chapter 12). These behave rather promiscuously in the *Symphonies,* without necessarily implicating the referential collections to which they belong (Ex. 18.27). They are "colors," bedizened in turn with all kinds of extra harmonic "nonessentials." Just as in *Svadebka,* the essential structure of the *Symphonies* inheres in its melodic dimension, the harmony (the thematically significant refrain chord alone excepted) being for the most part a decorative accessory. Thus did the *Symphonies* bring Stravinsky's Eurasian manner to final fruition, marking the peak of what is surely the most highly developed art of monophony the West had seen in centuries.

It was an art Stravinsky had by now exhausted—or perhaps one that had exhausted him. It signified for him the prospect of a Russian rebirth that, he now saw, would never come. Resolutely, he now faced westward, along with the reconstituted Ballets Russes of which he still felt himself very much a part. His next major work would be the one through which he would attempt to re-Europeanize his style once and for all.

74. Letter of 26 January 1948; in SelCorrI:230.

19 · ONTOGENY
RECAPITULATES PHYLOGENY

My pen is at the bottom of a page,
Which being finished, here the story ends;
'Tis to be wished it had been sooner done;
But stories somehow lengthen once begun.
—*Byron,* Beppo, *stanza 99, lines 5–8*

Who followed after Mavra as a cook then
And served the ladies next? It's not my worry:
To end this tale I'm rather in a hurry.
—*Pushkin,* Domik v Kolomne, *stanza 38, lines 5–8*[1]

I liked it all, then—poop—it ends too quickly.
—*Otto Kahn, after the première of* Mavra[2]

REPRISE DE CONTACT

Stravinsky's Turanian identity easily withstood the experience of composing *Pulcinella*. He was not about to turn down the first paying job Diaghilev had been able to offer him in five years, but the project had nothing to do with his own inclinations at the time. When it came along he was hard at the most quintessentially Turanian project of his life: the version of *Svadebka* with cimbaloms, harmonium, and pianola. True, he did not return to that endeavor; but the reason was less *Pulcinella* than a long letter from Ansermet, dated 12 June 1919 following a consultation with an "expert *pianoleur*," which cast grave doubt on the feasibility of the undertaking.[3] The hazards of coordinating the pianola with the rest of the ensemble, plus the scarcity of musically literate cimbalomists, eventually persuaded Stravinsky to put this most precious composition aside.[4] When he did return to it he was no longer the purebred Turanian he had been, and the sound of *Svadebka* was adjusted accordingly to a more "abstract" and "universal" conception in keeping with the composer's incipient "neoclassicism." Yet once again, it was not *Pulcinella* that had brought about the transformation.

On the contrary, wherever *Pulcinella* departs from "Pergolesi," it does so in ways that conform to the solid Turanian virtues of *drobnost'*, *nepodvizhnost'*, and *upro-*

---

1. Adapted from A. S. Pushkin, *Three Comic Poems,* trans. William Harkins (Ann Arbor: Ardis, 1977), 81.
2. Conv:III/99.
3. P&D:164–65. For some reason this very important letter was omitted from *Selected Correspondence,* vol. 1, where the section devoted to correspondence with Ansermet is the largest and (seemingly) most complete of all.
4. Nevertheless, as late as November 1921 he was still signaling his intention to complete the 1919 scoring. In a letter to Ansermet (22 November 1921; in SelCorrI:153) he even speaks of mechanizing the cimbalom.

shcheniye, qualities inimical to the linear, harmony-driven temporality of Western classical music. There is no real accommodation. What attracts the ear to *Pulcinella* is precisely the centrifugal tension arising out of the confrontation of irreconcilable forces.

Consider the very last section of the ballet, the coda to the finale, which is based with uncharacteristic freedom on "Pergolesi's" (that is, Domenico Gallo's) Trio Sonata No. 12 in E Major (Ex. 19.1). The harmonic *nepodvizhnost'* comes about not only through the primitive insistence on the tonic triad in the manner of the *Pièces faciles,* but also through the use of an extraordinary ersatz dominant chord made up of all the notes of an anhemitonic C scale right out of *Svadebka*—or *Petrushka,* from whose "Russkaya" the chord was actually borrowed. The two gaps in the scale are E and B. The first is present, of course, in the tonic triad, and its restoration is what gives a sense of resolution to the harmonic progression. The B, however—the leading tone, the cardinal definer of functional harmony—has been suppressed from the passage altogether. As a consequence both of the attenuated dominant function and the static repetitiveness of the whole (guaranteed by Stravinsky's fastidious stipulation "Sempre simile," which precludes the imposition of linearly directed dynamics or articulations), the passage turns into a typically stationary Turanian ostinato, one of those inertial automata that proceed, like the dances in *The Rite,* until acted upon by an outside force—in this case the conductor, who calls an arbitrary halt with his cutoff. There is even a suggestion of a musical "mobile" reminiscent of the Three Pieces for String Quartet in the three-beat ostinato in horn and trombone that crosscuts the four-beat cadential motive. If the conductor does his job properly, *Pulcinella* will end with the same kind of anticlassical jolt as the "Dance of the Earth."

Drobnost', meanwhile, is assured by the canny placement of the repeat sign, which coincides with the horn/trombone ostinato, but crosscuts and interrupts the melodic cadence, producing an *apocope* precisely analogous to the one that breaks up the word *kosa* at the very beginning of *Svadebka.* The entire finale is (dis)unified by brusque misplaced restatements of the motive with which the "Pergolesi" music begins, and with which the Stravinsky music both begins and ends.

As for *uproshcheniye,* consider the voice leading. In "Pergolesi," the penultimate note of the cadential motive is clearly heard as resolving to the lower note of the first-violin double-stop, the upper note serving as sonorous reinforcement of the harmony. With Stravinsky, the "top voice" is articulated melodically in a simplistic way that could never have happened in the eighteenth century except in the work of an inexperienced apprentice.

Another typically Turanian device in *Pulcinella* is the occasional suppression of tonally motivated triadic progressions in favor of anhemitonic, hence tonally non-implicative, ostinato harmonies. In Example 19.2, from the Andantino, an immobile (0 2 5 7) vamp (in another voicing it had provided the "*garmoshka*" ostinato at

EXAMPLE 19.1

a. Domenico Gallo, Trio Sonata No. 12 in E Major, III (Presto), m. 61–end

b. *Pulcinella,* fig. 202 –end

(continued)

EXAMPLE 19.1b (*continued*)

EXAMPLE 19.2

a. Gallo, Sonata No. 8 in E-flat Major, I, mm. 60–66 (transposed to facilitate comparison)

b. *Pulcinella,* Andantino, mm. 36–42

EXAMPLE 19.3 *Pulcinella,* fig. 20

the beginning of *Petrushka*) takes the place of "Pergolesi's" circle of fifths. Its four constituent tones being equivalent to the last four roots of the circle, a modicum of harmonic coherence is preserved despite anhemitonicization. In the little "Più vivo" that connects the Scherzino with the following Allegro (fig. [20]), "Pergolesi's" tune embodies a typical eighteenth-century swing to a dominant half-cadence. Stravinsky's harmony (Ex. 19.3) is just another static (0 2 5 7) concatenation, here contrived to resemble the din of tuning-up harmonics in the solo strings. Against such a background the G-sharp in the melody no longer sounds like the leading tone to the dominant but simply like a "modal" raised fourth degree. Again the music has been tonally denatured in good Turanian style.

Such passages in *Pulcinella,* where beady Scythian eyes seem to glint from behind the mask of European urbanity, are the more conspicuous for their rarity. They call attention to the mask and to the irreclaimable Turanian behind it. Having discharged the commission, the Scyth happily reverted to type. His next pair of works, the *Concertino* and the *Symphonies d'instruments à vent,* belie any hint that their creator had been altered for having accepted and executed the surprising commission he had received from his old impresario friend.

The impresario *was* an altered man, though, and eventually he got through to the composer. Diaghilev's reaction to the disruptions of war and revolution was very different from Stravinsky's. Where Stravinsky had been moved to create an imaginary, idealized Eurasia in his art, Diaghilev had turned westward more resolutely than ever, passionately embracing Trubetskoy's "pangermanoromanic chauvinism" (if for the time being with a strong preference for the "romanic" over the "germano") and, as always, valuing in Russia only what connected with Europe.

It was anything but a new attitude for the old *barin,* who had always identified with the Westernized elite in Russia. His postwar interests could be regarded as a *reprise de contact* with the aristocratic *Mir iskusstva* values from which the Ballets Russes had sprung, values we recall from Chapter 7, newly stripped of the gaudy neonationalist veneer the enterprise had affected for Europe's sake, owing to which—ironically—Diaghilev had sought and found Stravinsky in the first place. It was a return to the values of Bogdanovskoye, the Filosofov estate where Diaghilev had received his esthetic education; to the values that had informed his researches into the neoclassical portraiture of Levitsky, his grandiose Tauride portrait exhibition of 1905 in which the subjects had been mainly noble and the artists mainly foreign, and above all his first Parisian venture, the 1906 art show at the Salon d'Automne, where he had so brazenly snubbed the work of the Peredvizhniki.

Diaghilev would now turn decisively at last against "kuchkism." And he would carry Stravinsky along with him—out of the milieu from which the composer had emerged but which now rejected him, and on which Stravinsky would himself turn with a vengeance, both in venomous word and in exquisite musical deed. From purveyors of Slav exotica, Diaghilev and his troupe would become a fountainhead of postwar international (read: Parisian) modernism—and antimodernism. Of all the composers of the prewar period, only Stravinsky would survive the sea change.

Early glimmers of the new trend took the familiar, superficially paradoxical Miriskusnik form of historical retrospectivism. The old predilection now had a new and pressing poignancy. In an age of toppling thrones and rampant proletariats, retrospectives could offer a vicarious restoration. The initial fruits of the tendency were a quartet of spectacles based on old Italian music that Diaghilev had dug up in the libraries and conservatories of Rome and Naples. They were set by Leonid Massine (né Myasin, 1896–1979), the new chief choreographer of the Ballets Russes, to dances reconstructed from seventeenth- and eighteenth-century manuals Diaghilev had purchased for him at a Paris auction.[5]

The first was a ballet based on Carlo Goldoni's comedy *Le donne de buon'umore,* set to sonatas of Domenico Scarlatti as orchestrated by the Roman composer Vincenzo Tommasini.[6] It opened, as *Les femmes de bonne humeur,* at the Teatro Costanzi in Rome on 12 April 1917, where it shared the bill with a Futurist "ballet" to Stravinsky's *Fireworks*—actually just a painted curtain by Giacomo Balla that was subjected to a light show (devised and worked by Diaghilev himself) while Stravinsky's little orchestral sparkler was played. This was the occasion, too, for

5. On this phase of work see Leonid Massine, *My Life in Ballet,* ed. Phyllis Hartnall and Robert Rubens (London: Macmillan, 1968), 92–94.
6. Apparently Diaghilev approached Ravel for a "Scarlatti ballet" as early as 1913, but was rebuffed; Ravel to Stravinsky, 28 August 1913, in SelCorrIII:18.

which Stravinsky had prepared his consummately Turanian *Hymne à la nouvelle Russie*. At this point the "neoclassical" was but one of a variety of modernisms through which the Ballets Russes was seeking its postwar feet.

The other important novelty of the brief 1917 season was the Cocteau-Satie-Picasso-Massine *Parade,* the "ballet réaliste" that inaugurated the era of *choses en soi,* when, in Lincoln Kirstein's words, "the relics of *fin de siècle,* the pseudo-Oriental, the folkloristic, the last vestiges of the picturesque which saturated Diaghilev's first repertory [were] abandoned for Cocteau's rehabilitation of the commonplace."[7] As Diaghilev put it himself: "Not long ago, an apple orchard would have suggested to Rimsky-Korsakov, or even to the young Stravinsky, a secret, mysterious place, an impenetrable jungle, whereas in our day the poet seeks an ordinary apple on Olympus, an apple without artifice or complications, which is the most flavorful kind."[8] *Parade* had its first performance in Paris, at the Théâtre du Chatelet, on 18 May 1917. Its progeny were legion: *Les biches* (Poulenc), *Les fâcheux* (Auric), *Le train bleu* (Milhaud), and countless others.

The second "old-Italian" ballet was *La boutique fantasque,* to music by Rossini (the then-unpublished "Péchés de vieillesse," orchestrated by Respighi). In fact, it was none other than that dowdy old St. Petersburg favorite *Die Puppenfee,* the occasion of Leon Bakst's debut as theatrical designer in 1902, refurbished with a more fashionable score to replace Josef Bayer's, and with Bakst's costumes and designs supplanted, as the result of an unforeseen falling-out, by André Derain's.[9] This revival, introduced at the Alhambra Theater in London on 5 June 1919, was the first public inkling of Diaghilev's unexpected interest in restoring the art of the Imperial Theaters, the very establishment with which he had locked horns and against which Fokine had struck at the outset of their careers. But of course it was the empire itself he was symbolically restoring, not just its theatrical art.

Pulcinella, danced for the first time at the Paris Opera on 15 May 1920, was the third production in the new old-Italian line. It was followed twelve days later by *Le astuzie femminili,* an opera buffa by Cimarosa. Diaghilev, who had come across the score in Naples, once again engaged Respighi to do the reorchestration. The decision to produce the piece had rested on a curious misapprehension—a misapprehension of genius that determined the future course of the Ballets Russes and, indirectly, led Igor Stravinsky to his "second style."

———

Cimarosa had spent the years 1787–91 at St. Petersburg, in the service of Catherine the Great. *Le astuzie femminili,* composed in 1794 for Naples, has for its finale a rollicking "ballo russo," from which Diaghilev made the reasonable if erroneous

7. Lincoln Kirstein, "The Instigator," review of *Diaghilev* by Richard Buckle, *New York Review of Books,* 8 November 1979.
8. Letter to Boris Kochno, 21 July 1924; quoted in Kochno, *Diaghilev and the Ballets Russes,* 226.
9. For details of this misunderstanding, and of the production in general, see ibid., 126–29.

deduction that the piece had been written for Catherine. From this wrong conclusion came the inspired idea of staging the opera in the style of a St. Petersburg court spectacle. Cimarosa's *ballo russo,* which remained permanently in the Ballets Russes repertoire as the finale of a suite of danced extracts from *Le astuzie femminili* called "Cimarosiana," represented the earliest stratum of Westernized Russian music: the court music composed for Russian aristocratic consumption by itinerant Italian musicians, whose line would culminate in Catterino Cavos, Benois's maternal forebear. Their work, which often incorporated stylish adaptations of native motifs, was the exact musical equivalent of paintings by the Russian neoclassicists to whom Diaghilev had been devoted in his youth, who clothed their peasants (as Vernon Duke put it) in "a fanciful amalgam of peasant headgear and a Russian landowner's conception of Olympian fashions."[10]

Cimarosa's *ballo* featured just such a stylization, one that could not have been more conspicuous or, for Diaghilev, more suggestive: it took the form of a set of variations on the famous instrumental dance tune (*naígrïsh*) known as *Kamarinskaya,* the very "acorn" (in Chaikovsky's famous metaphor) from which—arranged half a century later by Glinka—the "oak" of Russian art music had sprouted.[11] What better way to achieve an end run around kuchkism than by locating the acorn *here,* in Cimarosa's Russo-Italianate divertissement, from which the growth of a different "oak"—that of Russian neoclassicism, the stuff of court entertainments and gentry drawing rooms—could be traced.

Diaghilev would show Europe that Russia was large and contained multitudes: multitudes of social classes and occupations, and multitudes of indigenous musical styles, not all of them "Asiatic" or peasant. There were also the musics of the nobility (*dvoryanye*), the landed gentry (*pomeshchiki*), and the urban upper crust (*meshchanye*), musics, as Stravinsky later put it, that "mingle[d] the Russian popular *melos* and the prevailing Italianism with the most carefree and charming ease."[12] It is no wonder that Diaghilev, who came—like Glinka, Dargomïzhsky, and Chaikovsky—from the *pomeshchik* class and loved its petty-aristocratic values, should have loved and honored its musical artifacts as well, and considered them representative of the best there was in Russia. Having bided his time and established himself as a tastemaker nonpareil, he could now, he felt, unveil such a Russia and such a music to the eyes and ears of Europe.

From now on, except for *Renard, Les noces,* and Prokofiev's *Chout*—all commissioned before *Les femmes de bonne humeur* and hence relics of another age (and also excepting the anomalous *Nuit sur le Mont chauve,* staged by Nijinska to Musorgsky's music and performed, in Monte Carlo only, in 1924)—all the "Russian" ballets the Ballets Russes would present to Europe would portray this European, neo-

10. *Passport to Paris,* 121.
11. See P. I. Chaikovsky, *Diaries of Tchaikovsky,* 250 (entry of 27 June 1888).
12. *Poetics of Music,* bilingual ed., 123.

classical, and (to Europe) unrecognizable Russia. *Zephyre et Floro* (1925, music by Dukelsky) purported to be a recreation of a famous neoclassical divertissement after Ovid by Charles Didelot (1767–1836), as enacted on the estate of an eighteenth-century Russian nobleman by a troupe of serf performers gotten up as mythological divinities. (Count Nikolai Sheremetyev, with his private theater at Ostankino near Moscow, was the unnamed noble prototype.) *Ode* (1928), one of the most celebrated of the late-period Diaghilev productions (less for Nicolas Nabokov's music than for its cinematic projections and neon lighting by Pavel Tchelitchew and Pierre Charbonnier), was a choreographic interpretation by Massine of a grandiose neoclassical eulogy in honor of the Empress Yelizaveta Petrovna by the court poet Mikhaíl Lomonosov.

The greatest spectacle along these lines, the watershed that inaugurated Diaghilev's second period, was a production that took everyone by surprise, and one Paris never saw. It was a revival of the work that, more than any other, had brought the whole European aristocratic line in Russian music to its culmination: Chaikovsky's *Sleeping Beauty*, as created for the Mariyinsky Theater in 1890 by Ivan Vsevolozhsky and Marius Petipa.

There was irony in this, since Diaghilev's original balletic alliance had been with the choreographer who had successfully challenged Petipa and ended his hegemony in Russian ballet. Defending Fokine and his first repertoire in 1911 against a detractor who had inveighed against the choreographer in the pages of the London *Times,* Diaghilev had even cast expedient aspersions upon "*The Sleeping Beauty,* that interminable ballet on a subject from a French fable, composed on French themes, and lacking any national element that might justify the idea of giving London this Franco-Italian fairy tale."[13]

While the sincerity of these remarks may be doubted, it is a fact that Petipa was always treated by the Miriskusniki with derision—here at least they were in agreement with the kuchkists and the Peredvizhniki. In the pages of *Mir iskusstva* itself, Benois (whose rapturous late memoirs of the original *Sleeping Beauty* would become famous) had written: "We won't deny that Mr. Petipa has talent. We know that some of his groupings, some of his khorovods are very elegantly conceived and very effective, yet we must nevertheless acknowledge that Mr. Petipa is a long way off from real art. It is very decently executed academic drawing, devoid of all soul, devoid of all artistic temperament."[14]

Now all at once the very qualities he and Benois had denigrated were indispensable to Diaghilev. The fact that the ultimate imperial Russian *Gesamtkunstwerk* was inspired by a French tale (Perrault), that it incorporated French themes, that its

13. "*La Belle au Bois Dormante,* ce ballet interminable au sujet tiré d'une fable française, composé sur des thèmes français, ne possède aucun élément national qui puisse justifier l'idée de donner à Londres cette féerie franco-italienne" (quoted in Macdonald, *Diaghilev Observed,* 28).

14. Alexandre Benois, "Novïye teatral'nïye postanovki," *Mir iskusstva,* 1902, no. 2, 28.

choreographer was French-born, that the very titles of its numbers were in French (which, lest we forget, was still unofficially the Russian court language)—what better earnest could there be that Russian culture was European culture after all? The fact that its chief qualities were elegance and academic workmanship—what better proof that not all Russians were peasants?

And there was also a fact Diaghilev and Benois had left unmentioned: *The Sleeping Beauty,* being based on a literary source from the *grand siècle,* had been given a period setting by the redoubtable intendant Vsevolozhsky, its original *metteur-en-scène,* and Chaikovsky had followed suit with a whole slew of neoclassical stylizations culminating in the penultimate number, a sarabande for the whole company right out of the old *ballet de cour.* This was the Russian Versailles of the old Miriskusnik dream in all its splendor, every bit as much a glorification of the now-vanished Romanov dynasty as Lomonosov's *Ode* had been.[15] Staging *The Sleeping Beauty* brought things full circle. Whatever anyone thought of Petipa's contribution to it, it was the spectacle of the ballet's first production that had, in the words of Benois's biographer, disclosed to the young Nevsky Pickwickians "the whole of the eighteenth century, Versailles, Louis XIV, and disclosed more than all the tomes and museums in the world."[16]

According to all observers, Diaghilev threw himself into this project with greater zeal and emotional investment than ever before or after.[17] It was his chance

15. Nor was this the only ancien régime evocation the staunchly monarchist and reactionary Chaikovsky willingly produced for the Imperial Theaters, which were supported (indeed, owned) by the only full-fledged autocracy left in Europe. His very next work for the stage, the opera *Pique dame,* would include a whole pastoral *intermède* in eighteenth-century style ("*Iskrennost' pastushki*"; roughly, "La bergère fidèle") alongside settings of texts by eighteenth-century Russian court poets, and even a direct quotation from Grétry. Chaikovsky was also among the Russian composers most given to writing suites and individual pieces of a more abstract character in a deliberately retrospective style. His orchestral suites contain an Introduzione e fuga (op. 43, no. 1), a Gavotte (op. 43, no. 6), and a Danse baroque (op. 53, no. 5), while the whole fourth suite, the familiar *Mozartiana,* consists of orchestrations—for an ensemble of eighteenth-century dimensions (but for the use of four horns)—of some particularly retrospective works of Mozart, beginning with the Gigue, K. 574. The beginnings of this tendency can be found in the work of Chaikovsky's teacher, Anton Rubinstein (the Grand Duchess Yelena Pavlovna's personal protégé), whose Suite for Piano, op. 38 (1855), consists of ten pieces: Prelude, Minuet, Gigue, Sarabande, Gavotte, Passacaglia, Allemande, Courante, Passepied, Bourrée. The trend would reach its final phase in the work of the Belyayevtsï. Glazunov, for example, wrote an entire ballet, *Barïshnya-Sluzhanka; or, "Les ruses d'amour"* (1898), in a deliberately Gallicizing "eighteenth-century" style; among his last works is a set of preludes and fugues for piano (op. 101, 1918–23). We have already taken note of the many retrospective "stylizations" among the "Chopsticks" paraphrases and the Fridays albums (see Chapter 1). An exploration of the relationship between the sentimental retrospectivism of the nineteenth century and the "neoclassicism" of the twentieth—especially as regards Stravinsky, who kept a copy of "Ruses d'amour" in his library until the day he died—is overdue. A beginning has been made by Messing, in *Neoclassicism in Music,* esp. chap. 1 ("Neoclassicism in France: 1870–1914"). On Stravinsky's personal collection of books and scores, see Robert Craft and Brett Shapiro, "Catalogue of Some Books and Music Inscribed to and/or Autographed and Inscribed to and/or Autographed and Annotated by Igor Stravinsky, and of Private Recordings and Test-Pressings Labelled by Him in the Estate of Vera Stravinsky" (typescript, New York, 1984); the Glazunov score is listed on p. 64.

16. Sergey Ernst, *Aleksandr Benua* (Petrograd, 1921), 22.

17. Not that Diaghilev hesitated to make his customarily ruthless cuts and substitutions (for all that the production was billed as an uncut restoration): several numbers from *The Nutcracker* were inserted, and the mimed numbers were either omitted or recast as dances. See Buckle, *Diaghilev,* 388; also Bronislava Nijinska, "Petipa pobedil," in Slonimsky et al. (eds.), *Marius Petipa,* 317–18.

to step at last into the shoes of Vsevolozhsky, the great *burin* of the Russian imperial stage and the great role model of Diaghilev's youth, and thus realize vicariously his old dream of becoming the intendant of the Imperial Theaters himself. Stravinsky had never seen his old friend work "with such ardor and love," and he described him after the première, in marked contrast to his other memoirs of the great impresario, with artless poignancy: "That night, probably because he had worked so hard and used so much vitality, he had a nervous breakdown. He sobbed like a child and all around him had difficulty calming him."[18]

Many were simply nonplussed by this apparent vagary and Diaghilev's frenzied commitment to it. Nijinska, who chose this moment to rejoin the Ballets Russes after a seven-year absence, was completely taken aback: "Diaghilev's determination to realize *The Sleeping Beauty* was interpreted as a deviation from his innovative path. I could not understand Diaghilev's enthusiasm, so unexpected and passionate, for a ballet of Petipa's that he had formerly disavowed."[19] Walter Nouvel, perhaps Diaghilev's closest confidant, described the production as a retreat from "modernism." This characterization, as significant as it was easily misunderstood, was undoubtedly something Nouvel had from Diaghilev himself—as were the typically pragmatic reasons, bordering on cynicism, that he went on to list: "At the time Diaghilev felt that the public had grown tired of modernism, and that this had been the reason why [Prokofiev's] *Chout* [premièred 17 May 1921] had failed. He proposed that a deviation in the form of a return to classicism was altogether timely and that just then he had the wherewithal to put on a spectacle that would be first-class in all respects."[20]

But the idea for the production had preceded the failure of *Chout* and was implicit in the direction the Ballets Russes had been taking for at least four years. It was a retreat from "modernism" only in the sense in which that word had come to be understood at the end of the First World War: viz., in terms of the anarchic radicalism of the Futurists and Dadaists and of clamorous spectacles on the order of *The Rite* (or *Chout,* its clumsy clone). Along with many other artists and esthetes of the period, Diaghilev sensed that the new newness would be an aristocratic retreat from the disorders that threatened civilization, that (to quote T. E. Hulme) "after a hundred years of romanticism we are in for a classical revival."[21]

The anarchic modernism of the immediate prewar period had been the decadent phase of Hulme's century of romanticism; the new modernism would be a new classicism, and Diaghilev was determined to help launch it with an example of the height to which an aristocratic, academic, neoclassical art could aspire in the last European autocracy, lately fallen. It was, in short, a new sort of Russian messian-

18. Stravinsky, "The Diaghilev I Knew," 34.
19. Nijinska, "Petipa pobedil," 317.
20. V. F. Nuvel', "Diaghilev" (unpublished memoir), quoted in Zilbershteyn and Samkov (eds.), *Diagilev* 2:438.
21. Hulme, "Romanticism and Classicism," 564.

ism that Diaghilev was promulgating with his "Sleeping Princess" (to give it the name he used). Where the Slavophiles had seen in Russia a new Rome, Diaghilev saw in her a new Versailles that had been martyred by the Bolsheviks, and he wanted all of Europe to see and recognize it too.

Needless to say, this was all a deranged miscalculation. The production, which opened in London's Alhambra Theater on 2 November 1921—whence it would be on to Paris and triumph—closed in London on 2 February 1922 after a horrible extended run of 115 performances, forced by the theater management in a hopeless effort to recoup its investment. It never went to Paris at all, save in the truncated form of a one-act divertissement drawn from Act IV, entitled "Aurora's Wedding." The Sleeping Princess came within a hair's breadth of ruining the Diaghilev enterprise once and for all, and persuaded the traumatized impresario never again to attempt a full-length spectacle.

Just as Diaghilev might have expected were he in his right mind, the critics despised and rejected his messianic exertions, tearing with particular mercilessness into poor Chaikovsky, who still represented to them a Russia that was not Russian. Ernest Newman surpassed himself in venom, calling the production the "suicide of the Russian Ballet," diagnosing the cause of death as "cerebral anaemia, after having become intellectually bankrupt," and mocking what he evidently took to be the production's bathetic sumptuousness by recalling the ending fizzle of Tennyson's *Enoch Arden:* "So passed the strong heroic soul away, / And when they buried him the little port / Had seldom seen a costlier funeral."[22]

But a broader historical view (alas, too broad for Diaghilev, who had only eight more years ahead of him) shows the impresario to have been right all along. His London *Sleeping Princess* was every bit the epoch-maker he had wanted it to be, though the epoch tarried a bit. As ballet historians have pointed out again and again, the production laid the foundation for the phenomenal (and entirely unexpected) revival of classical ballet in the West, which got under way in earnest a quarter of a century later with the Covent Garden *Sleeping Beauty* of 1946. More important (to us) is the fact that, by involving him heavily in the production from the very inception of the plan, Diaghilev succeeded in winning Igor Stravinsky over to the cause of the new classicism. A very eloquent page in the *Chroniques* testifies to the overwhelming effect his involvement in *The Sleeping Beauty* had on the composer, and what the classical ballet had come to mean to him by 1921. "Its essence," he wrote (through Nouvel), lay in "the beauty of its *ordonnance* and the aristocratic austerity of its forms," which "closely corresponds with my conception of art"—his conception, that is, by 1935, the year of writing. Stravinsky leaves no doubt as to the source of that conception:

For here in classical dancing, I see the triumph of studied conception over vague-

22. *Sunday Times,* 6 November 1921; quoted in Macdonald, *Diaghilev Observed,* 276.

ness, of rule over the arbitrary, of order over the haphazard. I am thus brought face to face with the eternal conflict in art between the Apollonian and the Dionysian principles. The latter assumes ecstasy to be the final goal—that is to say, the losing of oneself—whereas art demands above all the full consciousness of the artist. There can, therefore, be no doubt as to my choice between the two. And if I appreciate so highly the value of classical ballet, it is not simply a matter of taste on my part, but because I see exactly in it the perfect expression of the Apollonian principle.[23]

These are striking words, the more so since they came from the man who had brought prewar "modernism" to its Dionysian epitome. Their sincerity cannot be doubted, being backed up by 1935 with the output of a decade and a half of avowed, and in one case titularly explicit, Apollonianism. Like Diaghilev, like so many other artists in the aftermath of the Great War, Stravinsky became outwardly conservative, allying himself volubly and vehemently with the elite culture of the Western past, seeking to defend its purity against all that threatened to defile it, including his own early work. If he never actually disavowed *The Rite,* he nevertheless took great pains to distance it from the circumstances of its creation—as in an oft-cited interview on the eve of its postwar revival, where he stoutly maintained:

> I composed this work after *Petrushka.* Its embryo was a theme that came to me when I was just finishing *The Firebird.* Since this theme and all that followed from it was conceived in a strong, brutal manner, I took as pretext for its development what that very music evoked in my imagination, which was (since I am Russian) prehistoric Russia. But note well that the idea came from the music, not the music from the idea. I have written an architectonic work, not an anecdotal one. And it was an error to take it from the latter point of view, opposed [as it is] to the sense of the work itself.[24]

There was hardly a word of truth in this statement, and of course Stravinsky knew it. But he had just finished what would be his last piece of Turanian music, the *Symphonies,* and had no further use for "l'époque préhistorique russe." The Russia that mattered to him now was the Russia Diaghilev was in process of revealing to the world, at first through the music of Cimarosa, with Chaikovsky standing ready in the wings. The main task of this chapter will be to show how Stravinsky made his musical *prise de contact* with that Russia, and how it became

23. *An Autobiography,* 99–100.
24. "J'ai composé cette oeuvre après *Petrouchka.* L'embryon en est un thème qui m'est venu quand j'eus terminé *L'Oiseau de Feu.* Comme ce thème et ce qui en suivit étaient conçus dans une manière brutale, forte, je pris pour prétexte à développements l'évocation même de cette musique, soit, dans mon esprit, l'époque préhistorique russe, puisque je suis Russe. Mais considérez bien que cette idée vient de la musique et non la musique de cette idée. J'ai écrit une oeuvre architectonique et non anecdotique. Et ce fut l'erreur de l'avoir considérée de ce point opposé au sens même de l'oeuvre" (Michel Georges-Michel, "Les deux Sacres du printemps," *Comoedia* [11 December 1920]; cited in Bullard, "The First Performance of Stravinsky's *Sacre du Printemps,*" 1:2–3).

his passport out of Turania and into the mainstream of pangermanoromanic civilization.

LEADING TONES AND OPEN LETTERS

To understand the journey more fully, and the reasons why Stravinsky now wished to make it, we need to take a closer look at the circumstances of his life in 1920 and 1921. As Robert Craft has shrewdly observed, these circumstances created a need in Stravinsky "to formulate a philosophy of art, something that he had not needed before."[25] That philosophy, as we know, was a variant of the aristocratic theory of culture so widely propounded at the time. The inner ferment that made the composer receptive to it was a symptom of a larger malaise we would no doubt diagnose nowadays as a "midlife crisis," characterized by suddenly altered social and political views, wanderlust, domestic discontent, sexual restlessness (Craft calls the period "Stravinsky's years of *'chercher la femme'* "),[26] and a yearning for fresh starts on many levels of his existence. These factors had an at times startlingly palpable impact on his work.

With the 1920 defeat of the last "White" armies under Generals Denikin (April) and Wrangel (November), the Bolsheviks became the undisputed masters of Stravinsky's homeland, and his "loss of Russia" became complete. There would be no more romantic dreams of "États-unis slaves," no more celebrations of "notre chère Russie libérée." From an early sympathy with the bourgeois liberal aims of the Provisional Government (for which, as we recall, he even composed an anthem) and its Constitutional Democratic (Kadet) party,[27] Stravinsky recoiled into a hard-line monarchism typical of Russians from his social class. Disgusted and mortified by the Treaty of Brest-Litovsk, he shared the widespread suspicion of Lenin as a German puppet. The Stravinsky who left Switzerland for France was an embittered tsarist patriot who had given up waiting for the overthrow of the Bolshevik usurpers. In accepting a Nansen passport, the composer finally renounced his Russian nationality and joined the White emigration. (The decision actually to apply for French citizenship was taken—reluctantly—in July 1922, the main motive being the possibility of securing copyrights.[28] The country Stravinsky really wanted to join was Italy, partly out of admiration for the newly ascendent Mussolini.)[29]

For the uprooted composer, the twenties and thirties were a period not only of right-wing politics, but of social snobbery as well. To judge from innumerable photographs, his favored company of the Parisian years were the wealthy and the

25. P&D:209.
26. P&D:627n.11.
27. For favorable comments on Kerensky, Milyukov, and other Kadet leaders, see P&D:550.
28. See Stravinsky to Ansermet, 22 July 1922; in SelCorrI:155–56.
29. See P&D:551–52; for evidence of Stravinsky's continuing loyalty to the Duce, see SelCorrI:438–39n.

titled. Dagmar Godowsky's flighty but not altogether untrustworthy memoirs of the composer suggest that he took occasionally to promoting himself from the general class of *dvoryanin* to that of the actual titled nobility, a common affectation among White émigrés.[30] His position at the head of what seemed a veritable social clique and his virtually authoritarian prestige in musical Paris between the wars were profoundly interrelated. In both senses, as he approached his fortieth birthday Stravinsky had become a *maître,* a *grand seigneur,* and this meant a change in his musical as well as his social orientation: a flight from what he now perceived as a dangerous left wing. Authur Lourié did not exaggerate when he claimed, "What Scriabin was to a whole generation of musicians in Russia during the first decade of the twentieth century, that Stravinsky was to the young European composers. After beginning on the extreme left flank of the modernists, he went through a complex evolution and appeared on the extreme right of the position. In recent years he has been the dictator of the reaction against the anarchy into which modernism degenerated."[31]

Evidence to support such a view of Stravinsky between the wars can be found in any number of interviews and miscellaneous pronouncements. He loved to shock reporters by saying that "modernists have ruined modern music," to quote the banner of a typical interview from his first American tour (1925). He went on, pointedly: "The modernists set out to shock the bourgeoisie, sometimes they succeed only in pleasing the Bolshevists. I am not interested in either the bourgeoisie or the Bolshevists."[32] Any of his bemedaled neighbors in Biarritz could have seconded that last remark.

---

30. Dagmar Godowsky, *First Person Plural* (New York: Viking Press, 1958), 220: "Born Count Strava—the Strava River flowed through his family estates—Stravinsky was a snob like me." Corroboration of Stravinsky's insistence on being scion to "150 ans de la noblesse héréditaire" can be found in P&D:639n.170. In a publicity interview with Janet Flanner for the *New Yorker* at the time of his second American tour, he made a point of telling her that his father "descended from the Polish Counts of Soulima" and that "on both sides, the families were landed gentry or artists" (Flanner, "Profiles: Russian Firebird," *New Yorker,* 5 January 1935). Later, in M&C:15/17, Stravinsky again derived his name from the river Strava, but claimed no more for his family than that they "were landowners in eastern Poland, as far back as can be traced."

31. Arthur Lourié, *Sergei Koussevitzky and His Epoch* (New York: Alfred A. Knopf, 1931), 196.

32. Henrietta Malkiel, "Modernists Have Ruined Modern Music, Stravinsky Says," *Musical America,* 10 January 1925, 9. It was something Stravinsky was telling all the New York reporters that year. To the *Musical Courier* (15 January 1925, 7) he confided that his "modernists" were "the gentlemen who work with formulas instead of ideas"—the commonest form that philistine rejection of the Viennese atonalists took in those days—"[who] started out by trying to write so as to shock the Bourgeoisie and finished up by pleasing the Bolsheviki." One of Stravinsky's New York interviews appeared in translation in a German newspaper and was apparently the immediate provocation both of Schoenberg's anti-Stravinskian squib entitled "Der Restaurateur" (see Arnold Schoenberg, *Style and Idea,* ed. Leonard Stein [Berkeley and Los Angeles: University of California Press, 1984], 481–82) and of his little canon about "der kleine Modernsky" in *Drei Satiren,* op. 28. A clipping of the interview, pasted on larger sheets of paper to accommodate Schoenberg's infuriated marginalia, survives in his archive at the University of Southern California, and was described by Leonard Stein in a Stravinsky centennial talk that has been published, replete with facsimile, in Pasler (ed.), *Confronting Stravinsky,* 310–24. "I don't want to name names," Stravinsky insinuated, "but I could tell you about composers who spend all their time inventing a music of the future. But that is really very presumptuous. Where in all this does any integrity remain?" He went on to say that such composers "only intend to provoke the bourgeoisie and to achieve what pleases the Bolsheviks."

Other émigrés, especially older musicians who had known of Stravinsky in Russia, thought his new role a sham in both its related guises and grumbled indignantly at his snob appeal. One such musician, Nikolai Medtner, attended the legendary Koussevitzky concert at the Paris Opera (22 May 1924) at which Stravinsky unveiled his Concerto for Piano and Winds (the rest of the program consisting of all three prewar ballets!), and he described it in a letter to another, Sergey Rachmaninoff. At first, captivated by the *Firebird* suite, Medtner had been enjoying himself:

> But then the composer appeared with his new concerto and gave me such a box on the ear for my silly sentimentality that I couldn't bear to stay until the end of *The Rite of Spring,* the more so as it showed its stuff right from the start. I walked out. But the public, who had filled the Grand Opera to overflowing, this public who takes it as an insult if someone should appear in its midst in anything but tails or a smoking jacket (for which reason I had to hide myself and my little grey jacket in the highest loges)—this public steadfastly withstood every slap in the face and every humiliation, and what is more, rewarded the author with deafening applause. . . . What is all this?! . . . And you know, they say he, that is Stravinsky, has been summoned to America for the next season for enormous fees, so I will not be able to escape an encounter with this blasted boxer![33]

Stravinsky's social pretensions, his position as arbiter extraordinaire of musical fashion, the haughty emphasis on breeding as hallmark and bulwark of culture that would reach a peak in the *Poétique musicale*—all these received a powerful boost from Gabrielle (Coco) Chanel, the legendary couturière, who became the composer's unexpected benefactress as soon as he left Switzerland. Introduced to Diaghilev by Misia Sert in the summer of 1920, Chanel had agreed to sponsor the revival of *The Rite of Spring* as newly choreographed by Massine, and by September had installed its composer (together, at first, with his family) in her villa in the Paris suburb of Garches, the very command center of Paris chic. That fall, she and Stravinsky became lovers[34]—a liaison that apparently meant a great deal more to Stravinsky than it did to Chanel, who was collecting White Russians at the time,

33. Letter of 28 May 1924, in N. K. Medtner, *Pis'ma*, ed. Z. A. Apetyan (Moscow: Sovetskiy Kompozitor, 1973), 271. Sure enough, a photograph in *Expositions and Developments* (following p. 72/80) shows Stravinsky and Medtner seated side by side at a reception for Josef Hofmann in New York, 11 January 1925 (with Rachmaninoff not far off).

34. Reliable details of this affair are naturally hard to come by. It was first made known by Paul Morand in a biography of Chanel published half a decade after her death (and Stravinsky's) and which relied heavily on interviews with its aging and notoriously boastful subject (*L'allure de Chanel* [Paris: Hermann, 1976]). Later Arthur Gold and Robert Fizdale published the suppressed chapter on Chanel from the memoirs of Misia Sert, in which it had been asserted that when Chanel penetrated the Diaghilev circle, "Stravinsky in particular fell desperately in love with her," and that this had preceded the move to Garches (the implication being that the affair had been the motive for the composer's removal to France; see Gold and Fizdale, *Misia*, 199). Sert's surmise is seconded by Craft, who writes that Chanel and Stravinsky had been introduced by Misia herself in May 1920 (P&D:627n.8). More anecdotes can be found in Rubinstein, *My Many Years,* 151, which purports to give an account of the affair's end.

and whose primary interest was in the young grand duke Dmitri Romanov, grandson of Alexander II and favorite at the court of his cousin, the last tsar.

It may have wounded Stravinsky's pride that Chanel preferred grand dukes to great artists,[35] but his experience with her powerfully heightened his sense of solidarity with the exiled aristocracy. It cannot be a coincidence that upon leaving Garches, in May 1921, Stravinsky set up his family residence in the coastal resort town of Biarritz in the Basque country near the Spanish border. Not only was the place salubrious and possessed of good schools (the reasons Stravinsky gave in various memoirs), and not only did its remoteness free the composer to pursue his dalliances in the capital, ultimately with the woman he would one day marry (the reason Craft has given),[36] but Biarritz, always a favorite vacation spot for high-society Russians, was also the White nobility's gathering place in the decades following the Revolution. It was out of this milieu that Stravinsky made the short trip to Spain in the spring of 1921, there to be apprised of Diaghilev's plan to resurrect the ballet that more than any other work of art symbolized the world with which the composer now wished to identify himself.

His readiness to embrace the project was subtly signaled in the one opus he composed wholly at Garches, the little set of eight children's pieces for piano collectively entitled *Les cinq doigts,* completed on 18 February 1921. Compared with the *Pièces faciles* or the *Valse pour les enfants* of the Swiss decade, these opuscules already show a distinctly Europeanized style. In place of the calculated tonal ambiguity of Stravinsky's earlier white-key diatonicism, we now find major and minor keys that are cadentially articulated, if primitively so. The concluding Pesante (retitled "Tempo di tango" when the set was orchestrated as *Eight Instrumental Miniatures* in 1962), with its tangy mixed harmonies (tonic vying with the diminished triad on the leading tone), is the most frequently cited case in point, but the most poignant indication of a new direction comes in the third piece in the set, the Allegretto. It is not just a "white-key" piece; it is, despite its unconventional dissonance treatment, a composition in C major, as articulated by the descents to the leading tone, quite conventionally prepared and resolved from the linear standpoint, if not the vertical (Ex. 19.4a).

Although it is nowhere identified as such, the tune on which this little piece is based is none other than the venerable *Kamarinskaya,* synonymous with Russian "national" music since the time of Glinka, but prefigured, as we have seen, in Cimarosa's "ballo russo." It is to the latter, completely Westernized adaptation of the tune that Stravinsky's use of it here refers (Ex. 19.4b). The five-bar phrases in Stravinsky's *Kamarinskaya* possibly owe something to Beethoven's adaptation of the tune as the basis for "Twelve Variations on a Russian Dance from Wranitzky's

---

35. See Gold and Fizdale, *Misia,* 231. Chanel did remain a source of financial support for the Stravinskys all through the 1930s, as a letter reprinted in ibid., 230, attests.
36. P&D:210.

F I G .   1 9 . 1   Two *grands seigneurs:* Diaghilev and Stravinsky in Seville at the time of
The Sleeping Princess and *Mavra* (1921).

Das Waldmädchen," WoO71 (1797; Ex. 19.4c). Either way, we may observe the superb irony of Stravinsky now deliberately seeking Western models for his treatment of a "native" theme.

His little Allegretto is thus quietly momentous, contrasting not only with the
"cosmopolitan" white-key music of the war years, but (especially) with the *Pulcinella* extracts shown above. Where *Pulcinella* had been a Eurasianized version of
a Western music, here we have a pangermanoromanic setting of a Eurasian tune.
It is a little manifesto of Stravinsky's intention to let the ontogeny of his own music mirror the phylogeny of Russia's musical culture as it had made its initial fructifying contacts with the West under the auspices of the late, lamented Romanov
dynasty.

EXAMPLE 19.4

a. *Les cinq doigts*, Allegretto

b. Cimarosa, *Le astuzie femminili* (Paris: Escudier, n.d.), Act IV finale: pp. 274, 280 (orchestra only)

EXAMPLE 19.4 (*continued*)

c. Beethoven, "Twelve Variations on a Russian Dance from Wranitzky's *Das Waldmädchen*" (WoO71), Tema

Diaghilev put Stravinsky to work on the *Sleeping Beauty* revival in two capacities: as musical editor and as propagandist. Together in Seville they played over the music four-hands, decided on cuts and interpolations, and also resolved to reinstate some items that were traditionally omitted. Among the latter were two numbers from Act II that had been cut before the première and thus had never actually been performed in the theater. The first (no. 15b) was a variation (i.e., a solo turn) for Aurora, the Princess, who, according to Petipa's original scenario, appears to Prince Désiré in a dream vision the Lilac Fairy conjures up for him.[37] This extremely lightweight number was replaced in the first production, evidently at the request or for the sake of the ballerina (Carlotta Brianza), by the more emphatic waltz variation originally intended for the Gold Fairy in Act III (no. 23, var. 1).[38] Diaghilev reinstated it, but as a variation for the Lilac Fairy herself (in Petipa's version a mimed role), danced by "Lopokova" (Lydia Lopukhova), the London public's perky darling, to a new choreography by Nijinska.[39]

The other item to be reinstated was a big violin solo in the form of an entr'acte (no. 18)—scene-change music, really—meant originally to be played, with curtain down, by Leopold Auer, the imperial court violinist, whose contract obliged him to appear at ballet spectacles throughout the theatrical season (that is, from 1 September through the beginning of Lent). Because of the obligatory participation of a virtuoso violinist in ballet performances (before Auer, the post of

37. See the scenario, as translated by Wiley in *Tchaikovsky's Ballets,* 357 (no. 11).
38. Ibid., 153.
39. Nijinska, "Petipa pobedil," 318. Brianza, the original Aurora, played Carabosse in Diaghilev's revival.

imperial court violinist had been held, and the same obligation discharged, by Wieniawski and Vieuxtemps), it became customary to include a concertante violin movement in all full-evening ballet scores. Those that survived in the Soviet repertory (by Chaikovsky and Glazunov) are performed to this day with Auer's unwritten virtuoso embellishments, passed along from generation to generation by rote.[40]

Chaikovsky had accorded Auer two solos in *The Sleeping Beauty* (the other being Aurora's variation in the first act, replete with a flashy cadenza); hence, the Act II entr'acte could easily be discarded. Stravinsky himself repeated a story he had most likely heard from Diaghilev, to the effect that its omission had been personally requested by Tsar Alexander III after the ballet's first performance.[41] In fact the tsar never heard the piece: Vsevolozhsky had scratched it a week before the première, his stated reason being that, while beautiful, it slowed the action down too much.[42] R. John Wiley comments, "Omitting the *entr'acte* . . . implies the producers' confidence in the smooth operation of the stage machinery, malfunctions of which had caused several postponements of the premiere in the autumn of 1889." Diaghilev had no such confidence, which is why the entr'acte had to be reinstated.[43]

The only full score of *The Sleeping Beauty* at Diaghilev's disposal belonged to Nikolai Sergeyev (1876–1951), a former Mariyinsky régisseur, who had brought it with him when he emigrated in 1918, together with dance notations on the basis of which Petipa's choreography could be revived. Sergeyev's score conformed to the Mariyinsky performing version, of course, and hence was missing the two numbers Diaghilev wished to reinstate. Stravinsky was thus commissioned to orchestrate the newly christened "Variation de la Fée de lilas" and the entr'acte from Alexander Siloti's piano reduction.[44] He performed the task in a rush at the beginning of October 1921, just in time for the première.

For Stravinsky, these instrumentations are pretty routine. Chaikovsky had scored both the variation and the entr'acte lightly, using no brass except horns.

---

40. Lev Nikolayevich Raaben, *Leopol'd Semyonovich Auer: ocherk zhizni i deyatel'nosti* (Leningrad: Muzgiz, 1962), 107–8. Stravinsky himself recalled Auer in the capacity of "Soloist to His Majesty" in E&D:97/54: "I remember seeing him walk into the Mariyinsky pit, play the violin solos (standing, as though for a concerto), and then walk out again."

41. E&D:70/81, where the entr'acte with the violin solo is confused with the following number, the *Entr'acte symphonique*. The latter, which includes the awakening kiss, is obviously never cut. Diaghilev's version of the story can be found in Buckle, *Diaghilev,* 388–89.

42. See his telegram to Chaikovsky of 27 December 1889, quoted in Wiley, *Tchaikovsky's Ballets,* 152.

43. Ibid., 152; E&D:70/81.

44. In addition he retouched the orchestration of the coda to the Act III pas de deux, which Nijinska was rechoreographing as a Trepak for "The Three Ivans." This one departure from Petipa's choreography of the Act III divertissement became popular and was retained as part of "Aurora's Wedding." Finally, Stravinsky composed and orchestrated a brief transition in the Act I finale ("Aurore se pique") to cover a cut. The manuscript is in the Bibliothèque Nationale in Paris. In the unsigned preface to the Boosey & Hawkes study score of the Variation and Entr'acte (Hawkes Pocket Scores 959 [1979]) it is stated that the autograph of this bridge is dated October 1920. Confirmation that this date is off by one year can be found in SelCorrI:152n.

EXAMPLE 19.5

a. *Sleeping Beauty*, no. 15b (Variation), beginning

Stravinsky, evidently following without much reflection the general list of instruments at the head of the score, weighted both pieces down with trumpets, trombones, tuba, and timpani. Yet although his scorings are thus somewhat more conventional and generic than Chaikovsky's in overall timbre, he did not scruple when it came to occasional anachronistic usages, such as a trumpet solo in lyrical duet with the solo violin in the entr'acte (fig. [6]). (Chaikovsky always treated the trumpet as if it were a "natural" brass instrument; for him it was strictly for tuttis and fanfares.) And while Stravinsky added some alluring woodwind counterpoints to the texture in both pieces, there are also places where he followed the line of least resistance, mirroring the piano reduction in literalistic and orchestrally unidiomatic ways.

At the beginning of the variation, for example, Siloti, for the sake of a clean keyboard rendition, had replaced orchestral slurs connecting two voicings of a single vamping chord with ties. Stravinsky transferred the ties literally into his orchestration, producing a rhythmically static effect (Ex. 19.5). Even more literal was the opening of the entr'acte (Ex. 19.6). It was probably a deliberate eccentricity on Stravinsky's part to bring in the violin solo somewhat later than Chaikovsky had done (the two phrases in question being a parallel period), but when Stravinsky's violin does enter, its part reproduces the appearance of the piano reduction, which had been contrived to approximate the sound of an ascending arpeggio for the violin against a sustained chord in the winds. Later on, when the opening arpeggio comes back in the piano reduction in a form less occluded, Stravinsky again followed Siloti's notation literally, never turning back to bring the opening violin

EXAMPLE 19.5 (*continued*)

b. The same in Siloti's piano reduction

c. The same in Stravinsky's orchestration

EXAMPLE 19.6

a. *Sleeping Beauty,* no. 18 (Entr'acte), mm. 1–9

EXAMPLE 19.6 (*continued*)

b. Siloti's piano reduction

c. Stravinsky's orchestration

(*continued*)

EXAMPLE 19.6C (*continued*)

phrase into conformity with the later ones, even though they were obviously meant to be identical.

One more instance of this kind is worth citing: the most brilliant passage for the violin, consisting of sweeping broken chords preceding a cadenza (Ex. 19.7). When making the piano reduction, Siloti had to compress the range of these chords so as to keep the hands of the pianist out of each other's way. Stravinsky's figuration, once again, hews closely to the notation of his immediate source; he was content as before to follow the piano right hand rather than trying to regain a violinistic idiom for which he evidently had small feeling.

But then, one can never be fully sure of anyone's intentions. Was it just oversight or literalism, or was it a matter of deliberate style or taste that accounts (to cite one more troublesome point) for Stravinsky's failure to restore some of the long pedals Siloti was forced by pianistic limitations to eliminate from the reduction? We will never know; yet even after making every conceivable allowance, the mixture of nonchalance and dependency one encounters in the entr'acte arrangement casts Stravinsky in the very unaccustomed role of orchestral *routinier*, much as do Ravel's unaccountably clumsy 1914 orchestrations for Nijinsky of *Carnaval* and *Les sylphides*.

EXAMPLE 19.7

a. *Sleeping Beauty,* no. 18, mm. 44–47

EXAMPLE 19.7 (*continued*)

b. Siloti's piano reduction

c. Stravinsky's orchestration

The tiny variation is another story. Stravinsky obviously took a greater interest in the piece, possibly because it was going to be danced by Lopukhova, with whom he had dallied in Spain five years before and for whom he long retained a sentimental attachment.[45] His arrangement differed sufficiently from the original to require a separate piano reduction for rehearsals.[46] Not only did Stravinsky add some original countermelodies (cello solo before fig. [1]; flute, oboe, clarinet, and horn before [3]), but he also shortened the dance by a total of seventeen bars (omitted were Chaikovsky's mm. 2, 12–27). The ending was Stravinskianized in a fashion worth comparing with the end of the overture to *Mavra* (Ex. 19.8).

All in all, it does not seem that Stravinsky was especially stirred by his practical editorial work on *The Sleeping Beauty*. His propagandistic work, on the other hand, was vehement, personal, and indispensable to our understanding of the Stravinsky who emerged from it. This clamorous switching of historical allegiances (though of course its being a switch was fervently denied) was something Stravinsky evidently deemed necessary to his own transformation into a "European" composer.

The first item Stravinsky wrote at Diaghilev's request was an "open letter" dated Paris, 1 October 1921, printed (in Edwin Evans's English) in the *Times* of London three weeks later, and subsequently reprinted (in both English and the original French) in the program book for the whole run of the ballet at the Alhambra. It starts right off with a nostalgic glorification of the vanished Russian empire, the empire whose abolition Stravinsky had greeted with satisfaction some four and a half years earlier: "This work seems to me to be the most authentic expression of the epoch in our Russian life that we call the 'Petersburg period,' engraved in my memory by the matutinal vision of the horse-drawn carriage of Alexander III, the enormous Emperor and his enormous coachman, and with the boundless joy that awaited me in the evening: the spectacle of *The Sleeping Beauty.*" Next there is an encomium to Chaikovsky's "power of *melody* [puissance *mélodique*], a very rare and precious gift . . . and one that is altogether un-German." Glinka, too, is credited

45. See P&D:142.
46. Stravinsky presented Lopukhova with the autograph of this curious reduction of his scoring of Siloti's reduction of Chaikovsky's scoring, inscribing it "*Lopushke-predatel'nitse*" ("To Lopushka the Betrayer"; the manuscript is now at the Fitzwilliam Museum, Cambridge). Milo Keynes, Lopukhova's nephew, asked Anton Dolin for an explanation; the latter opined that it had to do with the departures from the original choreography (see Keynes [ed.], *Lydia Lopokova*, 8). It seems far likelier that the inscription was meant as a reference to their old flirtation and to the fact that she had just become involved with Maynard Keynes, the economist, whom she would marry in 1925. An additional sidelight on Stravinsky's affair with Lopukhova, and possibly the reasons for its ending, is contained in another comment recorded by Milo Keynes (ibid.): "Lydia once told me that Stravinsky seemed to have religious problems (about which she did not enlarge) which she thought had been a distinct handicap to the development of his personality."

EXAMPLE 19.8

a. *Sleeping Beauty,* no. 15b, original ending

b. Stravinsky's ending

c. *Mavra* overture, ending

with the spontaneous melodic gift, while "the Germans manufactured their music out of themes and leitmotifs in place of melodies."[47]

On the surface this last was a puzzling point, since, as anyone could hear, Chaikovsky's music for *The Sleeping Beauty* is saturated with themes that recur for identifying or dramaturgical purposes, of which at least two—those of the Lilac Fairy and the wicked fairy Carabosse—have to be regarded as full-fledged leitmotifs. And had not Stravinsky, a scant dozen years before, composed the most leitmotif-happy ballet in the whole history of the genre?[48] But he was using code. As his subsequent work and writings made clearer, what Stravinsky was really talking about was "numbers," not melodies—*drobnost'* as against the "organic" form of the Wagnerians.

Beyond that, the passage resonates with the notion, then so widespread, of the "two cultures of music," to cite the title of August Halm's influential tract of 1913,[49] according to which the Italo-French culture of stage music coexisted—but, increasingly, vied and interacted—with the Germanic instrumental tradition. The

47. "Cette oeuvre me semble être l'expression la plus authentique de l'époque de notre vie russe que nous appelons la 'période de Petersbourg,' gravée dans ma mémoire avec la vision matinale des traîneaux imperiaux d'Alexandre III, l'énorme Empereur et son énorme cocher, et la joie immense qui m'attendait le soir: le spectacle de *La Belle au Bois Dormant*. . . . Les Allemands fabriquaient de la musique avec des thèmes et des leit-motifs, les substituant à des mélodies." The apparition of the tsar and his equipage was revived in Conv:92–93/83.

48. The roles of the Lilac Fairy and Carabosse and their themes, as embodiments respectively of good and evil magic, are suggestive of *The Firebird*, and there may have been a musical echo of Chaikovsky's great ballet in Stravinsky's score as well: compare the opening of the *Sleeping Beauty* finale (no. 30) with one of the characteristic mime themes for the title character in *The Firebird* ([42]−2).

a. *Sleeping Beauty*, no. 30 (finale), opening

Allegro brillante (Tempo di mazurka)

b. *The Firebird*, 2 before [42]

49. August Halm, *Von zwei Kulturen der Musik* (1913; Stuttgart: Klett, 1947). Halm's ideas have been revived and applied to the historiography of nineteenth-century music by Carl Dahlhaus, in his *Nineteenth-Century Music,* trans. J. Bradford Robinson (Berkeley and Los Angeles: University of California Press, 1989), 8–15 and passim.

mainstay of the former was its self-sufficient, expressive vocal melody, which was given a clearly articulated rhythmic, metric, textural, and timbral support. The latter depended on the logic of its often exceedingly recondite harmonic and thematic relationships. What the former invited was enjoyment; what the latter demanded was "understanding."[50] It is easy enough for us now to see how the two cultures persisted into the twentieth century, with Stravinsky and Schoenberg at their respective heads. What is remarkable is the clarity with which Stravinsky saw the issues and his place within the scheme they describe. All this is encoded in his not-so-innocent use of the word *melody*. And yes, it did imply a rejection of the esthetic principles on which the musical structure of *The Firebird* had rested, as Stravinsky made explicit in notes accompanying his piano rolls (described in Chapter 9).

Then comes the nub and kernel, the remarkable passage in which Stravinsky defined Chaikovsky's place within Russian music and Russia's place within the two cultures:

> The music of Chaikovsky, which does not seem obviously Russian to everyone, is often more profoundly Russian than that which long ago received the superficial label of Muscovite picturesqueness.
>
> This music is every bit as Russian as Pushkin's verse or Glinka's songs. Without specifically cultivating "the Russian peasant soul" in his art, Chaikovsky imbibed *unconsciously* the true national sources of our race.
>
> And how characteristic were his preferences in older music, as well as the music of his time! He adored Mozart, Couperin, Glinka, Bizet: this leaves no doubt as to the quality of his taste. It's strange, but every time a Russian musician has been influenced by this Latin-Slav culture, and has seen clearly the line that divides the Austrian Catholic Mozart, with his Beaumarchais orientation, from the German Protestant Beethoven, inclined toward Goethe, the result has been striking.[51]

In part this assessment harks back to debates that had raged in Russia in days of yore. Hermann Laroche, Chaikovsky's conservatory classmate and long his principal advocate in the Russian press, touched, in his review of the first production of *The Sleeping Beauty*, on many of the same themes as did (Diaghilev and) Stravin-

---

50. The exposition of the "two cultures" here follows that given by Karol Berger, reviewing Asafyev's *Book About Stravinsky*, in *Journal of Music Theory* 28 (1984): 296.

51. "La musique de Tchaïkowsky, ne paraissant pas à tout le monde spécifiquement russe, est souvent plus profondément russe que celle qui, depuis longtemps a reçu l'étiquette facile du pittoresque moscovite. Cette musique est tout autant russe que le vers de Pouchkine, ou le chant de Glinka. Ne cultivant pas spécialement dans son art 'l'âme paysanne russe,' Tchaïkowsky puisait *inconsciemment* dans les vraies sources populaires de notre race. Et à quel point ses préférences dans la musique ancienne et de son temps étaient-elles caractéristiques! Il adorait Mozart, Couperin, Glinka, Bizet: voilà qui ne laisse nul doute sur la qualité de son goût. Chose étrange, chaque fois qu'un musicien russe s'influençait de cette culture latino-slave et voyait clairement la frontière entre l'Autrichien catholique Mozart tourné vers Beaumarchais, et l'Allemand protestant Beethoven, incliné vers Goethe, le résultat était marquant" (the text of the letter here follows that of the program book, as reproduced in Craft [ed.], *Igor and Vera Stravinsky: A Photograph Album*, 54).

sky a generation later. He in his time, like they in theirs, had been at pains to educe from the ballet the lesson that there was such a thing as an aristocratic taste in Russia that was no less Russian for its being aristocratic; that national character was not the same as local color (of *The Sleeping Beauty* he had written, "The local color is French, but the *style* is Russian"); and, most important of all, that the word *Russian* need not be equated with "peasant," for "the peasantlike, . . . recognized in its proper place, [is] but *part* of being Russian."[52]

The immediate purpose of Stravinsky's open letter was to forestall (unsuccessfully, as it turned out) a prejudiced reception of Chaikovsky's music. But it also contained, albeit between the lines and with benefit of hindsight, an announcement of the creative metamorphosis Stravinsky himself was undergoing—or, perhaps one should say, was planning to undergo. He was about to submit in full consciousness to "the influence of this Latino-Slav culture," and was naturally hoping for a "striking result."

More openly confessional was Stravinsky's front-page letter to *Le Figaro* in connection with the Paris première, on 18 May 1922, of "Aurora's Wedding" (titled in French "Le mariage de la Belle au bois dormant"). Stravinsky had had a small hand in this work, too: he had arranged the coda for Nijinska's "Three Ivans." For this his integrity had been impugned by those who saw him betraying the honorable heritage of his birthright for the sake of Diaghilev's commercial success. Stung by the charge of venality, Stravinsky retorted:

> I want to insist on the fact that I have always felt myself to be in communion with the spirit that animates the music of Chaikovsky, or, if you prefer, with the sense of his art. The love that I have managed to show for *Boris Godunov* or for a symphony by Borodin, and the esteem that I still have for them, in no way imply my adherence to the program of the Five, of which I have been, perhaps wrongly, viewed as the continuer. I feel much closer to a tradition that was founded by Glinka, Dargomïzhsky, and Chaikovsky. For the Russianism of the Five took the form mainly of opposition to the conventional Italianism that reigned in Russia in their day and found its outlet in a picturesqueness that easily captured the imagination of foreign audiences. But that day is over and gone: opposition to Italianism no longer has any raison d'être, and we find an altogether new flavor in works whose Russian nature is displayed not out of any need to oppose, and without the aid of that picturesqueness which by now seems to me to have itself become thoroughly conventional. . . .
>
> A few years ago people appreciated Russian music as if it were a sort of Negro music. No critic spoke of it without using the term "sauvage et raffiné." In those days the picturesqueness of the Five was something one valued. It is time to have done with it. Russian stage designs are no longer obliged to be Oriental tapestries. And Russian music can speak to us of other things besides the Russia that existed

---

52. Lengthy extracts from this important review (*Novosti i birzhevaya gazeta*, 2 January 1890) are given in Wiley, *Tchaikovsky's Ballets*, 190–92.

before Peter the Great. Those who cannot take this step and rid themselves of conventional notions are doomed to become what we call "Philistines."[53]

This was the earliest public manifestation of the position Stravinsky would maintain to the end of his life: in the *Chroniques,* in the *Poétique,* in the conversations, in countless interviews. Its essential falsity—especially as to the facts of Stravinsky's career up to the end of his Swiss period—has been exposed explicitly in the Introduction to this book and implicitly in the individual discussions of the masterworks dating from the period on which the composer was now turning his back. Its essential truth had to do with the conditions of musical politics in his adopted country, where Chaikovsky and the Five were dichotomized far more radically than in Russia, where the latter group had been canonized as a prime shaper of the modern French school, and where Chaikovsky was written off as "German." By emphasizing Chaikovsky's gift for *melody,* Stravinsky had hoped to dispose of that charge once and for all.

In his later writings he would even try to turn the tables on the conventional wisdom, shrewdly pointing out that the so-called nationalists of Russian music "Europeanized their music just as much [as Glinka, Dargomïzhsky, and Chaikovsky], but they were inspired by very different models—Wagner, Liszt, Berlioz"—that is, by what was known in their day as the New German School. Moreover, where the national character in Glinka and Chaikovsky "flow[ed] spontaneously from their very nature," with the Five it had been a matter of "a doctrinaire catechism they wished to impose," with the result that their music had "rapidly become academic and concentrated in the Belaieff circle under the domination of Rimsky-Korsakov and Glazunov."[54] We have already seen how high a premium Stravinsky placed on the "unconscious" wellsprings of Chaikovsky's nationality, as against the hothouse "nationalism" of the St. Petersburgers.

53. "Je désire insister sur le fait que je me suis toujours senti en communion avec l'esprit qui anime la musique de Tchaïkovsky, ou, si l'on préfère, avec le sens de son art. L'amour que j'ai pu ressentir pour *Boris Godunov* ou pour une symphonie de Borodine et l'estime que je leur conserve n'impliquent en rien mon adhésion à la tendance des *cinq,* dont on a eu peut-être tort de voir en moi un continuateur. Je me sens beaucoup plus près d'une tradition qui serait fondée par Glinka, Dargomijski et Tchaïkovsky. Car le russisme des Cinq s'est manifesté surtout en opposition à l'italianisme conventionnel qui régnait alors en Russie et a trouvé sa voie dans un pittoresque qui a facilement frappé l'imagination du public étranger. Mais cette époque est revolue: l'opposition à l'italianisme n'a plus de raison d'être et nous trouvons une toute nouvelle saveur à des oeuvres où s'est manifestée la nature russe en dehors de ce besoin d'opposition et sans l'aide de ce pittoresque qui me paraît lui-même aujourd'hui parfaitement conventionnel. . . . Il y a quelques années, on appreciait la musique russe comme une musique nègre. Pas un critique qui ne parlât d'elle en se servant du terme 'sauvage et raffiné.' A cette epoque, le pittoresque des *cinq* était de mise. Il est temps d'en finir. Les décors russes ne sont plus obligatoirement des tapis d'Orient. Et la musique russe peut nous parler d'autre chose que de la Russie d'avant Pierre le Grand. Ceux qui ne peuvent pas franchir ce pas et se détacher des notions convenues deviendront fatalement ce qu'on appelle des 'pompiers'" ("Une Lettre de Stravinsky sur Tchaïkovsky," *Figaro,* 18 May 1922; reprinted in *Revue musicale* 3, no. 9 [July 1922]: 87).

54. *An Autobiography,* 97, 98.

It therefore strikes an oddly ironic note when in the midst of the very same discussion in the *Chroniques,* Stravinsky accounts for his own stylistic reorientation in the following, perhaps too candid, terms:

> By his nature, his mentality, and his ideology Pushkin was the most perfect representative of that wonderful line which began with Peter the Great and which, by a fortunate alloy, has united the most characteristically Russian elements with the spiritual riches of the West. Diaghileff unquestionably belonged to this line, and all his activities have only confirmed the authenticity of that origin. As for myself, I had always been aware that I had in me the germs of this same mentality only needing development, and I subsequently deliberately cultivated them.[55]

Putting all these confessions together, we have what amounts to Stravinsky's explicit testimony that what Glinka and Chaikovsky meant to him above all was their link with the *barstvo,* the Russian high society of their day. Like Pushkin, from whose work the subject of *Mavra* would be drawn, and with whom Glinka and Chaikovsky made up the troika to whose memory that work would be dedicated (see Fig. 19.2), they had lived their lives among the aristocracy. (Glinka, in fact, was himself a landowning aristocrat.) Their work, implicitly by virtue of the genres they cultivated and explicitly by virtue of many of the texts they set and the patronage they invited, ardently upheld the values of the tsarist social structure. Although Glinka's historical reputation is that of the founder of the Russian national school, the "nationalism" (*narodnost'*) his art cultivated and exemplified was of the type that took its place alongside orthodoxy (*pravoslaviye*) and autocracy (*samoderzhaviye*) as one of the three pillars supporting the state ideology (the so-called Official Nationality) of the repressive Nikolai I regime, which coincided exactly with Glinka's artistic maturity.

The work (one of the very few works, it is important to add) in which Glinka had incorporated thematic material of peasant origin, the opera *A Life for the Tsar* (1836), was far from being for that reason the "liberal" or "progressive" work it is often made out to be (and not only by Soviet writers, alas). It is the story of a peasant who heroically sacrificed his life for the sake of the nascent Romanov dynasty, and the opera became for that reason the very emblem of the Russian ruling house, the obligatory season opener of the Imperial Theaters in both capitals, which, being funded by the office of the privy chancellor, were technically the personal property of the crown. Glinka's opera was therefore not so much nationalistic, in the sense the word later acquired, as it was patriotic, aimed at the glorification of the dynasty and the defense, in its day, of serfdom. Politically it was a profoundly reactionary work.

55. Ibid., 97.

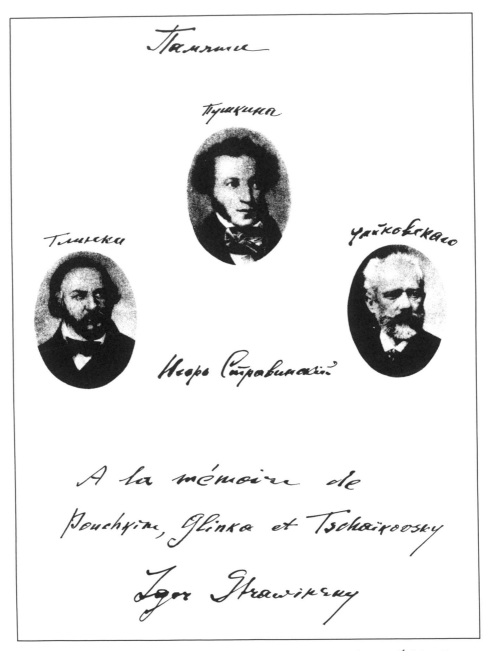

FIG. 19.2. Dedication page from first edition of *Mavra* (vocal score, Édition Russe de Musique, 1925).

As for Chaikovsky, by the end of his career he had become the closest thing old Russia ever had to an official court composer or composer laureate. His Mariyinsky ballets, commissioned by Vsevolozhsky on behalf of Tsar Alexander III, are already evidence of this fact; to them one may add such lesser commissions as his choral couplets based on the apotheosis from *A Life for the Tsar* combined contrapuntally with the "Tsarist Hymn" ("*Bozhe, Tsarya khrani*"), or his cantata *Moskva*, to a text by the poet and hardened Official Nationalist Apollon Nikolayevich Maikov, both composed for Alexander's coronation in 1883—making, together with an official Festival Coronation March, a total of three contributions to those dynastic festivities. Earlier (1866), Chaikovsky had composed a Festival Overture on the Danish national hymn to celebrate the future tsar's wedding to the Danish princess Dagmar, who would reign as the Empress Maria Fyodorovna. Chaikovsky was on intimate terms with several members of the imperial family, especially the Grand Dukes Konstantin (father and son). To the former, Konstantin Nikolayevich, brother of Alexander II, Chaikovsky dedicated his opera *The Oprichnik;* he also composed a choral setting of one of Konstantin Konstantinovich's religious verses (which was understandably omitted from the State Academic Edition of Chaikovsky's works, ostensibly completed in 1971). His many rococo pastiches further testify to a vigorously professed monarchism and to a political conservatism that if anything surpassed Glinka's, as do a number of startlingly violent letters: for example, that of 16/28 January 1882 to Mme von Meck, in which he asserted categorically that all "Nihilists" ought to be "exterminated."[56]

All this forms a crucial subtext to *Mavra*, the work through which Stravinsky sought so deliberately to reposition himself vis-à-vis Russia and the West alike. That seemingly innocent little *opéra bouffe* was, among other things, at once his "White émigré" manifesto, his proclamation of solidarity with the uprooted *barstvo,* and his pledge of pangermanoromanic allegiance. Since these aspects of *Mavra* were not of the slightest concern to the Parisian audience, it is no wonder that they took so little interest in the piece (though there were musical reasons for their indifference as well). *Mavra* was Stravinsky's first great public flop. Let this alone confound those who, in their ignorance, continue to claim that Stravinsky abandoned his earlier manner in an effort to keep up with Parisian chic.[57] On the contrary: by continuing to turn out exotic "Negro" pieces, Stravinsky could have maintained a facile success with the Parisians indefinitely. His switch was an act of

---

56. M. Chaikovsky, *Life and Letters of Peter Ilich Tchaikovsky* 2:418. The letter is double-dated because it was written in Rome.

57. E.g., Claudio Spies ("Conundrums, Conjectures, Construals," 134): "Once settled in France, he soon saw the futility and impracticality of continuing to produce compositions based on Russian texts or stories or folktunes, since these would have been bound to bear the stamp of mere exotic regionalism or quaint nationalism in a cultural milieu whose notion of *chic* had by then largely bypassed that trend." "Exotic regionalism" and "quaint nationalism" were just what Stravinsky's Parisian admirers, whose reviews we shall presently consider, wanted from him.

personal conviction that cost him heavily in the outward trappings of public esteem. Whatever we may now think of it, it was an act of courage.

MAVRA: ITS CONCEPTION

The *Mavra* fiasco was especially troubling in that with it Stravinsky encountered for the first time, as Craft has put it, "avant-garde as well as general-audience resistance."[58] Both the composer and his librettist Boris Kokhno (Kochno)—then Diaghilev's newly appointed secretary and all of seventeen years of age—have characterized the ill-fated piece as a spin-off from the *Sleeping Beauty* project, Stravinsky stating flat out that it was "inspired by the revival"[59] and Kochno actually attributing the idea for the work to Diaghilev, who wished to round out the *Sleeping Beauty* evening "with a curtain raiser and, with this in mind, asked Stravinsky to compose a short chamber opera."[60]

Kochno's version one can scarcely credit. In the first place, Chaikovsky's ballet, given practically uncut (as was the defiantly determined plan from the beginning), is a long evening all by itself. It left no room for a curtain raiser, and none was ever performed with it. In the second place, Stravinsky got down to work on *Mavra* in earnest only after returning from the *Sleeping Beauty* première.[61] To be sure, when "Aurora's Wedding" was unveiled in Paris on 18 May 1922 it did share the bill with "something modern" by Stravinsky; but that was *Renard,* in a new balletic production choreographed by Nijinska. When *Mavra* bowed on 3 June, it served as curtain raiser to *Petrushka* and *The Rite.* Next to *The Sleeping Beauty* it could only seem a parody.

Nor is it true that "*Mavra* is Tchaikovskian in period and style," even if, like *The Sleeping Beauty,* it did "show a different Russia to my non-Russian, and especially to my French, colleagues"[62]—which, of course, is precisely why it flopped. In period and style it is pre-Chaikovskian, except insofar as Chaikovsky wrote a couple of operas based, like *Mavra,* on Pushkin, in which he drew on the same fund of period music as Stravinsky would later do. What links *Mavra* with Chaikovsky is not a direct stylistic influx but a shared stylistic patrimony.

For all these reasons, Serge Grigoriev's version of the origin of *Mavra* as a Diaghilev spectacle is the most plausible of those available. Having impetuously dismissed Massine (ostensibly over the latter's affair with Vera Savina, a member

---

58. P&D:209.

59. E&D:71/81.

60. Kochno, *Diaghilev and the Ballets Russes,* 182. In an oral memoir paraphrased by Buckle (*Diaghilev,* 379), Kochno put it this way: "Because Diaghilev was afraid to give this old work [*The Sleeping Beauty*], or part of it, without something modern also in the programme, it was planned that there would be a short curtain-raiser in the form of an opera by Stravinsky to a libretto by Kochno."

61. See his postcard to Ansermet, dated sometime in December 1921 (SelCorrI:153), in which he writes, "I have been composing [*Mavra*] for two months now without a break."

62. E&D:72/82–83.

of the corps de ballet, whom Massine eventually married), Diaghilev was without a choreographer for the 1922 season. Nijinska arrived only just in time to help with the adaptation of "Aurora's Wedding" and to compose the dancing for the tiny *Renard*. "In addition to this," Grigoriev reports:

> Stravinsky was now [February 1922] hard at work on a one-act opera, the libretto of which was by Boris Kochno. Kochno, who had become Diaghilev's secretary in the previous year, was a well-educated and intelligent young man, given to writing poetry and eager to contribute to the work of the Ballet. This opera, which was called *Mavra*, was his first essay at a libretto; and Diaghilev decided to include it also in the Paris season.[63]

Mavra, then, was not commissioned by Diaghilev but merely co-opted by him, as an ostensible favor to Kochno but, more to the point, as a novelty that would not require a choreographer. Otherwise it is difficult to understand why Diaghilev should have been interested, at this stage in his career, in presenting an undanced opera, even one by Stravinsky.[64] Grigoriev's account is easy enough to reconcile with Stravinsky's recollection that "*Mavra* was conceived in the Savoy Hotel, London, in the spring of 1921, during the planning of *The Sleeping Beauty* revival,"[65] if we assume that only Stravinsky and Kochno were doing the conceiving at this point, and that the work was not directly related either to the Chaikovsky project or to the Diaghilev enterprise.

Then what was the stimulus that sparked conception? Enough scattered evidence points in an interesting and hitherto overlooked direction to permit the framing of an alternative hypothesis.

———

In December 1920, a Russian variety show opened at the Théâtre Femina on the Champs-Élysées, sporting the name "Le Théâtre de la Chauve-Souris à Moscou" (The Bat Theater of Moscow). It was a transplanted adaptation of a cabaret called *Letuchaya mïsh'* that had begun in 1908 as a modest postperformance farrago (what in Russian is called a *kapustnik*) of skits and songs in the cellar of the Moscow Art Theater. "At once," to quote its hyperbolic press releases, "it became the most intriguing, the most exclusive, the most expensive, and the most important night-spot theatre in Europe, the haunt of Russian artists, wits,

63. Grigoriev, *Diaghilev Ballet*, 175.

64. The only other operas performed under Diaghilev's auspices in the postwar period were *Le astuzie femminili*, which was presented as a sung ballet after the fashion of the 1914 *Coq d'or;* two by Gounod (*Le médecin malgré lui* and *Philémon et Baucis*), created in 1924 not as official Ballets Russes productions but as part of his contractual obligation to the Monte Carlo Opera; and the "opera-oratorio" *Oedipus Rex*, commissioned sight unseen from Stravinsky for a jubilee celebration marking the twentieth anniversary of Diaghilev's Paris enterprises—and in the expectation that it would be a ballet. See Kochno, *Diaghilev and the Ballets Russes*, 254.

65. E&D:71/81.

rakes and socialites and of all celebrities visiting Russia."[66] In Paris it took on more of the aspect of a conventional revue, specializing in picturesque glimpses of "la vieille Russie."

The Chauve-Souris was an immediate hit, not only in Paris, but (from 1921) in London and (from 1922) in America as well. It found favor not just in émigré communities but with the general theatergoing audience, thanks to the showmanship of its producer/director, a sometime Moscow Art Theater bit player named Nikita Baliyev (1877–1936) who acted as the cabaret's bug-eyed, roly-poly emcee. (Robert Benchley, who hated the show on its first American tour, nevertheless conceded that "Balieff" was "an excellent comedian and linguist—even through our tears of rage at the first performance we could see that he was funny.")[67] Another main attraction was the décor (sets and costumes), mostly the work of Sergey Sudeykin (Serge Soudeikine, 1882–1946), a well-known neonationalist painter with impeccable Abramtsevo and *Mir iskusstva* credentials. He had been close to Diaghilev since long before the latter's ballet enterprise was launched. At the impresario's invitation, Sudeykin had come to Paris in 1906 for the Salon d'Automne exhibition, at which his work was shown abroad for the first time. He had designed the very successful sets and costumes for Diaghilev's production of *La tragédie de Salomé* by Florent Schmitt in 1913, and had also helped execute Roerich's designs for *The Rite of Spring* that same season—work that brought him briefly into contact with Stravinsky. By the time of the Revolution, Sudeykin was one of the foremost theatrical designers in Russia; the highlight of his career in his homeland was his association with Alexander Taírov's Kamernïy (Chamber) Theater in Moscow, where he also fell in with Baliyev. For Taírov's 1915 production of Beaumarchais's *Marriage of Figaro,* Sudeykin supplied not only the sets and costumes, but also a Spanish dancer in the person of his wife, Vera (née de Bosset), with whom he had eloped to Paris two years before. Vera, too, was employed by Baliyev in 1920–21, in the atelier of the Chauve-Souris, where she helped execute her husband's costume designs.[68]

Among the friends the Sudeykins had made in the Crimea and the Caucasus— whither they had fled the Revolution in 1918, and whence they emigrated a year

66. Publicity release in the Theater Collection, Library and Museum of the Performing Arts, Lincoln Center, New York [hereafter cited as LMPA]. *Billboard* (24 January 1925), no doubt in reaction to this puff, characterized the Chauve-Souris as a "provincial Russian vaudeville, . . . sold as the pet High Art of discriminating European theatergoers."

67. "Chauve-Souris No. 2" (*Life*, 6 July 1922), clipping in the Theater Collection, LMPA.

68. Information on Sudeykin is from Bowlt, *Russian Stage Design,* 278; Craft (ed.), *Igor and Vera Stravinsky: A Photograph Album,* 33; and "La Chauve-Souris à Moscou de Nikita Balieff au Théâtre Femina," souvenir program (February 1921), inside front cover. Vera Sudeykina maintained her Chauve-Souris friendships well into the period of her marriage to Stravinsky. Her diary for 22 January 1941 notes the presence of "old acquaintances from Baliev's Chauve-Souris, like old times in Paris," among the audience at the première of the Balanchine-Tchelitchew ballet *Balustrade,* to the music of Stravinsky's violin concerto. In December 1942, in Hollywood, the Stravinskys entertained Zoya Karabanova, who may be seen in Figure 19.5 (Robert Craft, ed., *Dearest Bubushkin: Selected Letters and Diaries of Vera and Igor Stravinsky* [New York: Thames & Hudson, 1985], 118, 127).

FIG. 19.3. Nikita Baliyev (1877–1936), impresario and emcee of the Théâtre de la Chauve-Souris.

later—was the young poet Boris Kochno, who was part of the great wave of emigration from the Ukraine.[69] It was through Sergey Sudeykin that Kochno first met Diaghilev, whose inseparable companion he would remain for the rest of the impresario's life.[70] This was in February 1921. That same month, Baliyev, encouraged by the success of his Parisian venture, unveiled a new show, far more ambitious and "artistic" than the first. Through the Sudeykins he invited Diaghilev to see the dress rehearsal, and Diaghilev invited Stravinsky to come along. This is the show they saw, on the evening of 19 February 1921:

Overture: Rimsky-Korsakov, *Antar* (fragment)

  I. Les Tabatières des Grands Seigneurs russes
        a. Adieu d'un Cosaque russe
        b. La Marquise
        c. Voltaire
        d. Le Schah de Perse
 II. Romances de Rakhmaninoff
III. *C'était au mois de Mai*, duetto sentimental
 IV. Mazurka de Chopin
  V. Les Houzards noirs (Vieille Chanson des Houzards)
 VI. Katinka (Vieille Polka de l'époque 1860)

69. Craft (ed.), *Igor and Vera Stravinsky: A Photograph Album*, 45, 51.
70. See Kochno, "My First Meeting with Diaghilev," in *Diaghilev and the Ballets Russes*, 152–55. For Vera Stravinsky's (i.e., Sudeykina's) memoir of Kochno and Diaghilev, see Craft (ed.), *Dearest Bubushkin*, 13.

—Entr'acte—

VII. La Fontaine de Bakhtchisaraï

Poème de POUCHKINE, (le plus grand poète russe sous l'influence duquel se développa toute la littérature russe: Gogol, Dostoïewski, Tolstoï: né en 1799 et tué en duel, par Dantès, en 1837)

—Entr'acte—

VIII. Sous l'oeil des ancêtres (Ancienne Gavotte)
  IX. "Swetit mesiatz, Swetit iasni," danse populaire russe
   X. Mots historiques:
       a. Napoléon
       b. Louis XIV
       c. Louis XV
       d. Henri IV
       e. Jules César
  XI. Tard le soir dans la forêt, chanson populaire russe
 XII. La nuit chez les Tziganes. Au restaurant Yard, à Moscou, vers 1840.

One of Baliyev's headliners, whose presence was undoubtedly what lured Diaghilev to look in on the enterprise, was Vecheslav Svoboda (1892–1948), a prerevolutionary Bolshoy Theater soloist, who had danced briefly with the Ballets Russes a couple of seasons before. Nos. IV and IX were pas de deux for him and another former Bolshoy soloist, Elisabeth Anderson, with whom he had formed a team. (Diaghilev did not engage them.) "Swetit mesiatz" ("The Moon Shines Brightly") was the quintessential Russian "town song," without which no Muscovite Gypsy cabaret could have won its franchise. No nineteenth- or early twentieth-century ethnographer, though, would have deigned to pick up such a song with tweezers.

Of greatest interest to us are the skits and production numbers. We may form an idea of them from the brief descriptions printed in the Paris program books, plus (in some cases) the rather more detailed ones found in the programs of the American tours, where the audiences needed help following a show that was played exclusively in Russian and French (except for the running patter supplied by Baliyev himself, "whose failure to master the English language," according to his obituary, "made him one of the most popular of masters of ceremonies").[71] Most elaborate by far was the centerpiece, a musico-dramatic adaptation in two tableaux of the young Pushkin's extravagant romance of blood and thunder in the seraglio.[72] The program proudly proclaimed the production "the first time that a Russian classic author will be performed before a Paris audience."

Les Houzards noirs was an arrangement by Baliyev's musical director, Alexey

71. *New York Times,* 4 September 1936.
72. No composer is credited; the music was probably adapted from Arensky's incidental score (op. 46, 1899).

Water color by Soudeikine for the costumes of "Katinka."

FIG. 19.4. Sergey Sudeykin's design for "Katinka," the number with which Chauve-Souris dancer Zhenya Nikitina brought down the house, and which Stravinsky quoted in *Mavra* and elsewhere.

Arkhangelsky, of an old Hussar ballad, sung by a basso profondo accompanied by a male chorus. "Before leaving for battle," the program read, "the soldiers, pierced with the consciousness that they are going to meet inevitable death, wallow a while in that voluptuous melancholy of Gypsy chanting (*mélopées tziganes*) which reawakens in them the old Slav fatalism," etc. etc.

For the finale, "La Nuit chez les Tziganes," we have this description from the program of the Chauve-Souris's first American tour:

> The most striking feature of the night life in old Moscow were the Gypsies. Their passionate songs evoked happiness, comforted the sad and distressed, awakened men to a new life and inspired love. The greater portion of Russian society life was spent outside their homes, in luxurious restaurants, which were the abode of these Gypsies. Yard's was one of the largest and most renowned of these restaurants. You see here a group of Gypsies entertaining a young couple, spellbound by the beauty of their weird melodies.[73]

"Katinka," the first-act curtain, with music by Arkhangelsky based on "an old Russian polka of the sixties," was easily the most popular number in the show. The set (by Sudeykin) "was inspired," according to the American program, "by one of the wooden toy boxes made by Russian peasant artisans" (Fig. 19.4). The action

73. Century Roof Theater program, week of 18 September 1922 (Theater Collection, LMPA). The name "Yard's" is a transliteration, clumsily carried over from the French, of *Yar'*, the most famous of all the Muscovite Gypsy cabarets of the mid-nineteenth century.

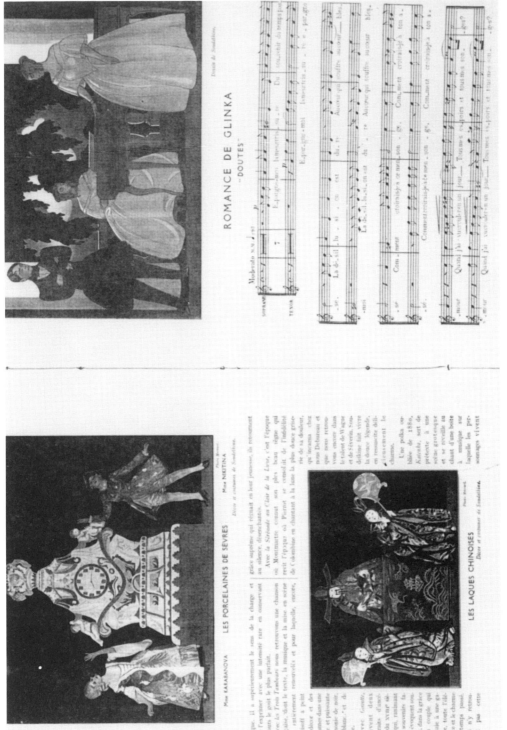

F I G . 1 9 . 5 . Chauve-Souris program book, February 1921. The dancer on the right in the illustration at the upper left is Zhenya Nikitina, briefly the object of Stravinsky's romantic interest. On the right, an illustration by Sergey Sudeykin above a romance by Glinka that typifies the stylistic rootstock of *Mavra*.

consisted of the following skit: "Katinka [= Katie or Cathy] is the too-modern daughter of old-fashioned Russian merchants. To her parents' displeasure she has learned to dance the polka at boarding school, and angers them furthermore by announcing her intention to marry an officer. They refuse to give their consent to such a marriage. Katinka then pretends to be dying, and the frightened parents yield to her wishes. She then expresses her happiness in an ecstatic dance."[74] To this description we may add some hype from the Paris souvenir program: "This scene, by virtue of its expressive power and its synthesis of colors, is a consummate theatrical expression of the twentieth century's all-consuming rhythm." But for the real secret of "Katinka's" popularity, we must turn to the memoirs of Arthur Rubinstein, who often attended the Chauve-Souris in Stravinsky's company: "The greatest success was obtained by a silly polka, played on an accordion by a bearded comic and danced by the most voluptuous blonde imaginable. A Rubens but with curves that were anything but flabby, she would appear showing most of her charms and would leave the audience agape."[75]

One more item should be mentioned, although it was not on the program in February 1921. For it was *in* the program—that is, the souvenir booklet, full of Sudeykin illustrations, which the painter and his wife must surely have given Stravinsky and Diaghilev. This was a number from the first Chauve-Souris bill entitled "Romance de Glinka," for which Sudeykin had done a set and costumes representing a *pomeshchik* salon, ca. 1825—that is, contemporaneous with the romance itself (Fig. 19.5). The music is given beneath Sudeykin's *maquette,* arranged as a soprano/tenor duet. It bears the French title "Doutes," and upon inspection it turns out to be Glinka's earliest published song, "Do Not Tempt Me Needlessly" ("*Ne iskushai menya bez nuzhdï*"), the composition with which, as Glinka put it in his memoirs, his musical career began. It is a perfect example of the so-called *bïtovoy romans,* the sentimental drawing-room romance of the early nineteenth century, a genre that amalgamated the Russian "town song," the Italianate aria, the French *ariette,* and the Gypsy cabaret song in a manner that was stylistically unmistakable—and therefore, for all its adulteration, identifiably Russian. The Chauve-Souris repertoire was saturated with these musical curios of a vanished Russia, for which Stravinsky, in years to come, repeatedly professed a special fondness.[76]

74. Shubert Theater program for the Chauve-Souris tour of 1925 (Theater Collection, LMPA).
75. Rubinstein, *My Many Years,* 106.
76. Besides the well-known passage from the *Poétique musicale,* cited above, about the mingling of the Russian and Italian *meloi,* there is a marvelous memoir by Nicolas Nabokov of the first audition of his *Ode* before Diaghilev and his "jury" in 1928: "I played the introductory chorus to *Ode* and then one of its lyrical ariettas, singing it in a mixture of bass and falsetto. Suddenly I saw Stravinsky lean forward and start helping me with his left hand, playing the bass part. His frown had given way to an amused and what seemed to me a pleased smile. When I stopped at the end of the first arietta, Stravinsky said, 'Continue, continue, this is quite good. I did not expect *ce truc-là.*' And so, with his help, I played another air of *Ode,* a duet, attempting to sing both the soprano and the bass parts. . . . When we came to the end of the piece, everybody laughed. Stravinsky turned to Diaghilev and said in a happy tone of voice, 'You know what it's like? It's as if it were written by a predecessor of Glinka, someone like [Al-

After the show, Stravinsky, Diaghilev, the Sudeykins (and Boris Kochno?) went for supper to an Italian restaurant in Montmartre. Robert Craft has written, "Vera Sudeykina had a pack of cards with her at that first meeting, and she told the composer's future, presumably saying something about the Queen of Hearts."[77]

Indeed, Stravinsky left the Chauve-Souris that evening smitten, but not with Vera Sudeykina. He had fallen for the voluptuous blonde who danced the "Katinka" polka, a young ballerina named Yevgeniya (Zhenya) Nikitina, who had trained at the Imperial Ballet School in St. Petersburg before the Revolution, and who would briefly be the toast of Paris.[78] Through the Sudeykins he was introduced to her, and, as Arthur Rubinstein recalled, "on a few evenings after the show we had the luck to have this beauty and her best friend, Vera Sudeikin, the wife of the painter, for supper at Fouquet's, where I was the happy host."[79] Through his liaison with Nikitina, Stravinsky became for a time quite intimately involved with the Chauve-Souris, and accepted a commission from Baliyev on the dancer's behalf to provide her with a prestigious vehicle—or so we may infer, in light of the evidence presented thus far, from Stravinsky's account in the *Chroniques* of the genesis of what eventually became his Suite No. 2 for Small Orchestra: "In the spring of 1921 a Paris music hall asked me if I could let them have a few pages of incidental music for a little sketch, within the range of their audience. It amused me to try my hand at that sort of thing, and I therefore orchestrated four pieces taken from my collections of Easy Duets."[80]

Proof that this "music hall" was the Chauve-Souris may be found in the third item in the suite, the Polka, which has been newly tricked out with an opening vamp and a coda. The latter incorporates an incongruous countermelody (incongruous, that is, in the sense that it forces a modification in the otherwise inviolate vamping ostinato); and this turns out to be a quotation from the "Katinka" polka, Zhenya Nikitina's theme song. Most surprising of all, the same tune surfaces again almost immediately in the overture to *Mavra* (Ex. 19.9).

---

exander] Gurilyov [1803–58] or [Alexander] Alyabiev [1787–1851] [both famous composers of *bïtovïye romansï*].' And then smilingly at me, 'From where do you know all this Russian salon music of the 1830s? It is unmistakably and naively Russian.' I did not know what to answer. Stravinsky got up and, turning to Diaghilev, said, 'Of course you should perform this music' " (N. Nabokov, *Bagazh*, 161–62). Alyabiev's "The Nightingale" ("*Solovey*"), the most famous Russian drawing-room romance of them all (arranged by Balakirev, Liszt, and others), was featured in the Chauve-Souris revues beginning in 1922 (see the Century Roof Theater program cited in note 73).

77. P&D:240.

78. See Lawrence Sullivan, "Nikita Baliev's Le Théâtre de la Chauve-Souris: An Avant-Garde Theater," *Dance Research Journal* 18, no. 2 (Winter 1986–87): 22. When the Chauve-Souris unveiled its "Troisième Spectacle" in March, critics and public alike protested the absence of "Katinka," and the number was reinstated. See Jean Bastia in *Comoedia* 15, no. 3019 (23 March 1921).

79. Rubinstein, *My Many Years*, 106. See also P&D:210, 627n.11, although many details, evidently imparted to Craft by Vera Stravinsky half a century after the fact, are a bit garbled (for example, the dancer is identified as a singer, and Katinka is given as her stage name rather than the name of the number that had brought her her notoriety). Somewhat later Rubinstein had an affair of his own with Nikitina. For details of Stravinsky's heavy infatuation (including a truly bizarre story of impotence and cure), as well as Rubinstein's light dalliance, see ibid., 106–8, 163.

80. *An Autobiography*, 93.

EXAMPLE 19.9

a. Suite No. 2 for Small Orchestra, Polka (last page, reduced; new interpolation on middle staff)

b. "Katinka (Balieff's Chauve-Souris)," music arr. Alexis Archangelsky, words trans. Itchok Czarovich [New York: Harms, 1922], parents' refrain

EXAMPLE 19.9 (*continued*)

c. *Mavra* overture, letter C

Now, this is enormously suggestive. It prompts the thought that Stravinsky and Kochno, introduced to each other by the Sudeykins, had the idea, or were actually commissioned, to collaborate on a musical skit for the Chauve-Souris, out of which the controversial *opéra bouffe* we know eventually emerged. Such a commission would have been entirely in keeping with Chauve-Souris traditions. While still in Russia the cabaret had mounted several quasi-operatic skits of its own creation, including a musical version of "Count Nulin," a humorous narrative poem by Pushkin very much on the order of "The Little House in Kolomna" ("*Domik v Kolomne*"), the source of *Mavra*'s plot.[81] The deal might even have been negotiated through Vera Sudeykina, who is known to have acted as go-between for Baliyev's stage director, one M. Vermeil, in approaching Stravinsky to collaborate on a different project (one involving a script by Francis Picabia).[82] In any event, a great deal of internal evidence supports the surmise that *Mavra* originated within the orbit of the Chauve-Souris. Thus, what seems a strange, practically inexplicable detour when viewed from the vantage point of the Ballets Russes and its traditions seems not just apt but inspired in its appropriateness to the Chauve-Souris repertoire, a repertoire that overflowed with precedents for the Stravinsky/Kochno collaboration.

Like "Count Nulin" or "La Fontaine de Bakhtchisaraï," *Mavra* is a dramatic ad-

81. Segel, *Turn-of-the-Century Cabaret,* 269. The list of "Répertoire de la Chauve-Souris" in the 1921 souvenir program includes musicalized skits based on a number of Russian literary classics: *La dame de pique* (Sept tableaux, d'après le roman de POUCHKINE [music by Arkhangelski]); *Le démon,* Drame en 2 tableaux (Lermontoff); *Le manteau,* Drame en 7 tableaux (Gogol); *La brouille d'Ivan Ivanovitch et d'Ivan Nikiforovitch,* Comédie en 2 actes (Gogol); *La mère,* Drame en 1 acte (Maxime Gorky); and—especially Mavresque, perhaps—*Roman avec contrebasse,* Satire en 1 acte (Tchekhoff).

82. See her letters to Stravinsky, dating from the month of September 1921, in Craft (ed.), *Dearest Bubushkin,* 14. The name is given there as Vermel; the correction is based on Chauve-Souris programs in the Theater Collection, LMPA.

aptation of a short narrative poem by Pushkin. Its principal dramatis personae consist of the "too-modern daughter of an old-fashioned Russian mother" (cf. Katinka) and a lover whom she smuggles into the house disguised as a cook. In Pushkin the young man is a prosaic "guardsman" (*gvardeyets*); Stravinsky and Kochno pointedly transformed him into a dashing "Houzard." The leading couple sing various interpolated songs not motivated directly by the Pushkin source. They all belong to typical Chauve-Souris genres: *duetto sentimentale, chanson populaire russe, bïtovoy romans, Chanson des Houzards, "mélopée tzigane."*

Like so many Chauve-Souris acts, *Mavra* is in effect a skit grown up around, enclosing, and as it were rationalizing a musical medley, not an "organically" motivated musical drama. In the eyes of its eventual audience this was its chief failing. In the eyes of its originally intended audience, perhaps, but surely in those of its creators, this was its chief merit. At any rate, it was *Mavra* that brought Stravinsky's art into fructifying contact with those musical genres of "la vieille Russie" that enabled him to chart an authentic course back to Europe. Although his period of interaction with it was short (Nikitina left the show by the end of May 1921;[83] by summer's end the composer's sights were fixed on Vera Sudeykina, who in 1940 would become the second Mme Stravinsky), nevertheless La Théâtre de la Chauve-Souris deserves recognition as one of the major catalysts of his career.

MAVRA: SOURCES AND STYLE

Pushkin's "Little House in Kolomna," usually said to derive from Byron's *Beppo,* has always been a favorite with Pushkinists of formalist bent, its maker having obviously been so much more interested in his telling than in his tale. "Its very conception is metapoetic," writes William Harkins, "a poem about the making of poetry and poetic esthetics."[84] Of its forty stanzas, only twenty-four (beginning with the ninth) are given over to the ostentatiously banal narrative about the mother, the daughter, and the smuggled lover, whose identity as such is revealed only implicitly, as a by-product of the absurdly abrupt dénouement in which the mother discovers the "cook" shaving in the kitchen.[85] For the rest there is a grandiloquent exordium in which the poet goes through elaborate motions of choosing a meter and a stanza; a coda in which an outrageously obtuse, Kozma-Prutkovian moral is drawn at "the reader's" insistence; and sundry gabby, gossipy asides as the poet ostensibly loses interest in his narrative.

83. *The New Witness,* 27 May 1921 (Theater Collection, LMPA): "M. Balieff [has] lost Mlle Nikitina, who has drifted to a Parisian music hall."

84. Pushkin, *Three Comic Poems,* 63. Nevertheless, Stravinsky and Kochno were not the first to base an opera on this unlikeliest of sources. They were preceded by Nikolai Solovyov (1846–1916), whose *Domik v Kolomne* remained unpublished and unperformed at his death.

85. According to Harkins (in Pushkin, *Three Comic Poems,* 63), many of Pushkin's contemporaries missed the point altogether and couldn't figure out what the poem was about.

A banal yarn drably spun, a pointless moral, a jaded author toying coyly with his rhymes and metrics—Pushkin's blasé pose, already spoofing Romanticism in the period of its first flush, had an obvious attraction for the anti-Romantics of a later age, wriggling free of the movement in the period of its dotage. The effortless classicism of the earlier author inspired the studied neoclassicism of the later ones. But problems of adaptation loomed large. The poem had little action and practically no dialogue. Virtually nothing in it could be transferred directly to the dramatic medium.

The solution was to string together a series of typical Chauve-Sourisian set pieces, with the Pushkin-derived action taking place in between as a series of skit-like "setups":

OVERTURE

1. "Chanson Russe" (Parasha), [1]–[6] (reprised at [27], [105]–[108])
2. Hussar's Gypsy song, [6]–[12]
    a. Dialogue: Parasha and the Hussar arrange a tryst ([12]–[27])
    b. Dialogue: Mother sends Parasha out to find a new cook ([28]–[34])
3. Mother's aria, [34]–[43]
    c. Dialogue: Neighbor drops in ([43]–[44])
4. Gossip-duet (Mother and Neighbor), [44]–[68]
    d. Dialogue: Parasha returns with "Mavra" ([68]–[75]+3)
5. Quartet (all dramatis personae), [75]+3–[93]
    e. Dialogue: Neighbor takes her leave, Mother exits after her ([93]–[96])
6. Love duet (waltz) (Parasha and Hussar), [96]+1–[133]
    f. Dialogue: Mother and daughter go out ([133]–[140])
7. "Mavra's" aria, [140]–[156]
    g. Dialogue: Shaving scene and dénouement ([156]–end)

The only dialogue taken over directly from Pushkin's *Domik v Kolomne* consists of a single clump, spread out through dialogues b and d, and running into the quartet (no. 5). The Mother sends Parasha out with a couplet ([30]+1) lifted from the end of Pushkin's stanza 28 (Ex. 19.10). Parasha's response, immediately following—*"Uznayu, mameñ'ka"* ("I'll go find out, mother dear")—quotes the first two words in stanza 29. At the end of the same stanza she returns with the words *"Vot ya kukharku privela"* ("Look, I've brought a cook"). These are not found in the score until 4 before [69] (Ex. 19.11). Four scattered repliques from stanzas 30 and 31 can be found, adapted, between [73] and [76] (Ex. 19.12). Finally, two and one-half ridiculous lines from stanza 31—*"Pokóynitsa Fyóklusha / Sluzhíla mne v*

EXAMPLE 19.10   *Mavra*, 1 after 30, setting of lines from Pushkin

Gde vzyat' ku-khar-ku? Sve-dai u so-sed-ki, ne
zna-yet li? De-sho-vï-ye tak red-ki.

[Where to get a cook? Go ask the neighbor if she knows. . . Cheap ones are so rare...]

EXAMPLE 19.11   *Mavra*, 4 before 69, Parasha's replique

Vot _____ ya — ku-khár-ku pri-ve-lá!

EXAMPLE 19.12   *Mavra*, 1 before 74 to 4 after 75, voice parts only

Cook
Chto bu-det vam u-god — no, su-da-rï-nya.

Mother
A kak _____ te-bya zo-vut? _____

Cook
                                                poco rit.   a tempo
A Mav - - - - - - roi, ___

[(Pay me) whatever you want, ma'am. – And what's your name? – Why, Mavra.]

kukhárkakh désyat' let, / Ni rázu dólga chésti ne narúsha" ("Dear departed Thecla served me in the capacity of cook for ten years, never once transgressing the bonds of honor")—are drawn out, the personal pronoun suitably pluralized, to form the basis for the first section of the quartet (Ex. 19.13).

That is all. Yet if Kochno's libretto of necessity made free with the letter of Pushkin's text, it was magnificently accurate when it came to reflecting the poem's spirit, precisely by virtue of the nonchalance with which the action, and particularly the dénouement, is dispatched.

Exactly like the poem, the musical setting is narcissistically preoccupied with its own style and rhetoric. Kochno was admirably adroit in contriving period flavor to support the style of the music, and in creating opportunities for varied, highly specific musical stylizations. Affected period style is already evident in the music

EXAMPLE 19.13 *Mavra,* 78 – 81

quoted above. In keeping with Glinka's canonized example, and like practically all his opera-composing countrymen, Stravinsky strove to keep his music hovering "on the borderline of arioso and cantilena," as Laroche had noted in a famous critique of *A Life for the Tsar* that had long since passed into the folklore of Russian opera.[86] The examples cited thus far could all be compared stylistically with the

86. Hermann Laroche, "Glinka i yego znacheniye v istorii muzïki" (1867), in *Sobraniye muzïkal'no-kriticheskikh statey,* vol. 1 (Moscow, 1913), 120.

EXAMPLE 19.14

a. Glinka, *A Life for the Tsar,* flourish from Antonida's cavatina (Act I)

b. Glinka, *Ruslan and Lyudmila,* flourish from Lyudmila's cavatina (Act IV)

Glinka romance in the Chauve-Souris program book, illustrated in Figure 19.5.

The working methods Stravinsky evolved for composing *Mavra,* as evinced by the many musical sketches in the Archive (Rothschild no. 77), insured a maximum of melodic interest. As he received the text piecemeal from Kochno, he would re-copy it along the tops of a bundle of printed manuscript sheets. On each page he would jot down melodies and accompanimental ideas pertaining to those words that appeared at the top. He would then work that much into a continuity draft before proceeding to the batch of words at the top of the next sheet.

At their most florid—as, for example, in the line by means of which the title character reveals "her" name (Ex. 19.12)—Stravinsky's melodies resemble the Italianate roulades with which Glinka decorated the heroines' roles in both his operas. Example 19.14, containing an example from each of them, circumscribes this style. Even at their most prosaic, Stravinsky's repliques have a lyrical basis that can be identified with Glinka's Russo-Italianate *melos,* especially as turned into *parlante* by Chaikovsky in *Eugene Onegin,* the opera that by virtue of its Pushkin source and its temporal setting lay closest to the repertoire from which Stravinsky drew his models.

The role of Parasha's Mother in *Mavra* is full of resonances with that of Larina, Tatyana's mother in *Eugene Onegin.* Also the widowed mistress of a household, Larina is confined throughout the opera to dialogue repliques, ensemble participation, and *parlante.* Her biggest moment in the opera comes in the first scene, an ingenious double duet in which Larina converses *parlante* with the Nanny to the overheard strains of a sentimental romance sung offstage by Tatyana and her sister. It is probably no coincidence that in the one replique in *Mavra* that is set verbatim to words taken directly from Pushkin's text (Ex. 19.10), Stravinsky practically

EXAMPLE 19.15

a. Chaikovsky, *Eugene Onegin,* Larina's replique before the Act I quartet

[I've got to go in and attend to matters about the house – you see to the guests. . .
I'll be right back!]

b. *Mavra,* fig. 28 (Mother)

[God grant you'll never lose a servant, daughter mine. . .]

quoted one of Larina's repliques from this double duet (Ex. 19.15a). The Mother's very first replique in *Mavra* (Ex. 19.15b) even has a similar accompaniment.[87]

Chaikovsky's device of setting the scene at the beginning of *Eugene Onegin* with an actual *bïtovoy romans* to a text by Pushkin may have guided Kochno toward finding the way of getting the scenic action started in *Mavra*. Pushkin also gave a clue. The action of the poem is not actually reflected in the libretto until the dialogue that introduces the Mother's aria, which corresponds, as we have seen, with Pushkin's stanza 28. Fourteen stanzas earlier, Pushkin had introduced his heroine to the reader by invoking one of the musical genres through which Stravinsky, with Kochno's help, was attempting to renovate his style. A natural starting point for the opera, it is also our natural starting point for a detailed investigation of the music and its stylistic sources.

Stanza 14 of "The Little House in Kolomna," in William Harkins's translation, runs as follows:

> She played guitar and sang through many a ditty:
> She knew by heart, "There coos the woodland dove,"
> "When I go to the brook," and tunes as pretty;
> All those which tedious winters by the stove
> Or autumns drear, by samovar long sitting,
> Or in the spring, while strolling through some grove,
> To sing so somberly our maids were born;
> Our Russian muse, you see, prefers to mourn.[88]

The two titles named in Pushkin's stanza were real. "*Stonet sizïy golubok*" (as Pushkin has it, or *golubochek;* lit., "There groans the blue-grey dovelet"), a famous *rossiyskaya pesnya* or imitation folk song to words composed in 1792 by Ivan Ivanovich Dmitriyev (1760–1837), was set to music by many composers (including Eduard Nápravník, the famous Mariyinsky conductor) over the next hundred years. Its first (anonymous) setting was published, also in 1792, in a collection "suitable for singing in parts or playing on gusli, clavichords, fiddles, or wind instruments." It offers a perfect illustration of the sentimental drawing-room genre known as *bïtovoy romans* at its very earliest stage of development (Ex. 19.16).

Stylistic points to note and ponder include, first of all, the use of the harmonic

---

87. This little tune could even be called the Mother's leitmotif. When Parasha officiously transmits her mother's orders to "Mavra" at fig. [134], she quotes it.

88. Pushkin, *Three Comic Poems*, 74. The next stanza goes on to tease the genre itself:

> I mean no metaphor; we are all doomed
> From drayman to top laureate, as a nation,
> To sing a dirge. Our favorite mood is gloom—
> And so our Russian song. Notorious allegation!
> 'Tis true: we start with hail! but of the tomb
> We sing before we're through. With desolation
> Our poems, like our songs, are all replete.
> And yet their melancholy mood is sweet.

EXAMPLE 19.16 *"Stonet sizïy golubochek"* (from *Noveyshiy rossiyskiy pesennik* [St. Petersburg, 1792]; rpt. Nikolai Findeyzen, *Ocherki po istorii muzïki v Rossii,* II [Moscow, 1929], vol. 2, ex. 115)

[The grey-blue dovelet moans day and night: his sweetheart has flown far away.
He coos no more, pecks no more grain, just grieves and silently sheds tears.]

[I'll go out to the brooklet, I'll look upon the swift (brook). Won't I see my beloved,
(My) sweetheart (there)?]

minor replete with leading tone, the most obvious (putative) Western import in sight. But this ought not blind us from noting the unconventional resolution of the seventh (e.g., at the end of m. 2 and analogous spots), the wayward harmonic rhythm (mm. 3–4), or the brusque dissonances that emerge from the doublings in thirds and sixths as they rub against the bass. Where a conventional editor might see these features as solecisms to be purged,[89] it is also possible to treasure them as stylistic ingredients specific to the genre. It will be useful to think of them that way in approaching the music of *Mavra*.

The other title cited by Pushkin—*"Vïydu l' ya na recheñ'ku"* (lit., "Shall I go out to the brooklet?"), a *rossiyskaya pesnya* (pub. 1776) by a St. Petersburg poet named Yuriy Neledinsky-Meletsky (1752–1829)—seems despite its urban origin to have entered the oral tradition, whence it was collected in various guises by late-eighteenth- and nineteenth-century ethnographers. In their great anthology of 1790, Lvov and Pratsch classified it as a dance song and published it in the form shown in Example 19.17. Even if collected in the field, though, the melody as pre-

89. For such a redaction of the piece see T. N. Trofimova and A. N. Drozdov, *Nachalo russkogo romansa* (Moscow: Muzgiz, 1936), 61.

sented in this form has obviously been arranged for the drawing room. Johann Gottfried Pratsch (Jan Bogumir Prač), a Czech musician who plied his trade in St. Petersburg for forty years until his death in 1818, specialized in turning actual folk songs into virtual *rossiyskiye pesni,* setting the tone for a whole generation of early-nineteenth-century collectors and arrangers. This particular setting, in which the unruly modal mutability (*peremennost'*) of the folk style has been accommodated to a typically "classical" swing to the relative minor, well illustrates Pushkin's satirical point (quoted in note 88) about "starting with 'hail' but singing of the tomb before we're through."

Kochno could easily have tracked down the text of either song Pushkin named to provide an opening number for his libretto, but he had a better idea. There was a typically sweet-sad *rossiyskaya pesnya*—its opening line, freely rendered into English, runs "Sweetheart mine, light of my life"—which Pushkin himself had jotted down in one of his notebooks, and which had been quite recently published for the first time in Semyon Vengerov's lavish collected edition of the poet's works. Although Vengerov had accepted the text at face value as that of an actual *narodnaya pesnya* (folk song), Kochno knew an urban simulacrum when he saw one and pounced. Here is the text of Parasha's aria, destined—in an independent arrangement for voice and orchestra (1923), but even more so in instrumental transcriptions actually entitled "Chanson russe" (= *rossiyskaya pesnya*)[90]—to become the hit tune from *Mavra,* as Kochno first encountered it:

1 Drug moi míliy, krásno sólnïshko moyó,	Sweetheart mine, my bright sun,
Sókol yásnïy, sizokrílïy moy oryól,	Bright falcon, my grey-winged eagle,
Uzh nedélyu ne vidálas' ya s tobóy,	It's been a week now since I've seen you,
Rovnó sem' dnéy, kak soználas' s góryem ya.	Seven days exactly since I became acquainted with grief.
5 Mne ne vzmílis' podrúzheñ'ki moí,	My girlfriends have not pleased me,
Igrï, plyaskí, khorovódï i myachí	Games, dancing, khorovods, and playing catch
Ne po nrávu, ne po mïsli mne prishlí.	No longer suit me. I have no thought of them.
Ya skitálas' po tyómnïm lesám,	I've been wandering in dark woods.
V tyómnom lése kinaréyechki poyút.	In the dark wood canaries sing.
10 Mne, devchónke, grust'-razlúku pridayút.	They fill me, maiden that I am, with parting-sorrow.
Tï ne poy kinaréyechka v sadú,	Don't you sing, canary, in the garden,
Ne daváï toskí serdéchku moyemú.[91]	Don't bring me heartaches.

90. For violin and piano, arranged by Stravinsky in collaboration with Samuel Dushkin (1937), and for cello in collaboration with Dmitry Markevitch.

91. S. A. Vengerov, ed., *Biblioteka velikikh pisateley: Pushkin,* vol. 4 (St. Petersburg: Brokgauz-Efron, 1910), 79. Kochno omitted lines 5–7, began line 8 with an inversion plus an interpolated monosyllable ("Tak skitalas' ya . . ."), and followed the penultimate line with a varied repeat, very much in the folk idiom: "Ne poy, moya rodimaya, v sadu" ("Don't sing, my own, in the garden").

Drug moy mi - lïy, kras - no sol - nïsh - ko __ mo - yo, __ So - kol
yas - nïy, __ si - zo - krï - lïy moy ____ o - ryol, . . .

Later editors of Pushkin have confirmed the canny Kochno's surmise as to this poem's literary provenance. One has even located a musical version the poet may have known. In 1821 the song was published in a volume entitled *The Latest Vanity-Table Songbook for Girls* (*Noveyshiy tualetnïy pesennik dlya devits*), with the heading "A New Song. To the tune, 'Time Was, I Had No Care in the World' ['*Ya ne znala o chom na svete tuzhit'*]."[92] In Example 19.18, the song that gets *Mavra* under way is set out to the tune to which it was sung in Pushkin's day, as set by Daniil Kashin (1770–1841), the leading arranger of the period.

With Kashin, whose setting of the wayward melody remains "tinctured," in Malcolm Brown's apt phrase, "by the contemporary romance,"[93] we make direct contact with Stravinsky. He owned a reprint of Kashin's anthology (published in Moscow in 1883 by Semyon Silivanovsky) and inscribed in it, in Russian, a phrase that conveys some of the bravado of the *Mavra* period: "A very rare book, one of the best collections of Russian songs."[94] As he knew very well, it was a book his teacher, for one, would have called one of the worst collections, and for the very reasons that made it now so precious to the latter's former pupil.

The *rossiyskiye pesni* quoted in Examples 19.16–18, chosen for display because of their fortuitous relevance to the textual source of Parasha's song, very neatly circumscribe the melodic style of Stravinsky's setting—or rather, they suggest the sources of what was innovative about that style in the context of Stravinsky's development. Most characteristic of all is a cadential phrase in which the borrowed leading tone is approached by the descending leap of a sixth, as exemplified in both of the Glinka citations in Example 19.14 (the first of them embellished) and with especial clarity in the very first item from Kashin's collection, a setting of a plaintive *protyazhnaya* called "As the Fog Settled on the Blue Sea" ("*Uzh kak pal tuman na sinyo morye*"; Ex. 19.19a). As Craft has noted, penciled adjustments to the harmony in Stravinsky's copy testify that he studied this song.[95] In fact, it became the

92. Blagoy et al. (eds.), *Pesni, sobrannïye pisatelyami,* 222.
93. M. H. Brown, "Native Song and National Consciousness," 77.
94. Craft (ed.), "Appendix: Selected Source Material," 350.
95. Ibid.

EXAMPLE 19.19

a. Kashin, *Russkiye narodnïye pesni,* no. 1: *"Uzh kak pal tuman na sinyo morye"*

Uzh kak pal tu - man Na si - nyo mo - rye, A zlo-

dey to - ska v re - ti - vo serd - tse.

b. *Mavra,* Parasha's aria, first phrase

Drug moy mi - lïy kras - no sol-nïsh - ko mo-yo

model for the oft-recurring first phrase in the vocal line of Parasha's aria (Ex. 19.19b).[96]

Thus Parasha's aria is a doubly authentic "Chanson russe" *à la Pouchkine.* The text was one Pushkin had copied out in his own hand, whereas the melody was modeled on the idiom of the romancelike "town songs" found in the very same anthology as the air to which the text was sung in Pushkin's time. Its "plaintive tune" (*zhalobnïy napev*) was therefore precisely the kind Pushkin must have had in mind when he wrote the fifteenth stanza of "The Little House in Kolomna."

When arranged by professionals for domestic singing, *rossiyskiye pesni* were often issued in contrasting pairs whose tempi are often said to reflect the "primo tempo" and cabaletta of the Italian opera aria. But the paired format was equally characteristic of the Gypsy singers who enjoyed such a tremendous vogue in the Russia of the 1830s and '40s, further adulterating the style of the Russian songs they performed. It was no doubt because of the stereotypical Gypsy sequence of *lassu* and *friss* that so many Russian musicians of the early to mid nineteenth century thought the world of folk music so limited in its expressive range. "Melancholy [*grust'*] and exuberance [*udal'stvo*]—that's it, that's the whole world," the young Alexander Serov had complained in 1842, a year falling within the period of *Mavra's* setting.[97]

96. The characteristic "Kashin cadence" turns up in many other places in *Mavra:* cf., albeit in the major, the middle section of the Mother's aria (two before fig. [38]).

97. Letter to V. V. Stasov, 15 March 1842; in *Muzïkal'noye nasledstvo,* vol. 1 (Moscow, 1962), 160.

Stravinsky and Kochno had their reasons for submitting to the stereotype, of course; and so Parasha's *grust'* gives way immediately to the Hussar Vasiliy's *udal'stvo* as he suddenly appears on stage to sing a song of his own. The text of the Hussar's song was another of Kochno's inspired finds—an imitation folk song that was actually composed, not just written down, by Pushkin. It dates from the year 1833:

1 Kolokól'chiki zvenyát,	Bells are jangling,
Barabánchiki gremyát,	Drums are booming,
A lyúdi-to lyúdi—	And the people, oh the people—
Oy lyúsheñ'ki-lyulí!	Hey peep-a-leep-a-leeple!
5 A lyúdi-to, lyúdi—	And the people, oh the people—
Na tsïgánochku glyadyát.	Gaze at the gypsy girl.
A tsïgánochka plyashót,	And the gypsy girl she dances,
V barabánchiki to b'yot,	She beats those little drums,
Golubóy shirínkoy mashót,	She waves her blue kerchief,
10 Zaliváyetsya-poyót:	And goes into her song:
"Ya plyasún'ya, ya pevítsa,	"I'm a dancer, I'm a singer,
Vorozhít' ya masterítsa."[98]	At telling fortunes I can't be beat."

Lines 3–5 of this little song are set to a variant of the "Katinka" polka, first heard in the Overture. The rest is a takeoff on that special genre of "dashing" (*molod-tsevatïy*) tenor-voice romance in polonaise rhythm, of which the preeminent example has always been Alexander Varlamov's setting (ca. 1840) of Mikhaíl Lermontov's "*Beleyet parus odinokiy*" ("White Sail"; Ex. 19.20a).[99] Stravinsky's setting avoids the metric regularity of the prototype, but the slashing string chords in the accompaniment (the violins and violas appearing for the first time in the orchestra) do suggest the swagger of the polonaise. Very characteristic (to anticipate the technical analysis of the music for a moment) is the way Stravinsky telescopes the stereotyped harmonic content of Varlamov's third measure into a single immediately hypostatized simultaneity to contrast with the tonic triad. (Example 19.20c is given without bar lines so that the distended vestiges of polonaise rhythm—see the brackets and braces—can show up with less interference from Stravinsky's irregular barring.)

Also telling is the final cadence, in which a sustained (in fact comically oversustained) sixth is prepared so that it clearly functions as a "dominant thirteenth," the sung D sounding an oblique diminished fourth against the accompaniment's downbeat A-sharp (Ex. 19.21). Melodically and harmonically emphasized sixths

98. A. S. Pushkin, *Sochineniya* (Moscow: Khudozhestvennaya Literatura, 1964), 1:338. The last two lines were not used in the libretto. The first and third lines of the second stanza are slightly altered: "*A tsïganochka-to plyashot, / . . . I shirinochkoy-to mashot.*"

99. That Stravinsky knew the poem and its famous setting goes without saying—no educated Russian does not. That he loved it (or them) enough to talk about them with Robert Craft is suggested by

EXAMPLE 19.20

a. Varlamov, *"Beleyet parus odinokiy"* (S. L. Ginzburg, *Istoriya russkoy muzïki v notnïkh obraztsakh* [Moscow: Muzïka, 1970], 3:246)

Be - le - yet pa - rus o - di - no - koy v tu - ma - ne

mo - rya go - lu - bom. Chto i - shchet on v stra - ne da -

lyo - koy? Chto ki - nul on v kra - yu rod - nom?

[A sail shows white amid the blue sea fog. What does it seek in far-off lands? What has it left behind at home?]

b. *Mavra,* fig. 6 (Hussar's aria)

Ko - lo - kol' - chi - ki zven -

EXAMPLE 19.20b (continued)

yat, ___ Ba-ra-ban - - -

- - - chi - ki gre - myat,

c. *Mavra*, fig. 9

A tsï-ga - - noch-ka - to plya-shet, v ba - ra - ban -

3/4   3/4

EXAMPLE 19.21 *Mavra*, 4 after 11

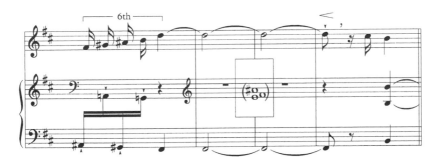

6th

(already encountered in Parasha's song with its "Kashin cadence") are so endemic to the repertoire of the sentimental Russian romance that a special term— *sekstovost'* ("sixthiness")—has been coined by Russian musicologists to mark the phenomenon.[100] The sixth was an interval with virtually no role to play in the tetrachordal music of Stravinsky's Turanian period (except by happy accident— see the discussion in Chapter 17 of the "Mitusov tune" in the fourth tableau of *Svadebka*). The texture of *Mavra,* by contrast, is absolutely saturated with sixths— sufficient testimony to the interval's pivotal significance in Stravinsky's work.

The model for the Mother's aria is obvious to anyone who knows the operas of Glinka. Its key, its vocal figuration, and its use of obbligato woodwinds all recall the first phrase of Antonida's cavatina in the first act of *A Life for the Tsar,* as does the carefully molded *sekstovost'* of the melody. The sixth degree of the F-minor scale forms the upper limit of the tune and always falls back upon the fifth. Meanwhile, anything lower than the tonic pitch is part of a melodic-minor cadence. The exceptional skip from the high D-flat in the fifth measure of Stravinsky's setting only "proves the rule": it is instantly perceived as a disruption and what follows as a backtracking, stability being achievable (and achieved) only when the D-flat falls back correctly on C (Ex. 19.22).

The difference between Glinka's approach and Stravinsky's is as clear as the similarity, and very telling as to what is "neo" about Stravinsky's classicism. Glinka's first phrase is followed by two others, one that initiates a *sekstovost'* construction from the fifth degree of the scale, making a direct and iconically "expressive" ascent of a minor sixth, then falling back through another emotionally charged interval, a diminished fourth, to the leading tone, after resolving which the cadential pull back to the starting point of the phrase can take place. The third phrase, which is the one given harmonic support, is yet another hexachordal construction that makes its cadence in what conventional theory calls the relative major. To Russian folklorists, as we know, Glinka's writing represents a tonalized version of the socalled *peremenniy lad,* the mutable-mode effect whereby two tone centers compete—or rather, peaceably oscillate—as stable points of melodic rest in the course of a song, it being impossible to predict which of the two will be the final.

In genuine melismatic folk songs (*protyazhniye*), the two centers are likeliest to be the tonics of a "D-scale" ("Russian minor" or "Dorian mode") and a "C-scale" (major). In a stylization like Glinka's, they are apt to be adjusted to conform to the more conventional "classical" disposition we find illustrated here, in which the har-

---

Craft's mentioning the poem in his diary of the 1962 Soviet tour (*Stravinsky: Chronicle of A Friendship,* 198); and this strengthens the probability that Varlamov's song was a specific, not merely a generic, model for the Hussar's song in *Mavra.*

100. See Boris Asafyev, *Yevgeniy Onegin: liricheskiye stseni P. I. Chaikovskogo* (Moscow: Muzgiz, 1944), 11, where the term seems to have been coined in connection with a discussion like the present one about the stylistic sources of a major masterpiece in the domestic genres of the nineteenth century.

EXAMPLE 19.22

a. *A Life for the Tsar,* beginning of Antonida's cavatina (Act I)

[I look out over the empty field...]

b. *Mavra,* Mother's aria at 34

[No, I'll never forget the departed]

monic/melodic minor—already an "impure" mode, ethnographically speaking—oscillates with its relative.[101] And yet the effect of Glinka's stylization remains extremely subtle and—to Western ears—exotic, owing to the relative strength and weakness with which the "tonic" and its relative major are articulated. The word *tonic* really needs the ironizing quotes in this connection because there is scarcely an F-minor triad to be heard in the course of Antonida's cavatina, not even at the end. F-minor cadences are effected by melodic means alone. Harmonic progressions underscore the departures to the relative key, and also mark tonic half-cadences (i.e., on the dominant). The very end of the aria is ambiguity itself. It is a half-cadence on C, approached by way of the relative major. When it arrives, however, the C is presented as a single pitch with octave doublings, not as a member of the dominant triad. It is sustained suspensefully for four bars before giving way to the Rondo, which is unambiguously in the classical tonality of A-flat major, even if approached, unconventionally, from the mediant. This arrival recasts the whole cavatina retrospectively in a tonally equivocal light. Its putative key of F minor is heard now in retrospect as a submediant anacrusis to the real tonic, that of the Rondo.

This elaborate description is meant to suggest the whole range of things Stravinsky elected *not* to do in his cavatina for the Mother. The outer sections of the aria are fixated entirely on the contents of Glinka's first phrase, given quintessentially hypostatic support from the very thing Glinka so conspicuously withheld: a blatant F-minor triad, repeated in a frozen metrical position through long sections of the piece, and of course returning to sign off at the end. The endings of each of the outer sections of the aria give tiny whiffs of *peremennost'* that only highly sensitized nostrils may discern. They are signaled in each case by the substitution of E-flat for E-natural beneath the tonic pitch, and initiate little sequential excursions into the territory of the relative major (though Stravinsky holds on to the tonic F as an inner-voice pedal even here; see Ex. 19.23).

It was the stringent reduction of model materials down to their atomic elements, such as we see not only here but also (and most of all) in Parasha's song, that gave many of Stravinsky's early neoclassic scores a "monumental" aspect in the eyes of the composer's admirers. The more a critic knew about the models, the more apt he was to view the achievement in these terms. Thus fellow émigré Schloezer called *Mavra* the first of Stravinsky's "type-works," to be followed by the *Octuor,* the *Concerto,* the *Sonate,* and so forth.[102]

As is so often the case, study of Stravinsky's sketches reveals that the impressively elemental quality was the result of an arduous process of refinement. One of the

101. Nevertheless, Glinka's cavatina does have a cadence on E-flat, the authentic "*peremennost'*" pitch (see mm. 33–40).

102. Boris de Schloezer, *Stravinsky: An Abridged Analysis,* trans. Ezra Pound, in *Igor Stravinsky: A Merle Armitage Book,* ed. Edwin Corle (New York: Duell, Sloan & Pearce, 1949), 71.

EXAMPLE 19.23 *Mavra*, 2 before 36, *peremennost'*

[She did the shopping and was friendly and merry]

EXAMPLE 19.24 *Mavra* sketches, jotting for the Mother's aria

earliest jottings for the Mother's aria shows Stravinsky experimenting doggedly with the idea of *peremennost'* (cadential oscillation), trying to turn the leading tone into a pivot so that, approached by an expressive diminished seventh, it might be reidentified (in place of the traditional "flat seventh") as tonic (Ex. 19.24). It is easy to see why Stravinsky abandoned the experiment: too obviously recherché, it sacrifices its aural connection with the ostensible model in Glinka, who never treated both his centers as tonics of melodic-minor scales. But the abortive sketch does show that the eventual strict adherence to a hexachordally conceived F minor was the product, not of stereotyped assumptions, but of a renunciation. It was a characteristically Stravinskian "second simplicity," with all the sharpness of focus and conviction that that implies.

The modulation that does occur in the middle section of the Mother's aria, in

EXAMPLE 19.25

a. *Mavra*, 4½ after 55 (voices only)

[Joy and sorrow are in the hands of the Lord]

b. Dargomïzhsky, *Rusalka,* vocal score (ed. Lamm [Moscow: Muzïka, 1960]), p. 28

c. Dargomïzhsky, *Rusalka,* p. 84

d. Dargomïzhsky, *Rusalka,* pp. 127–28

which F major vies with its relative minor on D, is very much within the canons of the model repertoire, and also retains a whiff of the old (0 3 6 9) common-tone linkage, also present in Parasha's song, which ties in the idiom of *Mavra,* to some vestigial extent, with the centric orbits of Stravinsky's earlier "Russian" music.

Prototypes for the delightful gossip-duet, as well as for the ensuing quartet, may be found in Dargomïzhsky, the recognized ensemble specialist among Russian composers of the immediate post-Pushkin period. The jolly tune that acts as refrain in the duet has an especially Dargomïzhskian cast, as a comparison with a few typical phrases from the ensembles in the first two acts of *Rusalka* will show (Ex. 19.25). The same polka-party geniality informs the quartet, again based on a theme with Dargomïzhskian affinities, though its angularity may appear superficially reminiscent of the "neobaroque" melodies Stravinsky would employ in works of slightly later vintage (Ex. 19.26).

Recognition of the polka rhythms underlying all these themes (another link with "Katinka"?) helps explain one of the most curious features in *Mavra,* one that early audiences found particularly bewildering—namely, the mixture of "Italo-Russian and black American styles," in Schloezer's indignant words.[103] After the ragtime pieces of the Swiss years, evidently, Stravinsky could leave no rapid duple meter unsyncopated (no polka un-*maxixe*d, one might say)—and this, to most listeners (and even in the composer's own late recollections), meant "jazz."[104] Compared even with the *Ragtime* of 1918, though, the "jazz" in *Mavra* is pale pro forma stuff, hardly more than a matter (in the duet) of elementary ties-across-the-bar and (in the quartet) of tightening rhythmic patterns so that they crosscut the meter hemiola-wise (Ex. 19.27).

The big love duet has two halves. The first is exultant, the lovers gloating over Parasha's successful ruse as the music parodies the duet for the title characters at their wedding feast in the Prologue to *Ruslan and Lyudmila* (Ex. 19.28). In the middle of this section, Parasha recalls her longing for the Hussar as she used to sit by the window, and her opening song is duly reprised. At the end of this

---

103. *Nouvelle revue française,* no. 106 (1922); quoted in SelCorrI:157n.

104. See E&D:71–71n./82n., where Jack Hylton's 1931 (not 1932) dance-band arrangements of the duet and quartet are recalled. Although later Stravinsky disavowed these arrangements, they were originally made at his enthusiastic request, and with his participation. See the extracts from letters by Stravinsky, Hylton, and Païchadze in SelCorrII:123–23n., as well as a photograph (after p. 338) that shows Stravinsky at a Hylton recording session (25 January 1931), baton in hand. Also compare the following account from the *Voice* (August 1930): "His meeting with Igor Stravinsky was one of the most memorable events of Jack Hylton's recent Continental tour. It was at a concert in Holland that the creator of 'Petrouchka' first heard Jack and his boys and he was so interested that he followed the band to the next city on their tour and attended the concert there. After the performance he went into the artists' room and spent over an hour with the wind and percussion players of the orchestra asking each man to demonstrate the capabilities and limitations of his instrument. He presented to Jack Hylton the manuscript of a work he had written specially for Europe's greatest dance band and played and sang to them a number of his own recent composition." The reference to the dance-band composition is puzzling and probably garbled, unless it was one of the Suites for Small Orchestra (but these were saxophoneless "theater orchestra" transcriptions, not dance-band arrangements).

EXAMPLE 19.26

a. *Mavra*, Parasha at 76

Parasha

Ya   du - ma - yu   po - le - zen   bïl   moy   trud

[I think my work was useful]

b. Dargomïzhsky, *Rusalka*, pp. 68–69

Natasha

Akh, tï   po - ve - dai   mne   pe - chal' svo - yu,   kho-chu de - lit' s to - boy ya

gor - ye

[Ah, let me know thy sadness, I would share thy woe]

c. Dargomïzhsky, *Rusalka*, pp. 18–19

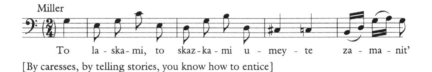

Miller

To   la - ska - mi,   to   skaz - ka - mi   u - mey - te   za - ma - nit'

[By caresses, by telling stories, you know how to entice]

d. Dargomïzhsky, *The Stone Guest*, vocal score (Moscow: Muzgiz, 1932), p. 9

Don Juan

ved'   ya   ne   go - su - dar - stven - nïy   pre - stup - nik

[I'm no political offender, after all]

EXAMPLE 19.27 *Mavra:* Beat pattern at 79

EXAMPLE 19.28

a. Glinka, *Ruslan and Lyudmila,* wedding duet (Prologue)

[O believe, Ruslan, Lyudmila is thine as long as life seethes in her breast!
I am thine, Lyudmila mine, as long as life seethes within me!]

b. *Mavra,* 2 after 97 , Parasha and "Mavra" only

[It is I, Vasily dear! What rapture!
Yes, my love, the present success is a regular military victory.]

EXAMPLE 19.29   *Mavra,* 3 after 107 , horns and trumpets omitted

[My memory will ne'er betray the present day]

interlude comes a wonderful commentary on the stylistic gulf separating *Mavra* from the music of the Swiss years. The final cadence is embellished with the only fully referable octatonic passage in the entire score, consisting of two complete Collection III melody scales ascending in the voice parts in parallel minor thirds, to an anapestic pattern that places the (0 3 6 9) nodes on the beats. Meanwhile the bass instruments rotate the nodes in the opposite direction, descending by minor thirds in full-beat quarter notes that in effect arpeggiate a diminished-seventh chord (Ex. 19.29). In other words, the passage displays precisely the kind of embellished diminished-seventh harmony that can crop up on the surface of the common practice as early as Bach, and that was therefore specifically dismissed from consideration in Chapter 4 as a forerunner to the octatonic tradition culminating in Stravinsky's "Russian" music.

Stravinsky, of course, was fully aware of the stylistic accommodation *Mavra* represented between his older harmonic usages and those of conventional tonality, and fully in control of it. That is precisely the point of the little cadenza we are looking at now: it neutralizes the harmonic potency of Stravinsky's earlier tonal praxis under the aegis of "classical" harmonic usage. Nowhere in *Mavra* do we see the composer more resolutely or self-consciously turning westward than in Example 19.29.

The second half of the love duet is tender, an anticipation of a nocturnal tryst. That it should take the form of a slow waltz is a foregone conclusion. The ballroom waltz was the favored genre for casting *bytovïye romansï* of an amorous sort (cf. Gurilyov's "Grust' devushki," discussed and illustrated in Chapter 17). Besides, a waltz number was virtually *de rigueur* in an early nineteenth-century opera. Glinka, for example, had found an easy pretext for one in the Polish ballroom scene (Act II) of *A Life for the Tsar* (No. 6b, notated, like many waltzes of the period, in 6/8 time). But he insisted on having one in *Ruslan,* too, nor did he hesitate to give it to his "oriental" Prince Ratmir (Act III, no. 14: Tempo di valse, again in 6/8 time), to the consternation of critics then and since.[105] Thus for Kochno and Stravinsky the question was not whether to include a waltz number, but where to put it. The spot selected was fortunate. The "Tempo commodo" (*sic*) is a welcome relief after three frantic ensembles in succession, and it is relaxed even further by the languid "duplets" in which Stravinsky cast much of the vocal writing. There is just such a duet for the romantic leads in *Rusalka* (again notated, according to the conventions of the period, in 6/8); there can be little doubt it provided Stravinsky with a model for one of *Mavra*'s most delicious moments (Ex. 19.30).

And now for the pièce de résistance: "Mavra's" aria. This most extended solo number in the opera, and arguably the greatest, was also the one number that was unquestionably a spoof. The genre so wickedly sent up here is the hyperemotional variety of romance known in its day as *zhestokiy* (lit., "cruel"), the genre that has bequeathed to the world such treasures as "Dark Eyes" ("*Ochi chornïye*") and "Two Guitars" ("*Dve gitari*"). Associated primarily with female Gypsy singers, such songs were distinguished not only by their musical content—wide, scooping intervals, often augmented or diminished—but also by their moaningly passionate mode of delivery, full of sobs, *rubato, messa di voce*—the works. This was the kind of music and singing one heard at the famous cabarets of old Russia like "Yard's," to recall the Chauve-Souris act that probably inspired Stravinsky's pen. The greatest contemporary connoisseur of such singing, the poet Apollon Grigor'yev (1822–64), found great release in *zhestokiye romansï,* accompanied by guitars and by a suitable dose of alcohol. "If you seek expression," he wrote in 1847,

> for that undefined, incomprehensible, sorrowful ennui [*khandra*], you make off to the gypsies, immerse yourself in the hurricane of these wild, passionate, oppressively-passionate songs. And even if total disillusion has you in its grip, I am willing to stake my head that you'll be pulled out of it (a characteristic of the Russian nature) when Masha starts to afflict your soul with a passionate song, or when a mad furious chorus takes up the last pure, clear, silvery sound of Styoshina's "Oh, do you hear, or do you ken?"[106]

Stravinsky and Kochno could not resist the prospect of having their Hussar-in-drag emulate Masha and Styoshina to the strains of a big guitar consisting of cellos and basses *secco e spiccato,* two bassoons, and timpani. The "oppressively-passionate" tune is first heard in the orchestra, crooned as a throaty contralto ob-

---

105. Even according to his most recent biographer, Glinka "betrayed Ratmir badly" by turning him into "a waltzing Westerner" (D. Brown, *Glinka*, 223).

106. Quoted by Ralph E. Matlaw in his introduction to Apollon Grigoryev, *My Literary and Moral Wanderings* (New York: E. P. Dutton, 1962), xi, slightly adapted.

EXAMPLE 19.30

a. Dargomïzhsky, *Rusalka,* vocal score, pp. 77–78

EXAMPLE 19.30a (*continued*)

bya, tol' — — ko b vi — de — la _____ te — bya!

nya pri — zï — va — yet me — nya pri — zï — va — yet me — nya!

[If only I might see you!
Sacred duty calls me!]

b. *Mavra*, figs. 126 – 128

Bï — — va — — yet nezh — nïy Ku — pi —

Bï — — va — — yet nezh — nïy Ku — pi —

don. _____ Kog — — — da v dvoy — —

don. _____ Kog — — — da v dvoy — —

nom so — yu — ze tret' — — im

nom so — yu — ze tret' — — im

[When in double union tender Cupid makes a third]

bligato by the rare trumpet in A, a band instrument fitted with a slide to give it an extra downward extension of range. The incongruous sound of the "cruel" romance emerging from the pit in a parade-ground timbre perfectly matches the incongruity of the stage situation. Stravinsky achieves the requisite performance style by notating the distended rhythms and impassioned dynamics with surgical precision, then directing the executant to play "tranquillo e molto rythmico" (*sic*). Volumes could be written—have been written, in fact—on the implied relationship between composer and performer that this fully prescribed "freedom" exemplifies, and its result in terms of twentieth-century performance esthetics.[107]

The singer's melody is notated the same way, the contrast between sustained, swelling tone and frenzied "graces" exaggerated beyond anything even a Gypsy would have countenanced. The melody is also overstuffed with "cruel" intervals—the augmented and diminished seconds and fourths (as well as sixths) that characterize the "real" *zhestokiy romans* (cf. Ex. 19.31a, from a genuine midcentury specimen called "He's Gone!"). When the phrase shown in Example 19.31b returns at the end of the song, the spoofing becomes even broader. The singer holds on to "her" D-flat "dominant thirteenth" so long that the band has to prod her with an extra "V_7" to get on with the cadence, which is then sung unaccompanied and followed by the baldest cadential signal-to-applaud ever put on paper (Ex. 19.31c). But of course the audience is given no chance to respond to the signal, Stravinsky having launched right into the chugging dénouement ostinato that will so shortly bring the opera to its sudden, anticlimactic close.

THE "CHANSON RUSSE" AS NEOCLASSICAL PARADIGM

Turning from the matter of style to that of facture, the accompaniment to Parasha's aria—the first item from the opera to be composed (as the Overture was the last)—offers the best entrée into *Mavra*'s fascinating interplay of old and new. The interplay is paradoxical, of course, and deliberately so: in the context of Stravinsky's development and of his audience's expectations, what was new was what was "old"—that is, the potted artifacts of nineteenth-century styles. These artifacts, unlike the *ur*-Slavic *popevki* in *Svadebka* or *The Rite*, are no longer archaistic; rather, they refer to the familiar, premodern common practice that had continued to coexist with modernism as an alternative—an alternative, moreover, that tended in the popular imagination to define the modern by negation (concepts of "atonality" or "asymmetry," for example, being parasitic on anterior notions of tonality and symmetry). A modernistic idiom like *Mavra*'s, which attempted to incorporate conspicuous elements lifted from common practice within an overall approach to

107. Cf. Nicholas Kenyon, ed., *Authenticity and Early Music* (Oxford: Oxford University Press, 1988), where Stravinsky comes in for a great deal of discussion, passim.

EXAMPLE 19.31

a. Sergey Donaurov (1838–97), *"On uyekhal"* (L. Mezentseva, ed.,
Napominaniye: starinnïye russkiye romansï [Moscow: Muzïka, 1972], 50),
piano prelude and postlude omitted

(continued)

EXAMPLE 19.31a (*continued*)

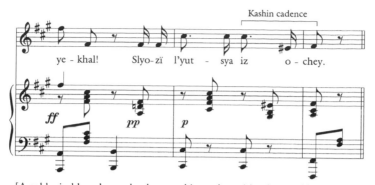

[A cold wind knocks on the door, and in my heart it's wintry cold. He's gone, my handsome one, never to return. No more will I hear his songs resounding, or his rapturous speech. He's gone! Tears flow from my eyes.]

b. "Mavra's" aria, fig. 142

[I wait submissively, beloved]

EXAMPLE 19.31 (*continued*)

c. "Mavra's" aria, fig. 155

[(Our kisses will) alternate with words.]

musical organization that was just as conspicuously unrelated to that practice, was bound to stir up problems of reception that were if anything more severe than those raised by earlier modernist idioms. The novel elements in late Scriabin or early Schoenberg, for example, could be far less problematically apprehended as surface features of a musical idiom that maintained a clear historical continuity with the immediate past. For all its apparent simplicity, then, the new Stravinsky style, in which the "past" elements seemed utterly disjunct from the "present" ones, created by far the greater sense of stylistic dichotomy and disruption.

The easy response was to regard it as wholly ironical—a trifling satire or parody of the past. The trifling plot of the *opéra bouffe* through which the new style was making its debut invited and seemed to justify such a response. *Mavra* seemed unworthy of Stravinsky: a dead end, a retrogression, a colossal talent run aground. By now we know that Stravinsky's accommodation to the common practice was far from wholly ironical. We have no trouble seeing in it a serious effort to establish contact with a needed source of artistic and spiritual renewal at a desperate time, an effort whose very sincerity may be gauged by the shield of irony behind which the composer sought at first to protect it. By now we know that the accommodation was anything but a dead end, that it conditioned the direction his work would take over the next three decades and would thus sustain him through the longest of his so-called periods. What we do not quite yet know is the precise technical and esthetic nature of Stravinsky's amalgamation of old and new, or what made it work so well. While a full investigation of this matter is the subject for another book, we can make a start by getting up close to this last of Stravinsky's Russian-texted pieces, which for that very reason is generally viewed, erroneously, as the end of his first period rather than as the beginning of his next one.

Let the accompaniment to Parasha's aria be our entrée, then. Its most conspicuously novel feature is the presence of a genuine resolving dominant harmony—something unheard in any major Stravinsky composition since his Rimsky-Korsakov days, a single exception being *Petrushka,* where functional harmony had operated quite normally, if within an overtly quotational (and therefore ironic) context. It could be argued that the role of the ostensibly functional tonal harmony in *Mavra* is still in a sense quotational; but unlike the harmonizations in *Petrushka,* the accompaniment to Parasha's aria is not by any means tonally functional. Indeed, it is not really a harmonization at all. Insofar as they are abstracted from their natural habitat and placed in synthetic relationships that are wholly of Stravinsky's making, the dominant harmonies in *Mavra* are like the *popevki* in *Svadebka* after all.

The relationship between chord sequence and bass line in Parasha's aria has evoked much comment. Stuart Campbell speaks for many when he calls the accompaniment "a four-beat ostinato pattern in the bass but with other parts out of step, so that tonic and dominant chords appear where the bass suggests the other"—an effect he characterizes as the "dissonances of a nonchalant vamper."[108] It is a good phrase, but the impression of nonchalance, while undeniable, seems more the product of the singer's precisely notated rubatos, composed, one feels certain, in imitation of the insinuating delivery of a Chauve-Souris chanteuse. The properly attuned Stravinskian ear immediately detects the rigidity that governs the accompaniment patterns, and indeed, a bit of scrutiny reveals a typical quasi-Turanian "mobile" construction.

In terms of the piano reduction (which doubtless represents the form in which Stravinsky's fingers first discovered it), the mobile consists, in the left hand, of a pattern of four beats, confined to the pitches of the tonic triad, starting on the root and ending on the lower fifth, so that each reiteration is enlivened by a little 5–1 cadential push. The right hand, meanwhile, has a six-beat pattern, clearly subarticulated by the harmonic progression into two three-beat groups, one ending on the dominant harmony, the other fully closing on the tonic, thus: T-D-D, T-D-T. The subdivision of the right-hand pattern is confirmed by the autonomous reiteration of the second group (one measure after fig. [2]). It is surely no coincidence that thanks precisely to this arbitrary alteration of the pattern the linear succession 5–1 in the left hand matches up for the first time with the harmonic pro-

108. Stuart Campbell, "The 'Mavras' of Pushkin, Kochno, and Stravinsky," *Music and Letters* 58 (1977): 313.

gression V_7–I in the right (it happens again two measures later). Stravinsky has in effect adjusted the focus screw on the key of B-flat minor.

Up to this point the lack of coincidence between cadential gestures in the two concurrent ostinati had had a magical defamiliarizing effect on what would otherwise have been completely utilitarian, hence virtually unnoticeable, diatonic harmony. The dissonant, fifthless dominant-seventh chords in the right hand (horns, in the orchestral scoring) are made to stand out with an unaccustomed force. We cannot take them for granted as they jar against the tonic roots and thirds in the bass pattern. We are thus made to take continual note of the hitherto quite un-Stravinskian leading tone.

Although the right-hand leading tones are always correctly resolved, hence "functional" in a local cadential sense, their deployment within a rigidly hypostatized pattern—one that takes cognizance neither of the concurrent antics of the bass below nor of the flexibly unfolding melody above—prevents their assimilation within the overall texture. They do not consistently ratify the harmonic tendencies of the bass, nor do they give direction to the melodic line. Indeed, the cadential leading tone in the voice part and in the right hand are often quite at odds (see in particular the measure right before fig. [2]). Thus, local harmonic functions are exercised in this piece only within the three separately unfolding strata of a deliberately unintegrated "mobile" texture. When functions do coincide among the strata one feels the event as a sort of planetary alignment, an accidental confluence of orbits. That is what makes the overall texture comparable to a mobile: its independently moving components do line up now and then, but often only by (apparent) chance.

The total texture, then, cannot be said to exemplify the functional harmony of the common practice; rather, the music in its elemental vocabulary (its phonology and morphology) is merely confined to a little repertoire of sonorities and local progressions normally associated with that practice. Nor can the accompaniment to Parasha's aria be described as a harmonization of the vocal melody. The most one can say is that it maps out or defines a diatonic tonal space within which that melody will unfold. (Nor is that unfolding without its ironies, the most significant being the playful variability of the sixth degree in its scale, forever oscillating between the "Russian minor" G-natural and the common-practice G-flat.)

Nevertheless, the deviations from normal tonal practice may not be described as random or casual; nor do they represent some putatively primitive stage of tonal organization. The organization of this music, based on the superimposition of ostinati, is of a different order from that governing tonality, viz., a hierarchical disposition of harmonies radiating outward from a tonic by fifths. Nonetheless, it is a rigorous order. And it displays one essential feature in common with functional tonality that is very much opposed to Stravinsky's Turanian idiom: its tonal coherence is generated and regulated by the bass.

EXAMPLE 19.32   Mobile structure in Parasha's aria (accompaniment)

To appreciate that coherence, we must take into account the structure of the whole song, up to the Hussar's entrance at fig. [6]. It falls into four sections, clearly demarcated by shifts of tone center and transpositions of the referential collection or scale—which is to say, by "modulations" in the conventional tonal sense. In each section the texture of the accompaniment resembles that of the first section: all are mobiles consisting of a left-hand pattern derived from the three constituent degrees of the tonic triad locally in force and a right-hand pattern of oscillations between two primary chords of the key defined by the bass (see Ex. 19.32).

The first modulation, by a minor third, is of a type familiar from Stravinsky's

EXAMPLE 19.33   Linkage of tonal centers in Parasha's aria

octatonic music, no doubt prompted by its congruence with his long-standing octatonic practice. That this was the most essential modulation in the piece is clear from the way Stravinsky prepared the reprise of the aria at fig. [27]. There, the key of B-flat minor is regained through G (mixed major/minor—another octatonic fingerprint), reversing and thus finally neutralizing the departure at fig. [3]. The first time through, however, a section in D minor intervenes between the G minor area and the reprise of the original key. Since D is the dominant of G, this interpolation might be looked upon as a traditional fifth-related "tonal" modulation, and a Stravinskian anomaly.

What the composer actually seems to be up to is a series of links based on common tones between the bass ostinati. Degree 1 of the B-flat–minor triad links with degree 3 in the G-minor triad. Three more such links would exhaust the (0 3 6 9) circle and achieve closure, but Stravinsky elects to short-circuit the process and achieve endgame in only two moves, thus: degree 5 in G minor = degree 1 in D minor; degree 3 in D minor = degree 5 in B-flat minor. This progression has the distinct virtue of never repeating the same configuration of linked degrees; the approach to the next key is always by way of a fresh interval (see Ex. 19.33; that the four tone centers combine to form the G-minor triad is an interesting by-product of the method, but does not appear to be of great moment in the tonal scheme). The overall circuit thus achieved, while fresher than the by-now jaded octatonic rotation, is nevertheless an outgrowth of the latter: the general idea of degree reidentification (that is, "common-tone modulation") is one with a long tradition in Russian music, even if chiefly (and ironically, given the *Mavra* ideology) confined to the kuchkist wing.

The fact that the bass line was the source of the harmonic linkages illustrated in Example 19.33 implies the primacy of the bass in the musical organization of the aria. This may be confirmed by observing that the bass patterns, shown in Example 19.32 without the distraction of bar lines, are always played out to the finish (the only exception being the very end of the piece, where, characteristically, the Hussar's aria crowds in with an interfering elided cadence exactly when the bass ostinato would have ended). The right-hand patterns, by contrast, always end with a "remainder," as represented in Example 19.32 by extra added quarter notes. That is, they are always interrupted in medias res. Not only that, but they are significantly more variable than the bass patterns.

We have seen how an element of unpredictability was introduced into the first section by repeating the second group from the right-hand pattern independently of the first. The same thing happens again in the last section of the song (the fourth and fifth measures before fig. [6]). Finally, when the original key returns, the original bass ostinato returns with it and continues unvaried, through fully a dozen reiterations, to the end. The right-hand pattern has a different second ("b") group from what it had at the beginning, and after three reiterations the first ("a") group is also modified, so that the whole six-chord pattern is different from what was heard at the outset. The phrasing of the voice part, meanwhile, is subjected to all kinds of "free" contractions and extensions so that it may conform to the lengths of the sections defined by each successive tone center. For all these reasons we may assert that the bassi ostinati, which are never varied within a section and are always brought to completion, truly set the rhythmic and harmonic parameters of this music, much as did the bass in the era of common practice.

BRINGING THINGS FULL CIRCLE: WHAT WAS ANTIMODERNISM?

Viewed solely in terms of its sources, its idiom, and its tone, *Mavra* seems hardly more than a mélange of amiably antiquated sundries: waltzes, polkas, sentimental ditties, and miscellaneous *musiquette*. Why, then, did Stravinsky excitedly refer to the work in progress as a "masterpiece"[109] and "the best thing I've done"?[110] What were the "musical ideas" he had "completely succeeded in realizing," as he put it later in the *Chroniques,* to the point where they determined what as of 1935 he could call the "whole subsequent course" of his work?[111]

Answers to these questions have to do with matters Stravinsky himself would not discuss coherently until the *Poétique musicale,* almost two decades later. Chief among them was the paradigmatic after-the-Great-War theme of defending "culture" against the mob, a defense that took the form of that authoritarian and reactionary stance we now call neoclassicism. As it related to opera, the neoclassic posture was given its full dogmatic exposition in the Third Lesson of the *Poétique,* where, taking off from an explicit reference to *Mavra,* the artificialities of operatic convention are defended against the "pathological" vulgarian depredations of the "music drama," the latter condemned for its lack of tradition, for its "*nouveau riche* smugness," and for the "terrible blow" it had inflicted upon music itself, which, in the aftermath of the Wagnerian miasma, could no longer be accepted without shame as a "purely sensual delight."[112] In the Second Lesson, meanwhile, Stravinsky had expounded a rigorous definition of melody—"the musical singing of a ca-

109. Letter to Ansermet, 2 December 1921; in SelCorrI:154.
110. Letter to Kochno, 11 January 1922; in Kochno, *Diaghilev and the Ballets Russes,* 184.
111. *An Autobiography,* 103–4.
112. *Poetics of Music,* bilingual ed., 77, 79.

denced phrase"—and affirmed that "melody must keep its place at the summit of the hierarchy of elements that make up music."[113] The word must be construed, of course, with its cultural and political subtext (see above) intact.

These were the breakthroughs he had achieved in *Mavra:* the rediscovery of the cadenced phrase after years spent building impressive structures out of open-ended *popevki,* and the reestablishment of the principle of cadenced construction at the higher levels of form. Like a true "pangermanoromanic chauvinist"—the more ardent for having been recently converted—Stravinsky now wished to rescue Europe from the cultural morass his own neoprimitivist work, among other things, had helped create; by the time he finished *Mavra,* he saw the work, whatever its humble origins, as a vessel of ecumenical regeneration, indeed of moral rearmament.

Or is all of this just an anachronistic extrapolation from a book that was composed as long after *Mavra* as *Mavra* itself was after the Symphony in E-flat? The outlandish importance with which Stravinsky invested his skit-turned-opera even as work on it progressed suggests otherwise; and so does a little-known literary document of the period. Practically the whole esthetic program of the *Poétique,* at least insofar as it may relate to *Mavra,* can be found prefigured in astonishingly complete form in an essay published in 1928 which shows that the program was even then an explicit part of the avowedly "antimodernist" message of Igor Stravinsky, and that *Mavra* had unquestionably been its crucible.

The essay was written by Artur Sergeyevich (or Arthur-Vincent) Lourié (1892–1966), one of the most interesting forgotten musicians of the twentieth century. A composition pupil of Glazunov in the period of Stravinsky's first fame (he graduated in 1913), Lourié later fell in with the Futurist poets (known in Russian as the *budetlyanye*) and became particularly close to Anna Akhmatova, whose verses he was among the first to set. Later he would serve as head of the music division (*Muzo*) of the Commissariat of Popular Enlightenment (*Narkompros*) under Lunacharsky in the earliest days of Soviet power, "distinguish[ing] himself by his leftist attitudes toward the classics."[114] Information on Lourié's Russian years is extremely hard to come by.[115] The manner of his emigration—he simply failed to return from an official visit (*komandirovka*) to Berlin in 1921—made him out a traitor in Soviet eyes. Consequently, until very recently Lourié has been a virtual un-

113. Ibid., 53, 55.

114. O. L. Dansker, annotation to *N. A. Mal'ko: vospominaniya, stat'i, pis'ma* (Leningrad: Muzïka, 1972), 354.

115. By far the most extensive source of information on Lourié's musical career is a series of publications by Detlef Gojowy. Besides his pioneering study *Neue sowjetische Musik der 20er Jahre* (Regensburg: Laaber-Verlag, 1980), where Lourié's works and activities are set in a broad context (see 97ff., 148ff., 187ff.), there is also his *Vie musicale en U.R.S.S. de 1900 à 1930* (Paris: IRCAM, n.d.), as well as a pair of specialized articles in (of all places) the *Hindemith-Jahrbuch* ("Arthur Lourié der Futurist," in 8 [1979]: 147–85 [pt. 1] and 12 [1983]: 116–57 [pt. 2]). Part 1 is accompanied (pp. 186–207) by "Arthur Sergeevič Lourié—biographische Notizen" (trans. from the Russian) by Irina Graham, Lourié's com-

FIG. 19.6. Artur Sergeyevich Lurye (Arthur-Vincent Lourié, 1892–1966), before his emigration. (Music Division, New York Public Library and Museum of the Performing Arts at Lincoln Center)

person in the Soviet press and scholarly literature.[116] By 1922 he had settled in Paris, where he became closely allied with Jacques Maritain, the neo-Thomist philosopher.[117] He was introduced to Stravinsky by Vera Sudeykina, who had known him well in Petrograd, Lourié and the Sudeykins having actually shared a home for a while.[118]

From 1924 to 1931, Arthur-Vincent Lourié was "one of the two or three most important associates in Stravinsky's life," in the well-qualified opinion of Robert Craft, another of them.[119] A virtual member of Stravinsky's household at this time,[120] Lourié performed such essential musical tasks as the preparation of piano reductions: the *Concertino,* the *Octuor,* and, most importantly, the *Symphonies d'instruments à vent* were published in Lourié's arrangements; the last, issued in 1926, remained the only available text until 1952. Most significantly for us, during this period Lourié acted, as Craft would later do, as Stravinsky's chief public interlocutor and mouthpiece.

By the time of the *Chroniques,* Lourié had fallen from grace owing to a feud with Vera Sudeykina and so became as much an unperson in the Stravinsky literature as in the Soviet, rating mention neither in the autobiography nor in any of the composer's later books of memoirs. It is evident, though, that his intellectual impact on Stravinsky was considerable, outlasting their period of personal intimacy. At the very least, Lourié had been Stravinsky's conduit to Maritain, whose enormous influence on the composer's "antimodernist" thinking may be gauged by the *Poétique musicale,* which so often lapses into virtual paraphrases of the French philosopher's *Art et scholastique* of 1921.[121] Not even a creative exchange can be

panion during his late American years. Other, more recent sources of information on which the present discussion has relied include Peter Deane Roberts, "Aspects of Modernism in Russian Piano Music, 1910–1929" (Thesis, Kingston Polytechnic, 1988), on some of the early music; and V. Markus (pseud.), "O dnyakh minuvshikh i prekrasnïkh: zapiski starogo moskvicha," *Muzïkal'naya zhizn',* no. 748 (January 1989): 27–30, on Lourié's career as a Soviet bureaucrat.

116. There is no entry under his name, for example, in the relevant volume of the standard Soviet encyclopedia of music (Yu. Keldïsh et al., eds., *Muzïkal'naya entsiklopediya,* vol. 3 [KORTO–OTKOL', 1976]). When Soviet reference to Lourié was unavoidable, its ticket of admission was massive gratuitous vituperation. The official, collectively authored *History of the Music of the Peoples of the USSR* follows up the necessary citation of his name in connection with *Muzo* with a quasi-reflexive stream of abuse: "An estheticizing decadent, a composer devoid of individuality, an eclectic but with pretensions to innovation and originality, Lourié used his official position for self-promotion and for supporting like-minded adventurists, concealing his motives behind loud, seemingly revolutionary declarations about the radical renovation of the language and forms of contemporary music" (Yu. Keldïsh et al., *Istoriya muzïki narodov SSSR,* vol. 1 [Moscow: Sovetskiy Kompozitor, 1970], 57).

117. That theirs was a mutual admiration is attested by Maritain's mystical appreciation "Sur la musique d'Arthur Lourié," *Revue musicale,* no. 165 (April 1936): 266–71.

118. Craft (ed.), *Dearest Bubushkin,* 20. Dates of Lourié's emigration and his arrival in Paris follow those given in an editorial footnote (by Carl Engel?) to an article by Lourié, "Musings on Music," *Musical Quarterly* 27 (1941): 235.

119. SelCorrI:217n.

120. Jacques Handschin, for example, closed a 1931 letter to Stravinsky with "regards to Yekaterina Gavrilovna, to your daughter, and to Arthur" (SelCorrIII:134).

121. Many telling parallels are traced in Andriessen and Schönberger, *Apollonian Clockwork,* 80–96.

ruled out: Lourié's massive *Concerto spirituale* of 1929 has many points of evident conceptual similarity with Stravinsky's *Symphonie de Psaumes,* composed the following year; and just when Stravinsky began his abortive setting of Petrarch's *Dialogue Between Joy and Reason* (in Charles-Albert Cingria's translation; some of this music eventually found a home in *Perséphone*), Lourié completed a setting of the same text for inclusion in his opera *Le festin pendant la peste* after Pushkin.[122]

Thus for seven years Arthur Lourié spoke for Stravinsky with an authority at least equal to that of Craft at a later time. From the plausible perspective of his own experience, Craft has suggested, with respect to the first wave of Stravinskian apologias in the 1920s, that "not all . . . were written by [the composer]," but that nevertheless "he seems to have initiated all of them and certainly kept them on a short leash."[123]

For all these reasons, then, Arthur Lourié's article "Two Operas by Stravinsky" ("*Dve operï Stravinskogo*"), dated Paris, May 1927, and published in its entirety only in Souvtchinsky's Eurasianist journal *Vyorstï,* is a document of unsurpassed importance.[124] The second part of it, on *Oedipus Rex,* was widely circulated in both French and German,[125] but the vociferous defense of *Mavra* has never been reprinted or translated, that opera having been written off even by 1927 as a dead letter of interest only to Russians. As the earliest extended exposition of Stravinsky's "neoclassicism," predating even the redoubtable "Avertissement" published over Stravinsky's signature in December 1927 (in which the term *neoclassic* was, to all Stravinskian intents and purposes, coined), Lourié's article deserves a close look; for it is already *La poétique musicale* in embryo.[126]

On behalf of what was far and away the least successful of Stravinsky's works, Lourié staked a public claim no less exalted than the claim Stravinsky expressed in private correspondence. While *Mavra* was superficially a "national Russian opera like *A Life for the Tsar* or *Eugene Onegin*," its real significance, according to Lourié, lay in the fact that it gave "renewed possibility to the rebirth of operatic form in the

---

122. On Lourié's *Concerto spirituale* and his Pushkin opera, see Henri Davenson's obituary in *Perspectives of New Music* 5, no. 2 (Spring–Summer 1967): 166–69.

123. P&D:219.

124. Artur Lourié, "Dve operï Stravinskogo," *Vyorstï* 3 (1928): 109–22 (all subsequent quotes come from within this page span). Lourié elaborated on the theme of Stravinsky's "antimodernism" in another article published in 1928, where "the camp of the modernists," easily identifiable as that of Schoenberg, is invidiously held up against the neoclassic Stravinsky of *Mavra* ("Neogothic and Neoclassic," *Modern Music* 5, no. 3 [March–April 1928], 3–8).

125. In French: "*Oedipus Rex* de Strawinsky," *Revue musicale* 8, no. 8 (August 1927): 240–53; in German: "Oedipus Rex. Opera-Oratorium nach Sophokles von Igor Strawinsky," *Blätter der Staatsoper* 8, no. 19 (1928): 9–13.

126. As mentioned in Chapter 18, however, the first actual use of the term neoclassic with regard to Stravinsky seems to have been by Schloezer, in a 1923 article that touched on the *Symphonies d'instruments à vent.*

West, that is, if opera is destined to be reborn at all." With mounting explicitness the argument is pursued:

> The decline of opera in the West is the result of the Wagnerian legacy. The so-called music drama has gradually swallowed up the pure forms of opera. Degenerating into a pseudo-Romanticism, the post-Wagnerian theater with its rhetorical emotionalism has destroyed the pure instrumental design [*plastika*] of the classical style. For Western opera *Mavra* may become a formal pivot. Despite the profoundly Russian character that defines the basis of *Mavra*'s musical language and its lyrico-epic atmosphere, thanks to the principles of its construction it can and must be apprehended from a non-nationalistic standpoint. The objective value of *Mavra* lies in the method of its formal system. . . . In reviving Russian national opera along classical lines, and at the same time putting a down payment on a new flowering of the same classical operatic forms in the West, Stravinsky returns us through *Mavra* to our pure original sources.

Next Lourié rehearses the story later repeated in the *Chroniques,* of how the mighty kuchka had misread Glinka's legacy, turning from the pure source to a "pseudo-Russian nationalism, nurtured by German scholasticism." Rimsky-Korsakov—inevitably—is named as chief culprit in this unfortunate "deviation": "Despite the superficial appearance of continuity with Glinka, [the latter's] legacy at this point in the history of Russian musical culture was subjected to revision and a seeming formal expansion—but it was anything but a development or an intensification of the pure line he had revealed. Glinka's essential line has found no continuation at all up to now." That is, up to *Mavra:*

> *Mavra* has revived the broken ties to Glinka's legacy, reconstituting it on a new basis. . . . Besides Glinka, *Mavra* returns to Chaikovsky, who has become through this work the connecting link between Glinka and Stravinsky. One could define *Mavra*'s genealogy thus: from *A Life for the Tsar* through Chaikovsky to the contemporary canon. For Stravinsky, the relationship to Glinka is a question of purely national tradition and a fundamental link. His common bond with Chaikovsky, on the other hand, is founded on what one might consider a familial blood tie, despite their manifest differences of temperament and taste.

It all came down to an end run around the "Asiatic" and the footless pseudo-Russianism that had been, in conjunction with other parvenu trends, so harmfully influential—through Diaghilev's first repertoire—on the music (and not only the music!) of the West. In a word, it came down to "antimodernism":

> Acknowledging his estrangement from musical modernism, glancing back at the Russian music of the past, Stravinsky was bound to ally himself with Chaikovsky. This was a natural reaction against an outdated modernism. His kinship with Chaikovsky, which always existed, was consciously revealed first in *Mavra,* then in

the *Octuor*. The return to Chaikovsky, the reevaluation of him that Stravinsky carried out at the time of *Mavra*, and the further consolidation of that position—all this has routed once and for all the old, already lifeless camp of the modernists.

The exigencies of resurrecting musical purity against the devastations wrought by "modernism" had conditioned the slightness of *Mavra*'s plot (and here Lourié/Stravinsky shows a genuine kinship with the author of "The Little House in Kolomna"). But the resurrection must be taken seriously withal, and treated with reverence!

> In *Mavra* the most astonishing thing is the insignificance of the subject, as it were its calculated insipidity. For the shortsighted, this poverty of scenic narration brought the work down to the level of a theatrical skit, a trifle unworthy of discussion. But in point of fact the subject of *Mavra* is not an anecdote lifted out of Pushkin's "Little House in Kolomna." Its subject is its purely musical, formal objective. *Mavra is constructed on a little anecdote for the sake of its scenic unfolding, but rises to the estate of national lyric epos in its musical unfolding.* It's just the opposite of all those innumerable operas built on the most complicated subjects—mythological, historical, symbolic, and so on—but in which the music has no life of its own. In *Mavra* the connection with the poem is intentionally minimal—it is just a point of departure. The plot of *Mavra* is just a springboard for leaping onto a musical trapeze, and this purpose it more than satisfies.

As to the musical retrogression Stravinsky's adoption of all the worst clichés of diatonic tonality seemed to imply, Lourié, at the composer's evident behest, insisted that, quite to the contrary,

> the primitivism in *Mavra* is intentional. The seeming poverty and squalor is the result of a ruthless creative will and full artistic consciousness. When the score is closely examined with "an armed eye" and checked by a tested ear, the unsophistication of *Mavra* stands revealed as the result of a synthesis of the kind that makes possible an authentic unsophisticatedness. *Mavra*, in all its simplicity, harbors within itself the whole of Stravinsky's past experience and is the consequence of ripe mastery.

The conclusion is a prophet's call: "The acceptance of *Mavra* will induce the excretion from the contemporary agenda of the whole Wagnerian theater, and with it the music drama along Wagnerian lines as his followers have maintained it, with Richard Strauss at their head in Europe, and Rimsky-Korsakov in Russia."

As history, not much of this will stand scrutiny, and the final jeremiad is contemptible in its forced jab at Stravinsky's old teacher, surely the strangest bedfellow Richard Strauss was ever assigned. Nor did Lourié or Stravinsky seem to know that Strauss had made his peace with the "Nummer-Oper" as far back as *Ariadne auf Naxos,* which is remarkably *Mavra*-esque as originally conceived in

1912. Most painful of all is the tone of the article, of which about one-quarter has been quoted. It is the tone Theodore Strawinsky captured so well when he compared his father after *Mavra* to a "vox clamans in deserto."[127] It would be hard to imagine a more unfamiliar role for the composer of *The Firebird* and *Petrushka*, or a more unwelcome one.

The trouble was, the "camp of the modernists" did not feel itself to have been routed; the general public greeted *Mavra* as it had greeted no earlier Stravinsky composition—with a yawn; and Stravinsky, who had always been able to count on a *succès de scandale* at the very least, found himself and his work being described, for the first time since he had achieved his international fame, as superfluous. It was after *Mavra* that he first had to contend with his lifelong bane, the judgment that cast him as something on the order of a musical Chanel, a purveyor of trifles to snobs. Were it not for the much-delayed première of *Svadebka* the next year, Stravinsky's reputation with the Parisian tastemakers might have suffered permanent damage.

Thus the failure of *Mavra* was without a doubt the most painful experience in Stravinsky's career, far more painful than the "failure" of *The Rite,* which had only enhanced his reputation among those who counted for him, and which was compensated with interest the following year. The fiasco of *Mavra* has never been compensated. The little opera remains to this day a stepchild among his works. More than that: it is to *Mavra* that all the many subsequent ambiguities concerning Stravinsky's reputation and his place in history must be traced.

RECEPTION

The ill-starred opera had its first public audition on what probably seemed a most auspicious day: 29 May 1922, the ninth anniversary of *The Rite of Spring.* The setting was the ballroom of the Hotel Continental in Paris, whither Diaghilev had summoned a distinguished audience to feast on a gala buffet and hear a program pointedly entitled "Musique russe en dehors des Cinq." *Mavra* formed the second half of the program, sung to the composer's piano accompaniment by a quartet of newly emigrated young singers headed, in the role of Parasha, by Oda Slobodskaya (1888–1970), who would enjoy a long and glorious career in England. The others were Yelena Sadoven (the Neighbor), Zoya Rosovskaya (the Mother), and the Polish tenor Stefan Belina-Skupiewski (1885–1962), appearing under the name Stepan Belina, in the role of the Hussar. On the first half of the program each of the sing-

127. Theodore Strawinsky, *The Message of Igor Strawinsky,* trans. Robert Craft and André Marion (London: Boosey & Hawkes, 1953), 47.

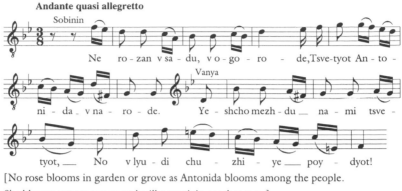

Andante quasi allegretto

Sobinin

Ne ro-zan v sa-du, v o-go-ro - de, Tsve-tyot An-to -

Vanya

ni - da v na - ro - de.   Ye - shcho mezh-du __ na - mi tsve -

tyot, __   No v lyu - di chu - zhi __ ye __ poy - dyot!

[No rose blooms in garden or grove as Antonida blooms among the people.

She blooms yet among us and will never join another race.]

ers took a solo turn, accompanied by Nikolai Kopeykin, Diaghilev's *répétiteur,* who led the concert off with a rendition of Glinka's song "The Lark" ("*Zhavronok*"), as arranged for piano by Balakirev (the "Cinq" after all!). There followed two arias from *Ruslan and Lyudmila:* Ratmir's waltz from Act III (the very one mentioned above in connection with Stravinsky's love duet), sung by Sadoven; and Gorislava's cavatina, sung by Slobodskaya. Rosovskaya and Belina followed, each with songs by Dargomïzhsky and Chaikovsky. Sadoven then returned with an especially tendentious selection: "Première et deuxième Chansons de Lel de l'opéra [*sic*!] *Snegurotchka,*" not the famous one by Rimsky-Korsakov, needless to say, which had been a favorite with French audiences since 1907, but the one by Chaikovsky—that is, his incidental music to Ostrovsky's play. To close the first half of the program, Slobodskaya, Sadoven, and Belina were joined by a basso named Constantin Kaidanoff to sing the Act III quartet from *A Life for the Tsar,* a piece bursting with melodies right out of *Mavra* (cf. the cadences in Ex. 19.34) and which includes a solemn prayer for the well-being of the house of Romanov.

It was an effective history lesson, and Stravinsky's opera, set in the context of its precise stylistic patrimony and played to a hand-picked audience, flattered to have been invited and handsomely fed, fared well. It was a different story five nights later when the same singers gave the opera its staged première on a tiny set by Leopold Survage, lost amid the vastitudes of the Palais Garnier stage, accompanied by some kind of ungainly brass band conducted by Grzegorz Fitelberg, and flanked—it could only seem invidiously—by the chefs d'oeuvre of Stravinsky's early fame, *Petrushka* and *The Rite.* According to Kochno, "The first duet, which had been received with an ovation at the Continental, met with no response at all from the Opéra audience; one might have supposed that the theater was empty. After a moment of attentive silence, people began to stir and speak to one another. If the house lights had not been turned up and the curtain lowered to signal the intermission, one would scarcely have noticed that the performance was over."[128]

One American correspondent compared the program that evening to "an inverted sandwich—i.e. a piece of bread between two pieces of meat."[129] Not even Diaghilev stood by Stravinsky this time. He mortally offended the composer by asking for a changed ending—a brilliant concluding quartet to replace the inspired "poop" that so perfectly reflected Pushkin's calculated anticlimax.[130]

We may gauge Stravinsky's mortification by comparing the two inscriptions he made—almost five years apart—on Kochno's copy of the souvenir program. The first, undated but presumably made on the occasion of the première, reads: "Boris: I really love your style in *Mavra*" ("*Boris: ya ochen' lyublyu vash stil' v Mavre*"). The second, dated Monte Carlo, 8 April 1927 (i.e., just when Lourié was writing his article on the opera), reads: "To Boris Kochno, my collaborator and witness to my excruciating sufferings on account of the public's stupidity" ("*Moyemu sotrudniku i svidetelyu moikh tyazhkikh perezhivaniy ot tuposti publiki Borisu Kokhno*").[131] As Louis Laloy, one of *Mavra*'s few Parisian sympathizers, commiserated, "A harsh judgment is subject to review; polite indifference is a condemnation that cannot be appealed."[132]

The critics were mostly dismissive indeed. The venerable Adolphe Julien, writing in the even more venerable *Journal des débats,* where Berlioz had preceded him as music critic, gave it all of one sentence: "As for *Mavra*, the most uncomical of comic operas, it is, despite the Pushkin trademark, and no matter how you look at it, of a poverty that is as pretentious as it is aggressive . . . ; poor singers, how I pity them!"[133] Deems Taylor titled his piece "Stravinsky Marks Time" and complained that "*Mavra* is so wanting even in Stravinsky's mannerisms, let alone his talent, that no one would dream he had written it were not his name on the programme."[134]

Many, put off by the surrounding propaganda, let a generalized refutation of the hype stand in place of a critique of the work. This sort of thing would become a commonplace in Stravinsky criticism, as would dark hints concerning the nefari-

128. Kochno, *Diaghilev and the Ballets Russes,* 185.
129. "Mavra Reveals New Stravinsky to Paris," *Musical America* 36, no. 10 (1 July 1922): 10.
130. Conv:III/99; corroborated by Kochno in conversation with Buckle (*Diaghilev,* 405).
131. Inscriptions transcribed from a photograph of the program inset as an illustration in Kochno, *Diaghilev and the Ballets Russes,* 182.
132. "Un jugement sévère est sujet à révision. L'indifférence polie est une condemnation sans appel" (Louis Laloy, "La musique," *Revue de Paris* 29, no. 4 [July–August 1922]: 192).
133. "Quant à l'opéra-comique de *Mavra*, aussi peu comique que possible, c'est, malgré l'estampille de Pouchkine et de quelque côté qu'on considère, une pauvreté aussi prétentieuse . . . ; pauvres chanteurs, que je les plains!" ("Chronique musicale," *Édition hebdomadaire du Journal des débats*, no. 1478 [23 June 1922]: 1031).
134. Deems Taylor, "Stravinsky Marks Time," *New York World,* 3 July 1922.

ous influence of unnamed acolytes. Thus the report of a certain Louis Schneider in the *Revue de France* becomes interesting as the prototype of innumerable reviews that would bedevil the second half of Stravinsky's career:

> The revolutionary Stravinsky has just pulled a stunt that, he hoped, would reconcile him with the upholders of tradition. He prepared for this about-face two weeks ago by publishing a manifesto in *Le Figaro* in which he asserted (I quote from memory) that Russian music ought to cultivate a Latin spirit and repudiate all German influence. And this German influence is represented, according to him, by whom? By the Five, by the Musorgskys, the Borodins, the Balakirevs, the Rimsky-Korsakovs, and the César Cuis. And who are the great Russian apostles of Latin music? The Glinkas, the Dargomïzhskys, and the Chaikovskys! This new classification was just a wee bit surprising, and so we awaited the advent of *Mavra*.
>
> The preface to [Victor Hugo's drama] *Cromwell* was Romanticism's declaration of war on classicism; but at least it was followed by *Hernani* and *Marion Delorme* in 1827. Here, Mr. Stravinsky's ultimatum seemed to be of somewhat lesser scope. . . .
>
> Igor Stravinsky evidently enjoyed himself greatly in putting this scenario to music; but he lacked invention and fastened on some orchestral tricks and some fairly puerile dissonances. In sum, he has renounced Rimsky-Korsakov, but he has not been able to improve on his teacher's work. He has already served the art of music too well not to enrich it further in some fashion, and we expect other things from him, and better ones. But in *Mavra* he has mistaken his path. Let us hope that in the future he will not take his bearings from the "Stravinskyites," more royalist than he, who can lead him only into error![135]

The fact that *Renard* was given its stage première during the same Ballets Russes season provided the text for many a sermon, as one can see even in one of the more tolerant notices, that of Maurice Brillant:

135. "Le révolutionnaire qu'est Strawinsky devait ensuite aboutir à une évocation qui, espérait-il, devait lui concilier les partisans de la tradition. Cette volte-face, il l'avait preparée quinze jours auparavant en publiant dans *Le Figaro* un manifeste où il affirmait,—je cite le sens et non le texte,—que la musique russe devait se rapprocher de l'esprit latin et s'éloigner de l'influence germanique. Or cette influence germanique est, selon lui, représentée par qui? Par les Cinq, les Moussorgsky, les Borodine, les Balakirew, les Rimsky-Korsakow, et les César Cui. Et quels sont les grands Russes apôtres de la musique latine? Les Glinka, les Dargomijsky, les Tschaïkowsky! On fut quelque peu surpris de cette classification nouvelle et on attendit l'apparition de *Mavra*. La préface de Cromwell avait été la déclaration de guerre du romantisme au classicisme; mais du moins avait-elle été suivie de l'apparition d'*Hernani* et de Marion Delorme en 1827. Ici, l'ultimatum de M. Strawinsky a semblé devoir être d'une portée moins ample. . . . M. Igor Strawinsky s'est évidemment beaucoup diverti à mettre ce scenario en musique; mais il a manqué d'invention, et il s'est attaché à des amusements d'orchestre, à des dissonances un peu puériles. En somme, il a renié Rimsky-Korsakow, mais il a été impuissant à parachever l'oeuvre de son maître. Il a déjà trop bien servi l'art de la musique pour ne pas l'enrichir encore de quelque façon, et nous attendons de lui autre chose, et mieux. Mais dans *Mavra* il s'est trompé de route. Souhaitons aussi qu'à l'avenir il ne demande pas son chemin aux 'strawinskystes,' plus royalistes que lui, et qui ne peuvent que l'induire en erreur!" (Louis Schneider, "M. Igor Strawinsky et les Ballets russes," *Revue de France* 2, no. 4 [July–August 1922]: 438–39). To straighten out M. Schneider's confusion of dates: the famous preface to *Cromwell* was published in 1827, *Hernani* followed in 1830, *Marion Delorme* in 1831.

The Ballets Russes sometimes enchant us with the harmony of their ensemble, in
which all elements are so precisely calculated to converge in a unique effect; . . .
and sometimes a violent discord—a deliberate one, mind you, as in the polytonalism of our young musicians—may seek to procure newer, rarer pleasures for us, or
fiercer ones. And this method, too, can sometimes please, but one must admit it is
far from surefire and its ways are not so normal. . . .

The two new works of M. Stravinsky belong respectively to the former and the
latter type. This great musician has precisely the characteristics we have noted in
the Diaghilev company: he has a horror of repeating himself and at every stage he
wishes to remake himself. A splendid, difficult aim. His ballet *Renard* . . . came before his panegyric to Chaikovsky; one can find there a Stravinsky we have known,
or at least one who comes fairly logically out of *Le sacre* and even more so out of
the *Pribaoutki*. . . . Poor *Renard* has been treated harshly. As for me, I'll admit I
was very amused, the way one is amused at any unpretentious farce. . . .

Renard was a sort of ballet with singing. . . . *Mavra* is not a ballet at all, but a
tiny *opéra-comique*. . . . It is certainly disconcerting to find out who signed it. . . .
This is no longer evolution (or if so the steps are well hidden); it is a brusque and
complete change of direction, a vehicle that turns without warning. Maybe after *Le
sacre* or *Renard* it was impossible to go further . . . I wouldn't know. It is also possible that a palate overexcited by peppery potables feels a need to taste some
syrup. . . . Thus M. Poulenc, "advanced" as he is, declares that nothing pleases him
like *Rigoletto*. . . .

As for me, was it because of walking in the lobby during intermission, overhear-
ing all the talk, M. Roland-Manuel's unhurried explanations, M. Poulenc's plain-
spoken affirmations—or was I simply touched by grace? For you see I am halfway
converted to *Mavra*. Just halfway. . . .

The first time I heard *Mavra* it was at a soirée of M. Diaghilev's. M. Stravinsky
accompanied at the piano. It seemed rather poor. I admit that I felt a little
stunned—and I was not the only one—despite the contentments of a fine buffet.
But at the Opéra there was the orchestra, which at first seemed odd but then, the
second time, remarkable. . . . But one perceives the clash deliberately sought—and
infallibly obtained—between the singing and the instruments. One might say: "It's
bel canto accompanied by a jazz band." This would be a bit of an exaggeration
(but when you want to be clear it is impossible to be precise). It would be better
to say, as M. Roland-Manuel did, very wittily: "Whereas the voices seem to be
singing in Italian . . . the orchestra is speaking Russian with a slight American accent." And that's distinctly "amusing," as long as one does not try to repeat the
experiment. The same speaker was perhaps right in saying, more or less, that
M. Stravinsky has accomplished exactly what he wished to, but that he is not sure
he was right to wish it. That's the voice of good sense. But now and then one may
pretend to renounce good sense.[136]

136. "Les *Ballets russes* tantôt nous enchantent par l'harmonie de l'ensemble où tous les elements s'ac-
cordent exactement pour concourir à un effet unique; . . . tantôt un désaccord violent, et d'ailleurs vo-
lontaire, comme dans la polytonalité de nos jeunes musiciens, cherche à nous procurer des plaisirs plus
nouveaux et plus raffinés—ou plus barbares; et cette méthode peut plaire quelquefois, mais il faut
avouer qu'elle est moins sûre et d'un art moins normal . . . Les deux oeuvres nouvelles de M. Stravinski
apartiennent respectivement à l'un et l'autre genre. Ce grand musicien a tout justement de caractère que
nous avons remarqué dans la compagnie de M. de Diaghilev: il a horreur de la répétition et à chaque

Surely the most celebrated *Mavra* review was a veritable cry of pain from Émile Vuillermoz, hitherto Stravinsky's most reliable champion in the French press. He felt himself betrayed, and lashed back with such a vengeance that the composer could not help but be impressed. Reacting with bravado, he pasted the offending notice right into his autograph score.[137] "Why this hateful 'backward march' in the time machine?" fumed the critic. A "Strawinsky" had no business trying to amuse:

This man of genius is not gay. He has nothing of the merry-andrew in him. His satire is heavy and forced.

. . . And the music is of a weight and a volume that deprives this "caricature" of all its ironic charm.

. . . And yet this risky business has, in a most unexpected way, brought some singularly instructive truths to the surface. One sees, to begin with, that Italian music is not so easily parodied as one might think. And then one realizes that Stravinsky, whose rhythmic genius is prodigious, is terribly lacking in melodic invention. His earlier works have hinted at this, but the present one leaves no doubt

---

étape il veut se renouveler. Beau et difficile dessein. Son ballet de *Renard* . . . est anterieur au panégyrique de Tchaïkowski; on y retrouve un Stravinski que nous connaissons ou du moins qui sort assez logiquement du *Sacre* et plus encore de *Pribaoutki*. . . . On a été sévère à ce pauvre *Renard*. J'avoue que, pour ma part, je m'y suis fort amusé, comme on s'amuse d'une farce sans prétention . . . *Renard* était une sorte de ballet avec chant. . . . *Mavra* n'est point du tout un ballet, mais un minuscule opéra-comique. . . . Il n'est pas douteux qu'elle déconcerte quand on sait qui l'a signée. . . . Ce n'est plus une évolution (supprima-t-elle bien des étapes), c'est un brusque et complet changement de direction, c'est la machine qui se retourne sans crier gare. Peut-être après le *Sacre* ou *Renard* était-il impossible d'aller plus loin . . . je n'en sais rien. Il est possible encore qu'un palais trop excité par des liqueurs trop poivrées sente le besoin de goûter quelque sirop . . . Ainsi M. Poulenc, si 'avancé' qu'il soit, déclare que rien ne lui fait plaisir comme *Rigoletto* . . . Quant à moi, est-ce la promenade dans le couloir, à l'entr'acte, où l'on bavarde tellement, les explications mésurées de M. Roland-Manuel, les affirmations plus nettes de M. Poulenc, ou bien ai-je simplement été touché par la grâce? Mais me voici à moitié converti à *Mavra*. A moitié seulement . . . La première fois que j'ai entendu *Mavra*, c'était au cours d'une soirée chez M. de Diaghilev. M. Strawinski accompagnait au piano. Cela paraissait assez pauvre. J'avoue que je me suis senti un peu abasourdi,—et je n'étais pas le seul,—malgré le réconfort d'un très bon buffet. Mais à l'Opéra il y avait l'orchestre, lequel m'a semblé d'abord curieux et puis, une seconde fois, remarquable . . . Mais on voit le désaccord cherché . . . et infailliblement obtenu, entre le chant et les instruments. On pourrait dire: 'C'est du *bel canto* accompagné par un orchestre de jazz-band.' Ce serait un peu exagéré (mais quand on veut être clair, il est impossible d'être en même temps exact). Il vaut mieux dire, très joliment, avec M. Roland-Manuel: 'Tandis que les voix semblent chanter en italien . . . l'orchestre parle russe avec un léger accent américain.' Et c'est évidemment 'amusant,' à condition d'ailleurs qu'on ne renouvelle pas l'expérience. Le même auteur a peut-être raison de dire encore ou à peu près que M. Stravinski a fait exactement ce qu'il a voulu, mais qu'il n'est pas sûr qu'il ait bien fait de le vouloir. C'est de bon sens qui parle. Mais du temps en temps on peut se donner la fantaisie de renoncer au bon sens" (Maurice Brillant, "Les oeuvres et les hommes," *Correspondent* 94, no. 1436 [25 July 1922]: 364–68). The quotation from Roland-Manuel refers to the latter's article "'Mavra' d'Igor Stravinsky," *Quinzaine musicale*, no. 13 (1 July 1922); clipping preserved in Stravinsky's scrapbook in the Archive (no. R56). In a "Letter from Paris," published in the London *Musical News and Herald* on 1 July 1922, Roland-Manuel sounded the "antimodernist" note: "His fanatical admirers, whirled along by the rapidity of the movement, are left embedded in the mire of atonalism and polytonalism, while the composer of the 'Sacre du Printemps' here forsakes his old track completely, and gives both his aesthetics and his technique an entirely new direction which nobody could foresee. There is an enormous difference between 'Oiseau de feu' and 'Renard,' yet it is not in any way comparable to the abyss which divides 'Renard' from 'Mavra'" (clipping in the Percy Scholes Collection, National Library of Canada). Poulenc to Stravinsky (31 July 1922): "Brillant's *Correspondent* article . . . shows a certain good will"; Stravinsky to Poulenc (9 September 1922): "It is as if Madame Manuel had written it" (SelCorrIII:201–2).

137. Darius Milhaud, *Notes Without Music*, trans. Donald Evans (New York: Alfred A. Knopf, 1953), 131.

of it. Let this great musician desist forthwith from wasting his time on such use-less jokes![138]

The remarks about melody must have been wounding, given Stravinsky's new line. (He would have to put up with them for the rest of his life, for his presumed lack of melodic invention became a time-honored cliché.) More wounding yet was the cruel review by Boris de Schloezer, Stravinsky's compatriot—who, if anyone, should have known what the composer was about—which appeared in the *Nouvelle revue française,* Jacques Rivière's old journal, whose support had meant so much to the composer in the past (see Chapter 13).[139] With the alacrity of a news-boy hawking an extra, Schloezer had rushed into print to announce Stravinsky's first failure:

> What is most striking in Stravinsky, what makes his activity especially valuable, it seems to me, is the fact that he does not exploit the riches he discovers, but leaves them generously to others, himself changing direction with every new work and opening new horizons to us. . . . Thus, each of his works is a test—but also a masterstroke. Up to now he has always succeeded; the initial astonishment and irritation passes and the listener always ends up convinced. Up to *Mavra,* that is, which, to my mind, is a failure. . . . The general impression is that of a pastiche, a sort of musical amusement whose principal fault is that it is not amusing enough. But that was certainly not Stravinsky's intention. He wants to pump new blood into old forms, he wants to renew those forms, so as to create a new comic opera style. In that case the subject was too puny, too frail: it crumbles to dust beneath its rich musical integument, where the two styles—Italo-Russian and black American—never succeed in meshing but only impede one another.[140]

138. "Pourquoi cette malicieuse 'marche-arrière' de la machine à explorer le temps? . . . Cet homme de génie n'est pas gai. Il n'a rien d'un amuseur. Sa caricature est lourde et appuyée . . . Et la musique est d'un poids et d'un volume qui enlèvent à cette 'charge' tout agrément ironique. . . . Et cette dangéreuse gageure fait apparaître de la façon la plus imprévue quelques vérités singulièrement instructives. On s'aperçoit, d'abord, que la musique italienne ne se parodie pas aussi facilement qu'on le croit. Et puis l'on constate que Strawinsky, dont le génie rythmique est prodigieux, manque terriblement d'invention mélodique. Ses ouvrages précédents nous l'avaient fait pressentir, mais celui-ci ne permet plus d'en douter. Que ce grand musicien cesse donc de se livrer à des facéties aussi inutiles" ("Mavra," *Excelsior,* 12 June 1922; transcript courtesy Scott Messing).

139. On Stravinsky's reaction to Schloezer's piece see SelCorrI:157 (letter to Ansermet, 11 August 1922; also cf. correspondence with Schloezer himself in footnote).

140. "Ce qui frappe le plus en Strawinsky, ce qui, à mon sens, doit nous rendre son action particu-lièrement précieuse, c'est qu'il n'exploite pas les richesses qu'il découvre, mais que les abandonnant généreusement à d'autres, lui-même à chaque oeuvre nouvelle change de direction et nous ouvre de nouveaux horizons. . . . Ainsi, chacune de ses oeuvres est un coup d'essai; mais ce sont aussi des coups de maître: jusqu'ici il les réussissait toujours; et le premier sentiment d'étonnement et d'inquiétude passé, l'auditeur devait s'avouer convaincu. Jusqu'ici, c'est-à-dire, jusqu'à *Mavra* qui, a mon avis, est un echec. . . . En effet, l'impression générale est celle d'un pastiche, d'une sorte de plaisanterie musicale dont le principal défaut serait de n'être pas suffisamment plaisante. Mais tel n'est certainement pas le dessein de Strawinsky: il s'agit d'infuser un sang nouveau à d'anciennes formes, il s'agit probablement de rénover ces formes, de créer ainsi un nouveau style d'opéra-comique. En ce cas le sujet est trop mince, trop fragile: il s'effrite en poussière sous son riche revêtement musical, où les deux styles—italo-russe et négro-américain—ne parviennent pas à se fondre et se gênent mutuellement" (Schloezer, "La musique," *Nouvelle revue française* 9, no. 106 [1 July 1922]: 116–18).

Who came to *Mavra*'s defense? The usual suspects: Satie, Cocteau, and the young—the very young—composers of Les Six, to whose faction Stravinsky had willy-nilly lent the enormous prestige of his name with his unexpected "petite plaisanterie," in the delighted words of Georges Auric, who went on to greet "a work that, after Satie, bearing the precious imprint of the young music of France, conveys to our hearts and minds its unforgettable pages, bound together like a bouquet whose fragrance will grow from day to day, far from all scholastic prejudice, esthetic argument, false bravado, or the cant of base disciples."[141] Indeed! As if the reception of any Stravinsky work in those days could be free of politics. "Think of it!" Cocteau exulted; "Stravinsky bringing the homage of his supreme contribution to the endeavors of Satie and our young musicians. Stravinsky the traitor. Stravinsky the deserter." And then a lovely sally at Messrs. Schloezer, Vuillermoz, et al.:

> It would never occur to any of them to think: Stravinsky the Fountain of Youth. For no one ever gives the masters credit. It would be simple to say to oneself, "He is stronger than I. His instinct is surer. He must be right. It would be wise to follow him!" No. Everybody thinks, "He is mistaken and I—clever fellow—am the only person who knows it." This downpour of drivel, of lava and ashes, is, however, a good thing for a work. Thus, the critics think to destroy it, but they only cover it up, they protect it and preserve it, and a long time afterwards an excavation brings the marble to light, intact.[142]

Inevitably, *Mavra* became the battle cry of the "jeune musique française." Milhaud, writing in the German press, where *neue Sachlichkeit* and *junge Klassizität* had become the catchwords of the avant-garde, proclaimed the fealty of the young musicians of France to their Russian elder: "*Mavra* will flourish wherever recognition is granted to the living school, the school that works, but upon which people look askance, with eyes dimmed by the contemplation of vain images or by too much reading of Rimsky-Korsakov's Handbook of Instrumentation."[143]

Far more substantial than these counterpuffs was a little essay in the Paris bimonthly *Feuilles libres* by the twenty-three-year-old Francis Poulenc, whose argu-

141. ". . . Un ouvrage qui, après Satie, avec les témoignages précieux de la jeune musique française apporte à notre coeur et à notre intelligence ses pages inoubliables, liées comme un bouquet, et dont la saveur de jour en jour augmentera bien loin des préjugés d'école, des polémiques esthétiques, des fausses hardiesses et des superstitions des mauvais disciples" ("Du 'Sacre du Printemps' à 'Mavra,'" *Nouvelles littéraires*, 6 January 1923, 4; transcript courtesy Scott Messing).

142. Jean Cocteau, "Critics and the Comic Spirit," *Vanity Fair* (1922); reprinted in Corle (ed.), *Stravinsky*, 23–24.

143. "Strawinskys neue Bühnenwerke," *Musikblätter des Anbruch* 4, no. 17 (November 1922); English translation in *Musical Times* 64, no. 1 (1 January 1923): 40.

ments on behalf of *Mavra* Maurice Brillant had found so charmingly persuasive in spite of himself that first night. It was an astonishingly perceptive piece—one that not only hit the mark where Stravinsky's stylistic evolution was concerned (and did so with impressively concrete technical observations), but pointed with equal precision to the nature of the influence this new Stravinskian manner would exercise on the musicians of Poulenc's generation. In a few spare sentences, the essence of Parisian "neoclassicism" is vividly laid bare:

> Ultimately it is the harmony in *Mavra* that is attacked in order to reproach [Stravinsky] for his lack of *originality*. It is amusing to observe in this regard that the musicians of the post-Debussy generation, drunk with their "rare harmonies," have got the habit of considering banal any resolution of perfect triads.
>   We have arrived at a period of leveling in which all chords seem to be on the same plane. It is elsewhere that one now must seek novelty.
>   In *Mavra*, Stravinsky has put all his effort into devising a system of modulation. It is by the horizontal juxtaposition of distant tones that he has obtained a music that is precise, frisky, and eminently tonal (a rare quality nowadays). No critic has noticed this.[144]

Indeed, it is tempting to view *Mavra* after all as Stravinsky's great seminal work of the twenties, despite its "sujet mince" and its lowly status as a "plaisanterie musicale." That very status constituted its chief significance. The reinstatement of *plaisanterie*—something made *pour plaire*—within the legitimate domain of art was a serious business for the postwar generation of "antimodernists," with Satie and now Stravinsky at their head—a generation whose stance now seems, with the advantage of six decades of hindsight, so much more modern than the "modernism," directly descended from Romanticism, with which it then contended.

Ortega y Gasset understood this first and best: three years after *Mavra* he wrote, "The symbol of art is seen again in the magic flute of the great god Pan which makes the young goats frisk at the edge of the grove. . . . All modern art begins to

144. "C'est enfin à l'harmonie de *Mavra* que l'on s'attaque pour . . . reprocher [Strawinsky] son peu d'*originalité*. Il est amusant de constater à ce propos que les musiciens de la génération post-Debussy grisés par les 'harmonies rares' ont pris l'habitude de considérer comme banale une résolution d'accords parfaits. Nous sommes à une époque de nivellement où tous les accords nous apparaissent sur le même plan. C'est donc dans un autre domaine qu'il faut chercher la nouveauté. Dans *Mavra*, Strawinsky a porté tous ses efforts sur le système de modulation. C'est par juxtaposition horizontale de tons éloignés qu'il a obtenu une musique précise, bondissante et éminemment tonale (qualité rare aujourd'hui). Aucun critique n'a remarqué cela" (Francis Poulenc, "La musique: à propos de 'Mavra' de Igor Strawinsky, *Feuilles libres*, no. 27 [June–July 1922]: 223–24). An extract in translation from the original typescript (SelCorrI:158n.) shows that before editing for publication, Poulenc's article had been even more technically astute: ". . . we must look, for novelty, to a composer who has reintroduced the dominant in our harmony." Many years later Poulenc averred that "it wasn't *Le Sacre du Printemps* that influenced me. I was influenced by works that are much more European like *Pulcinella*, *Le Baiser de la Fée*, *Jeu de Cartes*, *Mavra* . . ." (Francis Poulenc, *My Friends and Myself*, trans. James Harding [London: Dennis Dobson, 1978], 136).

appear comprehensible and in a way great when it is interpreted as an attempt to instil youthfulness into an ancient world."[145]

It was a new Enlightenment that reacted to its immediate forebear as the original Enlightenment had reacted against the heroics of the Baroque. To Dr. Burney, who passionately devoted his life to it, music had been "an innocent luxury, unnecessary, indeed, to our existence, but a great improvement and gratification of the sense of hearing."[146] To dedicate one's life to the cultivation of luxuries and the gratification of the senses was indeed the mark of aristocracy. To regard music as an ornament to one's existence, rather than a necessity or a livelihood, did honor to ornament and existence alike. The postwar antimodernist modernism exemplified in *Mavra* raised nonchalance—what the courtiers of the Renaissance called *sprezzatura*—to its former estate as the noblest of aristocratic values. The "purely" esthetic—what Ortega felt bound pleonastically to dub "artistic art"—came into its own again as the object of a properly aristocratic appreciation. *Mavra* was *Petrushka* minus the tears—that is, minus Petrushka—so that Benois's *smile* alone remained. This is what Stravinsky, unconsciously echoing Kant, would call loving music "for itself," rather than for what it might "express."[147]

Thus Ansermet was completely right to assert—though it only later became a "fact"—that with *Mavra,* Stravinsky entered "a new period, one in which music is divested of everything that has cramped it";[148] and Lourié was completely right (though of course the observation came from Stravinsky!) to draw a direct connection between *Mavra* and the *Octuor* that followed it, the composition with which the hard-core neoclassic phase is conventionally said to commence. In point of fact the music of the *Octuor,* however it may have struck its earliest listeners, is only superficially and sporadically "Bachian." What seemed to its earliest audiences "a mess of eighteenth-century mannerisms"[149] amounted to little more than a few ostentatious trills in the opening Sinfonia and a walking bass at the outset of the Finale, accompanying a self-conscious near-quotation from the *Well-Tempered Clavier*'s first C-minor fugue. Stylistically, the music of the *Octuor* is so consistently of a piece with the music of the predominantly wind-and-brass orchestra of *Mavra* that, were the singers to fall silent, the two works would often sound virtually interchangeable.

Whether "Russian," "Bachian," or "black American" in superficial affinity, the music of both pieces is characterized throughout by an insistent "monometric"

145. Ortega y Gasset, "Dehumanization of Art," 50.
146. Charles Burney, *A General History of Music* (1776), ed. Frank Mercer (New York: Dover Publications, 1957), 1:21.
147. See Stravinsky, "Quelques confidences sur la musique," in White, *Stravinsky: The Composer and His Works,* 535–39; the locus classicus for the attitude, of course, is the famous denigration of "expression" in the *Chroniques (An Autobiography,* 53–54).
148. SelCorrI:156n.
149. See Aaron Copland's memoir of the first performance (18 October 1923) in *The New Music, 1900–1960,* rev. and enlarged ed. (New York: W. W. Norton, 1968), 71–72.

rhythm, as Stravinsky called it at the time—that is, a rhythm organized around a subtactile equivalency, by now a very old story in his work.[150] The difference between the early "neoclassic" pieces and the "Russian" ones is largely a matter of the much greater extent to which the "monometrical pulse" is explicitly present on the sounding surface of the music, as it is in baroque music and in "jazz."

Beyond the general stylistic affinity, many specific devices link *Mavra* and the *Octuor*. The delayed tonic "sign-off" at the end of both pieces can be found also at the end of the *Mavra* overture, as well as in the latter's putative model, Stravinsky's arrangement of the *Variation de la Fée des lilas* (cf. Ex. 19.8b). The gag at the end of the March variation in the second movement of the *Octuor*—a "tacked-on" authentic cadence followed by an *attacca subito* into a new tempo—is copied right out of the end of Mavra's aria (fig. [156]; see Ex. 19.31c). The variations theme itself (Ex. 19.35) is a little masterpiece of slyly Europeanized Turanianism. One of the most extended wholly octatonic melodies Stravinsky ever wrote (fourteen bars, all strictly confined to Collection III) is accompanied by a quasi-functional harmonic progression centered on D, a nonreferable pitch. Melodic cadences are made on F-sharp, A, and C-sharp—the third, fifth, and leading tone. As the octatonic tune is subsumed within a diatonic harmonic texture, so "Turania" seems finally to surrender to pangermanoromanic hegemony. In texture and sonority the music of this theme is strikingly reminiscent of the Mother's aria in *Mavra*, etching all the more distinctly the stylistic line that runs from Stravinsky's last setting of his native language into the demonstratively cosmopolitan masterpieces of the twenties.

Mavra, then, was that rarity, a self-consciously and deliberately "transitional" work by a composer lately preoccupied to the point of obsession with his own stylistic evolution and his place in history. No wonder he set such store by it, and no wonder its public and critical rejection was such a blow; for it seemed a rejection of his bid for naturalization into the pangermanoromanic mainstream. Having lost Russia, he found himself shut out by Europe. Musically he was now as much a stateless person as, with his Nansen passport, he was stateless politically. "We'll have a good laugh about it five years from now," Poulenc had written him with reference to Schloezer's review.[151] But five years later the wound had not healed, as we may gather from Stravinsky's agonized inscription to Kochno. Nor would it ever: "For the rest of Stravinsky's life," Craft has written, "he would accept no criticism of the maligned *opéra-bouffe*, which he seems to have enjoyed composing

150. A sketchbook dated 1919–22, which pertains to some of the earliest "neoclassic" pieces (*Octuor*, *Sonate*), also contains notations for an unfinished set of "Cinq pièces monométriques." See the description of "Sketchbook G" in Shepard, "The Stravinsky *Nachlass*," 243. Also cf. Nicolas Nabokov: "Look at any one of [Stravinsky's] bars and you will find that it is not the measure closed in by bar lines (as it would be in Mozart, for example) but the monometrical unit of the measure, the single beat which determines the life of his musical organism" ("Stravinsky Now," *Partisan Review* 11, no. 3 [Summer 1944]: 332).

151. Letter of 31 July 1922; in SelCorrIII:201.

EXAMPLE 19.35 *Octuor* (1923), 2d movement, Tema

almost more than any other piece."[152] Yet despite the poor reception and the attendant trauma, he never flinched from the path on which he had embarked. For this he earned a special accolade from Werner Reinhart, his faithful friend and patron: "My greatest satisfaction in hearing *Mavra* last summer was the way in which you courageously followed your voice, not listening to what was said around you but obeying your inner voice only; this strength has been a quality of all the great creators."[153]

Seventy years later it is clear that the "excavation" to which Cocteau looked forward will not take place. Despite sporadic revivals and seeming periods of vogue, *Mavra* has never been rehabilitated, and its present reputation continues to obscure its huge importance. The full score was not even published until 1969, nearly half a century after the disastrous première, and only after the octogenarian composer had gone on his knees to his publisher: "Of course the music is not and will

152. P&D:626.
153. Letter of 6 June 1923; in SelCorrIII:146.

never be a success and there may be no demand or justification for printing it; and if I say that worse music than *Mavra* is performed you may say that better music is also not performed. Still, I would like to see the work in print."[154] As of the present writing it is out of print again.

Stravinsky's Russian period had ended—"poop"—with a whimper. His period of undisputed ascendancy in modern music circles was also over. For the duration of his neoclassic period he would be a figure of partisan controversy—a new kind of controversy requiring combat both on the right and on the left. He learned, in Cocteau's words, "qu'il est impossible de changer le peau sans déplaire": one cannot change one's skin without displeasing.[155]

Yet under the new skin there still beat a Russian heart, one that continued to make its presence felt in surprising ways. In the final chapter we shall have a look at some of them.

154. Letter to Stuart Pope, 10 April 1964; in SelCorrIII:446.
155. Cocteau to Elie Gagnebin, 21 June 1922; in P&D:626.

EPILOGUE:
THE TRADITIONS REVISITED

STIFLED SIGHS

"On this occasion the *Noces* would perhaps have cajoled them," wrote Cocteau of the critics who had refused to understand *Mavra*, "for the *Noces*, which precedes *Mavra* and *Renard* (another misunderstood and perfect work), is descended in a straight line from *Petrouchka* and *Le sacre*. But choral difficulties have transposed the chronological order of productions, and we shall hear the *Noces* later."[1] He may have had the reason wrong for the delay, but his diagnosis of the situation proved correct. On the evening of Wednesday, 13 June 1923—fully five years and eight months since the completion of its particell—*Svadebka* finally had its première on the stage of the Théâtre de la Gaîté-Lyrique in Paris. It was the single new production in the Ballets Russes spring season that year, and his friends and enemies all joined in welcoming back the old Stravinsky. Press opinion could once again divide along traditional party lines, the avant-garde hailing the composer as a "liberator,"[2] the old guard reproaching him for perpetrating "nothing but noise."[3]

Mavra, not revived, was gratefully forgotten. It had been a bad dream, "a useless gesture," in the words of Émile Vuillermoz, reviewing *Svadebka* with a great show of relief in the pages of the *Revue musicale*. *Mavra* had threatened to snap the musicians of France out of the Russian spell, the fecundating "dynamic influence" that, beginning with "Rimsky's revelatory orchestration and Musorgsky's blunt and powerful way of writing," had reached what seemed to

---

1. Cocteau, "Critics and the Comic Spirit," 23.
2. Erik Satie, "A Composer's Conviction," *Vanity Fair* (1923); reprinted in Corle (ed.), *Stravinsky*, 31.
3. Louis Schneider in the *Gaulois*, 17 June 1923; quoted in Buckle, *Diaghilev*, 412.

be its peak in *The Rite*. But now even *The Rite* had been surpassed: "After *Noces*, the magic vortex will extend to the very horizon." *Mavra* had been just a detour after all:

> The French public, which had resisted the deceptive *Mavra* ballyhoo, has been subdued and buffeted defenselessly in the rhythmic torrent of *Les noces*. Stravinsky has regained one of those magnificently rare successes that throw snobs, simpletons, the fastidious, the erudite, and the ignorant alike in one heap at an author's feet.... Such a brilliant victory, won under such conditions, puts Igor Stravinsky among the most powerful and irresistible geniuses music has ever boasted.

That "dazzling meteor that crosses our Western sky" was back on track, again beckoning the composers of France to follow in its life-giving train. Vuillermoz gave them a hearty send-off, plus a bit of fatherly advice: "It won't be by appropriating the technical inventions of *Le sacre* or *Les noces* that we will obtain a French Stravinsky: It will be by applying to our own folklore and our local traditions the creative and regenerative methods that this divine artist has magnificently developed."[4]

It was a masterpiece of wishful thinking based on a false chronology, this review; and perhaps, too, it was meant as a blandishment to help insure the fulfillment of the wish. But if it was that, it came far too late. The meteor had changed course irrevocably, and (what was worse) the composers of France were indeed following it (Cocteau fondly imagined they were leading it) in its new direction. The next Diaghilev season was one of the most prolific in terms of new productions, including a trio—Poulenc's *Les biches,* Auric's *Les fâcheux,* Milhaud's *Train bleu*—by the very composers who had declared themselves most vociferously for *Mavra*. Their work, as well as that of Rieti and Sauguet, whose compositions joined the Ballets Russes repertoire in 1925 and 1927, respectively, can be viewed along a line that passed through the opera of 1922, but not the "new" ballet of 1923. As we have observed, moreover, the *Octuor,* first performed four months after the *Svadebka* première, hooked up directly with *Mavra;* it can only have been the dazzling intervention of *Svadebka* itself that prevented contemporary observers from noticing the fact.

4. "... Un geste inutile ... influence active ... la révélation de l'orchestre de Rimsky et de l'écriture elliptique et puissante de Moussorgsky ... après *Noces,* la nuée tourbillonnante des envoûtes va s'étendre jusqu'aux confines de l'horizon.... Le public français, qui avait résisté au décevant partipris de *Mavra*, a été subjugué et roulé sans défense dans le torrent rythmique des *Noces*. Strawinsky a retrouvé là un de ces succès magnifiques, et si rares qui jettent pêle-mêle, aux pieds d'un auteur, les snobs, les simples, les délicats, les érudits et les ignorants.... Une victoire aussi brillante, remporté dans ces conditions, classe Igor Strawinsky parmi les génies les plus puissants et les plus irrésistibles dont se soit jamais glorifiée la musique ... bolide éblouissant qui traverse notre ciel musical d'Occident.... Ce n'est pas en utilisant les inventions techniques du *Sacre* ou des *Noces* que nous obtiendrons un Strawinsky français: c'est en appliquant à notre folklore et à nos traditions locales les méthodes créatrices et régénératrices que ce pieux artiste a magnifiquement utilisées" ("Noces—Igor Strawinsky," *Revue musicale* 4, no. 10 [August 1923]: 69–72).

What was mainly noticed about the *Octuor*, and about the piano works that followed it (the Concerto of 1923–24, the *Sonate* of 1924, the *Sérénade en la* of 1925), was the renunciation of national character in favor of a musical Esperanto with a lexicon heavily laced with self-conscious allusions to Bach, the perceived fountainhead of "universal" musical values. Within a few short years the "retour à Bach" would be absolutely *à l'ordre du jour* for musicians in the Parisian orbit. The phrase would come to signify the height of fashion, a fashion that would prove more durable than anyone at first suspected: "an art that wishes to be plain, brisk, nondescriptive, and even nonexpressive," in the words of one perceptive nonbeliever.[5] Yet because the lines of Stravinsky's development had been obscured by the misplaced *Svadebka* première, the *Octuor* produced for many a "general feeling of mystification . . . like a bad joke that left an unpleasant after-effect."[6] Among those who failed to take Stravinsky's neoclassical affectations seriously was Prokofiev, whose remarks (in letters to Myaskovsky) were both pungent and pertinent to our theme:

1 June 1924 (after the première of the Concerto): Stravinsky's Piano Concerto is fashioned after Bach and Handel, and that doesn't particularly appeal to me. . . . Here and there contemporary syncopated dance rhythms appear, which considerably freshens the scratched-up Bach. (Don't misunderstand me: I love old Sebastian, but I don't like faking him.)

5 March 1925: As to style and fashion, Stravinsky has been displaying a certain steadfastness of late: the Bachiness of this style could already be sensed in the octet, and now after the concerto a sonata has followed, once again in the same style. Stravinsky himself declares that he is creating a new epoch with this, and that this is the only way to write nowadays. For me personally *The Rite* and *Svadebka* are worth more.

4 August 1925: Stravinsky has delivered himself of a horrifying piano sonata, which he himself performs not without a certain chic. But the music itself sounds like Bach with smallpox.[7]

What seems remarkable is that even Prokofiev, Stravinsky's countryman, and one equally steeped in the heritage of the "Russian classics," should have been so distracted by the surface Bachiness as not only to lose sight of the stylistic and structural Russianisms that persisted in the Concerto and the *Sonate* (as they had in the *Octuor*), but even to miss the obvious thematic references with which both works abound. Alongside the pockmarked Bach and the contemporary dance rhythms, the first movement of the Concerto sports a thrice-recurring near-quotation from

5. "Un art qui se veut net, vigoureux, non descriptif, et même non expressif" (Charles Koechlin, "Le 'Retour à Bach,'" *Revue musicale* 8, no. 1 [November 1926]: 1–2).
6. Copland, *The New Music*, 72.
7. Kozlova and Yatsenko (eds.), *Prokof'yev i Myaskovskiy: perepiska*, 195, 211, 217–18.

EXAMPLE E.1

a. Chaikovsky, Fifth Symphony, II, mm. 67–68 (Moderato con anima), clarinet solo

b. Concerto, I, 3 before ⟨22⟩, oboe solo

the slow movement of the Chaikovsky Fifth Symphony, about as descriptive and expressive a piece as any (Ex. E.1). The second movement contains an incongruously wistful horn solo that unexpectedly reappears at a much faster tempo in the last movement of the horrifying *Sonate*. The tune in question has been likened by Casella to the music of Saint-Saëns,[8] and was also probably responsible for Edward Burlingame Hill's caustic comment on "a Stravinsky who, in striving to get 'back to Handel,' stalled on reaching César Franck"[9] (for it does sound a bit like the main theme of the Symphonic Variations). But it has a Chaikovskian resonance as well—and a particularly sentimental one at that, as a glance at such lachrymose effusions as the *Sérénade mélancolique* for violin or the *Tendres reproches* for piano (op. 72/3) will confirm (Ex. E.2).

It is striking to find sighs like these within the programmatically astringent Concerto, and they are what make credible (though Stravinsky didn't believe it) Leonard Bernstein's report that the piece had brought forth tears of nostalgia from Soviet audiences.[10] The way the sigh is turned into a pant in the *Sonate* perfectly illustrates the quality of irony that is such a necessary part of Stravinsky's early neoclassic style. But the nostalgia, however mocked or squeamishly disguised, was real enough; and however repressed or unacknowledged, it would be permanent.

Traces of Old Russia can be found in virtually any mid- or late-period Stravinsky piece, as Robert Craft has testified. Having resolved, after witnessing the composer's astonishing behavior on his Soviet visit in 1962, "to listen to his music . . . *sub specie patris* [*sic*]," Craft professed to have "discovered Russianisms even in *Pul-*

8. Alfredo Casella, *Igor Strawinski* (Rome: Formiggini, 1926), 133.
9. Edward Burlingame Hill, "The Young Composers' Movement," *Modern Music* 5, no. 4 (May–June 1928), 33.
10. D&D:200.

EXAMPLE E.2

a. Concerto, II, fig. 56, horn solo

mf cantabile

b. *Sonate*, III, mm. 26–30

staccatissimo

c. Chaikovsky, *Sérénade mélancolique*, entrance of soloist (m. 12)

d. Chaikovsky, *Tendres reproches*, op. 72/3

p molto espressivo

cinella," and observed further that "the Symphony in C seems to me now as nostalgically 'Russian' in its way as *Les Noces,* and Russia haunts Stravinsky's masterpiece *Oedipus Rex*."[11]

It would be wiser to take such covert Russianisms for granted than to attempt to catalogue them. Such a list would be too omnifarious to prove anything and too desultory to be of interest. Let us focus rather on those few items in Stravinsky's post-*Mavra* output that have an explicitly Russian content, and explore the relationship between that content and the style of the music, in hopes that such an inquiry will reflect some further illumination back upon the actual "Russian" period and provide a fitting conclusion to our study of it.

11. D&D:233.

Nineteen twenty-eight was the year in which Stravinsky's openly professed anti-modernism reached its peak. In that year he allowed himself to be described in print by Lourié as the leader of the "conservative and reactionary element" in contemporary music, the "antithesis" to the Schoenbergian "thesis," who sought "to affirm unity and unalterable substance" as against the ceaseless flux and disintegration of culture that was the inevitable consequence of modernist chaos. In the same article, Lourié made the unexpected declaration that "the order to return to Bach," issued by the leader only a few years earlier, had "had [its] day so far as movements are concerned." The chief surprise was the revelation that

> the musical heritage of the nineteenth century, so recently rejected, has acquired new recognition, it is being called upon to influence contemporary music. Hereafter the effort to create a new culture will probably be realized (if it is not already being achieved) by adapting and assimilating the elements of the earlier period into the later, without the sense of necessity to separate the one from the other. Our attitude toward the past century, moreover, has fundamentally changed. We are now far from looking back with scorn and condescension, conceding it only mediocre value. Today the opposite point of view has developed; we are, if anything, too reconciled, too inclined to exaggerate the importance of certain formulas of the past, some of which are banal and insignificant. We have even reached the point of raking up small fragments of that past simply because we find in them traces of good craftsmanship, of impersonality and perfected solidity, as, after an accident, we gather up the objects that have escaped destruction, especially those which may prove still to be of some use.[12]

This was a paragraph perfectly calculated to explain and justify the ballet on which Stravinsky had just begun work, one in which he was raking up some small fragments of Chaikovsky in which he had found traces of good impersonal craftsmanship, and putting them, he thought, to good use.

Like *Pulcinella,* with which it is often, if not quite justifiably, compared, *Le baiser de la fée* fell into Stravinsky's lap as an unanticipated commission (this time from Ida Rubinstein, who had set herself up as Diaghilev's rival) with a musical concept fully worked out in advance. That concept was the brainchild of Alexandre Benois, with whom Stravinsky had not collaborated since *The Nightingale.* Benois had written to the composer on 12 December 1927 with a proposal to "do something with Uncle Petya's music." He specified further that his idea was neither to adapt Chaikovsky's existing ballet music, nor to use excerpts from his symphonies, but rather "to choose certain piano pieces, which, together, would constitute a subject, or, better still, a base on which a subject could then be imposed, since the pieces would already be linked by purely musical affinities." He even proposed fourteen

12. Lourié, "Neogothic and Neoclassic," 5.

"candidates," of which Stravinsky ended up using more than half (they are designated by asterisks in Table 7).[13]

Evidently on the analogy with its ancestor, the Glazunov-Fokine *Chopiniana*, the project is referred to as "Tchaikovskyana" in Stravinsky's epistolary negotiations with Rubinstein.[14] It is unclear which of the parties came up with the idea of a scenario based on Andersen's "The Ice Maiden" ("La vierge des glaciers"), but it was Stravinsky who eventually changed the title to "The Fairy's Kiss." "Gradually," he wrote to Benois shortly before completing the piano score, "I find myself retaining only the skeleton of the story."[15] To his editor Païchadze he remarked, after finishing the full score, that "no hint of Andersen has survived."[16] In the end, it was indeed a "Tchaikovskyana" that he had composed.

The task of identifying the piano pieces that went, along with a few songs, into this score has been accomplished with great acumen by Lawrence Morton in a well-known article that also contains a great deal of shrewd commentary on Stravinsky's use of his borrowed goods.[17] Table 7 summarizes Morton's findings, meanwhile incorporating a few supplementary details and further identifications that have more recently surfaced both in the Soviet literature[18] and in the course of the present study.[19]

The formal organization of the ballet around the borrowed material—or more accurately, the deployment of the borrowed material to articulate the form of the ballet—will recall certain features of *Svadebka*. Both ballets end with reprises of their opening material, which thus attains a symbolic status. In *Le baiser de la fée* the effect is more nearly that of a conventional *Erinnerung*, the "Lullaby in the Storm" being so intimately bound up with the plot. (Indeed, the choice of the song may actually have determined the choice of subject.) In both ballets the first half of the second tableau consists of intercuttings between two preexistent items. Also familiar is the way the elements of op. 19/2 are reshuffled in the first part of the third tableau.

13. SelCorrI:172n.

14. P&D:283.

15. Letter of 12 August 1928; in P&D:284.

16. Letter of 26 October 1928; in P&D:638n.141.

17. "Stravinsky and Tchaikovsky: *Le Baiser de la Fée*," in *Stravinsky: A New Appraisal of His Work*, ed. Paul Henry Lang (New York: W. W. Norton, 1963), 47–60.

18. See Yarustovsky, *Stravinskiy*, 172; also Mikhaíl Mikhailov, "Esteticheskiy fenomen 'Potseluya fei,'" *Sovetskaya muzïka*, 1982, no. 8, 95–102.

19. Stravinsky's own recollections and his "checklist of sources," given first in the liner notes to his recording of the ballet with the Cleveland Orchestra (Columbia ML-5102 [1956]) and in expanded form in E&D:73–75/83–85, 158, have been superseded by the work of Morton et al. The main inaccuracies are twofold. One—attribution to himself of much that was derived from Chaikovsky—is characteristic of the composer; the other is highly uncharacteristic: he lists one source (*Scherzo à la russe*, op. 1, no. 1) that no one, not even Stravinsky, has ever been able to locate in the score (he may have been confusing Chaikovsky's *Scherzo à la russe* with his own). It must have been on Stravinsky's authority, moreover, that Schaeffner (*Strawinsky*, 116) asserted that the music at fig. [14] was "le seul thème que Strawinsky y ait inventé." Yet as Table 7 reveals, this passage was a development of music heard previously that can indeed be identified as Chaikovsky's.

TABLE 7
Chaikovsky in *Le baiser de la fée*

	Tableau I: Berceuse dans la tempête
0–[2], [3]–[10]	Op. 54/10, "*Kolïbel'naya pesn' v buryu*" ("Lullaby in the Storm"), words by Alexey Pleshcheyev (1883) (for opening melodic shape, cf. *Dumka* for Piano, op. 59 [1886], mm. 7–8):

	(for storm figuration cf. Tomsky's "Ballade of the Three Cards" in *The Queen of Spades*, Act I [no. 5])
[2]–[3], developed [14]–[18], [19]–[23]	Stravinsky claimed this melody for his own (E&D: 73/85), but Morton (p. 55) has argued plausibly that it is compounded of foreshadowings: motives from the Fifth Symphony (cf. [113] below) and from op. 6/3 (cf. [102]). For development figuration, cf. the Sixth Symphony, rehearsal letter I.
[13]–[14], [18], [23]+5–[25]	Op. 54/7, "*Zimniy vecher*" ("Winter Evening"), words by Pleshcheyev (1883): piano interlude
[25]−1 (and similar pickups), [27]–[31]	*Op. 40/10, "*Russkaya plyaska*" ("Russian Dance"), much altered. E.g.:

(Chaikovsky, mm. 12–14)

(Stravinsky, [28]−1)

[32]–[40]	Unidentified (i.e., neither claimed explicitly by Stravinsky nor found in Chaikovsky)
[40]–[42]	Op. 54/10 reprise
[42]–[43]	Op. 54/7 reprise
[43]–[44]+3	Op. 54/7, interlude figure inverted
	Tableau II: Une fête au village
[51]–[55], [75]–[78]	Winds: Op. 10/2, *Humoresque* (1871) Strings: *Op. 19/1, *Rêverie du soir* (1873)
55–63	Op. 10/2 (for string countermelody after [60], cf. Fourth Symphony, IV, 111–118)

TABLE 7 (*continued*)

[63]–[64], [68]–[70]	ᵏOp. 19/1, middle section
[64]–[68]	Op. 10/2
Countermelody at [64]+4	Op. 39/12 (1878), "*Muzhik na garmonike igrayet*" ("The Peasant Plays the Concertina")
[70]–[73]	*Op. 40/7, "*V derevne*" ("In the Village"), mm. 108ff.
[73]–[75], [89]–[91]	Unidentified. (In E&D:74/84 Stravinsky states, "No. 70 is my music, but no. 73 is Tchaikovsky." The reverse is likely to be true.)
[78]–[81], [82]+9 –[85]	*Op. 51/4, *Natha-Valse* (1882)
[82] (8 bars)	Op. 10/2 reprised as a waltz
[85]–[87]	Music at [73] reprised as a waltz
[87]–[89]	Op. 40/7 reprised as a waltz
[91]–[97]	Op. 10/2 reprised in original form
[97]–[101]	Op. 40/7, mainly mm. 14–21
[102]–[109], [114]–[120]	Op. 6/3, "*I bol'no i sladko*" ("Both Painful and Sweet"), words by Rostopchina (1869)
[113]–[114]	(first violins, cf. Fifth Symphony, II, m. 45)

Tableau III: Au moulin

[120]–[122]	*Op. 19/2, *Scherzo humoristique,* central episode of middle section
[122]–[131]	*Op. 19/2, main theme of middle section
[131]–[134], [140]–[143]	*Op. 19/2, beginning
[134]–[136]	*Op. 19/3, *Feuillet d'album,* mm. 24ff.
[143]–[146]	*Op. 19/3, beginning
[146]–[157]+3	≈[131]–[143] (Op. 19/2)
Pas de deux:	
Entrée: [156]–[166]	Op. 19/4, *Nocturne,* middle section. (At [160] Morton claims a fleeting citation of the middle section of op. 51/6, *Valse sentimentale.*)
Adagio: [167]–[175]	Op. 63/6, "Serenade," words by Grand Duke Konstantin Konstantinovich (1887)
Variation: [175]–[181]	Original?
Coda: [189]–[192]	*Op. 51/2, *Polka peu dansante* (1882), mm. 56ff. (also cf. *op. 51/1, *Valse de salon,* mm. 67ff.)
Scene:	
[205]–[213]	Op. 6/6 (1869), "*Net, tol'ko tot, kto znal*" ("None but the Lonely Heart"), words by Lev Mey, after Goethe ("Nur wer die Sehnsucht kennt")
[213]–[215]	Reprise of unidentified music at [37]–[39]

Tableau IV: Berceuse des demeures éternelles

[215]–end	Op. 54/10, reprise (for accompaniment figure, cf. Sixth Symphony, III, mm. 304ff.)

And yet there is a tremendous difference between the nature of Stravinsky's borrowings in his Chaikovsky ballet and his earlier habits of adaptation. Morton's comment that for Stravinsky, "Tchaikovsky's *oeuvre* is a storehouse of raw material, not unlike a collection of folk music,"[20] does not quite ring true; determining exactly why is instructive.

Partly it is because the Chaikovsky material in *Le baiser de la fée* is often so far from raw. Several fully elaborated passages, sections, and, in two cases (opp. 54/10 and 6/6), whole pieces are taken over from the older composer in a form almost as pristine as the "Pergolesi" items that went into *Pulcinella*. And yet the music of the *Fée* could never be described as an arrangement: Stravinsky's independent shaping hand intervenes at every turn, most dramatically perhaps from [14] to [23] in the first tableau, a lengthy passage that can fairly be described as an original development of Chaikovsky's themes (or to be pedantically precise, of a theme derived from two different melodies by Chaikovsky).

Partly it is because the borrowed material is stylistically so fully integrated with its surroundings. It never has the quality of a found object, like the Lanner and Spencer interpolations in *Petrushka*, to say nothing of the folk tunes. Nor is there ever a sense of stylistic jostling between the old model and its modern elaboration, as in parts of *Pulcinella*—or even *The Rite*, where the tension between the diatonic thematic surface and the octatonic harmonic texture gives the music so much of its characteristic flavor and evocative power. *Le baiser de la fée* lacks even the irony of what Prokofiev called the "Bachiness" of the *Octuor* or the Concerto.

And when irony goes, so does modernism. The melodic surface of the *Fée* is at one with its harmonic texture. Stravinsky seeks no shocks with his resolving dominants, as in *Mavra*. The harmony is not "éminentement tonale," as Poulenc had put it of the opera, it is tonal in a perfectly ordinary, unremarkable way. There is no dislocation, no defamiliarization. Nor, until the peroration on "None but the Lonely Heart," is there a single mixed or skewed harmony in the manner of *Pulcinella,* so full of pungent Turanian condiments and suppressed leading tones.

Moreover, while Morton's oft-quoted *mot* about the structure of the phrases— "instead of . . . Tchaikovsky's inevitable squares they are Stravinsky's rhomboids, scalenes, trapeziums or trapezoids"[21]—is surely justified with respect to the model, still, in comparison with the "Russian" Stravinsky the phraseology of the *Fée* is dowdy and most uncharacteristically prolix. The composer was obviously holding his rhythmic fantasy in check, allowing it exercise only within strictly delimited bounds, along tracks worn smooth by tradition, and—most un-Stravinskian of all—observing all the customary niceties of formal construction: transitions, developments, parallel periods, sequences. So much for *drobnost'*. As a result, and

20. Morton, "Stravinsky and Tchaikovsky," 59.
21. Ibid.

though it is rarely noted, *Le baiser de la fée* is Stravinsky's longest ballet; except for *Oedipus Rex* and *The Rake's Progress*, it is his longest work of any kind.

For Stravinsky borrowed from Chaikovsky far more than themes. To an extent unprecedented in his work he actually impersonated the style of his great compatriot. The *Fée* is deliberate, calculated imitation, nothing at all like the naïve imitations one finds in the earliest works, correctly described by critics of 1908 like Karatïgin with the word *priyomstvennost'* (reception), implying a natural assimilation. By 1928 there could be no question of *priyomstvennost'*, only *stilizatsiya:* "stylization," in the particular Russian sense of the word, implying a stylistic masquerade and a nullification of the self. Admittedly, Stravinsky possessed a self that not even he could extinguish, but he came closer to doing so in *Le baiser de la fée* than in any other piece he would ever write.

The matter went far beyond style. To a large (and openly acknowledged) extent, *Le baiser de la fée* was an outright imitation of *The Sleeping Beauty.* The orchestras are nearly identical.[22] While Stravinsky's usages are sometimes different from Chaikovsky's and reflective of his personal predilections—harp *près de la table* in the third-tableau Adagio; clarinets simultaneously staccato and legato in the immediately preceding Entrée; the obligatory lyrical solo for the trumpet in the Scène—more often his orchestration is of a studied Chaikovskianness (far more so than in his actual *Sleeping Beauty* orchestrations!), particularly as regards the "expressive" and most un-Stravinskianly soigné string writing, where his earlier hardboiled "neoclassic" manner had depended on the virtual suppression of the string section (*Mavra,* the Concerto, the *Octuor,* etc.).

By the orchestration alone Stravinsky was able to evoke certain specific passages in *The Sleeping Beauty*—passages he surely expected to be recognized. At the beginning of the third tableau, for example, he gave the *Scherzo humoristique,* op. 19/2, the exact colors of Chaikovsky's Entr'acte symphonique (no. 19), and in a more modest way accomplished a similar transformation in the Entrée, where Chaikovsky's *Nocturne,* op. 19/4, emerges sounding like a scaled-down version of the Panorama (no. 17).[23] The Grand pas d'action the Entrée introduces, moreover, with its pedantically labeled obligatory sections, each with its stereotyped beginning and ending formulas, goes beyond an imitation of *The Sleeping Beauty:* it is an elaborate obeisance to the formal requirements of the classical ballet à la Petipa—requirements thought outmoded since the time of Fokine (and by no one more

22. The only differences: Stravinsky has a third clarinet doubling bass clarinet; Chaikovsky has two cornets and two trumpets while Stravinsky has three trumpets; Chaikovsky's battery is larger, and includes a piano for an occasional special effect.

23. In *Expositions and Developments* Stravinsky evidently confused the Panorama with the Variation d'Aurore (no. 15b), one of the pieces he orchestrated for Diaghilev; by the same token, it must have been his recollection of having imitated Chaikovsky's Entr'acte symphonique in the *Fée* that led him to state erroneously that it had been one of the pieces he orchestrated for the 1921 "Sleeping Princess" (E&D:70, 74/81, 84).

than Stravinsky—see his letters to the Rimsky-Korsakov brothers quoted in Chapter 13).

In short, *Le baiser de la fée* was sheer pastiche, and a problem for critics (if not for audiences) since the *pasticheur* possessed so much more prestige at the time (and especially in the given place) than the *pastiché*. The usual way out has been to assert Stravinsky's mysterious transcendence of the conventions to which he was so ostentatiously submitting, and his magical success in correcting the shortcomings of his adopted preceptor. Henry Prunières, reviewing the first production for his *Revue musicale,* and making shrewd comparisons with *Pulcinella,* was already taking this tack:

> Yet this is not a ballet like *Pulcinella,* fabricated entirely out of fragments borrowed and laid end to end. *Pulcinella,* one has to say, is a miracle. This work, which may not contain as many as ten measures of Stravinsky, whose entire musical substance is by Pergolesi, is nevertheless one of Stravinsky's most personal compositions and one of those that have had the greatest influence on the fortunes of music. *Pulcinella* is no arrangement, but a creation.
>
> *Le baiser de la fée,* contrariwise, is nothing but a pastiche, one that is admirably done and that much surpasses the model. Never had Chaikovsky developed his ideas with such ingenuity and concision, never had he orchestrated with such care, guarding against fustian and triviality. Stravinsky here shows us how Chaikovsky ought to have written and struggles to avoid the habitual faults of his master.[24]

Thirty-four years later, Lawrence Morton was even more squeamish and intransigent: "At the very most, Stravinsky loves Tchaikovsky in spite of unforgivable faults. It is a love that is willed rather than inspired, a love *faute de mieux.* What Russian composer is there whom a Stravinsky could idealize? Thus it happens that the 'great artist' of the dedication has very little greatness and still less artistry in the score of *Le Baiser de la Fée.* All the virtues there are Stravinsky's." And stronger yet:

> Tchaikovsky's faults—his banalities and vulgarities and routine procedures—are composed *out* of the music, and Stravinsky's virtues are composed *into* it. Everywhere, Stravinsky invoked Tchaikovsky; everywhere he composed his own music.
>
> *Le Baiser de la Fée* is thus an act of criticism, criticism at its most rigorous. As a portrait of Tchaikovsky, it is no likeness at all, as that of Pergolesi was. . . . Neces-

24. "Il ne s'agit pas pourtant d'un ballet fabriqué entièrement comme *Pulcinella* avec des fragments empruntés et cousus bout à bout. *Pulcinella,* il faut bien le dire est un miracle. Cette oeuvre qui ne contient peut-être pas dix mesures de Strawinsky, dont toute la substance musicale est de Pergolèse, est quand même une des compositions les plus personnelles de Strawinsky et une de celles qui ont eu le plus d'influence sur les destinées de la musique. *Pulcinella* n'est pas un arrangement, mais une création. *Le Baiser de la Fée* au contraire n'est qu'un pastiche, pastiche admirablement fait et qui surpasse de beaucoup le modèle. Jamais Tchaikowsky n'a développé ses idées avec cette ingéniosité et cette concision[!], jamais il n'a orchestré avec tant de soin, se gardant des doublures et des trivialités. Strawinsky nous montre ici comment Tchaikowsky aurait dû écrire et s'efforce d'éviter les défauts habituels du maître" ("Les théâtres lyriques," *Revue musicale* 10, no. 3 [January 1929]: 243).

sarily, [Stravinsky] ignores the bulk of the music. For there is actually very little of which he can approve. . . . Even in the two categories to which Stravinsky limited his borrowings, there is not much acceptable music. When one goes through the complete piano music (a hundred-odd pieces) and the complete songs (another hundred), he sees how these works enlarge the figure of the tragic symphonist, the lachrymose sentimentalist—and, let it be said, the hack composer.[25]

To such a sycophantic screed one's first impulse is to offer a rejoinder in kind, such as Hans Keller's: "Tchaikovsky, though whole-heartedly accepted by naive music lovers and sophisticated composers alike, is still suspected by the West's intellectual lower middle class."[26] One hesitates only because one is sure that Morton inserted his odious remarks to appease his close friend, the Stravinsky of 1962, who probably found the Stravinsky of 1928 as incomprehensible as Morton so evidently did. The earlier Stravinsky had been thrilled with his restorative achievement in the *Fée* and proud to be found worthy of comparison on whatever terms with the premier composer of imperial Russia. He genuinely viewed as progress his great leap backward, as his 1929 New Year's greeting to Ansermet confirms: "Yes, you are right to say that this year, with *Apollo* and the *Fée,* was one of the most fruitful ones of my life, where my work is concerned, and one of the most significant in terms of development."[27]

To take the measure of that development one must compare the dreamily introspective *Fée,* nurtured and visually realized by charter Miriskusnik Benois, with the almost exactly contemporaneous *Pas d'acier,* Diaghilev's "Soviet" ballet, commissioned in opportunistic response to the strong Soviet showing at the Exposition internationale des arts décoratifs in 1925, with simplemindedly cacophonous music by Prokofiev and an impressive constructivist set by Georgiy Yakulov. We do not have Stravinsky's reaction to the *Pas,* but we have Benois's: "stupidity and affectation . . . something repulsive . . . cynical zeal."[28] Stravinsky's could not have been different. Indeed, his new undertaking with his old collaborator *was* in effect his reaction, in every sense of the word. Where the *Pas* fairly blared its actuality, contemporaneity, *Sachlichkeit,* the *Fée* was quintessentially and literally reactionary: a retreat into a blissful past—no longer an invented archaic world à la *Svadebka,* but the past as personally lived and experienced and enshrined in memory. No longer was it "Turania" but the actual Russia of the ancien régime for which Stravinsky now longed, and it was this he attempted to restore in his music.

And that is precisely why *Le baiser de la fée* has nothing to do with Stravinsky's "Russian" period, Russian though its sources happened to be. It was not merely because "Uncle Petya" was Russian that Stravinsky felt so close to him in 1928, but

25. Morton, "Stravinsky and Tchaikovsky," 49, 59–60.
26. Hans Keller, "Shostakovich's Twelfth Quartet," *Tempo,* no. 94 (Autumn 1970): 8.
27. SelCorrI:195.
28. Benois, *Reminiscences,* 381–82.

because he was, on planes both artistic and political, premodern. It was not the "tragic symphonist" that attracted Stravinsky, but the arbiter of the only classicism Russian music had ever known, the great master of what Balanchine so aptly called the "imperial style."[29] There was no irony in this attitude, nor was there any in the score, and no ambivalence—toward Chaikovsky, that is. We are all too apt nowadays to misunderstand the nature of the attitude, and of the relationship between the composer of *The Sleeping Beauty* and that of *Le baiser de la fée*. Theirs was above all else an affinity of class.

The last thing Chaikovsky meant to Stravinsky was "a symbol of the Russian music from which he himself stemmed, to which he has always remained umbilical."[30] As *Mavra* has taught us, that umbilical cord to Chaikovsky was a lifeline of Stravinsky's own making, and self-attached. He needed Chaikovsky most precisely when his true umbilical connections had snapped—even the one that joined him with Diaghilev. As Lourié put it, "Stravinsky had to connect himself with Chaikovsky; it was a natural reaction against outdated modernism."[31] The irony in the *Fée* is directed outward, not just at the "world of modernism" but at the whole modern world, and it is bitter. This gentle music was the fruit of crisis, of disillusion, and, it seemed, of exhaustion. Old enemies like Sabaneyev spoke gleefully of witnessing at last "the sunset of Stravinsky."[32]

The crisis was overcome by decade's end, in part through a renewal of religious faith. The *Symphony of Psalms* signaled relief: not only in its religious message but in the re-rejection of strings and the return to mobiles and octatonics. Stravinsky the *ur*-Russian and the modernist was back, and there was no longer a need for the Chaikovskian lifeline—until the next crisis, anyway, when the uprooted composer reattached it in Hollywood to write the *Danses concertantes* and the *Scènes de ballet*. Between 1920 and 1930 Stravinsky was Chaikovsky's votary, not his critic. One does not criticize one's life preserver until one has reached the shore.

THE RUSSIAN CHURCH CHORUSES (1926–34) AND *MASS* (1944–48)

On 9 April 1926 Stravinsky made confession and took communion for the first time in two decades. From then until the early American years, he would be a devoted son of the Orthodox church. He not only attended services; he also organized alms distributions, corresponded with priests (and even installed one in his house in Nice), contributed to monasteries, and studied religious books.[33] Like Chaikovsky

29. Solomon Volkov, *Balanchine's Tchaikovsky* (New York: Simon & Schuster, 1985), 127.

30. Morton, "Stravinsky and Tchaikovsky," 60.

31. Lourié, "Neogothic and Neoclassic," 8.

32. L. L. Sabaneyev, "Dawn or Dusk? Stravinsky's New Ballets," *Musical Times* 70 (1929): 406.

33. For details of Stravinsky's religious life during his Paris and early California years, see SelCorrII:40–45 (letters to Diaghilev); P&D:211–12, 628; and V. A. Ussachevsky, "My Saint Stravinsky," *Perspectives of New Music* 9, no. 2–10, no. 1 (1971): 34–38.

before him, and possibly in conscious emulation, Stravinsky was moved by his newfound religious zeal to make a musical offering to his church in the form of liturgical settings for actual service use ("*dlya tserkovnogo obikhoda*," as his manuscripts put it).[34]

The first of these settings, *Otche nash* (Pater Noster), is dated Paris, July 1926, shortly after Stravinsky's rededication. It is clear that the soprano part is modeled loosely on the traditional Orthodox chant melody (*znamenniy rospev*) for the Lord's Prayer, while the harmonic style, with its heavy emphasis on half-diminished cadential preparations ("subdominant plus sixth" in the minor), seems modeled on that of Chaikovsky's setting (Ex. E.3). The *Simvol verï* (Credo), dated Voreppe, 12 August 1932, is a sort of *falsobordone* in rapid-fire declamation, broadening at the ends of lines with occasional modest melismata. Comparison with the setting in Chaikovsky's *Liturgy of St. John Chrysostom*, op. 41 (1878), shows a basic similarity of approach, but in this case both composers were following the genre's traditional mode of delivery—necessary if the setting was to qualify for liturgical use. Stravinsky turns the restriction to good account. The patter and the line endings are temporally interrelated according to his characteristic habits of subtactile note-value equivalency. The result is a typically impersonal bit of Stravinskian ritual music, headed "Tutto molto metrico, non forte, non espress.," and thereafter devoid of dynamic or expression marks of any kind.

Bogoroditse devo, raduysya (Ave Maria), the last of the church choruses and the shortest, is dated "*Velikaya Sreda*" (Great Wednesday, i.e., Wednesday in Holy Week), 22 March/4 April 1934.[35] Like its companions a strictly homophonic "utilitarian" setting, it is musically far more distinguished. As an essay in pure diatonic modality it is worthy of setting beside such Swiss-period compositions as the fourth *Berceuse* or the "Volga Boatmen" harmonization. (The one chromatic touch, characteristically, is contrived to produce a recurring half-diminished cadential harmony.) The melody, not directly traceable to a preexistent model, recalls the *popevka* technique of *Svadebka*. Were it not for the pervasive cadential use of the D-minor triad, this piece could pass for a Russian-period composition.

The Stravinsky Archive contains a sketch for the beginning of a fourth chorus (R115), labeled by Stravinsky at some later date "in the Paris period" and—in "English"—"1930ties." A setting of the Cherubic Hymn (*Izhe Kheruvimi*), the ordinary chant that begins the Eucharist in the Orthodox Mass (*liturgiya*) and the portion of the Orthodox liturgy most frequently set by professional composers in the nineteenth century, this fourth chorus would have been the most elaborate of Stravinsky's church settings by far, judging by both the expansive treatment of the

---

34. The autographs (originals and revised versions of 1949 with Latin text), plus sketches, are collected together as a single item (Rothschild no. 96) in the Archive.

35. Craft notes (P&D:212) that the composer fell into the habit during this period of noting dates even in nonreligious scores according to the church calendar.

a. *Otche nash* (*znamenniy rospev*), transcribed from quadratic notation in *Obikhod notnago peniya* (Moscow: Sinodal'naya Tipografiya, 1775), through *"da priidet tsarstviye tvoye"* ("thy kingdom come")

b. Stravinsky setting (1926) up to the same words

c. Chaikovsky setting (1878) up to the same words

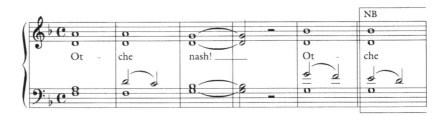

words and the freer deployment of the medium (Ex. E.4). The alto evidently carries as cantus firmus the "*Kievo-pecherskaya*" version of the traditional chant, i.e., the one used at the Crypt Monastery (*Pecherskaya lavra*) in Kiev, one of Orthodox Russia's holiest shrines.

Given their purpose, it is not surprising to find traces of traditional Slavic chant in these choruses, nor did the chants suffer any significant creative transformation such as the fifth-mode *dogmatik* from the Oktoechos underwent in becoming the central episode in the second tableau of *Svadebka* (see Chapter 17). Far more newsworthy was a young Soviet researcher's claim that ancient Russian and Georgian religious music was echoed in Stravinsky's Latin *Mass*, composed in the forties.[36] The hypothesis rested on evidence and materials with which we are long familiar: that the Swiss-period Stravinsky is known to have expressed (for instance, in a letter of 1916 to his mother) an interest in phonographically transcribed anthologies of Russian and Caucasian folk music and that he copied sixteen songs out of such an anthology around the same time (Archive, R25). Following Igor Blazhkov's commentary to the 1916 letter, the young researcher, Yelena Malïsheva, identified

36. Yelena Malïsheva, "O gruzinskikh istokakh messï," *Sovetskaya muzïka*, 1982, no. 7, 92–94.

a. Cherubic Hymn, excerpt (*Kievo-pecherskiy rospev*, transcribed from *Obikhod* of 1775)

b. Sketch for Kheruvimskaya (Paris, "1930-ties") in Stravinsky Archive, Rothschild no. 115

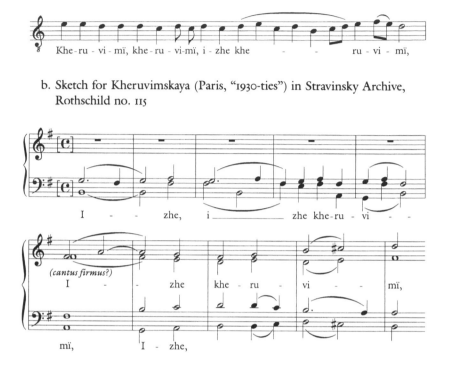

the source of the copied tunes as Arakishvili's publications in the first volume (1906) of the *Trudï MEK*. She then pointed to certain rhythmic, melodic, and harmonic resemblances between items in Arakishvili's collection and parts of Stravinsky's Gloria and Sanctus.

The evidence is as weak as the stylistic parallels. As noted in Chapter 17, the songs Stravinsky copied came not from Arakishvili's anthology but from a later one by Kargareteli; Malïsheva had simply accepted Blazhkov's speculations as fact. The copied songs do not exhibit the stylistic features cited as prototypes for the *Mass*. This in itself of course does not rule out the possibility that Stravinsky used the 1906 publication in its original form, since we have established the fact that he did at one time know and use the volume of the *Trudï* that contained Arakishvili's work.

What does rule out all the possibilities Malïsheva raises is the fact that at the time he wrote the *Mass*, Stravinsky did not have access to any of these sources—not even his own manuscript copies. His personal archive of musical scores had been left in Europe when he departed for America in 1939 (not, at the time, with any thought of emigrating, but merely to give the Norton Lectures at Harvard). The autographs were brought over by Soulima Stravinsky only in June 1948. The *Mass,* meanwhile, had been completed on 15 March. As for Stravinsky's folklore anthologies, they remained in the possession of his son Theodore Strawinsky in Geneva until the latter's death.

This is not the place for a detailed exposition of the matter, but the stylistic sources of the extremely archaistic *Mass* are to be found in the early Western music with which Stravinsky was becoming increasingly familiar during the 1930s and '40s, largely thanks to his contacts with Nadia Boulanger and Jacques Handschin in Europe and with academic musicologists in the United States beginning with Archibald T. Davison of Harvard, his frequent host during the period of the Norton Lectures, who was just then, together with Willi Apel, putting together the *Historical Anthology of Music* (*HAM*), doughty vade mecum to generations of American college music majors. Stravinsky was one of *HAM*'s most appetent pupils, and the *Mass* is the first of several late works that give evidence of the fact. Craft has called attention to "the influence of musicology on the composer," making special mention of Manfred Bukofzer of the University of California at Berkeley.[37] Correspondence with publishers in the Stravinsky Archive provides documentation that Stravinsky owned a broad range of musicological anthologies and scholarly editions, including such other standard classroom aids as Parrish and Ohl's *Masterpieces of Music Before 1750* and the Parrish *Treasury of Early Music.* The impact of such publications on Stravinsky's "American" work was far-reaching and deserves a special study. Suffice it to say here that the *Mass* was the earliest manifestation of this infatuation with the music of a remoter past than the one that had sustained his earlier "neoclassicism," and one of the most explicit.

SCHERZO À LA RUSSE AND SONATA FOR TWO PIANOS (1943–44)

After 22 June 1941 Stravinsky discovered, along with countless other White émigrés, that he was a Russian first and an anti-Bolshevik second. "He was the proudest Russian in Hollywood" during the war, writes Craft, "rejoicing in the victories of the Red Army, actively participating in Russian War Relief, and even going so far as to listen to Shostakovich's Symphony No. 7 when it was broadcast on July 19, 1942."[38] Vera Stravinsky's diaries record Soviet films enthusiastically viewed (including documentaries on Stalingrad and even speeches by Stalin himself), active fund-raising for the Russian American Actors' Mutual Aid Society, and participation in benefit concerts at the Shrine Auditorium in Los Angeles.[39] On 15 March 1944, at the request of the U.S. Office of War Information, Stravinsky dictated a

---

37. Craft, *Present Perspectives,* 311.
38. P&D:348.
39. Craft (ed.), *Dearest Bubushkin,* 130–33 passim.

message for publication overseas on the occasion of the hundredth anniversary of Rimsky-Korsakov's birth:

> With deepest emotion am I joining those who today commemorate the centenary of the great Russian master Nicolai Andreevich Rimsky-Korsakoff not only in a tribute to his genius but gratefully for his loving, unforgettable truly fatherly guidance in the very inception of my creative musical life.
> To the master and man whom I love I bow.
>
> Igor Stravinsky
Hollywood, March 1944[40]

More surprisingly, and apparently on his own initiative, Stravinsky sent a congratulatory telegram to Reinhold Glière, whom he had known only superficially in Russia, if at all, on the occasion of the seventieth birthday of the then-reigning dean of Soviet composers. The second sentence of this remarkable cable went well beyond the call of duty:

> 4 January 1945
>
> Let me join those numerous ones to congratulate you on your birthday celebration [the actual date of Glière's birth was 11 January]. Sincerely wish you strength and success for the furtherance of our Faterland's [*sic*] musical culture.
>
> Igor Strawinsky[41]

Those who only five years earlier had heard Stravinsky deliver his Harvard lectures, with their fierce repudiation of all Soviet art and music, would have been amazed at the reference to his Soviet Fatherland. They would have been even more amazed to see him enter into negotiations in 1942 with the Samuel Goldwyn studios for music to accompany *The North Star,* Lillian Hellman's socialist-realist film about guerrilla resistance to the fascist invaders in the first days of the "Great Patriotic War."[42] The movie was to be something of a musical à la *Alexander Nevsky,* with songs and choruses for which Ira Gershwin had been engaged to write lyrics. The project foundered over terms in January 1943,[43] but not before Stravinsky had sketched a considerable amount of music "on spec."

The Stravinsky Archive contains a draft (in R155) labeled "*Detskiy khorik*" ("Little Children's Chorus"), dated 18 January 1943, meticulously timed (to 1′08″) as film music must be (Ex. E.5). In another draft among the papers collected in R155, the same music appears in various more elaborate arrangements, including one for

---

40. Typescript in Stravinsky Archive.
41. IStrSM:493.
42. To his wife Stravinsky described Hellman's script as a *Schlafmittel*—a soporific (Craft [ed.], *Dearest Bubushkin,* 127).
43. Ibid.; also a *Time* magazine report (several years after the fact) of Stravinsky's negotiations with Goldwyn, reprinted in P&D:325–26. The commission finally went to Aaron Copland.

EXAMPLE E.5　*"Detskiy khorik"* ("Little Children's Chorus"), January 1943

1' 08''

two pianos (Ex. E.6). These sketches are unusual among the pencil drafts in Stravinsky's legacy in that they are written not on staves of his own ruling, but on standard-format music paper issued by the film studio for later submission to a subcontracted arranger. Although the time-saving but financially draining necessity of dividing the labor this way was one of the sticking points in Stravinsky's negotiations with Goldwyn, for a time at least he was evidently prepared to put up with it. It is easy to guess that the "*Detskiy khorik*" and its elaboration were intended for the last-day-of-school scene near the beginning of the picture: "*FULL SHOT: School Yard—Music over Sound Track*. About twenty-five children are hurrying into the building. There is much talk and much bustle."[44] What is somewhat less apparent is the fact that the chorus is a conflation of two authentic Russian dance songs, radically adapted to fit Gershwin's lyrics. The first is entitled "*U menya-l' vo sadochke*" ("In my little garden"), the second "*Vozle rechki, vozle mostu*" ("By the brook, by the bridge"). In Example E.7, the two songs are reproduced just as they are in the anthology from which Stravinsky took them, to show that he actually retained the keys of the original arrangements, exploiting their contrast, in characteristic fashion, as a *trouvaille*.

The source for these tunes was an old Jurgenson publication Stravinsky found and purchased (for $2.50) in a Los Angeles secondhand music shop in 1942: *Pesni russkogo naroda* (*Songs of the Russian People*), "collected and arranged for solo voice with piano accompaniment by M. Bernard," as the title page attests. The collector-arranger, Matvey (né Moritz) Ivanovich Bernard (1794–1871), was a pianist and composer of German-speaking Lettish stock who had emigrated to St. Petersburg where he studied with John Field and in 1829 founded a music magazine and a music publishing firm that became for a time the largest in Russia. His folk song anthology was first published in 1847 under his own imprint. The Jurgenson reprint was issued in 1886.

The collection is not one of the major Russian anthologies. In its breakdown of contents by genres it is modeled on the Lvov/Pratsch classic of 1790, and in the melodic-harmonic idiom of his arrangements, redolent of *rossiyskiye pesni,* Bernard stands in the tradition of Kashin (see Chapter 19). Stravinsky used the book strictly as a matter of convenience, the movie project having put him in need of Russian material in a hurry at a time when the anthologies he had formerly relied on were out of reach. The ample Bernard collection came first to hand and suited the immediate purpose well enough.

He mined the book extensively for *North Star;* and when the film project came to nought he transferred the music he had composed on the Bernard tunes, with customary frugality, to other pieces of the period. The "*Detskiy khorik,*" practically

44. Lillian Hellman, *The North Star: A Motion Picture About Some Russian People* (New York: Viking Press, 1943), 29.

EXAMPLE E.6   Trio II of *Scherzo à la russe,* arranged for two pianos on Maestro #108 12-staff piano transparencies (Rothschild no. 155). N.B.: Melody in brackets, mm. 16–23, inserted on the basis of an earlier pencil draft on film studio music paper

(continued)

EXAMPLE E.6 *(continued)*

EXAMPLE E.7

a. Matvey Bernard, *Pesni russkogo naroda,* p. 104

(continued)

[What have I in my pretty little garden, tra la la . . .]

b. Bernard, *Pesni,* p. 100

[By the river, by the bridge, the grass was growing . . .]

F I G . E . 1 . Pictorial title page and first section heading (*Pesni protyazhniye i tikhiye*) from *Pesni russkogo naroda*, an anthology by Matvey Ivanovich Bernard (1794–1871), first published in 1847. This was Stravinsky's main source of Russian folk tunes in the 1940s.

unchanged, became the Trio II in the *Scherzo à la russe,* a little potboiler (ostensibly named for Chaikovsky's op. 1/1) hurriedly assembled out of *North Star* shards on commission from Paul Whiteman's band.[45]

Although its sketches do not survive in the Archive, the canonic Trio I, with its delightful gusli tinkles in harp and piano, may be readily identified with one of the "Slow and Quiet Songs" ("*Pesni protyazhnïye i tikhiye*") in the first section of Bernard's anthology: "*U dorodnogo dobrogo molodtsa*" ("At the fine sleek lad's") (Ex. E.8).[46] As for the main scherzo theme, which many listeners find reminiscent of the "Russkaya" or the Coachmen's Dance in *Petrushka,* it does seem to echo the old "Along the Road to Piter" song (*Vdol' po Piterskoy*) made famous in the 1911 ballet—which, incidentally, Stravinsky had just recorded for Columbia, and which he would soon be reorchestrating from stem to stern. It is even closer, perhaps, to some of the Bernard tunes, as shown in Example E.9, where they are compared not with the scherzo theme as finally published, but with a loose jotting in R155 that ostensibly preserves the theme as it first occurred to the composer.

Even now that the entire thematic content of the *Scherzo à la russe* has been accounted for, we are by no means finished either with the *North Star* sketches or with the Bernard collection. Item R152 in the Archive contains a draft of some pastoral music for a chamber orchestra consisting of flute, oboe, English horn, two clarinets, two bassoons, trombone, and strings. That this was another sketch for *The North Star* follows not only from its having been written on film studio music paper, but also from the fact that it, too, is based on a "Slow and Quiet" song from Bernard (the ninth in that group), entitled "*Akh chto za milen'koy*" ("Ah, what a handsome lad"), with its metric structure subtly dislocated. What is even more remarkable, this film-score sketch eventually found a home in the first movement of the Sonata for Two Pianos, the earliest notations for which are dated 12 August 1943. In Example E.10 the Bernard tune is compared with Stravinsky's music in its more compact form, at m. 17 of the Sonata, where it furnishes the idyllic "second theme."

The existence of the second theme group from the Sonata in the form of an orchestral sketch—and the complementary existence of the Trio II from the *Scherzo à la russe* in a draft for two pianos replete with fingerings—suggest that the *Scherzo*

---

45. In M&C:102/108 Stravinsky went a little too far in asserting that the film music did not differ "in any way from its present concert form" (i.e., the *Scherzo*), as may be inferred from the fact that the prototype for the passage under discussion was vocal.

46. Having found a copy in Stravinsky's hand of another song from this section, identified by the anthologist's heading, Craft leapt to the erroneous conclusion that the composer was planning an original piece to be titled "Songs Lingering and Quiet" (*Present Perspectives,* 304). Bernard probably derived his section heading from the rubric "*protyazhno i tikho*" found in Russian liturgical books at moments of special solemnity (e.g., the *Vechnaya pamyat'* in the *panikhida* service, discussed in connection with the *Symphonies d'instruments à vent* in Chapter 18).

a. Bernard, *Pesni*, p. 15

[The sleek and jolly youth had . . .]

b. *Scherzo à la russe*, Trio I, 1 after ⬚11, piano and harp only

EXAMPLE E.9

a. Early jotting for *Scherzo à la russe,* main theme (Stravinsky Archive, Rothschild no. 155)

b. Bernard, *Pesni,* p. 105 (Quick and Dancing Songs, no. 27: "The Maids Went Walking in the Meadow")

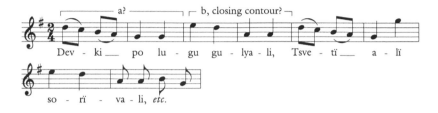

c. Bernard, *Pesni,* p. 42 (Slow and Quiet Songs, no. 38: "I'll Start Out Along the Street")

d. Bernard, *Pesni,* p. 66 (Slow and Quiet Songs, no. 62: "Oh, You Eyes")

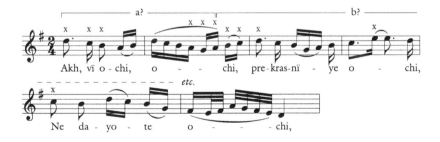

EXAMPLE E.10

a. Bernard, *Pesni,* p. 12 ("Akh, chto èto za mileñkoy")

[Ah, what a beauty . . .]

b. Sonata for Two Pianos, I, second theme

(continued)

and the Sonata were shaped out of a common fund of material, some of it in the form of particells, some in the form of two-piano drafts, all of it generated from the Bernard anthology for use in *The North Star.* Only a fraction of this material survives in the Archive today, but the accuracy of the surmise is supported by the surprising fact that all the thematic material in the Sonata, on its face surely one of the most chastely cosmopolitan of Stravinsky's neoclassical creations, can be traced to Bernard's anthology of Russian folk songs.

If we assume that the second-theme material cited in Example E.10 represents the earliest music to be developed out of Bernard for the first movement of the Sonata, it becomes easy to demonstrate the derivation of the first theme from the same source. The first three notes are taken from the ostinato that accompanies the second theme—in the context of the completed work, it is of course the ostinato that sounds like a derivation—while the rest is a cento of *popevki* drawn from no. 22 in the first section of Bernard, a *protyazhnaya* called "*Vspomni, moy lyubeznïy*" ("Remember, my beloved"; Ex. E.11).

The variations theme in the second movement, about which so much analytical ink has been spilled,[47] turns out to be another *protyazhnaya* from Bernard's "Slow and Quiet" section: no. 46, "*Ne poy, ne poy*" ("Sing not, sing not, my little nightingale"), transposed up a tone and transcribed in a manner that foreshadows the "isomelic" technique of the variations—that is, maintaining intervallic succession but with arbitrary alterations to rhythm and register.[48] Among the sketches for the Sonata is one, dated 30 January 1944, that shows the source melody in its original form and at its original pitch, followed immediately by a notation for what in the Sonata movement would become the third variation (Ex. E.12). There could be no better illustration of Stravinsky's technique of deriving new tunes isomelically from old.

The third movement is based straightforwardly on two "Slow and Quiet" melodies from Bernard. In the outer sections the source melody is an especially fa-

47. See Charles Burkhart, "Stravinsky's Revolving Canon," *Music Review* 29 (1968): 161–64, where the progressive expansion of the interval of imitation between *dux* and *comes* in the opening canon is discussed. An earlier article in the same journal—Donald C. Johns, "An Early Serial Idea of Stravinsky," *Music Review* 23 (1962): 305–13—had maintained that Stravinsky's variation technique in this movement, in which the pitch-class successions of the theme were held invariant while rhythm and register were freely manipulated, amounted to a sort of primitive row technique that utilized nothing but the prime form of a twenty-nine-note row, nor any transpositions save those along a traditional circle of fifths. (On such evidence any composition employing an ostinato might be called "serial.") Stravinsky's procedure might profitably be termed "isomelic," for this would point in the direction of the medieval pieces (in *HAM* and elsewhere) that probably gave him the idea.

48. This identification was first made by Lawrence Morton in his lecture at the International Stravinsky Symposium at the University of California, San Diego, in September 1982 (later published as "Stravinsky At Home" in Pasler [ed.], *Confronting Stravinsky,* 332–48). On the same occasion Morton identified the source of the theme of the trio section of the Sonata's last movement, to be discussed below. Morton was thus the first to reveal Stravinsky's dependence, in his works of the mid-1940s, on Bernard's folk song anthology. Quite strikingly, Mikhaíl Druskin (*Stravinskiy,* 68) singled out precisely the two spots in the Sonata for which Morton provided identifications from Bernard as having an "obviously Russian quality," even though he did not know the source, and even though they are far from the only themes in the Sonata that turn out to have Russian folk song antecedents.

a. Bernard, *Pesni,* p. 26 ("Vspomni, moy lyubeznïy")

[Recall, beloved, your former love, and how, beloved, you and she went out together.]

b. Sonata for Two Pianos, I, opening

EXAMPLE E.12

a. Sonata for Two Pianos, II, opening

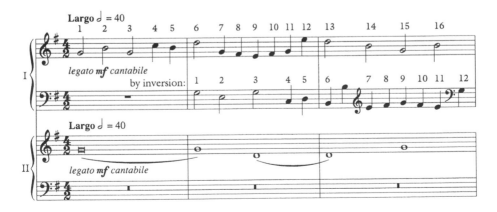

(*continued*)

b. Bernard, *Pesni*, p. 50 ("Ne poy, ne poy")

[Don't sing, my little nightingale. . .]

c. Sketch from Rothschild no. 152, dated 30 January 1944

mous *protyazhnaya* called "*Ne odna v polye dorozheń'ka*" ("There's more than one path across the field").[49] The tune migrates from voice to voice within Stravinsky's texture and is subjected to a certain amount of internal repetition and rhythmic distension. Nevertheless, the outlines of the familiar song emerge clearly enough to spark recognition in a properly expectant Russian ear. Stravinsky even allowed himself a couple of borrowings from Bernard's piano accompaniment this time: compare the ostinato in Stravinsky's mm. 2–6 (Ex. E.13a), allowing for the octave displacement, with the second group of four sixteenths in Bernard (Ex. E.13b), m. 7, left hand.

The trio, in the relative major, cites Bernard no. 16—a *protyazhnaya* entitled "*Akh, chto èto za serdtse*" ("Ah, what kind of a heart is this?")—more nearly literally than any other source tune in the Sonata (Ex. E.14). Therefore, this is the melody most likely to give its Russian origins away to a listener without preconceptions. Eric Walter White compared it to an "unexpected breeze from Volhynia," the guberniya in which the old Stravinsky estate at Ustilug had been located.[50]

Although White's observation was surely apt, and although, as Morton put it, "everyone who has played or even listened to the Sonata for Two Pianos is aware of some folk influence,"[51] it is no less true that by 1943 Stravinsky was approaching Russian folklore not as a neonationalist but very much from without, as one who, in Lourié's words, "no longer considers himself a Russian musician, but just a musician."[52] There is nothing to distinguish his opportunistic treatment of the Bernard tunes in the *Scherzo à la russe* from his adaptation of ten or a dozen melodies from "The Norway Music Album" for the *Four Norwegian Moods* composed the previous year as by-product of another aborted film project, *The Commandos Strike at Dawn*.[53] As for the Sonata, Stravinsky must have thought the provenance of its themes a nice private joke. He kept it from everyone: from Craft (who surely would have reported it), from Nadia Boulanger (who gave the première performance), from Alexandre Tansman (his California-period biographer), and from Lawrence Morton (who stumbled upon Bernard in the Stravinsky library while researching his long-awaited but alas unrealized monograph on the composer). He must have enjoyed the irony of the Sonata's reputation as "a model example of the neo-Classical style,"[54] to be understood in terms of its affinities with "the calm, poised, unpretentious and intimate instrumental style of the Viennese classical

49. For discussion and comparison of several variants of this tune and some earlier art-music adaptations, see Taruskin, " 'Little Star,' " 57–63.

50. White, *Stravinsky: The Composer and His Work*, 388.

51. Morton, "Stravinsky at Home," 335.

52. ". . . Ne se considère plus comme musicien russe, mais comme musicien tout court" (Arthur Lourié, "L'évolution de la musique russe," *Oeuvres nouvelles* 5 [1945]: 159–60).

53. For a discussion and a complete list of these borrowings, see Morton, "Stravinsky at Home," 337–41.

54. Paul Jacobs, liner notes to Nonesuch H-71347, "Igor Stravinsky: Music for Two Pianos and Piano Four Hands" (1978).

a. Sonata for Two Pianos, III, beginning

(continued)

EXAMPLE E.13 *(continued)*

b. Bernard, *Pesni*, p. 5 ("Ne odna v polye")

[More than one path crossed the field . . .]

a. Bernard, *Pesni,* p. 19 ("Akh, chto èto za serdtse!")

[Ah, what kind of heart is it that grieves within me, what kind of sweetheart torments me?]

b. Sonata for Two Pianos, III, middle section

(*continued*)

epoch,"[55] with "a pianistic style born of the toccatas and the violin sonatas of Bach," and even with Palestrinian cantus firmus technique.[56]

Yet there is a larger and deeper irony here as well. Now that we know the Sonata's thematic sources, the work emerges as a sort of metaphor of the Stravinskian condition as the composer approached what would be the biggest creative impasse of his career, a crisis described with characteristic one-sidedness, but not inaccurately, by Tikhon Khrennikov, the head of the Union of Soviet Composers, in a eulogy published two years after Stravinsky's death: "The drama of Stravinsky consisted in the fact that, living ... far from his homeland, he became ever more remote from the national source that had so fruitfully nourished his creative imagination during the first half of his life. The middle period of his career gave off several sparks of genius, . . . but after the thirties his inspiration gradually dissolved in the general 'universal' currents of European musical evolution."[57]

In just this way the Russian folk element that had formerly provided Stravinsky with his most potent avenues to musical innovation and his intransigently personal stylistic authenticity seems dissolved, in the Sonata for Two Pianos, into a generalized ambience of master-craftsmanly yet somewhat colorless purity. Stravinsky was now approaching folklore as his teacher had done half a century before: as a source of thematic material and nothing more. But where Rimsky-Korsakov had sought thematic material on two levels—that of musical substance and that of subject matter—and lovingly preserved the national coloration of his music (even if it was sometimes only a surface tint), Stravinsky, who had once sought a great deal more than thematics in folklore, now fastidiously denatured the national colora-

55. Robert Tangemann, "Stravinsky's Two-Piano Works" (1945), in *Stravinsky in "Modern Music," 1924–1946*, ed. Carol J. Oja (New York: Da Capo Press, 1982), 74.

56. Tansman, *Stravinsky,* 248–49.

57. IStrSM:8–9.

tion of his materials. For he had become the very spokesman of an extreme formalism that rejected the whole notion of "subject matter" in music.

He was assisted in this sterilizing project by the nature of his source, an anthology that had already subjected its contents to a degree of "Europeanization" in mode, phraseology, and harmonic affinity. Stravinsky was now attracted, moreover, precisely to the kind of ornately elaborate, "arty" folk song (epitomized by the *protyazhnaya*) that he had once explicitly rejected as irrelevant to his creative needs. For this type of Russian melody—especially as adapted by a Moritz Bernard— could play most innocuously on the surface of a smoothly decorative "pangermanoromanic" texture. For that very reason its presence was ultimately superfluous and its employment a peculiarly perverse *jeu d'esprit* of gratuitous concealment.

The Sonata for Two Pianos is a delightful essay *für Kenner und Liebhaber*. A connoisseur may always take pleasure and inspiration in watching a past master complete his appointed rounds. But its virtues, ironically enough, are quintessential "Belyayevets" virtues. In its formal and tonal orthodoxy, the Sonata is one Stravinsky work to which the adjective *academic* may be justly applied. That such a work should conceal traces of the same musical gunpowder Stravinsky had used to blast the foundations of that earlier academicism to which he had once subscribed does indeed define the "drama" of his career as of 1943—though one is surely entitled to add that it ill behooved Khrennikov, the official enforcer of a far more pronounced and retrogressive academicism, to point it out.

Yet however receptive we may be to the beauties of Stravinsky's forties output, and however hostile to the esthetic assumptions of a Khrennikov, we can hardly listen to the Sonata in light of its sources without sensing that the composer's powder was no longer altogether dry. Whatever his motives for saying so, Lourié was not wrong to conclude in 1945 that "Strawinsky s'est arrêté."[58]

Stravinsky's rejection of "modernism" caught up with him during the great modernist resurgence that followed the Second World War. *The Rake's Progress* left him exhausted, and its reception left him distraught. "After the première," Craft has recalled, "conducting concerts in Italy and Germany, Stravinsky found that he and Schoenberg were everywhere categorized as the reactionary and the progressive. What was worse, Stravinsky was acutely aware that the new generation was not interested in *The Rake*."[59] Where his self-proclaimed "reactionary" stance in the twenties had accorded with the temper of those times and had placed him at the forefront of a movement to which the youth of Europe could subscribe enthusiastically, with the beginnings of the Webern cult "Stravinsky, for the first time in his life, suffered from a fear that his music was being superseded."[60] The crisis, re-

58. Lourié, "L'évolution de la musique russe," 160.
59. Craft, "Assisting Stravinsky," 70.
60. Robert Craft to Joan Peyser, August 1982; quoted in Peyser, "Stravinsky-Craft, Inc.," *The American Scholar* 52 (1983): 516.

plete with breakdown and weeping, was reached in March 1952, after a performance of Schoenberg's Septet-Suite under Craft, who has pointed to the occasion as "the turning point in [Stravinsky's] later musical evolution."[61]

Craft's private story fits the public facts, for the influence of the Schoenberg composition on Stravinsky's own Septet, his first row composition, is obvious and has been frequently remarked.[62] But what is most poignant with respect to our present inquiry is that Craft's immediate prescription to Stravinsky, to help him over the crux, was to reinstrumentate the *Concertino* of 1920, "a work that the younger generation much admired."[63] This was a brilliant suggestion, bracketing as it did the whole "neoclassic" vagary, and putting Stravinsky back in touch with his "Russian" period, his "period of exploration and discovery," just as he was about to embark courageously upon another.

The question thus frames itself both naturally and urgently: is there any way in which the explorations and discoveries of the serial period can be related to those of the Russian? To what extent did Stravinsky recover his innovatory potency by returning to his roots?

REQUIEM CANTICLES (1966)

There is no work of Stravinsky after *Scherzo à la russe* with explicitly Russian thematic content, nor any yet discovered after the Sonata for Two Pianos with a hidden Russian source.[64] Nevertheless, the composer's deeply ingrained habits of Russian thinking and hearing continued to tell on the music of his last period, and even on its serial procedures. Pieter van den Toorn has shown how frequently the "Russian" T-S-T (0 2 3 5) tetrachord and especially the octatonic-specific (0 1 3 4) tetrachord crop up in Stravinskian rows, and also how Stravinsky continued to rely on the accumulated experience of fifty years' octatonic routine when it came to navigating his path from row form to row form in such early serial pieces as *Agon*

61. Craft, "Assisting Stravinsky," 71.

62. See, e.g., Leonard Stein, "Schoenberg and 'Kleine Modernsky,'" in Pasler (ed.), *Confronting Stravinsky*, 317. When delivering the paper orally at the International Stravinsky Symposium in San Diego, Stein was franker about the Septet's early reception among the Schoenbergians ("What a primitive piece!").

63. Craft, "Assisting Stravinsky," 71.

64. Excluded from this reckoning are arrangements or adaptations of older material like the "Russian Songs" (1953–54) or the Peasant Choruses (1954), likewise such revisitations of early works as the *Canon (On a Russian Popular Tune)* of 1965, a thirty-second "Concert Introduction or Encore" in which the main theme of the *Firebird* finale, reduced to a sequence of isochronous pitches, is made to run against itself at multiple levels ("prime form" in quarter notes, by inversion at the eleventh, by inversion and augmentation at the twelfth, by augmentation in syncopes at the octave, by augmentation at the lower fourth). The motivation for this strained concoction, so strangely lacking in Stravinskian finesse, is hard to fathom, unless it was to impress his friends at Princeton. It must have started out as a casual lark like the one (also dated 1965) shown in color in P&D: pl. 2, in which the "Danse russe" and the "Danse des nounous" from *Petrushka* are (somewhat more successfully) counterpointed. The latter has been recorded, incidentally, in an ad hoc instrumentation by Jürg Wyttenbach, on Tudor LP 73045 ("L'histoire de Strawinsky," a centennial commemoration originating at the Musikakademie, Basel).

and *Canticum sacrum*.[65] With reference to the riper twelve-tone works, Milton Babbitt has revealed the startling persistence of (0 3 6 9) and (0 4 8) symmetry as governors of "centricity" in music constructed according to Stravinsky's hexachordal transposition/rotation technique.[66] Such findings, more persuasively than any previously offered, testify to the essential continuity underlying what seemed the radical style-break of the early fifties, and specifically to the improbable resurfacing of Russian-period clichés in the serial music.[67]

It is thus not only appropriate but symbolic to close this book with a look at Stravinsky's last major work, the *Requiem Canticles,* considered in light not only of these suggestive analytical observations, but also in light of a remark by Nicolas Nabokov, an old pal from the Diaghilev days, who remained close to Stravinsky despite his inevitable estrangement from the music of the last period—which to Nabokov, as to most of Stravinsky's older acquaintances, "with a few exceptions . . . seemed remote and forbidding." And then all at once:

> Toward the very end of Stravinsky's life something changed. He wrote a piece, his last grand piece of music, the *Requiem Canticles.* Though in it he used the novel devices of serial technique, he somehow overpowered them. It was immediately, instinctively, totally lovable to me. I was able without any effort to penetrate into the essence of its tragic beauty. I was as fully taken and shaken by it as I used to be in the thirties and forties by every new composition of Stravinsky.[68]

In part this reaction must surely be attributed to sentiment: an aged, infirm composer at work on a requiem can mean only one thing. "*He* and *we* knew he was writing it for himself," as Vera Stravinsky put it to Robert Craft when they were planning the music for her husband's funeral.[69] By comparison with its immediate predecessors, moreover, from *Movements* (1959) to the orchestral *Variations* (1964), the *Requiem Canticles* are strikingly direct and uncomplicated in texture and rhythm. They are homophonic and pulsatile in the old Stravinsky manner. "What a shock," wrote an early reviewer, "after the intense, controlled densities of the marvelously inventive Variations to hear the almost ingenuous repeated-note fives of the Requiem Prelude!"[70] Gesturally the work is vivid, even obvious at times, with its tolling bells in the Postlude, suggestive of a church or a chiming clock, or the murmuring voices in the Libera me, where, in Craft's words, "the music leaves

65. Van den Toorn, *Music of Igor Stravinsky,* 402–26; also the discussion of the *Epitaphium* (1959) on pp. 433–35.

66. See Babbitt, "Order, Symmetry, and Centricity in Late Stravinsky," in Pasler (ed.), *Confronting Stravinsky,* 247–61, esp. the tables on pp. 252, 254, and 258, with their arresting vertical alignments of zeros, nines, and threes at the beginnings of hexachords (in *Movements*) and of zeros, fours, and eights plus octave-bisecting zeros and sixes (in the double-rowed *Requiem Canticles*).

67. It will be pertinent to recall the abundance of what, half a century later, Stravinsky would call symmetrically disposed "verticals" in the manipulation of the Firebird's leitmotif in his ballet of 1910 (see Chapter 9).

68. N. Nabokov, *Bagazh,* 179.

69. Craft, *Stravinsky: Chronicle of a Friendship,* 377.

70. Eric Salzman, "Current Chronicle: Princeton," *Musical Quarterly* 53 (1967): 81–83.

the concert hall and actually becomes part of a Requiem service."[71] For a composer whose music is so constantly labeled "hieratic" and compared with "ritual," the *Requiem Canticles* could hardly have seemed a more typical, not to say stereotypical, conception.

On the self-referential surface, the piece fairly reeks with nostalgia, quite belying the commonly expressed opinion that "Stravinsky kept no key to the past."[72] Those tolling bells in the Postlude recall a whole gamut of Stravinskiana, from the ending of *Svadebka* (the only previous Stravinsky composition to employ *campane*, orchestral tubular chimes) to the Graveyard scene in *The Rake's Progress*.[73] The *falsobordone* in the Libera me is a direct throwback to Stravinsky's 1932 setting of the Orthodox creed—and so is the actual harmony, ingeniously contrived to emphasize "liturgical" hollow fifths, octaves, and triads despite its strictly serial derivation (each chord being a verticalization of a transposed and cyclically permuted hexachord).[74] The litanic refrain harmony in the Interlude, consisting of a repeated chord always enunciated by flutes and horns (with timpani) in long-short pairs, is such an obvious reference to the *Symphonies d'instruments à vent* of 1920 that it is a wonder no critic or analyst seems yet to have reported the fact (the more so as the *Symphonies* shared the program with the "Requicles" on the latter's première performance at Princeton, 8 October 1966). Beyond these surface resemblances, Pierre Souvtchinsky has reflected on the *Svadebka*-like conclusion in a way that penetrates a bit beneath: it is "one of those endings, like that of *Les Noces*, which do not end, or end in infinity. And this is where Stravinsky adds a dimension to Western music."[75]

A quintessentially Stravinskian *nepodvizhnost'* pervades the *Requiem Canticles* and unquestionably refers back to his early manner. Those static punctuating chords in the Interlude are an example of this; but so is the habitual Stravinskian "stutter"—oscillation between contiguous pitches or simultaneities—that persists in the serial music, even across the boundaries between set forms (and nowhere more so than in the *Canticles*). It is one of Stravinsky's most characteristic "licenses" with respect to what is still often taken to be "classical" serial etiquette (Ex. E.15).

These are among the features that make the *Requiem Canticles* so uncommonly

71. Craft, *Chronicle of a Friendship*, 377.

72. Ernst Roth, "A Great Mind and a Great Spirit," *Tempo*, no. 81 (Summer 1967): 4.

73. Louis Andriessen and Elmer Schönberger took this evocative resonance as the springboard for an analysis of the Postlude's numerology that is both fascinating and moving (*Apollonian Clockwork*, chap. 2). Unfortunately, it is also inaccurate. The climactic Christological observation—that the "strokes of the clock" and the "chord of Death" come together for the first and only time in the last measure, at the thirty-third stroke of the clock and the thirty-third beat of the last section of the piece ("Wasn't there someone who died after 33 years?")—is based on a faulty count: the coincidence occurs either on the twenty-eighth or the thirty-first beat (depending on whether one starts to count from m. 298, a silent bar, or m. 299), not the thirty-third. The thirty-third beat is the last in the piece, and contains no attacks.

74. See Claudio Spies, "Notes on Stravinsky's Requiem Settings," in Cone and Boretz (eds.), *Perspectives on Schoenberg and Stravinsky*, 249.

75. Craft, *Stravinsky: Chronicle of a Friendship*, 329.

EXAMPLE E.15 *Requiem Canticles*

a. Exaudi, mm. 67–69, chorus only

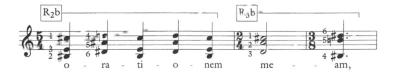

b. Dies Irae, mm. 88–89, flutes and xylophone only

c. Tuba mirum, mm. 125–35, bass soloist and bassoon

d. Lacrimosa, mm. 245–47

accessible to anyone who knows and cherishes Stravinsky's "Russian" manner. Just as surely, though, they are features incidental at best to row technique, and in some cases a bit at odds with it. Even with due recognition of the importance, to a composer like Stravinsky, of overcoming the "resistance" of his materials, it is neither a satisfying view of his serial music, nor one calculated to affirm its integrity, that considers what is personal and characteristic in the music to be the result of license or sly contrivance rather than the organic fruit of the method. The Libera me, especially, seems a strangely aberrant case if Stravinsky is thought to have, by dint of elaborate strategy, somehow wrested from the serial method a kind of harmony he might have composed without effort or qualm at an earlier phase of his career. That is why it is important to look further, to uncover the even more deeply embedded "Russian" features of the *Requiem Canticles* that may be brought to analytical consciousness only by probing Stravinsky's own characteristic and highly personal serial procedures.

———————

Although dodecaphony, in Stravinsky's own (dictated and edited) words, represented a rebirth of "rhythmic polyphony" and "melodic or intervallic construction" following the exhaustion of the "period of harmonic discovery,"[76] and although (in unedited conversation with a British journalist) Stravinsky the fledgling serialist declared himself to be "absolutely contrapunctical, like very few Russian composers even of the past,"[77] the fact remains that his late serial music is probably the most essentially harmonic—in the literal, vertical, chordal sense of the word—of any that may be found within the borders of the dodecaphonic

76. Conv:121/108–9.
77. Arthur Jacobs, "Talking with Igor Stravinsky," *Radio Times,* 21 May 1954, 8.

realm. Nor did he ever deny it: the 1959 *Conversations* abound in confessional remarks to the effect that "I compose vertically and that is, in one sense at least, to compose tonally"; that "I hear harmonically, of course, and I compose in the same way I always have"; and that his serial music was not only composed, it was also "intended to be heard vertically."[78] As will become clear in the necessarily brief description that follows of Stravinsky's methods of "composing vertically," they continued, even in his latest phase, to mark him as a Russian musical thinker, and point up deep-seated connections with his earlier—indeed, his earliest—musical and technical predilections.

This cannot be the place for a basic exposition of Stravinsky's late serial method.[79] Its most peculiar feature, possibly acquired in the first instance by studying certain compositions and theoretical writings by his Los Angeles neighbor Ernst Krenek,[80] consisted in partitioning the twelve-note series into two hexachords, which are then transposed in sequence by each of the intervals they contain. The standard way of effecting this sequence of transpositions is by "rotating" (or, as it is sometimes termed, "cyclically permuting") the hexachord so that each of the five transpositions will commence with the next order position in the series, transposed to the pitch of the first. So much Stravinsky may have picked up from Krenek. The operation about to be described, however, is uniquely Stravinskian.[81]

When an array of hexachordal transposition/rotations is arranged as a square, as in Example E.16, the columns reading up and down will yield five chords (plus a generating unison at the left). These chords—"verticals," in Stravinsky's nomenclature—consist of the collections of tones that stand in each respective order position within the six "rotated" hexachords. Their origin, as Stravinsky stressed in the one technical description he ever gave of the process, "lies not in an horizontal contrapunctical accord of different voices but in a vertical simultaneous clang (sounding?) of several notes belonging to a certain number of forms played together" (see Fig. E.2). As harmonic constructs they are only very tenuously related to the original series. In particular they have little or nothing to do with the series

---

78. Conv:22/24–25.

79. A good general introduction to the subject may be found in Van den Toorn, *Music of Igor Stravinsky,* chap. 14 (pp. 427–55), which contains detailed analyses of parts of *The Flood* and *Abraham and Isaac.* Briefer but especially lucid is the opening discussion in Paul Schuyler Phillips, "The Enigma of *Variations:* A Study of Stravinsky's Final Work for Orchestra," *Music Analysis* 3 (1984): 69–89. Milton Babbitt's more elliptical analyses of *Movements* in "Order, Symmetry, and Centricity" and in "Stravinsky's Verticals and Schoenberg's Diagonals: A Twist of Fate," in *Stravinsky Retrospectives,* ed. Ethan Haimo and Paul Johnson (Lincoln: University of Nebraska Press, 1987), 15–35, may then be tackled. The centric implications of Stravinsky's methods are explored in Charles Wuorinen and Jeffrey Kresky, "On the Significance of Stravinsky's Last Works," in Pasler (ed.), *Confronting Stravinsky,* 262–70.

80. See Babbitt, "Stravinsky's Verticals and Schoenberg's Diagonals," 19–20; also Catherine Hogan, " 'Threni': Stravinsky's Debt to Krenek," *Tempo,* no. 141 (1982): 22–25.

81. It has since been taken up by such composers as Oliver Knussen, Charles Wuorinen, and Peter Lieberson, son of Stravinsky's Columbia Records producer. Wuorinen has included a didactic exposition of it in his textbook *Simple Composition* (New York: Longman, 1979), 105–9.

a. Set 1 IRa, rotation/transpositions

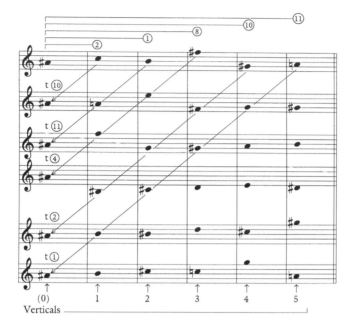

b. Set 2 IRa, rotation/transpositions

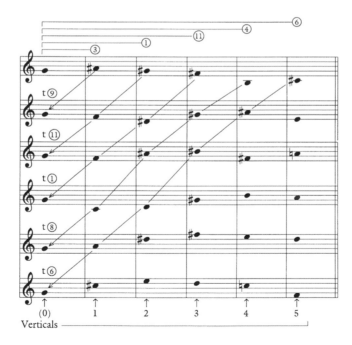

FIG. E.2. Stravinsky's own demonstration of his "transposition/rotation" method of cyclically permuting serial hexachords. An accompanying note reads, "Some stressed octaves and fifths and doubled intervals which could be found in this score [*Variations*] shouldn't contradict the serial (and not harmonical) basis of the composition; the origin of it lies not in an horisontal [*sic*] contrapunctical accord of different voices but in a vertical similtaneous [*sic*] clang (sounding?) of several notes belonging to a certain number of forms played together." Note that the resulting "vertical" chosen for illustration is an old Stravinskian "clang," the major/minor triad (0 3 4 7), referable to the octatonic collection.

qua series—that is, a temporally unfolding sequence or succession of intervals—and therefore have a rather ambiguous status as serial phenomena. Stravinsky nevertheless emphasized that for him "they shouldn't contradict the serial basis of the composition."[82]

In what is surely the shrewdest comment to date on this theoretically somewhat problematical innovation of Stravinsky's, Milton Babbitt has noted that if the " 'verticals' . . . have no predecessors in serial or preserial composition," they nevertheless have distinct "attitudinal" antecedents in Russian music. Citing Rimsky-Korsakov and Scriabin, Babbitt speaks of the Russian propensity for conceiving harmony in such a way that "the 'chord' is regarded more as a thing-in-itself, a collection, even as a spatial and temporal ordering of pitches, than in its tonally functional role," that is, within a directed progression.[83]

The "attitude" Babbitt describes, of course, is a manifestation of the same *drobnost'* we have been observing in Stravinsky's music since the time of his early piano sonata, always a distinguishing characteristic of the St. Petersburg strain of Russian music. Chaikovsky, though his description is framed as damagingly as he could manage, had put his finger on that trait as early as 1880: "What is the so-called New Russian School but the cult of varied and pungent harmonies, of original orchestral combinations and every kind of purely external effect? Musical ideas give place to this or that union of sounds. Formerly there was composition, creation; now (with few exceptions) there is only research and contrivance."[84] Stravinsky's own pseudohistorical description of the decline and fall of harmonic tonality, and of the place of harmony within his dodecaphonic technique, jibes perfectly both with Chaikovsky's complaint and with Babbitt's insight: "Harmony, considered as a doctrine dealing with chords and chord relations, has had a brilliant but short history. This history shows that chords gradually abandoned their direct function of harmonic guidance and began to seduce with the individual splendors of their harmonic effects. . . . When I say that I still compose 'harmonically' I mean to use the word in a special sense and without reference to chord relations."[85]

A sense of harmony devoid of reference to chord relations can only mean one that regards chords as static entities, products of "research and contrivance," as Chaikovsky says, or, as Babbitt puts it, self-referential "things in themselves": one thinks immediately of Scriabin's "mystic chord," as well as the *Petrushka* chord, the "Auguries" chord in *The Rite of Spring,* and all those other Stravinsky chords that have been given names. Babbitt continues:

82. Draft for a program note to *Abraham and Isaac* (1964), quoted in Craft (ed.), *Stravinsky Scrapbook,* 120.
83. Babbitt, "Stravinsky's Verticals and Schoenberg's Diagonals," 19.
84. To N. F. von Meck, 18/(30) July 1880; in M. Chaikovsky (ed.), *Life and Letters of Peter Ilich Tchaikovsky,* 382.
85. Conv:121/108–9.

The "chord" as compositional premise, as sonorous object, as "tonic sonority," as generative source was not exclusively Slavic, and Stravinsky's "verticals" stand in a different hierarchical position, as consequences rather than as antecedents, but the conceptual resemblance is unmistakable, and the relations necessarily induced by the successive transpositions are generalized instances of the notion of associative harmony, which is just "contextually coherent" harmony.[86]

Contextually coherent harmony: what better way to characterize the "triadic octatonicism" of *Sadko* (described in Chapter 4), the octatonically induced tonal relationships of Scriabin's Seventh Sonata (Chapter 11), the mirror writing in Stravinsky's own *Fireworks,* op. 4 (Chapter 5), or the elaborately symmetrical chromatic progressions in *Zvezdolikii,* with their circulations through the octatonic collections? And these principles of factitious harmonic coherence still survive, in an astonishingly concrete and specific way, in such passages in the *Requiem Canticles* as the final "cadence" of the Exaudi or, more elaborately, the whole Lacrimosa, which (like the fifth of the *Movements* for piano and orchestra) derives its structural coherence from an exhaustive "construction of twelve verticals"—in reality nothing more than the sums of the columns in the two hexachordal arrays generated from the original row as in Example E.16, sounded one element at a time, moving systematically from left to right across the board. "Associative harmony" indeed.

But of course there is more to it than that. Just how concrete and specific the relationship was between Stravinsky's earliest manner of harmonic research and contrivance and his latest will emerge from a few technical observations on the nature of "verticals" in general, and those in the *Requiem Canticles* in particular.

Let us return for a moment to Example E.16, where we see the complete array of transposition/rotations for the first hexachord of the inverted retrograde in each of the two sets used in the *Canticles*[87] (the inverted retrograde having been chosen for illustration because most of the verticals actually used in the piece happen to have been derived from it). As will be readily observed by comparing the intervals (computed in semitones) of the transpositions with those making up the content of the hexachords, the former are the inversions (or, in mathematical terms, the complements to sum 12) of the latter. This leads to the interesting situation whereby the verticals produced by any hexachordal transposition/rotation will invariably be arranged symmetrically around the generating pitch, the latter thus assuming the role of a tone center ("center" being construed here in its most literal sense). That is to say, verticals 1 + 5, 2 + 4, and 3 (self-inverting) in the array given in Example E.16a can be symmetrically displayed around the pitch class A-sharp,

---

86. Babbitt, "Stravinsky's Verticals and Schoenberg's Diagonals," 19.
87. The two sets are apportioned in the work as follows: Exaudi, Rex tremendae, and Lacrimosa are based on series 1; the Prelude, Dies irae, Tuba mirum, and Libera me are based on series 2. As will be demonstrated in detail below, the Interlude and Postlude make use of both sets, the former in alternation, the latter simultaneously.

EXAMPLE E.17 Symmetrical structure of verticals

a. Set 1

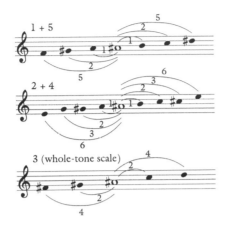

b. Set 2

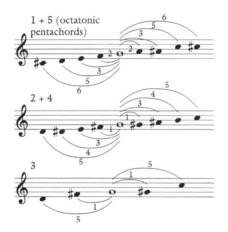

while their counterparts in Example E.16b will so arrange themselves around G, as demonstrated in Example E.17.[88]

Babbitt calls this phenomenon a "bonus . . . apparently unanticipated by Stravinsky."[89] On the contrary, it is hard to imagine what might have motivated Stravinsky so strongly to explore the transposition/rotation technique in the first place if not its potential for yielding inversionally symmetrical harmonies, includ-

88. For a formal description of the procedure, demonstrating how the inversional relations are an inherent function of the transpositional and permutational operations employed, see Babbitt, "Contemporary Music Composition and Music Theory as Contemporary Intellectual History," in *Perspectives in Musicology,* ed. Barry S. Brook et al. (New York: W. W. Norton, 1972), 166–67.

89. Babbitt, "Order, Symmetry, and Centricity," 259.

ing some Stravinskian perennials. It was a new entrée into what for him was most familiar and congenial harmonic terrain. In fact, it expanded the potential vocabulary of symmetrical harmonic constructs to which Stravinsky had methodical access, and offered a new perspective on those symmetrical pitch collections—whole tone and, of course especially, octatonic—that had furnished the stylistic bedrock of Stravinsky's Russian manner.

The self-inverting "middle" vertical (position 3) in each of the hexachords displayed in Example E.16 is nothing else but a French-sixth chord, familiar to us as the collection common to the whole-tone and octatonic scales. What is more, the actual pitch-class content of the two chords is identical, testifying to the close if hidden relationship between the two sets from which they derive. Nor will it be missed that the tetrachords on either side of the pivot in the sum of verticals 1 + 5 in Example E.17b are (0 1 3 4) octatonic half-scales. The (0 1 3 4) tetrachord, moreover, is the self-inverting "middle" vertical produced by the complementary hexachord of series 1, and the sum of verticals 1 + 5 in that hexachord yields the complete octatonic collection. Let it be also entered as evidence that vertical 1 in Example E.16a is a conspicuous subset of the octatonically referable *Petrushka* chord, and that when added to its reciprocal, vertical 5 (which is of course the inversion of the subset in question), it yields a six-note subset of the octatonic collection.

The abundance of traditionally Stravinskian material the *Requiem Canticle* sets generate upon hexachordal transposition/rotation seems little short of astonishing. But on reflection, it need not astonish; the whole-tone/octatonic bias is thoroughly researched and contrived, having been built into the structure of the sets themselves, the close relationship between which has been often remarked in the literature.[90] That structural relationship has always posed something of a riddle: if the two sets are indeed so close, why were they both needed to compose the piece? Let us defer the answer for now (there *will* be an answer) and consider the sets in light of the foregoing discussion.

In both sets (Ex. E.18), five notes in each hexachord refer to a single octatonic collection. The disposition is reciprocal: hexachords 1a and 2b refer to Collection III, their opposite numbers to Collection II. The opening trichord of 2a, moreover, is one intimately associated with Stravinsky's earlier octatonic usages; in Chapter 12 we christened it the "*Rite* chord."

These octatonic proclivities are very strongly asserted on the chordal surface of the Prelude. The pulsing harmonies in that movement are derived from a simple traversal of set 2, conjoined with its retrograde, so that the piece both begins and ends with the first trichord of the set, as shown in Example E.18. The first unbroken series of these pulses (mm. 1–7) is built on the first hexachord—with the ex-

90. Spies, "Notes," 233–34; Babbitt, "Order, Symmetry, and Centricity," 255, 258–59.

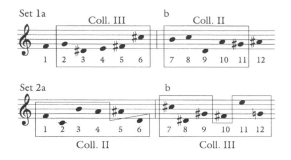

ception of note 5, the "odd" note (i.e., the single pitch class that is not referable to Collection II). Instead, the pitch class in question, A-sharp, is partitioned out to initiate the violin solo in m. 4. The partition invests the A-sharp with a double function: it simultaneously occupies the fifth position in the first hexachord of set 2 (hexachord 2a in the terminology of Stravinsky's serial charts as reproduced by Spies and adapted in Example E.18) and the first position in the first rotation/transposition of the opening hexachord of the same row's retrograde form (R_1a) at the further transposition of a tritone. That is why Stravinsky chose R_1a to furnish the pitch sequence for the violin solo in mm. 4–7. It is practically the unique instance in the *Requiem Canticles* of what is in any case an extreme rarity in Stravinsky's serial music: viz., the transposition of a "rotated" hexachord to a pitch level that is not the product of the rotation operation itself. The explanation for the anomaly must be sought, it seems, precisely in the need to filter the "foreign" pitch out of the pulsing prelude chords, leaving them wholly referable to the octatonic collection, and therefore "Stravinskian" in a way that a Nabokov (or a Haieff, or a Markevitch) could readily recognize and identify with.

Besides the emphatic *Rite* chord—which, in a fashion that fairly parodies the "Augures printaniers," is repeated thirty-two times to bring the Prelude to a conclusion (and which will resurface to stand alone in the choral echoes of the Dies Irae outbursts in mm. 83–84 and 98–102)—two other harmonies of long-standing Stravinskian pedigree are spotlit in the course of the brief opening movement. The accompanying pulses in mm. 25–33 (a total of forty-four iterations) comprise positions 1–4 in hexachord 2b (in context, positions 3–6 of the retrograde series), which as an aggregate yield the anhemitonic (0 2 5 7) tetrachord of *Petrushka*'s opening "*garmoshka*" music. After a silent bar, the pulse is resumed (mm. 35–46) with the last note of hexachord Ra plus the first two pitches of Rb (in terms of Example E.18, these are positions 5–7 in set 2), which combine to form the octatonic major/minor trichord (0 3 4). Between the notes of this chord and those of the concluding *Rite* chord, the series provides an intervening *A* (order position 4). Stravinsky nonchalantly omitted it (Ex. E.19), perhaps justifying the ploy on the

EXAMPLE E.19 Harmonies derived
from set 2 retrograde in Prelude

a. Mm. 25 – 33

b. Mm. 36 – 46

c. Mm. 47 – 54

grounds that the scamped pitch occurs several times in the parts running above. Can one doubt that he was bent on ferreting out harmonies calculated to evoke a shock of recognition from connoisseurs of his "Russian" idiom?

The Lacrimosa is at once the section of the *Requiem Canticles* most thoroughly composed out of transposition/rotations (involving the two IR—"inverted retrograde"—hexachords and the resultant "verticals" as shown in Example E.16) and, by no means coincidentally, the one most saturated with traditional octatonic sonorities. The vocal line begins with the retrograde of the fifth transposition/rotation of the "b" hexachord (that is to say, at the lower-right extremity of the chart from which Stravinsky worked) and snakes its way up through the array before switching over to the "a" hexachord and snaking its way back down.[91] Hexachord IR$_5$b has its "odd" note at the beginning, which perhaps explains why Stravinsky started at the end. For the first five of its notes, then, the vocal line in the Lacrimosa is referable to Collection II, and so are the accompanying "vertical" in the

91. For a complete description of this process, see Spies, "Notes," 245–48, with reference to the chart of rotations and verticals on p. 236.

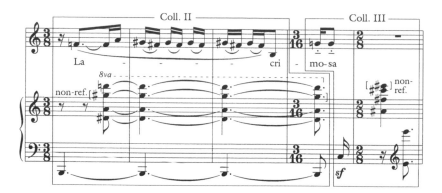

flutes and the bass note in the double bass and harp (the latter derived from the untransposed "a" hexachord of the retrograde). Moreover, the first four notes of the voice hexachord make up the (0 1 3 4) octatonic tetrachord, presented—just as it was, forty-three years earlier, in the Tema of the *Octuor* variations (see Ex. 19.35)—as a third (0 4) filled in by a second (1 3). Stravinsky underscores this reminiscence with a characteristic "stutter" (Ex. E.20).

At m. 232, both the voice part and the bass move to pitches referable to Collection III, as is (mostly) the accompanying flute "vertical." The harmony produced, in fact, is nothing other than a *Petrushka* chord (excepting only the E-sharp in the piccolo, which however can be referred back to Collection II). The bridging passage for the trombones at m. 234 (derived from I_1a) exactly duplicates the pitch content of the preceding vocal phrase, with the odd note similarly placed, so that we have in effect a return to Collection II. The next combination (m. 235), consisting of IR_4b in the voice, "vertical" no. 3 (from IRb) in the flutes, and notes 1–4 of Ra in the bass instruments, juxtaposes Collection III melody with Collection II harmony. And so it goes. The music in Example E.20 could almost have come out of *Zvezdolikiy*.

Alongside the verticals technique described by Babbitt and others, first employed in the *Movements,* and best exemplified within the *Requiem Canticles* by the Lacrimosa, there is another type of vertical construction in the *Requiem Canticles* that is unique to that composition, and even more explicit in its symmetric/centric properties, since it makes actual what is only virtual in the usual verticals technique: namely, literal pitch-class centricity as (in Babbitt's words) "the compositional point of convergence of all the symmetries."[92] As a serial operation it is so

92. Babbitt, "Stravinsky's Verticals and Schoenberg's Diagonals," 30.

artless that no analyst approaching Stravinsky from a Schoenbergian perspective has dreamed of looking for it; yet it perfectly epitomizes Stravinsky's brand of twelve-tone Turanian tonality.

At three points in the *Requiem Canticles* Stravinsky generates passages of four-part chordal harmony by simply running the basic untransposed forms of the complete set concurrently. The first of these takes place near the end of the first choral movement, the Exaudi (mm. 71–76). Series 1 in its prime form (P) is set against its own retrograde (R), the retrograde of its inversion (RI), and the peculiarly Stravinskian "retrograde of the inverted retrograde" (R/IR), the latter differing from what Stravinsky called the inversion only by its pitch level (in this case it is the lower major second or, in formal language, t10). In terms of Stravinsky's serial charts as reproduced by Spies,[93] these forms correspond to the prime and the retrograde read left to right, and the inversion and the inverted retrograde read right to left (see Ex. E.21, in which the set forms are distinguished by the shape of their note-heads: round for P, square for R, triangular for RI and diamond for R/IR).

Because we are dealing simultaneously with two inversionally related pairs (P and R/IR; R and RI) and with two reversibly related pairs (P and R; RI and R/IR), a situation like the one Babbitt described with respect to verticals again arises: symmetrically placed columns yield sums with inversionally/reversibly symmetrical intervallic content. But since there was no uniform starting point at "zero," there is consequently no single axis of symmetry. And since there is an even number of elements, there is no "middle vertical" that is itself inevitably self-inverting (though many of the individual columns do fortuitously produce such collections). Furthermore, while some of the sum-collections (namely, those referable to the whole-tone scales) have single axes of symmetry corresponding variously to the starting points of P and R, conditions are such that there is nothing to prevent the axis of symmetry from being a semitone pair (what Perle calls an "odd axis").[94] Under such circumstances there can be no inherent global centricity (although A-sharp is contextually singled out as the pitch of priority in the present case: the passage quoted is followed by one in which whole sequences of regular verticals produced by the IRa hexachord are sounded in succession over the "zero pitch" A-sharp, held as a pedal).

The next instance of the concurrent-set-forms device is an especially interesting one, because it accounts for the generation of the static *Symphonies*-like chord at the beginning of the Interlude. It has been claimed, by those eager to connect Stravinsky's serial technique with Schoenberg's, that this six-note chord is the sum of the initial trichord of set 1 and that of the combinatorially related transposition of its

93. Spies, "Notes," 236.

94. George Perle, *Twelve-Tone Tonality* (Berkeley and Los Angeles: University of California Press, 1977), 7–8.

EXAMPLE E.21   Exaudi: the last choral phrase (mm. 71–76) analyzed

a. The row forms

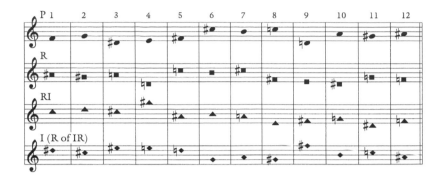

b. Their simultaneous deployment

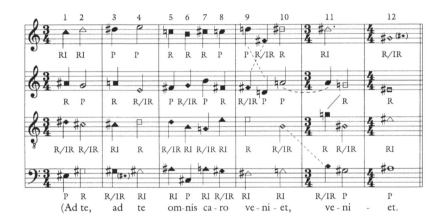

c. Symmetrical sums

inversion at the fourth.[95] However prevalent and potent in Schoenberg's music, the technique of combining inversionally related hexachords at transpositions that yield twelve-tone aggregates (what Babbitt has christened "combinatoriality") was rarely if ever exploited by Stravinsky, who was, in his concern for pitch centricity, extremely chary of transpositions generated by any other means than his own hexachordal rotation technique. There is no evidence that Stravinsky was even aware of Schoenberg's "combinatorial" practice, although he did pay occasional lip-service to Babbitt's term. As for the refrain chord in the Interlude, it is generated by a fourfold array of basic functions that is even simpler than the one just discussed: a mere concurrence of the P, R, I, and IR forms of set 1, just as they are found on the basic serial chart (Ex. E.22; note-heads differentiated as before).

In this case the simultaneities have been fudged to a degree, apparently so as to obtain a greater number of whole-tone chords than would otherwise have arisen. Since the only difference between this array and the preceding one involves the order of presentation of the third and fourth row-forms, not their content, the sum collections are just what they were the first time. Again, as there is no controlling "zero" pitch, there is no inherent center. Only the many repetitions serve factitiously to "tonicize" the refrain chord.

Several previous writers have claimed that only in the Interlude did Stravinsky at once display both of the sets that inform the *Requiem Canticles,* and have made much of what they perceived to be the symmetrical deployment of the two sets around that central movement (which was, significantly, the first to be composed).[96] In fact, the harmonies in the Postlude are derived from the sets in combination as well.[97] Not only does this make the Postlude a fitting harmonic summary, but it also enables Stravinsky to generate strings of as many as eleven harmonies derived from a single "zero" pitch, all of them consequently disposable around a single axis of symmetry—a single, literal center.

Thus, the eleven tolling chords in mm. 290–92 consist of the vertical concatenation of both primes and both inversions (Ex. E.23a–c). Given the similarity of the two sets, we have a near palindromic matrix of (by definition) self-inverting harmonies symmetrically disposed around the F that starts each of the row forms on its way, and which Stravinsky treats as a pedal, the way he had treated the "zero" pitches that control the hexachordal verticals in other movements. Only by deploy-

95. Spies, "Notes," 245.

96. Ibid., 234; Babbitt, "Order, Symmetry, and Centricity," 255; also idem, "Stravinsky's Verticals and Schoenberg's Diagonals," 31, 34: "[Stravinsky's] last large composition, *Requiem Canticles,* reveals two sets, whose appearances are symmetrically distributed around the Interlude, the centerpiece of the main body of the work, where the two sets appear, and simultaneously once, at the center of the centerpiece."

97. The first writer to note the precise relationship of the two series in the Postlude was Stephen Walsh (*Music of Stravinsky,* 275). Craft's lengthy analytical caption to fig. 268 in *A Stravinsky Scrapbook,* which shows a draft of the Postlude, while correctly stating that both series appear in it, is otherwise unaccountably inaccurate and irrelevant.

EXAMPLE E.22   Opening of Interlude analyzed

a. The row forms

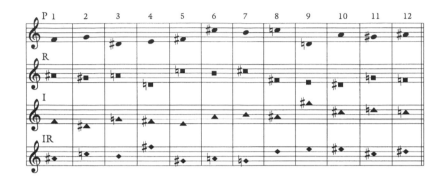

b. The refrain chord (mm. 136–39)
c. Simultaneous deployment of all row forms in mm. 140–43

b.   c.

EXAMPLE E.23 Simultaneous deployment of two sets in Postlude, mm. 289–92

a. The row forms
b. Bell chords analyzed

c. Their symmetrical disposition around F

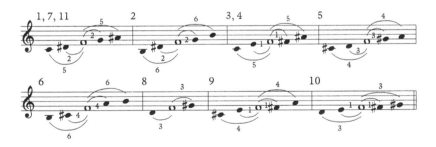

EXAMPLE E.23 (*continued*)

d. *The Firebird,* fig. $\boxed{5}$, reduced and analyzed to show symmetrical disposition of harmonies

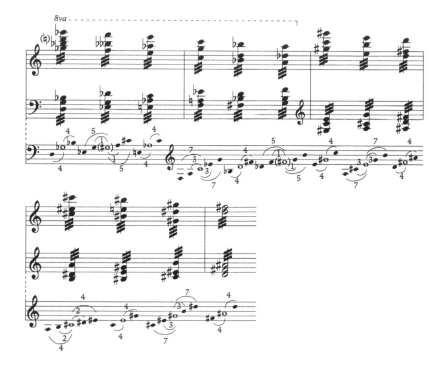

ing in tandem a pair of sets with a common starting point or "zero" factor could Stravinsky have generated such an impressive array of self-inverting harmonies—minor seventh chords, augmented triads, whole-tone segments, French sixths, diminished triads and sevenths, plus others without common-practice standing—all motivated by a new syntax governing their "contextual coherence" or "association," as Babbitt would say. And that must be why there are two different sets in the *Requiem Canticles* to begin with. Their use in tandem enabled a *reprise de contact* with a style of writing that had formed the backbone of Stravinsky's true "Russian" music—that is to say, the music he actually wrote in Russia—as comparison with a well-known passage in *The Firebird* will remind us (Ex. E.23d).

The sequence of chords at mm. 295–97 derives from the simultaneous deployment of the retrogrades and inverted retrogrades. The first notes in each series are omitted so that the sequence can once again number eleven chords in keeping with the numerological groundplan. Had Stravinsky chosen the retrograde inversion rather than the inverted retrograde (the difference is t10 in the case of set 1 and t4 in the case of set 2), he would have merely reproduced the chord sequence in Example E.23b in reverse. Instead he produced a noncentric and inconsistently symmetric concatenation which he felt the need arbitrarily to adjust at various points to improve the harmony; he actually substituted the second hexachord of the set 1 inversion for that of the inverted retrograde, so that the "second line" in Example E.24a actually doubles back on itself (at t2) at the midpoint. It follows, of course, that under these rather loose harmonic conditions the G-sharp pedal no longer plays any inherent structural role. No longer a true center, it seems to have been selected simply to match the lowest pitch of the first chord.

The final string of quarter-note tolling chords (mm. 300–302) is derived from the untransposed primes and retrogrades and therefore describes a perfect (though, in the event, arbitrarily telescoped and otherwise modified) palindrome. When the pedal B-sharp (C) is added to those verticals in the palindrome that do not already contain it, three pairs can be formed that yield inversionally symmetrical displays either around the pedal or around a central axis-dyad (Ex. E.25).

Is it mere coincidence that verticals 4 and 5 in Example E.25, omitted from the chord progression at m. 300, very nearly correspond in pitch-class content to the seven-member whole-note chord at the beginning of the Postlude? Probably so, for there is another way of accounting for that chord and its fellows at mm. 294, 299, and 304–5, the so-called Chords of Death.[98] They are combinations of hexachordal verticals referable to sets 1 and 2. Referring back to Example E.16, we recall that the "a" hexachords of both sets have the all-important self-inverting middle vertical in common, and that the latter is a subset of octatonic Collection II. If one of these verticals were rotated on an (0 3 6 9) axis (in keeping, let us say, with the progression from pedal F at the beginning of the Postlude to pedal G-sharp at m. 294), the collection would be exhausted. The opening Chord of Death, meanwhile, is in fact made up of seven of the eight pitches in Collection II (only B is missing). It seems reasonable, then, to consider it the product of such a rotation and, beyond that, as Stravinsky's fond (and in this funerary context, touching) farewell to the pitch field that had served him so long and so fruitfully.

The second Chord of Death is made up of six of the nine pitches found in the two second-position verticals in Example E.16. The third (m. 299) is the most massive, consisting of eight different pitch classes. They are all present and accounted for (with a single remainder) if the first-position vertical from the "a" hexachord of set 1 is combined with the corresponding vertical derived from the "b" hexachord of set 2. The fourth chord (m. 304) is wholly contained within the third-position vertical in the set 2b array (plus the B-sharp pedal). Finally, the enigmatic four-note chord that represents the point of intersection between the series of Chords of Death and that of the "tolling bells" in the last measure of the piece exactly corresponds in pitch-class content with the first-position vertical in the set 2a array, as already illustrated in Example E.16. Example E.26 summarizes the derivation of the Chords of Death.

98. For the name, see Craft, *Stravinsky: Chronicle of a Friendship*, 415.

EXAMPLE E.24   Simultaneous deployment of two sets in Postlude,
mm. 294–97

a. The row forms

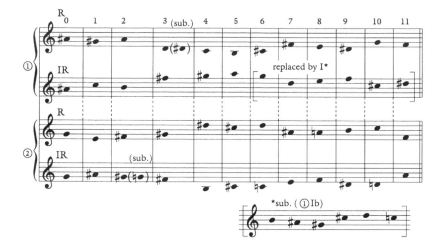

b. Bell chords analyzed

c. Their collectional affinities

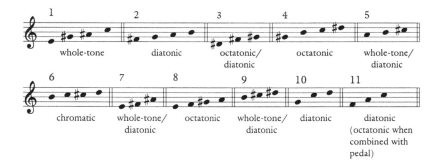

EXAMPLE E.25   Simultaneous deployment of two sets in Postlude, mm. 299–302

a. The row forms

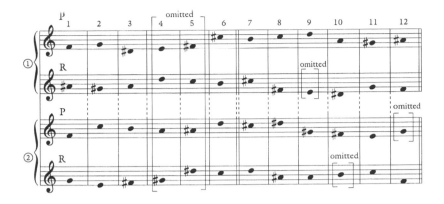

b. Bell chords analyzed

c. Symmetrical sums

a. "Middle" vertical of the "a" hexachord (cf. Ex. 20.15a) referred to Collection II and compared with the chord at m. 289

b. Chord at m. 294 compared with second-position vertical of set 1, hexachord "a" (i.e., hexachord 1a), and first-position vertical of set 2, hexachord "b" (hexachord 2b)

c. Chord at m. 299 compared with first-position vertical of hexachord 1a (cf. *Petrushka* chord) and first-position vertical of hexachord 2b

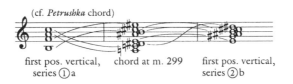

d. Chord at m. 304 compared with third-position vertical of hexachord 2b

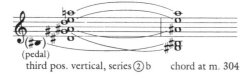

e. Chord at m. 305 compared with first-position vertical of hexachord 2a

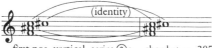

Whenever possible, Stravinsky voiced these chords in ways that emphasized triadic partitions at their tops and wide spacings at the bottoms suggesting harmonically stable roots. He was once again, at the very end of his career, up to the same tricks of *trompe l'oreille* "polyharmony" he had employed in the period of his first fame. Like those earlier "polychords," the Chords of Death in the *Requiem Canticles* are precisely the sort of thing Babbitt so perceptively described as "attitudinally Russian": chords as "things-in-themselves," as "sonorous objects." They are farewell Kisses of the Earth, and the composition in which they so surprisingly appear must surely be the most attitudinally Russian twelve-tone music ever composed.

Stravinsky's elaborately verticalized serial technique was something he guarded during his lifetime as if it were some kind of Belyayevets guild secret.[99] Yet it is ultimately possible to wonder whether his serialism was more than a marriage of convenience or one made for the sake of appearances, or whether, had he world enough and time, he might have found a more direct and theoretically better integrated route to the technique that produced his final style. For it is precisely the principle of strict intervallic order—the defining principle of serialism—that seems least relevant to Stravinsky's goals and predilections. Nor does he exhibit the least interest in exploring the twelve-tone aggregate "contrapuntally," whether by partitions, by juxtapositions of combinatorial row forms, or by "derivation" (i.e., the Webernian technique of embedding within the twelve-tone series trichords or tetrachords that are themselves related in intervallic contour). His hexachordally based (at times, as in the *Introitus* of 1965, even tetrachordally based) twelve-tone music shows a far greater affinity for what the pre-Schoenbergian atonalist Hauer would have called *Tropen* than for the Schoenbergian concept of a *Reihe*. When one observes him—in *Abraham and Isaac*, for example, as well as in the Lacrimosa from the *Canticles*—threading his strangely dogged and fatalistic way through his rotation charts in all directions, up, down, and from side to side (and this must be what that inscrutable "crystal" metaphor was all about), one sees that his concept of serialism really had little to do with order as such, and every-

---

99. Examples are notorious. "No theorist," he taunted (M&C:100/106), "could determine the spelling of the note order in, for example, the flute solo near the beginning [of *Movements*], or the derivation of the three Fs announcing the last movement simply by knowing the original order [of the series]." In place of an exposition of his transposition/rotation technique, Stravinsky offered gobbledygook about "the sixes, quadrilaterals, triangles, etc., . . . a construction of twelve verticals . . . while, at the same time, the six work in all directions as through a crystal." When this description was first printed, in the program of the world première of *Movements* under the composer's baton at a Stravinsky festival in New York's Town Hall (10 January 1960), literally no one in the audience (an audience that included Robert Craft and Milton Babbitt) knew what it meant, as Babbitt recalled in talks given at Stravinsky centennial symposia in La Jolla and Notre Dame in 1982. The laconic analytical example shown in Figure E.2 is Stravinsky's only known attempt to explicate his serial procedures technically.

thing to do with the perpetual arrangement and rearrangement of a fixed set of intervals around a center (and someone should really make a study to determine why that center was so often F).

In short, Stravinsky succeeded, just as Nabokov said he did, in "overpowering" the serial method—or rather, in foiling it. He figured out how to wheedle and cajole from it a new brand of the symmetrically disposed, centric but not tonally functional, music for which, as Arthur Berger was first to point out, Stravinsky had a long and stylistically determinant affinity. In terms of the *Poetics of Music,* he had found a new source of *complexes sonores*—complexes that now took the form of magic boxes: six-by-six intervallic arrays through which paths could be traced omnidirectionally, and which could thus lead to new and interesting tonal "polarities." In effect, Stravinsky was feeling his way to a kind of "twelve-tone tonality" comparable in certain aspects to that formulated by George Perle. Because his approach was inductive and in many ways irrelevant to the Schoenbergian technique he thought he was adopting, his methods were often cumbersome and—from the perspective of the analyst, if not of the listener—disconcertingly arbitrary. In the *Requiem Canticles,* though, he found his way at last to the "second simplicity" he had achieved in the music of the Swiss decade. It was a new and inspiring *uproshcheniye,* immediately perceived as such by Nabokov and the many others for whom the *Requiem Canticles* formed the great exception among Stravinsky's late serial pieces.

And this was not due only to whatever backward glances the *Canticles* may have embodied. One cannot shake the impression that in this last major work the dauntless octogenarian was standing on the threshold of what could have been a new period—a new "Russian period," if you please—that might have seen him cast off his excess Schoenbergian or Krenekite baggage and find his way to a settled and integrated idiom, one in which a newly refined and simplified technical means more nearly suited his creative ends.

CONCLUSION

At the age of eighty-four, then, Stravinsky was still a restless young composer—in fact, a newly young composer—feeling his way toward a future. The more we learn about this inexhaustible musical phoenix, the sharper the analytical lens we train on his work, and the deeper our historical perspective, the clearer become the connections between his pasts and his futures. He loved to hint at the presence of "serial tendencies" in *The Firebird*.[100] And they are surely there. But we may point just as surely to hints of *The Firebird* in his serialism.

If, as observed in the Introduction to this book, Stravinsky was an outsider to all

---

100. E.g., E&D:151/133.

traditions, that status was what enabled him to partake at pleasure whereof he would. His polymorphous adaptability has always provoked the lugubrious guardians of mainstreams. More recently, and even more irrelevantly, the same quality has been touted as presciently postmodern. But Stravinsky was no agent of cultural fragmentation. On the contrary, he was—with J. S. Bach (another outlander, in his day)—one of music's great centripetal forces, the crystallizer and definer of an age. Precisely because he did not inherit his patrimony but fashioned it on his own forge and, according to T. S. Eliot's prescription, "by great labour,"[101] his work possessed a strength of style, and his oeuvre a unity, that could accommodate an endless variety of surfaces. For all that variety, Stravinsky was the opposite of eclectic. His essential characteristics—his *drobnost'*, his *nepodvizhnost'*, above all his *uproshcheniye*—inform his mature work from first to last with rare authenticity and constancy.

And if one continues to insist on the Russian words, it is not only because they denote irreducibly Russian qualities for which there are no exact parallels in other nations and languages, but also because the esthetic outlook they collectively define, while wholly corresponding to no prior Russian outlook, had been formed in Russia by a Russian who made a profound and unique synthesis of his country's musical traditions, both those reflective of the high literate culture and those of folklore, and who at the end of a formidable cosmopolitan career finally acknowledged that his *slog*—that is to say, his morphology, his basic manner of self-expression, and something that goes far deeper than style—was *russkiy*.[102] To the extent that terms like *stasis, discontinuity, block juxtaposition, moment,* or *structural simplification* can be applied to modern music in general—a very great extent—and to the extent that Stravinsky is acknowledged as a source or an inspiration for the traits and traditions they signify—an even greater extent—the force of his example bequeathed a *russkiy slog* to the whole world of twentieth-century concert music. To that world Stravinsky related not by any "angle." He was the very stem.

101. Eliot, "Tradition and the Individual Talent," 38.
102. "Lyubite muzïku!" *Komsomolskaya pravda,* 27 September 1962 (unsigned interview).

The following Russian terms are defined on first appearance but used subsequently without translation. Accents indicate tonic stress.

ARTÉL Workers' cooperative; as applied ironically to a group of musicians (e.g. the Belyayevtsï; q.v.), the term connotes a faceless group identity.

BABA-YAGÁ The traditional Russian fairy-tale witch.

BÁIKA A fable.

BELYÁYEVETS (pl. BELYAYEVTSÏ) Member of the group organized ca. 1882 around the music publisher Mitrofan Petrovich Belyayev. As an attributive, the term has come to denote timid academicism.

BÏT Everyday life, life-as-lived.

BÓDROST' Cheerfulness, high spirits.

DEVÍCHNIK Bridal shower on the eve of a peasant wedding.

DRÓBNOST' Lit., "splinteredness"; the quality of being formally disunified, a sum-of-parts.

DVORYANÍN (pl. DVORYÁNYE) Nobleman.

GÚSLI Ancient Russian folk psaltery, associated with bards and skomorokhi (q.v.).

IVÁN-TSARÉVICH The "Prince Charming" character in Russian fairy tales (skazki).

IVÁNOVSKAYA Folk song associated with St. John's Eve or kupala (q.v.).

KALENDÁRNÏYE PÉSNI Folk songs pertaining to the ancient agrarian sun-worshipping calendar with its cycle of feasts such as semik and kupala (q.v.).

KIKÍMORA Goblin.

KHLÏST (pl. KHLÏSTÏ) Member of a Russian quasi-Pentecostal mystical sect, persecuted by the Orthodox church.

KHOROVÓD Group ceremonial dance.

KHUDÓZHESTVENNAYA PRÁVDA Artistic truth (i.e., license).

KNYAGÍNYA A married princess.

KNYAZHNÁ An unmarried princess.

KOLEDÁ Ancient Slavic midwinter festival.

KOLOKÓL (pl. KOLOKOLÁ) Bell.

KONYÓK-GORBUNÓK The Little Humpbacked Horse, fairy tale (skazka) that was the basis for a popular nineteenth-century ballet (music by Cesare Pugni).

KÓZMA PRUTKÓV A fictitious, proverbially bad poet, under whose name a group of Russian poets published satirical verse in the mid-nineteenth century.

KRASÁ or KRASOTÁ Beauty.

KÚCHKA Lit., "little heap." As used in this book the term refers to the sobriquet *mogúchaya kúchka,* "mighty little bunch," coined by Vladimir Stasov in 1867 to denote the younger school of Russian musicians, chiefly those gathered around Balakirev, otherwise known in nineteenth-century Russia as the Balakirev Circle or the "New Russian School." (The English sobriquet in common use, "The Mighty Five," is a conflation of *moguchaya kuchka* with *pyátero,* "The Five," referring specifically to Balakirev, Cui, Musorgsky, Rimsky-Korsakov, and Borodin.) In this book the Stasovian sobriquet is rendered as "mighty kuchka," whence "kuchkist" (a member of the group), "kuchkism" (their esthetic), etc.

KUL'TÚRA Civilized culture (cf. *stikhíya*).

KUM (fem. KUMÁ) Blood-brother, -sister.

KUPÁLA Ancient Slavic midsummer festival.

KUPCHÍSHKA Lit., "little tradesman"; derogatory aristocratic term for a capitalist or industrialist.

KUPÉCHESTVO The merchant class (chiefly Muscovite).

LIRNÍK Wandering mendicant singer (usually blind) who accompanied himself on the hurdy-gurdy (*líra*), once common in the Ukraine.

LITURGÍCHNOST' Liturgical quality.

LUBÓK (pl. LUBKÍ) A brightly colored peasant woodcut or broadside print.

MÁSLENITSA Shrovetide; *shirókaya m.,* Shrovetide greetings.

MIR ISKÚSSTVA "The World of Art," a magazine founded and edited by Diaghilev in 1898 and a concurrent series of art exhibits, whence *Miriskúsnik* (a member or fellow traveler of the Diaghilev circle), *Miriskusníchestvo* (their esthetic), etc.

MOGÚCHAYA KÚCHKA See *kuchka.*

MOLVÁ Tattle.

NAÍGRÏSH An instrumental dance tune.

NAPÉV A tune.

NENAGLYÁDNAYA KRASÁ The beautiful princess in Russian fairy tales (*skázki*).

NEPODVÍZHNOST' Immobility, stasis; as applied to form, the quality of being nonteleological, nondevelopmental.

OBIKHÓD As a musical term, the daily and yearly round of Orthodox church chants in common use, or the book containing them (compare the Roman Catholic *Liber usualis*).

OBLÓMOVSHCHINA Phlegmatic or fatalistic dawdling; named after the title character in Ivan Goncharov's novel *Oblómov* (1859).

OBRYÁDNAYA (or OBRYÁDOVAYA) PÉSNYA Folk song of a ritual nature, or one containing atavisms of folk rituals.

OPROSHCHÉNIYE Simplification, primitiveness (negative nuance); cf. *uproshcheniye.*

PANIKHÍDA The Russian Orthodox funeral or memorial service.

PEREDVÍZHNIK (pl. PEREDVÍZHNIKI) Member of the nineteenth-century Russian school of realist painters, whence *peredvizhníchestvo,* denoting their esthetic (the term, often mistranslated "wanderer" in English, derives from the group's organizational name: *Tovarishchestvo peredvizhnïkh khudozhestvennïkh vïstavok,* Association of Traveling Art Exhibitions).

POBÁSENKA Little fable in verse.

PODGOLÓSKI Lit., "undervoices"; the lines in Russian improvised folk part-singing.

PODGOLÓSOCHNAYA MNOGOGOLÓSIYE The scholarly term for the heterophonic texture produced by *podgoloski* (q.v.).

POPÉVKA A characteristic melodic turn or formula; a musical morpheme.

PRIBAÚTKA Jingle, nonsense rhyme.

PROTYÁZHNAYA (PESNYA) (pl. PROTYÁZHNÏYE) Lit., "drawn-out," "drawled"; a slow, melismatic folk song.

PRUTKÓV *See* Kozma Prutkov.

RADÚNITSA Folk holiday of ancestor commemoration.

RAZBÓR Lit., "analysis"; a detailed descriptive commentary or illustrated program note.

RMG *Russkaya muzïkal'naya gazeta,* a monthly (later weekly or biweekly) music magazine published by Nikolai Findeyzen from 1894 to 1918; St. Petersburg's musical periodical of record.

ROZHÓK (pl. ROZHKÍ) Russian peasant horn.

"RUSSKAYA" Short for *russkaya plyaska;* Russian (folk) dance, often of a strenuous, competitive nature, done squatting (*v prisyadku*).

RYÁZHENNÏYE Holiday mummers (cf. *ryazhéniye,* mummery).

SEKTÁNT General term for a member of a mystical sect such as *khlïstï* or *skoptsï* (q.v.).

SÉMIK Ancient Slavic springtime festival.

SEMÍTSKAYA A folk song associated with *semik* (q.v.).

SHIPÓVNIK Lit., "sweetbriar"; avant-garde publishing house.

SKÁZKA (pl. SKÁZKI) Fairy tale, folk tale.

SKOMORÓKH (pl. SKOMOROKHI) Russian folk minstrel, descendant of the ancient Slavic shamanistic priesthood.

SKOPÉTS (pl. SKÓPTSÏ) Member of a Russian mystical sect (cf. *khlïst*) practicing ritual castration.

SKOROGOVÓRKA Rapid patter.

SLOG Manner of expression or writing.

SOBÓRNOST' Community, collectivity, commonality (considered by Russian Symbolists to be the aim of art).

STIKHÍYA Elemental or natural dynamism; the opposite of *kul'tura* (q.v.).

SVÁDEBKA A fine peasant wedding.

SVYÁTKI Yuletide.

UPROSHCHÉNIYE Simplification (positive nuance); cf. *oproshcheniye.*

VAMPÚKA Stilted operatic convention. From *Vampuka; or, The African Bride,* a theatrical spoof by Vladimir Erenberg, mounted at Nikolai Yevreynov's Funhouse Mirror (*Krivoye zerkalo*) Theater in St. Petersburg in 1909; the title comes from a ridiculous-sounding line in the standard Russian translation of Meyerbeer's *Robert le diable.*

VOLOCHÓBNIKI Easter carolers who went door to door in rural Russia singing in return for eggs.

YAROVÓY Vernal.

ZARUBÉZHNÏY Lit., "beyond the frontiers"; foreign, outside of Russia.

ZOLOTÓYE RUNÓ "Golden Fleece," turn-of-the-century Moscow art magazine and publishing house.

ZVUKOSOZERTSÁNIYE Lit., "sound contemplation"; sound ideal, a musician's esthetic outlook.

The following proper names (of persons and places, as well as a few titles) are listed with accents to show tonic stress.

Abrámtsevo	Findéyzen	Kóposova
Afanásyev	Geórgiy	Koróvin
Akiménko	Glazunóv	Kramskóy
Aksákov	Goleníshchev-Kutúzov	Krúglikov
Alferáki	Golovín	Kustódiyev
Alyábiev	*Gólub*	Lavróv
Antípov	Goncharóva	Linyóva
Artsïbúshev	Grechanínov	Lomákin
Balákirev	Grigóriy	Lyádov
Balmónt	Grigóryev	Lyapunóv
Bilíbin	*Grozá*	Malkó
Bobrinskóy	Gurilyóv	Mámontov
Bogdánov-Berezóvsky	Ippolítov-Ivánov	Mariyínsky (Theater)
Bóndarenko	Ivanóv, Konstantín	Melgunóv
Borís Godunóv	Ivánov, Vyacheslác	Mélnikov
Borodín	Kalafáti	Mitúsov
Cherepnín	*Kamárinskaya*	Morózov
Chernígov	Karatïgin	Mosolóv
Dargomïzhsky	Kátinka	Músorgsky
Derzhanóvsky	Kítezh	Myásin
Deshevóv	Koltsóv	Nésterov
Filosófov	Kopïlov	*Nezabúdochka-tsvetóchek*

Nezhdánova

Nikíforov

Nikítina

Nikóleva

Nosénko

Núrok

Odóyevsky

Ossóvsky

Ostroúkhov (four syllables)

Pálchikov

Platónova

Pogozhóv

Pokhitónov

Pokróvsky

Polénova

Polónsky

Remízov

Répin

Románov

Roslávets

Rossíya

Rostisláv

Rubinshtéyn (= Rubinstein)

Rubtsóv

Ryabushínsky

Sandúlenko

Sarádzhev

Semyón

Senílov

Serebryákova

Seróv

Shestakóva

Shibánov

Shtéynberg (= Steinberg)

Silóti (pronounced Ziloti)

Smirnóv

Snegúrochka

Sóbinov

Sokálsky

Sokolóv

Solovyóv

Soróchintsï

Stásov

Stasyulévich

Sukhónin

Sumarókov

Taláshkino

Tanéyev

Tenísheva

Timoféyev

Tolstóy

Tredyakóvsky

Tretyakóv

Tsïganóv

Tyúmenev

Vasnetsóv

Vladímir

Vsevolózhsky

Yakúnchikova

Yakóvlev

Yarmólintsï

Yástrebtsev

Yérshov

Zhemchúzhnikov

Zherebtsóva

Zinaída (four syllables)

Zolotaryóv

Zolotóy petushók

Zvezdolíkiy

UNSIGNED ARTICLES AND REVIEWS

"Chauve-Souris no. 2." *Life,* 6 July 1922.

"Intsident mezhdu russkim kompozitorom i Venskim korolevskim orkestrom." *Peterburg-skaya gazeta,* 1913, no. 10 (11–24 January).

"Kamillo Everardi, 1825–1899." *Russkaya muzïkal'naya gazeta (RMG)* 6, no. 3 (16 January 1899), cols. 89–90.

"K 25-letiyu artisticheskoy deyatel'nosti F. I. Stravinskogo." *RMG* 8, no. 1 (January 1901), cols. 13–15.

"K desiatiletiyu 'Glinkinskikh Premii,' uchrezhdyonnïkh M. P. Belyayevïm." *Khronika zhurnala "Muzïkal'ny sovremennik,"* no. 12 (1915).

"Khronika: Peterburgskiye kontsertï." *RMG* 9, no. 8 (23 February 1902), cols. 243–44.

———. *RMG* 9, no. 10 (9 March 1902), cols. 304–5.

———. *RMG* 9, no. 14 (6 April 1902), col. 441.

———. *RMG* 9, no. 50 (15 December 1902), col. 1266.

———. *RMG* 11, no. 9 (29 February 1904), col. 241.

———. *RMG* 11, no. 14 (6 April 1902), col. 441.

———. *RMG* 12, no. 12 (20 March 1905), col. 355.

———. *RMG* 12, nos. 43–44 (23–30 October 1905), col. 1050.

———. *RMG* 14, no. 7 (8 February 1907), col. 221.

———. *RMG* 14, no. 11 (8 March 1907), col. 316.

———. *RMG* 14, no. 13 (22 March 1907), col. 383.

———. *RMG* 15, nos. 8–9 (24 February–2 March 1908), cols. 213–14.

———. *RMG* 15, no. 11 (16 March 1908), col. 331.

———. *RMG* 15, no. 42 (19 October 1908), col. 909.

———. *RMG* 16, no. 2 (11 January 1909), col. 54.

———. *RMG* 16, no. 4 (25 January 1909), col. 110.

———. *RMG* 16, no. 5 (1 February 1909), col. 147.

———. *RMG* 16, no. 10 (8 March 1909), col. 273.

———. *RMG* 16, no. 44 (1 November 1909), col. 1007.

———. *RMG* 16, no. 49 (6 December 1909), col. 1012.

———. *RMG* 17, no. 3 (17 January 1910), col. 79.

———. *RMG* 17, no. 12 (22 March 1910), col. 332.

———. *RMG* 18, no. 5 (29 January 1911), col. 137.

———. *RMG* 21, no. 49 (7 December 1914), col. 920.

———. *RMG* 22, no. 15 (12 April 1915), col. 282.

———. *RMG* 22, nos. 47–48 (22–29 November 1915), col. 745.

"Konflikt Shalyapin-Dyagilev." *Obozreniye teatrov,* 20 January 1913.

[Andrey Rimsky-Korsakov?]. "Kontsertnoye obozreniye." *Khronika zhurnala "Muzïkal'nïy sovremennik,"* no. 12 (1915).

"Mavra Reveals New Stravinsky to Paris." *Musical America* 36, no. 10 (1 July 1922).

"Na mogile F. I. Stravinskogo." *RMG* 15, no. 49 (6 December 1908), col. 1122.

"Neskol'ko slov o S. V. Malyutine." *Mir iskusstva,* no. 4 (1903).

"O kontsertnoy deyatel'nosti pridvornogo orkestra." *Khronika zhurnala "Muzïkal'nïy sovremennik,"* no. 19 (13 March 1916): 6–7.

"O nesostoyavshemsya balete Lyadova." *Muzïka,* no. 204 (1914).

Obituary for Nikita Baliev. *New York Times,* 4 September 1936.

"Poignée de nouvelles." *Excelsior,* no. 962 (4 July 1913).

"Raznïye izvestiya." *RMG* 21, nos. 36–37 (7–14 September 1914), col. 714.

Review of Baliev's Chauve-Souris. *New Witness,* 27 May 1921.

Review of *The Rite of Spring. Peterburgskiy listok,* 14–27 February 1914.

"Russkaya muzïka za granitsey." *RMG* 20, nos. 24–25 (16–23 June 1913), col. 573.

———. *RMG* 21, nos. 22–23 (1–8 June, 1914), col. 539.

"Simfonicheskoye sobraniye I.R.M.O." *Khronika zhurnala "Muzïkal'nïy sovremennik,"* no. 12 (1915).

[Sergey Pavlovich Diaghilev?]. "Slozhnïye voprosï." *Mir iskusstva,* 1899, nos. 1–2, 14–15, 52.

"Tol'ko faktï." *Muzïkal'naya zhizn',* no. 6 (1984): 3.

"25-letiye Pridvornogo orkestra." *RMG* 14, nos. 51–52 (23–30 December 1907), cols. 1181–87.

BOOKS AND ARTICLES

Abraham, Gerald. *100 Years of Music.* 4th ed. London: Duckworth, 1974.

———. ed. *The Music of Tchaikovsky.* New York: W. W. Norton, 1979.

Afanasyev, Alexander Nikolayevich. *Narodnïye russkiye skazki.* Vols. 1–2. Edited by M. K. Azadovsky, N. P. Andreyev, and Yu. M. Sokolov. Moscow: Academia, 1936–37.

———. *Narodnïye russkiye skazki.* Vol. 2. Edited by M. K. Azadovsky, N. P. Andreyev, and Yu. M. Sokolov. Moscow: Goslitizdat, 1938–40.

———. *Narodnïye russkiye skazki.* Vol. 1. Edited by V. Ya. Propp. Moscow: Gosudarstvennoye Izdatel'stvo Khudozhestvennoy Literaturï, 1957.

———. *Poèticheskiye vozzreniya slavyan na prirodu.* 3 vols. Moscow: K. Soldatenkov, 1865–69.

———. *Russian Fairy Tales.* Translated by Norbert Guterman. New York: Pantheon Books, 1945.

———. *Russkiye narodnïye skazki.* 5 vols. Edited by A. Gruzinsky. 4th ed. Moscow: Tip. Tovarishchestva I. D. Sïtina, 1913–14.

Agmon, Eytan. "Equal Division of the Octave in a Scarlatti Sonata." *In Theory Only* 11, no. 5 (May 1990): 1–8.

Albright, Daniel. *Stravinsky: The Music Box and the Nightingale*. New York: Gordon & Breach, 1989.

Alferov, A., and A. Gruzinsky. *Dopetrovskaya literatura i narodnaya poèziya*. 4th ed. Moscow: Sotrudnik Shkol, 1909.

Alfeyevskaya, Galina Sergeyevna, and Irina Yakovlevna Vershinina, eds. *I. F. Stravinskiy: stat'i, vospominaniya*. Moscow: Sovetskiy Kompozitor, 1985.

Allen, Warren Dwight. *Philosophies of Music History*. New York: Dover, 1962.

"A. N." (*see also* Nurok, A. P.; "Silèn"). "Frantsuzskiy kritik o russkoy muzïke." *Mir iskusstva*, 1902, no. 4.

———. "O nekotorïkh muzïkal'nïkh novinkakh." *Mir iskusstva*, 1902, no. 2, 51–52.

———. "Po kontsertam" (occasional essay). *Mir iskusstva*, 1904, no. 4, 80–83; no. 11, 68–72.

———. "Vensen d'Endi v Pavlovske." *Mir iskusstva*, 1904, no. 6, 123–24.

Andersen, Hans Christian. *The Complete Fairy Tales and Stories*. Translated by Erik Christian Haugaard. Garden City, N.Y.: Anchor Press/Doubleday, 1983.

Andriessen, Louis, and Elmer Schönberger. *Het apollinisch uurwerk: over Stravinsky*. Amsterdam: De Bezige Bij, 1983. English translation: *The Apollonian Clockwork: On Stravinsky*. Translated by Jeff Hamburg. Oxford: Oxford University Press, 1989.

Anichkov, Yevgeniy. *Yazïchestvo i drevnyaya Rus'*. St. Petersburg: M. M. Stasyulevich, 1914.

Ansermet, Ernest. *Les fondements de la musique dans la conscience humaine*. 2 vols. Neuchâtel: Baconnière, 1961.

———. "L'oeuvre d'Igor Strawinsky." *Revue musicale* 2, no. 9 (July 1921): 1–27.

———. "La naissance de 'Histoire du soldat.'" In C. F. Ramuz, *Lettres, 1900–1918*, 33–38. Lausanne: Éditions Clairefontaine, 1956.

Antheil, George. *Bad Boy of Music*. Garden City, N.Y.: Doubleday, Doran, 1945.

Antokoletz, Elliott. "Interval Cycles in Stravinsky's Early Ballets." *Journal of the American Musicological Society* 39 (1986): 578–614.

———. *The Music of Béla Bartók*. Berkeley and Los Angeles: University of California Press, 1984.

———. Review of *The Music of Igor Stravinsky*, by Pieter C. van den Toorn. *Journal of the American Musicological Society* 37 (1984): 428–36.

Apetyan, Zarui Apetovna, ed. *S. V. Rakhmaninov: pis'ma*. Moscow: Muzgiz, 1955.

Appleby, David P. *The Music of Brazil*. Austin: University of Texas Press, 1983.

Arakchiyev [Arakishvili], Dmitriy Ignatyevich. "Kratkiy ocherk razvitiya gruzinskoy, karatalino-kakhetinskoy, narodnoy pesni." In *Trudï MEK* 1:269–344.

———. "O gruzinskoy narodnoy muzïke." In *Trudï MEK* 1:319*bis*–360.

Arakchiyev, Dmitriy Ignatyevich, and Alexander Kastalsky et al. "Vïkriki i naígríshi." In *Trudï MEK* 2:386–88.

Asafyev, Boris Vladimirovich (*see also* Glebov, Igor). "Etyud o Cherepnine." *Muzïka*, no. 250 (19 March 1916).

———. *Yevgeniy Onegin: liricheskiye stsenï P. I. Chaikovskogo*. Moscow: Muzgiz, 1944.

Aslin, Elizabeth. *The Aesthetic Movement: Prelude to Art Nouveau*. New York: Excalibur Books, 1981.

Aston, W. G. *A History of Japanese Literature*. Rutland, Vt.: Charles E. Tuttle, 1972.

Auden, Wystan A. "Craftsman, Artist, Genius." *The Observer*, 11 April 1971.

Auric, Georges. "Du 'Sacre du Printemps' à 'Mavra.'" *Nouvelles littéraires*, 6 January 1923.

Austin, William W. *Music in the Twentieth Century*. New York: W. W. Norton, 1966.

Babbitt, Milton. "Contemporary Music Composition and Music Theory as Contemporary Intellectual History." In *Perspectives in Musicology*, edited by Barry S. Brook,

Edward O. Downes, and Sherman van Solkema, 151–84. New York: W. W. Norton, 1972.

———. "Order, Symmetry, and Centricity in Late Stravinsky." In *Confronting Stravinsky,* edited by Jann Pasler, 247–61. Berkeley and Los Angeles: University of California Press, 1986.

———. "Stravinsky's Verticals and Schoenberg's Diagonals: A Twist of Fate." In *Stravinsky Retrospectives,* edited by Ethan Haimo and Paul Johnson, 15–35. Lincoln: University of Nebraska Press, 1987.

Bachinskaya, Nina Mikhailovna. *Narodnïye pesni v tvorchestve russkikh kompozitorov.* Moscow: Muzgiz, 1962.

Baker, James M. *The Music of Alexander Scriabin.* New Haven: Yale University Press, 1986.

Bakhmetev, Nikolai Ivanovich, ed. *Obikhod notnogo peniya.* Vol. 2. Petrograd: Pridvornaya Pevcheskaya Kapèlla, 1869.

Bakst [Rosenberg], Lev [Leon] Nikolayevich. "Puti klassitsizma v isskustve." *Apollon,* 1909, nos. 2–3.

Balakirev, Miliy Alekseyevich. *Sbornik russkikh narodnïkh pesen.* St. Petersburg: Johansen, 1866; rpt. Leipzig: Belaïeff, 1895.

Balanchine, George. "The Dance Element in Stravinsky's Music." In *Stravinsky in the Theatre,* edited by Minna Lederman, 75–84. New York: Da Capo Press, 1975.

Balmont, Konstantin Dmitriyevich. *Poèziya kak volshebstvo.* Moscow: Skorpion, 1916.

———. *Svetozvuk v prirode i svetovaya simfoniya Skryabina.* Moscow: Rossiyskoye Muzïkal'noye Izdatel'stvo, 1917.

———. *Zelyonïy vertograd.* St. Petersburg, 1909.

Baltrushaitis, Jurgis Casimirovich, Alexandre Benois, et al. *Rerikh.* Petrograd, 1916.

Bancroft, David. "Stravinsky and the NRF (1910–20)." *Music and Letters* 53 (1972): 274–93; 55 (1974): 261–80.

Bárdos, Lajos. "Ferenc Liszt, the Innovator." *Studia musicologica* 17 (1975): 3–38.

Barkhudarov, S. G., et al. *Slovar' russkogo yazïka.* 4 vols. Moscow: Akademiya Nauk SSSR, Institut Russkogo Yazïka, 1959.

Barraqué, Jean. "Rythme et développement." *Polyphonie* 3 (1954): 47–58.

Barron, Stephanie, and Maurice Tuchman, eds. *The Avant-Garde in Russia, 1910–1930: New Perspectives.* Los Angeles: Los Angeles County Museum of Art, 1980.

Bastia, Jean. Review of Baliev's Chauve-Souris. *Comoedia* 15, no. 3019 (23 March 1921).

Batault, Georges. "Le règne du 'Cabotin.'" *Montjoie!* no. 7 (16 May 1913).

Beauquier, Charles. *Philosophie de la musique.* Paris, 1865.

Beckwith, Robert Sterling. "A. D. Kastal'skii (1856–1926) and the Quest for a Native Russian Choral Style." Ph.D. diss., Cornell University, 1969.

Belaiev [Belyayev], Victor. *Igor Stravinsky's "Les Noces": An Outline.* Translated by S. W. Pring. London: Oxford University Press, 1928. Original Russian text in Viktor Mikhailovich Belyayev, *Musorgskiy, Skryabin, Stravinskiy: sbornik statey.* Moscow: Muzïka, 1972.

Beletsky, Igor, and Igor Blazhkov. "Spisok proizvedeniy I. F. Stravinskogo." Appendix to Igor Stravinsky and Robert Craft, *Dialogi,* translated by V. A. Linnik, edited by M. S. Druskin. Leningrad: Muzïka, 1971.

Belikov, P., and V. Knyazeva. *Rerikh.* Moscow: Molodaya Gvardiya, 1972.

Belïy, Andrey. *Arabeski.* Moscow, 1911; rpt. Munich: Wilhelm Fink Verlag, 1969.

———. "Formï iskusstva." In *Simvolizm.* Moscow, 1910; rpt. (as Slavische Propyläen, no. 62) Munich: Wilhelm Fink Verlag, 1969.

———. *Mezhdu dvukh revolyutsiy.* Leningrad: Izdatel'stvo Pisateley, 1934; rpt. Chicago: Russian Language Specialties, 1966.

———. "O teurgii." *Novïy put',* 1903, no. 2, 100–123.

———. "Realiora." *Vesï* 5, no. 5 (May 1908): 59–62.

Belkin, Anatoliy A. *Russkiye skomorokhi.* Moscow: Nauka, 1975.

Belousov, Yevsey. "Muzïkal'naya khronika." *Russkiye vedomosti,* no. 115 (1913).

Benjamin, William. Review of *The Structure of Atonal Music,* by Allen Forte. *Perspectives of New Music* 13, no. 1 (1974): 170–90.

Benois [Benua], Alexandre. "Beseda o balete." In V. Meyerhold et al., *Teatr,* 100–121. St. Petersburg: Shipovnik, 1908.

———. "Iz chastnoy perepiski: pis'mo khudozhnika A. B. k D. S. Merezhkovskomu." *Novïy put',* 1903, no. 2, 157–59.

———. "Khudozhestvennïye èresi." *Zolotoye runo,* 1906, no. 10.

———. "Khudozhestvennïye pis'ma." *Rech',* 4 August 1911 [on *Petrushka*]; rpt. *Muzïka,* no. 39 (27 August 1911).

———. "Khudozhestvennïye pis'ma: russkaya maslenitsa." *Rech',* 10 February 1917.

———. "Khudozhestvennïye pis'ma: russkiye spektakli v Parizhe: 'Zhar-ptitsa.'" *Rech',* 18 July 1910.

———. *Memoirs.* Translated by Moura Budberg. 2 vols. London: Chatto & Windus, 1960.

———. *Moí vospominaniya.* 2 vols. Moscow: Nauka, 1980.

———. "Novïye teatral'nïye postanovki." *Mir iskusstva,* 1902, no. 2.

———. "The Origins of the Ballets Russes (1944)." In Boris Kochno, *Diaghilev and the Ballets Russes,* 2–21. New York: Harper & Row, 1970.

———. *Reminiscences of the Russian Ballet.* Translated by Mary Britnieva. London: G. P. Putnam's Sons, 1941.

———. *The Russian School of Painting* (1904). Translated by Avrahm Yarmolinsky. New York: Alfred A. Knopf, 1916.

———. "Russkiye spektakli v Parizhe." *Rech',* 25 July 1909.

———. "Sochineniye 'Petrushki.'" *Posledniye novosti* (Paris), no. 3285 (21 March 1930).

———. *Voznikoveniye "Mira iskusstva."* Leningrad: Komitet Populyarizatsii Khudozhestvennïkh Izdaniy pri Gosudarstvennoy Akademii Material'noy Kul'turï, 1928.

———. "Vrubel'." *Mir iskusstva,* 1903, no. 10, 35–45.

Bent, Ian D. Liner notes to London Records OS 25978, "Pergolesi/STRAVINSKY: *Pulcinella,* Complete Ballet with Song" (1966).

Berger, Arthur. "Problems of Pitch Organization in Stravinsky" (1963). In *Perspectives on Schoenberg and Stravinsky,* edited by Edward T. Cone and Benjamin Boretz, 123–55. Princeton: Princeton University Press, 1968.

Berger, Karol. Review of *A Book About Stravinsky,* by Boris Asafyev. *Journal of Music Theory* 28 (1984): 294–302.

Berkov, Pavel Naumovich, ed. *Russkaya narodnaya drama XVII–XX vekov.* Moscow: Iskusstvo, 1953.

Berlin, Isaiah. "A Note on 'Khovanshchina.'" *New York Review of Books,* 19 December 1985, 40–42.

Berlioz, Hector. *The Memoirs of Hector Berlioz.* Translated by David Cairns. New York: Alfred A. Knopf, 1969.

Berman, M. M. *See* Dvinsky, M.

Bernandt, Grigoriy Borisovich, and Izraíl Markovich Yampolsky. *Kto pisal o muzïke.* 4 vols. Moscow: Sovetskiy Kompozitor, 1971–89.

Bernshteyn [Bernstein], Nikolai Davïdovich. Review of *Petrushka*. *Sankt-peterburgskiye vedomosti*, 25 January 1913.

Bïkov, Alexey Vasilyevich, ed. *Iz arkhivov russkikh muzïkantov*. Moscow: Muzgiz, 1962.

Bilibin, Ivan Yakovlevich. "Narodnoye tvorchestvo russkogo severa." *Mir iskusstva*, 1904, no. 11.

Billington, James. *The Icon and the Axe*. New York: Alfred A. Knopf, 1966.

Birkan, Rafaíl. "O tematizme 'Svadebki' Stravinskogo." In *Iz istorii muzïki XX veka*, edited by Mikhaíl Semyonovich Druskin, 169–88. Moscow: Muzïka, 1971.

Blagoy, D. D., et al., eds. *Pesni, sobranniye pisatelyami*. Literaturnoye nasledstvo, no. 79. Moscow: Nauka, 1968.

Blesh, Rudi. *Shining Trumpets: A History of Jazz*. 2d ed. New York: Alfred A. Knopf, 1958.

———. *They All Played Ragtime*. 4th ed. New York: Oak Publications, 1971.

Blok, Alexander Alexandrovich. *Sobraniye sochineniy*. Vol. 5. Moscow: Gosudarstvennoye Izdatel'stvo Khudozhestvennoy Literaturï, 1962.

———. *Sobraniye sochineniy v shesti tomakh*. Vol. 5. Moscow: Izdatel'stvo "Pravda," 1971.

———. *Stikhotvoreniya–poèmï–teatr*. Vol. 1. Leningrad: Khudozhestvennaya Literatura, 1972.

Blum, Stephen. "Communication." *Journal of the American Musicological Society* 39 (1986): 212–15.

Blumenkranz-Onimus, Noëmi. "'Montjoie!' ou l'héroïque croisade pour une nouvelle culture." In *L'année 1913*, edited by L. Brion Guerry, 2:1105–16. Paris: Klincksieck, 1971.

"B-m." "Kontsertï v Petrograde." *Russkaya muzïkal'naya gazeta* 21, no. 50 (14 December 1914), col. 948.

Bogdanov-Berezovsky, Valerian Mikhailovich. *Fyodor Stravinskiy*. Moscow and Leningrad: Muzgiz, 1951.

———. "Igor' Stravinskiy i yego 'Khronika.'" In Igor Stravinsky, *Khronika moyey zhizni*, translated from the French by L. V. Yakovlevna-Shaporina, 5–30. Leningrad: Muzgiz, 1963.

Boguslavsky, Sergey. "Gusliar' S. P. Kolosov i yego repertuar." *Khronika zhurnala "Muzïkal'niy sovremennik"*, no. 17 (25 February 1917).

Bortnikova, Yevgeniya Yermolayevna, ed. *Vospominaniya o P. I. Chaikovskom*. Moscow: Muzgiz, 1962.

Boulez, Pierre. *Notes of an Apprenticeship*. Translated by Herbert Weinstock. New York: Alfred A. Knopf, 1968.

———. "Stravinsky demeure." In *Musique russe*, edited by Pierre Souvtchinsky, 1:151–224. Paris: Presses Universitaires de France, 1953.

———. "Trajectoires: Ravel, Stravinsky, Schönberg." *Contrepoints* 6 (1949): 122–42.

Bowlt, John E. *Russian Art, 1875–1975*. New York: Barnes & Noble, 1976.

———. *Russian Stage Design: Scenic Innovation, 1900–1930*. Jackson: Mississippi Museum of Art, 1982.

———. *The Silver Age: Russian Art of the Early Twentieth Century and the "World of Art" Group*. Newtonville, Mass.: Oriental Research Partners, 1979.

———. "Synthesism and Symbolism: The Russian *World of Art* Movement." In *Literature and the Plastic Arts*, edited by Ian Higgins, 35–48. New York: Barnes & Noble, 1973.

———. "The World of Art." In *The Silver Age of Russian Culture*, edited by Carl Proffer and Ellendea Proffer, 114–39. Ann Arbor: Ardis, 1975.

Brailoiu, Constantin. "Sur une mélodie russe." In *Musique russe*, edited by Pierre Souvtchinsky, 2:329–92. Paris: Presses Universitaires de France, 1953.

Brillant, Maurice. "Les oeuvres et les hommes." *Correspondent,* 94, no. 1436 (25 July 1922).

Brodsky, L. M. "Sledï professional'nïkh skazochnikov v russkikh skazkakh." *Etnograficheskoye obozreniye* 16 (1904): 2–18.

Brody, Elaine. "Viñes in Paris: New Light on Twentieth-Century Performance Practice." In *A Musical Offering: Essays in Honor of Martin Bernstein,* edited by Edward H. Clinkscale and Claire Brook, 45–62. New York: Pendragon Press, 1977.

Brown, David. *Mikhail Glinka: A Biographical and Critical Study.* London: Oxford University Press, 1974.

Brown, Malcolm H. "Native Song and National Consciousness." In *Art and Culture in Nineteenth-Century Russia,* edited by Theofanis George Stavrou, 57–84. Bloomington: Indiana University Press, 1983.

———. "Skriabin and Russian 'Mystic' Symbolism." *19th-Century Music* 3 (1979–80): 42–51.

Bruneau, Alfred. *Musiques de Russie et musiciens de France.* Paris: Bibliothèque Charpentier, 1903.

Brussel, Henri. "Avant la féerie." *Revue musicale* 11, no. 110 (December 1930): 33–41.

"Brut" (pseud.). "Okolo teatra." *Golos Moskvï,* no. 195 (26 August/8 September 1914).

Bryusov, Valeriy Yakovlevich. "Lishnyaya pravda?" *Mir iskusstva,* 1902, nos. 5–6, 58–61.

Buckle, Richard. *Diaghilev.* New York: Atheneum, 1979.

———. *Nijinsky.* New York: Simon & Schuster, 1971.

Bullard, Truman C. "The First Performance of Igor Stravinsky's *Sacre du Printemps.*" 3 vols. Ph.D. diss., University of Rochester, 1971.

———. "The Riot at the Rite: Not So Surprising After All." In *Essays on Music for Charles Warren Fox,* edited by Jerald C. Graue, 206–11. Rochester: Eastman School of Music Press, 1979.

Burkhart, Charles. "Stravinsky's Revolving Canon." *Music Review* 29 (1968): 161–66.

Call, Paul. *Vasily I. Kelsiev: An Encounter Between the Russian Revolutionaries and the Old Believers.* Belmont, Mass.: Nordland, 1979.

Calvocoressi, Michel-Dmitri. "La comédie musicale: aux concerts." *Comoedia illustré* 6, no. 9 (5 February 1914).

———. "M. Igor Stravinsky's Opera: 'The Nightingale.'" *Musical Times* 55 (1914): 372–74.

———. *Musicians Gallery.* London: Faber & Faber, 1932.

———. "Novaya redaktsiya 'Khovanshchinï.'" *Russkaya muzïkal'naya gazeta* 20, no. 39 (29 September 1913), cols. 827–33.

———. "A Russian Composer of To-Day: Igor Stravinsky." *Musical Times* 52 (1911): 511–12.

Campbell, Stuart. "The 'Mavras' of Pushkin, Kochno, and Stravinsky." *Music and Letters* 58 (1977): 304–21.

Carter, Elliott. Memoir in two-issue special edition entitled "Stravinsky: A Composers' Memorial." *Perspectives of New Music* 9, no. 2–10, no. 1 (1971): 1–6.

Casella, Alfredo. *Igor Strawinski.* Rome: Formiggini, 1926.

———. *Music In My Time.* Translated by Spencer Norton. Norman: University of Oklahoma Press, 1955.

Chaikovsky, Modest Ilyich. *Zhizn' P. I. Chaikovskogo.* 3 vols. Moscow: Jurgenson, 1901–3. Abridged English translation: *The Life and Letters of Peter Ilich Tchaikovsky.* Edited by Rosa Newmarch. London, 1906.

Chaikovsky, Pyotr Ilyich. *The Diaries of Tchaikovsky.* Translated and edited by Wladimir Lakond. New York: W. W. Norton, 1945.

———. *Polnoye sobraniye sochineniy: literaturnïye proizvedeniya i perepiska.* Vol. 5. Moscow: Muzgiz, 1959.

Chaliapin, Fyodor Ivanovich. *Pages from My Life*. New York: Harper, 1927.

———. *Chaliapin: An Autobiography as Told to Maxim Gorky*. Translated and edited by Nina Froud and James Hanley. New York: Stein & Day, 1967.

Champfleury [Jules Fleury-Husson]. "Pierrot, valet de la mort." In *Souvenirs des Funambules*. Paris: Michel Lévy Frères, 1859.

"La Chauve-Souris à Moscou de Nikita Balieff au Théâtre Femina." Souvenir program, February 1921.

Chennevière, Daniel. Review of the Ballets Russes production of *Le coq d'or*. *Montjoie!* 2, nos. 4–6 (April–June 1914): 22.

Cherepnin, Nikolai Nikolayevich. "Pod sen'yu moyey zhizni." Typescript.

———. *Vospominaniya muzïkanta*. Leningrad: Muzïka, 1976.

Chernïshevsky, Nikolai Gavrilovich. *The Esthetic Relations of Art to Reality*. In *Selected Philosophical Essays*. Moscow: Foreign Languages Publishing House, 1953.

Cheshikhin, Vsevolod Yevgrafovich. *Istoriya russkoy operï*. 2d ed. Moscow: Jurgenson, 1905.

Cholopov, Jurij N. *See* Kholopov, Yu. N.

Christensen, Thomas. "Stravinsky's *Zvesdoliki*." In *Abstracts of Papers Read at the Forty-eighth Annual Meeting of the American Musicological Society, Meeting Jointly with the Society for Music Theory*, ed. D. Kern Holoman, 40–41. Philadelphia: American Musicological Society, 1982.

Chuaqui, Miguel. "Stravinsky and Distortion in *Pulcinella*." Seminar report, University of California, Berkeley, 1990.

Cocteau, Jean. *Cock and Harlequin*. Translated by Rollo Myers. London: Egoist Press, 1921.

———. "Critics and the Comic Spirit." *Vanity Fair* (1922). Reprinted in *Igor Stravinsky: A Merle Armitage Book*, edited by Edwin Corle, 23–24. New York: Duell, Sloan & Pearce, 1949.

Collaer, Paul. *Strawinsky*. Brussels: Éditions "Équilibres," 1930.

Cone, Edward T. "Stravinsky: The Progress of a Method." *Perspectives of New Music* 1, no. 1 (Fall 1962): 18–26. Reprinted in *Perspectives on Schoenberg and Stravinsky*, edited by Benjamin Boretz and Edward T. Cone, 156–64. Princeton: Princeton University Press, 1968. And in Edward T. Cone, *Music: A View from Delft*, 293–301. Chicago: University of Chicago Press, 1989.

Cooper, Martin. "Aleksandr Skryabin and the Russian Renaissance." *Studi musicali* 1 (1972): 327–54.

Copland, Aaron. *Copland on Music*. New York: W. W. Norton, 1963.

———. *The New Music, 1900–1960*. Rev. and enlarged ed. New York: W. W. Norton, 1968.

Corle, Edwin, ed. *Igor Stravinsky: A Merle Armitage Book*. New York: Duell, Sloan & Pearce, 1949.

Costello, D. P., and I. P. Foote, eds. *Russian Folk Literature*. Oxford: Clarendon Press, 1967.

Craft, Robert. "Assisting Stravinsky: On a Misunderstood Collaboration." *Atlantic Monthly*, December 1982, 68–74.

———. "Commentary to the Sketches." Booklet published with Igor Stravinsky, *The Rite of Spring: Sketches, 1911–1913*. London: Boosey & Hawkes, 1969.

———. "Deux morceaux pour Debussy." In *Avec Stravinsky*. Monaco: Éditions du Rocher, 1958.

———. "*Histoire du soldat* (the Musical Revisions, the Sketches, the Evolution of the Libretto)." *Musical Quarterly* 66 (1980): 321–38.

———. "Jews and Geniuses." *New York Review of Books*, 16 February 1989, 35–37. Reprinted in *Small Craft Advisories*, 274–81. New York: Thames & Hudson, 1989.

———. "My Life With Stravinsky." *New York Review of Books,* 10 June 1982, 6, 8–10.

———. "A Personal Preface." *The Score and I.M.A. Magazine,* no. 20 (1957): 7–13.

———. *Prejudices in Disguise.* New York: Alfred A. Knopf, 1974.

———. *Present Perspectives.* New York: Alfred A. Knopf, 1984.

———. Review of *The Harmonic Organization of "The Rite of Spring,"* by Allen Forte. *Musical Quarterly* 64 (1978): 524–35.

———. "*The Rite:* Counterpoint and Choreography." *Musical Times* 129 (1988): 171–76.

———. " 'The Rite of Spring': Genesis of a Masterpiece." Introduction to Igor Stravinsky, *The Rite of Spring: Sketches, 1911–1913.* London: Boosey & Hawkes, 1969.

———. "*Le Sacre du Printemps:* The Revisions." *Tempo,* no. 122 (1977): 2–8.

———. *Small Craft Advisories.* London: Thames & Hudson, 1989.

———. "The Story Behind Stravinsky's Rejection by L'Institut de France." *Ovation* 3, no. 5 (June 1982): 12–14, 33.

———. *Stravinsky: Chronicle of a Friendship (1948–1971).* New York: Alfred A. Knopf, 1972.

———, ed. "Appendix: Selected Source Material from 'A Catalogue of Books and Music Inscribed to and/or Autographed and Annotated by Igor Stravinsky.' " In *Confronting Stravinsky,* edited by Jann Pasler, 349–57. Berkeley and Los Angeles: University of California Press, 1986.

———. *Dearest Bubushkin: Selected Letters and Diaries of Vera and Igor Stravinsky.* New York: Thames & Hudson, 1985.

———. *Igor and Vera Stravinsky: A Photograph Album (1921–1971).* London: Thames & Hudson, 1982.

———. *Stravinsky: Selected Correspondence* (SelCorr). 3 vols. New York: Alfred A. Knopf, 1982–85.

———. *A Stravinsky Scrapbook, 1940–1971.* London: Thames & Hudson, 1983.

Craft, Robert, with William Harkins. "Stravinsky's *Svadebka:* An Introduction." *New York Review of Books,* 14 December 1972, 23–29.

Craft, Robert, and Brett Shapiro. "Catalogue of Some Books and Music Inscribed to and/or Autographed and Annotated by Igor Stravinsky, and of Private Recordings and Test-Pressings Labelled by Him in the Estate of Vera Stravinsky." Typescript, 1984.

Croce, Arlene. "Footnotes in the Sands of Time." *New Yorker,* 23 November 1987.

Cross, Samuel Hazzard, and Olgerd P. Sherbowitz, trans. *The Russian Primary Chronicle.* Cambridge: Cambridge University Press, 1953.

Cui, César Antonovich. *Izbrannïye pis'ma.* Leningrad: Muzgiz, 1955.

———. *Izbrannïye stat'i.* Leningrad: Muzgiz, 1952.

———. *La musique en Russie.* Paris: Fischbacher, 1880.

Cyr, Louis. "*Le sacre du printemps:* petite histoire d'une grande partition." In *Stravinsky: études et témoignages,* edited by François Lesure, 91–147. Paris: Éditions Jean Claude Lattès, 1982.

Dahl [Dal'], Vladimir Ivanovich. *Poslovitsï russkogo naroda.* St. Petersburg, 1862.

———. *Tolkovïy slovar' zhivogo velikorusskogo yazïka* (1863–66). 4 vols. Rpt. Tokyo: Nauka Reprint Co., 1984.

Dahlhaus, Carl. *Between Romanticism and Modernism.* Translated by Mary Whittall. Berkeley and Los Angeles: University of California Press, 1980.

———. *Nineteenth-Century Music.* Translated by J. Bradford Robinson. Berkeley and Los Angeles: University of California Press, 1989.

———. *Realism in Nineteenth-Century Music.* Translated by Mary Whittall. Cambridge: Cambridge University Press, 1985.

Dansker, O. L., ed. *N. A. Mal'ko: vospominaniya, stat'i, pis'ma.* Leningrad: Muzïka, 1972.

Davenson, Henri. Obituary for Arthur Lourié. *Perspectives of New Music* 5, no. 2 (Spring–Summer 1967): 166–69.

"D. de R." (*see also* Derzhanovsky, V. V.; "Florestan"]. "Za rubezhom: novïye sochineniya Igorya Stravinskogo." *Muzïka,* no. 219 (18 April 1915).

Dent, Edward J. Review of *Pribaoutki. Athenaeum,* 30 July 1920.

Derzhanovsky, Vladimir Vladimirovich (*see also* "D. de R."; "Florestan"). "'Iz yaponskoy liriki' Ig. Stravinskogo." *Muzïka,* no. 159 (7 December 1913).

——. "K ispolneniyu prelyudii-kantatï 'Iz Gomera.'" *Muzïka,* no. 28 (10 June 1911): 603–4.

Diaghilev, Sergey Pavlovich. "Diaghileff Talks of Soul of the Ballet." *New York Post,* 24 January 1916.

——. *Exposition de l'art russe.* Paris: Salon d'Automne, 1906.

——. *Istoriya russkoy zhivopisi XVIII veka.* Vol. 1: *D. G. Levitskiy.* St. Petersburg, 1902.

——. "Neskol'ko slov o S. V. Malyutine." *Mir iskusstva,* 1903, no. 4.

——. "Otvet N. N. Rimskoy-Korsakovoy." *Rech',* 10 September 1910.

——. "Pis'mo v redaktsiyu." *Birzheviye vedomosti,* 4 February 1913.

——. "Portretist Shibanov." *Mir iskusstva,* 1904, no. 3, 125–37.

——. "Slozhnïye voprosï." *Mir iskusstva,* 1899, nos. 1–2, 14–15, 52.

——. "V chas itogov." *Vesï* 2, no. 4 (April 1905): 45–46.

Dianin, Serge [Sergey Alexandrovich]. *Borodin.* Translated by Robert Lord. London: Oxford University Press, 1963.

——, ed. *Pis'ma A. P. Borodina.* Vols. 2–3. Moscow: Muzgiz, 1936–49.

Dmitriyevsky, V. N., and E. R. Katernina. *Shalyapin v Peterburge-Petrograde.* Leningrad: Lenizdat, 1976.

Dobrotvorsky, Ivan. *Lyudi bozhii: russkaya sekta tak nazïvayemïkh dukhovnïkh khristian.* Kazan: University Press, 1869.

Dostoyevsky, Fyodor. *The Diary of a Writer.* Translated by Boris Brasol. Santa Barbara: Peregrine Smith, 1979.

Druskin, Mikhaíl Semyonovich. *Igor' Stravinskiy: lichnost', tvorchestvo, vzglyadï.* Leningrad: Sovetskiy Kompozitor, 1974. English translation: *Igor Stravinsky: His Personality, Works, and Views.* Translated by Martin Cooper. Cambridge: Cambridge University Press, 1983.

——. *Russkaya revolyutsionnaya pesnya.* Moscow: Muzgiz, 1954.

Duke, Vernon. *Passport to Paris.* Boston: Little, Brown, 1945.

Dvinsky, M. [M. M. Berman]. "O dyagilevskoy postanovki 'Khovanshchinï.'" *Birzheviye vedomosti,* 22 January 1913.

——. "U Igorya Stravinskogo." *Birzheviye vedomosti,* 25 September 1912.

Dvonchin, Georgette. *The Influence of French Symbolism on Russian Poetry.* Slavistische drukken en herdrukken, no. 19. The Hague: Mouton, 1958.

Dyachkova, L. S., ed., with Boris M. Yarustovsky. *I. F. Stravinskiy: stat'i i materialï* (IStrSM). Moscow: Sovetskiy Kompozitor, 1973.

Eliot, Thomas Stearns. "Tradition and the Individual Talent" (1919). In *Selected Prose of T. S. Eliot,* edited by Frank Kermode. New York: Harcourt Brace Jovanovich/Farrar, Straus, Giroux, 1975.

Engel, Yuliy Dmitriyevich [Joel]. *Glazami sovremennika.* Moscow: Sovetskiy Kompozitor, 1971.

Engelhardt, Jürgen. *Gestus und Verfremdung: Studien zum Musiktheater bei Strawinsky und Brecht/Weill.* Munich: Katzbichler Verlag, 1984.

Ernst, Sergey. *Aleksandr Benua.* Petrograd, 1921.

Evans, Edwin. *Stravinsky: "The Fire-Bird" and "Petrushka."* Oxford: Oxford University Press, 1933.

———. "The Stravinsky Debate." *Music Student,* no. 13 (December 1920).

Famintsïn, Alexander Sergeyevich. *"Gusli"—russkiy narodnïy muzïkal'nïy instrument.* Pamyatniki drevney pis'mennosti i iskusstva, no. 82. St. Petersburg, 1890.

———. *Skomorokhi na Rusi.* St. Petersburg, 1889.

Fels, Florent. "Un entretien avec Igor Stravinsky à propos de l'enregistrement au phonographe de *Pétrouchka.*" *Nouvelles littéraires,* 8 December 1928. Reprinted in *Stravinsky: études et témoignages,* edited by François Lesure. Paris: Éditions Jean Claude Lattès, 1982.

Fesenkova, Nadezhda Grigoryevna. Introduction and commentary to *Vosponimaniya,* by L. A. Kashperova. In *Muzïkal'noye nasledstvo,* vol. 2, pt. 2, 135–36, 166–67. Moscow: Muzïka, 1968.

Filosofov, Dmitriy Vladimirovich. "Russkaya tyazhba za granitsey." *Russkoye slovo,* 29 May 1914.

———. *Slova i zhizn': literaturnïye sporï noveyshego vremeni.* St. Petersburg, 1909.

Findeisen, Nicholas (*see also* Findeyzen, N. F.). "The Earliest Russian Operas." Translated by M. D. Calvocoressi. *Musical Quarterly* 19 (1933): 331–40.

Findeyzen, Nikolai Fyodorovich. *Ocherki po istorii muzïki v Rossii.* 2 vols. Moscow and Leningrad: Muzgiz, 1929.

———. "Pamyati F. I. Stravinskogo." *Russkaya muzïkal'naya gazeta* 9, no. 48 (1 December 1902), cols. 1199–1204.

———. *Petrovskiye kantï.* In *Izvestiya Akademii Nauk SSSR* (Moscow, 1927).

Flanner, Janet. "Profiles: Russian Firebird." *New Yorker,* 5 January 1935, 23–28.

"Florestan" (*see also* Derzhanovsky, V. V.; "D. de R."). "Igor' Stravinskiy (k segodnyashnemu konzertu)." *Utro Rossii,* 24 August 1912.

Fokine, Mikhail Mikhailovich. *Memoirs of a Ballet Master.* Translated by Vitale Fokine, edited by Anatole Chujoy. Boston: Little, Brown, 1961.

Forte, Allen. *The Harmonic Organization of "The Rite of Spring."* New Haven: Yale University Press, 1978.

———. "A Hymenopteran Response." *Music Analysis* 5 (1986): 321–37.

Francisque, Anthoine. *Le trésor d'Orphée.* Edited by Henri Quittard. Paris: Marcel Fortin, 1906.

Frankenstein, Alfred. "Victor Hartmann and Modeste Musorgsky." *Musical Quarterly* 25 (1939): 268–91.

Frazer, Sir James. *The Golden Bough: A Study in Magic and Religion.* Abridged ed. New York: Macmillan, 1947.

Frid, Emiliya Lazarevna, Yuliy Anatolyevich Kremlyov, and Anastasiya Sergeyevna Lyapunova, eds. *Miliy Alekseyevich Balakirev: issledovaniya i stat'i.* Leningrad: Muzgiz, 1961.

Fromrich-Bonéfant, Mme, ed. *Collection musicale André Meyer.* Abbéville: Imp. Paillart, 1961.

Garafola, Lynn. *Diaghilev's Ballets Russes.* New York: Oxford University Press, 1989.

Garden, Edward. *Balakirev.* New York: St. Martin's Press, 1967.

Gárdonyi, Zoltán. "Neue Tonleiter- und Sequenztypen in Liszts Frühwerken (zur Frage der 'Lisztschen Sequenzen')." *Studia musicologica* 11 (1969): 168–99.

Gautier, Théophile. *Complete Works.* Translated and edited by S. C. de Sumichrast. London: Athenaeum Press, n.d. [1904].

Ghéon, Henri. "Propos divers sur le Ballet Russe." *Nouvelle revue française* 4 (1910): 199–211.

Ginzburg, Semyon Lvovich. *Istoriya russkoy muzïki v notnïkh obraztsakh*. 3 vols. Moscow: Muzïka, 1969.

———, ed. *N. A. Rimskiy-Korsakov i muzïkal'noye obrazovaniye*. Leningrad: Muzgiz, 1959.

Glebov, Igor *(see also* Asafyev, B V.). *Kniga o Stravinskom*. Leningrad: Triton, 1929. Reprinted under the name B. Asafyev as *Kniga o Stravinskom*. Leningrad: Muzïka, 1977. English translation: Boris Asaf'yev. *A Book About Stravinsky*. Translated by Richard French. Ann Arbor: UMI Research Press, 1982.

———. "Soblaznï i preodoleniya." *Melos*, no. 1 (1917).

Glezer, Raísa Vladimirovna, ed. *M. F. Gnesin: stat'i, vospominaniya, materialï*. Moscow: Sovetskiy Kompozitor, 1961.

Glière, Reinhold Moritzevich. "Vstrechi s belyayevskim kruzhkom." *Sovetskaya muzïka*, 1949, no. 8, 65–68.

Glinka, Mikhaíl Ivanovich. "Zapiski" (Autobiography). In *Literaturnïye proizvedieniya i perepiska*, vol. 1. Moscow: Muzgiz, 1973. English translation: *Memoirs*. Translated by Richard B. Mudge. Norman: University of Oklahoma Press, 1963.

Glumov, Alexander. *Muzïka v russkom dramaticheskom teatre*. Moscow: Muzgiz, 1955.

Gnesin, Mikhaíl Fabianovich. "Maksimilian Shteynberg." *Sovetskaya muzïka*, 1946, no. 12, 27–31.

———. *Mïsli i vospominaniya o N. A. Rimskom-Korsakove*. Moscow: Muzgiz, 1956.

———. "N. A. Rimskiy-Korsakov: pedagog i chelovek." *Sovetskaya muzïka*, 1945, no. 3, 202–5.

Godowsky, Dagmar. *First Person Plural*. New York: Viking Press, 1958.

Gojowy, Detlef. "Arthur Lourié der Futurist." *Hindemith-Jahrbuch* 8 (1979): 147–85; and 12 (1983): 116–57.

———. *Neue sowjetische Musik der 20er Jahre*. Regensburg: Laaber-Verlag, 1980.

———. *La vie musicale en U.R.S.S. de 1900 à 1930*. Paris: IRCAM, n.d.

Gold, Arthur, and Robert Fizdale. *Misia: The Life of Misia Sert*. New York: Alfred A. Knopf, 1980.

Goldshteyn, Mikhaíl. "Zwei Briefe von Igor Strawinsky." *Musik des Ostens* 7 (1975): 280–83.

Goldwater, Robert. *Symbolism*. New York: Harper & Row, 1979.

Golovinsky, Grigoriy Lvovich. "Stravinskiy i fol'klor: nablyudeniya i zametki." In *I. F. Stravinskiy: stat'i, vospominaniya*, edited by G. Alfeyevskaya and I. Vershinina, 68–93. Moscow: Sovetskiy Kompozitor, 1985.

Golub, Spencer. *Evreinov: The Theatre of Paradox and Transformation*. Ann Arbor: UMI Research Press, 1984.

Golubinsky, Yevgeniy. *Istoriya kanonizatsii svyatïkh v russkoy tserkvi*. 2d ed. Moscow: Universitetskaya Tipografiya, 1903.

Gorodetsky, Sergey Mitrofanovich. "Moy put'." In *Sovetskiye pisateli: avtobiografii v dvukh tomakh*, 1:317–35. Moscow: Sovetskiy Pisatel', 1959.

———. *Stikhotvoreniya i poèmï*. Edited by E. I. Prokhorov. Leningrad: Sovetskiy Pisatel', 1974.

———. *Yar': stikhi liricheskiye i liro-èpicheskiye*. St. Petersburg: Kruzhok Molodïkh, 1907.

Gorodetsky, Sergey Mitrofanovich, Victor Grigoryevich Valter, and Iosif Ivanovich Vitol. *A. N. Lyadov*. Petrograd: Izdatel'stvo Popechitel'nogo Soveta dlya Pooshchreniya Russkikh Kompozitorov [M. P. Belyayev], 1916.

Gozenpud, Abram Akimovich. *Russkiy opernïy teatr XIX veka*. Vols. 1–3. Leningrad: Muzïka, 1969–73.

———. *Russkiy opernïy teatr i Shalyapin, 1890–1904*. Leningrad: Muzïka, 1974.

————. *Russkiy operniy teatr mezhdu dvukh revolyutsiy, 1905–1917*. Leningrad: Muzïka, 1975.

Grabar, Igor Emmanuilovich. "Teatr i khudozhniki." *Vesï* 5, no. 4 (April 1908).

Graham, Irina. "Arthur Sergeevič Lourié—biographische Notizen." *Hindemith-Jahrbuch* 8 (1979): 186–207.

Gray, Camilla. *The Russian Experiment in Art, 1863–1922*. London: Thames & Hudson, 1962.

Grechaninov, Alexander Tikhonovich, et al. "Vïkriki raznoschikov v zapisyakh A. T. Grechaninova, A. M. Listopadova, N. A. Nevstruyeva, N. A. Yanchuka i D. I. Arak-chiyeva." *Trudï MEK* 1:497–516.

Grigoriev, S. L. [Sergey Leonidovich Grigoryev]. *The Diaghilev Ballet, 1909–1929*. London: Constable, 1953.

Grigoryev, Apollon Alexandrovich. *My Literary and Moral Wanderings*. New York: E. P. Dutton, 1962.

————. "Russkiy teatr v Peterburge." *Epokha*, 1864, no. 3.

Grimm's Fairy Tales. Translated by E. V. Lucas, Lucy Crane, and Marian Edwards. New York: Grosset & Dunlap, 1945.

Grosheva, Yelena Andreyevna, ed. *Fyodor Ivanovich Shalyapin*. 2 vols. Moscow: Iskusstvo, 1957–58; 2d ed., 1970–77.

Grover, Stuart. "Savva Mamontov and the Mamontov Circle, 1870–1905: Art Patronage and the Rise of Nationalism in Russian Art." Ph.D. diss., University of Wisconsin, 1971.

"Gr. Pr." (*see also* Prokofiev, G. P.). "Teatr i muzïka." *Russkiye vedomosti*, 24 August 1912, 4.

"G. T." (*see also* Timofeyev, G. N.). "Vecher 'muzïkal'nïkh novostey.'" *Rech'*, 29 January [11 February] 1908, 4.

Gumilyov, Nikolai Stepanovich. "Novïye sborniki stikhov." *Vesï* 5, no. 12 (December 1908): 57–61.

Guseva, A. "Pamyati M. O. Shteynberga." *Sovetskaya muzïka*, 1984, no. 12, 133–34.

Guyau, Jean-Marie. *Les problèmes de l'esthétique contemporaine*. Paris: Alcan, 1884.

Hahl-Koch, Jelena, ed. *Arnold Schoenberg/Wassily Kandinsky: Letters, Pictures, and Documents*. Translated by John C. Crawford. London: Faber & Faber, 1984.

Haimo, Ethan, and Paul Johnson, eds. *Stravinsky Retrospectives*. Lincoln: University of Nebraska Press, 1987.

Halm, August. *Von zwei Kulturen der Musik* (1913). 3d ed. Stuttgart: Klett, 1947.

Halperin, Charles J. "Russia and the Steppe: George Vernadsky and Eurasianism." *Forschungen zur osteuropäischen Geschichte* 36 (1985): 55–194.

Hamilton, David. "Igor Stravinsky: A Discography of the Composer's Performances." *Perspectives of New Music* 9, no. 2–10, no. 1 (1971): 163–79.

Hamm, Charles, ed. *Petrushka*. Norton Critical Scores. New York: W. W. Norton, 1967.

Harding, James. *Erik Satie*. New York: Praeger, 1975.

Harkins, William E. "The Text of Stravinsky's *Les Noces*." Typescript.

Harris, Simon. "Chord-Forms Based on the Whole-Tone Scale in Early Twentieth-Century Music." *Music Review* 41 (1980): 36–51.

Harrison, Jane Ellen. *Ancient Art and Ritual* (1913). Bradford-on-Avon: Moonraker Press, 1978.

Haskell, Arnold, with Walter Nouvel. *Diaghileff: His Artistic and Private Life*. New York: Simon & Schuster, 1935; rpt. New York: Da Capo Press, 1978.

Hasty, Christopher F. "On the Problem of Succession and Continuity in Twentieth-Century Music." *Music Theory Spectrum* 8 (1986): 58–74.

Hellman, Lillian. *The North Star: A Motion Picture About Some Russian People*. New York: Viking Press, 1943.

Herodotus. *The Persian Wars*. Translated by Alfred Denis Godley. London: W. Heinemann, 1963.

Heyman, Barbara B. "Stravinsky and Ragtime." *Musical Quarterly* 68 (1982): 543–62.

Hill, Edward Burlingame. "The Young Composers' Movement." *Modern Music* 5, no. 4 (May–June 1928).

Hodeir, André. *Since Debussy: A View of Contemporary Music*. Translated by Noel Burch. New York: Grove Press, 1961.

Hodson, Millicent. "The Fascination Continues: Searching for Nijinsky's *Sacre*." *Dance Magazine* 54, no. 6 (June 1980): 64–66, 71–75.

———. "Nijinsky's Choreographic Method: Visual Sources from Roerich for *Le Sacre du Printemps*." *Dance Research Journal* 18, no. 2 (Winter 1986–87): 7–15.

———. "Nijinsky's New Dance: Rediscovery of Ritual Design in *Le Sacre du Printemps*." Ph.D. diss., University of California, Berkeley, 1985.

———. "*Sacre*: Searching for Nijinsky's Chosen One." *Ballet Review* 15, no. 3 (Fall 1987): 53–66.

Hoffman, Stephani Hope. "Scythianism: A Cultural Vision in Revolutionary Russia." Ph.D. diss., Columbia University, 1975.

Hogan, Catherine. "'Threni': Stravinsky's Debt to Krenek." *Tempo*, no. 141 (1982): 22–25.

Hucher, Yves. *Florent Schmitt*. Paris: Éditions le Bon Plaisir, 1953.

Hulme, Thomas Ernest. "Romanticism and Classicism." In *Criticism: The Major Texts*, enlarged ed., edited by Walter Jackson Bate. New York: Harcourt Brace Jovanovich, 1970.

———. *Speculations*. Edited by Herbert Read. London: Kegan Paul, Trench, Trubner, 1936.

Ilyashenko, Andrey Stepanovich. "O 'Vesne svyashchennoy' I. Stravinskogo." *Russkaya muzïkal'naya gazeta* 21, no. 6 (9 February 1914), col. 155.

Imbrie, Andrew. "One Measure of Eternity." *Perspectives of New Music* 9, no. 2–10, no. 1 (1971): 51–57.

Istomin, Fyodor Mikhailovich, and Georgiy Ottonovich Dyutsh. *Pesni russkogo naroda, sobranï v guberniyakh Arkhangel'skoy i Olonetskoy v 1886 godu. Zapisali slova F. M. Istomin, napevï G. O. Dyutsh*. St Petersburg: Imperial Russian Geographical Society, 1894.

Istomin, Fyodor Mikhailovich, and Sergey Mikhailovich Lyapunov. *Pesni russkogo naroda, sobranï v guberniyakh Vologodskoy i Kostromskoy v 1893 godu. Zapisali slova F. M. Istomin, napevï S. M. Lyapunov*. St. Petersburg: Imperial Russian Geographical Society, 1899.

Ivanov, Georgiy Konstantinovich. *Russkaya poèziya v otechestvennoy muzïke (do 1917 goda): spravochnik*. 2 vols. Moscow: Sovetskiy Kompozitor, 1966–69.

Ivanov, Vyacheslav Ivanovich. "O narisovannïkh glazakh: o Shalyapine i o 'Khovanshchine' v Bol'shom Teatre." *Muzïka*, no. 108 (15 December 1912).

———. "Vechera sovremennoy muzïki." *Muzïka*, no. 165 (18 January 1914).

Ivanov, Vyacheslav Ivanovich, and Mikhaíl Gershenzon. "A Corner-to-Corner Correspondence," translated by Gertrude Vakar. In *Russian Intellectual History: An Anthology*, edited by Marc Raeff, 372–401. New York: Harcourt, Brace & World, 1966.

Jacobs, Arthur. "Talking with Igor Stravinsky." *Radio Times*, 21 May 1954.

Jacobs, Paul. Liner notes to Nonesuch H-71347, "Igor Stravinsky: Music for Two Pianos and Piano Four Hands" (1978).

Jakobson, Roman. "On Russian Fairy Tales." Commentary to [A. N. Afanasyev], *Russian Fairy Tales*, translated by Norbert Guterman. New York: Pantheon Books, 1945.

Jakobson, Svatáva Pirková. "Slavic Folklore." In *Funk & Wagnall's Standard Dictionary of Folklore, Mythology, and Legend*, vol. 2. New York: Funk & Wagnall, 1950.

Jankelevitch, Vladimir. *Ravel*. Translated by Margaret Crosland. New York: Grove Press, 1959.

Johns, Donald C. "An Early Serial Idea of Stravinsky." *Music Review* 23 (1962): 305–13.

Johnsson, Bengt. "Modernities in Liszt's Works." *Svensk tidskrift för musikforskning* 46 (1964): 83–117.

Joseph, Charles M. *Stravinsky and the Piano*. Ann Arbor: UMI Research Press, 1983.

———. "Stravinsky's Piano Scherzo (1902) in Perspective: A New Starting Point." *Musical Quarterly* 67, no. 1 (January 1981): 82–93.

Julien, Adolphe. "Chronique musicale." *Édition hebdomadaire du Journal des débats,* no. 1478 (23 June 1922).

Just, Martin. "Tonordnung und Thematik in Strawinskys 'Feu d'artifice,' op. 4." *Archiv für Musikwissenschaft* 40 (1983): 61–72.

Juszkiewicz, Anton. *Melodie ludowe litewskie (Litauische Volks-Weisen)*. Cracow, 1900. Reprinted as *Litovskiye svadebnïye pesni*. Vilnius, 1955.

Kalachov, Nikolai. *Arkhiv istoriko-yuridicheskikh svedeniy otnosyashchikhsya do Rossii*. Vol. 1. St. Petersburg: A. E. Landau, 1876.

Karasyov, Pavel Alexeyevich. "Besedï s Nikolayem Andreyevichem Rimskim-Korsakovïm." *Russkaya muzïkal'naya gazeta* 15, no. 49 (7 December 1908), cols. 1117–22.

———. "Narodnoye tvorchestvo, russkaya muzïka i N. A. Rimskiy-Korsakov." *Trudï MEK* 2:365–77.

"Kar." (*see also* Karatïgin, V. G.). "Teatr i muzïka." *Stolichnaya pochta*, no. 220 (25 January [7 February] 1908): 6.

Karatïgin, Vyacheslav Gavrilovich (*see also* "Kar."). *Izbrannïye stat'i*. Moscow: Muzïka, 1965.

———. " 'Khovanshchina' i yeyo avtorï." *Muzïkal'nïy sovremennik* 2, nos. 5–6 (1917): 192–218.

———. "Kontsertnoye obozreniye." *Yezhegodnik imperatorskikh teatrov*, no. 4 (1910): 153–69.

———. "Molodïye russkiye kompozitorï." *Apollon*, 1910, no. 11, 33–41.

———. "Pamyati N. A. Sokolova." *Orfey* (Petrograd) 1 (1922).

———. "Sed'moy kontsert Kusevitskogo." *Rech'*, 25 January 1913.

———. "Teatr i muzïka." *Rech'*, 7 May 1914.

———. "Vechera sovremennoy muzïki." *Vesï* 3, nos. 3–4 (1906): 70–73.

———. " 'Vesna svyashchennaya.' " *Rech'*, 16 February 1914.

Karlinsky, Simon. "The Composer's Workshop." *The Nation,* 15 June 1970.

———. "Igor Stravinskii—East and West." *Slavic Review* 27, no. 3 (September 1968): 452–58.

———. "A Pocket Full of Buttered Figs." *Times Literary Supplement,* 5 July 1985.

———. *Russian Drama from Its Beginnings to the Age of Pushkin*. Berkeley and Los Angeles: University of California Press, 1985.

———. "The Repatriation of Igor Stravinsky." *Slavic Review* 33, no. 3 (September 1974): 528–32.

———. "Stravinsky and Russian Pre-literate Theater." *19th-Century Music* 6, no. 3 (Spring 1983): 232–40.

Karsavin, Lev Platonovich. *Vostok, zapad i russkaya ideya*. Petrograd: Ogni, 1922.

Karsavina, Tamara Platonovna. *Theatre Street*. London: Heinemann, 1930.

Kashkin, Nikolai Dmitriyevich. "Teatr i muzïka." *Russkoye slovo,* 20 January 1915.

Kashperova, Leokadia Alexandrovna. *Vospominaniya*. In *Muzïkal'noye nasledstvo*, vol. 2, pt. 2, 135–68. Moscow: Muzïka, 1968.

Kastalsky, Alexander Dmitriyevich. "Iz zapisok." In *I. F. Stravinskiy: stat'i i materialï* (IStrSM), edited by L. S. Dyachkova, 207–13. Moscow: Sovetskiy Kompozitor, 1973.

Kazanskaya, Larisa. "Stepan Mitusov." *Sovetskaya muzïka,* 1990, no. 12, 80–84.

Kean, Beverly Whitney. *All the Empty Palaces.* New York: Universe Books, 1983.

Keldïsh, Yuriy Vsevolodovich. *Ocherki i issledovaniya po istorii russkoy muzïki.* Moscow: Sovetskiy Kompozitor, 1978.

Keller, Hans. "Shostakovich's Twelfth Quartet." *Tempo,* no. 94 (Autumn 1970): 6–15.

Kelly, Catriona. *Petrushka: The Russian Carnival Puppet Theatre.* Cambridge: Cambridge University Press, 1990.

Kelsiyev, Vasiliy Ivanovich. *Sbornik pravitel'stvennïkh svedeniy o raskol'nikakh.* 4 vols. London: Trübner, 1862.

Kenyon, Nicholas, ed. *Authenticity and Early Music.* Oxford: Oxford University Press, 1988.

Kerman, Joseph. "A Romantic Detail in Schubert's *Schwanengesang.*" *Musical Quarterly* 48 (1962): 36–49.

Keynes, Milo, ed. *Lydia Lopokova.* New York: St. Martin's Press, 1982.

Kholopov, Yuriy Nikolayevich. "Diatonicheskiye ladï i tertsovïye khromaticheskiye sistemï v muzïke Prokof'yeva." In *Ot Lyulli do nashikh dney,* edited by Valentina Dzhosefovna Konen. Moscow: Muzïka, 1967.

——— . "Simmetrichnïye ladï v teoreticheskikh sistemakh Yavorskogo i Messiana." *Muzïka i sovremennost'* 7 (1971): 247–93.

——— [Jurij N. Cholopov]. "Symmetrische Leitern in der russischen Musik." *Musikforschung* 28 (1975): 379–407.

Kielian-Gilbert, Marianne. "Relationships of Symmetrical Pitch-Class Sets and Stravinsky's Metaphor of Polarity." *Perspectives of New Music* 21 (1982–83): 210–21.

Kinkulkina, Natalya. "Pis'ma I. F. Stravinskogo i F. I. Shalyapina k A. A. Saninu." *Sovetskaya muzïka,* 1978, no. 6, 92–96.

Kireyevsky, Pavel Vasilyevich. *Pesni, sobrannïye P. V. Kireyevskim. Novaya seriya. Izdanï Obshchestvom Lyubiteley Rossiyskoy Slovesnosti pri Imperatorskom Moskovskom Universitete.* Vol. 1: *Pesni obryadovïye.* Edited by V. F. Miller and M. N. Speransky. Moscow: Pechatnya A. I. Snegiryovoy, 1911.

Kirstein, Lincoln. *Movement and Metaphor: Four Centuries of Ballet.* New York: Praeger, 1970.

——— . "The Instigator." Review of *Diaghilev,* by Richard Buckle. *New York Review of Books,* 8 November 1979, 3–5.

Kiselyov, Vasiliy Alexandrovich, ed. *M. A. Balakirev: perepiska s N. G. Rubinshteynom i s M. P. Belyayevïm.* Moscow: Muzgiz, 1956.

Klimovitsky, Abram Iosifovich. "Dve 'Pesni o Blokhe'—Betkhovena i Musorgskogo— v instrumentovke Stravinskogo (k izucheniyu rukopisnogo naslediya i tvorcheskoy biografii Stravinskogo)." In *Pamyatniki kul'turï: novïye otkrïtiya, 1984,* 196–216. Leningrad: Nauka, 1986.

——— . "Ob odnom neizvestnom avtografe I. Stravinskogo (k probleme tvorcheskogo formirovaniya kompozitora)." In *Pamyatniki kul'turï: novïye otkrïtiya, 1986,* 227–36. Leningrad: Nauka, 1987.

Kolberg, O. *Piesni ludu litewskiego.* Cracow, 1879.

Kochno, Boris Petrovich. *Diaghilev and the Ballets Russes.* New York: Harper & Row, 1970.

Kodryanskaya, Natalya. *Remizov v svoikh pis'makh.* Paris: Private printing, 1978.

Koechlin, Charles. "Le 'Retour à Bach.'" *Revue musicale* 8, no. 1 (November 1926).

Koptyayev, Alexander Petrovich. Review of *Petrushka. Vechernyaya birzhevaya gazeta,* 24 January 1913.

——— . Review of *Petrushka. Birzhevïye vedomosti,* 12/25 December 1913.

———. Review of *The Rite of Spring*. *Birzheviye vedomosti*, 14/27 February 1914.

Kostïlyov, Nikolai. "Nashe iskusstvo vo Parizhe." *Russkaya molva*, 24 May 1913.

Kozlova, Miralda Georgiyevna, and Nina Romanovna Yatsenko, eds. *S. S. Prokof'yev i N. YA. Myaskovskiy: perepiska*. Moscow: Sovetskiy Kompozitor, 1977.

Krader, Barbara. "Ethnomusicology." In *The New Grove Dictionary of Music and Musicians*, 6:275–82. London: Macmillan, 1980.

Kramer, Jonathan D. "Moment Form in Twentieth-Century Music." *Musical Quarterly* 64 (1978): 177–94.

———. "New Temporalities in Music." *Critical Inquiry* 7 (1981): 539–56.

———. *Time and the Meanings of Music*. New York: Schirmer Books, 1988.

Krasovskaya, Vera Mikhailovna. *Nijinsky*. Translated by John E. Bowlt. New York: Schirmer Books, 1979.

———. *Russkiy baletnïy teatr nachala XX veka*. 2 vols. Leningrad: Iskusstvo, 1971–72.

Kroó, György. *Rácz Aladár*. Budapest: Zenemükiadó, 1979.

Kryukov, Andrey Nikolayevich, ed. *Vospominaniya o B. V. Asaf'yeve*. Leningrad: Muzïka, 1974.

Kurdyumov, Yuriy. *See* "Yu. K."

Kutateladze, Larisa Mikhailovna, and Abram Akimovich Gozenpud, eds. *F. Stravinskiy: stat'i, pis'ma, vospominaniya*. Leningrad: Muzïka, 1972.

Kutateladze, Larisa Mikhailovna, and Lev Nikolayevich Raaben, eds. *Aleksandr Il'yich Ziloti, 1863–1945: vospominaniya i pis'ma*. Leningrad: Muzgiz, 1963.

Kutepov, Konstantin. *Sektï khlïstov i skoptsov*. 2d ed. Stavropol, 1900.

Kuznetsov, Anatoliy. "V zerkale russkoy kritiki." *Sovetskaya muzïka*, 1982, no. 6, 69–75.

Kuznetsov, Yevgeniy, ed. *Russkiye narodnïye gulyaniya po rasskazam A. Ya. Alekseyeva-Yakovleva*. Leningrad: Iskusstvo, 1948.

Kuznetsova, I. S., ed. *Fyodor Ivanovich Shalyapin: sbornik*. 2 vols. Moscow: Iskusstvo, 1958.

Krzhimovskaya, Yekaterina Leonidovna. "Skryabin i russkiy simvolizm." *Sovetskaya muzïka*, 1985, no. 2, 82–86.

Laloy, Louis. "Le mois." *Revue musical S.I.M.*, no. 5 (June 1909).

———. "La musique." *La revue de Paris* 29, no. 4 (July–August 1922).

Lambert, Constant. *Music Ho! A Study of Music in Decline* (1934). 3d ed. London: Hogarth Press, 1985.

Lamm, Pavel. "Ot redaktora/Einleitung des Herausgebers." In M. P. Musorgsky, *Polnoye sobraniye sochineniy*, vol. 2. Moscow/Vienna: Muzgiz/Universal-Edition, 1931; rpt. New York: Edwin F. Kalmus, n.d. (as vol. 4).

Laroche, Hermann [German Avgustovich Larosh]. *Sobraniye muzïkal'no-kriticheskikh statey*. Vol. 1. Moscow, 1913.

Laudon, Robert T. *The Sources of the Wagnerian Synthesis*. Munich: Katzbichler Verlag, 1978.

Lawson, Rex. "Stravinsky and the Pianola." In *Confronting Stravinsky*, edited by Jann Pasler, 284–301. Berkeley and Los Angeles: University of California Press, 1986.

Lederman, Mina, ed. *Stravinsky in the Theater*. New York: Dance Index, 1949; rpt. Da Capo Press, 1975.

Lenin, Vladimir Ilyich. *Selected Works*. New York: International Publishers, 1971.

Lerdahl, Fred, and Ray Jackendoff. *A Generative Theory of Tonal Music*. Cambridge, Mass.: MIT Press, 1983.

Lerma, Dominque René de. *Igor Fedorovitch Stravinsky: A Practical Guide to Publications of His Music*. Kent, Ohio: Kent State University Press, 1974.

Lessem, Alan Philip. *Music and Text in the Works of Arnold Schoenberg*. Ann Arbor: UMI Research Press, 1979.

Lesure, François, ed. *Igor Stravinsky: la carrière européenne*. Paris: Musée d'Art Moderne de la Ville de Paris, 1980.

———. *Igor Stravinsky, "Le sacre du printemps": dossier de presse*. Geneva: Éditions Minkoff, 1980.

———. *Stravinsky: études et témoignages*. Paris: Éditions Jean Claude Lattès, 1982.

Lesure, François, and Roger Nichols, eds. *Debussy Letters*. Translated by R. Nichols. Cambridge, Mass.: Harvard University Press, 1987.

Levarie, Siegmund. "Tonal Relations in Verdi's *Un Ballo in maschera*." *19th-Century Music* 2 (1978): 143–47.

Levinson, Andrey Yakovlevich. *Ballet Old and New* (1918). Translated by Susan Cook Summer. New York: Dance Horizons, 1982.

———. *Bakst: The Story of the Artist's Life*. London: Bayard Press, 1923.

———. "Russkiy balet v Parizhe." *Rech'*, 3 June 1913.

Leyda, Jay, and Sergei Bertensson (eds.). *The Musorgsky Reader*. New York: W. W. Norton, 1947.

Leyfert, A. V. *Balaganï*. Petrograd: Yezhenedel'nik Petrogradskikh Gosudarstvennïkh Akademicheskikh Teatrov, 1922.

Lichtenhahn, E., and T. Seebass, eds. *Musikhandschriften aus der Sammlung Paul Sacher*. Basel: F. Hoffmann–La Roche, 1976.

Lieven, Peter, Prince. *The Birth of the Ballets-Russes*. London: George Allen & Unwin, 1936.

Lifar, Serge. *Serge Diaghilev: His Life, His Work, His Legend*. New York: G. P. Putnam's Sons, 1940.

Likhtenberger, G. "Vzglyadï Vagnera na iskusstve." *Mir iskusstva*, 1899, nos. 7–8, 195–206. Excerpts in Russian translation from the French: Henri Lichtenberger. *Richard Wagner: poète et penseur*. Paris, 1898.

Lindlar, Heinrich. "Die frühen Lieder von Strawinsky." *Musica* 23 (1969): 116–18.

———. *Igor Strawinskys sakraler Gesang*. Regensburg: Gustav Bosse Verlag, 1957.

Linyova [Lineff], Yevgeniya Eduardovna. "Mïsli V. V. Stasova o narodnosti v muzïke." *Trudï MEK* 2:379–85.

———. "Opït zapisi fonografom ukraínskikh narodnïkh pesen." *Trudï MEK* 1:221–66.

———. *Velikorusskiye pesni v narodnoy garmonizatsii*. 2 vols. St. Petersburg: Imperatorskaya Akademiya Nauk, 1904–9. English translation: *The Peasant Songs of Great Russia as They Are in the Folk's Harmonization: Collected and Transcribed from Phonograms by Eugenie Lineff*. St. Petersburg, 1905–12.

———. "Yu. N. Mel'gunov kak novator-issledovatel' narodnoy pesni." *Russkaya muzïkal'naya gazeta* 10, no. 2324 (8–15 June 1903), col. 563.

Listopadov, Alexander Mikhailovich. "Narodnaya kazach'ya pesnya na Donu. Donskaya èkspeditsiya 1902–1903 gg." *Trudï MEK* 1:159–218.

———. "Zapisi narodnïkh pesen v 1904 godu. Poyezdka v Donskuyu oblast' dlya sobiraniya kasach'yikh u malorusskikh pesen i zapisi velikorusskikh pesen Orlovskoy i Penzenskoy guberniy. S prilozheniyem 30 pesen v narodnoy garmonizatsii." *Trudï MEK* 2: 341–63.

Lockspeiser, Edward. *Debussy: His Life and Mind*. 2 vols. 2d ed. Cambridge: Cambridge University Press, 1966.

Loewenberg, Alfred. *Annals of Opera, 1597–1940*. 3d ed. Totowa, N.J.: Rowman & Littlefield, 1978.

Loguine, Tatiana, ed. *Gontcharova et Larionov*. Paris: Klincksieck, 1971.

Lopokova, Lydia. "Memories of the Russian Ballet." In *Lydia Lopokova,* edited by Milo Keynes. New York: St. Martin's Press, 1982.

Lourié, Arthur-Vincent [Artur Sergeyevich Lur'ye]. "Dve operï Stravinskogo." *Vyorstï,* no. 3 (1928): 109–21.

———. "L'évolution de la musique russe." *Oeuvres nouvelles* 5 (1945).

———. "Neogothic and Neoclassic." *Modern Music* 5, no. 3 (March–April 1928): 3–8.

———. "*Oedipus Rex* de Strawinsky." *Revue musicale* 8, no. 8 (August 1927): 240–53. German translation: "Oedipus Rex. Opera-Oratorium nach Sophokles von Igor Strawinsky." *Blätter der Staatsoper* 8, no. 19 (1928): 9–13.

———. "Musings on Music." *Musical Quarterly* 27 (1941): 235–42.

———. "Muzïka Stravinskogo." *Vyorstï,* no. 1 (1926): 119–35.

———. *Sergei Koussevitzky and His Epoch.* New York: Alfred A. Knopf, 1931.

Lowe, David. "Vladimir Odoevskii as Opera Critic." *Slavic Review* 41 (1982): 306–15.

Luening, Otto. Memoir in the special issue entitled "Stravinsky: A Composers' Memorial." *Perspectives of New Music* 9, no. 2–10, no. 1 (1971): 131–33.

Lunacharsky, Anatoliy Vasilyevich. *Teatr i revolyutsiya.* Moscow: Gosudarstvennoye Izdatel'stvo, 1924.

Lyapunov, Sergey Mikhailovich. "Otchot ob ѐkspeditsii dlya sobiraniya russkikh narodnïkh pesen s napevami v 1893 godu." *Izvestiya russkogo geograficheskogo obshchestva* 30, no. 3 (1894): 347–54.

———, ed. "Perepiska M. A. Balakireva i N. A. Rimskiy-Korsakov (1868–1898)." *Muzïkal'nïy sovremennik,* no. 1 (1915); no. 7 (1916).

Lyapunova, Anastasiya Sergeyevna, ed. *M. A. Balakirev i V. V. Stasov: perepiska.* Vol. 2. Moscow: Muzïka, 1971.

Macdonald, Nesta. *Diaghilev Observed by Critics in England and the United States, 1911–1929.* New York/London: Dance Horizons/Dance Books, 1975.

McQuere, Gordon D. "Concepts of Analysis in the Theories of B. L. Yavorsky." *Music Review* 41 (1980): 278–88.

———, ed. *Russian Theoretical Thought in Music.* Ann Arbor: UMI Research Press, 1983.

Maeterlinck, Maurice. *The Life of the Bee.* Translated by Alfred Sutro. London: George Allen, 1904.

Makovsky, Sergey Konstantinovich. "L'art décoratif des ateliers de la princesse Tenichef." In *Talachkino,* translated by N. Izerguine. St. Petersburg: Sodruzhestvo, 1906.

Malïsheva, Yelena. "O gruzinskikh istokakh messï." *Sovetskaya muzïka,* 1982, no. 7, 92–94.

Malkiel, Henrietta. "Modernists Have Ruined Modern Music, Stravinsky Says." *Musical America,* 10 January 1925, 9.

Maritain, Jacques. "Sur la musique d'Arthur Lourié." *Revue musicale,* no. 165 (April 1936): 266–71.

Mark, Jeffrey. "The Fundamental Qualities of Folk Music." *Music and Letters* 10 (1929): 285–95.

Markov, Vladimir. "Balmont: A Reappraisal." *Slavic Review* 28 (1969): 221–64.

Markus, V. (pseud.). "O dnyakh minuvshikh i prekrasnïkh: zapiski starogo moskvicha." *Muzïkal'naya zhizn',* no. 748 (January 1989): 27–30.

Marr, Nikolai Yakovlevich. "Mïsli o religioznom penii Drevnago Vostoka: po povodu gruzinskogo dukhovnogo kontserta v zale Dvoryanskogo sobraniya 16-go marta." *Rech',* 16/29 March 1914.

Maslenikov, Oleg A. *The Frenzied Poets.* Berkeley and Los Angeles: University of California Press, 1952.

Maslov, Alexander Leont'yevich. "Illyustrirovannoye opisaniye muzïkal'nïkh instrumentov, khranyashchikhsya v Dashovskom Etnograficheskom Muzeye v Moskve." *Trudï MEK* 2:205–68.

Massine, Leonid. *My Life in Ballet*. Edited by Phyllis Hartnall and Robert Rubens. London: Macmillan, 1968.

Matlaw, Ralph E. Introduction to *My Literary and Moral Wanderings*, by Apollon Grigor'yev. New York: E. P. Dutton, 1962.

Mazo, Margarita. "Stravinsky's *Les Noces* and Russian Folk Wedding Ritual." *Journal of the American Musicological Society* 43 (1990): 99–142.

Medtner, Nikolai Karlovich. *Pis'ma*. Edited by Z. A. Apetyan. Moscow: Sovetskiy Kompozitor, 1973.

Melgunov, Yuliy Nikolayevich. "O ritme i garmonii russkikh pesen: iz posmertnïkh bumag Yu. N. Melgunova." *Trudï MEK* 1:361–99.

———. *Russkiye pesni neprosredstvenno s golosov naroda i s ob"yasneniyami izdannïye*. Moscow: Tip. E. Lissner & Yu. Roman, 1879.

Mellers, Wilfred. *Man and His Music*. Vol. 4. New York: Schocken Books, 1969.

Messing, Scott. *Neoclassicism in Music: From the Genesis of the Concept Through the Schoenberg/ Stravinsky Polemic*. Ann Arbor: UMI Research Press, 1988.

Mikhailov, Mikhaíl. "Esteticheskiy fenomen 'Potseluya fei.'" *Sovetskaya muzïka*, 1982, no. 8, 95–102.

Milhaud, Darius. *Notes Without Music*. Translated by Donald Evans. New York: Alfred A. Knopf, 1953.

———. "Strawinskys neue Bühnenwerke." *Musikblätter des Anbruch* 4, no. 17 (November 1922). English translation: "Milhaud on Stravinsky." *Musical Times* 64, no. 1 (1 January 1923): 40.

Miller, Vsevolod Fyodorovich. "Pushkin kak poèt-etnograf." *Etnograficheskoye obozreniye* 11, no. 4 (1899): 129–34.

Mirsky, D. S. *See* Sviatopolk-Mirsky, D. P.

Moevs, Robert. Review of *The Harmonic Organization of "The Rite of Spring,"* by Allen Forte. *Journal of Music Theory* 24 (1980): 103–14.

Montagu-Nathan, Montagu. "Belaiev—Maecenas of Russian Music." *Musical Quarterly* 4, no. 3 (July 1918): 450–65.

Monter, Barbara Heldt. *Koz'ma Prutkov: The Art of Parody*. The Hague: Mouton, 1972.

Morand, Paul. *L'allure de Chanel*. Paris: Hermann, 1976.

———. *Journal d'un attaché d'ambassade, 1916–1917*. Paris: Gallimard, 1963.

Morton, Lawrence. "Footnotes to Stravinsky Studies: 'Le Sacre du printemps.'" *Tempo*, no. 128 (1979): 9–16.

———. "Stravinsky and Tchaikovsky: *Le Baiser de la Fée*." *Musical Quarterly* 48 (1962): 313–26. Reprinted in *Stravinsky: A New Appraisal of His Work*, edited by Paul Henry Lang, 47–60. New York: W. W. Norton, 1963.

———. "Stravinsky at Home." In *Confronting Stravinsky*, edited by Jann Pasler, 332–48. Berkeley and Los Angeles: University of California Press, 1986.

Musorgsky, Modest Petrovich. *Kartinki s vïstavki* (facsimile edition). Moscow: Muzïka, 1975.

———. *Literaturnoye naslediye*. Edited by Mikhaíl Samoylovich Pekelis and Alexandra Anatolyeva Orlova. 2 vols. Moscow: Muzïka, 1971–72.

Myaskovsky, Nikolai Yakovlevich. "I Stravinskiy. Op. 9, No. 1 'Dushu skovali,' No. 2 'Gde v lunnom svete'; dlya peniya i fortepiano, na sl. P. Verlena. Izd P. Yurgensona. Ts. 60 k." *Muzïka*, no. 65 (25 February 1912).

———. "O 'Vesne Svyashchennoi' Ig. Stravinskogo." *Muzïka,* no. 167 (1 February 1914): 106–12.

———. "Peterburgskiye pis'ma" (occasional essay). *Muzïka,* no. 53 (3 December 1911); no. 103 (10 November 1912).

———. " 'Petrushka,' balet Ig. Stravinskogo." *Muzïka,* no. 59 (14 January 1912).

———. "Simfoniya I. Stravinskogo." *Muzïka,* no. 91 (22 August 1912).

Myuller, Teodor Fridrikhovich, ed. *Voprosï teorii muzïki.* Vol. 3 Moscow: Muzgiz, 1975.

Nabokov, Nicolas. *Bagazh: Memoirs of a Russian Cosmopolitan.* New York: Atheneum, 1975.

———. *Old Friends and New Music.* Boston: Little, Brown, 1951.

———. "The Peasant Marriage (*Les Noces*) by Igor Stravinsky." *Slavic Studies of the Hebrew University of Jerusalem* 3 (1978): 272–81.

———. "Stravinsky Now." *Partisan Review* 11, no. 3 (Summer 1944): 324–34.

Nabokov, Vladimir. Commentary to *The Song of Igor's Campaign,* translated by V. Nabokov. New York: Vintage Books, 1960.

Nestyev, Izraíl Vladimirovich. *Prokofiev.* Translated by Florence Jonas. Palo Alto: Stanford University Press, 1960.

———. "Skryabin i yego russkiye 'antipodï.' " In *Muzïka i sovremennost'* 10 (Moscow: Muzïka, 1976), 79–112.

———. "Vo obshchenii s sovremennikami." *Sovetskaya muzïka,* 1967, no. 4, 77–85.

———. *Zvyozdï russkoy èstradï.* 2d ed. Moscow: Sovetskiy Kompozitor, 1974.

Nettl, Bruno. "Words and Music: English Folk Songs in the United States." In Charles Hamm, Bruno Nettl, and Ronald Byrneside, *Contemporary Music and Music Cultures.* Englewood Cliffs, N.J.: Prentice-Hall, 1975.

Newmarch, Rosa. *The Russian Opera.* New York: Dutton, n.d. [1914].

Nijinska, Bronislava. *Early Memoirs.* Translated and edited by Irina Nijinska and Jean Rawlinson. New York: Holt, Rinehart & Winston, 1981.

———. "Petipa pobedil." In *Marius Petipa: materialï, vospominaniya, stat'i,* edited by Yu. I. Slonimsky et al., 315–19. Leningrad: Iskusstvo, 1971.

Nijinsky, Romola. *Nijinsky.* New York: Simon & Schuster, 1934.

Nikiforov, A. I. "Narodnaya detskaya skazka dramaticheskogo zhanra." In *Skazochnaya komissiya v 1927 g.,* edited by S. F. Oldenburg, 49–63. Leningrad: Gosudarstvennoye Russkoye Geograficheskoye Obshchestvo, 1928.

Nikolskaya, Lyubov Borisovna. "Opït khudozhnika." *Sovetskaya muzïka,* 1963, no. 8.

"N. Minsky" [N. M. Vilenkin]. "Pis'mo iz Parizha: prazdnik vesnï." *Utro Rossii,* 30 May 1913.

———. "Soyedineniye iskusstv: pis'mo iz Parizha." *Utro Rossii,* 24 May 1914.

Noble, Jeremy. "Debussy and Stravinsky." *Musical Times* 108 (1967): 22–24.

Nordau, Max. *Degeneration.* 5th ed. New York: D. Appleton, 1895.

Norman, Gertrude, and Miriam Lubell Shrifte. *Letters of Composers.* New York: Grosset & Dunlap, n.d.

Norris, Geoffrey. *Rakhmaninov.* London: J. M. Dent & Sons, 1976.

Nulman, Macy. *Concise Encyclopedia of Jewish Music.* New York: McGraw-Hill, 1975.

Nurok, Alfred Pavlovich (*see also* "A. N."; "Silèn"). "Kontsertï Ziloti." *Apollon,* 1910, no. 4, 68–69.

———. "Muzïkal'naya khronika." *Apollon,* 1910, no. 4, 112–13.

Odoyevsky, Vladimir Fyodorovich, Prince. *Muzïkal'no-literaturnoye naslediye.* Moscow: Muzgiz, 1956.

Orlova, Alexandra Anatolyevna. *Stranitsï zhizni N. A. Rimskogo-Korsakova.* Vol. 4. Leningrad: Muzïka, 1974.

————. *Trudï i dni M. P. Musorgskogo.* Moscow: Muzgiz, 1963.

Orlova, Alexandra Anatolyevna, and Vladimir Nikolayevich Rimsky-Korsakov. *Stranitsï zhizni N. A. Rimskogo-Korsakova.* Vol. 2. Leningrad: Muzïka, 1971.

Orlova, Yelena Mikhailovna. *B. V. Asaf'yev.* Leningrad: Muzïka, 1964.

Ornstein, Arbie. *Ravel: Man and Musician.* New York: Columbia University Press, 1975.

Ortega y Gasset, José. "The Dehumanization of Art" (1925). In *The Dehumanization of Art and Other Essays on Art, Culture, and Literature,* translated by H. Weil, 3–56. Princeton: Princeton University Press, 1968.

Ossovsky, Alexander Vyacheslavovich. *Muzïkal'no-kriticheskiye stat'i.* Leningrad: Muzïka, 1971.

Otsup, Nikolai. *Sovremenniki.* Paris: YMCA, 1961.

"O. V-va" [A. V. Ossovsky?]. "Sovremennïye muzïkal'nïye deyateli: F. I. Stravinskiy." *Russkaya muzïkal'naya gazeta* 5, no. 3 (March 1898): 272–80.

Owen, Thomas C. *Capitalism and Politics in Russia: A Social History of the Moscow Merchants, 1855–1905.* Cambridge: Cambridge University Press, 1981.

Pahissa, Jaime. *Manuel de Falla: His Life and Works.* London: Museum Press, 1954.

Paísov, Yuriy Ivanovich. "Russkiy fol'klor v vokal'no-khorovom tvorchestve Stravinskogo." In *I. F. Stravinskiy: stat'i, vospominaniya,* edited by G. Alfeyevskaya and I. Vershinina, 94–127. Moscow: Sovetskiy Kompozitor, 1985.

Palchikov, Nikolai Yevgrafovich. *Krest'yanskiye pesni, zapisannïye v sele Nikolayevke Menzelinskogo uyezda Ufimskoy gubernii.* St. Petersburg: A. E. Palchikov, 1888.

Paliashvili, Zakhariy Petrovich. *Kartuli khalkhuri simgerebi.* Tiflis, 1910.

Parilova, G. N., and A. D. Soymonov. "P. V. Kireyevskiy i sobrannïye im pesni." In *Pesni, sobrannïye pisatelyami,* edited by D. D. Blagoy et al., Literaturnoye nasledstvo, no. 79. Moscow: Nauka, 1968.

Parny, Évariste Désiré Desforges, Chevalier du. *Oeuvres choisies de Parny.* Paris: Roux-Dufort Frères, 1826.

Pasler, Jann. "Stravinsky and the Apaches." *Musical Times* 123 (1982): 403–5.

————, ed. *Confronting Stravinsky.* Berkeley and Los Angeles: University of California Press, 1986.

Pasternak, Leonid. *The Memoirs of Leonid Pasternak.* Translated by Jennifer Bradshaw. London: Quartet Books, 1982.

Pekelis, Mikhaíl Samoylovich. *Dargomïzhskiy i narodnaya pesnya.* Moscow and Leningrad: Muzgiz, 1951.

Perle, George. "Berg's Master Array of the Interval Cycles." *Musical Quarterly* 62 (1977): 1–30.

————. "The Musical Language of *Wozzeck*." *Music Forum* 1 (1967): 204–59.

————. "Scriabin's Self-Analyses." *Music Analysis* 3 (1984): 101–24.

————. *Serial Music and Atonality* (1962). 5th ed. Berkeley and Los Angeles: University of California Press, 1981.

————. *Twelve-Tone Tonality.* Berkeley and Los Angeles: University of California Press, 1977.

Peyser, Joan. "Stravinsky-Craft, Inc." *American Scholar* 52 (1983): 513–18.

Phillips, Paul Schuyler. "The Enigma of *Variations:* A Study of Stravinsky's Final Work for Orchestra." *Music Analysis* 3 (1984): 69–89.

Pipes, Richard. *Russia Under the Old Regime.* New York: Charles Scribner's Sons, 1974.

Plevitskaya-al'bom: sobraniye russkikh pesen repertuara izvestnoy ispolnitel'nitsï Nadezhdï Vasil'yevnï Plevitskoy. St. Petersburg: Zimmerman, n.d. [ca. 1910].

Poggioli, Renato. *Poets of Russia, 1890–1930*. Cambridge, Mass.: Harvard University Press, 1960.

Polonsky, Yakov Petrovich. *Polnoye sobraniye stikhotvoreniy*. Vol. 1. St. Petersburg: A. F. Marx, 1896.

Polyakova, Yelena. *Nikolai Rerikh: zhizn' v iskusstve*. Moscow: Iskusstvo, 1973.

Popova, Tatyana Vasilyevna. *Osnovï russkoy narodnoy muzïki*. Moscow: Muzïka, 1977.

———. *Russkoye narodnoye muzïkal'noye tvorchestvo*. 4 vols. Moscow: Muzgiz, 1955–58.

———. *Russkoye narodnoye muzïkal'noye tvorchestvo*. Vol. 2, revised and expanded. Moscow: Muzïka, 1964.

Potyomkin, Pyotr Petrovich. *Izbrannïye stranitsï*. Paris: Taïr, 1928.

Poueigh, Jean. "A travers la quinzaine." *Revue musicale S.I.M.* 10, no. 3 (1 February 1914).

Poulenc, Francis. "La musique: à propos de 'Mavra' de Igor Strawinsky." *Feuilles libres*, no. 27 (June–July 1922): 223–25.

———. *My Friends and Myself*. Translated by James Harding. London: Dennis Dobson, 1978.

Proffer, Carl, and Ellendea Proffer, eds. *The Silver Age of Russian Culture*. Ann Arbor: Ardis, 1975.

Prokofiev, Grigoriy Petrovich (*see also* "Gr. Pr."). "Teatr i muzïka." *Russkiye vedomosti*, 24 August 1912; 6 July 1914.

Prokofiev, Sergey Sergeyevich (*see also* "S."). *Avtobiografiya*. Edited by M. G. Kozlova. Moscow: Sovetskiy Kompozitor, 1973. English translation: *Prokofiev by Prokofiev: A Composer's Memoir*, edited by David H. Appel, translated by Guy Daniels. Garden City, N.Y.: Doubleday, 1979.

Propert, W. A. *The Russian Ballet in Western Europe, 1909–1920*. London: Bodley Head, 1921.

Propp, Vladimir. *Morphology of the Folktale* (1928). Edited by Svatava Pirkova-Jakobson, translated by Laurence Scott. Bloomington: Indiana University Research Center in Anthropology, Folklore, and Linguistics, 1968.

———. *Russkiye agrarnïye prazdniki*. Leningrad: Izdatel'stvo Leningradskogo Universiteta, 1963.

Prunières, Henry. "Les théâtres lyriques." *Revue musicale* 10, no. 3 (January 1929).

Pryashnikova, Margarita, and Olga Tompakova, eds. *Letopis' zhizni i tvorchestva A. N. Skryabina*. Moscow: Muzïka, 1985.

Pushkin, Alexander Sergeyevich. *Eugene Onegin: A Novel in Verse by Aleksandr Pushkin, Translated from the Russian, with a Commentary, by Vladimir Nabokov*. Bollingen Series 72. 3 vols. New York: Pantheon Books, 1964.

———. *Sochineniya*. Vol. 1. Moscow: Khudozhestvennaya Literatura, 1964.

———. *Three Comic Poems*. Translated by William E. Harkins. Ann Arbor: Ardis, 1977.

Pushkina, S. "Tol'ko li diatonika?" *Sovetskaya muzïka*, 1967, no. 3, 102–4.

Raaben, Lev Nikolayevich. *Leopol'd Semyonovich Auer: ocherk zhizni i deyatel'nosti*. Leningrad: Muzgiz, 1962.

———, ed. *V. M. Bogdanov-Berezovskiy: stat'i, vospominaniya, pis'ma*. Leningrad: Sovetskiy Kompozitor, 1978.

Rabinovich, Vadim Lvovich, ed. *Russkiy romans*. Moscow: Izdatel'stvo "Pravda," 1987.

Rachmaninoff's Recollections as Told to Oskar von Riesemann. Translated by Dolly Rutherford. New York: Macmillan, 1934; rpt. New York: Books for Libraries, 1979.

Racz-Barblan, Yvonne. "Igor Stravinsky vu par le cymbaliste Aladar Racz." *Feuilles musicales* (Lausanne), special issue on Stravinsky (March–April 1962).

Ralston, W. R. S. *The Songs of the Russian People*. London: Ellis & Green, 1872.

Rambert, Marie. *Quicksilver*. London: Macmillan, 1972.

Ramuz, Charles Ferdinand. *Lettres, 1900–1918*. Lausanne: Éditions Clairefontaine, 1956.

———. *Souvenirs sur Igor Strawinsky*. In *Oeuvres complètes*, vol. 14. Lausanne: H. L. Mermod, 1941.

Ravel, Maurice. "Les nouveaux spectacles de la saison russe: *Le Rossignol*." *Comoedia illustré* 6, no. 17 (5 June 1914): 400–402. Reprinted in part as "Stravinsky défendu par Ravel." *Revue musicale* 5, no. 2 (December 1923): 191. English translation in *A Ravel Reader*, edited by Arbie Ornstein, 380–82. New York: Columbia University Press, 1990.

———. "O parizhskoy redaktsii 'Khovanshchinï.'" *Muzïka*, no. 129 (14 May 1913): 338–42.

Reeder, Roberta, ed. and trans. *Down Along the Mother Volga: An Anthology of Russian Folk Lyrics with an Introductory Essay by V. Ja. Propp*. Philadelphia: University of Pennsylvania Press, 1975.

———. "Stravinsky's *Les Noces*." *Dance Research Journal* 18, no. 2 (Winter 1986–87): 31–53.

Reff, Theodore. "Harlequins, Saltimbanques, Clowns, and Fools." *Artforum* 10 (October 1971): 30–43.

Reilly, Edward R. *The Music of Musorgsky: A Guide to the Editions*. New York: Musical Newsletter, 1980.

Remizov, Alexey Mikhailovich. "A. M. Remizov o svoyey 'Rusalii.'" *Muzïka*, no. 217 (1915).

———. "Peterburgskaya Rusaliya." In *Plyashushchiy demon*. Paris: Private printing, 1949.

———. *Sochineniya Alekseya Remizova*. Vol. 6. St. Petersburg: Shipovnik, 1912; rpt. Munich: Wilhelm Fink Verlag, 1971.

Rémy, Tristan. *Les clowns*. Paris: Bernard Grasset, 1945.

Repin, Ilya Yefimovich. *Dalyokoye blizkoye*. Moscow, 1944.

Restout, Denise, ed. *Landowska on Music*. New York: Stein & Day, 1964.

Reznikoff, Natalie. *Ognennaya pamyat': vospominaniya o Alekseye Remizove*. Modern Russian Literature and Culture: Studies and Texts, vol. 4. Berkeley: Berkeley Slavic Specialties, 1980.

Riasanovsky, Nicholas V. "The Emergence of Eurasianism." *California Slavic Studies* 4 (1967).

Ridenour, Robert C. *Nationalism, Modernism, and Personal Rivalry in Nineteenth-Century Russian Music*. Ann Arbor: UMI Research Press, 1981.

Riesemann, Oskar von. Review of *Tri stikhotvoreniya iz yaponskoy liriki*. *Moskauer Deutsche Zeitung*; rpt. *Muzïka*, no. 168 (8 February 1914).

Rimskaya-Korsakova, Nadezhda Nikolayevna. "Otkrïtoye pis'mo S. P. Dyagilevu." *Rech'*, 25 July 1910.

Rimsky-Korsakov, Andrey Nikolayevich. "7-y simfonicheskiy kontsert S. Kusevitskogo." *Russkaya molva*, no. 45 (25 January–7 February 1913).

———. "Baletï Igorya Stravinskogo." *Apollon*, 1915, no. 1, 46–57.

———. "'Khovanshchina' M. P. Musorgskogo i S. Dyagilev." *Russkaya molva*, no. 101 (23 March 1913); rpt. in *Muzïka*, no. 123 (30 March 1913): 230–32.

———. "Lettre de M. André Rimsky-Korsakow." *Comoedia illustré* 5, no. 22 (20 August 1913).

———. "Lichnost' Lyadova." *Muzïkal'nïy sovremennik* 2, no. 1 (September 1916): 80–97.

———. *Maksimilian Shteynberg*. Moscow: Muzgiz, 1928.

———. *N. A. Rimskiy-Korsakov: zhizn' i tvorchestvo*. Vols. 3–5. Moscow: Muzgiz, 1936–46.

———. "O novom narodnom gimne." *Khronika zhurnala "Muzïkal'nïy sovremennik,"* no. 18 (21 March 1917).

———. "O 'Solov'ye' Igorya Stravinskogo." *Muzïkal'nïy sovremennik* 1, no. 1 (1915–16).

———. "Ot redaktora." *Muzïkal'nïy sovremennik* 2, no. 4 (December 1916).

———. "Russkiye opernïye i baletnïye spektakli v Parizhe." *Russkaya molva,* no. 193 (27 June 1913).

———. " 'Zolotoy petushok' na parizhskoy i londonskoy stsenakh," *Apollon,* 1914, nos. 6–7.

———, ed. *Musorgskiy: pis'ma i dokumentï.* Moscow: Muzgiz, 1932.

Rimsky-Korsakov, Andrey Nikolayevich, et al., eds. *V. G. Karatïgin: zhizn', deyatel'nost, stat'i i materialï.* Leningrad: Academia, 1927.

Rimsky-Korsakov, Nikolai Andreyevich. *My Musical Life.* Translated by Judah A. Joffe. London: Eulenberg Books, 1974.

———. *Notnïye zapisnïye knizhki.* Edited by A. S. Lyapunova and E. E. Yazovitsky. In *Polnoye sobraniye sochineniy: literaturnïye proizvedeniya i perepiska,* vol. 4, suppl. Moscow: Muzïka, 1970.

———. "O muzïkal'nom obrazovanii." In *Muzïkal'nïye stat'i i zametki (1869–1907),* edited by Nadezhda Nikolayevna Rimskaya-Korsakova. St. Petersburg: Tip. M. Stasyulevicha, 1911.

———. *Osnovï orkestrovki s partiturnïmi obraztsami iz sobstvennïkh sochineniy.* Edited by M. Steinberg. Berlin: Rossiyskoye Muzïkal'noye Izdatel'stvo, 1913. English translation: *Principles of Orchestration,* translated by Edward Agate. Berlin: Russische Musikverlag, 1922; rpt. New York: Dover, 1964.

———. *Polnoye sobraniye sochineniy: literaturnïye proizvedeniya i perepiska.* Vols. 1–8b. Moscow: Muzgiz/Muzïka, 1955–82.

———. *Sbornik russkikh narodnïkh pesen.* Paris: Bessel, n.d.

Rivière, Jacques. *Nouvelles études.* Paris: Gallimard, 1947.

Roberts, Peter Deane. "Aspects of Modernism in Russian Piano Music, 1910–1929." Thesis, Kingston Polytechnic, 1988.

Rodriguez, Natalia, and Malcolm Hamrick Brown. "Prokofiev's Correspondence with Stravinsky and Shostakovich." In *Slavonic and Western Music: Essays for Gerald Abraham,* edited by M. H. Brown and R. John Wiley, 271–92. Ann Arbor/Oxford: UMI Research Press/Oxford University Press, 1985.

Roerich [Rerikh], Nikolai Konstaninovich. *Adamant.* New York: Corona Mundi, 1923.

———. *Iz literaturnogo naslediya.* Moscow: Iskusstvo, 1974.

———. "Novïy balet—'Vesna Svyashchennaya.' " *Rech',* 22 November 1912.

———. "Pamyati M. K. Tenishevoy." In M. Tenisheva, *Emal' i inkrustatsiya.* Prague, 1930.

———. *Pervaya kniga.* Moscow: I. D. Sïtin, 1914.

———. "Radost' iskusstvu." *Vestnik Yevropï,* 1909, no. 2, 508–33.

———. *Realm of Light.* New York: Roerich Museum Press, 1931.

Roland-Manuel, Alexis. " 'Jeux,' ballet de Claude Debussy." *Montjoie!* no. 8 (29 May 1913): 6.

———. "Letter from Paris." *Musical News and Herald,* 1 July 1922.

———. " 'Mavra' d'Igor Stravinsky." *Quinzaine musicale,* no. 13 (1 July 1922).

———. "Le sacre du printemps." *Montjoie!* nos. 9–10 (14–29 June 1913): 13.

Rolland, Romain. *Journal des années de guerre, 1914–1919.* Paris: Éditions Albin Michel, 1952.

Rosenthal, Bernice Glatzer. Review of *Russian Modernism,* edited by George Gibian and H. W. Tjalsma. *Russian History* 4 (1977): 207–10.

———. "Theater as Church: The Vision of the Mystical Anarchists." *Russian History* 4 (1977): 122–41.

———. "The Transmutation of the Symbolist Ethos: Mystical Anarchism and the Revolution of 1905." *Slavic Review* 36 (1977): 610–26.

Roslavleva, Natalia. *The Era of the Russian Ballet*. London: Victor Gollancz, 1966.

Rostislav [Feofil Matveyevich Tolstoy]. *Novaya opera A. N. Serova Vrazh'ya sila*. St. Petersburg, 1871.

Roth, Ernst. "A Great Mind and a Great Spirit." *Tempo*, no. 81 (Summer 1967): 4–5.

Rothmüller, Aron Marko. *The Music of the Jews*. Translated by H. S. Stevens. South Brunswick, N.J.: Thomas Yoseloff, 1967.

Rovinsky, Dmitriy Alexandrovich. *Russkiye narodnïye kartinki*. Vol. 5. Sbornik otdeleniya russkogo yazïka i slovesnosti Imperatorskoy Akademii Nauk, vol. 27. St. Petersburg: Tipografiya Imperatorskoy Akademii Nauk, 1881; rpt. Liechtenstein: Knaus, 1966.

Rozanov, Vasiliy Vasilyevich. *Apokalipsicheskaya sekta (khlïstï i skoptsï)*. St. Petersburg: Vaisberg & Gershunin, 1914.

Rozhdestvensky, T. S., and M. I. Uspensky. *Pesni russkikh sektantov mistikov*. Zapiski Imperatorskogo russkogo geograficheskogo obshchestva po otdeleniyu ètnografii, vol. 35. St. Petersburg, 1912.

Rubinstein, Arthur. *My Many Years*. New York: Alfred A. Knopf, 1980.

Rubtsov, Feodosiy Antonovich. *Osnovï ladovogo stroeniya russkoy narodnoy pesni*. Leningrad: Muzïka, 1964.

———. *Stat'i po muzïkal'nomu fol'kloru*. Leningrad: Sovetskiy Kompozitor, 1973.

Rudneva, Anna Vasilyevna. *Narodnïye pesni Kurskoy oblasti*. Moscow, 1957.

"S." (*see also* Prokofiev, S. S.). "Za rubezhom." *Muzïka*, no. 216 (28 March 1915).

Sabaneyev, Leonid Leonidovich. "Dawn or Dusk? Stravinsky's New Ballets." *Musical Times* 70 (1929): 403–6.

———. "Kontsert iz proizvedeniy Stravinskogo." *Golos Moskvï*, 23 August 1912.

———. *Modern Russian Composers*. Translated by Judah A. Joffe. New York: International Publishers, 1927; rpt. New York: Da Capo Press, 1975.

———. Review of *Tri stikhotvoreniya iz yaponskoy liriki*. *Golos Moskvï*, no. 19 (1914); rpt. *Muzïka*, no. 167 (1 February 1914).

———. "Sed'maya sonata Skryabina." *Muzïka*, no. 64 (18 February 1912).

———. "The Stravinsky Legends." *Musical Times* 69 (1928): 785–87.

———. "'Vesna svyashchennaya.'" *Golos Moskvï*, 8 June 1913.

———. *Vospominaniya o Skryabine*. Moscow: Muzïkal'nïy Sektor Gosudarstvennogo Izdatel'stva, 1925.

Sakharov, Ivan Petrovich. *Skazaniya russkogo naroda*. 3 vols. in 1. 3d ed. St. Petersburg, 1841.

Salazar, Adolfo. *Music in Our Time*. Translated by Isobel Pope. New York: W. W. Norton, 1946.

Salzman, Eric. "Current Chronicle: Princeton." *Musical Quarterly* 53 (1967): 81–83.

Saminsky, Lazare. *Music of Our Day*. 2d ed. New York: Thomas Y. Crowell, 1939.

Satie, Erik. "Igor Strawinsky: A Tribute to the Great Russian Composer by an Eminent French Confrère." *Vanity Fair*, 1923, no. 10, 33–38. Reprinted as "A Composer's Conviction" in *Igor Strawinsky: A Merle Armitage Book*, edited by Edwin Corle, 25–32. New York: Duell, Sloan & Pearce, 1949.

Savitskaya, T. A., ed. *N. K. Rerikh: zhizn' i tvorchestvo: sbornik statey*. Moscow: Izdatel'stvo "Izobratitel'noye Iskusstvo," 1978.

Schaeffner, André. "Au fil des esquisses du 'Sacre.'" *Revue de musicologie* 57 (1971): 179–90.

———. *Strawinsky*. Paris: Éditions Rieder, 1931.

———. "Variations Schoenberg." *Contrepoints* 7 (1950): 110–29.

Schiff, David. *The Music of Elliott Carter*. London: Eulenberg Books, 1983.

Schloezer, Boris de. *Igor Stravinsky.* Paris: Éditions Claude Aveline, 1929. English translation: *Stravinsky: An Abridged Analysis.* Translated by Ezra Pound. In *Igor Stravinsky: A Merle Armitage Book,* edited by Edwin Corle, 33–91. New York: Duell, Sloan & Pearce, 1949.

———. "La musique." *Nouvelle revue française* 9, no. 106 (1 July 1922).

———. "Zapiski B. F. Shletsera o Predvaritel'nom Deystvii." In *Russkiye propilei,* vol. 6, edited by Mikhaíl Gershenzon. Moscow: M. & S. Sabashnikov, 1919.

Schlumberger, Jean. "Considérations." *Nouvelle revue française* 1 (Paris, 1909); rpt. (of early run of journal) New York: Kraus Reprint Co., 1968, 9–11.

Schmitt, Florent. "Les concerts" (occasional essay). *France,* 19 November 1912; 21 January 1913.

Schnabel, Artur. *My Life and Music.* London: Longmans, 1961.

Schneider, Herbert. Preface to *Fireworks,* by I. Stravinsky. Eulenberg pocket scores, no. 1396 (1984).

Schneider, Louis. "M. Igor Strawinsky et les Ballets russes." *Revue de France* 2, no. 4 (July–August 1922).

Schoenberg, Arnold. *Harmonielehre.* Vienna: Universal-Edition, 1911. English translation: *Theory of Harmony.* Translated by Roy E. Carter. Berkeley and Los Angeles: University of California Press, 1978.

———. *Style and Idea.* Edited by Leonard Stein. Berkeley and Los Angeles: University of California Press, 1984.

Schouvaloff, Alexander, and Victor Borovsky. *Stravinsky on Stage.* London: Stainer & Bell, 1982.

Schulenberg, David. "Modes, Prolongations, and Analysis." *Journal of Musicology* 4 (1985–86): 303–27.

Schumann, Robert. *Gesammelte Schriften über Musik und Musiker.* Leipzig, 1854.

Scriabin, Alexander Nikolayevich. *Pis'ma.* Edited by A. V. Kholopov. Moscow: Muzïka, 1965.

Seaman, Gerald. *History of Russian Music.* Vol. 1. New York: Praeger, 1967.

———. "Stravinsky and Russian Folk Music." Typescript, 1969; rev. 1981.

Segel, Harold B. *Turn-of-the-Century Cabaret.* New York: Columbia University Press, 1987.

Serov, Alexander Nikolayevich. "Pis'ma k V. V. i D. V. Stasovïm." Edited by A. A. Gozenpud and V. A. Obram. In *Muzïkal'noye nasledstvo,* 1:65–312. Moscow: Muzgiz, 1962.

———. "Russkaya narodnaya pesnya, kak predmet nauki" (1869). In *Izbrannïye stat'i,* 1:81–108. Moscow: Muzgiz, 1950.

Serov, Valentin Alexandrovich. *Paintings, Graphic Works, Stage Designs.* New York: Harry N. Abrams, 1982.

———. *Perepiska, 1884–1911.* Leningrad: Iskusstvo, 1937.

Shanet, Howard. Liner notes to Columbia Records MS 6329, "Stravinsky: *Pulcinella* Suite" (ca. 1960).

Shattuck, Roger. "The Devil's Dance: Stravinsky's Corporal Imagination." In *The Innocent Eye,* 318–33. New York: Washington Square Press, 1986.

Shaw, J. Thomas. *The Letters of Alexander Pushkin.* Madison: University of Wisconsin Press, 1967.

Shead, Richard. *Music in the 1920s.* New York: St. Martin's Press, 1976.

Shepard, John. "The Stravinsky *Nachlass:* A Provisional Checklist of Music Manuscripts." *MLA Notes* 40 (1983–84): 719–50.

Sheyn, Pavel Vasilyevich. *Russkiye narodnïye pesni.* Pt. 1: *Pesni plyasovïye i besednïye.* In *Chteniya v Imperatorskom obshchestve istorii i drevnostey rossiyskikh* 67 (1868).

———. *Velikoruss v svoikh pesnyakh, obïchayakh, verovaniyakh i t.p.* St. Petersburg, 1898.

Shlifshteyn, Semyon Isaakovich, ed. *N. Ya. Myaskovskiy: sobraniye materialov v dvukh tomakh.* 2 vols. 2d ed. Moscow: Muzïka, 1964.

———. *N. Ya. Myaskovskiy: stat'i, pis'ma, vospominaniya.* 2 vols. Moscow: Sovetskiy Kompozitor, 1960.

———. *S. S. Prokof'yev: notograficheskiy spravochnik.* Moscow: Sovetskiy Kompozitor, 1962.

Shteynpress, Boris Solomonovich. *Opernïye prem'yerï XX veka.* Moscow: Sovetskiy Kompozitor, 1983.

"Silèn" (*see also* Nurok, A. P.; "A. N."). "Muzïkal'naya artel'." *Mir iskusstva,* nos. 21–22 (1899): 71–74.

Siohan, Robert. *Stravinsky.* Translated by Eric Walter White. London: Calder & Boyars, 1965.

Skrebkov, Sergey Sergeyevich. "K voprosu o stile sovremennoy muzïki ('Vesna svyashchennaya' Stravinskogo)." In *Muzïka i sovremennost',* vol. 6, edited by Valentina Konen, 3–53. Moscow: Muzïka, 1969.

Slonimsky, Nicolas. *Music Since 1900.* 4th ed. New York: Charles Scribner's Sons, 1971.

———, ed. *Baker's Biographical Dictionary of Musicians.* 6th ed. New York: Schirmer Books, 1978.

Slonimsky, Yuriy Iosifovich, et al., eds. *Marius Petipa: materialï, vospominaniya, stat'i.* Leningrad: Iskusstvo, 1971.

Small, Ian, ed. *The Aesthetes: A Sourcebook.* London: Routledge & Kegan Paul, 1979.

Smirnov, Boris Fyodorovich. *Iskusstvo Vladimirskikh rozhechnikov.* 2d ed., revised and expanded. Moscow: Muzïka, 1965.

Smirnov, S. "Babï bogomerzkiye." In *Sbornik statey posvyashchonnïkh V. O. Klyuchevskomu,* 217–43. Moscow: S. I. Yakovlev, 1909.

Smirnov, Valeriy. "A. N. Benua—librettist 'Petrushki.'" In *I. F. Stravinskiy: stat'i i materialï,* edited by L. S. Dyachkova, with Boris M. Yarustovsky, 155–61. Moscow: Sovetskiy Kompozitor, 1973.

———. "Stravinsky: vsled za Musorgskim." *Sovetskaya muzïka,* 1989, no. 3, 86–91.

———. "Tvorcheskaya vesna Igorya Stravinskogo." In *Rasskazï o muzïki i muzïkantakh,* edited by M. G. Aranovsky, 55–79. Leningrad: Sovetskiy Kompozitor, 1973.

———. *Tvorcheskoye formirovaniye I. F. Stravinskogo.* Leningrad: Muzïka, 1970.

———. "U istokov kompozitorskogo puti I. Stravinskogo." In *Voprosï teorii i èstetiki muzïki,* vol. 8, edited by Yuriy Kremlyov, Lev Raaben, and Feodosii Rubtsov, 85–95. Leningrad: Sovetskiy Kompozitor.

Smolensky, Stepan Vasilyevich. "Znacheniye XVII veka i yego kantov v oblasti sovremennogo tserkovnogo peniya tak nazïvayemogo 'prostogo napeva.'" In *Muzïkal'naya starina,* vol. 5. St. Petersburg, 1911.

Snegiryov, I. M. *Russkiye prostonarodnïye prazdniki i suyevernïye obryadï.* Vol. 1. Moscow: University Press, 1837.

Sokalsky, Pyotr Petrovich. *Russkaya narodnaya muzïka, velikorusskaya i malorusskaya, v yeyo stroyenii melodicheskom i ritmicheskom i otlichiya yeyo ot osnov sovremennoy garmonicheskoy muzïki.* Kharkov, 1888. Ukrainian translation: *Rus'ka narodna muzïka....* Translated by M. Khomichevsky. Kiev, 1959. Extracts reprinted in *Russkaya mïsl' o muzïkal'nom fol'klore,* edited by Pavel Alexandrovich Vulfius, 140–51. Moscow: Muzïka, 1979.

Sokolov, Yuriy. *Russkiy fol'klor*. Moscow, 1938. English translation: *Russian Folklore*. Translated by Catherine Ruth Smith. Hatboro, Pa.: Folklore Associates, 1966.

Sologub, Fyodor [Fyodor Kuzmich Teternikov]. "Nochnïye plyaski." *Russkaya mïsl* 29, no. 12 (December 1908).

Somfai, László. "*Symphonies of Wind Instruments* (1920): Observations on Stravinsky's Organic Construction." *Studia musicologica* 14 (1972): 355–83.

Souvtchinsky, Pierre. "Stravinsky as a Russian." *Tempo*, no. 81 (Summer 1967): 5–6.

———, ed. *Iskhod k Vostoku*. Sofia: Rossiysko-bolgarskoye Knigoizdatel'stvo, 1921.

Speransky, M. N. "P. V. Kireyevskiy i yego sobraniye pesen." In P. V. Sperensky, *Pesni sobrannïye P. V. Kireyevskim. Novaya seriya*, vol. 1: *Pesni obryadnïye*, edited by V. F. Miller and M. N. Speransky. Moscow: Pechatnya A. I. Snegiryovoy, 1911.

Spies, Claudio. "Conundrums, Conjectures, Construals; or, 5 v. 3: The Influence of Russian Composers on Stravinsky." In *Stravinsky Retrospectives*, edited by Ethan Haimo and Paul Johnson, 76–140. Lincoln: University of Nebraska Press, 1987.

———. "Notes on Stravinsky's Requiem Settings." In *Perspectives on Schoenberg and Stravinsky*, edited by Edward T. Cone and Benjamin Boretz, 233–50. Princeton: Princeton University Press, 1968.

Sreznevsky, Izmail I. *Issledovaniya o yazïcheskom bogosluzhenii drevnikh slavyan*. St. Petersburg: Tip. Zhernakova, 1848.

———. *Svedeniya i zametki o maloizvestnïkh i neizvestnïkh pamyatnikakh*. Part 2. St. Petersburg, 1876.

Stalin, Iosif Vissarionovich. *Voprosy Leninizma*. Moscow: Gospolitizdat, 1931.

Stanislavski, Constantin. *My Life in Art*. Translated by J. J. Robbins. New York: Meridian Books, 1956.

Stark, Eduard Alexandrovich. *Peterburgskaya opera i yeyo mastera*. Leningrad, 1940.

Stasov, Vladimir Vasilyevich. *Izbrannïye sochineniya*. 3 vols. Moscow: Iskusstvo, 1952.

———. "Pavel Mikhailovich Tret'yakov i yego kartinnaya gallereya." *Russkaya starina* 80, no. 2 (1893): 583–95.

———. *Pis'ma k rodnim*, vol. 1, pt. 2–vol. 3, pt. 2. Moscow: Muzgiz, 1954–62.

———. "Proiskhozhdeniye russkikh bïlin." *Vestnik Yevropï* 3 (1868): 169–221.

———. *Russkiy narodnïy ornament*. St. Petersburg: Obshchestvo Pooshreniya Khudozhestv, 1872.

———. "Slavyanskiy kontsert g. Balakireva." *Sankt-peterburgskiye vedomosti*, 13 May 1867.

———. *Sobraniye sochineniy V. V. Stasova, 1847–1886*. 4 vols. St. Petersburg, 1894–1906.

———. *Stat'i o muzïke*. Vols. 4–5a. Moscow: Muzïka, 1978–80.

Steele, Robert, trans. *The Russian Garland of Fairy Tales*. New York: Robert M. McBride, 1916; rpt. New York: Kraus Reprint Co., 1971.

Stein, Jack M. *Richard Wagner and the Synthesis of the Arts*. Detroit: Wayne State University Press, 1960.

Stein, Leonard. "Schoenberg and 'Kleine Modernsky.'" In *Confronting Stravinsky*, edited by Jann Pasler, 310–24. Berkeley and Los Angeles: University of California Press, 1986.

Steinberg, Ada. *Word and Music in the Novels of Andrey Bely*. Cambridge: Cambridge University Press, 1982.

Sternfeld, Frederick W. "Some Russian Folk Songs in Stravinsky's *Petrouchka*." *Music Library Association Notes* 2 (1945): 98–104. Reprinted in *Petrushka* (Norton Critical Scores), edited by Charles Hamm, 203–15. New York: W. W. Norton, 1967.

Stockhausen, Karlheinz. *Texte zur elektronischen und instrumentalen Musik*. Vol. 1. Cologne: Verlag M. Du Mont Schauberg, 1963.

Straus, Joseph. "Stravinsky's Tonal Axis." *Journal of Music Theory* 26 (1982): 264.

Stravinskaya, Kseniya Yuryevna. *O I. F. Stravinskom i yego blizkikh.* Leningrad: Muzïka, 1978.

Stravinsky, Igor. *An Autobiography.* New York: W. W. Norton, 1962. Anonymous English translation (first published 1936) of *Chroniques de ma vie.* 2 vols. Paris: Denoel & Steele, 1935–36.

———. "Ce que j'ai voulu exprimer dans 'Le sacre du printemps.'" *Montjoie!* no. 8 (29 May 1913). English translation: "What I Wished to Express in 'The Rite of Spring.'" Translated by Edward Burlingame Hill. *Boston Evening Transcript,* 12 Februay 1916. Anonymous Russian translation: "To chto ya khotel vïrazit' v 'Vesne svyashchennoy.'" *Muzïka,* no. 141 (3 August 1913).

———. "A Cure for V.D." *Listen: A Music Monthly* 1, no. 5 (September–October 1964): 1–2.

———. "The Diaghilev I Knew." Translated by Mercedes de Acosta. *Atlantic Monthly,* November 1953.

———. Interview. *Ogonyok,* 14 October 1912.

———. Letter to the editor. *The Nation,* 3 August 1970.

———. "Une lettre de Stravinsky sur Tchaikovsky." *Figaro,* 18 May 1922; rpt. *Revue musicale* 3, no. 9 (July 1922).

———. "Lyubite muzïku!" *Komsomolskaya pravda,* 27 September 1962.

———. "M. Igor Strawinsky nous parle de 'Perséphone.'" *Excelsior* 29 (April 1934). Reprinted in Eric Walter White, *Stravinsky: The Composer and His Works.* Berkeley and Los Angeles: University of California Press, 1966.

———. "Pis'mo I. Stravinskogo." *Muzïka,* no. 159 (7 December 1913).

———. *Poetics of Music in the Form of Six Lessons.* Bilingual ed., English translation from the original French by Arthur Knodel and Ingolf Dahl. Cambridge, Mass.: Harvard University Press, 1970.

———. *Themes and Conclusions.* Berkeley and Los Angeles: University of California Press, 1982.

Stravinsky, Igor, and Robert Craft. "35 Antworten auf 35 Fragen." *Melos* 24 (June 1957): 161–76.

———. "Answers to 34 Questions: An Interview with Igor Stravinsky." *Encounter* 9, no. 7 (July 1957): 3–14.

———. *Conversations with Igor Stravinsky* (Conv). Garden City, N.Y.: Doubleday, 1959; rpt. Berkeley and Los Angeles: University of California Press, 1980.

———. *Dialogues.* Berkeley and Los Angeles: University of California Press, 1982.

———. *Dialogues and a Diary* (D&D). Garden City, N.Y.: Doubleday, 1963.

———. *Expositions and Developments* (E&D). Garden City, N.Y.: Doubleday, 1962; rpt. Berkeley and Los Angeles: University of California Press, 1981.

———. *Memories and Commentaries* (M&C). Garden City, N.Y.: Doubleday, 1960; rpt. Berkeley and Los Angeles: University of California Press, 1981.

———. *Retrospectives and Conclusions* (R&C). New York: Alfred A. Knopf, 1969.

———. *Themes and Episodes.* New York: Alfred A. Knopf, 1966.

Stravinsky, Vera, and Robert Craft. *Stravinsky in Pictures and Documents* (P&D). New York: Simon & Schuster, 1978.

Strawinsky: sein Nachlass, sein Bild. Basel: Kunstmuseum, 1984.

Strawinsky, Theodore. *Catherine and Igor Stravinsky: A Family Album.* London: Boosey & Hawkes, 1973.

———. *The Message of Igor Strawinsky.* Translated by Robert Craft and André Marion. London: Boosey & Hawkes, 1953.

Street, Donald. "A Forgotten Firebird." *Musical Times* 119 (1978): 674–77.

————. "The Modes of Limited Transposition." *Musical Times* 117 (1976): 801–20.

Suben, Joel Eric. "Debussy and Octatonic Pitch Structure." Ph.D. diss., Brandeis University, 1980.

Sullivan, Lawrence. "Nikita Baliev's Le Théâtre de la Chauve-Souris: An Avant-Garde Theater." *Dance Research Journal* 18, no. 2 (Winter 1986–87).

Sviatopolk-Mirsky, Dmitriy Petrovich, Prince. "The Eurasian Movement." *Slavonic and East European Review* 6 (1927–28): 312–20.

————. *A History of Russian Literature*. Edited and abridged by Francis J. Whitfield. New York: Alfred A. Knopf, 1949.

————. *Pushkin*. New York: E. P. Dutton, 1963.

Swan, Alfred J. *Russian Music and Its Sources in Chant and Folk Song*. New York: W. W. Norton, 1973.

————. *Six Russian Folksongs from Gorodishche, Pechorsky District, Estonia*. Leipzig: Belaïeff, 1939.

Swerkoff, E. L. *See* Zverkov, Ye. L.

Tangemann, Robert. "Stravinsky's Two-Piano Works" (1945). In *Stravinsky in "Modern Music," 1924–1946*, edited by Carol J. Oja. New York: Da Capo Press, 1982.

Tansman, Alexandre. *Igor Stravinsky: The Man and His Music*. Translated by Therese Bleefield and Charles Bleefield. New York: G. P. Putnam's Sons, 1949.

Taruskin, Richard. "*Chez Petrouchka:* Harmony and Tonality *chez* Stravinsky." *19th-Century Music* 10, no. 3 (Spring 1987): 265–86.

————. "The Dark Side of Modern Music." *New Republic*, 5 September 1988, 28–34.

————. "From Fairy Tale to Opera in Four Not-So-Simple Moves." *English National Opera Programme*, December 1989.

————. "Handel, Shakespeare, and Musorgsky: The Sources and Limits of Russian Musical Realism." In *Studies in the History of Music* 1 (New York: Broude Bros., 1984): 247–68.

————. "How the Acorn Took Root: A Tale of Russia." *19th-Century Music* 6, no. 3 (Spring 1983): 189–212.

————. Letter to the editor. *Musical Times* 129, no. 1746 (August 1988): 385.

————. " 'Little Star': An Étude in the Folk Style." In *Musorgsky: In Memoriam, 1881–1981*, edited by Malcolm H. Brown, 57–84. Ann Arbor: UMI Research Press, 1982.

————. "Musorgsky vs. Musorgsky: The Versions of *Boris Godunov*." *19th-Century Music* 8 (1985): 91–118, 245–72.

————. "Opera and Drama in Russia: The Case of Serov's *Judith*." *Journal of the American Musicological Society* 32 (1979): 74–117.

————. *Opera and Drama in Russia as Preached and Practiced in the 1860s*. Ann Arbor: UMI Research Press, 1981.

————. "The Present in the Past: Russian Opera and Russian Historiography, ca. 1870." In *Russian and Soviet Music: Essays for Boris Schwarz*, edited by Malcolm H. Brown, 74–143. Ann Arbor: UMI Research Press, 1984.

————. "Realism as Preached and Practiced: The Russian *Opéra Dialogué*." *Musical Quarterly* 56 (1970): 431–54.

————. Review of *The Music of Alexander Scriabin*, by J. Baker, and *Scriabin: Artist and Mystic*, by B. Schloezer. *Music Theory Spectrum* 10 (1988): 143–69.

————. "Russian Folk Melodies in *The Rite of Spring*." *Journal of the American Musicological Society* 33 (1980): 501–43.

————. "Serov and Musorgsky." In *Slavonic and Western Music: Essays for Gerald Abraham*, edited by Malcolm H. Brown and R. John Wiley, 139–62. Ann Arbor/Oxford: UMI Research Press/Oxford University Press, 1985.

———. "Some Thoughts on the History and Historiography of Russian Music." *Journal of Musicology* 3 (1984): 321–39.

Taruskin, Richard, and Robert Craft. "Jews and Geniuses: An Exchange." *New York Review of Books,* 15 June, 1989, 57–58.

Taylor, Deems. *Of Men and Music.* New York: Simon & Schuster, 1937.

———. "Stravinsky Marks Time." *New York World,* 3 July 1922.

"Teatral." "Beseda s baletmeysterom B. G. Romanovïm." *Peterburgskaya gazeta,* 1 June 1914.

———. "U kompozitora I. F. Stravinskogo," *Peterburgskaya gazeta,* 27 September 1912.

———. "U T. P. Karsavinoy." *Peterburgskaya gazeta,* no. 197 (21 July 1910).

———. "Vdova N. A. Rimskogo-Korsakova o 'Zolotom petushke.' " *Peterburgskaya gazeta,* 17 May 1914.

Tenisheva, Maria Klavdiyevna. *Vpechatleniya moyey zhizni.* Paris: Russkoye Istoriko-genealogicheskoye Obshchestvo vo Frantsii, 1933.

Tereshchenko, A. V. *Bït russkogo naroda.* 7 vols. St. Petersburg, 1848.

Threlfall, Robert. "The Stravinsky Version of *Khovanshchina.*" *Studies in Music* 15 (1981): 106–15.

Timofeyev, Grigoriy Nikolayevich (*see also* "G. T."). "Iz muzïkal'noy khroniki." *Vestnik Yevropï,* no. 5 (1909): 755–62.

———. "Iz peterburgskoy muzïkal'noy zhizni." *Russkaya mïsl'* 32, no. 2 (February 1911).

———. "Muzïkal'nïy obzor: Peterburgskaya muzïkal'naya zhizn' v 1908 g." *Russkaya mïsl'* 30, no. 2 (February 1909).

———. [Gregoire Timoféev]. "Les nouveautés de la musique russe." *Revue musicale S.I.M.* 5 (1909).

Tïrkova, A. V. *Anna Pavlovna Filosofova i yeyo vremya.* Sbornik pamyati Annï Pavlovnï Filoso-fovoy, vol. 1. Petrograd: Galiks & Vilborg, 1915.

Todd, R. Larry. "Liszt, Fantasy and Fugue for Organ on 'Ad nos, ad salutarem undam.' " *19th-Century Music* 4 (1981): 250–61.

Trofimova, Tatyana Nikolayevna, and Anatoliy Nikolayevich Drozdov. *Nachalo russkogo ro-mansa.* Moscow: Muzgiz, 1936.

Trubetskoy, Nikolai Sergeyevich, Prince. *K probleme russkogo samopoznaniya.* Paris: Yevraziyskoye Knigoizdatel'stvo, 1927.

———. *Yevropa i chelovechestvo.* Sofia: Rossiysko-bolgarskoye Knigoizdatel'stvo, 1920.

Trudï muzïkal'no-ètnograficheskoy komissii, sostoyashchei pri ètnograficheskom otdele Imperator-skogo obshchestva lyubiteley yestestvoznaniya, antropologii i etnografii (*Trudï MEK*). Vol. 1: Izvestiya Imperatorskogo obshchestva lyubiteley yestestvoznaniya, antropologii i et-nografiii, sostoyashchego pri Imperatorskom Moskovskom universitete, vol. 113; Trudï etnograficheskogo otdela, vol. 15. Moscow: Tip. K. L. Men'shova, 1906. Vol. 2: vols. 114, 16. Moscow: Tovarishchestvo Skoropechatii A. A. Levenson, 1911.

Tugenhold, Yakov. "Itogi sezona (pis'mo iz Parizha)." *Apollon,* 1911, no. 6.

———. "Russkiy sezon' v Parizhe." *Apollon,* 1910, no. 10.

Turnell, Martin. *Jacques Rivière.* Cambridge: Bowes & Bowes, 1953.

Turner, J. Rigbie. "Nineteenth-Century Music Manuscripts in the Pierpont Morgan Li-brary: A Check List (II)." *19th-Century Music* 4 (1980–81): 157–83.

Tyuneyev, Boris Dmitriyevich. "I. Stravinskiy." *Russkaya muzïkal'naya gazeta,* 20, no. 5 (2 February 1913), cols. 132–36.

———. "O Cherepnine (dialog)." *Russkaya muzïkal'naya gazeta* 22, no. 15 (12 April 1915), cols. 275–76.

————. "S.-Peterburgskiye kontsertï." *Russkaya muzïkal'naya gazeta* 17, no. 44 (31 October 1910), col. 974.

————. "V. Senilov: materialï." *Russkaya muzïkal'naya gazeta* 23, nos. 8–9 (21–28 February 1916), cols. 180–84.

Uspensky, Nikolai Dmitriyevich. *Obraztsï drevnerusskogo pevcheskogo iskusstva.* 2d ed., Leningrad: Muzïka, 1971.

Ussachevsky, Vladimir Alexeyevich. "My Saint Stravinsky." *Perspectives of New Music* 9, no. 2–10, no. 1 (1971): 34–38.

Valkenier, Elizabeth K. *Russian Realist Art.* Ann Arbor: Ardis, 1977.

Valter, Viktor Grigoryevich. "O 'Vesne svyashchennoy' Igorya Stravinskogo." *Birzheviye vedomosti,* 22 February/7 March 1914.

Van den Toorn, Pieter C. *The Music of Igor Stravinsky.* New Haven: Yale University Press, 1983.

————. *Stravinsky and "The Rite of Spring": The Beginnings of a Musical Language.* Berkeley and Los Angeles: University of California Press, 1987.

————. "Stravinsky Rebarred." *Music Analysis* 7, no. 2 (July 1988): 165–96.

Varunts, Viktor, ed. *I. Stravinskiy—publitsist i sobesednik.* Moscow: Sovetskiy Kompozitor, 1988.

Vasilenko, Sergey Nikiforovich. *Vospominaniya.* Moscow: Sovetskiy Kompozitor, 1979.

Vengerov, Semyon Afanasyevich, ed. *Biblioteka velikikh pisateley: Pushkin.* Vol. 4. St. Petersburg: Brokgauz-Efron, 1910.

Vernadsky, George. *Kievan Russia.* 2d ed. New Haven: Yale University Press, 1973.

————. *The Origins of Russia.* London: Oxford University Press, 1959.

Vershinina, Irina Yakovlevna. *Ranniye baletï Stravinskogo.* Moscow: Nauka, 1967.

————, ed. "Pis'ma I. Stravinskogo N. Rerikhu." *Sovetskaya muzïka,* 1966, no. 8, 57–63.

Vilenkin, Nikolai Maximovich. *See Minsky, N.*

Villebois [Vil'boa], Konstantin Ivanovich. *Sto russkikh narodnïkh pesen.* St. Petersburg: Stellovsky, 1860.

Vitol, Jazep [Wihtol, Iosif]. *Vospominaniya, stat'i, pis'ma.* Leningrad: Muzïka, 1969.

Vlad, Roman. "Reihenstrukturen im 'Sacre du Printemps.'" *Musik-Konzepte* 34–35 (January 1984).

————. *Stravinsky.* 3d ed. London: Oxford University Press, 1978.

Volkonsky, Sergey Mikhailovich, Prince. *Otkliki teatra.* Petrograd: Sirius, 1914.

————. "Russkiy balet v Parizhe." *Apollon,* 1913, no. 6.

Volkov, Solomon. *Balanchine's Tchaikovsky.* New York: Simon & Schuster, 1985.

————. "The 'New Folkloristic Wave' in Contemporary Soviet Music as a Sociological Phenomenon." In *Report of the 12th Congress [of the International Musicological Society], Berkeley, 1977,* edited by Daniel Heartz and Bonnie Wade, 49–52. Kassel: Bärenreiter, 1981.

Voloshin, Maximilian Alexandrovich. "Arkhaízm v russkoy zhivopisi." *Apollon,* 1910, no. 5.

Vuillermoz, Émile. "Mavra." *Excelsior,* 12 June 1922.

————. "Noces—Igor Strawinsky." *Revue musicale* 4, no. 10 (August 1923): 69–72.

————. "Strawinsky." *Revue musicale S.I.M.* 8, no. 5 (1912): 12–18.

Vulfius, Pavel Alexandrovich, ed. *Russkaya mïsl' o muzïkal'nom fol'klorye.* Moscow: Muzïka, 1979.

Wagner, Richard. *Gesammelte Schriften und Dichtungen.* Vol. 3. Leipzig, 1871.

Walsh, Stephen. *The Music of Stravinsky.* London: Routledge, 1988.

Warner, Elizabeth A. *The Russian Folk Theatre.* The Hague: Mouton, 1977.

Wellesz, Egon. *A History of Byzantine Music and Hymnography.* 2d ed. Oxford: Clarendon Press, 1962.

Westphal, Rudolf. *Allgemeine Theorie der musikalischen Rhythmik seit J. S. Bach auf Grundlage der Antiken.* Leipzig, 1880.

White, Eric Walter. *Stravinsky: The Composer and His Works.* Berkeley and Los Angeles: University of California Press, 1966.

———. *Stravinsky: A Critical Survey.* New York: Philosophical Library, 1948.

———. "Stravinsky in Interview." *Tempo,* no. 97 (1971): 6–9.

———. *Stravinsky's Sacrifice to Apollo.* London: Hogarth Press, 1930.

Whittall, Arnold. "Music Analysis as Human Science? *Le Sacre du Printemps.*" *Music Analysis* 1 (1982): 33–53.

Wild, Roger, ed. *Maurice Ravel par quelques-uns de ses familiers.* Paris: Éditions du Tambourinaire, 1939.

Wiley, Roland John. *Tchaikovsky's Ballets.* Oxford: Clarendon Press, 1985.

———. "The Tribulations of Nationalist Composers: A Speculation Concerning Borrowed Music in *Khovanshchina.*" In *Musorgsky: In Memoriam, 1881–1981,* edited by Malcolm H. Brown, 163–78. Ann Arbor: UMI Research Press, 1982.

Wise, C. Stanley. "Impressions of Igor Strawinsky." *Musical Quarterly* 2 (1916): 249–56.

Wuorinen, Charles. Untitled tribute. *Perspectives of New Music* 9, no. 2–10, no. 1 (1971): 128–29.

———. *Simple Composition.* New York: Longman, 1979.

Wuorinen, Charles, and Jeffrey Kresky. "On the Significance of Stravinsky's Last Works." In *Confronting Stravinsky,* edited by Jann Pasler, 262–70. Berkeley and Los Angeles: University of California Press, 1986.

Yankovsky, Mark Osipovich, et al., eds. *Glazunov: issledovaniya, materialï, publikatsiy, pis'ma.* 2 vols. Leningrad: Muzgiz, 1959–60.

———. *Rimskiy-Korsakov: issledovaniya, materialï, pis'ma.* 2 vols. Moscow: Izdatel'stvo Akademii Nauk SSSR, 1954.

Yarustovsky, Boris Mikhailovich. "I. Stravinskiy: eskiznaya tetrad' (1911–1913 gg.): nekotorïye nablyudeniya i razmïshleniya." In *I. F. Stravinskiy: stat'i i materialï,* edited by L. S. Dyachkova, with Boris M. Yarustovsky, 162–206. Moscow: Sovetskiy Kompozitor, 1973.

———. *Igor' Stravinskiy.* 2d ed. Moscow: Sovetskiy Kompozitor, 1969.

Yastrebtsev, Vasiliy Vasilyevich. "K yubileyu N. A. Rimskogo-Korsakova." *Russkaya muzïkal'naya gazeta* 7, no. 51 (17 December 1900), cols. 1267–71.

———. *N. A. Rimskiy-Korsakov: vospominaniya 1886–1908.* 2 vols. Edited by Alexander V. Ossovsky. Leningrad: Muzgiz, 1959–60. English translation (abridged): *Reminiscences of Rimsky-Korsakov.* Edited and translated by Florence Jonas. New York: Columbia University Press, 1985.

———. "O slukhovïkh zabluzhdeniyakh." *Russkaya muzïkal'naya gazeta* 16, nos. 22–23 (30 May–6 June 1909).

Yaunzem, Irma Petrovna. "Rozhdeniye pesni." *Sovetskaya muzïka,* 1963, no. 8.

Yavorsky, Boleslav Leopoldovich. "Neskol'ko mïsley v svyazi s yubileyem Frantsa Lista." *Muzïka,* no. 45 (8 October 1911): 961–64.

Youens, Susan. "Excavating an Allegory: The Texts of *Pierrot Lunaire.*" *Journal of the Arnold Schoenberg Institute* 8, no. 2 (November 1984): 96–101.

"Yu. K." [Yuriy Kurdyumov]. "Pridvornïy orkestr." *Peterburgskiy listok,* 24 January 1908, 4.

Yuzhakov, S. N., ed. *Bol'shaya èntsiklopediya.* Vol. 22 (supplement). St. Petersburg: Prosveshcheniye, 1909.

"Zabïtoye interv'yu s P. I. Chaikovskim." *Sovetskaya muzïka,* 1949, no. 7, 60–63.

Zaporozhets, Nataliya Vladimirovna. *A. K. Lyadov: Zhizn' i tvorchestvo.* Moscow: Muzgiz, 1954.

Zatsarnïy, Yuriy Andreyevich, ed. *Russkiye narodnïye pesni: pesennik.* Vol. 7. Moscow: Sovetskiy Kompozitor, 1987.

Zemtsovsky, Izaliy Iosifovich. *Melodika kalendarnïkh pesen.* Leningrad: Muzïka, 1975.

———. *Russkaya protyazhnaya pesnya: opït issledovaniya.* Leningrad: Muzïka, 1967.

Zguta, Russell. *Russian Minstrels: A History of the Skomorokhi.* Philadelphia: University of Pennsylvania Press, 1978.

———. *"Skomorokhi:* The Russian Minstrel-Entertainers." *Slavic Review* 31 (1972): 297–313.

Zhitiya svyatïkh. Vol. 10. Moscow: Sinodal'naya Tipografiya, 1908.

Zhuravleva, L. S. "K stoletiyu so dnya rozhdeniya M. K. Tenishevoy (istoriko-biograficheskiy ocherk)." *Materialï po izucheniyu Smolenskoy oblasti* 7 (1970).

Zilbershteyn, Ilya Samoylovich, and Vladimir Alexeyevich Samkov, eds. *Sergey Dyagilev i russkoye iskusstvo.* 2 vols. Moscow: Izobratitel'noye Iskusstvo, 1982.

———. *Valentin Serov v vospominaniyakh, dnevnikakh i perepiske sovremennikov.* Vol. 1. Leningrad: Khudozhnik RSFSR, 1960.

Zverkov [Swerkoff], Ye. L. *Sbornik populyarneyshikh russkikh narodnïkh pesen.* Leipzig: Zimmermann, 1921.

Arensky, Anton Stepanovich *(continued)*
ostinato" (op. 5/5), 11n; *Cléopâtre (Yegipetskiye nochi)*, 546, 972; Concerto for Violin and Orchestra, 10; *Dream on the Volga (Son na Volge)*, 11, 914n; *Fountain of Bakchisarai (Bakchisaraiskiy fontan)*, 1542n; *Nal and Damayanti*, 10–11; String Quartet No. 2, 9; Symphony No. 1, 10; Trio in D minor (op. 32), 60

Argutinsky-Dolgorukov, Vladimir Nikolayevich, 1184n

Aristotle, 427

Aristoxenus, 723

Arkhangelsky, Alexey, 1542–43, 1548n; "Katinka," 1543, 1545, 1546–47 (incl. Ex. 19.19b), 1561

Arnaud, Yvonne, 643

Arnold, Yuriy Karlovich, 64

Artemyevna, Zinaída, 845n

art nouveau, 513

Artsïbushev, Nikolai Vasilyevich, 50 (Fig. 1.2), 57, 61, 250–51, 360n; as Belyayev trustee, 73

Asafyev, Boris (Igor Glebov), 37, 315, 365, 498–99, 578, 767, 900n, 906, 1027n, 1121. 1124; on *Baika*, 1237–38, 1242; *A Book About Stravinsky*, 1124, 1237, 1299, 1323n, 1483, 1532n; on Cherepnin, 456; on *Histoire du soldat*, 1292; on *Khovanshchina*, Stravinsky's final chorus to, 1053; on *Poèmes de Verlaine*, 652; on *Svadebka*, 1385

Astruc, Gabriel, 982

Astruc, Yvonne, 1446

Auden, W. H., 1198, 1236

Auer, Leopold Semyonovich, 1045n, 1302, 1520–21

aukaniye, 364n

Auric, Georges, 777; *Les fâcheux*, 1507, 1606; on *Mavra*, 1598

"authenticity" in performance, 1576n

autodidactism, 24–25, 40

"Avdeyeva, Mme": *Russkiye skazki dlya detey* (Russian Folktales for Children), 1248–50, 1253

Azanchevsky, Mikhaíl Pavlovich, 29

Aztecs, 881n

Baba-yaga (Russian folktale witch), 565

Babbitt, Milton, 3n, 1649, 1653n, 1656, 1658, 1662, 1665n, 1673, 1673n

Bach, Carl Philipp Emanuel, 257

Bach, Johann Sebastian, 1572, 1675; English Suite No. 3 in G minor, Sarabande, 269 (Ex. 4.14); "retour à," 1607–8, 1614

Bach, Wilhelm Friedemann, 979

Bachinskaya, Nina Mikhailovna, 695n, 1330n

Bakst (*né* Rosenberg), Lev Samoylovich, 524, 569, 577, 662, 820n, 983n, 1184n; caricatured, 520 (Fig. 8.9); and Imperial Theaters, 539, 1507; on *Metamorphoses* (Steinberg), 1109–10; and *Mir iskusstva*, 513, 516n; *Mir iskusstva* logo designed by, 440, 517–18 (incl. Fig. 8.8b); as "Nevsky Pickwickian," 430, 433; *Le sacre du printemps* christened by, 861n; and "saisons russes," 550; and *Shéhérazade*, 663, 739–40; and Stravinsky's "Souvenir d'une marche boche," 1133. Works: "Paths of Classicism in Art" *(Puti klassitsizma v iskusstve)*, 855; *Terror Antiquus*, 443

balaganï (fairground showbooths), 665, 671, 683, 690, 760

Balakirev, Miliy Alexeyevich, 49, 66, 262, 267, 734, 894n, 1594; and Belyayev, compared as "group leaders," 53–54, 446; as folklorist, 1212; as folk song harmonist, 1381; and Glazunov, 36; latter-day career of, 37–38; and Mighty Kuchka, 23, 31; and Rimsky-Korsakov, 6, 33; and "Russian minor," 1173. Works: "Ey, ukhnem!" (Volga Boatmen's Song, arr.), 1184–86 (incl. Ex. 15.14a), 1188; *Firebird* (projected opera), 623–25 (incl. Ex. 9.34); First Overture on Russian Themes, 261, 955; Hymn to the Dowager Empress, 73; Overture to *King Lear*, 283; *Sbornik russkikh narodnïkh pesen* (folk song anthology), 111, 133, 145, 148–49 (Ex. 2.20c), 498, 606, 609 (Ex. 9.22b), 724, 1054n, 1175, 1184–86 (incl. Ex. 15.14a), 1188, 1208–10 (incl. Ex. 15.24), 1214 (Ex. 15.28); Second Overture on Russian Themes *(Rus')*, 38, 261; "Solovey" (The Nightingale; Alyabiev, arr.), 1546n; Sonata for piano in B minor, 99; Symphony No. 1 in C, 409n, 410; Symphony No. 2 in D minor, 646; *Thamar*, 639, 646, 1010; "Zhavronok" (The Lark; Glinka, arr.), 1592

balalaikas, at Paris Exposition (1900), 522; evoked in *Petrushka*, 735

Balanchine, George (Georgiy Melitonovich Balanchivadze), 1229, 1540n

Baliyev, Nikita, 1540–42 (incl. Fig. 19.3), 1546, 1549n

Balla, Giacomo, 8, 1320n, 1506

ballet: creative process in, 585; estheticist rediscovery of, 487, 535–42; nineteenth-century decline of, 535–36; "with singing" *(balet s peniyem)*, 1087

Ballets russes, 16, 450, 1595; incorporated, 660. Productions: "Aurora's Wedding" (after Chaikovsky, *Sleeping Beauty*), 1512, 1533, 1538–39; *Cimarosiana*, 1508; *Cléopâtre*

(*Yegipetskiye nochi*), 546, 550–51, 970, 972, 1047; *Les femmes de bonne humeur*, 1506, 1508; *Le festin*, 548–49; *Liturgiya* (project), 496, 1321, 1379n; *Nuit sur le Mont chauve*, 1508; *Les orientales*, 548; *Papillons* (Schumann, orch. Cherepnin, chor. Fokine), 1112; "Scènes et danses polovtsiennes" (after Borodin, *Prince Igor*, designed by Roerich), 851–52, 863, 1048; *Shéhérazade* (after Rimsky-Korsakov), 663, 739–40, 759, 970, 972, 1010, 1039–41, 1047, 1074–75; *Le spectre de la rose* (after Weber), 759; *Les sylphides*, 546–48, 549, 761, 970; *Les tentations de la bergère* (Montéclair, chor. Nijinska), 368

Balmont, Konstantin Dmitriyevich, 308, 364, 372, 378, 463, 779, 780, 782–91 (incl. Fig. 11.1), 1151, 1206

—Works:
 Firebird (*Zhar-ptitsa*), 557, 858; frontispiece by Somov, 559 (Fig. 9.1a), 786, 789
 "Poetry as Magic" (*Poèziya kak volshebstvo*), 849
 Zelyoniy vertograd, 784–89, 1152; "The Dove" from, 786–87; "Zvezdolikiy" from, 787, 789–91 (incl. Fig. 11.3)
 Zovi drevnosti, 856

Baltrushaitis, Jurgis, 780n, 789
Bancroft, David, 992
bandura, banduristï, 1192, 1196
Barère, Simon, 50
Bartók, Béla, 14, 15, 727n, 803n, 940n, 1212, 1282, 1419, 1462n; Stravinsky on, 8
Batault, Georges, 999
Bat Theater of Moscow. *See* Chauve-Souris, Théâtre de la
Baudelaire, Charles, 373
Bayer, Josef: *Die Puppenfee*, 1507
Beardsley, Aubrey, 374, 826n
bears, trained, 665–66 (incl. Fig. 10.1), 1242–43
Beaumarchais, Pierre Augustin Caron de, 1532; *Marriage of Figaro*, 1540
Bechet, Sidney, 1483n
Beckwith, R. S., 1166
Beecham, Thomas, 759n
Beethoven, Ludwig van, 54, 1532. Works: "Jena" Symphony (actually by Witt), 979; Piano Concerto No. 4 in G, 268; Symphony No. 5 in C minor, 1475–76 (incl. Ex. 18.10); Symphony No. 6 in F, "Pastoral," 257–58 (incl. Ex. 4.3); Symphony No. 7 in A, 258–59; "Twelve Variations on a Russian Dance from Wranitzky's *Das Waldmädchen*," 1517–18, 1520 (Ex. 19.4c); Variations for piano, op. 34, 259
Belanovsky, S. P., 972n

Belina-Skupiewski, Stefan, 1591
Belïy, Andrey (*né* Bugayev, Boris Nikolayevich), 437, 438n, 489, 571, 781, 855, 856, 1319, 1333, 1379
Belkin, A. A., 1243
Bellaigue, Camille, 551
Bellay, Joachim du, 989
Bellini, Vincenzo: *Norma*, 865
bells and bell-ringing, 348, 463, 499, 1430
Belousov, Yevsey Yakovlevich, 842; on *Rite of Spring*, 1013
Belsky, Vladimir Nikolayevich, 359, 405, 464, 496, 1079, 1110, 1322n
Belyankin, Grigoriy Pavlovich (brother-in-law), 40n, 1333
Belyayev Charter, 58–60
Belyayev Circle ("Belyayevtsï"), 4, 6, 50 (Fig. 1.2) 52–58, 446, 719, 765, 1493, 1510n, 1534, 1647, 1673; academicism of, 58, 67; and Conservatory, 56; "New Russian School," compared with, 51–52, 53–54, 67; Quartet Fridays, 48–49, 61
—Collective orchestral compositions:
 "Variations on a Russian Theme" (Rimsky-Korsakov, Glazunov, Lyadov, Artsïbushev, Wihtol, Sokolov), 111
—Collective quartet compositions:
 "B-La-F" quartet (Borodin, Rimsky-Korsakov, Lyadov, Glazunov), 61, 68
 "Jour de fête" (*Imeninï*) (Rimsky-Korsakov, Lyadov, Glazunov), 61
 "Variations on a Russian Folk Song" (Artsïbushev, Wihtol, F. Blumenfeld, Ewald, Winkler, Sokolov, Scriabin), 61
 Les Vendredis, 61, 63 (Fig. 1.4b), 377
Belyayev, Mitrofan Petrovich, 47–52 (incl. Figs. 1.1–2), 90, 380, 651; and chamber music, 60–62; and "denationalization" of Russian music, 60–64; Glinka Prizes awarded by, 60, 315; promotional concert series, *see* Russian Symphony Concerts; and Russian concerts at Paris Exposition (1889), 524; and Tretyakov compared, 60
Belyayev, Victor Mikhailovich, 15, 1357, 1385
Belyayev publishing house ("Édition M. P. Belaïeff, Leipzig"), 49, 56, 60–61, 503; Board of Trustees, 58–59 (incl. Fig. 1.3), 68, 392; predominance of instrumental music in catalogue, 65
Benchley, Robert, 1540
Benfey, Theodor, 622–23n
Benjamin, William, 1473n, 1485n
Benois, Alexander Nikolayevich, 373, 429, 433, 434n, 445, 453, 535, 649, 796, 820n, 969, 970,

in E-flat, 253; Symphony No. 2 in B minor, 38, 202, 213, 646

Bossé, Gualter, 651–52

Boulanger, Nadia, 224n, 1623, 1641

Boulez, Pierre, 4, 824n, 963, 1376n, 1487n; *Relévés d'apprenti*, 4n

Bowlt, John, 436, 446n

Boyarsky, Ilya, 414n

"Bozhe, Tsarya khrani!" (Tsarist anthem), 1183, 1537

Brahms, Johannes, 65, 375; Symphony No. 3 in F, 259n

Brailoiu, Constantin, 1384–85n

Brandt, A., 835

Brianza, Carlotta, 1520

Brillant, Maurice, 1594–95, 1596n

Britten, Benjamin, 547n

Brown, David, 1573n

Brown, Malcolm H., 438n, 1354n

Bruckner, Anton: Symphony No. 7 in E, 259n

Bruneau, Alfred, 172, 974; on Chaikovsky, 527

Brussel, Robert, 641

Bryullov, Karl Pavlovich, 441

Bryusov, Valeriy Yakovlevich, 438, 441, 655n, 782, 789, 856

Buckle, Richard, 677–78, 846n, 851–52, 1007

bugle, keyed (flugelhorn), 1458

Bukofzer, Manfred, 1623

Bullard, Truman C., 1007

Burkhart, Charles, 1637n

Burney, Charles, 1600

Buslayev, Fyodor Ivanovich, 883n, 1333, 1335–37

Buslayev, Vasiliy (epic hero), 971

Byron, George Gordon, Lord: *Beppo*, 1501, 1549

cabotin/cabotinage, 999, 1003

calendar songs. See *kalendarnïye pesni*

Calvocoressi, Michel-Dimitri, 28, 357, 358n, 527, 551, 646, 978–79, 1013, 1040, 1083; on *Firebird*, 639–40, 823, 1155–56; on *Khovanshchina* (Diaghilev production), 1051–53; on *Nightingale*, 1107

Campbell, Stuart, 1580

Canudo, Ricciotto, 877, 996–99 (incl. Fig. 13.5), 1112

Capet, Lucien, 1022

Caplet, André, 1446

Carter, Elliott, 1246, 1349

Cary, Mary Flagler, Music Collection, 1142

Casadesus, Henri, 367–68

Casals, Pablo, 416

Casella, Alfredo, 842, 1444, 1447, 1608

Casella, Hélène, 826

Castiglione, Baldesar, 427

Catherine (Yekaterina) II (The Great), 443, 924, 1507

Catoire (Katuar), Georgiy Lvovich, 377

Cavos, Alberto Camille (Albert Catterinovich), 426

Cavos, Catterino, 426, 624n, 1508. Works: *Firebird*, 426, 624n; *Ivan Susanin*, 426; *Zéphyre et Flore*, 426

Cecchetti, Enrico, 75, 537

Chabrier, Emmanuel, 308

Chaikovsky, Modest Ilyich, 36, 364n; as librettist, 542

Chaikovsky, Pyotr Ilyich, 3, 5, 6, 9–10, 11, 26–27, 139, 315, 396, 624, 767, 914, 1513, 1534, 1536 (Fig. 19.2), 1589, 1594–95; and *Baiser de la fée*, 1611–13 (incl. Table 7); as ballet composer, 536, 584–85; on Delibes, 540; on Glinka, 717, 1508; and folklore, 1136; folk song arrangements, 697; on form, 138, 956; French and English prejudice against, 526–27, 1512; and French music, 308; Glazunov's memoir of, 37–38; as "most Russian" composer, 424, 1532–33; on "New Russian School," 30–31, 35–36, 1656; on opera, 534; orchestrational style, 206; on professionalism, 167; and Rimsky-Korsakov, 30–31, 206, 241; Stravinsky on, 1532–36 (incl. Fig. 19.2); and F. I. Stravinsky, 81; as unofficial court composer, 46, 1537, 1618; and young St. Petersburg composers, 39–40
—Works:

"Both Painful and Sweet" (*I bol'no i sladko*, op. 6/3), 1612–13

Capriccio italien, 111

Dumka for piano, 1612

Enchantress, 81, 157, 159–60 (incl. Ex. 2.28b)

Eugene Onegin, 241, 1553–55 (incl. Ex. 19.15), 1588

Festival Coronation March, 1537

Festival Overture on the Danish National Hymn, 1537

Feuillet d'album (op. 19/3), 1613

Francesca da Rimini, 37, 526

Grande sonate (op. 37), 115, 116–17 (incl. Ex. 2.5), 125–26 (incl. Ex. 2.10a)

Humoresque (op. 10/2), 1612

"In the Village" (*V derevne*, op. 40/7), 1613

Iolanta, 39

Liturgy of St. John Chrysostom, 1619

"Lullaby in the Storm" (*Kolïbel'naya pesn' v buryu*, op. 54/10), 1612–13

Manfred Symphony, 37

Moscow (cantata), 1537

Mozartiana, 1510n

Natha-Valse (op. 51/4), 1613

Chevillard, Camille, 310, 524

"Chicher-yacher" (children's song), 216, 229

Chopin, Frédéric, 166, 367, 979, 1451, 1541;
   Polonaise-Fantaisie (op. 61), 268

Christensen, Thomas, 819n

Christoff, Boris, 414n

Chudnovsky, Valerian, 789

Chukovsky, Korney Ivanovich, 855

Cimarosa, Domenico, 1513; *Le astuzie femminili*,
   1507–8; *Le astuzie femminili*, "ballo russo"
   from, 1517, 1519 (Ex. 19.4b), 1539n

cimbalom, 1152, 1196, 1239n, 1303–1304 (incl. Fig.
   16.4), 1426, 1457–58

Cingria, Charles-Albert, 1588

circles of thirds, 166, 197, 211, 255–71 (incl. Exx.
   4.1–16), 273, 283, 297, 319, 320 (Ex. 5.2b), 327,
   481–82, 657, 1572, 1582–83; in *Firebird*, 589–91
   (incl. Ex. 9.6); in *Rite of Spring*, 937–38; in
   Two Poems of Balmont, 801–2 (incl. Ex. 11.2); in
   Baika, 1280–89

Ciurlionis, Mikolajus, 380

civil war, Russian, 16

Claudel, Paul, 1199

Coates, Albert, 973, 975, 978n, 1038, 1085n;
   Ashurbanipal, 1085n

Cocteau, Jean, 991, 1007, 1322n, 1507, 1598, 1603,
   1605–6; *Le coq et l'arlequin*, 777

Collaer, Paul, 655

collage, 1452, 1455

Commedia dell'Arte, 672–73 (incl. Fig. 10.3), 677

Cone, Edward T., 956, 1487n

Conlan, Barnett, 864

Conservatories: ethos of, replaces autodidactism,
   40–41; Moscow, 26, 31; St. Petersburg, 25–26,
   46; St. Petersburg composition curriculum,
   172

Cooper (Kuper), Emil Albertovich, 409, 767,
   1046

Copland, Aaron, 781, 1624; on *Octuor*, 1600, 1607

Corelli, Arcangelo, 297

Cortes, Ramiro, 1456n

Cortot, Alfred, 979

Couperin, François, 1532

Court Chapel Choir [School] *(Pridvornaya
   kapèlla)*, 163

Court Orchestra *(Pridvorniy orkestr)*, 222–24
   (incl. Fig. 3.2), 251, 792

Craft, Robert, 2, 371, 669n, 671, 740, 799n, 959,
   1122, 1143–44, 1149, 1215n, 1293, 1357, 1446,
   1488n, 1619n, 1623, 1632n, 1641, 1673n; on
   "Dostoevskian dinner" in Moscow, 12; and
   guzla (misnomer), 1251n; and Hulme, 1182n;
   on *Japanese Lyrics*, 824n; on Lourié, 1587; on
   Mavra, 1559, 1601–2; on *Montjoie!* affair, 998;

on pianola, 1453; on *Piano-Rag-Music*, 1455; on
prospects for Stravinsky research, 13–14; on
Pulcinella, 1608–9; on *Rake's Progress*, 1647; on
Requiem Canticles, 1649, 1665n; on *Rite of
Spring*, 776, 858n; and "Saucers" (misnomer),
1153; and Souvtchinsky, Pierre, 3–4, 18; on
Stravinsky's funeral, 1495n; as Stravinsky's
literary collaborator, 6–7, 12–13n, 797; on
Stravinsky's midlife crisis, 1514, 1516n, 1546; on
Stravinsky's text-setting, 1198; on *Svadebka*,
1323n, 1340n, 1379, 1385; and *Svadebka*,
reconstruction of preliminary version, 1456n;
on *Symphonies d'instruments à vent*, sketches,
1483n. Publications: "Catalogue of
Manuscripts in Stravinsky's Possession," 138,
1142, 1246n, 1258; "Catalogue of Source Books
and Music Inscribed to and/or Autographed
and Annotated by Igor Stravinsky" (with B.
Shapiro), 571n, 1473n, 1510n; *A Stravinsky
Scrapbook 1940–1971*, 1136, 1444

"cruel" romances. See *zhestokiye romansï*

cubism, 1452

Cui, César Antonovich, 11, 31, 33, 50 (Fig. 1.2),
   66, 81, 87, 96, 392, 499, 639, 718, 765, 1234,
   1594; and Belyayev Circle, 51–53; on
   declamation, 1199–1201, 1205–7; ghost of, 1226;
   on *Khovanshchina* (Diaghilev production),
   1043; on *The Power of the Fiend* (Serov),
   734–35; and Russian Musical Society, 53n; on
   Rite of Spring, 1023–24; on *Scherzo fantastique*,
   409–10; on Steinberg, 411. Works: "Fathers
   and Sons," 52–53; *La musique en Russie*, 526,
   551n; *Paraphrases*, contributions to, 35 (see also
   Paraphrases); Romanov Tercentenary Cantata,
   73; *Scherzo* for orchestra (op. 1), 102, 323;
   William Ratcliff, 87

Dada, 1511

Dahl (Dal'), Vladimir Ivanovich, 1333; *Poslovitsï
   russkogo naroda*, 1148, 1263; *Tolkoviy slovar'
   zhivogo velikorusskogo yazïka*, 1141–42, 1145,
   1148, 1277n, 1324–27, 1342, 1385, 1423–25, 1428

Dahlhaus, Carl, 16n, 1531n

Danilov, Kirsha, 1135

Danilov, V. V., 1265

Danto, Arthur C., 778

Dargomïzhsky, Alexander Sergeyevich, 23, 45,
   534, 987n, 1125, 1207, 1508, 1533–34, 1594;
   Rusalka, 1568–70 (incl. Exx. 19.25–26), 1573–75
   (incl. Ex. 19.30a); *Stone Guest*, 81, 261, 534, 1201,
   1570 (Ex. 19.26d)

Davïdov, Karl Yulyevich, 52

Davison, Archibald T., 1623

Dawe, George, 444, 445n

Firebird *(continued)*
552–53, 556, 567; parallel in Grimm fairy tales, 569; tale of summarized by Stasov, 562, 564–65
Fitelberg, Grzegorz, 1592
Fizdale, Robert, 1516
Flanner, Janet, 1515
Flonzaley Quartet, 1444, 1446, 1484
Florenz, Karl Adolf, 835
Fokine, Mikhaíl Mikhaílovich, 543–44, 546, 549, 556, 563 (Fig. 9.3), 663, 739, 820n, 990, 1507, 1509, 1615; *Carnaval* ballet, 677–78, 761, 970, 973, 1010; *Coq d'or* choreographed by for Diaghilev, 1069, 1076n; and *Firebird* scenario, 558, 561–62, 571, 622; on Lyadov, 577; *Papillons* ballet, 1112; and Remizov, 574n; *Rite of Spring*, intended choreographer of, 863, 875n, 969; "Second Chopiniana" (after Glazunov after Chopin), 546, 1611; working relationsip with Stravinsky, 575, 579–80, 583–86, 970
folk art: low repute of in nineteenth century, 497–99; reevaluation of by *Mir iskusstva*, 518
folklore: artistic treatment of, 355–56; esthetics of, 994; and modernity, 1167; urban vs. rural, 734, 1542
folk song anthologies: Balakirev's, 111, 133, 145, 148–49 (Ex. 2.20c), 498, 606, 609 (Ex. 9.22b), 724, 1054n, 1175, 1184–86 (incl. Ex. 15.14a), 1208–10 (incl. Ex. 15.24), 1214 (Ex. 15.28); Bernard's, 1626, 1629–47 (incl. Exx. E.7–14, Fig. E.1); Chaikovsky's (piano four-hands), 914; *Gusel'ki* (The Little Psalterion), 139–43 (incl. Fig. 2.9), 1217–18 (incl. Ex. 15.29c); Istomin-Dyutsh *(Pesni russkogo naroda)*, 1141, 1143, 1365 (Fig. 17.4b), 1372, 1375 (Fig. 17.6c), 1383, 1423, 1431, 1435; Istomin-Lyapunov *(Pesni russkogo naroda)*, 903–4 (incl. Exx. 12.4–5), 924, 926 (Ex. 12.20e), 1138, 1143, 1167–69 (incl. Ex. 15.5), 1371–72 (incl. Ex. 17.11); Kashin's, 1559–60 (incl. Ex. 19.19a), 1626; Linyova's, 1059–62 (incl. Ex. 14.2b), 1184, 1186–88 (incl. Ex. 15.14b); Lvov-Pratsch, 707n, 724, 1354, 1356 (Ex. 17.1a), 1557 (Ex. 19.17), 1626; Rimsky-Korsakov's, 145, 148 (Ex. 2.20b), 627–28 (incl. Ex. 9.36b), 632, 696–97, 698–99 (incl. Ex. 10.2a), 707, 710, 712 (Ex. 10.9), 724n, 869–70, 912 (Ex. 12.11b), 914, 959, 1155–56, 1354; Villebois's, 914n
Forte, Allen, 934n, 938, 940, 1022n, 1487n, 1493
Francisque, Anthoine: *Le trésor d'Orphée*, 368
Franck, César, 309, 376, 979, 1608; *Chasseur maudit*, 1022; Symphonic Variations for piano and orchestra, 1608; Symphony in D minor, 187
Franco-Russian alliance, 520–21

Frazer, Sir James, 880; *Golden Bough*, 881n, 883n
Free Music School, 27, 36, 86, 163
Free Theater (Moscow), 1077–84
French art, Russian discovery of, 521
French music: defined by Stravinsky as a minor tradition, 3; Stravinsky's early contact with, assessed, 307–15
Friedenburg, Boris, 504
Frishman, Dmitriy, 924n
Frolov, Vladimir Konstantinovich, 174
Fuchs, Georg, 975n
Furtwängler, Wilhelm, 1009
Futurism/Futurists, 8, 707n, 963, 1027–28, 1076n, 1237–38, 1320n, 1511, 1585

Gabel, Stanislav Ivanovich, 1043n
Gabrilowitsch, Osip, 978n
Gallo, Domenico, 1464–65, 1502
gamma ton-poluton. See octatonic scale
Garafola, Lynn, 881n
garmoshka (concertina), 734–35, 757, 766–67, 934
"garmoshka effect," 758, 1451, 1502, 1660
Gartman (Hartmann), Victor Alexandrovich, 504, 507–10 (incl. Figs. 8.4–5)
Gauguin, Paul, 521
Gautier, Théophile, 542; *Omphale*, or "Le gobelin en amour," 542n
Gay, John: *Beggar's Opera*, 1330n
Gedeonov, Stepan Alexandrovich, 536
Georges-Michel, Michel, 865n
Georgian folk and religious singing, 1413–16 (incl. Ex. 17.40)
German traditions, 3
Gershenzon, Mikhaíl, 854–55, 951
Gershwin, George: *An American in Paris*, 1478 (Fig. 18.7b)
Gershwin, Ira, 1624, 1626
"Gesamtkunstwerk" as *Mir iskusstva* ideal, 780, 1509; Diaghilev's version of emphasizes visual, 496, 534; dismantling of, 865, 1207
Ghéon, Henri, 638, 990
Gide, André, 989, 1199, 1236
Gilyanov, Mikhaíl Artemyevich, 580n
Gippius (Hippius), Zinaída, 441, 844
Giraud *(né Kayenbergh)*, Albert, 674
Girshman, Vladimir Osipovich, 366n
Glazunov, Alexander Konstantinovich, 381n, 855, 971n, 987n, 1049, 1125, 1202, 1585; academicism of, 34, 75, 1534; as ballet composer, 39, 536, 584–85; and M. P. Belyayev, 48–49; and Belyayev Circle, 50 (Fig. 1.2), 53, 56, 58, 68; as Belyayev trustee, 59 (Fig. 1.3), 416; and Chaikovsky, 10, 31–32, 37–38, 39–40; circle of thirds in, 298; and Diaghilev, 524–25;

Lyadov, Anatoliy Konstantinovich *(continued)*
conductor, 66; Chaikovsky, relationship with, 38–40; contrapuntal virtuosity of, 36; epigonism of, 73; and *Firebird* commission, 575–78, 579, 1080; octatonicism in, 298, 303; as teacher, 385. Works: *Baba-yaga,* 68, 323, 453, 575; *Bride of Messina,* 34; Canons (1898), 100; *Detskiye pesni* (Children's songs), 1162–66 (incl. Exx. 15.3–4), 1211–12 (incl. Ex. 15.27b), 1248, 1250 (Ex. 16.1b); *Eight Russian Folk Songs,* 413, 575–76, 632; Fugue on "B-la-F," 72 (Fig. 1.5); Fugue for string quartet, 61; Fugues for piano (op. 41), 36; "Hymn" (op. 54), 36; *Kikimora,* 323; *Leyla i Alaley,* 298n, 574n; *Magical* (or *Enchanted*) *Lake* (*Volshebnoye ozero*), 576; "Of Olden Days" *(Pro starinu),* 36; *Paraphrases,* contributions to, 35 (see also *Paraphrases*); Polonaise in D (op. 55), 36, 576; Sarabande for string quartet, 61; Scherzo in D (1879), 323; *Les sylphides,* contribution to, 547; *Zoryushka,* 298–99 (incl. Ex. 4.43), 303, 574n
Lyapunov, Sergey Mikhailovich, 37, 41, 50 (Fig. 1.2), 525, 696, 734, 903–4; Concerto for piano and orchestra, 60

Maeterlinck, Maurice, 7, 316; *La vie des abeilles,* 7, 318–19, 321–23, 419
Mahler, Gustav: *Lieder eines fahrenden Gesellen,* 247
"mainstream," Germanic, 2
Makovsky, Sergey Konstantinovich, 493, 513
Malevich, Kazimir Severinovich, 1298n
Malipiero, Gian Francesco, 1462n
Malïsheva, Yelena, 1621–22
Maliszewski, Witold, 68–69, 75
Malko, Nikolai Andreyevich, 370 (Fig. 6.1), 654 (Fig. 9.6b), 1123
Mallarmé, Stéphane, 323, 1235
Malyutin, Sergey Vasilyevich, 442, 446n, 495, 513–14 (incl. Fig. 8.7), 516, 522
Mamontov, Savva Ivanovich, 46, 382, 446, 490–97 (incl. Figs. 8.1–2), 503, 534; Abramtsevo, estate of and arts colony at, 490, 493, 497, 504, 507, 510–11 (incl. Fig. 8.5), 516, 1073, 1540; and *Mir iskusstva,* 496, 516, 520 (Fig. 8.9); Russian Private Opera Company of, 511, 1038n, 1077; and Tenisheva, compared, 511; and Tretyakov, compared, 507
Mamontova, Maria, 139
Mamontova, Yelizaveta, 510
Mardzhanov (Mardzhanishvili), Konstantin Alexandrovich, 1077, 1081–83, 1085n
Maria Fyodorovna, Empress, 1537

Marinetti, Emilio, 1320n
Maritain, Jacques, 1587
Mariyinsky (Kirov) Theater (St. Petersburg), 10, 360n, 494, 1509
Markévitch, Dmitry, 1558n
Markévitch, Igor, 1660
Markov, Vladimir, 557n, 786–87
Marlowe, Sylvia, 1198n
Marnold, Jean, 526
Marr, Nikolai Yakovlevich, 1413
Martín y Soler, Vicente, 924
maslenichnaya (Shrovetide song), 919, 921 (Ex. 12.16g)
maslenitsa (Shrovetide fair), 665, 671, 689–95 (incl. Fig. 10.4, Ex. 10.1), 698, 1242
Massine (Myasin), Leonid Fyodorovich, 891n, 1008, 1321, 1379n, 1506–7, 1509, 1516, 1538–39
Matinsky, Mikhaíl Alexeyevich, 1330
Matlaw, Ralph, 1573n
Matyushin, Mikhaíl, 75n
Maurer, Ludwig Wilhelm, 48
maxixe (Brazilian polka), 1475, 1477–78 (incl. Fig. 18.7), 1481 (Ex. 18.12)
Mayakovsky, Vladimir Vladimirovich, 75
Mazo, Margarita, 1353, 1423–24, 1427
Meck, Nadezhda von, 40n, 46, 167; and Mitrofan Belyayev, compared, 49
Medem, Alexander Davidovich, 308n, 309, 374, 654
Medtner, Emiliy Karlovich, 781
Medtner, Nikolai Karlovich, 381, 437n, 781–82, 798, 1123, 1516
Mei-Figner, Medea, 77
MEK. *See* Musico-Ethnographic Commission of Moscow University
Melgunov, Yuliy Nikolayevich, 64, 498, 723–27 (incl. Fig. 10.8), 915, 1059, 1213, 1330; *Russian Songs Transcribed Directly from the Voices of the People* (1879), 724
Mellers, Wilfrid, 1301n
Melnikov, Ivan Alexandrovich, 78n, 86
Melos (magazine), 1124–25
memory hole, Orwellian, 1
Mendelssohn, Felix, 315, 624
merchant class, Russian, 41–42
merchant patronage: of art, 41–45; of music, 45, 47
Merezhkovsky, Dmitriy Sergeyevich, 371n, 416, 437, 439, 439n, 441, 461, 851
Messiaen, Olivier, 963, 1487n; modes of limited transposition, 268
Messing, Scott, 1510
Mey, Lev Alexandrovich, 163, 1613
Meyer, André, 1018, 1143–44

Meyerbeer, Giacomo, 534

Meyerhold, Vsevolod Emilyevich, 371n, 372, 676, 1298n

Meytus, Yuliy Sergeyevich: *Dneprostroy,* 963

Michelangelo (Buonarotti), 973

"Mighty Five" (*Moguchaya kuchka,* lit. "Mighty Little Heap"), 6, 24, 39, 424, 752, 1533, 1594; lack of snob appeal, 528; name coined, 24n; and Peredvizhniki, 498, 525

Milhaud, Darius, 371n, 841, 1446; on *Mavra,* 1598; *Le train bleu,* 1507, 1606

Miller, Vsevolod Fyodorovich, 1337

Milyukov, Pavel Nikolayevich, 1514n

Minkus, Ludwig, 536, 585

"Minsky, N." (Nikolai Maximovich Vilenkin), 1010–12, 1070

"Miriskusnichestvo" (*Mir isskustva*-ism), 424, 428, 1104, 1332, 1342, 1506; and *Baiser de la fée,* 1617; and "decorativism," 447; and estheticism, 438–42; and neonationalism, 445, 487, 528; and *sprezzatura,* 427; and Symbolism, distinguished, 438; and synthesism, 445, 487, 528. *See also* neonationalism; synthesism

Mir iskusstva (magazine), 57, 69, 372, 375, 377, 438, 441, 446n, 513, 516, 519, 521–22, 543, 1509; inaugural editorial ("Complicated Questions"), 440; layout of, 490; logo (designed by Bakst), 440, 517–18 (incl. Fig. 8.8b); Stasov on, 435–6 (incl. Fig. 7.3); and Wagnerian synthesis, 489

Mir iskusstva (World of Art), 15, 18, 307, 368, 418, 423, 426, 429–30, 880, 950, 1540; antiliterary esthetics of, 532–35, 759–60, 782, 1072–73, 1090; and ballet, 538; and Belyayev Circle, 445, 447; and myth of Firebird, 557; portrait exhibition (1905), 443–45; reputation enhanced by Stasov's attacks, 436–37; retrospectivism of, 443, 446, 1510

Mirsky, D. S. (Dmitry Petrovich Svyatopolk-Mirsky, Prince), 234, 438, 859, 1133, 1134n

Mitusov, Stepan Stepanovich, 100, 113, 308, 381, 389, 580n, 795, 893, 1145n, 1322; as librettist of *The Nightingale,* 464–68, 1078n, 1085n, 1086–90, 1104; as source for *Svadebka,* 1372–75 (incl. Fig. 17.6), 1383, 1389, 1418, 1431, 1435; as translator of *Poèmes de Verlaine,* 655, 1206

Mlada (collectively composed opera-ballet), 536

"mobile" form, 1449, 1452, 1502, 1580, 1618

Moevs, Robert, 939n

"moment" form, 1451–52

Monday Evening Concerts (Los Angeles), 367

Monte Carlo Opera, 1539n

Montéclair, Michel Pignolet de, 367–68; "Les plaisirs champêtres" (arr. Casadesus), 367; *Les tentations de la bergère,* 368

Monteux, Pierre, 877n, 978n, 1008; conducts concert première of *Rite of Spring,* 1031–33

Monteverdi, Claudio, 367

Montjoie! (magazine), 877, 995–96, 999–1006 (incl. Figs. 13.6–7), 1112–13 (incl. Fig. 14.5)

Monza, Carlo Ignazio, 1464

Morand, Paul, 1184n, 1516n

Moreau, Gustave, 516

Morozov, Ivan Abramovich, 397, 410, 521

Morris, William, 504

Morton, Lawrence, 895, 1611–14, 1616–18, 1637n, 1638

Moskvityanin (magazine), 1149

Mosolov, Alexander Vasilyevich, 75; *Zavod* (Iron Foundry), 963

Mottl, Felix, 397

Mozart, Wolfgang Amadeus, 1532; Fugue in C minor for two pianos (K. 426), 1453n; Sonata for piano in C (K. 309), 268–69

Musico-Ethnographic Commission of Moscow University (MEK), 697, 718, 1135, 1166; *Trudï* (papers of), 733, 921, 1163, 1176–77, 1370–71 (incl. Ex. 17.10), 1413–14, 1622

Musorgsky, Modest Petrovich, 66, 524, 768, 1006, 1125, 1144n, 1145n, 1189, 1242, 1594; antipathy of to chamber music, 60; as idol of the French, 639, 642; as model for Stravinsky, 143, 1381, 1409; prose settings of, 1270–71; realism of, 438; Rimsky-Korsakov on, 33, 40, 382; and F. I. Stravinsky, 86–88; on symphonic development, 137, 955

—Works:

"The Billy Goat" (*Kozyol),* 243

Boris Godunov, 40, 348–49, 639–40, 731, 741, 965, 1035, 1041, 1533; "Clapping Game," 1162, 1267; Coronation bells, chord progression, 283–84 (incl. Ex. 4.28a), 740; Inn scene, 1200; staged by Diaghilev at Paris Opera (1908), 528–35 (incl. Fig. 8.10), 552, 1040, 1042; staged by Russian Private Opera (Mamontov), 495; Varlaam's song, 150, 152 (Ex. 2.22); Yurodivïy's lament, 1290

Fair at Sorochintsï, 1077, 1123; "Hopak" from, 549; "Peasant Lad's Dumka" and *Rite of Spring* (Intro.), 935–37 (incl. Ex. 12.29); "Red jacket" leitmotif from (quoted), 720n

Khovanshchina, 358, 359n; Persian Dances from, 546; revised by Stravinsky and Ravel for Diaghilev, 826, 978n, 1013, 1015, 1035, 1038–51, 1074; Rimsky-Korsakov redaction, 1036–38

Musorgsky, Modest Petrovich *(continued)*
"King Saul," 87, 150, 152–53 (incl. Ex. 2.23)
Marriage (Zhenit'ba), 386, 1077, 1202–3 (incl. Ex. 15.19b)
Mlada, contribution to, 536–37
Night on Bald Mountain, 884n, 1508
"Picking Mushrooms" *(Po gribï)*, 145–46 (incl. Ex. 2.18)
Pictures from an Exhibition, 507; "Bydlo" from, 1184; "Hut on Hen's Legs" from, 453
"Pride" *(Spes')*, 143–44 (incl. Ex. 2.17)
Scherzo in B-flat (orchestra), 102, 262, 323
"Song of the Flea" (orch. Stravinsky), 334
Songs and Dances of Death, 646; "Trepak" from, 145, 147 (Ex. 2.19)
Sunless (song cycle), 472
"Where Art Thou, Little Star!" *(Gde tï, zvyozdochka)*, 349, 1355–56 (incl. Ex. 17.1c)
Mussolini, Benito, 1514
Muzika (magazine), 817, 840, 845, 1319–20
Muzikal'nïy sovremennik (magazine), 1121–25, 1183
Myaskovsky, Nikolai Yakovlevich, 14, 231n, 392, 423, 654, 706, 767, 842–44 (incl. Fig. 11.6), 1018, 1114, 1116, 1123, 1322n, 1607; on *Firebird,* 644–45; on generations of Russian composers, 381n; on *Japanese Lyrics,* 835–36, 840–41; on *Khovanshchina,* final chorus (Stravinsky), 1053; on *Petrushka,* 762–63; on *Poèmes de Verlaine* (Stravinsky), 652n; on *Rite of Spring,* 1020–23; and *Rite of Spring,* "dedication" of, 1018–19n; on Schmitt, 846n; and Stravinsky, 1019–21; on Stravinsky's reputation, 988; on *Svadebka,* 1323; on Symphony in E-flat (Stravinsky), 227, 229–33, 334. Works: *The Idiot* (projected opera), 1126n; Symphony No. 2, 1124

Nabokov, Nicolas, 15, 1322n, 1323n, 1601n, 1649, 1660, 1674; *Ode,* 1509, 1545n
Nabokov, Vladimir Dmitriyevich, 428
Nabokov, Vladimir Vladimirovich, 1153, 1159, 1324, 1326
naígrish(i) (instrumental dance tune[s]), 669, 923, 1370, 1465, 1508; *Timon'ya,* 932n
napevï, 1135, 1163, 1166–67, 1244, 1326, 1332, 1367, 1375, 1438. See also *popevki*
Nápravník, Eduard Frantsevich, 52, 81, 492, 972, 974, 1038; *Dubrovsky,* 364n; "Stonet sizïy golubochek," 1555
Nash, Ogden, 713
national character ("Russianness") of Russian music, 133, 137, 232, 363, 1532–33; as subject matter and ethos, 497

nationalism: as Western historiographical cliché, 28, 1534; diminishes in Russian music, 60–64; vs. patriotism, 1535
naturalism and modernism, 445–46
Nazism, 1134
nega, 469, 857
Neighbour, Oliver, 1041n
Neledinsky-Meletsky, Yuriy, 1557
Nemirovich-Danchenko, Vladimir Ivanovich, 1086
neoclassicism, 367, 1318, 1443, 1447, 1459, 1462, 1485–86, 1501, 1507, 1511, 1550, 1564, 1588; adumbrated by Rivière, 994–95; as appropriation of phonology and morphology of common practice, 1581; as authoritarian, reactionary stance, 1584; and irony, 1608; as "rediscovery of cadenced phrase," 1585; as "retour à Bach," 1607–8, 1614; as "stilizatsiya," 1615; as stylistic disjunction, 1579–84
neonationalism, 364, 445, 449 (Fig. 7.4b), 493, 496, 499, 502–18, 660, 760, 786, 791, 847, 950, 1132; and *Coq d'or* (Diaghilev production), 1073; defined by Tugenhold, 502; vs. Europeanism, 519; in *Histoire du soldat,* 1312–15; in *Khovanshchina* chorus (Stravinsky), 1059–63, 1065; and "kuchkism," compared, 910–11; as methodology, 915; musical, 718–35, 905–33; in *Petrushka,* 713–17, 770; prefigured, 355–56, 363; in *Rite of Spring,* 905–33, 937–50, 965; in symbiosis with synthesism, 528
neonationalist architecture, 503–10 (incl. Figs. 8.3–5)
neoprimitivist painting, 949
nepodvizhnost' (immobility), as Stravinskian characteristic, 954–55, 1449–52, 1458–59, 1465, 1501–2, 1650, 1675
Nesterov, Mikhaíl Vasilyevich, 442, 446n, 463, 520 (Fig. 8.9)
Nestor Letopisets (Nestor the Chronicler), 884, 910, 951–52
neue Sachlichkeit, 1598, 1617
Neumann, Angelo, 490
"Nevsky Pickwickians," 430, 1510
"New Folkloristic Wave" *(Novaya fol'kloristiche-skaya volna)*, 16n
Newman, Ernest (William Roberts), 1512
Newmarch, Rosa, 6, 28
"New Russian School," 23, 27; Chaikovsky on, 31–32; controversy about, 28; *embourgeoisement* of, 54, 56; latter-day parochialism of, 69; Rimsky-Korsakov on, 33–34; Stasov, characterized by, 24, 28–29
New Vienna School, 3, 1206

with, 1511, 1513, 1515, 1585, 1587, 1589–90, 1599, 1610, 1647; "monometric" rhythm in, 1600–1601; monophony in, 1171; as most famous twentieth-century composer, 1; as "nationalist" heir presumptive, 640–41, 642; on "naturalism," 6; "neoclassicism" of, 17, 1648 (*see also* neoclassicism); *nepodvizhnost'* (immobility) in, 954–55; and nobility pretense, 1515n; on opera, 971, 982, 1107; on orchestration, 210; as outsider *(zarubezhnïy)*, 14, 16; and pangermanoromanic chauvinism, 2; as performer, 1453n, 1465; as "piano composer," 817n; and pianola, 1452–55 (incl. Fig. 18.3), 1458, 1501; "polytonalism" of, 406, 595, 657, 748–49, 756–57, 858n, 948, 1173–74; on professionalism, 169; projected "Poe" ballet, 662; and "pure music," 8, 11; recherché vocabulary of, 2; religious activities, 1618–19; on Rimsky-Korsakov, 292; on Rimsky-Korsakov, centenary tribute, 1624; and Rimsky-Korsakov, efforts to surpass, 315; and Rimsky-Korsakov, lessons with, 109, 109n, 165–69, 171–72; Rimsky-Korsakov family, attachment to, 110–13; Russian folk poetry, settings of, 1136–47 (incl. Table 2, Ex. 15.1); and Russian traditions, 3, 12, 13, 18, 1675; and Schoenberg, compared, 1021–22, 1022n, 1029; and Scriabin, 791–99 (incl. Fig. 11.4); serial technique, 1649n, 1652–59 (incl. Exx. E.16–17, Fig. E.2); and *Sleeping Beauty* (Chaikovsky, prod. Diaghilev), 1512–13, 1517, 1529; M. Steinberg, jealousy of, 389–91, 394–95, 423; technique, respect for, 75; on theory, 171; "vamping pieces," 1447, 1449, 1456, 1502; and vocal score of *Legend of the Invisible City of Kitezh*, 360; on Vsevolozhsky, 539n; as "Wagner's Antichrist," 247; as "walled-in" artist, 74; wartime patriotism of, 1623

—Musical works:

Abraham and Isaac, 1653n, 1673

Agon, 1171, 1648

Apollon musagètes, 1229, 1513; prefigured, 1112

"Aus Goethe's Faust" [Song of the Flea], (Beethoven, orch. Stravinsky), 398 (Fig. 6.6), 412–15 (incl. Ex. 6.8), 1024

Ave Maria (*Bogoroditse devo, raduysya*), 1619

Baika pro lisu, petukha, kota da barana (*Renard*), 14, 733, 1136, 1144, 1199, 1215n, 1237–92, 1310, 1484, 1508; assembly of text out of Afanasyev *skazki*, 1245–69 (incl. Table 3); cimbalom in, 1152; "The Cock's Whine," 1257, 1281–82 (incl. Ex. 16.22); Cocteau on, 1605; Diaghilev production (1922, chor. Nijinska, designed by

Laryonov), 949n, 1538–39, 1594–95; earliest musical sketches, 1246–47, 1247n (quoted), 1251–52 (incl. Exx. 16.2–3); "First Song of the Cat and the Ram," 1259–62 (incl. Exx. 16.5–6), 1269n, 1277, 1279 (Ex. 16.18), 1282–87 (incl. Exx. 16.24–28), 1431; folklore sources of, summarized, 1139; harmonic and tonal structure, 1280–89 (incl. Exx. 16.22–31), 1388; nonlinear presentation of story in, 1332; première performance, 1132; *pribautki* in, 1137, 1149, 1162, 1247–48, 1267–69 (incl. Ex. 16.7), 1275–77 (incl. Exx. 16.15–17); prosody in, 1269–80 (incl. Exx. 16.8–19); "salto mortale" in, 1122, 1189; "Song to the Gusli," 1272–74 (incl. Ex. 16.13)

Le baiser de la fée, 103, 213, 1610–18 (incl. Table 7); and *Sleeping Beauty* (Chaikovsky), 1615–16

Berceuses [*du chat*]. See *Kolïbel'nïye*, below

Bogoroditse devo, raduysya, 1619

Canon (On a Russian Popular Tune), 1648n

Canticum sacrum, 698, 1205, 1649

"Cat's Cradle Songs." See *Kolïbel'nïye*, below

Chant du rossignol, 1090, 1130, 1132, 1137, 1453

Cherubic Hymn (*Izhe kheruvimi*), sketch, 1619, 1621–22 (incl. Ex. E.4)

Les cinq doigts, 1517; arr. orchestra (*Eight Instrumental Miniatures*), 1517; no. 3 (Allegretto), 1517–19 (incl. Ex. 19.4a)

Cinq pièces faciles for piano four-hands, 1445, 1446; no. 5 (Galop), 1475–76 (incl. Ex. 18.9), 1485

Concertino (string quartet), 1446, 1484–85 (incl. Ex. 18.17), 1505; arranged for twelve instruments, 1648; piano reduction by A. Lourié, 1587

Concerto per due pianoforti soli, 303, 1233–34 (incl. Ex. 15.37b), 1453n

Concerto for piano and winds, 3n, 962, 1516, 1566, 1607–9 (incl. Exx. E.1–2), 1614, 1615

Credo (Simvol verï), 1619

Danses concertantes, 1618

"Detskiy khorik." See *Scherzo à la russe*, below

Detskiye pesenki (Trois histoires pour enfants), 1136–37, 1140, 1144; "Gusi-lebedi" (no. 2), 1151, 1174–75, 1455 (Fig. 18.3b); "Medved' " (no. 3), 1149, 1245, 1246–47; "Tilim-bom" (no. 1), 139, 1145–47 (incl. Ex. 15.1), 1163, 1166, 1317; "Tilim-bom" (rev. 1954), 1166n

Detskiye pesni (early sketches for *Baika*), 1246–47

Dialogue Between Joy and Reason (Petrarch), sketch, 1588

"The Dove" (*Golub*). See Two Poems of Balmont, *below*

Compositor:	BookMasters, Inc., and Clarinda
Music setter:	Dennis Riley
Text:	10/14 Galliard
Display:	Galliard
Printer:	Malloy Lithographing, Inc.
Binder:	John H. Dekker & Sons